Lecture Notes in Computer Science 3722

Commenced Publication in 1973
Founding and Former Series Editors:
Gerhard Goos, Juris Hartmanis, and Jan van Leeuwen

T0189550

Dang Van Hung   Martin Wirsing (Eds.)

Theoretical Aspects of Computing – ICTAC 2005

Second International Colloquium
Hanoi, Vietnam, October 17-21, 2005
Proceedings

 Springer

Volume Editors

Dang Van Hung
United Nations University
International Institute for Software Technology
P.O. Box 3058, Macao SAR, China
E-mail: dvh@iist.unu.edu

Martin Wirsing
Universität München, Institut für Informatik
Oettingenstr. 67, 80538 München, Germany
E-mail: wirsing@informatik.uni-muenchen.de

Library of Congress Control Number: 2005933498

CR Subject Classification (1998): F.1, F.3, F.4, D.3, D.2, C.2.4

ISSN   0302-9743
ISBN-10   3-540-29107-5 Springer Berlin Heidelberg New York
ISBN-13   978-3-540-29107-7 Springer Berlin Heidelberg New York

Springer is a part of Springer Science+Business Media

springeronline.com

© Springer-Verlag Berlin Heidelberg 2005
Printed in Germany

Typesetting: Camera-ready by author, data conversion by Scientific Publishing Services, Chennai, India
Printed on acid-free paper   SPIN: 11560647   06/3142   5 4 3 2 1 0

Preface

This volume contains the proceedings of ICTAC 2005, the second ICTAC, *International Colloquium on Theoretical Aspects of Computing*. ICTAC 2005 took place in Hanoi, Vietnam, October 17–21, 2005.

ICTAC was founded by the International Institute for Software Technology of the United Nations University (UNU-IIST) to serve as a forum for practitioners, lecturers and researchers from academia, industry and government who are interested in theoretical aspects of computing and rigorous approaches to software engineering. The colloquium is aimed particularly, but not exclusively, at participants from developing countries. We believe that this will help developing countries to strengthen their research, teaching and development in computer science and engineering, improve the links between developing countries and developed countries, and establish collaboration in research and education. By providing a venue for the discussion of common problems and their solutions, and for the exchange of experiences and ideas, this colloquium supports research and development in computer science and software technology. ICTAC is attracting more and more attention from more and more countries.

Topics covered by ICTAC include:
- automata theory and formal languages,
- principles and semantics of programming languages,
- logic and its applications,
- software architectures and their description languages,
- software specification, refinement and verification,
- model checking and theorem proving,
- formal techniques in software testing,
- models of object and component systems,
- coordination and feature interaction,
- integration of formal and engineering methods,
- service-oriented and document-driven development,
- models of concurrency, security and mobility,
- theory of parallel, distributed and Internet-based (grid) computing,
- real-time and embedded systems,
- type and category theory in computer science.

Research papers in these topics are always considered by ICTAC.

ICTAC 2005 received 122 paper submissions from 29 countries, and accepted 35 papers. We would like to thank the authors of all submitted papers.

Selecting papers for a program from the large number of submissions in a fair and competent manner is a hard job. Luckily, ICTAC 2005 had an excellent Program Committee with highly qualified members from diverse backgrounds to carry out the job. Each submission was reviewed carefully by at least three referees working in relevant fields. Borderline papers were further discussed during an intensive on-line meeting of the Program Committee. We believe that the program resulting from this excellent job of the Program Committee was scientifically very strong. In addition to the contributed papers, the proceedings also include contributions from invited speakers: Reiko Heckel, Zhiming Liu, José Meseguer, Rocco De Nicola, and Do Long Van.

Five tutorials were selected as affiliated events of ICTAC 2005. The abstracts of the tutorials are also included in the proceedings. We express our thanks to all of the people who submitted tutorial proposals.

Special thanks are due to the Program Committee members and all the referees, whose names are listed on the following pages, for their assistance in reviewing and selecting papers. The help from the Advisory Committee, especially Zhiming Liu, was invaluable. We express our appreciation to the Organizing Committee, especially Ho Si Dam, Le Hai Khoi, Le Quoc Hung and Bui The Duy, and the Publicity Chair, Bernhard Aichernig, for their efforts in making ICTAC 2005 such a successful and enjoyable event. We would particularly like to thank Kitty Iok Sam Chan of UNU-IIST for her hard work in maintaining the conference administration system. We would also like to express our thanks to all UNU-IIST staff for their active support of ICTAC 2005. Last but not least we are grateful to Springer for its helpful collaboration and quick publication.

October 2005   Dang Van Hung and Martin Wirsing

Organization

ICTAC 2005 was organized by the International Institute for Software Technology of the United Nations University, the College of Technology of the Vietnam National University, Hanoi, and the Institute of Information Technology of the Vietnam Academy of Science and Technology.

Conference Chairs

Program Co-chair	Dang Van Hung (UNU-IIST, Macau, China)
	Martin Wirsing (University of Munich, Germany)
Organizing Committee Co-chair	Ho Si Dam (College of Technology, Vietnam)
	Le Hai Khoi (Institute of Information Technology, Vietnam)
Publicity Chair	Bernhard K. Aichernig (UNU-IIST, Macau, China)

Advisory Committee

Dines Bjørner	Technical University of Denmark, Denmark
Manfred Broy	Technische Universität München, Germany
José Luiz Fiadeiro	University of Leicester, UK
Jifeng He	UNU-IIST, Macau, China
Mathai Joseph	TRDDC/TCS, India
Shaoying Liu	Hosei University, Japan
Zhiming Liu	UNU-IIST, Macau, China
Zohar Manna	Stanford University, USA
Tobias Nipkow	Technische Universität München, Germany
Mike Reed	UNU-IIST, Macau, China
Jim Woodcock	York University, UK

Program Committee

Marc Aiguier	University of Evry, France
Keijiro Araki	Kyushu University, Japan
J.O.A. Ayeni	University of Lagos, Nigeria
Jay Bagga	Ball State University, USA
Hubert Baumeister	LMU, Munich, Germany
Michel Bidoit	CNRS & ENS de Cachan, France

Jonathan Bowen   London South Bank University, UK
Victor A. Braberman   University of Buenos Aires, Argentina
Cristian S. Calude   University of Auckland, New Zealand
Ana Cavalcanti   University of York, UK
Yifeng Chen   University of Leicester, UK
Jim Davies   Oxford University, UK
János Demetrovics   MTA-SZTAKI, Hungary
Henning Dierks   University of Oldenburg, Germany
Jin Song Dong   NUS, Singapore
Marcelo F. Frias   University of Buenos Aires, Argentina
Wan Fokkink   CWI, The Netherlands
Valentin Goranko   University of Witwatersrand, Johannesburg,
                                     South Africa
Susanne Graf   VERIMAG, France
Dimitar P. Guelev   Bulgarian Academy of Science, Bulgaria
Michael R. Hansen   DTU, Lyngby, Denmark
Nguyen Cat Ho   IoIT, Hanoi, Vietnam
Jozef Hooman   Embedded Systems Institute, Eindhoven,
                                     The Netherlands
Ngo Quang Hung   State University of New York at Buffalo, USA
Purush Iyer   North Carolina State University, USA
Ryszard Janicki   McMaster University, Ontario, Canada
Takuya Katayama   JAIST, Japan
Maciej Koutny   University of Newcastle upon Tyne, UK
Xuandong Li   Nanjing University, China
Antonia Lopes   University of Lisbon, Portugal
Andrea Maggiolo-Schettini   University of Pisa, Italy
Antoni Mazurkiewicz   Institute of Computer Science of PAS, Poland
Hrushikesha Mohanty   University of Hyderabad, India
Paritosh Pandya   TIFR, Mumbai, India
Jean-Eric Pin   LIAFA, CNRS and University Paris 7, France
Narjes Ben Rajeb   INSAT, Tunisia
R. Ramanujam   Institute of Mathematical Sciences, Chennai,
                                     India
Anders P. Ravn   Aalborg University, Denmark
Gianna Reggio   University of Genoa, Italy
Wolfgang Reif   Augsburg, Germany
Riadh Robbana   LIP2/EPT, Tunisia
Mark Ryan   University of Birmingham, UK
Zaidi Sahnoun   UMC, Algeria
Augusto Sampaio   Federal Univ. of Pernambuco, Recife, Brazil
Don Sannella   University of Edinburgh, UK
Bernhard Schätz   TU München, Germany
Carolyn Talcott   RI International, USA

P. S. Thiagarajan   NUS, Singapore
Do Long Van   Institute of Mathematics, Vietnam
Ji Wang   National Laboratory for Parallel
                               and Distributed Processing, China
Mingsheng Ying   Tsinghua University, Beijing, China
Jian Zhang   Chinese Academy of Sciences, Beijing,
                               China
Hongjun Zheng   Semantics Designs Inc., USA

Referees

Femi Agboola	Marcin Dziubinski	Kenneth MacKenzie
Luca Aceto	Eugene Eberbach	Ian Mason
Aderemi O. Adewumi	Martin Escardo	Paulo Mateus
Bernhard K. Aichernig	Hugues Fauconnier	Ralph Matthes
Nazareno Aguirre	Ansgar Fehnker	Anne Micheli
Jean Philippe Babeau	Pascale Le Gall	Paolo Milazzo
Diane Bahrami	Christophe Gaston	Michael Mislove
Rilwan Olayinka Basanya	Vincenzo Gervasi	Carroll Morgan
Andreas Bauer	P. Gouveia	Akira Mori
Peter Baumgartner	Johannes Grünbauer	Ben Moszkowski
Adel Benzina	James Harland	I. Nunes
Lennart Beringer	Joos Heintz	Edward Ochmanski
Nicole Bidoit	Rolf Hennicker	Atsushi Ohori
Javier Blanco	Gabriel Infante-Lopez	Adegboyega Ojo
Tomek Borzyszkowski	Alan Jeffrey	Alfredo Olivero
O.K. Boyinbode	Ole Høgh Jensen	Mizuhito Ogawa
Marius Bozga	Ata Kaban	Savas Parastatidis
Vasco Brattka	Wolfram Kahl	Adriano Peron
Andrew Brown	Hiroyasu Kamo	Diego Piemonte
Mario Bravetti	Kamel Karoui	Alessandra Di Pierro
Franck Capello	Tran Dinh Khang	Sophie Pinchinat
Jacques Carette	Victor Khomenko	Andre Platzer
Paul Caspi	Kais Klai	Pascal Poizat
Antonio Ceron	Michal Konečný	John Power
Bob Coecke	Moez Krichen	Stefan Ratschan
Frédéric Cuppens	Antonin Kucera	James Riely
Stefan Dantchev	Christian Laforest	Jan Romberg
Steve Dawson	K. Lakshmanan	Dominique Rossin
Carole Delporte	Eric Laporte	Jonathan Rowe
Josée Desharnais	Reinhold Letz	Domenico Sacca
Raymond Devillers	Paul B. Levy	Fernando Schapachnik
Enrica Duchi	Zhiming Liu	Laura Semini
Phan Thi Ha Duong	Bas Luttik	Guillermo Simari

B.A. Sawyerr
Emil Sekerinski
Amilcar Sernadas
Michael Soltys
Volker Sorge
Meng Sun
Makoto Takeyama
Andrzej Tarlecki
Hendrik Tews
Ho Thuan
Nguyen Thanh Thuy

Simone Tini
David Trachtenherz
Emina Torlak
Tayssir Touilli
Marek Tudruj
Sebastian Uchitel
Irek Ulidowski
Martín Urtasun Charles
O. Uwadia
V. Vasconcelos
S. Vial

Alan Wassyng
Heike Wehrheim
Jozef Winkowski
Bozena Wozna
Dobieslaw Wroblewski
Zhang Yan
Naijun Zhan
Yunquan Zhang
Jianhua Zhao
Huibiao Zhu

Sponsoring Institutions

International Institute for Software Technology of the United Nations University
Vietnam National University, Hanoi
Vietnam Academy of Science and Technology

Table of Contents

Program Construction

Real-Time Systems

Concurrency and Refinement

Software Security

Quantitative Logics

Object-Orientation and Component Systems

Model-Checking and Algorithms

Applied Logics and Computing Theory

Tutorials at ICTAC 2005

A Rewriting Logic Sampler

José Meseguer

University of Illinois at Urbana-Champaign, USA

Abstract. Rewriting logic is a simple computational logic very well suited as a *semantic framework* within which many different models of computation, systems and languages can be naturally modeled. It is also a flexible *logical framework* in which many different logical formalisms can be both represented and executed. As the title suggests, this paper does not try to give a comprehensive overview of rewriting logic. Instead, after introducing the basic concepts, it focuses on some recent research directions emphasizing: (i) extensions of the logic to model real-time systems and probabilistic systems; and (ii) some exciting application areas such as: semantics of programming languages, security, and bioinformatics.

1 Introduction

Rewriting logic is now a teenager; a *quinceañera*, as they call adolescent women reaching 15 in Spain and Latin America. There are hundreds of papers; five rewriting logic workshops have already taken place and a sixth will meet in Vienna next March; and a host of tools and applications have been developed. Taking pictures of this "young person" as it grows up is a quite interesting intellectual exercise, one that can help other people become familiar with this field and its possibilities. I, with the help of others, have done my share of picture taking in earlier stages [69,70,72,67]. In particular, the "roadmap" [67] that Narciso Matí-Oliet and I wrote, gives a brief but comprehensive overview and cites 328 papers in the area as of 2002. This paper takes a different tack. I will *not* try to give you an overview. I will give you a *sampler*, some rewriting logic *tapas* if you will, to tease your curiosity so that hopefully you may find some things that you like and excite your interest.

I should of course say something about my choice of topics for the sampler; and about some important developments that I do not cover. At the theoretical level, one of the interesting questions to ask about a formalism is: how *general, flexible and extensible* is it? For example, how does it compare in generality to other formalisms? how can it deal with new application areas? how well can it be extended in new directions? can it represent its own metalevel? I address some of these questions by my choice of topics, but I consciously omit others. The most glaring omission is the theoretical extension from ordinary rewrite theories to *generalized rewrite theories* [10], that substantially extend the logic's expressive power. For the sake of a simpler exposition, this whole development

D.V. Hung and M. Wirsing (Eds.): ICTAC 2005, LNCS 3722, pp. 1–28, 2005.

is relegated here to Footnote 1. I do however discuss two other important theoretical extensions, namely, *real-time rewrite theories* [87] (Section 3.2), which extend rewriting logic to deal with real-time and hybrid systems; and *probabilistic rewrite theories* [63,64,2] (Section 3.3), that bring probabilistic systems, as well as systems exhibiting both probabilistic and nodeterministic behavior, within the rewriting logic fold. In both cases, the generality aspect is quite encouraging, in the sense that many models of real time and of probabilistic systems appear as special cases. However, to keep the exposition short, I do not discuss all those models except in passing, and refer to [87] and [63] for detailed comparisons. For the generality of rewriting logic itself see [67]. Reflection, that allows rewriting logic to represent its own metalevel, is of such great theoretical and practical importance that I also discuss it in Section 2.3.

At the practical level, one can ask questions such as: how well is this formalism supported by *tools*? (this I briefly answer in Section 2.4); and what are some exciting application areas? I have chosen three such areas for the sampler: (1) semantics of programming languages and formal analysis of programs (Section 3.1); (2) security (Section 3.4); and (3) bioinformatics (Section 3.5). Enjoy!

2   What Is Rewriting Logic?

A *rewrite theory*[1] is a tuple $\mathcal{R} = (\Sigma, E, R)$, with:

- (Σ, E) an equational theory with function symbols Σ and equations E; and
- R a set of *labeled rewrite rules* of the general form

$$r : t \longrightarrow t'$$

with t, t' Σ-terms which may contain variables in a countable set X of variables which we assume fixed in what follows; that is, t and t' are elements of the term algebra $T_\Sigma(X)$. In particular, their corresponding sets of variables, $vars(t)$, $vars(t')$ are both contained in X.

---

[1] To simplify the exposition I present here the simplest version of rewrite theories, namely, *unconditional* rewrite theories over an *unsorted* equational theory (Σ, E). In general, however, the equational theory (Σ, E) can be many-sorted, order-sorted, or even a membership equational theory [71]. And the rules can be *conditional*, having a conjunction of rewrites, equalities, and even memberships in their condition, that is, they could have the general form

$$r : t \longrightarrow t' \ \text{ if } \ (\bigwedge_i u_i = u'_i) \wedge (\bigwedge_j v_j : s_j) \wedge (\bigwedge_l w_l \longrightarrow w'_l)$$

Furthermore, the theory may also specify an additional mapping $\phi : \Sigma \longrightarrow \mathcal{P}(\mathbb{N})$, assigning to each function symbol $f \in \Sigma$ (with, say, n arguments) a set $\phi(f) = \{i_1, \ldots, i_k\}$, $1 \leq i_1 < \ldots < i_k \leq n$ of *frozen argument positions* under which it is forbidden to perform any rewrites. Rewrite theories in this more general sense are studied in detail in [10]; they are clearly more expressive than the simpler unconditional and unsorted version presented here. This more general notion is the one supported by the Maude language [17,18].

Intuitively, $\mathcal{R}$ specifies a *concurrent system*, whose states are elements of the initial algebra $T_{\Sigma/E}$ specified by (Σ, E), and whose *concurrent transitions* are specified by the rules R. The equations E may decompose as a union $E = E_0 \cup A$, where A is a (possibly empty) set of structural axioms (such as associativity, commutativity, and identity axioms). To give a flavor for how concurrent systems are axiomatized in rewriting logic, I discuss below a fault-tolerant communication protocol example specified as a Maude [17,18] module[2]

```
mod FT-CHANNEL is
protecting NAT .
sorts NatList Msg MsgSet Channel .
subsorts Nat < NatList .
subsorts Msg < MsgSet .
op nil : -> NatList .
op _;_ : NatList NatList -> NatList [assoc id: nil] .
op null : -> MsgSet .
op __ : MsgSet MsgSet -> MsgSet [assoc comm id: null] .
op [_,_]_[_,_] : NatList Nat MsgSet NatList Nat -> Channel .
op {_,_} : Nat Nat -> Msg .
op ack : Nat -> Msg .

vars N M I J K : Nat .
vars L P Q R : NatList .
var MSG : Msg .
var S : MsgSet .

rl [send] : [J ; L,N] S [P,M] => [J ; L,N] {J,N} S [P,M] .
rl [recv] : [J ; L,N] {J,K} S [P,M] =>
              if K == M then [J ; L,N] S ack(M) [P ; J,s(M)]
                      else [J ; L,N] S ack(K) [P,M] fi .
rl [ack-recv] : [J ; L,N] ack(K) S [P,M] =>
                  if K == N then [L,s(N)] S [P,M]
                          else [J ; L,N] S [P,M] fi .
rl [loss] : [L,N] MSG S [P,M] => [L,N] S [P,M] .
endm
```

This rewrite theory imports the natural numbers module NAT and has an order-sorted signature Σ specified by its sorts, subsorts, and operations. All its equations are *structural axioms* A, which in Maude are not specified explicitly as equations, but are instead declared as attributes of their corresponding operator: here the list concatenation operator `_;_` has been declared associative and

---

[2] The Maude syntax is so close to the corresponding mathematical notation for defining rewrite theories as to be almost self-explanatory. The general point to keep in mind is that each item: a sort, a subsort, an operation, an equation, a rule, etc., is declared with an obvious keyword: **sort**, **subsort**, **op**, **eq** (or **ceq** for conditional equations), **rl** (or **crl** for conditional rules), etc., with each declaration ended by a space and a period. Another important point is the use of "mix-fix" user-definable syntax, with the argument positions specified by underbars; for example: if_then_else_fi.

having `nil` as its identity element with the `assoc` and `id:` keywords. Similarly, the multiset union operator has been declared with empty syntax (juxtaposition) `__` and with associativity, commutativity (`comm`), and identity axioms, making `null` its identity element. The rules R are `send`, `recv`, `ack-recv`, and `loss`; they are applied *modulo* the structural axioms A, that is, we get the effect of rewriting in A-equivalence classes. This theory specifies a fault-tolerant communication protocol in a bidirectional faulty channel, where messages can be received out of order and can be lost. The sender is placed at the left of the channel and has a list of numbers to send and a counter. The receiver is placed at the right, with also a list of numbers to receive and another counter. The contents of the channel in the middle is a multiset of messages (since there can be several repeated copies of the same message). The protocol is *fault-tolerant*, in that it will work even when some messages are permuted or lost, provided the `recv` and `ack-recv` rules are applied in a *fair* way (for fairness in rewriting logic see [74]).

2.1 Rewriting Logic Deduction

Given $\mathcal{R} = (\Sigma, E, R)$, the sentences that $\mathcal{R}$ proves are rewrites of the form, $t \longrightarrow t'$, with $t, t' \in T_\Sigma(X)$, which are obtained by finite application of the following *rules of deduction*:

- **Reflexivity.** For each $t \in T_\Sigma(X)$, $\quad \dfrac{}{t \longrightarrow t}$

- **Equality.** $\dfrac{u \longrightarrow v \quad E \vdash u = u' \quad E \vdash v = v'}{u' \longrightarrow v'}$

- **Congruence.** For each $f : k_1 \ldots k_n \longrightarrow k$ in Σ, and $t_i, t'_i \in T_\Sigma(X)$, $1 \leq i \leq n$,

$$\frac{t_1 \longrightarrow t'_1 \quad \ldots \quad t_n \longrightarrow t'_n}{f(t_1, \ldots, t_n) \longrightarrow f(t'_1, \ldots, t'_n)}$$

- **Replacement.** For each substitution $\theta : X \longrightarrow T_\Sigma(X)$, and for each rule $r : t \longrightarrow t'$ in R, with, say, $vars(t) \cup vars(t') = \{x_1, \ldots, x_n\}$, and $\theta(x_l) = p_l$, $1 \leq l \leq n$, then

$$\frac{p_1 \longrightarrow p'_1 \quad \ldots \quad p_n \longrightarrow p'_n}{\theta(t) \longrightarrow \theta'(t')}$$

where for $1 \leq i \leq n$, $\theta'(x_i) = p'_i$, and for each $x \in X - \{x_1, \ldots, x_n\}$, $\theta'(x) = \theta(x)$.

- **Transitivity.**

$$\frac{t_1 \longrightarrow t_2 \quad t_2 \longrightarrow t_3}{t_1 \longrightarrow t_3}$$

We can visualize the above inference rules as follows:

Reflexivity

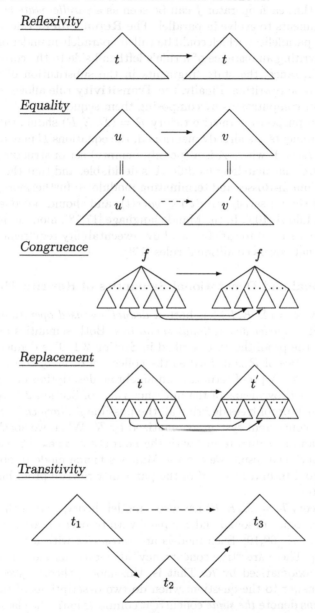

Equality

Congruence

Replacement

Transitivity

The notation $\mathcal{R} \vdash t \longrightarrow t'$ states that the sequent $t \longrightarrow t'$ is *provable* in the theory $\mathcal{R}$ using the above inference rules. Intuitively, we should think of the inference rules as different ways of *constructing* all the (finitary) *concurrent computations* of the concurrent system specified by $\mathcal{R}$. The **Reflexivity** rule says that for any state t there is an *idle transition* in which nothing changes. The **Equality** rule specifies that the states are in fact equivalence classes modulo the equations E. The **Congruence** rule is a very general form of "sideways parallelism," so that each operator f can be seen as a *parallel state constructor*, allowing its arguments to evolve in parallel. The **Replacement** rule supports a different form of parallelism, which could be called "parallelism under one's feet," since besides rewriting an instance of a rule's lefthand side to the corresponding righthand side instance, the state fragments in the substitution of the rule's variables can also be rewritten. Finally, the **Transitivity** rule allows us to build longer concurrent computations by composing them sequentially.

For execution purposes, a rewrite theory $\mathcal{R} = (\Sigma, E, R)$ should satisfy some additional requirements. As already mentioned, the equations E may decompose as a union $E = E_0 \cup A$, where A is a (possibly empty) set of structural axioms. We should require that matching modulo A is decidable, and that the equations E_0 are ground Church-Rosser and terminating modulo A; furthermore, the rules $r : t \longrightarrow t'$ in R should satisfy $vars(t') \subseteq vars(t)$, and should be coherent with respect to E modulo A [109]. In the Maude language [17,18], modules are rewrite theories that are assumed to satisfy the above executability requirements (in an extended form that covers conditional rules [17]).

2.2 Operational and Denotational Semantics of Rewrite Theories

A rewrite theory $\mathcal{R} = (\Sigma, E, R)$ has both a *deduction-based operational semantics*, and an *initial model denotational semantics*. Both semantics are defined naturally out of the proof theory described in Section 2.1. The deduction-based operational semantics of $\mathcal{R}$ is defined as the collection of *proof terms* [69,10] of the form $\alpha : t \longrightarrow t'$. A proof term α is an algebraic description of a proof tree proving $\mathcal{R} \vdash t \longrightarrow t'$ by means of the inference rules of Section 2.1. As already mentioned, all such proof trees describe all the possible *finitary concurrent computations* of the concurrent system axiomatized by $\mathcal{R}$. When we specify $\mathcal{R}$ as a Maude module and rewrite a term t with the `rewrite` or `frewrite` commands, obtaining a term t' as a result, we can use Maude's `trace` mode to obtain what amounts to a proof term $\alpha : t \longrightarrow t'$ of the particular rewrite proof built by the Maude interpreter.

A rewrite theory $\mathcal{R} = (\Sigma, E, R)$ has also a model theory, so that the inference rules of rewriting logic are sound and complete with respect to satisfaction in the class of models of $\mathcal{R}$ [69,10]. Such models are *categories* with a (Σ, E)-algebra structure [69,10]. These are "true concurrency" denotational models of the concurrent system axiomatized by $\mathcal{R}$. That is, this model theory gives a precise mathematical answer to the question: when do two descriptions of two concurrent computations denote *the same* concurrent computation? The class of models of a rewrite theory $\mathcal{R} = (\Sigma, E, R)$ has an *initial model* $\mathcal{T}_{\mathcal{R}}$ [69,10]. The initial model semantics is obtained as a *quotient* of the just-mentioned deduction-based operational semantics, precisely by axiomatizing algebraically when two proof terms $\alpha : t \longrightarrow t'$ and $\beta : u \longrightarrow u'$ denote the same concurrent computation. Of course, α and β should have identical beginning states and identical ending states. By the **Equality** rule this forces $E \vdash t = u$, and $E \vdash t' = u'$. That is, the objects of the category $\mathcal{T}_{\mathcal{R}}$ are E-equivalence classes $[t]$ of ground Σ-terms, which denote the states of our system. The arrows or morphisms in $\mathcal{T}_{\mathcal{R}}$ are *equivalence classes of proof terms*, so that $[\alpha] = [\beta]$ iff both proof terms denote the same concurrent computation according to the "true concurrency" axioms. Such axioms are very natural. They for example express that the **Transitivity** rule behaves as an arrow composition and is therefore associative. Similarly, the **Reflexivity** rules provides an identity arrow for each object, satisfying the usual identity laws.

As discussed in Section 4.1 of [67], rewriting logic is a very general *semantic framework* in which a wide range of concurrency models such as process calculi, Petri nets, distributed object systems, Actors, and so on, can be naturally axiomatized as specific rewrite theories. Furthermore, as also explained in Section 4.1 of [67], the algebraically-defined true concurrency models of rewriting logic include as special cases many other true concurrency models such as residual models of term rewriting, parallel λ-calculus models, process models for Petri nets, proved transition models for CCS, and partial order of events models for object systems and for Actors. Note, however, that a rewrite rule

$$r : t \longrightarrow t'$$

has *two complementary readings, one computational, and another logical.* Computationally, as already explained, it axiomatizes a parametric family of *concurrent transitions* in a system. Logically, however, it represents and *inference rule*[3] in a *logic*, whose inference system is axiomatized by $\mathcal{R}$. It turns out that, with this second reading, rewriting logic has very good properties as a *logical framework*, in which many other logics can be naturally represented, so that we can simulate deduction in a logic as rewriting deduction in its representation [66].

2.3 Reflection

Reflection is a very important property of rewriting logic [22,15,23,24]. Intuitively, a logic is reflective if it can represent its metalevel at the object level in a sound and coherent way. Specifically, rewriting logic can represent its own theories and their deductions by having a finitely presented rewrite theory $\mathcal{U}$ that is *universal*, in the sense that for any finitely presented rewrite theory $\mathcal{R}$ (including $\mathcal{U}$ itself) we have the following equivalence

$$\mathcal{R} \vdash t \rightarrow t' \quad \Leftrightarrow \quad \mathcal{U} \vdash \langle \overline{\mathcal{R}}, \overline{t} \rangle \rightarrow \langle \overline{\mathcal{R}}, \overline{t'} \rangle,$$

---

[3] The use of conditional rewrite rules is of course very important in this logical reading. Logically, we would denote a conditional rewrite rule

$$r : t \longrightarrow t' \text{ if } (\bigwedge_i u_i = u_i') \wedge (\bigwedge_j v_j : s_j) \wedge (\bigwedge_l w_l \longrightarrow w_l')$$

as an inference rule

$$\frac{(\bigwedge_i u_i = u_i') \wedge (\bigwedge_j v_j : s_j) \wedge (\bigwedge_l w_l \longrightarrow w_l')}{t \longrightarrow t'}$$

where $\overline{\mathcal{R}}$ and $\overline{t}$ are terms representing $\mathcal{R}$ and t as data elements of $\mathcal{U}$. Since $\mathcal{U}$ is representable in itself, we can achieve a "reflective tower" with an arbitrary number of levels of reflection [15,16].

Reflection is a very powerful property: it allows defining rewriting strategies by means of metalevel theories that extend $\mathcal{U}$ and guide the application of the rules in a given object-level theory $\mathcal{R}$ [15]; it is efficiently supported in the Maude implementation by means of *descent functions* [16]; it can be used to build a variety of theorem proving and theory transformation tools [15,19,20,25]; it can endow a rewriting logic language like Maude with powerful theory composition operations [40,35,37,42]; and it can be used to prove metalogical properties about families of theories in rewriting logic, and about other logics represented in the rewriting logic (meta-)logical framework [5,21,4].

2.4   Maude and Its Formal Tools

Rewrite theories can be executed in different languages such as CafeOBJ [53], and ELAN [7]. The most general support for the execution of rewrite theories is currently provided by the Maude language [17,18], in which rewrite theories with very general conditional rules, and whose underlying equational theories can be membership equational theories [71], can be specified and can be executed, provided they satisfy the already-mentioned requirements. Furthermore, Maude provides very efficient support for rewriting *modulo* any combination of associativity, commutativity, and identity axioms. Since an equational theory (Σ, E) can be regarded as a degenerate rewrite theory of the form $(\Sigma, E, \varnothing)$, equational logic is naturally a sublogic of rewriting logic. In Maude this sublogic is supported by *functional modules* [17], which are theories in membership equational logic.

Besides supporting efficient execution, typically in the order of several million rewrites per second, Maude also provides a range of formal tools and algorithms to analyze rewrite theories and verify their properties. A first very useful formal analysis feature is its *breadth-first search* command. Given an initial state of a system (a term), we can search for all reachable states matching a certain pattern and satisfying an equationally-defined semantic condition P. By making $P = \neg Q$, where Q is an invariant, we get in this way a *semi-decision procedure* for finding failures of invariant safety properties. Note that there is no finite-state assumption involved here: any executable rewrite theory can thus be analyzed. For systems where the set of states reachable from an initial state are finite, Maude also provides a linear time temporal logic (LTL) model checker. Maude's is an explicit-state LTL model checker, with performance comparable to that of the SPIN model checker [58] for the benchmarks that we have analyzed [45,46].

As already pointed out, *reflection* is a key feature of rewriting logic, and is efficiently supported in the Maude implementation through its META-LEVEL module. One important fruit of this is that it becomes quite easy to build new formal tools and to add them to the Maude environment. Indeed, such tools by their very nature manipulate and analyze rewrite theories. By reflection, a rewrite theory $\mathcal{R}$ becomes a *term* $\overline{\mathcal{R}}$ in the universal theory, which can be efficiently manipulated by the descent functions in the META-LEVEL module. As a consequence, Maude formal tools have a reflective design and are built in Maude as suitable extensions of the META-LEVEL module. They include the following:

- the Maude Church-Rosser Checker, and Knuth-Bendix and Coherence Completion tools [19,41,38,36]
- the Full Maude module composition tool [35,42]
- the Maude Predicate Abstraction tool [88]
- the Maude Inductive Theorem Prover (ITP) [15,19,25]
- the Real-Time Maude tool [82] (more on this in Section 3.2)
- the Maude Sufficient Completeness Checker (SCC) [57]
- the Maude Termination Tool (MTT) [39].

3   Some Research Directions

3.1   The Rewriting Logic Semantics Project

The fact that rewriting logic specifications provide an easy and expressive way to develop executable formal definitions of languages, which can then be subjected to different tool-supported formal analyses, is by now well established [107,8,108,103,98,73,105,14,91,106,51,49,59,9,75,76,13,12,50,26,93,3,99,27,77]. In fact, the just-mentioned papers by different authors are contributions to a collective ongoing research project which we call the *rewriting logic semantics project*. What makes this project promising is the combination of three interlocking facts:

1. that rewriting logic is a flexible and expressive *logical framework* that unifies denotational semantics[4] and SOS in a novel way, avoiding their respective limitations and allowing very succinct semantic definitions (see [77]);
2. that rewriting logic semantic definitions are *directly executable* in a rewriting logic language such as Maude [17], and can thus become quite efficient interpreters (see [76,77]) ; and
3. that *generic formal tools* such as the Maude LTL model checker [45], the Maude inductive theorem prover [19,25], and new tools under development such as a language-generic partial order reduction tool [50], allow us to amortize tool development cost across many programming languages, that can thus be endowed with powerful program analysis capabilities; furthermore, *genericity does not necessarily imply inefficiency*: in some cases the analyses so obtained outperform those of well-known language-specific tools [51,49].

For the most part, equational semantics and SOS have lived separate lives. Although each is very valuable in its own way, they are "single hammer" approaches and have some limitations [77]. Would it be possible to seamlessly

---

[4] I use in what follows the broader term *equational semantics* —that is, semantics based on *semantic equations*— to emphasize the fact that higher-order denotational and first-order algebraic semantics have many common features and can both be viewed as instances of a common equational semantics framework.

unify them within a more flexible and general framework? Could their respective limitations be overcome when they are thus unified? Rewriting logic does indeed provide one such unifying framework. The key to this, indeed very simple, unification is what Grigore Roșșu and I call rewriting logic's *abstraction knob*. The point is that in equational semantics' model-theoretic approach entities are *identified by the semantic equations*, and have unique *abstract denotations* in the corresponding models. In our knob metaphor this means that in equational semantics the abstraction knob is *always turned all the way up to its maximum position*. By contrast, one of the key features of SOS is providing a very detailed, step-by-step formal description of a language's evaluation mechanisms. As a consequence, most entities —except perhaps for built-in data, stores, and environments, which are typically treated on the side— are *primarily syntactic*, and computations are described in full detail. In our metaphor this means that in SOS the abstraction knob is *always turned down to its minimum position*.

How is the unification and corresponding availability of an abstraction knob achieved? Since a rewrite theory (Σ, E, R) has an underlying equational theory (Σ, E) with Σ a signature of operations and sorts, and E a set of (possibly conditional) equations, and with R a set of (possibly conditional) rewrite rules, equational semantics is then obtained as the special case in which $R = \varnothing$, so we only have the semantic equations E and the abstraction knob is turned up to its maximum position. Roughly speaking,[5] SOS is then obtained as the special case in which $E = \varnothing$, and we only have (possibly conditional) rules R rewriting purely syntactic entities (terms), so that the abstraction knob is turned down to the minimum position.

Rewriting logic's "abstraction knob" is precisely its crucial distinction between equations E and rules R in a rewrite theory (Σ, E, R). *States of the computation* are then E-equivalence classes, that is, *abstract elements* in the initial algebra $T_{\Sigma/E}$. Because of rewriting logic's **Equality** inference rule (see Section 2.1) a rewrite with a rule in R is understood as a transition $[t] \longrightarrow [t']$ between such abstract states. The knob, however, can be turned up or down. We can turn it *all the way down to its minimum* by converting all equations into rules, transforming (Σ, E, R) into $(\Sigma, \varnothing, R \cup E)$. This gives us the most concrete, SOS-like semantic description possible. Instead, to make a specification *as abstract as possible* we can identify a subset $R_0 \subseteq R$ such that: (1) $R_0 \cup E$ is Church-Rosser; and (2) R_0 is biggest possible with this property. In actual language specification practice this is not hard to do. Essentially, we can use semantic equations for most of the sequential features of a programming language: only when interactions with memory could lead to nondeterminism (particularly if the language has threads, or they could later be added to the language in an extension) or for intrinsically concurrent features are rules (as opposed to

---

[5] I gloss over the technical difference that in SOS all computations are "one-step" computations, even if the step is a big one, whereas in rewriting logic, because of its built-in **Transitivity** inference rule (see Section 2.1) the rewriting relation is always transitive. For a more detailed comparison see [76].

equations) really needed. In this way, we can obtain drastic search space reductions, making formal analyses much more scalable than if we used only rules.

Many languages have already been given semantics in this way using Maude. The language definitions can then be used as interpreters, and —in conjunction with Maude's search command and its LTL model checker— to formally analyze programs in those languages. For example, large fragments of Java and the JVM have been specified in Maude this way, with the Maude rewriting logic semantics being used as the basis of Java and JVM program analysis tools that for some examples outperform well-known Java analysis tools [51,49]. A similar Maude specification of the semantics of Scheme at UIUC yields an interpreter with .75 the speed of the standard Scheme interpreter on average for the benchmarks tested. The specification of a C-like language and the corresponding formal analyses are discussed in detail in [77]. A semantics of a Caml-like language with threads was discussed in detail in [76], and a modular rewriting logic semantics of CML has been given by Chalub and Braga in [13]. d'Amorim and Roşu have given a definition of the Scheme language in [27]. Other language case studies, all specified in Maude, include: bc [9], CCS [107,108,9], CIAO [99], Creol [59], ELOTOS [105], MSR [11,97], PLAN [98,99], and the pi-calculus [103]. In fact, the semantics of large fragments of conventional languages are by now routinely developed by UIUC graduate students as course projects in a few weeks, including, besides the languages already mentioned: Beta, Haskell, Lisp, LLVM, Pict, Python, Ruby, and Smalltalk.

Besides search and model checking analyses, it is also possible to use a language's semantic definition to perform semantics-based deduction analyses either on programs in that language, or even about the correctness of a given logic of programs with respect to the language's rewriting semantics. Work in this direction includes [93,3,26,108,105].

Modularity of semantic definitions, that is, the property that a feature's semantics does not have to be redefined when a language is extended, is notoriously hard to achieve. To solve this problem for SOS, Peter Mosses has proposed the *modular structural operational semantics* (MSOS) methodology [80]. This inspired C. Braga and me to develop a similar modular methodology for rewriting logic semantics [75,9]. This has had the pleasant side-effect of providing a Maude-based execution environment for MSOS specifications, namely the Maude MSOS Tool developed at the Universidade Federal Fluminense in Brazil by F. Chalub and C. Braga [12], which is available on the web at http://mmt.ic.uff.br/.

3.2   Real-Time Rewrite Theories and Real-Time Maude

In many reactive and distributed systems, real-time properties are essential to their design and correctness. Therefore, the question of how systems with real-time features can be best specified, analyzed, and proved correct in the semantic framework of rewriting logic is an important one. This question has been investigated by several authors from two perspectives. On the one hand, an extension of rewriting logic called *timed rewriting logic* has been investigated, and has been applied to some examples and specification languages [62,84,96]. On the other hand, Peter Ölvecky and I have found a simple way to express real-time and hybrid system specifications *directly* in rewriting logic [85,87]. Such specifications are called *real-time rewrite theories* and have rules of the form

$$\{t\} \xrightarrow{r} \{t'\} \ if \ C$$

with r a term denoting the *duration* of the transition (where the time can be chosen to be either discrete or continuous), $\{t\}$ representing the *whole* state of a system, and C an equational condition. Peter Ölvecky and I have shown that, by making the clock an explicit part of the state, these theories can be *desugared* into semantically equivalent ordinary rewrite theories [85,87,82]. That is, in the desugared version we can model the state of a real-time or hybrid system as a pair (t, r), with t the current state, and with r the current global clock time. Rewrite rules can then be either *instantaneous rules*, that take no time and only change some part of the state t, or *tick rules*, that advance the global time of the system according to some time expression r and may also change the state t. By characterizing equationally the enabledness of each rule and using conditional rules and *frozen* operators [10], it is always possible to define tick rules so that instantaneous rules are always given higher priority; that is, so that a tick rule can never fire when an instantaneous rule is enabled [82]. When time is continuous, tick rules may be *nondeterministic*, in the sense that the time r advanced by the rule is not uniquely determined, but is instead a parametric expression (however, this time parameter is typically subjected to some equational condition C). In such cases, tick rules need a *time sampling strategy* to choose suitable values for time advance. Besides being able to show that a wide range of known real-time models, (including, for example, timed automata, hybrid automata, timed Petri nets, and timed object-oriented systems) and of discrete or dense time values, can be naturally expressed in a direct way in rewriting logic (see [87]), an important advantage of our approach is that one can use an existing implementation of rewriting logic to execute and analyze real-time specifications. Because of some technical subtleties, this seems difficult for the alternative of timed rewriting logic, although a mapping into our framework does exist [87].

Real-Time Maude [83,86,82], is a specification language and a formal tool built in Maude by reflection. It provides special syntax to specify real-time systems, and offers a range of formal analysis capabilities. The Real-Time Maude 2.0 tool [82] systematically exploits the underlying Maude efficient rewriting, search, and LTL model checking capabilities to both execute and formally analyze real-time specifications. Reflection is crucially exploited in the Real-Time Maude 2.0 implementation. On the one hand Real-Time Maude specifications are internally desugared into ordinary Maude specifications by transforming their meta-representations. On the other, reflection is also used for execution and analysis purposes. The point is that the desired modes of execution and formal properties to be analyzed have real-time aspects with no clear counterpart at the Maude level. To faithfully support these real-time aspects a *reflective transformational approach* is adopted: the original real-time theory and query (for either execution or analysis) are simultaneously transformed into a semantically equivalent pair of a Maude rewrite theory and a Maude query [82]. In practice, this makes those executions and analyses quite efficient and allows scaling up to highly nontrivial specifications and case studies.

In fact, both the naturalness of Real-Time Maude to specify large nontrivial real-time applications (particularly for distributed object-oriented real-time systems) and its effectiveness in simulating and analyzing the formal properties of such systems have been demonstrated in a number of substantial case studies, including the specification and analysis of advanced scheduling algorithms and of: (1) the AER/NCA suite of active network protocols [83,81]; (2) the NORM multicast protocol [65]; and (3) the OGDC wireless sensor network algorithm [104]. The Real-Time Maude tool is a mature and quite efficient tool freely available (with source code, a tool manual, examples, case studies, and papers) from http://www.ifi.uio.no/RealTimeMaude.

3.3 Probabilistic Rewrite Theories and PMaude

Many systems are probabilistic in nature. This can be due either to the uncertainty of the environment in which they must operate, such as message losses and other failures in an unreliable environment, or to the probabilistic nature of some of their algorithms, or to both. In general, particularly for distributed systems, both probabilistic and nondeterministic aspects may coexist, in the sense that different transitions may take place nondeterministically, but the outcomes of some of those transitions may be probabilistic in nature. To specify systems of this kind, rewrite theories have been generalized to *probabilistic rewrite theories* in [63,64,2]. Rules in such theories are *probabilistic rewrite rules* of the form

$$l : t(\boldsymbol{x}) \to t'(\boldsymbol{x}, \boldsymbol{y}) \ \ if \ \ cond(\boldsymbol{x}) \ \ with \ probability \ \ \boldsymbol{y} := \pi_r(\boldsymbol{x})$$

where the first thing to observe is that the term t' has new variables $\boldsymbol{y}$ disjoint from the variables $\boldsymbol{x}$ appearing in t. Therefore, such a rule is *nondeterministic*; that is, the fact that we have a matching substitution θ such that $\theta(cond)$ holds does not uniquely determine the next state fragment: there can be many different choices for the next state, depending on how we instantiate the extra variables $\boldsymbol{y}$ in t'. In fact, we can denote the different such next states by expressions of the form $t'(\theta(\boldsymbol{x}), \rho(\boldsymbol{y}))$, where θ is fixed as the given matching substitution, but ρ ranges along all the possible substitutions for the new variables $\boldsymbol{y}$. The probabilistic nature of the rule is expressed by the notation: *with probability* $\boldsymbol{y} := \pi_r(\boldsymbol{x})$, where $\pi_r(\boldsymbol{x})$ is a probability distribution *which may depend on the matching substitution* θ. We then choose the values for $\boldsymbol{y}$, that is, the substitution ρ, probabilistically according to the distribution $\pi_r(\theta(\boldsymbol{x}))$.

The fact that the probability distribution may depend on the substitution θ can be illustrated by means of a simple example. Consider a battery-operated clock. We may represent the state of the clock as a term clock(T,C), with T a natural number denoting the time, and C a positive real denoting the amount of battery charge. Each time the clock ticks, the time is increased by one unit, and the battery charge slightly decreases; however, the lower the battery charge, the greater the chance that the clock will stop, going into a state of the form broken(T,C'). We can model this system by means of the probabilistic rewrite rule

```
rl [tick]: clock(T,C) => if B then clock(s(T),C - (C / 1000))
                         else broken(T,C (C / 1000))
                  fi
      with probability B := BERNOULLI(C / 1000) .
```

that is, the probability of the clock breaking down instead of ticking normally *depends on the battery charge*, which is here represented by the battery-dependent bias of the coin in a Bernoulli trial. Note that here the new variable on the rule's righthand side is the Boolean variable B, corresponding to the result of tossing the biased coin. As shown in [63], probabilistic rewrite theories can express a wide range of models of probabilistic systems, including continuous-time Markov chains [100], probabilistic non-deterministic systems [90,94], and generalized semi-Markov processes [54]; they can also naturally express probabilistic object-based distributed systems [64,2], including real-time ones.

The PMaude language [64,2] is an experimental specification language whose modules are probabilistic rewrite theories. Note that, due to their nondeterminism, probabilistic rewrite rules *are not directly executable*. However, probabilistic systems specified in PMaude *can be simulated in Maude*. This is accomplished by transforming a PMaude specification into a corresponding Maude specification in which actual values for the new variables appearing in the righthand side of a probabilistic rewrite rule are obtained by *sampling* the corresponding probability distribution functions. This theory transformation uses three key Maude modules as basic infrastructure, namely, COUNTER, RANDOM, and SAMPLER. The built-in module COUNTER provides a built-in strategy for the application of the nondeterministic rewrite rule

```
rl counter => N:Nat .
```

that rewrites the constant counter to a natural number. The built-in strategy applies this rule so that the natural number obtained after applying the rule is exactly the successor of the value obtained in the preceding rule application. The RANDOM module is a built-in Maude module providing a (pseudo-)random number generator function called random. The SAMPLER module supports sampling for different probability distributions. It has a rule

```
rl [rnd] : rand => float(random(counter + 1) / 4294967296) .
```

which rewrites the constant rand to a floating point number between 0 and 1 pseudo-randomly chosen according to the uniform distribution. This floating point number is obtained by converting the rational number random(counter + 1) / 4294967296 into a floating point number, where 4294967296 is the maximum value that the random function can attain. SAMPLER has rewrite rules supporting sampling according to different probability distributions; this is based on first sampling a floating point number between 0 and 1 pseudo-randomly chosen according to the uniform distribution by means of the above rnd rule.

For example, to sample the Bernoulli distribution we use the following operator and rewrite rule in SAMPLER:

```
op BERNOULLI : Float -> Bool .
rl BERNOULLI(R) => if rand < R then true else false fi .
```

that is, to sample a result of tossing a coin with bias R, we first sample the uniform distribution. If the sampled value is strictly smaller than R, then the answer is true; otherwise the answer is false. Any discrete probability distribution on a finite set can be sampled in a similar way. The ordinary Maude specification that *simulates* the PMaude specification for a clock with the above tick probabilistic rewrite rule imports COUNTER, RANDOM, and SAMPLER, and has then a corresponding Maude rewrite rule

```
rl [tick] : clock(T,C) => if BERNOULLI(C / 1000.0)
                  then clock(s(T),C - (C / 1000.0))
                  else broken(T,C - (C / 1000.0))
              fi .
```

For a continuous probability distribution π with differentiable density function d_π, and with cumulative distribution function $F_\pi(x) = \int_{-\infty}^{x} d_\pi(y)dy$, we can use the well-known fact (see for example [89], Thm 8A, pg. 314) that if U is a random variable uniformly distributed on $[0,1]$, then $F_\pi^{-1}(U)$ is a random variable with probability distribution π, to sample elements according to the distribution π by means of a rewrite rule

$$sample_\pi \longrightarrow F_\pi^{-1}(\mathtt{random})$$

Of course, π may not be a fixed probability distribution, but a *parametric family* $\pi(p)$ of distributions depending on some parameters p, so that the above rule will then have extra variables for those parameters.

In general, provided that sampling for the probability distributions used in a PMaude module are supported in the underlying SAMPLER module, we can associate to it a corresponding Maude module. We can then use this associated Maude module to perform Monte Carlo simulations of the probabilistic systems thus specified. As explained in [2], provided all nondeterminism has been eliminated from the original PMaude module[6], we can then use the results of such Monte Carlo simulations to perform a *statistical model checking analysis* of the

---

[6] The point is that, as explained above, in general, given a probabilistic rewrite theory and a term t describing a given state, there can be several different rewrites, perhaps with different rules, at different positions, and with different matching substitutions, that can be applied to t. Therefore, the choice of rule, position, and substitution is *nondeterministic*. To eliminate all nondeterminism, at most one rule at exactly one position and with a unique substitution should be applicable to any term t. As explained in [2], for many systems, including probabilistic real-time object-oriented systems, this can be naturally achieved, essentially by scheduling events at real-valued times that are all different, because we sample a continuous probability distribution on the real numbers.

given system to verify certain properties. For example, for a PMaude specification of a TCP/IP protocol variant that is resistant to Denial of Service (DoS) attacks, we may wish to establish that, even if an attacker controls 90% of the network bandwith, it is still possible for the protocol to establish a connection in less than 30 seconds with 99% probability. Properties of this kind, including properties that measure quantitative aspects of a system, can be expressed in the QATEX probabilistic temporal logic, [2], and can be model checked using the VeStA tool [95]. See [1] for a substantial case study specifying a DoS-resistant TCP/IP protocol as a PMaude module, performing Monte Carlo simulations by means of its associated Maude module, and formally analyzing in VeStA its properties, expressed as QATEX specifications, according to the methodology just described.

3.4   Security Applications and Narrowing

Security is a concern of great practical importance for many systems, making it worthwhile to subject system designs and implementations to rigorous formal analysis. Security, however, is *many-faceted*: on the one hand, we are concerned with properties such as *secrecy*: malicious attackers should not be able to get secret information; on the other, we are also concerned with properties such as *availability*, which may be destroyed by a (DoS) attack: a highly reliable communication protocol ensuring secrecy may be rendered useless because it spends all its time checking spurious signatures generated by a DoS attacker. Rewriting logic has been successfully applied to analyze security properties, including both secrecy and availability, for a wide range of systems. More generally, using distributed object-oriented reflection techniques [28,78], it is possible to analyze *tradeoffs* between different security properties, and between them and other system properties; and it is possible to develop system composition and adaptation techniques allowing systems to behave adequately in changing environments.

Work in this general area includes: (1) work of Denker, Meseguer, and Talcott on the specification and analysis of cryptographic protocols using Maude [29,30] (see also [92]); (2) work of Basin and Denker on an experimental comparison of the advantages and disadvantages of using Maude versus using Haskell to analyze security protocols [6]; (3) work of Millen and Denker at SRI using Maude to give a formal semantics to their new cryptographic protocol specification language CAPSL, and to endow CAPSL with an execution and formal analysis environment [31,32,33,34]; (4) work of Gutierrez-Nolasco, Venkatasubramanian, Stehr, and Talcott on the Secure Spread protocol [56]; (5) work of Gunter, Goodloe, and Stehr on the formal specification and analysis of the L3A security protocol [55]; (6) work of Cervesato, Stehr, and Reich on the rewriting logic semantics of the MSR security specification formalism, leading to the first executable environment for MSR [11,97]; and (7) the already-mentioned work by Agha, Gunter, Greenwald, Khanna, Meseguer, Sen, and Thati on the specification and analysis of a DoS-resistant TCP/IP protocol using probabilistic rewrite theories [1].

A related technique with important security applications is *narrowing*, a symbolic procedure like rewriting, except that rules, instead of being applied by matching a subterm, are applied by unifying the lefthand side with a nonvariable subterm. Traditionally, narrowing has been used as a method to solve equations in a confluent and terminating equational theory. In rewriting logic, narrowing has been generalized by Meseguer and Thati to a semi-decision procedure for *symbolic reachability analysis* [79]. That is, instead of solving equational goals $\exists \boldsymbol{x}.\ t = t'$, we solve reachability goals $\exists \boldsymbol{x}.\ t \longrightarrow t'$. The relevant point for security applications is that, since narrowing with a rewrite theory $\mathcal{R} = (\Sigma, E, R)$ is performed *modulo* the equations E, this allows more sophisticated analyses than those performed under the usual Dolev-Yao "perfect cryptography assumption". It is well-known that protocols that had been proved secure under this assumption can be broken if an attacker uses knowledge of the algebraic properties satisfied by the underlying cryptographic functions. In rewriting logic we can specify a cryptographic protocol as a rewrite theory $\mathcal{R} = (\Sigma, E, R)$, and can model those algebraic properties as equations in E. Under suitable assumptions that are typically satisfied by cryptographic protocols, narrowing then gives us a complete semidecision procedure to find attacks *modulo* the equations E; therefore, any attack making use algebraic properties can be found this way [79]. Very recent work in this direction by Escobar, Meadows and Meseguer [47] is using rewriting logic and narrowing to give a precise rewriting semantics to the inference system of one of the most effective analysis tools for cryptographic protocols, namely the NRL Analyzer [68]. Further recent work on narrowing with rewrite theories focuses on: (1) generalizing the procedure to so-called "back-and-forth narrowing," so as to ensure completeness under very general assumptions about the rewrite theory $\mathcal{R}$ [102]; and (2) efficient lazy strategies to restrict as much as possible the narrowing search space [48].

3.5   Bioinformatics Modeling and Analysis

Biology lacks at present adequate mathematical models that can provide something analogous to the analytic and predictive power that mathematical models provide for, say, Physics. Of course, the mathematical models of Chemistry describing, say, molecular structures are still applicable to biochemistry. The problem is that they *do not scale up* to something like a cell, because they are too low-level. One can of course model biological phenomena at different *levels of abstraction*. Higher, more abstract levels seem both the most crucial and the least supported. The most abstract the level, the better the chances to scale up.

All this is analogous to the use of different levels of abstraction to model digital systems. There are great scaling up advantages in treating digital systems and computer designs at a *discrete* level of abstraction, above the continuous level provided by differential equations, or, even lower, the quantum electrodynamics (QED) level. The discrete models, when they can be had, can also be more *robust and predictable*: there is greater difficulty in predicting the behavior of a system that can only be modeled at lower levels. Indeed, the level at which biologists like to reason about cell behavior is typically the discrete level; however, at present descriptions at this level consist of semi-formal notations for the elementary reactions, together with informal and potentially ambiguous notations for things like pathways, cycles, feedback, etc. Furthermore, such notations are static and therefore offer little predictive power. What are needed are *new computable mathematical models of cell biology* that are at a high enough level of abstraction so that they fit biologist's intuitions, make those intuitions mathematically precise, and provide biologists with the *predictive power* of mathematical models, so that the consequences of their hypotheses and theories can be analyzed, and can then suggest laboratory experiments to prove them or disprove them.

Rewriting logic seems ideally suited for this task. The basic idea is that we can *model a cell as a concurrent system* whose concurrent transitions are precisely its biochemical reactions. In fact, the chemical notation for a reaction like $A\,B \longrightarrow C\,D$ is *exactly* a rewriting notation. In this way we can develop *symbolic bioinformatic models* which we can then analyze in their dynamic behavior just as we would analyze any other rewrite theory.

Implicit in the view of modeling a cell as a rewrite theory (Σ, E, R) is the idea of modeling the cell states as elements of an algebraic data type specified by (Σ, E). This can of course be done at different levels of abstraction. We can for example introduce basic sorts such as `AminoAcid`, `Protein`, and `DNA` and declare the most basic building blocks as constants of the appropriate sort. For example,

```
ops T U Y S K P : -> AminoAcid .
ops 14-3-3 cdc37 GTP Hsp90 Raf1 Ras : -> Protein .
```

But sometimes a protein is *modified*, for example by one of its component amino acids being phosphorylated at a particular *site* in its structure. Consider for example the c-Raf protein, denoted above by `Raf1`. Two of its S amino acid components can be phosphorilated at sites, say, 259 and 261. We then obtain a modified protein that we denote by the symbolic expression,

```
[Raf1 \ phos(S 259) phos(S 621)]
```

A fragment, relevant for this example, of the signature Σ needed to symbolically express and analyze such modified proteins is given by the following sorts, subsorts, and operators:

```
sorts Site Modification ModSet .
subsort Modification < ModSet .

op phos : Site -> Modification .
op none : -> ModSet .
op __ : ModSet ModSet -> ModSet [assoc comm id: none] .
op __ : AminoAcid MachineInt -> Site .
op [_\_] : Protein ModSet -> Protein [right id: none] .
```

Proteins can stick together to form *complexes*. This can be modeled by the following subsort and operator declarations

```
sort Complex .
subsort Protein < Complex .
op _:_ : Complex Complex -> Complex [comm] .
```

In the cell, proteins and other molecules exist in "soups," such as the cytosol, or the soups of proteins inside the cell and nucleus membranes, or the soup inside the nucleus. All these soups, as well as the "structured soups" making up the different structures of the cell, can be modeled by the following fragment of sort, subsort, and operator declarations,

```
sort Soup .
subsort Complex < Soup .
op __ : Soup Soup -> Soup [assoc comm] .
op cell{_{_}} : Soup Soup -> Soup .
op nucl{_{_}} : Soup Soup -> Soup .
```

that is, soups are made up out of complexes, including individual proteins, by means of the above binary "soup union" operator (with juxtaposition syntax) that combines two soups into a bigger soup. This union operator models the fluid nature of soups by obeying *associative and commutative* laws. A *cell* is then a *structured soup*, composed by the above cell operator out of two subsoups, namely the soup in the membrane, and that inside the membrane; but this second soup is itself also structured by the cytoplasm and the nucleus. Finally, the nucleus itself is made up of two soups, namely that in the nucleus membrane, and that inside the nucleus, which are composed using the above nucl operator. Then, the following expression gives a partial description of a cell:

```
cell{cm  (Ras : GTP) {cyto
       (([Raf1 \ phos(S 259)phos(S 621)] : (cdc37 : Hsp90)) : 14-3-3)
                                               nucl{nm{n}}}}
```

where cm denotes the rest of the soup in the cell membrane, cyto denotes the rest of the soup in the cytoplasm, and nm and n likewise denote the remaining soups in the nucleus membrane and inside the nucleus.

Once we have cell states defined as elements of an algebraic data type specified by (Σ, E), the only missing information has to do with cell *dynamics*, that is, with its biochemical reactions. They can be modeled by suitable rewrite rules R, giving us a full model (Σ, E, R). Consider, for example, the following reaction described in a survey by Kolch [61]:

> "Raf-1 resides in the cytosol, tied into an inactive state by the binding of a 14-3-3 dimer to phosphosterines-259 and -621. When activation ensues, Ras-GTP binding ... brings Raf-1 to the membrane."

We can model this reaction by the following rewrite rule:

```
rl[10]: {CM  (Ras : GTP) {CY
(([Raf1 \ phos(S 259)phos(S 621)] : (cdc37 : Hsp90)) : 14-3-3) }}
=>
{CM ((Ras : GTP) :
(([Raf1 \ phos(S 259)phos(S 621)] : (cdc37 : Hsp90)) : 14-3-3))
                                               {CY}} .
```

where CM and CY are variables of sort Soup, representing, respectively, the rest of the soup in the cell membrane, and the rest of the soup inside the cell (including the nucleus). Note that in the new state of the cell represented by the righthand side of the rule, the complex has indeed migrated to the membrane.

Given a type of cell specified as a rewrite theory (Σ, E, R), rewriting logic then allows us to reason about the *complex changes* that are possible in the system, given the basic changes specified by R. That is, we can then use (Σ, E, R) together with Maude and its supporting formal tools to simulate, study, and analyze *cell dynamics*. In particular, we can study in this way *biological pathways*, that is, complex processes involving chains of biological reactions and leading to important cell changes. In particular we can:

- observe progress in time of the cell state by *symbolic simulation*, obtaining a corresponding trace;
- answer questions of *reachability* from a given cell state to another state satisfying some property; this can be done both *forwards* and *backwards*;
- answer more complex questions by *model checking* LTL properties; and
- do *meta-analysis* of proposed models of the cell to weed out spurious conjectures and to identify *consequences* of a given model that could be settled by *experimentation*.

Since the first research in this direction [43], on which the above summary is based, this line of research has been vigorously advanced, both in developing more sophisticated analyses of cell behavior in biological pathways, and in developing useful notations and visualization tools that can represent the Maude-based analyses in forms more familiar to biologists [44,101]. In particular, [101] contains a good discussion of related work in this area, using other formalisms, such as Petri nets or process calculi, that can also be understood as particular rewrite theories; and shows how cell behavior can be modeled with rewrite rules and can be analyzed *at different levels of abstraction*, and even across such levels. In fact, I view this research area as ripe for bringing in more advanced specification and analysis techniques —for example, techniques based on real-time and probabilistic rewrite theories as introduced in this paper— so as to develop a *range of complementary models* for cell biology. In this way, aspects such as the probabilistic nature of cell reactions, their dependence on the concentration of certain substances, and their real-time behavior could also be modeled, and even more sophisticated analyses could be developed.

4   Where to Go from Here?

This finishes the sampler. I have tried to give you a feeling for some of the main ideas of rewriting logic, some of its theoretical extensions to cover entire new areas, and some of its exciting application areas. I did not promise an overview: only an appetizer. If you would like to know more, I would recommend the roadmap in [67] for a good overview: it is a little dated by now, and there are many new references that nobody has yet managed to gather together, but this sampler puts the roadmap up to date in some areas; and reading both papers together is the best suggestion I can currently give for an introduction.

Acknowledgments. This research has been supported by ONR Grant N00014-02-1-0715 and NSF Grant CCR-0234524. I thank the ICTAC05 organizers for kindly giving me the opportunity of presenting these ideas. Many of them have been developed in joint work with students and colleagues; and many other ideas are not even my own work. Besides the credit given in each case through the references, I would like to point out that: (1) the recent work on foundations of rewriting logic is joint work with Roberto Bruni; (2) the work on Maude is joint work with all the members of the Maude team at SRI, UIUC, and the Universities of Madrid and Málaga; (3) the work on Maude tools is joint work with Manuel Clavel, Francisco Durán, Joseph Hendrix, Salvador Lucas, Claude Marché, Hitoshi Ohsaki, Peter Ölveczky, Miguel Palomino, and Xavier Urbain; (4) the work on the rewriting logic semantics project is a fairly wide collective effort, in which I have collaborated most closely with Feng Chen, Azadeh Farzan, and Grigore Roşu at UIUC, and with Christiano Braga at the Universidade Federal Fluminense in Brazil; (5) my part of the work on real-time rewrite theories is joint work with Peter Ölveczky at the University of Oslo; (6) the work on probabilistic rewrite theories is joint work with Gul Agha, Nirman Kumar, and Koushik Sen at UIUC; (7) security applications is again a wide effort in which I have collaborated most closely with Santiago Escobar, Grit Denker, Michael Greenwald, Carl Gunter, Sanjiv Khanna, Cathy Meadows, Koushik Sen, Carolyn Talcott, and Prasanna Thati; and (8) I was only involved in the early stages of the bioinformatics work, which has been continued by the Pathway Logic Team at SRI International.

References

1. G. Agha, C. Gunter, M. Greenwald, S. Khanna, J. Meseguer, K. Sen, and P. Thati. Formal modeling and analysis of DoS using probabilistic rewrite theories. In *Workshop on Foundations of Computer Security (FCS'05) (Affiliated with LICS'05)*, 2005.
2. G. Agha, J. Meseguer, and K. Sen. PMaude: Rewrite-based specification language for probabilistic object systems. In *3rd Workshop on Quantitative Aspects of Programming Languages (QAPL'05)*, 2005.
3. W. Ahrendt, A. Roth, and R. Sasse. Automatic validation of transformation rules for Java verification against a rewriting semantics. Manuscript, June 2005.
4. D. Basin, M. Clavel, and J. Meseguer. Reflective metalogical frameworks. *ACM Transactions on Computational Logic*, 2004.
5. D. Basin, M. Clavel, and J. Meseguer. Rewriting logic as a metalogical framework. In S. Kapoor and S. Prasad, editors, *Twentieth Conference on the Foundations of Software Technology and Theoretical Computer Science, New Delhi, India, December 13–15, 2000, Proceedings*, volume 1974 of *Lecture Notes in Computer Science*, pages 55–80. Springer-Verlag, 2000.

6. D. Basin and G. Denker. Maude versus Haskell: An experimental comparison in security protocol analysis. In Futatsugi [52], pages 235–256. http://www.elsevier.nl/locate/entcs/volume36.html.
7. P. Borovanský, C. Kirchner, H. Kirchner, and P.-E. Moreau. ELAN from a rewriting logic point of view. *Theoretical Computer Science*, 285:155–185, 2002.
8. C. Braga. *Rewriting Logic as a Semantic Framework for Modular Structural Operational Semantics*. PhD thesis, Departamento de Informática, Pontificia Universidade Católica de Rio de Janeiro, Brasil, 2001.
9. C. Braga and J. Meseguer. Modular rewriting semantics in practice. in Proc. *WRLA'04*, ENTCS.
10. R. Bruni and J. Meseguer. Generalized rewrite theories. In J. Baeten, J. Lenstra, J. Parrow, and G. Woeginger, editors, *Proceedings of ICALP 2003, 30th International Colloquium on Automata, Languages and Programming*, volume 2719 of *Springer LNCS*, pages 252–266, 2003.
11. I. Cervesato and M.-O. Stehr. Representing the msr cryptoprotocol specification language in an extension of rewriting logic with dependent types. In P. Degano, editor, *Proc. Fifth International Workshop on Rewriting Logic and its Applications (WRLA'2004)*. Elsevier ENTCS, 2004. Barcelona, Spain, March 27 - 28, 2004.
12. F. Chalub. An implementation of modular SOS in maude. Master's thesis, Universidade Federal Fluminense, May 2005. http://www.ic.uff.br/~frosario/dissertation.pdf.
13. F. Chalub and C. Braga. A Modular Rewriting Semantics for CML. *Journal of Universal Computer Science*, 10(7):789–807, July 2004. http://www.jucs.org/jucs_10_7/a_modular_rewriting_semantics.
14. F. Chen, G. Roşu, and R. P. Venkatesan. Rule-based analysis of dimensional safety. In *Rewriting Techniques and Applications (RTA'03)*, volume 2706 of *Springer LNCS*, pages 197–207, 2003.
15. M. Clavel. *Reflection in Rewriting Logic: Metalogical Foundations and Metaprogramming Applications*. CSLI Publications, 2000.
16. M. Clavel, F. Durán, S. Eker, P. Lincoln, N. Martí-Oliet, and J. Meseguer. Metalevel computation in Maude. In Kirchner and Kirchner [60], pages 3–24. http://www.elsevier.nl/locate/entcs/volume15.html.
17. M. Clavel, F. Durán, S. Eker, P. Lincoln, N. Martí-Oliet, J. Meseguer, and J. Quesada. Maude: specification and programming in rewriting logic. *Theoretical Computer Science*, 285:187–243, 2002.
18. M. Clavel, F. Durán, S. Eker, P. Lincoln, N. Martí-Oliet, J. Meseguer, and C. Talcott. Maude 2.0 Manual. June 2003, http://maude.cs.uiuc.edu.
19. M. Clavel, F. Durán, S. Eker, and J. Meseguer. Building equational proving tools by reflection in rewriting logic. In *CAFE: An Industrial-Strength Algebraic Formal Method*, pages 1–31. Elsevier, 2000. http://maude.cs.uiuc.edu.
20. M. Clavel, F. Durán, S. Eker, J. Meseguer, and M.-O. Stehr. Maude as a formal meta-tool. In J. M. Wing, J. Woodcock, and J. Davies, editors, *FM'99 — Formal Methods, World Congress on Formal Methods in the Development of Computing Systems, Toulouse, France, September 20–24, 1999 Proceedings, Volume II*, volume 1709 of *Lecture Notes in Computer Science*, pages 1684–1703. Springer-Verlag, 1999.
21. M. Clavel, F. Durán, and N. Martí-Oliet. Polytypic programming in Maude. In Futatsugi [52], pages 339–360. http://www.elsevier.nl/locate/entcs/volume36.html.

22. M. Clavel and J. Meseguer. Reflection and strategies in rewriting logic. In J. Meseguer, editor, *Proceedings First International Workshop on Rewriting Logic and its Applications, WRLA'96, Asilomar, California, September 3-6, 1996*, volume 4 of *Electronic Notes in Theoretical Computer Science*, pages 125-147. Elsevier, Sept. 1996. http://www.elsevier.nl/locate/entcs/volume4.html.

23. M. Clavel and J. Meseguer. Reflection in conditional rewriting logic. *Theoretical Computer Science*, 285:245-288, 2002.

24. M. Clavel, J. Meseguer, and M. Palomino. Reflection in membership equational logic, many-sorted equational logic, horn logic with equality, and rewriting logic. In F. Gadducci and U. Montanari, editors, *Proc. 4th. Intl. Workshop on Rewriting Logic and its Applications*. ENTCS, Elsevier, 2002.

25. M. Clavel and M. Palomino. The ITP tool's manual. Universidad Complutense, Madrid, April 2005, http://maude.sip.ucm.es/itp/.

26. M. Clavel and J. Santa-Cruz. ASIP+ITP: A verification tool based on algebraic semantics. To appear in *Proc. PROLE'05*, http://maude.sip.ucm.es/~clavel/pubs/.

27. M. d'Amorim and G. Roşu. An Equational Specification for the Scheme Language. In *Proceedings of the 9th Brazilian Symposium on Programming Languages (SBLP'05)*, to appear 2005. Also Technical Report No. UIUCDCS-R-2005-2567, April 2005.

28. G. Denker, J. Meseguer, and C. Talcott. Rewriting semantics of meta-objects and composable distributed services. ENTCS, Elsevier, 2000. Proc. 3rd. Intl. Workshop on Rewriting Logic and its Applications.

29. G. Denker, J. Meseguer, and C. L. Talcott. Protocol specification and analysis in Maude. In N. Heintze and J. Wing, editors, *Proceedings of Workshop on Formal Methods and Security Protocols, June 25, 1998, Indianapolis, Indiana*, 1998. http://www.cs.bell-labs.com/who/nch/fmsp/index.html.

30. G. Denker, J. Meseguer, and C. L. Talcott. Formal specification and analysis of active networks and communication protocols: The Maude experience. In D. Maughan, G. Koob, and S. Saydjari, editors, *Proceedings DARPA Information Survivability Conference and Exposition, DISCEX 2000, Hilton Head Island, South Carolina, January 25-27, 2000*, pages 251-265. IEEE Computer Society Press, 2000. http://schafercorp-ballston.com/discex/.

31. G. Denker and J. Millen. CAPSL and CIL language design: A common authentication protocol specification language and its intermediate language. Technical Report SRI-CSL-99-02, Computer Science Laboratory, SRI International, 1999. http://www.csl.sri.com/~denker/pub_99.html.

32. G. Denker and J. Millen. CAPSL intermediate language. In N. Heintze and E. Clarke, editors, *Proceedings of Workshop on Formal Methods and Security Protocols, FMSP'99, July 1999, Trento, Italy*, 1999. http://www.cs.bell-labs.com/who/nch/fmsp99/program.html.

33. G. Denker and J. Millen. CAPSL integrated protocol environment. In D. Maughan, G. Koob, and S. Saydjari, editors, *Proceedings DARPA Information Survivability Conference and Exposition, DISCEX 2000, Hilton Head Island, South Carolina, January 25-27, 2000*, pages 207-222. IEEE Computer Society Press, 2000. http://schafercorp-ballston.com/discex/.

34. G. Denker and J. Millen. The CAPSL integrated protocol environment. Technical Report SRI-CSL-2000-02, Computer Science Laboratory, SRI International, 2000. http://www.csl.sri.com/~denker/pub_99.html.

35. F. Durán. A reflective module algebra with applications to the Maude language. Ph.D. Thesis, University of Málaga, 1999.

36. F. Durán. Coherence checker and completion tools for Maude specifications. Manuscript, Computer Science Laboratory, SRI International, http://maude.cs.uiuc.edu/papers, 2000.

37. F. Durán. The extensibility of Maude's module algebra. In T. Rus, editor, *Algebraic Methodology and Software Technology, 8th International Conference, AMAST 2000, Iowa City, Iowa, USA, May 20–27, 2000, Proceedings*, volume 1816 of *Lecture Notes in Computer Science*, pages 422–437. Springer-Verlag, 2000.

38. F. Durán. Termination checker and Knuth-Bendix completion tools for Maude equational specifications. Manuscript, Computer Science Laboratory, SRI International, http://maude.cs.uiuc.edu/papers, 2000.

39. F. Durán, S. Lucas, J. Meseguer, C. Marché, and X. Urbain. Proving termination of membership equational programs. In P. Sestoft and N. Heintze, editors, *Proc. of ACM SIGPLAN 2004 Symposium on Partial Evaluation and Program Manipulation, PEPM'04*, pages 147–158. ACM Press, 2004.

40. F. Durán and J. Meseguer. An extensible module algebra for Maude. In Kirchner and Kirchner [60], pages 185–206. http://www.elsevier.nl/locate/entcs/volume15.html.

41. F. Durán and J. Meseguer. A Church-Rosser checker tool for Maude equational specifications. Manuscript, Computer Science Laboratory, SRI International, http://maude.cs.uiuc.edu/papers, 2000.

42. F. Durán and J. Meseguer. On parameterized theories and views in Full Maude 2.0. In K. Futatsugi, editor, *Proc. 3rd. Intl. Workshop on Rewriting Logic and its Applications*. ENTCS, Elsevier, 2000.

43. S. Eker, M. Knapp, K. Laderoute, P. Lincoln, J. Meseguer, and K. Sonmez. Pathway logic: Symbolic analysis of biological signaling. In *Proceedings of the Pacific Symposium on Biocomputing*, pages 400–412, January 2002.

44. S. Eker, M. Knapp, K. Laderoute, P. Lincoln, and C. Talcott. Pathway Logic: executable models of biological networks. In F. Gadducci and U. Montanari, editors, *Proc. 4th. Intl. Workshop on Rewriting Logic and its Applications*. ENTCS, Elsevier, 2002.

45. S. Eker, J. Meseguer, and A. Sridharanarayanan. The Maude LTL model checker. In F. Gadducci and U. Montanari, editors, *Proc. 4th. Intl. Workshop on Rewriting Logic and its Applications*. ENTCS, Elsevier, 2002.

46. S. Eker, J. Meseguer, and A. Sridharanarayanan. The Maude LTL model checker and its implementation. In *Model Checking Software: Proc. 10th Intl. SPIN Workshop*, volume 2648, pages 230–234. Springer LNCS, 2003.

47. S. Escobar, C. Meadows, and J. Meseguer. A rewriting-based inference system for the NRL Protocol Analyzer. Submitted for publication, 2005.

48. S. Escobar, J. Meseguer, and P. Thati. Natural narrowing for general term rewriting systems. In J. Giesl, editor, *Proceedings of the 16th Intl. Conference on Term Rewriting and Applications, RTA 2005*, pages 279–293. Springer LNCS Vol. 3467, 2005.

49. A. Farzan, F. Cheng, J. Meseguer, and G. Roşu. Formal analysis of Java programs in JavaFAN. in Proc. CAV'04, Springer LNCS, 2004.

50. A. Farzan and J. Meseguer. Partial order reduction for rewriting semantics of programming languages. Technical Report UIUCDCS-R-2005-2598, CS Dept., University of Illinois at Urbana-Champaign, June 2005.

51. A. Farzan, J. Meseguer, and G. Roşu. Formal JVM code analysis in JavaFAN. in Proc. *AMAST'04*, Springer LNCS 3116, 132–147, 2004.

52. K. Futatsugi, editor. *Proceedings Third International Workshop on Rewriting Logic and its Applications, WRLA 2000, Kanazawa, Japan, September 18–20, 2000*, volume 36 of *Electronic Notes in Theoretical Computer Science*. Elsevier, 2000. http://www.elsevier.nl/locate/entcs/volume36.html.

53. K. Futatsugi and R. Diaconescu. *CafeOBJ Report*. World Scientific, AMAST Series, 1998.

54. P. Glynn. The role of generalized semi-Markov processes in simulation output analysis, 1983.

55. C. Gunter, A. Goodloe, and M.-O. Stehr. Formal prototyping in early stages of protocol design. In *In* Proceedings of the Workshop on Issues in the Theory of Security (WITS'05). January 10-11, 2005, Long Beach, California. To appear in the ACM Digital Library. Paper available at http://formal.cs.uiuc.edu/stehr/l3a-wits.pdf.

56. S. Gutierrez-Nolasco, N. Venkatasubramanian, M.-O. Stehr, and C. L. Talcott. Exploring adaptability of secure group communication using formal prototyping techniques. In *Proceedings of the 3rd Workshop on Reflective and Adaptive Middleware (RM2004)*. October 19, 2004, Toronto, Ontario, Canada. To appear in ACM Digital Library. Extended version available at http://formal.cs.uiuc.edu/stehr/spread_eng.html.

57. J. Hendrix, J. Meseguer, and M. Clavel. A sufficient completeness reasoning tool for partial specifications. In J. Giesl, editor, *Proceedings of the 16th Intl. Conference on Term Rewriting and Applications, RTA 2005*, pages 165–174. Springer LNCS Vol. 3467, 2005.

58. G. Holzmann. *The Spin Model Checker - Primer and Reference Manual*. Addison-Wesley, 2003.

59. E. B. Johnsen, O. Owe, and E. W. Axelsen. A runtime environment for concurrent objects with asynchronous method calls. In N. Martí-Oliet, editor, *Proc. 5th. Intl. Workshop on Rewriting Logic and its Applications*. ENTCS, Elsevier, 2004.

60. C. Kirchner and H. Kirchner, editors. *Proceedings Second International Workshop on Rewriting Logic and its Applications, WRLA'98, Pont-à-Mousson, France, September 1-4, 1998*, volume 15 of *Electronic Notes in Theoretical Computer Science*. Elsevier, 1998. http://www.elsevier.nl/locate/entcs/volume15.html.

61. W. Kolch. Meaningful relationships: the regulation of the Ras/Raf/MEK/ERK pathway by protein interactions. *Biochem. J.*, 351:289–305, 2000.

62. P. Kosiuczenko and M. Wirsing. Timed rewriting logic with application to object-oriented specification. Technical report, Institut für Informatik, Universität München, 1995.

63. N. Kumar, K. Sen, J. Meseguer, and G. Agha. Probabilistic rewrite theories: Unifying models, logics and tools. Technical Report UIUCDCS-R-2003-2347, University of Illinois at Urbana-Champaign, May 2003.

64. N. Kumar, K. Sen, J. Meseguer, and G. Agha. A rewriting based model of probabilistic distributed object systems. Proc. of Formal Methods for Open Object-Based Distributed Systems, FMOODS 2003, Springer LNCS Vol. 2884, 2003.

65. E. Lien. Formal modeling and analysis of the NORM multicast protocol in Real-Time Maude. Master's thesis, Dept. of Linguistics, University of Oslo, 2004. http://wo.uio.no/as/WebObjects/theses.woa/wo/0.3.9.

66. N. Martí-Oliet and J. Meseguer. Rewriting logic as a logical and semantic framework. In D. Gabbay and F. Guenthner, editors, *Handbook of Philosophical Logic, 2nd. Edition*, pages 1–87. Kluwer Academic Publishers, 2002. First published as SRI Tech. Report SRI-CSL-93-05, August 1993.

67. N. Martí-Oliet and J. Meseguer. Rewriting logic: roadmap and bibliography. *Theoretical Computer Science*, 285:121–154, 2002.
68. C. Meadows. The NRL protocol analyzer: An overview. *Journal of Logic Programming*, 26(2):113–131, 1996.
69. J. Meseguer. Conditional rewriting logic as a unified model of concurrency. *Theoretical Computer Science*, 96(1):73–155, 1992.
70. J. Meseguer. Rewriting logic as a semantic framework for concurrency: a progress report. In *Proc. CONCUR'96, Pisa, August 1996*, pages 331–372. Springer LNCS 1119, 1996.
71. J. Meseguer. Membership algebra as a logical framework for equational specification. In F. Parisi-Presicce, editor, *Proc. WADT'97*, pages 18–61. Springer LNCS 1376, 1998.
72. J. Meseguer. Research directions in rewriting logic. In U. Berger and H. Schwichtenberg, editors, *Computational Logic, NATO Advanced Study Institute, Marktoberdorf, Germany, July 29 – August 6, 1997*. Springer-Verlag, 1999.
73. J. Meseguer. Software specification and verification in rewriting logic. In M. Broy and M. Pizka, editors, *Models, Algebras, and Logic of Engineering Software, NATO Advanced Study Institute, Marktoberdorf, Germany, July 30 – August 11, 2002*, pages 133–193. IOS Press, 2003.
74. J. Meseguer. Localized fairness: A rewriting semantics. In J. Giesl, editor, *Proceedings of the 16th Intl. Conference on Term Rewriting and Applications, RTA 2005*, pages 250–263. Springer LNCS Vol. 3467, 2005.
75. J. Meseguer and C. Braga. Modular rewriting semantics of programming languages. in Proc. AMAST'04, Springer LNCS 3116, 364–378, 2004.
76. J. Meseguer and G. Roşu. Rewriting logic semantics: From language specifications to formal analysis tools. In *Proc. Intl. Joint Conf. on Automated Reasoning IJCAR'04, Cork, Ireland, July 2004*, pages 1–44. Springer LNAI 3097, 2004.
77. J. Meseguer and G. Roşu. The rewriting logic semantics project. In *Proc. of SOS 2005*. Elsevier, ENTCS, 2005. To appear.
78. J. Meseguer and C. Talcott. Semantic models for distributed object reflection. In *Proceedings of ECOOP'02, Málaga, Spain, June 2002*, pages 1–36. Springer LNCS 2374, 2002.
79. J. Meseguer and P. Thati. Symbolic reachability analysis using narrowing and its application to the verification of cryptographic protocols. In N. Martí-Oliet, editor, *Proc. 5th. Intl. Workshop on Rewriting Logic and its Applications*. ENTCS, Elsevier, 2004.
80. P. D. Mosses. Modular structural operational semantics. *J. Log. Algebr. Program.*, 60–61:195–228, 2004.
81. P. Ölveczky, M. Keaton, J. Meseguer, C. Talcott, and S. Zabele. Specification and analysis of the AER/NCA active network protocol suite in Real-Time Maude. In *Proc. of FASE'01, 4th Intl. Conf. on Fundamental Approaches to Software Engineering*, Springer LNCS. Springer-Verlag, 2001.
82. P. Ölveczky and J. Meseguer. Real-Time Maude 2.0. in *Proc. WRLA'04*, ENTCS.
83. P. C. Ölveczky. *Specification and Analysis of Real-Time and Hybrid Systems in Rewriting Logic*. PhD thesis, University of Bergen, Norway, 2000. http://maude.csl.sri.com/papers.
84. P. C. Ölveczky, P. Kosiuczenko, and M. Wirsing. An object-oriented algebraic steam-boiler control specification. In J.-R. Abrial, E. Börger, and H. Langmaack, editors, *The Steam-Boiler Case Study Book*, pages 379–402. Springer-Verlag, 1996. Vol. 1165.

85. P. C. Ölveczky and J. Meseguer. Specifying real-time systems in rewriting logic. In J. Meseguer, editor, *Proc. First Intl. Workshop on Rewriting Logic and its Applications*, volume 4 of *Electronic Notes in Theoretical Computer Science*. Elsevier, 1996.
    http://www.elsevier.nl/cas/tree/store/tcs/free/noncas/pc/volume4.htm.
86. P. C. Ölveczky and J. Meseguer. Real-Time Maude: a tool for simulating and analyzing real-time and hybrid systems. ENTCS, Elsevier, 2000. Proc. 3rd. Intl. Workshop on Rewriting Logic and its Applications.
87. P. C. Ölveczky and J. Meseguer. Specification of real-time and hybrid systems in rewriting logic. *Theoretical Computer Science*, 285:359–405, 2002.
88. M. Palomino. A predicate abstraction tool for maude. Documentation and tool available at http://maude.sip.ucm.es/~miguelpt/bibliography.html.
89. E. Parzen. *Modern Probability Theory and its Applications*. Wiley, 1960.
90. M. Puterman. *Markov Decision Processes: Discrete Stochastic Dynamic Programming*. John Wiley and Sons, 1994.
91. G. Roşu, R. P. Venkatesan, J. Whittle, and L. Leustean. Certifying optimality of state estimation programs. In *Computer Aided Verification (CAV'03)*, pages 301–314. Springer, 2003. LNCS 2725.
92. D. E. Rodríguez. Case studies in the specification and analysis of protocols in Maude. In Futatsugi [52], pages 257–275.
    http://www.elsevier.nl/locate/entcs/volume36.html.
93. R. Sasse. Taclets vs. rewriting logic – relating semantics of Java. Master's thesis, Fakultät für Informatik, Universität Karlsruhe, Germany, May 2005. Technical Report in Computing Science No. 2005-16,
    http://www.ubka.uni-karlsruhe.de/cgi-bin/psview?document=ira/2005/16.
94. R. Segala. *Modelling and Verification of Randomized Distributed Real Time Systems*. PhD thesis, Massachusetts Institute of Technology, 1995.
95. K. Sen, M. Viswanathan, and G. Agha. On statistical model checking of stochastic systems. In *17th conference on Computer Aided Verification (CAV'05)*, volume 3576 of *Lecture Notes in Computer Science (To Appear)*, Edinburgh, Scotland, July 2005. Springer.
96. L. Steggles and P. Kosiuczenko. A timed rewriting logic semantics for SDL: a case study of the alternating bit protocol. *Proc. 2nd Intl. Workshop on Rewriting Logic and its Applications*, ENTCS, Vol. 15, North Holland, 1998.
97. M.-O. Stehr, I. Cervesato, and S. Reich. An execution environment for the MSR cryptoprotocol specification language.
    http://formal.cs.uiuc.edu/stehr/msr.html.
98. M.-O. Stehr and C. Talcott. PLAN in Maude: Specifying an active network programming language. In F. Gadducci and U. Montanari, editors, *Proc. 4th. Intl. Workshop on Rewriting Logic and its Applications*. ENTCS, Elsevier, 2002.
99. M.-O. Stehr and C. L. Talcott. Practical techniques for language design and prototyping. In J. L. Fiadeiro, U. Montanari, and M. Wirsing, editors, *Abstracts Collection of the Dagstuhl Seminar 05081 on Foundations of Global Computing. February 20 – 25, 2005. Schloss Dagstuhl, Wadern, Germany.*, 2005.
100. W. J. Stewart. *Introduction to the Numerical Solution of Markov Chains*. Princeton, 1994.
101. C. Talcott, S. Eker, M. Knapp, P. Lincoln, and K. Laderoute. Pathway logic modeling of protein functional domains in signal transduction. In *Proceedings of the Pacific Symposium on Biocomputing*, January 2004.
102. P. Thati and J. Meseguer. Complete symbolic reachability analysis using back-and-forth narrowing. To appear in *Proc. CALCO 2005*, Springer LNCS, 2005.

103. P. Thati, K. Sen, and N. Martí-Oliet. An executable specification of asynchronous Pi-Calculus semantics and may testing in Maude 2.0. In F. Gadducci and U. Montanari, editors, *Proc. 4th. Intl. Workshop on Rewriting Logic and its Applications.* ENTCS, Elsevier, 2002.
104. S. Thordvalsen. Modeling and analysis of the OGDC wireless sensor network algorithm in Real-Time Maude. Master's thesis, Dept. of Informatics, University of Oslo, 2005. http://heim.ifi.uio.no/~peterol/RealTimeMaude/OGDC/.
105. A. Verdejo. *Maude como marco semántico ejecutable.* PhD thesis, Facultad de Informática, Universidad Complutense, Madrid, Spain, 2003.
106. A. Verdejo and N. Martí-Oliet. Executable structural operational semantics in Maude. Manuscript, Dto. Sistemas Informáticos y Programación, Universidad Complutense, Madrid, August 2003.
107. A. Verdejo and N. Martí-Oliet. Implementing CCS in Maude. In *Proc. FORTE/PSTV 2000*, pages 351–366. IFIP, vol. 183, 2000.
108. A. Verdejo and N. Martí-Oliet. Implementing CCS in Maude 2. In F. Gadducci and U. Montanari, editors, *Proc. 4th. Intl. Workshop on Rewriting Logic and its Applications.* ENTCS, Elsevier, 2002.
109. P. Viry. Equational rules for rewriting logic. *Theoretical Computer Science,* 285:487–517, 2002.

Codes and Length-Increasing Transitive Binary Relations

Do Long Van[1], Kieu Van Hung[2], and Phan Trung Huy[3]

[1] Institute of Mathematics, 18 Hoang Quoc Viet Road, 10307 Hanoi, Vietnam
dlvan@math.ac.vn
[2] Hanoi Pedagogical University No.2, Xuan Hoa, Phuc Yen, Vinh Phuc, Vietnam
hungkv@hn.vnn.vn
[3] Hanoi Polytechnic University, 1 Dai Co Viet Street, Hanoi, Vietnam
phanhuy@hn.vnn.vn

Abstract. Classes of codes defined by binary relations are considered. It turns out that many classes of codes can be defined by length-increasing transitive binary relations. By introducing a general embedding schema we show that the embedding problem can be solved in a unified way for many classes of codes defined in such a way. Several among these classes of codes can be characterized by means of variants of Parikh vectors. This is very useful in constructing many-word concrete codes, maximal codes in corresponding classes of codes. Also, this allows to establish procedures to generate all maximall codes as well as algorithms to embed a code in a maximal one in some classes of codes.

Keywords: Code, binary relation, embedding problem, Parikh vector.

1 Introduction

Throughout the paper about codes we mean length-variable codes whose theory has been initiated by M. P. Shützenberger and then developed by many others. This theory has now become a part of theoretical computer science and of formal languages, in particular. A code is a language such that every text encoded by words of the language can be decoded in a unique way or, in other words, every coded message admits only one facterization into code-words. A simple application of Zorn's Lemma showed that every code is included in a maximal code. For thin codes, regular codes in particular, the maximality is equivalent to the completeness, which concerns with optimal use of transmission alphabet. Thus maximal codes are important in both theoretical and practical points of view. For background of the theory of codes we refer to [1,11,17].

Every regular code is included in a maximal code, which is still regular [4]. There exist however finite codes, which cannot be included in any finite maximal code [13,15]. These facts lead to a general question of whether, for a given class C of codes, every finite (regular) code in C can be included in a code maximal in C (not necessarily maximal as a code) which is still finite (regular, resp.). We call this the *embedding problem* for the class C of codes. Until now answer for the

D.V. Hung and M. Wirsing (Eds.): ICTAC 2005, LNCS 3722, pp. 29–48, 2005.

embedding problem is only known for several cases using different combinatorial techniques. For prefix codes the answer is positive for the finite case (folklore, see [1]). The embedding procedure is simple: given a finite prefix code X, it suffices to add the lacking leaves to the tree associated with X [1]. The regular case can be solved similarly by using deterministic finite automaton associated with X [2,16]. From a well-known result of M. P. Schützenberger (see [1]) it follows that it is impossible to embed a finite code with deciphering delay $d \neq 0$ into a maximal finite code with deciphering delay $d' \neq 0$. For the regular case, the embedding problem for these codes has been solved positively in [3]. There is finite bifix code, which cannot be included in any finite maximal bifix code [1] whereas every regular bifix code is included in a regular maximal bifix code [23]. This generalizes the construction in [14]. The finite case for infix codes is solved positively in [10] and later by another way in [12] together with the regular case, etc.

H. Shyr and G. Thierrin [18] were the first who observed that several classes of codes can be defined by binary relations on words (see also [17,9]). This idea comes from the notion of independent sets in universal algebra [5]. Our work is a further development of this idea. The paper is organized as follows. Section 2 presents some basic notions which will be used in the sequel. In Section 3 we show that many classes of codes, well-known as well as new, can be defined by length-increasing transitive binary relarions. In Section 4 we propose a general embedding schema for the classes of codes defined by length-increasing transitive binary relations (Theorem 1). Using this schema, positive solutions for the embedding problem are obtained in a unified way for many classes of codes, well-known as well as new. In Section 5 it is shown that Parikh vectors and their appropriate generalizations can be used to characterize several among introduced kinds of codes (namely, supercodes, superinfix codes, p-superinfix codes, s-superinfix codes and corresponding maximal codes). This is very usefull in constructing many-word concrete codes, maximal codes in corresponding classes of codes. Also, this allows to construct procedures to generate all maximal codes as well as algorithms to embed a code in a maximal one in some classes of codes.

2   Preliminaries

Let A throughout be a non-empty finite alphabet. Let A^* be the free monoid generated by A, that is the set of words over A. The empty word is denoted by 1 and $A^+ = A^* - 1$. The number of occurrences of letters in a word u is the *length* of u, denoted by $|u|$. Any set of words over A is a *language* over A. A language X is a *code* if for any $n, m \geq 1$ and any $x_1, \ldots, x_n, y_1, \ldots, y_m \in X$, the condition

$$x_1 x_2 \ldots x_n = y_1 y_2 \ldots y_m$$

implies $n = m$ and $x_i = y_i$ for $i = 1, \ldots, n$. A code X over A is *maximal* if X is not properly contained in any other code over A. Let C be a class of codes over A. A code $X \in C$ is *a maximal code in* C (not necessarily maximal as a code) if it is not properly contained in any other code in C.

Given a binary relation $\prec$ on A^*. A subset X in A^* is an *independent set* with respect to the relation $\prec$ if any two elements of X are not in this relation. A class C of codes is said to be *defined by* $\prec$ if these codes are exactly the independent sets w.r.t. $\prec$. The class C is then denoted by $C_\prec$. When the relation $\prec$ characterizes some property α of words, instead of $\prec$ we write $\prec_\alpha$, and also C_α stands for $C_{\prec_\alpha}$. We denote by $\preceq$ the reflexive closure of $\prec$, i.e. for any $u, v \in A^*, u \preceq v$ iff $u = v$ or $u \prec v$.

A word u is called an *infix* (a *prefix*, a *suffix*) of a word v if there exist words x, y such that $v = xuy$ ($v = uy$, $v = xu$, resp.). The infix (prefix, suffix) is *proper* if $xy \neq 1$ ($y \neq 1$, $x \neq 1$, resp.). A word u is a *subword* of a word v if, for some $n \geq 1, u = u_1 \ldots u_n, v = x_0 u_1 x_1 \ldots u_n x_n$ with $u_1, \ldots, u_n, x_0, \ldots, x_n \in A^*$. If $x_0 \ldots x_n \neq 1$ then u is called a *proper subword* of v.

Definition 1. *Let A be an alphabet and $X \subseteq A^+$.*

(i) X *is a prefix code (suffix code) if no word in X is a proper prefix (proper suffix, resp.) of another word in X;*
(ii) X *is a bifix code if it is both a prefix code and a suffix code;*
(iii) X *is an infix code (a p-infix code, a s-infix code) if no word in X is an infix of a proper infix (a proper prefix, a proper suffix, resp.) of another word in X;*
(iv) X *is a hypercode if no word in X is a proper subword of another word in it.*

The classes of prefix codes, suffix codes, bifix codes, infix codes, p-infix codes, s-infix codes and hypercodes are denoted respectively by C_p, C_s, C_b, C_i, $C_{p.i}$, $C_{s.i}$ and C_h. It is easy to see that these classes of codes are defined respectively by the relations which satisfy, for any $u, v \in A^*$, the following corresponding conditions:

$$u \prec_p v \Leftrightarrow v = ux, \text{ with } x \neq 1;$$
$$u \prec_s v \Leftrightarrow v = xu, \text{ with } x \neq 1;$$
$$u \prec_b v \Leftrightarrow (u \prec_p v) \vee (u \prec_s v);$$
$$u \prec_i v \Leftrightarrow v = xuy, \text{ with } xy \neq 1;$$
$$u \prec_{p.i} v \Leftrightarrow v = xuy, \text{ with } y \neq 1;$$
$$u \prec_{s.i} v \Leftrightarrow v = xuy, \text{ with } x \neq 1;$$
$$u \prec_h v \Leftrightarrow \exists n \geq 1 : u = u_1 \ldots u_n \wedge v = x_0 u_1 x_1 \ldots u_n x_n, \text{ with } x_0 \ldots x_n \neq 1.$$

Prefix codes, suffix codes and bifix codes play a fundamental role in the theory of codes (see [1,17]). For more details about infix codes, p-infix codes and s-infix codes we refer to [9,17]. Hypercodes, a special kind of infix codes, have some interesting properties, especially, all hypercodes are finite (see [17]). Relationship between these classes of codes can be resumed in the following proposition.

Proposition 1. *Over any alphabet consisting of at least two letters, the followings hold true.*

(i) $C_b \subset C_p, C_b \subset C_s, C_b = C_p \cap C_s, C_h \subset C_i$;

(ii) $C_i \subset C_{p.i}, C_i \subset C_{s.i}, C_i = C_{p.i} \cap C_{s.i}, C_i \subset C_b, C_{p.i} \subset C_p, C_{s.i} \subset C_s$.

3 New Classes of Codes Defined by Binary Relations

3.1 Definitions and Examples

We introduce in this section some new classes of codes which can be defined by binary relations. Definitions of these codes are based on appropriate combinations of the basic notions such as prefix, subfix, infix, subword, permutation, and cyclic permutation of a word. All such classes of codes, as we shall see later (Proposition 4), are subclasses of prefix codes or suffix codes.

Given $u, v \in A^+$. Let u be a subword of v, $u = u_1 \ldots u_n, v = x_0 u_1 x_1 \ldots u_n x_n$. As $u \neq 1$, we may assume $u_i \neq 1$ for all i. Then, we call u a *right-proper subword* of v if $x_1 \ldots x_n \neq 1$. Dually, if $x_0 \ldots x_{n-1} \neq 1$ then u is a *left-proper subword* of v. A word u is called a *permutation* of a word v if $|u|_a = |v|_a$ for all $a \in A$, where $|u|_a$ denotes the number of occurrences of the letter a in u. And u is a *cyclic permutation* of v if there exist two words x, y such that $u = xy$ and $v = yx$.

Definition 2. *Let A be an alphabet and $X \subseteq A^+$.*

(i) *X is a subinfix (p-subinfix, s-subinfix) code if no word in X is a **sub**word of a proper **infix** (**p**refix, **s**uffix, resp.) of another word in X;*

(ii) *X is a p-hypercode (s-hypercode) if no word in X is a right-proper (left-proper) subword of another word in X;*

(iii) *X is a superinfix (p-superinfix, s-superinfix) code if no word in X is a **sub**word of a **per**mutation of a proper **infix** (**p**refix, **s**uffix, resp.) of another word in X;*

(iv) *X is a sucyperinfix (p-sucyperinfix, s-sucyperinfix) code if no word in X is a **sub**word of a **cy**clic **per**mutation of a proper **infix** (**p**refix, **s**uffix, resp.) of another word in X;*

(v) *X is a supercode (sucypercode) if no word in X is a proper **sub**word of a **per**mutation (**cy**clic **per**mutation, resp.) of another word in it.*

This definition itself explains the way we named the new kinds of codes. It is easy to see that these classes of codes have as defining relations the following, respectively.

$$u \prec_{si} v \Leftrightarrow \exists w \in A^* : w \prec_i v \wedge u \preceq_h w;$$
$$u \prec_{p.si} v \Leftrightarrow \exists w \in A^* : w \prec_p v \wedge u \preceq_h w;$$
$$u \prec_{s.si} v \Leftrightarrow \exists w \in A^* : w \prec_s v \wedge u \preceq_h w;$$
$$u \prec_{p.h} v \Leftrightarrow \exists n \geq 1 : u = u_1 \ldots u_n \wedge v = x_0 u_1 x_1 \ldots u_n x_n, \text{ with } x_1 \ldots x_n \neq 1;$$
$$u \prec_{s.h} v \Leftrightarrow \exists n \geq 1 : u = u_1 \ldots u_n \wedge v = x_0 u_1 x_1 \ldots u_n x_n, \text{ with } x_0 \ldots x_{n-1} \neq 1;$$
$$u \prec_{spi} v \Leftrightarrow (\exists v' : v' \prec_i v)(\exists v'' \in \pi(v')) : u \preceq_h v'';$$
$$u \prec_{p.spi} v \Leftrightarrow (\exists v' : v' \prec_p v)(\exists v'' \in \pi(v')) : u \preceq_h v'';$$
$$u \prec_{s.spi} v \Leftrightarrow (\exists v' : v' \prec_s v)(\exists v'' \in \pi(v')) : u \preceq_h v'';$$
$$u \prec_{scpi} v \Leftrightarrow (\exists v' : v' \prec_i v)(\exists v'' \in \sigma(v')) : u \preceq_h v'';$$
$$u \prec_{p.scpi} v \Leftrightarrow (\exists v' : v' \prec_p v)(\exists v'' \in \sigma(v')) : u \preceq_h v'';$$

$$u \prec_{s.scpi} v \Leftrightarrow (\exists v' : v' \prec_s v)(\exists v'' \in \sigma(v')) : u \preceq_h v'';$$
$$u \prec_{sp} v \Leftrightarrow \exists v' \in \pi(v) : u \prec_h v';$$
$$u \prec_{scp} v \Leftrightarrow \exists v' \in \sigma(v) : u \prec_h v';$$

where $\pi(v)$ and $\sigma(v)$ are the sets of all permutations and cyclic permutations of v respectively.

Example 1. Consider the subsets $X_1 = \{aba, bab^2a\}$, $X_1^R = \{aba, ab^2ab\}$, $X_2 = ab^*a$, $X_3 = \{a, ba\}$, $X_3^R = \{a, ab\}$, $X_4 = \{ab, b^3a\}$, $X_4^R = \{ba, ab^3\}$, $X_5 = \{abab, a^2b^3\}$ and $X_6 = \{ab, b^2a\}$ over the alphabet $A = \{a, b\}$. It is easy to check that the followings hold true

$$X_1 \in C_{p.si} - C_{si}, X_1^R \in C_{s.si} - C_{si}, X_2 \in C_{si} \cap C_{spi} \cap C_{scpi};$$
$$X_3 \in C_{p.h} - C_h, X_3^R \in C_{s.h} - C_h, X_6 \in C_h - C_{scp};$$
$$X_4 \in C_{p.spi} - C_{scpi}, X_4^R \in C_{s.spi} - C_{scpi}, X_5 \in C_{scpi} \cap C_{scp} - C_{spi}.$$

Although, as we shall see below (Proposition 4), the class of p-hypercodes (s-hypercodes) strictly contains the class of hypercodes, the former codes however are still finite.

Proposition 2. *All the p-hypercodes and s-hypercodes over a finite alphabet are finite.*

A binary relation $\prec$ is said to be *length-increasing* if for any $u, v \in A^*$: $u \prec v$ implies $|u| < |v|$. From now on, we denote by Ω the set $\{p, s, p.i, s.i, i, p.si, s.si, si, p.scpi, s.scpi, scpi, p.spi, s.spi, spi, p.h, s.h, h, scp, sp\}$ and $\Omega' = \Omega - \{p.h, s.h, h, scp, sp\}$.

Proposition 3. *The relations $\prec_\alpha$, $\alpha \in \Omega$ are all transitive and length-increasing.*

Note that the relation $\prec_b$ is length-increasing but not transitive. That's the reason why, as we shall see later, Theorem 1 cannot be applied to solve the embedding problem for bifix codes.

3.2 Relative Positions of the Classes of Codes

Relationship between the classes of codes under consideration can be resumed in the following proposition.

Proposition 4. *Over any alphabet consisting of at least two letters, the followings hold true*

 (i) $C_{si} \subset C_{p.si}$, $C_{si} \subset C_{s.si}$, $C_{si} = C_{p.si} \cap C_{s.si}$, $C_{si} \subset C_i$,
   $C_{p.si} \subset C_{p.i}$, $C_{s.si} \subset C_{s.i}$;
 (ii) $C_{scpi} \subset C_{p.scpi}$, $C_{scpi} \subset C_{s.scpi}$, $C_{scpi} = C_{p.scpi} \cap C_{s.scpi}$,
   $C_{scpi} \subset C_{si}$, $C_{p.scpi} \subset C_{p.si}$, $C_{s.scpi} \subset C_{s.si}$;
 (iii) $C_{spi} \subset C_{p.spi}$, $C_{spi} \subset C_{s.spi}$, $C_{spi} = C_{p.spi} \cap C_{s.spi}$, $C_{spi} \subset C_{scpi}$,
   $C_{p.spi} \subset C_{p.scpi}$, $C_{s.spi} \subset C_{s.scpi}$;
 (iv) $C_h \subset C_{p.h}$, $C_h \subset C_{s.h}$, $C_h \subset C_{si}$, $C_{p.h} \subset C_{p.si}$, $C_{s.h} \subset C_{s.si}$,
   $C_h = C_{p.h} \cap C_{s.h} = C_{p.h} \cap C_{s.si} = C_{p.si} \cap C_{s.h}$;
 (v) $C_{sp} \subset C_{scp} \subset C_h$, $C_{scp} \subset C_{scpi}$, $C_{sp} \subset C_{spi}$.

Remark 1. Consider the languages $X = \{abab, a^2b^3\}$, $Y = \{ba, b^3a\}$, $Z = \{a, ba\}$ and $T = \{bab, ab^3a\}$. It is easy to verify that $X \in C_{scp} - C_{p.spi} \cup C_{s.spi}$, $T \in C_h - C_{p.scpi} \cup C_{s.scpi}$, $Z \in C_{p.h} - C_s$, $Z^R \in C_{s.h} - C_p$, $Y \in C_{p.spi} - C_s$ and $Y^R \in C_{s.spi} - C_p$. It follows that, except for the inclusions mentioned in Proposition 4, there is no any more inclusion between the classes of codes under consideration.

By virtue of Propositions 1, 4 and Remark 1, the relative positions of the classes of codes under consideration can be illustrated in the Figure 1, where

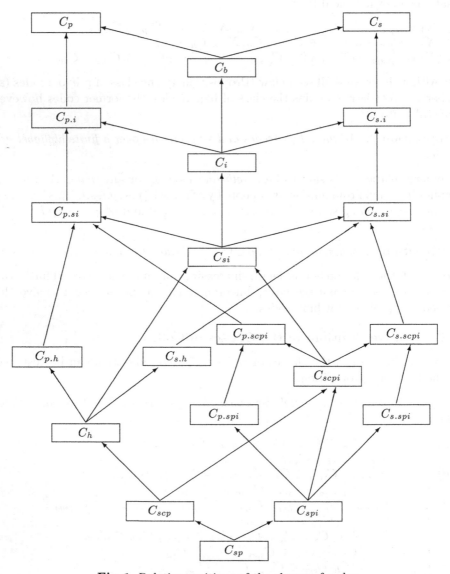

Fig. 1. Relative positions of the classes of codes

the arrow $\to$ stands for a strict inclusion. It is worthy to note that if we restrict ourselves to considering only one-letter alphabets then all the classes of codes represented in the Figure 1 coincide.

4   Embedding Problem

4.1   A General Embedding Schema

In this section we present a general embedding schema for the classes of codes defined by length-increasing transitive binary relations which will be used in the sequel.

Let $\prec$ be a binary relation on A^* and $u, v \in A^*$. We say that u *depends* on v if $u \prec v$ or $v \prec u$ holds. Otherwise, u is *independent* of v. These notions can be extended to subsets of words in a standard way. Namely, a word u is dependent on a subset X if it depends on some word in X. Otherwise, u is independent of X. For brevity, we shall adopt the following notations

$$u \prec X \rightleftharpoons \exists v \in X : u \prec v; \quad X \prec u \rightleftharpoons \exists v \in X : v \prec u.$$

An element u in X is *minimal* in X if there is no word v in X such that $v \prec u$. When X is finite, by $\max X$ we denote the maximal wordlength of X.

Now, for every subset X in A^* we denote by D_X, I_X, L_X and R_X the sets of words dependent on X, independent of X, non-minimal in I_X and minimal in I_X, respectively. In notations

$$D_X = \{u \in A^* \mid u \prec X \vee X \prec u\};$$
$$I_X = A^* - D_X;$$
$$L_X = \{u \in I_X \mid I_X \prec u\};$$
$$R_X = I_X - L_X.$$

When there is no risque of confusion, for brevity we write simply D, I, L, R instead.

The following theorem has been first formulated in [19] (see also [20]). Another proof of it is presented in [21]. An extension of this result has been made in [7].

Theorem 1. *Let $\prec$ be a length-increasing transitive binary relation on A^* which defines the class $C_\prec$ of codes. Then, for any code X in $C_\prec$, we have*

(i) *R_X is a maximal code in $C_\prec$ which contains X;*
(ii) *If moreover the relation $\prec$ satisfies the condition*

$$\exists k \geq 1 \forall u, v \in A^+ :(|v| \geq |u| + k) \wedge (u \not\prec v) \Rightarrow \exists w:(|w| \geq |u|) \wedge (w \prec v) \quad (*)$$

then the finiteness of X implies the finiteness of R_X, and $\max R_X \leq \max X + k - 1$.

4.2   Embedding Problem for Regular Case

In this section we apply Theorem 1 to solve the embedding problem for the classes of codes introduced above in the regular case. The main lemmas needed for this are the following.

Lemma 1. *For any $X \subseteq A^*$, $\pi(X)$ and $\sigma(X)$ are regular if so is X.*

For any set X we denote by $\mathcal{P}(X)$ the family of all subsets of X. Recall that a *substitution* is a mapping f from B into $\mathcal{P}(C^*)$, where B and C are alphabets. If $f(b)$ is regular for all $b \in B$ then f is called a *regular substitution*. When $f(b)$ is a singleton for all $b \in B$ it induces a *homomorphism* from B^* into C^*. Let $\#$ be a new letter not being in A. Put $A_\# = A \cup \{\#\}$. Let's consider the regular substitutions S_1, S_2 and the homomorphism h defined as follows

$S_1 : A \to \mathcal{P}(A_\#^*)$, where $S_1(a) = \{a, \#\}$ for all $a \in A$;
$S_2 : A_\# \to \mathcal{P}(A^*)$, with $S_2(\#) = A^+$ and $S_2(a) = \{a\}$ for all $a \in A$;
$h : A_\#^* \to A^*$, with $h(\#) = 1$ and $h(a) = a$ for all $a \in A$.

Factually, as we will see later, the substitution S_1 will be used to mark the occurrences of letters to be deleted from a word. The homomorphism h realizes the deletion by replacing $\#$ by the empty word. The inverse homomorphism h^{-1} "chooses" in a word the positions where the words of A^+ may be inserted, while S_2 realizes the insertions by replacing $\#$ by A^+. Notice that regular languages are closed under regular substitutions, homomorphisms and inverse homomorphisms (see [8]).

Lemma 2. *Given $\alpha \in \Omega$ and $X \in C_\alpha$. Then R_X can be computed by the following expressions according to the case*

(i)   *Case of prefix codes:* $R = I - IA^+$, *where* $I = A^* - XA^- - XA^+$ *and* A^- *stands for* $(A^+)^{-1}$.

(ii) *Case of suffix codes:* $R = I - A^+I$, *where* $I = A^* - A^-X - A^+X$.

(iii) *Case of p-infix codes:* $R = I - (IA^+ + A^+IA^+)$, *where* $I = A^* - XA^- - A^-XA^- - XA^+ - A^+XA^+$.

(iv) *Case of s-infix codes:* $R = I - (A^+I + A^+IA^+)$, *where* $I = A^* - A^-X - A^-XA^- - A^+X - A^+XA^+$.

(v)   *Case of infix codes:* $R = I - (IA^+ + A^+I + A^+IA^+)$, *where* $I = A^* - XA^- + A^-X + A^-XA^- - XA^+ - A^+X - A^+XA^+$.

(vi) *Case of p-subinfix codes:* $R = I - S_2(h^{-1}(I) \cap A_\#^*\{\#\})$, *where* $I = A^* - h(S_1(X) \cap A_\#^*\{\#\}) - S_2(h^{-1}(X) \cap A_\#^*\{\#\})$.

(vii) *Case of s-subinfix codes:* $R = I - S_2(h^{-1}(I) \cap \{\#\}A_\#^*)$, *where* $I = A^* - h(S_1(X) \cap \{\#\}A_\#^*) - S_2(h^{-1}(X) \cap \{\#\}A_\#^*)$.

(viii) *Case of subinfix codes:* $R = I - S_2(h^{-1}(I) \cap (\{\#\}A_\#^* \cup A_\#^*\{\#\}))$, *where* $I = A^* - h(S_1(X) \cap (\{\#\}A_\#^* \cup A_\#^*\{\#\})) - S_2(h^{-1}(X) \cap (\{\#\}A_\#^* \cup A_\#^*\{\#\}))$.

(ix) *Case of p-sucyperinfix codes:* $R = I - S_2(h^{-1}(\sigma(I)) \cap A_\#^*\{\#\})$, *where* $I = A^* - \sigma(h(S_1(X) \cap A_\#^*\{\#\})) - S_2(h^{-1}(\sigma(X)) \cap A_\#^*\{\#\})$.

(x) *Case of s-sucyperinfix codes:* $R = I - S_2(h^{-1}(\sigma(I)) \cap \{\#\}A_\#^*)$, *where* $I = A^* - \sigma(h(S_1(X) \cap \{\#\}A_\#^*)) - S_2(h^{-1}(\sigma(X)) \cap \{\#\}A_\#^*)$.

(xi) *Case of sucyperinfix codes:* $R = I - S_2(h^{-1}(\sigma(I)) \cap (\{\#\}A_\#^* \cup A_\#^*\{\#\}))$, *where* $I = A^* - \sigma(h(S_1(X) \cap (\{\#\}A_\#^* \cup A_\#^*\{\#\}))) - S_2(h^{-1}(\sigma(X)) \cap (\{\#\}A_\#^* \cup A_\#^*\{\#\}))$.

(xii) *Case of p-superinfix codes:* $R = I - S_2(h^{-1}(\pi(I)) \cap A_\#^*\{\#\})$, *where* $I = A^* - \pi(h(S_1(X) \cap A_\#^*\{\#\})) - S_2(h^{-1}(\pi(X)) \cap A_\#^*\{\#\})$.

(xiii) *Case of s-superinfix codes:* $R = I - S_2(h^{-1}(\pi(I)) \cap \{\#\}A_\#^*)$, *where* $I = A^* - \pi(h(S_1(X) \cap \{\#\}A_\#^*)) - S_2(h^{-1}(\pi(X)) \cap \{\#\}A_\#^*)$.

(xiv) *Case of superinfix codes:* $R = I - S_2(h^{-1}(\pi(I)) \cap (\{\#\}A_\#^* \cup A_\#^*\{\#\}))$, *where* $I = A^* - \pi(h(S_1(X) \cap (\{\#\}A_\#^* \cup A_\#^*\{\#\}))) - S_2(h^{-1}(\pi(X)) \cap (\{\#\}A_\#^* \cup A_\#^*\{\#\}))$.

(xv) *Case of p-hypercodes:* $R = I - S_2(h^{-1}(I) \cap (A_\#^*\{\#\}A_\#^* - \{\#\}^+A^+))$, *where* $I = A^* - h(S_1(X) \cap (A_\#^*\{\#\}A_\#^* - \{\#\}^+A^+)) - S_2(h^{-1}(X) \cap (A_\#^*\{\#\}A_\#^* - \{\#\}^+A^+))$.

(xvi) *Case of s-hypercodes:* $R = I - S_2(h^{-1}(I) \cap (A_\#^*\{\#\}A_\#^* - A^+\{\#\}^+))$, *where* $I = A^* - h(S_1(X) \cap (A_\#^*\{\#\}A_\#^* - A^+\{\#\}^+)) - S_2(h^{-1}(X) \cap (A_\#^*\{\#\}A_\#^* - A^+\{\#\}^+))$.

(xvii) *Case of hypercodes:* $R = I - S_2(h^{-1}(I) \cap (A_\#^*\{\#\}A_\#^*))$, *where* $I = A^* - h(S_1(X) \cap (A_\#^*\{\#\}A_\#^*)) - S_2(h^{-1}(X) \cap (A_\#^*\{\#\}A_\#^*))$.

(xviii) *Case of sucypercodes:* $R = I - \sigma(S_2(h^{-1}(I) \cap (A_\#^*\{\#\}A_\#^*)))$, *where* $I = A^* - h(S_1(\sigma(X)) \cap (A_\#^*\{\#\}A_\#^*)) - \sigma(S_2(h^{-1}(X) \cap (A_\#^*\{\#\}A_\#^*)))$.

(xix) *Case of supercodes:* $R = I - \pi(S_2(h^{-1}(I) \cap (A_\#^*\{\#\}A_\#^*)))$, *where* $I = A^* - h(S_1(\pi(X)) \cap (A_\#^*\{\#\}A_\#^*)) - \pi(S_2(h^{-1}(X) \cap (A_\#^*\{\#\}A_\#^*)))$.

The following result, which follows from Proposition 3, Theorem 1, Lemma 1 and Lemma 2, has been proved partially in [19,6]. For more details see [21].

Theorem 2. *For any $\alpha \in \Omega'$, every regular code in C_α, is contained in a maximal code in C_α which is still regular.*

4.3 Embedding Problem for Finite Case

Our aim in this section is to solve the embedding problem for the mentioned above classes of codes in the finite case. Namely, we will exhibit algorithms to construct, for every finite code X in a class C_α, $\alpha \in \Omega$, a finite maximal code in the same class which contains X.

The following theorem, whose proof is based on Proposition 3, Theorem 1 and Lemma 2, has been proved partially in [19,20,6]. For more details see also [21].

Theorem 3. *For any $\alpha \in \Omega$, every finite code X in C_α, , is contained in a finite maximal code Y in C_α with $\max Y = \max X$.*

Denote by $A^{[n]}$ the set of all the words in A^* whose length is less than or equal to n. As an immediate consequence of Lemma 2 and Theorem 3 we have

Corollary 1. *Given $\alpha \in \Omega$ and $X \in C_\alpha$ with $\max X = n$. Then the maximal code R_X in C_α which contains X can be computed by the following "restricted" expressions according to the case.*

(i) *Case of prefix codes:* $R = I - IA^+ \cap A^{[n]}$, *where* $I = A^{[n]} - XA^- - XA^+ \cap A^{[n]}$.

(ii) *Case of suffix codes:* $R = I - A^+I \cap A^{[n]}$, *where* $I = A^{[n]} - A^-X - A^+X \cap A^{[n]}$.

(iii) *Case of p-infix codes:* $R = I - (IA^+ + A^+IA^+) \cap A^{[n]}$, *where* $I = A^{[n]} - XA^- - A^-XA^- - (XA^+ + A^+XA^+) \cap A^{[n]}$.

(iv) *Case of s-infix codes :* $R = I - (A^+I + A^+IA^+) \cap A^{[n]}$, *where* $I = A^{[n]} - A^-X - A^-XA^- - (A^+X + A^+XA^+) \cap A^{[n]}$.

(v) *Case of infix codes:* $R = I - (IA^+ + A^+I + A^+IA^+) \cap A^{[n]}$, *where* $I = A^{[n]} - XA^- + A^-X + A^-XA^- - (XA^+ + A^+X + A^+XA^+) \cap A^{[n]}$.

(vi) *Case of p-subinfix codes:* $R = I - S_2(h^{-1}(I) \cap A_{\#}^{[n-1]}\{\#\}) \cap A^{[n]}$, *where* $I = A^{[n]} - h(S_1(X) \cap A_{\#}^*\{\#\}) - S_2(h^{-1}(X) \cap A_{\#}^{[n-1]}\{\#\}) \cap A^{[n]}$.

(vii) *Case of s-subinfix codes:* $R = I - S_2(h^{-1}(I) \cap \{\#\}A_{\#}^{[n-1]}) \cap A^{[n]}$, *where* $I = A^{[n]} - h(S_1(X) \cap \{\#\}A_{\#}^*) - S_2(h^{-1}(X) \cap \{\#\}A_{\#}^{[n-1]}) \cap A^{[n]}$.

(viii) *Case of subinfix codes:* $R = I - S_2(h^{-1}(I) \cap (\{\#\}A_{\#}^{[n-1]} \cup A_{\#}^{[n-1]}\{\#\})) \cap A^{[n]}$, *where* $I = A^{[n]} - h(S_1(X) \cap (\{\#\}A_{\#}^* \cup A_{\#}^*\{\#\})) - S_2(h^{-1}(X) \cap (\{\#\}A_{\#}^{[n-1]} \cup A_{\#}^{[n-1]}\{\#\})) \cap A^{[n]}$.

(ix) *Case of p-sucyperinfix codes:* $R = I - S_2(h^{-1}(\sigma(I)) \cap A_{\#}^{[n-1]}\{\#\}) \cap A^{[n]}$, *where* $I = A^{[n]} - \sigma(h(S_1(X) \cap A_{\#}^*\{\#\})) - S_2(h^{-1}(\sigma(X)) \cap A_{\#}^{[n-1]}\{\#\}) \cap A^{[n]}$.

(x) *Case of s-sucyperinfix codes:* $R = I - S_2(h^{-1}(\sigma(I)) \cap \{\#\}A_{\#}^{[n-1]}) \cap A^{[n]}$, *where* $I = A^{[n]} - \sigma(h(S_1(X) \cap \{\#\}A_{\#}^*)) - S_2(h^{-1}(\sigma(X)) \cap \{\#\}A_{\#}^{[n-1]}) \cap A^{[n]}$.

(xi) *Case of sucyperinfix codes:* $R = I - S_2(h^{-1}(\sigma(I)) \cap (\{\#\}A_{\#}^{[n-1]} \cup A_{\#}^{[n-1]}\{\#\})) \cap A^{[n]}$, *where* $I = A^{[n]} - \sigma(h(S_1(X) \cap (\{\#\}A_{\#}^* \cup A_{\#}^*\{\#\}))) - S_2(h^{-1}(\sigma(X)) \cap (\{\#\}A_{\#}^{[n-1]} \cup A_{\#}^{[n-1]}\{\#\})) \cap A^{[n]}$.

(xii) *Case of p-superinfix codes:* $R = I - S_2(h^{-1}(\pi(I)) \cap A_{\#}^{[n-1]}\{\#\}) \cap A^{[n]}$, *where* $I = A^{[n]} - \pi(h(S_1(X) \cap A_{\#}^*\{\#\})) - S_2(h^{-1}(\pi(X)) \cap A_{\#}^{[n-1]}\{\#\}) \cap A^{[n]}$.

(xiii) *Case of s-superinfix codes:* $R = I - S_2(h^{-1}(\pi(I)) \cap \{\#\}A_{\#}^{[n-1]}) \cap A^{[n]}$, *where* $I = A^{[n]} - \pi(h(S_1(X) \cap \{\#\}A_{\#}^*)) - S_2(h^{-1}(\pi(X)) \cap \{\#\}A_{\#}^{[n-1]}) \cap A^{[n]}$.

(xiv) *Case of superinfix codes:* $R = I - S_2(h^{-1}(\pi(I)) \cap (\{\#\}A_{\#}^{[n-1]} \cup A_{\#}^{[n-1]}\{\#\})) \cap A^{[n]}$, *where* $I = A^{[n]} - \pi(h(S_1(X) \cap (\{\#\}A_{\#}^* \cup A_{\#}^*\{\#\}))) - S_2(h^{-1}(\pi(X)) \cap (\{\#\}A_{\#}^{[n-1]} \cup A_{\#}^{[n-1]}\{\#\})) \cap A^{[n]}$.

(xv) *Case of p-hypercodes:* $R = I - S_2(h^{-1}(I) \cap (A_{\#}^*\{\#\}A_{\#}^* - \{\#\}^+A^+) \cap A_{\#}^{[n]}) \cap A^{[n]}$, *where* $I = A^{[n]} - h(S_1(X) \cap (A_{\#}^*\{\#\}A_{\#}^* - \{\#\}^+A^+)) - S_2(h^{-1}(X) \cap (A_{\#}^*\{\#\}A_{\#}^* - \{\#\}^+A^+) \cap A_{\#}^{[n]}) \cap A^{[n]}$.

(xvi) *Case of s-hypercodes:* $R = I - S_2(h^{-1}(I) \cap (A_{\#}^*\{\#\}A_{\#}^* - A^+\{\#\}^+) \cap A_{\#}^{[n]}) \cap A^{[n]}$, *where* $I = A^{[n]} - h(S_1(X) \cap (A_{\#}^*\{\#\}A_{\#}^* - A^+\{\#\}^+)) - S_2(h^{-1}(X) \cap (A_{\#}^*\{\#\}A_{\#}^* - A^+\{\#\}^+) \cap A_{\#}^{[n]}) \cap A^{[n]}$.

(xvii) *Case of hypercodes:* $R = I - S_2(h^{-1}(I) \cap (A_{\#}^* \{\#\} A_{\#}^*) \cap A_{\#}^{[n]}) \cap A^{[n]}$, where
$I = A^{[n]} - h(S_1(X) \cap (A_{\#}^* \{\#\} A_{\#}^*)) - S_2(h^{-1}(X) \cap (A_{\#}^* \{\#\} A_{\#}^*) \cap A_{\#}^{[n]}) \cap A^{[n]}$.

(xviii) *Case of sucypercodes:* $R = I - \sigma(S_2(h^{-1}(I) \cap (A_{\#}^* \{\#\} A_{\#}^*) \cap A_{\#}^{[n]}) \cap A^{[n]})$, where $I = A^{[n]} - h(S_1(\sigma(X)) \cap (A_{\#}^* \{\#\} A_{\#}^*)) - \sigma(S_2(h^{-1}(X) \cap (A_{\#}^* \{\#\} A_{\#}^*) \cap A_{\#}^{[n]}) \cap A^{[n]})$.

(xix) *Case of supercodes:* $R = I - \pi(S_2(h^{-1}(I) \cap (A_{\#}^* \{\#\} A_{\#}^*) \cap A_{\#}^{[n]}) \cap A^{[n]})$, where $I = A^{[n]} - h(S_1(\pi(X)) \cap (A_{\#}^* \{\#\} A_{\#}^*)) - \pi(S_2(h^{-1}(X) \cap (A_{\#}^* \{\#\} A_{\#}^*) \cap A_{\#}^{[n]}) \cap A^{[n]})$.

Example 2. Consider the p-subinfix code $X = \{a^2, ba^2\}$ over $A = \{a, b\}$. Since $\max X = 3$, by Corollary 1(vi), R_X can be computed by the formula

$$R = I - S_2(h^{-1}(I) \cap A_{\#}^{[2]} \{\#\}) \cap A^{[3]},$$

where $I = A^{[3]} - h(S_1(X) \cap A_{\#}^* \{\#\}) - S_2(h^{-1}(X) \cap A_{\#}^{[2]} \{\#\}) \cap A^{[3]}$. We may now compute R_X step by step as follows.

$S_1(X) \cap A_{\#}^* \{\#\} = \{a\#, \#^2, ba\#, b\#^2, \#a\#, \#^3\}$;

$h(S_1(X) \cap A_{\#}^* \{\#\}) = \{1, a, b, ba\}$;

$h^{-1}(X) \cap A_{\#}^{[2]} \{\#\} = \{a^2 \#\}$;

$S_2(h^{-1}(X) \cap A_{\#}^{[2]} \{\#\}) \cap A^{[3]} = a^2 A = \{a^3, a^2 b\}$;

$I = A^{[3]} - \{1, a, b, ba\} - \{a^3, a^2 b\} = \{a^2, ab, b^2, aba, ab^2, ba^2, bab, b^2 a, b^3\}$;

$h^{-1}(I) \cap A_{\#}^{[2]} \{\#\} = \{a^2 \#, ab \#, b^2 \#\}$;

$S_2(h^{-1}(I) \cap A_{\#}^{[2]} \{\#\}) \cap A^{[3]} = a^2 A + abA + b^2 A = \{a^3, a^2 b, aba, ab^2, b^2 a, b^3\}$;

$R = I - \{a^3, a^2 b, aba, ab^2, b^2 a, b^3\} = \{a^2, ab, b^2, ba^2, bab\}$.

Example 3. For the sucypercode $X = \{acb, a^2 b^2, cabc\}$ over $A = \{a, b, c\}$, in a similar way, using formulas in Corollary 1(xviii) with $n = 4$ instead, we obtain the maximal sucypercode $R = \{a^3, a^2 c, aca, acb, bac, b^3, b^2 c, bcb, ca^2, cba, cb^2, c^3, a^2 b^2, abab, ab^2 a, abc^2, ba^2 b, baba, b^2 a^2, bc^2 a, cabc, c^2 ab\}$, which contains X.

4.4 Tree Representations

Sometime a graph-theoretic representation of codes defined by binary relations seems to be useful. Like the case of prefix codes, it facilitates the construction of examples of codes and in many cases maximal codes containing a given code. Moreover, as we shall see below, it makes more intuitive in understanding and proving facts.

First, to every transitive binary relation $\prec$ on A^* we associate an infinite oriented graph as follows. The alphabet A is totally ordered, and words of equal length are ordered lexicographically. Each word represents a node of the graph. Words of small length are to the left of words of greater length, and words of equal length are disposed vertically according to lexical ordering. For any nodes u, v, there is an edge $u \rightarrow v$ iff $u \prec v$ and there is no w such that $u \prec w \prec v$.

Throughout we restrict ourself to length-increasing relations only. Thus, the corresponding graph is a tree in some large sense, called the *tree of A^* w.r.t.* $\prec$, denoted by $\mathcal{T}(A^*, \prec)$, or simply $\mathcal{T}$ when there is no risque of confusion. In the case of the relation $\prec_p$ this is nothing but the *literal representation* of A^* [1]. ¿From now on, we refer indifferently to a node in $\mathcal{T}$ and the word it represents. For example, one may say of the length of a node which means the length of the word it represents, etc.

To a given subset X of A^* we associate a subtree of $\mathcal{T}(A^*, \prec)$ as follows. We keep just the nodes representing the words of X and of $\{u \mid u \prec v, v \in X\}$, and all related edges. The tree obtained in this way is the *tree of X w.r.t.* $\prec$, denoted by $\mathcal{T}(X, \prec)$ (see Figure 2).

A set X of nodes is *node-independent* if there is no path from one node to another. The set X is *maximal* if it is included properly in no node-independent set. In other words, a node-independent set X is maximal if it becomes no more a node-independent set by adding a new node. The following fact establishes relationship between the codes defined by $\prec$, that is the independent sets w.r.t. $\prec$, and the node-independent sets of the tree $\mathcal{T}(A^*, \prec)$.

Proposition 5. *Let $\prec$ be a length-increasing transitive binary relation on A^* which defines a class $C_\prec$ of codes. Let $\mathcal{T}(A^*, \prec)$ be the tree of A^* w.r.t. $\prec$. Then, for any $X \subseteq A^*$, X is a (maximal) code in $C_\prec$ iff the corresponding nodes in $\mathcal{T}(A^*, \prec)$ constitute a (maximal, resp.) node-independent set.*

Remark 2. Proposition 5 can be used to obtain another proof [19], more intuitive, of the item (i) in Theorem 1.

As seen in the above examples (Section 4.3), even for a small code X, computing R_X is not simple in practice. It is however much easier when using tree representation of A^* with respect to $\prec$ as shown in the following example.

Example 4. Consider again the p-subinfix code $X = \{a^2, ba^2\}$. As $\max X = 3$, for finding R_X we may restrict to considering the tree $\mathcal{T}(A^3, \prec_{p.si})$ of the full uniform code A^3 w.r.t. $\prec_{p.si}$. By virtue of Theorem 1 and Proposition 5, R_X can be obtained by applying the following algorithm: First, mark the nodes represented by the words in X (namely: aa, baa). Then, delete all the nodes depending on X (namely: $1, a, b, ba, aaa, aab$). Next, among the rest (namely: $ab, bb, aba, abb, bab, bba, bbb$) keep just the minimal nodes (namely: ab, bb, bab), which together with X constitute R_X, i.e. $R_X = \{a^2, ab, b^2, ba^2, bab\}$ (see Figure 2).

5   Characterizations of Some Classes of Codes

5.1   Vector Characterizations

The results in the rest of the paper have been obtained partially in [20,6]. For more details see also [22].

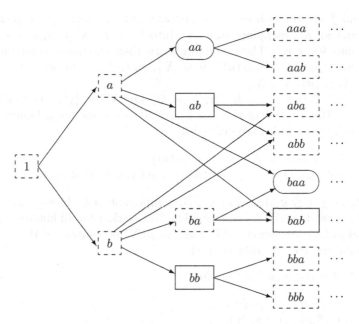

Fig. 2. Computing $R_X, X = \{a^2, ba^2\}$, by using the tree $T(A^3, \prec_{p.si})$

Let $A = \{a_1, a_2, \ldots, a_k\}$ and $K = \{1, 2, \ldots, k\}$. For every $u \in A^*$, we denote by $p(u)$ the Parikh vector of u, namely

$$p(u) = (|u|_{a_1}, |u|_{a_2}, \ldots, |u|_{a_k}).$$

where $|u|_{a_i}$ denotes the number of occurrences of a_i in u. Thus p is a mapping from A^* into the set V^k of all the k-vectors of non-negative integers.

For any subset $X \subseteq A^*$ we denote by $p(X)$ the set of all Parikh vectors of the words in X, $p(X) = \{p \in V^k \mid p = p(u) \text{ for some } u \in X\}$.

The following result gives a simple characterization of supercodes.

Theorem 4. *For any subset $X \subseteq A^+$ the following assertions are equivalent*

(i) X *is a supercode;*
(ii) $\pi(X)$ *is a supercode;*
(iii) $p(X)$ *is an independent set w.r.t. the relation $<$ on V^k.*

Similarly, for sucypercodes we have

Proposition 6. *For any subset X of A^+, X is a sucypercode iff so is $\sigma(X)$.*

Now, to every $u \in A^+$ we associate two elements of the cartesian product $V^k \times K$, denoted by $p_L(u)$ and $p_F(u)$, and one element of $V^k \times K^2$, denoted by $p_{LF}(u)$, which are defined as follows

$$p_L(u) = (p(u), l); \quad p_F(u) = (p(u), f); \quad p_{LF}(u) = (p(u), l, f);$$

where l and f are the indices of the last and the first letter in u, respectively. Thus p_L and p_F are mappings from A^+ into $V^k \times K$, while p_{LF} is a mapping from A^+ into $V^k \times K^2$. These mappings are then extended to languages in a standard way: $p_L(X) = \{p_L(u) \mid u \in X\}$, $p_F(X) = \{p_F(u) \mid u \in X\}$ and $p_{LF}(X) = \{p_{LF}(u) \mid u \in X\}$.

Put $U = \{(\xi, i) \in V^k \times K \mid p_i(\xi) \neq 0\}$ and $W = \{(\xi, i, j) \in V^k \times K^2 \mid p_i(\xi), p_j(\xi) \neq 0\}$. To each of the sets U and W we associate a binary relation, denoted both by $\prec$, which are defined by

$$(\xi, i) \prec (\eta, j) \Leftrightarrow (\xi \leq \eta) \wedge (p_j(\xi) < p_j(\eta)),$$
$$(\xi, m, n) \prec (\eta, i, j) \Leftrightarrow (\xi \leq \eta) \wedge (p_i(\xi) < p_i(\eta) \vee p_j(\xi) < p_j(\eta)),$$

where $p_i(\xi), 1 \leq i \leq k$, denotes the i-th component of ξ. These relations on U and on W, as easily verified, are transitive. Notice that for all language $X \subseteq A^+$, $p_L(X)$ and $p_F(X)$ are subsets of U while $p_{LF}(X)$ is a subset of W.

The following fact is easily verified.

Lemma 3. *For any $u, v \in A^+$ we have*

(i) $u \prec_{p.spi} v$ *iff* $p_L(u) \prec p_L(v)$;
(ii) $u \prec_{s.spi} v$ *iff* $p_F(u) \prec p_F(v)$;
(iii) $u \prec_{spi} v$ *iff* $p_{LF}(u) \prec p_{LF}(v)$.

To every subset X of A^+, we associate the sets

$$E_X = \{x \in X \mid \exists y \in X : p(y) < p(x)\} \text{ and } O_X = X - E_X.$$

Clearly, if $E_X = \emptyset$ then X is a supercode.

Let u be a word in A^+, we define the following operations

$$\pi_L(u) = \pi(u')b, \text{ with } u = u'b, b \in A;$$
$$\pi_F(u) = a\pi(u'), \text{ with } u = au', a \in A;$$
$$\pi_{LF}(u) = \begin{cases} a\pi(u')b, & \text{if } |u| \geq 2 \text{ and } u = au'b, \text{ with } a, b \in A; \\ u, & \text{if } u \in A; \end{cases}$$

which are extended to languages in a normal way: $\pi_L(X) = \bigcup_{u \in X} \pi_L(u)$, $\pi_F(X) = \bigcup_{u \in X} \pi_F(u)$ and $\pi_{LF}(X) = \bigcup_{u \in X} \pi_{LF}(u)$.

Lemma 4. *Let X be a subset of A^+. If $p_L(X)$ $(p_F(X))$ is an independent set w.r.t. the relation $\prec$ on U then so is $p_L(\pi(O_X) \cup \pi_L(E_X))$ $(p_F(\pi(O_X) \cup \pi_F(E_X))$, resp.). If $p_{LF}(X)$ is an independent set w.r.t. the relation $\prec$ on W then so is $p_{LF}(\pi(O_X) \cup \pi_{LF}(E_X))$.*

The last two lemmas allow us to prove the following characterizations of p-superinfix codes, s-superinfix codes and superinfix codes (see also [22]).

Theorem 5. *For any subset X of A^+, the following assertions are equivalent*

(i) *X is a p-superinfix code (resp., a s-superinfix code, a superinfix code);*

(ii) $\pi(O_X) \cup \pi_L(E_X)$ *is a p-superinfix code (resp., $\pi(O_X) \cup \pi_F(E_X)$ is a s-superinfix code, $\pi(O_X) \cup \pi_{LF}(E_X)$ is a superinfix code);*
(iii) $p_L(X)$ *is an independent set w.r.t. the relation $\prec$ on U (resp., $p_F(X)$ is an independent set w.r.t. the relation $\prec$ on U, $p_{LF}(X)$ is an independent set w.r.t. the relation $\prec$ on W).*

Example 5. Consider the language $X = \{a^2ba, aba^2, ab^3, ba^3, bab^2, b^2ab, a^2b^2a,$ $a^2b^3, ababa, abab^2, ab^2a^2, ab^2ab, ba^2ba, ba^2b^2, baba^2, babab, b^2a^3, b^2a^2b\}$ over the alphabet $A = \{a, b\}$. It is easy to check that $p_L(X) = \{((3,1),1), ((3,2),1),$ $((2,3),2), ((1,3),2)\}$ and that it is an independent set w.r.t. $\prec$ on $U = \{(\xi, j) \in$ $V^2 \times \{1,2\} \mid p_j(\xi) \neq 0\}$. By Theorem 5, X is a p-superinfix code.

5.2 Maximality

First we formulate a characterization of the maximal supercodes by means of independent sets w.r.t. the relation $<$ on V^k.

Theorem 6. *For any subset X of A^+, X is a maximal supercode iff $p(X)$ is a maximal independent set w.r.t. $<$ on V^k and $\pi(X) = X$.*

Next we characterize the maximal p-superinfix, s-superinfix and superinfix codes by means of independent sets w.r.t. the relation $\prec$ on U and on W.

Theorem 7. *For any subset X of A^+, we have*

(i) *X is a maximal p-superinfix (s-superinfix) code iff $p_L(X)$ (resp., $p_F(X)$) is a maximal independent set w.r.t. the relation $\prec$ on U and $\pi(O_X) \cup \pi_L(E_X) = X$ (resp., $\pi(O_X) \cup \pi_F(E_X) = X$).*
(ii) *X is a maximal superinfix code iff $p_{LF}(X)$ is a maximal independent set w.r.t. the relation $\prec$ on W and $\pi(O_X) \cup \pi_{LF}(E_X) = X$.*

Example 6. (i) Let $X = \{a^3, ab^2, bab, b^2a, b^3, a^2ba, a^2b^2, aba^2, abab, ba^3, ba^2b\}$. It is easy to see that $X = \pi(O_X) \cup \pi_L(E_X)$ and $p_L(X) = \{((3,0),1), ((3,1),1),$ $((2,2),2), ((1,2),1), ((1,2),2), ((0,3),2)\}$, which is easily verified to be a maximal independent set w.r.t. $\prec$ on $U = \{(\xi, i) \in V^2 \times \{1,2\} \mid p_i(\xi) \neq 0\}$. By virtue of Theorem 7(i), we may conclude that X is a maximal p-superinfix code over $A = \{a, b\}$.

(ii) Let's consider the set $X = \{a^3, a^2ba, aba^2, b^4, a^2b^2a, ababa, ab^2a^2,$ $bab^3, b^2ab^2, b^3ab, a^2b^3a, abab^2a, ab^2aba, ab^3a^2, ba^2b^3, babab^2, bab^2ab, b^2a^2b^2,$ $b^2abab, b^3a^2b\}$ over $A = \{a, b\}$. We have evidently $O_X = \{a^3, b^4\}$. A simple verification leads to $X = \pi(O_X) \cup \pi_{LF}(E_X)$ and also $p_{LF}(X) = \{((3,0),1,1),$ $((3,1),1,1), ((3,2),1,1), ((3,3),1,1), ((2,4),2,2), ((1,4),2,2) ((0,4),2,2)\}$. It is easy to see that the latter is a maximal independent set w.r.t. $\prec$ on $W = \{(\xi, i, j) \in V^2 \times \{1,2\}^2 \mid p_i(\xi), p_j(\xi) \neq 0\}$. By Theorem 7(ii), it follows that X is a maximal superinfix code over A.

The following result establishes relationship between maximal p-superinfix (s-superinfix, superinfix) codes and p-infix (s-infix, sucyperinfix, resp.) codes.

Theorem 8. *For any subset X of A^+, we have*

(i) *X is a maximal p-superinfix (s-superinfix, resp.) code iff X is a maximal p-infix (s-infix, resp.) code and $\pi(O_X) \cup \pi_L(E_X) = X$ $(\pi(O_X) \cup \pi_F(E_X) = X$, resp.).*

(ii) *X is a maximal superinfix code iff X is a maximal sucyperinfix code and $\pi(O_X) \cup \pi_{LF}(E_X) = X$ $(\pi(O_X) \cup \pi_F(E_X) = X$, resp.).*

As a direct consequence of Theorem 8 we obtain

Corollary 2. *For any subset X of A^+, X is a maximal p-superinfix (s-superinfix, resp.) code iff X is a maximal p-subinfix/p-sucyperinfix (s-subinfix/s-sucyperinfix, resp.) code and $\pi(O_X) \cup \pi_L(E_X) = X$ $(\pi(O_X) \cup \pi_F(E_X) = X$, resp.).*

We have moreover

Corollary 3. *Every maximal p-superinfix (s-superinfix) code is a maximal code.*

This corollary together with Theorem 2 and Theorem 3 imply immediately

Corollary 4. *Every finite (regular) p-superinfix code (s-superinfix code) is included in a finite (regular, resp.) p-superinfix code (s-superinfix code) which is maximal as a code.*

Remark 3. While, as seen above, a maximal p-superinfix code (s-superinfix code) is always a maximal prefix code (suffix code, resp.), a maximal superinfix code is not necessarily a maximal subinfix code. Indeed, consider the code $X = ab^*a$ over the alphabet $A = \{a, b\}$ which is easily verified to be a maximal superinfix code. But it is not a maximal subinfix code because $X \cup \{bab\}$ is still a subinfix code.

Relationship between maximal supercodes, sucypercodes and hypercodes is pointed out in the following result.

Theorem 9. *For any subset X of A^+, we have the following*

(i) *X is a maximal supercode iff X is a maximal hypercode and $\pi(X) = X$.*

(ii) *X is a maximal sucypercode iff X is a maximal hypercode and $\sigma(X) = X$.*

(iii) *X is a maximal supercode iff X is a maximal sucypercode and $\pi(X) = \sigma(X)$.*

5.3   Supercodes Over Two-Letter Alphabets

Let's fix a two-letter alphabet $A = \{a, b\}$. On V^2 we introduce the relation $\prec_{2.v}$ defined by

$$u \prec_{2.v} w \Leftrightarrow p_1(u) > p_1(w) \wedge p_2(u) < p_2(w),$$

where $p_i(u)$ denotes the i-th component of u. For simplicity, in this section we write $\prec$ instead of $\prec_{2.v}$.

A finite sequence (may be empty) S: $u_1, u_2, \ldots, u_n$ of elements in V^2 is a *chain* if

$$u_1 \prec u_2 \prec \cdots \prec u_n.$$

The chain S is *full* if

$$\forall i, 1 \le i \le n-1, \not\exists v : u_i \prec v \prec u_{i+1}.$$

If the full chain S satisfies moreover the condition

$$p_2(u_1) = p_1(u_n) = 0,$$

then it is said to be *complete*. A finite subset T of V^2 is *complete* if it can be arranged to become a complete chain. For $1 \le i < j \le n$ we denote by $[u_i, u_j]$ the subsequence $u_i, u_{i+1}, \ldots, u_j$ of the sequence S.

Theorem 10. *For any finite subset X of A^+, X is a maximal supercode iff $p(X)$ is complete and $X = \pi(X)$.*

Example 7. For any $n \ge 1$, the sequence

$$(n,0), (n-1,2), \ldots, (n-i, 2i), \ldots, (0, 2n)$$

is obviously a complete chain. Therefore, the set $V_n = \{(n,0), (n-1,2), \ldots, (0,2n)\}$ is complete. With $n = 3$ for example, $V_3 = \{(3,0), (2,2), (1,4), (0,6)\}$. By Theorem 10 it follows that the set $X = \pi(\{a^3, a^2b^2, ab^4, b^6\}) = \{a^3, a^2b^2, abab, ab^2a, ba^2b, baba, b^2a^2, ab^4, bab^3, b^2ab^2, b^3ab, b^4a, b^6\}$ is a maximal supercode.

By Theorem 10, in order to characterize the maximal supercodes over $A = \{a, b\}$ we may characterize the complete sets instead. For this we first consider some transformations on complete chains. Let $S: u_1, u_2, \ldots, u_n$ be a complete chain.

(T1) (*extension*). It consists in doing consecutively the following:
- Add on the left of S a 2-vector u with $p_1(u) > p_1(u_1)$;
- Delete from S all the u_is with $p_2(u_i) \le p_2(u)$;
- If u_{i_0} is the first among the u_is remained, then insert between u and u_{i_0} any chain such that $[u, u_{i_0}]$ is a full chain;
- If there is no such a u_{i_0}, then add on the right of u any chain ending with a v, $p_1(v) = 0$, and such that $[u, v]$ is a full chain;
- Add on the left of u any chain begining with a v, $p_2(v) = 0$, and such that $[v, u]$ is a full chain.

(T2) (*replacement*). The following steps will be done successively:
- Replacing some element u_i in S by an element u with $p_1(u) = p_1(u_i)$;
- If $p_2(u) < p_2(u_i)$, then delete all the u_js on the left of u with $p_2(u_j) \ge p_2(u)$;
- If u_{j_0} is the last among the u_j remained, then insert between u_{j_0} and u any sequence such that $[u_{j_0}, u]$ is a full chain;
- If there is no such a u_{j_0}, then add on the left of u any chain commencing with a v, $p_2(v) = 0$, and such that $[v, u]$ is a full chain;
- If $i < n$ then insert between u and u_{i+1} any chain such that $[u, u_{i+1}]$ is a full chain;

• If $p_2(u) > p_2(u_i)$, then delete all the u_js on the right of u with $p_2(u_j) \leq p_2(u)$;

• If u_{j_0} is the first among the u_js remained, then insert between u and u_{j_0} any chain such that $[u, u_{j_0}]$ is a full chain;

• If there is no such a u_{j_0}, then add on the right of u any chain ending with a v, $p_1(v) = 0$, and such that $[u, v]$ is a full chain;

• If $i > 1$ then insert between u_{i-1} and u any chain such that $[u_{i-1}, u]$ is a full chain;

• If $i = 1$ then add on the left of u any chain begining with a v, $p_2(v) = 0$, and such that $[v, u]$ is a full chain.

(T3) (*insertion*). This consists of the following successive steps:

• For some i, insert in the middle of u_i and u_{i+1}, $1 \leq i \leq n - 1$, an element u with $p_1(u_i) > p_1(u) > p_1(u_{i+1})$;

• If $p_2(u) \leq p_2(u_i)$, then delete all the u_js on the left of u with $p_2(u_j) \geq p_2(u)$;

• If u_{j_0} is the last among the u_js remained, then insert between u_{j_0} and u any chain such that $[u_{j_0}, u]$ is a full chain;

• If there is no such a u_{j_0}, then add on the left of u any chain commencing with a v, $p_2(v) = 0$, and such that $[v, u]$ is a full chain;

• Insert between u and u_{i+1} any chain such that $[u, u_{i+1}]$ is a full chain;

• If $p_2(u) \geq p_2(u_{i+1})$, then delete all the u_js on the right of u with $p_2(u_j) \leq p_2(u)$;

• If u_{j_0} is the first among the u_js remained, then insert between u and u_{j_0} any chain such that $[u, u_{j_0}]$ is a full chain;

• If there is no such u_{j_0}, then add on the right of u any sequence ending with a v, $p_1(v) = 0$, and such that $[u, v]$ is a full chain;

• Insert between u_i and u any chain such that $[u_i, u]$ become a full chain.

Theorem 11. *The following assertions hold true*

(i) *The transformations (T1)-(T3) preserve the completeness of a chain.*

(ii) *Any complete chain can be obtained from another one by a finite number of applications of the transformations (T1)-(T3).*

(iii) *Every chain S can be embedded in a complete chain by a finite number of applications of the transformations (T1)-(T3).*

Example 8. Consider the chain $S : (5, 2), (3, 4), (1, 7)$. We try to embed S in a complete chain by using (T1)-(T3). For this, we choose an arbitrary complete chain S', say $S' : (2, 0), (1, 2), (0, 4)$, and manipulate like this:

• Applying (T1) to S' with $u = (5, 2)$ we obtain from step to step the following sequences, where underline indicates the 2-vectors added in every step.

$\underline{(5, 2)}, (2, 0), (1, 2), (0, 4)$;
$\overline{(5, 2)}, (0, 4)$;
$(5, 2), \underline{(2, 3)}, (0, 4)$;
$\underline{(6, 0)}, \overline{(5, 2)}, (2, 3), (0, 4)$;

- Applying (T3) to the last chain with $u = (3, 4)$ we obtain successively:

$(6, 0), (5, 2), \underline{(3, 4)}, (2, 3), (0, 4);$
$(6, 0), (5, 2), \overline{(3, 4)};$
$(6, 0), (5, 2), (3, 4), \underline{(1, 5)}, \underline{(0, 6)};$
$(6, 0), (5, 2), \underline{(4, 3)}, \overline{(3, 4)}, \overline{(1, 5)}, (0, 6);$

- Applying (T2) to the last chain with $u = (1, 7)$ we obtain:

$(6, 0), (5, 2), (4, 3), (3, 4), \underline{(1, 7)}, (0, 6);$
$(6, 0), (5, 2), (4, 3), (3, 4), \overline{(1, 7)};$
$(6, 0), (5, 2), (4, 3), (3, 4), (1, 7), \underline{(0, 8)};$
$(6, 0), (5, 2), (4, 3), (3, 4), \underline{(2, 6)}, \overline{(1, 7)}, (0, 8).$

The last chain is a complete chain containing S.

As a consequence of Theorem 11 we have

Theorem 12. *Let A be a two-letter alphabet. Then, we have*

(i) *There exists a procedure to generate all the maximal supercodes over A starting from an arbitrary given maximal supercode.*

(ii) *There is an algorithm allowing to construct, for every supercode X over A, a maximal supercode Y containing X.*

Example 9. Let $X = \{b^2 a^2 bab, a^3 ba^2 b, b^4 ab^3\}$. Since $p(X) = \{(3, 4), (5, 2), (1, 7)\}$ is an independent set w.r.t. $<$ on V^2, by Theorem 4, X is a supercode over $A = \{a, b\}$. The corresponding chain of $p(X)$ is $S : (5, 2), (3, 4), (1, 7)$. As has been shown in Example 8, the sequence

$$S' : (6, 0), (5, 2), (4, 3), (3, 4), (2, 6), (1, 7), (0, 8)$$

is a complete chain containing S. The corresponding complete set of S' is

$$T = \{(6, 0), (5, 2), (4, 3), (3, 4), (2, 6), (1, 7), (0, 8)\}.$$

So $Y = p^{-1}(T)$ is a maximal supercode containing X. More explicitly, $Y = \pi(Z)$ with $Z = \{a^6, a^5 b^2, a^4 b^3, a^3 b^4, a^2 b^6, ab^7, b^8\}$.

References

1. J. BERSTEL, D. PERRIN, *Theory of Codes.* Academic Press, New York, 1985.
2. V. BRUYÈRE, M. LATTEUX, Variable-length maximal codes. *Theoretical Computer Science* **98** (1992), 321–337.
3. V. BRUYÈRE, L. WANG, L. ZHANG, On completion of codes with finite deciphering delay. *European Journal of Combinatorics* **11** (1990), 513–521.
4. A. EHRENFEUCHT, G. ROZENBERG, Each regular code is included in a maximal regular code. *RAIRO Theoretical Informatics and Applications* **20** (1986), 89–96.
5. G. GRÄTZER, *Universal Algebra.* Van Nostrand, Princeton, NJ, 1968.

48   D.L. Van, K.V. Hung, and P.T. Huy

6. K. V. Hung, P. T. Huy, D. L. Van, On some classes of codes defined by binary relations. *Acta Mathematica Vietnamica* **29** (2004), 163–176.
7. K. V. Hung, P. T. Huy, D. L. Van, Codes concerning roots of words. *Vietnam Journal of Mathematics* **32** (2004), 345–359.
8. J. Hopcroft, J. Ullman, *Formal Languages and Their Relation to Automata*. Addison-Wesley Publishing Company, Massachussetts, 1969.
9. M. Ito, H. Jürgensen, H. Shyr, G. Thierrin, Outfix and infix codes and related classes of languages. *Journal of Computer and System Science* **43** (1991), 484–508.
10. M. Ito, G. Thierrin, Congruences, infix and cohesive prefix codes. *Theoretical Computer Science* **136** (1994), 471–485.
11. H. Jürgensen, S. Konstatinidis, Codes. In: G. Rozenberg, A. Salomaa (eds.), *Handbook of Formal Languages*. Springer, Berlin, 1997, 511–607.
12. N. H. Lam, Finite maximal infix codes. *Semigroup Forum* **61** (2000), 346–356.
13. A. A. Markov, An example of an independent system of words which cannot be included in a finite complete system. *Matematicheskie Zametki* **1** (1967), 87–90 (in Russian).
14. D. Perrin, Completing biprefix codes. *Theoretical Computer Science* **28** (1984), 329–336.
15. A. Restivo, On codes having no finite completion. *Discrete Mathematics* **17** (1977), 309–316.
16. A. Restivo, S. Salemi, T. Sportelli, Completing codes. *RAIRO Theoretical Informatics and Applications* **23** (1989), 135–147.
17. H. Shyr, *Free Monoids and Languages*. Hon Min Book Company, Taichung, 1991.
18. H. Shyr, G. Thierrin, Codes and binary relations. *Lecture Notes 586 "Sèminarie d'Algèbre, Paul Dubreil, Paris (1975-1976)"*, Springer-Verlag, 180–188.
19. D. L. Van, Embedding problem for codes defined by binary relations. *Preprint 98/A22*, Institute of Mathematics, Hanoi, 1998.
20. D. L. Van, On a class of hypercodes. In: M. Ito, T. Imaoka (eds.), *Words, Languages and Combinatorics III*. World Scientific, 2003, 171–183.
21. D. L. Van, K. V. Hung, On codes defined by binary relations, Part I: Embedding problem (submitted).
22. D. L. Van, K. V. Hung, On codes defined by binary relations, Part II: Vector characterizations and maximality (submitted).
23. L. Zhang, Z. Shen, Completion of recognizable bifix codes. *Theoretical Computer Science* **145** (1995), 345–355.

Languages and Process Calculi for
Network Aware Programming
- Short Summary -

Rocco De Nicola

Dipartimento di Sistemi e Informatica,
Università di Firenze
denicola@dsi.unifi.it

Abstract. We describe motivations and background behind the design of KLAIM, a process description language that has proved to be suitable for describing a wide range of applications distributed over wide area networks with agents and code mobility. We argue that a drawback of KLAIM is that it is neither a programming language, nor a process calculus. We then outline the two research directions we have recently pursued. On the one hand we have evolved KLAIM to a full-fledged language for highly distributed mobile programming. On the other hand we have distilled the language to a number of simple calculi that we have used to define new semantic theories and equivalences and to test the impact of new operators for network aware programming.

1 Introduction

In the last decade, programming computational infrastructures available globally for offering uniform services has become one of the main issues in Computer Science. The challenges come from the necessity of dealing at once with issues like communication, co-operation, mobility, resource usage, security, privacy, failures, etc., in a setting where demands and guarantees can be very different for the many different components. This has stimulated research on concepts, abstractions, models and calculi that could provide the basis for the design of systems "sound by construction", predictable and analyzable.

One of the abstractions that appears to be very important is *mobility*. This feature deeply increases flexibility and, thus, expressiveness of programming languages for network-aware programming. Evidence of the success of this programming style is provided by the recent design of commercial/prototype programming languages with primitives for moving code and processes, Java, T-Space, Oz, Pict, Oblique, Odyssey ... that have seen the involvement of several important industrial and academic research institutions.

The first foundational calculus dealing with mobility has been the π-calculus, a simple and expressive calculus aiming at capturing the essence of name passing with the minimum number of basic constructs. If considered from a network-aware perspective, one could say that π-calculus misses an explicit notion of locality and/or domain where

D.V. Hung and M. Wirsing (Eds.): ICTAC 2005, LNCS 3722, pp. 49–52, 2005.

computations take place. To overcome this deficiency of π-calculus, several foundational formalisms, presented as process calculi or strongly based on them, have been developed. We want to mention, among the others, Ambient calculus, $D\pi$-calculus, DJoin, Nomadic Pict, ... A major problem that has been faced in their development has been the search for the appropriate abstractions that can be considered an acceptable compromise between expressiveness, elegance, and implementability. A paradigmatic example is the Ambient calculus: it is very elegant and expressive, but a reasonable distributed implementation is still problematic.

2   A Kernel Language for Agents Interaction and Mobility

KLAIM (A Kernel Language for Agents Interaction and Mobility) is a formalism specifically designed to describe distributed systems made up of several mobile interacting components that is positioned along the same lines of the above mentioned calculi. The distinguishing features of the approach is the explicit use of localities for accessing data or computational resources. The choice of its primitives was heavily influenced by *CCS* and π-calculus and by Linda. Indeed, KLAIM stemmed from our work on process algebras with localities [4] and our work on the formalization of the semantics of Linda as a process algebra [10].

Linda is a coordination language that relies on an asynchronous and associative communication mechanism based on a shared global environment called *tuple space*, a multiset of *tuples*. Tuples are ordered sequence of information items (called *fields*). There can be *actual fields* (i.e., expressions, processes, localities, constants, identifiers) and *formal fields* (i.e., variables). Tuples are *anonymous* and *content-addressable*. The basic interaction mechanism is *pattern–matching* that is used to select tuples from tuple spaces. Linda has four primitives for manipulating tuple spaces: two blocking operations that are used for accessing and removing tuples and two non-blocking ones that are used for adding tuples.

KLAIM can be seen as an asynchronous higher–order process calculus whose basic actions are the original Linda primitives enriched with explicit information about the location of the nodes where processes and tuples are allocated. Communications take place through distributed repositories and remote operations. The primitives allow programmers to distribute and retrieve data and processes to and from the different localities (nodes) of a net. Localities are first-class citizens that can be dynamically created and communicated. Tuples can contain both values and code that can be subsequently accessed and evaluated. An allocation environment, associating logical and physical localities, is used to avoid the programmers to consider the precise physical allocation of the distributed tuple spaces.

The main drawback of KLAIM is that it is neither a real programming language nor a process calculus. We have thus, more recently, worked along two directions. On the one hand, we have evolved KLAIM to a full-fledged language (X-KLAIM) to be used for distributed mobile programming. On the other hand, we have distilled the language into a number of simpler calculi that we have used to define new semantic theories and equivalences and to assess the expressive power of tuple based communications and evaluate the theoretical impact of new linguistic primitives.

3   A Programming Language Based on KLAIM

X-KLAIM (eXtended Klaim) [1] is an experimental programming language that has bee specifically designed to program distributed systems with several components interacting through multiple tuple spaces and mobile code (possibly object-oriented). X-KLAIM has been implemented on the top of a run-time system that was developed in Java for the sake of portability [2]. The linguistic constructs of KLAIM have proved to be appropriate for programming a wide range of distributed applications with agents and code mobility that, once compiled in Java, can run over different platforms.

4   KLAIM-Based Calculi

From KLAIM we have distilled μKLAIM, CKLAIM and LCKLAIM) and we have studied the encoding of each of them into a simpler one [7]. μKLAIM is obtained from KLAIM by eliminating the distinction between logical and physical localities (*no allocation environment*) and the possibility of higher order communication (*no process code in tuples*). CKLAIM, is obtained from μKLAIM by only considering *monadic* communications and by removing the read action, the non destructive variant of the in basic actions. LCKLAIM is obtained from CKLAIM by removing also the possibility of performing remote inputs and outputs. In LCKLAIM communications is only local and process migration is exploited to use remote resources.

This work on core calculi has also stimulated and simplified the search for other variants of KLAIM that better model more sophisticated settings for network aware programming. In [6] and in [8] we have considered TOPOLOGICAL-KLAIM a variant of CKLAIM that permits explicit creation of inter-node connections and their destruction and thus considering two typical features of global computers, namely *dynamic inter-node connections* and *failures*. In [9] we have developed more flexible (but still easily implementable) forms of pattern matching.

For the simpler calculi we have instantiated the theory developed in [3] and have introduced two abstract semantics: *barbed congruence* and *may testing*. They are obtained as the closure under operational and contexts reduction of the extensional equivalences induced by what can be considered a natural *basic observable* for global computers:

A specific site is up and running
(when requested, the site provides a data of some kind).

For the two equivalences obtained as context closures, we have also provided alternative characterizations that permit a better appreciation of their discriminating power and the development of proof techniques that avoid universal quantification over contexts. Indeed, we have established their correspondence with a bisimulation-based and a trace-based equivalence over the labelled transition system used to describe the semantics for the different variants of KLAIM.

5   Miscellanea

Starting from KLAIM, other lines of research have been pursued. We have considered extensions of KLAIM for dealing with issues of security, quality of services and performance evaluation. We have studied logics for reasoning about mobile code. We have proposed type systems for controlling access to shared resources. Additional information, software and papers related to KLAIM and to the KLAIM Project can be retrieved at: http://music.dsi.unifi.it/klaim.html.

Acknowledgements

The KLAIM Project is a collective effort. It is the result of the Ph.D. thesis of Lorenzo Bettini, Michele Loreti and Daniele Gorla and of joint work with many other researchers: Viviana Bono, Gianluigi Ferrari, Joost-Peeter Katoen, Diego Latella, Mieke Massink, Eugenio Moggi, Ugo Montanari, Rosario Pugliese, Emilio Tuosto and Betti Venneri. I would like to thank all of them for the contribution to the project and for what they have taught me.

References

1. L. Bettini, R. De Nicola. Interactive Mobile Agents in X-KLAIM. In *SFM-05:Moby,* 5th *International School on Formal Methods for the Design of Computer, Communication and Software Systems: Mobile Computing*, volume 3465 of *LNCS*, pages 29–68, Spinger, 2005 .
2. L. Bettini, R. De Nicola, and R. Pugliese. KLAVA: a Java Package for Distributed and Mobile Applications. *Software – Practice and Experience*, 32:1365–1394, 2002.
3. Michele Boreale, Rocco De Nicola, and Rosario Pugliese. Basic observables for processes. *Inf. Comput.*, 149(1):77–98, 1999.
4. Flavio Corradini and Rocco De Nicola. Locality based semantics for process algebras. *Acta Inf.*, 34(4):291–324, 1997.
5. R. De Nicola, G. Ferrari, and R. Pugliese. KLAIM: a Kernel Language for Agents Interaction and Mobility. *IEEE Trans. on Software Engineering*, 24(5):315–330, 1998.
6. R. De Nicola, D. Gorla, and R. Pugliese. Basic observables for a calculus for global computing. Tech. Rep. 07/2004, Dip. di Informatica, Università di Roma "La Sapienza". Short version to appear in the *Proc. of ICALP'05*.
7. R. De Nicola, D. Gorla, and R. Pugliese. On the expressive power of KLAIM-based calculi. To appera in TCS. Short version in *Proc. of EXPRESS'04*, ENTCS 128(2):117–130. Elsevier, 2004.
8. R. De Nicola, D. Gorla, and R. Pugliese. Global computing in a dynamic network of tuple spaces. In *Proc. of COORDINATION'05*, volume 3454 of *LNCS*, pages 157–172. Springer, 2005.
9. R. De Nicola, D. Gorla, and R. Pugliese. Pattern matching over a dynamic network of tuple spaces. In *Proc. of FMOODS'05*, volume 3535 of *LNCS*, pages 1–14. Springer.
10. Rocco De Nicola and Rosario Pugliese. Linda-based applicative and imperative process algebras. *Theor. Comput. Sci.*, 238(1-2):389–437, 2000.

Stochastic Analysis of Graph Transformation Systems: A Case Study in P2P Networks

Reiko Heckel*

Department of Computer Science, University of Leicester, United Kingdom

Abstract. In distributed and mobile systems with volatile bandwidth and fragile connectivity, non-functional aspects like performance and reliability become more and more important. To formalise, measure, and predict these properties, *stochastic methods* are required. At the same time such systems are characterised by a high degree of architectural reconfiguration. Viewing the architecture of a distributed system as a graph, this is naturally modelled by *graph transformations*.

To address these two concerns, stochastic graph transformation systems have been introduced associating with each rule its application rate—the rate of the exponential distribution governing the delay of its application. Deriving continuous-time Markov chains, Continuous Stochastic Logic is used to specify reliability properties and verify them through model checking.

In particular, we study a protocol for the reconfiguration of P2P networks intended to improve their reliability by adding redundant connections. The modelling of this protocol as a (stochastic) graph transformation system takes advantage of negative application and conditions path expressions. This ensuing high-level style of specification helps to reduce the number of states and increases the capabilities for automated analysis.

1   Introduction

Non-functional requirements, concerning the quality or resources of a system, are often difficult to capture, measure, and predict. At the same time they are usually critical for success. Many failures of software engineering projects have been attributed to a lack of understanding of non-functional aspects in the early stages of development [9].

With the success of Internet and mobile technology, properties like the reliability of connections, available bandwidth and computing resources become an even greater concern. Since individual occurrences of failures are generally unpredictable, stochastic concepts are required to formalise such properties. Many specification formalisms provide corresponding extensions, including stochastic transition systems (or Markov chains [2,21]), stochastic Petri nets [1,4,19,20] or process algebras [5,7]. Most of these formalisms specialise in describing behaviour

---

* European Community's Human Potential Programme under contract HPRN-CT-2002-00275, SegraVis.

D.V. Hung and M. Wirsing (Eds.): ICTAC 2005, LNCS 3722, pp. 53–69, 2005.

in terms of orderings of events, neglecting aspects like data transformations and changes to software architecture or network topology.

A noticeable exception is the π-calculus [18], which allows communication of channel names between interacting processes. It is thus possible to describe changes of data structures or network topologies. The stochastic π-calculus [22], extending the original by assigning rates to the communication actions of a process, allows to address non-functional aspects. However, while the π-calculus is an adequate semantic framework for programming, it is too low-level for expressing requirements in the early stages of a project. Here communication between developers and clients requires a direct, diagrammatic description of *what* changes are required, instead of a detailed description of *how* they are achieved.

A more abstract style of specification is provided by rewriting-based formalisms like Rewriting Logic or Graph Transformation [17,24]. Here, rules specify pre- and post-conditions of operations (*what* should be achieved) in terms of complex patterns, while the underlying mechanisms for pattern matching and implementing these changes are hidden from the user. Graph transformation, in particular, supports a visual representation of rules which is reminiscent of to the intuitive way in which engineers would sketch, for example, network reconfigurations.

In order to account for the non-functional aspects, we introduced *stochastic* graph transformation systems [11]. Associating an exponentially distributed application delay with each rule, we derive continuous-time Markov chains (CTMCs), the standard model for stochastic analysis. This enables us to establish a link to continuous stochastic logic (CSL) to express and verify properties like the probability of being connected within 20 seconds after start-up, the long-term probability for connectedness, etc.

This paper is devoted to a case study, a simplified version of a protocol for the reconfiguration of Peer-to-Peer networks [16], to validate the practicability of the approach. P2P networks are decentralised overlay networks that use a given transport infrastructure like the Internet to create a self-organising network. Due to the lack of global control and potential unreliability of the infrastructure, P2P networks are prone to dependability problems. The standard solution consists in creating sufficient redundancy so that, when a node unexpectedly leaves the network, its role in the routing of information can be taken over by other nodes.

Mariani [16] proposes an algorithm which, executed asynchronously by each peer, adds redundant connections to the network to guarantee that the disappearance of a peer does not unduly affect the overall performance and routing capabilities of the network. It does so by querying the local context of a node up to a given depth to expose potential weaknesses in the network topology. The assumption is that this happens fast enough to prevent loss of connectivity due to the disappearance of the node before extra links could be added. The desired result is an increased fault tolerance.

We are going to validate these assumptions and compare the level of fault tolerance achieved with the one obtained by the simpler solution of just adding a limited number of references at random. To this purpose, we shall model the protocol as a stochastic graph transformation systems and analyse different variants of it. To develop a satisfactory model, we will require advanced features for controlling the application of rules, like negative application conditions and path expressions. We give an introduction to the basic approach and its extensions and discuss their relevance w.r.t. the model checking problem.

The paper is structured as follows. Below, in Sect. 2 we introduce typed graph transformation systems and provide a functional model model of the P2P network. In Sect. 3 we extend definitions and examples to stochastic graph transformation systems, including the derivation of Markov chains, stochastic logic and model checking. Their application to the case study is reported in Sect. 4. Sect. 5 concludes the paper with a discussion of tools and relevant theoretical problems.

2   Graph Transformation Systems

In this section we will first focus on the basic ideas of typed graph transformation systems, followed by a survey of the more advanced concepts required by our case study. We follow the so-called algebraic single-pushout (SPO) approach [15] to the transformation of typed graphs [13,6].

2.1   Type and Instance Graphs

Graphs provide the most basic mathematical model for entities and relations. A graph consists of a set of vertices V and a set of edges E such that each edge e in E has a source and a target vertex $s(e)$ and $t(e)$ in V, respectively.

In this paper, graphs shall represent configurations of a Peer-to-Peer (P2P) network, modelling network nodes as vertices and links between them as edges. We distinguish two different kinds of nodes in our networks, labelled by P for peers and R for registry, as well as edge types l and r representing links and registrations, respectively. The idea is that new peers participating in the network have to login with a central registry server. Afterwards, they can connect and communicate directly, without using any central infrastructure.

The graph in the upper right of Fig. 2.1 represents a network with a single participant and the registry, while the one in the upper left has two connected participants. Our graphs are directed, but in the case of links we use undirected l-edges edges to denote symmetric pairs of directed ones.

Like a network configuration, also a collection of interrelated types may be represented as a graph. In the bottom, Figure 2.1 shows the type graph of the P2P model, providing the types for the instance graphs in the top. The relation between types and their occurrences in configurations is formally captured by the notion of *typed graphs*: A fixed *type graph* TG represents the type level and its *instance graphs* the individual snapshots.

Definition 1 (typed graphs). *A directed (unlabelled) graph is a four-tuple* $G = \langle G_V, G_E, src^G, tar^G \rangle$ *with a set of vertices* G_V, *a set of edges* G_E, *and functions* $src^G : G_E \rightarrow G_V$ *and* $tar^G : G_E \rightarrow G_V$ *associating to each edge*

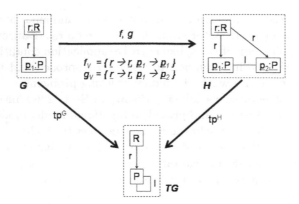

Fig. 1. Type and instance graphs

its source and target vertex. A graph homomorphism $f : G \to H$ is a pair of functions $\langle f_V : G_V \to H_V, f_E : G_E \to H_E \rangle$ preserving source and target, i.e., such that $f_V \circ src^G = src^H \circ f_E$ and $f_V \circ tar^G = tar^H \circ f_E$.

Fixing a type graph TG, an instance graph $\langle G, tp^G \rangle$ over TG is a graph G equipped with a graph homomorphism $tp^G : G \to TG$. A morphism of typed graphs $h : \langle G_1, g_1 \rangle \to \langle G_2, g_2 \rangle$ is a graph homomorphism $h : G_1 \to G_2$ that preserves the typing, that is, $tp^{G_2} \circ h = tp^{G_1}$.

We us the notation of the Unified Modelling Language (UML) for class and object diagrams to capture the distinction between types and instances: $r : R$ denotes an element of an instance graph $\langle G, tp^G \rangle$ such that its type $tp^G(r) = R$. The expression is underlined to stress that it is considered part of a system configuration (rather than a rule as we shall see below). Morphisms between typed graphs $\langle G, tp^G \rangle$ and $\langle H, tp^H \rangle$ are exemplified in Fig. 2.1. Morphism f represents a subgraph inclusion while g, combining inclusion and renaming, is an injective homomorphism or subgraph isomorphism.

2.2   Single-Pushout Graph Transformation

Having modelled configurations as instance graphs, we are turning to the specification of instance graph transformations by means of rules. A rule can be seen as a representative example of all transformations, modelling them by means of patterns for pre and post states.

For a given type graph TG, a *graph transformation rule* $p : L \to R$ consists of a name p and a pair of graphs typed over TG. The left-hand side L represents the pre-condition of the operation specified by the rule while the right-hand side R describes the post-condition. A correspondence between elements in L and R is given by the identities of the nodes (sometimes omitted, assuming that the intention is obvious from the layout).

The rules for the P2P network model are shown in Fig. 2 and 5. Rule *new* creates a new peer. This requires to look up the registration of an existing peer at the registry server, represented by the r-edge from $r : R$ to $p : P$, to create a

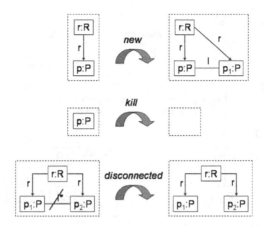

Fig. 2. Rules for creating and killing peers

new peer $p_1 : P$ with corresponding registration, and to link it to p with a new edge of type l.

Rule *kill* models the deletion of a peer with all its ingoing and outgoing edges. This may cause the network to become disconnected, except for registrations, which are not used for communication. The rule *disconnected* in the bottom is provided to detect such situations. The rule is applicable if there are two registered nodes which are *not connected* by a path of l-edges, but the application does not have any effect on the graph. This rule combines two interesting features: Negative application conditions and path expressions, both to be introduced below in more detail.

Rules generate transformations by replacing in a given graph a match for the left-hand side with a copy of the right-hand side. Thus, a *graph transformation* from a pre-state G to a post-state H, denoted by $G \overset{p(m)}{\Longrightarrow} H$, is performed in three steps.

1. *Find* a match of the left-hand side L in the given graph G, represented by an injective graph morphism $m : L \to G$, and check if it satisfies the application conditions, if any;
2. *Delete* from G all vertices and edges matching $L \setminus R$;
3. *Paste* to the result a *copy* of $R \setminus L$, yielding the derived graph H.

In Fig. 3 the application of a rule is shown which creates a new peer, but unlike *new* in Fig. 2 passes on the registration from the existing to the new peer. The match m of the rule's left-hand side is indicated by the boldface nodes and edges in G. The transformation deletes the r-edge from $\underline{r : R}$ to $\underline{p_2 : P}$, because it is matched by an edge in the left-hand side L, which does not occur in R. To the graph obtained after deletion, we paste a copy of the node $p_1 : P$ in L, renaming it to $\underline{p_3}$ to avoid a name conflict, as well as copies of the l-edge from $p : P$ to $p_1 : P$ and the r-edge from $r : R$ to p_1. The match m tells us where these edges must be added, e.g., $p \mapsto \underline{p_2}$ means that the new l-edge is attached to $\underline{p_2}$ rather than to $\underline{p_1}$ in H. However, this is not the only possibility for applying this

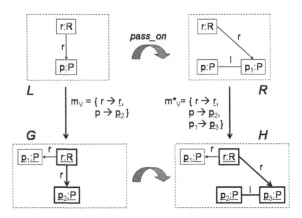

Fig. 3. Transformation step using rule *collect*

rule. Another option would be to match p by $\underline{p}_1$, attaching the link to a different peer. That means, there are two causes of non-determinism: choosing the rule to be applied (e.g., *new* or *pass_on*) and the match at which it is applied. (In this case, both transformations lead to graphs that are isomorphic, i.e., differ only up to renaming.)

The example of Fig. 3 is not entirely representative of the problems that may be caused by deleting elements in a graph during step 2. In fact, we have to make sure that the remaining structure is still a valid graph, i.e., that no edges are left dangling because of the deletion of their source or target vertices. The problem is exemplified by the step in Fig. 4. The deletion of $\underline{p}_2: P$ would leave the attached r and l edges "dangling".

There exist two solutions to this problem: a radical and a conservative one. The first gives priority to deletion, removing the vertex along with the dangling edges. The conservative alternative consists in assuming a standard applications condition which excludes the depicted situation as valid transformation. This application condition is known as the *dangling condition*, and it is characteristic of the algebraic DPO (double-pushout) approach to graph transformation [8].

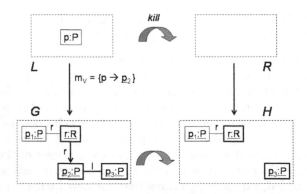

Fig. 4. More interesting example

We adopt the more radical Single-Pushout (SPO) approach [15] because it provides a more realistic representation of the behaviour we intend to model: It may not be possible to stop a peer from leaving the network, even if it is still connected to other peers. The SPO approach owes its name to the fact that the construction of applying a transformation rule can be formalised as a pushout (a gluing construction) in the category of graphs and partial graph homomorphisms [15]. A partial graph morphism $g : G \to H$ is a total morphisms from some subgraph $dom(g)$ of G to H. We consider the simplified case of injective matching, where the left-hand side is essentially a subgraph of the graph to be transformed, rather than an arbitrary homomorphic image.

Definition 2 (rule, match, transformation). *A rule $p : L \xrightarrow{r} R$ consists of a rule name p and a partial graph morphism r. A match for $r : L \to R$ into some graph G is a total injective morphism $m : L \to G$. Given a rule p and a match m for p in a graph G the direct (SPO-) transformation from G with p at m, written $G \xRightarrow{p(m)} H$, is the pushout of r and m in the category of graphs and partial graph morphisms.*

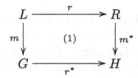

The typing $G, L \xrightarrow{r} R$, and $L \xrightarrow{m} G$ over TG induces a unique typing for the derived graph H as well as for the tracking morphism r^* and the co-match m^*. Intuitively, all elements that are preserved get their typing from G via r^* and all new elements inherit their typing from R via m^*. Pushout properties of (1) imply that there are no further elements in H (i.e., r^* and m^* are jointly surjective) and for all elements that are in the image of both morphisms, there exists a common pre-image in L so that commutativity of the diagram and type compatibility of r and m ensure that they inherit the same types from R and G.

2.3   Application Conditions and Path Expressions

Quite often, plain graph matching is not enough to express sophisticated application conditions. An example is the dangling edge condition, requiring that there are no edges incident to nodes that are to be deleted, except for those that are already part of the rule.

User defined negative application conditions [10] can "sense" the existence or non-existence of connections in the vicinity of the match. As examples, Fig. 5 shows the rules for creating redundant links in the network to achieve a higher fault tolerance in case a node is unexpectedly deleted. Using *smart* in the bottom, a shortcut is introduced if the two neighbours of a peer are not otherwise connected by a direct link or via a third peer. This is expressed by two negative context conditions: the crossed out l-edge and the crossed out P-node with its two attached edges.

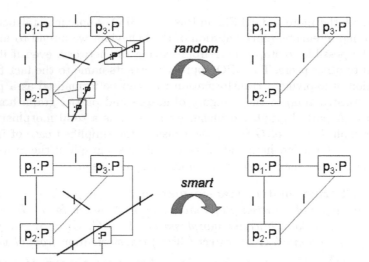

Fig. 5. Rules for introducing short-cuts in the network

The rule should be applicable at match m only if m can *not* be extended to include any of the two forbidden structures, i.e., neither the crossed out l-edge nor the P-node with its two edges. They are represented in Fig. 6 by two injective morphisms l_1 and l_2 outgoing from the left-hand side L. Extension l_i is present in graph G if an injective morphism n_i can be found which coincides with m on L, i.e., the corresponding sub-diagram commutes.

Definition 3 (application conditions). *A constraint over L is an injective typed graph morphism $L \xrightarrow{l} \hat{L}$. Given a a match (injective morphism) $L \xrightarrow{m} G$, match m satisfies l, written $m \models_L l$, if there is an injective morphism $\hat{L} \xrightarrow{n} G$,*

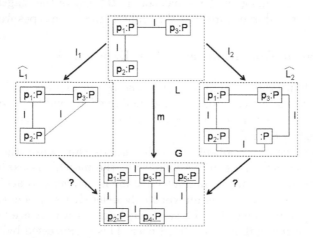

Fig. 6. Satisfaction of shortcut constraints as graph morphisms

such that $n \circ l = m$. *An* application condition *is a Boolean expression using constraints over L as atomic propositions. Satisfaction is defined as usual, based on the satisfaction of constraints.*

A conditional transformation step *is a transformation step where the match satisfies the application conditions associated with the rule.*

The negative application in Fig. 6 is thus of the structure $N = \neg l_1 \wedge \neg l_2$. Its satisfaction does not only depend on the graph G, but also on the chosen match m. Consider, for example, $m_1 = \{p_i \mapsto \underline{p}_i\}$, $m_2 = \{p_1 \mapsto \underline{p}_3, p_2 \mapsto \underline{p}_4, p_3 \mapsto \underline{p}_5\}$, and $m_3 = \{p_1 \mapsto \underline{p}_3, p_2 \mapsto \underline{p}_1, p_3 \mapsto \underline{p}_5\}$. Then $m_1, m_2 \not\models_L N$, but $m_3 \models_L N$.

The rule *random* in Fig. 5 models the naive approach of adding links at random as long as the number of additional l-edges attached to either p_3 or p_4, beyond the ones linking them to p_1, do not exceed two. Hence, the rule will not increase the degree of any node beyond three. This condition is expressed by negative constraints, too. Note that injectivity of $\hat{L} \xrightarrow{n} G$ is essential here, because this enables us to count the number of nodes in a graph which would have been confused otherwise.

Path expressions specifying the (non-)existence of certain paths support the navigation within graphs and are generally useful if non-local graph properties shall be expressed. For instance, rule *disconnected* in Fig. 2 detects disconnected parts of the graph.

For vertices $v, w \in G_V$, a *path* from v to w is a sequence of edges $s = (e_1, e_2, \ldots, e_n) \in G_E$ such that $tar^G(e_i) = src^G(e_{i+1})$ for all $i \in \{1, \ldots, n-1\}$ (the target vertex of one edge is the source of its successor), $v = src^G(e_1)$ and $w = tar^G(e_n)$. If G is typed over TG by tp^G, the type of s is is defined by extending tp^G to sequences, i.e., $tp^G(s) = tp^G_E(e_1), tp^G_E(e_2), \ldots, tp^G_E(e_n)$.

A path expressions p is a regular expression over the alphabet TG_E of edge types. Labelling an edge e in the left-hand side of a rule, it is satisfied by a match $m : L \to G$ if there exists a path s from $m(src^L(e))$ to $m(tar^L(e))$ such that $tp^G(s) = p$.

Path expressions are formally subsumed by Def. 3 if we allow for a countably infinite set of constraints and infinitary Boolean expressions as application conditions. An expression stating the non-existence of a path labelled by l-edges, like in rule *disconnected* in Fig. 2, is then represented by a conjunction $\neg l_1 \wedge \neg l_2 \wedge \ldots$ where the l_i are constraints specifying paths of length i.

2.4   Graph Transformation Systems

Rules over the same type graph are collected in a graph transformation system. Given a graph to start with, they can generate any of the usual state-based models, like sets of traces, labelled transition systems, event structures. We will be particularly interested in a variant of transition systems.

Definition 4 (graph transformation system). *A* graph transformation system *$\mathcal{G} = \langle TG, P \rangle$ consists of a type graph TG and a set of (conditional) graph transformation rules $p : L \xrightarrow{r} R \in P$. The application condition of p is denoted by $AP(p)$.*

A transformation sequence in $\mathcal{G}$

$$G_0 \overset{p_1(m_1)}{\Longrightarrow} G_1 \overset{p_2(m_2)}{\Longrightarrow} \cdots \overset{p_k(m_k)}{\Longrightarrow} G_k$$

is a sequence of consecutive transformation steps with $p_i \in P$, briefly denoted by $G_0 \Longrightarrow_{\mathcal{G}}^* G_k$.

The graph transformation systems we shall be interested in are

- $\mathcal{G}_{random} = \langle TG, \{new, kill, disconnected, random\} \rangle$
- $\mathcal{G}_{smart} = \langle TG, \{new, kill, disconnected, smart\} \rangle$

with TG being the type graph shown in the bottom of Fig. 2.1 and the rules given in Fig. 2 and 5.

A labelled transition graph is the multi-graph equivalent of a labelled transition system, allowing for more than one transition between a given pair of states, defined as isomorphism classes of the graphs reachable from the initial one.

Definition 5 (induced labelled transition graph). *Let $\mathcal{G} = \langle TG, P \rangle$ be a graph transformation system and G_0 a graph typed over TG. Assume a fixed mapping χ associating to each isomorphism class C of typed graphs a representative G, i.e. $\chi(C) = G$ with $C = [G] := \{H \mid H \cong G\}$. The labelled transition graph induced by $\mathcal{G}$ and G_0 is given by $LTG(\mathcal{G}, G_0) = \langle L, S, T, pre, post, lab \rangle$, where*

- $L = P$ *is the set of rule names of $\mathcal{G}$;*
- S *is the set of all isomorphism classes of graphs reachable from G_0, i.e. $S = \{ [G_n] \mid G_0 \Longrightarrow_{\mathcal{G}}^* G_n \}$;*
- T *is the set of transformations $t = (G \overset{p(m)}{\Longrightarrow} H)$ with $\chi(s) = G$ and $\chi(s') = H$ for some $s, s' \in S$. In this case, $pre(t) = s$, $post(t) = s'$, $lab(t) = p$ and we write briefly $s \overset{p}{\Longrightarrow} s'$.*

Multiple transitions are of interest when in the following section labelled transition graphs are used to derive Markov chains.

3   Stochastic Graph Transformation

In this section, we introduce stochastic graph transformations extending typed graph transformation systems in the SPO approach by rates associated with rule names. We show how to derive a Continuous-Time Markov Chain (CTMC) from the generated transition system, thus providing the basis for stochastic logic and model checking in Section 3.3.

3.1   Markov Chains

First we provide some basic notions adopting the Q-matrix, a kind of "incidence matrix" of the Markov Chain, as elementary notion (cf. [21]).

Definition 6 (Q-matrix). *Let S be a countable set. A Q-matrix on S is a real-valued matrix $Q = Q(s, s')_{s,s' \in S}$ satisfying the following conditions:*

(i) $0 \leq -Q(s,s) < \infty$ *for all* $s \in S$,
(ii) $Q(s,s') \geq 0$ *for all* $s \neq s'$,
(iii) $\sum_{s' \in S} Q(s,s') = 0$ *for all* $s \in S$.

The Q-matrix is also called *transition rate matrix*. We use Q-matrices in order to define random processes. A random process is a family of random variables $X(t)$ where t is an indexing parameter. Depending on whether t is taken from a discrete or continuous set, we speak of a discrete- or continuous-time process, respectively.

We consider continuous-time random processes in which the number of times the random variables $X(t)$ changes value is finite or countable. Let $t_1, t_2, t_3, \ldots$ be the times at which the state changes occur. If we ignore how long the random process remains in a given state, we can view the sequence $X(t_1), X(t_2), X(t_3), \ldots$ as a discrete-time process embedded in the continuous-time process, the so called *jump chain* [21, 2.2].

Definition 7 (CTMC). *A continuous-time Markov chain (CTMC) is a continuous-time, discrete-state random process such that*

1. *The jump chain is a discrete-time Markov chain, i.e. a random process in which the current state depends only on the previous state in the chain.*
2. *The time between state changes is a random variable T with a memoryless distribution, i.e.* $\mathbb{P}(T > t + \tau \mid T > t) = \mathbb{P}(T > \tau)$ *for all* $t, \tau > 0$.

A Q-matrix on a countable set of states S defines a CTMC in the following way:

If $s \neq s'$ and $Q(s, s') > 0$, then there is a transition from s to s'. If the set $\{s' \mid Q(s,s') > 0\}$ is not a singleton, then there is a competition between the transitions originating in s. The probability that transition $s \to s'$ wins the "race" is $-\frac{Q(s,s')}{Q(s,s)}$. This defines the jump chain.

The time T for leaving a state s to another state is exponentially distributed with rate $Q(s) = -Q(s,s)$ *(the total exit rate)*, i.e. $\mathbb{P}(T > t) = e^{-Q(s) \cdot t}$. The exponential distribution is well-known to enjoy the memoryless-property [21, 2.3.1]. Thus a Q-matrix defines a Continuous-Time Markov Chain:

Definition 8 (CTMC with generating matrix Q). *Let Q be a Q-matrix on a countable set of states S. Then the continuous-time random process with jump chain and state-change times as decried above is the Continuous-Time Markov Chain with generator matrix Q.*

Let Q be a Q-matrix on S and Q' be a Q-matrix on S'. We call the CTMCs generated by Q and Q' *isomorphic* if there is a bijective mapping $\phi : S \to S'$ such that $Q'(\phi(s), \phi(t)) = Q(s, t)$ for all states $s, t \in S$. The transition probability matrix $P(t) = (P_{ss'}(t))_{s,s' \in S}$ describes the dynamic behaviour. It is the minimal non-negative solution of the equation

$$P'(t) = QP(t), \quad P(0) = I.$$

The (s, s')-indexed entry of $P(t)$ specifies the probability that the system is in state s' after time t if it is in state s at present. Given an initial distribution $\pi(0)$, the *transient solution* $\pi(t) = (\pi_s(t))_{s \in S}$ is then

$$\pi(t) = \pi(0)P(t).$$

In the finite case, $P(t)$ can be computed by the matrix exponential function, $P(t) = e^{Qt}$, but the numerical behaviour of the matrix exponential series is rather unsatisfactory [25]. Apart from the transient solution, which specifies the behaviour as time evolves, the *steady state* or *invariant distribution* is of great interest. It is a distribution, i.e. a map $\pi : S \to [0,1]$ with $\sum_{s \in S} \pi_s = 1$, such that $\pi Q = 0$ holds. The steady state gives information about the long term behaviour of the Markov Chain.

3.2   Stochastic Graph Transformation Systems

A stochastic graph transformation system associates with each rule name a positive real number representing the rate of the exponentially distributed delay of its application.

Definition 9 (stochastic GTS). *A stochastic graph transformation system* $SG = \langle TG, P, \rho \rangle$ *consists of a graph transformation system* $\langle TG, P \rangle$ *and a function* $\rho : P \to \mathbb{R}^+$ *associating with every rule its application rate* $\rho(p)$.

For the rules of our sample systems G_{random}, G_{smart}, fixed rates shall be given by $\rho(new) = \rho(kill) = 1$ and $\rho(disconnected) = 0$, while the rates of $random, smart$ shall range over 10^x for $x = 1 \ldots 4$. That means, *disconnected* shall never actually be applied, while the frequency of applying the rules for creating shortcuts will vary considerably between the experiments. This will allow us to answer the question if and under which conditions the protocol proposed in [16] is superior to a random addition of links.

Next we show how a stochastic graph transformation system gives rise to a Markov Chain, so that the analysis techniques described in Sect. 3.1 can be applied.

Definition 10 (induced Markov chain). *Let* $SG = \langle TG, P, \rho \rangle$ *be a stochastic graph transformation system with start graph* G_0 *and let the induced labelled transition graph* $LTG(\mathcal{G}, G_0) = \langle L, S, T, pre, post, lab \rangle$ *be finitely-branching. Assume for all* $s \in S$ *that* $\rho(p) = 0$ *if* $p \in R(s, s)$.

Then the Q-matrix on S, *generating the* induced Markov chain *of* SG *is defined by*

$$Q(s, s') = \begin{cases} \sum_{s \xrightarrow{p} s'} \rho(p) & , \text{ for } s \neq s' \\ -\sum_{t \neq s} Q(s, t) & , \text{ for } s = s'. \end{cases}$$

The initial distribution $\pi(0)$ is given by $\pi_s(0) = 1$ for $s = [G_0]$ and $\pi_s(0) = 0$ else. For a proof that this is well-defined, see [11].

Note that there may be multiple transitions linking two given states. As the Q-matrix can hold only a single entry for every pair of states, the rates of all these transitions have to be added up. Hence our notion of equality on transitions determines the rate in the Q-matrix. We regard two transitions as equal only if the same rule is applied at the same match. For example, if two different peers can decide to terminate themselves, these decisions should be independent, lead to two different transitions, and finally add up to a higher rate.

3.3   Stochastic Temporal Logic

We use extended Continuous Stochastic Logic **CSL** as presented in [3] to describe properties of CTMCs. Suppose that a labelling function $L : S \to 2^{AP}$ is given, associating to every state s the set of atomic propositions $L(s) \subseteq AP$ that are valid in s. The syntax of **CSL** is:

$$\Phi ::= tt \mid a \mid \neg\Phi \mid \Phi_1 \wedge \Phi_2 \mid S_{\triangleleft p}(\Phi) \mid \mathcal{P}_{\triangleleft p}(\Phi_1 \mathcal{U}^I \Phi_2)$$

where $\triangleleft \in \{\leq, \geq\}$, $p \in [0, 1]$, $a \in AP$ and $I \subseteq \mathbf{R}$ is an interval. The other boolean connectives are defined as usual, i.e., $ff = \neg tt$, $\Phi \vee \Psi = \neg(\neg\Phi \wedge \neg\Psi)$ and $\Phi \to \Psi = \neg\Phi \wedge \Psi$. The steady-state operator $S_{\triangleleft p}(\Phi)$ asserts that the steady-state probability of the formula Φ meets the bound $\triangleleft p$. The operator $\mathcal{P}_{\triangleleft p}(\Phi_1 \mathcal{U}^I \Phi_2)$ asserts that the probability measure of the paths satisfying $\Phi_1 \mathcal{U}^I \Phi_2$ meets the bound $\triangleleft p$.[1]

For example, the formula $\mathcal{P}_{\geq 0.02}(true\ \mathcal{U}^{[0,10]}\ disconnected)$ expresses the fact that the probability of reaching a state labelled *disconnected* within 10 time units is at most 0.02, while $S_{\leq 0.01}(disconnected)$ that the long-term probability of being in a state labelled *disconnected* is less than 0.01. Both operators are also available as queries, asking for the probability of a certain formula to be true. For example, $S_{=?}(disconnected)$ would return the probability of being in a *disconnected*-labelled state, rather than true or false.

In order to use **CSL** for analysing stochastic graph transformation systems, we have to define the atomic propositions AP and the labelling function L.

Definition 11 (interpreting CSL over labelled transition graphs). *Let $LTG = \langle L, S, T, pre, post \rangle$ be the labelled transition graph of a (stochastic) graph transformation system $\mathcal{G}$ with initial graph G_0. We define $AP = L$ to be the set of transition labels (rule names of $\mathcal{G}$), and the labelling of states*

$$L(s) = \{p \in AP \mid \exists t : pre(t) = s\}$$

to be given by the sets of labels of outgoing transitions.

Thus we can reason about the applicability of rules. Coming back to the above example, a state labelled *disconnected* is therefore one where the rule *disconnected* is applicable (which has an outgoing transition with that label). $S_{=?}(disconnected)$ therefore queries the transition system for the probability of being in a disconnected state.

Recall that rule *disconnected* does not have any effect on the state, i.e., it is exclusively used to represent a state property. The transition rates of such property rules are set to 0, so that they do not affect the Q-matrix.

---

[1] The other path and state operators can be derived. Details are given in [3].

4 Application

We have constructed an experimental tool chain consisting of GROOVE [23] for generating the labelled transition graph of a graph transformation system, and PRISM [14] for probabilistic model checking. An adapter connects both tools by translating the transition graph generated by GROOVE into a PRISM transition system specification, incorporating the transition rates ρ as specified in a separate file [2].

As usual, the size of the state space to be generated and analysed is a limiting factor. Presently the main bottleneck is not the actual state space generation in GROOVE, which can handle up to 10^6 states, but its import into the PRISM model checker, which reaches its limits at a few thousand states. The actual model checking, once the model is successfully imported, takes no more than a few seconds.

The problem is caused by the low-level presentation of transition systems generated by the transformation tool, which uses a single state variable s only. Transitions are represented as conditional assignments as in the listing below, where [new]s=176->1*new_rate:(s'=80) defines a transition from state 176 to state 80 using rule *new* at rate *new_rate* $= 1$. The enumeration at the end defines the labelling of states by atomic propositions ($=$ rule names).

```
stochastic
// 605 Nodes
// 14322 Transitions
const int kill_rate=1;
const int smart_rate=1000;
const int new_rate=1;
const int disconnected_rate=0;
module M s :   [0..604] init 438;
    [new] s=176 -> 1*new_rate:(s'=80);
    [kill] s=359 -> 2*kill_rate:(s'=537);
    ...
    [disconnected] s=101 -> 4*disconnected_rate:(s'=422);
endmodule
// label "smart" = (s= 227, 159, 587, 247, 194);
// label "kill" = (s= 359, 174, 202, 151, 264, 126, ...);
// label "new" = (s= 176, 341, 324, ...);
// label "disconnected" = (s= 95, 364, 302, 116, 402, ...);
```

The limitation in the number of states requires a style of specification where all operations are specified by single rules, rather than breaking them down into smaller steps. The latter would lead to simpler rules, but create intermediate states. The use of path expressions and application conditions is essential for this style of specification.

The results of applying the tool chain to the two stochastic graph transformation systems defined in the previous section are visualised in Fig. 7.

---

[2] http://www.ls10.de/sgt

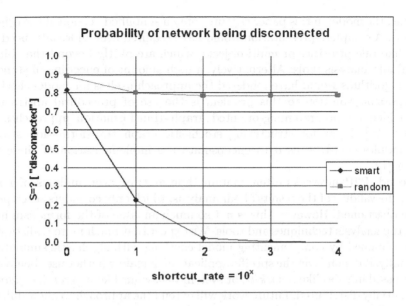

Fig. 7. Results of stochastic model checking

Both systems have been restricted to a maximum of 7 peers and one registry. The bottom graph represents the behaviour of $\mathcal{G}_{smart}$ whose transition graph has 798 states and 16293 transitions.

We observe that, increasing the rate of rule *smart* by a factor of 10 we decrease the long-term probability for a disconnected network by about the same factor: from 0.225300 for $\rho(smart) = 10$ to 0.000244 for $\rho(smart) = 10000$. Indeed, for rates at least 10 times higher than those of *kill* and *new*, the probability seems to go against $2.4 \cdot \rho(smart)^{-1}$. That means, an estimate of the average time it takes to execute (the implementation of) *smart* in relation with the rate of peers entering and leaving the system would provide us with an estimate of the networks reliability.

The upper graph in Fig. 7 represents the system $\mathcal{G}_{random}$ which has 487 states and 9593 transitions. We observe that the added redundancy does not have a relevant effect on the reliability, even if the number of additional edges created is roughly the same as in the other system (the overall number of states is only slightly smaller). This shows the superiority of the first system.

5   Conclusion

In this paper we have developed a case study in stochastic graph transformation to validate the practicability of the approach and understand its limitations. The problem addressed, a protocol for adding redundant links in a P2P network, has been modelled and analysed using an experimental tool chain. Let us conclude this paper by discussing some of the issues and lessons learned in this exercise.

First, the model in this paper captures only a simplified version of the original protocol. A complete presentation would have required even more advanced features, like rule priorities or multi-objects, which are partly beyond the abilities of available analysis tools. Alternatively, a high amount of encoding of standard graph algorithms would have rendered the approach useless for model checking.

A possible solution to this problem is the use of procedural abstractions as provided by programming-oriented graph transformation approaches like FUJABA [26]. Ideas for structuring stochastic graph transformation systems into modules could be used to encapsulate the implementation of these procedures [12].

Second, P2P networks often contain thousands or even millions of nodes. Hence, the validity of the results of our analysis, which only considers seven peers, can be questioned. However, this is not so much an issue of the formalism itself, but of the analysis techniques and tools. We expect that much more realistic data can be obtained by complementing model checking with stochastic simulation.

Finally, it depends on the specific application domain whether user behaviour, as expressed in rules like *new*, *kill*, or system behaviour like in *smart*, *random* is exponentially distributed. Future work will extend the approach to allow different kinds of distributions.

Acknowledgement. The author wishes to express his gratitude to Arend Rensink for numerous new versions of GROOVE to cater for the needs of the case study, Sebastian Menge for his support with the transformation tool from GROOVE to PRISM transition systems, as well as Thomas Erlebach, Georgios Laijos, and Leonardo Mariani for comments and discussions.

References

1. M. Ajmone-Marsan, G. Balbo, G. Conte, S. Donatelli, and G. Franceschinis. *Modelling with Generalized Stochastic Petri Nets*. Wiley Series in Parallel Computing. John Wiley and Sons, 1995.
2. William G. Anderson. *Continuous-Time Markov Chains*. Springer, 1991.
3. Christel Baier, Boudewijn R. Haverkort, Holger Hermanns, and Joost-Pieter Katoen. Model checking continuous-time markov chains by transient analysis. In *Computer Aided Verification*, pages 358–372. Springer, 2000.
4. Falko Bause and Pieter S. Kritzinger. *Stochastic Petri Nets*. Vieweg Verlag, 2nd edition, 2002.
5. E. Brinksma and H. Hermanns. Process algebra and Markov chains. In J.-P. Katoen E. Brinksma, H. Hermanns, editor, *FMPA 2000*, number 2090 in LNCS, pages 183–231. Springer, 2001.
6. A. Corradini, U. Montanari, and F. Rossi. Graph processes. *Fundamenta Informaticae*, 26(3,4):241–266, 1996.
7. P.R. D'Argenio. *Algebras and Automata for Timed and Stochastic Systems*. IPA Dissertation Series 1999-10, CTIT PhD-Thesis Series 99-25, University of Twente, November 1999.
8. H. Ehrig, M. Pfender, and H.J. Schneider. Graph grammars: an algebraic approach. In *14th Annual IEEE Symposium on Switching and Automata Theory*, pages 167–180. IEEE, 1973.

9. T. Gilb. *Principles of Software Engineering Management*. Addison-Wesley, 1988.
10. A. Habel, R. Heckel, and G. Taentzer. Graph grammars with negative application conditions. *Fundamenta Informaticae*, 26(3,4):287 – 313, 1996.
11. R. Heckel, G. Lajios, and S. Menge. Stochastic graph transformation systems. In H. Ehrig, G. Engels, F. Parisi-Presicce, and G. Rozenberg, editors, *Proc. 2nd Intl. Conference on Graph Transformation (ICGT'04), Rome, Italy*, volume 3256 of *LNCS*, pages 210 – 225. Springer-Verlag, October 2004.
12. R. Heckel, G. Lajios, and S. Menge. Modulare Analyse Stochastischer Graphtransformationssysteme. In P. Liggesmeyer, K. Pohl, and M. Goedicke, editors, *Software Engineering 2005, Essen, Germany*, volume 64 of *Lecture Notes in Informatics*, pages 141 – 152. GI, March 2005.
13. M. Korff and L. Ribeiro. Concurrent derivations as single pushout graph grammar processes. In *Proc. Joint COMPUGRAPH/SEMAGRAPH Workshop on Graph Rewriting and Computation (SEGRAGRA)*, volume 2 of *Electronic Notes in TCS*, pages 113–122. Elsevier Science, 1995.
14. M. Kwiatkowska, G. Norman, and D. Parker. PRISM: Probabilistic symbolic model checker. In T. Field, P. Harrison, J. Bradley, and U. Harder, editors, *Proc. 12th Int. Conf. on Modelling Techniques and Tools for Computer Performance Evaluation (TOOLS'02)*, volume 2324 of *LNCS*, pages 200–204. Springer, 2002.
15. M. Löwe. Algebraic approach to single-pushout graph transformation. *Theoret. Comput. Sci.*, 109:181–224, 1993.
16. L. Mariani. Fault-tolerant routing for p2p systems with unstructured topology. In *Proc. International Symposium on Applications and the Internet (SAINT 2005)*, Trento (Italy), 2005. IEEE Computer Society.
17. J. Meseguer. Conditional rewriting logic as a unified model of concurrency. *Theoret. Comput. Sci.*, 96:73–155, 1992.
18. R. Milner. *Communication and Concurrency*. Prentice-Hall, 1989.
19. M. K. Molloy. *On the Integration of Delay and Throughput Measures in Distributed Processing Models*. PhD thesis, University of California, 1981.
20. S. Natkin. *Les Réseaux de Petri Stochastiques et leur Application à l'Evaluation des Systèmes Informatiques*. PhD thesis, CNAM Paris, 1980.
21. James R. Norris. *Markov Chains*. Cambridge University Press, 1997.
22. C. Priami. Stochastic π-calculus. *The Computer Journal*, 38:578 – 589, 1995. Proc. PAPM '95.
23. A. Rensink. The GROOVE simulator: A tool for state space generation. In J.L. Pfaltz, M. Nagl, and B. Böhlen, editors, *Applications of Graph Transformation with Industrial Relevance Proc. 2nd Intl. Workshop AGTIVE'03, Charlottesville, USA, 2003*, volume 3062 of *Lecture Notes in Computer Science*. Springer-Verlag, Berlin, 2004.
24. G. Rozenberg, editor. *Handbook of Graph Grammars and Computing by Graph Transformation, Volume 1: Foundations*. World Scientific, 1997.
25. W. Stewart. *Introduction to the Numerical Solution of Markov Chains*. Princeton University Press, 1994.
26. University of Paderborn Software Engineering Group. The Fujaba Tool Suite. www.fujaba.de.

Component-Based Software Engineering*
The Need to Link Methods and Their Theories

He Jifeng[1,**], Xiaoshan Li[2], and Zhiming Liu[1,***]

[1] International Institute for Software Technology,
United Nations University, Macao SAR, China
{hjf, lzm}@iist.unu.edu
[2] Faculty of Science and Technology, University of Macau, Macao SAR, China
xsl@umac.mo

Abstract. We discuss some of the difficulties and significant issues that we need to consider when developing a formal method for component-based software engineering. We argue that to deal with the challenges, there is a need in research to link existing theories and methods of programming for effective support to component-based software engineering. We then present our initiative on a unified multi-view approach to modelling, design and analysis of component systems, emphasising the integration of models for different views.

Keywords: Components, Interfaces, Contracts, Protocols, Functionality, Consistency, Composition, Refinement, Simulation.

1 Introduction

The idea to exploit and reuse components to build and to maintain software systems goes back to "structured programming" in the 70s. It was a strong argument for development of object oriented methods and languages in the 80s. However, it is today's growing complexity of systems that forces us to turn this idea into practice [5].

While component-based software development is understood to require reusable components that interact with each other and fit into system architectures, there is so far no agreement on standard technologies for designing and creating components, nor on methods of composing them. Finding appropriate formal approaches for describing components, the architectures for composing them, and the methods for component-based software construction, is correspondingly challenging. It seems component-based programming is now in the similar situation of object-oriented programming in the 80s:

> My guess is that object-oriented programming will be in the 1980s what structured programming was in the 1970s. Everyone will be in favor of it. Every manufacture will promote his products as supporting it. Every manager will

---

* Partly supported as a research task of E-Macao Project funded by the Macao Government.

** On leave from East China Normal University, Shanghai, China. The work is partially supported by the 211 Key project of the Ministry of Education, and the 973 project 2002CB312001 of the Ministry of Science and Technology of China.

*** Corresponding author.

D.V. Hung and M. Wirsing (Eds.): ICTAC 2005, LNCS 3722, pp. 70–95, 2005.
© Springer-Verlag Berlin Heidelberg 2005

pay lip service to it. Everyone programmer will practice it (differently). And no one will know just what it is [32].   – T. Rentsch, September 1982

In this paper, we discuss some of the concepts and issues that are important for a formal method to support component-based software engineering (CBSE). We argue that there is a need to integrate existing theories and methods of programming. We then propose a unified multi-view modelling approach that is intended to support separation of concerns. Different concerns are described in different viewpoints of a system at different levels of abstraction, including those of the syntactic dependency among components, static behavior, dynamic behavior and interactions of components. We show how in the model to integrate a state-based model of functional behavior and an event-based model of inter-component interactions. The state-based model is for white-box specification to support component design and the event-based model is for black-box specification used when composing components. Linking the theories will also shed light on the integration of tools, such as model checkers, theorem provers and testing tools, for system verification.

An integrated approach allows knowledge sharing among different people in a component system development, such as requirement engineers and analysts, system assemblers, component designers, component certifiers and system verifiers. Different people play different roles and are only concerned with and use the models of aspects relevant to their jobs.

After this introduction, we will discuss in Section 2 the concepts of components, interfaces and architectures. These are the three most primary concepts, on which people have not yet reached an agreement. In Section 3, we will give an overview about the recent frameworks for component systems modelling, and argue about the need to link methods. We will in Section 4 give an outline of the framework that is being developed at UNU-IIST, and point out its difficulties and limitations. We will conclude in Section 5 with a discussion about future work.

2   Components, Interfaces and Architectures

The notions of components, interfaces and architectures are the most important, but not yet commonly defined three concepts in CBSE. This section discusses how different views on these concepts can be reconciled.

2.1   Components

Looking into Oxford Advanced Learners Dictionary, we can find:

A component is any part of which something is made.

In software engineering, this would allow a software system to have as "components" assembly language instructions, sub-routines, procedures, tasks, modules, objects, classes, software packages, processes, sub-systems, etc[1]. This definition obviously is

---

[1] Notice these entities have very different natures.

too general for CBSE to provide anything new. To decide what is to be ruled in and what is to be ruled out, we first clarify the purposes of using "components" in software development, and then study their implications or necessary properties.

As we said earlier, the widely accepted goal of component-based development is to build and maintain software systems by using existing software components, e.g. [38,34,29,21,33,13,8]. It is understood that the components are required to be reusable components. They must interact with each other in a system architecture [36,4,29,12,40,33]. This goal of CBSE implies four orthogonal properties for a truly reusable component [38]:

P1 contractually specified *interfaces*,
P2 fully explicit context dependencies,
P3 independent deployment,
P4 third party composition.

Based on these conditions, it is argued in [20] that an assembly language instruction and software packages should not be treated as components, but classes in a class library are components. However, classes can hardly be components if we require **P3** when composing components without access to the source code. On the other hand, we can lift a class to make it usable as a component, by providing a description of its required classes and methods.

The usage of a component in a software system includes using it to replace an out of date component to upgrade the system or a failed component to repair the system, adding it to the system to extend the system services, or composing it into the system while the system itself is still being built. Some researchers insist on a component being reusable during dynamic reconfiguration. The implications of properties **P1-P4** are different when a component is used in different applications, for different purposes or in different kinds of systems. This is the main reason why some people give more stringent definitions than others (e.g. [8,34]). In [8], a component is defined by the following three axioms :

A1 A component is capable of performing a task in isolation; i.e. without being composed with other components.
A2 Components may be developed independently from each other.
A3 The purpose of composition is to enable cooperation between the constituent components.

These properties are in fact those required for a "sub-system" in [37].

The paper [8] argues that the three axioms further imply a number of more properties, called corollaries of components:

C1 A component is capable of acquiring input from its environment and/or of presenting output to its environment.
C2 A component should be independent from its environment.
C3 The addition or removal of a component should not require modification of other components in the composition.
C4 Timeliness of output of a component should be independent from timeliness of input.

C5 The functioning of a component should be independent of its location in a composition.

C6 The change of location of a component should not require modifications to other components in the composition.

C7 A component should be a unit of fault-containment.

The implication of the corollaries from the axioms is only argued informally. Property **C2** implies that a component has no state and this is also insisted on in [38]. This is now generally understood to be only required in some limited circumstances, such as for dynamic reconfiguration. Property **C4** only applies to real-time systems and properties **C5&C6** are only relevant to distributed mobile systems. We do not see why **C7** is needed at all unless a component is to be used to replace another during the runtime of the system. In fact, in many applications coordinators or managers can be used to coordinate fault-prone components to achieve fault-tolerance [25].

On the other hand, it is argued in [34] that a software component itself is a static abstraction with plugs which are not only used to provide services, but also to require them. This implies that components are not usually used in isolation, but according to a software architecture that determines how components are plugged together. This in fact is the kind of component called a *module* in [37].

2.2 Interfaces

Although there is no consensus on what components are, all definitions agree on the importance of *interfaces* of components, and interfaces are for composition without the access to source code of components. This indicates that the differences are mainly reflected in decisions on what information should be included in the interface of a component.

We further argue that interfaces for different usages and different applications in different environments may contain different information, and have different properties:

- An interface for a component in a sequential system is obviously different from one in a communicating concurrent system. The later requires the interface to include a description of the communicating protocol while the former does not.
- An interface for a component in a real-time application will need to provide the real-time constraints of services, but an untimed application does not.
- Components in distributed, mobile or internet-based systems require their interfaces to include information about their locations or addresses.
- An interface (component) should be stateless when the component is required to be used dynamically and independently from other components.
- A service component has different features from a middleware component.

Therefore, it is the interface that determines the external behavior and features of the component and allows the component to be used as a black box.

Based on the above description, our framework defines the notion of an *interface* for a component as a description of what is needed for the component be *used* in building and maintaining software systems. The description of an interface must contain information about all the viewpoints among, for example functionality, behavior, protocols, safety, reliability, real-time, power, bandwidth, memory consumption and communication mechanisms, that are needed for composing the component in the given architecture for the application of the system. However, this description can be incremental in the sense that newly required properties or view points can be added when needed according to the application.

2.3 Architecture

The main concerns about programming in the small are the flow of control and the data structure. The specifications, design and verification all focus on the algorithm and the data structure of the program.

For programming in the large, the major concerns are components and their consistent integration in an architectural context. The architectural design becomes a critical issue because of the important roles it plays in communication among different stakeholders, system analysis and large-scale reuse [4].

There are numerous definitions of software architecture, such as [2,4,29,37]. The common basis of all of them is that an architecture describes a system as structural decomposition of the system into subsystems and their connections. Architecture Description Languages (ADLs), such as [2,4,29], are proposed for architecture description. The basic elements of ADLs are components and connectors. An ADL also provides rules for putting (composing) components together with connectors. They suffer from the disadvantage that they can only be understood by language experts – they are inaccessible to domain and application specialists. Informal and graphical notations, such as UML, are now also widely used by practical software developers for architecture specification [10,33]. However, the semantic foundation for these UML-based models has not yet been firmly established.

A mere structural description of a system is not enough in supporting further system analysis, design, implementation, verification, and reconfiguration. More expressive power is needed for an ADL [5]. In particular, an ADL should also support the following kinds of views:

Interaction: the interaction protocol and mechanisms,
Functionality and Behavior: functional services, key properties of its components (e.g. safety and reliability),
Resources and Quality of Service: hardware units required, real-time, power, bandwidth, etc. These details allow analysis and critical appraisal, such as the quality of service.

It is a great advantage if an architectural description supports the separation of these concerns and allows them to be consistently integrated for system analysis.

One of the biggest challenges in formal CBSE is to develop a model that effectively supports the separation of the views for analysis of different concerns, while they can be consistently linked or combined in a whole system development process.

3   State of the Art of Formal Theories

This section gives an overview of existing component-based models, and summarises the common requirements on component-based models.

3.1 Models of Architectures

Most of the early theories, such as [27,26,39,1,29], focus on modelling system architectures. All these models of architectures deal with coordinations among components, in an event-based approach. They can also be used for specification of connectors and coordinators. However, they do not go to the level of component design, implementation and deployment. This might be reason why ADLs still do not play any major role in practical software engineering.

Recently, more delicate models are proposed for describing behavior of components and their coordinations, such as [3,13]. Reo [3] is a channel-based model with synchronous communication. The composition of components (and connectors) are defined in terms of a few operators. The model is defined operationally and thus algebraic reasoning and simulation are supported for analysis. The disadvantage of this approach is that it is not clear how it can be extended to deal with other viewpoints, such as timing and resources. Also, being even-based, the model in [13] considers a layered architecture for composition, provided by connectors (glueing operations). It considers real-time constraints and scheduling analysis. The behavior of a component is defined in a form of a timed automaton. This provides a good low level model of execution of a component. However, the use of local clocks for modelling delays can hardly be said to be component-based. We need talk about a component at a higher level of granularity.

The Stream Calculus [6,7,41] is a denotational framework, but otherwise similar to those of [3,13] for being a channel-based model. In general a denotational model supports the notion of stepwise development by *refinement* and links specifications at different levels of abstraction better. With the scream calculus, Broy also proposes a multi-view modelling to include *interface model, state machine model, process model, distributed system model,* and *data model* [6,7].

The main disadvantage of message/event based approaches is that changes of the data states of a component are not specified directly. While they are good at modelling behavior of electronic devices and communicating protocols, they are not inclined to the software engineering terminology and techniques. The relation of these models to program implementations is not clear and practical software design techniques, such as design patterns, is not well supported. These lead to difficulties in understanding the consistency between the interaction protocol and the functionality.

3.2 The Need to Link Methods and Theories

The grand aim of CBSE is to support independently development of components and compositional design, analysis and verification of overall systems.

To achieve this aim, it is essential that the approach provides a notation for multi-view modelling, that allows separation of concerns and supports modelling and reasoning about properties at different levels of abstraction. The nature of multi-view and separation of concerns allows us to independently identify, describe and compose different correctness conditions/aspects [19] of different views of components, including syntactic interfaces, static and functional behavior, dynamic and synchronization behavior, interaction protocols, timing and resource constraints, etc. Separation is the key principle to ensure the simplicity of the model [21].

It is crucial that the model supports abstraction with information hiding so that we can develop refinement and transformation based design techniques [21,6,11]. This will provide a theoretical foundation for the integration of formal design techniques with practical engineering development methods. Design in this way can preserve correctness to a certain level of abstraction and support code generation that ensures certain correctness properties (i.e. being correct by construction [30]).

Refinement in this framework characterises the *substitutability* of one component for another. It involves the substitutability of all the aspects, but we should be able to define and carry out refinement for different features separately, without violating the correctness of the other aspects. The integration of event-based simulation and state-based refinement facilitates assurance of *global refinement* by *local refinement*. Global refinement is specified as set containment of system behavior (such as the failure-divergence semantics of CSP). Global refinement is verified in a deductive approach supported possibly with support of a theorem prover. Local refinement is specified in terms of pre and post conditions of operations and verified by simulation often supported by a model checker. Also, refinement in CBSE must be compositional in order to *global reasoning about the system* can be done by *local reasoning about the components* [7].

We would also like the refinement calculus to support *incremental and iterative* design, analysis and verification. This is obviously important for scaling up the application of the method to large scale software development, and for the development of efficient tool support. We believe being incremental and iterative is closely related and complementary to being compositional, and important for lowering the amount of specification and verification and reducing the degree of automation [30].

To benefit the advantages of different methods for dealing with different aspects of component systems, an integration of these methods is needed so that their theories and tools are linked to ensure the consistency of the different views of a system. For example, the static functionality described by pre- and post conditions, dynamic behavior by state machines (or transition systems) and interaction protocols by traces have to be consistent.

Summary. A number of formal notations and theories have been well-established and proved themselves effective as tools for the treatment of different aspects of computer systems. Operational simulation techniques and model checking tools are believed to be effective for checking correctness, consistency and refinement of interaction protocols, while deductive verification and theorem provers are found better suited for reasoning about denotational functionality specification. For CBSE, analysis and verification of different aspects of correctness and substitutability can thus be carried out with different techniques and tools. However, integration of components requires the integration of the methods for ensuring different aspects of correctness and substitutability. The integration requires an underlying execution model of component software systems.

A component may not have to be designed and implemented in an object-oriented framework. However, the current component technologies such as COM, CORBA, and Enterprise JavaBeans are all built upon object-oriented programming. Object programs are now widely used in applications and many of them are safety critical. This leads to the need to investigate the techniques of modelling, design and verification of object systems and the construction of component systems on underlying object systems.

Also, the unification of the theories of imperative programming and object-oriented programming is naturally achievable [16,24,14].

4 rCOS

At UNU-IIST, we are developing a model and calculus, called rCOS, for component and object systems. In this section, we focus on the main theme and features of this model, instead of technical details.

Based on discussion the previous sections, we intend to formalize the characteristics of a component in a model with the following elements and notions which serve different purposes for different people at different stages of a system development:

- *interfaces:* describe the structural nature of a system and are only used for checking syntactic dependencies and compositionality. They are represented in terms of signatures of service operations.
- *contracts:* are semantic specifications of interfaces. A contract relates an interface to an application by specifying the (abstract) data model, functionality of the service operations, synchronization protocols, and other required qualities of service (QoS) depending on the application.
  The model also provides a definition of consistency among these views and and method for checking this consistency. A contract can be extended *horizontally* by adding more services, more properties (e.g. QoS). In this paper, we are only concerned with functionalities and protocols.
- *components:* are implementations of contracts. The execution model of component is defined. The relation of a component to a contract is defined for the correctness of the component.
- *operations:* are defined for interfaces, contracts and components so that they can be composed in different ways.
- *substitutability:* is defined in terms of refinement which covers and relates state-based refinement and even-based simulation.
- *coordination:* is defined as predicates on protocols to glue and manage a group of components.
- *class model:* is used to define the data model that is more general than pure data types and makes it easier to link a contract to a component with an object-oriented implementation.

Interfaces and contracts are used by assemblers to check compatibilities of components when assembling or maintaining a system. If components do not match with each other, assemblers can consider to write connectors with glue code to put them together. Connectors can sometimes be built as components. The protocols in the contracts are used to avoid deadlock when putting components together. The functional specification of the operations are used to ensure that the user (the other components) provides correct inputs and the component returns with correct outputs.

The designer of a component has to ensure that the component satisfies its contract, in particular to avoid livelock and design errors. The verifier (certifier) must have access to the code of the component to verify the satisfaction of the contract by the component.

4.1   UTP: The Semantic Basis

rCOS is based on Hoare and He's Unifying Theories of Programming (UTP) [18]. UTP takes an approach to modelling the execution of a program in terms of a relation between the *states* of the program. Here, a state of a program P is defined over a set of variables called the *alphabet* of the program, denoted by $\alpha(P)$ (simply α when there is no confusion). Given an alphabet α, a *state* of α is a (well-typed) mapping from α to the value space of the alphabet.

Programs as Designs. For an imperative sequential program, we are interested in observing the values of the input variables $in\alpha$ and output variables $out\alpha$. We use a Boolean variable ok to denote whether a program is *started properly* and its primed version ok' to represent whether the execution has terminated. The alphabet α is defined as the union $in\alpha \cup out\alpha \cup \{ok, ok'\}$, and a design is of the form

$$(p(x) \vdash R(x, y')) \stackrel{def}{=} ok \wedge p(x) \Rightarrow ok' \wedge R(x, y')$$

where

- p is the *precondition*, defining the initial states
- R is the *postcondition*, relating the initial states to the final states in terms the of input value x and the output value y'. Note that some variable x is modified by a program and in this case we say $x \in in\alpha$ and the primed version $x' \in out\alpha$.
- ok and ok': describe start and termination, they do **not** appear in expressions or assignments in program texts

The design represents a *contract* between the "user" and the program such that if the program is started properly in a state satisfying the precondition it will terminate in a state satisfying the postcondition.

A design is often *framed* in the form

$$\beta : (p \vdash R) \stackrel{def}{=} p \vdash (R \wedge \underline{w}' = \underline{w})$$

where $\underline{w}$ contains all the variables in $in\alpha - \beta$, which are the variables in in but not in β.

We can use the conventional operations on programs statements for designs too.

- Given two designs such that the output alphabet of P is the same as the primed version of the input alphabet of Q, the sequential composition

$$P(in\alpha_1, out\alpha_1); Q(in\alpha_2, out\alpha_2) \stackrel{def}{=} \exists m \cdot P(in\alpha_1, m) \wedge Q(m, out\alpha_2)$$

- Conditional choice: $(D_1 \triangleleft b \triangleright D_2) \stackrel{def}{=} (b \wedge D_1) \vee (\neg b \wedge D_2)$
- Demonic and angelic choice operators:

$$D_1 \sqcap D_2 \stackrel{def}{=} D_1 \vee D_2 \quad D_1 \sqcup D_2 \stackrel{def}{=} D_1 \wedge D_2$$

- while b do D is defined as the weakest fixed point of

$$X = ((D; X) \triangleleft b \triangleright skip)$$

We can now define the meaning of primitive program commands as framed designs in Table 1. Composite statements are then defined by operations on designs.

Table 1. Basic commands as designs

command: c	design: $[\![c]\!]$	description
skip	$\{\} : true \vdash true$	does not change anything, but terminates
chaos	$\{\} : false \vdash true$	anything, including non-termination, can happen
$x := e$	$\{x\} : true \vdash x' = val(e)$	side-effect free assignment; updates x with the value of e
$m(e; v)$	$[\![\mathbf{var}\ in, out]\!];$ $[\![in{:}{=}e]\!]; [\![body(m)]\!]; [\![v{:}{=}out]\!];$ $[\![\mathbf{end}\ in, out]\!]$	$m(in; out)$ is the signature with input parameters *in* and output parameters *out*; $body(m)$ is the body command of the procedure/method

Refinement of Designs. The refinement relation between designs is then defined to be logical implication. A design $D_2 = (\alpha, P_2)$ is a **refinement** of design $D_1 = (\alpha, P_1)$, denoted by $D_1 \sqsubseteq D_2$, if P_2 entails P_1

$$\forall x, x', \ldots, z, z' \cdot (P_2 \Rightarrow P_1)$$

where $x, x', \ldots, z, z'$ are variables contained in α. We write $D_1 = D_2$ if they refine each other.

If they do not have the same alphabet, we can use data refinement. Let ρ be a mapping from α_2 to α_1. Design $D_2 = (\alpha_2, P_2)$ is a **refinement** of design $D_1 = (\alpha_1, P_1)$ under ρ, denoted by $D_1 \sqsubseteq_\rho D_2$, if $(\rho; P_1) \sqsubseteq (P_2; \rho)$. It is easy to prove that *chaos* is the worst program, i.e. *chaos* $\sqsubseteq P$ for any program P. For more algebraic laws of imperative programs, please see [18].

The following theorem is the basis for the fact that the notion of designs can be used for defining the semantics of programs.

Theorem 1. *The notion of designs is closed under programming constructors:*

$$((p_1 \vdash R_1); (p_2 \vdash R_2)) = ((p_1 \wedge \neg(R_1; \neg p_2)) \vdash (R_1; R_2))$$
$$((p_1 \vdash R_1) \sqcap (p_2 \vdash R_2)) = ((p_1 \wedge p_2) \vdash (R_1 \vee R_2))$$
$$((p_2 \vdash R_1) \sqcup (p_2 \vdash R_2)) = ((p_1 \vee p_2) \vdash ((p_1 \Rightarrow R_1) \wedge (p_2 \Rightarrow R_2)))$$
$$((p_1 \vdash R_1) \triangleleft b \triangleright (p_2 \vdash R_2)) = ((p_1 \triangleleft b \triangleright p_2) \vdash (R_1 \triangleleft b \triangleright R_2))$$

Linking Designs with Predicate Transformers. A widely used method for program analysis and design is the calculus of predicate transformers [9]. The link from the design calculus to the theory of predicate transformers is given by the following definition

$$\mathbf{wp}(p \vdash R, q) \stackrel{def}{=} p \wedge \neg(R; \neg q)$$

It gives the weakest precondition for the design $p \vdash R$ to ensure the post condition q. Design $p \vdash R$ is *feasible* iff $\mathbf{wp}(p \vdash R, false) = false$, or equivalently

$$\forall v \bullet (p(v) \Rightarrow \exists v' \bullet R(v, v'))$$

meaning $p \vdash R$ can deliver a result whenever its execution terminates.

In [15], we show this definition of **wp** ensures validity of all the algebraic rules of the **wp** transformer. For example

$$\mathbf{wp}(true \vdash x' = f(x), q(x)) = q[f(x)/x] \quad \text{assignment}$$
$$\mathbf{wp}(D_1 \vee D_2, q) = \mathbf{wp}(D_1, q) \wedge \mathbf{wp}(D_2, q) \ \text{disjunction /non-determinism}$$

4.2 Interfaces

In our framework, the notion of *interface* is different from that in Section 2.2. There, an "interface" is actually an interface specification and the same as the notion of *contracts* that we are to define in the next subsection.

A *primitive interface* is a collection of *features* where a feature can be either a *field* or a *method*. We thus define a primitive interface as a pair of feature declaration sections:

$$I = \langle FDec, MDec \rangle$$

where *FDec* is a set of *field declarations*, denoted by *I.FDec*, and *MDec* a set of *method declarations*, denoted by *I.MDec*, respectively.

A member of *FDec* has the form $x : T$ where x and T represent respectively the name and type of this declared field. It is forbidden to declare two fields with the same name.

A method $op(\text{in } inx, \text{out } outx)$ in *MDec* declares the name op, the list of input parameters inx and the list of output parameters of the method. Each input or output parameter declaration is of the form $u : U$ giving the name and type of the parameter.

The method name together with the numbers and types of its input and output parameters forms the *signature* of a method. In general both inx and $outx$ can be empty. For simplicity and without losing any generality in the theory, we assume a method has one input parameter and one output parameter and thus can be represented in the form $op(in : U, out : V)$ by removing the key words **in** and **out**. Notice that the names of parameters are irrelevant. Thus, $op(in_1 : U, out_1 : V)$ and $op(in_2 : U, out_2 : V)$ are treated as the same method.

Interface Inheritance and Hiding Operations. Inheritance is a useful means for reuse and incremental programming. When a component provides only part of the services that one needs or some of the provided operations are not quite suitable for the need, we may still use this component by rewriting some of the operations or extending it with some operations and attributes.

Definition 1. (**Interface inheritance**) *Let I_i ($i = 1, 2$) be interfaces. I_1 and I_2 are composable if no field of I_i is redefined in I_j for $i \neq j$. When they are composable, notation $I_2 \oplus I_1$ represents an interface with the following field and method sectors*

$$FDec \overset{def}{=} FDec_1 \cup FDec_2$$
$$MDec \overset{def}{=} MDec_2 \cup \{op(in : U, out : V) | op \in MDec_1 \wedge op \notin MDec_2\}$$

To enable us to provide different services to different clients of a component, we allow to hide operations in an interface to make them invisible when the component is composed with certain components. Hiding operations provides the opposite effect to interface inheritance and is to be used to restrict an interface. In a graphical notation like UML, this can be achieved by the notation of generalization alone.

Definition 2. (**Hiding**) *Let I be an interface and S a set of method names. The notation $I \backslash S$ denotes the interface I after removal of methods of S from its method declaration sector.*

$$FDec \overset{def}{=} I.FDec, \quad MDec \overset{def}{=} I.MDec \setminus S$$

The hiding operator enjoys the following properties.

1. Hiding two sets of operations separately is the same as hiding all of the operations in the two set together, $(I \backslash S_1) \backslash S_2 = I \backslash (S_1 \cup S_2)$. Thus, the order in which two sets of operations are hidden is inessential too.
2. Hiding distributes among operands of interface inheritance

$$(I \oplus J) \backslash S = (I \backslash S) \oplus (J \backslash S)$$

4.3 Contract

A contract gives the functional specification of an interface.

Definition 1. *(Contract) A contract is a pair Ctr = (I, MSpec), where*

1. *I is an interface,*
2. *MSpec maps each method op(in : U, out : V) of I to a specification of op that is a design with the alphabet*

$$in\alpha \overset{def}{=} \{in\} \cup I.FDec, \quad out\alpha \overset{def}{=} \{out'\} \cup I.FDec'$$

For a contract $Ctr = (I, MSpec)$, we will use $Ctr.I$, $Ctr.FDec$, $Ctr.MDec$ and $Ctr.MSpec$ to denote respectively I, $I.FDec$, $I.MDec$ and $MSpec$.

Two contracts can be composed to extend both of them only when their interfaces are composable and the specifications of the common methods are *consistent*. This composition will be used to calculate the provided and required services when components are composed.

Definition 2. *(Composable contracts) Contracts $Ctr_i = (I_i, MSpec_i)$, $i = 1, 2$, are composable if*

1. *I_1 and I_2 are composable, and*
2. *for any method op occurring in both I_1 and I_2,*

$$MSpec_1(op(x : U, y : V)) = \\ MSpec_2(op(u : U, v : V))[x, x', y, y'/u, u', v, v']$$

In this case their composition $Ctr_1 \| Ctr_2$ is defined by

$$I \overset{def}{=} I_1 \oplus I_2, \quad MSpec \overset{def}{=} MSpec_1 \oplus MSpec_2$$

where $MSpec_1 \oplus MSpec_2$ denotes the overriding $MSpec_1(op)$ with $MSpec_2(op)$ if op occurs in both I_1 and I_2.

Notice that for the purpose of compositional reasoning, condition (2) makes the composition *conservative extension* and serves as a limited form of UML generalization.

Based on this definition, a calculus of refinement of contracts and components is developed in [23]. In the rest of this section, we present the generalized notion of contracts and components.

4.4   Reactive Contracts

A contract defined in the previous subsection specifies the *static functionality* of a component that does not require synchronization when the operations are used. Such components are often used in the functional layer [11]. Business process and rules are, however, accomplished by invoking particular sequences of operations. This means a protocol of using the function operation must be imposed, often by composing a component in the functional layer and a component in the system layer [11]. The component then becomes *reactive* and only reacts to the calls of the operation that come in the right order. To describe synchronisation, we introduce two Boolean observables *wait* and *wait'* to the alphabet of an operation $op(in : U, out : V)$ in a contract. A design D on such an extended alphabet is called *reactive* if $\mathcal{W}(D) \equiv D$ holds for the linking function

$$\mathcal{W}(D) \stackrel{def}{=} (true \vdash wait') \lhd wait \rhd D$$

And we extend the specification *MSpec(op)* to a *guarded design* (α, g, D) denoted as $g\&D$, where

- g is boolean expression over *I.FDec* and represents the firing guard of *op*
- D is a *reactive design* over $\alpha = \{in, wait, ok\} \cup I.FDec \cup \{out', ok', wait'\} \cup I.FDec'$.

The semantics of a guarded design $g\&D$ is defined as $(true \vdash wait') \lhd \neg g \rhd D$. The following theorem forms the theoretical basis for using reactive designs as the semantic domain of a programming language.

Theorem 1. *(Reactive designs are closed under programming constructors)*

1. *For any design $p \vdash R$, $\mathcal{W}(p \vdash R)$ is a design.*
2. *$\mathcal{W}$ maps a design to a reactive design: $\mathcal{W}^2(D) \equiv \mathcal{W}(D)$*
3. *If D is a reactive design, so is the g-guarded version $g\&D$.*
4. *$\mathcal{W}$ is monotonic: $\mathcal{W}(D_1) \sqsubseteq \mathcal{W}(D_2)$ iff $(\neg wait \Rightarrow (D_2 \Rightarrow D_1))$. So, all reactive designs form a complete lattice.*
5. *Reactive designs are closed under the conventional programming operators.*

We can now formally define a reactive contract.

Definition 3. *(Reactive Contract) A reactive contract is tuple Ctr=(I, Init, MSpec, Prot), where*

- *I is an interface*
- *Init is a design that initialises the state and is of the form*

  $$true \vdash Init(v') \wedge \neg wait', \text{ where Init is a predicate}$$

- *MSPec assigns each operation to a guarded design (α, g, D).*
- *Prot, called the* protocol, *is a set of sequences of call events. Each is of the form*

  $$?op_1(x_1), \ldots, ?op_k(x_k)$$

  where $?op_i(x_i)$ is a (receipt of) call to operation op_i in I.MDec with an input value x_i.

We use guard(op) to denote the guard in MSPec(op) for an operation $op \in MDec$.

Notice that a contract defined in Section 4.3 can be used as the model of the static behavior of the component, and can seen as special case of reactive contract with all the guards of the operations being *true*, and the protocol being the whole set of sequences of the operations $MDec^*$.

Definition 4. *(Semantics of Contracts) The* dynamic behavior *of Ctr is described by the triple* $(Prot, \mathcal{F}(Ctr), \mathcal{D}(Ctr))$, *where*

– *the set* $\mathcal{D}(Ctr)$ *consists of the sequences of interactions between Ctr and its environment which lead the contract to a divergent state*

$$\mathcal{D}(Ctr) \stackrel{def}{=} \{\langle ?op_1(x_1), op_1(y_1)!, \ldots, ?op_k(x_k), op_k(y_k)!, ?op_{k+1}(x_{k+1})\rangle \cdot s \mid$$
$$\exists v, v', wait' \bullet (Init; g_1 \& D_1[x_1, y_1/in_1, out_1'];$$
$$\ldots;$$
$$g_k \& D_k[x_k, y_k/in_k, out_k'])[true/ok][false/ok']\}$$

where $op_i(y_i)!$ *represents the return event generated at the end of execution of* op_i *with the output value* y_i, in_1 *and* out_i *are the input and output parameters of* op_i, *and* $g_i \& D_i$ *is the guarded design of method* op_i.

– $\mathcal{F}(Ctr)$ *is the set of pairs* (s, X) *where* s *is a sequence of interactions between C and its environment, and X denotes a set of methods which the contract may refuse to respond to after it has engaged all events in* s.

$$rej \stackrel{def}{=} (true, false, true, false/ok, wait, ok', wait')$$
$$rej_1 \stackrel{def}{=} (true, false, true, true/ok, wait, ok', wait')$$
$$\mathcal{F}(Ctr) \stackrel{def}{=} \{(\langle\rangle, X) \mid \exists v' \bullet Init[rej] \wedge \forall ?op \in X \bullet \neg guard(op)[v'/v]\}$$

$$\cup \left\{ \begin{array}{l} (\langle ?op_1(x_1), op_1(y_1)!, \ldots, ?op_k(x_k), op_k(y_k)!\rangle, X) \mid \\ \exists v' \bullet (Init; g_1 \& D_1[x_1, y_1/in_1, out_1']; \\ \ldots; \\ g_k \& D_k[x_k, y_k/in_k, out_k'])[rej] \wedge \forall ?op \in X \bullet \neg guarad(op)[v'/v] \end{array} \right\}$$

$$\cup \left\{ \begin{array}{l} (\langle ?op_1(x_1), op_1(y_1)!, \ldots, ?op_k(x_k), op_k(y_k)!\rangle, X) \mid \\ \exists v' \bullet (Init; g_1 \& D_1[x_1, y_1/in_1, out_1']; \\ \ldots; \\ g_k \& D_k[x_k, y_k/in_k, out_k'])[rej] \wedge op_k! \notin X \end{array} \right\}$$

$$\cup \left\{ \begin{array}{l} (\langle ?op_1(x_1), op_1(y_1)!, \ldots, ?op_k(x_k)\rangle, X) \mid \\ \exists v' \bullet (Init; g_1 \& D_1[x_1, y_1/in_1, out_1']; \\ \ldots; \\ g_{k-1} \& D_{k-1}[x_{k-1}, y_{k-1}/in_{k-1}, out_{k-1}'])[rej]; g_k \& D_k[x_k/in_k][rej_1] \end{array} \right\}$$

$$\cup \ \{s, X) \mid s \in \mathcal{D}(Ctr) \wedge \forall ?op \in X \bullet \neg g_i[v'/v]\}$$

$\mathcal{F}(Ctr)$ defines fives cases when events may be refused and thus deadlock may occur if the environment only offers these refusals:

1. The first subset of the refusals records the cases when the operation call events $?op$ in X cannot occur because their guards do not hold in the initial state.
2. The second subset identifies those cases where after a sequence of calls executed, the system may reach a state where the guards of the events in X are false.
3. The third case is when the execution of an operation op_k is waiting to output its result.

4. The fourth case defines the scenarios when the execution of an operation op_k enters a waiting state.
5. Finally, the fifth case takes the divergent traces into account.

We define the traces of a contract as those traces in the failure set

$$T(Ctr) \stackrel{def}{=} \{s \mid \exists X \bullet (s, X) \in \mathcal{F}(Ctr)\}$$

which are prefix closed.

Notice that the guarded designs of the operations defines a state-based model of the dynamic behavior of the component. It corresponds to a state transition system [28,17] and it has a clear link to temporal logic approaches for analysis and verification [22,25]. When the state space can be reduced to a finite one, the specification of the operations can be represented by a finite state machine or automaton, that model checking tools are based on. From the guarded designs, we can obtain a the model of the static behavior too. This is how a contract model combines the event-based model of the protocol, the stated based model dynamic behavior and the pre- and postcondition specification of the static behavior of a component. However, the protocol and the functional specification of the operations have to be consistent.

Definition 5. (Consistency) *A contract Ctr is consistent, denoted by Consistent(Ctr), if it will never enter a deadlock state if its environment interacts with it according to the protocol. That is for all* $\langle ?op_1(x_1), \ldots, ?op_k(x_k) \rangle \in Prot$,

$$\mathbf{wp}(Init; g_1 \& D_1[x_1/in_1]; \ldots; g_k \& D_k[x_k/in_k], \neg wait \wedge \exists op \in MDec \bullet guard(op)) = true$$

It is shown in [15] that a contract *Ctr* is consistent if and only if for all sequences *tr* in *Prot*

1. there is a trace *s* in $T(Ctr)$ whose projection[2] on operation calls $s{\downarrow}\{?\}$ equals *tr*, and
2. for any failure $(s, X) \in \mathcal{F}(Ctr)$, if $s{\downarrow}\{?\}$ is a prefix of *tr* then not all operations and operation returns are refusals, that is $X \neq \{?op, op! \mid op \in MDec\}$.

The following useful properties of consistency are proved in [15]:

1. The union of consistent protocols is a consistent protocol (with respect to a specification for the operations), that is, if $Ctr_i = (I, Init, MSPec, Prot_i)$, $i = 1, 2$, are consistent, so is $Ctr = (I, Init, MSPec, Prot_1 \cup Prot_2)$.
2. If contract $Ctr_1 = (I, Init, MSPec, Prot_1)$ is consistent and $Prot_2 \subseteq Prot_1$, then contract $Ctr_1 = (I, Init, MSPec, Prot_2)$ is consistent. This allows us to restrict the services of a component.
3. For contracts $Ctr_i = (I, Init_i, MSPec_i, Prot)$, $i = 1, 2$, if Ctr_1 is consistent, $Init_1 \sqsubseteq Init_2$, and $MSPec_1(m) \sqsubseteq MSPec_2(m)$, for all $m \in I.MDec$, then Ctr_2 is consistent.

Therefore, for a given $(I, Init, MSPec)$, there is more than one protocol consistent with it. We call the largest one the *weakest* consistent protocol, denoted as $WProt(I, Init, MSPec)$, such that

$$Consitent(I, Init, MSPec, Prot) \Rightarrow Prot \subseteq WProt(I, Init, MSPec)$$

---

[2] We use ${\downarrow}$ for the projection (or restriction) operator in general.

The weakest consistent protocol can be directly defined as

$$WProt \stackrel{def}{=} \{\langle ?op_1(x_1),\ldots,?op_k(x_k)\rangle | \mathbf{wp}(Init; g_1 \& D_1[x_1/in_1];\ldots;g_k \& D_k[x_k/in_k],$$
$$\neg wait \wedge \exists op \in MDec \bullet guard(op))\}$$

We can prove that $WProt$ is prefix closed [15]. We, for simplicity, use $(I, Init, MSpec)$ to denote $(I, Init, MSpec, WProt)$.

Example 1. Consider a one-place buffer with an interface

$$BI = \langle empty : Boolean, \{put(in : Item), get(out : Item))\}\rangle$$

Given $MSpec$ to assign put and get as

$$MSpec(put) \stackrel{def}{=} empty\&(true \vdash \neg empty'), \quad MSpec(get) \stackrel{def}{=} \neg empty\&(true \vdash empty')$$

With the initial condition $Init \stackrel{def}{=} empty$, we can calculate the weakest consistent protocol to be $(?put, ?get)^*$ which is the set of alternating sequences of put and get, starting with a put. An n-place buffer can be similarly defined.

Definition 6. *(Contract Refinement) Contract Ctr_1 is refined by contract Ctr_2, denoted by $Ctr_1 \sqsubseteq Ctr_2$, if*

1. *Ctr_2 provides no less services than Ctr_1:$Ctr_1.MDec \subseteq Ctr_2.MDec$*
2. *Ctr_2 is not more likely to diverge than Ctr_1: $\mathcal{D}(Ctr_1) \supseteq \mathcal{D}(Ctr_2)\lfloor Ctr_1.MDec$, and*
3. *Ctr_2 is not more likely to deadlock than Ctr_1: $T(Ctr_1) \supseteq T(Ctr_2)\lfloor Ctr_1.MDec$.*

Notice that refinement allows us to add new services. The following two theorems (see [15] for the proofs) link the notions of simulation and refinement and combine event-based and state-based modelling.

Theorem 2. *(Refinement by Downwards Simulation) Let $Ctr_i = (I_i, Init_i, MSpec_i)$ be two contracts. $Ctr_1 \sqsubseteq Ctr_2$, if there exists a total mapping $\rho(u, v')$ from the fields $FDec_1$ of Ctr_1 to the fields $FDec_2$ of Ctr_2 such that the following conditions are satisfied*

1. *ρ preserves the initial condition: $Init_2 \Rightarrow (Init_1; \rho)$*
2. *ρ preserves the guards of all operations: $\rho \Rightarrow (guard_1(op) = guard_2(op))$ for all $op \in MDec_1$.*
3. *The function specification of each operation by Ctr_1 is preserved by Ctr_2: for each $op \in MDec_1$*

$$MSpec_1(op); \rho \sqsubseteq \rho; MSpec_2(op)$$

Notice that the state mapping ρ is used as a design which does not change wait.

Theorem 3. *(Refinement by Upwards Simulation) Let $Ctr_i = (I_i, Init_i, MSpec_i)$ be two contracts. $Ctr_1 \sqsubseteq Ctr_2$, if there exists a surjective mapping $\rho(v, u')$ from the fields $FDec_2$ of Ctr_2 to the fields $FDec_1$ of Ctr_1 such that the following conditions are satisfied*

1. ρ *preserves the initial condition:* $(Init_2; \rho) \Rightarrow Init_1$
2. ρ *preserves the guards of all operations:* $\rho \Rightarrow (guard_1(op) = guard_2(op))$ *for all* $op \in MDec_1$.
3. *The function specification of each operation by* Ctr_1 *is preserved by* Ctr_2: *for each* $op \in MDec_1$

$$MSpec_2(op); \rho \sqsupseteq \rho; MSPec_1(op)$$

The same results can be found about transitions systems and the temporal logic of actions [22,25].

Theorem 4. *(**Completeness of simulations***) If* $Ctr_1 \sqsubseteq Ctr_2$, *then there exists a contract* Ctr *such that*

1. *There is an upwards simulation from* Ctr *to* Ctr_1.
2. *There is a downwards simulation from* Ctr *to* Ctr_2.

Contract Operations. All the operations defined by an interface are *public*, i.e, they are directly accessible by the environment of the interface. We can remove cervices from a contract as we did for an interface.

Definition 7. *(**Removing Services***) Let* $Ctr = (I, Init, MSPec)$ *be a contract and* S *a subset of the operations MDec, then contract* $Crt \backslash S \stackrel{def}{=} (I \backslash S, Init, MSPec \lfloor (MDec - S))$, *where we use* "$-$" *for set difference.*

The behavior of $Ctr \backslash S$ is defined by

$$\mathcal{D}(Ctr \backslash S) = \{s \mid s \in \mathcal{D}(Crt) \wedge s \in \{?op, op! \mid op \in MDec - S\}^*\}$$
$$\mathcal{F}(Ctr \backslash S) = \{(s, X) \mid (s, X) \in \mathcal{F}(Crt) \wedge s \in \{?op, op! \mid op \in MDec - S\}^* \wedge$$
$$X \subseteq \{?op, op! \mid op \in MDec - S\}\}$$

When a component is to be implemented, an operation can be used in the code of another. We would like to be able to remove the former from the interface but at the same the implementation of the latter method should still work without the need for any modification. To handle this problem, we introduce in this section the notion of *private* (or *internal*) *methods/operations*, which are not available to the public, but can be used by the component itself. For this we need to generalize the notation of contracts to *general contracts*.

Definition 8. *(**General Contract***) A general contract GCtr extends a contract Ctr with a set of private methods declarations PriMDec and their specification PriMSPec*

$$GCtr = (Ctr, PriMDec, PriMSPec)$$

The behavior of GCtr is defined to be that of Ctr.

Now we can hide a *public operation* in *MDec* of a general contract to make it internal.

Definition 9. *(Hiding Service) Let GCtr = (Ctr, PriMDec, PriMSPec) be a general contract, and S a subset of the public methods MDec. The restricted contract GCtr\S is defined as*

$$(Ctr\backslash S, PriMDec \cup S, PriMSPec \cup MSPec|S)$$

We are now ready to define the composition of two general contracts.

Definition 10. *(Composition of Contracts) Let GCtr$_i$, i = 1, 2 be two general contracts such that*

1. *all shared fields have the same types,*
2. *all shared methods have the same specification*
3. *the initial conditions of the two contracts are consistent, that is satisfiable.*

The composition GCtr$_1$∥GCtr$_2$ is the general contract

$$GCtr = ((I, MSPec), PriMDec, PriMSPec)$$

where

$$I.FDec \stackrel{def}{=} I_1.FDec \cup I_2.FDec \qquad \textit{union of the fields}$$
$$I.MDec \stackrel{def}{=} I_1.MDec \cup I_2.MDec \qquad \textit{union of the public methods}$$
$$MSPec \stackrel{def}{=} MSpec_1 \oplus MSPec_2 \qquad \textit{overriding union of the specifications}$$
$$PriMDec \stackrel{def}{=} PriMDec_1 \cup PriMDec_2 \qquad \textit{union of the private methods}$$
$$PriMSPec \stackrel{def}{=} PriMSpec_1 \oplus PriMSPec_2 \quad \textit{overriding union of the specifications}$$

Properties of the operations on contracts can be found in [15].

4.5 Components and Their Compositions

A component is an implementation of a contract. The implementation of an operation, however, may call operations of other components. Therefore, a component may optionally have a required interface as well as a provided interface and executable code.

Definition 11. *(Component) A component C is a tuple*

$$(I, MCode, PriMDec, PriMCode, InMDec)$$

where

1. *I is an interface.*
2. *PriMDec is a set of method declarations which are private to the component.*
3. *The tuple (I, MCode, PriMDec, PriMCode) has the same structure as a general contract, except that the functions MCode and PriMCode map each method op in the sets I.MDec and PriMDec respectively to a guarded command of the form g $\longrightarrow$ c, where g is called the guard, denoted as guard(op) and c is a command, denoted as body(op).*
4. *InMDec denotes the set of input methods which are called by public or internal methods, but not defined in MDec $\cup$ PriMDec.*

We use $C.I$, $C.Init$, $C.MCode$, $C.PriMDec$, $C.PriMCode$ and $C.InMDec$ to denote the corresponding parts of C.

The semantics of a component is defined to be a function that given a contract for the required interface, returns a general contract calculated from the code of the operations.

Definition 12. *(Semantics of Components) Let $InCtr$ be a contract such that its interface methods are the same as the required methods of C, $InCtr.MDec = C.InMDec$. The behavior $C(InCtr)$ of C with respect to $InCtr$ is the general contract*

$$((I, MSPec), Init, PriMDec, PriMSPec)$$

where

$$
\begin{array}{ll}
I.FDec & \stackrel{def}{=} C.FDec \cup InCtr.FDec \\
I.MDec & \stackrel{def}{=} C.MDec \cup InCtr.MDec \\
MSPec & \stackrel{def}{=} \Phi \lfloor MDec \\
PriMSPec & \stackrel{def}{=} \Phi \lfloor PriMDec \\
Init & \stackrel{def}{=} C.Init \wedge InCtr.Init
\end{array}
$$

where function Φ assign each operation in $Mdec \cup PriMDec$ the guarded design calculated from the code:

$$\Phi(op) \stackrel{def}{=} guard(op) \& [\![body(op)]\!]$$

where if $m \in InMDec$ is called in $body(op)$, the specification of op assigned by $InCtr$ is used in the calculation [15].

It is easy to show that if $InCtr_1 \sqsubseteq InCtr_2$, then $C(InCtr_1) \sqsubseteq C(InCtr_2)$

Definition 13. *(Component Refinement) A component C_1 is refined by component C_2, denoted by $C_1 \sqsubseteq C_2$, if $C_1.MDec \subseteq C_2.MDec$, $C_1.InMDec \supseteq C_2.InMDec$, and the contract refinement $C_1(InCtr) \sqsubseteq C_2(InCtr)$ holds for all the input contracts $InCtr$.*

Composition of Components. The most natural composition is to plug the provided operations of one component into the required operation of the other to *chain* these two together.

Definition 14. *(Chaining) Let C_1 and C_2 be components such that*

1. *none of the provided or private methods of C_2 appears in C_1,*
2. *C_1 and C_2 have disjoint field declarations.*

The chain $C_1 \rangle\rangle C_2$ of C_1 with C_2 is the component, which has

- *the fields $C_1 FDec \cup C_2.FDec$.*
- *the required operations $C_1.InMDec \cup C_2.InMDec - C_1.MDec \cap C_2.InMDec$*
- *the provide operation $C_1.MDec \cup C_2.MDec - C_1.MDec \cap C_2.InMDec$*
- *the initial condition $C_1 Init \wedge C_2.Init$*
- *the code $C_1.Code \cup C_2.Code$*
- *the private code $C_1.PriCode \cup C_2.PriCode$*

Theorem 5. *For any given input contract InCtr*

$$(C_1\rangle\rangle C_2)(InCtr) \stackrel{def}{=} (C_1(InCtr_1)\|C_2(InCtr_2))\backslash(C_1.MDec \cap C_2.InMDec)$$

where

$$InCtr_1 \stackrel{def}{=} InCtr\lfloor C_1.InMDec$$

$$InCtr_2 \stackrel{def}{=} InCtr\lfloor(C_2.InMDec - C_1.MDec)\|C_1(InCtr_1)\lfloor(C_1.MDec \cap C_2.InMDec)$$

The chaining operator is monotonic and commutes with the hiding operator [15]. The other often used composition is *disjoint parallel composition*.

Definition 15. *(**Disjoint Composition**)* *Let C_1 and C_2 be components such that they do not share fields, public operations. Then $C_1 \otimes C_2$ is defined to be the composite component which has the provided operations of C_1 and C_2 as its provided operations, and the required operations of C_1 and C_2 as its required operations:*

$$(C_1 \otimes C_2)(InCtr) \stackrel{def}{=} C_1(InCtr\lfloor C_1.InMDec)\|C_2(InCtr\lfloor C_2.InMDec)$$

Obviously, chaining $C_1\rangle\rangle C_2$ is the same as disjoint parallel composition $C_1 \otimes C_2$ when the provided services of C_1 are disjoint from the required services of C_2.

We also allow a provided operation to call another (possibly the same) provided operation, so as to link a required a operation to a provided operation.

Definition 16. *(**Feedback**)* *Let C be a component and $m \in C.MDec$ and $n \in C.InMDec$. $C[m \hookrightarrow n]$ is the component such that for any InCrt*

$$C[m \hookrightarrow n](InCtr) \stackrel{def}{=} C(InCtr.MSPec \oplus \{n \mapsto (g\&[\![c]\!]\})\backslash\{m\}$$

$C.MCode(m) = g \longrightarrow c$. *Notice here the design $[\![c]\!]$ is the weakest fixed point of a recursive equation if it calls other methods [15].*

Putting Components Together. Please notice that the conditions for disjoint parallel composition can be easily checked and carried out by either assemblers or designers.

When an putting two components together using the chaining composition $C_1\rangle\rangle C_2$, one may not have access to the codes. In this case, a *black box specification* of C_i must be given for C_i in the form of a pair of $\langle PCtr_i, RCtr_i \rangle$ of a *provided* (or *promising*) contract and a *required* (or *relied*) contract for the components C_i. They are provided by the designer who has checked to ensure

$$C_i(RCtr_i) \sqsupseteq PCtr_i$$

In fact, in these black box specifications, it is not necessary for the specification of operations to include the guards of the operations. The guards are only used by the designers to ensure the consistency of the protocol and the functional behavior.

When C_1 and C_2 are to be chained, we need to check to ensure the *compatibility* of $PCtr_1$ and $RCtr_2$, i.e. $PCtr_1 \sqsupseteq RCtr_2$, so that the protocol in the required contract $RCtr_2$ agrees with that in the provided protocol, and the functional designs of the operations in the provided contract $PCtr_1$ refine those in $RCtr_2$.

Furthermore, the components we have considered so far are *passive components*. Therefore, we treat sequences in the *required protocol in $RCtr_2$ as non-deterministic choices*, but *the provided protocol in $PCtr_1$ as providing deterministic choice*.

Let $Spec_i = \langle PCtr_i, RCtr_i \rangle$, $i = 1, 2$, be two black box specifications, $PProt_i$ and $RProt_i$ the provided protocol and required protocol, and $MDec_i$ and $InMDec_i$ the provided and required operations, respectively. We define

$$PProt_1 / RProt_2 \stackrel{def}{=} \{s | \exists t_1 \in PProt_1, t_2 \in RProt_2 \bullet (t_1 \lfloor (InMDec_2)[!/?] = t_2 \wedge \\ t_1 \lfloor (MDec_1 - InMDec_2) = s\}$$

Definition 17. *(**Interaction compatibility**) For a provided protocol $PProt_1$ and a required protocol $RProt_2$ given in the previous paragraph, we say they are compatible if $PProt_1 \lfloor InMDec_2 \supseteq RProt_2[?op/!op \mid op \in InMDec]$, where a sequence in the required protocol is of the form $\langle !op_1(x_1), \ldots, !op_k(x_k) \rangle$ and $!op_i(x_i)$ is the call out event[3] to operation op.*

Furthermore, when they are compatible, we define the (largest) provided protocol after the provided operations are plugged in the required operations

$$PProt_1 \rangle\rangle RProt_2 \stackrel{def}{=} PProt_1 / RProt_2$$

Example 2. For the one-place buffer, the provided protocol is $(?put, ?get)^*$. Assume a producer requires to interact with the buffer to place items into the buffer only three times. The required protocol would be $\{ \langle !put, !put, !put \rangle \}$. It is compatible with the provided protocol, and the protocol $(?put, ?get)^* / \{ \langle !put, !put, !put \rangle \} = \{ \langle !get, !get, !get \rangle \}$. So a consumer that can be composed in must have such a required protocol.

When we have a number of components requiring services from following $PProt_1$, the chaining compositions can be done (compatibility checking too) one by one

$$PProt_1 \rangle\rangle RProt_2 \rangle\rangle \ldots \rangle\rangle RProt_k$$

The black box specifications of components are in fact the interfaces in UML. They represent the static structural dependency among components as illustrated in Figure 1, which is from the example in [23].

For general system assembly, the model of components needs to be extended by adding the notion of *ports* to represent the Service Access Points (SAPs) [35]. Each port is attached with a pair of provided and required interfaces specified by their contracts $\langle PCtr, RCtr \rangle$, either can be optionally empty. We require that interfaces at different ports are independent. For interaction between two components, a binding has to be established between the required interface at a port of one component and a compatible provided interface at a port of another. This extension allows us to refine a component by adding ports.

4.6   Active Components and Connectors

The components (and contracts) we have studied so far are only passive components. When a provided service is called (according to the protocol), the component starts to

---

[3] It is different from $op(y)!$ which is the return of the method op.

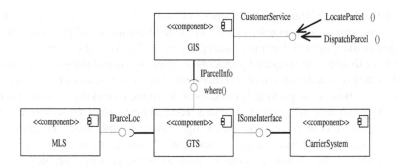

Fig. 1. Static dependency among components

execute and during the execution it may call services of other components. In general a component may be *active* (i.e. an actor in the sense of ROOM [35]) and have its own control and once it is started it can execute its internal actions, call services of other components, and wait to be called by other components. For purely active components, we can simply give the specification of the required contracts, including the protocol. The sequences in the protocol do not have to be non-deterministic choices in general. However, it is always safe to assume the worst case, i.e. the choice over input (namely method calls) is non-deterministic. Otherwise, the failure set must be given to describe when a choice is in the refusal set.

For a more general active component the provided and required operations may be tightly related and it is not always possible to separate the provided protocol and required protocol by projections.

For example, an active producer that uses the buffer in Example 2 only produces the next item after receiving an acknowledgement of the receipt of the previous one from the consumer. The protocols of the producer *Prd* and the consumer *Con* are given respectively as

$$Prd \stackrel{def}{=} (!put, ?ack)^*, \quad Con \stackrel{def}{=} (!get, !ack)^*$$

Again, we can introduce ports into the mode of active components to represent independently defined interfaces that allows components to be connected in arbitrary configuration.

If we changed *Prd* to a pair of provided and required protocols by projections, we would have the provided protocol $(!put)^*$ and the required protocol $(?ack)^*$. With these, we would not have been able to check deadlock freedom when composing it with the producer and the buffer.

We believe composing this kind of active element with *gray box specifications* will require the full power of a theory of concurrency, such as a process algebra (CSP or CCS) or automata theory. In fact, most of the existing models adopt such a gray box specification approach, e.g. [2,6,3,13].

Connectors are often treated as first class elements in component-based architecture description languages. In our framework, the simple connectors are defined by the operations of chaining, disjoint parallel composition and hiding. More general connectors are defined as predicates of protocols of the form $C(Prot_1, \ldots, Prot_k, Prot)$, where $Prot_1, \ldots, Prot_k$ can be seen as *roles* that are mapped to components' protocols and $Prot$ can be seen as the *glue* which is the resulting protocol [2]. We call C a *connector* if the roles are to be linked to the required protocols of components and the resulting protocol is linked to the provided protocol of a component. C is a *coordinator* or *manager* if the roles are to be linked to the provided protocols of components and the resulting protocol is used as a provided protocol (i.e. linked to a required protocol). Connectors and coordinators for passive components are often simple. More complicated coordinators and glues can be defined for general active components. Again the need of writing complicated glue codes would push the users away from using component-based development.

4.7   Component-Based and Object-Oriented Methods

In most books on component-based design in the UML framework, e.g. [10,31], a components is taken as a family of collaborating objects (or class at the level of templates or styles) without being formally defined. Some papers, e.g. [6,3], are critical to object-orientation and think that objects or classes are not composable and thus cannot be treated as objects. To some extent, this is true as objects or classes do not specify their required interfaces. On the other hand, all the existing component technologies, such as JavaBeans, EJB, .NET and COM, are based on object-oriented methods. Therefore, it is useful to investigate the integration of the models of components and objects.

In our framework, we can take a class and translate it to primitive components easily by calculating the required methods from the code of the class methods. However, in general, a component in our proposed model can be realized by a family of collaborating classes. Therefore, for a component C, we treat the interface methods of C and the protocol as the specification of the use cases of the component and the components in environment of C as the actors of these use cases. The design and implementation of this component can then be carried out in a UML-based object-oriented framework.

The types of the fields in interfaces and components can be classes. The classes and their associations form the information (data) model. This model can be represented as a UML class diagram and formalized as class declaration in rCOS [16,14,24]. The implementation of a contract in a component is based on the implementation of the class model. Also, for example UML2.0, a port of a component is realized by a class too (a port in an active component is realized by an active class). The component-based part of rCOS presented here and its object-oriented part in [16,14,24] form a consistent combination.

5   Conclusion and Future Work

We have discussed the basic concepts of components and argued for the need to link methods and their theories for programming. The link will go in two dimensions. In the horizontal direction, we need the integration of theories of state-based functional refinement [18], event-based interaction simulation, real-time [17,25,13], fault-tolerance [25], security, mobility and general QoS. In the vertical dimension, we need to link the theories of domain and requirements analysis, system construction by assembly of components, component construction, and component deployment.

So far most models focus on the theories of interfaces and coordination models to support system construction by composing components. The link of these theories and model to software technology for component construction is still weak. We have provided some initial results towards this direction in rCOS. More work needed in the areas of component-based domain and requirements analysis and component deployment. In the horizontal direction, it is still a long way to deal with general QoS issues. Another challenge is the combination of synchronous communication and asynchronous communication. This could be done by adding message queues at the end of the receiving components or allowing shared fields in components. However, it is not clear whether there is any better way at a higher level of abstraction.

We have presented the ongoing research on rCOS to support this argument. We realize the tradeoff between the simplicity of the model required for the support to CBSE and the expressiveness of the model. While linking methods will help to ease the difficulties by localising a method to a stage of the development, the need to develop sophisticated 'glueware' to coordinate components in applications is one reason why the saving from using "off-the-shelf" components is sometimes not as great as anticipated. If general active components and coordinators among them have to be all covered, the formal method and theory of CBSE cannot be expected to be simpler than those established for general concurrent and distributed systems. On the other hand, linking methods and their theories is useful for general software and system engineering.

Acknowledgement

We would like to thank Chris George, Liu Xiaojian, Chen Xin and Rodrigo Ramos for their comments on earlier versions of the paper.

References

1. R. Allen. *A Formal Approach to Software Architecture*. PhD thesis, Carnegie Mellon, School of Computer Science, 1997.
2. R. Allen and D Garlan. A formal basis for architectural connection. *ACM Transactions on Software Engineering and Methodology*, 6(3):213 – 249, 1997.
3. F. Arbab. Reo: A channeled based coordination model for components composition. *Mathematical Structures in Computer Science*, 14(3):329–366, 2004.
4. L. Bass, P. Clements, and R. Kazman. *Software Architecture in Practice*. Addison-Wesley, 1999.
5. G. Beneken and U. Hammerschall *et al.* Componentware - sate of the art 2003. Background Paper for *Understanding Components Workshop* of the CUE Initiative, 2003.
6. M. Broy. Multi-view modeling of software systems. In Z.Liu and J. He, editors, *Mathematical Frameworks for Component Software: Models for Analysis and Synthesis*. World Scientific, to appear.
7. M. Broy and K. Stølen. *Specification and Development of Interactive Systems: FOCUS on Streams, Interfaces, and Refinement*. Springer, 2001.
8. M.R.V. Chaudron and E. de Jong. Components are from Mars. In *Proc. 15 IPDPS 2000 Workshops on Parallel and Distributed Processing, Lecture Notes In Computer Science; Vol. 1800*, pages 727 – 733, 2000.

9. E.W. Dijkstra. *A Discipline of Programming*. Prentece-Hall, INC, 1976.
10. D. D'Souza and A.C. Wills. *Objects, Components and Framework with UML: The Catalysis Approach*. Addison-Wesley, 1998.
11. Hartmut Ehrig, Werner Damm, Jörg Desel, Martin Große-Rhode, Wolfgang Reif, Eckehard Schnieder, and Engelbert Westkämper, editors. *Integration of Software Specification Techniques for Applications in Engineering, Priority Program SoftSpez of the German Research Foundation (DFG), Final Report*, volume 3147 of *Lecture Notes in Computer Science*. Springer, 2004.
12. D. Garlan, R.T. Monroe, and D. Wile. Acme: Architectural description of component-based systems. In G.T. Leavens and M. Sitaraman, editors, *Foundations of Component-Based Systems*, pages 47–68. Cambridge University Press, 2000.
13. G. Gössler and J. Sifakis. Composition for component-based modeling. *Science of Computer Programming*, 55(1-3), 2005.
14. J. He, Z. Liu, and X. Li. rCOS: A refinement calculus for object systems. Technical Report UNU-IIST Report No 322, UNU-IIST, P.O. Box 3058, Macau, March 2005.
15. J. He, Z. Liu, and X. Li. A theory of contracts. Technical Report UNU-IIST Report No 327, UNU-IIST, P.O. Box 3058, Macau, July 2005.
16. J. He, Z. Liu, X. Li, and S. Qin. A relational model of object oriented programs. In *Proceedings of the Second ASIAN Symposium on Programming Languages and Systems (APLAS04)*, Lecture Notes in Computer Science 3302, pages 415–436, Taiwan, March 2004. Springer.
17. T. Henzinger, Z. Manna, and A. Pnueli. Temporal proof methodologies for real-time systems. In *Proceedings of the 8th ACM Annual Symposium on Principles of Programming Languages*, pages 269–276, U.S.A, 1991. ACM Press.
18. C.A.R. Hoare and J. He. *Unifying theories of programming*. Prentice-Hall International, 1998.
19. Tony Hoare. The verifying compiler: A grand challenge for computer research. *Journal of the ACM*, 50(1):63–69, 2003.
20. J.P. Holmegaard, J. Knudsen, P. Makowski, and A.P. Ravn. Formalization in component based development. In Z.Liu and J. He, editors, *Mathematical Frameworks for Component Software: Models for Analysis and Synthesis*. World Scientific, to appear.
21. D. Hybertson. A uniform component modeling space. *Informatica*, 25:475–482, 2001.
22. L. Lamport. *Specifying Systems: The TLA+ Language and Tools for Hardware and Software Engineers*. Pearson Education, Inc., 2002.
23. Z. Liu, J. He, and X. Li. Contract-oriented development of component software. In *Proc. 3rd IFIP International Conference on Theoretical Computer Science*.
24. Z. Liu, J. He, and X. Li. rCOS: Refinement of component and object systems. Invited Talk at 3rd International Symposium on Formal Methods for Component and Object Systems. To Appear in Lecture Notes of Computer Science, 2005.
25. Z. Liu and M. Joseph. Specification and verification of fault-tolerance, timing and scheduling. *ACM Transactions on Languages and Systems*, 21(1):46–89, 1999.
26. D.C. Luckham and J. Vera. An event-based architecture definition language. *IEEE Transactions on Software Engineering*, 21(9):717–734, 1995.
27. J. Magee, N. Dulay, S. Eisenbach, and J. Kramer. Specifying distributed software architectures. In *Proc. of 5th European Software Engineering Conference (ESEC95)*, pages 137–153. Springer-Verlag, 1995.
28. Z. Manna and A. Pnueli. *The Temporal Logic of Reactive and Concurrent Systems: Specification*. Springer-Verlag, New York, 1991.
29. N. Medvidovic and R.N. Taylor. A classification and comparison framework for software architecture description languages. *IEEE Transactions on Software Engineering*, 26(1):70–93, 2000.

30. A. Pnueli. Looking ahead. Workshop on The Verification Grand Challenge February 21–23, 2005 SRI International, Menlo Park, CA.

31. R. Pooley and P. Steven. *Using UML: Software Engineering with Objects and Component.* Addison-Wesley, 1999.

32. T. Rentsch. Object-oriented programming. *SIGPLAN Notices*, 17(2):51, 1982.

33. R. Roshandel, B. Schmerl, N. Medvidovic, D. Garlan, and D. Zhang. Understanding trade-offs among different architectural modeling approaches. In *Proceedings of the Fourth Working IEEE/IFIP Conference on Software Architecture (WICSA04)*.

34. J.-G. Schneider and O. Nierstrasz. Components, scripts and glue. In L. Barroca, J. Hall, and P. Hall, editors, *Software Architectures Advances and Applications*, pages 13 – 25. Springer, 1999.

35. B. Selic, G. Gullekson, and P.T. Ward. *Real-Time object-oriented modeling.* Wiley, 1994.

36. M. Shaw and D. Garlan. *Software Architectures: Perspectives on an Emerging Discipline.* Prentice Hall, 1996.

37. I. Sommerville. *Software Engineering (6th Edition).* Addison-Wesley, 2001.

38. C. Szyperski. *Component Software: Beyond Object-Oriented Programming.* Addison-Wesley, 1997.

39. R.N. Taylor, N. Medvidovic, K.M. Anderson, E. J. Whitehead Jr., J.E. Robbins, K.A. Nies, P. Oreizy, and D.L. Dubrow. A component- and message-based architectural style for gui software. *IEEE Transactions on Software Engineering*, 22(6):390 – 406, 1996.

40. A. van de Hoek, M. Rakic, R. Roshandel, and N. Medvidovic. Taming architecture evolution. In *Proceedings of the 6th European Software Engineering Conference (ESEC) and the 9th ACM SIGSOFT Symposium on the Foundations of Software Engineering (FSE-9)*, 2001.

41. M. Wirsing and M. Broy. Algebraic state machines. In T. Rus, editor, *Proc. 8th Internat. Conf. Algebraic Methodology and Software Technology, AMAST 2000. LNCS 1816*, pages 89–118. Springer, 2000.

Outfix-Free Regular Languages and Prime Outfix-Free Decomposition*

Yo-Sub Han and Derick Wood

Department of Computer Science,
The Hong Kong University of Science and Technology
{emmous, dwood}@cs.ust.hk

Abstract. A string x is an outfix of a string y if there is a string w such that $x_1 w x_2 = y$, where $x = x_1 x_2$ and a set X of strings is outfix-free if no string in X is an outfix of any other string in X. We examine the outfix-free regular languages. Based on the properties of outfix strings, we develop a polynomial-time algorithm that determines the outfix-freeness of regular languages. We consider two cases: A language is given as a set of strings and a language is given by an acyclic deterministic finite-state automaton. Furthermore, we investigate the prime outfix-free decomposition of outfix-free regular languages and design a linear-time prime outfix-free decomposition algorithm for outfix-free regular languages. We demonstrate the uniqueness of prime outfix-free decomposition.

1 Introduction

Codes play a crucial role in many areas such as information processing, date compression, cryptography, information transmission and so on [14]. They are categorized with respect to different conditions (for example, *prefix-free, suffix-free, infix-free* or *outfix-free*) according to the applications [11,12,13,15]. Since a code is a set of strings, it is a *language*. The conditions that classify code types define proper subfamilies of given language families. For regular languages, for example, prefix-freeness defines the family of prefix-free regular language, which is a proper subfamily of regular languages.

Based on such subfamilies of regular language, researchers have investigated properties of these languages as well as their decomposition problems. A decomposition of a language L is a catenation of several languages $L_1, L_2, \ldots, L_k$ such that $L = L_1 L_2 \cdots L_k$ and $k \geq 2$. If L cannot be further decomposed except for $L \cdot \{\lambda\}$ or $\{\lambda\} \cdot L$, where λ is the null-string, we say that L a *prime* language.

Czyzowicz et al. [5] studied prefix-free regular languages and the prime prefix-free decomposition problem. They showed that the prime prefix-free decomposition of a prefix-free language is unique and demonstrated the importance of prime prefix-free decomposition in practice. Prefix-free regular languages are often used in the literature: to define the determinism of generalized automata [6] and of expression automata [10], and to represent a pattern set [9].

---

* The authors were supported under the Research Grants Council of Hong Kong Competitive Earmarked Research Grant HKUST6197/01E.

D.V. Hung and M. Wirsing (Eds.): ICTAC 2005, LNCS 3722, pp. 96–109, 2005.

Recently, Han et al. [8] studied infix-free regular languages and developed an algorithm to determine whether or not a given regular expression defines an infix-free regular language. They also designed an algorithm for computing the prime infix-free decomposition of infix-free regular languages and showed that the prime infix-free decomposition is not unique. Infix-free regular languages give rise to faster regular-expression text matching [2]. Infix-free languages are also used to compute forbidden words [1,4].

As a continuation of our investigations of subfamilies of regular languages, it is natural to examine outfix-free regular languages and the prime outfix-free decomposition problem. Note that Ito and his co-researchers [12] showed that an outfix-free regular language is finite and Han et al. [7] demonstrated that the family of outfix-free regular languages is a proper subset of the family of simple-regular languages. On the other hand, there was no known efficient algorithm to determine whether or not a given finite set of strings is outfix-free apart from using brute force. Furthermore, the decomposition of a finite set of strings is not unique and the computation of the decomposition is believed to be NP-complete [17]. Therefore, our goal is to develop an efficient algorithm for determining outfix-freeness of a given finite language and to investigate the prime outfix-free decomposition and its uniqueness.

We define some basic notions in Section 2 and propose an efficient algorithm to determine outfix-freeness in Section 3. Then, in Section 4, we show that an outfix-free regular language has a unique prime outfix-free decomposition and the unique decomposition can be computed in linear time in the size of the given finite-state automaton. We suggest some open problems and conclude this paper in Section 5.

2   Preliminaries

Let Σ denote a finite alphabet of characters and Σ^* denote the set of all strings over Σ. A language over Σ is any subset of Σ^*. The character $\emptyset$ denotes the empty language and the character λ denotes the null string. Given a string $x = x_1 \cdots x_n$, $|x|$ is the number of characters in x and $x(i,j) = x_i x_{i+1} \cdots x_j$ is the substring of x from position i to position j, where $i \leq j$. Given two strings x and y in Σ^*, x is said to be an *outfix* of y if there is a string w such that $x_1 w x_2 = y$, where $x = x_1 x_2$. For example, abe is an outfix of $abcde$. Given a set X of strings over Σ, X is *outfix-free* if no string in X is an outfix of any other string in X. Given a string x, let x^R be the reversal of x, in which case $X^R = \{x^R \mid x \in X\}$.

A finite-state automaton A is specified by a tuple $(Q, \Sigma, \delta, s, F)$, where Q is a finite set of states, Σ is an input alphabet, $\delta \subseteq Q \times \Sigma \times Q$ is a (finite) set of transitions, $s \in Q$ is the start state and $F \subseteq Q$ is a set of final states. Let $|Q|$ be the number of states in Q and $|\delta|$ be the number of transitions in δ. Then, the size $|A|$ of A is $|Q| + |\delta|$. Given a transition (p, a, q) in δ, where $p, q \in Q$ and $a \in \Sigma$, we say p has an *out-transition* and q has an *in-transition*. Furthermore, p is a *source state* of q and q is a *target state* of p. A string x over Σ is accepted by A if there is a labeled path from s to a final state in F that spells out x. Thus, the language $L(A)$ of a finite-state automaton A is the set of all strings spelled out by paths from s to a final state in F. We define A to be *non-returning* if the start state of A does not have any in-transitions and A to be *non-exiting* if a final state of A does not have any out-transitions. We assume that A has only *useful* states; that is, each state appears on some path from the start state to some final state.

3   Outfix-Free Regular Languages

We first define outfix-free regular expressions and languages, and then present an algorithm to determine whether or not a given language is outfix-free. Since prefix-free, suffix-free, infix-free and outfix-free languages are related to each other, we define all of them and show their relationships.

Definition 1. *A language L is*

- prefix-free *if, for all distinct strings* $x, y \in \Sigma^*$, $x \in L$ *and* $y \in L$ *imply that* x *and* y *are not prefixes of each other.*
- suffix-free *if, for all distinct strings* $x, y \in \Sigma^*$, $x \in L$ *and* $y \in L$ *imply that* x *and* y *are not suffixes of each other.*
- bifix-free *if L is prefix-free and suffix-free.*
- infix-free *if, for all distinct strings* $x, y \in \Sigma^*$, $x \in L$ *and* $y \in L$ *imply that* x *and* y *are not substrings of each other.*
- outfix-free *if, for all distinct strings* $x, y, z \in \Sigma^*$, $xz \in L$ *and* $xyz \in L$ *imply* $y = \lambda$.
- hyper *if L is infix-free and outfix-free.*

For further details and definitions, refer to Ito et al. [12] or Shyr [18].

We say that a regular expression E is outfix-free if $L(E)$ is outfix-free. The language defined by such an outfix-free regular expression is called an *outfix-free regular language*. In a similar way, we can define prefix-free, suffix-free and infix-free regular expressions and languages.

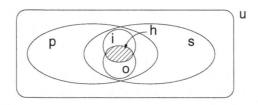

Fig. 1. A diagram to show inclusions of families of languages, where p,s,i,o and h denote prefix-free, suffix-free, infix-free , outfix-free and hyper families, respectively, and u denotes Σ^*. Note that the outfix-free family is a proper subset of the prefix-free and suffix-free families and the hyper family is the common intersection between the infix-free family and the outfix-free family.

Let $A = (Q, \Sigma, \delta, s, F)$ denote a deterministic finite-state automaton (DFA) for L. Han and Wood [10] showed that if A is non-exiting, then L is prefix-free. Han et al. [8] proposed an algorithm to determine whether or not a given regular expression E is infix-free in $O(|E|^2)$ worst-case time. This algorithm can also solve the prefix-free and suffix-free cases as well. Therefore, it is natural to design an algorithm to determine whether or not a given regular language is outfix-free. Since an outfix-free regular language L is finite [12,14], the problem is decidable by comparing all pairs of strings in L, although it is certainly undesirable to do so.

3.1   Prefix-Freeness

Since the family of outfix-free regular languages is a proper subfamily of prefix-free regular languages as shown in Fig. 1, we consider prefix-freeness of a finite language first.

Given a finite set of strings $W = \{w_1, w_2, \ldots, w_n\}$, where n is the number of strings in W, we construct a trie T for W. A trie is an ordered tree data structure that is used to store a set of strings and each edge in the tree has a single character label. For details on tries, refer to data structure textbooks [3,19]. Assume that w_i is a prefix of w_j, where $i \neq j$; it implies that $|w_i| < |w_j|$. Then, w_i and w_j must have the common path in T from the root to the ith node q that spells out w_i. Therefore, if we reach q while constructing the path for w_j in T, we recognize that w_i is a prefix of w_j. Let us consider the case when we construct a path for w_j first and, then, construct a path for w_i in T. The path for w_i ends at the $|w_i|$th node q that already has a child node for the path for w_j. Therefore, we know that w_i is a prefix of some other string. Note that we can construct a trie for W in $O(|w_1| + |w_2| + \cdots |w_n|)$ time, which is linear in the size of W.

Lemma 1. *Given a finite set W of strings, we can determine whether or not W is prefix-free in linear time in the size of W by constructing a trie for W. We can also determine suffix-freeness of W in the same runtime by constructing a trie for W^R.*

3.2   Outfix-Freeness

We now consider outfix-freeness. Assume that we have two distinct strings w_1 and w_2 and w_2 is an outfix of w_1. It implies that $w_1 = xyz$ for some strings x, y and z such that $w_2 = xz$ and $y \neq \lambda$. Moreover, w_1 and w_2 have the common prefix x and the common suffix z. Fig. 2 illustrates it.

Based on these observations, we determine whether or not one string w_1 is an outfix of another string w_2 for two given strings w_1 and w_2, where $|w_1| \geq |w_2|$. We compare two characters, one from w_1 and the other from w_2, from left to right (from 1 to $|w_2|$) until two compared characters are different; say the ith characters are different. If we completely read w_2, then we recognize that w_2 is a prefix of w_1 and, therefore, w_2 is an outfix of w_1. We repeat these character-by-character comparisons from right to left (from $|w_2|$ to 1) until we have two

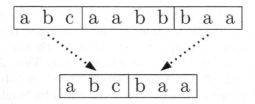

Fig. 2. A graphical illustration of an outfix string; *abcbaa* is an outfix of *abcaabbbaa*

different characters. Assume that the jth characters are different. If $i > j$, then w_2 is an outfix of w_1. Otherwise, w_2 is not an outfix of w_1. For example, $i = 4$ and $j = 3$ in Fig. 2.

Lemma 2. *Given two strings w_1 and w_2, where $|w_1| \geq |w_2|$, w_2 is an outfix of w_1 if and only if there is a position i such that $w_2(1, i)$ is a prefix of w_1 and $w_2(i + 1, |w_2|)$ is a suffix of w_1.*

Let us consider the trie T for w_1 and w_2. Since w_1 and w_2 have the common prefix, both strings share the common path from the root to a node q of height i that spells out $w_2(1, i)$. Moreover, the path for $w_2(i+1, |w_2|)$ in T is a suffix-path for $w_1(i + 1, |w_1|)$ in T. For example, in Fig. 3, the path for x is the common prefix-path and the path for z is the common suffix-path. Thus, if a given finite set W of strings is not outfix-free, then there is such a pair of strings. Since a node $q \in T$ gives the common prefix for all strings that pass through q, we only need to check whether some path from q to a leaf is a suffix-path for some other path from q to another leaf.

Let $T(q)$ be the subtree of T rooted at $q \in T$. Then, we can determine whether or not a path from q is a suffix-path for another path from q in $T(q)$ by determining the suffix-freeness of all paths from q to a leaf in $T(q)$ based on the same algorithm for Lemma 1. The running time is linear in the the size of $T(q)$.

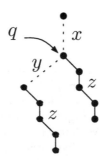

Fig. 3. An example of a trie for strings $w_1 = xyz$ and $w_2 = xz$. Note that both paths end with the same subpath sequence in the trie since w_1 and w_2 have the common suffix z.

3.3   Complexity of Outfix-Freeness

The subfunction is_prefix-free(T) in Fig. 4 determines whether or not the set of strings represented by a given trie T is prefix-free. Note that is_prefix-free(T) runs in $O(|T|)$ time, where $|T|$ is the number of nodes in T.

Given a finite set $W = \{w_1, w_2, \ldots, w_n\}$ of strings, we can construct a trie T in $O(\sum_{i=1}^{n} |w_i|)$ time and space, which is linear in the size of W, where $n \geq 1$. Prefix-freeness and suffix-freeness can be verified in linear time. Thus, the total running time for the algorithm Outfix-freeness (OFF) in Fig. 4 is

$$O(|T|) + \sum_{q \in T} |T(q)|,$$

where q is a node that has more than one child. In the worst-case, we have to examine all nodes in T; for example, T is a complete tree, where each internal node has the same number of children. To compute the size of $\sum |T(q)|$, let us consider a string $w_i \in W$ that makes a path P from the root to a leaf in T. If a node $q \in T$ of height j in path P has more than one child, then the suffix $w_i(j + 1, |w_i|)$ of w_i that starts from q is used in is_suffix-free($T(q)$) in OFF. In the worst-case, all suffixes of w_i can be used by is_suffix-free($T(q)$). Therefore, w_i contributes $O(|w_i|^2)$ to the total running time of OFF. Fig. 5 illustrates a worst-case example.

Therefore, the total time complexity is $O(|w_1|^2 + |w_2|^2 + \cdots + |w_n|^2)$ in the worse case. If the size of w_i is $O(k)$, for some k, then the running time is $O(k^2 n)$. On the other hand, the all-pairs comparison approach gives $O(kn^2)$ worst-case running time. Note that the size of each string in W is usually much smaller than the number of strings in W; namely, $k \ll n$.

Theorem 1. *Given a finite set $W = \{w_1, w_2, \ldots, w_n\}$ of strings, we can determine whether or not W is outfix-free in $O(\sum_i^n |w_i|^2)$ time using $O(\sum_i^n |w_i|)$ space in the worse-case.*

Outfix-freeness($W = \{w_1, w_2, \ldots, w_n\}$)

Construct a trie T for W

if (is_prefix-free(T) = no)
    then return no
if (is_suffix-free(T) = no)
    then return no

    for each $q \in T$ that has more than one child
        if (is_suffix-free($T(q)$) = no)
            then return no

return yes

Fig. 4. An outfix-freeness checking algorithm for a given finite set of strings

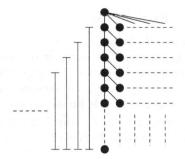

Fig. 5. All suffixes of a string w in T are used to determine the outfix-freeness by OFF. The size of the sum of all suffixes is $O(|w|^2)$.

Now we characterize the family of outfix-free (regular) languages in terms of closure properties.

Theorem 2. *The family of outfix-free (regular) languages is closed under catenation and intersection but not under union, complement or star.*

Proof. We only prove the catenation case. The other cases can be proved straightforwardly.

Assume that $L = L_1 \cdot L_2$ is not outfix-free whereas L_1 and L_2 are outfix-free. Then, there are two distinct strings s and $t \in L$, where t is an outfix of s. Namely, $s = xyz$, $t = xz$ and $y \neq \lambda$. Since s and t are catenation of two strings from L_1 and L_2, s and t can be partitioned into two parts; $s = s_1 s_2$ and $t = t_1 t_2$, where $s_i, t_i \in L_i$ for $i = 1, 2$. From the assumption that t is an outfix of s, s and t have the common prefix and the common suffix as shown in Fig. 6. If we decompose s and t into $s_1 s_2$ and $t_1 t_2$, then we have one of the following four cases:

1. s_1 is a prefix of t_1.
2. t_1 is a prefix of s_1.
3. s_2 is a suffix of t_2.
4. t_2 is a suffix of s_2.

Let us consider the first case as illustrated in Fig. 6. Since s_1 is a prefix of t_1 and $s_1, t_1 \in L_1$, L_1 is not outfix-free — a contradiction. We can use a similar argument for the other three cases. □

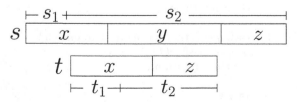

Fig. 6. The figure illustrates the first case in the proof of Theorem 2, where s_i and $t_i \in L_i$ for $i = 1, 2$. Since s_1 is a prefix of t_1, L_1 is not outfix-free.

3.4 Outfix-Freeness of Acyclic Deterministic Finite-State Automata

Acyclic deterministic finite-state automata (ADFAs) are a proper subfamily of DFAs that define finite languages. For example, a trie is an ADFA. Since ADFAs represent finite languages, they are often used to store a finite number of strings. Moreover, ADFAs require less space than tries. For instance, we use $O(|\Sigma|^5)$ space to store all strings of length 5 over Σ in a trie. On the other hand, we use 6 states with $5 \times |\Sigma|$ transitions in an ADFA. We consider outfix-freeness of a language given by an ADFA $A = (Q, \Sigma, \delta, s, f)$. Given A and a state $q \in Q$, we define the *right language* $L_{\overrightarrow{q}}$ to be the set of strings spelled out by paths from q to f.

Assume that two strings $w_1 = xyz$ and $w_2 = xz$ are accepted by A, where w_2 is an outfix of w_1. Note that w_1 and w_2 have the common prefix x and the common suffix z and there is a unique path from s to a state q that spells out x in A since A is deterministic. Then, yz and z are accepted by $A_{\overrightarrow{q}}$. It means that $L_{\overrightarrow{q}}$ is not suffix-free.

Lemma 3. *Given an ADFA $A = (Q, \Sigma, \delta, s, f)$, $L(A)$ is outfix-free if and only if $L_{\overrightarrow{q}}$ is suffix-free for any state $q \in Q$.*

Proof.
$\Longrightarrow$ Assume that $L_{\overrightarrow{q}}$ is not suffix-free. Then, there are two strings w_1 and w_2 in $L_{\overrightarrow{q}}$, where w_2 is a suffix of w_1. Since A has only useful states, there must be a path from s to q that spells out a string x. It implies that A accepts both xw_1 and xw_2, where xw_2 is an outfix of xw_1 — a contradiction. Therefore, if $L(A)$ is outfix-free, then $L_{\overrightarrow{q}}$ is suffix-free for any state $q \in Q$.

$\Longleftarrow$ Assume that $L(A)$ is not outfix-free. Then, there are two strings $w_1 = xyz$ and $w_2 = xz$ accepted by A, where w_2 is an outfix of w_1. There is a unique path from s to q that spells out x in A. Then, there are two distinct paths, one is for yz and the other is for z, from q since A accepts w_1 and w_2. It implies that $A_{\overrightarrow{q}}$ accepts yz and z and $L_{\overrightarrow{q}}$ is not suffix-free — a contradiction. Therefore, if $L_{\overrightarrow{q}}$ is suffix-free for any state $q \in Q$, then $L(A)$ is outfix-free. $\square$

Recently, Han et al. [8] proposed algorithms to determine prefix-freeness, suffix-freeness, bifix-freeness and infix-freeness of a given a (nondeterministic) finite-state automaton $A = (Q, \Sigma, \delta, s, f)$ in $O(|Q|^2 + |\delta|^2)$ time. We use their algorithm to check suffix-freeness for each state. Given an ADFA $A = (Q, \Sigma, \delta, s, f)$ and a state $q \in Q$, the size of $A_{\overrightarrow{q}}$ is at most the size of A; namely, $|A_{\overrightarrow{q}}| \leq |A|$. Since it takes $O(|Q|^2 + |\delta|^2)$ time for each state to check suffix-freeness and there are $|Q|$ states, the total time complexity to determine outfix-freeness of A is $O(|Q|^3 + |Q||\delta|^2)$. Since a DFA has a constant number of out-transitions from a state, we obtain the following result.

Theorem 3. *Given an ADFA $A = (Q, \Sigma, \delta, s, f)$, we can determine outfix-freeness of $L(A)$ in $O(|Q|^3)$ worst-case time.*

Furthermore, we determine infix-freeness of $L(A)$ after an outfix-freeness test. If $L(A)$ is infix-free and outfix-free, then $L(A)$ is hyper. Since the time complexity for the infix-freeness test is $O(|Q|^2)$ for A [8], we can determine hyperness of $L(A)$ in $O(|Q|^3)$ time as well.

Theorem 4. *Given an ADFA $A = (Q, \Sigma, \delta, s, f)$, we can determine hyperness of $L(A)$ in $O(|Q|^3)$ worst-case time.*

4   Prime Outfix-Free Regular Languages and Prime Decomposition

Decomposition is the reverse operation of catenation. If $L = L_1 \cdot L_2$, then L is the catenation of L_1 and L_2 and $L_1 \cdot L_2$ is a decomposition of L. We call L_1 and L_2 *factors* of L. Note that every language L has a decomposition, $L = \{\lambda\} \cdot L$, where L is a factor of itself. We call $\{\lambda\}$ a *trivial* language. We define a language L to be *prime* if $L \neq L_1 \cdot L_2$ for any two non-trivial languages. Then, the prime decomposition of L is to decompose L into $L_1 \cdot L_2 \cdot \ldots \cdot L_k$, where $L_1, L_2, \ldots, L_k$ are prime languages and $k \geq 1$ is a constant.

Mateescu et al. [16,17] showed that the primality of regular languages is decidable and the prime decomposition of a regular language is not unique even for finite languages. Furthermore, they pointed out that no star language L ($L = K^*$, for some K) can possess a prime decomposition. Czyzowicz et al. [5] considered prefix-free regular languages and showed that the prime prefix-free decomposition for a prefix-free regular language L is unique and the unique decomposition for L can be computed in $O(m)$ worst-case time, where m is the size of the minimal DFA for L. Recently, Han et al. [8] investigated the prime infix-free decomposition of infix-free regular languages and demonstrated that the prime infix-free decomposition is not unique.

We examine prime outfix-free regular languages and decomposition. Even though outfix-free regular languages are finite [12], the primality test for finite languages is believed to be NP-complete [17]. Thus, the decomposition problem for finite languages is not trivial at all. We design a linear-time algorithm to determine whether or not a given finite language L is prime outfix-free. We investigate prime outfix-free decompositions and uniqueness.

4.1   Prime Outfix-Free Regular Languages

Definition 2. *A regular language L is a* prime outfix-free language *if $L \neq L_1 \cdot L_2$ for any outfix-free regular languages L_1 and L_2.*

From now on, when we say prime, we mean prime outfix-free. Since we are dealing with outfix-free regular languages, there are no back-edges in finite-state automata for such languages. Furthermore, these finite-state automata are always non-exiting and non-returning. Note that if a finite-state automaton is non-exiting and has several final states, then all final states are equivalent and, therefore, are merged into a single final state.

Definition 3. *We define a state b in a DFA A to be a* bridge state *if the following two conditions hold:*

1. *State b is neither a start nor a final state.*
2. *For any string $w \in L(A)$, its path in A must pass through b. Therefore, we can partition A at b into two subautomata A_1 and A_2.*

Given a DFA $A = (Q, \Sigma, \delta, s, f)$ and a bridge state $b \in Q$, where $L(A)$ is outfix-free, we can partition A into two subautomata A_1 and A_2 as follows: $A_1 = (Q_1, \Sigma, \delta_1, s, b)$ and $A_2 = (Q_2, \Sigma, \delta_2, b, f)$, where Q_1 is a set of states of A that appear on some path from s to b in A, $Q_2 = Q \setminus Q_1 \cup \{b\}$, δ_2 is a set of transitions of A that appear on some path from b to f in A and $\delta_1 = \delta \setminus \delta_2$. Fig. 7 illustrates a partition at a bridge state.

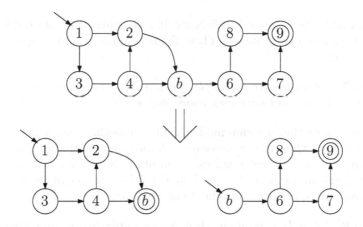

Fig. 7. An example of partitioning of an automaton at a bridge state b

It is easy to verify that $L(A) = L(A_1) \cdot L(A_2)$ from the second requirement in Definition 3.

Lemma 4. *If a minimal DFA A has a bridge state, where $L(A)$ is outfix-free, then $L(A)$ is not prime.*

Proof. Since A has a bridge state b, we can partition A into A_1 and A_2 at b. We establish that $L(A_1)$ and $L(A_2)$ are outfix-free and, therefore, $L(A)$ is not prime. Assume that $L(A_1)$ is not outfix-free. Then, there are two distinct strings u and v accepted by A_1, where v is an outfix of u; namely, $u = xyz$ and $v = xz$ for some strings x, y and z. Let w be a string from $L(A_2)$. Since $L(A) = L(A_1) \cdot L(A_2)$, both $uw = xyzw$ and $vw = xzw$ are in $L(A)$. It contradicts the assumption that $L(A)$ is outfix-free. Therefore, if $L(A)$ is outfix-free, then $L(A_1)$ should be outfix-free as well. With a similar argument, we can show that $L(A_2)$ should be outfix-free. Hence, if A has a bridge state, then $L(A)$ can be decomposed as $L(A_1) \cdot L(A_2)$, where $L(A_1)$ and $L(A_2)$ are outfix-free, and, therefore, $L(A)$ is not prime. □

Lemma 5. *If a minimal DFA A does not have any bridge states and $L(A)$ is outfix-free, then $L(A)$ is prime.*

Proof. Assume that L is not prime. Then, L can be decomposed as $L_1 \cdot L_2$, where L_1 and L_2 are outfix-free. Czyzowicz et al. [5] showed that given prefix-free languages A, B and C such that $A = B \cdot C$, A is regular if and only if B and C are regular. Thus, if L is regular, then L_1 and L_2 must be regular since all outfix-free languages are prefix-free. Let A_1 and A_2 be minimal DFAs for L_1 and L_2, respectively. Since A_1 and A_2 are non-returning and non-exiting, there are only one start state and one final state for each of them. We catenate A_1 and A_2 by merging the final state of A_1 and the start state of A_2 as a single state b. Then, the catenated automaton is the minimal DFA for $L(A_1) \cdot L(A_2) = L$ and has a bridge state b — a contradiction.   □

We can rephrase Lemma 4 as follows: If L is prime, then its minimal DFA does not have any bridge states. Then, from Lemmas 4 and 5, we obtain the following result.

Theorem 5. *An outfix-free regular language L is prime if and only if the minimal DFA for L does not have any bridge states.*

Lemma 4 shows that if a minimal DFA A for an outfix-free regular language L has a bridge state, then we can decompose L into a catenation of two outfix-free regular languages using bridge states. In addition, if we have a set B of bridge states for A and decompose A at b, then $B \setminus \{b\}$ is the set of bridge states for the resulting two automata after the decomposition.

Theorem 6. *Let A be a minimal DFA for an outfix-free regular language that has k bridge states. Then, $L(A)$ can be decomposed into $k + 1$ prime outfix-free regular languages, namely, $L(A) = L_1 L_2 \cdots L_{k+1}$ and $L_1, L_2, \ldots, L_{k+1}$ are prime.*

Proof. Let $(b_1, b_2, \ldots, b_k)$ be the sequence of bridge states from s to f in A. We prove the statement by induction on k. It is sufficient to show that $L(A) = L'L''$ such that L' is accepted by a DFA A' with $k - 1$ bridge states and L'' is a prime outfix-free regular language.

We partition A into two subautomata A' and A'' at b_k. Note that $L(A')$ and $L(A'')$ are outfix-free languages by the proof of Lemma 4. Since A'' has no bridge states, $L'' = L(A'')$ is prime by Theorem 5. By the definition of bridge states, all paths must pass through $(b_1, b_2, \ldots, b_{k-1})$ in A' and, therefore, A' has $k - 1$ bridge states. Thus, if A has k bridge states, then $L(A)$ can be decomposed into $k + 1$ prime outfix-free regular languages.   □

Note that Theorem 6 guarantees the uniqueness of prime outfix-free decomposition. Furthermore, finding the prime decomposition of an outfix-free regular language is equivalent to identifying bridge states of its minimal DFA by Theorems 5 and 6.

We now show how to compute a set of bridge states defined in Definition 3 from a given minimal DFA A in $O(m)$ time, where m is the size of A. Let $G(V, E)$ be a labeled directed graph for a given minimal DFA $A = (Q, \Sigma, \delta, s, f)$, where $V = Q$ and $E = \delta$. We say that a path in G is *simple* if it does not have a cycle.

Lemma 6. *Let $P_{s,f}$ be a simple path from s to f in G. Then, only the states on $P_{s,f}$ can be bridge states of A.*

Proof. Assume that a state q is a bridge state and is not on $P_{s,f}$. Then, it contradicts the second requirement of bridge states. □

Assume that we have a simple path $P_{s,f}$ from s to f in $G = (V, E)$, which can be computed in $O(|V| + |E|)$ worst-case time. All states on $P_{s,f}$ form a set of candidate bridge states (CBS); namely, $CBS = (s, b_1, b_2, \ldots, b_k, f)$.

We use DFS to explore G from s. We visit all states in CBS first. While exploring G, we maintain the following two values, for each state $q \in Q$,

anc: The index i of a state $b_i \in CBS$ such that there is a path from b_i to q and there is no path from $b_j \in CBS$ to q for $j > i$. The **anc** of b_i is i.

max: The index i of a state $b_i \in CBS$ such that there is a path from q to b_i and there is no path from q to b_j for $i < j$ without visiting any state in CBS.

The **max** value of a state q means that there is a path from q to $b_{\mathbf{max}}$. If b_i has a **max** value and $\mathbf{max} \neq i + 1$, then it means that there is another simple path from b_i to $b_{\mathbf{max}}$ without passing through b_{i+1}.

When a state $q \in Q \setminus CBS$ is visited during DFS, q inherits **anc** of its preceding state. A state q has two types of child state: One type is a subset T_1 of states in CBS and the other is a subset T_2 of $Q \setminus CBS$; namely, all states in T_1 are candidate bridge states and all states in T_2 are not candidate bridge states. Once we have explored all children of q, we update **max** of q as follows:

$$\mathbf{max} = \max(\max_{q \in T_1}(q.\mathbf{anc}), \max_{q \in T_2}(q.\mathbf{max})).$$

Fig. 8 provides an example of DFS after updating (**anc**, **max**) for all states in G.

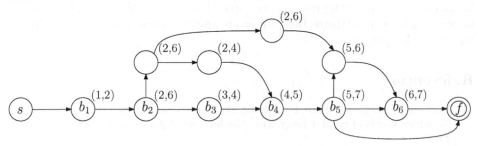

Fig. 8. An example of DFS that computes (**anc**, **max**), for each state in G, for a given $CBS = (s, b_1, b_2, b_3, b_4, b_5, b_6, f)$

If a state $b_i \in CBS$ does not have any out-transitions except a transition to $b_{i+1} \in CBS$ (for example, b_6 in Fig. 8), then b_i has $(i, i+1)$ when DFS is completed. Once we have completed DFS and computed $(\mathbf{anc}, \mathbf{max})$ for all states in G, we remove states from CBS that violate the requirements to be bridge states. Assume $b_i \in CBS$ has (i, j), where $i < j$. We remove $b_{i+1}, b_{i+2}, \ldots, b_{j-1}$ from CBS since that there is a path from b_i to b_j; that is, there is another simple path from b_i to f. Then, we remove s and f from CBS. For example, we have $\{b_1, b_2\}$ after removing states that violate the requirements from CBS in Fig. 8. This algorithm gives the following result.

Theorem 7. *Given a minimal DFA A for an outfix-free regular language:*

1. *We can determine the primality of $L(A)$ in $O(m)$ time,*
2. *We can compute the unique outfix-free decomposition of $L(A)$ in $O(m)$ time if $L(A)$ is not prime,*

where m is the size of A.

5   Conclusions

We have investigated the outfix-free regular languages. First, we suggested an algorithm to verify whether or not a given set $W = \{w_1, w_2, \ldots, w_n\}$ of strings is outfix-free. We then established that the verification takes $O(\sum_{i=1}^{n} |w_i|^2)$ worst-case time, where n is the number of strings in W. We also considered the case when a language L is given by an ADFA. Moreover, we have extended the algorithm to determine hyperness of L by checking infix-freeness using the algorithm of Han et al. [8].

We have demonstrated that an outfix-free regular language L has a unique outfix-free decomposition and the unique decomposition can be computed in $O(m)$ time, where m is the size of the minimal DFA for L.

As we have observed, outfix-free regular languages are finite sets. However, this observation does not hold for the context-free languages. For example, the non-regular language, $\{w \mid w = a^i c b^i, i \geq 1\}$ is context-free, outfix-free and infinite. The decidability of outfix-freeness for context-free languages is open as is the prime decomposition problem. Moreover, there are non-context-free languages that are outfix-free; for example, $\{w \mid w = a^i b^i c^i, i \geq 1\}$. Thus, it is reasonable to investigate the properties and the structure of the family of outfix-free languages.

References

1. M.-P. Béal, M. Crochemore, F. Mignosi, A. Restivo, and M. Sciortino. Computing forbidden words of regular languages. *Fundamenta Informaticae*, 56(1-2):121–135, 2003.
2. C. L. A. Clarke and G. V. Cormack. On the use of regular expressions for searching text. *ACM Transactions on Programming Languages and Systems*, 19(3):413–426, 1997.

3. T. H. Cormen, C. E. Leiserson, R. L. Rivest, and C. Stein. *Introduction to Algorithms*. McGraw-Hill Higher Education, 2001.

4. M. Crochemore, F. Mignosi, and A. Restivo. Automata and forbidden words. *Information Processing Letters*, 67(3):111–117, 1998.

5. J. Czyzowicz, W. Fraczak, A. Pelc, and W. Rytter. Linear-time prime decomposition of regular prefix codes. *International Journal of Foundations of Computer Science*, 14:1019–1032, 2003.

6. D. Giammarresi and R. Montalbano. Deterministic generalized automata. *Theoretical Computer Science*, 215:191–208, 1999.

7. Y.-S. Han, G. Trippen, and D. Wood. Simple-regular expressions and languages. In *Proceedings of DCFS'05*, 146–157, 2005.

8. Y.-S. Han, Y. Wang, and D. Wood. Infix-free regular expressions and languages. To appear in International Journal of Foundations of Computer Science, 2005.

9. Y.-S. Han, Y. Wang, and D. Wood. Prefix-free regular-expression matching. In *Proceedings of CPM'05*, 298–309. Springer-Verlag, 2005. Lecture Notes in Computer Science 3537.

10. Y.-S. Han and D. Wood. The generalization of generalized automata: Expression automata. *International Journal of Foundations of Computer Science*, 16(3):499–510, 2005.

11. M. Ito, H. Jürgensen, H.-J. Shyr, and G. Thierrin. N-prefix-suffix languages. *International Journal of Computer Mathematics*, 30:37–56, 1989.

12. M. Ito, H. Jürgensen, H.-J. Shyr, and G. Thierrin. Outfix and infix codes and related classes of languages. *Journal of Computer and System Sciences*, 43:484–508, 1991.

13. H. Jürgensen. Infix codes. In *Proceedings of Hungarian Computer Science Conference*, 25–29, 1984.

14. H. Jürgensen and S. Konstantinidis. Codes. In G. Rozenberg and A. Salomaa, editors, *Word, Language, Grammar*, volume 1 of *Handbook of Formal Languages*, 511–607. Springer-Verlag, 1997.

15. D. Y. Long, J. Ma, and D. Zhou. Structure of 3-infix-outfix maximal codes. *Theoretical Computer Science*, 188(1-2):231–240, 1997.

16. A. Mateescu, A. Salomaa, and S. Yu. On the decomposition of finite languages. Technical Report 222, TUCS, 1998.

17. A. Mateescu, A. Salomaa, and S. Yu. Factorizations of languages and commutativity conditions. *Acta Cybernetica*, 15(3):339–351, 2002.

18. H.-J. Shyr. *Lecture Notes: Free Monoids and Languages*. Hon Min Book Company, Taichung, Taiwan R.O.C, 1991.

19. D. Wood. *Data structures, algorithms, and performance*. Addison-Wesley Longman Publishing Co., Inc., Boston, MA, USA, 1993.

Solving First Order Formulae
of Pseudo-Regular Theory

Sébastien Limet and Pierre Pillot

LIFO, Université d'Orléans, France
{limet, pillot}@lifo.univ-orleans.fr

Abstract. In this paper[1], we study the class of pseudo-regular relations which is an extension of regular relations that weakens some restrictions on the "synchronization" between tuple components of the relation. We choose logic programming as formalism to describe tree tuple languages (i.e. relations) and logic program transformation techniques for computing operations on them. We show that even if pseudo-regular cs-programs are syntactically less restrictive than regular ones, they define the same class of tree tuple languages. However, pseudo-regular relations allow one to define classes of term rewrite systems the transitive closure of which is a regular relation. We apply this result to give a decidable class of first order formulae based on the joinability predicate $\downarrow_R^?$ where R is a pseudo-regular term rewrite system.

1 Introduction

Term rewrite systems (TRS) are fundamental to fields like theorem proving, system verification, or functional-logic programming. Applications there require decision procedures e.g. for R-unifiability (for terms t and t', are there a substitution σ and a term u such that $t\sigma \rightarrow_R^* u \ _R^* \leftarrow t'\sigma$?) or for reachability (is term t' reachable from term t by a rewriting derivation?). In this paper, we are interested in solving formulae where the only predicate is the R-joinability $\downarrow_R^?$ where R is a term rewrite system. R-joinability coincides with R-unification for confluent rewrite systems.

Solving a single equation $s \downarrow_R^? t$ is known to be undecidable without any strong restrictions on the TRS [4,5]. Some positive results have been shown restricting the TRS to obtain a finitary equational problem (i.e. insuring that the set of minimal solutions is finite). For example shallow or standard theories [3,12] impose that the depth of all variables in the (un-oriented) TRS is one. In fact standard property weakens a little this restriction by allowing variables at depth more than one when they are not under a defined function symbol. For infinitary theories (i.e. theories where the set of solutions of an equation $s \downarrow_R^? t$ may be infinite) many results have been given to decide the existence of solutions using the reachability problem (e.g. [14,15]) but very few of them [5,8] give a finite representation of the solutions and even less go beyond solving a single equation.

---

[1] A full version can be found in the LIFO RR-2005-2 at the following URL
http://www.univ-orleans.fr/lifo/prodsci/rapports/RR2005.htm.en

D.V. Hung and M. Wirsing (Eds.): ICTAC 2005, LNCS 3722, pp. 110–124, 2005.
© Springer-Verlag Berlin Heidelberg 2005

In order to reach our aim, we have first to solve the problem of the representation of a possibly infinite set of solutions of an equation $s \downarrow_R^? t$. The most common tools used for such a representation are tree languages recognizers [2] such as tree automata or tree grammars. In our context, a tree language is a set of ground terms that is represented by a logic program as in e.g. [6,11]. More precisely, we use the class of cs-programs of [6].The operations on the languages are computed thanks to logic program transformations inspired from [13].

Many of the tree tuple languages are not closed under all the set operations. As far as we know the only class that is closed under those operation and have decidable emptiness and membership tests are the regular relations [2]. Pseudo-regular relations are tree tuple languages that allow some kind of duplications between the components of the tuple. In [6], the emptiness and membership tests as well as the intersection, projection, union and join (which can be seen as a composition of relations) of pseudo-regular relations have been described in term of logic program transformations, but no result about the complement of a pseudo-regular relation is given. In this paper, we give an algorithm that computes the complement of pseudo-regular relations.

Once the finite representation of infinite sets of solutions has been chosen, we have to give an algorithm to compute a representation of the solutions of equations $s \downarrow_R^? t$. We use the method described in [7], where a term rewrite system is transformed into a logic program that encodes the transitive closure of the rewrite relation $\rightarrow_R^*$. Thanks to this transformation, we can define a class of TRS which corresponding logic programs are pseudo-regular. Then thanks to the closure of pseudo-regular relation under the set operations, we can compute the solutions of any formulae where $\downarrow_R^?$ is the only predicate when R belongs to this class.

2   Preliminaries

We recall some basic notions and notations concerning terms, term rewrite systems and logic programming; for details see [1,9].

Let Σ be a finite set of symbols with arity, Var be an infinite set of variables, and $T(\Sigma, Var)$ be the first-order term algebra over Σ and Var. A term is *linear* if no variable occurs more than once in it and a term without variable is called a *ground term*. Σ consists of three disjoint subsets: the set $\mathcal{F}$ of *defined function symbols*, the set $\mathcal{C}$ of *constructor symbols* and the set Pr of *predicate symbols*. The terms of $T(\mathcal{C}, Var)$ are called *data-terms* and those of the form $P(\vec{t})$ where P is a predicate symbol of arity n and $\vec{t}$ is a vector of $T(\mathcal{F} \cup \mathcal{C}, Var)^n$ are called *atoms*.

A *position* p is a list of integers which length is denoted by $|p|$. For a term t, $Pos(t)$ denotes the set of *positions* in t, $|t| = |Pos(t)|$ the size of t, and $t|_u$ the *subterm* of t at position u. The term $t[u \leftarrow s]$ is obtained from t by replacing the subterm at position u by s. $Var(t)$ is the set of variables occurring in t. The set $\Sigma Pos(t) \subseteq Pos(t)$ denotes the set of non-variable positions, i.e., $t|_u \notin Var$ for $u \in \Sigma Pos(t)$ and $t|_u \in Var$ for $u \in Pos(t) \setminus \Sigma Pos(t)$. The *depth of a term* $t \in T(\mathcal{F} \cup \mathcal{C}, Var)$ denoted $Depth(t)$ is 0 if $t \in Var$ and $Max(\{ |p| \mid p \in \Sigma Pos(t) \}$

otherwise. The *depth of an atom* $P(\vec{t})$ denoted $Depth(P(\vec{t}))$ is $Max(\{\, Depth(s) \mid s \in \vec{t}\,\})$.

A *substitution* is a mapping from Var to $T(\Sigma, Var)$, which extends trivially to a mapping from $T(\Sigma, Var)$ to $T(\Sigma, Var)$. The *domain* of a substitution σ, $Dom(\sigma)$, is the set $\{\, x \in Var \mid x\sigma \neq x \,\}$. For $V \subseteq Var$, $\sigma|_V$ denotes the *restriction of σ* to the variables in V, i.e., $x\sigma|_V = x\sigma$ for $x \in V$ and $x\sigma|_V = x$ otherwise. If $\forall x \in Dom(\sigma)$, $x\sigma$ is a data-term then σ is called a *data substitution*. If term t is an *instance* of term s, i.e. $t = s\sigma$, we say that t *matches* s and s *subsumes* t.

Let $CVar = \{\, \square_i \mid i \geq 1 \,\}$ be the set of *context variables* distinct from Var, a *n-context* is a term t in $T(\Sigma, Var \cup CVar)$ such that each $\square_i$ $1 \leq i \leq n$ occurs once and only once in t and no other element of $CVar$ occurs in t. $\square_1$ (also denoted $\square$) is called the *trivial context*. For an n-context C, the expression $C[t_1, \ldots, t_n]$ denotes the term $C\{\, \square_i \mapsto t_i \mid 1 \leq i \leq n \,\}$.

A *term rewrite system* (TRS) is a finite set of oriented equations built over $T(\mathcal{F} \cup \mathcal{C}, Var)$ and called *rewrite rules*. Lhs and rhs are shorthands for the left-hand and right-hand side of a rule, respectively. A TRS is *constructor based* iff every rule is of the form $f(t_1, \ldots, t_n) \to r$ where all t_i's are data-terms and f is a defined function symbol. For a TRS R, the *rewrite relation* is denoted by $\to_R$ and is defined by $t \to_R s$ iff there exists a rule $l \to r$ in R, a non-variable position u in t, and a substitution σ, such that $t|_u = l\sigma$ and $s = t[u \leftarrow r\sigma]$. Such a step is written as $t \to_{[u, l \to r]} s$. If σ is a data-substitution then the step is called a *data-step*. If a term t cannot be reduced by any rewriting rule, it is said to be *irreducible*. The reflexive-transitive closure of $\to_R$ is denoted by $\to_R^*$.

The *joinability relation* $\downarrow_R$ is defined by $t \downarrow_R s$ iff $t \to_R^* u$ and $s \to^* u$ for some term u. Notice that R-joinability is equivalent to R-unifiability for confluent rewrite systems. In the context of constructor based TRS, a *data-solution* of a joinability equation $s \downarrow_R^? t$ is a data-substitution σ such that $s\sigma \to_R^* u$ and $t\sigma \to_R^* u$ where u is a data term and all rewriting steps are data-steps.

If $H, A_1, \ldots, A_n$ are atoms then $H \leftarrow A_1, \ldots, A_n$ is a *Horn clause*, H is called the *head* and $A_1, \ldots, A_n$ is called the *body* of the clause. The elements of $Var(A_1, \ldots, A_n) \setminus Var(H)$ are called *existential variables*. A *logic program* is a set of Horn clauses. The body of the clause $H \leftarrow \mathcal{B}$ is said linear iff every variable occurs at most once in $\mathcal{B}$. A clause is said to be *linear* if both the head and the body are linear. The *Herbrand domain* is the set of all ground atoms. A set of ground atoms S is an *Herbrand model* of the clause $H \leftarrow \mathcal{B}$ iff $\forall \sigma$ such that $\mathcal{B}\sigma \subseteq S$, $H\sigma \in S$. S is an Herbrand model of the logic program $\mathcal{P}$ if it is a model of all clauses of $\mathcal{P}$. For a logic program $\mathcal{P}$ and a ground atom A we write $\mathcal{P} \models A$ if A belongs to the least Herbrand model of $\mathcal{P}$. The language described by a n-ary predicate symbol P w.r.t. a program $\mathcal{P}$ is the set $\{\, (t_1, \ldots, t_n) \mid \mathcal{P} \models P(t_1, \ldots, t_n) \,\}$ of n-tuples of ground terms.

3   Pseudo-Regular Relations

This section first presents the logic programming formalism we use to represent the tree tuple languages and then some new results about pseudo-regular relations.

3.1 Representing Tree Tuple Languages

A *cs-program* is simply a logic program consisting in Horn clauses with linear bodies and without function symbols. [6] introduces two subclasses of cs-programs, called respectively regular and pseudo-regular programs. The first class corresponds to the regular relations of [2], and the second one weakens the syntax of regular programs.

Definition 1. *Let $H \leftarrow \mathcal{B}$ be a clause such that $\mathcal{B}$ contains no function symbols.*

- *$H \leftarrow \mathcal{B}$ is called* pseudo-regular-like *(PR-like for short) iff each argument of H is of the form $f(x_1, \dots, x_{\mathrm{ar}(f)})$ where f is a function symbol and the x_is are pairwise distinct variables and there exists a mapping $\pi \colon Var \mapsto I\!N$ such that $\pi(x_l) = l$ for all $l = 1, \dots, \mathrm{ar}(f)$ and $\pi(x) = \pi(y)$ for all variables x and y occurring in the same body atom.*
- *$H \leftarrow \mathcal{B}$ is called* pseudo-regular *(PR for short) iff it is PR-like and $\mathcal{B}$ is linear.*
- *$H \leftarrow \mathcal{B}$ is called* regular *(R for short) iff it is PR and H is linear.*
- *$H \leftarrow \mathcal{B}$ is called* shared pseudo-regular *(shared-PR for short) iff it is PR-like and contains no existential variables.*
- *$H \leftarrow \mathcal{B}$ is called* shared regular *(shared-R for short) iff it is shared-PR and H is linear.*

A program is PR-like, PR, R, shared-PR or shared-R if all its clauses are of the corresponding type.

Example 1. The clause $P(c(x_1, y_1), c(x_1, y_2)) \leftarrow P_1(y_1), P_2(x_1, y_2)$ is not PR-like since x_1 and y_2 occur in the same body atom but they do not occur at the same position in arguments of the head of the clause.

The clause $P(c(x_1, y_1), c(x_1, y_2)) \leftarrow P_2(y_1, z), P_2(y_2, y_1)$ is PR-like but it is neither PR because the body is not linear nor shared-PR since z is an exitential variable.

The following logic program is PR. Notice that the clauses defining Id_2 are regular since their heads are linear

$P_f(s(x_1), s(x_2), s(x_3)) \leftarrow Q(x_1, x_2, x_3)$ $Id_2(c(x_1, y_1), c(x_2, y_2)) \leftarrow Id_2(x_1, x_2),$
$ Id_2(y_1, y_2)$
$P_f(0, 0, 0) \leftarrow$ $ Id_2(s(x), s(y)) \leftarrow Id_2(x, y)$
$P_g(s(x), s(x))$ $ Id_2(0, 0) \leftarrow$
$Q(c(x_1, y_1), c(x_1, y_2), c(x_2, y_3)) \leftarrow P_g(x_1, x_2) P_f(y_1, y_2, y_3)$

Decidability of membership and emptiness tests as well as closure under intersection of pseudo-regular relations have been shown in [6] using the logic program transformation rules summarized below (see [6] for more details).

Definition 2. *A definition is an equivalence of the form $H \leftrightarrow \mathcal{B}$ (abusively written $H \leftarrow \mathcal{B}$) where H is a single atom of depth 0 and $\mathcal{B}$ is a set of atoms.*

A set of definitions, $\mathcal{D}$ is compatible with a logic program $\mathcal{P}$, if all predicate symbols occurring in the heads of the definitions occur in exactly one head and

nowhere else in D and $\mathcal{P}$ the only exception are tautological definitions of the form $P(x) \leftarrow P(x)$ where P may occur without restriction throughout D and $\mathcal{P}$.
   A definition $H \leftarrow \mathcal{B}$ is called a general join-definition *if H is linear and $H, \mathcal{B}$ do not contain function symbols.*

The rules transform states $\langle \mathcal{P}, \mathcal{D}_{\mathrm{new}}, \mathcal{D}_{\mathrm{done}}, \mathcal{C}_{\mathrm{new}}, \mathcal{C}_{\mathrm{out}} \rangle$ where $\mathcal{P}$ is the input logic program, $\mathcal{D}_{\mathrm{new}}$ are definitions not yet unfolded, $\mathcal{D}_{\mathrm{done}}$ are definitions already processed but still used for simplifying clauses, $\mathcal{C}_{\mathrm{new}}$ are clauses generated from definitions by unfolding, and $\mathcal{C}_{\mathrm{out}}$ is the cs-program generated so far.

We write $S \Rightarrow S'$ if S' is a state obtained from state S by applying one of the rules *unfolding* or *definition introduction* defined below. An *initial state* is of the form $\langle \mathcal{P}, \mathcal{D}, \emptyset, \emptyset, \emptyset \rangle$ where $\mathcal{D}$ is compatible with $\mathcal{P}$. A *final state* is of the form $\langle \mathcal{P}, \emptyset, \mathcal{D}', \emptyset, \mathcal{P}' \rangle$. $\mathcal{P}$ and $\mathcal{D}$ are called the input of a derivation, $\mathcal{P}'$ its output. A derivation is *complete* if its last state is final.

Unfolding.

$$\frac{\langle \mathcal{P},\ \mathcal{D}_{\mathrm{new}} \,\dot{\cup}\, \{L \leftarrow \mathcal{R}\dot{\cup}\{A_1, \ldots, A_k\}\},\ \mathcal{D}_{\mathrm{done}},\ \mathcal{C}_{\mathrm{new}},\ \mathcal{C}_{\mathrm{out}} \rangle}{\langle \mathcal{P},\ \mathcal{D}_{\mathrm{new}},\ \mathcal{D}_{\mathrm{done}} \cup \{L \leftarrow \mathcal{R}\cup\{A_1, \ldots, A_k\}\},\ \mathcal{C}_{\mathrm{new}} \cup \mathcal{C},\ \mathcal{C}_{\mathrm{out}} \rangle}$$

where $\mathcal{C}$ is the set of all clauses $(L \leftarrow \mathcal{R} \cup \mathcal{B}_1 \cup \cdots \cup \mathcal{B}_k)\mu$ such that $H_i \leftarrow \mathcal{B}_i$ is a clause in $\mathcal{P}$ for $i = 1, \ldots, k$, and such that the simultaneous most general unifier μ of $(A_1, \ldots, A_k)$ and $(H_1, \ldots, H_k)$ exists.

Definition Introduction.

$$\frac{\langle \mathcal{P},\ \mathcal{D}_{\mathrm{new}},\ \mathcal{D}_{\mathrm{done}},\ \mathcal{C}_{\mathrm{new}} \,\dot{\cup}\, \{H \leftarrow \mathcal{B}_1\dot{\cup}\cdots\dot{\cup}\mathcal{B}_k\},\ \mathcal{C}_{\mathrm{out}} \rangle}{\langle \mathcal{P},\ \mathcal{D}_{\mathrm{new}} \cup \mathcal{D},\ \mathcal{D}_{\mathrm{done}},\ \mathcal{C}_{\mathrm{new}},\ \mathcal{C}_{\mathrm{out}} \cup \{H \leftarrow L_1, \ldots, L_k\} \rangle}$$

where $\mathcal{B}_1, \ldots, \mathcal{B}_k$ is a maximal decomposition of $\mathcal{B}_1 \cup \cdots \cup \mathcal{B}_k$ into non-empty variable-disjoint subsets,

$$L_i = \begin{cases} L\eta^{-1} & \text{if } (L\leftarrow\mathcal{B}_i)\eta \in \mathcal{D}_{\mathrm{done}} \text{ for some var. renaming } \eta \\ P_i(x_1, \ldots, x_n) & \text{otherwise, } \{x_1, \ldots, x_n\} \text{ being the vars. of } \mathcal{B}_i. \end{cases}$$

for $1 \leq i \leq k$ and new predicate symbols P_i, and where $\mathcal{D}$ is the set of all $L_i \leftarrow \mathcal{B}_i$ such that L_i contains a new predicate symbol.

The closure of pseudo-regular relations under intersection can be proved thanks to the following result of [6].

Theorem 1. *[6] Let $\mathcal{P}$ be a PR program, and let D_p a general join definition. Any complete derivation with input $\mathcal{P}$ and $\{D_p\}$ that unfolds in each unfolding step all atoms simultaneously is finite and its output is a PR program.*

Example 2. Let us consider the PR program of Example 1. The general join definition $I(x,y) \leftarrow P_g(x,y), Id_2(x,y)$ defines the intersection of the relations defined respectively by P_g and Id_2. The $\Rightarrow$-derivation with input program $\mathcal{P}$

and the former join definition can be summarized as follows $\mathcal{D}_{\text{done}}$ is omitted and the last column indicates which rule has been applied:

$\mathcal{D}_{\text{new}}$	$\mathcal{C}_{\text{new}}$	$\mathcal{C}_{\text{out}}$	rule
$I(x,y) \leftarrow P_g(x,y),$ $Id_2(x,y)$			U
	$I(s(x),s(x)) \leftarrow Id_2(x,x)$		D
$I'(x) \leftarrow Id_2(x,x)$		$I(s(x),s(x)) \leftarrow I'(x)$	U
	$I'(0) \leftarrow$ $I'(s(x)) \leftarrow Id_2(x,x)$ $I'(c(x,y)) \leftarrow Id_2(x,x),$ $Id_2(y,y)$		D
		$I'(0) \leftarrow$ $I'(s(x)) \leftarrow I'(x)$ $I'(c(x,y)) \leftarrow I'(x), I'(y)$	

The output program consists in the clauses of $\mathcal{C}_{\text{out}}$.

The decidability of membership test and emptiness test of language defined by PR programs come from the fact that PR-programs are cs-programs which have these properties [6]. The closure under union is obvious.

3.2   Shared Pseudo-Regular Programs

In this section, we show how to compute the complement of a pseudo-regular language using logic program transformation techniques. For that we use the class of shared-PR programs. A program of this class can be transformed into a PR program. Moreover if the clause heads of the input program are all linear then the result is a regular program. This result proves the equivalence of pseudo-regular relations and regular relations.

Theorem 2. *Let $\mathcal{P}$ be a shared-PR program, and let $\mathcal{D}_p$ the set of all tautologies $P(x) \leftarrow P(x)$ such that P occurs in $\mathcal{P}$. Any $\Rightarrow$-derivation with input $\mathcal{P}$ and $\mathcal{D}_{\mathcal{P}}$ is finite and its output is a PR program. If the input program $\mathcal{P}$ is shared regular then the result is a regular program.*

The proof of this theorem is closed to the proof of Theorem 1 given in [6]. The differences are that one has to verify that no existential variables are introduced during the $\Rightarrow$-derivation and to slightly modify the termination argument. This result has several interesting consequences.

Corollary 1. *Any shared regular (resp. PR) program $\mathcal{P}$ can be transformed into an equivalent regular (resp. PR) program.*

If the input set of join definitions is the set of all tautologies $P(\vec{x}) \leftarrow P(\vec{x})$ such that P occurs in $\mathcal{P}$, then the $\Rightarrow$-derivation produces a regular (or PR) program that defines the same predicates as $\mathcal{P}$.

Corollary 2. *Any PR program can be transformed into an equivalent finite regular program.*

Proof. Without loss of generality we can consider that the PR program does not contain clauses with existential variables[2]. Let us observe that any PR clause $H \leftarrow \mathcal{B}$ is equivalent to the shared regular clause $H' \leftarrow \mathcal{B}' \mathbin{\dot{\cup}} Id$ where

- H' is a linear atom such that $H = H'\sigma$ where σ is a substitution from Var to Var, $\mathcal{B} = \mathcal{B}'\sigma$ and
- $Id = \{Id_n(x_1, \ldots, x_n) | n > 1$ and $\{x_1, \ldots, x_n\}$ is the set of variables that have the same image by $\sigma\}$ where each Id_i are predicates defined by R programs and define the set of i-tuples of identical terms.

$H' \leftarrow \mathcal{B}' \mathbin{\dot{\cup}} Id$ is a shared regular since it has no existential variables, H' is linear and $\forall x, y \in Var(A)$ with $A \in \mathcal{B}' \mathbin{\dot{\cup}} Id$, x and y occur at the same position in the arguments of H'. This shared-R program can be transformed into a R program.

The equivalence of regular relations and pseudo-regular relations does not decrease the interest for PR programs since they are syntactically less restrictive than regular ones as Section 4 will show.

Now shared-PR programs are used to give an algorithm that computes the complement of tree tuple language defined by a predicate P of a PR program $\mathcal{P}$ using the $\Rightarrow$ transformation. This algorithm is useful to compute the solutions of pseudo-regular formulae thanks to logic programs transformations. It consists in two steps. The first step computes from $\mathcal{P}$ a new shared regular program $\overline{\mathcal{P}}$ that defines the complement of P. The second step uses Corollary 1 to obtain a regular program equivalent to $\overline{\mathcal{P}}$.

Let P be a predicate defined by the PR program $\mathcal{P}$. Without loss of generality we can consider that $\mathcal{P}$ has neither unproductive clauses (i.e. clauses that do not contribute to the least Herbrand model), nor clauses with existential variables. Then $\mathcal{P}$ is transformed into the shared regular program $\mathcal{P}'$ by the technique used in proof of Corollary 2.

For each predicate Q of arity n of $\mathcal{P}'$ and each n-tuple $(f_1, \ldots, f_n)$ of $\mathcal{C}^n$ we define the set of all clauses of $\mathcal{P}$ which head is $Q(f_1(\vec{x}_1), \ldots, f_n(\vec{x}_n))$ as $AC(Q, (f_1, \ldots, f_n)) = \{Q(f_1(\vec{x}_1), \ldots, f_n(\vec{x}_n)) \leftarrow \mathcal{B} \in \mathcal{P}'\}$. Notice that since the clause heads of $\mathcal{P}'$ are linear all the clause heads of $AC(Q, \vec{f})$ are equal up to a variable renaming. In the following we consider them equal. For an atom $A = P(\vec{t})$, $\overline{A}$ stands for $\overline{P}(\vec{t})$.

Let $\vec{f} = f_1, \ldots f_n$, $\vec{x}_i$ ($1 \le i \le n$) be pairwise distinct vectors of distinct variables and $AC(Q, \vec{f}) = \{H \leftarrow \mathcal{B}_1, \ldots, H \leftarrow \mathcal{B}_k\}$. We define

$$\overline{AC}(Q, \vec{f}) = \begin{cases} \emptyset & \text{if } H \leftarrow \in AC(Q, \vec{f}) \\ Q(f_1(\vec{x}_1), \ldots, f_n(\vec{x}_n)) \leftarrow & \text{if } AC(Q, \vec{f}) = \emptyset \\ \{\overline{H} \leftarrow \overline{A_1}, \ldots, \overline{A_k} \mid \forall i \in [1, k] A_i \in \mathcal{B}_i\} & \text{otherwise} \end{cases}$$

Example 3. Let consider the logic program consisting in the three following clauses $P(c(x_1, y_1), c(x_2, y_2)) \leftarrow P(x_1, x_2)$, $P(c(x_1, y_1), c(x_2, y_2)) \leftarrow P(y_1, y_2)$ and $P(0, 0) \leftarrow$

---

[2] In the full version of the present paper we give an algorithm to eliminate existential variables of R and PR programs.

$$AC(P, (0, c)) = \emptyset$$
$$AC(P, (c, 0)) = \emptyset$$
$$AC(P, (0, 0)) = \{P(0, 0) \leftarrow\}$$
$$AC(P, (c, c)) = \{$$
$$P(c(x_1, y_1), c(x_2, y_2)) \leftarrow P(x_1, x_2),$$
$$P(c(x_1, y_1), c(x_2, y_2)) \leftarrow P(y_1, y_2)\}$$

$$\overline{AC}(P, (0, c)) = \{\overline{P}(0, c(x, y)) \leftarrow\}$$
$$\overline{AC}(P, (c, 0)) = \{\overline{P}(c(x, y), 0) \leftarrow\}$$
$$\overline{AC}(P, (0, 0)) = \emptyset$$
$$\overline{AC}(P, (c, c)) = \{\ \overline{P}(c(x_1, y_1), c(x_2, y_2)) \leftarrow$$
$$\overline{P}(x_1, x_2), \overline{P}(y_1, y_2)\}$$

Lemma 1. *Let $\mathcal{P}$ be a shared regular program without any unproductive clauses. The program $\overline{\mathcal{P}}$ consisting in the set of clauses $\bigcup_{P \in \mathcal{P}, \vec{f} \in \mathcal{C}^n} \overline{AC}(P, \vec{f})$ is such that $\forall P \in \mathcal{P}, \forall (t_1, \ldots, t_n) \in T_{\mathcal{C}}^n, \mathcal{P} \models P(t_1, \ldots, t_n)$ iff $\overline{\mathcal{P}} \models \overline{P}(t_1, \ldots, t_n)$.*

Proof. We show that $\overline{\mathcal{P}}$ is obtained from $\mathcal{P}$ just using logical equivalences. Let us denote $H \leftarrow$ by $H \leftarrow true$. $\mathcal{P}$ is equivalent to $\{H \leftarrow false \bigvee_{H \leftarrow \mathcal{B} \in \mathcal{P}} \mathcal{B} \mid H = P(f_1(\vec{x}_1), \ldots, f_n(\vec{x}_n)), P \in \mathcal{P}, (f_1, \ldots, f_n) \in \mathcal{C}^n\}$ i.e. for any possible atom $H = P(f_1(\vec{x}_1), \ldots, f_n(\vec{x}_n))$, we collect the set of bodies of the clauses which have the head H. These bodies are connected by the logical operator or. Notice that since the clauses head are linear the symbol $\leftarrow$ here is indeed an equivalence $\leftrightarrow$. The negation of these formulae are $\{\overline{H} \leftrightarrow true \bigwedge_{H \leftarrow \mathcal{B} \in \mathcal{P}} \neg \mathcal{B}\}$. If one $\mathcal{B}$ is the constant $true$ then $\overline{H}$ is equivalent to false, therefore no clause is headed by $\overline{H}$ in $\overline{\mathcal{P}}$. If the definition is reduced to $H \leftarrow false$ meaning that none of the ground instances of H are in the model of $\mathcal{P}$ then $\overline{H} \leftarrow$ is in $\overline{\mathcal{P}}$, meaning that all ground instances of $\overline{H}$ are in the model of $\overline{\mathcal{P}}$. Finally, in the other cases, $true \bigwedge_{H \leftarrow \mathcal{B} \in \mathcal{P}} \neg \mathcal{B}$ is reduced into a disjunction of conjunctions of negative atoms. Each conjunction is of the form $\neg A_1 \wedge \ldots \wedge \neg A_k$ where each A_i belongs to one different $\mathcal{B}_i$. These definitions produce the clauses $\{\overline{Q}(f_1(\vec{x}_1), \ldots, f_n(\vec{x}_n)) \leftarrow \overline{A_1}, \ldots, \overline{A_k} \mid AC(Q, (f_1, \ldots, f_n)) = \{H \leftarrow \mathcal{B}_1, \ldots, H \leftarrow \mathcal{B}_k\}$ and $\forall i \in [1, k] A_i \in \mathcal{B}_i\}$ of $\overline{\mathcal{P}}$.

Lemma 2. *Let $\mathcal{P}$ be a shared regular program without any unproductive clauses. The program $\overline{\mathcal{P}}$ is a shared regular program.*

The proof of this lemma is obvious since no substitution but variable renamings is used to define $\overline{\mathcal{P}}$ so the mappings used to check the shared regularity of $\mathcal{P}$ are preserved in $\overline{\mathcal{P}}$.

Theorem 3. *Pseudo-regular relations are closed under complement*

Proof. Let $\mathcal{L}$ be a pseudo-regular relation defined by the PR program $\mathcal{P}$. First compute an equivalent regular program $\mathcal{P}'$ without neither unproductive clauses nor existential variables in the body of the clauses. $\overline{\mathcal{P}'}$ defines the complement of $\mathcal{L}$ in $T_{\mathcal{C}}^n$ if $\mathcal{L}$ is of arity n.

For two languages $\mathcal{L}_1$ and $\mathcal{L}_2$ we have $\mathcal{L}_1 \setminus \mathcal{L}_2 = \overline{\mathcal{L}_2} \cap \mathcal{L}_1$ therefore we have the following corollary.

Corollary 3. *Let $\mathcal{P}_1$ and $\mathcal{P}_2$ two PR programs, $\mathcal{L}_1$ and $\mathcal{L}_2$ two languages defined by the predicates $P_{\mathcal{L}_1}$ of $\mathcal{P}_1$ and $P_{\mathcal{L}_2}$ of $\mathcal{P}_2$. The program that represents the language $\mathcal{L}_1 \setminus \mathcal{L}_2$ is computed in two phases. First compute the program $\overline{\mathcal{P}_2}$ and then compute $\mathcal{P}_1 \cap \overline{\mathcal{P}_2}$ from $\mathcal{P}_1 \cup \overline{\mathcal{P}_2}$ and the definition $P_{\mathcal{L}_1 \setminus \mathcal{L}_2}(\vec{x}) \leftarrow P_{\mathcal{L}_1}(\vec{x}), P_{\overline{\mathcal{L}_2}}(\vec{x})$ using $\Rightarrow$-derivation.*

Notice that the input definition of the second point is a general join definition.

3.3   Non-greibach Logic Programs

Even if PR programs are less restrictive than regular ones, their syntax is still very strict. This section aims at defining a class of logic programs that can be transformed into a finite PR one. Our aim is to allow more than one function symbol in the clause heads.

Definition 3. *A Horn clause is called* non-Greibach *(NG for short) if at least one of the arguments of the head is of depth more than one. Let $H \leftarrow \mathcal{B}$ be a clause such that $\mathcal{B}$ contains no function symbols.*

- *$H \leftarrow \mathcal{B}$ is called* NGPR-like *iff none of the arguments of H are variables and there exists a mapping $\pi \colon Var \mapsto I\!N^+$ such that $\pi(x) = u$ then all occurrences of x in the arguments of H are at position u and $\pi(x) = \pi(y)$ for all variables x and y occurring in the same body atom.*
- *$H \leftarrow \mathcal{B}$ is called* NGPR *iff it is NGPR-like and $\mathcal{B}$ is linear.*
- *$H \leftarrow \mathcal{B}$ is called* NGR *iff it is NGPR and H is linear.*
- *$H \leftarrow \mathcal{B}$ is called* NG-shared-PR *iff it is NGPR-like and it contains no existential variables.*
- *$H \leftarrow \mathcal{B}$ is called* NG-shared-R *iff it is NG-shared-PR and H is linear.*

A program is NGPR-like, NGPR, R, NG-shared-PR or NG-shared-R if all its clauses are of the corresponding type.

For example, the clause $P(c(s(x), y), s(s(z))) \leftarrow P(x, z), Q(y)$ is NGPR since x and z occur both at occurrence 1.1 in the arguments of the head. (It is more precisely NGR since the head is linear).

Lemma 3. *Any NG-xxx clause $H \leftarrow B$ has an equivalent finite set of xxx clauses (xxx being either PR or shared-PR or R or shared-R).*

Proof. Let $P(f_1(\vec{t_1}), \ldots, f_n(\vec{t_n})) \leftarrow \mathcal{B}, \mathcal{B}_1 \,\dot\cup\, \ldots \,\dot\cup\, \mathcal{B}_k$ be a NGPR-like clause where $\mathcal{B}$ is the set of atoms the variables of which occur all at depth one in the argument of the head and each $\mathcal{B}_i$ is the set of atoms not occurring in $\mathcal{B}$ and the variables of which have an image by π of the form $i.u$ ($u \neq \varepsilon$).

Let us consider the atom $P(f_1(\vec{x_1}), \ldots, f_n(\vec{x_n}))$ where $\vec{x_i}|_j = \vec{t_i}|_j$ if $\vec{t_i}|_j$ is a variable and $\vec{x_i}|_j$ is a new variable [3] otherwise. Let σ be a substitution such that $P(f_1(\vec{x_1}), \ldots, f_n(\vec{x_n}))\sigma = P(f_1(\vec{t_1}), \ldots, f_n(\vec{t_n}))$

$P(f_1(\vec{t_1}), \ldots, f_n(\vec{t_n})) \leftarrow \mathcal{B}, \mathcal{B}_1 \,\dot\cup\, \ldots \,\dot\cup\, \mathcal{B}_k$ is equivalent to the set of clauses $\{P(f_1(\vec{x_1}), \ldots, f_n(\vec{x_n})) \leftarrow \mathcal{B}, P_1(\vec{y_1}), \ldots, P_k(\vec{y_k})\} \bigcup_{i \in [1,k]} \{P_i(\vec{y_i})\sigma \leftarrow \mathcal{B}_i\}$ where the P_is are new predicate symbols and $\vec{y_i}$ is the vector of all the variables z occurring at position i in $P(f_1(\vec{x_1}), \ldots, f_n(\vec{x_n}))$ and such that $z\sigma \neq z$.

The clause $P(f_1(\vec{x_1}), \ldots, f_n(\vec{x_n})) \leftarrow \mathcal{B}, P_1(\vec{y_1}), \ldots, P_k(\vec{y_k})$ is PR-like by construction and the clauses $P_i(\vec{y_i})\sigma \leftarrow \mathcal{B}_i$ are NGPR-like and have heads of depth strictly inferior to the depth of $P(f_1(\vec{t_1}), \ldots, f_n(\vec{t_n}))$. Therefore iterating this process, we obtain a set of PR-like clauses. One can remark that

---

[3] I.e. new introduced variables are pairwise different and also different from the variables of $P(f_1(\vec{t_1}), \ldots, f_n(\vec{t_n}))$.

- no existential variable is introduced by the process so if the initial clause is NG-shared-PR, the resulting clauses are all NG-shared-PR,
- the new variables introduced by the process are all different, therefore if $P(f_1(\vec{t_1}), \ldots, f_n(\vec{t_n})) \leftarrow \mathcal{B}, \mathcal{B}_1 \ \dot{\cup} \ \ldots \ \dot{\cup} \ \mathcal{B}_k$ is NGPR so are the resulting clauses and moreover if $P(f_1(\vec{t_1}), \ldots, f_n(\vec{t_n}))$ is linear the heads of the new clauses are also linear.

Example 4. Consider the NG-shared-PR clause

$$P_f(s(c(x_1, y_1)), s(c(x_1, y_2)), s(c(x_2, y_3))) \leftarrow P_f(y_1, y_1, y_3), P_g(x_1, x_2)$$

the equivalent set of shared-PR clauses is

$$P_f(s(x), s(y), s(z)) \leftarrow P_1(x, y, z)$$
$$P_1(c(x_1, y_1), c(x_1, y_2), c(x_2, y_3)) \leftarrow P_f(y_1, y_1, y_3), P_g(x_1, x_2).$$

4   Solving Pseudo-Regular Formulae

In this section, we show how our results on pseudo-regular relations can be used in the context of term rewriting theory. The aim is to solve formulae based on joinability equations for the class of pseudo-regular TRS. First we define the class of TRS and the type of formulae we deal with and then we give an algorithm to solve such formulae.

4.1   Pseudo-Regular TRS and Formulae

The next definition uses the notion of possible redex for constructor based rewrite system[4], i.e. subterms of a term that may be rewritten.

Let R be a TRS and t a term. A position u in t is called a *possible redex position* if $t|_u$ is of the form $f(C_1, \ldots, C_k)[f_1(\vec{t_1}), \ldots, f_n(\vec{t_n})]$ where $f, f_1, \ldots f_n \in \mathcal{F}$ and $C_1, \ldots, C_k \in T(\Sigma, Var \cup CVar)$. $f(C_1, \ldots, C_k)$ is called the *possible redex* at occurrence u of t. The context C that does not contain any possible redex and that is such that $t = C[t_1, \ldots, t_n]$ where u_i for $1 \leq i \leq n$ is a possible redex position, is called the *irreducible part* of t and is denoted $Irr_R(t)$.

Definition 4. *A constructor based TRS R is called pseudo-regular if for all rule $f(t_1, \ldots, t_n) \to r \in R$:*

- *there exists a mapping $\pi\colon Var \mapsto \mathbb{N}^+$, such that $\pi(x) = u$ implies that all occurrences of x in each $t_1, \ldots, t_n$ and $Irr(r)$ are at position u,*
- *each possible redex C at position u of r is of the form $f(x_1, \ldots, x_n)$ where $\forall 1 \leq i \leq n \ x_i \in Var(f(t_1, \ldots, t_n))$ and $\pi(x_i) = u$.*

Example 5. $R = \{f(s(c(x, y)), s(c(x, z))) \to p(c(g(x), f(y, y))), f(s(0), s(0)) \to 0, g(s(x)) \to s(x)\}$ is pseudo-regular. The irreducible part of the lhs of the first rule is $p(c(\Box_1, \Box_2))$ and it contains two possible redex positions namely 1.1 and 1.2 corresponding to the possible redexes $g(x)$ and $f(y, y)$. Notice that Definition 4 does not forbid duplicated variables in a single possible redex.

---

[4] A similar notion was introduced in [7] for general TRS.

Definition 5. *Let R be a pseudo regular TRS. A pseudo-regular joinability equation $s \downarrow_R^? t$ is an equation such that s and t are built over $T(\mathcal{F}, Var)$.*

Let R be a pseudo-regular TRS, pseudo-regular R-formulae are defined by the following grammar: $e ::= s \downarrow_R^? t | \neg e | e \vee e | e \wedge e | \exists x e | \forall x e$
where $s \downarrow_R^? t$ is a pseudo-regular joinability equation.

The set of solutions of such a formula is defined as follows:

$SOL(s \downarrow_R^? t)$ is the set of data-solutions of $s \downarrow_R^? t$

$SOL(\neg e) = \{ \sigma \mid \sigma \notin SOL(e) \}$

$SOL(e_1 \wedge e_2) = \{ \sigma \mid Dom(\sigma) = Var(e_1 \wedge e2), \sigma|_{Var(e_1)} \in SOL(e_1), \sigma|_{Var(e_2)} \in SOL(e_2) \}$

$SOL(e_1 \vee e_2) = \{ \sigma \mid Dom(\sigma) = Var(e_1 \vee e_2), \sigma|_{Var(e_1)} \in SOL(e_1) \text{ or } \sigma|_{Var(e_2)} \in SOL(e_2) \}$

$SOL(\exists x e) = \{ \sigma \mid Dom(\sigma) = Var(e) \setminus \{x\}, \exists \sigma' \in SOL(e), \sigma = \sigma'|_{Var(e) \setminus \{x\}} \}$

$SOL(\forall x e) = \{ \sigma \mid Dom(\sigma) = Var(e) \setminus \{x\}, \forall \sigma' \in SOL(e), \sigma = \sigma'|_{Var(e) \setminus \{x\}} \}$

Even if the constructors are forbidden in the joinability equations, many wanted properties for TRS can be expressed by a pseudo-regular formula. Among them we can cite

- confluency $\forall x, y \neg (f(x,y) \downarrow_R^? z \wedge f(x,y) \downarrow_R^? z') \vee z \downarrow_R^? z'$,
- commutativity $\forall x, y f(x,y) \downarrow_R^? f(y,x)$,
- associativity $\forall x, y, z f(x, f(y,z)) \downarrow_R^? f(f(x,y),z)$,
- idempotency $\forall x g(g(x)) \downarrow_R^? x$,
- fixed points of a function $g(x) \downarrow_R^? x$.
- search for neutral elements $\forall x f(x,y) \downarrow_R^? x$.

4.2 Solving Pseudo-Regular Formulae

Our algorithm is based on the results given in Section 3. The first step consists in computing the solutions of a pseudo-regular joinability equation. For that we use a technique introduced in [7] that encodes the rewrite relation by a logic program. This translation intends to obtain logic programs that preserve as best as possible syntactic properties of the TRS. It works for any term rewrite system but the obtained logic program encodes only a subset of the rewriting relation called basic rewriting. Fortunately, basic rewriting and rewriting relations coincide when considering only data-steps.

Table 1 specifies the rules for transforming terms and rewrite rules to clause logic. For a TRS R, let $\mathcal{LP}(R)$ denote the logic program consisting of the clauses obtained by applying the fourth rule to all rewrite rules in R. For sake of simplicity, we will denote by x_u the fresh variable introduced in the third rule for the subterm $f(s_1, \ldots, s_n)$ at occurrence u of a rhs s and A_u the atom produced by this rule.

For example, the first rewrite rule of Example 5 is transformed into

$$P_f(s(c(x,y)), s(c(x,z)), p(c(x_1, x_2))) \leftarrow P_g(x, x_1), P_f(y, y, x_2).$$

Theorem 4. *Let R be a TRS, s a term such that $s \rightsquigarrow \langle s', \mathcal{G} \rangle$. $s \rightarrow^* t$ iff t is a data-term $\mathcal{LP}(R), \models \mathcal{G}\mu$ and $t = s'\mu$ where μ is a data substitution.*

Table 1. Converting rewrite rules to clause logic

$$\frac{\top}{v \rightsquigarrow \langle v, \emptyset \rangle} \quad \text{if } v \in Var$$

$$\frac{s_1 \rightsquigarrow \langle t_1, \mathcal{G}_1 \rangle \ldots s_n \rightsquigarrow \langle t_n, \mathcal{G}_n \rangle}{f(s_1, \ldots, s_n) \rightsquigarrow \langle f(t_1, \ldots, t_n), \bigcup_i \mathcal{G}_i \rangle} \quad \text{if } f \in \mathcal{C}$$

$$\frac{s_1 \rightsquigarrow \langle t_1, \mathcal{G}_1 \rangle \ldots s_n \rightsquigarrow \langle t_n, \mathcal{G}_n \rangle}{f(s_1, \ldots, s_n) \rightsquigarrow \langle x, \bigcup_i \mathcal{G}_i \bigcup \{P_f(t_1, \ldots, t_n, x)\} \rangle} \quad \text{if } f \in \mathcal{F}$$

$$\frac{s \rightsquigarrow \langle t, \mathcal{G} \rangle}{f(s_1, \ldots, s_n) \rightarrow s \rightsquigarrow P_f(s_1, \ldots, s_n, t) \leftarrow \mathcal{G}} \quad \text{if } f(s_1, \ldots, s_n) \rightarrow s \in \mathcal{R}$$

The rules of Table 1 slightly differ from those presented in [7] because [7] deals with general TRS whereas we are working on constructor based TRS in the present paper. Theorem 4 in [7] is also a little bit different because in [7] the set of clauses $\mathcal{P}_{Id}$ is added to $\mathcal{LP}(R)$ to be able to stop rewrite derivation at any step. For computing data-solutions of a joinability equation, we need to compute rewrite derivation until reaching a data term so $\mathcal{P}_{Id}$ has been removed.

Lemma 4. *Let R be a pseudo-regular TRS then $\mathcal{LP}(R)$ is a NG-shared-PR logic program.*

Proof. Each rule of a pseudo regular TRS is of the form
$$f(t_1, \ldots, t_n) \rightarrow C[f_1(\vec{x}_1), \ldots, f_k(\vec{x}_k)]$$
where C is the irreducible part of the lhs of the rule, and $f, f_1, \ldots, f_k$ are function symbols. C and each t_i contain no defined function symbols. Therefore the clause produced for this rule is
$$P_f(t_1, \ldots, t_n, C[x_{u_1} \ldots, x_{u_k}]) \leftarrow P_{f_1}(\vec{x}_1, x_{u_1}), \ldots, P_{f_k}(\vec{x}_k, x_{u_k})$$
Since all variables of $f_1(\vec{x}_1), \ldots, f_k(\vec{x}_k)$ are variables of $f(t_1, \ldots, t_n)$, the clause contains no existential variables. By extending the mapping π of the pseudo-regular rewrite rule $f(t_1, \ldots, t_n) \rightarrow C[f_1(\vec{x}_1), \ldots, f_k(\vec{x}_k)]$ to $\pi' = \pi \cup_{1 \leq i \leq k} \{x_{u_i} \mapsto u_i\}$ we obtain that the clause is NG-shared-PR.

The data solutions of pseudo-regular joinability equations expressed as a pseudo-regular language can be computed using the following algorithm.

Algorithm 1. *Let R be a pseudo-regular TRS and $s \downarrow_R^? t$ a pseudo-regular joinability equation, $\vec{x}$ the variables occurring in $s \downarrow_R^? t$. Let $\mathcal{LP}(s \downarrow_R^? t) = Id_2(x_s, x_t), G_s, G_t$ where $s \rightsquigarrow (x_s, G_s)$ and $t \rightsquigarrow (x_t, G_t)$ (see Table 1) and Id_2 is a pseudo regular predicate that define equality of terms like in Example 1.*

1. Compute $\mathcal{LP}(R)$
2. Compute $\mathcal{LP}(s \downarrow_R^? t)$
3. Use $\Rightarrow$ and Lemma 3 to compute a pseudo-regular program $\mathcal{P}$ from $\mathcal{LP}(R)$.
4. Use $\Rightarrow$ to compute from $\mathcal{P}$ and the join definition $P_{s\downarrow_R^? t, \vec{x}}(\vec{x}) \leftarrow \mathcal{LP}(s \downarrow_R^? t)$ the PR program $\mathcal{P}_{s\downarrow_R^? t}$.

Theorem 5. *Let R be a pseudo-regular TRS and $s \downarrow_R^? t$ a pseudo-regular join-ability equation and $\mathcal{P}_{s\downarrow_R^? t}$ the resulting program of Algorithm 1.*
$$\mathcal{P}_{s\downarrow_R^? t} \models \mathcal{P}_{s\downarrow_R^? t, \vec{x}}(\vec{t}) \text{ iff } \{\, \vec{x}|_i \mapsto \vec{t}|_i \mid 1 \le i \le length(\vec{x}) \,\} \in SOL(s \downarrow_R^? t).$$

Proof. From Lemma 4, we know that $\mathcal{LP}(R)$ is a NG-shared-PR program. According to Lemma 3 and Theorem 2, point 3 of Algorithm 1 produces a finite PR program that is equivalent to $\mathcal{LP}(R)$. The definition $\mathcal{P}_{s\downarrow_R^? t, \vec{x}}(\vec{x}) \leftarrow \mathcal{LP}(s \downarrow_R^? t)$ is a general join definition since all predicates of $\mathcal{LP}(s \downarrow_R^? t)$ are defined by a PR program and $\mathcal{LP}(s \downarrow_R^? t)$ contains no function symbols since s and t contain no constructor symbol. Therefore, from Theorem 1, the point 4 of the algorithm produces a finite PR program.

From Theorem 4 we know that for any predicate P_f of $\mathcal{LP}(R)$, $\mathcal{LP}(R) \models P_f(t_1, \ldots, t_n, t)$ iff $f(t_1, \ldots, t_n) \to^* t$. $P_f(\ldots, x_u, \ldots)$ and $P_g(\vec{x}, x_u)$ belong to $\mathcal{LP}(s \downarrow_R^? t)$ iff either s or t contains the subterm $f(\ldots, g(\vec{t}), \ldots)$ thus $\mathcal{LP}(s \downarrow_R^? t)$ simulates the composition of functions contained in s and t. Moreover the atom $Id_2(x_s, x_t)$ insures that the respective results of the rewrite derivations from s and t are equal.

Solving pseudo-regular formulae can be done using the following algorithm

Algorithm 2. *Let R be a pseudo-regular TRS and e a pseudo-regular formula.*

1. *Solve each elementary formula $s \downarrow_R^? t$ by computing $\mathcal{P}_{s\downarrow_R^? t}$*
2. *If $\mathcal{P}_e$ defines $SOL(e)$ then $\overline{\mathcal{P}_e} = \mathcal{P}_{\neg e}$ defines $SOL(\neg e)$.*
3. *If $\mathcal{P}_{e_1}$ and $\mathcal{P}_{e_2}$ define respectively $SOL(e_1)$ and $SOL(e_2)$ then the program $\mathcal{P}_{e_1 \wedge e_2}$ obtained by a complete derivation of $\Rightarrow$ with inputs $\mathcal{P}_{e_1} \cup \mathcal{P}_{e_2}$ and $\mathcal{P}_{e_1 \wedge e_2, \vec{x}}(\vec{x}) \leftarrow P_{e_1, \vec{x}_1}(\vec{x}_1), P_{e_2, \vec{x}_2}(\vec{x}_2)$ where $\vec{x} = Var(e_1 \wedge e_2)$, is a PR program that defines $SOL(e_1 \wedge e_2)$*
4. *If $\mathcal{P}_{e_1}$ and $\mathcal{P}_{e_2}$ define respectively $SOL(e_1)$ and $SOL(e_2)$ then the program $\mathcal{P}_{e_1 \vee e_2}$ obtained by a complete derivation of $\Rightarrow$ with inputs $\mathcal{P}_{e_1} \cup \mathcal{P}_{e_2}$ and $\{P_{e_1 \vee e_2, \vec{x}}(\vec{x}) \leftarrow P_{e_1, \vec{x}_1}(\vec{x}_1), P_{e_1 \vee e_2, \vec{x}}(\vec{x}) \leftarrow P_{e_2, \vec{x}_2}(\vec{x}_2)\}$ where $\vec{x} = Var(e_1 \wedge e_2)$, is a PR program that defines $SOL(e_1 \vee e_2)$.*
5. *If $\mathcal{P}_e$ defines $SOL(e)$ then the program $\mathcal{P}_{\exists x e}$ obtained from $\mathcal{P}_e$ by a complete $\Rightarrow$-derivation with $P_{\exists x e, \vec{y}}(\vec{y}) \leftarrow P_{e, \vec{x}'}(\vec{x}')$ as input definition is a PR program that defines $SOL(\exists x e)$ since it is a projection on all arguments of $P_{e, \vec{x}'}$ but the one defining the variable x.*

Solving a $\forall x e$ can be done by using well-known identity $\forall x e \equiv \neg \exists \neg e$.

Theorem 6. *Let R be a pseudo-regular TRS and e a pseudo-regular formula and $\mathcal{P}_e$ the resulting program of Algorithm 2. $\mathcal{P}_e \models P_{e, \vec{x}}(\vec{t})$ iff $\{\, \vec{x}|_i \mapsto \vec{t}|_i \mid 1 \le i \le length(\vec{x}) \,\} \in SOL(e)$.*

Proof. It is done by an easy induction on the structure of the formula. From Theorem 5, we know that for each elementary formula $s \downarrow_R^? t$, $\mathcal{P}_{s\downarrow_R^? t} \models \mathcal{P}_{s\downarrow_R^? t, \vec{x}}(\vec{t})$ iff $\{\, \vec{x}|_i \mapsto \vec{t}|_i \mid 1 \le i \le length(\vec{x}) \,\} \in SOL(s \downarrow_R^? t)$. Let e_1 and e_2 be two formulae such that $\mathcal{P}_{e_1}$ and $\mathcal{P}_{e_2}$ computes the solutions of e_1 and e_2 respectively.

- From Theorem 3, we know that $\mathcal{P}_{\neg e_1}$ defines $SOL(\neg e_1)$ and is regular.
- $P_{e_1 \wedge e_2, \vec{x}}(\vec{x}) \leftarrow P_{e_1, \vec{x}_1}(\vec{x}_1), P_{e_2, \vec{x}_2}(\vec{x}_2)$ is a general join definition since $P_{e_1, \vec{x}_1}$ and $P_{e_2, \vec{x}_2}$ are defined by a PR program, therefore from Theorem 1 $\mathcal{P}_{e_1 \wedge e_2}$ is a PR program that defines the solutions of $e_1 \wedge e_2$.
- $P_{e_1 \vee e_2, \vec{x}}(\vec{x}) \leftarrow P_{e_1, \vec{x}_1}(\vec{x}_1)$ and $P_{e_1 \vee e_2, \vec{x}}(\vec{x}) \leftarrow P_{e_2, \vec{x}_2}(\vec{x}_2)$ are general join definitions since $P_{e_1, \vec{x}_1}$ and $P_{e_2, \vec{x}_2}$ are defined by a PR program, therefore from Theorem 1 $\mathcal{P}_{e_1 \wedge e_2}$ is a PR program that defines the solutions of $e_1 \vee e_2$.
- $P_{\exists x e_1, \vec{y}}(\vec{y}) \leftarrow P_{e_1, \vec{x}'}(\vec{x}')$ is a general join definition since $P_{e_1, \vec{x}'}(\vec{x}')$ is defined by a PR program, therefore from Theorem 1 $P_{\exists x e_1, \vec{y}}$ is defined by a PR program. Moreover $P_{\exists x e_1, \vec{y}}(\vec{y})$ defines the solutions of $\exists x e_1$ since $P_{e_1, \vec{x}'}(\vec{x}')$ defines $SOL(e_1)$ and therefore $P_{\exists x e_1, \vec{y}}(\vec{y})$ defines $SOL(e_1)|_{\{x\}}$.

5   Conclusion and Future Work

The main contributions of this paper are the definition of an algorithm to compute the complement of a pseudo-regular relation represented by a logic program and the use of pseudo-regular relations to solve pseudo-regular formulae. The representation of tree tuple languages by logic programs simplifies the connection between term rewriting systems and tree languages. Indeed, it would have been quite difficult to obtain the definition of pseudo regular TRS and pseudo-regular formulae without NG-Shared-PR logic programs.

Since we know other classes of logic programs that can be transformed into a finite pseudo-regular one, allowing some function symbols in the body of the clauses, it would be possible to weaken some restrictions on the possible redexes of the pseudo-regular TRS as well as on the pseudo-regular joinability equations.

We should study the actual expressiveness of pseudo-regular TRS by encoding some problems coming from fields like theorem proving or system verification. For example, we already have encoded the semantics of the so-called process algebra of [10] by a regular TRS. We intend to study what pseudo-regularity can bring to the model checking of process algebra.

It would be also interesting to implement the resolution of pseudo-regular formulae. A prototype should be soon available since $\Rightarrow$ and $\rightsquigarrow$ (the transformation of a TRS into a logic program) have already been implemented in Prolog.

References

1. F. Baader and T. Nipkow. *Term Rewriting and All That.* Cambridge University Press, United Kingdom, 1998.
2. H. Comon, M. Dauchet, R. Gilleron, D. Lugiez, S. Tison, and M. Tommasi. *Tree Automata Techniques and Applications (TATA).*
   http://www.grappa.univ-lille3.fr/tata, 1997.
3. H. Comon, M. Haberstrau, and J.-P. Jouannaud. Syntacticness, cycle-syntacticness, and shallow theories. *Information and Computation*, 111(1):154–191, 1994.

4. Heinz Faßbender and Sebastian Maneth. A strict border for the decidability of e-unification for recursive functions. *Journal of Functional and Logic Programming*, 1998(4), 1998.
5. S. Limet and P. Réty. E-unification by means of tree tuple synchronized grammars. *Discrete Mathematics and Theoretical Computer Science*, 1:69–98, 1997.
6. S. Limet and G. Salzer. Manipulating tree tuple languages by transforming logic programs. Technical Report RR-2004-01, LIFO, Université d'Orléans, 2003.
7. S. Limet and G. Salzer. Proving properties of term rewrite systems via logic programs. In V. van Oostrom, editor, *Proc. 15th Int. Conf. on Rewriting Techniques and Applications (RTA'04)*, volume 3091 of *LNCS*, pages 170–184. Springer, 2004.
8. S. Limet and F. Saubion. A general framework for R-unification. In C. Palamidessi, H. Glaser, and K. Meinke, editors, *proc of the Conf. on Principle of Declarative Programming (PLILP-ALP)*, volume 1490 of *LNCS*, pages 266–281. Springer, 1998.
9. J.W. Lloyd. *Foundations of Logic Programming*. Springer, 1984.
10. D. Lugiez and Ph. Schnoebelen. The regular viewpoint on PA-processes. *Theoretical Computer Science*, 274(1-2):89–115, 2002.
11. F. Nielson, H. Riis Nielson, and H. Seidl. Normalizable horn clauses, strongly recognizable relations and spi. In *Proc. SAS'02*, number 2477 in Lecture Notes in Computer Science, pages 20–35. Springer-Verlag, 2002.
12. Robert Nieuwenhuis. Decidability and complexity analysis by basic paramodulation. *Information and Computation*, 147:1–21, 1998.
13. M. Proietti and A. Pettorossi. Unfolding-definition-folding, in this order, for avoiding unnecessary variables in logic programs. *Theoretical Computer Science*, 142(1):89–124, 1995.
14. P. Réty. Regular sets of descendants for constructor-based rewrite systems. In *Proc. of the 6th conference LPAR*, number 1705 in LNAI. Springer, 1999.
15. T. Takai, Y. Kaji, and H. Seki. Right-linear finite path overlapping term rewriting systems effectively preserve recognizability. In *Proc. 11th Int. Conf. on Rewriting Techniques and Applications (RTA'00)*, volume 1833 of *LNCS*, pages 270–273. Springer, 2000.

Splicing Array Grammar Systems

K.G. Subramanian[1], A. Roslin Sagaya Mary[2], and K.S. Dersanambika[3,*]

[1] Department of Mathematics, Madras Christian College,
Chennai - 600 059, India
kgsmani1948@yahoo.com
[2] Rovira I Virgili University,
Pl. Imperial Tarraco 1, 43005 Tarragona, Spain
[3] Department of Computer Science and Engineering,
Indian Institute of Technology, Madras, Chennai - 600 036, India
dersanapdf@yahoo.com

Abstract. Splicing Array Grammar Systems (SAGS) generating pictures of rectangular arrays of symbols are introduced. The components consist of two-dimensional tabled matrix Grammars working in parallel and arrays generated in two different components of the SAGS are allowed to be "cut" and "pasted" according to array splicing domino rules. This model is motivated by the study of Dassow and Mitrana (1996) on string splicing grammar systems. Certain properties of SAGS are obtained.

1 Introduction

Grammar systems are known to provide a formal framework for modelling distributed complex systems [2]. A grammar system consists of several grammars or other language identifying mechanisms, that cooperate according to some well-defined protocol. Among a variety of grammar system models, Parallel Communicating Grammar Systems, in which the components are generative grammars working on their own sentential forms in parallel and communicating with each other by sending their sentential forms by request, have been of intensive study [1] and [2].

Head [7] and [8] defined the operation of splicing of strings while studying the behaviour of DNA sequences under the action of restriction enzymes and ligases. Making use of this operation, a new type of grammar system, called Splicing Grammar System has been introduced in [3]. The component grammars work in parallel in this system as in a parallel communicating grammar system but communication between components is done by splicing of strings.

Several two-dimensional grammars have been proposed and studied [10] in syntactic approaches to generation and recognition of picture patterns, considered as digitized arrays. As a simple and effective extension of the operation of splicing on strings, a new method of splicing on rectangular arrays is introduced in [9] . The idea here is that each of two rectangular arrays is "cut" between two

---

* This work is partially supported by University Grants Commission, India.

D.V. Hung and M. Wirsing (Eds.): ICTAC 2005, LNCS 3722, pp. 125–135, 2005.

specified columns (respectively rows) and the "left" ('upper") part of the first array is "pasted" with the "right" ("lower")part of the second array, resulting in a new array and the "cut" and "paste" operations are according to a set of domino splicing rules.

Freund [5] has introduced and investigated cooperating distributed array grammar systems extending the concept of cooperation in string grammar systems and using array grammars. Here, motivated by the study of Dassow and Mitrana [3], we consider Grammar Systems that describe Pictures of rectangular arrays. The components of these Grammar systems consist of two-dimensional (2d) tabled matrix grammars [12] and domino splicing rules [9] with the grammars working in parallel and splicing rules acting on arrays of two components yielding rectangular arrays of symbols. The resulting systems are called Splicing Array Grammar Systems (SAGS). Properties such as generative power, comparison etc. are obtained.

2   Preliminaries

The basic notions and notations on arrays are now recalled [6] and [11].

Let Σ be a finite alphabet. Σ^* is the set of all words over Σ including the empty word λ. A picture A over Σ is a rectangular $m \times n$ array of elements of Σ of the form

$$A = \begin{bmatrix} a_{11} & \cdots & a_{1n} \\ \vdots & \ddots & \vdots \\ a_{m1} & \cdots & a_{mn} \end{bmatrix}$$

or in short $A = [a_{ij}]_{m \times n}$. We write an array A without enclosing it in square brackets when there is no confusion. The set of all pictures is denoted by Σ^{**}. A picture language or a two dimensional language over Σ is a subset of Σ^{**}.

Definition 1. *For an array A of dimension $m \times n$ and an array B of dimension $m' \times n'$, the column catenation $A \Phi B$ is defined only when $m = m'$ and the row catenation $A \Theta B$ is defined only when $n = n'$. Informally speaking, in row catenation $A \Theta B$, B is attached below A. In column catenation $A \Phi B$, B is attached to the right of X. We refer to [6] and [11] for a formal definition of column and row catenations of rectangular arrays.*

We now recall the definition of a Two-dimensional(2d) tabled matrix grammar [12].

Definition 2. *A 2d **tabled matrix grammar** is a $3-tuple$ $G = (G_1, G_2, \Omega)$ where*
$G_1 = (H_1, I_1, P_1, S)$ is a Regular, CF or CS grammar,
H_1 is a finite set of horizontal nonterminals,
$I_1 = \{S_1, S_2, \cdots, S_k\}$, a finite set of intermediates, $H_1 \cap I_1 = \emptyset$,
P_1 is a finite set of production rules called horizontal production rules,
S is the start symbol, $S \in H_1$,
$G_2 = (G_{21}, G_{22}, \cdots, G_{2k})$ where

$G_{2i} = (V_{2i}, T, P_{2i}, S_i), 1 \leq i \leq k$ *are regular grammars,*
V_{2i} *is a finite set of vertical nonterminals,* $V_{2i} \cap V_{2j} = \emptyset$, $i \neq j$,
T *is a finite set of terminals,*
P_{2i} *is a finite set of right linear production rules of the form* $X \longrightarrow aY$ *or*
$X \longrightarrow a$ *where* $X, Y \in V_{2i}, a \in T$
$S_i \in V_{2i}$ *is the start symbol of* G_{2i}.
$\Omega = \{t_1, ..., t_n\}$ *for some* $n \geq 1$; *Each* $t_j \subseteq \cup P_{2i}$ *is a table of rules so that either*
all the rules in t_j *are of the form* $X \longrightarrow aY$ *or all the rules in* t_j *are of the form*
$X \longrightarrow a$.

The type of G_1 *gives the type of* G *, so we speak about regular, context-free, context sensitive 2d matrix grammars if* G_1 *is regular, context-free, context sensitive respectively.*

Derivations are defined as follows: First a string $S_{i1}S_{i2} \cdots S_{in} \in I_1^*$ *is generated horizontally using the horizontal production rules of* P_1 *in* G_1. *That is,* $S \Rightarrow S_{i1}S_{i2} \cdots S_{in} \in I_1^*$. *Vertical derivations proceed as follows: We write*

$$A_{i1} \cdots A_{in}$$
$$\Downarrow$$
$$a_{i1} \cdots a_{in}$$
$$B_{i1} \cdots B_{in}$$

if $A_{ij} \to a_{ij}B_{ij}$ *are rules in a table* t_j. *The derivation terminates if* $A_{ij} \to a_{mj}$ *are all terminal rules in in a table* t_j.

The set $L(G)$ *of all matrices generated by* G *consists of all* $m \times n$ *arrays* $[a_{ij}]$ *such that* $1 \leq i \leq m$, $1 \leq j \leq n$ *and* $S \Rightarrow_{G_1}^* S_{i1}S_{i2} \cdots S_{in} \Rightarrow_{G_2}^* [a_{ij}]$. *We denote the picture language classes of regular, CF, CS 2d Tabled Matrix grammars by 2dTRML, 2dTCFML, 2dTCSML respectively.*

Remark 1. When the number of tables in Ω is just two, with one consisting of all rules of the form $X \longrightarrow aY$ and the other consisting of all rules of the form $X \longrightarrow a$, then G in Definition 2 is a two-dimensional matrix grammar [11].

We now recall the notions of domino splicing rules and Splicing of arrays using these rules [9].

Definition 3. *Let* V *be an alphabet.* #, $ *are two special symbols, not in* V. *A domino over* V *is of the form* $\boxed{\begin{array}{c} a \\ b \end{array}}$ *or* $\boxed{a\,b}$ *for some* $a, b \in V$ *A domino column splicing rule over* V *is of the form* $r = \alpha_1 \# \alpha_2 \$ \alpha_3 \# \alpha_4$ *where each* $\alpha_i = \boxed{\begin{array}{c} a \\ b \end{array}}$ *for some* $a, b \in V \cup \{\#\}$. *A domino row splicing rule over* V *is of the form* $r = \beta_1 \# \beta_2 \$ \beta_3 \# \beta_4$ *where each* $\beta_i = \boxed{a\,b}$ *for some* $a, b \in V \cup \{\#\}$.

We refer to $\alpha_1, \alpha_2, \alpha_3, \alpha_4$ *of a column splicing rule* $r = \alpha_1 \# \alpha_2 \$ \alpha_3 \# \alpha_4$ *as the first, second, third and fourth dominoes of* r *respectively. Similarly for a row splicing rule* $r = \beta_1 \# \beta_2 \$ \beta_3 \# \beta_4$. $\beta_1, \beta_2, \beta_3, \beta_4$ *are the first, second, third and fourth dominoes of* r *respectively.*

Given two arrays X and Y of sizes $m \times p$ and $m \times q$ respectively,

$$X = \begin{matrix} a_{11} & \cdots & a_{1,j} & a_{1,j+1} & \cdots & a_{1p} \\ a_{21} & \cdots & a_{2,j} & a_{2,j+1} & \cdots & a_{2p} \\ \vdots & \ddots & \vdots & \vdots & \ddots & \vdots \\ a_{m1} & \cdots & a_{m,j} & a_{m,j+1} & \cdots & a_{mp} \end{matrix},$$

$$Y = \begin{matrix} b_{11} & \cdots & b_{1,k} & b_{1,k+1} & \cdots & b_{1q} \\ b_{21} & \cdots & b_{2,k} & b_{2,k+1} & \cdots & b_{2q} \\ \vdots & \ddots & \cdots & \vdots & \ddots & \vdots \\ b_{m1} & \cdots & b_{m,k} & b_{m,k+1} & \cdots & b_{mq} \end{matrix}$$

$a_{ir}, b_{is} \in V$, *for* $1 \leq i \leq m$, $1 \leq r \leq p$, $1 \leq s \leq q$. *We write* $(X, Y) \mid^{\Phi} Z$ *if there is a sequence* $r_1, r_2, \ldots r_m$ *of column splicing rules (not necessarily all different) such that*

$$r_i = \boxed{\begin{matrix} a_{i,j} \\ a_{i+1,j} \end{matrix}} \quad \# \quad \boxed{\begin{matrix} a_{i,j+1} \\ a_{i+1,j+1} \end{matrix}} \quad \$ \quad \boxed{\begin{matrix} b_{i,k} \\ b_{i+1,k} \end{matrix}} \quad \# \quad \boxed{\begin{matrix} b_{i,k+1} \\ b_{i+1,k+1} \end{matrix}}$$

for all i, $1 \leq i \leq m-1$ *and for some* j, k $1 \leq j \leq p-1$, $1 \leq k \leq q-1$ *and*

$$Z = \begin{matrix} a_{11} & \cdots & a_{1,j} & b_{1,k+1} & \cdots & b_{1q} \\ a_{21} & \cdots & a_{2,j} & b_{2,k+1} & \cdots & b_{2q} \\ \vdots & \ddots & \vdots & \vdots & \ddots & \vdots \\ a_{m1} & \cdots & a_{m,j} & b_{m,k+1} & \cdots & b_{mq} \end{matrix}$$

In other words, we can imagine that a 2×1 window is moved down the jth column of X The sequence of dominoes collected are the first dominoes of the rules $r_1, r_2, \ldots, r_m$ (not all necessarily different). When a 2×1 window is moved down the $j + 1^{st}$ column of X the sequence of dominoes collected are the second dominoes of the rules $r_1, r_2, \ldots, r_m$. Likewise for the kth and $k + 1^{st}$ columns of Y When such rules exist in the system, the column splicing of the arrays X and Y amounts to the array X being vertically "cut" between j^{th} and $j + 1^{st}$ columns and the array Y between k^{th} and $k + 1^{st}$ columns and the resulting left subarray of X "pasted" (column catenated) with the right subarray of Y to yield Z We now say that Z is obtained from X and Y by domino column splicing in parallel. We can similarly define row splicing operation of two arrays U and V of sizes $p \times n$ and $q \times n$, using row splicing rules to yield an array W.

$$U = \begin{matrix} c_{11} & c_{12} & \cdots & c_{1n} \\ \vdots & \vdots & \ddots & \vdots \\ c_{r,1} & c_{r,2} & \cdots & c_{r,n} \\ c_{r+1,1} & c_{r+1,2} & \cdots & c_{r+1,n} \\ \vdots & \vdots & \ddots & \vdots \\ c_{p1} & c_{p2} & \cdots & c_{pn} \end{matrix}, \qquad V = \begin{matrix} d_{11} & d_{12} & \cdots & d_{1n} \\ \vdots & \vdots & \ddots & \vdots \\ d_{s,1} & d_{s,2} & \cdots & d_{s,n} \\ d_{s+1,1} & d_{s+1,2} & \cdots & d_{s+1,n} \\ \vdots & \vdots & \ddots & \vdots \\ d_{q1} & d_{q2} & \cdots & d_{qn} \end{matrix}$$

$c_{rj}, d_{sj} \in V$, *for* $1 \leq j \leq n$, $1 \leq r \leq p$, $1 \leq s \leq q$.

We write (U, V) $\mid\!\underline{\Theta}$ W *if there is a sequence* $r_1, r_2, \cdots r_n$ *of row splicing rules (not necessarily all different) such that*

$$r_j = \boxed{c_{r,j}\,c_{r,j+1}} \quad \# \quad \boxed{c_{r+1,j}\,c_{r+1,j+1}} \quad \$ \quad \boxed{d_{s,j}\,d_{s,j+1}} \quad \# \quad \boxed{d_{s+1,j}\,d_{s+1,j+1}}$$

for all j, $1 \leq j \leq n-1$ *and for some* r, s $1 \leq r \leq p-1$, $1 \leq s \leq q-1$ *and*

$$W = \begin{matrix} c_{11} & c_{12} & \cdots & c_{1n} \\ \vdots & \vdots & \ddots & \vdots \\ c_{r,1} & c_{r,2} & \cdots & c_{r,n} \\ d_{s+1,1} & d_{s+1,2} & \cdots & d_{s+1,n} \\ \vdots & \vdots & \ddots & \vdots \\ d_{q1} & d_{q2} & \cdots & d_{qn} \end{matrix}$$

As done for the column splicing of arrays, we can imagine 1×2 windows being moved over respective rows. The row splicing of the arrays U and V can be thought of as U being horizontally "cut" between the rth and $r + 1^{st}$ rows and V between s^{th} and $s + 1^{st}$ rows and the upper subarray of U "pasted" (row catenated) to the lower subarray of V to yield W We now say that W is obtained from U and V by domino row splicing in parallel.

We illustrate with an example.

Example 1. Let $V = \{a, b\}$,

$$R_c = \{p_1 : \boxed{\begin{matrix} a \\ b \end{matrix}} \quad \# \quad \$ \quad \# \quad \boxed{\begin{matrix} b \\ a \end{matrix}}$$

$$p_2 : \boxed{\begin{matrix} b \\ a \end{matrix}} \quad \# \quad \$ \quad \# \quad \boxed{\begin{matrix} a \\ b \end{matrix}} \quad \}$$

$$R_r = \{q_1 : \boxed{a\,b} \quad \# \quad \$ \quad \# \quad \boxed{b\,a}$$

$$q_2 : \boxed{b\,a} \quad \# \quad \$ \quad \# \quad \boxed{a\,b} \quad \}$$

Column splicing in parallel of an array with itself using the rules given is shown below:

$$\begin{matrix} a & b \\ b & a \end{matrix} \left|\begin{matrix} a & b \\ b & a \end{matrix}\right. \quad \mid\!\underline{\Phi} \quad \begin{matrix} a & b & a & b \\ b & a & b & a \end{matrix}$$

Likewise, row splicing in parallel of an array with itself using the rules given is shown below:

$$\begin{matrix} a\,b\,a\,b\,\overline{a\,b\,a\,b} \\ b\,a\,b\,a\,b\,a\,b\,a \end{matrix} \quad \mid\!\underline{\Theta} \quad \begin{matrix} a\,b\,a\,b \\ b\,a\,b\,a \\ a\,b\,a\,b \\ b\,a\,b\,a \end{matrix}$$

A vertical bar '$\mid$' or a horizontal bar '——' indicates the place where splicing is done.

3   Splicing Array Grammar Systems

We now introduce the notion of Splicing array grammar system in which the component grammars consist of rules of 2d tabled matrix grammars.

Definition 4. *A Splicing Array Grammar system (SAGS) is a construct*
$\Gamma = (V_h, \Sigma_I, V_v, T, (S_1, R_1^h, R_1^v), ..., (S_n, R_n^h, R_n^v), M)$ *where,*
V_h *is a finite set of variables called horizontal variables;*
V_v *is a finite set of variables called vertical variables;*
$\Sigma_I \subseteq V_v$ *is a finite set of intermediates;*
T *is a finite set of terminals;*
$S_i, 1 \leq i \leq n$ *is the start symbol of the corresponding horizontal component;*
$R_i^h, 1 \leq i \leq n$ *is a finite set of rules called horizontal productions
and the rules can be regular or context free or context sensitive;*
$R_i^v, 1 \leq i \leq n$ *is a finite set tables of right linear rules called vertical productions;The productions in a table are all either of the form $A \rightarrow aB$ or of the form $A \rightarrow a$;*
M *is a finite set of domino column or row splicing rules of the form*

$$m = \alpha_1 \# \alpha_2 \$ \alpha_3 \# \alpha_4 \text{ or } \beta_1 \# \beta_2 \$ \beta_3 \# \beta_4$$

where $\alpha_i = \boxed{\begin{array}{c} a \\ b \end{array}}$ and $\beta_i = \boxed{c\,d}$ for some $a, b, c, d \in V_v \cup \{T\} \cup \{\lambda\}$.

The derivations take place in two phases as follows :

Each component grammar generates a word called intermediate word, over intermediates starting from its own start symbol and using its horizontal production rules ; the derivations in this phase are done with the component grammars working in parallel.

In the second phase any of the following steps can take place :

(i) *each component grammar can rewrite as in a two dimensional matrix grammar using the tables of vertical rules, starting from its own intermediate word generated in the first phase. (The component grammars rewrite in parallel and the rules of a table are applied together). Note that the component grammars together terminate or together continue rewriting in the vertical direction.*

(ii) *At any instant the array X generated in the ith component for some $1 \leq i \leq n$ and the array Y generated in the jth component for some $1 \leq j \leq n$ can be spliced using column / row domino splicing rules as in definition 4, thus yielding array Z in i^{th} component and W in the jth component; In fact Z will have a prefix of X column concatenated with a suffix of Y and W will have a prefix of Y, column concatenated with a suffix of X, the prefixes and suffixes being given by the splicing rules. In any other components (other than i^{th}, j^{th} components), the arrays generated at this instant will remain unchanged during this splicing process.*

There is no priority between steps (i) and (ii).

The language $L_i(\Gamma)$ generated by the ith component of Γ consists of all arrays, generated over T, by the derivations described above.

This language will be called the individual language of the system and we may choose this to be the language of the first component and $L_t(\Gamma) = \bigcup_{i=1}^{n} L_i(\Gamma)$ as the total language. The family of individual languages generated by SAGS with n components of type X for $X \in \{REG, CF\}$ is denoted by $I_{sags}L_n(X)$, and the corresponding family of total languages by $T_{sags}L_n(X)$ respectively and $Y_{sags}L_n(X)$ when $Y \in \{I, T\}$. We basically deal with individual languages although the results obtained apply to total languages as well.

Remark 2. The image splicing grammar system (ISGS)introduced in [4] in which the component grammars are 2d Matrix grammars [12]is a special case of SAGS.

Example 2. Let $\Gamma = (\{S, X, Y, Z\}, \{A, B, E, C\}, \{A, B, C, D, E, F, T, U\}\{., x\},$
$\qquad (S, R^h, R^v), (S, R^h, R^v), (S, R^h, R^v), M)$
where
$R^h = \{S \to AX, X \to BX, X \to BY, Y \to EZ, Z \to C\}$
$R^v = \{t_1, t_2, ..., t_6\}$
$t_1 = \{A \to xA, B \to .B, E \to .E, C \to xC\}.$
$t_2 = \{A \to xA, B \to .D, E \to .F, C \to xC\}.$
$t_3 = \{A \to xA, D \to .D, F \to .F, C \to xC\}.$
$t_4 = \{A \to xA, D \to xT, F \to yU, C \to xC\}$
$t_5 = \{A \to xA, T \to .T, U \to .U, C \to xC\}$
$t_6 = \{A \to x, T \to ., U \to ., C \to x\}$

The horizontal rules in a component generate intermediate words of the form $AB^n EC$ with the same value of $n \geq 1$ at a time. The vertical rules of the components generate from an intermediate word rectangular pictures of digitized token H surrounded in the left and right by x's and the bottom border of the form $AT^n UC$. At this stage with domino splicing rules, column splicing of the array in a component with the array in another component can take place before rewriting is terminated in the components with terminating vertical rules. In fact any picture generated in the individual language of this splicing array grammar system will be rectangular pictures in which any row, except a middle row, will be of the form $x(.)^{kn} x$ and a middle row will be of the form $x((x)^n y)^k x$ for some $k\epsilon\{1, 2, 3\}$. One such picture obtained is shown in Figure 1.

```
x . . . . . . . . . . . x
x . . . . . . . . . . . x
x x x x y x x x y x x x y x
x . . . . . . . . . . . x
x . . . . . . . . . . . x
x . . . . . . . . . . . x
```

Fig. 1. A Picture of Example 2

Example 3. Let $\Gamma = (\{S, X\}, \{A, B, E\}, \{A, B, C, D, E\} \{., x\}, (S, R^h, R^v),$
$(S, R^h, R^v), (S, R^h, R^v), M)$ where

$R^h = \{S \to EXE, X \to AXB, X \to AB\}$
$R^v = \{t_1, t_2, t_3, t_4, t_5\}$
$t_1 = \{A \to .A, B \to .B, E \to xE\}$
$t_2 = \{A \to .C, B \to .D, E \to xE, \}$
$t_3 = \{C \to aY, D \to bZ, E \to xE, \}$
$t_4 = \{Y \to .Y, Z \to .Z, E \to xE, \}$
$t_5 = \{Y \to ., Z \to ., E \to x\}$

and $M = \{$
$\begin{array}{|c|} \hline b \\ \hline . \\ \hline \end{array}$ # $\begin{array}{|c|} \hline x \\ \hline x \\ \hline \end{array}$ \$ $\begin{array}{|c|} \hline x \\ \hline x \\ \hline \end{array}$ # $\begin{array}{|c|} \hline a \\ \hline . \\ \hline \end{array}$

$\begin{array}{|c|} \hline . \\ \hline b \\ \hline \end{array}$ # $\begin{array}{|c|} \hline x \\ \hline x \\ \hline \end{array}$ \$ $\begin{array}{|c|} \hline x \\ \hline x \\ \hline \end{array}$ # $\begin{array}{|c|} \hline . \\ \hline a \\ \hline \end{array}$

$\begin{array}{|c|} \hline . \\ \hline . \\ \hline \end{array}$ # $\begin{array}{|c|} \hline x \\ \hline x \\ \hline \end{array}$ \$ $\begin{array}{|c|} \hline x \\ \hline x \\ \hline \end{array}$ # $\begin{array}{|c|} \hline . \\ \hline . \\ \hline \end{array}$

$\begin{array}{|c|} \hline . \\ \hline Z \\ \hline \end{array}$ # $\begin{array}{|c|} \hline x \\ \hline E \\ \hline \end{array}$ \$ $\begin{array}{|c|} \hline x \\ \hline E \\ \hline \end{array}$ # $\begin{array}{|c|} \hline . \\ \hline Y \\ \hline \end{array}$ $\}$

The horizontal rules generate in a component intermediate words of the form EA^nB^nE with the same value of $n \geq 1$ at a time. The vertical rules of the components generate from an intermediate word rectangle pictures of (.)'s with a middle row of the form xa^mb^mx, and the bottom row of the form EC^mD^mE, the leftmost column being a column of x's ending with E and the rightmost column being a column of x's ending with E. At this stage with domino splicing rules, column splicing of the array in a component with the array in another component can take place before rewriting is terminated in the components with terminating vertical rules. One such picture obtained is shown in Figure 2.

```
x . . . . . . . . . . x
x . . . . . . . . . . x
x . . . . . . . . . . x
x a a b b a a b b a a b b x
x . . . . . . . . . . x
x . . . . . . . . . . x
```

Fig. 2. A Picture of Example 3

Theorem 1. *For $Y \in \{I, T\}$,*

1. $2dRML = Y_{isgs}L_1(REG) \subset 2dTRML = Y_{sags}L_1(REG)$
2. $2dRML \subset Y_{isgs}L_2(REG)$
3. $2dCFML = Y_{isgs}L_1(CF) \subset 2dTCFML = Y_{sags}L_1(CF)$
4. $2dTRML \subset Y_{sags}L_2(REG)$
5. $2dTCFML \subset Y_{sags}L_2(CF)$
6. $Y_{sags}L_3(REG) - CS \neq \phi$.

Proof. The equalities in statements (1) and (3) are clear from definitions and the proper inclusions are known [12]. Statement (2) is proved in [4]. Inclusions in statement (4)and(5) are clear. The proper inclusion in statement (4) is a consequence of Example 2. In fact the picture language of the Example 2 even with $k = 2$, cannot be generated by any $2dTRMG$ as the rules in both the horizontal and vertical phases are only regular rules. Likewise the proper inclusion in statement (5) is a consequence of Example 3even with two components since the rules in the horizontal phase of a $2dCFMG$ are only CF rules but the pictures generated will require CS rules.The last statement follows from example 2 as the the pictures in Figure 1 require CS rules in the first phase to generate these.

Example 4. [4]
Let $\Gamma = (\{S_1, \cdots S_n, X\}, \{A_1, \cdots, A_n, B_1, \cdots, B_n, C_1, \ldots, C_n, \},$
$\{A_1, \cdots, A_n, B_1, \cdots, B_n, C_1, \ldots, C_n, D_1, \ldots, D_n\},$
$\{., x, a, b\}, (S, R^{h_1}, R^{v_1}), (S, R^{h_2}, R^{v_2}), \cdots, (S, R^{h_n}, R^{v_n}), M)$

where
$R^{h_1} = \{S_1 \to A_1 X, X \to B_1 X, X \to C_1\}$
$R^{v_1} = \{A_1 \to xA_1, A_1 \to x, B_1 \to aD_1, D_1 \to .D_1, D_1 \to a, C_1 \to xC_1, C_1 \to$
$x, D_i \to a$ *if* $i \geq 2$ *and* i *odd*, $D_i \to b$ *if* $i \geq 2$ *and* i *even*, $C_i \to x\}$.

For $i > 1$ and i even
$R^{h_i} = \{S_i \to A_i X, X \to B_i X, X \to C_i\}$
$R^{v_i} = \{A_i \to xA_i, A_i \to x, B_i \to bD_i, D_i \to .D_i, C_i \to xC_i, \}$.
For $i > 1$ and i odd $R^{h_i} = \{S_i \to A_i X, X \to B_i X, X \to C_i\}$
$R^{v_i} = \{A_i \to xA_i, A_i \to x, B_i \to aD_i, D_i \to .D_i, C_i \to xC_i, \}$.

$$M = \{ \begin{array}{|c|} \hline a \\ \hline . \\ \hline \end{array} \quad \# \quad \begin{array}{|c|} \hline x \\ \hline x \\ \hline \end{array} \quad \$ \quad \# \quad \begin{array}{|c|} \hline x \\ \hline x \\ \hline \end{array}$$

$$\begin{array}{|c|} \hline b \\ \hline . \\ \hline \end{array} \quad \# \quad \begin{array}{|c|} \hline x \\ \hline x \\ \hline \end{array} \quad \$ \quad \# \quad \begin{array}{|c|} \hline x \\ \hline x \\ \hline \end{array}$$

$$\begin{array}{|c|} \hline . \\ \hline . \\ \hline \end{array} \quad \# \quad \begin{array}{|c|} \hline x \\ \hline x \\ \hline \end{array} \quad \$ \quad \# \quad \begin{array}{|c|} \hline x \\ \hline x \\ \hline \end{array}$$

$$\begin{array}{|c|} \hline . \\ \hline D_i \\ \hline \end{array} \quad \# \quad \begin{array}{|c|} \hline x \\ \hline C_i \\ \hline \end{array} \quad \$ \quad \# \quad \begin{array}{|c|} \hline x \\ \hline A_i \\ \hline \end{array} \}$$

We note that the top and bottom rows of the rectangular arrays generated in the individual language will be of the form $xa^m x b^m x a^m x b^m ...x$ as there are n component grammars.

Theorem 2. *For* $Y \in \{I, T\}$,

1. $2dRML = Y_{isgs}L_1(REG) \subset Y_{isgs}L_2(REG) \subset$
   $$\cdots \subset Y_{isgs}L_n(REG) \subset \cdots$$
2. $2dCFML = Y_{isgs}L_1(CF) \subset Y_{isgs}L_2(CF) \subset$
   $$\cdots \subset Y_{isgs}L_n(CF) \subset \cdots$$
3. $2dTRML = Y_{sags}L_1(REG) \subset Y_{sags}L_2(REG) \subset$
   $$\cdots \subset Y_{sags}L_n(REG) \subset \cdots$$
4. $2dTCFML = Y_{sags}L_1(CF) \subset Y_{sags}L_2(CF) \subset$
   $$\cdots \subset Y_{sags}L_n(CF) \subset \cdots$$

The first statement has been proved in [4] using the Example 4. The remaining statements can be seen similarly.

4   Conclusion

The splicing array grammar system introduced in this paper turns out to be a powerful means of generating picture arrays. It extends the image grammar system in [4] to tabled matrix grammars. It remains to compare other picture generating mechanisms with these systems.

Acknowledgement. The authors thank the referees for their useful comments.

References

1. E. Csuhaj-Varjú: Grammar systems: 12 years, 12 problems (short version), In R. Freund and A. Kelemenov (Eds.), Proceedings of the International Workshop on Grammar Systems 2000, **2000**, 77-92, Silesian University, Opava.
2. E. Csuhaj-Varjú, J. Dassow, J. Kelemen and Gh. Păun: Grammar systems: A grammatical approach to distribution and cooperation, Gordon and Breach Science Publishers, 1994.
3. J. Dassow and V. Mitrana: Splicing grammar systems, Computers and Artificial Intelligence, **15**, 1996, 109-122.
4. K.S. Dersanambika, K.G. Subramanian, A. Roslin Sagaya Mary: Image Splicing grammar systems,Proc. Grammar systems Week 2004
5. R. Freund : Array Grammar Systems, Journal of Automata, Languages and Combinatorics, **5**,1, 2000, 13-29.
6. D. Giammarresi and A. Restivo: Two-dimensional languages, In "Handbook of Formal Languages" Vol.3, Eds. G. Rozenberg and A. Salomaa, Springer Verlag, 1997, 215-267.
7. T. Head, Formal language theory and DNA: an analysis of the generative capacity of specific recombinant behaviours, Bull. Math. Biology, **49**, 1987, 737-759.
8. T. Head, Gh. Păun and D. Pixton: Language theory and molecular genetics: Generative mechanisms suggested by DNA recombination, In "Handbook of Formal Languages" Vol.2, Eds. G. Rozenberg and A. Salomaa, Springer Verlag, 1997, 295 - 360.
9. P. Helen Chandra, K.G. Subramanian, and D.G. Thomas: Parallel Splicing on Images, Int. J. of pattern recognition and artificial intelligence, 2004.

10. A. Rosenfeld and R. Siromoney: Picture languages - a survey, Languages of design, **1**, 1993, 229–245.
11. G. Siromoney, R. Siromoney and K. Krithivasan: Abstract families of matrices and picture languages, Computer Graphics and Image Processing, **1**, 1972, 234-307.
12. R. Siromoney, K.G. Subramanian, K. Rangarajan: Parallel /Sequential Rectangular Arrays with Tables, Inter. J. Computer Math., **6**, 1977, 143-158.

Compositionality of Fixpoint Logic with Chop

Naijun Zhan[1,*] and Jinzhao Wu[2]

[1] Lab. of Computer Science, Institute of Software,
Chinese Academy of Sciences, 100080 Beijing, P.R. China
[2] Lehrstuhl für Praktische Informatik II, Fakultät für Mathematik und Informatik,
Universität Mannheim, D7,27, 68163, Mannheim, Deutschland

Abstract. Compositionality plays an important role in designing reactive systems as it allows one to compose/decompose a complex system from/to several simpler components. Generally speaking, it is hard to design a complex system in a logical frame in a compositional way because it is difficult to find a connection between the structure of a system to be developed and that of its specification given by the logic. In this paper, we investigate the compositionality of the Fixpoint Logic with Chop (FLC for short). To this end, we extend FLC with the nondeterministic choice "+" (FLC$^+$ for the extension) and then establish a correspondence between the logic and the basic process algebra with deadlock and termination (abbreviated BPA$_\delta^\epsilon$). Subsequently, we show that the choice "+" is definable in FLC.

As an application of the compositionality of FLC, an algorithm is given to construct characteristic formulae of BPA$_\delta^\epsilon$ up to strong bisimulation directly from the syntax of processes in a compositional manner.

Keywords: FLC, compositionality, verification, bisimulation, characteristic formula, basic process algebra.

1 Introduction

As argued in [2], compositionality is very important in developing reactive systems for at least the following reasons. Firstly, it allows modular design and verification of complex systems so that the complexity is tractable. Secondly, during re-designing a verified system only the verification concerning the modified parts should be re-done rather than verifying the whole system from scratch. Thirdly, compositionality makes it possible to partially specify a large system. When designing a system or synthesizing a process, it is possible to have undefined parts of a process and still to be able to reason about it. For example, this technique can be applied for revealing inconsistencies in the specification or proving that with the choices already taken in the design no component supplied for the missing parts will ever be able to make the overall system satisfy the original specification. Finally, it can make possible the *reuse* of verified components; their previous verification can be used to show that they meet the requirements on the components of a large system.

---

* This work is supported in part by CNSF-60493200 and CNSF-60421001.

D.V. Hung and M. Wirsing (Eds.): ICTAC 2005, LNCS 3722, pp. 136–150, 2005.

The μ-calculus [15] is a popular modal logic as most of modal and temporal logics can be defined in it. However, [8] proved that only "regular" properties can be defined in the μ-calculus, meanwhile [14] proved that all bisimulation invariant properties of Monadic Second Order Logic can be defined in the modal μ-calculus. In order to specify non-regular properties, [21] extended the μ-calculus with the chop operator (denoted by ";"). It seems that the chop operator ";" was first introduced in process logics [12,6], then adopted as the unique primitive modality in interval-based logics, see [11,28,7], for example. In an interval-based logic, it is easy to interpret a formula like $\phi; \psi$ by partitioning the given interval into two parts such that ϕ is satisfied in the first segment and ψ is held in the second one. But it is hard to interpret the operator in modal logics. Therefore, in [21] the meaning of FLC is interpreted in second-order. [21] proved that FLC is strictly more expressive than the μ-calculus as non-regular properties can be expressed in FLC by showing that characteristic formulae of context-free processes can be defined in FLC. Since then, FLC has attracted more attentions in computer science because of its expressiveness. For example, [16,17] investigated the issues of FLC model checking on finite-state processes.

Let us assume a setting in which the behavior of systems are modeled by some process algebra and behavioral properties of systems are specified by some specification logic. In order to exploit the compositionality inherent in the process algebra it is desirable to be able to mimic the process algebra operators in the logic (see [10]). That is, for any program constructor *cons* there should be an operator **cons** of the logic such that

(a) $P_i \models \phi_i$ for $i = 1, \cdots, n$ implies $cons(P_1, \cdots, P_n) \models \mathbf{cons}(\phi_1, \cdots, \phi_n)$;

(b) $cons(P_1, \cdots, P_n) \models \mathbf{cons}(\phi_1, \cdots, \phi_n)$ is the strongest assertion which can be deduced from $P_i \models \phi_i$ for $i = 1, \cdots, n$.

It seems that FLC does not meet the above conditions. For example, the $+$ operator of process algebra has no counterpart in FLC and in addition it is still an open problem if it is possible to derive a property from ϕ and ψ that holds in $P + Q$ in FLC, where $P \models \phi$ and $Q \models \psi$.

To achieve the goal, we first introduce the non-deterministic choice "$+$" that was proposed in [10,18] as a primitive and denote the extension of FLC by FLC$^+$. Intuitively, $P \models \phi + \psi$ means that there exist P_1 and P_2 such that $P \sim P_1 + P_2$, $P_1 \models \phi$ and $P_2 \models \psi$. Thus, it is easy to see that we can use $\phi + \psi$ as a specification for the combined system $P + Q$. Then we show that the constructors of the basic process algebra with termination and deadlock (BPA$_\delta^\epsilon$ for short) correspond to the connectives of FLC$^+$. Subsequently, we prove that the choice "$+$" can be defined essentially by conjunction and disjunction in FLC.

As a result, we can use FLC to specify systems modeled by BPA$_\delta^\epsilon$ in an algebraical way, typically, this may allow much more concise descriptions of concurrent systems and more easy composing/decomposing the verification of a large systems from/to some similar and simpler ones of the subsystems. As an example, we now show that using "$+$" as an auxiliary operator could make senses in practice:

i) It means one more step to the goal to exploit the structure of process terms for model checking.

ii) It enables a precise and compact specification of certain nondeterministic systems.

iii) It is very easy to modify the specification of a system when additional alternatives for the behavior of the system should be admitted.

iv) It enhances the possibility of modularity in model checking which is useful in redesigning of systems.

i) depends on if it is possible to work out a syntax-directed model checker for FLC on finite-state processes. In fact, we believe that it may be done exploiting the connection between FLC^+ and BPA_δ^ϵ that is presented in this paper. To explain the issues ii), iii) and iv), we present the following example: Consider a car factory that wants to establish an assembly line shown in the Fig. 1.,

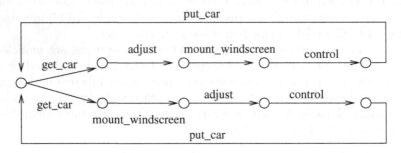

Fig. 1. The Process P

which we denote by the process P, for one production step. If there is a car available for P then P will either get the car, adjust the motor, mount the windscreen, control the car, and then put the car on the conveyer belt or P will get the car, mount the windscreen, adjust the motor, control the car, and then put it back. Afterwards P may start again. The first option can be specified by

$$\text{Spec}_1 \cong [\text{get\_car}]; \langle\text{adjust}\rangle; \langle\text{mount\_windscreen}\rangle; \langle\text{control}\rangle; \langle\text{put\_car}\rangle$$
$$\wedge\langle\text{get\_car}\rangle; \text{true},$$

whereas the second is described by

$$\text{Spec}_2 \cong [\text{get\_car}]; \langle\text{mount\_windscreen}\rangle; \langle\text{adjust}\rangle; \langle\text{control}\rangle; \langle\text{put\_car}\rangle$$
$$\wedge\langle\text{get\_car}\rangle; \text{true}.$$

We are now looking for a specification that admits only such systems that offer both alternatives and that can be easily constructed from Spec_1 and Spec_2. Obviously, $\text{Spec}_1 \wedge \text{Spec}_2$ is not suitable whereas $\text{Spec}_1 \vee \text{Spec}_2$ allows for implementations that exhibit only one of the behavior. $\text{Spec}_1 + \text{Spec}_2$ describes the behavior we have in mind and a system that offers this behavior repeatedly is described by $\text{Spec} \cong \nu X.(\text{Spec}_1 + \text{Spec}_2); X$.

It is easy to show that $rec\ x.(P_1 + P_2); x \models \text{Spec}$, where

$$P_1 \triangleq \text{get\_car; adjust; mount\_windscreen; control; put\_car}$$
$$P_2 \triangleq \text{get\_car; mount\_windscreen; adjust; control; put\_car}.$$

Let us now assume that the system specification should be modified to allow for a third alternative behavior Spec_3, then this specification may be simply "added" to form

$$\text{Spec}' \triangleq \nu X.(\text{Spec}_1 + \text{Spec}_2 + \text{Spec}_3); X.$$

If we establish $P_3 \models \text{Spec}_3$ then we obtain immediately that

$$rec\ x.(P_1 + P_2 + P_3); x \models \text{Spec}'.$$

In addition, if we have to modify Spec_1 to Spec'_1 such that $P'_1 \models \text{Spec}'_1$, and obtain

$$rec\ x.(P'_1 + P_2 + P_3); x \models \nu X.(\text{Spec}'_1 + \text{Spec}_2 + \text{Spec}_3); X.$$

Some preliminary results of this paper have been reported in [27].

The remainder of this paper is structured as follows: Section 2 briefly reviews $\text{BPA}^\epsilon_\delta$. In Section 3, FLC^+ is established and some preliminary results are given. Section 4 establishes a connection between the constructors of $\text{BPA}^\epsilon_\delta$ and the connectives of FLC^+. Section 5 is devoted to showing that the choice "+" can be defined in FLC. In Section 6, we sketch how to construct a formula Ψ_P for each process $P \in \text{BPA}^\epsilon_\delta$ according to its syntax and then show the formula obtained by eliminating "+" in Ψ_P is the characteristic formula of P. Finally, a brief conclusion is provided in Section 7.

2   Basic Process Algebra with Termination and Deadlock

Let $Act = \{a, b, c, \cdots\}$ be a set of (atomic) actions, and $\mathcal{X} = \{x, y, z, ...\}$ a countable set of process variables. *Sequential process terms*, written $\mathcal{P}^s$, are those which do not involve parallelism and communication, which are generated by the following grammar:

$$E ::= \delta \mid \epsilon \mid x \mid a \mid E_1; E_2 \mid E_1 + E_2 \mid rec\ x.E$$

Intuitively, the elements of $\mathcal{P}^s$ represent programs: δ stands for a deadlocked process that cannot execute any action and keeps idle for ever; ϵ denotes a terminated process that cannot proceed, but terminates at once; the other constructors can be understood as the usual ones.

In order to define an operational semantics for expressions of the form $E_1; E_2$, we need to define a special predicate $\mathcal{T}$ over $\mathcal{P}^s$ to indicate if a given process term is terminated or not. Formally, $\mathcal{T} \subset \mathcal{P}^s$ is the least set which contains ϵ and is closed under the following rules: (i) if $\mathcal{T}(E_1)$ and $\mathcal{T}(E_2)$ then $\mathcal{T}(E_1; E_2)$ and $\mathcal{T}(E_1 + E_2)$; (ii) if $\mathcal{T}(E)$ then $\mathcal{T}(rec\ x.E)$.

$$\text{Act } \frac{}{a \xrightarrow{a} \epsilon} \qquad \text{Rec } \frac{E[rec\ x.E/x] \xrightarrow{a} E'}{rec\ x.E \xrightarrow{a} E'} \qquad \text{Seq-1 } \frac{E_1 \xrightarrow{a} E_1'}{E_1; E_2 \xrightarrow{a} E_1'; E_2}$$

$$\text{Seq-2 } \frac{E_2 \xrightarrow{a} E_2' \wedge \mathcal{T}(E_1)}{E_1; E_2 \xrightarrow{a} E_2'} \qquad \text{Nd } \frac{E_1 \xrightarrow{a} E_1'}{E_1 + E_2 \xrightarrow{a} E_1', \quad E_2 + E_1 \xrightarrow{a} E_1'}$$

Fig. 2. The Operational Semantics of $\mathcal{P}^s$

An occurrence of a variable $x \in \mathcal{X}$ is called *free* in a term E iff it does not occur within a sub-term of the form $rec\ x.E'$, otherwise called *bound*. We will use $fn(E)$ to stand for all variables which have some free occurrence in E, and $bn(E)$ for all variables which have some bound occurrence in E. A variable $x \in \mathcal{X}$ is called *guarded* within a term E iff every occurrence of x is within a sub-term F where F is prefixed with a subexpression F^* via ";" such that $\neg \mathcal{T}(F^*)$. A term E is called *guarded* iff all variables occurring in it are guarded. The set of all closed and guarded terms of $\mathcal{P}^s$ essentially corresponds to the *basic process algebra* (BPA) with the terminated process ϵ and the deadlocked process δ, denoted by $\text{BPA}_\delta^\epsilon$, ranged over by $P, Q, \cdots$, where BPA is a fragment of ACP [5].

An operational semantics of $\mathcal{P}^s$ is given in the standard Plotkin's style, yielding a transition system $(\mathcal{P}^s, \rightarrow)$ with $\rightarrow \subseteq \mathcal{P}^s \times Act \times \mathcal{P}^s$ that is the least relation derived from the rules in the Fig.2.

Definition 1. *A binary relation $\mathcal{S} \subseteq \text{BPA}_\delta^\epsilon \times \text{BPA}_\delta^\epsilon$ is called a strong bisimulation if $(P, Q) \in \mathcal{S}$ implies:*

- $\mathcal{T}(P)$ iff $\mathcal{T}(Q)$;
- *whenever $P \xrightarrow{a} P'$ then, for some $Q', Q \xrightarrow{a} Q'$ and $(P', Q') \in \mathcal{S}$ for any $a \in Act$;*
- *whenever $Q \xrightarrow{a} Q'$ then, for some $P', P \xrightarrow{a} P'$ and $(P', Q') \in \mathcal{S}$ for any $a \in Act$.*

Given two processes $P, Q \in \text{BPA}_\delta^\epsilon$, we say that P and Q are strongly bisimilar, written $P \sim Q$, if $(P, Q) \in \mathcal{S}$ for some strong bisimulation $\mathcal{S}$. We can extend the definition of $\sim$ over $\mathcal{P}^s$ as: let $E_1, E_2 \in \mathcal{P}^s$ and $fn(E_1) \cup fn(E_2) \subseteq \{x_1, \cdots, x_n\}$, if $E_1\{P_1/x_1, \cdots, P_n/x_n\} \sim E_2\{P_1/x_1, \cdots, P_n/x_n\}$ for any $P_1, \cdots, P_n \in \text{BPA}_\delta^\epsilon$, then $E_1 \sim E_2$.

Convention: From now on, we use $\mathcal{A}\ op\ \mathcal{B}$ to stand for $\{E_1\ op\ E_2 \mid E_1 \in \mathcal{A} \text{ and } E_2 \in \mathcal{B}\}$, $\mathcal{A}\ op\ E$ for $\mathcal{A}\ op\ \{E\}$, where $E \in \mathcal{P}^s, \mathcal{A} \subseteq \mathcal{P}^s, \mathcal{B} \subseteq \mathcal{P}^s$, and $op \in \{+, ;\}$.

3   FLC with the Nondeterministic Operator "+" (FLC$^+$)

FLC, due to Markus Müller-Olm [21], is an extension of the modal μ-calculus that can express non-regular properties, and is therefore strictly more powerful than the μ-calculus. In order to study the compositionality of FLC, we extend

FLC with the nondeterministic operator "+", which is proposed as a primitive operator in [10,18].

Let $X, Y, Z, \cdots$ range over an infinite set *Var* of *variables*, *tt* and *ff* be *propositional constants* as usual, and $\sqrt{}$ another special propositional constant that is used to indicate if a process is terminated. Formulae of FLC$^+$ are generated by the following grammar:

$$\phi ::= tt \mid ff \mid \sqrt{} \mid \tau \mid X \mid [a] \mid \langle a \rangle \mid \phi_1 \wedge \phi_2 \mid \phi_1 \vee \phi_2 \mid \phi_1 ; \phi_2 \mid \phi_1 + \phi_2 \mid \mu X.\phi \mid \nu X.\phi$$

where $X \in Var$ and $a \in Act$. The fragment of FLC$^+$ without "+" is called FLC [21]. In what follows, we use @ to stand for $\langle a \rangle$ or $[a]$, p for tt, ff or $\sqrt{}$, and σ for ν or μ.

Some notations can be defined as in the modal μ-calculus, for example *free* and *bound* occurrences of variables, *closed* and *open* formulae etc. The two *fixpoint operators* μX and νX are treated as quantifiers. We will use $fn(\phi)$ to stand for all variables which have some free occurrence in ϕ and $bn(\phi)$ for all variables that have some bound occurrence in ϕ.

Definition 2. *In the following, we define what it means for a formula to be a guard:*

1. *@ and p are guards;*
2. *if ϕ and ψ are guards, so are $\phi \wedge \psi$, $\phi \vee \psi$ and $\phi + \psi$;*
3. *if ϕ is a guard, so are $\phi; \psi$ and $\sigma X.\phi$, where ψ is any formula of FLC$^+$.*

X is said to be guarded *in ϕ if each occurrence of X is within a subformula ψ that is a guard. If all variables in $fn(\phi) \cup bn(\phi)$ are guarded, then ϕ is called* guarded. *A formula ϕ is said to be* strictly guarded *if ϕ is guarded and for any $X \in fn(\phi) \cup bn(\phi)$, there does not exist a subformula of the forms $X + \psi$, $(X \odot \chi) + \psi$, $(X; \varphi) + \chi$ or $(X; \varphi \odot \chi) + \psi$, where $\odot \subseteq \{\vee, \wedge\}$.*

Intuitively, a variable X is said to be *guarded* means that each occurrence of X is within the scope of a modality @ or a propositional letter p.

Example 1. Formulae $\langle a \rangle; X; Y, \nu X.(\langle a \rangle \vee \langle b \rangle); X; (Y + Z), ff; X$ are guarded, but $X, \langle a \rangle \wedge X, \mu X.(X + Y) \vee [a], \mu X.(\langle a \rangle; X \vee \langle b \rangle); \mu Y.(Y + \langle a \rangle)$ are not. $\langle a \rangle; X; Y$ and $ff; X$ are strictly guarded, however, $\nu X.(\langle a \rangle \vee \langle b \rangle); X; (Y + Z)$ is not.

We will use $\mathcal{L}_{\text{FLC}^+}$ to denote all formulae of FLC$^+$ that are closed and guarded, and $\mathcal{L}_{\text{FLC}}$ for the fragment of $\mathcal{L}_{\text{FLC}^+}$ without +. In the sequel, we are only interested in closed and guarded formulae.

As in FLC, a formula of FLC$^+$ is interpreted as a *predicate transformer* which is a mapping $f : 2^{\text{BPA}_\delta^\epsilon} \to 2^{\text{BPA}_\delta^\epsilon}$. We use MPT$_T$ to represent all these predicate transformers over BPA$_\delta^\epsilon$.

The meaning of variables is given by a *valuation* ρ: $Var \to (2^{\text{BPA}_\delta^\epsilon} \to 2^{\text{BPA}_\delta^\epsilon})$ that assigns variables to functions from sets to sets. $\rho[X \rightsquigarrow f]$ agrees with ρ except for associating f with X.

Definition 3. *The meaning of a formula ϕ, under a valuation ρ, denoted by $[\![\phi]\!]_\rho$, is inductively defined as follows:*

$$[\![tt]\!]_\rho(\mathcal{A}) = \text{BPA}^\epsilon_\delta$$
$$[\![ff]\!]_\rho(\mathcal{A}) = \emptyset$$
$$[\![\sqrt{}]\!]_\rho(\mathcal{A}) = \{P \in \text{BPA}^\epsilon_\delta \mid \mathcal{T}(P)\}$$
$$[\![\tau]\!]_\rho(\mathcal{A}) = \mathcal{A}$$
$$[\![X]\!]_\rho(\mathcal{A}) = \rho(X)(\mathcal{A})$$
$$[\![[a]]\!]_\rho(\mathcal{A}) = \{P \in \text{BPA}^\epsilon_\delta \mid \neg\mathcal{T}(P) \wedge \forall P' \in \text{BPA}^\epsilon_\delta . P \xrightarrow{a} P' \Rightarrow P' \in \mathcal{A}\}$$
$$[\![\langle a \rangle]\!]_\rho(\mathcal{A}) = \{P \in \text{BPA}^\epsilon_\delta \mid \exists P' \in \text{BPA}^\epsilon_\delta . P \xrightarrow{a} P' \wedge P' \in \mathcal{A}\}$$
$$[\![\phi_1 \wedge \phi_2]\!]_\rho(\mathcal{A}) = [\![\phi_1]\!]_\rho(\mathcal{A}) \cap [\![\phi_2]\!]_\rho(\mathcal{A})$$
$$[\![\phi_1 \vee \phi_2]\!]_\rho(\mathcal{A}) = [\![\phi_1]\!]_\rho(\mathcal{A}) \cup [\![\phi_2]\!]_\rho(\mathcal{A})$$
$$[\![\phi_1 ; \phi_2]\!]_\rho = [\![\phi_1]\!]_\rho \cdot [\![\phi_2]\!]_\rho$$
$$[\![\phi_1 + \phi_2]\!]_\rho(\mathcal{A}) = \{P \in \text{BPA}^\epsilon_\delta \mid P \sim P_1 + P_2 \wedge P_1 \in [\![\phi_1]\!]_\rho(\mathcal{A}) \wedge P_2 \in [\![\phi_2]\!]_\rho(\mathcal{A})\}$$
$$[\![\mu X.\phi]\!]_\rho = \sqcap\{f \in \text{MPT}_\text{T} \mid [\![\phi]\!]_{\rho[X \rightsquigarrow f]} \subseteq f\}$$
$$[\![\nu X.\phi]\!]_\rho = \sqcup\{f \in \text{MPT}_\text{T} \mid [\![\phi]\!]_{\rho[X \rightsquigarrow f]} \supseteq f\}$$

where $\mathcal{A} \subseteq \text{BPA}^\epsilon_\delta$, and $\cdot$ *stands for the composition operator over functions.*

Note that because ϵ and δ have different behaviour in the presence of ;, they should be distinguished in FLC^+. To this end, we interpret $[a]$ differently from in [21]. According to our interpretation, $P \models [a]$ only if $\neg\mathcal{T}(P)$, whereas in [21] it is always valid that $P \models [a]$ for any $P \in \mathcal{P}^s$. Thus, it is easy to show that $\epsilon \not\models \bigwedge_{a \in Act}[a]; ff$, while $\bigwedge_{a \in Act}[a]; ff$ is the characteristic formula of δ.

As the meaning of a closed formula ϕ is independent of any environment, we sometimes write $[\![\phi]\!]$ for $[\![\phi]\!]_\rho$, where ρ is an arbitrary environment. We also abuse $\phi(\mathcal{A})$ to stand for $[\![\phi]\!]_\rho(\mathcal{A})$ if ρ is clear from the context.

The set of processes *satisfying* a given closed formula ϕ is $\phi(\text{BPA}^\epsilon_\delta)$. A process P is said to satisfy ϕ iff $P \in [\![\phi]\!]_\rho(\text{BPA}^\epsilon_\delta)$ under some valuation ρ, denoted by $P \models_\rho \phi$. If ρ is clear from the context, we directly write $P \models \phi$. $\phi \Rightarrow \psi$ means that $[\![\phi]\!]_\rho(\mathcal{A}) \subseteq [\![\psi]\!]_\rho(\mathcal{A})$ for any $\mathcal{A} \subseteq \text{BPA}^\epsilon_\delta$ and any ρ. $\phi \Leftrightarrow \psi$ means $(\phi \Rightarrow \psi) \wedge (\psi \Rightarrow \phi)$. The other notations can be defined in the standard way.

Given a formula ϕ, the set of the atomic sub-formulae *at the end* of ϕ, denoted by $\text{ESub}(\phi)$, is: $\{\phi\}$ if $\phi = p, \tau, X$ or @; $\text{ESub}(\phi_1) \cup \text{ESub}(\phi_2)$ if $\phi = \phi_1$ *op* ϕ_2 where *op* $\in \{\wedge, \vee, +\}$; if $\phi = \phi_1; \phi_2$ then if $\tau \notin \text{ESub}(\phi_1)$ then $\text{ESub}(\phi_2)$ else $(\text{ESub}(\phi_2) \backslash \{\tau\}) \cup \text{ESub}(\phi_1)$; $\text{ESub}(\phi')$ if $\phi = \sigma X.\phi'$. It is said that $\sqrt{}$ only occurs at the end of ϕ if $\sqrt{}$ can only be in $\text{ESub}(\phi)$ as a sub-formula of ϕ.

As [16] proved that FLC has the tree model property, we can also show that FLC^+ has such property as well, i.e.,

Theorem 1. *Given* $P, Q \in \text{BPA}^\epsilon_\delta$, $P \sim Q$ *iff for any* $\phi \in \mathcal{L}_{\text{FLC}^+}$, $P \models \phi$ *iff* $Q \models \phi$.

4   A Connection Between $\text{BPA}^\epsilon_\delta$ and FLC^+

In this section, we discuss how to relate the primitives of $\text{BPA}^\epsilon_\delta$ to the connectives of FLC^+.

4.1 Nondeterminism

From Definition 3, it is clear that "+" of $\text{BPA}_\delta^\epsilon$ corresponds to "+" of FLC^+. The connection can be expressed as follows:

Proposition 1. *For any $P, Q \in \text{BPA}_\delta^\epsilon$, if $P \models \phi$ and $Q \models \psi$ then $P + Q \models \phi + \psi$.*

4.2 Sequential Composition

In this subsection, we show that under some conditions, the sequential composition ";" of $\text{BPA}_\delta^\epsilon$ can be related to the chop ";" of FLC^+.

From the definition of the semantics of $\text{BPA}_\delta^\epsilon$, it is clear that as far as the execution of the process $P; Q$ is concerned, Q starts to be executed only if P finishes the execution. A similar requirement on properties concerning P must be considered in order to derive a combined property for $P; Q$ from the properties for P and Q. For example, let $P = a; b$, $Q = c; d$, and it is therefore clear that $P \models \langle a \rangle$ and $Q \models \langle c \rangle$, however $P; Q \not\models \langle a \rangle; \langle c \rangle$. So, we require that the property about P must specify full executions of P, that is, $P \models \phi; \sqrt{}$.

On the other hand, it is easy to see that ϵ is a neutral element of ";" in $\text{BPA}_\delta^\epsilon$. However, $\sqrt{}$, the counterpart of ϵ in FLC, is not the neutral element of the chop ";". Thus, we have to replace $\sqrt{}$ occurring in properties of P with τ in order to give a connection between ";" of $\text{BPA}_\delta^\epsilon$ and the chop ";" of FLC^+. E.g., let $P = a; \epsilon$ and $Q = b; \delta$, $\phi = \langle a \rangle; \sqrt{}$, and $\psi = \langle b \rangle$. It's obvious that $P \models \phi; \sqrt{}$ and $Q \models \psi$, but $P; Q \not\models \phi; \psi$. Furthermore, it is required that $\sqrt{}$ can only appear at the end of properties of P, because from Definition 3 $\sqrt{}$ as a subformula of ϕ makes all subformulae following it with ; no sense during calculating the meaning of ϕ, but they will play a nontrivial role in the resulting formula. E.g. $\epsilon \models \sqrt{}; [a]; \langle b \rangle$ and $a; c \models \langle a \rangle; \langle c \rangle$, but $\epsilon; (a; c) \not\models (\tau; [a]; \langle b \rangle); (\langle a \rangle; \langle c \rangle)$. In fact, such a requirement can be always satisfied because all formulae can be transformed to such kind of the form equivalently.

In summary, the following theorem indicates the connection between the sequential composition ";" of $\text{BPA}_\delta^\epsilon$ and the chop ";" of FLC^+.

Theorem 2. *For any $\phi, \psi \in \mathcal{L}_{\text{FLC}^+}$ and any $P, Q \in \text{BPA}_\delta^\epsilon$, if $\sqrt{}$ only occurs at the end of ϕ, $P \models \phi; \sqrt{}$ and $Q \models \psi$ then $P; Q \models \phi\{\tau/\sqrt{}\}; \psi$.*

Remark 1. Generally speaking, the converse of Theorem 2 is not valid.

4.3 Recursion

In this subsection, we sketch how to relate $rec\ x$ to νX. Thus, in the rest of this sub-section all fixed point operators occurring in formulae will be referred to ν if not otherwise stated. To this end, we first employ a relation called *syntactical confirmation* between processes and formulae, with the type $\mathcal{P}^s \times FLC^+ \mapsto \{\text{tt}, \text{ff}\}$, denoted by $\models_{sc}$.

Definition 4. *Given a formula ϕ, we associate a map from $2^{\mathcal{P}^s}$ to $2^{\mathcal{P}^s}$ with it, denoted by $\widehat{\phi}$, constructed by the following rules:*

$$\widehat{\surd}(\mathcal{E}) \mathrel{\widehat{=}} \{E \mid E \in \mathcal{P}^s \wedge T(E)\}$$

$$\widehat{tt}(\mathcal{E}) \mathrel{\widehat{=}} \mathcal{P}^s$$

$$\widehat{ff}(\mathcal{E}) \mathrel{\widehat{=}} \emptyset$$

$$\widehat{\tau}(\mathcal{E}) \mathrel{\widehat{=}} \mathcal{E}$$

$$\widehat{X}(\mathcal{E}) \mathrel{\widehat{=}} \{x; E \mid E \in \mathcal{E}\}$$

$$\widehat{\langle a \rangle}(\mathcal{E}) \mathrel{\widehat{=}} \{E \mid \exists E' \in \mathcal{E}.E \xrightarrow{a} E'\}$$

$$\widehat{[a]}(\mathcal{E}) \mathrel{\widehat{=}} \{E \mid \neg T(E) \wedge E \text{ is guarded } \wedge \forall E'.E \xrightarrow{a} E' \Rightarrow E' \in \mathcal{E}\}$$

$$\widehat{\phi_1 \wedge \phi_2}(\mathcal{E}) \mathrel{\widehat{=}} \widehat{\phi_1}(\mathcal{E}) \cap \widehat{\phi_2}(\mathcal{E})$$

$$\widehat{\phi_1 \vee \phi_2}(\mathcal{E}) \mathrel{\widehat{=}} \widehat{\phi_1}(\mathcal{E}) \cup \widehat{\phi_2}(\mathcal{E})$$

$$\widehat{\phi_1 + \phi_2}(\mathcal{E}) \mathrel{\widehat{=}} \{E \mid \exists E_1, E_2.E = E_1 + E_2 \wedge E_1 \in \widehat{\phi_1}(\mathcal{E}) \wedge E_2 \in \widehat{\phi_2}(\mathcal{E})\}$$

$$\widehat{\phi_1; \phi_2}(\mathcal{E}) \mathrel{\widehat{=}} \widehat{\phi_1} \cdot \widehat{\phi_2}(\mathcal{E})$$

$$\widehat{\sigma X.\phi}(\mathcal{E}) \mathrel{\widehat{=}} \{(rec\ x.E_1); E_2 \mid E_1 \in \widehat{\phi}(\{\epsilon\}) \wedge E_2 \in \mathcal{E}\}$$

where $\mathcal{E} \subseteq \mathcal{P}^s$.

$\models_{sc} (E, \phi) = \text{tt}$ iff $E \in \widehat{\phi}(\{\epsilon\})$; otherwise, $\models_{sc} (E, \phi) = \text{ff}$. In what follows, we denote $\models_{sc} (E, \phi) = \text{tt}$ by $E \models_{sc} \phi$ and $\models_{sc} (E, \phi) = \text{ff}$ by $E \not\models_{sc} \phi$.

Informally, $P \models_{sc} \phi$ means that P and ϕ have a similar syntax, e.g.,

Example 2. Let $E_1 \mathrel{\widehat{=}} (a; x; x) + d$, $E_2 \mathrel{\widehat{=}} x; (b + c); y$, $E_3 \mathrel{\widehat{=}} a; b; c$, $\phi \mathrel{\widehat{=}} \langle a \rangle; X; X$, $\psi \mathrel{\widehat{=}} X; \langle b \rangle; Y$ and $\varphi \mathrel{\widehat{=}} [a]; \langle b \rangle; \langle c \rangle$. We have $E_1 \models_{sc} \phi$, $E_2 \models_{sc} \psi$, $E_3 \models_{sc} \varphi$.

The following theorem states that $\models_{sc}$ itself is compositional as well.

Theorem 3. *Let $\surd$ only appear at the end of ϕ_1, ϕ_2 and ϕ. Then,*

i) if $E_1 \models_{sc} \phi_1$ and $E_2 \models_{sc} \phi_2$ then $E_1 + E_2 \models_{sc} \phi_1 + \phi_2$;

ii) if $E_1 \models_{sc} \phi_1$ and $E_2 \models_{sc} \phi_2$ then $E_1; E_2 \models_{sc} \phi_1\{\tau/\surd\}; \phi_2$;

iii) if $E \models_{sc} \phi$ then $rec\ x.E \models_{sc} \sigma X.\phi\{\tau/\surd\}$.

Example 3. In Example 2, according to Theorem 3, we obtain $E_1 + E_2 \models_{sc} \phi + \psi$, $E_3; (E_1 + E_2) \models_{sc} \varphi; (\phi + \psi)$ and $rec\ x.\ rec\ y.E_3; (E_1 + E_3) \models_{sc} \nu X.\nu Y.(\varphi; (\phi + \psi))$.

Theorem 4 establishes a connection between $\models_{sc}$ and $\models$, so that $rec\ x$ is related to νX.

Theorem 4. *If $P \in \text{BPA}_\delta^\epsilon$, $\surd$ only occurs at the end of ϕ and $P \models_{sc} \phi$, then $P \models \phi; \surd$.*

Theorem 4 provides the possibility to compositionally verify a complex system and even this can be done syntactically.

Example 4. For instance, let E_1, E_2, E_3 and ϕ, ψ, φ be as defined in Example 2. In order to verify $rec\ x.\ rec\ y.E_3; (E_1 + E_3) \models \nu X.\nu Y.(\varphi; (\phi + \psi))$, we only need to prove $E_1 + E_2 \models_{sc} \phi + \psi$ and $E_3; (E_1 + E_2) \models_{sc} \varphi; (\phi + \psi)$. This proof can further be reduced to $E_1 \models_{sc} \phi$, $E_2 \models_{sc} \psi$ and $E_3 \models_{sc} \varphi$. From Example 2, this is true.

5 Reducing $\mathcal{L}_{\text{FLC+}}$ to $\mathcal{L}_{\text{FLC}}$

In this section, we will show that as far as closed and guarded formulae are concerned, the $+$ of FLC$^+$ can be defined essentially by conjunction and disjunction, that is, for any $\phi \in \mathcal{L}_{\text{FLC+}}$, there exists a formula $\phi' \in \mathcal{L}_{\text{FLC}}$ such that $\phi \Leftrightarrow \phi'$. This can be obtained via the following three steps: firstly, we show that in some special cases "$+$" can be defined by conjunction and disjunction essentially; then we prove that the elimination of "$+$" in a strictly guarded formula ϕ of FLC$^+$ can be reduced to one of the above special cases; and finally, we complete the proof by showing that for any $\phi \in \mathcal{L}_{\text{FLC+}}$ there exists a strictly guarded formula $\phi' \in \mathcal{L}_{\text{FLC+}}$ such that $\phi \Leftrightarrow \phi'$.

The following lemma claims that in some special cases, "$+$" can be defined essentially by conjunction and disjunction.

Lemma 1. *Let* $n, k \leq m, \{a_1, \cdots, a_n\}$ *and* $\{c_1, \cdots, c_k\}$ *be subsets of* $\{b_1, \cdots, b_m\}$, *where* $b_i \neq b_j$ *if* $i \neq j$. *Assume* $< a_1, \cdots, a_n >\!\!\prec\!\!< b_1, \cdots, b_n >$ *and* $< c_1, \cdots, c_k >$ $= < b_{l_1}, \cdots, b_{l_k} >$, *where* $l_j \in \{1, \cdots, m\}$ *for* $j = 1 \cdots k$. *Then*

$$\left(\bigwedge_{i=1}^{n} \bigwedge_{j=1}^{n_i} \langle a_i \rangle; \phi_{i,j} \wedge \bigwedge_{i=1}^{m} [b_i]; \psi_i \wedge q_1\right) + \left(\bigwedge_{i=1}^{k} \bigwedge_{j=1}^{k_i} \langle c_i \rangle; \varphi_{i,j} \wedge \bigwedge_{i=1}^{m} [b_i]; \chi_i \wedge q_2\right)$$

$$\Leftrightarrow \bigwedge_{i=1}^{n} \bigwedge_{j=1}^{n_i} \langle a_i \rangle; (\phi_{i,j} \wedge \psi_i) \wedge \bigwedge_{i=1}^{k} \bigwedge_{j=1}^{k_i} \langle c_i \rangle; (\varphi_{i,j} \wedge \chi_{l_i}) \wedge \bigwedge_{i=1}^{m} [b_i]; (\psi_i \vee \chi_i) \wedge q_1 \wedge q_2$$

where $q_1 \Leftrightarrow tt$ *or* $q_1 \Leftrightarrow \tau$, *and* $q_2 \Leftrightarrow tt$ *or* $q_2 \Leftrightarrow \tau$.

Proof (Sketch). According to Definition 3, it is easy to see that $+$ and $;$ both are monotonic. On the other hand, it is not hard to prove that 1. if $P \models \langle a \rangle; \phi$, then $P + Q \models \langle a \rangle; \phi$ for any $Q \subset \text{BPA}_\delta^\epsilon$; 2. $P \models [a]; \phi$ and $Q \vdash [a]; \psi$, then $P + Q \models [a]; (\phi \vee \psi)$; 3. $([a]; \phi \wedge \langle a \rangle; \psi) \Rightarrow (\langle a \rangle; (\phi \wedge \psi) \wedge [a]; \phi)$. Thus, it is not hard to prove the forward direction.

For the converse direction, we first prove that given a $P \in \text{BPA}_\delta^\epsilon$, there exists a $Q \in \text{BPA}_\delta^\epsilon$ of the form $\sum_{a \in Act} \sum_{j=1}^{i_a} a; Q_{a,j}$ or δ such that $P \sim Q$; then by Theorem 1, P satisfies the formula of the right hand in the lemma iff Q also meets it; subsequently, we design an algorithm to partition all summands of Q into two parts $\mathcal{Q}_1$ and $\mathcal{Q}_2$ such that $\sum \mathcal{Q}_1$ satisfies the first operand of "$+$" in the left formula of the lemma, $\sum \mathcal{Q}_2$ meets the second operand. Obviously, $\sum \mathcal{Q}_1 + \sum \mathcal{Q}_2 \sim P$. Therefore, the converse direction has been proved.   ⊣

By applying the above lemma, induction on the given formula ϕ, we can show that if ϕ is strictly guarded, then there exists ϕ' such that $\phi \Leftrightarrow \phi'$ and no $+$ occurs in ϕ', i.e.

Lemma 2. *For any* ϕ *of* FLC$^+$, *if* ϕ *is strictly guarded, then there exists* ϕ' *of* FLC *such that* $\phi' \Leftrightarrow \phi$.

In the below, we will apply some rewriting techniques to prove that for any closed and guarded formula ϕ of FLC$^+$, there exists ϕ' that is strictly guarded such that $\phi \Leftrightarrow \phi'$, namely

Lemma 3. *For any $\phi \in \mathcal{L}_{FLC^+}$, there is $\phi' \in \mathcal{L}_{FLC^+}$ that is strictly guarded such that $\phi \Leftrightarrow \phi'$.*

Proof (Sketch). In order to prove the lemma, we need to show the following equations:

$$\mu X.\phi_1[@; \phi_2[(X \odot \phi_3) + \phi_4]] \Leftrightarrow \mu X.\phi_1[@; \phi_2[\mu Y.(\phi_1[@; \phi_2[Y]] \odot \phi_3) + \phi_4]] \quad (1)$$

$$\nu X.\phi_1[@; \phi_2[(X \odot \phi_3) + \phi_4]] \Leftrightarrow \nu X.\phi_1[@; \phi_2[\nu Y.(\phi_1[@; \phi_2[Y]] \odot \phi_3) + \phi_4]] \quad (2)$$

$$\mu X.\phi_1[@; \phi_2[(X; \phi_3 \odot \phi_4) + \phi_5]] \Leftrightarrow \mu X.\phi_1[@; \phi_2[\mu Y.(\phi_1[@; \phi_2[Y]]; \phi_3 \odot \phi_4) + \phi_5]] \quad (3)$$

$$\nu X.\phi_1[@; \phi_2[(X; \phi_3 \odot \phi_4) + \phi_5]] \Leftrightarrow \nu X.\phi_1[@; \phi_2[\nu Y.(\phi_1[@; \phi_2[Y]]; \phi_3 \odot \phi_4) + \phi_5]] \quad (4)$$

where $\odot \in \{\wedge, \vee\}$, $\phi_i[\ ]$ stands for a formula with the hole $[\ ]$, the formula at the left side of each equation is guarded.

We will only prove (3) as an example, the others can be proved similarly. Since $\phi_1[@; \phi_2[(X; \phi_3 \odot \phi_4) + \phi_5]]$ is guarded, by Knaster-Tarski Theorem, it is clear that $\mu X.\phi_1[@; \phi_2[(X; \phi_3 \odot \phi_4) + \phi_5]]$ is the unique least solution of the equation

$$X = \phi_1[@; \phi_2[(X; \phi_3 \odot \phi_4) + \phi_5]] \quad (5)$$

Let Y be a fresh variable and $Y = (X; \phi_3 \odot \phi_4) + \phi_5$. It is easy to see the least solution of (5) is equivalent to the X-component of the least solution of the following equation system:

$$X = \phi_1[@; \phi_2[(X; \phi_3 \odot \phi_4) + \phi_5]]$$
$$Y = (X; \phi_3 \odot \phi_4) + \phi_5$$

Meanwhile, exploiting some rewriting techniques, it is easy to transform solving the least solution of the above equation system to the following one equivalently,

$$X = \phi_1[@; \phi_2[(X; \phi_3 \odot \phi_4) + \phi_5]]$$
$$Y = (\phi_1[@; \phi_2[Y]]; \phi_3 \odot \phi_4) + \phi_5$$

It is not hard to obtain the least solution of the above equation system as $(\mu X.\phi_1[@; \phi_2[\mu Y.(\phi_1[@; \phi_2[Y]]; \phi_3 \odot \phi_4) + \phi_5]], \mu Y.(\phi_1[@; \phi_2[Y]]; \phi_3 \odot \phi_4) + \phi_5)$. Therefore, (3) follows.

Repeatedly applying (1)–(4), for any given formula $\phi \in \mathcal{L}_{FLC^+}$, we can rewrite it to ϕ' which is strictly guarded such that $\phi \Leftrightarrow \phi'$.   ⊣

Remark 2. In the proof for Lemma 3, we only consider the cases that a variable is guarded by a modality@, and ignore the cases that a variable is guarded by a propositional letter p, because according to Definition 3 it is easy to show that $p; \phi \Leftrightarrow p$.

From the above lemmas, the following result is immediate.

Theorem 5. *For any $\phi \in \mathcal{L}_{FLC^+}$, there exists $\phi' \in \mathcal{L}_{FLC}$ such that $\phi' \Leftrightarrow \phi$.*

We use the following example to demonstrate how to translate a closed and guarded formula ϕ of FLC$^+$ into a formula ϕ' of FLC by applying the above procedure.

Example 5. Let $\phi = \mu X.\nu Y.\langle a\rangle; (X+Y); X; Y; \langle b\rangle \vee \langle c\rangle$. Applying (1), it follows

$$\phi \Leftrightarrow \mu X.\nu Y.\langle a\rangle; [\mu Z.(\nu V.\langle a\rangle; Z; X; V; \langle b\rangle \vee \langle c\rangle) + Y]; X; Y; \langle b\rangle \vee \langle c\rangle \;\hat{=}\; \phi'$$

where $\phi_1[\;]\hat{=}\nu Y.[\;]; X; Y; \langle b\rangle \vee \langle c\rangle$, $\phi_2[\;]\hat{=}[\;]$, $\phi_3\hat{=} \begin{cases} tt & \text{if } \odot = \wedge \\ ff & \text{o.w.} \end{cases}$, $\phi_4\hat{=}Y$. Furthermore, applying (2), we can get

$$\phi' \Leftrightarrow \mu X.\nu Y.\langle a\rangle; [\mu Z.\nu W.(\langle a\rangle; W; X; Y; \langle b\rangle \vee \langle c\rangle) + (\nu V.\langle a\rangle; Z; X; V; \langle b\rangle \vee \langle c\rangle)];$$
$$X; Y; \langle b\rangle \vee \langle c\rangle \;\hat{=}\; \phi''$$

where $\phi_1[\;] \;\hat{=}\; [\;]; X; Y; \langle b\rangle \vee \langle c\rangle$, $\phi_2[\;] \;\hat{=}\; \mu Z.[\;]$, $\phi_3 \;\hat{=}\; \begin{cases} tt & \text{if } \odot = \wedge \\ ff & \text{o.w.} \end{cases}$,

$\phi_4 \;\hat{=}\; \nu V.\langle a\rangle; Z; X; V; \langle b\rangle \vee \langle c\rangle$. Thus, using Lemma 2, we can eliminate "+" in
ϕ'' as follows:

$$\phi'' \Leftrightarrow \mu X.\nu Y.\langle a\rangle; [\mu Z.\nu W. \begin{pmatrix} (\langle a\rangle; W; X; Y; \langle b\rangle + \langle c\rangle)\vee \\ (\langle a\rangle; W; X; Y; \langle b\rangle + \\ \nu V.\langle a\rangle; Z; X; V; \langle b\rangle)\vee \\ (\nu V.\langle a\rangle; Z; X; V; \langle b\rangle + \langle c\rangle)\vee \\ (\langle c\rangle + \langle c\rangle) \end{pmatrix}]; X; Y; \langle b\rangle \vee \langle c\rangle$$

$$\Leftrightarrow \mu X.\nu Y.\langle a\rangle; [\mu Z.\nu W. \begin{pmatrix} ((\langle a\rangle; W; X; Y; \langle b\rangle \wedge \langle c\rangle)\vee \\ (\langle a\rangle; W; X; Y; \langle b\rangle\wedge \\ \nu V.\langle a\rangle; Z; X; V; \langle b\rangle)\vee \\ (\nu V.\langle a\rangle; Z; X; V; \langle b\rangle \wedge \langle c\rangle)\vee \\ \langle c\rangle \end{pmatrix} ; X; Y; \langle b\rangle \vee \langle c\rangle$$

$$\hat{=}\; \phi^*$$

It is easy to see that $\psi \Leftrightarrow \phi^*$ and no + occurs in ϕ^*.   ⊣

In what follows, we will use $en(\phi)$ to denote the resulting formula by applying
the above procedure to ϕ in which + is eliminated.

6   Constructing Characteristic Formulae for Context-Free Processes Compositionally

Given a binary relation $\mathcal{R}$ over processes, which may be an equivalence or a
preorder, the characteristic formula for a process P up to $\mathcal{R}$ is a formula ϕ_P such
that for any process Q, $Q \models \phi_P$ if and only if $Q\mathcal{R}P$. [21] presented a method to
derive the characteristic formula for a context-free process up to strong (weak)
bisimulation by solving the equation system induced by the rewrite system of
the process in FLC. In this section, we present an algorithm to construct the
characteristic formula for a process of $\text{BPA}_\delta^\epsilon$ up to strong bisimulation directly
from its syntax in a compositional manner based on the above results, in contrast
to the semantics-based method given in [21]. We believe that our approach also
works for weak bisimulation, but it is necessary to re-interpret modalities of
FLC.

It is easy to see that $\bigwedge_{a \in Act}[a]; ff$ (Φ_δ for short) is the characteristic formula for δ, and $\sqrt{}$ for ϵ.

For simplicity, $\bigwedge_{a \in Act-A}[a]; ff$ will be abbreviated as Φ_{-A} from now on.

Definition 5. *Given a process term $E \in \mathcal{P}^s$, we associate with it a formula denoted by Ψ_E derived by the following rules:*

$$
\begin{array}{llll}
\Psi_\delta & \hat{=} \Phi_\delta, & \Psi_\epsilon & \hat{=} \sqrt{}, \\
\Psi_x & \hat{=} X, & \Psi_a & \hat{=} \Phi_{-\{a\}} \wedge (\langle a \rangle \wedge [a]), \\
\Psi_{E_1;E_2} & \hat{=} \Psi_{E_1}\{\tau/\sqrt{}\}; \Psi_{E_2}, & \Psi_{E_1+E_2} & \hat{=} \Psi_{E_1} + \Psi_{E_2}, \\
\Psi_{rec\ x.E} & \hat{=} \nu X.\Psi_E\{\tau/\sqrt{}\}.
\end{array}
$$

Regards Definition 5, we have

Lemma 4. 1. *For any $E \in \mathcal{P}^s$, $\sqrt{}$ only occurs at the end of Ψ_E;*
2. *For any $E \in \mathcal{P}^s$, $E \models_{sc} \Psi_E$ and $E \models_{sc} \Psi_E; \sqrt{}$;*
3. *For any $P \in \mathrm{BPA}^\epsilon_\delta$, $\Psi_P; \sqrt{}$ is closed and guarded.*

The following theorem states if two processes are strong bisimilar then the derived formulae are equivalent.

Theorem 6 (Completeness). *If $E_1 \sim E_2$, then $\Psi_{E_1} \Leftrightarrow \Psi_{E_2}$.*

We can show that $en(\Psi_P; \sqrt{})$ is the characteristic formula of P up to $\sim$ for each $P \in \mathrm{BPA}^\epsilon_\delta$.

Theorem 7. *For any $P \in \mathrm{BPA}^\epsilon_\delta$, $en(\Psi_P; \sqrt{})$ is the characteristic formula of P up to $\sim$.*

Remark 3. In Theorem 7, the condition that P is guarded is essential. Otherwise, the theorem is not true any more. For instance, $\nu X.(X + (\langle a \rangle \wedge [a] \wedge \Phi_{-\{a\}}))$ is equivalent to $\Psi_{rec\ x.(x+a)}$, nevertheless, $(\nu X.(X + (\langle a \rangle \wedge [a] \wedge \Phi_{-\{a\}}))); \sqrt{}$ is not the characteristic formula of $rec\ x.(x + a)$, since $rex\ x.(x + b + a)$ meets the formula, but $rex\ x.(x + b + a) \not\sim rec\ x.(x + a)$.

Example 6. Let $P \hat{=} a; \epsilon$ and $Q \hat{=} b; \delta$. Then, $\Psi_P \hat{=} (\langle a \rangle \wedge [a] \wedge \Phi_{-\{a\}}); \sqrt{}$, and , $\Psi_Q \hat{=} (\langle b \rangle \wedge [b] \wedge \Phi_{-\{b\}}); \Phi_\delta$ by Definition 5.

It's obvious that $en(\Psi_P; \sqrt{}) = \Psi_P; \sqrt{}$ is the characteristic formula of P and $en(\Psi_Q; \sqrt{}) = \Psi_Q; \sqrt{}$ is the one of Q. Furthermore, by Definition 5,

$$
en(\Psi_{rec\ x.(P;x;x;Q+P)}; \sqrt{})
$$
$$
\hat{=} en([\nu X. \left(\begin{array}{l} (\langle a \rangle \wedge [a] \wedge \Phi_{-\{a\}}); X; X; (((\langle b \rangle \wedge [b] \wedge \Phi_{-\{b\}}); \Phi_\delta)) \\ + (\langle a \rangle \wedge [a] \wedge \Phi_{-\{a\}}) \end{array} \right)]; \sqrt{}
$$
$$
\Leftrightarrow [\nu X. \left(\begin{array}{l} \langle a \rangle; X; X; ((\langle b \rangle \wedge [b] \wedge \Phi_{-\{b\}}); \Phi_\delta \wedge \langle a \rangle \wedge \\ [a]; (\tau \vee X; X; ((\langle b \rangle \wedge [b] \wedge \Phi_{-\{b\}}); \Phi_\delta) \wedge \Phi_{-\{a\}} \end{array} \right)]; \sqrt{}
$$

which is exactly the characteristic formula of $rec\ x.(a; x; x; b; \delta + a; \epsilon)$. $\dashv$

7   Concluding Remarks

In this paper, we investigated the compositionality of FLC. To this end, inspired by [10,18], we first extended FLC with the non-deterministic choice "+" and then established a connection between the primitives of BPA_δ^ϵ and the connectives of FLC^+, and finally, we proved that as far as closed and guarded formulae are concerned, "+" can be defined essentially by conjunction and disjunction in FLC.

Although introducing "+" cannot improve the expressive power of FLC, using it as an auxiliary can be applied to compositional specification and verification of a complex system, some advantages have been argued in the Introduction. As an application of the compositionality of FLC, we presented an algorithm to construct the characteristic formula of each process of BPA_δ^ϵ directly according to its syntax in contrast to the method in [21] which derives the characteristic formula for a process from the transition graph of the process. We believe that our approach also works for weak bisimulation, but it is necessary to re-interpret modalities of FLC.

Various work concerning compositionality of modal and temporal logics have been done, for example, [9,18] directly introduced the non-deterministic operator "+" into the modal μ-calculus like logics so that the resulted logics have compositionality; [3,4] discussed the compositionality of linear temporal logic [23] by introducing the chop into the logic, while [24] investigated some logic properties of the extension; [19,20] studied the compositionality of μ-calculus; [26] investigated the compositionality of a fixpoint logic in assume-guarantee style. Comparing with the previous work, the logics studied in previous work can only express regular properties, but FLC which is investigated in this paper can define non-regular properties. [9] gave a method to define characteristic formulae for finite terms of CCS up to observational congruence, [25] furthered the work by presenting an approach to define characteristic formulae for regular processes up to some preorders; Moreover, [21] gave a method to define characteristic formulae for context-free processes up to some preorders based on the rewriting system of a given process. In contrast to [21], in our approach characteristic formulae of BPA_δ^ϵ are constructed directly from syntax.

As future work, it is worth investigating the parallel operator and establishing a proof system for FLC.

References

1. L. Aceto and M. Hennessy. Termination, deadlock, and divergence. *Journal of ACM*, Vol. 39, No.1: 147-187. January, 1992.
2. H.R. Andersen, C. Stirling, G. Winskel. A compositional proof system for the modal mu-Calculus. LICS'94, pp.144-153.
3. H. Barringer, R. Kuiper, A. Pnueli. Now you may compose temporal logic specifications. In Proc. 16th STOC, pp. 51-63. 1984.
4. H. Barringer, R. Kuiper, A. Pnueli. A compositional temporal approach to a CSP-like language. In Proc. IFIP conference, The Role of Abstract Models in Information Processing, pp. 207-227. 1985.

5. J.A. Bergstra and J.W. Klop. Algebra of communication processes with abstraction. *Theoretical Computer Science*, 37:77-121. 1985.
6. A. Chandra, J. Halpern, A. Meyer and R. Parikh. Equations between regular terms and an application to process logic. In Proc. 13th STOC, pp.384-390. 1981.
7. B. Dutertre. On first order interval logic. LICS'95, pp. 36-43, 1995.
8. E.A. Emerson and C.S. Jutla. Tree automata, μ-calculus, and determinacy. In Proc. 33rd FOCS, pp.368-377. 1991.
9. S. Graf and J. Sifakis. A modal characterization of observational congruence on finite terms of CCS. *Information and Control*, 68:125-145. 1986.
10. S. Graf and J. Sifakis. A logic for the description of non-deterministic programs and their properties. *Information and Control*, 68:254-270. 1986.
11. J. Halpern, B. Moskowski, and Z. Manna. A hardware semantics based on temporal intervals. ICALP'83, LNCS 154, pp. 278-291, 1983.
12. D. Harel, D. Kozen and R. Parikh. Process Logic: Expressiveness, decidability, completeness. In IEEE FOCS'80, pp. 129-142. 1980.
13. C.A.R. Hoare. *Communicating Sequential Processes*. Prentice-Hall, 1985.
14. D. Janin and I. Walukiewicz. On the expressive completeness of the propositional μ-calculus with respect to monadic second order logic. CONCUR'96, LNCS 1119, pp.263-277. 1996.
15. D. Kozen. Results on the propositional mu-calculus. *Theoretical Computer Science*, 27:333-354. 1983.
16. M. Lange and C. Stirling. Model checking fixed point logic with chop. FOSSACS'02, LNCS 2303, pp. 250-263. 2002.
17. M. Lange. Local model checking games for fixed point logic with chop. CONCUR'02, LNCS 2421, pp. 240-254. 2002.
18. K.G. Larsen and B. Thomsen. A modal process logic. In the proc. of LICS'88, pp.203-210. 1988.
19. K.G. Larsen and X.X. Liu. Compositionality through an operational semantics of contexts. ICALP'90, LNCS 443, pp.526-539. 1990.
20. K.G. Larsen and X.X. Liu. Equation solving using modal transition systems. LICS'90, pp. 108-107. 1990.
21. M. Müller-Olm. A modal fixpoint logic with chop. STACS'99, LNCS 1563, pp.510-520. 1999.
22. R. Milner. *Communication and Concurrency.* Prentice Hall, 1989.
23. A. Pnueli. The temporal logic of programs. In Proc. 18th STOC, pp.232-239. 1977.
24. R. Rosner and A. Pnueli. A choppy logic. In the proc. of LICS'86, pp.306-313. 1986.
25. B. Steffen, A. Ingólfsdóttir. Characteristic formulae for processes with divergence. *Information and Computation*, 110:149-163. 1994.
26. M. Viswanathan and R. Viswanathan. Foundations for circular compositional reasoning. ICALP'01, LNCS 2076, pp. 835-847, 2001.
27. Naijun Zhan. Compositional properties of sequential processes. In the proc. of SVV'03, *ENTCS* 118, pp.111-128. 2005.
28. C.C. Zhou, C.A.R. Hoare, and A. Ravn. A calculus of durations. *Information Processing Letters*, 40(5):269-276, 1991.

An SLD-Resolution Calculus
for Basic Serial Multimodal Logics

Linh Anh Nguyen

Institute of Informatics, University of Warsaw,
ul. Banacha 2, 02-097 Warsaw, Poland
nguyen@mimuw.edu.pl

Abstract. We develop semantics for modal logic programs in basic serial multimodal logics, which are parameterized by an arbitrary combination of generalized versions of axioms T, B, 4, 5 (in the form, e.g.,
$4 : \Box_i \varphi \rightarrow \Box_j \Box_k \varphi$) and $I : \Box_i \varphi \rightarrow \Box_j \varphi$. We do not assume any special
restriction for the form of programs and goals. Our fixpoint semantics
and SLD-resolution calculus are defined using the direct approach and
closely reflect the axioms of the used modal logic. We prove that our
SLD-resolution calculus is sound and complete.

1 Introduction

Classical logic programming is very useful in practice and has been thoroughly
studied by many researchers. There are three standard semantics for definite
logic programs: the least model semantics, the fixpoint semantics, and the SLD-
resolution calculus (a procedural semantics) [9]. SLD-resolution was first described by Kowalski [8] for logic programming. It is a top-down procedure for
answering queries in definite logic programs. On the other hand, the fixpoint semantics of logic programs is a bottom-up method for answering queries and was
first introduced by van Emden and Kowalski [16] using the direct consequence
operator T_P. This operator is monotonic, continuous, and has the least fixpoint
$T_P \uparrow \omega = \bigcup_{n=0}^{\omega} T_P \uparrow n$, which forms the least Herbrand model of the given logic
program P.

Multimodal logics are useful in many areas of computer science. For example,
multimodal logics are used in knowledge representation and multi-agent systems
by interpreting $\Box_i \varphi$ as "agent i knows/believes that φ is true". Modal extensions
have been proposed for logic programming. There are two approaches to modal
logic programming: the direct approach [6,1,2,10,13] and the translational approach [4,14]. The first approach directly uses modalities, while the second one
translates modal logic programs to classical logic programs.

In [4], Debart *et al.* applied a functional translation technique for logic programs in multimodal logics which have a finite number of modal operators $\Box_i$
and $\Diamond_i$ of any type among KD, KT, $KD4$, $KT4$, KF and interaction axioms
of the form $\Box_i \varphi \rightarrow \Box_j \varphi$. The technique is similar to the one used in Ohlbach's
resolution calculus for modal logics [15]. Extra parameters are added to pred-
icate symbols to represent paths in the Kripke model, and special unification

D.V. Hung and M. Wirsing (Eds.): ICTAC 2005, LNCS 3722, pp. 151–165, 2005.
© Springer-Verlag Berlin Heidelberg 2005

algorithms are used to deal with them. In [14], Nonnengart proposed a semi-functional translation. His approach uses accessibility relations for translated programs, but with optimized clauses for representing properties of the accessibility relations, and does not modify unification. Nonnengart [14] applied the approach for modal logic programs in basic serial monomodal logics. He also gave an example in a multimodal logic of type $KD45$.

The translational approach seems attractive: just translate and it is done. However, the problem is more complicated. Using modal logics adds more non-determinism to the search process, which cannot be eliminated but must be dealt with in some way. In the functional translation [4], the modified unification algorithm may return many substitutions, which causes branching. In the semi-functional translation [14], additional nondeterminism is caused by clauses representing frame restrictions of the used modal logic. In the direct approach considered shortly, additional nondeterminism is caused by modal rules which are used as meta clauses. Our point of view is that the direct approach is justifiable, as it deals with modalities more closely and "modalities allow us to separate object-level and epistemic-level notions nicely".

Using the direct approach for modal logic programming, Balbiani et $al.$ [1] gave a declarative semantics and an SLD-resolution calculus for a class of logic programs in the monomodal logics KD, T, and $S4$. The work assumes that the modal operator $\Box$ does not occur in bodies of program clauses and goals. In [2], Baldoni et $al.$ gave a framework for developing declarative and operational semantics for logic programs in multimodal logics which have axioms of the form $[t_1] \ldots [t_n]\varphi \to [s_1] \ldots [s_m]\varphi$, where $[t_i]$ and $[s_j]$ are universal modal operators indexed by terms t_i and s_j, respectively. In that work, existential modal operators are disallowed in programs and goals.

In [10], we developed a fixpoint semantics, the least model semantics, and an SLD-resolution calculus in a direct way for modal logic programs in all of the basic serial monomodal logics KD, T, KDB, B, $KD4$, $S4$, $KD5$, $KD45$, and $S5$. We also extended the SLD-resolution calculus for the almost serial monomodal logics KB, $K5$, $K45$, and $KB5$. There are two important properties of our approach in [10]: no special restriction on occurrences of $\Box$ and $\Diamond$ is assumed and the semantics are formulated closely to the style of classical logic programming (as in Lloyd's book [9]).

The aim of this paper is to generalize the methods and results of our above-mentioned work for the whole class of $basic$ $serial$ $multimodal$ $logics$ (BSMM). A BSMM logic is an extension of the multimodal logic K_m with the axioms of seriality $D : \Box_i\varphi \to \Diamond_i\varphi$ and any combination of axioms of the form $T : \Box_i\varphi \to \varphi$ or $I : \Box_i\varphi \to \Box_j\varphi$ or $\varphi \to \Box_i\Diamond_j\varphi$ or $\Box_i\varphi \to \Box_j\Box_k\varphi$ or $\Diamond_i\varphi \to \Box_j\Diamond_k\varphi$, where i, j, k can be arbitrary or related somehow. Note that the last three schemata are generalized versions of the axioms B, 4, and 5, respectively.

Using the framework presented in our manuscript [13], we give a fixpoint semantics, the least model semantics, and an SLD-resolution calculus for modal logic programs in any BSMM logic. We prove that the calculus is sound and complete. Due to the lack of space, we do not present proofs involving with the fixpoint semantics and the least model semantics.

From the view of SLD-resolution, our idea is to use labeled existential modal operators to break a complex goal into simple goal atoms and to use modal axioms as meta clauses. For example, we cannot break $\leftarrow \Diamond_i(A \wedge B)$ into $\leftarrow \Diamond_i A, \Diamond_i B$, but if we label the operator $\Diamond_i$ by X then we can safely break $\leftarrow \langle X \rangle_i(A \wedge B)$ into $\leftarrow \langle X \rangle_i A, \langle X \rangle_i B$. Additionally, for example, we use the axiom $\Diamond_i \varphi \rightarrow \Box_j \Diamond_k \varphi$ (and their reverse $\Diamond_j \Box_k \varphi \rightarrow \Box_i \varphi$) in the form of meta clauses $\triangle \Box_j \Diamond_k \triangle' E \leftarrow \triangle \Diamond_i \triangle' E$ and $\triangle \Box_i \triangle' E \leftarrow \triangle \Diamond_j \Box_k \triangle' E$, where $\triangle$ and $\triangle'$ are sequences of modal operators and E is a classical atom.

2 Preliminaries

2.1 Syntax and Semantics of Quantified Multimodal Logics

A language for quantified multimodal logics is an extension of the language of classical predicate logic with modal operators $\Box_i$ and $\Diamond_i$, for $1 \leq i \leq m$ (where m is fixed). The modal operators $\Box_i$ and $\Diamond_i$ can take various meanings. For example, $\Box_i$ can stand for "the agent i believes" and $\Diamond_i$ for "it is considered possible by agent i". The operators $\Box_i$ are called universal modal operators, while $\Diamond_i$ are called existential modal operators. Terms and formulas are defined in the usual way, with the addition that if φ is a formula then $\Box_i \varphi$ and $\Diamond_i \varphi$ are also formulas.

A *Kripke frame* is a tuple $\langle W, \tau, R_1, \ldots, R_m \rangle$, where W is a nonempty set of possible worlds, $\tau \in W$ is the *actual world*, and R_i for $1 \leq i \leq m$ is a binary relation on W, called the *accessibility relation* for the modal operators $\Box_i, \Diamond_i$. If $R_i(w, u)$ holds then we say that u is accessible from w via R_i.

A *fixed-domain Kripke model with rigid terms*, hereafter simply called a Kripke model or just a model, is a tuple $M = \langle D, W, \tau, R_1, \ldots, R_m, \pi \rangle$, where D is a set called the *domain*, $\langle W, \tau, R_1, \ldots, R_m \rangle$ is a Kripke frame, and π is an interpretation of constant symbols, function symbols and predicate symbols. For a constant symbol a, $\pi(a)$ is an element of D, denoted by a^M. For an n-ary function symbol f, $\pi(f)$ is a function from D^n to D, denoted by f^M. For an n-ary predicate symbol p and a world $w \in W$, $\pi(w)(p)$ is an n-ary relation on D, denoted by $p^{M,w}$.

A *model graph* is a tuple $\langle W, \tau, R_1, \ldots, R_m, H \rangle$, where $\langle W, \tau, R_1, \ldots, R_m \rangle$ is a Kripke frame and H is a function that maps each world of W to a set of formulas.

Every model graph $\langle W, \tau, R_1, \ldots, R_m, H \rangle$ corresponds to a Herbrand model $M = \langle \mathcal{U}, W, \tau, R_1, \ldots, R_m, \pi \rangle$ specified by: $\mathcal{U}$ is the Herbrand universe (i.e. the set of all ground terms), $c^M = c$, $f^M(t_1, \ldots, t_n) = f(t_1, \ldots, t_n)$, and $((t_1, \ldots, t_n) \in p^{M,w}) \equiv (p(t_1, \ldots, t_n) \in H(w))$, where $t_1, \ldots, t_n$ are ground terms. We will sometimes treat a model graph as its corresponding model.

A *variable assignment* V w.r.t. a Kripke model M is a function that maps each variable to an element of the domain of M. The value of $t^M[V]$ for a term t is defined as usual.

Given some Kripke model $M = \langle D, W, \tau, R_1, \ldots, R_m, \pi \rangle$, some variable assignment V, and some world $w \in W$, the *satisfaction relation* $M, V, w \vDash \psi$ for a formula ψ is defined as follows:

$$M, V, w \vDash p(t_1, \ldots, t_n) \quad \text{iff} \quad (t_1^M[V], \ldots, t_n^M[V]) \in p^{M,w};$$
$$M, V, w \vDash \Box_i \varphi \qquad \text{iff} \quad \text{for all } v \in W \text{ such that } R_i(w, v), M, V, v \vDash \varphi;$$
$$M, V, w \vDash \forall x. \varphi \qquad \text{iff} \quad \text{for all } a \in D, (M, V', w \vDash \varphi),$$
$$\text{where } V'(x) = a \text{ and } V'(y) = V(y) \text{ for } y \neq x;$$

and as usual for the other cases (treating $\Diamond_i \varphi$ as $\neg \Box_i \neg \varphi$, and $\exists x. \varphi$ as $\neg \forall x. \neg \varphi$). We say that M satisfies φ, or φ is true in M, and write $M \vDash \varphi$, if $M, V, \tau \vDash \varphi$ for every V. For a set Γ of formulas, we call M a model of Γ and write $M \vDash \Gamma$ if $M \vDash \varphi$ for every $\varphi \in \Gamma$.

If the class of admissible interpretations contains all Kripke models (with no restrictions on the accessibility relations) then we have a quantified multimodal logic which has a standard Hilbert-style axiomatization denoted by K_m. Other *normal (multi)modal logics* are obtained by adding certain axioms to K_m. Mostly used axioms are ones that correspond to a certain restriction on the Kripke frame defined by a classical first-order formula using the accessibility relations. For example, the axiom $(D) : \Box_i \varphi \to \Diamond_i \varphi$ corresponds to the frame restriction $\forall x \, \exists y \, R_i(x, y)$. Normal modal logics containing this axiom (for all $1 \leq i \leq m$) are called *serial* modal logics.

For a normal modal logic L whose class of admissible interpretations can be characterized by classical first-order formulas of the accessibility relations, we call such formulas L-*frame restrictions*, and call frames with such properties L-*frames*. We call a model M with an L-frame an L-*model*. We say that φ is L-*satisfiable* if there exists an L-model of φ, i.e. an L-model satisfying φ. A formula φ is said to be L-*valid* and called an L-*tautology* if φ is true in every L-model. For a set Γ of formulas, we write $\Gamma \vDash_L \varphi$ and call φ a *logical consequence* of Γ in L if φ is true in every L-model of Γ.

2.2   Basic Serial Multimodal Logics

A normal multimodal logic can be characterized by axioms extending the system K_m. Consider the class $BSMM$ of basic serial multimodal logics specified as follows. A $BSMM$ logic is a normal multimodal logic parameterized by relations $AD/1, AT/1, AI/2, AB/2, A4/3, A5/3$ on the set $\{1, \ldots, m\}$, where the numbers on the right are arities and AD is required to be full. These relations specify the following axioms:

$$\begin{aligned}
\Box_i \varphi \to \Diamond_i \varphi & \qquad \text{if } AD(i) \\
\Box_i \varphi \to \varphi & \qquad \text{if } AT(i) \\
\Box_i \varphi \to \Box_j \varphi & \qquad \text{if } AI(i, j) \\
\varphi \to \Box_i \Diamond_j \varphi & \qquad \text{if } AB(i, j) \\
\Box_i \varphi \to \Box_j \Box_k \varphi & \qquad \text{if } A4(i, j, k) \\
\Diamond_i \varphi \to \Box_j \Diamond_k \varphi & \qquad \text{if } A5(i, j, k)
\end{aligned}$$

It can be shown that the above axioms correspond to the following frame restrictions in the sense that by adding some of the axioms to the system K_m

we obtain an axiomatization system which is sound and complete with respect to the class of admissible interpretations that satisfy the corresponding frame restrictions.

Axiom	Corresponding Condition
$\Box_i\varphi \to \Diamond_i\varphi$	$\forall u\, \exists v\, R_i(u,v)$
$\Box_i\varphi \to \varphi$	$\forall u\, R_i(u,u)$
$\Box_i\varphi \to \Box_j\varphi$	$R_j \subseteq R_i$
$\varphi \to \Box_i\Diamond_j\varphi$	$\forall u,v\ (R_i(u,v) \to R_j(v,u))$
$\Box_i\varphi \to \Box_j\Box_k\varphi$	$\forall u,v,w\ (R_j(u,v) \wedge R_k(v,w) \to R_i(u,w))$
$\Diamond_i\varphi \to \Box_j\Diamond_k\varphi$	$\forall u,v,w\ (R_i(u,v) \wedge R_j(u,w) \to R_k(w,v))$

For a $BSMM$ logic L, we define the set of L-frame restrictions to be the set of the frame restrictions corresponding to the tuples of the relations AD, AT, AI, AB, $A4$, $A5$. We also use $BSMM$ to denote an arbitrary logic belonging to the $BSMM$ class.

For further reading on first-order modal logic, see, e.g., [3,7].

2.3 Modal Logic Programs

A *modality* is a sequence of modal operators, which may be empty. A *universal modality* is a modality containing only universal modal operators. We use $\triangle$ to denote a modality and $\boxdot$ to denote a universal modality. Similarly as in classical logic programming, we use the clausal form $\boxdot(\varphi \leftarrow \psi_1, \ldots, \psi_n)$ to denote the formula $\forall(\boxdot(\varphi \vee \neg\psi_1 \ldots \vee \neg\psi_n))$. We use E to denote a classical atom.

A *program clause* is a formula of the form $\boxdot(A \leftarrow B_1, \ldots, B_n)$, where $n \geq 0$ and $A, B_1, \ldots, B_n$ are formulas of the form E, $\Box_i E$, or $\Diamond_i E$. $\boxdot$ is called the *modal context*, A the *head*, and $B_1, \ldots, B_n$ the *body* of the program clause. An *MProlog program* is a finite set of program clauses.

An *MProlog goal atom* is a formula of the form $\boxdot E$ or $\boxdot\Diamond_i E$. An *MProlog goal* is a formula written in the clausal form $\leftarrow \alpha_1, \ldots, \alpha_k$, where each α_i is an MProlog goal atom. We denote the *empty goal* (the *empty clause*) by $\diamond$.

Let P be an MProlog program and $G = \leftarrow \alpha_1, \ldots, \alpha_k$ be an MProlog goal. An *answer* θ for $P \cup \{G\}$ is a substitution whose domain is the set of all variables of G. We say that θ is a *correct answer* in L for $P \cup \{G\}$ if θ is an answer for $P \cup \{G\}$ and $P \vDash_L \forall((\alpha_1 \wedge \ldots \wedge \alpha_k)\theta)$.

It is shown in [11] that MProlog has the same expressiveness power as the general Horn fragment in normal modal logics.

3 Semantics of MProlog Programs in BSMM

In this section, we present a fixpoint semantics, the least model semantics, and an SLD-resolution calculus for MProlog programs in a BSMM logic L.

3.1 Labeled Modal Operators

When applying the direct consequence operator $T_{L,P}$ for an MProlog program P in L, if we obtain an "atom" of the form $\triangle\Diamond_i E$, where $\triangle$ is a sequence of modal operators, then to simplify the task we label the modal operator $\Diamond_i$. Labeling allows us to address the chosen world(s) in which this particular E must hold. A natural way is to label $\Diamond_i$ by E to obtain $\langle E \rangle_i$. On the other hand, when dealing with SLD-derivation, we cannot change a goal $\leftarrow \Diamond_i(A \wedge B)$ to $\leftarrow \Diamond_i A, \Diamond_i B$. But if we label the operator $\Diamond_i$, let's say by X, then we can safely change $\leftarrow \langle X \rangle_i(A \wedge B)$ to $\leftarrow \langle X \rangle_i A, \langle X \rangle_i B$.

We will use the following notations:

- $\top$: the *truth* symbol, with the usual semantics;
- E, F : classical atoms (which may contain variables) or $\top$;
- X, Y, Z : variables for classical atoms or $\top$, called *atom variables*;
- $\langle E \rangle_i$, $\langle X \rangle_i$: $\Diamond_i$ labeled by E or X;
- ∇ : $\Box_i$, $\Diamond_i$, $\langle E \rangle_i$, or $\langle X \rangle_i$, called a modal operator;
- $\triangle$: a (possibly empty) sequence of modal operators, called a *modality*;
- $\boxdot$: a *universal modality*;
- A, B : formulas of the form E or ∇E, called *simple atoms*;
- α, β : formulas of the form $\triangle E$, called *atoms*;
- φ, ψ : *(labeled) formulas* (i.e. formulas that may contain $\langle E \rangle_i$ and $\langle X \rangle_i$).

We use subscripts beside ∇ to indicate modal indexes in the same way as for $\Box$ and $\Diamond$. To distinguish a number of modal operators we use superscripts of the form (i), e.g. $\Box^{(1)}$, $\Box^{(2)}$, $\nabla^{(i)}$, $\nabla^{(i')}$.

A *ground formula* is a formula with no variables and no atom variables. A modal operator is said to be *ground* if it is $\Box_i$, $\Diamond_i$, or $\langle E \rangle_i$ with E being $\top$ or a ground classical atom. A *ground modality* is a modality that contains only ground modal operators. A *labeled modal operator* is a modal operator of the form $\langle E \rangle_i$ or $\langle X \rangle_i$.

Denote $EdgeLabels = \{\langle E \rangle_i \mid E \in \mathcal{B} \cup \{\top\}$ and $1 \leq i \leq m\}$, where $\mathcal{B}$ is the Herbrand base (i.e. the set of all ground classical atoms). The semantics of $\langle E \rangle_i \in EdgeLabels$ is specified as follows. Let $M = \langle D, W, \tau, R_1, \ldots, R_m, \pi \rangle$ be a Kripke model. A $\Diamond$-*realization function on* M is a partial function $\sigma :$ $W \times EdgeLabels \to W$ such that if $\sigma(w, \langle E \rangle_i) = u$, then $R_i(w, u)$ holds and $M, u \vDash E$. Given a $\Diamond$-realization function σ, a world $w \in W$, and a ground formula φ, the satisfaction relation $M, \sigma, w \vDash \varphi$ is defined in the usual way, except that $M, \sigma, w \vDash \langle E \rangle_i \psi$ iff $\sigma(w, \langle E \rangle_i)$ is defined and $M, \sigma, \sigma(w, \langle E \rangle_i) \vDash \psi$. We write $M, \sigma \vDash \varphi$ to denote that $M, \sigma, \tau \vDash \varphi$. For a set I of ground atoms, we write $M, \sigma \vDash I$ to denote that $M, \sigma \vDash \alpha$ for all $\alpha \in I$; we write $M \vDash I$ and call M a model of I if $M, \sigma \vDash I$ for *some* σ.

3.2   Model Generators

A modality is in *labeled form* if it does not contain modal operators of the form $\Diamond_i$ or $\langle \top \rangle_i$. An atom is in *labeled form* (resp. *almost labeled form*) if it is of the form $\triangle E$ (resp. $\triangle A$) with $\triangle$ in labeled form.

A *model generator* is a set of ground atoms not containing $\Diamond_i$, $\langle \top \rangle_i$, $\top$.

We will define the *standard L-model* of a model generator I so that it is a *least L-model* of I (where a model M is *less than or equal to* a model M' if

Table 1. A schema for semantics of MProlog in $BSMM$

$L = BSMM$

Rules specifying Ext_L and Sat_L:

$$\triangle\langle E\rangle_i\alpha \rightarrow \triangle\diamondsuit_i\alpha \tag{1}$$
$$\triangle\square_i\alpha \rightarrow \triangle\diamondsuit_i\alpha \tag{2}$$
$$\triangle\square_i\alpha \rightarrow \triangle\alpha \quad \text{if } AT(i) \tag{3}$$
$$\triangle\alpha \rightarrow \triangle\diamondsuit_i\alpha \quad \text{if } AT(i) \tag{4}$$
$$\triangle\square_i\alpha \rightarrow \triangle\square_j\alpha \quad \text{if } AI(i,j) \tag{5}$$
$$\triangle\diamondsuit_j\alpha \rightarrow \triangle\diamondsuit_i\alpha \quad \text{if } AI(i,j) \tag{6}$$
$$\triangle\alpha \rightarrow \triangle\square_i\diamondsuit_j\alpha \quad \text{if } AB(i,j) \tag{7}$$
$$\triangle\diamondsuit_i\square_j\alpha \rightarrow \triangle\alpha \quad \text{if } AB(i,j) \tag{8}$$
$$\triangle\square_i\alpha \rightarrow \triangle\square_j\square_k\alpha \quad \text{if } A4(i,j,k) \tag{9}$$
$$\triangle\diamondsuit_j\diamondsuit_k\alpha \rightarrow \triangle\diamondsuit_i\alpha \quad \text{if } A4(i,j,k) \tag{10}$$
$$\triangle\diamondsuit_i\alpha \rightarrow \triangle\square_j\diamondsuit_k\alpha \quad \text{if } A5(i,j,k) \tag{11}$$
$$\triangle\diamondsuit_j\square_k\alpha \rightarrow \triangle\square_i\alpha \quad \text{if } A5(i,j,k) \tag{12}$$

Rules specifying $rSat_L$:

$$\triangle\diamondsuit_i\alpha \leftarrow \triangle\langle X\rangle_i\alpha \quad \text{where } X \text{ is a fresh atom variable} \tag{1}$$
$$\triangle\nabla_i\alpha \leftarrow \triangle\square_i\alpha \tag{2}$$

plus a rule $\alpha \leftarrow \beta$ for each k-th rule $\beta \rightarrow \alpha$ specifying Sat_L,
$\quad k \geq 3$, with the same accompanying condition $\qquad$ (3)..(12)

Comments w.r.t. [13]:
$\quad \preceq_L$ is denoted by $\preceq$ and defined in page 158.
$\quad$ No restrictions on L-normal form of modalities.
$\quad$ No rules specifying NF_L and rNF_L.

---

for every positive ground formula φ without labeled operators, if $M \vDash \varphi$ then $M' \vDash \varphi$). In the construction we will use the operator Ext_L defined below.

A *forward rule* is a schema of the form $\alpha \rightarrow \beta$, while a *backward rule* is a schema of the form $\alpha \leftarrow \beta$. A rule can be accompanied with some conditions specifying when the rule can be applied.

The *operator* Ext_L is specified by the corresponding forward rules given in Table 1. Given a model generator I, $Ext_L(I)$ is the least extension of I that contains all ground atoms in labeled form that are derivable from some atom of I using the rules specifying Ext_L.

Define $Serial = \{\square\langle\top\rangle_i\top \mid 1 \leq i \leq m\}$.

Let I be a model generator. The *standard L-model* of I is defined as follows. Let $W' = EdgeLabels^*$ (i.e. the set of finite sequences of elements of $\{\langle E\rangle_i \mid E \in \mathcal{B} \cup \{\top\}$ and $1 \leq i \leq m\}$), $\tau = \epsilon$, $H(\tau) = Ext_L(I) \cup Serial$. Let $R'_i \subseteq W' \times W'$ and $H(u)$, for $u \in W'$, $u \neq \tau$, be the least sets such that:

- if $\langle E\rangle_i\alpha \in H(w)$, then $R'_i(w, w\langle E\rangle_i)$ holds and $\{E, \alpha\} \subseteq H(w\langle E\rangle_i)$;
- if $\square_i\alpha \in H(w)$ and $R'_i(w, w\langle E\rangle_i)$ holds, then $\alpha \in H(w\langle E\rangle_i)$.

Let R_i, for $1 \leq i \leq m$, be the least extension of R_i' such that $\{R_i \mid 1 \leq i \leq m\}$ satisfies all the L-frame restrictions except seriality (which is cared by $Serial$)[1]. Let W be W' without worlds not accessible directly nor indirectly from τ via the accessibility relations R_i. We call the model graph $\langle W, \tau, R_1, \ldots, R_m, H \rangle$ the *standard L-model graph* of I, and its corresponding model M the *standard L-model* of I. $\{R_i' \mid 1 \leq i \leq m\}$ is called the *skeleton* of M. By the *standard $\Diamond$-realization function on M* we call the $\Diamond$-realization function σ defined as follows: if $R_i'(w, w\langle E \rangle_i)$ holds then $\sigma(w, \langle E \rangle_i) = w\langle E \rangle_i$, else $\sigma(w, \langle E \rangle_i)$ is undefined.

It is shown in [11] that *the standard L-model of a model generator I is a least L-model of I.*

3.3 Fixpoint Semantics

We now consider the direct consequence operator $T_{L,P}$. Given a model generator I, how can $T_{L,P}(I)$ be defined? Basing on the axioms of L, I is first extended to the *L-saturation* of I, denoted by $Sat_L(I)$, which is a set of atoms. Next, *L-instances of program clauses* of P are *applied* to the atoms of $Sat_L(I)$. This is done by the operator $T_{0L,P}$. Then $T_{L,P}(I)$ is defined as $T_{0L,P}(Sat_L(I))$.

To compare modal operators we define $\preceq$ to be the least reflexive and transitive binary relation between modal operators such that $\Diamond_i \preceq \langle E \rangle_i \preceq \Box_i$ and $\Diamond_i \preceq \langle X \rangle_i \preceq \Box_i$.

An atom $\nabla^{(1)} \ldots \nabla^{(n)} \alpha$ is called an *instance* of an atom $\nabla^{(1')} \ldots \nabla^{(n')} \alpha'$ if there exists a substitution θ such that $\alpha = \alpha' \theta$ and $\nabla^{(i)} \preceq \nabla^{(i')} \theta$ for all $1 \leq i \leq n$ (treating $\nabla^{(i')}$ as an expression). For example, $\langle X \rangle_1 \Diamond_2 E$ is an instance of $\Box_1 \langle F \rangle_2 E$.

A modality $\triangle$ is called an *instance* of $\triangle'$, and we also say that $\triangle'$ is *equal to* or *more general in L than* $\triangle$ (hereby we define a *pre-order between modalities*), if $\triangle E$ is an instance of $\triangle' E$ for some ground classical atom E.

Let $\boxdot$ and $\boxdot'$ be universal modalities. We say that $\boxdot$ is an *L-context instance* of $\boxdot'$ if $\boxdot' \varphi \to \boxdot \psi$ is L-valid (for every ψ). This is defined semantically, and in general, the problem of checking whether $\boxdot$ is an L-context instance of $\boxdot'$ for an *input* BSMM logic L is perhaps undecidable. However, the problem is decidable for many modal logics, including basic monomodal logics, multimodal logics of belief [11], and regular grammar logics [5].

Let φ and φ' be program clauses with empty modal context. We say that $\boxdot \varphi$ is an *L-instance* of (a program clause) $\boxdot' \varphi'$ if $\boxdot$ is an L-context instance of $\boxdot'$ and there exists a substitution θ such that $\varphi = \varphi' \theta$.

We now give definitions for Sat_L and $T_{0L,P}$.

The *saturation operator Sat_L* is specified by the corresponding forward rules given in Table 1. Given a model generator I, $Sat_L(I)$ is the least extension of I that contains all ground atoms in *almost* labeled form that are derivable from some atom in I using the rules specifying Sat_L. (Note that the rules specifying Sat_L are the same as the rules specifying Ext_L, but these operators are different.)

---

[1] The least extension exists due to the assumption that all L-frame restrictions not concerning seriality are classical first-order Horn formulas.

When computing the least fixpoint of a modal logic program, whenever an atom of the form $\triangle \Diamond_i E$ is introduced, we "fix" the $\Diamond$ by replacing the atom by $\triangle \langle E \rangle_i E$. This leads to the following definition. The *forward labeled form* of an atom α is the atom α' such that if α is of the form $\triangle \Diamond_i E$ then $\alpha' = \triangle \langle E \rangle_i E$, else $\alpha' = \alpha$.

Let P be an L-MProlog program. The *operator* $T_{0L,P}$ is defined as follows: for a set I of ground atoms in almost labeled form, $T_{0L,P}(I)$ is the least (w.r.t. $\subseteq$) model generator such that if $\boxdot (A \leftarrow B_1, \ldots, B_n)$ is a ground L-instance of some program clause of P and $\triangle$ is a maximally general[2] ground modality *in labeled form* such that $\triangle$ is an L-instance of $\boxdot$ and $\triangle B_i$ is an instance of some atom of I for every $1 \leq i \leq n$, then the forward labeled form of $\triangle A$ belongs to $T_{0L,P}(I)$.

Define $T_{L,P}(I) = T_{0L,P}(Sat_L(I))$. By definition, the operators Sat_L and $T_{0L,P}$ are both increasingly monotonic and compact. Hence the operator $T_{L,P}$ is monotonic and continuous. By the Kleene theorem, it follows that $T_{L,P}$ has the least fixpoint $T_{L,P} \uparrow \omega = \bigcup_{n=0}^{\omega} T_{L,P} \uparrow n$, where $T_{L,P} \uparrow 0 = \emptyset$ and $T_{L,P} \uparrow n = T_{L,P}(T_{L,P} \uparrow (n-1))$ for $n > 0$.

Denote the least fixpoint $T_{L,P} \uparrow \omega$ by $I_{L,P}$ and the standard L-model of $I_{L,P}$ by $M_{L,P}$. It is shown in [11] that $M_{L,P}$ *is a least L-model of P.*

Example 1. Consider the multimodal logic L specified by $m = 2$, $AD = \{1, 2\}$, $AT = \{1\}$, $AI = \{(2,1)\}$, and $AB = A4 = A5 = \emptyset$. In other words, the logic is characterized by the axioms: $\Box_1 \varphi \rightarrow \Diamond_1 \varphi$; $\Box_2 \varphi \rightarrow \Diamond_2 \varphi$; $\Box_1 \varphi \rightarrow \varphi$; and $\Box_2 \varphi \rightarrow \Box_1 \varphi$. Consider the following program P:

$$\varphi_1 = \Diamond_2 p(a) \leftarrow$$
$$\varphi_2 = \Box_2(\Box_1 q(x) \leftarrow \Diamond_2 p(x))$$
$$\varphi_3 = \Box_2(r(x) \leftarrow p(x), q(x))$$

We have $T_{L,P} \uparrow 1 = \{\langle p(a) \rangle_2 p(a)\}$ and

$$Sat_L(T_{L,P} \uparrow 1) = \{\langle p(a) \rangle_2 p(a), \langle p(a) \rangle_2 \Diamond_1 p(a), \langle p(a) \rangle_2 \Diamond_2 p(a)\}$$

The program clause φ_2 has two L-instances applicable to $Sat_L(T_{L,P} \uparrow 1)$: the clause φ_2 itself and $\Box_1 q(x) \leftarrow \Diamond_2 p(x)$. Applying these clauses to $Sat_L(T_{L,P} \uparrow 1)$, we obtain $T_{L,P} \uparrow 2 = T_{L,P} \uparrow 1 \cup \{\langle p(a) \rangle_2 \Box_1 q(a), \Box_1 q(a)\}$. Observe that the set $Sat_L(T_{L,P} \uparrow 2)$ contain both $\langle p(a) \rangle_2 p(a)$ and $\langle p(a) \rangle_2 q(a)$. Hence, by applying the program clause φ_3, we have $\langle p(a) \rangle_2 r(a) \in T_{L,P} \uparrow 3$ and arrive at

$$I_{L,P} = T_{L,P} \uparrow 3 = \{\langle p(a) \rangle_2 p(a), \langle p(a) \rangle_2 \Box_1 q(a), \Box_1 q(a), \langle p(a) \rangle_2 r(a)\}$$

3.4 SLD-Resolution

The main work in developing an SLD-resolution calculus for MProlog in L is to specify a reverse analogue of the operator $T_{L,P}$. The operator $T_{L,P}$ is a composition of Sat_L and $T_{0L,P}$. So, we have to investigate reversion of these operators.

---

[2] W.r.t. the pre-order between modalities described earlier.

A *goal* is a clause of the form $\leftarrow \alpha_1, \ldots, \alpha_k$, where each α_i is an atom.

The following definition concerns reversion of the operator $T_{0L,P}$.

Let $G = \leftarrow \alpha_1, \ldots, \alpha_i, \ldots, \alpha_k$ be a goal and $\varphi = \square(A \leftarrow B_1, \ldots, B_n)$ a program clause. Then G' is *derived* from G and φ in L using mgu θ, and called an *L-resolvent* of G and φ, if the following conditions hold:

- $\alpha_i = \triangle' A'$, with $\triangle'$ *in labeled form*, is called the *selected atom*, and A' is called the *selected head atom*;
- $\triangle'$ is an instance of a universal modality $\square'$ and $\square'(A \leftarrow B_1, \ldots, B_n)$ is an L-instance of the program clause φ;
- θ is an mgu of A' and the forward labeled form of A;
- G' is the goal $\leftarrow (\alpha_1, \ldots, \alpha_{i-1}, \triangle' B_1, \ldots, \triangle' B_n, \alpha_{i+1}, \ldots, \alpha_k)\theta$.

As a reverse analogue of the operator Sat_L, we provide the operator $rSat_L$, which is specified by the corresponding backward rules given in Table 1. We say that $\beta = rSat_L(\alpha)$ *using an $rSat_L$ rule* $\alpha' \leftarrow \beta'$ if $\alpha \leftarrow \beta$ is of the form $\alpha' \leftarrow \beta'$. We write $\beta = rSat_L(\alpha)$ to denote that "$\beta = rSat_L(\alpha)$ using some $rSat_L$ rule".

Let $G = \leftarrow \alpha_1, \ldots, \alpha_i, \ldots, \alpha_k$ be a goal. If $\alpha'_i = rSat_L(\alpha_i)$ using an $rSat_L$ rule φ, then $G' = \leftarrow \alpha_1, \ldots, \alpha_{i-1}, \alpha'_i, \alpha_{i+1}, \ldots, \alpha_k$ is *derived* from G and φ, and we call G' an *(L-)resolvent* of G and φ, and α_i the *selected atom* of G.

Observe that $rSat_L$ rules are similar to program clauses and the way of applying them is similar to the way of applying classical program clauses, except that we do not need mgu's.

We now define SLD-derivation and SLD-refutation.

Let P be an MProlog program and G a goal. An *SLD-derivation* from $P \cup \{G\}$ in L consists of a (finite or infinite) sequence $G_0 = G, G_1, \ldots$ of goals, a sequence $\varphi_1, \varphi_2, \ldots$ of variants of program clauses of P or $rSat_L$ rules, and a sequence $\theta_1, \theta_2, \ldots$ of mgu's such that if φ_i is a variant of a program clause then G_i is derived from G_{i-1} and φ_i in L using θ_i, else $\theta_i = \varepsilon$ (the empty substitution) and G_i is derived from G_{i-1} and (the $rSat_L$ rule variant) φ_i. Each φ_i is called an *input clause/rule* of the derivation.

We assume *standardizing variables apart* as usual (see [9]).

An *SLD-refutation* of $P \cup \{G\}$ in L is a finite SLD-derivation from $P \cup \{G\}$ in L which has the empty clause as the last goal in the derivation.

Let P be an MProlog program and G a goal. A *computed answer* θ in L of $P \cup \{G\}$ is the substitution obtained by restricting the composition $\theta_1 \ldots \theta_n$ to the variables of G, where $\theta_1, \ldots, \theta_n$ is the sequence of mgu's used in an SLD-refutation of $P \cup \{G\}$ in L.

Example 2. Reconsider the modal logic L and the program P given in Example 1. Let $G = \leftarrow \Diamond_2 r(x)$. We give below an SLD-refutation of $P \cup \{G\}$ in L with computed answer $\{x/a\}$.

Goals	Input clauses/rules	MGUs
$\leftarrow \Diamond_2 r(x)$		
$\leftarrow \langle X \rangle_2 r(x)$	(1)	
$\leftarrow \langle X \rangle_2 p(x), \langle X \rangle_2 q(x)$	φ_3	$\{x_2/x\}$

$$\leftarrow \langle p(a)\rangle_2 q(a) \qquad \varphi_1 \qquad \{X/p(a), x/a\}$$
$$\leftarrow \langle p(a)\rangle_2 \square_1 q(a) \qquad (3)$$
$$\leftarrow \langle p(a)\rangle_2 \Diamond_2 p(a) \qquad \varphi_2 \qquad \{x_5/a\}$$
$$\leftarrow \langle p(a)\rangle_2 \Diamond_1 p(a) \qquad (6)$$
$$\leftarrow \langle p(a)\rangle_2 p(a) \qquad (4)$$
$$\Diamond \qquad\qquad\qquad \varphi_1$$

4   Soundness and Completeness of SLD-Resolution

In this section, we prove soundness and completeness of the SLD-resolution calculus given for MProlog in BSMM, which are stated as follows.

Theorem 1. *Let L be a BSMM logic, P an MProlog program, and G an MProlog goal. Then every computed answer in L of $P \cup \{G\}$ is a correct answer in L of $P \cup \{G\}$. Conversely, for every correct answer θ in L of $P \cup \{G\}$, there exists a computed answer γ in L of $P \cup \{G\}$ which is more general than θ (i.e. $\theta = \gamma\delta$ for some δ).*

4.1   How to Prove?

In [13], we presented a general framework for developing fixpoint semantics, the least model semantics, and SLD-resolution calculi for logic programs in multimodal logics and proved that under certain expected properties of a concrete instantiation of the framework for a specific multimodal logic, the SLD-resolution calculus is sound and complete. The semantics of MProlog in BSMM presented in the previous section and summarized in Table 1 are based on and compatible with the framework given in [13]. For $L = BSMM$, we have applied the following simplifications w.r.t. [13]:

- There are no restrictions on L-normal form of modalities and the normalization operator NF_L and it reverse rNF_L are just identity operators. The word *L-normal* is also omitted in "L-normal model generator".
- There are no restrictions on BSMM-MProlog, i.e. every MProlog program (resp. goal) is a BSMM-MProlog program (resp. goal).
- The index L is omitted in the notations $Serial_L$, $\preceq_L$, and "L-instance" (of an atom or a modality).

By the results of [13], to prove soundness and completeness of SLD-resolution for MProlog in BSMM, we can prove Expected Lemmas 4 – 10 of [13] (w.r.t. the schema given in Table 1). The Expected Lemma 6 is trivial. The Expected Lemma 10 and the part of Expected Lemma 8 involving with NF_L/rNF_L can be omitted because NF_L and rNF_L are identity operators. The Expected Lemmas 7 and 9 and the remaining part of Expected Lemma 8, which concern properties of the operators Sat_L and $rSat_L$, can be verified in a straightforward way. The remaining Expected Lemmas 4 and 5 are given below as Lemmas 1 and 2, respectively, and will be proved in this section.

A model generator I is called an *L-model generator of P* if $T_{L,P}(I) \subseteq I$.

Lemma 1. *Let P be an MProlog program and I an L-model generator of P. Then the standard L-model of I is an L-model of P.*

Lemma 2. *Let I be a model generator, M the standard L-model of I, and α a ground MProlog goal atom. Suppose that $M \vDash \alpha$. Then α is an instance of some atom of $Sat_L(I)$.*

4.2   Extended L-Model Graphs

To proceed we need extended L-model graphs and some properties of them. Let I be a model generator. Define Ext'_L to be the operator such that $Ext'_L(I)$ is the least set of atoms extending I and closed w.r.t. the rules specifying Ext_L. Note that we allow $Ext'_L(I)$ to contain atoms not in labeled form and have that $Ext_L(I) \subseteq Ext'_L(I)$. The *extended L-model graph* of I is defined in the same way as the standard L-model graph of I but with $Ext'_L(I)$ in the place of $Ext_L(I)$.

We need the two following auxiliary lemmas.

Lemma 3. *Let I be a model generator, M the standard L-model graph of I, and M' the extended L-model graph of I. Then M' has the same frame as M, and furthermore, if $M = \langle W, \tau, R_1, \ldots, R_m, H \rangle$ and $M' = \langle W, \tau, R_1, \ldots, R_m, H' \rangle$ then for every $w \in W$, $H(w) \subseteq H'(w)$ and $H'(w) - H(w)$ is a set of formulas containing some unlabeled existential modal operators.*

The proof of this lemma is straightforward.

If a modality $\triangle$ is obtainable from $\triangle'$ by replacing some (possibly zero) ∇_i by $\square_i$ then we call $\triangle$ a $\square$-*lifting form* of $\triangle'$. If $\triangle$ is a $\square$-lifting form of $\triangle'$ then we call an atom $\triangle\alpha$ a $\square$-*lifting form* of $\triangle'\alpha$. For example, $\square_1\langle p(a)\rangle_1\square_2 q(b)$ is a $\square$-lifting form of $\langle X\rangle_1\langle p(a)\rangle_1\diamondsuit_2 q(b)$.

Lemma 4. *Let I be a model generator and $M = \langle W, \tau, R_1, \ldots, R_m, H \rangle$ be the extended L-model graph of I. Let $w = \langle E_1\rangle_{i_1} \ldots \langle E_k\rangle_{i_k}$ be a world of M and $\triangle = w$ be a modality. Then for α (resp. A) not containing $\top$, $\alpha \in H(w)$ (resp. $A \in H(w)$) iff there exists a $\square$-lifting form $\triangle'$ of $\triangle$ such that $\triangle'\alpha \in Ext'_L(I)$ (resp. $\triangle'A \in Sat_L(I)$).*

This lemma can be proved by induction on the length of $\triangle$ in a straightforward way. We give below the main lemma of this subsection.

Lemma 5. *Let I be a model generator and $M = \langle W, \tau, R_1, \ldots, R_m, H \rangle$ be the extended L-model graph of I. Then for any w and u such that $R_i(w, u)$ holds:*

- *if $\square_i\alpha \in H(w)$ then $\alpha \in H(u)$,*
- *if $\alpha \in H(u)$ then $\diamondsuit_i\alpha \in H(w)$.*

Proof. Let $\{R'_j \mid 1 \le j \le m\}$ be the skeleton of M. We prove this lemma by induction on the number of steps needed to obtain $R_i(w, u)$ when extending $\{R'_j \mid 1 \le j \le m\}$ to $\{R_j \mid 1 \le j \le m\}$.

Consider the first assertion. Suppose that $\square_i\alpha \in H(w)$. By Lemma 4, there exists a $\square$-lifting form $\triangle$ of w such that $\triangle\square_i\alpha \in Ext'_L(I)$. Since $R_i(w, u)$ holds, there are the following cases to consider:

- Case $u = w\langle E\rangle_i$ and $R'_i(w, w\langle E\rangle_i)$: The assertion holds by the definition of M.
- Case $AT(i)$ holds and $u = w$: Since $\triangle\square_i\alpha \in Ext'_L(I)$, we have $\triangle\alpha \in Ext'_L(I)$, and by Lemma 4, $\alpha \in H(u)$.
- Case $AI(i,j)$ holds and $R_i(w, u)$ is created from $R_j(w, u)$: Since $\triangle\square_i\alpha \in Ext'_L(I)$, we have $\triangle\square_j\alpha \in Ext'_L(I)$, and by Lemma 4, $\square_j\alpha \in H(w)$. Hence, by the inductive assumption, $\alpha \in H(u)$.
- Case $AB(j,i)$ holds and $R_i(w, u)$ is created from $R_j(u, w)$: Since $\square_i\alpha \in H(w)$, by the inductive assumption, $\diamond_j\square_i\alpha \in H(u)$. By Lemma 4, there exists a $\square$-lifting form $\triangle'$ of u such that $\triangle'\diamond_j\square_i\alpha \in Ext'_L(I)$. Thus $\triangle'\alpha \in Ext'_L(I)$. Hence, by Lemma 4, $\alpha \in H(u)$.
- Case $A4(i,j,k)$ holds and $R_i(w, u)$ is created from $R_j(w, v)$ and $R_k(v, u)$: Since $\triangle\square_i\alpha \in Ext'_L(I)$, we have $\triangle\square_j\square_k\alpha \in Ext'_L(I)$, and by Lemma 4, $\square_j\square_k\alpha \in H(w)$. Hence, by the inductive assumption, $\square_k\alpha \in H(v)$ and $\alpha \in H(u)$.
- Case $A5(j,k,i)$ holds and $R_i(w, u)$ is created from $R_j(v, u)$ and $R_k(v, w)$: Since $\square_i\alpha \in H(w)$, by the inductive assumption, $\diamond_k\square_i\alpha \in H(v)$. Hence, by Lemma 4, there exists a $\square$-lifting form $\triangle'$ of v such that $\triangle'\diamond_k\square_i\alpha \in Ext'_L(I)$. Hence $\triangle'\square_j\alpha \in Ext'_L(I)$, and by Lemma 4, $\square_j\alpha \in H(v)$. By the inductive assumption, it follows that $\alpha \in H(u)$.

The second assertion can be proved in a similar way (see [11]).

4.3   Remaining Proofs

We also need the following lemma (labeled Expected Lemma 2 in [13]), which states that the standard L-model of I is really an L-model of I.

Lemma 6. *Let I be a model generator, M the standard/extended L-model graph of I, and σ the standard $\diamond$-realization function on M. Then M is an L-model and $M, \sigma \vDash I$.*

Proof. By Lemma 3, it suffices to prove for the case when M is the standard L-model graph of I. By the definition, M is an L-model. It can be proved by induction on the length of α that for any $w \in W$, if $\alpha \in H(w)$, then $M, \sigma, w \vDash \alpha$. The cases when α is a classical atom or $\alpha = \langle E\rangle_i\beta$ are trivial. The case when $\alpha = \square_i\beta$ is solved by Lemmas 3 and 5. Hence $M, \sigma \vDash I$.

Proof of Lemma 1. Let I' be the least extension of I such that, if $\boxdot\varphi$ is a program clause of P, $\varphi = (A \leftarrow B_1, \dots, B_n)$, and ψ is a ground instance of φ, then $\boxdot p_\psi \in I'$, where p_ψ is a fresh 0-ary predicate symbol. Let M and M' be the extended L-model graphs of I and I', respectively. It is easy to see that these model graphs have the same frame. Let $M = \langle W, \tau, R_1, \dots, R_m, H\rangle$ and $M' = \langle W, \tau, R_1, \dots, R_m, H'\rangle$. Clearly, M is an L-model. By Lemma 3, it suffices to show that $M \vDash P$.

Let $\boxdot\varphi$ be a program clause of P, $\varphi = (A \leftarrow B_1, \dots, B_n)$, and ψ a ground instance of φ. By Lemma 6, $M' \vDash \boxdot p_\psi$. To prove that $M \vDash P$ it is sufficient to show that for any $w \in W$, if $p_\psi \in H'(w)$ then $M, w \models \psi$. Suppose that $p_\psi \in H'(w)$.

Let $\triangle = w$ and $\boxdot' = \Box_{i_1} \ldots \Box_{i_k}$ be a $\Box$-lifting form of $\triangle$. By Lemma 4, some $\Box$-lifting form of $\triangle p_\psi$ belongs to $Sat_L(I')$. This $\Box$-lifting form must be $\boxdot' p_\psi$. Thus $\boxdot' p_\psi \in Sat_L(\{\boxdot p_\psi\})$. Hence $\boxdot p_\psi \rightarrow \boxdot' p_\psi$ is L-valid and the program clause $\boxdot' \psi$ is a ground L-instance of $\boxdot \varphi$.

Let $\psi = (A' \leftarrow B'_1, \ldots, B'_n)$ and suppose that $M, w \models B'_i$ for all $1 \leq i \leq n$. We need to show that $M, w \models A'$. For this, we first show that a $\Box$-lifting form of $\triangle B'_i$ belongs to $Sat_L(I)$ for every $1 \leq i \leq n$. Consider the following cases:

- Case B'_i is a classical atom: The assertion follows from Lemma 4.
- Case B'_i is of the form $\Box_j E$: Since $M, w \models B'_i$, it follows that $M, w\langle \top \rangle_j \models E$, and by Lemma 4, some $\Box$-lifting form of $\triangle\langle \top \rangle_j E$ belongs to $Sat_L(I)$, which means that some $\Box$-lifting form of $\triangle B'_i$ belongs to $Sat_L(I)$.
- Case B'_i is of the form $\Diamond_j E$: Since $M, w \models B'_i$, there exists a world u such that $R_j(w, u)$ holds and $M, u \models E$. By Lemma 5, it follows that $\Diamond_j E \in H(w)$. Hence, by Lemma 4, some $\Box$-lifting form of $\triangle B'_i$ belongs to $Sat_L(I)$.

Therefore, by the definition of $T_{0L,P}$, some $\Box$-lifting form α of $\triangle A''$, where A'' is the forward labeled form of A', belongs to $T_{0L,P}(Sat_L(I))$. Since $T_{0L,P}(Sat_L(I)) = T_{L,P}(I) \subseteq I$, by Lemma 6, we have that $M, \sigma \models \alpha$, where σ is the standard $\Diamond$-realization function on M. Hence $M, w \models A'$. Thus $M, w \models \psi$, which completes the proof.

Proof of Lemma 2. Let $M' = \langle W, \tau, R_1, \ldots, R_m, H \rangle$ be the extended L-model graph of I, $\boxdot = \Box_{i_1} \ldots \Box_{i_k}$ and $w = \langle \top \rangle_{i_1} \ldots \langle \top \rangle_{i_k}$. Suppose that α is of the form $\boxdot E$. Since $M \models \alpha$, by Lemma 3, we have $M', w \models E$. By Lemma 4, it follows that $\boxdot E \in Sat_L(I)$. Now suppose that α is of the form $\boxdot \Diamond_i E$. Since $M \models \alpha$, we have $M, w \models \Diamond_i E$, and by Lemma 3, $M', w \models \Diamond_i E$. There exists u such that $R_i(w, u)$ holds and $M', u \models E$. By Lemma 5, it follows that $\Diamond_i E \in H(w)$. Hence $\boxdot \Diamond_i E \in Sat_L(I)$ (by Lemma 4).

We have proved Lemmas 1 and 2, which completes the proof of Theorem 1.

5   Conclusions

We have developed semantics for MProlog programs in BSMM and proved that the given SLD-resolution calculus is sound and complete. The class BSMM of basic serial multimodal logics is much larger than the class of multimodal logics considered by Debart *et al.* using the translational approach [4] and is very different from the class of grammar modal logics considered by Baldoni *et al.* [2].

This paper is an extension of our previous paper on programming in monomodal logics [10] and is an instantiation of our general framework given in [13]. The SLD-resolution calculus for BSMM presented in this paper together with its soundness and completeness is, however, a strong and essential result.

The $Sat_L/rSat_L$ rules given for semantics of MProlog in BSMM are based directly on the axioms of the used modal logic. This makes our fixpoint semantics and SLD-resolution calculus intuitive. The clarity of the rules suggests that our methods can be extended for other multimodal logics.

Our SLD-resolution calculus for MProlog in BSMM is elegant like a Hilbert-style axiom system, but similarly to using a Hilbert-style axiom system for automatic reasoning, it is not very efficient. For more specific modal logics, as reported in [12,13], we have implemented the modal logic programming system MProlog. It uses optimization techniques like normalization of modalities, better orderings of modal operators, options for restricting the search space.

In summary, we have successfully applied the direct approach for modal logic programming in a large class of basic multimodal logics, while not assuming any special restriction on the form of logic programs and goals.

References

1. Ph. Balbiani, L. Fariñas del Cerro, and A. Herzig. Declarative semantics for modal logic programs. In *Proceedings of the 1988 International Conference on Fifth Generation Computer Systems*, pages 507–514. ICOT, 1988.
2. M. Baldoni, L. Giordano, and A. Martelli. A framework for a modal logic programming. In *Joint International Conference and Symposium on Logic Programming*, pages 52–66. MIT Press, 1996.
3. M.J. Cresswell and G.E. Hughes. *A New Introduction to Modal Logic*. Routledge, 1996.
4. F. Debart, P. Enjalbert, and M. Lescot. Multimodal logic programming using equational and order-sorted logic. *Theoretical Comp. Science*, 105:141–166, 1992.
5. S. Demri. The complexity of regularity in grammar logics and related modal logics. *Journal of Logic and Computation*, 11(6):933–960, 2001.
6. L. Fariñas del Cerro. Molog: A system that extends Prolog with modal logic. *New Generation Computing*, 4:35–50, 1986.
7. M. Fitting and R.L. Mendelsohn. *First-Order Modal Logic*. Springer, 1998.
8. R.A. Kowalski. Predicate logic as a programming language. In J.L. Rosenfeld, editor, *Information Processing 74, Proc. of IFIP Congress 74*, pages 569–574, 1974.
9. J.W. Lloyd. *Foundations of Logic Programming, 2nd Ed.* Springer-Verlag, 1987.
10. L.A. Nguyen. A fixpoint semantics and an SLD-resolution calculus for modal logic programs. *Fundamenta Informaticae*, 55(1):63–100, 2003.
11. L.A. Nguyen. Multimodal logic programming and its applications to modal deductive databases. Manuscript (served as a technical report), available on Internet at http://www.mimuw.edu.pl/~nguyen/papers.html, 2003.
12. L.A. Nguyen. The modal logic programming system MProlog. In J.J. Alferes and J.A. Leite, editors, *Proceedings of JELIA 2004, LNCS 3229*, pages 266–278. Springer, 2004.
13. L.A. Nguyen. The modal logic programming system MProlog: Theory, design, and implementation. Available at http://www.mimuw.edu.pl/~nguyen/mprolog, 2005.
14. A. Nonnengart. How to use modalities and sorts in Prolog. In C. MacNish, D. Pearce, and L.M. Pereira, editors, *Proceedings of JELIA'94, LNCS 838*, pages 365–378. Springer, 1994.
15. H.J. Ohlbach. A resolution calculus for modal logics. In E.L. Lusk and R.A. Overbeek, editors, *Proc. of CADE-88, LNCS 310*, pages 500–516. Springer, 1988.
16. M.H. van Emden and R.A. Kowalski. The semantics of predicate logic as a programming language. *Journal of the ACM*, 23(4):733–742, 1976.

Upside-Down Transformation in SOL/Connection Tableaux and Its Application*

Koji Iwanuma[1], Katsumi Inoue[2], and Hidetomo Nabeshima[1]

[1] University of Yamanashi,
4-3-11 Takeda, Kofu-shi,Yamanashi 400-8511, Japan
{iwanuma, nabesima}@iw.media.yamanashi.ac.jp
[2] National Institute of Informatics,
2-1-2 Hitotsubashi, Chiyoda-ku, Tokyo 101-8430, Japan
ki@nii.ac.jp

Abstract. In this paper, we study an upside-down transformation of a branch in SOL/Connection tableaux and show that SOL/Connection tableaux using the folding-up operation can always accomplish a size-preserving transformation for any branch in any tableau. This fact solves the exponentially-growing size problem caused both by the order-preserving reduction and by an incremental answer computation problem.

1 Introduction

Given an axiom set, the task of *consequence-finding* [2] is to find out some theorems of interest.[1] To efficiently compute interesting consequences, Inoue [3] defined *SOL resolution*, which is an extension of the *Model Elimination* (ME) calculus [11] by adding the *Skip rule* to ME. When the Skip rule is applied to the selected literal in SOL, it is just "skipped". When a deduction with the top clause C is completed, those skipped literals are collected and output. This output clause is a logical consequence of $\Sigma \cup \{C\}$. Iwanuma et.al [5] proposed SOL Tableaux, which is a reformulation of SOL within the framework of connection tableaux [8,1,10].

In this paper, we study an upside-down transformation of a branch in SOL/ Connection tableaux. SOL/Connection tableau calculus suffers from redundant duplicate computation which is induced by many contrapositives of an axiom clause. Thus, the upside-down transformation studied here can shed some new light on redundancy/efficiency of Connection (and thus, SOL) tableaux. We show that SOL/Connection tableaux using the folding-up operation can always accomplish a size-preserving transformation for any branch in any tableau. This fact solves the size-growing problem caused both by the order-preserving reduction and by an incremental answer computation problem.

---

* This research was partially supported by the Grant-in-Aid from The Ministry of Education, Science and Culture of Japan ((A)(1) No.13358004) and (B)(1) No.17300051.
[1] A survey of consequence-finding in propositional logic is given in Marquis [12], and an application of consequence-finding to abduction is summarized in [4].

D.V. Hung and M. Wirsing (Eds.): ICTAC 2005, LNCS 3722, pp. 166–179, 2005.

This paper is organized as follows: Section 2 gives several definition of SOL/ Connection tableaux, In Section 3, we study an upside-down transformation of a branch in a tableau. In Section 4, we investigate some application of the upside-down transformation to two open problems in automated deduction.

2   SOL Tableaux

We follow several definition of Connection Tableaux [8], thus define a clause as a *multiset* of literals. We write $\subseteq_{ms}$ to denote the inclusion relation over multisets which is defined as usual.

Definition 1 (Subsumption). Let C and D be clauses, i.e., multisets of literals. C *subsumes* D if there is a substitution θ such that $C\theta \subseteq_{ms} D$. We say C *properly subsumes* D if C subsumes D but D does not subsume C. For a set of clauses Σ, $\mu\Sigma$ denotes the set of clauses in Σ not properly subsumed by any clause in Σ.

Definition 2 (Production Field [3]). A *production field* $\mathcal{P}$ is a pair $\langle \mathbf{L}, Cond \rangle$, where $\mathbf{L}$ is a set of literals closed under instantiation from the Herbrand Universe, and $Cond$ is a certain condition to be satisfied. When $Cond$ is not specified, $\mathcal{P}$ is just denoted as $\langle \mathbf{L} \rangle$. A clause C *belongs to* $\mathcal{P} = \langle \mathbf{L}, Cond \rangle$ if every literal in C belongs to $\mathbf{L}$ and C satisfies $Cond$. When Σ is a set of clauses, the set of logical consequences of Σ belonging to $\mathcal{P}$ is denoted as $Th_{\mathcal{P}}(\Sigma)$.

For example, if $\mathcal{L}^+$ is the set of positive literals in a language, and $\mathcal{P}_1$ is a production field $\langle \mathcal{L}^+ \rangle$, then $Th_{\mathcal{P}_1}(\Sigma)$ is the set of all positive clauses derivable from Σ. Notice that the empty clause ϕ is the unique clause in $\mu Th_{\mathcal{P}}(\Sigma)$ if and only if Σ is unsatisfiable. This means that proof-finding is a special case of consequence-finding.

Definition 3 (Connection Tableau [8]).

1. A *clausal tableau* T is a labeled ordered tree, where every non-root node of T is labeled with a literal. If no confusion arises, we shall identify a node with its label in T. If the immediate successor nodes of a node N are nodes. i,e., literals, $L_1, \ldots, L_n$, then the clause $L_1 \vee \cdots \vee L_n$ is called the *tableau clause below* N; the tableau clause below the root is called the *top clause*. T is said to be a *clausal tableau for* a set Σ of clauses if every tableau clause C in T is an instance of a clause D in Σ. Additionally, in such a case, D is called an *origin clause of* C in Σ. Finally, the *size* of a clausal tableau T is the number of nodes in T.
2. A *connection tableau* T is a clausal tableau such that, for every non-leaf node L (except the root), there is an immediate successor of L which is labeled with the complement $\overline{L}$. A *marked tableau* is a clausal tableau T such that some leaf nodes are marked with the labels closed or skipped. The unmarked leaf nodes are called *subgoals*. T is *solved* if all leaf nodes are marked. The literal of a node L in T is called a *skipped literal* if L is marked with skipped. We denote the set of skipped literals in T as $skip(T)$.

Notice that $skip(T)$ is a *set*, not a multiset. $skip(T)$ is sometimes identified with a clause. In the following, we abbreviate a marked connection tableau as a tableau if no confusion arises.

Definition 4 (Regularity, Skip-regularity and TCS-freeness). A marked tableau T is *regular* if no two nodes on a branch in T are labeled with the same literal. T is *tautology-free* if any tableau clause in T does not have a pair of complementary literals. T is *complement-free* if no two non-leaf nodes on a branch in T are labeled with complementary literals. A marked tableau T is *skip-regular* if no node N in T is labeled with literal L such that the complement $\overline{L}$ belongs to $skip(T)$. T is *TCS-free (Tableau Clause Subsumption free)* for a clause set Σ if no tableau clause C in T is subsumed by any clause in Σ other than origin clauses of C.

Notice that skip-regularity is effective all over a tableau, so that it is effective not only for subgoals but also for non-leaf and/or solved nodes in a tableau.

Definition 5 (SOL Tableau Calculus [5]). Let Σ be a set of clauses, C a clause, and $\mathcal{P}$ a production field. An *SOL-deduction deriving a clause S from $\Sigma + C$ and $\mathcal{P}$* consists of a sequence of tableaux $T_0, T_1, \ldots, T_n$ satisfying that:

1. T_0 is a tableau consisting of the start clause C only. All leaf nodes of T_0 are unmarked.
2. T_n is a solved tableau, and $skip(T_n) = S$.
3. For each T_i ($i = 0, \ldots, n$), T_i is regular, tautology-free, complement-free, skip-regular and TCS-free for $\Sigma \cup \{C\}$. Moreover, the clause $skip(T_i)$ belongs to $\mathcal{P}$.
4. T_{i+1} is constructed from T_i as follows. Select a subgoal K, then apply one of the following rules to T_i to obtain T_{i+1}:
   (a) **Skip:** If $skip(T_i) \cup \{K\}$ belongs to $\mathcal{P}$, then mark K with label skipped.
   (b) **Skip-Factoring:** If $skip(T_i)$ contains a literal L, and K and L are unifiable with mgu θ, then mark K with label skipped, and apply θ to T_i.
   (c) **Extension:** Select a clause B from $\Sigma \cup \{C\}$ and obtain a variant $B' = L_1 \vee \cdots \vee L_m$ by renaming variables in B. If there is a literal L_j such that $\overline{K}$ and L_j are unifiable with mgu θ, then first attach new nodes $L_1, \ldots, L_m$ to K as the immediate successors. Next, mark the node L_j with label closed and apply θ to all literals in the extended tableau. We say, the node L_j is the *entering point* of the new tableau clause $L_1 \vee \cdots \vee L_m$.
   (d) **Reduction:** If K has an ancestor node L on the branch from the root to K, and $\overline{K}$ and L are unifiable with mgu θ, then mark K with label closed, and apply θ to T_i.

The following theorem is due to [3,5].

Theorem 1 (Soundness and Completeness of SOL).
For the SOL tableau calculus, the following results hold [5].

1. *If a clause S is derived by an SOL-deduction from $\Sigma + C$ and $\mathcal{P}$, then S belongs to $Th_{\mathcal{P}}(\Sigma \cup \{C\})$.*
2. *If a clause F does not belong to $Th_{\mathcal{P}}(\Sigma)$ but belongs to $Th_{\mathcal{P}}(\Sigma \cup \{C\})$, then there is an SOL-deduction deriving a clause S from $\Sigma + C$ and $\mathcal{P}$ such that S subsumes F.*

A *skeleton* of a tableau T is a labeled ordered tree obtained from T by eliminating any arc of which destination node is not an entering node. The skeleton of a tableau is significantly helpful for understanding the upside-down transformation proposed later. If no confusion arises, we identify a tableau with its skeleton throughout this paper.

Example 1. Let us consider the set Σ of the following clauses:

(1) $\neg goal \vee U \vee \neg Q$,   (2) $T \vee Q \vee \neg P$,   (3) $S \vee P \vee \neg goal$,
(4) $\neg P \vee \neg T$,   (5) $\neg P \vee \neg Q \vee \neg U$,   (6) $\neg S$,   (7) $goal$

The skeleton of a tableau for Σ is depicted in Fig.1, where the clause (7) is used as the top clause. Each solid (or broken) line denotes an extension (or respectively, reduction) operation. Each rectangle expresses a tableau clause, and every incoming solid line indicates an entering point, i.e., a literal used for an extension in a tableau clause.

3   Upside-Down Transformation

In this section, we investigate an upside-down transformation of a branch in an SOL tableau. Connection tableau calculus suffers from redundant duplicate computation which is caused by many contrapositives of a clause. For example, the SOL tableau in Fig.2 is an alternative solved tableau for the same set Σ of clauses in Ex.1, which can be easily constructed with contrapositive clauses in

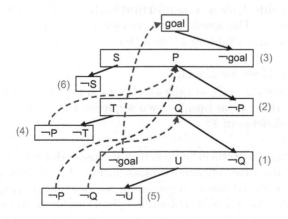

Fig. 1. The skeleton of an SOL tableau

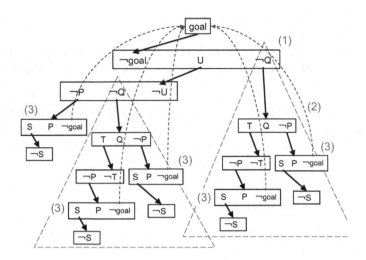

Fig. 2. Another SOL tableau satisfying the order-preserving condition

general. This tableau is obviously redundant because of duplicate occurrences of some tableau clauses, whereas the tableau in Fig.1 has the *minimal* size among all solved SOL tableaux.

Notice that each of the right-most branches in the two tableaux has an upside-down form for each other. The right-most branch of the tableau in Fig.1 consists of the tableau clauses No.3, 2 and 1, whereas the right-most branch in Fig.2 consists of the clauses No.1, 2 and 3 in the upside-down order. This is an very important relationship between both SOL tableaux, which can clarify certain redundancy hidden in SOL/Connection Tableaux. Thus, the *size-preserving upside-down transformation theorem*, shown later, can shed some new light on redundancy/efficiency of Connection (and thus, SOL) Tableaux.

Definition 6 (Upside-Down Trasnformation). Let T be a solved tableau for a set Σ of clauses. The *upside-down transformation* of T is the operation which transforms T into a tableau T' such that

1. T' is a solved tableau for Σ and,
2. for an sequence $C_1, \ldots, C_k$ of tableau clauses appearing in a branch in the skeleton of T, there is an upside-down sequence $C_k, \ldots, C_1$ occurring in a branch in the skeleton of T'.

Figure 3 illustrates a problem to be solved in upside-down transformation of an SOL tableau. Given the left-hand tableau in Fig. 3, the right-hand tableau is obtained from the initial one by transposing the right-most branch in a naive manner. The problem is that some reduction operations are no longer possible in the upside-down branch of a resulting tableau. In the approach of this paper, we replace such broken reductions with extensions in order to avoid such a problem.

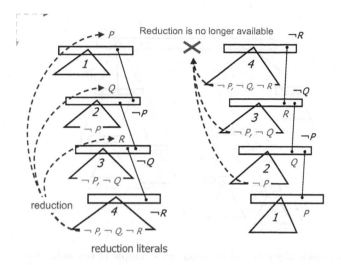

Fig. 3. A naive upside-down transformation of an SOL tableau

Figure 4 and 5 show how to recursively replace broken reductions with extensions using some copies of subtableaux which are already completed in early induction steps.

Figure 4 depicts the basic transformation step, where the broken reduction for the literal $\neg P$ in the subtableau No.2 is replaced with the extension for the subtableau No.1. Figure 5 explains the induction step for the upside-down transformation. The broken reduction for the literal $\neg Q$ in the subtableau No.3 is replaced with the extension for the subtableau rooted by $\neg Q$ which is completed in the previous induction step, i.e., in the step depicted in Fig.4. The broken reduction for $\neg P$ in the subtableau No.3 is similarly compensated. These repairing operations are always applicable to any upside-down branch in any transformed tableau. Thus we have the following:

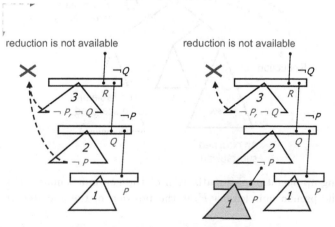

Fig. 4. Upside-down transformation: an example of the base step

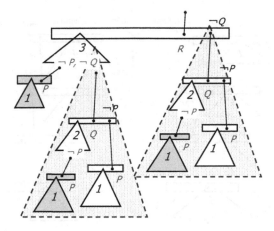

Fig. 5. Upside-down transformation: an example of the induction step

Lemma 1 (Upside-Down Transformation). *In SOL and Connection tableaux, the upside-down transformation is always possible for any branch in any solved tableau.*

Notice that new serious drawback occurs after the above repairing operations, that is, the size of resulting tableau grows up exponentially. We shall prevent such an ill-growth of the size of a tableau by introducing a sort of lemmatization, i.e., the folding-up operation [8]. Figure 6 and 7 explain the folding-up operation in Connection/SOL tableaux, which consists of two phases: the first is for lemma extraction and its embedding in a tableau branch; the second phase is for using

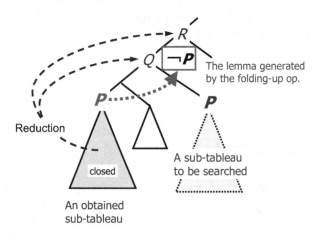

Fig. 6. Folding-up operation: lemmatization of the non-unit lemma $\neg P \leftarrow Q \wedge R$ by embedding the pseudo unit lemma P at the position of the ancestor literal Q in a branch

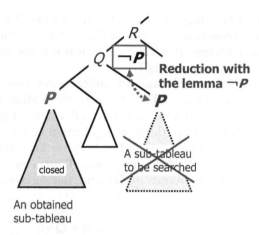

Fig. 7. Folding-up operation: reduction with an embedded non-unit lemma for other subtableau

an embedded lemma in the form of the ordinary reduction, where an embedded lemma plays a role of an ordinary ancestor literal in Connection Tableaux.

Let us consider an example depicted in Fig.6. Assume here that the subtableau under the left occurrence of the literal P is closed, and also that the literals Q and R are all ancestor literals which are used in reductions and appear in the branch from the root to P. In this situation, we can generate the non-unit lemma $(\neg P \leftarrow Q \wedge R)$ from the solved subtableau below P in Fig.6. Thus the folding-up operation embeds the lemma $\neg P \leftarrow Q \wedge R$ as a pseudo unit lemma P on the literal Q in a tableau. Notice that Q is the literal occurring at the lowest position among the antecedent literals Q and R in the branch from

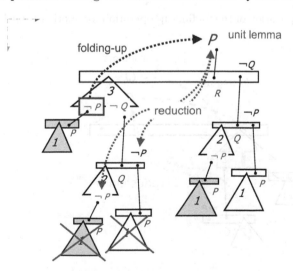

Fig. 8. The first application of the folding-up operation for an upside-down branch in shown in Fig.5

the root. At the later stages, the pseudo unit lemma P is used as an ancestor literal for pseudo reduction as shown in Fig.7. Such a reduction operation prevents unnecessary computation for an identical subtableau under the literal P appearing in the right part in Fig.7.

Now we can eliminate all duplicate subtableaux appearing in the previous upside-down branch depicted in Fig.5 by using the folding up operation. Assume here that the tableau construction is performed under a depth-first and leftmost-first strategy. Figure 8 shows the first application of the folding-up to the left most occurrence of the literal $\neg P$ and the succeeding reductions to the second and third occurrences of $\neg P$. Figure 9 also illustrates the second folding-up operation for the left occurrence of $\neg Q$ and the succeeding reduction for the

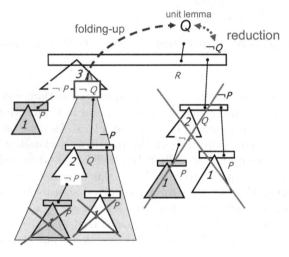

Fig. 9. The second application of the folding-up operation for another branch in shown in Fig.5

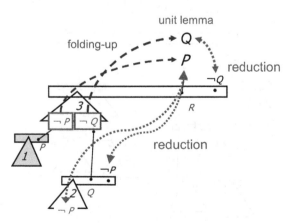

Fig. 10. The final tableau of the upside-down transformation with the folding-up operation

right occurrence of $\neg Q$ with the embedded lemma Q. Eventually, the upside-down transformation with the folding-up operation produces the very concise small tableau shown in Fig.10. The readers can easily verify that the subtableaux No.1, 2 and 3 appear just once in the final tableau in Fig.10, respectively.

Strictly speaking, the tableau shown in Fig.10 has no exact upside-down branch in it: the subtableau No.1 is not below in the subtablau No.2. This is the reason why we need the following modified definition.

Definition 7 (Essentially Upside-Down Trasnformation). Let T be a solved tableau for a set Σ of clauses. The *essentially upside-down transformation* of T is the operation which transforms T into a tableau T' such that

1. T' is a solved tableau for Σ and,
2. for an sequence $C_1, \ldots, C_k$ of tableau clauses appearing in a branch in the skeleton of T, there is a subtableau T'' in T' satisfying that
   (a) the top clause of T'' is C_k and
   (b) $C_{k-1}, \ldots, C_1$ occur in T'' as tableau clauses.

Now, we have the following main theorem:

Theorem 2 (Size-Preserving Essentially Upside-Down Transformation). *In SOL and Connection tableaux with the folding up operation, the essentially upside-down transformation is always possible for any branch in any solved tableau. Moreover the size of the upside-down tableau is identical with the one of the original tableau.*

We shall omit the formal proof here, because the space allowed to us is limited. Precisely speaking, in all examples shown in this paper, the original branch does not involve the folding up operation. However, the same upside-transformation is always applicable for a branch containing the folding-up without any difficulty.

4   Application

In this section, we investigate some application of the upside-down transformation to some open problems in the research field of automated deduction.

4.1   Order-Preserving Reduction

The order-preserving reduction [10] and the foothold refinement of ME calculus [13] were proposed as remedies for redundant duplicate computations appearing in the Connection (or Model Elimination) calculus. The both methods can eliminate, without losing the completeness, some redundancy which is induced by contrapositive clause of a initial clause. Unfortunately, the allowed and remaining tableaux are sometimes exponentially larger than the eliminated tableaux. This is a serious shortcoming in practical automated deduction.

Definition 8. Let Σ be a set of clauses, T a tableau for Σ and L a literal in a tableau clause C in T. Suppose that C' is the origin clause of C in Σ and $L' \in C'$ is the literal corresponding with $L \in C$. We denote L' as L^Σ. Given an ordering $\prec$ over the literal occurrences in Σ, the *extension ordering* $\prec_T$ for T is defined as the ordering on the literal occurrences in T such that, for any two literal occurrences L_i and L_j in T,

1. $L_i \prec_T L_j$ iff $L_i^\Sigma \prec L_j^\Sigma$, and
2. L_i and L_j are equal in $\prec_T$ if $L_i^\Sigma = L_j^\Sigma$

The order-preserving reduction preserves the completeness of SOL tableaux [5].

Definition 9 (Order-preserving reduction [10]). Let $\prec_T$ be an extension ordering over literal occurrences in a tableau T. A reduction step for a subgoal L using an ancestor node N is said to *preserve the extension ordering* $\prec_T$ if the literal occurrence L is not greater than the literal occurrence L', which is the entering point of the tableau clause below N.

Let us reconsider the clause set Σ in Example 1 and the SOL tableau T depicted in Fig.1. We define here the ordering $\prec$ over the literal occurrences in Σ as follows: Let L and L' be literal occurrences in clauses C and C', respectively.

1. $L \succ L'$ iff the identity number of C is less than the one of C'.
2. if C and C' are identical, then $L \succ L'$ iff L occurs at the left-hand side of L' in C.

For example, the literal $\neg goal$ in the clause (1) is greater than $\neg goal$ in the clause (3), and the literal $\neg P$ in clause (2) is greater than the literal occurrence $\neg P$ appearing in clauses (4) and (5).

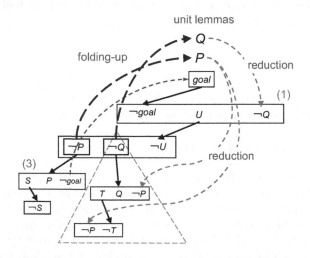

Fig. 11. An SOL tableau compressed with the folding-up operation

In the tableau T in Fig.1, the reduction for $\neg goal$ in the clause (1) to the ancestor literal $goal$ in the top clause *violates* the order-preserving condition, because the literal $\neg goal$ in the clause (1) is greater than the literal $\neg goal$ in the clause (3), at which the tableau clause (3) is entered.

The upside-down transformation without the folding-up operation can produce another closed SOL tableau T^C, already shown in Fig.2, where the branch of the tableau clause (3) to the clause (1) in Fig.1 is inversely transposed. In the tableau T^C in Fig.2, all performed reductions satisfy the order-preserving condition. Notice that no folding-up operation is applied in T^C. Thus the size of T^C increases exponentially. This is a typical example of a serious drawback of the order-preserving reduction and the foothold refinement [13].

If we apply the folding-up operation, then all duplication of subtableaux can be eliminated. We can obtain the tableau T^C_{FD} depicted in Fig.11 with the folding-up operation. Notice that the tableau T^C_{FD} has the exactly same size as T in Fig.1.

Therefore, the following is an immediate consequence of Theorem 1.

Lemma 2. *The order-preserving reduction does not increase the minimal size of a closed SOL/Connection tableau if the folding-up operation is used together with the order-preserving reduction.*

4.2 Incremental Answer Computation

We studied answer computation in a multi-agent environment [6], where the communication between agents is incomplete, e.g., answers/replies returned from agents may be delayed and also be tentative, so answers might be changed at a later stage. In such an communication environment, an incremental answer computation becomes extremely important, because complete information is never available before starting answer computation.

The use of answer literals proposed by Green is a well-known method for computing correct answers [1]. A *query* $\leftarrow Q(X)$ is a clause of the form $\leftarrow L_1 \wedge \cdots \wedge L_n$ where each L_i is a literal. Let $\neg Q(X)$ denote the disjunction $\neg L_1(X) \vee \cdots \vee \neg L_n(X)$.

Proposition 1. *[7] Let Σ be a set of clauses, $\leftarrow Q(X)$ a query and ANS a new predicate symbol not appearing in Σ nor Q. For any disjunctive answer $Q(X)\theta_1 \vee \cdots \vee Q(X)\theta_n$ of $\leftarrow Q(X)$, the following are equivalent:*

1. $\Sigma \models \forall(Q(X)\theta_1 \vee \cdots \vee Q(X)\theta_n)$.
2. $\Sigma \cup \{\neg Q(X) \vee ANS(X)\} \models \forall(ANS(X)\theta_1 \vee \cdots \vee ANS(X)\theta_n)$.

Suppose that the production field $\mathcal{P}$ is the set of all positive literals of the predicate ANS. Then SOL tableaux is complete to find out all disjunctive answers provided that an appropriate clause is chosen as the top clause.

Now reconsider the incremental answer computation problem in a multi-agent system. When new information P arrives at an agent in a certain stage, the agent tries to compute an answer for a query $Q(X)$ which is related to

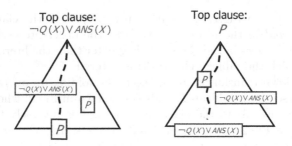

Fig. 12. Two SOL tableaux of different top clauses

this new information P. In other words, the agent has no interest in computing any answers irrelevant to the new information P. In order to achieve an efficient answer computation, we have to investigate the selection problem of a top clause in SOL tableaux. We have two alternatives for a top clause: one is the clause P which is newly added to the agent; the other is the answer clause $\neg Q(X) \lor ANS(X)$ (see Fig.12).[2]

The question is which form is better for efficient answer computation. In this paper, we suppose that the search strategy of SOL tableaux is the ordinary iterative deepening strategy which is very common in automated theorem proving. There are several important factors to be considered in the search space.

1. The most important factor is the size of minimal tableaux each of which produces a new answer being relevant to a newly informed fact P.
2. The second is the number of solved tableau irrelevant to a new fact P

The second question can be immediately solved as follows; SOL tableaux with the top clause $\neg Q(X) \lor ANS(X)$ quite often produces redundant answers which are irrelevant to the new fact P, because there are lots of minimal solved tableaux not containing any occurrences of P, in general. On the other hand, if we use a newly added clause P as a top clause, then the solved SOL tableaux must contain at least one occurrence for each of P and the answer clause, thus never produce answers being irrelevant to the new information P.

Theorem 2 solves the first difficult question. That is, Theorem 2 clearly shows that the size of minimal solved tableaux is identical for both cases of the newly added clause P and the answer clause $\neg Q(X) \lor ANS(X)$ as a top-clause.

5   Conclusion

In this paper, we studied the upside-down transformation of SOL/Connection tableau branch, and showed that SOL/Connection tableaux using the folding-up operation can always accomplish a size-preserving transformation for any branch in any tableau. This fact solves some open problems with respect to the order-preserving reduction and also an incremental answer computation problem.

---

[2] The both top clauses are admissible/complete for finding out all answers in SOL tableaux.

References

1. Baumgartner, P., U. Furbach, and F. Stolzenburg. Computing answers with model elimination. *Artificial Intelligence*, Vol.90, pp.135–176, 1997.
2. Lee, C. T. A completeness theorem and computer program for finding theorems derivable from given axioms. Ph.D. thesis, Department of Electrical Engineering and Computer Science, University of California, Berkeley, CA, 1967.
3. Inoue, K. Linear resolution for consequence finding. *Artificial Intelligence*, Vol.56, pp.301–353, 1992.
4. Inoue, K. Automated abduction. In: A. C. Kakas and F. Sadri, editors, *Computational Logic: Logic Programming and Beyond—Essays in Honor of Robert A. Kowalski, Part II*, LNAI 2408, pp.311–341, Springer, 2002.
5. Iwanuma, K., Inoue, K., and Satoh, K. Completeness of pruning methods for consequence finding procedure SOL. In: P. Baumgartner and H. Zhang, editors, *Proceedings of the 3rd International Workshop on First-Order Theorem Proving*, pp.89–100, 2000.
6. Inoue, K. and Iwanuma, K. Speculative Computation Through Consequence-Finding in Multi-agent Environments. *Ann. Math. Artif. Intell.*, Vol.42, No.1-3, 2004.
7. Kunen, K. The semantics of Answer Literals, *J. Automated Reasoning*, Vol.17, pp.83–95, 1996.
8. Letz, R., C. Goller, and K. Mayr. Controlled integration of the cut rule into connection tableau calculi. *Journal of Automated Reasoning*, Vol.13, pp.297–338, 1994.
9. Letz, R. Clausal tableaux. In: W. Bibel, P. H. Schmitt, editors, *Automated Deduction: A Basis for Applications*, Volume 1, pp.39–68, Kluwer, 1998.
10. Letz, R. Using Mating for Pruning Connection Tableaux, *Proceedings of 15th. Inter. Conf. on Automated Deduction (CADE-15) LNCS* Vol.1421, pp.381–396, 1998.
11. Loveland, D. W. *Automated Theorem Proving: A Logical Basis*. North-Holland, Amsterdam, 1978.
12. Marquis, P. Consequence finding algorithms. In: Dov M. Gabbay and Philippe Smets, editors, *Handbook for Defeasible Reasoning and Uncertain Management Systems*, Vol.5, pp.41–145, Kluwer Academic, 2000.
13. Spencer, B. Avoiding Duplicate Proofs with the Foothold Refinement. *Ann. Math. Artif. Intell.*, Vol.12 No.1-2, pp.117–140, 1994.

On the Stability Semantics
of Combinational Programs

Tran Van Dung

Hanoi University of Communication and Transport
tvdzung@hn.vnn.vn

Abstract. In this paper we prove some properties of combinational programs which is an improvement of the results presented in our previous work. We prove the derivation of loop-programs for combinational ones by both event semantics and stability semantics. We give a normal form for syntactically well-formed combinational programs, and show that for them Dimitrov's multiple parallel approach and Zhu's shared store parallel approach are equivalent.

1 Introduction

The VERILOG hardware description language [4] has simulation-oriented semantics based on *events* [1]. This *event semantics* can actually model detailed asynchronous behaviour, but is too fine-grained and does not support formal verification. There are some attempts to give operational and denotational semantics for Verilog in [8] and [9] to serve as a formal foundation for understanding and verification of Verilog programs. The first [8] uses shared store parallel operation between threads and the latter [9] uses fully parallel operation between them. They both capture a large class of hardware programs, but are too complex for our purposes. To use standard software verification techniques, in [7] we restricted ourselves to a small subset of hardware programs, and gave relational semantics to the programs in this class. We considered a class of combinational programs, which can model the behaviour of some kinds of sequential circuits. In that work, for each variable in a program, we have to use an additional variable called a signal variable for showing the change of its value. Therefore, the number of variables may be large for a large program. To overcome these disadvantages in this paper we introduced the stability control in term of variables, and show that combinational programs are indeed loop-programs with stability control. Then using relational calculus in [2], [3] we derive and prove some properties of these kind of programs. We then show the equivalence of two types of parallel operations for the subclass of combinational programs which do not have any dependency cycle.

The paper is organized as follows: in the next section, we briefly recall the definition of combinational programs and their relational semantics [7]. In the third section, we introduce the concept of stability condition and stability control. Then, first, we prove that the stability condition and the stability control

D.V. Hung and M. Wirsing (Eds.): ICTAC 2005, LNCS 3722, pp. 180–194, 2005.

are loop invariant for combinational programs. Secondly, we show that for them the relational semantics and the stability semantics coincide. Then we can use standard software verification techniques to prove the correctness of combinational programs. In the fourth section, we generalize the definition of syntactic combinational programs with no dependency cycle on variables, and improve on some results in our previous work [7]. We give a more formal proof for the termination and uniqueness of the final states for these kind of programs. We also show that for syntactic combinational programs the synchronous behaviour and the asynchronous behaviour coincide. So, inside their atomic execution there is no need for a clock, and threads can be connected arbitrarily with one another.

2   Combinational Programs and Relational Semantics

A sequential program is generated from multiple assignments and the **SKIP** program by sequential composition, conditional and non-deterministic choice. Global variables on index of the program are used to keep track of its execution.

Definition 1. *(sequential program and index)*

1. *A finite sequential program is generated by the following grammar:*

$$S ::= \Pi \mid \overline{v} := \overline{E} \mid S; S \mid S \lhd b \rhd S \mid S \sqcap S,$$

   where
   - *Π stands for the **SKIP** program, i.e., the program does nothing,*
   - *$\overline{v}$ a vector of Boolean variables*
   - *$\overline{E}$ a vector of Boolean expressions having the same length as $\overline{v}$ and*
   - *$\sqcap$ a non-deterministic choice.*

2. *In sequential program, different assignments are indexed by different natural numbers. Define*
   index$(P \, op \, Q) =_{df}$ **index**$(P) \cup$ **index**(Q) *for $op \in \{;, \lhd b \rhd, \sqcap\}$*

For each Boolean variable, a signal Boolean variable is introduced to mark the change of its during the execution. Combinational circuits are usually activated by some kinds of input changes. The input changes are shown by signal rising variables and signal falling variables. An event control marks the change of variables or program inputs, and is defined as a disjunction of their signal variables and some expected kind of signal inputs.

Definition 2. *(signal variable and event control)*

1. *The signal Boolean variable of a Boolean variable x is denoted by $\sim x$ and defined as: when x changes its value, $\sim x =$**true**. When x is a global variable, the $\sim x$ is a dimensioned logical vector, each its component $\sim x[i]$ is used to inform a change of x for the subprogram indexed by i.*

2. *An event control $g(S)$ of a program S is defined as*
   - *Let*
     - *S be an assignment $\overline{x} := \overline{E}$ with index i,*

- $\overline{x} = (x_1, \ldots, x_k)$ *contains those variables which can occur on either the left or right hand sides of S,*
- $p_1, \ldots, p_l$ *be those inputs which occur only in the expression $\overline{E}$, and*
- $\uparrow p$ *be Boolean variable expressing the rising of the value of input p and $\downarrow p$ be Boolean variable expressing the falling of the value of p.*

- *Define $g(S) =_{df} \sim x_1[i] \vee \sim x_2[i] \vee \ldots \vee \sim x_k[i] \vee t(p_1)[i] \vee \ldots \vee t(p_l)[i]$, where $t(z)$ is $\uparrow z$ or $\downarrow z$ or $\sim z$ or ff and i an index of S. The ith components of signal variables are used to keep information about changes of the corresponding variables for the program S. So event control $g(S)$ of the program S shows there is or not any change of variables used in S still triggering its execution.*
- *Define $g(P \, op \, Q) =_{df} g(P) \vee g(Q)$ for $op \in \{;, \triangleleft \, b \, \triangleright, \sqcap\}$.*

Sequential programs are used to simulate combinational circuits. To consider some properties of sequential circuits we introduce a parallel composition of programs. Clearly, it is commutative, associative and distributed over nondeterministic choices and conditional statements.

Definition 3. *(parallel composition)*

1. *Parallel composition of two programs P and Q with disjoint index sets is defined as*
$$P \| Q =_{df} (g(P) \to P) \sqcap (g(Q) \to Q)$$
2. *Define $g(g(P) \to P) =_{df} g(P)$ and $\mathbf{index}(g(P) \to P) =_{df} \mathbf{index}(P)$. So $g(P \| Q) = g(P) \vee g(Q)$ and $\mathbf{index}(P \| Q) = \mathbf{index}P \cup \mathbf{index}Q$.*

By an appearance of the definition at most one of P or Q will be executed, but its iteration simulates asynchronous parallel composition of them. Now we deal with sequential circuits which are somehow synchronous outside and asynchronous inside. It means that they are built from combinational circuits which may have a feedback and are connected with one another in some way so a change of outside inputs to the whole circuit can trigger its execution only when it is waiting for supplying new input, but any change of shared stored level can affect any part using it at any instant of time. The event control of a program is used to repeat its execution. This is formalized in the following definition.

Definition 4. *(combinational program)*

1. *Combinational program has the form $@ \, g(S) \, S$, where $S = P_1 \| P_2 \| \ldots \| P_m$, and $P_1, P_2, \ldots, P_m$, called threads of S, are sequential or combinational programs with disjoint index sets.*
2. *Define $g(@ \, g(S) \, S) =_{df} g(S)$ and $\mathbf{index}(@ \, g(S) \, S) =_{df} \mathbf{index}(S)$.*

If a change of some variable x makes $g(P_i)$ changing from ff to tt, then we say the new value of x triggers the event control $g(P_i)$, and the thread P_i becomes enabled.

In [1] the behaviour of a combinational program with some threads is described by an infinite sequence of simulation steps as:

1. At the beginning of each simulation step a value for each input is supplied. The new values of inputs may trigger some event controls. Corresponding threads become enabled.
2. The environment chooses non-deterministically one of enabled threads to execute.
3. The execution of a chosen enabled thread P_i, which we call *atomic step*, consists of following steps:
   (a) Execute the program P_i.
   (b) Clear the event control to indicate that it has been used to trigger the chosen thread.
   (c) Broadcast the change over variables caused by the execution of P_i.
4. If there are no more enabled threads, this *simulation step* terminates and waits for the next input. If there is always at least one enabled thread after the execution of every atomic step, then this simulation step does not terminate.

The behaviour of a simulation step can be modeled by an iteration of non-deterministic choice of threads accompanied with some actions to clear and record changes of variables. This internal *atomic action* of the executing thread is called an *event*. The signal Boolean variable with index of executing thread is set to **false** if the execution does not bring any change of the variable. At the same time signal Boolean variables with all indexes of changed variables are set to **true** to trigger all threads using them. In our paper [7], we provided a relational description to it.

Definition 5. *(event semantics) Let @ $g(S)$ S be a combinational program with n variables $v_1, \ldots, v_n$ and m different indexes. Suppose that one of its threads P has an index set I. Its event semantics with index set I is defined by*

$$(g(P) \to P_{e,I}) =_{df} (g[P])^{\top} ; (P \|_{DIS} \mathbf{event}(P, I)),$$

where

1. *The assumption $b^{\top} =_{df} II \lhd b \rhd \top$, where $\top$ is the miracle program, i.e., the program is impossible to carry out. Here $g[P]$ is the assumption to start the program P.*
2. *$P \|_{DIS} Q$ represents the disjoint parallel composition of P and Q [3].*
3. *Program $\mathbf{event}(P, I)$ is used to clear the event control once the thread P is executed and broadcast the changes of variables caused by the execution of P:*
   $\mathbf{event}(P, I) =_{df} \exists v'_1, \ldots, v'_n \bullet result(P) \ \wedge \forall k : 1 \leq k \leq n \ \bullet$
   $\quad \sim v'_k := (\sim v_k \wedge \mathbf{clear}(I)) \vee (\mathbf{bool}(v_k \neq v'_k))^m$
   where
   − *the bullet symbol means that bound variables satisfy a following statement;*
   − *$result(P)$ is a predicate describing the program P, which mentions values of its variables $v_1, \ldots, v_n$ before the execution and their new values after the execution by the corresponding dash variables $v'_1, \ldots, v'_n$;*

- m is the number of different indexes;
- the Boolean expression **bool**(b) has the value tt if b is true, otherwise it takes the value ff;
- the m dimensioned logical vector $(\textbf{bool}(b))^m$ dimensioned logical vector has all component values of **bool**(b) and
- **clear**(I) is a m dimensioned logical vector such that
  clear$(I)[i] = f\!f$ if $i \in I$, otherwise **clear**$(I)[i] = tt$

The program **event**(P, I) compares new and old value of every variable used in P; if these values are same then it sets all components of this signal variables' vector with indexes in I to be ff, i.e., clears them; if these values are different then it sets all m components of this signal variables' vector to be tt, i.e., broadcasts the change of the variable.

4. We use a denotation $P_{e,I} =_{df} (P\|_{DIS}\textbf{event}(P, I))$

Now as in [7] we give a formal description to *simulation step* - an execution of the whole combinational program from previous waiting and receiving new values of inputs through its executing till to the next waiting. Indeed *Simulation step* is an iteration of events executed by enable threads until all of them have not been triggered. The program waits for new values of inputs and then starts the next simulation step. Results of simulation steps give us external observations of a program. A formal description of simulation step of a combinational program fully characterizes it.

Definition 6. *(simulation step) Let* @ $g(S)$ S *be a combinational program, where* $S = P\| \ldots \|Q$ *with disjoint index sets* $I, \ldots, J$, *respectively. Define its simulation step by the corresponding iteration of events made by enable threads*

$$@\, g(S)\ S =_{df} (g(P) \vee \ldots \vee g(Q)) * (g(P) \to P_{e,I} \sqcap \ldots \sqcap g(Q) \to Q_{e,J})$$

or shortly

$$@\, g(S)\ S =_{df} g(S) * S_e \text{ and we also use a notaion } Comb\ S =_{df} g(S) * S_e$$

where $g(S) = g(P) \vee \ldots \vee g(Q)$ *and* $S_e = g(P) \to P_{e,I} \sqcap \ldots \sqcap g(Q) \to Q_{e,J}$.

For simplicity we omit variable's declarations in this paper and suppose all variables are global.

3   Combinational Programs and Stability Semantics

The actual behaviour of a hardware device available for an implementation of a control system can be simulated by a program, and hence the same for the behaviour of combinational gates. This allows the correctness of a hardware device to be proved by standard software techniques. Now we introduce the concept of stability control of combinational programs, i.e., control is stable if variables do not change their values and then we use it to check their effectiveness.

Definition 7. *(stability control) The stability control of a combinational program is defined syntactically as follows*

1. $r(\overline{x} := \overline{E}) =_{df} \textbf{bool}(\overline{x} \neq \overline{E})$ *or for abbreviation* $r(\overline{x} := \overline{E}) =_{df} (\overline{x} \neq \overline{E})$.
2. $r(P \, op \, Q) =_{df} r(P) \vee r(Q)$ *for* $op \in \{; , \sqcap, \|\}$.
3. $r(P \triangleleft b \triangleright Q) = (b \wedge r(P)) \vee (\neg b \wedge r(Q))$.

A stability control can be used as a test for a proper execution of the corresponding sequential program. If the variables did not change, but the assignment is still done, then there is no effect.

Lemma 1. *If* S *is a sequential program with* $I = \textbf{index}(S)$, *then*

1. $S = S \triangleleft r(S) \triangleright \Pi$
2. $S_{e,I} = S_{e,I} \triangleleft r(S) \triangleright \Pi_{e,I}$

Proof. 1. Let S be an assignment $\overline{x} := \overline{E}$, then

$$
\begin{aligned}
S \triangleleft r(S) \triangleright \Pi \qquad &\qquad \{P \triangleleft b \triangleright Q = b \to P \sqcap \neg b \to Q\} \\
= r(S) \to S \sqcap \neg r(S) \to \Pi \qquad &\qquad \{\text{By Definition } 7\} \\
= \overline{x} \neq \overline{E} \to \overline{x} := \overline{E} \sqcap \overline{x} = \overline{E} \to \Pi \quad &\quad \{(\overline{x} = \overline{E})^\top; \Pi = (\overline{x} = \overline{E})^\top; (\overline{x} := \overline{E})\} \\
= \overline{x} \neq \overline{E} \to \overline{x} := \overline{E} \sqcap \overline{x} = \overline{E} \to \overline{x} := \overline{E} \quad &\quad \{b \to P \sqcap c \to P = (b \vee c) \to P\} \\
= (\overline{x} \neq \overline{E} \vee \overline{x} = \overline{E}) \to \overline{x} := \overline{E} \qquad &\qquad \{b \vee \neg b = \textbf{true}\} \\
- \textbf{true} \to \overline{x} := \overline{E} \\
= \overline{x} := \overline{E} \\
= S
\end{aligned}
$$

Similarly for other cases.

2. Let $S_{e,I} = S\|_{DIS}\textbf{event}(S, I))$, then

$$
\begin{aligned}
S_{e,I} \triangleleft r(S) \triangleright \Pi_{e,I} \\
= r(S) \to S_{e,I} \sqcap \neg r(S) \to \Pi_{e,I} \qquad &\qquad \{\text{By Definition } 5\} \\
= r(S) \to S_{e,I} \sqcap \neg r(S) \to (\Pi\|_{DIS}\textbf{event}(\Pi, I)) \quad &\quad \{\neg r(S)^\top; S = \neg r(S)^\top; \Pi\} \\
&\quad \{\textbf{event}(\neg r(S)^\top; S, I) = \neg r(S)^\top; \textbf{event}(\Pi, I)\} \\
= r(S) \to S_{e,I} \sqcap \neg r(S) \to (S\|_{DIS}\textbf{event}(S, I)) \qquad &\qquad \{\text{By Definition } 5\} \\
= r(S) \to S_{e,I} \sqcap \neg r(S) \to S_{e,I} \\
= (r(S) \vee \neg r(S)) \to S_{e,I} \\
= \textbf{true} \to S_{e,I} \\
= S_{e,I}
\end{aligned}
$$

The state of a program is defined as a vector of values of its variables and it becomes stable with respect to a program, when its execution brings no change of variables.

Definition 8. *(stability) Given a combinational program* $Comb\,S$. *Let* $\textbf{VAR}$ *the set of all variables and* $STATE: \textbf{VAR} \to \{0, 1\}$.

1. *(stable state) A state* $s \in STATE$ *is stable with respect to* $Comb\,S$ *if* $\langle \neg r(S) \rangle s = \textbf{true}$, *where the Boolean expression* $\langle \neg r(S) \rangle s$ *is obtained by replacing all free occurrences of variable* x *in* $\neg r(S)$ *by value* x *in state* s.
2. *(stability condition) A stability condition* $c(S)$ *for a program* S *is defined as*
   (a) *If* $S = (\overline{x} := \overline{E})$, *then* $c(S) =_{df} (\neg g(S) \Rightarrow \neg r(S))$.
   (b) *If* $S = P \, op \, Q$, *then* $c(S) =_{df} c(P) \wedge c(Q)$ *for* $op \in \{; , \triangleleft b \triangleright, \sqcap, \|\}$.
   (c) $c(Comb \, S) = c(S)$

If the stability condition of a program is its assumption, then it is waiting for new inputs only at its stable state. The next lemma shows that stability condition is invariant for an event executed by some thread of combinational program.

Lemma 2. *Given a combinational program Comb $S = @g(S)S$. Let $c = c(S)$ and $S'_e = S_e \lhd g(S) \rhd \Pi$. Then*

$$c^\top; S'_e = c^\top; S'_e; c_\perp$$

where $\perp$ is the program responsible for a failure and the assertion $c_\perp$ is defined as $c_\perp =_{df} \Pi \lhd c \rhd \perp$. That means after execution of S'_e the assertion c is achieved.

Proof. It is sufficient to prove for combinational program *Comb S*, where $S = P\|Q$. We use following abbreviation in the rest of the paper, when we deal with a program $S = P\|Q$.

$$
\begin{aligned}
s' &= g(S) & s &= r(S)\\
p' &= g(P) & p &= r(P)\\
q' &= g(Q) & q &= r(Q)\\
c_1 &= p' \to p & c_2 &= q' \to q\\
I &= \mathbf{index}(P) & J &= \mathbf{index}(Q)\\
P' &= P_{e,I} & Q' &= Q_{e,J}
\end{aligned}
$$

$\Pi_1 = \Pi_{e,I}$ and $\Pi_2 = \Pi_{e,J}$
$\Pi' = (p' \to \Pi_1 \sqcap q' \to \Pi_2) \lhd s' \rhd \Pi$

At first we show that event control p' and q' can be replaced by the stability controls p and q: $c^\top; S'_e = c^\top; (p \to P' \sqcap q \to Q') \lhd s \rhd \Pi'$. And then it follows the invariant of stability condition.

$$
\begin{aligned}
&c^\top; S'_e && \{\text{Definition } 6\}\\
={}& c^\top; (p' \to P' \sqcap q' \to Q') \lhd s' \rhd \Pi && \{\text{Lemma } 1\}\\
={}& c^\top; (p' \to (P' \lhd p \rhd \Pi_1) \sqcap q' \to (Q' \lhd q \rhd \Pi_2)) \lhd s' \rhd \Pi\{c = c_1 \wedge c_2\}\\
={}& c^\top; c_1^\top; c_2^\top; (p' \wedge p \to P' \sqcap p' \wedge \neg p \to \Pi_1 \sqcap && \{c_1 \wedge p' \wedge p = c_1 \wedge p\}\\
& q' \wedge q \to Q' \sqcap q' \wedge \neg q \to \Pi_2) \lhd s' \rhd \Pi && \{c_2 \wedge q' \wedge q = c_2 \wedge q\}\\
={}& c^\top; (p \to P' \sqcap q \to Q' \sqcap p' \wedge \neg p \to \Pi_1 \sqcap q' \wedge \neg q \to \Pi_2) \lhd s' \rhd \Pi\\
& \qquad\qquad \{s = p \vee q \text{ and by Lemma } 1 \ \neg p; \Pi_1 = \neg p; \Pi_{e,I}\}\\
={}& c^\top; ((p \to P' \sqcap q \to Q') \lhd s \rhd (p' \to \Pi_{e,I} \sqcap q' \to \Pi_{e,J})) \lhd s' \rhd \Pi\\
={}& c^\top; ((p \to P' \sqcap q \to Q') \lhd s \rhd \Pi') \lhd s' \rhd \Pi && \{\neg s'^\top; \Pi = \neg s'^\top; \Pi'\}\\
={}& c^\top; (p \to P' \sqcap q \to Q') \lhd s \wedge s' \rhd \Pi' && \{c \wedge s \wedge s' = c \wedge s\}\\
={}& c^\top; (p \to P' \sqcap q \to Q') \lhd s \rhd \Pi' && \{p \to P' = p \to P'; p'_\perp\}\\
={}& c^\top; (p \to P'; p'_\perp \sqcap q \to Q'; q'_\perp) \lhd s \rhd \Pi' && \{p'_\perp = p'_\perp; c_\perp\}\\
={}& c^\top; ((p \to P'; c_\perp \sqcap q \to Q'; c_\perp) && \{\neg s^\top; \Pi' = \neg s^\top; \Pi'; \neg s_\perp\}\\
& \lhd s \rhd \neg s_\perp; \Pi'; c_\perp) && \{\neg s_\perp = \neg s_\perp; c_\perp\}\\
={}& c^\top; ((p \to P' \sqcap q \to Q') \lhd s \rhd \Pi'); c_\perp\\
={}& c^\top; S'_e; c_\perp
\end{aligned}
$$

The stability condition is a loop invariant for whole combinational program, too. A combinational program executes from a stable state to a stable state, which have been proved in [6]:

Theorem 1. *For any combinational program CombS with* $c = c(S)$ *and* $s = r(S)$:

1. $c^\top; Comb\ S = c^\top; Comb\ S; c_\perp$
2. $c^\top; Comb\ S = c^\top; Comb\ S; \neg s_\perp$

Adding the stability control to the event control of a combinational program has no effect on its behaviour as shown in [6]:

Lemma 3. *For any combinational program CombS with* $c = c(S), s' = g(S)$ *and* $s = r(S)$:

$$c^\top; Comb\ S = c^\top; (s' \vee s) * S'_e$$

Proof. We have

$$
\begin{aligned}
& c^\top; (s' \vee s) * S'_e && \{(b \vee c) * R = b * R; (b \vee c) * R\} \\
= & c^\top; s' * S'_e; (s' \vee s) * S'_e && \{\text{ Theorem 1}\} \\
= & c^\top; s' * S'_e; c_\perp; \neg s'_\perp; (s' \vee s) * S'_e && \{c_\perp; \neg s'_\perp = c_\perp; \neg s'_\perp; \neg s_\perp\} \\
= & c^\top; s' * S'_e; \neg s'_\perp; \neg s_\perp; (s' \vee s) * S'_e && \{b_\perp; c_\perp = (b \wedge c)_\perp\} \\
= & c^\top; Comb\ S; (\neg s' \wedge \neg s)_\perp; (s' \vee s) * S'_e && \{\neg b_\perp; b * R = \neg b_\perp\} \\
= & c^\top; Comb\ S
\end{aligned}
$$

The stability control can replace the event control as a loop condition for combinational programs. This loop program is really a software program with no signal variables. From the stable state new input values are supplied and the stability is broken. Next the simulation step occurs, it starts running and continues the execution until reaching the next stable state.

Definition 9. *(loop program) Iteration of a program S and its stability are defined as* $S^* =_{df} r(S) * S$ *and* $r(S^*) =_{df} r(S)$.

A loop program is used to describe one simulation step of the considered kind of sequential circuits as the iteration of events made by executions of the enabled threads. Then the loop program fully characterizes the whole corresponding combinational program. Finally, hardware combinational programs can be derived to equivalent software loop programs with stability control as loop condition.

Theorem 2. *For any combinational program Comb S with* $c = c(S)$ *and* $s = r(S)$:

$$c^\top; Comb\ S = c^\top; s * S$$

Proof. Clearly

$$
\begin{aligned}
&c^\top; Comb\ S && \{\text{Definition 6}\}\\
&= c^\top; s' * S'_e && \{\text{Lemma 3}\}\\
&= c^\top; (s' \vee s) * S'_e && \{\text{Theorem 1}\}\\
&= c^\top; s * S'_e; (s' \vee s) * S'_e && \{\text{ Lemma 2}\}\\
&= c^\top; s * S'_e; c_\perp; \neg s_\perp; (s' \vee s) * S'_e && \{c_\perp; \neg s'_\perp = c_\perp; \neg s'_\perp; \neg s_\perp\}\\
&= c^\top; s * S'_e; \neg s'_\perp; \neg s_\perp; (s' \vee s) * S'_e && \{\neg s'_\perp; \neg s_\perp = (\neg s' \wedge \neg s)_\perp\}\\
&= c^\top; s * S'_e; \neg(s' \vee s)_\perp; (s' \vee s) * S'_e && \{\neg b_\perp; b * R = \Pi\}\\
&= c^\top; s * S'_e && \{\text{Signal variables are redundant}\}\\
&= c^\top; s * S
\end{aligned}
$$

Then for combinational programs the relational event semantics and the stability semantics are equivalent. Now we can use software techniques for formal verification as in the next section . If in the simulation step of a combinational program we give the priority of choosing enable threads to recently executing thread, i.e., every thread or composition of some threads continuously runs until it does not become enabled in execution of the combinational program, then it leads to deeper results.

Lemma 4. *Suppose $Comb\ S = Comb\ (P_1 \| P_2 \| \ldots \| P_k \| \ldots \| P_n)$ a combinational program and $Q \sqsubseteq R$ to stand for the improvement ordering, comparing Q with R (see [3]). Then*

1. *$Comb\ S \sqsubseteq Comb\ (Comb\ (P_1 \| P_2 \| \ldots \| P_k) \| \ldots \| P_n)$*
2. *$Comb\ S \sqsubseteq Comb\ (Comb\ P_1 \| Comb\ P_2 \| \ldots \| Comb\ P_n)$*

Proof. Clearly by the event semantics of combinational program.

4   Syntactic Combinational Programs

The assembly of combinational circuits is subject to the constraint that the output wire of each circuit can be connected only to the input some other gate, and that a chain of gates connected in this way must never form a cycle. Partial order on variables ensures that the first occurrence of each output wire name is on the left hand side of its defining equation, and that the behaviour of the device can be simulated by executing the equations as a sequence of assignments in a high level language. The constraint is syntactic checkable and can be formalized.

At first we investigate the subclass of combinational programs, whose threads are idempotent.

Definition 10. *(idempotent program) A program P is idempotent if $P; P = P$*

After execution of an idempotent program its state becomes stable. Clearly, combinational programs have this property.

Lemma 5. *Given any program P and any combinational program $Comb\ S$. Then*

1. *The program P is idempotent, if and only if $P = P; r(P)_\perp$.*
2. *The combinational program $Comb\ S$ is idempotent.*

Proof. Obvious by Theorem 2 and the law $s * S = s * S; (\neg s)_\perp$.

If all threads are combinational circuits or sequential circuits which are simulated by combinational programs, then by the previous Lemma these components are idempotent. So combinational programs with idempotent threads take an important role.

Definition 11. *(component-idempotent program) A combinational program is component-idempotent if all its threads are idempotent.*

In [6] we show that from an initial stable state component-idempotent combinational program with two threads can start from any component and follows by another until it does not reach a stable state. That means in this case we can eliminate parallel composition used in definition of a combinational program.

Theorem 3. *Let $S = P \| Q$, where P and Q are idempotent programs, then*
$$c^\top; Comb\, S = c^\top; Comb\,(P; Q \sqcap Q; P)$$

Each gate has private input and output wires, and each wire has its separate name. This can be formalized as follows:

Definition 12. *(input, output variables) Given a program P in a normal form of the parallel assignment $(v_1, \ldots, v_k := E_1, \ldots, E_k)$. Define*

$$\mathbf{Out}(P) =_{df} \{v_1, \ldots, v_k\}$$

i.e., $\mathbf{Out}(P)$ is a set of all variables which occur on the left hand side of the expressions of a normal form of P. We suppose that none of variables occurs more than once on the left hand side of assignments of P.

$$\mathbf{In}(P) =_{df} \{v_j | v_j \text{ appears in } E_i, \forall i : 1 \leq i \leq k\}$$

i.e., $\mathbf{In}(P)$ is a set of all variables which occur on the right hand side of the expressions of a normal form of P.
The pairs (v_i, E_i) are called updates of the program P.

Combinational circuits are connected via variables, output variables of previous circuits are include in input of next ones.

Definition 13. *(precedence relation) Given a collection of programs $\{P_i, i = 1, \ldots, n\}$. Define a binary relation $\preceq$ on programs as follows*

$$P_i \preceq P_j \quad \text{if and only if} \quad \mathbf{Out}(P_i) \cap \mathbf{In}(P_j) \neq \emptyset$$

i.e., some outputs of P_i are within inputs of P_j.

Naturally, sequential circuits are expected to terminate and behave correctly. It is fine if these properties are syntactically checkable. Now we give a definition of such class of component-idempotent combinational programs that all their threads do not form a Precedence cycle and some of their threads may have a feedback.

Definition 14. *(component syntactic combinational program) Given a collection of idempotent programs $\{P_i \mid i = 1, \ldots, n\}$, where $Out(P_i) \cap Out(P_j) = \emptyset$ for all pairs of different threads. Then a combinational $Comb\ (P_1\|P_2\|\ldots\|P_n)$ is called a component syntactic, if*

1. *The closure of the binary relation $\preceq$ is a partial order on the set $\{P_i \mid i = 1, \ldots, n\}$ and*
2. *All non-minimal threads P_i with respect to $(\preceq)^*$ have no feedback: $In(P_i) \cap Out(P_i) = \emptyset$ and only its minimal threads may have a feedback.*

For simplicity we always suppose that $P_i \preceq P_j \Rightarrow i \leq j$.

Definition 15. *(syntactic combinational program) Given a collection of updates $U = \{(v_i, E_i) \mid i = 1, \ldots, m\}$ and every update is used only for one of the programs $P_1, P_2, \ldots, P_n$. Then a combinational $Comb\ (P_1\|P_2\|\ldots\|P_n)$ is said to be syntactical, if*

1. *A combinational program $Comb\,((v_1 := E_1)\|(v_2 := E_2)\|\ldots\|(v_m := E_m))$ is a component syntactic, and*
2. *Every thread P_i is constructed from some of these updates by any sequential or multiple parallel or combinational compositions.*

Given a component syntactic combinational program with threads in the form of single assignments, i.e. given a collection of single idempotent updates with no dependency cycle and only first precedence updates may have a feedback. Then any combinational program reconstructed from them by some kinds of compositions in some way is syntactical. We will show that a way, how threads are built from these updates, does not effect to the final results.

Execution of a syntactic combinational program inside simulation step preserves variable's stability and their iteration brings the new variable to stable states according to the associated partial order.

Lemma 6. *Let $Comb\ S = Comb\ (P_1\|P_2\|\ldots\|P_n)$ be a component syntactic combinational program. Then*

1. $(\wedge_{i \leq k} \neg r(P_i))^\top ; P_j = (\wedge_{i \leq k} \neg r(P_i))^\top ; P_j ; (\wedge_{i \leq k} \neg r(P_i))_\perp, \ \forall j.$
2. $(\wedge_{i < j} \neg r(P_i))^\top ; P_j = (\wedge_{i < j} \neg r(P_i))^\top ; P_j ; (\wedge_{i \leq j} \neg r(P_i))_\perp$

Proof. Obvious by properties of a component syntactic combinational program.

If after each execution of single multiple assignment at least one of variables becomes stable, then all variables will be stable during its iteration. Because enable thread of a syntactic combinational program should be executed, then every variable should become stable during execution of a syntactic combinational program. It follows its termination.

Theorem 4. *Any syntactic combinational program terminates.*

Proof. If there is only single component-thread $(\overline{v} := \overline{E}) = (v_1, \ldots, v_h := E_1, \ldots, E_h)$, then without loss of generality we assume that $v_i \preceq v_j \Rightarrow i \leq j$. It follows that $(\overline{v} := \overline{E}) = (v_h := E_h); \ldots; (v_2 := E_2); (v_1 := E_1)$. Then using it and by Lemma 6 (2) we have

$$
\begin{aligned}
& c^\top; Comb\ (\overline{v} := \overline{E}) \\
= {} & c^\top; (\overline{v} := \overline{E}); Comb\ (\overline{v} := \overline{E}) \\
= {} & c^\top; (v_h := E_h); \ldots; (v_1 := E_1); Comb\ (\overline{v} := \overline{E}) && \{\text{Lemma 6 (2)}\} \\
= {} & c^\top; (v_h := E_h); \ldots; (v_1 := E_1); (v_1 = E_1)_\perp; Comb\ (\overline{v} := \overline{E}) && \{\text{Similarly}\} \\
= {} & c^\top; (\overline{v} := \overline{E})^2; (v_1 = E_1 \wedge v_2 = E_2)_\perp; Comb\ (\overline{v} := \overline{E}) && \{\text{Lemma 6 (1)}\} \\
= {} & c^\top; (\overline{v} := \overline{E})^h; (\wedge_{1 \leq i \leq h} v_i = E_i)_\perp; Comb\ (\overline{v} := \overline{E}) && \{\text{Theorem 2}\} \\
= {} & c^\top; (\overline{v} := \overline{E})^h
\end{aligned}
$$

Let n be a number of components. Suppose by induction we have proved the theorem for fewer number of components and m be a number such that for all combinations R of $n-1$ components of the program: $R^m = R^{m-1}$. By first part of the proof for any component P_i let h_i be a number such that $P_i^{h_i+1} = P_i^{h_i}$ and $h = \max h_i$. Denote $k = (m+1).h$. Then

$$
\begin{aligned}
& c(S)^\top; Comb\ S && \{\text{Theorem 2}\} \\
= {} & c(S)^\top; S^* \\
= {} & c(S)^\top; S^k; S^* && \{\text{By the assumption}\} \\
= {} & c(S)^\top; S^{(m+1)h}; S^* && \{P_1 \text{ appears at least } h \text{ times}\} \\
= {} & c(S)^\top; S^{m_1}; P_1; \ldots; S^{m_h}; P_1; S^* && \{\text{Lemma 6 and } P_1^h = P_1^h; \neg r(P_1)\} \\
= {} & c(S)^\top; S^k; (\neg r(P_1))_\perp; S^* \\
= {} & c(S)^\top; S^k; (\neg r(P_1))_\perp; S^k; S^* && \{\text{Lemma 6 and } P_2^h = P_2^h; \neg r(P_2)\} \\
= {} & c(S)^\top; S^k; (\neg r(P_1))_\perp; S^k; (\neg r(P_2))_\perp; S^* \\
= {} & c(S)^\top; S^{2k}; (\neg r(P_1) \wedge \neg r(P_2))_\perp; S^* && \{\text{By the iteration}\} \\
= {} & c(S)^\top; S^{nk}; (\neg r(P_1) \wedge \ldots \wedge \neg r(P_n))_\perp; S^* && \{b_\perp; c_\perp = (b \wedge c)_\perp\} \\
= {} & c(S)^\top; S^{nk}; (\neg r(S))_\perp; r(S) * S \\
= {} & c(S)^\top; S^{nk}; (\neg r(S))_\perp
\end{aligned}
$$

Lemma 7. *A component syntactic combinational program terminates*

Proof. Similar to second part of the previous proof.

In general different combinational constructions from single assignments give differentially behaved programs as following example shows.

Example 1. Given two single assignments: $x := p \wedge \neg y$ and $y := p \wedge \neg x$. Using them we construct following combinational programs $Comb\ ((x := p \wedge \neg y) \| (y := p \wedge \neg x))$ and $Comb\ (x, y) := (p \wedge \neg y, p \wedge \neg x)$, where p is used as an input and x, y as variables. In the first one we use the shared store parallel composition and in second - the synchronous parallel or multiple assignment. From the initial state with $x = y = \textbf{false}$ and $p = \textbf{false}$ the new value of input $p = \textbf{true}$ will trigger both threads of two combinational programs.

1. In the shared store parallel approach the program $Comb\,((x := p \wedge \neg y) \| (y := p \wedge \neg x))$ terminates, but its final state is not deterministic:
   - If first thread executes first and then second one: $x := \mathbf{true} \wedge \neg\mathbf{false} = \mathbf{true}$ and $y := \mathbf{true} \wedge \neg\mathbf{true} = \mathbf{false}$. The stable state ($x = \mathbf{true}, y = \mathbf{false}$) is reached.
   - If the second thread executes first and then first one: $y := \mathbf{true} \wedge \neg\mathbf{false} = \mathbf{true}$ and $x := \mathbf{true} \wedge \neg\mathbf{true} = \mathbf{false}$. The stable state ($x = \mathbf{false}, y = \mathbf{true}$) is reached.

2. In the multiple parallel approach the program $Comb\,(x, y) := (p \wedge \neg y, p \wedge \neg x)$ does not terminate. At first $(x, y) := (\mathbf{true} \wedge \neg\mathbf{false}, \mathbf{true} \wedge \neg\mathbf{false}) = (\mathbf{true}, \mathbf{true})$ and then $(x, y) := (\mathbf{true} \wedge \neg\mathbf{true}, \mathbf{true} \wedge \neg\mathbf{true}) = (\mathbf{false}, \mathbf{false})$. It does not reach a stable state.

Clearly, the behaviours of the two programs are not equivalent. There is a dependency cycle on variables in two assignments.

But if a given set of updates is partially ordered by the precedence relation, then any syntactic combinational program leads to the same result. At first we show that component syntactic combinational program behaves like a sequential composition of threads in order consistent with the dependency order.

Theorem 5. *Given a component syntactic combinational program $Comb\,S = Comb\,(P_1 \| P_2 \| \dots \| P_n)$, where $P_i \preceq P_j \Rightarrow i \leq j$. Then*

1. $c(S)^\top ; Comb\,S = c(S)^\top ; P_1 ; P_2 ; \dots ; P_n$
2. $c(S)^\top ; Comb\,S = c(S)^\top ; Comb\,(P_{i_1} ; P_{i_2} ; \dots ; P_{i_n})$, *where $i_1, i_2, \dots, i_n$ is some permutation of $1, 2, \dots, n$.*
3. $c(S)^\top ; Comb\,S = c(S)^\top ; Comb\,(P_1 \|_S P_2 \|_S \dots \|_S P_n)$
4. $c(S)^\top ; Comb\,S = c(S)^\top ; Comb\,(Comb\,(P_1 \| \dots \| P_k) \| \dots \| P_n)$

Where $\|_S$ is synchronous parallel composition of two output disjoint programs.

Proof. 1. Suppose $P_i \preceq P_j \Rightarrow i \leq j$.

$$c(S)^\top ; Comb\,S \qquad\qquad\qquad\qquad\qquad \{\text{Theorem 2}\}$$
$$= c(S)^\top ; S^* \qquad\qquad\qquad\qquad\qquad\qquad \{\text{Lemma 1}\}$$
$$= c(S)^\top ; S^* ; (\neg r(S))_\perp \qquad\qquad \{\,(a \wedge b)_\perp = a_\perp ; b_\perp\}$$
$$= c(S)^\top ; S^* ; (\neg r(P_1))_\perp ; (\neg r(S))_\perp \qquad\qquad \{\text{Lemma 1}\}$$
$$= c(S)^\top ; S^* ; (\neg r(P_1))_\perp ; P_1 ; (\neg r(S))_\perp$$
$$= c(S)^\top ; S^* ; P_1 ; (\neg r(P_2))_\perp ; (\neg r(S))_\perp \qquad\qquad \{\text{Lemma 1}\}$$
$$= c(S)^\top ; S^* ; P_1 ; (\neg r(P_2))_\perp ; P_2 ; (\neg r(S))_\perp$$
$$= c(S)^\top ; S^* ; P_1 ; P_2 ; (\neg r(S))_\perp \qquad\qquad \{\text{By the induction}\}$$
$$= c(S)^\top ; S^* ; P_1 ; P_2 ; \dots ; P_n \qquad \{\text{By the termination from Theorem 4}\}$$
$$= c(S)^\top ; S^k ; P_1 ; P_2 ; \dots ; P_n \qquad \{\text{By syntactical properties of } Comb\,S :$$
$$(x := e; z := g; x := f) = (z := g; x := f),\ x \text{ not in } g\}$$
$$= c(S)^\top ; P_1 ; P_2 ; \dots ; P_n$$

2. We denote $Comb\ Q = Comb\ (P_{i_1}; \ldots; P_{i_{n-1}}; P_{i_n})$

$$
\begin{aligned}
& c(S)^\top; Comb\ (P_{i_1}; \ldots; P_{i_{n-1}}; P_{i_n}) \\
={}& c(S)^\top; (P_{i_1}; \ldots; P_{i_{n-1}}; P_{i_n}); Comb\ Q && \{\text{Lemma } 6(1)\} \\
={}& c(S)^\top; (P_{i_1}; \ldots; P_{i_{n-1}}; P_{i_n}); (\neg r(P_1); Comb\ Q && \{\text{Lemma } 6\} \\
={}& c(S)^\top; (P_{i_1}; \ldots; P_{i_{n-1}}; P_{i_n})^n; (\neg r(P_1) \wedge \ldots \wedge \neg r(P_n))\bot; Comb\ Q && \\
={}& c(S)^\top; (P_{i_1}; \ldots; P_{i_{n-1}}; P_{i_n})^n; (\neg r(P_1) \wedge \ldots \wedge \neg r(P_n))\bot && \{\text{Lemma } 6(2)\} \\
={}& c(S)^\top; (P_{i_1}; \ldots; P_{i_{n-1}}; P_{i_n})^n; (\neg r(P_1) \wedge \ldots \wedge \neg r(P_n))\bot; P_1; P_2; \ldots; P_n && \\
={}& c(S)^\top; (P_{i_1}; \ldots; P_{i_{n-1}}; P_{i_n})^n; P_1; P_2; \ldots; P_n && \{\text{idempotent of minimal}\} \\
& \qquad \{(x := e; z := g; x := f) = (z := g; x := f),\ x \text{ not in } g\} \\
={}& c(S)^\top; P_1; P_2; \ldots; P_n && \{\text{Part 1 of this Theorem}\} \\
={}& c(S)^\top; Comb\ (P_1 \| \ldots \| P_{n-1} \| P_n) &&
\end{aligned}
$$

3. Clearly

$$
\begin{aligned}
& c(S)^\top; Comb\ (P_1 \| \ldots \| P_{n-1} \| P_n) && \{\text{Part 2 of this Theorem}\} \\
={}& c(S)^\top; Comb\ (P_n; P_{n-1}; \ldots; P_2; P_1) && \{P_n; \ldots; P_1 = P_1 \|_S \ldots \|_S P_n\} \\
={}& c(S)^\top; Comb\ (P_1 \|_S P_2 \|_S \ldots \|_S P_n) &&
\end{aligned}
$$

4. Obvious from Lemma 4.

Equivalent sequential executions of threads of a syntactic combinational program are uniquely defined by their Precedence relation. It leads to its normal form by a multiple parallel assignment.

Corollary 1. *(normal form) Given a syntactic combinational program $Comb\ S = Comb\ (P_1 \| P_2 \| \ldots \| P_n)$ with the collection of updates $U = \{(v_i, E_i) \mid i = 1, \ldots, m\}$ such that $v_i \preceq v_j \Rightarrow i \leq j$. Then*

$$
c(S)^\top; Comb\ S = c(S)^\top; (\overline{v} := \overline{F})
$$

where $F_1 =_{df} E_1$, $F_{k+1} =_{df} E_{k+1}[F_1, \ldots, F_k / v_1, \ldots, v_k]$.

Proof. Clearly by the definition of a syntactic combinational program, every thread P_i can be constructed from some of these updates by any sequential or multiple parallel or combinational compositions.

$$
\begin{aligned}
& c(S)^\top; (\overline{v} := \overline{F}) \\
& \qquad\qquad\qquad\qquad\qquad\qquad\qquad\qquad\qquad \{\text{By definition of } F_k\} \\
={}& c(S)^\top; (v_1 := E_1); (v_2 := E_2); \ldots; (v_k := E_k); \ldots; (v_m := E_m) \\
& \qquad\qquad\qquad\qquad\qquad\qquad\qquad\qquad\qquad\qquad \{\text{Theorem } 5\} \\
={}& c(S)^\top; Comb\ ((v_1 := E_1) \| (v_2 := E_2) \| \ldots \| (v_k := E_k) \| \ldots \| (v_m := E_m)) \\
& \qquad\qquad \{\text{Construction according to } P_i \text{ and by Theorem } 5\} \\
={}& c(S)^\top; Comb\ (P_1 \| P_2 \| \ldots \| P_n)
\end{aligned}
$$

So all syntactic combinational programs with the same collection of updates have the same normal form by the multiple assignment. Then the effect of a syntactic combinational program is based on the collection of updates with no dependency cycle from which it is constructed but does not depend on a way how it is built of. It follows for them fully parallel and shared store parallel coincide.

Corollary 2. *(equivalence of asynchronous and synchronous parallel) Given a syntactic combinational program* $Comb\,S = Comb\,(P_1\|P_2\|\dots\|P_n)$. *Then*

$$c(S)^\top; Comb\,(P_1\|P_2\|\dots\|P_n) \;=\; c(S)^\top; Comb\,(P_1\|_S P_2\|_S\dots\|_S P_n)$$

where $\|_S$ *is synchronous parallel composition of two output disjoint programs.*

5 Conclusion

The paper [1] describes an event semantics of combinational circuits so that the execution of a combinational device, which is triggered by the change over its input wires, will lead to a stable state. A well-designed sequential circuit always terminates, and its behaviour is solely captured by the stable states. In papers [6] and [7] the relational semantics to event and simulation step of some kinds of sequential circuits is introduced where signal variables have been considered in accompany with each state variable to keep information of its changes during the execution. To overcome this disadvantage and fully use standard software verification techniques in [2], [3] this paper presents stability semantics to these sequential circuits and shows it is equivalent to the relational event semantics. We examine some properties of combinational programs. We give more formal proofs to some known results such that a syntactic combinational program terminates and reaches unique stable state. The behaviour of a combinational program depends on collection of updates from which it is built but not on how they are combined if there is no dependency cycle on these updates. In this way the paper presents their normal form and shows that for them Dimitrov's multiple parallel approach [9] and Zhu's shared store parallel approach [8] are equivalent.

The author would like to thank He JiFeng for his valuable advises and UNU/IIST for great support.

References

1. M. Gordon. Event and Cycle Semantics of Hardware Description Languages. University of Cambridge Computer Laboratory, (1998).
2. C.A.R Hoare *et al.* Laws of Programming. Comm. of the ACM 30 (8): 672-686 (1987).
3. C.A.R. Hoare and He Jifeng. Unifying Theory of Programming. Prentice - Hall International, (1998).
4. Open VERILOG International. VERILOG Hardware Description Language Reference Manual, Version 1.0.
5. D.E. Thomas and P.R. Mooby. The VERILOG Hardware Description Language. Kluwer Academic Publishers, (1995)
6. T.V. Dung and He JiFeng. A Theory of Combinational Programs. UNU/IIST Report No 162.
7. T.V. Dung and He JiFeng. A Theory of Combinational Programs. Proceedings, APSEC 2001, 325-328.
8. Z. Huibiao, J. Bowen and He JiFeng. Deriving Operational Semantics from Denotational Semantics for Verilog. Proceedings, APSEC 2001, 177-184.
9. J. Dimitrov. Operational semantics for Verilog. Proceedings, APSEC 2001, 161-168.

Generating C Code from LOGS Specifications

Jianguo Zhou[1] and Yifeng Chen[2]

[1] Depart. of Computer Science, University of Leicester, Leicester LE1 7RH, UK
J.Zhou@mcs.le.ac.uk
[2] Depart. of Computer Science, Durham University, Durham DH1 3LE, UK
Yifeng.Chen@dur.ac.uk

Abstract. This paper introduces a tool that automatically translates a concrete form of specifications into C code linked with BSPlib. The translation tool is rigorously developed with important safety properties proved. A LOGS specification for Bulk-Synchronous Parallelism is a relation of an initial state, a final state and some intermediate states. Nondeterminism and parallelism correspond to disjunction and conjunction respectively. Various advanced specification commands can be derived from the basic ones. The translator checks syntax, freedom of communication interference, type consistency and communication dependencies before generating the target code. Static analysis (including both static checkings and translation) is presented in abstract interpretation. It is shown that a few laws are complete for transforming any specification into a normal form. These laws are satisfied by the abstract functions. We demonstrate the actual effects of the abstract functions by applying them on the normal form. The approach has been implemented using an object-oriented language.

1 Introduction

Bulk-Synchronous Parallelism [13] is a programming paradigm based on variable sharing and global synchronisation. In BSP, processes are synchronised at corresponding synchronisation commands issued by individual processes. Arbitrarily many local computation commands are allowed between consecutive synchronisations. Most communications are delayed until the following synchronisation point at which their delivery is guaranteed. Synchronization points partition the execution of any BSP program into so-called *supersteps*. BSP has a simple model for complexity analysis. However the main challenge still lies in parallel program development [12]. The following BSP program consists of one superstep comprising two processes in parallel:

$$(x := 1 \; ; \; \mathtt{put}\; y := x - 1 \; ; \; \mathtt{get}\; x := y + 1 \; ; \; \mathtt{sync}) \; \| \; (y := 2 \; ; \; \mathtt{sync})$$

We have omitted the syntax declaring x to be local to the first program and y to be local to the second; put is a communication command that writes a value (calculated locally) to a remote variable, and get is a command that reads the value (immediately before the following synchronization) of a remote variable. Any communication is completed at the following sync commands. Thus the final values of x and y are 3 and 0 respectively.

Traditionally BSP programs are developed in the SPMD style. One program is run on multiple processors, each of which may process a segment of the input data. The

D.V. Hung and M. Wirsing (Eds.): ICTAC 2005, LNCS 3722, pp. 195–210, 2005.

length and relative position of each segment in a large array must be calculated dynamically by the parallel program according the dynamic process's pid. Such code is difficult to write, as the size of the input data may not be exactly aligned for a particular partitioning method. Programmers must not only worry about the computation but also the actual communications and the detailed partitioning. We try to develop tools to automate these non-computation aspects of parallel programming in this paper.

Existing BSP implementations [9] actually allow MIMD programming. For example, we can store different C procedures (as function pointers) in an array and use a single program to call one of them according to the dynamic process's pid number. This is essentially MIMD programming: different processors run different program procedures in execution.

A BSPlib-C program is a normal C program linked with BSPlib [9] that supports several function calls. Command bsp_pushregister registers a piece of memory to be shared for communications; command bsp_poporegister releases a piece of memory from registration; command bsp_sync synchronises with other processes' bsp_sync commands; command bsp_put sends some data from a local address to an address on a remote process, and the communication is delivered at the following synchronisation; command bsp_get requests some data from an address on a remote process to to a local address, and the data arrives at the following synchronisation.

Chen and Sanders [3] introduced an intermediate specification language LOGS supporting MIMD program development in BSP and PRAM [7] styles. It makes explicit the intermediate global states at synchronisation points. Communications are abstracted in LOGS. A number of algebraic and refinement laws have been identified for the language and applied to the reasoning and refinement of (data-parallel) matrix multiplication and (task-parallel) dining philosopher problem. For a vector w of program variables, the primitives of LOGS are commands on w taking n steps. The refinement of specifications corresponds to removal of nondeterminism. The following table lists the primitive commands of LOGS.

$\langle p \rangle_n$	n-step command
$P \,\fatsemi\, Q$	sequential composition
$P \sqcap Q$	nondeterministic choice (disjunction)
$P \sqcup Q$	parallel composition (conjunction)
ϕf	recursion

An n-step command is written $\langle p \rangle_n$ where $p = p(\overleftarrow{w}, w_0, \ldots, w_{n-1}, \overrightarrow{w})$. In it each w_k with $k < n$ denotes the state at the $(k+1)$-th intermediate synchronisation point. For example, $\langle \overleftarrow{x} + 1 = x_0 = \overrightarrow{x} - 1 \rangle_1$ is a 1LOGS command in which the program variable x is increased by 1 before its first intermediate synchronisation point x_0 and increased by 1 again by termination. Another example of 0-step command $\langle \overleftarrow{x}^2 + \overrightarrow{x}^2 \leqslant 4 \rangle_0$ represents a local computation without synchronisation, and the final state of x is implicitly related to its initial state by an inequation. The sequential composition of two processes merges into a longer one in which the final state of the first process is associated with the initial state of the second process, and then the interface is hidden. No additional synchronisation point is inserted by sequential composition. This reflects the fact that, in BSP, the sequential composition can be placed either at a synchronisation point or between two consecutive synchronisation points. The nondeterministic choice between two nLOGS commands is the disjunction of their internal predicates. The parallel composition of two nLOGS commands is the conjunction of their internal predicates. More useful commands can be derived from the primitive ones, including binary conditional, loop, repetitions, safety and liveness specifications.

A specification is concrete, if it is composed of only sequential and parallel compositions and a finite number of 0-step commands, each explicitly expressed as $\langle \overrightarrow{w} = f(\overleftarrow{w}) \rangle_0$, and 1-step commands, each expressed as $\langle w = g(\overleftarrow{w}) \wedge \overrightarrow{w} = h(\overleftarrow{w}, w) \rangle_1$ where f, g and h are expressions. The refinement from abstract specifications to concrete ones requires decision makings and is normally done manually [3]. A concrete specification can be automatically transformed into program code. Chen and Sanders [2] studied the refinement laws from LOGS to a simplified BSP language. The method is mainly suitable for manual calculation.

In this paper concrete LOGS specifications are directly transformed into MIMD code for BSPLib in C. The resulting code has the appearance of a common SPMD program. However the single main function calls different sub-programs (stored in an array) on different machines according to the pid of the machine. In short, different programs execute different commands during the same superstep and hence form a MIMD program. Program code is generated for each machine separately. This allows the translator to calculate the approximated values of some expressions (e.g. indices of array access) for specific individual processes during the phase of static analysis and hence results in faster and safer code. Compared to other code generation methods for executable specifications, our approach does automate a few aspects of coding that otherwise are difficult to write manually. They include the automation of inserting code for registration/communication/synchronisation, pre-defined data partitioning and distributing, and individual process based safety and consistency checking. The resulting C code is impossible to write manually, because for example the boundary constants of the loops are already pre-determined (and safety-checked) by the translator for each individual processor (resulting code whose length grows with the number of processes).

Before generating target code, the translator needs to check the syntax, freedom of communication interference, type consistency and communication dependencies between processes. The methods are presented in abstract interpretation. Abstract interpretation [5,6] is a theoretical foundation of static-analysis methods based on denotational semantics. For example, syntactical checking can be defined as an abstract boolean function on program constructs. Code generation becomes an abstract function that transforms a program into a string in the target language.

Communication interference occurs in any shared-memory parallelism. It is represented as infeasibility and inconsistency in LOGS [3], modelled as nondeterminism in most BSP semantic models [2,8], and implemented as runtime exception in BSPlib [9]. It is possible to check communication interference for basic LOGS specifications statically. Advanced commands such as multiple parallel composition and loops may require some degree of approximation (see section 3).

Traditional type systems are founded in proof theory and defined with inference rules in the style of operational semantics. Cousot [4] showed that types can be checked using abstract interpretation. Simple (stateless) type inference rules directly correspond to abstract functions on types, which can be regarded as abstract values. If type inference rules depend on the context (i.e. the state of the type checker), it is still possible to encode the context as an argument of an abstract function.

How do we know that the definition of an abstract function is appropriate? Normal form is a widely used technique in relational/predicative semantics [10,11]. Under some algebraic laws, the syntax of a language may collapse to a normal form. This is known as the *completeness* of the laws with respect to the normal form in *algebraic semantics*. In this paper, we try to demonstrate the effect of an abstract function by applying it to the normal form of LOGS specifications and calculate the result. This suffices to show the effect of the function on *every* specification, if every specification can be reduced to the normal form, and the abstract function satisfies the algebraic laws.

1-step LOGS commands (those containing only one global synchronization) represent stepwise design of both PRAM and BSP programs with synchronisations, while 0-step commands is a specific characteristic of BSP's local computation without synchronisations. Here, we use two special 1-step commands:

$$\lceil p(\overleftarrow{w}, \overrightarrow{w}) \rceil = \langle p \wedge w = \overrightarrow{w} \rangle_1 \quad \text{early transition}$$
$$\lfloor p(\overleftarrow{w}, \overrightarrow{w}) \rfloor = \langle p \wedge \overleftarrow{w} = w \rangle_1 \quad \text{late transition.}$$

An *early* transition (implementable with bsp_put()) is a 1-step command that may change state before the synchronisation point but maintains a stable state between the intermediate and final states. For example, the specification

$$\lceil \overrightarrow{x} = \overleftarrow{y} + 1 \rceil \sqcup \lceil \overrightarrow{y} = \overleftarrow{x} - 1 \rceil \tag{1}$$

is a parallel composition of two early transitions. The values of x and y are changed at the synchronisation point. The new values remain unchanged in the final state. Most numeric computations with data parallelism can be characterised with early transitions. A *late* transition (implementable with bsp_get()) keeps a stable state up to the synchronisation point but may have a different final state from the intermediate state. Other processes can access a process's initial state by observing its first intermediate state at the synchronisation point. This is particularly convenient for task-parallel computations such as the dining-philosopher problem [3].

A concrete 1-step specification $\langle x = g(\overleftarrow{x}) \wedge \overrightarrow{x} = h(\overleftarrow{x}, x) \rangle_1$ can always be transformed into the sequential composition of an early transition and a 0-step command with a fresh temporary variable y: $\lceil \overrightarrow{x} = g(\overleftarrow{x}) \wedge \overrightarrow{y} = \overrightarrow{y} \rceil \ \S \ \langle \overrightarrow{x} = h(\overleftarrow{x}, \overrightarrow{y}) \rangle_0$, or similarly, the sequential composition of a 0-step command and a late transition. We deal only with early transitions in this paper, although 0-step commands are already implemented in our translator. The inconsistency in the original concrete specification can be detected automatically, subject to a certain degree of abstraction (e.g. the abstract interval analysis of array indices).

The LOGS translator is implemented in a highly flexible Object-Oriented language language called FLEXIBO [1]. Although FLEXIBO is untyped, it simulates the behaviours of types, allows *ad hoc* user-defined types (as objects) and checks type consistency in runtime. Program constructs of the language can be inherited and extended for translation from a given source language (e.g. LOGS) into a more efficient target language (e.g. C/C++). Runtime checkings (e.g. type checking) performed by the FLEXIBO program actually become static analysis for the source language. For example, FLEXIBO's if-then-else statements are objects of a class called `SemBinaryConditional`. Pre-defined methods such as evaluation and printing can be overridden in its subclasses. When a reflected program is evaluated, user-defined evaluation method instead of the pre-defined method will be invoked. FLEXIBO provides a platform on which various static-analysis methods can be systematically developed in an Object-Oriented manner.

2 Translation of Basic LOGS Commands

2.1 Syntactical Checking

FLEXIBO is essentially free of syntactical restrictions. For example, the operator $F_1 \# F_2$ represents a method invocation of F_1 with argument F_2. F_1 and F_2 can be arbitrary expressions. Even an expression like $1 \# 2$ is syntactically correct, although its evaluation would generate a runtime exception, since the integer 1 cannot provide the service of a method. If we ignore syntactical restrictions for priority order and parenthesis, FLEXIBO's syntax is completely flat:

$$F ::= F \parallel F \mid F \,\mathbf{\S}\, F \mid \text{if } F \text{ then } F \text{ else } F \mid \textbf{early } F \mid F \otimes F \mid$$
$$\textbf{after } F = F \mid F + F \mid F \wedge F \mid \neg F \mid \textbf{before } F \mid x \mid v.$$

The program operators are, in order, the parallel composition $\parallel$ (MIMD parallelism), sequential composition $\mathbf{\S}$, binary conditional `if-then-else`, early transition, logical *and* $\otimes$ between internal predicates of early transitions, internal predicate in which $\textbf{after } F$ stands for the final state of an individual program variable F, arithmetic plus $+$, boolean and $\&$, boolean negation $\neg$, initial state $\textbf{before } F$ of a variable F, program variable $x \in \mathcal{X}$ and constant value $v \in \mathcal{V}$. Note that we have listed only the basic program constructs used by LOGS. The operators $+$, $\wedge$ and $\neg$ are merely representatives of arithmetic and logical operators allowed in LOGS. The specification (1) can be written in the above syntax as follows:

$$P_{ex} \mathrel{\widehat{=}} \textbf{early}\,(\textbf{after } x = \textbf{before } y + 1) \parallel \textbf{early}\,(\textbf{after } y = \textbf{before } x + 2).$$
$$(2)$$

To facilitate effective static analysis and translation, we need more syntactical restrictions. A *well-formed* LOGS specification has the following hierarchical syntax:

$$
\begin{aligned}
P &::= P \parallel P \mid S \\
S &::= S \,\mathbf{\S}\, S \mid \text{if } S \text{ then } S \text{ else } S \mid S \sqcap S \mid E \rhd S \mid T \\
T &::= \textbf{early } I \\
I &::= I \otimes I \mid W \\
W &::= A = E \\
A &::= \textbf{after } X \\
E &::= E + E \mid E \wedge E \mid \neg E \mid \textbf{before } X \mid X \mid V \\
X &::= x \\
V &::= v.
\end{aligned}
$$

Note that we have added two operators: nondeterministic choice $\sqcap$ and conditional magic $E \triangleright S$ (i.e. a partial "if-then" command becoming infeasible with false condition). They are by-products of static analysis and only appear in the normal form of specifications (see section 2.2). For example, an `if-then-else` command can be decomposed as the nondeterministic choice between two exclusive conditional magics [10]. Let $\mathcal{P}, \mathcal{S}, \mathcal{T}, \mathcal{I}, \mathcal{E}, \mathcal{X}$ denote the sets of specifications, sequential processes, early transitions, internal predicates, expressions and variables, respectively. Obviously, we have $\mathcal{T} \subseteq \mathcal{S} \subseteq \mathcal{P}$ and $\mathcal{X} \subseteq \mathcal{E}$. As a convention, we use $P, P_1, P_2, \cdots$ to denote individual specifications in $\mathcal{P}$, and let $S, S_1, S_2, \cdots$ denote individual sequential processes in $\mathcal{S}$ and so on. We also use $\mathcal{S}_0$ to denote the set of sequential processes without the two additional operators. The above syntactical restrictions can be formalised with abstract boolean functions $\alpha, \alpha_S, \alpha_I, \alpha_E, \alpha_X : \mathcal{F} \rightarrow \{\texttt{true}, \texttt{false}\}$. A FLEXIBO expression F is a well-formed LOGS specification if and only if $\alpha(F) = \texttt{true}$.

Def 1.
$$\alpha(F_1 \parallel F_2) = \alpha(F_1) \wedge \alpha(F_2) \qquad \alpha(F_1 \, \text{\textsemicolon} \, F_2) = \alpha_S(F_1 \, \text{\textsemicolon} \, F_2)$$
$$\alpha(\texttt{if } F_1 \texttt{ then } F_2 \texttt{ else } F_3) = \alpha_S(\texttt{if } F_1 \texttt{ then } F_2 \texttt{ else } F_3)$$
$$\alpha(\texttt{early } F) = \alpha_S(\texttt{early } F)$$
$$\alpha_S(\texttt{if } F_1 \texttt{ then } F_2 \texttt{ else } F_3) = \alpha_E(F_1) \wedge \alpha_S F_2 \wedge \alpha_S(F_3)$$
$$\alpha_S(F_1 \, \text{\textsemicolon} \, F_2) = \alpha_S(F_1) \wedge \alpha_S(F_2) \qquad \alpha_S(\texttt{early } F) = \alpha_I(F)$$
$$\alpha_I(F_1 \otimes F_2) = \alpha_I(F_1) \wedge \alpha_I(F_2) \qquad \alpha_I(F_1 = F_2) = \alpha_W(F_1 = F_2)$$
$$\alpha_W(F_1 = F_2) = \alpha_A(F_1) \wedge \alpha_E(F_2)$$
$$\alpha_A(\texttt{after } F) = \alpha_X(F)$$
$$\alpha_E(F_1 + F_2) = \alpha_E(F_1 \wedge F_2) = \alpha_E(F_1) \wedge \alpha_E(F_2)$$
$$\alpha_E(\neg F) = \alpha_E(F)$$
$$\alpha_E(\texttt{before } F) = \alpha_X(F)$$
$$\alpha_E(x) = \alpha_E(v) = \texttt{true}$$
$$\alpha_X(x) = \texttt{true}$$

We assume that, by default, every boolean function returns `false` for any expression undefined in the above rules. For example, $\alpha(P_{ex}) = \texttt{true}$. This syntactical restrictions can be implemented with a polymorphic method without side effect in FLEXIBO:

```
var LOGS:= class Reflection (
    var SemExp:= class (superclass.SemExp) (
        var alphaP := method [] false;
        var alphaS := method [] false;
        var alphaW := method [] false;
        var alphaE := method [] false;
        var alphaA := method [] false;
        var alphaX := method [] false;
    );
    var SemOpOr:= class (superclass.SemOpOr) (
        var alphaP := method []
            e1.alphaP[] && e2.alphaP[];
    );
    ......
); LOGS.flexibo[];
```

The above FLEXIBO program provides a real example how static analysis is implemented in the language. `Reflection` is the root reflection system, a class containing internal classes that represent program constructs. By extending `Reflection`, LOGS also becomes a reflection system whose internal classes extend the original classes for program constructs. The reflection system LOGS can then be used as a template to convert syntactical constructs. Methods like `alphaP[]` will be re-directed to the corresponding classes in LOGS through dynamic binding.

2.2 Basic Assumptions, Normal Form and Completeness

Static analysis methods based on abstract interpretation are defined recursively for every program constructs. We shall use the technique of normal form to demonstrate that the abstract functions are indeed properly defined. The following laws are assumed to be true for basic LOGS specifications.

Law 1 (Basic assumptions).

(1) *associativity of* $(\cdot \parallel \cdot)$, $(\cdot \, \fatsemi \, \cdot)$, $(\cdot \sqcap \cdot)$ *and* $(\cdot \otimes \cdot)$

(2) *distributivity of* $(\cdot \, \fatsemi \, \cdot)$ *into* $(\cdot \sqcap \cdot)$

(3) `if` E `then` S_1 `else` $S_2 = (E \rhd S_1) \sqcap (\neg E \rhd S_2)$

(4) $E \rhd (S_1 \sqcap S_2) = (E \rhd S_1) \sqcap (E \rhd S_2)$

(5) $E \rhd (S_1 \, \fatsemi \, S_2) = (E \rhd S_1) \, \fatsemi \, S_2$

(6) $E_1 \rhd (E_2 \rhd S) = (E_1 \wedge E_2) \rhd S$

(7) `true` $\rhd S = S$.

The above list is not a complete list of all laws satisfied by the concrete semantics of LOGS specifications. For example, parallel composition also has commutativity in the concrete semantics of dynamic behaviour. Nevertheless the list is complete for the static-analysis methods in this paper.

Under the above assumed laws, LOGS syntax collapses to the following normal form where $\prod_{j=1}^{n} K_j \,\hat{=}\, K_1 \, \fatsemi \, K_2 \, \fatsemi \, \cdots \, \fatsemi \, K_n$ and $\bigotimes_{i=1}^{m} A_i \,\hat{=}\, A_1 \otimes A_2 \otimes \cdots \otimes A_m$.

Norm 1. $P ::= \parallel_{l=1}^{t} \prod_{k=1}^{s} S_{kl}$

$S ::= \prod_{j=1}^{n} K_j$

$K ::= E \rhd T$

$T ::= \text{early } \bigotimes_{i=1}^{m} \text{ after } x_i = E_i$

The above normal form can be merged into one line where nondeterministic choices are located in the outmost layer, and then parallel compositions, sequential compositions, conditionals and finally, early transitions. The collapse of the syntax stops at the level of LOGS expressions, which are not further reducible:

$$\overset{t}{\underset{l=1}{\parallel}} \, \overset{s}{\underset{k=1}{\prod}} \, \overset{n}{\underset{j=1}{\prod}} E_{jkl} \rhd \left(\text{early } \overset{m}{\underset{i=1}{\bigotimes}} \text{ after } x_{ijkl} = E_{ijkl} \right) \tag{3}$$

where t is a constant, but $s = s(t)$, $n = n(s,t)$ and $m = m(n,s,t)$ are dependent functions. The proof of this following theorem in included in the appendix.

Theorem 1 (Completeness of basic assumptions). *Any well-formed basic LOGS specification can be reduced to the above normal form under the laws of basic assumptions.*

2.3 Detecting Communication Interference

We first introduce an abstract function $\beta : (\mathcal{P} \cup \mathcal{I}) \to \mathbb{P}(\mathcal{X})$ to check interference for the first superstep of all processes. In fact checking and analysing the set of variables accessed during the first superstep are done at the same time. For example, if there is interference between any two variables from the sets collected from two specifications, the parallel composition will return the infinite set $\mathcal{X}$ indicating the occurrence of interference. Any interference-free specification, however, returns a finite set of variables.

The interference relation is denoted: $\bowtie \subseteq \mathcal{X} \times \mathcal{X}$. Primitive variables interfere iff they are identical. We use the operator $\uplus$ to merge sets of variables: for any $\mathcal{X}_1, \mathcal{X}_2 \subseteq \mathcal{X}$, if there exist $X_1 \in \mathcal{X}_1$ and $X_2 \in \mathcal{X}_2$ such that $X_1 \bowtie X_2$ then $\mathcal{X}_1 \uplus \mathcal{X}_2 = \mathcal{X}$; otherwise, $\mathcal{X}_1 \uplus \mathcal{X}_2 = \mathcal{X}_1 \cup \mathcal{X}_2$.

Def 2.
$$\beta(P_1 \parallel P_2) = \beta(P_1) \uplus \beta(P_2) \qquad \beta(S_1 \,\fatsemi\, S_2) = \beta(S_1)$$
$$\beta(\text{if } E \text{ then } S_1 \text{ else } S_2) = \beta(S_1 \sqcap S_2) = \beta(S_1) \cup \beta(S_2)$$
$$\beta(E \rhd S) = \beta(S) \qquad \beta(I_1 \otimes I_2) = \beta(I_1) \uplus \beta(I_2)$$
$$\beta(\text{early } I) = \beta(I) \qquad \beta(\text{after } x = E) = \{x\}$$

For example, $\beta(P_{ex}) = \{x, y\}$. Note that since sequential processes in a nondeterministic choice or a binary conditional do not run at the same time, they will not interfere with each other.

Proposition 2. *The abstract function β satisfies all laws in* **Law 1**.

Lemma 3. *A well-formed specification P contains communication interference in its first superstep iff $\beta(P) = \mathcal{X}$.*

Proof. For any P in normal form (3), if there exist i_1, k_1, l_1 and i_2, k_2, l_2 such that $i_1 \neq i_2$ or $l_1 \neq l_2$ and $x_{i_1 1 k_1 l_1} \bowtie x_{i_2 1 k_2 l_2}$, then $\beta(P) = \mathcal{X}$; otheriwse, $\beta(P) = \{x_{i1kl} \mid l \leqslant t,\, k \leqslant s,\, i \leqslant m\}$.   □

We also need an abstract function $\gamma : \mathcal{P} \to \mathcal{P} \cup \{\mathrm{I\!I}\}$ to strip the first superstep and get the tail of a specification. The tail of a specification with only one superstep is a special construct $\mathrm{I\!I}$ called skip. If there are unbalanced processes, the translator can either report an error or simply ignore the shorter processes. We choose the latter approach in the following definition. For example, we have $\gamma(P_{ex}) = \mathrm{I\!I}$.

Def 3.

$$\gamma(P_1 \parallel P_2) \qquad = \gamma(P_1) \parallel \gamma(P_2) \quad (\gamma(P_1) \neq \mathrm{I\!I},\, \gamma(P_2) \neq \mathrm{I\!I})$$
$$\gamma(P_1 \parallel P_2) \qquad = \gamma(P_1) \qquad\quad (\gamma(P_2) = \mathrm{I\!I})$$
$$\gamma(P_1 \parallel P_2) \qquad = \gamma(P_2) \qquad\quad (\gamma(P_1) = \mathrm{I\!I})$$
$$\gamma(\text{if } E \text{ then } S_1 \text{ else } S_2) = \gamma(S_1 \sqcap S_2)$$
$$\gamma(S_1 \,\fatsemi\, S_2) \qquad = \gamma(S_1) \,\fatsemi\, S_2 \quad\ (\gamma(S_1) \neq \mathrm{I\!I})$$
$$\gamma(S_1 \,\fatsemi\, S_2) \qquad = S_2 \qquad\qquad (\gamma(S_1) = \mathrm{I\!I})$$
$$\gamma(S_1 \sqcap S_2) \qquad = \gamma(S_1) \sqcap \gamma(S_2) \quad (\gamma(S_1) \neq \mathrm{I\!I},\, \gamma(S_2) \neq \mathrm{I\!I})$$
$$\gamma(S_1 \sqcap S_2) \qquad = \gamma(S_1) \qquad\quad (\gamma(S_2) = \mathrm{I\!I})$$
$$\gamma(S_1 \sqcap S_2) \qquad = \gamma(S_2) \qquad\quad (\gamma(S_1) = \mathrm{I\!I})$$
$$\gamma(E \rhd S) \qquad\quad = \gamma(S)$$
$$\gamma(\text{early } I) \qquad\ = \mathrm{I\!I}$$

Proposition 4. *The abstract function γ satisfies all laws in* **Law 1**.

Lemma 5. *The abstract function γ returns the tail of a given well-formed specification.*

Proof.   For any P in normal form (3), $\gamma(P) = \|_{l=1}^{t} \prod_{k=1:\ n(s,t)>1}^{s} \prod_{j=2}^{n} K_{jkl}$. $\square$

The abstract function $\delta: \mathcal{P} \cup \{\Pi\} \rightarrow \{\texttt{true}, \texttt{false}\}$ combines β and γ and checks the whole specification superstep by superstep recursively: $\delta(S)=\texttt{true}$, $\delta(\Pi) = \texttt{true}$, $\delta(P) = \texttt{false}$ if $\beta(P) = \mathcal{X}$, and $\delta(P) = \delta(\gamma(P))$ otherwise. For example, $\delta(P_{ex}) = \texttt{true}$ indicating the freedom of communication interference in P_{ex}.

Theorem 6. *A well-formed specification has communication interference iff the function δ returns false.*

Proof.   Shown from **Lemma 3** and **5**. $\square$

2.4   Type Checking

Simple (stateless) typing rules directly correspond to an abstract function. For example, Int and Bool are the types of integers and booleans. The following rules can be used to infer the types of expressions and directly correspond to implementation consisting of if-then-else conditional statements in structured programming style:

$$\frac{E_1 :: \text{Int} \quad E_2 :: \text{Int}}{E_1 + E_2 :: \text{Int}} \qquad \frac{E_1 :: \text{Bool} \quad E_2 :: \text{Bool}}{E_1 \wedge E_2 :: \text{Bool}} \qquad \frac{E :: \text{Bool}}{\neg E :: \text{Bool} .}$$

Alternatively, we may regard types as (abstract) values and introduce functions for type calculation: $\text{Int} \hat{+} \text{Int} = \text{Int}$, $\text{Bool} \hat{\wedge} \text{Bool} = \text{Bool}$ and $\hat{\neg} \text{Bool} = \text{Bool}$. Typing rules can then be modelled as an abstact function $\epsilon: \mathcal{E} \rightarrow \text{TYPE}: \epsilon(E_1 + E_2) = \epsilon(E_1) \hat{+} \epsilon(E_2)$, $\epsilon(E_1 \wedge E_2) = \epsilon(E_1) \hat{\wedge} \epsilon(E_2)$ and $\epsilon(\neg E) = \hat{\neg} \epsilon(E)$. Unlike inference rules, abstract interpretation directly corresponds to implmentation in Object-Oriented programming style with polymorphism. The abstract function can be implemented as an overloaded method without side effect.

Let $\text{TYPE} \hat{=} \{\text{Int, Bool, True, False}\} \cup \text{RANGE}$ be the set of all types in Logs. The inferred type of an expression is True or False if its truth-value can be determined statically; the inferred type is Bool if the precise type cannot be determined statically. RANGE is a set of interval types each $\text{Range}(a, b)$ of which represents a range between integers a and b where $a \leqslant b$. Interval types are used in range analysis (e.g. for array index). In particular, if the inferred type is $\text{Range}(a, a)$, that means the dynamic value of the expression is constant and can be determined statically. The constant a will directly appear in the generated target code. The additional definitions of type calculation are as follows:

$$\text{Range}(a_1, b_1) + \text{Range}(a_2, b_2) = \text{Range}(a_1 + a_2, b_1 + b_2) .$$
$$\text{Int} \hat{+} \text{Range}(a, b) = \text{Range}(a, b) \hat{+} \text{Int} = \text{Int}$$
$$\text{False} \hat{\wedge} T = T \hat{\wedge} \text{False} = \hat{\neg} \text{True} = \text{False}$$
$$\text{True} \hat{\wedge} T = T \hat{\wedge} \text{True} = T$$
$$\text{Bool} \hat{\wedge} \text{Bool} = \text{Bool}$$
$$\hat{\neg} \text{Bool} = \text{Bool}$$

where $T = \text{Bool, True, False}$. If an expression's type is undefined, in the FLEXIBO implementation, the translator program directly reports a *runtime* error, which is actually a *compilation* error for the source language Logs.

The primitive types are primitive values in FLEXIBO. The rules of calculation are already embedded in the language and can be inherited by the translator. Many more types and arithmetic/logical/comparative operators are supported in FLEXIBO. RANGE is implemented as a class in the translator. Each object of the class has two attributes a and b. Type calculation rules and type checking become the methods of the class.

The type of an expression may depend on a context, i.e. the state of the type checker. For example, the most accurate inferred type of an uninitialised variable is its declared type. After initialising it to an integer 1, its inferred type may be changed to $\text{Range}(1, 1)$. This can be easily represented using state-dependent inference rules in the style of operational semantics. In abstract interpretation, it can be encoded as an additional argument of abstract functions. In FLEXIBO, it is directly implemented as a (polymorphic) method allowing side effects.

Let $\rho : \mathcal{X} \to \text{TYPE}$ denote the mapping from variables to their types at the current point of static analysis, $\mu : \mathcal{X} \to \mathcal{V}$ a mapping from variables to their initial values, $\tau : \mathcal{X} \to \text{TYPE}$ a mapping from variables to their declared types, and $\pi : \mathcal{V} \to \text{TYPE}$ a mapping from constant values to their inferred types. We assume $\pi(n) = \text{Range}(n, n)$ for any integer n, $\pi(\texttt{true}) = \text{True}$ and $\pi(\texttt{false}) = \text{False}$.

The abstract function $\epsilon : \mathcal{E} \to \text{TYPE}$ evaluates the type of an expression in a given state ρ.

Def 4.

$$\epsilon(E_1 + E_2) = \epsilon(E_1) \hat{+} \epsilon(E_2) \qquad \epsilon(E_1 \wedge E_2) = \epsilon(E_1) \hat{\wedge} \epsilon(E_2)$$
$$\epsilon(\neg E) = \hat{\neg} \epsilon(E) \qquad\qquad \epsilon(\texttt{before } x) = \tau(x)$$
$$\epsilon(x) = \rho(x) \qquad\qquad \epsilon(v) = \pi(v)$$

Note that the inferred type of a variable of communication (in $\texttt{before } y$) is always its declared type $\tau(x)$, while that of an independent variable is context-related. For example, suppose $\tau(x) = \text{Int}$, then $\epsilon(\texttt{before } y + 1) = \tau(y) \hat{+} \text{Range}(1, 1) = \text{Int}$. Another example is $\epsilon(1 + 1) = \text{Range}(1, 1) \hat{+} \text{Range}(1, 1) = \text{Range}(2, 2)$.

Before defining the type checking for LOGS, we introduce a subtyping partial ordering $\preccurlyeq$. For example, the command $\texttt{after } x = E$ tries to write to variable x remotely. It requires that the inferred type of E be a subtype of the decalred type of x. We assume that $\text{Range}(a_1, b_1) \preccurlyeq \text{Range}(a_2, b_2) \preccurlyeq \text{Int}$ if $a_2 \leqslant a_1 \leqslant b_1 \leqslant b_2$ and $\text{True}, \text{False} \preccurlyeq \text{Bool}$. The abstract function $\varepsilon : (\mathcal{P} \cup \mathcal{I}) \to \{\texttt{true}, \texttt{false}\}$ checks whether a specification is type-consistent in a given state of static analysis.

Def 5.

$$\varepsilon(P_1 \parallel P_2) = \varepsilon(P_1) \wedge \varepsilon(P_2) \qquad\qquad \varepsilon(S_1 \, \fatsemi \, S_2) = \varepsilon(S_1) \wedge \varepsilon(S_2)$$
$$\varepsilon(\texttt{if } E \texttt{ then } S_1 \texttt{ else } S_2) = \epsilon(E) \preccurlyeq \text{Bool} \wedge \varepsilon(S_1) \wedge \varepsilon(S_2)$$
$$\varepsilon(S_1 \sqcap S_2) = \varepsilon(S_1) \wedge \varepsilon(S_2) \qquad\qquad \varepsilon(E \triangleright S) = \epsilon(E) \preccurlyeq \text{Bool} \wedge \varepsilon(S)$$
$$\varepsilon(\texttt{early } I) = \varepsilon(I) \qquad\qquad \varepsilon(T_1 \otimes T_2) = \varepsilon(T_1) \wedge \varepsilon(T_2)$$
$$\varepsilon(\texttt{after } x = E) = \epsilon(E) \preccurlyeq \tau(x)$$

The condition in a conditional must be a boolean, and the inferred type of the expression E must be a subtype of the declared type of the accessed variable x in $\texttt{after } x = E$.

Proposition 7. *The abstract function ε satisfies all laws in* **Law 1.**

Proof.   Only need to check **Law 1**(6), which can be proved from **Def 4**.   □

In FLEXIBO, LOGS type checking is implemented as a (polymorphic) method that returns boolean value. We can assume $\rho = \tau$ for basic specifications, as they do not modify the types of variables. For example, if x and y are declared as integers, we then have:

$$\begin{aligned} \varepsilon(P_{ex}) =\ & \epsilon(\texttt{before } y + 1) \preccurlyeq \tau(x) \ \wedge\ \epsilon(\texttt{before } x + 2) \preccurlyeq \tau(y) \\ =\ & (\text{Int} \mathbin{\hat{+}} \text{Range}(1,1)) \preccurlyeq \text{Int} \ \wedge\ (\text{Int} \mathbin{\hat{+}} \text{Range}(2,2)) \preccurlyeq \text{Int} \\ =\ & \text{Int} \preccurlyeq \text{Int} \ \wedge\ \text{Int} \preccurlyeq \text{Int} \\ =\ & \texttt{true}\,. \end{aligned}$$

2.5   Variable Registration for Communication

In BSPlib, variables involved in communication (either read or written) need to be registered at the beginning of each process.

We first define an abstract function $\omega : \mathcal{E} \to \mathbb{P}(\mathcal{X})$ that collects the set of all variables to be read in a given expression.

Def 6.
$$\begin{array}{ll} \omega(E_1 + E_2) = \omega(E_1) \cup \omega(E_2) & \omega(E_1 \wedge E_2) = \omega(E_1) \cup \omega(E_2) \\ \omega(\neg E) = \omega(E) & \omega(\texttt{before } x) = \{x\} \\ \omega(x) = \{\,\} & \omega(v) = \{\,\} \end{array}$$

To generate the code for variable registration, we introduce an abstract function $\zeta : (\mathcal{P} \cup \mathcal{I}) \to \mathbb{P}(\mathcal{X})$ to collect the set of all variables that are either in $\texttt{after } x$ or $\texttt{before } x$. For example, $\zeta(P_{ex}) = \{x, y\}$.

Def 7.
$$\begin{array}{ll} \zeta(P_1 \parallel P_2) = \zeta(P_1) \cup \zeta(P_2) & \zeta(S_1 \mathbin{\fatsemi} S_2) = \zeta(S_1) \cup \zeta(S_2) \\ \zeta(\texttt{if } E \texttt{ then } S_1 \texttt{ else } S_2) = \zeta(S_1) \cup \zeta(S_2) & \zeta(S_1 \sqcap S_2) = \zeta(S_1) \cup \zeta(S_2) \\ \zeta(E \rhd S) = \omega(E) \cup \zeta(S) & \zeta(\texttt{early } I) = \zeta(I) \\ \zeta(I_1 \otimes I_2) = \zeta(I_1) \cup \zeta(I_2) & \zeta(\texttt{after } x = E) = \{x\} \cup \omega(E) \end{array}$$

Proposition 8. *The abstract function ζ satisfies all the laws in* **Law 1**.

Theorem 9. *The set of all variables in* $\texttt{after } x$ *and* $\texttt{before } x$ *of a well-formed specification P is $\zeta(P)$.*

Proof.   For any P in normal form (3), we have $\zeta(P) = \bigcup_{ijkl} (\omega(E_{jkl}) \cup \{x_{ijkl}\} \cup \omega(E_{ijkl}))$. $\square$

2.6   Analysis of Communication Dependencies

If a process writes a new value to a variable, it issues a $\texttt{bsp\_put}$ communication to every process that reads it. In this paper, we assume that the writing process will send the new value to every process that may ever read the variable (not just in the subsequent supersteps).

Before analysing the dependencies, we use an abstract function $\theta : \mathcal{P} \to \mathbb{N}$ to count the total number of sequential processes in a specification. For example, $\theta(P_{ex}) = 2$.

Def 8.
$$\begin{aligned} \theta(P_1 \parallel P_2) &= \theta(P_1) + \theta(P_2) \\ \theta(S) &= 1 \end{aligned}$$

Proposition 10. *The abstract function θ satisfies all the laws in* **Law 1**.

Theorem 11. *The total number of sequential processes in any well-formed specification P is $\theta(P)$.*

Proof.   For any P in normal form (3), we have $\theta(P) = t$. $\square$

The process *id* of the communication destination must be identified for a `bsp_put` command. Process *id* numbers are absolute numbers relevant to the whole process. We use an abstract function $\eta : \mathbb{N} \times \mathbb{N} \times (\mathcal{P} \cup \mathcal{I}) \to \mathbb{P}(\mathcal{X})$ to collect the set of all variables (in `before` x of process i) to be read. The first argument is the absolute process *id*, the second argument is the relative starting process *id* of the specification, and the last argument is a specification that may include several sequential processes. This design guarantees the compositionality for the operation.

Def 9. $\eta(i, n, P_1 \parallel P_2) \ = \ \eta(i, n, P_1) \cup \eta(i, n + \theta(P_1), P_2)$

$\eta(i, n, S) \ = \ \{\,\}$ $\hspace{5cm}$ $(i \neq n)$

$\eta(i, n, \text{if } E \text{ then } S_1 \text{ else } S_2) \ = \ \omega(E) \cup \eta(i, n, S_1 \sqcap S_2)$ $\hspace{0.8cm}$ $(i = n)$

$\eta(i, n, S_1 \sqcap S_2) \ = \ \eta(i, n, S_1 \,\fatsemi\, S_2) \ = \ \eta(i, n, S_1) \cup \eta(i, n, S_2)$ $\hspace{0.3cm}$ $(i = n)$

$\eta(i, n, E \rhd S) \ = \ \eta(i, n, E) \cup \eta(i, n, S)$ $\hspace{2.9cm}$ $(i = n)$

$\eta(i, n, \text{early } I) \ = \ \eta(i, n, I)$ $\hspace{4.2cm}$ $(i = n)$

$\eta(i, n, I_1 \otimes I_2) \ = \ \eta(i, n, I_1) \cup \eta(i, n, I_2)$ $\hspace{2.6cm}$ $(i = n)$

$\eta(i, n, \text{after } x = E) \ = \ \omega(E)$ $\hspace{4cm}$ $(i = n)$

For example, $\eta(i, i, P_{ex}) = \{y\}$, $\eta(i, i+1, P_{ex}) = \{x\}$, but $\eta(i, n, P_{ex}) = \{\,\}$ if $n \notin \{i, i+1\}$.

Proposition 12. *The function η satisfies all laws in* **Law 1**.

Proof.   Only need to check the associativity of $(\cdot \parallel \cdot)$:

$\eta(i, n, P_1 \parallel (P_2 \parallel P_3))$

$= \ \eta(i, n, P_1) \cup \eta(i, n + \theta(P_1), (P_2 \parallel P_3))$

$= \ \eta(i, n, P_1) \cup \eta(i, n + \theta(P_1), P_2) \cup \eta(i, n + \theta(P_1) + \theta(P_2), P_3)$

$= \ \eta(i, n, P_1 \parallel P_2) \cup \eta(i, n + \theta(P_1) + \theta(P_2), P_3)$

$= \ \eta(i, n, (P_1 \parallel P_2) \parallel P_3)$. $\square$

Theorem 13. *The abstract function $\eta(i, n, P)$ collects the set of all variables read by process i, a sequential process in a well-formed specification P with starting process id n.*

Proof.   For any P in normal form (3), if $n' \leqslant i' < n' + t$, we let $l \mathrel{\widehat{=}} i' - n' + 1$, and then $\eta(i', n', P) = \bigcup_{ijk} (\omega(E_{jkl}) \cup \omega(E_{ijkl}))$; otherwise, $\eta(i', n', P) = \{\,\}$. $\square$

A process writing to a shared variable must issue a `bsp_put` communication to every process that may read another variable interfering with the shared variable.

2.7   Generating Code for Expressions

We use an abstract function $\phi : \mathcal{E} \to \text{String}$ to translate a LOGS expression into a C expression (as a string). The operator $str_1 \frown str_2$ denotes string concatenation.

If the dynamic value of an sub-expression can be determined statically in type calculation, the generated code for that sub-expression will be the static value itself; otherwise, the sub-expression is converted to a string in C syntax. Specifically, if the inferred type is a singleton range: $\epsilon(E) = \mathrm{Range}(a, a)$, then we let $\phi(E)$ be "a", a string converted from the integer a; if $\epsilon(E) = \mathrm{True}$ or $\epsilon(E) = \mathrm{False}$, then $\phi(E) = $ "1" (i.e. the boolean `true` in C) or $\phi(E) = $ "0" (i.e. the boolean `false` in C) respectively; otherwise, the abstract function follows the following definition:

Def 10.
$$\phi(E_1 + E_2) \;=\; \phi(E_1)\,\widehat{\;}\,\text{``+''}\,\widehat{\;}\,\phi(E_2)$$
$$\phi(E_1 \wedge E_2) \;=\; \phi(E_1)\,\widehat{\;}\,\text{``\&\&''}\,\widehat{\;}\,\phi(E_2)$$
$$\phi(\neg E) \;=\; \text{``!''}\,\widehat{\;}\,\phi(E)$$
$$\phi(\texttt{before } x) \;=\; \phi(x) \;=\; \text{``}x\text{''}$$
$$\phi(v) \;=\; \text{``}v\text{''}.$$

For example, if $\tau(y) = \mathrm{Int}$, then $\phi(\texttt{before } y + 1) = $ "$y + 1$", as $\epsilon(\texttt{before } y + 1) = \mathrm{Int} \;\hat{+}\; \mathrm{Range}(1, 1) = \mathrm{Int}$; on the other hand, $\phi(1 + 1) = $ "2", because its value can be determined statically in type calculation: $\epsilon(1 + 1) = \mathrm{Range}(1, 1) \;\hat{+}\; \mathrm{Range}(1, 1) = \mathrm{Range}(2, 2)$.

2.8   Generating Code for Communications

The code for a sequential process that writes into a shared variable may involve other processes in parallel. Thus the abstract function $\psi : (\mathcal{S}_0 \cup \mathcal{I}) \times \mathcal{P} \to \mathrm{String}$ of communication code generation must have the whole specification as an argument. Let $\lambda(x, P)$ denote the set of id numbers of the processes that may read variable x:

$$\lambda(x, P) \;\hat{=}\; \{\, i < \theta(P) \mid \exists y \in \eta(i, 0, P) \cdot x \bowtie y \,\}.$$

For example, we have $\lambda(x, P_{ex}) = \{1\}$, $\lambda(y, P_{ex}) = \{0\}$, and for any other variable z, $\lambda(z, P_{ex}) = \{\,\}$. In the following definition, we use $\int$ to denote collective string concatenation. For example, $\int_{i \in \{1,3,4\}} str_i = str_1 \,\widehat{\;}\, str_3 \,\widehat{\;}\, str_4$. Note that code generation does not have to deal with nondeterministic choice and conditional magic, which are by-products of static analysis.

Def 11.
$$\psi(\texttt{if } E \texttt{ then } S_1 \texttt{ else } S_2, P) \;=\; \text{``if''}\,\widehat{\;}\,\phi(E)\,\widehat{\;}\,\text{``\{''}\,\widehat{\;}\,\psi(S_1, P)\,\widehat{\;}\,\text{``\}''}\,\widehat{\;}$$
$$\text{``else \{''}\,\widehat{\;}\,\psi(S_2, P)\,\widehat{\;}\,\text{``\}''}$$
$$\psi(S_1 \,\fatsemi\, S_2, P) \;=\; \psi(S_1, P)\,\widehat{\;}\,\psi(S_2, P)$$
$$\psi(\texttt{early } I, P) \;=\; \psi(I, P)\,\widehat{\;}\,\text{``bsp\_sync();''}$$
$$\psi(I_1 \otimes I_2, P) \;=\; \psi(I_1, P)\,\widehat{\;}\,\psi(I_2, P)$$
$$\psi(\texttt{after } x = E, P) \;=\; \text{``}x\texttt{:=''}\,\widehat{\;}\,\phi(E)\,\widehat{\;}\,\text{``;''}\,\widehat{\;}$$
$$\int_{i : \lambda(x, P)} \text{``bsp\_put}(i, x, x, 0, \texttt{sizeof}(\tau(x)));\text{''}$$

For example, $\psi(\texttt{early } (\texttt{after } x = \texttt{before } y + 1), P_{ex})$ generates C code:

```
x:=y+1; bsp_put(1, x, x, 0, sizeof(int)); bsp_sync();
```

The actual implementation of the above abstract function is a (polymorphic) method that directly prints out the code as output.

2.9   Generating Code for Processes

A sequential process starts from `bsp_pushregister` of shared variables and ends with their release by `bsp_popregister`. The function $\kappa : (\mathbb{N} \times \mathcal{P} \times \mathcal{P}) \to \mathrm{String}$

generates the code for each process n. The first argument is the relative starting process *id*, the second one is the sub-specification to be translated, and the last one is the whole specification.

Def 12. $\kappa(n, P_1 \parallel P_2, P) = \kappa(n, P_1, P) \frown \kappa(n + \theta(P_1), P_2, P)$
    $\kappa(n, S, P) = $"void process n {"$\frown$
        $\int_{x\,:\,\varsigma(P)}$ "bsp_pushregister(&x, sizeof($\tau(x)$));"$\frown$
        $\psi(S, P)\frown$
        $\int_{x\,:\,\varsigma(P)}$ "bsp_pushregister(&x);"$\frown$
        "}"

If a specification P passes syntactical checking, communication interference checking and type checking, the target C code can be generated in the following structure:

"#include $\cdots$"$\frown \kappa(0, P, P)\frown$ "void main() $\cdots$"

where we assume that $\rho = \tau$.

3   Advanced Commands

Due to the length limit of this paper, we are unable to discuss in details the translation and static analysis of advanced LOGS commands, although they are already implemented.

SPMD parallelism corresponds to a command par x from E_1 to E_2 do S. The values of the expressions E_1 and E_2 must be natural numbers statically determinable during type calculation; otherwise, a typing error is reported. The command generates a number of sequential processes in parallel in the target code. For each process, the variable x takes a different singleton range $\mathrm{Range}(a, a)$ where a is any number between the values of E_1 and E_2. Communication interference, type consistency and communication dependencies are checked for each process independently.

To facilitate static analysis, the translator supports only a restricted form of iteration for x from E_1 to E_2 do S. Again, E_1 and E_2 must be statically determinable. Such a command always terminates and can be translated to a for-loop in C. Communication interference is checked superstep by superstep after unfolding the iteration. If there are too many supersteps, a decision must be made on a limit n: the static analyser will only check the freedom of communication interference for the first n supersteps. Types and communication dependencies, on the other hand, are analysed without unfolding the iteration. The range between the values of E_1 and E_2 will be used as the inferred type of x recorded in the new state of the static analyser. The body of the for-loop will be type-checked under the abstraction.

Note that both of the above commands may change the static analyser's state. Thus advanced specifications have an extended normal form incorporating an additional command that allows the state of the analyser to be changed before each early transition. Both commands can then be decomposed into the normal form with that additional command.

Early transition is a characteristic of both BSP and PRAM programming. 0-step command local I, representing local computation without synchronisation, is specific to BSP paradigm. 0-step commands can be included in the translation and has been implemented. They tend to complicate the abstract functions with more exceptional cases.

The operator $x\#E$ can be overridden to represent the access of array x at the index E. Range analysis is important for the safety of the index expression. Two array accesses interfere if they are on the same array and the type-inferred ranges of the index expressions overlap with each other.

Partitionings can be defined as FLEXIBO classes. The choice of a particular partitioning method can be inserted into a LOGS specification as an operator $x: Partition$ of an array x. Various checkings and the related code generation can be defined as methods of the classes. This has opened a door to systematic studies on partitioning methods in a class library.

4   Conclusions and Future Work

In this paper, we have introduced the basic static-analysis methods for generating C code from LOGS specifications. The tool is still at an early experimental stage of development. The syntax adopted is restrictive, but it already covers most numeric applications, supports powerful static-analysis methods and generates fast and safe BSPlib-C code. The technique of normal form proves to be an illustrative tool for verifying the correctness of the translator. The authors are not aware of any previous application of the technique in abstract interpretation. This paper is to demonstrate the construction of translators and their formal verification. Many algorithms (e.g. communication dependencies) are subject to further refinement. The translator provides useful assistance to human programmers by automatically adding communication commands, generating code for each process, optimising expressions and partitioning data structures. Although this paper is primarily presented in abstract interpretation, the actual implementation sometimes "conveniently" deviates from the style of denotational semantics. For example, it is convenient to allow side effect on the state of the static analyser during type checking (especially for advanced commands), which is conveniently presented using inference rules in the style of operational semantics. Nevertheless both styles can be straightforwardly supported by Object-Oriented programming. This perhaps highlights the integrating power of OO framework for static analysis. The translator generates a separate code for every processor. This approach may not be applicable to massively parallel machines. Systematic studies on partitioning methods in OO style is an interesting area of future research.

References

1. Y. Chen. A language of flexible objects. Technical Report 29, Department of Computer Science, Leicester University, 2004.
2. Y. Chen and J.W. Sanders. Top-down design of BSP programs. *Parallel Processing Letters*, 13(3):389–400, 2003.
3. Y. Chen and J.W. Sanders. Logic of global synchrony. *ACM Transactions on Programming Languages and Systems*, 26(2):221–262, 2004.

4. P. Cousot. Types as abstract interpretations. In *Proceedings of POPL*, pages 316–331. ACM, 1997.
5. P. Cousot. Abstract interpretation based formal methods and future challenges. In *In Informatics, 10 Years Back - 10 Years Ahead*, volume 2000 of *LNCS*, pages 138–156, 2001.
6. P. Cousot and R. Cousot. Abstract interpretation: A unified lattice model for static analysis of programs by construction or approximation of fixedpoints. In *Proceedings of 4th POPL*, pages 238–252. ACM, 1977.
7. S. Fortune and J. Wyllie. Parallelism in random access machines. In *10th Annual ACM Symposium on Theory of Computing*, pages 114–118. ACM Press, 1978.
8. J. He, Q. Miller, and L. Chen. Algebraic laws for BSP programming. In *Euro-Par'96*, volume 1124 of *Lecture Notes in Computer Science*, pages 359–367. Springer-Verlag, 1996.
9. J. M. D. Hill and et al. BSPlib: The BSP programming library. *Parallel Computing*, 24(14):1927–2148, 1998.
10. C. A. R. Hoare and et al. Laws of programming. *Communications of the ACM*, 30(8):672–686, 1987.
11. C. A. R. Hoare and J. He. *Unifying Theories of Programming*. Prentice Hall, 1998.
12. W. F. McColl. Compositional systems. In *Symposium in Celebration of the work of C.A.R. Hoare*. 1999.
13. L.G. Valiant. A bridging model for parallel computation. *Communications of the ACM*, 33(8):103–111, 1990.

Formalizing the Debugging Process in Haskell*

Alberto de la Encina, Luis Llana, and Fernando Rubio

Departamento de Sistemas Informáticos y Programación,
Universidad Complutense de Madrid, Spain
{albertoe, llana, fernando}@sip.ucm.es

Abstract. Due to its absence of side effects, it is usually claimed that reasoning about functional programs is simpler than reasoning about their imperative counterparts. Unfortunately, due to the absence of practical debuggers, finding bugs in lazy functional languages has been much more complex until quite recently. One of the easiest to use Haskell debuggers is Hood, whose behavior is based on the concept of observation of intermediate data structures. However, it can be hard to understand how it works when dealing with complex situations.

In this paper, we introduce debugging facilities in the STG abstract machine. Our goal is to obtain debugging information as close to the one obtained by the Hood debugger as possible. By extending the STG abstract machine, we do not only provide a formal framework to the debugging process, but also an alternative method to implement debuggers.

Keywords: Functional programming, debugging, abstract machines.

1 Introduction

The debugging of lazy functional programs is currently an active area of research. Although not much attention was paid to it in the past (see e.g. [17]), during the last years there have been several proposals for incorporating execution traces to lazy functional languages. In particular, we can highlight the work done with Hat [16,18], HsDebug [5], the declarative debuggers Freja [10,11] and Buddha[14], and specially the work done with the Haskell Object Observation Debugger (Hood) [6,15]. All of them are designed to be used with the language Haskell [13], the *de facto* standard in the lazy-evaluation functional programming community.

The approaches followed in each of the previous debuggers are quite different, both from the point of view of the user of the system and from the implementation point of view. For instance, from an implementation point of view, most of them strongly depend on the compiler being used, while that is not the case in Hood. From the user point of view, Freja and Buddha are question-answer systems that directs the programmer to the cause of an incorrect value, while Hat allows the user to travel backwards from a value along the redex history leading to it. In this paper we will not concentrate on those differences (the interested reader can find a detailed comparison between Freja, Hat and Hood in [1]). In contrast, we will concentrate on how to improve one of them.

---

* Research supported by the Spanish MCYT project TIC2003–07848–C02–01, and the Marie Curie project MRTN-CT-2003-505121/TAROT.

D.V. Hung and M. Wirsing (Eds.): ICTAC 2005, LNCS 3722, pp. 211–226, 2005.

Among all of the Haskell debuggers, Hood has an interesting advantage over the rest, as it is the only one that can be used with different Haskell compilers. The reason is that it is implemented as an independent library that can be used from any Haskell compiler, provided that the compiler implements some quite common extensions. Hood can currently be used with the Glasgow Haskell Compiler, Hugs98, the Snowball Haskell compiler, and also with nhc98. Due to its portability, Hood has become one of the most used Haskell debugger.

The way Hood works is relatively simple. First, the programmer instruments the program marking the variables he wants to observe and, after finishing the execution of the program, the system produces a printing of their final value. Let us remark that *final value* does not necessarily mean normal form, but evaluation to the degree required by the computation. Unfortunately, it is sometimes tricky to understand what should be observed by using Hood in special situations. In fact, as the author recognizes in [6], the semantics of observe (the main debugging combinator of Hood) should be clearly defined to help understanding these situations.

The problem can get more complicated when we consider different implementations of Hood. For instance, the Hugs interpreter currently incorporates an observe combinator that differs from that of the original version of Hood. Both the original debugging strategy and the debugging strategy implemented in Hugs are useful and have advantages over each other. However, both of them lack a formalization allowing to reason what should be expected about concrete executions. Moreover, although both strategies are interesting, only one of them can be used in each environment.

In this paper we propose an extension of the STG abstract machine [12] for it to have debugging capabilities. We present three extensions in order to approach gradually the behavior of the Hood debugger. By doing so, we obtain several benefits. First, the semantics of the observations are clearly defined in terms of the semantics of the STG abstract machine. Second, the implementation can be trivially derived from the modified rules of the STG machine, overcoming some limitations of the current Hood implementation.[1] In this sense, we have reused the work done in [4] to implement our versions of the Hood debugger. Following the ideas of that paper we have proved [2] the the correctness of our modifications to the standard STG machine. And third, by encoding the observations inside the STG machine, we can easily study different types of observations. Thus, variations of the Hood observe combinator can be introduced. Let us remark that, when introducing such variations, we will trivially obtain its semantics. Moreover, the implementation will also be obtained by modifying accordingly the one of the STG machine. In fact, we have already implemented all the variations appearing in the paper (and also others not shown).

Summarizing, we propose a cleaner and more modular approach to the trace problem in lazy functional programming, allowing to easily provide both implementations and formal foundations for them.

---

[1] The sharing of closures is partially lost when using the original implementation of Hood.

The rest of the paper is structured as follows. In the next section we introduce the main characteristics of Hood. In Section 3 we briefly review the main characteristics of the STG machine. Then, in Section 4 we present how to modify the STG machine to include Hood-like observations. In sections 5 and 6 we study variations of the Hood observations that can be obtained by modifying the STG rules. Finally, in Section 7 we present our conclusions and lines for future work.

2   An Introduction to Hood

In this section we show the basic ideas behind Hood. The interested reader is referred to [6,7] for more details about it.

When debugging programs written in an imperative language, the programmer can explore not only the final result of the computation, but also the intermediate values stored in the variables being used by the program. Moreover, it is simple to follow how the value of each variable changes over time.

Unfortunately, this task is not that simple when dealing with lazy functional languages. However, Hood allows the programmer to observe something similar to it. In fact, Hood allows the programmer to observe any intermediate structure appearing in a program. Moreover, by using GHood [15] we can also observe the evolution in time of the evaluation of the structures under observation.

In order to illustrate what kind of observations can be obtained by using Hood, let us consider an example. It will be complex enough to highlight important aspects of Hood, but also relatively simple to be easily understandable without requiring knowledge about Haskell. Given a natural number, the following Haskell function returns the list of digits of that number:

```
natural = reverse . map ('mod' 10)
          . takeWhile (/= 0) . iterate ('div' 10)
```

That is, `natural` 3408 returns the list `3:4:0:8:[]`, where `[]` denotes the empty list and `:` denotes the list constructor. Let us remark that, in order to compute the final result, three intermediate lists were produced in the following order:

```
-- after iterate
3408:340:34:3:0:_
-- after takeWhile
3408:340:34:3:[]
-- after map
8:0:4:3:[]
```

Notice that the first intermediate list is infinite, although only the first five elements are computed. As the rest of the list does not need to be evaluated, it is represented as _ (the underscore char).

By using Hood we can annotate the program in order to obtain the output shown before. In order to do that, we have to use the `observe` combinator that is the core of Hood. The type declaration of this combinator is: `observe ::` `String -> a -> a`.   From the evaluation point of view, `observe` only returns its second value. That is, `observe s a = a`. However, as a side effect, the value associated to `a` will be squirrelled away, using the label `s`, in a file that will be analyzed after the evaluation finishes. It is important to remark that `observe` returns its second parameter in a completely lazy, demand driven manner. That is, the evaluation degree of `a` is not modified by introducing the observation, in the same way that it is not modified when applying the identity function `id`. Thus, as the evaluation degree is not modified, Hood can deal with infinite lists like the one appearing after applying `iterate` (`'div'` 10).

If we consider again our previous example, we can observe all of the intermediate structures by introducing three observations as follows:

```
natural = reverse
        . observe "after map"       . map ('mod' 10)
        . observe "after takeWhile" . takeWhile (/= 0)
        . observe "after iterate"   . iterate ('div' 10)
```

After executing `natural 3408`, we will obtain the desired result. Hood does not only observe simple structures like those shown before. In fact, it can observe anything appearing in a Haskell program. In particular, we can observe functions. For instance,

```
observe "sum" sum (4:2:5:[])
```

will observe the application of function `sum` to its parameter, returning

```
-- sum
  { \ (4:2:5:[]) -> 11  }
```

Notice that what we observe can be read as *when the function receives as input the list 4:2:5:[], it returns as output the value 11*. The elements 4, 2 and 5 appear explicitly because they were really demanded to evaluate the output. However, when observing something like

```
observe "length" length (4:2:5:[])
```

we will obtain the following observation:

```
-- length
  { \ (_:_:_:[]) -> 3 }
```

That is, we are observing a function that when it receives a list with three elements it returns the number 3 without evaluating the concrete elements appearing in the list. Note that only the number of elements is relevant, but not the *concrete* elements.

As it can be expected, higher-order functions can also be observed. This is done in a similar way as in the previous cases. For instance, in our initial example, instead of observing the intermediate structures, we can observe the higher-order function `iterate`:[2]

```
natural = reverse
        . map ('mod' 10) . takeWhile (/= 0)
        . observe "iterate" iterate ('div' 10)
```

In this situation, when applying `natural` to 3408, Hood returns

```
-- iterate
  { \ { \ 3 -> 0 , \ 34 -> 3 ,
        \ 340 -> 34 , \ 3408 -> 340  } 3408
        -> 3408 : 340 : 34 : 3 : 0 : _  }
```

---

[2] This higher-order function applies infinite times the first function it receives. For instance, applying `iterate (+3) 1` returns the infinite list `1:4:7:10:13:...`

That is, it observes that it is a function that returns `3408:340:34:3:0:_` when it receives as second parameter `3408` and as first parameter a function (`'div' 10`) that has been observed with four different input values: 3408, 340, 34 and 3.

Let us finally comment a drawback of Hood implementation. Even though it is guaranteed that `observe` does not modify the evaluation degree of the observed values, it does not completely preserve the sharing of closures. That is, each time a structure is observed, the corresponding closure is cloned, and its computation takes place without sharing the closure with the rest of the program. Obviously, this is an inefficiency in terms of memory and also in terms of runtime. However, by doing so, the implementation was easier.

It is important to remark that, as expressions under observation do not share closures with other parts of the program, it is easier to decide who was the responsible of evaluating each thing. That is, if we are observing a structure in a given environment, we are not interested in the parts of the structure that were evaluated due to other environments. For instance, if we are observing function `length` in the following example

```
let xs = take 5 (1:2:3:4:5:6:7:[])
in (observe "length" length xs) + (sum xs)
```

we will obtain the output

```
-- length
  { \ (_:_:_:_:_:[]) -> 5 }
```

That is, even though all the elements of the list `xs` were actually computed (due to function `sum`), they were not needed at all to compute any application of the function `length`

However, the Hugs interpreter provides a modified version of Hood whose behavior is quite different in this situation. In fact, when observing function length in exactly the same situation as before, the observation that it returns is

```
-- length
  { \ (1:2:3:4:5:[]) -> 5 }
```

That is, Hugs does not observe what was really demanded by function `length`. The main advantage of using Hugs-like observations instead of Hood is that the sharing of closures is not lost in Hugs. Moreover, we obtain information about the actual degree of evaluation of each structure. However, no information is provided about what function was responsible for each evaluation, while Hood does obtain it.

Summarizing, both the original version of Hood and the version implemented in Hugs have advantages over each other. So, it is interesting to try to obtain the best of both worlds.

3   The STG Abstract Machine

In this section we briefly describe a slightly modified version of the STG abstract machine. The interested reader is referred to [12] for a very detailed description of it and to [2,3] for details about the differences.

3.1 The Basic Language

Before starting the description of the rules governing our STG machine, let us firstly present the core functional language used in the machine. The syntax of this language, called FUN, is shown in Figure 1, where we assume n, k and m to be integers such that $n > 0$, $k \geq 0$ and m is an unboxed integer. We also assume $\overline{x_i}^n$ to represent n variables.

As it can be seen, FUN is a normalized λ-calculus, extended with recursive **let**, constructor applications, **case** expressions and unboxed integers. The normalization process forces constructor applications to be saturated and all applications to only have variables or unboxed values as arguments. Weak head normal forms are lambda abstractions, constructions or unboxed integers.

Let us note that **case** expressions are not required to be saturated. In this sense, two types of default alternatives are introduced. The difference between them is that in the second one the result of the discriminant will be bound to variable v, while in the first case it will be discarded. Let us also note that applications are done to n arguments at once, not one by one. Finally, note that the language includes unboxed integers. We would like to remark that it is not possible to bind an unboxed value.

3.2 The STG Abstract Machine

A configuration in the STG machine is a quadruple of the form (Γ, e, E, S) where Γ represents the heap, e is the control expression, E is the environment, and S is the stack. The environment E binds the free variables of the control expression e with the corresponding pointers. The heap Γ binds pointers to closures which are presented by a pair (lf, F) where lf is a lambda expression and E represents the environment which maps the free variables of lf to the corresponding pointers. The stack S stores three kinds of objects: arguments p_i of pending applications (that should be unboxed values or pointers), case alternatives $(alts, E)$ of pending pattern matches, and marks $\#p$ of pending updates.

The reason why we need the environments is that control expressions, lambda expressions and alternatives keep their original variables and in execution we need to know their associated pointers.

The STG machine starts with an expression to be evaluated in an empty heap, environment and stack. Its execution follows the rules shown in Figure 2.

$$
\begin{array}{llll}
e & \rightarrow e\ \overline{atom_i}^n & \text{-- application} & lf \rightarrow \lambda\ \overline{x_i}^n.e & \text{-- lambda abstraction}\\
 & \mid op\ \overline{atom_i}^n & \text{-- saturated built-in op} & \mid C\ \overline{x_i}^k & \text{-- constructor application}\\
 & \mid atom & \text{-- variable or literal} & \mid e & \text{-- expression}\\
 & \mid \textbf{let}\ \overline{x_i = lf_i}^n\ \textbf{in}\ e & \text{-- let} & & \\
 & \mid \textbf{letrec}\ \overline{x_i = lf_i}^n\ \textbf{in}\ e & \text{-- recursive let} & atom \rightarrow x & \text{-- variable}\\
 & \mid \textbf{case}\ e\ \textbf{of}\ alts & \text{-- case expression} & \mid m & \text{-- primitive integers}\\
\end{array}
$$

$$
\begin{array}{lll}
alts & \rightarrow \overline{C_i\ \overline{x_j}^{k_i} \mapsto e_i}^k.default & \text{-- algebraic alternative}\\
 & \mid \overline{m_i \mapsto e_i}^k.default & \text{-- primitive alternative}\\
\end{array}
\qquad op \rightarrow +\# \mid -\# \mid *\# \mid /\# \text{-- primitive integer op}
$$

$$
\begin{array}{ll}
default & \rightarrow \textbf{default} \mapsto e & \text{-- default alternative}\\
 & \mid v \mapsto e\\
 & \mid \phi\\
\end{array}
$$

Fig. 1. FUN language

Heap	Control	Environment	Stack	rule
Γ	**let** $\{x_i = lf_i\}$ **in** e	E	S	let (^{1})
$\Rightarrow \Gamma \cup [\overline{q_i \mapsto (lf_i, E)}]$	e	E'	S	
Γ	**letrec** $\{\overline{x_i = lf_i}\}$ **in** e	E	S	letrec (^{2})
$\Rightarrow \Gamma \cup [\overline{q_i \mapsto (lf_i, E')}]$	e	E'	S	
Γ	**case** e **of** $alts$	E	S	case1
$\Rightarrow \Gamma$	e	E	$(alts, E) : S$	
$\Gamma[q \mapsto (C_k \ \overline{x_i}, \{\overline{x_i \mapsto p_i}\})]$	x	$E\{x \mapsto q\}$	$(alts, E') : S$	case2 (^{3})
$\Rightarrow \Gamma$	e_k	$E' \cup \{\overline{y_{ki} \mapsto p_i}\}$	S	
$\Gamma[q \mapsto (C_k \ \overline{x_i}, \{\overline{x_i \mapsto p_i}\})]$	x	$E\{x \mapsto q\}$	$(alts.\textbf{default}-> e, E') : S$	case2d (^{4})
$\Rightarrow \Gamma$	e	E'	S	
$\Gamma[q \mapsto (C_k \ \overline{x_i}, \{\overline{x_i \mapsto p_i}\})]$	x	$E\{x \mapsto q\}$	$(alts.v-> e, E') : S$	case2v (^{4})
$\Rightarrow \Gamma$	e	$E' \cup \{v \mapsto q\}$	S	
Γ	$e \ \overline{x_i}^n$	$E\{\overline{x_i \mapsto p_i}\}$	S	app1
$\Rightarrow \Gamma$	e	E	$\overline{p_i}^n : S$	
$\Gamma[q \mapsto (\lambda \overline{x_i}^n.e, E')]$	x	$E\{x \mapsto q\}$	$\overline{p_i}^n : S$	app2
$\Rightarrow \Gamma$	e	$E' \cup \{\overline{x_i \mapsto p_i}^n\}$	S	
$\Gamma \cup [p \mapsto (e, E')]$	x	$E\{x \mapsto p\}$	S	var1
$\Rightarrow \Gamma$	e	E'	$\#p : S$	
$\Gamma[p \mapsto (\lambda \overline{x_i}^k.\lambda \overline{y_i}^n.e, E')]$	x	$E\{x \mapsto p\}$	$\overline{p_i}^k : \#q : S$	var2 (^{5})
$\Rightarrow \Gamma \cup [q \mapsto (x \ \overline{x_i}^k, E'')]$	x	E	$\overline{p_i}^k : S$	
$\Gamma[q \mapsto (C_k \ \overline{x_i}, E')]$	x	$E\{x \mapsto q\}$	$\#p : S$	var3
$\Rightarrow \Gamma \cup [p \mapsto (C_k \ \overline{x_i}, E')]$	x	$\{x \mapsto p\}$	S	
Γ	x	$E\{x \mapsto k\}$	S	int#
$\Rightarrow \Gamma$	k	$\{\}$	S	
Γ	k	E	$(alts, E') : S$	case2# (^{3})
$\Rightarrow \Gamma$	e_k	E'	S	
Γ	k	E	$(alts.\textbf{default}-> e, E') : S$	case2d# (^{4})
$\Rightarrow \Gamma$	e	E'	S	
Γ	k	E	$(alts.v-> e, E') : S$	case2v# (^{4})
$\Rightarrow \Gamma$	e	$E' \cup \{v \mapsto k\}$	S	
Γ	$op \ x_1 \ x_2$	E	S	op# (^{6})
$\Rightarrow \Gamma$	$k_1 op \ k_2$	$\{\}$	S	

(^{1}) $\overline{q_i}$ are distinct and fresh w.r.t. Γ, **let** $\{x_i = lf_i\}$ **in** e, and S. $E' = E \cup \{\overline{x_i \mapsto q_i}\}$
(^{2}) $\overline{q_i}$ are distinct and fresh w.r.t. Γ, **letrec** $\{\overline{x_i = lf_i}\}$ **in** e, and S. $E' = E \cup \{\overline{x_i \mapsto q_i}\}$
(^{3}) Expression e_k corresponds to the k-th alternative of $\overline{C_j \ \overline{y_{ji}} \to e_j}$ in $alts$
(^{4}) C_k not in $alts$
(^{5}) $E'' = \{x \mapsto p, \overline{x_i \mapsto p_i}^k\}$
(^{6}) $k_i =$ if $isInt(x_i)$ then x_i else $E(x_i)$

Fig. 2. The STG abstract machine

The STG machine presented above has some differences from the original one [12] and they are deeply discussed in [4].

We will use the following notation to describe the rules. x and y represent variables, while p and q represent pointers in the heap. From now on we will use the term *lambda forms* to refer to both λ-abstractions and constructor application. By using $\Gamma \cup [p \mapsto w]$ we denote that we are adding to the heap Γ a new closure w, and we are locating it at position p; we assume that the pointer p is not bound to any closure w in Γ. In contrast, $\Gamma[p \mapsto w]$ means that closure w is already in the position p of the heap. The same notation used for the heap is also used with the environments. That is, $E\{x \mapsto p\}$ means that variable x is bound to pointer p in the environment. Moreover, if variable x was not bound, by using $E \cup \{x \mapsto p\}$ we add a new binding so that variable x is now bound to

$$lf \rightarrow \lambda \ \overline{x_i}^n.e \ \text{-- lambda abstraction}$$
$$| \ C \ \overline{x_i}^k \ \text{-- constructor application}$$
$$| \ e \ \text{-- expression}$$
$$| \ x^{@str} \ \text{-- observed variable}$$

Fig. 3. Introducing observations in FUN

pointer p. In case x was already bound to something else, by using $E \cup \{x \mapsto p\}$ we replace such previous binding with the new one.

As in the STG machine, lambda forms do not appear in control expressions. The main reason for that is efficiency: we do not want to move continuously lambda forms from heap to control and the other way around. Because of that, weak head normal forms corresponds to pointers pointing to lambda forms. It is easy to demonstrate that this is invariant under the application of all rules.

Let us briefly comment the transitions shown in Figure 2. The first two rules (*let*, *letrec*) deal with **let** and **letrec** expressions. In this case, the body of the **let** and **letrec** will be evaluated after adding to the heap all the bindings corresponding to their local definition. The evaluation of **case** (rules *case*1, *case*2, *case*2d, *case*2v) expressions requires two steps: The first rule stores the list of alternatives in the stack, and goes on evaluating the discriminant. After finishing its computation, a weak head normal form will be obtained. In that moment, it will be compared with the alternatives stored in the stack to decide what alternative of the case matches the result. In order to do that, three different rules are needed (*case*2, *case*2d, *case*2v): one for applying conventional alternatives, and two for applying each kind of default alternative. The case of the applications is also split into two steps (*app*1, *app*2): first, the arguments are stored in the stack until the function is computed, and then it is applied to those arguments. We have three cases when evaluating a variable: if it is not evaluated (rule *var*1), we put an update mark on the stack and start to evaluate the corresponding expression; on the other hand if it is in normal form we update the heap with the corresponding normal form (rules *var*2, *var*3). Finally, the last five rules deal with unboxed integers.

4   Encoding Hood in the STG Abstract Machine

Let us consider now how to introduce Hood-like observations at STG level. Let us remember that Hood users can annotate their programs to mark which structures are to be observed. Thus, in our case we also have to be able to annotate any structure. This can be trivially done by allowing to annotate as *observable* any variable bound in a **letrec**. Thus, we only need to modify slightly the FUN language to include an extra construction as shown in Figure 3. Notice that $x^{@str}$ is the equivalent to the Hood expression **observe str x**.

Once the language allows us to include observations, we have to deal with them in the abstract machine. The main idea is that each rule will have the possibility of generating a side effect to write some observations in a log file. By using this basic idea, we need to rewrite some of the transitions. In Figure 4, the new transitions needed to model the observations are shown. We will need a

Heap	Control	Environment	Stack	Side Effect	rule
$\Gamma[q \mapsto closure]$	$x^{@str}$	$E\{x \mapsto q\}$	S		var1@$_1$
$\Rightarrow \Gamma \cup [q' \mapsto closure]$	x	$\{x \mapsto q'^{@<str>}\}$	S	$\emptyset$	
$\Gamma[q \mapsto closure]$	$x^{@str}$	$E\{x \mapsto q^{@<strs>}\}$	S		var1@$_2$
$\Rightarrow \Gamma \cup [q' \mapsto closure]$	x	$\{x \mapsto q'^{@<str + strs>}\}$	S	$\emptyset$	
$\Gamma \cup [q \mapsto (C_k\ \overline{x_i}, \{\overline{x_i \mapsto p_i}\})]$	x	$E\{x \mapsto q^{@<strs>}\}$	S		observer@ (^{1})
$\Rightarrow \Gamma'$	x	$\{x \mapsto q\}$	S	$(strs, q \mapsto C_k\ \overline{p_i})$	
$\Gamma[q \mapsto (\lambda\overline{x_i}^n.e, E')]$	x	$E\{x \mapsto q^{@<strs>}\}$	$\overline{p_i}^n : S$		app2@ (^{2})
$\Rightarrow \Gamma'$	x	$\{x \mapsto q'^{@<strs>}\}$	S	$(strs, q \mapsto (\lambda\overline{p_i}^n.q'))$	
$\Gamma[q \mapsto (\lambda\overline{x_i}^k.\lambda\overline{y_i}^n.e, E')]$	x	$E\{x \mapsto q\}$	$\overline{p_i}^k : \#q'^{@<strs>} : S$		var2@$_1$ (^{3})
$\Rightarrow \Gamma \cup [q' \mapsto (x\ \overline{x_i}^k, E'')]$	x	$\{x \mapsto q^{@<strs>}\}$	$\overline{p_i}^k : S$	$\neg(strs, q \mapsto \overline{p_i}^k)$	
$\Gamma[q \mapsto (\lambda\overline{x_i}^k.\lambda\overline{y_i}^n.e, E')]$	x	$E\{x \mapsto q^{@<strs>}\}$	$\overline{p_i}^k : \#q'^{@<strs'>} : S$		var2@$_2$ (^{4})
$\Rightarrow \Gamma \cup [q' \mapsto (x\ \overline{x_i}^k, E'')]$	x	$\{x \mapsto q^{@<strs + strs'>}\} \overline{p_i}^k : S$		$\neg(strs', q \mapsto \overline{p_i}^k)$	

$(^1)\ \Gamma' = \Gamma \cup [\overline{p_i' \mapsto \Gamma(p_i)}] \cup [q \mapsto (C_k\ \overline{x_i}, \{\overline{x_i \mapsto p_i'^{@<strs>}}\})]$
$(^2)\ \Gamma' = \Gamma \cup [\overline{p_i' \mapsto \Gamma(p_i)}] \cup [q' \mapsto (e, E' \cup \{\overline{x_i \mapsto p_i'^{@<strs>}}\}^n)]$
$(^3)\ E'' = \{x \mapsto q^{@<strs>}, \overline{x_i \mapsto p_i}^k\}$
$(^4)\ E'' = \{x \mapsto q^{@<strs + strs'>}, \overline{x_i \mapsto p_i}^k\}$

Fig. 4. Including the original version of Hood in the STG abstract machine

completely new rule (*observer*) to deal with the observation of the constructors, and we will also have to add modifications of the rules *var1*, *var2* and *app2* of the STG machine.

In Figure 4 it can be seen that there is an extra column containing the side effects of the rules. Let us remark that the side effects are produced at the same time as the evaluation of the program takes place. Thus, observations can be obtained even in the case that the program does not finish its computation.

Before describing the concrete rules, we must introduce some notation. As Hood allows to annotate with a string each observed structure, our pointers can also be annotated with sets of strings (the notation $< str >$ represents a set of strings). We use sets of strings instead of only one string because the same closure could be observed in different environments with different marks.

As our pointers can now contain annotations, in the stack we can have two different types of pointers: Normal pointers and pointers under observation. As both types of pointers are still pointers, the transitions of the STG machine equally apply to both types. However, in some situations we will be interested in distinguishing both of them. In order to do that in a compact way, we will use as notation that q refers to non-observed pointers, while p refers to any type of pointer (under observation or not).

Let us describe the main differences with the STG machine shown in the previous section. First, when a variable under observation is entered, the corresponding closure is cloned, and then this new closure is observed (this is done in the first two rules shown in Figure 4). It is important to remark that what we are doing is to copy the behavior of Hood. In Hood, closures under observation are not shared with other parts of the program. By doing so, it is easier to decide who was the responsible for evaluating each part of the structure.

In order to better understand the rules, we assume $x^{@str}$ to represent a closure that is to be observed under the name str, but that has not already been cloned.

It is worth to point out that this kind of closures can only be created by the programmer. That is, once the original program is introduced, it is not possible that new closures of this style appear due to the effects of the transitions of the machine. In contrast, we would use $p^{@<strs>}$ to represent a cloned closure that is being observed under the set of names $strs$.

Let us describe the modified rules one by one. Rules $var1@_1$ and $var1@_2$ clone an observed closure and annotate the pointer to the cloned closure as an observed pointer. By doing so, we can remember that the closure has already been cloned. Moreover, when the closure is reduced to weak head normal form (whnf), the machine will be able to detect that a side effect has to be performed to observe such a whnf. In addition to that, in the same moment, it will be necessary to clone the closures appearing in such whnf, and also to annotate them as observables.

The rule $observer@$ corresponds to the observation of a constructor applied to a list of arguments. When obtaining the constructor, a side effect is produced. Then, the closures corresponding to the arguments of the constructor are cloned. Finally, those cloned closures are marked as observables.

From that moment, the evaluation goes on, but what is being evaluated is not necessarily a variable associated to a pointer under observation. The reason is that the observation has already been performed. Thus, the variable under evaluation will only be under observation again when entering a closure that has been marked appropriately.

Let us remark that the rule $observer@$ does not modify the stack, as its only purpose is to perform an observation, not an evaluation.

As it can be seen, observing constructors is relatively simple. However, observing applications of functions will be a little bit more complex. In fact, such observations are done at the same time as the normal computation, by using rules $app2@$, $var2@_1$ and $var2@_2$.

Rule $app2@$ is used to observe a total application, that is, the application of a function to all the arguments it requires. Let us remind that, due to efficiency issues, the STG machine assumes that partial applications are never done.

In this $app2@$ rule, we have something of the form $\lambda \overline{x_i}^n.e$ (where $e \neq \lambda$) that is being observed under the set of strings $strs$. Moreover, this function is going to be applied to its arguments $\overline{p_i}^n$. Observe that in this situation what we need to do to behave as Hood is to observe both the arguments of the function and the result of the application. Thus, we proceed to observe both things: We clone the closures of the arguments marking the new closures as observables; and we create a new closure corresponding to the body of the lambda form, but marking as observables all the arguments. Notice that, in case any of the p_i are already being observed due to another mark, then the corresponding p_i' will have both observation marks.

Rules $var2@_1$ and $var2@_2$ correspond to updates of partial applications. In this case, closure q has been reduced to a partial application to its first k parameters of the λ-abstraction stored at position p of the heap. In this situation, an observation is generated indicating that we are not really observing the first

k parameters, and we go on evaluating the λ-abstraction marked as observable. Notice that we need to record that it is an *intermediate* step needed before the actual observation, but we do not want to show this intermediate step to the user (this is represented in the rules by using the $\neg$ symbol). Thus, by using this strategy we are obtaining more information than expected by the Hood user. However, by using this kind of special intermediate marks, after the end of the execution we can trivially postprocess the log file obtaining only those observations corresponding to the actual behavior of Hood.

Let us finally comment that in rules $var2@_2$ and $var@_2$ we deal with the situation where a closure is observed with several marks. Rule $var2@_2$ join the two sets of marks corresponding to the marks that were already attached to the closure and to the marks of the new observation. Similarly, $var@_2$ adds the new mark to the previous set of marks. For the sake of simplicity, we use the same symbol ($+\!\!+$) to denote both the union of sets and adding an element to a set.

5 Sharing Closures: Hugs-Like Debugging

As we said in Section 2, when observing a structure in Hood, the sharing of closures is completely lost. This implies that more memory is needed to run the program, and it also implies that some computations can be duplicated. Thus, both the runtime and the space efficiency are reduced.

In Section 2 we commented that the Haskell interpreter Hugs includes a different version of Hood. One of the advantages of this version is that the sharing of closures is not lost due to the observations. However, the results obtained when using Hugs are not the same as when using Hood with other compilers. The difference is that Hugs does not record who was responsible for each evaluation, it only records whether a value was computed or not.

We can easily embed this variant of Hood by slightly modifying the rules we introduced in the previous section. The new rules are shown in Figure 5. Notice that rules $var1@_1$ and $var1@_2$ are nearly the same as in the previous implementation, the difference being that now we do not clone any closure. Rule $observerH@$ has also been modified to remove the duplication of the closure under evaluation. By removing such duplications, we keep the sharing of closures, like Hugs does.

Rule $app2@$ is also slightly modified to avoid cloning the closures corresponding to the parameters of the application. However, it is necessary to use a new pointer to bind the body of the lambda abstraction. This is done to be able to observe the lambda form it evaluates to. However, we would like to remark that we are not cloning the closure. That is, sharing is kept.

Finally, rules $var2@_1$ and $var2@_2$ are not changed at all. That is, they are exactly the same as in the previous section. The reason is that the only difference with the previous implementation is that we do not want to clone closures. However, we do not care about keeping the behavior of the original version of Hood. The reason is that we are marking all the closures that are under observation, but we are not taking care about the closures that are observing those observed closures. Thus, in case function `length` is observed in a program like

Heap	Control	Environment	Stack	Side Effect	rule
Γ	$x^{@str}$	$E\{x \mapsto q\}$	S		var1@$_1$
$\Rightarrow \Gamma$	x	$\{x \mapsto q^{@<str>}\}$	S	$\emptyset$	
Γ	$x^{@str}$	$E\{x \mapsto q^{@<str>}\}$	S		var1@$_2$
$\Rightarrow \Gamma$	x	$\{x \mapsto q^{@<str \#\!\!+ strs>}\}$	S	$\emptyset$	
$\Gamma \cup [q \mapsto (C_k\ \overline{x_i}, \{\overline{x_i \mapsto p_i}\})]$	x	$E\{x \mapsto q^{@<strs>}\}$	S		observerH@
$\Rightarrow \Gamma \cup [q \mapsto (C\ \overline{x_i}, \{x_i \mapsto p_i^{@<strs>}\})]$	x	$\{x \mapsto q\}$	S	$(strs, q \mapsto C\ \overline{p_i})$	
$\Gamma[q \mapsto (\lambda \overline{x_i}^n.e, E')]$	x	$E\{x \mapsto q^{@<strs>}\}$	$\overline{p_i}^n : S$		app2@
$\Rightarrow \Gamma \cup [q' \mapsto (e, E' \cup \{x_i \mapsto p_i^{@<strs>}\})]$	x	$\{x \mapsto q'^{@<strs>}\}$	S	$(strs, q \mapsto (\lambda \overline{p_i}^n.q'))$	
$\Gamma[q \mapsto (\lambda \overline{x_i}^k.\lambda \overline{y_i}^n.e, E')]$	x	$E\{x \mapsto q\}$	$\overline{p_i}^k : \#q^{@<strs>} : S$		var2@$_1$ $(^1)$
$\Rightarrow \Gamma \cup [q' \mapsto (x\ \overline{x_i}^k, E'')]$	x	$\{x \mapsto q^{@<strs>}\}$	$\overline{p_i}^k : S$	$\neg(strs, q \mapsto \overline{p_i}^k)$	
$\Gamma[q \mapsto (\lambda \overline{x_i}^k.\lambda \overline{y_i}^n.e, E')]$	x	$E\{x \mapsto q^{@<strs>}\}$	$\overline{p_i}^k : \#q^{@<strs'>} : S$		var2@$_2$ $(^2)$
$\Rightarrow \Gamma \cup [q' \mapsto (x\ \overline{x_i}^k, E'')]$	x	$\{x \mapsto q^{@<strs \#\!\!+ strs'>}\}\ \overline{p_i}^k : S$		$\neg(strs', q \mapsto \overline{p_i}^k)$	

$(^1)\ E'' = \{x \mapsto q^{@<strs>}, \overline{x_i \mapsto p_i}^k\}$

$(^2)\ E'' = \{x \mapsto q^{@<strs \#\!\!+ strs'>}, \overline{x_i \mapsto p_i}^k\}$

Fig. 5. The Hugs-Hood abstract machine

```
let xs = take 5 (1:2:3:4:5:6:7:[])
in (observe "length" length xs) + (sum xs)
```

we have that xs is being observed, being function **length** its observer. Moreover, xs is completely evaluated due to the demand of function **sum**. Then, although function **length** only demands the spine of xs, the observation obtained would be

```
-- length
 { \ (1:2:3:4:5:[]) -> 5 }
```

That is, we obtain the same type of observations as Hugs, not that of the original Hood. The reason is that the abstract machine is not considering who is the observer of the observed structures. Thus, in case an observed closure is demanded, its evaluation will be observed even if the reason of the computation is not related with the observer function.

6   Hood Sharing Closures

As we showed in Section 4, by encoding Hood in the STG abstract machine we can do exactly the same as in Hood. In fact, we have followed an approach that was also losing the sharing of closures. Thus, it had the same efficiency disadvantages.

In the previous section we have shown another implementation keeping the sharing of closures. However, its behavior was not equivalent to that of the original version of Hood.

Fortunately, when working at the level of the abstract machines we can easily overcome the previous problems. In fact, in this section we show how we can embed Hood in the STG abstract machine without reducing the sharing of closures. That is, the observed programs will run using the same space as it would be required to run the program without observations.

In Figure 6, the new transitions needed to model the observations are shown. Before explaining them in detail, we would like to remark that there is no rule where closures are cloned. That is, sharing of closures will be preserved.

As closures are not being cloned, it is now very important to clearly understand not only what closure is being observed, but also what other closure is observing it. For instance, in the expression **letrec** $x = y^{@str} \ldots$ **in** e, we have that y is a closure that is being observed, while x is the closure that is observing it. That is, x is the observer of y. In this situation, even though we must remember that y is being observed with the mark str, when updating a value the observation marks should be attached to the pointer corresponding to variable x, and not to the pointer corresponding to variable y. That is, what we need to do is to associate the observations to the entity that is observing, not to the one that is being observed.

Following the previous ideas, $x^{@str}$ means that closure x is being observed by other closure. Similarly, $q^{@<strs>}$ means that the closure located at position q of the heap is being observed from other closures by using the set of marks $strs$. As a consequence, closure q must be stored in the heap without any observation mark.

Rules $var2@_1$ and $var2@_2$ are exactly the same as in Section 4, that is, when sharing was not preserved, except that now it is not necessary to add $@<strs>$ to the closure q' added to the heap because annotation $@<strs>$ means that another closure is observing q'. However, rules $var1@_1$, $var1@_2$ and $app2@$ need to be slightly rewritten, the only difference being that now we do not have to clone any closure. That is, we have to use exactly the same rules as in the Hugs-like machine.

Notice that in the new abstract machine we can not use the rules $observer@$ or $observerH@$. Rule $observer$ is incorrect because closure p corresponds to the closure that is being observed, not to the closure that is observing it. In the first machine, as closure p was a copy of the original closure, we could mark it without any risk, as it was only possible to enter this closure from the closures that were observing it. However, now p is not cloned, and it can be entered both from a closure that is observing it or from any other closure. Due to this reason, now we need more rules to be able to distinguish both situations. Let us remark that rule $observerH$ is also incorrect in this situation, as it was not taking into account who was the observer of each observed closure.

Let us describe the rest of the new rules, that are needed to substitute rule $observer$. As we need to take care of both the observer and the observed closures, we need to track the evolution of the computation transmitting the marks corresponding to the closures under observation. Observe that rules $case2@$, $case2d@$, $case2v@$ and $var3@$ are exactly the same as in the original STG machine, but transmitting the marks and generating side effects.

Rules $case2@$, $case2d@$ and $case2v@$ deal with closures that has been reduced to a constructor application, and that are being observed with the set of strings $strs$. Thus, a side effect has to be generated to observe the constructor, and then the machine has to go on evaluating the corresponding alternative of the outer case expression. Notice that all the pointers appearing in the application of the constructor are also marked as observable, so that we can actually observe them when appropriate.

Heap	Control	Environment	Stack	Side Effect	rule
Γ	$x^{@str}$	$E\{x \mapsto q\}$	S		var1@$_1$
$\Rightarrow \Gamma$	x	$\{x \mapsto q^{@<str>}\}$	S	$\emptyset$	
Γ	$x^{@str}$	$E\{x \mapsto q^{@<strs>}\}$	S		var1@$_2$
$\Rightarrow \Gamma$	x	$\{x \mapsto q^{@<str + strs>}\}$	S	$\emptyset$	
$\Gamma[q \mapsto (\lambda \overline{x_i}^n.e, E')]$	x	$E\{x \mapsto q^{@<strs>}\}$	$\overline{p_i}^n : S$		app2@([1])
$\Rightarrow \Gamma'$	x	$\{x \mapsto q'^{@<strs>}\}$	S	$(strs, q \mapsto (\lambda \overline{p_i}^n.q'))$	
$\Gamma[q \mapsto (\lambda \overline{x_i}^k.\lambda \overline{y_i}^n.e, E')]$	x	$E\{x \mapsto q\}$	$\overline{p_i}^k : \#q'^{@<strs>} : S$		var2@$_1$ ([2])
$\Rightarrow \Gamma \cup [q' \mapsto (x\ \overline{x_i}^k, E'')]$	x	$\{x \mapsto q^{@<strs>}\}$	$\overline{p_i}^k : S$	$\neg(strs, q \mapsto \overline{p_i}^k)$	
$\Gamma[q \mapsto (\lambda \overline{x_i}^k.\lambda \overline{y_i}^n.e, E')]$	x	$E\{x \mapsto q^{@<strs>}\}$	$\overline{p_i}^k : \#q'^{@<strs'>} : S$		var2@$_2$ ([3])
$\Rightarrow \Gamma \cup [q' \mapsto (x\ \overline{x_i}^k, E'')]$	x	$\{x \mapsto q^{@<strs + strs'>}\}$	$\overline{p_i}^k : S$	$\neg(strs', q \mapsto \overline{p_i}^k)$	
$\Gamma[q \mapsto (C_k\ \overline{x_i}, \{\overline{x_i \mapsto p_i}\})]$	x	$E\{x \mapsto q^{@<strs>}\}$	$(alts, E') : S$		case2@ ([4])
$\Rightarrow \Gamma$	e_k	$E' \cup \{y_{ki} \mapsto p_i^{@<strs>}\}\ S$		$(strs, q \mapsto C_k\ \overline{p_i})$	
$\Gamma[q \mapsto (C_k\ \overline{x_i}, \{\overline{x_i \mapsto p_i}\})]$	x	$E\{x \mapsto q^{@<strs>}\}$	$(alts.\textbf{default}->e, E') : S$		case2d@ ([5])
$\Rightarrow \Gamma$	e	E'	S	$(strs, q \mapsto C_k\ \overline{p_i})$	
$\Gamma[q \mapsto (C_k\ \overline{x_i}, \{\overline{x_i \mapsto p_i}\})]$	x	$E\{x \mapsto q^{@<strs>}\}$	$(alts.v->e, E') : S$		case2v@ ([5])
$\Rightarrow \Gamma$	e_k	$E' \cup \{v \mapsto q^{@<strs>}\}\ S$		$(strs, q \mapsto C_k\ \overline{p_i})$	
$\Gamma[q \mapsto (C\ \overline{x_i}, \{\overline{x_i \mapsto p_i}\})]$	x	$E\{x \mapsto q^{@<strs>}\}$	$\#p : S$		var3@ ([6])
$\Rightarrow \Gamma'$	x	$\{x \mapsto p\}$	S	$(strs, q \mapsto C\ \overline{p_i})$	

([1]) $\Gamma' = \Gamma \cup [q' \mapsto (e, E' \cup \{x_i \mapsto p_i^{@<strs>''}\})]$
([2]) $E'' = \{x \mapsto q, \overline{x_i \mapsto p_i}^k\}$
([3]) $E'' = \{x \mapsto q^{@<strs>}, \overline{x_i \mapsto p_i}^k\}$
([4]) Expression e_k corresponds to alternative $\overline{C_j\ \overline{y_{ji}} \to e_j}$ in $alts$
([5]) C_k not in $alts$
([6]) $\Gamma' = \Gamma \cup [p \mapsto (C\ \overline{x_i}, \overline{\{x_i \mapsto p_i^{@<strs>}\}})]$

Fig. 6. The Hood abstract machine sharing closures

Rule $var3@$ deals with the update of closures. In this case, p is updated recording the appropriate observation, the corresponding side effect is produced, and the machine goes on evaluating p.

Let us finally remark that, although the new machine is not so simple as the one presented in Section 4, it is still presented in a relatively simple an compact way.

7 Conclusions and Future Work

In this paper we have presented a new view of the Hood debugger allowing both to clarify its formal foundations and to easily implement different variations of it. In particular, we have described how to embed Hood inside the STG abstract machine, showing different possible implementations of it. In fact, by encoding it at STG level we have shown how to improve the efficiency of the implementation, as observations can now be done without cloning closures.

Note that the approach we use to embed Hood inside the STG machine can also be done to embed any other Haskell debugger. In this sense, it could be used as a common framework for describing (and also implementing) all of them.

As future work, we plan to extend our framework to deal with parallel extensions of Haskell. In this sense, we will pay special attention to the language Eden[9], whose abstract machine is an extension of the STG machine. An interesting feature of Eden is that it uses eager evaluation when sending values from one process to another process. Due to this reason, unnecessary computations are sometimes done, and it can be hard to discover how much data was produced speculatively. By using an extension of Hood we could detect the amount of speculation, as we could see how much data was produced and how much was actually demanded.

A more general framework to deal with different parallel extensions of Haskell could also be used. Unfortunately, there does not exist a common abstract machine shared by different parallel languages. In this sense, the best choice is to try to embed the debugging method inside the Jauja language[8], a very simple parallel functional language that has already been used as a common framework to describe three different languages, namely GpH, Eden and pH.

References

1. O. Chitil, C. Runciman, and M. Wallace. Freja, Hat and Hood — a comparative evaluation of three systems for tracing and debugging lazy functional programs. In *Implementation of Functional Languages (IFL'00)*, LNCS 2011, pages 176–193. Springer-Verlag, 2001.
2. A. Encina, L. Llana, and F. Rubio. Formalizing the debugging process in Haskell (extended version). http://dalila.sip.ucm.es/miembros/albertoe/, 2005.
3. A. Encina and R. Peña. Proving the correctness of the STG machine. In *Implementation of Functional Languages (IFL'01)*, LNCS 2312, pages 88–104. Springer-Verlag, 2001.
4. A. Encina and R. Peña. Formally deriving an STG machine. In *Principles and Practice of Declarative Programming (PPDP'03)*, pages 102–112. ACM, 2003.
5. R. Ennals and S. Peyton Jones. HsDebug: Debugging lazy programs by not being lazy. In *7th Haskell Workshop*, pages 84–87. ACM, 2003.
6. A. Gill. Debugging Haskell by observing intermediate data structures. In *4th Haskell Workshop*. Technical Report of the University of Nottingham, 2000.
7. A. Gill. Hood homepage. http://www.haskell.org/hood, 2005.
8. M. Hidalgo-Herrero and Y. Ortega-Mallén. Continuation semantics for parallel Haskell dialects. In *First Asian Symposium on Programming Languages and Systems (APLAS'03)*, LNCS 1058, pages 303–321. Springer-Verlag, 2003.
9. U. Klusik, R. Loogen, S. Priebe, and F. Rubio. Implementation skeletons in Eden: Low-effort parallel programming. In *Implementation of Functional Languages (IFL'00)*, LNCS 2011, pages 71–88. Springer-Verlag, 2001.
10. H. Nilsson. Declarative debugging for lazy functional languages. PhD thesis, Dpt. Computer and Information Science, Linköping University, Sweden, 1998.
11. H. Nilsson. How to look busy while being as lazy as ever: The implementation of a lazy functional debugger. *Journal of Functional Programming*, 11(6):629–671, Nov 2001.
12. S. Peyton Jones. Implementing lazy functional languages on stock hardware: The spineless tagless G-machine, version 2.5. *Journal of Functional Programming*, 2(2):127–202, 1992.
13. S. Peyton Jones and J. Hughes, editors. *Report on the Programming Language Haskell 98*. URL http://www.haskell.org, February 1999.
14. B. Pope and L. Naish. Practical aspects of declarative debugging in Haskell 98. In *Principles and Practice of Declarative Programming (PPDP'03)*, pages 230–240. ACM, 2003.

15. C. Reinke. GHood — graphical visualization and animation of Haskell object observations. In *5th Haskell Workshop*, volume 59 of *ENTCS*. Elsevier Science, 2001.
16. J. Sparud and C. Runciman. Tracing lazy functional computations using redex trails. In *Programming Languages, Implementations, Logics and Programs (PLILP'97)*, LNCS 1292, pages 291–308. Springer-Verlag, 1997.
17. P. Wadler. Functional programming: Why no one uses functional languages. *SIGPLAN Notices*, 33(8):23–27, August 1998. Functional Programming Column.
18. M. Wallace, O. Chitil, T. Brehm, and C. Runciman. Multipleview tracing for Haskell: a new Hat. In *5th Haskell Workshop*, pages 151–170, 2001.

Finding Resource Bounds in the Presence of Explicit Deallocation*

Hoang Truong and Marc Bezem

Department of Informatics, University of Bergen,
PB. 7800, N-5020 Bergen, Norway
{hoang, bezem}@ii.uib.no

Abstract. A software program requesting a resource that is not available usually raises an out-of-resource exception. Component software is software that has been assembled from standardized, reusable components which, in turn, may also composed from other components. Due to the independent development and reuse of components, component software has a high risk of causing out-of-resource exceptions. We present a small component language and develop a type system which can statically prevent this type of errors .

This work continues our previous works [3,18] by including explicit deallocation. We prove that the type system is sound with respect to safe deallocation and that sharp resource bounds can be computed statically.

1 Introduction

Component software is built from various components, possibly developed by third-parties [15,17,8]. These components may in turn use other components. Upon execution instances of these components are created. For example, when we launch a web browser application it may create an instance of a dial-up network connection, an instance of a menubar and several instances of a toolbar, among others. Each toolbar may in turn create its own control instances such as buttons, addressbars, bookmarks, and so on.

The process of creating an instance of a component x does not only mean the allocation of memory space for x's code and data structures, the creation of instances of x's subcomponents (and so on), but possibly also the binding of other system and hardware resources. Usually, these resources are limited and components are required to have only a certain number of simultaneously active instances. In the above example, there should be only one instance of a menubar and one instance of a modem for network connection. Other examples come from the singleton pattern and its extensions (multitons), which have been widely discussed in literature [10,9]. These patterns limit the number of objects of a certain class dynamically, at runtime.

* This research was supported by the Research Council of Norway.

D.V. Hung and M. Wirsing (Eds.): ICTAC 2005, LNCS 3722, pp. 227–241, 2005.

When building large component software it can easily happen that different instances of the same component are created. Creating more active instances than allowed can lead to errors or even a system crash, when there are not enough resources for them. An example is resource-exhaustion DoS (Denial of Service) attacks which cause a temporary loss of services. There are several ways to meet this challenge, ranging from testing, runtime checking [9], to static analysis.

Type systems are a branch of static analysis. Type systems have traditionally been used for compile-time error-checking, cf. [1,4,11]. Recently, there are several works on using type systems for certifying important security properties, such as performance safety, memory safety, control-flow safety [14,6,5,12]. In component software, typing has been studied in relation to integrating components such as type-safe composition [21] or type-safe evolution [13]. In this paper we explore the possibility of a type system which allows one to detect *statically* whether or not the number of simultaneously active instances of specific components exceeds the allowed number. Note that here we only control resources by the number of instances. However, we can extend to more specific resources, such as memory, by adding annotations to components using such resources.

For this purpose we have designed a component language where we have abstracted away many aspects of components and have kept only those that are relevant to instantiation, deallocation and composition. In the previous work [3,18], the main features are instantiation and reuse, sequential composition, choice, parallel composition and scope and the deallocation of instances is controlled by scope mechanism. In this work, we consider sequencing and parallel composition, choice and scope, add an explicit deallocation primitive, which allows us to imperatively remove an instance in the same scope. For the sake of simplicity, we do not consider the reuse primitive. However, we believe that the combination of all the features is feasible.

Though abstract, the strength of the primitives for composition is considerable. Choice allows us to model both conditionals and non-determinism. It can also be used when a component have several compatible versions and the system can choose one of them at runtime. Scope is a mechanism to deallocate instances but it can also be used to model method calls. Parallel composition allows several threads of execution. Sequential composition is associative.

We use a small-step operational semantics and as a result, we can prove the soundness of our type system using the standard technique of Wright and Felleisen [20].

The type inference algorithm for this system is almost the same as in [3]. We still have a polynomial time type inference algorithm. Polynomial type inference is of crucial importance since examining all possible executions of the operational semantics is (at least) exponential.

The paper is organized as follows. Section 2 introduces the component language and a small-step operational semantics. In Section 3 we define types and the typing relation. The soundness and several other properties of the system are presented in Section 4. Finally, we outline some future directions.

2 A Component Language

2.1 Syntax

Component programs, declarations and expressions are defined in Table 1. In the definition we use extended Backus-Naur Form with the following meta-symbols: infix | for choice and overlining for Kleene closure (zero or more iterations).

Table 1. Syntax

$Prog$	$::= Decls; E$	Program
$Decls$	$::= \overline{x \prec E}$	Declarations
E	$::=$	Expression
	$\mid \ \epsilon$	Empty
	$\mid \ \textbf{new} x$	Instantiation
	$\mid \ \textbf{del} x$	Deallocation
	$\mid \ (E + E)$	Choice
	$\mid \ (E \parallel E)$	Parallel
	$\mid \ \{E\}$	Scope
	$\mid \ E\ E$	Sequencing

Let $a, \ldots, z$ range over component names and $A, \ldots, E$ range over expressions. We collect all component names in a set $\mathbb{C}$.

The main ingredients in the component language are component declaration and expression. We have two primitives (**new** and **del**) for creating and deleting an instance of a component, and four primitives for composition (sequential composition denoted by juxtaposition, + for choice, $\parallel$ for parallel, and $\{\ldots\}$ for scope). Together with the empty expression ϵ these generate so-called *component expressions*. A *declaration* $x \prec E$ states how the component x depends on subcomponents as expressed in the component expression E. If x uses no subcomponents then E is ϵ and we call x a *primitive component*. A *component program* consists of declarations and ends with a *main expression* which sparks off the execution, see Section 2.2.

The following example is a well-formed component program. In this example, d and e are primitive components. Component a is the parallel composition of $\{\textbf{new} d\}\textbf{new} e$ and $\textbf{new} d$ followed by a deallocation of d. Component b has a choice expression before deleting an instance of e.

$$d \prec \epsilon \quad e \prec \epsilon$$
$$a \prec (\{\textbf{new} d\}\textbf{new} e \parallel \textbf{new} d)\textbf{del} d$$
$$b \prec (\textbf{new} a + \textbf{new} e\,\textbf{new} d)\textbf{del} e;$$
$$\textbf{new} b$$

2.2 Operational Semantics

Informally, expression E can be viewed as a sequence of commands of the form $\mathtt{new}\,x$, $\mathtt{del}\,x$, $(A + B)$, $(A \parallel B)$, $\{A\}$ in imperative programming languages and the execution is sequential from left to right. In the operational semantics E is paired with a local store, modelled by a multiset. The first three commands act locally. When executing a command of the form $\mathtt{new}\,x$, a new instance of x is created in the local store and the execution continues with the 'body' A, if the declaration of x is $x \prec A$ and $A \neq \epsilon$. If $A = \epsilon$ the execution proceeds to the next command after $\mathtt{new}\,x$. Executing $\mathtt{del}\,x$ simply removes a x in the local store then continues with the next command. Executing $(A + B)$ means to choose A or B to execute with the same store.

When the current command is of the form $\{E\}$ the execution of the commands after $\{E\}$, say A, is suspended, and the execution is transferred to E with a new empty local store. When the execution of the new pair $([], E)$ terminates in pair (M, ϵ), the instances in M are *discarded* and the execution resumes to the expression A and its local store. We will use stacks for this scope mechanism.

Executing $(E_1 \parallel E_2)$ suspends the execution of the commands after it and creates two new empty stores for each E_1 and E_2 and these two new pairs $([], E_1)$ and $([], E_2)$, called child threads, are executed concurrently. When a thread terminates in the pair (M, ϵ) the instances in M are *returned* to the store at the top of its parent thread. When all the child threads terminated, the execution resumes to the parent thread. The formal model is detailed as follows.

The operational semantics is defined by a rewriting system [16] of *configurations*. A configuration is a binary tree $\mathbb{T}$ of threads. A thread is a stack ST of pairs of a local store and an expression (M, E), where M is a multiset over component names $\mathbb{C}$, and E is an expression as defined in Table 1. A thread is *active* if it is a leaf thread. A configuration is *terminal* if it has only one (root) thread of the form (M, ϵ). Figure 1 illustrates stacks and configurations. The syntax of stacks and configurations is as follows.

$$
\begin{array}{lll}
ST & ::= (M_1, E_1) \circ \ldots \circ (M_n, E_n) & \text{Stack} \\
\mathbb{T}, \mathbb{S} & ::= & \text{Configurations} \\
& \quad \mathsf{Lf}(ST) & \text{Leaf} \\
& \mid \mathsf{Nd}(ST, \mathbb{T}) & \text{Node with one branch} \\
& \mid \mathsf{Nd}(ST, \mathbb{T}, \mathbb{T}) & \text{Node with two branches}
\end{array}
$$

The above stack ST has n elements where (M_1, E_1) is the bottom, (M_n, E_n) is the top of the stack, and 'o' is the stack separator. A node in our binary trees may have no child nodes $\mathsf{Lf}(ST)$, or one branch $\mathsf{Nd}(ST, \mathbb{T})$, or two branches $\mathsf{Nd}(ST, \mathbb{T}, \mathbb{T})$.

We assign to each node in our tree a *location*, illustrated in Figure 1. Let α, β range over locations. A location is a sequence over $\{l, r\}$. The root is assigned the empty sequence. The locations of two direct nodes from the root are l and r. The locations of the two direct child nodes of l are ll and lr, and so on. In

Stack/thread	Binary tree of stacks	Locations of a tree

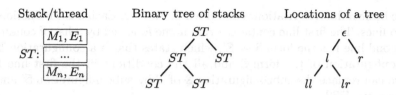

Fig. 1. Illustration of a tree of stacks

general, αl and αr are the locations of the direct children of α. We write $\alpha \in \mathbb{T}$ when α is a valid location in tree $\mathbb{T}$.

By $\mathbb{T}[\ ]_\alpha$ we denote a tree with a hole at the leaf location α. Filling this hole with another tree $\mathbb{S}$ is denoted by $\mathbb{T}[\mathbb{S}]_\alpha$. One step reduction is defined first by choosing an arbitrary active thread. Then depending on the pattern of the chosen thread and the state of the configuration, the appropriate rewrite rule can be applied. The rewriting rules for these patterns or subconfigurations, notation $\mathbb{S} \rightsquigarrow \mathbb{S}'$, are called the basic reduction relation. The configuration $\mathbb{T}[\mathbb{S}]_\alpha$ can take a step to $\mathbb{T}[\mathbb{S}']_\alpha$, notation $\mathbb{T}[\mathbb{S}]_\alpha \longrightarrow \mathbb{T}[\mathbb{S}']_\alpha$, if $\mathbb{S} \rightsquigarrow \mathbb{S}'$. As usual, $\longrightarrow^*$ is the reflexive and transitive closure of $\longrightarrow$.

Table 2. Basic reduction rules

(osNew) $x \prec A \in Decls$
$\mathsf{Lf}(ST \circ (M, \mathtt{new}\, xE)) \rightsquigarrow \mathsf{Lf}(ST \circ (M + x, AE))$

(osDel) $x \in M$
$\mathsf{Lf}(ST \cup (M, \mathtt{del}\, xE)) \rightsquigarrow \mathsf{Lf}(ST \circ (M - x, E))$

(osChoice) $i \in \{1, 2\}$
$\mathsf{Lf}(ST \circ (M, (A_1 + A_2)E)) \rightsquigarrow \mathsf{Lf}(ST \circ (M, A_i E))$

(osPush)
$\mathsf{Lf}(ST \circ (M, \{A\}E)) \rightsquigarrow \mathsf{Lf}(ST \circ (M, E) \circ ([\,], A))$

(osPop)
$\mathsf{Lf}(ST \circ (M, E) \circ (M', \epsilon)) \rightsquigarrow \mathsf{Lf}(ST \circ (M, E))$

(osParIntr)
$\mathsf{Lf}(ST \circ (M, (A \parallel B)E)) \rightsquigarrow \mathsf{Nd}(ST \circ (M, E), \mathsf{Lf}(([\,], A)), \mathsf{Lf}(([\,], B)))$

(osParElimL)
$\mathsf{Nd}(ST \circ (M, E), \mathsf{Lf}((M', \epsilon)), \mathbb{S}) \rightsquigarrow \mathsf{Nd}(ST \circ (M + M', E), \mathbb{S})$

(osParElimR)
$\mathsf{Nd}(ST \circ (M, E), \mathbb{S}, \mathsf{Lf}((M', \epsilon))) \rightsquigarrow \mathsf{Nd}(ST \circ (M + M', E), \mathbb{S})$

(osParElim)
$\mathsf{Nd}(ST \circ (M, E), \mathsf{Lf}((M', \epsilon))) \rightsquigarrow \mathsf{Lf}(ST \circ (M + M', E))$

The basic reduction relation is described in Table 2. Each basic reduction rule has two lines. The first line contains a rule name followed by a list of conditions. The second line has the form $\mathbb{S} \rightsquigarrow \mathbb{S}'$, which states that if a configuration $\mathbb{T}$ has a subconfiguration of the form $\mathbb{S}$ and all the conditions in the first line hold, then we can replace the subconfiguration $\mathbb{S}$ of $\mathbb{T}$ by subconfiguration $\mathbb{S}'$ and get the new state $\mathbb{T}[\mathbb{S}']$.

Multisets are denoted by $[\ldots]$, where sets are denoted, as usual, by $\{\ldots\}$. $M(x)$ is the multiplicity of element x in the multiset M and $M(x) = 0$ if $x \notin M$. The operation $\cup$ is union of multisets: $(M \cup N)(x) = max(M(x), N(x))$. The operation $+$ or $\uplus$ is additive union of multisets: $(M + N)(x) = M(x) + N(x)$. We write $M + x$ for $M + [x]$ and when $x \in M$ we write $M - x$ for $M - [x]$.

By the rules osNew, osDel, and osChoice we only rewrite the pair at the top of a leaf stack. The rule osNew first creates a new instance of component x in the local store. Then if x is a primitive component it continues to execute the remaining expression E; otherwise, it continues to execute A before executing the remaining expression E. The rule osDel deallocates an instance of x in the local store if there exists one. If there exists no instance of x in the local store, the execution is stuck. Note that here we have abstracted away the specific instance that will be deleted. The rule osChoice selects a branch to execute.

The next two rules change the shape of a leaf stack. Rule osPush pushes an element on the top of the leaf stack. The rule osPop pops the stack when the stack has at least two elements. That means no stack in any configuration is empty. The last four rules change the tree structure of the configuration. By the rule osParIntr, a leaf is replaced by a branch of a node and two leaves. In contrast, by the rules osParElimR, osParElimL, osParElim, a leaf is removed from the tree and the instances left at the leaf are returned to the store at the top of the parent thread. When appropriate, the parent node may be promoted to be an active thread (osParElim).

The example at the end of Section 2.1 is used to illustrate the operational semantics. There are many possible runs of the program due to the choice composition and when a configuration has more than one leaf thread, the number of possible runs can be exponential as active threads have the same priority. Here we only show one of the possible runs. To make it easier to follow, we represent the trees graphically instead of using the formal syntax; '$\llcorner$' and '$\langle$' denote branches with one and two child nodes, respectively. At the starting point, the configuration has one leaf $Lf([\,], \mathbf{new}\,b)$. After the first step, there are two possibilities by the rule osChoice.

$$
\begin{array}{lll}
(\text{Start}) & ([\,], \mathbf{new}\,b) & \\
(\text{osNew}) \longrightarrow & ([b], (\,\mathbf{new}\,a + \mathbf{new}\,e\,\mathbf{new}\,d)\,\mathbf{del}\,e) & \\
(\text{osChoice}) \longrightarrow & ([b], \mathbf{new}\,a\,\mathbf{del}\,e) & (\text{or }([b], \mathbf{new}\,e\,\mathbf{new}\,d\,\mathbf{del}\,e))
\end{array}
$$

Now we continue with the first possibility. When the tree grows two more leaves we draw a box around the leaf which is to be executed in the next step.

$$([b], \mathbf{new}\, a\, \mathbf{del}\, e)$$

$$(\mathsf{osNew}) \longrightarrow ([b,a], (\{\, \mathbf{new}\, d\}\, \mathbf{new}\, e \parallel \mathbf{new}\, d)\, \mathbf{del}\, d\, \mathbf{del}\, e)$$

$$(\mathsf{osParIntr}) \longrightarrow ([b,a], \mathbf{del}\, d\, \mathbf{del}\, e) \left\langle \frac{([\,], \{\, \mathbf{new}\, d\}\, \mathbf{new}\, e)}{\boxed{([\,], \mathbf{new}\, d)}} \right.$$

$$(\mathsf{osNew}) \longrightarrow ([b,a], \mathbf{del}\, d\, \mathbf{del}\, e) \left\langle \frac{\boxed{([\,], \{\, \mathbf{new}\, d\}\, \mathbf{new}\, e)}}{([d], \epsilon)} \right.$$

$$(\mathsf{osPush}) \longrightarrow ([b,a], \mathbf{del}\, d\, \mathbf{del}\, e) \left\langle \frac{\boxed{([\,], \mathbf{new}\, e) \circ ([\,], \mathbf{new}\, d)}}{([d], \epsilon)} \right.$$

$$(\mathsf{osNew}) \longrightarrow ([b,a], \mathbf{del}\, d\, \mathbf{del}\, e) \left\langle \frac{([\,], \mathbf{new}\, e) \circ ([d], \epsilon)}{\boxed{([d], \epsilon)}} \right.$$

$$(\mathsf{osParElimL}) \longrightarrow ([b,a,d], \mathbf{del}\, d\, \mathbf{del}\, e) \leftarrow ([\,], \mathbf{new}\, e) \circ ([d], \epsilon)$$

$$(\mathsf{osPop}) \longrightarrow ([b,a,d], \mathbf{del}\, d\, \mathbf{del}\, e) \leftarrow ([\,], \mathbf{new}\, e)$$

$$(\mathsf{osNew}) \longrightarrow ([b,a,d], \mathbf{del}\, d\, \mathbf{del}\, e) \leftarrow ([e], \epsilon)$$

$$(\mathsf{osParElim}) \longrightarrow ([b,a,d,e], \mathbf{del}\, d\, \mathbf{del}\, e)$$

$$(\mathsf{osDel}) \longrightarrow ([b,a,e], \mathbf{del}\, e)$$

$$(\mathsf{osDel}) \longrightarrow ([b,a], \epsilon) \quad (\text{terminal})$$

As mentioned in Section 1, here we have abstracted resources by the number of instances. When we want to account for specific resources, we can annotate the source program with the resource consumption of relevant component. Then the maximum resources the component program will use can be computed from our inferred types and the annotation. Another way to find how much resources a component program will probably use is declaring the specific resources as primitive components. Other components will then instantiate these resources in their declarations if they use the resources. Then our type system in the next section can tell us the maximum resources the program needs.

3   Type System

We have two main goals in designing the type system. The first one comes from the rule osDel of the dynamic semantics, where the program is stuck if the next operation is a deallocation of a component and there exists no instance of that component in the local store. In other words, the type system must guarantee the safety of the deallocation operation. We solve the problem by keeping a store in the typing environment, a technique inspired by linear type systems [19,12]. For the second goal, we want to find the upper bounds of resources that a program may request. Since we have abstracted the specific resources in the instances, the upper bounds become the maximum numbers of simultaneously active instances. In the rest of this section, we first define types and explain them informally; Then then we present the formal typing rules and some typing examples.

Before defining types, we extend the notion of multiset in Section 2 to the notion of *signed multiset*. Recall, a multiset over a set of elements S can be viewed as a map from S to the set of natural numbers $\mathbb{N}$. Similarly, a signed multiset M, also denoted by $[...]$, over a set S is a map from S to the set of integers $\mathbb{Z}$. The analogous operations of multisets are overloaded for signed multisets. $M(x)$ is the 'multiplicity' of x (can be negative); $M(x) = 0$ when x is not an element of M, notation $x \notin M$. Let M, N be signed multisets, then we define additive union: $(M + N)(x) = M(x) + N(x)$; substraction: $(M - N)(x) = M(x) - N(x)$; union: $(M \cup N)(x) = max(M(x), N(x))$; intersection: $(M \cap N)(x) = min(M(x), N(x))$; inclusion: $M \subseteq N$ if $M(x) \leq N(x)$ for all $x \in M$. For example, $[x, -y, -y]$ is a signed multiset where the multiplicity of x is 1 and the multiplicity of y is -2.

Definition 1 (Types). *Types of component expressions are tuples*

$$X = \langle X^i, X^o, X^l \rangle$$

where X^i is a multiset and X^o, X^l are signed multisets.

Intuitively, the meaning of each part of a type triple is as follows. Suppose X is the type of an expression E. Then X^i is the upper bound of the number of simultaneously active instances for all components during the execution of E. Multisets are the right data structure to store this information. Next, X^o is the maximum number of instances that 'survive' at the end of the execution when executing E alone, as in [3,18]. In this paper, we have the deallocation primitive and its behaviour is opposite to instantiation so we use signed multisets. Moreover we want compositionality of typing, so in composition X^o is the maximal net effect (with respect to the change in the number of instances) to the runtime environment *before* and *after* the execution of E. Similarly, X^i in composition is the effect on the maximum during the execution. The pair $\langle X^i, X^o \rangle$ is enough to calculate the upper bound.

Besides, we want the safety of the deallocation primitives in composition. When sequencing E and $\mathtt{del}\, x$ the safety of $\mathtt{del}\, x$ depends on the minimum outcome of E. Therefore we need X^l, which is the minimum number of surviving instances after the execution of E. Like X^o, in composition, X^l is the minimal net effect to the runtime environment before and after the execution of E. The discrepancy between X^o and X^l is caused by choice composition $+$. More explanation is given shortly in the exposition of typing rules below.

A *basis* is a list of declarations: $x_1 \prec E_1, \ldots, x_n \prec E_n$. Empty basis is denoted by $\varnothing$. Let Γ, Δ range over bases. The domain of basis $\Gamma = x_1 \prec E_1, \ldots, x_n \prec E_n$, notation $\mathbf{dom}(\Gamma)$, is the set $\{x_1, \ldots, x_n\}$. A *store* is a multiset (no negative multiplicities) of component names. Let σ range over stores. An *environment* is a pair of a store and a basis. A typing judgment is a tuple of the form

$$\sigma, \Gamma \vdash E : X$$

and it asserts that expression E has type X in the environment σ, Γ.

Definition 2 (Valid typing judgments). *Valid typing judgments $\sigma, \Gamma \vdash A : X$ are derived by applying the typing rules in Table 3 in the usual inductive way.*

Table 3. Typing rules

(Axiom)

$$\frac{}{[],\varnothing \vdash \epsilon : \langle [],[],[]\rangle}$$

(WeakenB)

$$\frac{\sigma_1,\Gamma \vdash A:X \quad \sigma_2,\Gamma \vdash B:Y \quad x \notin \mathsf{dom}(\Gamma)}{\sigma_1,\Gamma, x \prec B \vdash A:X}$$

(WeakenS)

$$\frac{\sigma,\Gamma \vdash A:X \quad \sigma \subseteq \sigma_1}{\sigma_1,\Gamma \vdash A:X}$$

(New)

$$\frac{\sigma,\Gamma \vdash A:X \quad x \notin \mathsf{dom}(\Gamma)}{\sigma,\Gamma, x \prec A \vdash \mathsf{new}\, x : \langle X^i + x, X^o + x, X^l + x\rangle}$$

(Del)

$$\frac{\sigma,\Gamma \vdash A:X \quad x \in \mathsf{dom}(\Gamma)}{[x],\Gamma \vdash \mathsf{del}\, x : \langle [],[-x],[-x]\rangle}$$

(Seq)

$$\frac{\sigma_1,\Gamma \vdash A:X \quad \sigma_2,\Gamma \vdash B:Y \quad A,B \neq \epsilon}{\sigma_1 \cup (\sigma_2 - X^l),\Gamma \vdash AB : \langle X^i \cup (X^o + Y^i), X^o + Y^o, X^l + Y^l\rangle}$$

(Choice)

$$\frac{\sigma_1,\Gamma \vdash A:X \quad \sigma_2,\Gamma \vdash B:Y}{\sigma_1 \cup \sigma_2,\Gamma \vdash (A+B) : \langle X^i \cup Y^i, X^o \cup Y^o, X^l \cap Y^l\rangle}$$

(Parallel)

$$\frac{[],\Gamma \vdash A:X \quad [],\Gamma \vdash B:Y}{[],\Gamma \vdash (A \parallel B) : \langle X^i + Y^i, X^o + Y^o, X^l + Y^l\rangle}$$

(Scope)

$$\frac{[],\Gamma \vdash A:X}{[],\Gamma \vdash \{A\} : \langle X^i, [],[]\rangle}$$

These typing rules deserve some further explanation. The most critical rule is Seq because sequencing two expressions can lead to increase in instances of the composed expression. First, the semantics of the store in the typing judgment requires that the store always has enough elements for deallocation commands in the expression. So we need to increase the store when the minimum outcome of A and its store, $X^l + \sigma_1$, is not enough for σ_2. Consider a component x. The premise of the rule Seq tells us that we need a store σ_1 for executing A. Thereafter, we have at least $X^l(x)$ instances of x, where $X^l(x) \in \mathbb{Z}$. Again by the premise of the rule Seq we need $\sigma_2(x)$ instances for safely executing B. Therefore we must start the execution of AB with at least $(\sigma_2 - X^l)(x)$ in the store (more than $\sigma_2(x)$ if $X^l(x) < 0$). Second, in the type expression of AB, the maximum is the maximum of A or of the outcome of A together with the maximum of B. So the first part of the type of AB is $X^i \cup (X^o + Y^i)$. The remaining parts, $X^o + Y^o$ and $X^l + Y^l$, are easy referring to the semantics of these parts of the types.

Other typing rules are straightforward. The rule Axiom is used for startup. The rules WeakenB allows us to extend the type environments so that the rules Seq, Choice, Parallel may be applied. The rule WeakenS plays a technical role in some proofs and is a natural rule anyway: enlarging the store should preserve typing. The rule New accumulates a new instance in type expression while the rule Del reduces by one instance. The first signed multiset in the type of $\mathsf{del}\, x$ is empty since it has no effect to the maximum in composition, but the last two multisets are both $[-x]$ since $\mathsf{del}\, x$ reduces the local stores by one x. The judgment $\sigma,\Gamma \vdash A:X$ in the premise of this rule only guarantees that the basis Γ

is legal. The rules Parallel and Scope require an empty store in the environment because the semantics of deallocation applies to local store only.

Now we can define the notion of *well-typed program* with respect to our type system. Basically, a program is well-typed if we can derive a type for the main expression of the program from an empty store and a list of the program declarations. As mentioned in the Introduction Section 1, we have an polynomial algorithm (cf. [3]) which can automatically decide whether a program is well-typed or not, and if so, infer a type.

Definition 3 (Well-typed programs). *Program Prog = Decls; E is well-typed if there exists a reordering Γ of declarations in Decls such that $[\,], \Gamma \vdash E : X$.*

Using the example in Section 2.1 we derive type for **new** b. Note that we omitted some side conditions as they can be checked easily and we shortened the rule names to the first two characters (we do not use the rule WeakenS so WeakenB is abbreviated to We). The signed multisets are simplified as well. The elements of a signed multiset are listed in a string with the multiplicities as superscripts, multiplicity 1 is not shown as supperscript and elements with multiplicity 0 are not shown. The rule Axiom is also simplified.

$$
\text{We} \cfrac{\text{Sc} \cfrac{\text{Ne} \cfrac{[\,], \varnothing \vdash \epsilon : \langle [\,], [\,], [\,] \rangle}{[\,], d \prec \epsilon \vdash \textbf{new } d : \langle d, d, d \rangle}}{[\,], d \prec \epsilon \vdash \{\textbf{new } d\} : \langle d, [\,], [\,] \rangle} \quad \text{We} \cfrac{[\,], \varnothing \vdash \epsilon : \langle [\,], [\,], [\,] \rangle \quad [\,], \varnothing \vdash \epsilon : \langle [\,], [\,], [\,] \rangle}{[\,], d \prec \epsilon \vdash \epsilon : \langle [\,], [\,], [\,] \rangle}}{[\,], d \prec \epsilon, e \prec \epsilon \vdash \{\textbf{new } d\} : \langle d, [\,], [\,] \rangle} \tag{1}
$$

$$
\text{Se} \cfrac{(1) \quad \text{Ne} \cfrac{\text{We} \cfrac{[\,], \varnothing \vdash \epsilon : \langle [\,], [\,], [\,] \rangle \quad [\,], \varnothing \vdash \epsilon : \langle [\,], [\,], [\,] \rangle}{[\,], d \prec \epsilon \vdash \epsilon : \langle [\,], [\,], [\,] \rangle}}{[\,], d \prec \epsilon, e \prec \epsilon \vdash \textbf{new } e : \langle e, e, e \rangle}}{[\,], d \prec \epsilon, e \prec \epsilon \vdash \{\textbf{new } d\} \textbf{new } e : \langle de, e, e \rangle} \tag{2}
$$

$$
\text{Pa} \cfrac{(2) \quad \text{We} \cfrac{\text{Ne} \cfrac{[\,], \varnothing \vdash \epsilon : \langle [\,], [\,], [\,] \rangle}{[\,], d \prec \epsilon \vdash \textbf{new } d : \langle d, d, d \rangle} \quad [\,], \varnothing \vdash \epsilon : \langle [\,], [\,], [\,] \rangle}{[\,], d \prec \epsilon, e \prec \epsilon \vdash \textbf{new } d : \langle d, d, d \rangle}}{[\,], d \prec \epsilon, e \prec \epsilon \vdash (\{\textbf{new } d\} \textbf{new } e \parallel \textbf{new } d) : \langle d^2 e, de, de \rangle} \tag{3}
$$

$$
\text{Ne} \cfrac{\text{Se} \cfrac{(3) \quad \text{De} \cfrac{(3) \quad d \in \text{dom}(d \prec \epsilon, e \prec \epsilon)}{[d], d \prec \epsilon, e \prec \epsilon \vdash \textbf{del } d : \langle [\,], d^{-1}, d^{-1} \rangle}}{[\,], d \prec \epsilon, e \prec \epsilon \vdash (\{\textbf{new } d\} \textbf{new } e \parallel \textbf{new } d) \textbf{del } d : \langle d^2 e, e, e \rangle}}{[\,], d \prec \epsilon, e \prec \epsilon, a \prec (\{\textbf{new } d\} \textbf{new } e \parallel \textbf{new } d) \textbf{del } d \vdash \textbf{new } a : \langle ad^2 e, ae, ae \rangle} \tag{4}
$$

Similarly, we can derive $\Gamma \vdash \textbf{new } b : \langle abd^2 e, abd, b \rangle$ where $\Gamma = d \prec \epsilon, e \prec \epsilon, a \prec (\{\textbf{new } d\} \textbf{new } e \parallel \textbf{new } d) \textbf{del } d, b \prec (\textbf{new } a + \textbf{new } e \textbf{new } d) \textbf{del } e$.

By the example we illustrate how we can infer the specific resources. If component a and d each creates a database connection, then from the type of **new** b, we know that the program, in particular the main expression **new** b, may need three database connections (one by a and two by d). From another point of view, we regard d as a database connection component, then we know that the program needs maximum two database connections.

4   Formal Properties

4.1   Type Soundness

A fundamental property of static type systems is *type soundness* or *safety* [4]. It states that well-typed programs cannot cause type errors. In our model, type errors occur when the program tries to delete an instance which is not in the local store or when the program tries to instantiate a component x but there is no declaration of x. We will prove that these two situations will not happen. Besides, we will prove an additional important property which guarantees that a well-typed program will not create more instances than a certain maximum stated in its type.

Our proof of the type soundness is based on the approach of Wright and Felleisen [20]. We will prove two main lemmas: Preservation and Progress. The first lemma states that well-typedness is preserved under reduction. The latter guarantees that well-typed programs cannot get stuck, that is, move to a non-terminal state, from which it cannot move to another state. In order to use this technique, we need to define the notion of *well-typed configuration*. We start with some auxiliary definitions.

First, since the location of a parent node is a subsequence of the location of its children (direct and indirect), we define the following binary prefix ordering relation $\leq$ over locations. For location $\alpha = s_0 s_1..s_n$ where $s_i \in \{l, r\}$, $\alpha' \leq \alpha$ if $\alpha' = s_0 s_1..s_m$, $0 \leq m \leq n$. The set of all locations in a tree and this binary relation form a partially ordered set [7]. A maximal element of this partially ordered set is the location of a leaf. We denote by leaves($\mathbb{T}$) the set of locations of all the leaves of $\mathbb{T}$ and $\mathbb{T}(\alpha)$ the stack at location α in $\mathbb{T}$.

Second, we call $\alpha.k$ the *position* of the kth element (from the bottom) of the stack $\mathbb{T}(\alpha)$. Again the set of all positions $\alpha.k$ in tree $\mathbb{T}$ is a partially ordered set with the following binary relation. $\alpha_1.k_1 \leq \alpha_2.k_2$ if either $\alpha_1 = \alpha_2$ and $k_1 \leq k_2$, or $\alpha_1 < \alpha_2$.

Next, we formalize the notion of *subtree*. Given a tree $\mathbb{T}$. The set of positions $\mathcal{L} = \{\alpha_i.k_i \in \mathbb{T} \mid 1 \leq i \leq m\}$ is *valid* if $\alpha_i.k_i \not\leq \alpha_j.k_j$ for all $i \neq j$. The tree $\mathbb{T}'$ obtained from $\mathbb{T}$ by removing all elements at positions $\alpha.k \geq \alpha_i.k_i$ for all $1 \leq i \leq m$ is a subtree of $\mathbb{T}$, notation $\mathbb{T}' \sqsubseteq_{\mathcal{L}} \mathbb{T}$ or $\mathbb{T}' = \mathbb{T}|_{\mathcal{L}}$. Consequently, $\mathbb{T}'$ has the same root as $\mathbb{T}$. When $\mathcal{L}$ is empty, we get $\mathbb{T}' = \mathbb{T}$.

We denote by hi(ST) the height of the stack ST. By $\mathbb{T}(\alpha.k) = (M, E)$ we denote that the element at position $\alpha.k$ is the pair (M, E). We denote by $[\mathbb{T}(\alpha.k)]$ the store M at position $\alpha.k$, by $[\mathbb{T}(\alpha)]$ the additive union of all stores in the stack at location α, and by $[\mathbb{T}]$ the multiset of all active instances in the tree $\mathbb{T}$, i.e. $[\mathbb{T}] = \biguplus_{\alpha \in \mathbb{T}} [\mathbb{T}(\alpha)]$.

Now we calculate the multiset of instances that will be returned to a position $\alpha.k$. Due to the non-determinism of osChoice, we can only calculate the upper bound and the lower bound of the collection. The minimal number of instances returned to a position $\alpha.k$, denoted by function retl$_{\mathbb{T}}(\alpha.k)$, is zero if k is not the top of the stack at location α, or α is a leaf. Otherwise, it contains those in the multisets at the bottom of its child nodes and the minimal number of instances which survive the expressions there. Since the bottom of a child node of $\alpha.k$ may receive instances from its child nodes (osParElimL, osParElimR, osParElim) and so on, we need to call the function recursively.

$$\mathsf{retl}_{\mathbb{T}}(\alpha.k) = \begin{cases} [\,], & \text{if } k < \mathsf{hi}(\mathbb{T}(\alpha)) \text{ or } \alpha \in \mathsf{leaves}(\mathbb{T}) \\ \biguplus_{\beta \in \{\alpha l, \alpha r\}}(M + X^l + \mathsf{retl}_{\mathbb{T}}(\beta.1)), & \text{otherwise} \end{cases}$$

where $\mathbb{T}(\beta.1) = (M, E)$ and $M + \mathsf{retl}_{\mathbb{T}}(\beta.1), \Gamma \vdash E : X$. Note that this recursive definition is well-defined since first it is well-defined for all the positions at all leaves. Then it is well-defined for the top position of the parents of all leaves. And so on until the root.

The maximal number of instances that will be returned to a position $\alpha.k$, denoted by function $\mathsf{reto}_{\mathbb{T}}(\alpha.k)$, is calculated analogously.

$$\mathsf{reto}_{\mathbb{T}}(\alpha.k) = \begin{cases} [\,], & \text{if } k < \mathsf{hi}(\mathbb{T}(\alpha)) \text{ or } \alpha \in \mathsf{leaves}(\mathbb{T}) \\ \biguplus_{\beta \in \{\alpha l, \alpha r\}}(M + X^o + \mathsf{reto}_{\mathbb{T}}(\beta.1)), & \text{otherwise} \end{cases}$$

where $\mathbb{T}(\beta.1) = (M, E)$ and $M + \mathsf{retl}_{\mathbb{T}}(\beta.1), \Gamma \vdash E : X$.

By Lemma 5 below, these two functions always return multisets even though signed multisets X^l, X^o appear in their definitions.

Now we can define the notion of well-typed configuration. It guarantees that the local store always has enough elements for typing its executing expression. Hence deallocation operations are always safe to execute.

Definition 4 (Well-typed configuration). *Configuration* $\mathbb{T}$ *is well-typed with respect to a basis* Γ, *notation* $\Gamma \models \mathbb{T}$, *if for all pair* (M, E) *at position* $\alpha.k \in \mathbb{T}$ *there exists* X *such that*

$$M + \mathsf{retl}_{\mathbb{T}}(\alpha.k), \Gamma \vdash E : X$$

Having the definition of well-typed configuration, the two main lemmas mentioned at the beginning of the section are stated as follows.

Lemma 1 (Preservation). *If* $\Gamma \models \mathbb{T}$ *and* $\mathbb{T} \longrightarrow \mathbb{T}'$, *then* $\mathbb{T}'$ *is well-typed.*

Lemma 2 (Progress). *If* $\Gamma \models \mathbb{T}$, *then either* $\mathbb{T}$ *is terminal or there exists a configuration* $\mathbb{T}'$ *such that* $\mathbb{T} \longrightarrow \mathbb{T}'$.

Next, we show some additional invariants which allow us to infer the resource bounds of a well-typed program. Then we state the soundness theorem which contains both goals mentioned at the beginning of the section.

Consider the pair (M, E) at position $\alpha.k$ in a well-typed configuration $\mathbb{T}$. By Definition 4 we have $M + \mathsf{retl}_{\mathbb{T}}(\alpha.k), \Gamma \vdash E : X$ for some X. The maximum number of instances involved in the execution of the pair (M, E) is computed by:

$$\mathsf{io}_{\mathbb{T}}(\alpha.k) = M + \mathsf{reto}_{\mathbb{T}}(\alpha.k) + X^i$$

Lemma 3 (Invariants of retl, reto, and io). *If* $\Gamma \models \mathbb{T}$ *and* $\mathbb{T} \longrightarrow \mathbb{T}'$, *then for all positions* $\alpha.k$ *in both configurations* $\mathbb{T}$ *and* $\mathbb{T}'$ *we have:*

1. $\mathsf{retl}_{\mathbb{T}}(\alpha.k) \subseteq \mathsf{retl}_{\mathbb{T}'}(\alpha.k)$,
2. $\mathsf{reto}_{\mathbb{T}}(\alpha.k) \supseteq \mathsf{reto}_{\mathbb{T}'}(\alpha.k)$,
3. $\mathsf{io}_{\mathbb{T}}(\alpha.k) \supseteq \mathsf{io}_{\mathbb{T}'}(\alpha.k)$.

Note that the inclusions are related to choice: less options means smaller maxima and larger minima.

The maximum number of instances of a subtree $\mathbb{T}|_{\mathcal{L}}$ includes the maximum of its leaves and all the active instances in all the stores inside the subtree.

$$\mathsf{maxins}(\mathbb{T}|_{\mathcal{L}}) = \biguplus_{\alpha.k < \mathcal{L}'} [\mathbb{T}(\alpha.k)] + \biguplus_{\alpha.k \in \mathcal{L}'} \mathsf{io}_{\mathbb{T}}(\alpha.k)$$

where $\mathcal{L}'$ is the set of all positions at the top of leaves of subtree $\mathbb{T}|_{\mathcal{L}}$, i.e. $\mathcal{L}' = \{\alpha.\mathsf{hi}(\mathbb{T}|_{\mathcal{L}}(\alpha)) \mid \alpha \in \mathsf{leaves}(\mathbb{T}|_{\mathcal{L}})\}$.

By the monotonicity of the function io, the function *maxins* also has this property.

Lemma 4 (Invariant of maxins**).** *If* $\Gamma \models \mathbb{T}$ *and* $\mathbb{T} \longrightarrow \mathbb{T}'$, *then for all valid set of positions* $\mathcal{L}'$ *of* $\mathbb{T}'$ *there exists a valid set of positions* $\mathcal{L}$ *of* $\mathbb{T}$ *such that*

$$\mathsf{maxins}(\mathbb{T}|_{\mathcal{L}}) \supseteq \mathsf{maxins}(\mathbb{T}'|_{\mathcal{L}'})$$

Now we can state the soundness property together with the upper bounds of instances that a well-typed program always respects.

Theorem 1 (Soundness). *If program Prog = Decls; E is well-typed, then there exists a multiset M such that for every sequence of reductions* $\mathsf{Lf}([], E) \longrightarrow^* \mathbb{T}$ *we have* $\mathbb{T}$ *is not stuck and* $[\mathbb{T}] \subseteq M$.

4.2 Typing Properties

This section lists some properties of the type system. They are needed to prove the lemmas and theorem in the previous section. We start with some definitions.

Let $\Gamma = x_1 \prec A_1, \dots, x_n \prec A_n$ be a basis. Γ is called *legal* if $\sigma, \Gamma \vdash A : X$ for some store σ, expression A and type X. A declaration $x \prec A$ *is in* Γ, notation $x \prec A \in \Gamma$, if $x \equiv x_i$ and $A \equiv A_i$ for some i. Δ is an *initial segment* of Γ, if $\Delta = x_1 \prec A_1, \dots, x_j \prec A_j$ for some $1 \leq j \leq n$.

We use X^* for any of X^i, X^o and X^l. Recall X^* are maps, we denote by $\mathsf{dom}(X^*) = \{x \mid X^*(x) \neq 0\}$ the domain of X^*. For multiset M we denote $\mathsf{dom}(M) = \{x \mid M(x) \neq 0\}$. Let $\mathsf{var}(E)$ denote the set of variables occurring in an expression:

$$\mathsf{var}(\mathtt{new}\,x) = \mathsf{var}(\mathtt{del}\,x) = \{x\}, \quad \mathsf{var}(\{A\}) = \mathsf{var}(A),$$
$$\mathsf{var}(AB) = \mathsf{var}((A+B)) = \mathsf{var}((A \parallel B)) = \mathsf{var}(A) \cup \mathsf{var}(B)$$

The following lemma collects a number of simple properties of a valid typing judgment.

Lemma 5 (Legal typing). *If* $\sigma, \Gamma \vdash A : X$, *then*

1. $\mathsf{var}(A) \subseteq \mathsf{dom}(\Gamma)$, $\mathsf{dom}(X^*) \subseteq \mathsf{dom}(\Gamma)$,
2. *every variable in* $\mathsf{dom}(\Gamma)$ *is declared only once in* Γ,

3. $X^i \supseteq X^o \supseteq X^l$, $X^i \supseteq []$,
4. $\sigma + X^* \supseteq []$.

The following lemmas show the associativity of the sequential composition and the significance of the order of declarations in a legal basis.

Lemma 6 (Associativity). *If $\sigma_i, \Gamma \vdash A_i : X_i$, for $i \in \{1, 2, 3\}$, then the typing judgments for $(A_1 A_2) A_3$ and $A_1 (A_2 A_3)$ are the same.*

The following lemma is important in that it allows us to find a syntax-directed derivation of the type of an expression. This lemma is sometimes called the *inversion lemma of the typing relation* [11].

Lemma 7 (Generation).

1. *If $\sigma, \Gamma \vdash \mathbf{new}\, x : X$, then there exist bases Δ, Δ' and expression A such that $\Gamma = \Delta, x \prec A, \Delta'$, and $\sigma, \Delta \vdash A : Y$ with $X = \langle Y^i + x, Y^o + x, Y^l + x \rangle$.*
2. *If $\sigma, \Gamma \vdash \mathbf{del}\, x : X$, then $x \in \sigma$, $x \in \mathsf{dom}(\Gamma)$ and $X = \langle [], [-x], [-x] \rangle$.*
3. *If $\sigma, \Gamma \vdash AB : Z$ with $A, B \neq \epsilon$, then there exist X, Y such that $\sigma, \Gamma \vdash A : X$, $\sigma + X^l, \Gamma \vdash B : Y$ and $Z = \langle X^i \cup (X^o + Y^i), X^o + Y^o, X^l + Y^l \rangle$.*
4. *If $\sigma, \Gamma \vdash (A + B) : Z$, then there exist X, Y such that $\sigma, \Gamma \vdash A : X$ and $\sigma, \Gamma \vdash B : Y$ and $Z = \langle X^i \cup Y^i, X^o \cup Y^o, X^l \cap Y^l \rangle$.*
5. *If $\sigma, \Gamma \vdash (A \parallel B) : Z$, then there exist X, Y such that $[], \Gamma \vdash A : X$ and $[], \Gamma \vdash B : Y$, and $Z = \langle X^i + Y^i, X^o + Y^o, X^l + Y^l \rangle$.*
6. *If $\sigma, \Gamma \vdash \{A\} : Z$, then there exist multisets X^o and X^l such that $[], \Gamma \vdash A : X$ and $Z = \langle X^i, [], [] \rangle$.*

5　Conclusions and Research Directions

This work follows a more liberal approach compared to our previous works [3,18] where the resource bounds, i.e. the maximum number of instances for each component, are known in advance and the type system checks these bounds in typing rules. The dynamic semantics of the deallocation primitive here applies to local stores only. Even though this style is rather common in practice, we plan to extend the semantics of deallocation so that it can operate beyond scopes and even threads. We are well aware of the level of abstraction of the component language and plan to incorporate more language features. These include recursion in component declarations, communication among threads and location of resources.

References

1. H. Barendregt. Lambda Calculi with Types. In: Abramsky, Gabbay, Maibaum (Eds.), *Handbook of Logic in Computer Science*, Vol. II, Oxford University Press. 1992.
2. M. Bezem and H. Truong. A Type System for the Safe Instantiation of Components. In *Electronic Notes in Theoretical Computer Science* Vol. 97, July 2004.

3. M. Bezem and H. Truong. Counting Instances of Software Components, In *Proceedings of LRPP'04*, July 2004.
4. L. Cardelli. Type systems. In A. B. Tucker, editor, *The Computer Science and Engineering Handbook*, chapter 103, pages 2208-2236. CRC Press, 1997.
5. K. Crary, D. Walker, and G. Morrisett. Typed Memory Management in a Calculus of Capabilities. In *Twenty-Sixth ACM SIGPLAN-SIGACT Symposium on Principles of Programming Languages*, pages 262-275, San Antonio, TX, USA, January 1999.
6. K. Crary and S. Weirich. Resource Bound Certification. In *the Twenty-Seventh ACM SIGPLAN-SIGACT Symposium on Principles of Programming Languages*, pages 184-198, Boston, MA, USA, January 2000.
7. B. Dushnik and E. W. Miller. *Partially Ordered Sets*, American Journal of Mathematics, Vol. 63, 1941.
8. R. Englander. *Developing Java Beans*. 1st Edition, ISBN 1-56592-289-1, June 1997.
9. E. Gamma, R. Helm, R. Johnson, and J. Vlissides. *Design Patterns - Elements of Reusable Object-Oriented Software*, Addison-Wesley, ISBN 0201633612, 1994.
10. E. Meijer and C. Szyperski. Overcoming Independent Extensibility Challenges, *Communications of the ACM*, Vol. 45, No. 10, pp. 41–44, October 2002.
11. B. Pierce. *Types and Programming Languages*. MIT Press, ISBN 0-262-16209-1, February 2002.
12. B. Pierce. *Advanced Topics in Types and Programming Languages*. MIT Press, ISBN 0-262-16228-8, January 2005.
13. J. C. Seco. Adding Type Safety to Component Programming. In *Proc. of The PhD Student's Workshop* in FMOODS'02, University of Twente, the Netherlands, March 2002.
14. F. Smith, D. Walker and G. Morrisett. Alias Types. In *European Symposium on Programming*, Berlin, Germany, March 2000.
15. C. Szyperski. *Component Software: Beyond Object-Oriented Programming*, 2nd edition, Addison-Wesley, ISBN 0201745720, 2002.
16. Terese. *Term Rewriting Systems*, Cambridge Tracts in Theoretical Computer Science, Vol. 55, Cambridge University Press, 2003
17. T. Thai, H. Lam. *.NET Framework Essentials*. 3nd Edition, ISBN 0-596-00302-1, August 2003.
18. H. Truong. Guaranteeing Resource Bounds for Component Software. Martin Steffen, Gianluigi Zavattaro, editors. In *Proceedings of FMOODS'05*, Athens, Greece, June 2005. *LNCS 3535*, Springer, ISBN: 3-540-26181-8. pp. 179-194, May 2005.
19. P. Wadler. Linear types can change the world! In M. Broy and C. Jones, editors, *Programming Concepts and Methods*, Sea of Galilee, Israel, April 1990. North Holland. IFIP TC 2 Working Conference.
20. A. K. Wright and M. Felleisen, A Syntactic Approach to Type Soundness. In *Information and Computation*, Vol. 115, No. 1, pp. 38–94, 1994.
21. M. Zenger, Type-Safe Prototype-Based Component Evolution. In *Proceedings of the European Conference on Object-Oriented Programming*, Malaga, Spain, June 2002.

The Timer Cascade: Functional Modelling and Real Time Calculi

Raymond Boute[1] and Andreas Schäfer[2]

[1] INTEC, Universiteit Gent, Belgium
Raymond.Boute@intec.UGent.be
[2] Department für Informatik, Universität Oldenburg, Germany
Andreas.Schaefer@informatik.uni-oldenburg.de

Abstract. Case studies can significantly contribute towards improving the understanding of formalisms and thereby to their applicability in practice. One such case, namely a cascade of the familiar 24-hour timers (in suitably generalized form) provides interesting gedanken experiments and illustrations for presenting, illustrating and comparing various formalisms for modelling real-time behaviour of systems.

The timer cascade is first modelled in a general-purpose functional formalism (Funmath) and various properties are derived, including an interesting algebraic monoid structure of timer programs. Then it is described and analyzed in duration calculus, thereby highlighting, similarities and differences in the approach to modelling and reasoning, and also the link between the formalisms.

Future work consists in using this case as a running example for exploring the same issues for other formalisms intended for real time and hybrid systems. The underlying idea is that other authors join this effort and contribute towards extending it, finally arriving at a broad comparative survey of such formalisms.

Index Terms — Automata, cascade connection, Duration Calculus, functional description, Funmath, hybrid systems, real time systems, systems modelling, timers.

1   Introduction: Motivation and Overview

Hybrid systems formalisms have become increasingly important for modelling interacting continuous and discrete aspects [2,9,16,23]. Research was especially fruitful in the past two decades, but the very wealth of techniques resulting from these efforts may be a problem for integration into practice. We briefly elaborate.

A basis for comparison is the wide and problem-free integration of mathematical software such as Maple, Mathematica, Matlab and Mathcad throughout all branches of engineering. This is possible because the mathematics is classical (linear algebra, differential and integral calculus etc.) with long-standing notational and calculational conventions. Standard high school and college mathematics suffice for direct use of such software, and engineers educated 50 years

D.V. Hung and M. Wirsing (Eds.): ICTAC 2005, LNCS 3722, pp. 242–256, 2005.
© Springer-Verlag Berlin Heidelberg 2005

ago apply it without further ado, yet quite reliably. Admittedly, use in discrete mathematics is less safe due to errors as pointed out in [19] and remedied in [7].

The situation alters drastically as soon as nontrivial elements from logic enter into the picture, as needed for software, digital hardware and hybrid systems. The relevant concepts are neither supported by common mathematical software, nor part of classical engineering background. Computer science students have difficulties with logic [1], and in industry, applications with logic software often requires external support by consultants (private or university researchers).

Quick introductions or trying to learn logic via tools are ill-advised. Habrias [14] aptly warns against using tools without sufficient awareness. Safe use requires a solid background in logic, including understanding as can be fostered only by serious pencil-and-paper problem solving similar to common practice in analysis and algebra. This holds for students, but even more for industrial users.

As mentioned, the wealth of formalisms is a complicating factor. Notational and calculational conventions are far less uniform than in classical mathematics; hence commonality in software support is still remote. Choosing one tool excludes possibly crucial features present in an other one. Given this situation, the (ideal) hybrid systems engineer must master several quite different formalisms, awaiting the emergence of a common framework.

Meanwhile, there is no universal solution, only ways for alleviation.

In particular, case studies provide a good starting point for understanding and comparing formalisms [16]. A widely studied example is the steam boiler [22], which has proved a useful testbed for various systems aspects. However, the crucial aspects to be highlighted are often diluted by other details.

Here we propose a case chosen to be as simple as possible and concentrating on the time aspect in its purest form, while still offering interesting ramifications: the 24 hour timer (somewhat generalized) and timer cascades. This turns out to be very appropriate for studying how time is handled in different formalisms.

An important side issue is how well formalisms "scale down" in the sense that simple systems can be described in a comparably simple way. Indeed, whereas industrial applicability often relies on scaling up (to "large" systems with many details), the intrinsic design quality and intellectual value of a formalism is often characterized by its downscaling potential in the aforesaid sense.

Overview. Section 2 informally introduces the timer and the timer cascade. Section 3 provides a formal description in the functional formalism Funmath and illustrates the calculational derivation of interesting algebraic properties. In section 4, similar issues are studied using Duration Calculus (DC). The link between the two is briefly discussed in section 5, followed by an outline of future work and suggestions for contributions by others.

2   The Timer Cascade: Informal Introduction

The 24-hour timer is a "common household" device that is plugged into a wall outlet in order to supply power during predetermined time intervals (Fig. 1).

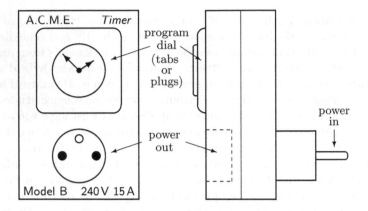

Fig. 1. A 24-hour timer

An interesting configuration arose by coincidence when storing a few of these timers, while reducing the volume by inserting them into each other (Fig. 2). This immediately raises the question what would be the behavior of the resulting cascade, and what would be the best way to describe and analyze it. The idea to use this as a testbed for real time formalisms came up during a session at ICTAC 2004 in Guiyang, where several such formalisms were presented.

We make some basic assumptions explicit. Depending on the kind of timer, the "power on" intervals are programmed by pushing tabs or inserting plugs (for the analog variant with a timing motor) or via pushbuttons and a small screen (for the digital variant with electronic clock). Some digital variants support programs for longer periods (week, month) and have a battery that preserves the program during power failures. However, the battery also keeps the timer going during power out intervals, making the behavior of cascades uninteresting.

Hence our abstract model follows the analog variant: removal of power does not erase the program (which is mechanical) but pauses the timer. We also make

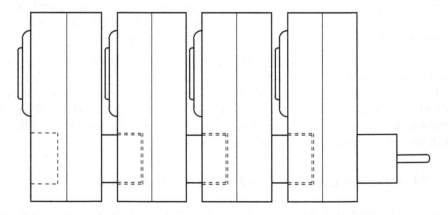

Fig. 2. A timer cascade

the model generic by supporting infinitely long programs. This is done WLOG, since a finite program can be modelled by a periodic infinite one. Conversely, a cascade of 24-hour timers can realize certain programs with longer periods, but such "practical" application is not envisaged since digital timers support longer programs in a less challenging way. Here we only want interesting behavior.

3   Functional Modelling of the Timer Cascade

3.1   The Formalism Used

By *formalism* we mean a language (or notation) together with formal manipulation rules. In this section we shall use *Funmath* (*Functional mathematics*).

The language of Funmath [4] consists of only 4 constructs: *identifier*, *application*, *abstraction* and *tupling*. These suffice to synthesize common mathematical conventions while removing all defects (ambiguities, inconsistencies) and to support new and very useful styles of expression, in particular point-free ones.

The calculation rules of Funmath [5] equip all these forms of expression, including those that are rather loose in conventional mathematics, with a precise formal basis for symbolic manipulation, "making the symbols do the work". This means that calculation is guided by the shape of the expressions [11,13].

The two main elements are: (i) a *functional predicate calculus* [5,7], enabling engineers to calculate with predicates and quantifiers as fluently as they have learned for derivatives and integrals; (ii) *concrete generic functionals* [5,6], providing similar fluency with higher order functions (functionals), with the point-free style, and with smooth transition between styles.

Here we use Funmath mostly in the "conservative mode" of synthesizing conventions familiar to readers with modest mathematical background and no prior acquaintance with our formalism. The references provide further detail.

3.2   Modelling the (Abstract) Timer and the Timer Cascade

Conventions. We do not model power inputs and outputs as AC waveforms, but as binary signals taking the values 0 ("off") and 1 ("on"). Signals are themselves functions of time. We assume the time domain $\mathbb{T} := \mathbb{R}_{\geq 0}$ and value domain $\mathbb{B} := \{0, 1\}$, which is a subset of $\mathbb{R}$. We prefer this over $\{F, T\}$ for various reasons. Adherents of $\{F, T\}$ can adapt the sequel via a *characteristic function* $c : \{F, T\} \to \{0, 1\}$ with $c\,F = 0$ and $c\,T = 1$ (or simply $c := (F, T)^-$ in Funmath) .

Timer Model. Our first signal space is the set of $\mathbb{B}$-valued functions (predicates)

$$\mathsf{Sig} := \{P : \mathbb{T} \to \mathbb{B} \mid P \text{ is p.c.}\} \ . \tag{1}$$

The usual notion of piecewise continuity over a closed interval is assumed generalized to possibly infinite intervals: a function is piecewise continuous (p.c.) over an interval iff in every finite closed subinterval it has at most a finite number of discontinuities, and left and right limits exist at each discontinuity (plus right limit at the start and left limit at the end of each of the subintervals). If the interval of interest is not stated explicitly, it is taken to be the domain of the function. For the predicates at hand, p.c. amounts to piecewise constant. Calculational reasoning about limits and derivatives using functional predicate calculus is illustrated in [5,7].

Timer programs also have type Sig. In view of cascading timers, it does not suffice to express behavior as the output signal with the program as the only input parameter. Doing so would only model a single timer plugged into an outlet (without power failures), i.e., an uninteresting autonomous system. Rather, we model behaviors as input-output system functions of type $\mathsf{Bvr} := \mathsf{Sig} \to \mathsf{Sig}$ and take programs as parameters, formalizing intuitive understanding by defining

$$\textbf{def } \mathsf{Tmr} : \mathsf{Sig} \to \mathsf{Bvr} \textbf{ with } \mathsf{Tmr}\, P\, I\, t \;\equiv\; I\, t \wedge P\, (\textstyle\int I\, t) \quad . \tag{2}$$

We chose mnemonic names P (program), I (input), t (time), so $\mathsf{Tmr}\, P\, I\, t$ is the timer output at time t for program P and input I. The operator $\int : \mathsf{Sig} \to \mathsf{Sig}$ is defined by $\int f\, t = \int_0^t f\tau \cdot \mathrm{d}\tau$ for piecewise continuous (hence, integrable) f. Note that $\int I\, t$ remains constant whenever $I\, t = 0$ and grows with t whenever $I\, t = 1$.

A proof obligation raised by (2) is that $\mathsf{Tmr}\, P\, I$ as specified by the r.h.s. is indeed of type Sig, leading to a refinement beyond the scope of this discussion.

Cascade Model. Parametrized by a list of programs, with the convention that indexing starts from the output side, the behavior of a cascade is modelled by

$$\textbf{def } \mathsf{Csc} : \mathsf{Sig}^* \to \mathsf{Bvr} \textbf{ with } \mathsf{Csc}\, p = \bigcirc j : \mathcal{D}\, p \,.\, \mathsf{Tmr}\, (p\, (\# p - 1 - j)) \tag{3}$$

where $\bigcirc$ is the elastic extension of function composition, extending $\circ$ in the same way as $\sum$ extends $+$. For instance, if $p = p_0, p_1$ then $\mathsf{Csc}\, p = (\mathsf{Tmr}\, p_1) \circ (\mathsf{Tmr}\, p_0)$. hence $\mathsf{Csc}\, p\, I = \mathsf{Tmr}\, p_1\, (\mathsf{Tmr}\, p_0\, I)$ and $\mathsf{Csc}\, p\, I\, t \equiv \mathsf{Tmr}\, p_1\, (\mathsf{Tmr}\, p_0\, I)\, t$.

3.3   Deriving Properties: A Few Typical Examples

Signal Flow Model. As outlined in [6], the signal flow model is obtained by eliminating the time variable t from $\mathsf{Tmr}\, P\, I\, t \equiv I\, t \wedge P\, (\int I\, t)$, since time is not a structural element. In the calculation, the generic operator $\widehat{}$ denotes *direct extension* for 2-place functions $\star$ such that $(f \mathbin{\widehat{\star}} f')\, t = f\, t \star f'\, t$, and $^-$ does the same for 1-place functions g, i.e., $\overline{g}\, f\, t = g\, (f\, t)$ (note: $\overline{g}\, f = g \circ f$). For full definitions (with types) of these and other generic functionals, see [6]. Now

$$
\begin{aligned}
\mathsf{Tmr}\, P\, I\, t \;&\equiv\; \langle \text{Def. Tmr} \rangle && I\, t \wedge P\, (\textstyle\int I\, t) \\
&\equiv\; \langle \text{Def. } \circ \rangle && I\, t \wedge (P \circ \textstyle\int I)\, t \\
&\equiv\; \langle \text{Def. } ^- \rangle && I\, t \wedge \overline{P}\, (\textstyle\int I)\, t \\
&\equiv\; \langle \text{Def. } \circ \rangle && I\, t \wedge (\overline{P} \circ \textstyle\int)\, I\, t \\
&\equiv\; \langle \text{Def. } \widehat{} \rangle && (I \mathbin{\widehat{\wedge}} (\overline{P} \circ \textstyle\int)\, I)\, t
\end{aligned}
$$

and, by function equality, $\mathsf{Tmr}\, P\, I = I \mathbin{\widehat{\wedge}} (\overline{P} \circ \int)\, I$. The structural interpretation is the signal flow circuit in figure 3, letting the direct extension symbols (for the memoryless devices $\wedge$ and P) be implicit in the boxes.

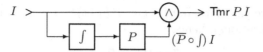

Fig. 3. Signal flow model of a timer

The model of the timer cascade is the cascade of stages, each with its program.

State Space Model. A large class of systems [17] is modelled by a *state function* stf and an *output function* out relating state s, input i, output u by

$$D s t = \mathsf{stf}(s t, i t) \quad \text{and} \quad u t = \mathsf{out}(s t, i t) \tag{4}$$

where $D s$ is the derivative of s. E.g., for linear circuits these functions are of the form $\mathsf{stf}(s t, i t) = a t \cdot s t + b t \cdot i t$ etc. or similar matrix expressions in case there are several state, input or output variables.

A timer is not linear (due to the way in which it depends on P), but fits into the generic model of (4) as follows, the state being the integrator output.

$$D s t \equiv I t \quad \text{and} \quad U t \equiv I t \wedge P(s t) \quad . \tag{5}$$

For an n-stage cascade, the state s is an n-tuple (of integrator outputs) with $\forall k : \square n . (D s_k t \equiv i_k t) \wedge (u_k t \equiv i_k t \wedge p_k(s_k t)) \wedge (k \neq 0 \Rightarrow i_k t = u_{k-1} t)$ and $I, U = i_0, u_{n-1}$. For the *block*: $\square n = \{j : \mathbb{N} \mid j < n\}$. The state space model is

$$\forall k : \square n . D s_k t \equiv I t \wedge \forall j : \square k . p_j(s_j t)$$
$$U t \equiv I t \wedge \forall j : \square n . p_j(s_j t) \quad . \tag{6}$$

The calculation is based on logic only; linearity neither holds nor is assumed.

Convention. Since $\mathbb{B} = \{0, 1\}$, we replace $\wedge$ by $\cdot$, so $\mathsf{Tmr}\, P I t = I t \cdot P(\int I t)$. For (5), this yields $U t = I t \cdot P(s t)$, whereas (6) can be written

$$\forall k : \square n . D s_k t = I t \cdot \prod_{j=0}^{k-1} p_j(s_j t) \quad \text{and} \quad U t = I t \cdot \prod_{j=0}^{n-1} p_j(s_j t) \quad . \tag{7}$$

Algebraic Properties: Program Composition and the Program Monoid Since the behavior of a timer is fully characterized by its program, we look for operators on programs in order to reduce reasoning to programs only. Specifically, we wish to study timer cascades via two-argument operators on programs.

A cascade of 2 timers with programs P and P' has behavior $\mathsf{Tmr}\, P \circ \mathsf{Tmr}\, P'$. The question is: can we calculate a program Q such that $\mathsf{Tmr}\, Q = \mathsf{Tmr}\, P \circ \mathsf{Tmr}\, P'$ or, equivalently, an operator $\triangleright : \mathsf{Sig}^2 \to \mathsf{Sig}$ satisfying the following condition?

$$\text{DESIGN REQUIREMENT FOR } \triangleright : \quad \mathsf{Tmr}\,(P \triangleright P') = \mathsf{Tmr}\, P \circ \mathsf{Tmr}\, P' \tag{8}$$

Algebraic Derivation. Clearly, a timer plugged into a non-interrupted outlet reflects its own program at the output. Formally, for the constant signal $\underline{1} := \mathbb{T}^{\bullet} 1$

and any $P : \mathsf{Sig}$ we calculate $\mathsf{Tmr}\, P\, \underline{1}\, t = P\, (\int \underline{1}\, t) \cdot \underline{1}\, t = P\, t \cdot 1 = P\, t$ (omitting the obvious justifications), hence

$$\mathsf{Tmr}\, P\, \underline{1} = P \quad . \tag{9}$$

So, $\mathsf{Tmr}\, P = \mathsf{Tmr}\, P' \Rightarrow \langle \text{Leibniz} \rangle \ \mathsf{Tmr}\, P\, \underline{1} = \mathsf{Tmr}\, P'\, \underline{1} \Rightarrow \langle \mathsf{Tmr}\, P\, \underline{1} = P \rangle \ P = P'$, from which we conclude the injectivity of Tmr. Therefore the inverse Tmr^- satisfies $\mathsf{Tmr}^-\, (\mathsf{Tmr}\, P) = P$ for any $P : \mathsf{Sig}$ and, by the preceding reasoning, an explicit formula for Tmr^- is $\mathsf{Tmr}^-\, b = b\, \underline{1}$ for any behavior b in $\mathcal{R}\, \mathsf{Tmr}$, the range of Tmr.

If programs P and P' satisfy $\mathsf{Tmr}\, P \circ \mathsf{Tmr}\, P' \in \mathcal{R}\, \mathsf{Tmr}$ (hypothesis) and we impose on $\triangleright : \mathsf{Sig}^2 \to \mathsf{Sig}$ the design requirement $\mathsf{Tmr}\, (P \triangleright P') = \mathsf{Tmr}\, P \circ \mathsf{Tmr}\, P'$ (for any P, P'), then

$$
\begin{aligned}
P \triangleright P' &= \langle \mathsf{Tmr}^-\, (\mathsf{Tmr}\, P) = P \rangle \ \mathsf{Tmr}^-\, (\mathsf{Tmr}\, (P \triangleright P')) \\
&= \langle \text{Dsgn. requirement} \rangle \ \mathsf{Tmr}^-\, (\mathsf{Tmr}\, P \circ \mathsf{Tmr}\, P') \\
&= \langle \text{Hyp.,}\ \mathsf{Tmr}^-\, b = b\, \underline{1} \rangle \ (\mathsf{Tmr}\, P \circ \mathsf{Tmr}\, P')\, \underline{1} \\
&= \quad \langle \text{Definition} \circ \rangle \qquad \mathsf{Tmr}\, P\, (\mathsf{Tmr}\, P'\, \underline{1}) \\
&= \quad \langle \mathsf{Tmr}\, P\, \underline{1} = P \rangle \qquad \mathsf{Tmr}\, P\, P'
\end{aligned}
$$

This yields an explicit formula for $\triangleright$ namely $P \triangleright P' = \mathsf{Tmr}\, P\, P'$, depending on the condition $\mathsf{Tmr}\, P \circ \mathsf{Tmr}\, P' \in \mathcal{R}\, \mathsf{Tmr}$. Next we verify that it is always satisfied.

Analytic Verification. It suffices proving that $\triangleright$ defined by $P \triangleright P' = \mathsf{Tmr}\, P\, P'$ satisfies the design requirement (8). Before doing so, observe that, when generalizing Sig to $\mathsf{Sig} := \{ f : \mathbb{R} \to \mathbb{R} \mid f \text{ is p.c.} \}$ and $\int$ and Tmr accordingly while maintaining the image definition $\mathsf{Tmr}\, f\, g\, x = f\, (\int g\, x) \cdot g\, x$, everything done since replacing $\wedge$ by $\cdot$ remains valid, because the proofs nowhere relied on any restriction to $\mathbb{B}$.

THEOREM: $\mathsf{Tmr}\, (\mathsf{Tmr}\, f\, g) = \mathsf{Tmr}\, f \circ \mathsf{Tmr}\, g$ for any signals f, g.

PROOF: The successive domains are clearly equal. Also, for $h : \mathsf{Sig}$ and $x : \mathbb{T}$,

$$
\begin{aligned}
\mathsf{Tmr}\, (\mathsf{Tmr}\, f\, g)\, h\, x &= \langle \text{Def. Tmr} \rangle \ \mathsf{Tmr}\, f\, g\, (\int h\, x) \cdot h\, x \\
&= \langle \text{Def. Tmr} \rangle \ f\, (\int g\, (\int h\, x)) \cdot g\, (\int h\, x) \cdot h\, x \\
&= \langle \text{Def. Tmr} \rangle \ f\, (\int g\, (\int h\, x)) \cdot \mathsf{Tmr}\, g\, h\, x \\
&= \langle \text{Lemma} \rangle \ f\, (\int (\mathsf{Tmr}\, g\, h)\, x) \cdot \mathsf{Tmr}\, g\, h\, x \\
&= \langle \text{Def. Tmr} \rangle \ \mathsf{Tmr}\, f\, (\mathsf{Tmr}\, g\, h)\, x \\
&= \langle \text{Def.} \circ \rangle \ (\mathsf{Tmr}\, f \circ \mathsf{Tmr}\, g)\, h\, x
\end{aligned}
$$

Thus far, the lemma justifying $\int g\, (\int h\, x) = \int (\mathsf{Tmr}\, g\, h)\, x$ is "wishful thinking", guided by the shape of $\mathsf{Tmr}\, g\, h\, x$ to enable the next step. Now we prove it.

LEMMA: $\int f \circ \int g = \int (\mathsf{Tmr}\, f\, g)$ for p.c. f and g.

PROOF: We shall invoke some properties for the derivative D, namely

(i) Fundamental theorem of calculus: $\mathrm{D}\, (\int f) = f \rceil \mathcal{D}\, (\mathrm{D}\, (\int f))$ for p.c. f.

(ii) Leibniz's rule: $\mathrm{D}\, (f \circ g) = \mathrm{D}\, f\, (g\, x) \cdot \mathrm{D}\, g\, x$ provided the derivatives are p.c..

(iii) Delegation of equality to derivative: $f = g \equiv f\, 0 = g\, 0 \wedge \mathrm{D}\, f = \mathrm{D}\, g$ (idem).

In applying (iii), $(\int f \circ \int g)\, 0 = \int (\mathsf{Tmr}\, f\, g)\, 0$ is trivial since $\int f\, 0 = 0$ for p.c. f.

For the derivatives, the domains exclude undefined points and discontinuities do not affect the integral [3, p. 311]. The images for x in the domain obey

$$
\begin{aligned}
D\left(\textstyle\int f \circ \textstyle\int g\right) x &= \langle\text{Leibniz's rule}\rangle \; D\left(\textstyle\int f\right)\left(\textstyle\int g\, x\right) \cdot D\left(\textstyle\int g\right) x \\
&= \langle\text{Fundam. thm.}\rangle \; f\left(\textstyle\int g\right) x \cdot g\, x \\
&= \langle\text{Definition Tmr}\rangle \; \mathsf{Tmr} f\, g\, x \\
&= \langle\text{Fundam. thm.}\rangle \; D\left(\textstyle\int(\mathsf{Tmr} f\, g)\right) x
\end{aligned}
$$

We call $\int(\mathsf{Tmr} f\, g)$ the *timer integral* for obvious reasons.

Algebraic Properties of Program Composition. Having fulfilled all proof obligations, we can now assert that $\triangleright$ defined (for f and g in the generalized Sig) by

$$
\text{DEFINITION OF } \triangleright : \quad f \triangleright g = \mathsf{Tmr} f\, g \tag{10}
$$

satisfies

$$
\text{HOMOMORPHISM:} \quad \mathsf{Tmr}\left(f \triangleright g\right) = \mathsf{Tmr} f \circ \mathsf{Tmr} g \quad . \tag{11}
$$

Recall also that Tmr is injective. We now derive some properties.

(a) The operator $\triangleright$ is associative. Indeed,

$$
\begin{aligned}
f \triangleright (g \triangleright h) &= \langle\text{Defin. } \triangleright\rangle \; \mathsf{Tmr} f\, (\mathsf{Tmr} g\, h) \\
&= \langle\text{Defin. } \circ\rangle \; (\mathsf{Tmr} f \circ \mathsf{Tmr} g)\, h \\
&= \langle\text{Prop. (11)}\rangle \; \mathsf{Tmr}\, (f \triangleright g)\, h \\
&= \langle\text{Defin. } \triangleright\rangle \; (f \triangleright g) \triangleright h
\end{aligned}
$$

(b) The operator $\triangleright$ has $\underline{1} := \mathbb{R} \bullet 1$ as left and right identity. Indeed,

$$
\begin{aligned}
(\underline{1} \triangleright f)\, x &= \langle\text{Defin. } \triangleright\rangle \; \mathsf{Tmr}\, \underline{1}\, f\, x \\
&= \langle\text{Def. Tmr}\rangle \; \underline{1}\left(\textstyle\int f\, t\right) \cdot f\, x \\
&= \langle\text{Defin. } \underline{1}\rangle \; f\, x \\
(f \triangleright \underline{1})\, x &= \langle\text{Def. Tmr}\rangle \; f\left(\textstyle\int \underline{1}\, x\right) \cdot \underline{1}\, x \\
&= \langle\text{Defin. } \underline{1}\rangle \; f\left(\textstyle\int \underline{1}\, x\right) \\
&= \langle\textstyle\int \underline{1}\, x = x\rangle \; f\, x
\end{aligned}
$$

This makes Sig a monoid under $\triangleright$ and Tmr an injective monoid homomorphism.

3.4   Conclusions

It is clear that Tmr and $\triangleright$ have many algebraic properties, about which only the tip of the iceberg has been explored.

One of the issues deserving further investigation is the periodicity of periodic programs and (as a gedanken experiment) program synthesis by cascades of periodic programs (which model the behavior of finite programs).

4   Modelling Using Duration Calculus

Duration Calculus (DC) [10,15] is an interval temporal logic. It incorporates the integral operator and is thus able to reason about durations of system states. This is a particular convenient feature for modelling and reasoning about the timer cascade as each timer is in fact a stop-watch. As in the previous section we investigate how a cascade of two timers can be expressed using only one timer. Although DC is equipped with a powerful proof system, we put emphasis on automatic verification using model-checking techniques. Modelling and the automatic verification are performed on a more concrete level than in the functional modelling with Funmath.

4.1   Duration Calculus

The behavior of systems is described by time-dependent variables, so called observables which have in most cases finite domains. For each timer in the cascade we use two observables power_in and power_out. The observable power_in models that the timer is connected to current and power_out models that it supplies current at its output. As we use only boolean observables in this example the semantics of an observable is a function of type Sig thus $\mathcal{I}(X) : \mathbb{T} \to \mathbb{B}$. For the integrals to exist, we further require the functions to be piecewise constant.

Boolean combinations of observables, so called state assertions are used to to specify the state of the system for a certain point in time.

Duration Calculus is interpreted over time intervals. Therefore DC terms associate a real number to each interval. An integral operator can be applied to state assertions in order to measure its duration. Furthermore DC provides global rigid variables and the special symbol ℓ, denoting the length of the interval.

Formally, the set of DC terms is defined by the following EBNF

$$\theta ::= x \mid f(\theta_1, \ldots, \theta_n) \mid \int P \mid \ell$$

where x denotes a global time-independent variable, f an n-ary function symbol and P a state assertion. As usual, the value of a rigid variable is determined by a valuation $\mathcal{V}$. In addition to first order quantifiers and boolean connectives, Duration Calculus uses a special modality $\frown$ called "chop". A formula $F \frown G$ is true on an interval, iff this interval can be partitioned into two subintervals, such that F holds on the first part and G holds on the second part. Formally, DC formulas are generated from the following EBNF

$$F ::= \neg F \mid F_1 \wedge F_2 \mid F_1 \frown F_2 \mid p(\theta_1, \ldots, \theta_n) \mid \forall x.F.$$

As usual, the other logical connectives can be derived as abbreviations. Additionally, we introduce the following abbreviations, to denote the point interval,

$$\lceil\rceil \overset{df}{=} \ell = 0$$

To denote that the state assertion P is true almost everywhere on a non-point interval, we use

$$\lceil P \rceil \overset{df}{=} \int P = \ell \wedge \ell > 0$$

The modalities $\Diamond^{DC}$, $\Box^{DC}$ and $\Box_0^{DC}$ are derived by

$$\Diamond^{DC} F \overset{df}{=} true^\frown F^\frown true \qquad \Box^{DC} F \overset{df}{=} \neg\Diamond^{DC}\neg F \qquad \Box_0^{DC} F \overset{df}{=} \neg(\neg F^\frown true)$$

The modality $\Diamond^{DC}$ reads as "on some subinterval", $\Box^{DC}$ as "on every subinterval" and $\Box_0^{DC}$ as "on every subinterval starting at point zero".

4.2 Modelling the Timer Cascade

As mentioned in the introduction, we employ two boolean observables power_in and power_out to model the state of one timer in the cascade. Additionally, we use the auxiliary observable pass to denote whether current can pass through the timer or not. We use the index i to indicate the i-th timer. For each timer we use three parameters,

- $cycle_i$, the cycle time of the i-th timer,
- $start_i$ the start time of the i-th timer,
- $stop_i$ the stop time of the i-th timer.

We specify the behavior of a timer cascade using the following DC formulas.

If the duration of power_in$_i$ is below the start value, pass has to be false, i.e.

$$\Box_0^{DC}((\textstyle\int \mathsf{power\_in}_i \bmod cycle_i < start_i) \Rightarrow true^\frown \lceil \neg\mathsf{pass}_i \rceil)$$

If the value is between start and stop, pass is true.

$$\Box_0^{DC}((start_i \le \textstyle\int \mathsf{power\_in}_i \bmod cycle_i \le stop_i) \Rightarrow true^\frown \lceil \mathsf{pass}_i \rceil)$$

Above the stop value, the observable pass has to be false again.

$$\Box_0^{DC}((\textstyle\int \mathsf{power\_in}_i \bmod cycle_i > stop_i) \Rightarrow true^\frown \lceil \neg\mathsf{pass}_i \rceil)$$

If power can pass through the timer and it is connected to current, the outlet is powered.

$$\lceil \; \rceil \vee \lceil (\mathsf{power\_in}_i \wedge \mathsf{pass}) \Leftrightarrow \mathsf{power\_out}_i \rceil$$

The observables power_out and power_in of two consecutive timers are connected.

$$\lceil \; \rceil \vee \lceil \mathsf{power\_in}_{i+1} \Leftrightarrow \mathsf{power\_out}_i \rceil$$

As the first timer in the cascade should always be connected to the power supply, we assume

$$\lceil \; \rceil \vee \lceil \mathsf{power\_in}_0 \rceil$$

The behavior of the complete cascade is specified by the DC formula TC which is defined to be the conjunction of all the formulas given above.

4.3   Refinement

Duration Calculus can be used to describe systems at several levels of detail in different phases of the design process. Especially, it can be used to establish a refinement relationship between a more abstract specification and a more concrete implementation level.

In this section we investigate how a single abstract timer of cycle time $cycle^A$ with program start $start^A$ and stop $stop^A$ where $start^A \le stop^A$ can be implemented by two concrete timers having the same shorter cycle-time $cycle^C$.

To derive an implementation, we introduce the following abbreviation

$$\Delta^A \stackrel{df}{=} stop^A - start^A$$

denoting the length of the program. At first, we compute how many cycles of the concrete the cascade has to wait until the program should start. We denote by div and rem the result of the division and the remainder respectively of the start time $start^A$ by the cycle time $cycle^C$ of the implementation, i.e.

$$start^A = div \cdot cycle^C + rem$$

such that $0 \le rem < cycle^C$. We can now implement the abstract timer by a cascade of two concrete timers using the program

$$start_0^C \stackrel{df}{=} rem$$

$$stop_0^C \stackrel{df}{=} rem + \frac{cycle^C}{m}$$

$$start_1^C \stackrel{df}{=} div \cdot \frac{cycle^C}{m}$$

$$stop_1^C \stackrel{df}{=} div \cdot \frac{cycle^C}{m} + \Delta^A$$

for $m = \frac{cycle^A}{cycle^C} \in \mathbb{N}$ with the additional constraint that $\frac{cycle^C}{m} > \Delta^A$. The program of timer 0 must have a duration of $\frac{cycle^C}{m}$ to ensure that both timers are in zero position after the first timer has completed m cycles. During the first div cycles of timer 0, power_out$_1^C$ is not activated. Only after $div \cdot cycle^C + rem$ time units power_out$_1$ becomes true for Δ^A time units. This is ensured by the extra condition $\frac{cycle^C}{m} > \Delta^A$. It is not always possible to find an implementation of the abstract timer, by two concrete ones. For example if the duration Δ^A of the abstract timer is greater than the cycle time of the concrete timers, it is impossible to find an implementation. The definition above does not yield a valid program in these cases, as the value of $stop_1^C$ exceeds the cycle time. Nevertheless, if all time bounds are below the cycle time, we get a correct implementation of the abstract specification. This is to be verified formally.

Let TC^A denote the specification of the abstract timer and TC^C be the specification of the concrete implementation, then we have to show the refinement requirement e.g.

$$TC^C \wedge TC^A \Rightarrow \lceil \text{power\_out}_1^C \Leftrightarrow \text{power\_out}^A \rceil.$$

4.4   Verification

Duration Calculus is equipped with numerous proof rules to facilitate this kind of proofs. As we have shown such a calculation by hand in the previous section, we concentrate on the application of tools here. DC is decidable for discrete time domain – and undecidable for continuous time domain. A model-checker called DCValid [18] is available, so we employ this tool for the verification of the refinement requirement. As DCValid does not allow arbitrary computation, we verify the refinement of one 24-hour timer by a cascade of two 12h timers. Henceforth, we assume our two systems are defined by the following parameters.

$$start^A = 15, \qquad stop^A = 17, \qquad cycle^A = 24,$$
$$start_0^C = 3, \qquad stop_0^C = 9,$$
$$start_1^C = 6, \qquad stop_1^C = 8, \qquad cycle^C = 12.$$

As DCValid does not incorporate calculation of remainders, this calculation has to be eliminated. To this end, we introduce 3 fresh observables $zero^A$, $zero_1^C$, and $zero_2^C$ to mark all points on which the respective timer is in zero position. We specify that zero has to be true for one time unit after the timer having power_in activated for its cycle time. To this end, we define lower and upper bound for zero by the following DC formulas.

$$\neg \lozenge^{DC}(((\lceil zero \rceil ^\frown \lceil \neg zero \rceil) \wedge (\textstyle\int power\_in < cycle))^\frown \lceil zero \rceil)$$
$$\neg(((\lceil \neg power\_in \rceil \vee \lceil \rceil)^\frown \lceil power\_in \wedge \neg zero \rceil)^\frown true)$$
$$\neg \lozenge^{DC}(\lceil zero \rceil \wedge \ell > 1)$$
$$\neg \lozenge^{DC}(((\lceil zero \rceil ^\frown \lceil \neg zero \rceil) \wedge \textstyle\int power\_in > cycle)$$

As we use *discrete* DC for automatic verification, we need not to specify a lower bound on the duration of zero as a phase $\lceil zero \rceil$ cannot have a duration below one time unit. Having introduced these auxiliary observables, we can modify the specification. Instead of looking at all intervals starting at the beginning and calculating the measure of power_in modulo the cycle time, we can just measure the amount of time power_in is true since the last phase on which zero holds.

Every interval starting with a phase on which zero is true and the measure of power_in is below the start of the timer, on the end of the interval pass does not hold.

$$\square^{DC}(((\lceil zero \rceil \wedge \ell = 1^\frown (\lceil \neg zero \rceil \vee \lceil \rceil))$$
$$\wedge (\textstyle\int power\_in \leq start))$$
$$\Rightarrow (true^\frown \lceil \neg pass \rceil))$$

If the measure is between *start* and *stop* the interval must end in a phase satisfying pass.

$$\square^{DC}(((\lceil zero \rceil \wedge \ell = 1^\frown (\lceil \neg zero \rceil \vee \lceil \rceil))$$
$$\wedge (\textstyle\int power\_in > start \wedge \textstyle\int power\_in \leq stop))$$
$$\Rightarrow (true^\frown \lceil pass \rceil))$$

If the measure is above *stop* it has to end in ¬pass.

$$\Box^{DC}((([\text{zero}] \wedge \ell = 1^\frown([\neg\text{zero}] \vee \lceil\rceil)) \wedge (\int \text{power\_in} > stop))$$
$$\Rightarrow (true^\frown[\neg\text{pass}]))$$

Using this definition, the refinement requirement can be automatically verified. DCValid takes 4.16 seconds on a 1.8 GHz Athlon XP 2200+ machine to verify the validity. We employed manual optimisations exploiting the fact, that power_in^A and power_in$_2^C$ are always true and therefore instead of calculating the measure $\int$ power_in^A and $\int$ power_in$_2^C$ respectively, one can use the length of the interval directly.

4.5 Conclusion

We presented how a specification of a timer cascade can be formalised in Duration Calculus. As DC incorporates the $\int$-operator, it allows natural modelling of stop watches and henceforth the whole timer cascade. Duration Calculus can be used in various stages of the design process. So we presented how an abstract timer cascade can be refined and how the correctness of the refinement can be automatically verified.

5 Final Remarks and Future Work

5.1 Linking Formalisms

Linking formalisms in a clear, formal way always contributes to a better understanding of all formalisms involved.

A promising approach to linking Duration Calculus as used in section 4 with the functional approach as used in section 3 is similar to the one used for linking R. Dijkstra's *Computation Calculus* [12] to Calculational Semantics in [8].

Within the scope of this paper, only an outline can be given. Define the set of intervals over a totally ordered time domain $\mathbb{T}$ by $\mathcal{I} := \{[a, b] \mid a, b : (\mathbb{T}^2)_\leq\}$. Various styles of DC can be defined in Funmath. Here are two of them.

- Interval style: predicates of type IP $:= \mathcal{I} \to \mathbb{B}$ (predicates on intervals)
- Computation style: predicates of type CP $:= \mathcal{C} \to \mathbb{B}$ where the set of *computations* is defined by $\mathcal{C} := \bigcup I : \mathcal{I} . I \to \mathbb{S}$, given a suitable state space $\mathbb{S}$.

In this outline, we concentrate on "chop" ($^\frown$), the pivotal operator in DC.

- Interval style: $^\frown$ has type IP$^2 \to$ IP, map $(P^\frown Q) I \equiv \exists t : I . P I_{\leq t} \wedge Q I_{\geq t}$
- Computation style: type CP$^2 \to$ CP, map $(P^\frown Q) \gamma \equiv \exists t : \mathcal{D} \gamma . P \gamma_{\leq t} \wedge Q \gamma_{\geq t}$

Note: *filtering* ($\downarrow$) is defined for any set S by $S \downarrow P = \{x : S \cap \mathcal{D} P \mid P x\}$ and for any function f by $\mathcal{D} f_P = \{x : \mathcal{D} f \cap \mathcal{D} P \mid P x\}$ with $\forall x : \mathcal{D} f_P . f_P x = f x$; in both cases P is any predicate. Abbreviating $a \downarrow b$ as a_b (and $a \uparrow b$ as a^b), together with so-called *partial application* (as in $\leq t$) explains the notation formally.

Crucial remark   Parameters like I and γ appear only in basic definitions and calculations where axioms of the axiomatic formulations of DC are derived as theorems. In subsequent use, the formulas can be written in exactly the same form as in the axiomatic formulations, and calculations are "point-free". The difference between interval style and computation style then becomes hidden.

For instance, associativity of "chop", namely $(P^\frown Q)^\frown R = P^\frown (Q^\frown R)$, is easily proven from either definition using functional predicate calculus.

Another example: let $\lozenge$ be defined in the interval style by[1] $\lozenge P\, I \equiv \exists P_{\subseteq I}$. Defining $\mathrm{T} := \mathcal{I} \bullet 1$ ("1 for any interval"), one proves similarly $\lozenge P = \mathrm{T}^\frown P^\frown \mathrm{T}$.

While this is only an outline, it captures the flavor of the approach.

5.2 Future Work

Obviously, the most immediate task is the complete elaboration of the link between the functional and the DC models of the timer.

However, this paper is only a first step in a more ambitious effort towards a broad comparative survey of formalisms for real time and hybrid systems. To this effect, we shall study several other formalisms in a similar way, elaborating for each two examples: one that highlights its strong points (dependent on the formalism), and the timer cascade (the same running example for all). Most importantly, links and the possibility of a common framework will be investigated. Another issue is the interaction between tools supporting various formalisms.

We hope that other researchers join this effort, most conveniently by providing a brief outline of their preferred formalism and two examples as described. For those who are interested, we will prepare a more extensive discussion of the kind of specifications and verification obligations that would be most helpful.

References

1. Vicki L. Almstrum, "Investigating Student Difficulties With Mathematical Logic", in: C. Neville Dean, Michael G. Hinchey, eds, *Teaching and Learning Formal Methods*, pp. 131–160. Academic Press (1996)
2. Rajeev Alur, Thomas A. Henzinger, Eduardo D. Sontag, eds., *Hybrid Systems III*, LNCS 1066. Springer-Verlag, Berlin Heidelberg (1996)
3. Robert G. Bartle, *The Elements of Real Analysis*. Wiley, New York (1964)
4. Raymond T. Boute, *Funmath illustrated: A Declarative Formalism and Application Examples*. Declarative Systems Series No. 1, Computing Science Institute, University of Nijmegen (1993)
5. Raymond Boute, *Functional Mathematics: a Unifying Declarative and Calculational Approach to Systems, Circuits and Programs — Part I: Basic Mathematics*. Course text, Ghent University (2002)
6. Raymond T. Boute, "Concrete Generic Functionals: Principles, Design and Applications", in: Jeremy Gibbons, Johan Jeuring, eds., *Generic Programming*, pp. 89–119, Kluwer (2003)

---

[1] In the functional predicate calculus, quantifiers are predicates over predicates, viz., $\forall P \equiv P = \mathcal{D} P \bullet 1$ and $\exists P \equiv P \neq \mathcal{D} P \bullet 0$. We write $S \bullet e$ for the constant function mapping all elements of set S to e. Note: $\exists P_{\subseteq I} \equiv \exists J : \mathcal{I} . J \subseteq I \wedge P J$ for P in $\mathbb{IP}$.

7. Raymond Boute, "Functional declarative language design and predicate calculus: a practical approach", to appear in *ACM Trans. Prog. Lang. and Syst.*

8. Raymond Boute, "Calculational semantics: deriving programming theories from equations by functional predicate calculus", to appear in *ACM Trans. Prog. Lang. and Syst.*

9. J. Buck, S. Ha, E. A. Lee, D. G. Messerschmitt, "Ptolemy: a framework for simulating and prototyping heterogeneous systems", *International Journal of Computer Simulation*, spec. issue on Simulation Software Development (Jan. 1994)

10. Zhou Chaochen, C.A.R. Hoare, and A.P. Ravn. A calculus of durations. *IPL*, 40(5):269–276, 1991.

11. Edsger W. Dijkstra, "Under the spell of Leibniz's dream", *EWD1298* (April 2000).

12. Rutger M. Dijkstra, "Computation calculus: Bridging a formalization gap", in: Johan Jeuring, ed., *Mathematics of Program Construction*, pp. 151–174. LNCS 1422, Springer (1998)

13. David Gries, "The need for education in useful formal logic", *IEEE Computer 29*, 4, pp. 29–30 (April 1996)

14. Henri Habrias and Sébastien Faucou, "Linking Paradigms, Semi-formal and Formal Notations", in: C. Neville Dean and Raymond T. Boute, eds., *Teaching Formal Methods*, pp. 166–184, Springer LNCS 3294 (Nov. 2004)

15. M. R. Hansen and Zhou Chaochen. *Duration Calculus: A Formal Approach to Real-Time Systems*. EATCS: Monographs in Theoretical Computer Science. Springer, 2004.

16. Thomas Krilavičius, "Bestiarium of Hybrid Systems" (draft, Mar. 2005) `http://wwwhome.cs.utwente.nl/~krilaviciust/publications/bestiarium.pdf`

17. Edward A. Lee and Pravin Varaiya. *Structure and Interpretation of Signals and Systems*. Addison-Wesley (2003)

18. P.K. Pandya, Specifying and deciding qauntified discrete-time duration calculus formulae using dcvalid. Technical report, Tata Institute of Fundamental Research, 2000.

19. William Pugh, "Counting Solutions to Presburger Formulas: How and Why", *ACM SIGPLAN Notices 29*, 6, pp. 121–122 (June 1994)

20. Andreas Schäfer, "Combining Real-Time Model-Checking and Fault Tree Analysis", in: D. Mandrioli and K. Araki and S. Gnesi, eds., *FM 2003: 12th International FME Symposium*. LNCS 2805, Springer (2003) `http://csd.Informatik.Uni-Oldenburg.DE/pub/Papers/as03.pdf`

21. Andreas Schäfer, "A Calculus for Shapes in Time and Space", in: Z. Liu and K. Araki, eds., *Proc. ICTAC 2004*. LNCS 3407, Springer (2005)

22. Graeme Smith, "Specifying Mode Requiremens of Embedded Systems", in: Michael Oudshoorn, ed., *ACSC2002*, pp. 251–257 (Jan.–Feb. 2002). Also: `http://www.itee.uq.edu.au/~smith/papers/acsc2002.pdf`

23. Frits W. Vaandrager, Jan H. van Schuppen, eds., *Hybrid Systems: Computation and Control*, LNCS 1569. Springer-Verlag, Berlin Heidelberg (1999)

A Robust Interpretation of Duration Calculus

Martin Fränzle[1] and Michael R. Hansen[2]

[1] Carl von Ossietzky Universität Oldenburg,
FK II, Dpt. Informatik, D-26111 Oldenburg, Germany
Phone: +49-441-9722 566
fraenzle@informatik.uni-oldenburg.de

[2] Informatics and Mathematical Modelling, Technical University of Denmark,
Richard Petersens Plads, Bldg. 322, DK-2800 Kgs. Lyngby, Denmark
Phone: +45-4525 3727
mrh@imm.dtu.dk

Abstract. We transfer the concept of robust interpretation from arithmetic first-order theories to metric-time temporal logics. The idea is that the interpretation of a formula is robust iff its truth value does not change under small variation of the constants in the formula. Exemplifying this on Duration Calculus (DC), our findings are that the robust interpretation of DC is equivalent to a multi-valued interpretation that uses the real numbers as semantic domain and assigns Lipschitz-continuous interpretations to all operators of DC. Furthermore, this continuity permits approximation between discrete and dense time, thus allowing exploitation of discrete-time (semi-)decision procedures on dense-time properties.

Keywords: Metric-time temporal logic; Robust interpretation; Discrete time vs. dense time.

1 Introduction

As embedded systems become more and more complex, early availability of unambiguous specification of their intended behaviour has become an important factor for quality and timely delivery. Consequently, the quest for automatic analysis methods for specifications arises. This quest becomes even more pronounced if specifications are to be formal, because formal specifications are often found to be particularly hard to write and maintain. Therefore, decision procedures for entailment between specifications, satisfiability of specifications, etc., may be extremely helpful in their design process. The price to be paid for such procedures is, however, a firmly constrained expressiveness of the specification formalisms: one has to sacrifice all elements that could give rise to undecidability.

However, the logically motivated notions of entailment between specifications, satisfiability of specifications, etc., have often been criticized from an engineering standpoint, as their validity or invalidity may well depend on the *exact* values of certain constants (e.g., the exact length of a steering rod relative to the exact distance of two joints), while any technical realization of these constants can only be approximate. In system design, the role of any decision problem

D.V. Hung and M. Wirsing (Eds.): ICTAC 2005, LNCS 3722, pp. 257–271, 2005.
© Springer-Verlag Berlin Heidelberg 2005

prone to changing its truth value under arbitrarily small variations of constants may be considered questionable. Based on this insight, research has in recent years addressed more "robust" notions of property satisfaction, where a property is considered to be *robustly (in-)valid* iff it does not change its validity under small variation of constants and/or values of variables [6,8,3,1,4,9,10]. The ultimate hope is that, besides being more relevant to engineering problems, such robust notions enhance decidability as, e.g., existence of non-computable reals cannot influence their validity.

With respect to design of embedded systems, such robust properties have by now mainly been investigated in the automata-based modeling context. Starting with Gupta's, Henzinger's, and Jagadeesan's [6] as well as Puri's [8] investigation of timed automata, the idea has been to exploit topological properties of systems in order to obtain robust answers. Asarin and Bouajjani [1] have applied this approach to reach set computation of, a.o., hybrid automata and Turing machines. Fränzle introduced a variant thereof in [3] by applying the concept to decision problems about hybrid automata instead of reach-set computation, e.g. invariance of a first-order property over hybrid states [3] or progress [4], thereby obtaining automatic analysis procedures that succeed in all robust cases, even such which are undecidable wrt. non-robust notions of property satisfaction.

Independently, constraint solving technology for numerical constraints over the real numbers was developed that has perfectly corresponding properties: one can solve otherwise undecidable constraints (containing functions over the real numbers other than polynomials [14]), provided they are robust, in the sense that their solvability does not change under small perturbations of the constants the constraints contain [9,10,11]. Even in cases where constraints are decidable, robust constraints can be solved much more efficiently.

In this paper, we unite above two lines of research by addressing logical models of embedded systems. In Section 3, we provide a robust interpretation of a very expressive metric-time temporal logic, Duration Calculus [17,15], and show its equivalence to a multi-valued interpretation that uses the real numbers as semantic domain and assigns Lipschitz-continuous interpretations to all operators of DC in Section 4. Sections 5 and 6 deal with approximation of the multi-valued truth value, in particular discrete-time approximation of the dense-time interpretation, and with decidability issues.

2   Duration Calculus

Duration Calculus (abbreviated DC in the remainder) is a real-time logic that is specially tailored towards reasoning about durational constraints on time-dependent Boolean-valued states. Since its introduction in [17], many variants of Duration Calculus have been defined [15]. Aiming at a mechanizable design calculus, we present a slight syntactic subset of the Duration Calculus as defined in [17]. Our subset allows full treatment of the gas burner case study [13], the primary case study of the ProCoS project. This indicates that our subset offers an interesting vocabulary for specifying embedded real-time controllers.

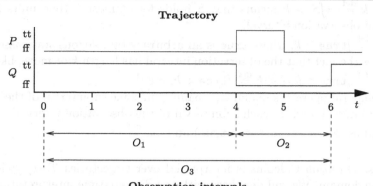

The formula $\int Q > 3$ holds on observation interval $O_1 = [0, 4]$, as the accumulated duration of Q being true over this interval exceeds 3. Analogously, $\int (P \wedge \neg Q) \geq 1$ holds on observation interval $O_2 = [4, 6]$. Consequently, the formula $(\int Q > 3) \frown (\int (P \wedge \neg Q) \geq 1)$ holds on the catenation $O_3 = [0, 6]$ of the other two observation intervals.

Fig. 1. The meaning of $\int S \sim k$ and of the chop modality

Syntax. The syntax of DC used in this paper is as follows.

$$\phi ::= \int S \geq c \mid \int S > c \mid \neg \phi \mid (\phi \wedge \phi) \mid (\phi \frown \phi)$$
$$S ::= P \mid \neg S \mid (S \wedge S)$$
$$P ::\in Varname$$
$$c ::\in \mathbb{R} \ ,$$

where *Varname* is a countable set of state-variable names. Note that, in contrast to other expositions of DC, we allow negative constants as this makes the theory more homogeneous.

Formulae are interpreted over trajectories providing Boolean-valued valuation of state variables that vary finitely, in the sense of featuring only finitely many changes over any finite interval of time. For a given bounded and closed time interval, also called an "observation interval", a formula is either true or false. While the meaning of the Boolean connectives used in DC formulae should be obvious, the temporal connective $\frown$ (pronounced "chop") may need some explanation. A formula $\phi \frown \psi$ is true of an observation interval iff the observation interval can be split into a left and a right subinterval s.t. ϕ holds of the left part and ψ of the right part. A duration formula $\int S \geq k$ is true of an observation interval iff the state assertion S, interpreted over the trajectory, is true for an accumulated duration of at least k time units within the observation interval. Fig. 1 provides an illustration of the meaning of these formulae.

Despite its simple syntax, DC is very expressive, as can be seen from the following abbreviations frequently used in formulae:

- $\int S < k \stackrel{\text{def}}{=} \neg \int S \geq k$ means that S holds for strictly less than k time units in the current observation interval;

- $\int S \leq k \overset{\text{def}}{=} \neg \int S > k$ means that S holds for at most k time units in the current observation interval,
- $\ell \geq k \overset{\text{def}}{=} \int \text{true} \geq k$, where true is an arbitrary tautologous state assertion, denotes the fact that the observation interval has length k or more; likewise, $\ell \leq k \overset{\text{def}}{=} \int \text{true} \leq k$, $\ell < k \overset{\text{def}}{=} \int \text{true} < k$, etc.;[1]
- the temporal operators $\Diamond$ and $\Box$, meaning 'in some subinterval of the observation interval' and 'in each subinterval of the observation interval', can be defined as $\Diamond \phi \overset{\text{def}}{=} (\text{true} \frown \phi \frown \text{true})$ and $\Box \phi \overset{\text{def}}{=} \neg \Diamond \neg \phi$.

Semantics. Duration Calculus is interpreted over trajectories Traj_T, where T is the time domain. We will deal here with the discrete-time interpretation (i.e. $T = \mathbb{N}$), the rational-time interpretation (i.e. $T = \mathbb{Q}_{\geq 0}$), and the real-time interpretation (i.e. $T = \mathbb{R}_{\geq 0}$) of DC. The definition of trajectories is as follows:

$$\mathit{Traj}_T \overset{\text{def}}{=} \mathbb{R}_{\geq 0} \rightarrow \mathit{Varname} \rightarrow \mathbb{B} ,$$

where for every $tr \in \mathit{Traj}_T$, we require for each function $\underline{P}(t) = tr(t)(P)$, where $P \in \mathit{Varname}$, that the discontinuity points of $\underline{P}$ belongs to T, and the function $\underline{P}$ is finitely varied, in the sense that it has at most a finite number of discontinuity points in every bounded and closed interval.

Satisfaction of a formula ϕ by a trajectory tr is defined as a limit property over a chain of finite chunks from tr called *observations*, where an observation is a pair $(tr, [a,b]) \in \mathit{Obs}_T \overset{\text{def}}{=} \mathit{Traj}_T \times \mathit{TimeInterval}_T$ with $\mathit{TimeInterval}_T$ being the set of bounded and closed time intervals $\{ [a,b] \subseteq \mathbb{R}_{\geq 0} \mid a, b \in T \}$.

First, we will define when an *observation* $(tr, [a,b])$ *satisfies a formula* ϕ when interpreted over time domain T, denoted $tr, [a,b] \models_T \phi$. For atomic duration formulae $\int S \geq k$ or $\int S > k$, this is defined by

$$tr, [a,b] \models_T \int S \geq k \quad \text{iff} \quad \int_{t=a}^{b} \chi \circ [\![S]\!] \circ tr(t) \, dt \geq k ,$$

$$tr, [a,b] \models_T \int S > k \quad \text{iff} \quad \int_{t=a}^{b} \chi \circ [\![S]\!] \circ tr(t) \, dt > k ,$$

where $[\![S]\!](\sigma)$ canonically lifts a Boolean-valued interpretation $\sigma : \mathit{Varname} \rightarrow \mathbb{B}$ of state variables to an interpretation of the state assertion S, e.g. $[\![P \wedge \neg Q]\!](\sigma) = \sigma(P) \wedge \neg \sigma(Q)$, and χ maps truth values to $\{0, 1\}$ according to the convention $\chi(\text{false}) = 0$ and $\chi(\text{true}) = 1$. I.e., $\int S \geq k$ holds on $(tr, [a,b])$ iff S holds for an accumulated duration of at least k time units within $[a,b]$.

The interpretation of Boolean connectives is classical:

$$tr, [a,b] \models_T \neg \phi \quad \text{iff} \quad tr, [a,b] \not\models_T \phi ,$$
$$tr, [a,b] \models_T \phi \wedge \psi \quad \text{iff} \quad tr, [a,b] \models_T \phi \text{ and } tr, [a,b] \models_T \psi .$$

---

[1] Note that ℓ in $\ell \sim k$ is not a state variable, but a piece of concrete syntax that denotes the length of the current observation interval.

Satisfaction of a chop formula $\phi \frown \psi$, finally, requires that the observation interval can be split into two subintervals $[a, m]$ and $[m, b]$ s.t. ϕ resp. ψ hold on the two subintervals:

$$tr, [a, b] \models_T \phi \frown \psi \quad \text{iff} \quad \exists m \in T \cap [a, b] . \; (tr, [a, m] \models_T \phi \text{ and } tr, [m, b] \models_T \psi) \; .$$

A trajectory tr *satisfies a formula* ϕ, which is denoted by $tr \models_T \phi$, iff any prefix-observation of tr satisfies ϕ — formally, $tr \models_T \phi$ iff $tr, [0, t] \models_T \phi$ for each $t \in T$. For notational convenience, we denote the set of models of ϕ over time domain T (where $T \in \{\mathbb{N}, \mathbb{Q}_{\geq 0}, \mathbb{R}_{\geq 0}\}$), i.e. the set of trajectories satisfying ϕ wrt. to that interpretation, by $\mathcal{M}_T[\![\phi]\!]$. As usual, we say that ϕ *is valid over* T, denoted $\models_T \phi$, iff $\mathcal{M}_T[\![\phi]\!] = Traj_T$.

3   Robust Interpretation of DC

From an engineering perspective, arguments that become invalid when an infinitesimally small change to the constants occurring in the argument appears, are at least doubtful, if not even useless. Hence, we define a formula to be *robustly valid* iff it remains valid under some small variation of constants:

Definition 1 (Robust validity). *A DC formula ϕ is robustly valid over time domain T iff there is $\varepsilon > 0$ such that $\models_T \phi'$ holds for each $\phi' \in \mathcal{N}(\phi, \varepsilon)$, where $\mathcal{N}(\phi, \varepsilon)$ is the set of all DC formulae that are structurally equal to ϕ, yet may differ from ϕ in the constants of the individual atomic formulae by at most ε.*

I.e., $\mathcal{N}(\phi, \varepsilon)$ is the ε-neighborhood of ϕ with respect to the following recursively defined metrics on DC formulae:

$$d(\textstyle\int S_1 \geq k, \int S_2 \geq l) = \begin{cases} |k - l| & \text{if } S_1 = S_2, \\ \infty & \text{otherwise}; \end{cases}$$

$$d(\textstyle\int S_1 > k, \int S_2 > l) = \begin{cases} |k - l| & \text{if } S_1 = S_2, \\ \infty & \text{otherwise}; \end{cases}$$

$$d(\neg\phi, \neg\psi) = d(\phi, \psi) \; ;$$

$$d(\phi_1 \wedge \phi_2, \psi_1 \wedge \psi_2) = \max\{d(\phi_1, \psi_1), d(\phi_2, \psi_2)\} \; ;$$

$$d(\phi_1 \frown \phi_2, \psi_1 \frown \psi_2) = \max\{d(\phi_1, \psi_1), d(\phi_2, \psi_2)\} \; ;$$

$$d(\phi, \psi) = \infty \text{ if } \phi \text{ and } \psi \text{ disagree on the outermost operator}.$$

In analogy to robust validity, we define *robust satisfaction* of formulae by observations and by trajectories as follows:

Definition 2 (Robust satisfaction).

1. *A formula ϕ is robustly satisfied (over time domain T) by an observation $obs \in Obs_T$ iff there is $\varepsilon > 0$ such that $obs \models_T \phi'$ holds for each $\phi' \in \mathcal{N}(\phi, \varepsilon)$.*
2. *A formula ϕ is robustly satisfied (over time domain T) by a trajectory $tr \in Traj_T$ iff there is $\varepsilon > 0$ such that $tr \models_T \phi'$ holds for each $\phi' \in \mathcal{N}(\phi, \varepsilon)$.*

Note that this definition in fact yields a three-valued interpretation of satisfaction by observations, as an observation may fail to robustly satisfy both ϕ and $\neg\phi$, while in classical DC, exactly one of $obs \models_T \phi$ or $obs \not\models_T \phi$ does inevitably hold. On the levels of satisfaction by trajectories or of validity, no fundamental differences do arise. It is, however, a consequence of the definitions that robust validity is more discriminative than classical validity: classical validity is a necessary, yet not sufficient, condition for robust validity.

Unfortunately, the existential quantification of ε in the three definitions yields that the relation between satisfaction by an observation, satisfaction by a trajectory, and validity is different from the classical setting. Thus, the following statements (which follow immediately from the definitions) are just single-sided implications, while they are equivalences in the classical setting:

Lemma 1 (Satisfaction vs. validity).

1. *For each trajectory $tr \in Traj_T$ it holds that ϕ is robustly satisfied (over time domain T) by all observations of the form $(tr, [0, e])$ if ϕ is robustly satisfied (over time domain T) by tr.*
2. *ϕ is robustly satisfied (over time domain T) by all trajectories tr if ϕ is robustly valid (over time domain T).*

4   Multi-valued Interpretation

As the definition of robust satisfaction or validity has an extra quantification over formula neighborhoods, the robust interpretation is structurally more complex than the standard semantics of DC. Fortunately, an equivalent semantics can be derived by more direct means, namely by a multi-valued interpretation of DC. The idea is to assign to each (sub-)formula a real-number denoting its *slackness* in the following sense: each formula is mapped to the upper bound of variation in constants it can take on the current observation without changing its truth value. Such slackness information can be lumped together with the formula's truth value by mapping it to a signed slackness value: if the formula is satisfied by the observation then we assign the slackness as its multi-valued "truth" value; otherwise we assign minus its slackness. We will now define a truth-functional version of this multi-valued interpretation and will then show that it coincides with the robust interpretation.

In a first step, we define a real-valued interpretation $\mathcal{M}_T[\![\cdot]\!] : DC \to Obs_T \to \mathbb{R}$ of formulae on observations $obs \in Obs_T$ and over time domain T as follows:

$$\mathcal{M}_T[\![\textstyle\int S \geq k]\!](tr, [a, b]) = \int_{t=a}^{b} \chi \circ [\![S]\!] \circ tr(t)\, dt - k$$

$$\mathcal{M}_T[\![\textstyle\int S > k]\!](tr, [a, b]) = \int_{t=a}^{b} \chi \circ [\![S]\!] \circ tr(t)\, dt - k$$

$$\mathcal{M}_T[\![\neg\phi]\!]obs = -\mathcal{M}_T[\![\phi]\!](obs)$$

$$\mathcal{M}_T[\![\phi \wedge \psi]\!]obs = \min\{\mathcal{M}_T[\![\phi]\!](obs), \mathcal{M}_T[\![\psi]\!](obs)\}$$

$$\mathcal{M}_T[\![\phi \frown \psi]\!](tr, [a, b]) = \sup_{m \in T \cap [a,b]} \min\{\mathcal{M}_T[\![\phi]\!](tr, [a, m]), \mathcal{M}_T[\![\psi]\!](tr, [m, b])\} \ .$$

In fact, the supremum operator in $\mathcal{M}_T[\![\phi \frown \psi]\!](tr, [a, b])$ could be replaced by the maximum over interval $[a, b]$, as Corollary 3 below shows the semantics to be continuous such that closedness of the observation interval $[a, b]$ implies that the maximum exists (and trivially coincides with the supremum).

Finally, we overload the symbol $\mathcal{M}_T[\![\cdot]\!]$ by defining the multi-valued interpretations $\mathcal{M}_T[\![\cdot]\!] : DC \to Traj_T \to \mathbb{R}$ over individual trajectories and $\mathcal{M}_T[\![\cdot]\!] : DC \to \mathbb{R}$ over the universe of trajectories to be

$$\mathcal{M}_T[\![\phi]\!](tr) = \inf_{e \in T} \mathcal{M}_T[\![\phi]\!](tr, [0, e]),$$

$$\mathcal{M}_T[\![\phi]\!] = \inf_{tr \in Traj_T} \mathcal{M}_T[\![\phi]\!](tr)$$

This multi-valued semantics corresponds closely to the standard semantics:

Lemma 2 (Multi-valued semantics vs. classical semantics).

1. If $\mathcal{M}_T[\![\phi]\!](obs) > 0$ then $obs \models_T \phi$;
2. if $\mathcal{M}_T[\![\phi]\!](obs) < 0$ then $obs \not\models_T \phi$;
3. if $\mathcal{M}_T[\![\phi]\!](tr) > 0$ then $tr \models_T \phi$;
4. if $\mathcal{M}_T[\![\phi]\!](tr) < 0$ then $tr \not\models_T \phi$;
5. if $\mathcal{M}_T[\![\phi]\!] > 0$ then $\models_T \phi$;
6. if $\mathcal{M}_T[\![\phi]\!] < 0$ then $\not\models_T \phi$.

I.e., positivity of the multi-valued semantics is a sufficient, yet not necessary, condition for satisfaction or validity (depending on the variant of $\mathcal{M}_T[\![\phi]\!]$ used), while negativity is a sufficient, yet not necessary, condition for dissatisfaction or invalidity. Despite this close correspondence, the multi-valued interpretation has a number of interesting properties that distinguish it from the standard interpretation:

Lemma 3 (Lipschitz-continuity). *For any DC formula ϕ, the semantic mapping $\mathcal{M}_T[\![\phi]\!] : Obs_T \to \mathbb{R}$ is Lipschitz continuous with constant 1 with respect to the metrics*

$$d\left((tr_1, [b_1, e_1]), (tr_2, [b_2, e_2])\right) \stackrel{\text{def}}{=}$$

$$\max \left\{ \begin{array}{l} |b_1 - b_2|, \\ |e_1 - e_2|, \\ \int_{t=\max\{b_1,b_2\}}^{\min\{e_1,e_2\}} \chi \circ (tr_1 \neq tr_2)(t)\, dt \end{array} \right\}$$

on observations.

This Lipschitz continuity, together with the following linearity properties, will allow us to develop approximation schemes for $\mathcal{M}_T[\![\phi]\!]$.

Lemma 4 (Linearity of multi-valued semantics). *Let $obs = (tr, [b, e])$ be an observation, let $c \in \mathbb{R}$ and $d \in \mathbb{R}_{>0}$. If $\mathcal{M}_T[\![\phi]\!](obs) = x$ then*

1. $\mathcal{M}_T[\![\phi_{+c}]\!](obs) = x + c$, where ϕ_{+c} is the formula obtained from ϕ by replacing each positive occurrence of an atomic formula $\int S \geq k$ (or $\int S > k$) by $\int S \geq k - c$ (by $\int S > k - c$, resp.) and each negative occurrence by $\int S \geq k + c$ (by $\int S > k + c$, resp.),

2. $\mathcal{M}_{d \cdot T}[\![\phi_{\cdot d}]\!](obs') = xd$, where $d \cdot T = \{dt \mid t \in T\}$ and $\phi_{\cdot d}$ is the formula obtained from ϕ by replacing each occurrence of $\int S \geq k$ by $\int S \geq kd$ and each occurrence of $\int S > k$ by $\int S > kd$, and observation $obs' = \left(t \mapsto tr\left(\frac{t}{d}\right), [bd, ed]\right)$.

Given these properties, which help in building verification support, as e.g. the continuity property allows to remove whole parts (namely a ball of radius δ in the observation space around obs) from the search space of a satisfiability search once an observation obs with truth value $\mathcal{M}_T[\![\phi]\!](obs) = -\delta$ has been found, it is interesting to see that the multi-valued semantics is in fact tightly linked to the robust interpretation:

Theorem 1 (Robustness vs. multi-valued).

1. $\mathcal{M}_T[\![\phi]\!](obs) > 0$ iff obs robustly satisfies ϕ;
2. $\mathcal{M}_T[\![\phi]\!](tr) > 0$ iff tr robustly satisfies ϕ;
3. $\mathcal{M}_T[\![\phi]\!] > 0$ iff ϕ is robustly valid.

Proof. We show only (1.); the other cases are analogous:

As $\mathcal{M}_T[\![\phi]\!](obs)$ assigns the slackness of the constants, i.e. corresponds to the amount of variation of constants that can be applied without invalidating satisfaction by obs, it is straightforward to show by induction on the structure of ϕ that $\mathcal{M}_T[\![\phi]\!](obs) > 0$ implies that all formulae ϕ' with $d(\phi, \phi') < \mathcal{M}_T[\![\phi]\!](obs)$ are satisfied by obs. I.e., $\mathcal{M}_T[\![\phi]\!](obs) > 0$ implies that obs robustly satisfies ϕ.

Vice versa, if $\mathcal{M}_T[\![\phi]\!](obs) \leq 0$ then $\mathcal{M}_T[\![\phi_{+(-\varepsilon)}]\!](obs) < 0$ for each $\varepsilon > 0$. I.e., according to Lemma 2, $obs \not\models \phi_{+(-\varepsilon)}$ for all $\varepsilon > 0$. As $d(\phi, \phi_{+(-\varepsilon)}) = \varepsilon$, this shows that obs does not robustly satisfy ϕ.   □

5   Approximability

Due to the Lipschitz continuity of the multi-valued semantics and due to its correspondence to the robust interpretation, it turns out that the robust interpretation is approximable in a variety of ways. E.g., we find that the discrete-time interpretation approximates the real-time interpretation with a quantifiable tolerance. Note that such results do inherently build on the multi-valued interpretation.

5.1   Real Time Versus Rational Time

Before we can start with discrete-time approximation, we show that robust DC cannot distinguish between real-valued and rational-valued time in the sense that a robustly satisfying observation over real-valued time exists iff a robustly satisfying observation over rational time exists:[2]

---

[2] The same is, btw., true for the standard interpretation, yet for different reasons: for every $n \in \mathbb{N}$, existence of an observation with n discontinuities satisfying ϕ can be expressed as a formula in $FOL(\mathbb{R}, +, <)$. As $FOL(\mathbb{R}, +, <)$ cannot distinguish between rationals and reals, ϕ has a rational-time model with n state changes iff it has a real-time model with n state changes.

Lemma 5 (Rational time vs. real time). $\mathcal{M}_{\mathbb{R}\geq 0}[\![\phi]\!] = \mathcal{M}_{\mathbb{Q}\geq 0}[\![\phi]\!]$.

Proof. Let $tr \in Traj_{\mathbb{R}\geq 0}$ and $e \in \mathbb{R}_{\geq 0}$. Due to density of $\mathbb{Q}$ in $\mathbb{R}$,

$$\inf_{tr' \in Traj_{\mathbb{Q}\geq 0}, e' \in \mathbb{Q}\geq 0} d((tr, [0, e]), (tr', [0, e'])) = 0 \ .$$

Similarly, real-valued chop points can be arbitrarily closely approximated by rational ones. Given the continuity of $\mathcal{M}_T[\![\phi]\!]$, as expressed in Lemma 3, an easy induction over the structure of ϕ thus shows

$$\mathcal{M}_{\mathbb{R}\geq 0}[\![\phi]\!]$$

$$= \inf_{tr \in Traj_{\mathbb{R}\geq 0}, e \in \mathbb{R}} \mathcal{M}_{\mathbb{R}\geq 0}[\![\phi]\!](tr, [0, e]) \qquad \text{[Def. of } \mathcal{M}_{\mathbb{R}\geq 0}[\![\phi]\!]]$$

$$= \inf_{tr \in Traj_{\mathbb{Q}\geq 0}, e \in \mathbb{Q}} \mathcal{M}_{\mathbb{Q}\geq 0}[\![\phi]\!](tr, [0, e]) \qquad \text{[Density of } \mathbb{Q} \text{ in } \mathbb{R}]$$

$$= \mathcal{M}_{\mathbb{Q}\geq 0}[\![\phi]\!] \qquad \text{[Def. of } \mathcal{M}_{\mathbb{Q}\geq 0}[\![\phi]\!]]$$

$\square$

5.2   Approximation of Real Time Interpretation by the Discrete Time Interpretation

Given the equivalence of the real-valued time and the rational-time interpretation expressed by Lemma 5, we can proceed towards approximation of real time by discrete time:

Lemma 6 (Upper approximation by discrete time). *Let ϕ be a DC formula and let $depth(\phi)$ denote the nesting depth of chop operators in ϕ. Then*

$$\mathcal{M}_{\mathbb{R}\geq 0}[\![\phi]\!] \leq \mathcal{M}_{\mathbb{N}}[\![\phi]\!] + \frac{depth(\phi)}{2} \ .$$

Proof. Let $obs = (tr, [a, b]) \in Obs_{\mathbb{N}}$ be a discrete-time (and hence also a real-time) observation. We show by induction on the structure of ϕ that

$$\mathcal{M}_{\mathbb{R}\geq 0}[\![\phi]\!](obs) \in \mathcal{M}_{\mathbb{N}}[\![\phi]\!](obs) \pm \frac{depth(\phi)}{2} \ ,$$

where $x \pm y$ denotes the set $[x - y, x + y]$.

Base case: $\phi = \int S \geq k$ or $\phi = \int S > k$. Is simple as $depth(\phi) = 0$ and $\mathcal{M}_{\mathbb{R}\geq 0}[\![\phi]\!](obs) = \int_{t=a}^{b} \chi \circ [\![S]\!] \circ tr(t) \, dt - k = \mathcal{M}_{\mathbb{N}}[\![\phi]\!](obs)$.

Induction steps $\phi = \neg\psi_1$ and $\phi = \psi_1 \wedge \psi_2$ follow from the corresponding properties of ψ_i.

Induction step: $\phi = \psi_1 \frown \psi_2$. We establish the upper bound for $\mathcal{M}_{\mathbb{R}\geq 0}[\![\phi]\!](obs)$ below. The lower bound is established similarly.

$$\mathcal{M}_{\mathbb{R}\geq 0}[\![\phi]\!](obs)$$

$$= \sup_{m\in[a,b]} \min \left\{ \begin{array}{l} \mathcal{M}_{\mathbb{R}\geq 0}[\![\psi_1]\!](tr,[a,m]), \\ \mathcal{M}_{\mathbb{R}\geq 0}[\![\psi_2]\!](tr,[m,b]) \end{array} \right\} \qquad [\text{Def. } \mathcal{M}_{\mathbb{R}\geq 0}[\![\phi]\!]]$$

$$\leq \sup_{m\in\mathbb{N}\cap[a,b]} \min \left\{ \begin{array}{l} \mathcal{M}_{\mathbb{R}\geq 0}[\![\psi_1]\!](tr,[a,m]), \\ \mathcal{M}_{\mathbb{R}\geq 0}[\![\psi_2]\!](tr,[m,b]) \end{array} \right\} + \frac{1}{2} \qquad [\text{Lemma 3, } d(\mathbb{N},\mathbb{R}_{\geq 0}) = \tfrac{1}{2}]$$

$$\leq \sup_{m\in\mathbb{N}\cap[a,b]} \min \left\{ \begin{array}{l} \mathcal{M}_{\mathbb{N}}[\![\psi_1]\!](tr,[a,m]) + \frac{depth(\psi_1)}{2}, \\ \mathcal{M}_{\mathbb{N}}[\![\psi_2]\!](tr,[m,b]) + \frac{depth(\psi_2)}{2} \end{array} \right\} + \frac{1}{2} \qquad [\text{Induction}]$$

$$\leq \sup_{m\in\mathbb{N}\cap[a,b]} \min \left\{ \begin{array}{l} \mathcal{M}_{\mathbb{N}}[\![\psi_1]\!](tr,[a,m]) + \frac{depth(\phi)}{2}, \\ \mathcal{M}_{\mathbb{N}}[\![\psi_2]\!](tr,[m,b]) + \frac{depth(\phi)}{2} \end{array} \right\} \qquad [depth(\psi_i)+1 \leq depth(\phi)]$$

$$= \mathcal{M}_{\mathbb{N}}[\![\phi]\!](obs) + \frac{depth(\phi)}{2} \qquad [\text{Def. } \mathcal{M}_{\mathbb{N}}[\![\phi]\!]]$$

Thus, $\mathcal{M}_{\mathbb{R}\geq 0}[\![\phi]\!](obs) \in \mathcal{M}_{\mathbb{N}}[\![\phi]\!](obs) \pm \frac{depth(\phi)}{2}$ holds for $\phi = \psi_1 \frown \psi_2$, which ends the induction.

As a consequence, $\mathcal{M}_{\mathbb{R}\geq 0}[\![\phi]\!](obs) \leq \mathcal{M}_{\mathbb{N}}[\![\phi]\!](obs) + \frac{depth(\phi)}{2}$ holds for arbitrary formulae ϕ and arbitrary discrete-time observations $obs \in Obs_{\mathbb{N}}$. As the universe $Traj_{\mathbb{N}}$ of discrete-time trajectories is properly included in the universe $Traj_{\mathbb{R}\geq 0}$ of real-time trajectories, we have:

$$\mathcal{M}_{\mathbb{R}\geq 0}[\![\phi]\!]$$

$$= \inf_{tr\in Traj_{\mathbb{R}\geq 0}, e\in\mathbb{R}_{\geq 0}} \mathcal{M}_{\mathbb{R}\geq 0}[\![\phi]\!](tr,[0,e]) \qquad [\text{Def. } \mathcal{M}_{\mathbb{R}\geq 0}[\![\phi]\!]]$$

$$\leq \inf_{tr\in Traj_{\mathbb{N}}, e\in\mathbb{N}} \mathcal{M}_{\mathbb{R}\geq 0}[\![\phi]\!](tr,[0,e]) \qquad [\mathbb{N} \subset \mathbb{R}_{\geq 0}]$$

$$\leq \inf_{tr\in Traj_{\mathbb{N}}, e\in\mathbb{N}} \mathcal{M}_{\mathbb{N}}[\![\phi]\!](tr,[0,e]) + \frac{depth(\phi)}{2} \qquad [\text{above induction}]$$

$$= \mathcal{M}_{\mathbb{N}}[\![\phi]\!] + \frac{depth(\phi)}{2} \qquad [\text{Def. } \mathcal{M}_{\mathbb{N}}[\![\phi]\!]]$$

$$\square$$

Therefore, dense-time formulae can be falsified using discrete-time reasoning: if $\mathcal{M}_{\mathbb{N}}[\![\phi]\!] + \frac{depth(\phi)}{2}$ is negative then ϕ is certainly robustly invalid, as $\mathcal{M}_{\mathbb{R}\geq 0}[\![\phi]\!] < 0$ follows.

In case above approximation is too inexact, linearity of the multi-valued semantics allows for scaling, thus yielding tighter approximation by using higher "sampling rates":

Corollary 1 (Discr. approx. with higher sampling rate). *For any* $n \in \mathbb{N} \setminus \{0\}$,

$$\mathcal{M}_{\mathbb{R}\geq 0}[\![\phi]\!] \leq \mathcal{M}_{\frac{1}{n}\cdot\mathbb{N}}[\![\phi]\!] + \frac{depth(\phi)}{2n} .$$

Proof. Follows directly from the previous lemma together with Lemma 4 and the fact that $depth(\phi) = depth(\phi_{\cdot n})$:

$$\mathcal{M}_{\mathbb{R}\geq 0}[\![\phi]\!]$$

$$= \frac{1}{n}\mathcal{M}_{\mathbb{R}\geq 0}[\![\phi._n]\!] \hspace{4cm} \text{[Lemma 4]}$$

$$\leq \frac{1}{n}\left(\mathcal{M}_{\mathbb{N}}[\![\phi._n]\!] + \frac{depth(\phi._n)}{2}\right) \hspace{2.5cm} \text{[Lemma 6]}$$

$$= \frac{1}{n}\mathcal{M}_{\mathbb{N}}[\![\phi._n]\!] + \frac{depth(\phi)}{2n} \hspace{2cm} [depth(\phi) = depth(\phi._n)]$$

$$= \mathcal{M}_{\frac{1}{n}\cdot\mathbb{N}}[\![\phi]\!] + \frac{depth(\phi)}{2n} \hspace{3cm} \text{[Lemma 4]}$$
$$\square$$

Unfortunately, the previous lemma and its corollary do only provide *upper* approximations of the real-valued time interpretation $\mathcal{M}_{\mathbb{R}\geq 0}[\![\phi]\!]$ by discrete time with arbitrary sampling rates $\mathcal{M}_{\frac{1}{n}\cdot\mathbb{N}}[\![\phi]\!]$. Yet, these upper approximations are complemented by a tightness result concerning rational time:

Lemma 7. $\inf_{k\geq l,k\in\mathbb{N}}\mathcal{M}_{\frac{1}{k!}\cdot\mathbb{N}}[\![\phi]\!] \leq \mathcal{M}_{\mathbb{Q}\geq 0}[\![\phi]\!]$ *holds for each DC formula* ϕ *and each* $l \in \mathbb{N}$.

Proof. Assume, on the contrary, that $x \stackrel{\text{def}}{=} \inf_{k\geq l,k\in\mathbb{N}}\mathcal{M}_{\frac{1}{k!}\cdot\mathbb{N}}[\![\phi]\!] > \mathcal{M}_{\mathbb{Q}\geq 0}[\![\phi]\!]$. Then there is a rational-time observation $obs \in Obs_{\mathbb{Q}\geq 0}$ with $x > \mathcal{M}_{\mathbb{Q}\geq 0}[\![\phi]\!](obs)$. But as $obs = (tr, [a, b])$ is a rational-time observation, there is $m \in \mathbb{N}$ with $m \geq l$ such that $a, b \in \frac{1}{m}\cdot\mathbb{N}$ and tr is constant on $[\frac{i}{m}, \frac{i+1}{m})$ for each $i \in \mathbb{N}$ and that, furthermore, all chop points characterizing (i.e., yielding the suprema in) $\mathcal{M}_{\mathbb{Q}\geq 0}[\![\phi]\!]$ are in $\frac{1}{m}\cdot\mathbb{N}$. Therefore, $\mathcal{M}_{\frac{1}{n}\cdot\mathbb{N}}[\![\phi]\!](obs_n) = \mathcal{M}_{\mathbb{Q}\geq 0}[\![\phi]\!](obs)$ holds for all multiples n of m, where $obs_n = (tr_n, [a, b])$ is the natural restriction of obs to over-sampled discrete time obtained using the restriction tr_n of tr to domain $\frac{1}{n}\cdot\mathbb{N}$. With $n = m!$, this yields the contradiction $x > \mathcal{M}_{\mathbb{Q}\geq 0}[\![\phi]\!](obs) = \mathcal{M}_{\frac{1}{n}\cdot\mathbb{N}}[\![\phi]\!](obs_n) \geq \inf_{obs'\in Obs_{\frac{1}{n}\cdot\mathbb{N}}}\mathcal{M}_{\frac{1}{n}\cdot\mathbb{N}}[\![\phi]\!](obs') = \mathcal{M}_{\frac{1}{n}\cdot\mathbb{N}}[\![\phi]\!] \geq \inf_{k\geq l,k\in\mathbb{N}}\mathcal{M}_{\frac{1}{k!}\cdot\mathbb{N}}[\![\phi]\!] = x$. Consequently, the assumption that $\inf_{k\geq l,k\in\mathbb{N}}\mathcal{M}_{\frac{1}{k!}\cdot\mathbb{N}}[\![\phi]\!] > \mathcal{M}_{\mathbb{Q}\geq 0}[\![\phi]\!]$ must be wrong, which proves $\inf_{k\geq l,k\in\mathbb{N}}\mathcal{M}_{\frac{1}{k!}\cdot\mathbb{N}}[\![\phi]\!] \leq \mathcal{M}_{\mathbb{Q}\geq 0}[\![\phi]\!]$. $\square$

However, using Lemma 5, this tightness result carries over to real-valued time:

Corollary 2 (Asymptotic tightness of disc.-time approx.).
$\inf_{k\geq l,k\in\mathbb{N}}\mathcal{M}_{\frac{1}{k!}\cdot\mathbb{N}}[\![\phi]\!] \leq \mathcal{M}_{\mathbb{R}\geq 0}[\![\phi]\!]$ *holds for each DC formula* ϕ *and each* $l \in \mathbb{N}$.

5.3   Discrete Time with Different Sampling Rates

Given above approximation results between discrete time and real-valued time, the rate of convergence of the discrete time interpretation when using increasingly larger sampling rates becomes interesting. A close look at the proofs of Lemma 6 and Corollary 1 reveals that they carry over from real-valued time to using discrete time (with different sampling rates) on both sides. When replacing $\mathcal{M}_{\mathbb{R}\geq 0}[\![\phi]\!]$ by $\mathcal{M}_{\frac{1}{k}\cdot\mathbb{N}}[\![\phi]\!]$ for some arbitrary $k \in \mathbb{N}\setminus\{0\}$, we obtain

Lemma 8 (Approximation by sub-sampling). *Let ϕ be a DC formula and let $k \in \mathbb{N} \setminus \{0\}$. Then*

$$\mathcal{M}_{\frac{1}{k} \cdot \mathbb{N}}[\![\phi]\!] \leq \mathcal{M}_{\mathbb{N}}[\![\phi]\!] + \frac{depth(\phi)}{2} \ .$$

Proof. Substitute $\mathcal{M}_{\mathbb{R}\geq 0}[\![\phi]\!]$ with $\mathcal{M}_{\frac{1}{k} \cdot \mathbb{N}}[\![\phi]\!]$ in the proof of Lemma 6. $\square$

Again, we can scale this result using the linearity properties from Lemma 4, thus obtaining a discrete-time variant of Corollary 1:

Corollary 3 (Sampling-rate conversion). *For any $m, n \in \mathbb{N} \setminus \{0\}$,*

$$\mathcal{M}_{\frac{1}{mn} \cdot \mathbb{N}}[\![\phi]\!] \leq \mathcal{M}_{\frac{1}{n} \cdot \mathbb{N}}[\![\phi]\!] + \frac{depth(\phi)}{2n} \ .$$

Proof. Repeat the proof of Corollary 1 with $\mathcal{M}_{\mathbb{R}\geq 0}[\![\phi]\!]$ replaced by $\mathcal{M}_{\frac{1}{mn} \cdot \mathbb{N}}[\![\phi]\!]$ and Lemma 6 substituted with Lemma 8. $\square$

Note that this implies that independently of the formula structure, finer sampling cannot yield arbitrary changes in the multi-valued truth value. When moving to an over-sampling, the possible increase in truth value is bounded by $\frac{depth(\phi)}{2n}$, where n is the base sampling rate. In particular, the possible increase converges against 0 for growing sampling rates.

6   Decidability

We will now turn to decidability and semi-decidability results over integer and real-valued time.

6.1   Decidability over Discrete Time

In order to obtain a decision procedure for robust validity over discrete time, we present a reduction of robust validity over discrete time to conventional validity over discrete time. A simple induction shows

Lemma 9 (Robust vs. classical satisfaction). *For each DC formula ϕ and each observation $obs \in Obs_{\mathbb{N}}$, the equivalence $\mathcal{M}_{\mathbb{N}}[\![\phi]\!](obs) > 0$ iff $obs \models_{\mathbb{N}} \phi^{\circ}$ holds, where ϕ° is the formula ϕ with all positive occurrences of $\int S \geq k$ replaced by $\int S > k$ and all negative occurrences of $\int S > k$ replaced by $\int S \geq k$.*

As $\mathcal{M}_{\mathbb{N}}[\![\cdot]\!]$ maps formulae to integers, a corresponding reduction of robust validity to classical validity can be derived.

Lemma 10 (Robust vs. classical validity). *For a DC formula ϕ with integer constants, $\mathcal{M}_{\mathbb{N}}[\![\phi]\!] > 0$ iff $\models_{\mathbb{N}} \phi^{\circ}$. I.e., ϕ is robustly valid over discrete time iff ϕ° is valid over discrete time in the classical sense.*

Proof. It follows from the definition of $\mathcal{M}_{T}[\![\cdot]\!]$ that $\mathcal{M}_{\mathbb{N}}[\![\phi]\!](obs) \in \mathbb{Z} \pm C$ for each $obs \in Obs_{\mathbb{N}}$, where C is the set of constants occurring in ϕ and $M \pm N = \{m + n \mid m \in M, n \in N\} \cup \{m - n \mid m \in M, n \in N\}$. Therefore,

$$\mathcal{M}_N[\![\phi]\!] > 0$$

$$\text{iff} \quad \inf_{tr \in Traj_N, e \in \mathbb{N}} \mathcal{M}_N[\![\phi]\!](tr, [0, e]) > 0 \qquad\qquad [\text{Def. } \mathcal{M}_T[\![\phi]\!]]$$

$$\text{iff} \ \forall tr \in Traj_N, e \in \mathbb{N}. \ \big(\mathcal{M}_N[\![\phi]\!](tr, [0, e]) > 0\big)$$
$$[\mathcal{M}_N[\![\phi]\!](obs) \in \mathbb{Z} \pm C, \text{ which has no accumulation point}]$$

$$\text{iff} \ \forall tr \in Traj_N, e \in \mathbb{N}. \ \big((tr, [0, e]) \models_N \phi^\circ\big) \qquad\qquad [\text{Lemma 9}]$$

$$\text{iff} \ \models_N \phi^\circ \qquad\qquad\qquad\qquad [\text{Def. of classical validity}]$$

$$\square$$

Thus, robust validity of ϕ over discrete time can be reduced to classical validity of ϕ° over discrete time.

Theorem 2 (Decidability of robust validity over discrete time). *It is decidable whether a DC formula ϕ with integer constants is robustly valid over discrete time.*

Proof. According to Lemma 10 it suffices to decide classical validity of ϕ° instead. This problem is known to be decidable via a reduction to an emptiness problem of extended regular expressions; see [7] for details. [3] $\qquad\qquad \square$

6.2   Semi-Decidability Over Dense Time

Using the approximation scheme between discrete and dense time exposed in Section 5, above discrete-time decidability result does immediately generalize to a dense-time semi-decision procedure:

Theorem 3 (Semi-decidab. of dense time rob. invalidity). *If ϕ contains rational constants only then it is semi-decidable whether $\mathcal{M}_{\mathbb{R} \geq 0}[\![\phi]\!] < 0$, i.e. whether ϕ is robustly invalid over real-valued time.*

Proof. W.l.o.g. we may assume that ϕ contains integer constants only[4] such that $\mathcal{M}_N[\![\phi._n]\!] \in \mathbb{Z}$ for each $n \in \mathbb{N}$. According to Corollaries 1 and 2, inequation $\mathcal{M}_{\mathbb{R} \geq 0}[\![\phi]\!] < 0$ holds iff $\mathcal{M}_{\frac{1}{n} \cdot N}[\![\phi]\!] < -\frac{depth(\phi)}{2n}$ for some $n \in \mathbb{N} \setminus \{0\}$. However,

$$\mathcal{M}_{\frac{1}{n} \cdot N}[\![\phi]\!] < -\frac{depth(\phi)}{2n}$$

$$\text{iff} \ \mathcal{M}_N[\![\phi._n]\!] < -\frac{depth(\phi)}{2} \qquad\qquad\qquad\qquad [\text{Lemma 4}]$$

---

[3] Strictly speaking, we need to extend the procedure from reference [7] to handle arbitrary integer constants in duration inequations $\int S \sim k$, as [7] deals with non-negative constants only. However, given that durations $\int S$ can only yield non-negative values, this extension is straightforward: validity of an arbitrary formula ϕ is equivalent to validity of its variant ϕ_N, where ϕ_N is derived from ϕ by replacing each occurrence of $\int S \geq k$ or $\int S > k$ with $k < 0$ by $\int S \geq 0$.

[4] If ϕ contains non-integer rational constants then we can use $\phi._d$, with d being a common denominator of all constants in ϕ, instead. According to Lemma 4, the formulae ϕ and $\phi._d$ are equivalent wrt. robust validity over dense time.

iff $\mathcal{M}_\mathbb{N}[\![\phi.n]\!] + 1 \leq - \left\lfloor \dfrac{depth(\phi)}{2} \right\rfloor$ $\qquad\qquad$ $[\mathcal{M}_\mathbb{N}[\![\phi.n]\!] \in \mathbb{Z}]$

iff $\mathcal{M}_\mathbb{N}[\![(\phi.n)_{+\left(1+\lfloor \frac{depth(\phi)}{2} \rfloor\right)}]\!] \leq 0$ $\qquad\qquad$ [Lemma 4]

iff $(\phi.n)_{+\left(1+\lfloor \frac{depth(\phi)}{2} \rfloor\right)}$ is not robustly valid over discrete time.

$\qquad\qquad\qquad\qquad\qquad\qquad\qquad\qquad\qquad\qquad$ [Def. of robust validity]

The latter is decidable according to Theorem 2. Hence, in order to semi-decide whether ϕ is robustly invalid over real-valued time, it suffices to decide robust validity of $(\phi.n)_{+\left(1+\lfloor \frac{depth(\phi)}{2} \rfloor\right)}$ over discrete time for successively larger $n \in \mathbb{N}\backslash\{0\}$ until an invalid instance is found. $\qquad\qquad\qquad\qquad\qquad\qquad\qquad\qquad$ $\square$

7 Discussion

We have developed the concept of robust interpretation for the interval temporal logic Duration Calculus, and we have shown an equivalence result relating robust interpretation to a multi-valued semantics, where real numbers is used as semantic domain and Lipschitz continuous functions are associated with the operators of Duration Calculus.

The multi-valued semantics provides insight concerning robustness of the formula, as the meaning of a formula describes how much the constants in the formula may be varied without changing the truth value of the formula. Furthermore, this semantics was shown to provide a nice framework for studying the relationship between different time domains.

Based on the multi-valued semantics, we have studied how a real-time semantics of Duration Calculus can be approximated by a discrete-time semantics. This extends dicrete-time approximation, as suggested by Chakravorty and Pandya [2], to an interval-based temporal logic featuring accumulated durations. In our setting, an asymptotically tight upper-bound approximation constitutes the basis for a semi-decision procedure. A similar lower-bound approximation would give a decidability result. Unfortunately we do not have a corresponding lower-bound approximation result yet, although it is likely that such do at least hold for those fragments of Duration Calculus, where chop is confined to occur in only one polarity (i.e., either in only positive or in only negative contexts).

Acknowledgements. The authors would like to thank Stefan Ratschan for his detailed comments on an earlier draft of this paper. Work of the first author was partly supported by the German Research Council (DFG) as part of the Transregional Collaborative Research Center "Automatic Verification and Analysis of Complex Systems" (SFB/TR 14 AVACS, www.avacs.org).

References

1. Eugene Asarin and Ahmed Bouajjani. Perturbed turing machines and hybrid systems. In *Proceedings of the Sixteenth Annual IEEE Symposium on Logic in Computer Science (LICS 2001)*. IEEE, 2001.

2. G. Chakravorty and P. K. Pandya. Digitizing Interval Duration Logic. In *Proceedings of CAV 2003*, LNCS 2725, pages 167–179, Springer-Verlag 2003.
3. Martin Fränzle. Analysis of hybrid systems: An ounce of realism can save an infinity of states. In Jörg Flum and Mario Rodríguez-Artalejo, editors, *Computer Science Logic (CSL'99)*, LNCS 1683, pages 126–140. Springer-Verlag, 1999.
4. Martin Fränzle. What will be eventually true of polynomial hybrid automata. In Naoki Kobayashi and Benjamin C. Pierce, editors, *Theoretical Aspects of Computer Software (TACS 2001)*, LNCS 2215, pages 340–359. Springer-Verlag, 2001.
5. Martin Fränzle and Michael R. Hansen. A Robust Interpretation of Duration Calculus (Extended abstract). In Paul Pettersson and Wang Yi, editors, *Nordic Workshop on Programming Theory*, Technical report 2004-041, Department of Information Technology, Uppsala University, pages 83–85, 2004.
6. Vineet Gupta, Thomas A. Henzinger, and Radha Jagadeesan. Robust timed automata. In Oded Maler, editor, *Proceedings of the First International Workshop on Hybrid and Real-Time Systems (HART 97)*, LNCS 1201, pages 331–345. Springer-Verlag, 1997.
7. Michael R. Hansen. Model-checking discrete duration calculus. *Formal Aspects of Computing*, 6(6A):826–845, 1994.
8. Anuj Puri. Dynamical properties of timed automata. In Ravn and Rischel [12], pages 210–227.
9. Stefan Ratschan. Continuous first-order constraint satisfaction. In J. Calmet, B. Benhamou, O. Caprotti, L. Henocque, and V. Sorge, editors, *Artificial Intelligence, Automated Reasoning, and Symbolic Computation*, LNCS 2385, pages 181–195. Springer, 2002.
10. Stefan Ratschan. Quantified constraints under perturbations. *Journal of Symbolic Computation*, 33(4):493–505, 2002.
11. Stefan Ratschan. Search heuristics for box decomposition methods. *Journal of Global Optimization*, 24(1):51–60, 2002.
12. A. P. Ravn and H. Rischel, editors. *Formal Techniques in Real-Time and Fault-Tolerant Systems (FTRTFT'98)*, LNCS 1486, Springer-Verlag, 1998.
13. Anders P. Ravn, Hans Rischel, and Kirsten M. Hansen. Specifying and verifying requirements of real-time systems. *IEEE Transactions on Software Engineering*, 19(1):41–55, January 1993.
14. Alfred Tarski. A decision method for elementary algebra and geometry. RAND Corporation, Santa Monica, Calif., 1948.
15. Zhou Chaochen and Michael R. Hansen. *Duration Calculus — A Formal Approach to Real-Time Systems*. EATCS monographs on theoretical computer science. Springer-Verlag, 2004.
16. Zhou Chaochen, Michael R. Hansen, and Peter Sestoft. Decidability and undecidability results for duration calculus. In P. Enjalbert, A. Finkel, and K. W. Wagner, editors, *Symposium on Theoretical Aspects of Computer Science (STACS 93)*, LNCS 665, pages 58–68. Springer-Verlag, 1993.
17. Zhou Chaochen, C. A. R. Hoare, and Anders P. Ravn. A calculus of durations. *Information Processing Letters*, 40(5):269–276, 1991.

Symbolic Model Checking of Finite Precision Timed Automata[*]

Rongjie Yan[1,2], Guangyuan Li[1], and Zhisong Tang[1]

[1] Laboratory of Computer Science, Institute of Software,
Chinese Academy of Sciences, Beijing 100080, China
[2] Graduate School of the Chinese Academy of Sciences,
Beijing 100039, China
{yrj, ligy}@ios.ac.cn

Abstract. This paper introduces the notion of finite precision timed automata (FPTAs) and proposes a data structure to represent its symbolic states. To reduce the state space, FPTAs only record the integer values of clock variables together with the order of their most recent resets. We provide constraints under which the reachability checking of a timed automaton can be reduced to that of the corresponding FPTA, and then present an algorithm for reachability analysis. Finally, the paper reports some preliminary experimental results, and analyzes the advantages and disadvantages of the new data structure.

Keywords: Finite precision timed automata, model checking, symbolic methods.

1 Introduction

Timed automata (TAs) [1] provide a formal framework for the automatic analysis and verification of real-time systems, and in the past few years several tools for the model checking of TAs have been developed and used, including Uppaal [20], Kronos [15,11], Red [22,23,24] and Rabbit [9].

State space explosion is likely to be the most serious problem that any model checker has to deal with. Within the model checking community, there were many different attempts to reduce memory consumption and to accelerate the speed of exploration, including symmetry reduction [10,18], partial order reduction [6] and active clock reduction [16] (all based on the structural characteristics of the system being verified), as well as region equivalence partition of state space [1], and the discretization of time models [3,9].

In addition to the approaches mentioned above, many works were based on symbolic representations of the state space. The region equivalence of [1] is the precursor of the symbolic methods in which the state space is covered

---

[*] Supported by 973 Program of China under Grant No. 2002cb312200; and the National Natural Science Foundation of China under Grant Nos. 60273025, 60223005, 60421001.

D.V. Hung and M. Wirsing (Eds.): ICTAC 2005, LNCS 3722, pp. 272–287, 2005.

using regions with the same integer parts of clock values and the ordering of fractional parts. As a result, an infinite state space may then become finite. A zone, based on region equivalence, uses a set of clock difference constraints to represent all the states satisfying these constraints. Currently, most of verifiers, like Uppaal, Kronos, and Red, use zones to represent symbolic states. And there exist different data structures to describe the constraint sets, for example, DBM (difference bound matrices) [5] and BDD-like (binary decision diagrams) [13] data structures. In DBMs, employed by Uppaal and Kronos, a constraint set is expressed as a weighted, directed graph with vertices corresponding to all the clock variables and a zero-vertex 0. In BDD-like data structures, a node of the decision tree represents a clock difference, an edge is labelled with an integral interval, and a node together with an outgoing edge represents a constraint. Uppaal and Kronos implemented such data structures too [4,12].

Discrete timed automata [2] may achieve higher efficiency in analysis and verification due to having fewer states, but they are not suitable to describe asynchronous systems. On the other hand, timed automata with continuous semantics [1] are appropriate to both synchronous and asynchronous systems, but the complexity remains very high. To apply the mature techniques in discrete time models to improve the efficiency of model checking, we try to discretize the continuous time.

The present paper introduces a finite precision timed automaton (FPTA) together with a data structure, different from DBMs and BDDs, for a symbolic representation of the state space (note that *Finite precision* means that the clocks have integral valuations). It can be shown that the reachability problem of TA may be reduced to that of the corresponding FPTA under certain constraints (see Theorm 1). The paper also develops a reachability analysis algorithm for the FPTAs, and shows some initial experimental results.

The paper is organized as follows. In section 2, we briefly recall the definition of TAs and their semantics. In section 3, we introduce FPTAs. In section 4, we discuss the reachability problem equivalence for the TAs and FPTAs. In section 5, we present the new symbolic data structure and the reachability analysis algorithm for the FPTAs. In section 6, we give some experiment results. In the concluding section, we discuss related work.

2   Timed Automata

A timed automaton (TA), proposed by Alur and Dill [1], is a finite state automaton extended with a finite set of real-valued clock variables. Nodes of a TA represent locations, and arcs represent transitions between them. Clock constraints within a node (invariants) restrict the time that can elapse in it. Constraints labelling arcs act as guards for transitions between the nodes.

Definition 1. *(Syntax of Timed Automata). Let X be a finite set of clocks, and $C(X)$ be the clock constraint set over X, given by the syntax:*

$$\phi ::= (x \sim c) \mid \phi_1 \wedge \phi_2 \mid true$$

where $x \in X$, $\sim \in \{<, \leq, >, \geq\}$ *and* $c \in \mathbb{N}^+$ *($\mathbb{N}^+$ is the set of non-negative integers).*

A timed automaton *over* X *is a tuple* $A = \langle L, l_0, \Sigma, X, I, E \rangle$, *where*

- L *is a finite set of locations, and* $l_0 \in L$ *is the initial location,*
- I *is a mapping that labels each location* $l \in L$ *with some constraint in* $C(X)$, *and* $I(l)$ *is called the invariant of* l,
- Σ *is a finite set of synchronization labels, and*
- $E \subseteq L \times C(X) \times \Sigma \times 2^X \times L$ *is the set of transitions.*

A transition $(l, \phi, \sigma, Y, l') \in E$ means that one can move from the location l to l' through a transition labelled with $\sigma \in \Sigma$. Moreover, ϕ the guard must be satisfied by the current clock values, and all the clocks in Y ($Y \subseteq X$) are reset to 0.

A clock valuation is a function $\mu : X \mapsto \mathbb{R}^+$, where $\mathbb{R}^+$ is the set of non-negative reals. μ_X denotes the set of all clock valuations over X. For $t \in \mathbb{R}^+$, $\mu + t$ denotes the clock valuation such that $\mu(x+t) = \mu(x)+t$, for all $x \in X$. For $Y \subseteq X$, $\mu[Y := 0]$ denotes the clock valuation such that $\mu[Y := 0](x) = 0$, for all $x \in Y$ and otherwise $\mu[Y := 0](x) = \mu(x)$. μ satisfies a constraint $\phi \in C(X)$, denoted by $\mu \models \phi$, if ϕ evaluates to *true* under the assignment given by μ.

The continuous semantics of a timed automaton $A = \langle L, l_0, \Sigma, X, I, E \rangle$ over X is defined as a transition system $[\![A]\!]_C = \langle S, s_0, \Sigma \cup \mathbb{R}^+, \rightarrow \rangle$, where $S = L \times \mu_X$; $s_0 = (l_0, \mu_0)$ is the initial state where $\mu_0(x) = 0$ for all $x \in X$; and the transition relation $\rightarrow$ comprises two kinds of moves:

- delay transition: $(l, \mu) \xrightarrow{\delta} (l, \mu+\delta)$, if $\delta \in \mathbb{R}^+$ and $\mu \models I(l)$ and $\mu + \delta \models I(l)$;
- discrete transition: $(l, \mu) \xrightarrow{\sigma} (l', \mu[Y := 0])$, if $(l, \phi, \sigma, Y, l') \in E$ and $\mu \models \phi$ and $\mu[Y := 0] \models I(l')$.

In the transition system of $A = \langle L, l_0, \Sigma, X, I, E \rangle$, for a state $s_k = (l, \mu)$ where $l \in L$, if there exists a transition sequence such that $s_0 \xrightarrow{\alpha_0} s_1 \xrightarrow{\alpha_1} \cdots \xrightarrow{\alpha_{k-1}} s_k$, then s_k is called reachable in the continuous semantics of A where $\alpha_i \in \Sigma \cup \mathbb{R}^+$. Given a location l and a clock constraint ϕ, if there exists a reachable state (l, μ) such that $\mu \models \phi$, then (l, ϕ) is called reachable in A.

3   Finite Precision Timed Automata

The syntax of FPTAs is the same as that of TAs. The feature that differentiates an FPTA from a discrete time TA is that it can distinguish the ordering of clock resets, by the introduction of an *order*. To define the semantics of FPTAs, we introduce the notion of *order* firstly.

Definition 2. *(Order). An order over X is a mapping $o : X \mapsto \mathbb{N}^+$, and the set of all such mappings is denoted by o_X. For $x_1, x_2 \in X$ with $o(x_1) < o(x_2)$, we say that the order of x_1 is less than that of x_2.*

Since different order valuations may represent the same ordering relationship between the clocks, we introduce order normalization.

Definition 3. *(Order Normalization).*

1. *An order o over X is normalized if the image $o(X)$ is an initial interval of $\mathbb{N}^+$.*
2. *Two orders, o and o', are equivalent if $o(x) \leq o(y)$ iff $o'(x) \leq o'(y)$, for all $x, y \in X$.*
3. *For each order o, we denote by $norm(o)$ the unique normalized order which is equivalent to o.*

For example, the normalization of the order $o_1 = (1, 0, 3, 4, 3)$ is $norm(o_1) = (1, 0, 2, 3, 2)$.

For an FPTA $A = \langle L, l_0, \Sigma, X, I, E \rangle$, a clock valuation is a mapping $v : X \mapsto \mathbb{N}^+$, and the set of all such valuations is denoted by v_X. A state of A is $s = (l, (v, o))$ where $l \in L$, $v \in v_X$ is a clock valuation, $o \in o_X$ is a normalized order, and (v, o) is the clock information of the state. For a state $s = (l, (v, o))$ and a constraint $\phi \in C(X)$, if $v \models \phi$, we say that s satisfies (l, ϕ), denoted by $s \models (l, \phi)$.

The semantics of A is the transition system $[\![A]\!]_{FP} = \langle S, s_0, \Sigma, \rightarrow \rangle$, where $S = L \times (v_X \times o_X)$; $s_0 = (l_0, (v_0, o_0))$ is the initial state where $v_0(x) = o_0(x) = 0$ for all $x \in X$; and the transition relation $\rightarrow$ comprises two kinds of moves:

- delay transition: $(l, (v, o)) \xrightarrow{\epsilon} (l, (v, o) \oplus k)$ (or simply $(l, (v, o)) \rightarrow (l, (v, o) \oplus k)$), if $k \in \mathbb{N}^+$ and $(v, o) \oplus k \models I(l)$, where $((v, o) \oplus k)(x) = (v(x) + (o(x) + k) \text{ div } m, (o(x) + k) \bmod m)$ for $m = 1 + \max o(X)$;
- discrete transition: $(l, (v, o)) \xrightarrow{\sigma} (l', (v', o'))$, if there exists $(l, \phi, \sigma, Y, l') \in E$ such that $v \models \phi$ and $v' \models I(l')$ and $(v', o') = reset((v, o), Y)$ where $reset((v, o), Y) = (v[Y := 0], norm((o + 1)[Y := 0]))$ and for each $x \in X$:

$$v[Y := 0](x) = \begin{cases} 0 & \text{if } x \in Y \\ v(x) & \text{if } x \in X - Y, \end{cases}$$

$$(o + 1)[Y := 0](x) = \begin{cases} 0 & \text{if } x \in Y \\ o(x) + 1 & \text{if } x \in X - Y. \end{cases}$$

A run of an FPTA A is an infinite sequence of its discrete and delay transitions:

$$(l_0, (v_0, o_0)) \xrightarrow{\alpha_0} (l_1, (v_1, o_1)) \xrightarrow{\alpha_1} (l_2, (v_2, o_2)) \xrightarrow{\alpha_2} (l_3, (v_3, o_3)) \xrightarrow{\alpha_3} \dots$$

where $\alpha \in \Sigma \cup \{\epsilon\}$.

Here we show one of runs for the FPTA in Figure 1. For convenience, in Figure 1, the discrete transition from l_0 to l_1 is called t_1; the other is called t_2.

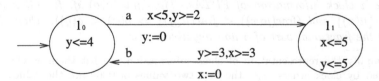

Fig. 1. A simple timed automaton

Example 1. One of the runs for the FPTA in Figure 1 is:[1] $(l_0, 0000) \to (l_0, 1100) \to$ $(l_0, 2200) \xrightarrow{a} (l_1, 2010) \to (l_1, 3001) \to (l_1, 3110) \to (l_1, 4101) \to (l_1, 4210) \to$ $(l_1, 5201) \to (l_1, 5310) \xrightarrow{b} (l_0, 0301) \to \cdots$

Before discrete transitions, all the clock values will increase by one after every time unit and the orders will not change. When the state $(l_0, 2200)$ is generated, the guard of t_1 is satisfied, and its occurrence leads to $(l_1, 2010)$. Now the guard of t_2 is not satisfied, and time elapses in location l_1 on condition that its invariant is satisfied. When $(l_1, 5310)$ is generated, transition t_2 can occur and generate successive states. □

Since safety and bounded liveness properties can be expressed in terms of reachability [8], many model checkers for real-time systems concentrate on the latter. The reachability checker of FPTAs will analyze whether (l, ϕ) is reachable.

Definition 4. *(The Reachable State of FPTAs). Let A be an FPTA. For a state $(l_n, (v_n, o_n))$, if there is a finite state sequence such that*

$$(l_0, (v_0, o_0)) \xrightarrow{\alpha_0} (l_1, (v_1, o_1)) \xrightarrow{\alpha_1} (l_2, (v_2, o_2)) \xrightarrow{\alpha_2} \ldots \xrightarrow{\alpha_{n-1}} (l_n, (v_n, o_n))$$

then $(l_n, (v_n, o_n))$ is called reachable. Given a location l and a clock constraint ϕ, if there exists a reachable state $(l, (v, o))$ in A such that $v \models \phi$, we say that (l, ϕ) is reachable in A.

4   The Relationship Between FPTAs and TAs

In this section, we investigate the relationship between reachability in FPTAs and TAs. We have left proofs of Lemma 1 and 2 to Appendix A.

Definition 5. *(Left Closed and Right Open Timed Automata). A clock constraint ϕ generated by the syntax*

$$\phi ::= x \geq c \mid x < c \mid \phi_1 \wedge \phi_2 \mid true$$

is called left-closed and right-open (lcro-constraint). If all the constraints of a TA are of this kind, we call it an lcro-TA.

With the lcro-constraint ϕ, the clock valuation of TAs $\mu \models \phi$ iff $\lfloor \mu \rfloor \models \phi$ (where $\lfloor \mu \rfloor$ is the mapping which assigns every $x \in X$ an integer $\lfloor \mu(x) \rfloor$). Let A be an lcro-TA, we will investigate the relationship between the continuous semantics $[\![A]\!]_C$ and the finite precision semantics $[\![A]\!]_{FP}$.

Definition 6. *(Relation ▷). Let $\mu : X \mapsto \mathbb{R}^+$ be a clock valuation of TAs, and (v, o) be a clock information of FPTAs. Then $\mu \vartriangleright (v, o)$ if, for all $x, y \in X$, $v(x) = \lfloor \mu(x) \rfloor$ and $(frac(\mu(x)) < frac(\mu(y)) \Rightarrow o(x) < o(y))$, where $frac(r)$ denotes the fractional part of a non-negative real r.*

---

[1] To simplify the representation of clock information, we list them as clock values followed by clock orders, e.g., the first two values of 0000 are the values of clock variable x and y, the last two values are their orders.

Lemma 1. *For an lcro-TA A, if (l, μ) is reachable in $[\![A]\!]_C$, then there exists (v, o) such that $(l, (v, o))$ is reachable in $[\![A]\!]_{FP}$, and $\mu \triangleright (v, o)$.*

Definition 7. *(Relation $\backsimeq$). Let $\mu : X \mapsto \mathbb{R}^+$ be a clock valuation of TAs, and (v, o) be a clock information of FPTAs. Then $\mu \backsimeq (v, o)$ if, for all $x, y \in X$, $v(x) = \lfloor \mu(x) \rfloor$ and $(frac(\mu(x)) < frac(\mu(y)) \Leftrightarrow o(x) < o(y))$.*

Lemma 2. *For an lcro-TA A, if $(l, (v, o))$ is reachable in $[\![A]\!]_{FP}$, then there exists μ such that (l, μ) is reachable in $[\![A]\!]_C$, and $(v, o) \backsimeq \mu$.*

Let $Reach_C(A) = \{(l, \phi) | l \in L, \phi \in C(X)$, and (l, ϕ) is reachable in the continuous semantics$\}$, and $Reach_{FP}(A) = \{(l, \phi) | l \in L, \phi \in C(X)$, and (l, ϕ) is reachable in the finite precision semantics$\}$.

Theorem 1. *Let A be an lcro-TA, ϕ be an lcro-constraint, then $(l, \phi) \in Reach_C(A)$ iff $(l, \phi) \in Reach_{FP}(A)$.*

Proof. "$\Rightarrow$:" If (l, ϕ) is reachable in $[\![A]\!]_C$, then there exists a state (l, μ) such that (l, μ) is reachable in $[\![A]\!]_C$ and $\mu \models \phi$. Followed from the claim of Lemma 1, there exists a state $(l, (v, o))$ such that it is reachable in $[\![A]\!]_{FP}$, and $\mu \triangleright (v, o)$. Therefore, $v \models \phi$ by the Definition 6, then $(l, \phi) \in Reach_{FP}(A)$.

"$\Leftarrow$:" The proof is similar to the above using Lemma 2 and Definition 7. $\square$

In FPTAs, state equivalence is determined by the clock value and its order, which is different from the region equivalence in TAs [1]. The clock information of FPTAs $(v, o) \backsimeq (v', o')$, if they hold the following relation:

- for all $x \in X$, either $v(x) = v'(x)$, or $(v(x) \geq c_x + 1) \wedge (v'(x) \geq c_x + 1$ [2]$)$,
- for all $x \in X, o(x) = o'(x)$

The equivalence classification can ensure the finiteness of the state space. When the clock value of x is equal to or greater than $c_x + 1$, it is recorded as $c_x + 1$, which prevents the infiniteness of the state space. The models proposed in [22,23] are similar to FPTAs, which use integer to record clock values and orders. However, they are based on the continuous semantics.

5   Reachability Analysis of FPTAs

One of the most common properties being checked by the verifiers is the reachability whose analysis is based on the exploration of the graph. There are two kinds of search strategies during state space exploration: forward and backward search. Currently our tool uses the forward search technique.

To relieve the state space explosion problem, verifiers usually use symbolic methods to record set of states. And the key issue is how to represent them. Different from the constraint based symbolic methods, the checker of FPTAs

---

[2] c_x is the maximal constant in clock constraints on x in the automaton.

uses a data structure to describe the state set explicitly, meaning that all the sequences created by time delays are enumerated.

In this section, according to the characteristics of state space generation, we first analyze the features and the representation of a sequence of states created by time delays (called delay sequence). Then, based on the relation of the states generated from a segment of delay sequence by the discrete transition, we propose a data structure to represent the set of states symbolically. Thirdly, we present the symbolic transition systems of FPTAs. Finally, we introduce the algorithm for reachability analysis.

Let us fix for the rest of this section an FPTA $A = \langle L, l_0, \Sigma, X, I, E \rangle$.

5.1   Representation of States in the Delay Sequence

The generation of the state space is started from the initial state $(l_0, (v_0, o_0))$. Whenever allowed by the invariant of l_0, the sequence $(l_0, (v_0, o_0)) \rightarrow (l_0, (v_0, o_0) \oplus 1) \rightarrow \ldots$ can be generated by time delays, where $((v_0, o_0) \oplus i) \models I(l_0), i \geq 0$. Here we introduce a symbolic representation for this kind of sequence.

Definition 8. *(Symbolic Representation of Delay Sequence).*

- *Let* $(l, (v, o), k)$ *denote the set of states* $\{(l, (v, o) \oplus 0), (l, (v, o) \oplus 1), \ldots, (l, (v, o) \oplus (k-1))\}$, *where* $k \in \mathbb{N}^{>0}$ *($\mathbb{N}^{>0}$ is the set of positive integers).*
- *Let* $(l, (v, o), \infty)$ *denote the set of states* $\{(l, (v, o) \oplus 0), (l, (v, o) \oplus 1), \ldots\}$. *Based on the equivalence relation, for all* $x \in X$, *all the clock valuations greater than* $c_x + 1$ *are treated as* $c_x + 1$. *Therefore, though time can progress infinitely, the number of states in the delay sequence is finite.*

We say that $(l, (v, o), k)$ *is a delay sequence(DS) generated by delay transitions from the state* $(l, (v, o))$, *where* $k \in \mathbb{N}^{>0} \cup \{\infty\}$.

In a delay sequence, when some states satisfy the guard of a transition, the corresponding discrete transition can be taken, leading to the new states. From these new states, the execution of delay or discrete transitions will be continued. So it is necessary to judge which state will satisfy the guard of the discrete transition. To compare every state with the guard is time-consuming. In this paper, we can get a set of such states rapidly according to the form of inequations in the guards.

According to the Definition 1, the guard is the conjunction of the inequations of the form $x \sim c, \sim \in \{<, \leq, >, \geq\}$. The inequations in the forms of $x > c$ and $x \geq c$ determine the minimum value the clock variable should be to switch to other locations; and inequations in the forms of $x < c$ and $x \leq c$ determine the maximal clock value to take discrete actions. By computing the sets of states satisfying the two kinds of constraints, we can get those that satisfy the guard of the discrete transition. Then the successors can be generated.

Next, we will generalize the features of the delay sequence. For example, the delay sequence formed from the initial state in Figure 1 is

$$(l_0, 0000, 5) = \{(l_0, 0000), (l_0, 1100), (l_0, 2200), (l_0, 3300), (l_0, 4400)\}.$$

With the increase of i, we can compute every state in the sequence respectively with $(v, o) \oplus i, 0 \le i < 5$. Moreover, there is an ordering between the clock information of the states. Because of the convex nature of the constraints, if we find the state with the maximal clock value satisfying the constraints in the form of $x < c$ or $x \le c$, all its pre-states in the delay sequence will meet the constraints too. Similarly, when we get the state with the minimum clock value satisfying the constraints in the form of $x > c$ or $x \ge c$, all its subsequent states in the delay sequence will satisfy this kind of constraints. The following definition describes how to determine the delay sequence restricted by constraints.

To facilitate the computation, let $c \in \mathbb{N}^+$, we assume that $\infty - c = \infty$, and $\infty > c$.

Definition 9. *(Constrained Delay Sequence). Let $(l, (v, o), k)$ be a delay sequence, and $\phi \in C(X)$ be the constraint, the constrained delay sequence $(l, (v, o), k)|_\phi$ is defined recursively as follows.*

1. *if ϕ is true, $(l, (v, o), k)|_\phi$ is $(l, (v, o), k)$.*
2. *if ϕ is $(x \le c)$, let $l_c = \min\{(c - v(x)) * m + m - o(x), k\}$ where $m = 1 + \max o(X)$, then $(l, (v, o), k)|_{x \le c}$ is $(l, (v, o), l_c)$.*
3. *if ϕ is $(x \ge c)$, let $d = (c - v(x)) * m - o(x)$, if $0 \le d < k$, let $(v', o') = (v, o) \oplus d, g_c = k - d$, then $(l, (v, o), k)|_{x \ge c}$ is $(l, (v', o'), g_c)$. If $d \ge k$, then $(l, (v, o), k)|_{x \ge c}$ is empty. When $v(x) \ge c$, the original sequence keeps unchanged.*
4. *if $\phi = \phi_1 \wedge \phi_2$, $(l, (v, o), k)|_\phi$ is $((l, (v, o), k)|_{\phi_1})|_{\phi_2}$.*

Now let us consider the model in Figure 1 again, to interpret the function of the above computation in the state space generation process.

Example 2. Computation on the Constrained Delay Sequence.

Here, we try to determine the states capable of switching to l_1 by discrete transition t_1, with the guard $x < 5$ and $y \ge 2$. Since $I(l_0)$ is $y \le 4$, the delay sequence started from the initial state is $(l_0, 0000, 5)$. First, the result of constrained delay sequence by $x < 5$ is $(l_0, 0000, 5)$; $(l_0, 2200, 3)$ is the result of $(l_0, 0000, 5)$ being constrained by $y \ge 2$, whose states can take discrete transition t_1. □

To check whether $(v_1, o_1) \in ((v, o), k)$, we can judge whether there exists k' such that $(v, o) \oplus k' = (v_1, o_1)$ and $k' < k$, where $k' = \max\{(v_1(x) - v(x)) * m + o_1(x) - o(x)|x \in X$ and $v_1(x) \le c_x\}$. Let $(l, (v, o), k)$ and $(l, (v_1, o_1), k_1)$ be two sets of states, if $(v, o) \in ((v_1, o_1), k_1)$ or $(v_1, o_1) \in ((v, o), k)$, then the intersection of the two sets is not empty.

5.2   The Formation of Symbolic States

In the last subsection we have analyzed the features and the representation of the delay sequence. If we use it as the symbolic method to record the state space, the number of the symbolic states is still larger. However, if we can organize them into a coarser data structure, based on some relationship between these delay sequences, the number of the symbolic states can be reduced effectively.

In Figure 1, started from the initial state, the segment that can take discrete transition t_1 is $(l_0, 2200, 3) = \{(l_0, 2200), (l_0, 3300), (l_0, 4400)\}$. The occurrence of t_1 leads to the new set $\{(l_1, 2010), (l_1, 3010), (l_1, 4010)\}$. Among the new states, the clock information of y is $(0, 0)$ at every state, and the clock value of x increases monotonically.

Then given a state generated by the discrete transition, we can compute all other new successors from the states in the same delay sequence. Let (v_r, o_r) be the clock information after a discrete transition, where Y is the reset clock set. The clock information of the ith state from (v_r, o_r) is $(v_{ir}, o_{ir}) = ((v_r, o_r) \circledast i) \backslash Y$, where $(((v, o) \circledast i) \backslash Y)(x) =$

$$\begin{cases} (v(x) + (o(x) - 1 + i) \text{ div } m', (o(x) + i - 1) \text{ mod } m' + 1) & \text{if } x \notin Y \text{ and } Y \neq \emptyset \\ (0, 0) & \text{if } x \in Y \text{ and } Y \neq \emptyset \ , \\ (v(x), o(x)) & \text{if } Y = \emptyset \end{cases}$$

and $m' = \max o(X)$.

Definition 10. *(Series of Delay Sequences). Let $(l, (v, o))$ be a state, $\theta \in \mathbb{N}^{>0}$ and $Y \subseteq X$, we use $(l, (v, o), \theta, Y)$ as the symbolic representation for the set of states $\{(l, (v', o')) | (v', o') = ((v, o) \circledast i) \backslash Y, 0 \leq i < \theta\}$. We call this representation the series of delay sequence (SDS). When $Y = \emptyset$, $(l, (v, o), \theta, Y)$ is $(l, (v, o), 1, \emptyset)$.*

For instance, $(l_1, 2010, 3, \{y\}) = \{(l_1, 2010), (l_1, 3010), (l_1, 4010)\}$ is a set of states in the example of Figure 1.

A symbolic state consists of a set of so-called start states, which are generated from states in the same delay sequence by a discrete transition. And new delay sequences will be generated from these start states.

In certain cases, some start states of the symbolic state may not satisfy the invariant of the new location. So we should determine the start states that meet the new invariant.

Definition 11. *(Constrained Symbolic State by Invariants $(l', (v, o), \theta, Y) \lfloor_{I(l')}$).* *Let $(l', (v, o), \theta, Y)$ be a symbolic state, and $\phi = I(l')$ be the invariant of l'.*

- *if $Y = \emptyset$, assume that $(l', (v, o), \infty) |_\phi = (l', (v', o'), g)$, then $(l', (v, o), \theta, Y) \lfloor_\phi$ is $(l', (v', o'), 1, \emptyset)$.*
- *if $Y \neq \emptyset$.*
  - *if ϕ is true, then $(l', (v, o), \theta, Y) \lfloor_\phi$ is $(l', (v, o), \theta, Y)$.*
  - *if ϕ is $x \leq c$, and $x \notin Y$, let $\theta' = min\{\theta, (c - v(x)) * m' + m' - o(x) + 1\}$, then $(l', (v, o), \theta, Y) \lfloor_{x \leq c}$ is $(l', (v, o), \theta', Y)$.*
  - *if ϕ is $x \geq c$, and $x \notin Y$, let $d = (c - v(x)) * m' + 1 - o(x)$. If $0 \leq d < \theta'$, let $(v', o') = ((v, o) \circledast d) \backslash Y, \theta'' = \theta' - d$, then $(l', (v, o), \theta', Y) \lfloor_{x \geq c}$ is $(l', (v', o'), \theta'', Y)$. If $d \geq \theta'$, $(l', (v, o), \theta', Y) \lfloor_{x \geq c}$ is empty.*
  - *if $\phi = \phi_1 \wedge \phi_2$, then $(l', (v, o), \theta, Y) \lfloor_\phi$ is $((l', (v, o), \theta, Y) \lfloor_{\phi_1}) \lfloor_{\phi_2}$.*

The inclusion relation between the series of delay sequences can be judged quickly, which is similar to the judgement between delay sequences.

Let $(l, (v_1, o_1)), (l, (v_2, o_2))$ be two states which are generated from a delay sequence by the same discrete transition (with reset clock set $Y \neq \emptyset$), and $v_1(x) \leq v_2(x)$ for all $x \in X$. To simplify the representation, we introduce a function $len((v_1, o_1), (v_2, o_2), Y) =$

$$\begin{cases} \max\{(v_2(x) - v_1(x)) * m' + o_2(x) - o_1(x)|x \in Z\} & \text{if } Z \neq \emptyset \\ \max\{(c_x - v_1(x)) * m' + m' - o_1(x)|x \in X - Y\} & \text{if } Z = \emptyset \end{cases},$$

where $Z = \{x|v_2(x) \leq c_x, \text{and } x \in X - Y\}, m' = \max o_1(X)$.

Let $(l, (v, o), k)$ be a delay sequence meeting the guards of a discrete transition (l, ϕ, σ, Y, l'). Then the successor generated from $(l, (v, o), k)$ with transition (l, ϕ, σ, Y, l') is $(l', (v_r, o_r), \theta, Y)$, where

- $(v_r, o_r) = reset((v, o), Y)$,
- $\theta = dist((v, o), k, Y)$,
- $dist((v, o), k, Y) =$

$$\begin{cases} 1 & \text{if } Y = \emptyset \text{ or } Y = X \\ len((v_r, o_r), reset((v, o) \oplus (k - 1), Y)) + 1 & \text{else if } k \neq \infty \\ \max\{(c_x - v_r(x) + 1) * m' - o_r(x)|x \in X - Y\} + 1 & \text{else} \end{cases},$$

- $m' = \max o_r(X)$.

For example, when the discrete transition t_1 in Figure 1 is taken, the delay sequence $(l_0, 2200, 3)$ will generate the new symbolic state $(l_1, 2010, 3, \{y\})$.

5.3   The Symbolic Transition Systems of FPTAs

The symbolic transition system of FPTA $A = \langle L, l_0, \Sigma, X, I, E \rangle$ is $\langle S, s_0, \Sigma, \leadsto \rangle$. $S = L \times D$ is the set of symbolic states where $D = \{((v, o), \theta, Y)|(v, o) \in (v_X \times o_X), Y \subseteq X, \theta \in \mathbb{N}^{>0}\}$. $s_0 = (l_0, D_0)$ is the initial symbolic state, where $l_0 \in L, D_0 = ((v_0, o_0), 1, \emptyset) \in D$ is the initial symbolic clock information. The symbolic transition relation $\leadsto$ is defined as follows, which explains how the symbolic successor is created.

Definition 12. *(Symbolic Transition Relation $\leadsto$). Let $(l, D), (l', D') \in L \times D$ be two symbolic states, where $D = ((v, o), \theta, Y), D' = ((v', o'), \theta', Y')$. We say $((l, D), (l', D')) \in \leadsto$, if there exist an integer $i \in \{0, 1, 2, \ldots, \theta - 1\}$ and a transition $e = (l, \phi, \alpha, Y', l') \in E$, such that $((v', o'), \theta', Y') = ((v_r, o_r), \theta_r, Y') \downharpoonright_{I(l')}$, where*

- $(v_r, o_r) = reset((v'', o''), Y')$,
- $\theta_r = dist((v'', o''), g_\phi, Y'),$ *and*
- $((v'', o''), g_\phi) = (((v, o) \circledast i) \setminus Y, \infty)|_{I(l) \wedge \phi}.$

With the state equivalent relation in FPTAs, the symbolic semantics results in a finite symbolic state space.

Example 3. The Generation of Symbolic States of the Model in Figure 1.

The initial symbolic state is $s_0 = (l_0, 0000, 1, \emptyset)$. Then it just has one delay sequence $(l_0, 0000, 5)$, in which some states can take discrete transition t_1. The occurrence of t_1 leads to the symbolic state $s_1 = (l_1, 2010, 3, \{y\})$. Time can elapse in l_1 when its invariant is satisfied. Among the states resulting from time delays, only the state $(l_1, 5310)$ created from the start state $(l_1, 2010)$ can meet the guard of t_2. So the next symbolic state is $s_2 = (l_0, 0301, 1, \{x\}) \ldots$. $\square$

5.4   Algorithms for Reachability Analysis

In this subsection we firstly present a reachability analysis algorithm. Then we list the generated symbolic states during the state space exploration in the example of Figure 1.

During the forward search of the state space, we use two lists W and P to record the states waiting for checking and being examined respectively. Another function of P is to avoid revisiting parts of the state space. W and P are empty in the beginning. Then the initial symbolic state is pushed into W. In every repetition, if the popped symbolic state from W has not been examined, the satisfiability of (l, ϕ) is checked. If it is satisfied, the whole process is completed. Otherwise, it is stored in P, and then successors are generated and pushed into W. The process can be described as Algorithm 1.

Algorithm 1 ReachabilityAnalysis

SDS: wa;
List of State: $Succ$;
List of SDS:$P, W := \emptyset$;
$wa := (l_0, (v_0, o_0), 1, \emptyset)$;
$W := \{wa\}$;
while $W \neq \emptyset$ **do**
　get wa from W;
　if $wa \notin P$ **then**
　　if Satisfy(wa, l, ϕ) **then**
　　　$return(true)$
　　else
　　　Add(wa, P);
　　　$Succ :=$Unfolding(wa);
　　　CreateSuccessive$(Succ)$
　　end if
　end if
end while

In Algorithm 1, *Satisfy* is *true* if there exists a state s in a delay sequence of a start state in wa such that $s \models (l, \phi)$. *Succ* stores the start states unfolded from the symbolic state by the *unfolding* function, which computes all the start states meeting the invariant of the current location. *CreateSuccessive* computes the successive symbolic states from the start states in $Succ$. If the new symbolic states have no inclusion relation with the states in P, they are pushed into W.

Here we use the example in Figure 1 to explain how the whole state space is generated. The steps to compute the symbolic states can refer to the definitions and examples above. We just list the symbolic states in P and W during the reachability analysis process in Table 1.

Table 1. Symbolic states in W and P

Step	W	P
1	$\{(l_0, 0000, 1, \emptyset)\}$	$\{\}$
2	$\{(l_1, 2010, 3, \{y\})\}$	$\{(l_0, 0000, 1, \emptyset)$
3	$\{(l_0, 0301, 1, \{x\})\}$	$\{(l_0, 0000, 1, \emptyset), (l_1, 2010, 3, \{y\})$
4	$\{(l_1, 0010, 2, \{y\})\}$	$\{(l_0, 0000, 1, \emptyset), (l_1, 2010, 3, \{y\}), (l_0, 0301, 1, \{x\})\}$
5	$\{(l_0, 0401, 1, \{x\})\}$	$\{(l_0, 0000, 1, \emptyset), (l_1, 2010, 3, \{y\}), (l_0, 0301, 2, \{x\}), (l_1, 0010, 2, \{y\})\}$
6	$\{\}$	$\{(l_0, 0000, 1, \emptyset), (l_1, 2010, 3, \{y\}), (l_0, 0301, 2, \{x\}), (l_1, 0010, 2, \{y\})\}$

In the 5th step of Table 1, the successor of $(l_1, 0010, 2, \{y\})$ is $(l_0, 0301, 2, \{x\})$. However, it includes the state $(l_0, 0301, 1, \{x\})$ in P. After P is updated, the unexamined part $(l_0, 0401, 1, \{x\})$ is pushed into W. The generated state in step 6 is already in P, so W is empty. Then the whole state space is generated.

6   Experiment

We have implemented a prototype to support the verification of real-time systems with multi-processes, synchronizations, and broadcasts. The tool is available at http://lcs.ios.ac.cn/~xyz/FPTA. Due to the page limit, we only use Fischer's mutual exclusive protocol [19] (see Figure 2) as the example. We compare the results with those of Uppaal 3.4.6 in various assignments of a and b, when the whole state space is created in breadth first search strategy. The environment is Intel P4 2.60GHz Dell PC with 512MB memory. In Table 2, we list the time consumption in seconds and the number of generated symbolic states (zones or SDSs) in the passed list. "-" indicates that the verification did not terminate within 600 seconds, and "N/A" stands for "not available".

The time and space consumption of Uppaal will not be quite different with various assignments of a and b. However, our prototype may be sensitive to the

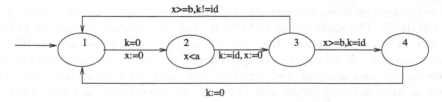

Fig. 2. Fischer's mutual exclusive protocol

Table 2. Results with Fischer's mutual exclusive protocol

no	Uppaal(a=2,b=4)		FPTA(a=2,b=4)		FPTA(a=9,b=19)	
	Time(s)	Zones	Time(s)	SDSs	Time(s)	SDSs
2	0.12	21	0	23	0.02	23
3	0.12	145	0.06	271	0.22	413
4	0.14	1073	0.61	1907	69.24	15185
5	1.13	8581	27.13	27155	-	N/A
6	41.09	75385	-	497980	-	N/A

maximal constant of the constraints. And with the increasing number of processes or clock variables, the performance of FPTA checker is not so well as that of Uppaal, which has employed many methods to improve the efficiency of model checking [17]. Currently, except for the active clock reduction method [16], our prototype does not use other techniques to reduce the state space, or to compress the data yet. From this point of view, there is a great gap between the prototype and Uppaal. Though there are lots of work to be done, the discretization of FPTA is still a promising attempt, based on the preliminary results.

7   Related Work and Conclusion

Though FPTAs have integer clock valuations, they are different from the discrete time models, which do not concern about the ordering of events in a time unit. The model in [21] uses a global clock as the reference. The ordering of events happened in one time unit is distinguishable. But when the global clock reaches an integer point, all clock values will increase by 1. Then the ordering information disappears. FPTAs can keep the ordering until the next reset happens. The model in [14] uses integer clock valuations too. In its model, if no clock is reset in a discrete transition, all clock values will increase by 1. Otherwise, only reset clocks will be set to 0, and others will not change.

As to the data structures, recording time constraints in a DBM can reduce the sensitivity to the maximal constant of clock constraints. However, it can only express convex zones, and is not suitable for the data sharing. The BDD-like structures, like CDDs [4], REDs [22,23], and CRDs [24], can express non-convex zones, and are easy to share the existed data. But the ordering between variables will affect the memory consumption greatly. An SDS enumerates all the delay sequences in the state space, which is different from the structures based on the constraints. Compared with DBMs, memory consumption is low in SDSs. And all operations on SDSs are very simple with linear complexity, lower than that of DBMs [7]. The shortcoming of SDSs is that the number of states described by one SDS may be smaller than that by a DBM. Compared with BDD-like data structures, SDSs avoid state space explosion caused by the inappropriate ordering between processes and variables. And they need not consider the normalization of different forms. But SDSs are sensitive to the number of clocks variables.

Based on the discussion, our future work will be as follows. Firstly, the performance of the prototype must be improved and more industrial examples should be carried out. Then the research on the features of FPTAs will be continued. Finally, the data structure needs to be adjusted to facilitate the data sharing, and to reduce the sensitivity to the number of clock variables and the maximal constant. SDSs are just an attempt as one of data structures of FPTAs, we will apply more mature techniques in discrete time models such as BDD data structure in the checker.

Acknowledgements. Thanks to Maciej Koutny for suggestions not only to the English but also to some technical content, and Yubo Xu and Chunming Liu for the implementation of the prototype. We also thank the anonymous referees for their helpful criticisms, comments, and suggestions.

References

1. Alur, R., Dill, D.L.: A Theory of Timed Automata. Theoretical Computer Science 126(2), (1994) 183-235
2. Alur, R., Henzinger, T.A.: A Really Temproal Logic. IEEE FOCS (1989) 164-169
3. Asarin, E., Bozga, M., Kerbrat, A., Maler, O., Pnueli, A., Rasse, A.: Data-Structures for the Verification of Timed Automata. In Proceedings of the International Workshop on Hybrid and Real-Time Systems, LNCS 1201 (1997) 346-360
4. Behrmann, G., Larsen, K.G., Weise, C., Wang, Y., Pearson, J.: Efficient Timed Reachability Analysis Using Clock Difference Diagrams. CAV (1999) 341-353
5. Bellman, R.: Dynamic Programming. Princeton University Press (1957)
6. Bengtsson, J., Jonsson, B., Lilius, J., Wang, Y.: Partial Order Reductions for Timed System. CONCUR (1998) 485-500
7. Bengtsson, J., Wang,Y.: Timed Automata: Semantics, Algorithms and Tools. LNCS 3098 (2004) 87-124
8. Berard, B., Bidoit, M., Finkel, A., Laroussinie, F., Petit, A., Petrucci, L., Schnoebelen, P.: Systems and Software Verification: Model-Checking Techniques and Tools. Springer (2001)
9. Beyer, D., Lewerentz, C., Noack, A.: Rabbit: A Tool for BDD-based Verification of Real-Time Systems. CAV (2003) 122-125
10. Bosnacki, D., Dams, D., Holenderski, L.: A Heuristic for Symmetry Reductions with Scalarsets. LNCS 2021, FME (2001) 518-533
11. Bozga, M., Daws, C., Maler, O., Olivero, A., Tripakis, S., Yovine, S.: Kronos: a Model-Checking Tool for Real-Time Systems. LNCS 1427, CAV (1998) 298-302
12. Bozga, M., Maler, O., Pnueli, A., Yovine, S.: Some Progress in the Symbolic Verification of Timed Automata. LNCS 1254, CAV (1997) 179-190
13. Bryant, R.: Graph-based Algorithms for Boolean Function Manipulation. IEEE Transactions on Computers, 35(8) (1986) 677-691
14. Dang, Z., Ibarra, O.H., Bultan, T., Kemmerer, R.A., Su, J.: Binary Reachability Analysis of Discrete Pushdown Timed Automata. LNCS 1855, CAV (2000) 69-84
15. Daws, C., Olivero, A., Tripakis, S., Yovine, S.: The tool KRONOS. Hybrid Systems III, LNCS 1066 (1996) 208-219
16. Daws, C., Yovine, S.: Reducing the Number of Clock Variables of Timed Automata. IEEE RTSS (1996) 73-81

17. Gerd, B., Johan, B., Alexandre, D., Larsen, K.G., Paul, P., Wang, Y.: UPPAAL Implementation Secrets. FTRTFT (2002) 3-22
18. Hendriks, M., Behrmann, G., Larsen, K.G., Vaandrager, F.: Adding Symmetry Reduction to Uppaal. FORMATS (2003) 46-59
19. Lamport, L.: A Fast Mutual Exclusion Algorithm. ACM Transactions on Computer Systems, 5(1), (1987) 1-11
20. Larsen, K.G., Pettersson, P., Wang, Y.: UPPAAL in a Nutshell. International Journal on Software Tools for Technology Transfer, 1(1/2), (1997) 134-152
21. Raskin, J.F., Schoebbens, P.: Real-Time Logics: Fictitious Clock as an Abstraction of Dense Time. LNCS 1217, TACAS (1997) 165-182
22. Wang, F.: Efficient Data Structure for Fully Symbolic Verification of Real-Time Software Systems. TACAS (2000) 157-171
23. Wang, F.: Region Encoding Diagram for Fully Symbolic Verification of Real-Time Systems. COMPSAC (2000) 509-515
24. Wang, F: Efficient Verification of Timed Automata with BDD-like Data-Structures. VMCAI (2003) 189-205
25. Wang, F.: Formal Verification of Timed Systems: A Survery and Perspective. In Proceedings of the IEEE, 92(8), (2004) 1283-1307

A   Proofs of Lemma 1 and 2

A.1   Lemma 1

Proof. According to the definition of transition relations, it suffices to show the following:

- if $\mu \triangleright (v, o)$, then for all $d \in \mathbb{R}^+$, there exists $k \in \mathbb{N}^+$ such that $(\mu + d) \triangleright (v, o) \oplus k$.
- if $\mu_1 \triangleright (v_1, o_1)$ and $(l_1, \mu_1) \xrightarrow{\sigma} (l_2, \mu_2)$, then there exists (v_2, o_2) such that $\mu_2 \triangleright (v_2, o_2)$ and $(l_1, (v_1, o_1)) \xrightarrow{\sigma} (l_2, (v_2, o_2))$.

Firstly, we prove that the states resulting from delay transitions in FPTAs and TAs satisfy the $\triangleright$ relation. Suppose this is not true, and $\mathcal{D}$ is the set of all d such that there is no $k \in \mathbb{N}^+$ such that $(\mu + d) \triangleright (v, o) \oplus k$. Let d_0 be the infimum of $\mathcal{D}$, then $d_0 \in \mathcal{D}$.

Let $Z = \{x \in X \mid \mathrm{frac}(\mu(x) + d_0) = 0\}$, then Z is the set of clocks whose values will become integer after x increased by d_0. If Z is empty, no clocks will be integer when time increased by d_0. Then $(\mu + d_0) \triangleright (v, o)$, contrary to the hypothesis. So Z is nonempty.

Since clock values increased by d_0 will cause the change of fractional parts of clock values, so will the ordering. Let $\delta_2 = \frac{1}{2}\min\{\{1\} \cup \{\mathrm{frac}(\mu(x) + d_0) \mid x \in X - Z\}\}$, then $(\mu + d_0 - \delta_2)$ will not affect the ordering of the fractional parts.

If there exists k_1, such that $(\mu + d_0 - \delta_2) \triangleright (v, o) \oplus k_1$, then let $k_2 = 1 + \max\{o_1(x) - o_1(y) \mid x, y \in Z\}$, where $o_1 = o \oplus k_1$. Therefore, $(\mu + d_0) \triangleright (v, o) \oplus (k_1 + k_2)$, contrary to the fact that $d_0 \in \mathcal{D}$.

It is straightforward to prove the states generated by discrete transitions hold the relation. Let $(v_2, o_2) = \mathrm{reset}((v_1, o_1), Y)$, then $\mu_2 \triangleright (v_2, o_2)$, where Y is the reset clock set in the transition.   □

A.2   Lemma 2

Proof. According to the definition of transition relations, it suffices to show the following:

- if $(v, o) \simeq \mu$, then for all $k \in \mathbb{N}^+$, there exists $d \in \mathbb{R}^+$ such that $(v, o) \oplus k \simeq (\mu + d)$.
- if $(v_1, o_1) \simeq \mu_1$ and $(l_1, (v_1, o_1)) \xrightarrow{\sigma} (l_2, (v_2, o_2))$, then there exists $d \in \mathbb{R}^+$ such that $(v_1, o_1) \simeq (\mu_1 + d)$, $(l_1, \mu_1 + d) \xrightarrow{\sigma} (l_2, \mu_2)$ and $(v_2, o_2) \simeq \mu_2$.

Firstly we prove that the states resulting from delay transitions in FPTAs and TAs satisfy the $\simeq$ relation. Assume this is not true, and $\mathcal{K}$ is the set of all k such that there is no $d \in \mathbb{R}^+$ such that $(v, o) \oplus k \simeq (\mu + d)$. Let k_0 be the least element in $\mathcal{K}$, then $k_0 > 0$ (otherwise $(v, o) \oplus 0 \simeq \mu$, then $k_0 \notin \mathcal{K}$, contrary to the fact that $k_0 \in \mathcal{K}$).

If there exists d_1, such that $(v, o) \oplus (k_0 - 1) \simeq (\mu + d_1)$, then let $d_2 = \min\{1 - \text{frac}(\mu(x) + d_1) \mid x \in X\}$. So after time increased by $d_1 + d_2$, the clock value with the largest fractional part will become integer. Therefore, $(v, o) \oplus (k_0 - 1 + 1) = (v, o) \oplus k_0 \simeq (\mu + d_1 + d_2)$, contrary to the fact that $k_0 \in \mathcal{K}$.

Now we prove the second claim. Let $d = \frac{1}{2} \min\{1 - \text{frac}(\mu(x)) \mid x \in X\}$. Since $\min\{1 - \text{frac}(\mu(x))\}$ is the real number that causes some clock values to become integer, $\mu + d$ will not affect the relative ordering of fractional parts of clock values. So $(v_1, o_1) \simeq (\mu_1 + d)$.

Let $\mu_2 = (\mu_1 + d)[Y := 0]$ where Y is the clock set to be reset, then $(l_1, \mu_1 + d) \xrightarrow{\sigma} (l_2, \mu_2)$ and $(v_2, o_2) \simeq \mu_2$. $\qquad \square$

Covarieties of Coalgebras: Comonads and Coequations

Ranald Clouston and Robert Goldblatt*

Centre for Logic, Language and Computation,
Victoria University of Wellington, New Zealand

Abstract. Coalgebras provide effective models of data structures and state-transition systems. A *virtual covariety* is a class of coalgebras closed under coproducts, images of coalgebraic morphisms, and subcoalgebras defined by split equalisers. A *covariety* has the stronger property of closure under all subcoalgebras, and is *behavioural* if it is closed under domains of morphisms, or equivalently under images of bisimulations. There are many computationally interesting properties that define classes of these kinds.

We identify conditions on the underlying category of a comonad $\mathbb{G}$ which ensure that there is an exact correspondence between (behavioural/virtual) covarieties of $\mathbb{G}$-coalgebras and *subcomonads* of $\mathbb{G}$ defined by comonad morphisms to $\mathbb{G}$ with natural categorical properties. We also relate this analysis to notions of *coequationally defined* classes of coalgebras.

1   Introduction

Coalgebras of functors on the category of sets have proven effective in modelling various computational systems, including data structures (infinite lists, streams, trees), state-based systems (automata, labelled transition systems, process algebras) and classes in object-oriented programming languages [1,2,3,4,5,6]. Consequently, the study of coalgebras has developed as a distinctive theme in the theory of computing over the last decade.

One significant notion is that of a *behavioural covariety*: a class of coalgebras that is closed under coproducts and images of bisimulation relations. A *covariety* is defined by the weaker requirement of closure under coproducts, images of coalgebraic morphisms, and subcoalgebras. Historically, the concept of covariety arose by dualising that of a *variety* as being a class of universal algebras closed under products, subalgebras and homomorphic images. A famous theorem of Garrett Birkhoff [7] characterised varieties as being those classes of algebras that are definable by *equations*.

Behavioural covarieties correspond to computationally significant behaviours. For example, suppose the coalgebras in question are state-transition systems

* The authors acknowledge support from a Logic and Computation programme funded by the New Zealand Institute of Mathematics and its Applications.

D.V. Hung and M. Wirsing (Eds.): ICTAC 2005, LNCS 3722, pp. 288–302, 2005.

having a Hennessy-Milner style logic [8] for specifying their behaviour. Then the class of all models of a logical formula, or set of formulas, will in general be a behavioural covariety.

This paper generalises and extends work of the second author [9] that gave a comonadic characterisation of behavioural covarieties of coalgebras for certain endofunctors $T : \mathbf{Set} \to \mathbf{Set}$ on the category of sets. Under the assumption that the forgetful functor on T-coalgebras has a right adjoint, it was shown that there is a bijective correspondence between behavioural covarieties of T-coalgebras and certain subcomonads of the comonad $\mathbb{G}^T$ induced on $\mathbf{Set}$ by this adjunction. The subcomonads corresponding to behavioural covarieties were identified by the requirement that the natural transformations on which they are based be *cartesian*, i.e. all their naturality squares are pullbacks.

Here we replace $\mathbf{Set}$ by an abstract category $\mathbf{C}$ and seek to analyse the conditions on $\mathbf{C}$ that are needed for this bijective correspondence to obtain. Moreover we work with classes of $\mathbb{G}$-coalgebras for an arbitrary comonad $\mathbb{G}$ on $\mathbf{C}$, rather than classes of T-coalgebras for an endofunctor $T : \mathbf{C} \to \mathbf{C}$. This covers the work of [9] as a special case, since if $\mathbb{G}^T$ is the comonad induced on $\mathbf{Set}$ as above, then the category of T-coalgebras is isomorphic to the category of $\mathbb{G}^T$-coalgebras.

Furthermore we go beyond the analysis of [9] to give a comonadic character-isation of covarieties themselves. For this we must confront the fact that there has been more than one notion of "covariety" developed in work that dualises Birkhoff's theorem, depending on how "subcoalgebra" is interpreted. Over $\mathbf{Set}$, a subcoalgebra is given by an inclusion function that is a coalgebraic morphism. But abstracting this to the concept of subobject, i.e. monomorphism, allows pathological cases, since there can be monomorphisms that are not injective. In fact over $\mathbf{Set}$ a T-morphism is injective iff it is a *regular* mono, i.e. an equaliser in the category of T-coalgebras [10, 3.4] and experience has shown that it is this concept of *regular subobject* that provides the most suitable notion of subcoal-gebra in the abstract.

Awodey and Hughes [11,12,13] showed, in a suitable setting, that covarieties given by this regular notion of subcoalgebra are precisely those classes defined, in a certain way, by *coequations*. They defined a coequation to be a regular mono whose codomain is injective for regular monos. This dualised the analysis of Banaschewski and Herrlich [14], who observed that equations for classical algebras can be identified with regular epis (coequalisers) having a free algebra as domain, and then replaced the free algebras by their more intrinsic property of being an algebra that is projective for regular epis.

Adámek and Porst [15] focused on coequations as regular monos with cofree codomain. Working with an endofunctor T on a suitable category $\mathbf{C}$, they showed that classes of T-coalgebras defined by such coequations are precisely those that are closed under coproducts, images of morphisms and *retracts*, where $\mathcal{A}$ is a retract of $\mathcal{B}$ when there is a regular mono $\mathcal{A} \to \mathcal{B}$ whose underlying arrow splits (has a left inverse) in $\mathbf{C}$. These closure conditions define what we will call a *virtual* covariety.

It will be shown below that under certain general conditions on a comonad G on $\mathbf{C}$, virtual covarieties of G-coalgebras correspond bijectively to all subcomonads of G, while covarieties (closed under all regular subcoalgebras and not just retracts) correspond bijectively to subcomonads whose underlying transformation is cartesian *for regular monos only*. Behavioural covarieties continue, as in the **Set**-case, to correspond to subcomonads that are fully cartesian-based. We also show in the final Section how these characterisations relate to the work that has been done on coequations.

These ideas are illustrated (in Section 6) by properties of non-deterministic acceptors, represented as coalgebras for a power-object functor on a category that models the starting-state and accepting-state structure of such systems.

2   Coalgebras, Comonads, Covarieties

Given a category $\mathbf{C}$ with an endofunctor $G : \mathbf{C} \to \mathbf{C}$, a *$G$-coalgebra* $\mathcal{A} = (A, \alpha_{\mathcal{A}})$ consists of an underlying $\mathbf{C}$-object A and a $\mathbf{C}$-arrow $\alpha_{\mathcal{A}} : A \to GA$ that is sometimes called the *transition (structure)* of the coalgebra. A *G-morphism* $f : \mathcal{A} \to \mathcal{B} = (B, \alpha_{\mathcal{B}})$ is given by a $\mathbf{C}$-arrow $f : A \to B$ that preserves transitions in the sense that $\alpha_{\mathcal{B}} \circ f = Gf \circ \alpha_{\mathcal{A}}$. The G-coalgebras and their morphisms form a category $\mathbf{C}_G$ with a forgetful functor $U_G : \mathbf{C}_G \to \mathbf{C}$ that acts by $U_G \mathcal{A} = A$ on objects and $U_G f = f$ on arrows (so we often write f when we mean $U_G f$). U_G creates and preserves any kind of *colimit* that exists in $\mathbf{C}$. Thus if $\mathbf{C}$ has coproducts, then any set $\{\mathcal{A}_i : i \in I\}$ of G-coalgebras has a coproduct $\Sigma_I \mathcal{A}_i$ in $\mathbf{C}_G$ whose underlying object is the coproduct $\Sigma_I A_i$ in $\mathbf{C}$.

We will need to know how U_G treats epi arrows. Since U_G is faithful (injective on hom-sets), it reflects epis, i.e. $U_G f$ epi in $\mathbf{C}$ implies f epi in $\mathbf{C}_G$. But it seems some condition on $\mathbf{C}$ is needed for *preservation* of epis. A category is said to *have cokernel pairs* if for each arrow f there is a pair of arrows g, g' making a pushout of f with itself:

$$
\begin{array}{ccc}
\bullet & \xrightarrow{f} & \bullet \\
f \downarrow & \quad & \downarrow g' \\
\bullet & \xrightarrow[g]{} & \bullet
\end{array}
$$

In particular, f is epi iff it has a cokernel pair with $g = g'$. So if f is a $\mathbf{C}_G$-epi and f has a cokernel pair (g, g') in $\mathbf{C}$, then since such $\mathbf{C}$-colimits are created by U_G, it follows readily that $g = g'$. This implies

Lemma 1. *If $\mathbf{C}$ has cokernel pairs, then U_G preserves epis.*   □

A *comonad* $\mathbb{G} = (G, \varepsilon, \delta)$ on $\mathbf{C}$ consists of a functor $G : \mathbf{C} \to \mathbf{C}$ and two natural transformations $\varepsilon : G \to 1$ and $\delta : G \to GG$ such that the following diagrams commute for each $\mathbf{C}$-object A:

$$
\begin{array}{ccc}
GA & \xrightarrow{\delta_A} & G^2 A \\
\delta_A \downarrow & & \downarrow \delta_{GA} \\
G^2 A & \xrightarrow[G\delta_A]{} & G^3 A
\end{array}
\qquad\qquad
\begin{array}{c}
GA \\
{}^{1}\swarrow \ \ \downarrow \delta_A \ \ \searrow^{1} \\
GA \xleftarrow[G\varepsilon_A]{} G^2 A \xrightarrow[\varepsilon_{GA}]{} GA
\end{array}
\qquad (2.1)
$$

A $\mathbb{G}$-*coalgebra* is a G-coalgebra $\mathcal{A}$ for which the following commute:

$$
\begin{array}{ccc}
A & \xrightarrow{\;\alpha_A\;} & GA \\
{\scriptstyle \alpha_A}\downarrow & & \downarrow{\scriptstyle \delta_A} \\
GA & \xrightarrow[\;G\alpha_A\;]{} & G^2 A
\end{array}
\qquad\qquad
\begin{array}{ccc}
A & & \\
{\scriptstyle \alpha_A}\downarrow & \searrow^{1} & \\
GA & \xrightarrow[\;\varepsilon_A\;]{} & A
\end{array}
\tag{2.2}
$$

For example, (2.1) implies that $\mathcal{G}A = (GA, \delta_A)$ is a $\mathbb{G}$-coalgebra for any A: it is the *cofree* $\mathbb{G}$-coalgebra over A. The square in (2.2) states that the transition α_A is itself a G-morphism $\alpha_A : \mathcal{A} \to \mathcal{G}A$.

We denote by $\mathbf{C}_{\mathbb{G}}$ the full subcategory of $\mathbf{C}_G$ consisting of the $\mathbb{G}$-coalgebras. Arrows in $\mathbf{C}_{\mathbb{G}}$, i.e. G-morphisms between $\mathbb{G}$-coalgebras, may be referred to as $\mathbb{G}$-*morphisms*. The assignment $A \mapsto \mathcal{G}A$ is the object part of a functor $\mathcal{G} : \mathbf{C} \to \mathbf{C}_{\mathbb{G}}$ that is right adjoint to the forgetful functor $U_{\mathbb{G}} : \mathbf{C}_{\mathbb{G}} \to \mathbf{C}$, which accounts for the cofreeness of $\mathcal{G}A$. The transition-morphisms $\alpha_A : \mathcal{A} \to \mathcal{G}A$ are the components of the unit $1 \to \mathcal{G} \circ U_{\mathbb{G}}$ of this adjunction. Since $U_{\mathbb{G}}$ is a left adjoint it preserves colimits, so altogether a $\mathbb{G}$-morphism is epi in $\mathbf{C}_{\mathbb{G}}$ iff it is epi in $\mathbf{C}$. $U_{\mathbb{G}}$ also creates any colimits that exist in $\mathbf{C}$ [16, dual of Proposition 4.3.1]. This implies that if $\mathbf{C}$ has coproducts, then every set of $\mathbb{G}$-coalgebras has a coproduct in $\mathbf{C}_{\mathbb{G}}$ that is the same as its coproduct in $\mathbf{C}_G$, i.e. $\mathbf{C}_{\mathbb{G}}$ is closed under coproducts in $\mathbf{C}_G$.

Assume from now on that $\mathbb{G}$ is a comonad on a category $\mathbf{C}$ that has cokernel pairs and a coproduct of any set of $\mathbf{C}$-objects. Let $\mathbf{D}$ be any full subcategory of $\mathbf{C}_G$, and K a class of $\mathbf{D}$-objects. K is called a *quasi-covariety in* $\mathbf{D}$ if it is closed under coproducts and under codomains of epis in $\mathbf{D}$. The latter means that for any $\mathbf{D}$-epi $\mathcal{A} \twoheadrightarrow \mathcal{B}$, if $\mathcal{A} \in K$ then $\mathcal{B} \in K$.

A regular mono $m : \mathcal{A} \to \mathcal{B}$ in $\mathbf{D}$ will be called a *subcoalgebra* of $\mathcal{B}$ in $\mathbf{D}$. In that case, $\mathcal{A}$ is a *retract* of $\mathcal{B}$ in $\mathbf{D}$ if Um splits in $\mathbf{C}$, i.e. if there is a $\mathbf{C}$-arrow $g : B \to A$ with $g \circ m = 1_A$. If K is a quasi-covariety in $\mathbf{D}$, then:

- K is a *virtual covariety in* $\mathbf{D}$ if it is closed under retracts in $\mathbf{D}$;
- K is a *covariety in* $\mathbf{D}$ if it is closed under subcoalgebras in $\mathbf{D}$; and
- K is a *behavioural covariety in* $\mathbf{D}$ if it is closed under domains of $\mathbf{D}$-morphisms, i.e. for any $\mathbf{D}$-arrow $\mathcal{A} \to \mathcal{B}$, if $\mathcal{B} \in K$ then $\mathcal{A} \in K$.

It can be shown that a class K is a behavioural covariety in $\mathbf{D}$ iff it is closed under coproducts and under images of bisimulation relations in $\mathbf{D}$ (see [11], [9, 2.1]). The present definition is easier to work with.

Theorem 1. $\mathbf{C}_{\mathbb{G}}$ *is a virtual covariety in* $\mathbf{C}_G$.

Proof. In [9, 5.1] it is shown that if $\mathbf{C} = \mathbf{Set}$, then $\mathbf{C}_{\mathbb{G}}$ is a *covariety* in $\mathbf{C}_G$. Closure of $\mathbf{C}_{\mathbb{G}}$ under coproducts holds as there, as explained above. The proof of closure under codomains of epis depends on a $\mathbf{C}_G$-epi being epi in $\mathbf{C}$, and that is provided here by our Lemma 1. The proof that a $\mathbf{C}_G$-subcoalgebra $m : \mathcal{A} \to \mathcal{B}$ of $\mathcal{B} \in \mathbf{C}_{\mathbb{G}}$ has $\mathcal{A} \in \mathbf{C}_{\mathbb{G}}$ depends on $G^2 m$ being mono in $\mathbf{C}$. In $\mathbf{Set}$ we can use the fact that any endofunctor on $\mathbf{Set}$ preserves monos with non-empty domain. Here, if we assume instead that m splits in $\mathbf{C}$, then $G^2 m$ will also split in $\mathbf{C}$ and hence be mono. So the proof adapts to show that $\mathbf{C}_{\mathbb{G}}$ is closed under *retracts*. $\square$

3   Coregular Factorisations and Inverse Images

A category has *coregular factorisations* if each arrow f factors as $f = m \circ e$ with m a regular mono and e an epi. Such a factorisation is unique up to a unique isomorphism: if $m' \circ e'$ is a second such factorisation of f, then there is a unique iso arrow $i : \operatorname{dom} m \to \operatorname{dom} m'$ factoring m through m' and e' through e.

Hughes [12, Section 1.2.3] gives results about the lifting of coregular factorisations from $\mathbf{C}$ to $\mathbf{C}_G$ and their preservation by U_G. Here are the corresponding versions of these results for $\mathbf{C}_{\mathbb{G}}$ and $U_{\mathbb{G}}$.

Theorem 2.

(1) If $G : \mathbf{C} \to \mathbf{C}$ takes regular monos to monos, then $U_{\mathbb{G}}$ reflects regular monos.
(2) If $\mathbf{C}$ has coregular factorisations, and $G : \mathbf{C} \to \mathbf{C}$ preserves regular monos, then $\mathbf{C}_{\mathbb{G}}$ has coregular factorisations which are preserved and reflected by $U_{\mathbb{G}}$. Moreover, $U_{\mathbb{G}}$ preserves regular monos.   □

Theorem 3. If $\mathbf{C}$ has coregular factorisations, and $G : \mathbf{C} \to \mathbf{C}$ preserves regular monos, then $\mathbf{C}_{\mathbb{G}}$ is a covariety in $\mathbf{C}_G$.

Proof. Take a $\mathbf{C}_{\mathbb{G}}$-subcoalgebra $m : \mathcal{A} \to \mathcal{B}$ with $\mathcal{B} \in \mathbf{C}_{\mathbb{G}}$. In the proof of Theorem 1 we noted that $\mathcal{A} \in \mathbf{C}_{\mathbb{G}}$ if $G^2 m$ is a $\mathbf{C}$-mono. By the dual of [12, 1.2.15], U_G preserves regular monos, so m is regular mono in $\mathbf{C}$, hence so is $G^2 m$. Thus $\mathbf{C}_{\mathbb{G}}$ is closed under subcoalgebras.   □

Given a regular mono $m : A \to B$ and an arrow $f : C \to B$, an *inverse image* of m with respect to f is a pullback of m along f:

$$
\begin{array}{ccc}
D & \xrightarrow{f^*} & A \\
{\scriptstyle m^*}\big\downarrow & & \big\downarrow{\scriptstyle m} \\
C & \xrightarrow{f} & B
\end{array}
$$

A category *has inverse images* if all such pullbacks exist. A functor H *preserves inverse images* if the H-image of any such pullback is also a pullback and Hm is a regular mono. With the help of Theorem 2(2) we can show:

Theorem 4. If $\mathbf{C}$ has coregular factorisations and inverse images, and G preserves regular monos and inverse images, then $\mathbf{C}_{\mathbb{G}}$ has inverse images preserved by $U_{\mathbb{G}}$.   □

4   Comonad Morphisms

From now on we assume $\mathbf{C}$ has coregular factorisations as well as cokernel pairs and coproducts. A *morphism* from comonad $\mathbb{F} = (F, \varepsilon^F, \delta^F)$ to comonad $\mathbb{G} = (G, \varepsilon^G, \delta^G)$ on $\mathbf{C}$ [17, Section 3.6] is a natural transformation $\sigma : F \to G$ making the diagrams

$$FA \xrightarrow{\sigma_A} GA \qquad\qquad FA \xrightarrow{\delta_A^F} FFA$$

$$\begin{array}{ccc} FA \xrightarrow{\sigma_A} GA & & FA \xrightarrow{\delta_A^F} FFA \\ {\scriptstyle \varepsilon_A^F} \searrow \quad \downarrow {\scriptstyle \varepsilon_A^G} & & {\scriptstyle \sigma_A} \downarrow \qquad \downarrow {\scriptstyle (\sigma_A)^2} \\ \qquad A & & GA \xrightarrow{\delta_A^G} GGA \end{array} \qquad (4.1)$$

commute for all $\mathbf{C}$-objects A, where $(\sigma_A)^2 = G\sigma_A \circ \sigma_{FA} = \sigma_{GA} \circ F\sigma_A$:

$$\begin{array}{ccc} FFA & \xrightarrow{\sigma_{FA}} & GFA \\ {\scriptstyle F\sigma_A}\downarrow & & \downarrow{\scriptstyle G\sigma_A} \\ FGA & \xrightarrow{\sigma_{GA}} & GGA \end{array} \qquad (4.2)$$

We will see later that, under some natural assumptions on $\mathbf{C}$, any quasi-covariety K in $\mathbf{C}_\mathbb{G}$ gives rise to such a comonad morphism to $\mathbb{G}$. This will be constructed from a "coreflection" functor $\mathbf{C}_\mathbb{G} \to K$ which takes each $\mathbb{G}$-coalgebra to its largest subcoalgebra that belongs to K.

A comonad morphism $\sigma : \mathbb{F} \to \mathbb{G}$ is *cartesian* if the diagram

$$\begin{array}{ccc} FA & \xrightarrow{Ff} & FB \\ {\scriptstyle \sigma_A}\downarrow & & \downarrow{\scriptstyle \sigma_B} \\ GA & \xrightarrow{Gf} & GB \end{array}$$

is a pullback in $\mathbf{C}$ for any $\mathbf{C}$-arrow $f : A \to B$. σ is *cartesian for regular monos* if this square is a pullback whenever f is a regular mono in $\mathbf{C}$. σ is *regularly monomorphic* if all of its components σ_A are regular monos in $\mathbf{C}$.

Now any morphism $\sigma : \mathbb{F} \to \mathbb{G}$ induces a mapping $\varphi\sigma$ from $\mathbf{C}_\mathbb{F}$ to $\mathbf{C}_\mathbb{G}$, taking each $\mathbb{F}$-coalgebra $\mathcal{A}$ to the $\mathbb{G}$-coalgebra $\varphi\sigma\mathcal{A} = (A, \sigma_A \circ \alpha_A : A \to FA \to GA)$ on the same underlying object. We write $\mathrm{Im}\varphi\sigma$ for the full subcategory of $\mathbf{C}_\mathbb{G}$ based on the class of all $\mathbb{G}$-coalgebras of the form $\varphi\sigma\mathcal{A}$ for some $\mathbb{F}$-coalgebra $\mathcal{A}$. In [9, Section 6] it is verified that $\varphi\sigma\mathcal{A}$ is a $\mathbb{G}$-coalgebra and that $\varphi\sigma$ becomes a functor $\mathbf{C}_\mathbb{F} \to \mathbf{C}_\mathbb{G}$ that leaves the underlying $\mathbf{C}$-arrow of morphisms unchanged ($U_\mathbb{G}\varphi\sigma f = f$), and so is faithful (injective on hom-sets). Furthermore, if σ is regularly monomorphic then $\varphi\sigma$ is also full (surjective on hom-sets) and injective on objects, making $\mathbf{C}_\mathbb{F}$ isomorphic to $\mathrm{Im}\varphi\sigma$.

This $\varphi\sigma$ construction is functorial in the sense that $\varphi(\sigma \circ \tau) = \varphi\sigma \circ \varphi\tau$ whenever σ and τ are comonad morphisms whose composition $\sigma \circ \tau$ is defined. The map $\sigma \mapsto \varphi\sigma$ gives a *bijection* between comonad morphisms $\mathbb{F} \to \mathbb{G}$ and those functors $\mathbf{C}_\mathbb{F} \to \mathbf{C}_\mathbb{G}$ that commute with the forgetful functors to $\mathbf{C}$ [17, Section 3.6].

Theorem 5. *If $\sigma : \mathbb{F} \to \mathbb{G}$ is regularly monomorphic and G preserves regular monos, then:*

(1) $\mathrm{Im}\varphi\sigma$ *is a virtual covariety in $\mathbf{C}_\mathbb{G}$.*
(2) *If σ is cartesian for regular monos, then $\mathrm{Im}\varphi\sigma$ is a covariety in $\mathbf{C}_\mathbb{G}$.*
(3) *If σ is cartesian, then $\mathrm{Im}\varphi\sigma$ is a behavioural covariety in $\mathbf{C}_\mathbb{G}$.*

Proof. (1) In [9, 6.3] it is shown that $\mathrm{Im}\varphi\sigma$ is a quasi-variety when $\mathbb{G}$ is any comonad on **Set**. Closure of $\mathrm{Im}\varphi\sigma$ under coproducts continues to hold here, as $\Sigma_I\varphi\sigma\mathcal{A}_i = \varphi\sigma\Sigma_I\mathcal{A}_i$. The proof that any $\mathbf{C}_{\mathbb{G}}$-epi $f : \varphi\sigma\mathcal{B} \to \mathcal{A}$ has $\mathcal{A} \in \mathrm{Im}\varphi\sigma$ requires that f is epi in $\mathbf{C}$, which holds as $U_{\mathbb{G}}$ preserves epis, and that $G\sigma_A$ is mono, which holds now by our assumptions on σ and G. It also requires that there is a $\mathbf{C}$-arrow β making a commuting diagram

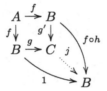

This holds by diagonalization in $\mathbf{C}$ because f is epi and σ_A is regular mono. It can then be shown that (A, β) is an F-coalgebra with $\mathcal{A} = \varphi\sigma(A, \beta) \in \mathrm{Im}\varphi\sigma$, by the argument of [9] and using that $G\sigma_A$ is mono.

Now for something new. Suppose $\mathcal{A}$ is a *retract* of $\varphi\sigma\mathcal{B}$, with a regular mono $f : \mathcal{A} \to \varphi\sigma\mathcal{B}$ that has a left inverse $h : \mathcal{B} \to \mathcal{A}$ in $\mathbf{C}$. Let $g, g' : \mathcal{B} \to \mathcal{C}$ be a cokernel pair for f in both $\mathbf{C}_{\mathbb{G}}$ and $\mathbf{C}$. By the universal property of pushouts, g has a left inverse j in $\mathbf{C}$ with $j \circ g' = f \circ h$:

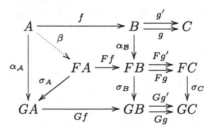

This means that $A \xrightarrow{f} B \underset{g}{\overset{g'}{\rightrightarrows}} C$ is (the dual of) a *split fork* and so is an absolute equaliser: any functor H on $\mathbf{C}$ makes Hf an equaliser of Hg and Hg' [18, VI.6]. Consider the diagram

$$
\begin{array}{ccccc}
A & \xrightarrow{\quad f \quad} & B & \overset{g'}{\underset{g}{\rightrightarrows}} & C \\
& \searrow^{\beta} & \downarrow^{\alpha_B} & \overset{Fg'}{} & \\
\alpha_A \downarrow & FA \xrightarrow{Ff} & FB & \overset{Fg'}{\underset{Fg}{\rightrightarrows}} & FC \downarrow^{\sigma_C} \\
& \sigma_A \swarrow & \downarrow^{\sigma_B} & \overset{Gg'}{} & \\
GA & \xrightarrow{\quad Gf \quad} & GB & \overset{Gg'}{\underset{Gg}{\rightrightarrows}} & GC
\end{array}
$$

From some diagram chasing and the fact that σ_C is mono, we get $Fg \circ (\alpha_B \circ f) = Fg' \circ (\alpha_B \circ f)$, and hence, because Ff equalises Fg and Fg', there is a unique $\beta : A \to FA$ as shown making $\alpha_B \circ f = Ff \circ \alpha$. Then $Gf \circ \alpha_A = Gf \circ \sigma_A \circ \beta$, so as G preserves the regular mono f, $\alpha_A = \sigma_A \circ \beta$ and $\mathcal{A} = \varphi\sigma(A, \beta)$. It can be checked that (A, β) is an F-coalgebra, and we conclude that $\mathrm{Im}\varphi\sigma$ is closed under retracts.

(2) Given a regular $\mathbf{C}_{\mathbb{G}}$-mono $f : \mathcal{A} \to \varphi\sigma\mathcal{B}$, f is a regular $\mathbf{C}$-mono by Theorem 2(2), so the lower quadrangle of the diagram

$$\begin{array}{ccc}
A & \xrightarrow{\ f\ } & B \\
\end{array}$$

is a pullback as σ is cartesian for regular monos. Hence the arrow β exists as shown to make the whole diagram commute. It can be checked that (A, β) is an $\mathbb{F}$-coalgebra. Then $\mathcal{A} = \varphi\sigma(A, \beta)$, so we conclude that $\mathrm{Im}\varphi\sigma$ is closed under subcoalgebras in $\mathbf{C}_{\mathbb{G}}$.

(3) If σ is cartesian, then the lower quadrangle of the diagram in (2) is a pullback for any $\mathbf{C}_{\mathbb{G}}$-morphism $f : \mathcal{A} \to \varphi\sigma B$, so we get that $\mathrm{Im}\varphi\sigma$ is closed under domains of all such morphisms. $\qquad\Box$

There is an equivalence $\sigma_1 \simeq \sigma_2$ between regularly monomorphic $\sigma_i : \mathbb{F}_i \to \mathbb{G}$ that holds when there exists a morphism $\tau : \mathbb{F}_1 \to \mathbb{F}_2$ that factors σ_1 through σ_2, i.e. $\sigma_1 = \sigma_2 \circ \tau$, and likewise a morphism $\tau' : \mathbb{F}_2 \to \mathbb{F}_1$ factoring σ_2 through σ_1. If such τ, τ' exist then they are unique, because the components of the σ_i are mono, and are mutually inverse, giving a natural isomorphism between the underlying functors of $\mathbb{F}_1$ and $\mathbb{F}_2$. The functoriality of the $\varphi\sigma$ construction then gives a commuting functor diagram

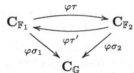

which implies that $\mathrm{Im}\varphi\sigma_1 = \mathrm{Im}\varphi\sigma_2$. Conversely if $\mathrm{Im}\varphi\sigma_1 = \mathrm{Im}\varphi\sigma_2$, then from $\varphi\sigma_i : \mathbf{C}_{\mathbb{F}_i} \cong \mathrm{Im}\varphi\sigma_i$ we get isomorphisms between $\mathbf{C}_{\mathbb{F}_1}$ and $\mathbf{C}_{\mathbb{F}_2}$ that are of the form $\varphi\tau$ and $\varphi\tau'$ for some τ, τ' that establish $\sigma_1 \simeq \sigma_2$.

Now two equivalent regularly monomorphic $\sigma_i : \mathbb{F}_i \to \mathbb{G}$ can be regarded as representing the same *subcomonad* of $\mathbb{G}$, so in this sense the map $\sigma \mapsto \mathrm{Im}\varphi\sigma$ injectively assigns virtual covarieties in $\mathbf{C}_{\mathbb{G}}$ to regularly monomorphic comonad morphisms with codomain $\mathbb{G}$. In the next sections we will identify further conditions on $\mathbf{C}$ and $\mathbb{G}$ that ensure this map is surjective and gives a bijective correspondence between virtual covarieties in $\mathbf{C}_{\mathbb{G}}$ and subcomonads of $\mathbb{G}$. We will also show that it restricts to give a bijection between covarieties and subcomonads whose morphism σ is cartesian for regular monos, as well as a bijection between behavioural covarieties and subcomonads with fully cartesian σ.

5   Coreflective Subcategories

We assume from now on that

- $\mathbf{C}$ has coregular factorisations, cokernel pairs, coproducts and inverse images.
- $\mathbf{C}$ is *regularly well-powered*, i.e. for each object A there is a *set* of representatives of all the isomorphism classes of regular subobjects of A.
- $\mathbb{G} = (G, \varepsilon, \delta)$ is a comonad on $\mathbf{C}$ with G preserving regular monos and inverse images.

Recall that the adjunction $U_{\mathrm{G}} \dashv \mathcal{G} : \mathbf{C}_{\mathrm{G}} \to \mathbf{C}$ has counit ε, and unit η with components $\eta_{\mathcal{A}} = \mathcal{A} \xrightarrow{\alpha_{\mathcal{A}}} \mathcal{G}\mathcal{A}$ for all G-coalgebras $\mathcal{A}$.

Let K be a *quasi-covariety* of G-coalgebras, regarded as a full subcategory of $\mathbf{C}_{\mathrm{G}}$. Then K is a *regular-mono-coreflective subcategory of* $\mathbf{C}_{\mathrm{G}}$, which means that the inclusion functor $I : K \hookrightarrow \mathbf{C}_{\mathrm{G}}$ has a right adjoint (coreflector) $R : \mathbf{C}_{\mathrm{G}} \to K$ whose counit ε^R has regular mono components (coreflections) $\varepsilon_{\mathcal{B}}^R : R\mathcal{B} \rightarrowtail \mathcal{B}$ for all G-coalgebras $\mathcal{B}$. This is a well-known result (essentially the dual of [19, 37.1]). Briefly, R is constructed by taking a set $\{\mathcal{A}_j \xrightarrow{m_j} \mathcal{B} : j \in J\}$ representing all the subcoalgebras of $\mathcal{B}$ with domain $\mathcal{A}_j$ in K, and taking $\varepsilon_{\mathcal{B}}^R$ to be the regular-mono part of the coregular factorisation of the coproduct arrow $\Sigma_J \mathcal{A}_j \xrightarrow{\Sigma_J m_j} \mathcal{B}$. The important point for us is that if $\mathcal{A} \in K$, then any G-morphism $f : \mathcal{A} \to \mathcal{B}$ factors uniquely through $\varepsilon_{\mathcal{B}}^R$:

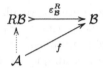

In particular, $\varepsilon_{\mathcal{B}}^R$ is the *largest* subcoalgebra of $\mathcal{B}$ with domain in K.

By composing the adjunctions $K \underset{I}{\overset{R}{\rightleftarrows}} \mathbf{C}_{\mathrm{G}} \underset{U_{\mathrm{G}}}{\overset{\mathcal{G}}{\rightleftarrows}} \mathbf{C}$ we obtain the functor $\mathcal{G}^K = R \circ \mathcal{G} : \mathbf{C} \to K$ right adjoint to the forgetful functor $U_K = U_{\mathrm{G}} \circ I : K \to \mathbf{C}$. For each $\mathbf{C}$-object A, let σ_A^K be the coreflection morphism $\varepsilon_{\mathcal{G}A}^R$. This associates with K a natural transformation $\sigma^K : \mathcal{G}^K \to \mathcal{G}$, with the regular-mono component σ_A^K giving the largest K-subobject of $\mathcal{G}A$.

Now let $\mathbb{G}^K = (G^K, \varepsilon^K, \delta^K)$ be the comonad on $\mathbf{C}$ induced by the adjunction $U_K \dashv \mathcal{G}^K$. Thus $G^K = U_K \circ \mathcal{G}^K : \mathbf{C} \to \mathbf{C}$, and ε^K is the counit of this adjunction. We write η^K for its unit, with components $\eta_A^K : A \to \mathcal{G}^K A$. Applying the forgetful functor to the components of σ^K defines a natural transformation $G^K \to G$ which we will also denote by σ^K. Standard calculations for composition of adjunctions [18, IV.8] give the formulas

$$\varepsilon_A \circ \sigma_A^K = \varepsilon_A^K \tag{5.1}$$

$$\sigma_A^K \circ \eta_A^K = \eta_A = \alpha_A \tag{5.2}$$

The transformation δ^K has components $\delta_A^K = \eta_{G^K A}^K : G^K A \to G^K G^K A$, which is a G-morphism $\mathcal{G}^K A \to \mathcal{G}^K G^K A$ for each A, the unique one factoring the identity on $\mathcal{G}^K A$ through $\varepsilon_{G^K A}^K$, so

$$\varepsilon_{G^K A}^K \circ \delta_A^K = 1_{G^K A}, \tag{5.3}$$

and thus by (5.2),

$$\sigma_{G^K A}^K \circ \delta_A^K = \alpha_{\mathcal{G}^K A}. \tag{5.4}$$

By the reasoning of [9, 6.1], $\sigma^K : G^K \to G$ is a (regularly monomorphic) comonad morphism from $\mathbb{G}^K$ to $\mathbb{G}$. Hence, by the work of Section 4, σ^K induces a functor

$\varphi\sigma^K : \mathbf{C}_{\mathbb{G}^K} \to \mathbf{C}_{\mathbb{G}}$ making $\mathbf{C}_{\mathbb{G}^K}$ isomorphic to $\mathrm{Im}\varphi\sigma^K$. The theory of comonads also provides the quasi-covariety K with a *comparison functor* $\chi^K : K \to \mathbf{C}_{\mathbb{G}^K}$ that acts on objects by $\chi^K \mathcal{A} = (A, \eta_A^K)$, and leaves the underlying $\mathbf{C}$-arrow of morphisms unchanged.

Theorem 6. *If K is a virtual covariety in $\mathbf{C}_{\mathbb{G}}$, then χ^K is an isomorphism of categories with inverse $\varphi\sigma^K$, and so $K = \mathrm{Im}\varphi\sigma^K$:*

$$\mathbf{C}_{\mathbb{G}^K} \underset{\varphi\sigma^K}{\overset{\chi^K}{\rightleftarrows}} K \hookrightarrow \mathbf{C}_{\mathbb{G}}$$

□

By this Theorem, the correspondence $\sigma \mapsto \mathrm{Im}\varphi\sigma$ from subcomonads of $\mathbb{G}$ to virtual covarieties in $\mathbf{C}_{\mathbb{G}}$ is surjective: every virtual covariety is of the form $\mathrm{Im}\varphi\sigma$. Together with our earlier work it follows that the correspondence is bijective. It remains to show that it also gives a bijection between covarieties and subcomonads whose morphism σ is cartesian for regular monos, as well as a bijection between behavioural covarieties and subcomonads with cartesian σ. This is provided by the following results together with parts 2 and 3 of Theorem 5.

Theorem 7. *If K is a covariety, then σ^K is cartesian for regular monos. If K is a behavioural covariety, then σ^K is cartesian.*

Proof. Given a regular mono $\mathbf{C}$-arrow $f : A \to B$, consider the diagram

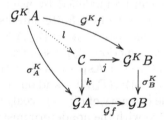

The inner square is a pullback giving an inverse image k of σ_B^K along $\mathcal{G}f$ in $\mathbf{C}_{\mathbb{G}}$. This exists by Theorem 4. k is a subcoalgebra of $\mathcal{G}A$, being a pullback of a regular mono. The outer perimeter of the diagram commutes by naturality of σ^K, so a unique $\mathbb{G}$-morphism l exists as shown to make the subcoalgebra σ_A^K factor through k. We will show that l is an isomorphism.

Now $\mathcal{G}$ preserves limits, being a right adjoint, so $\mathcal{G}f$ is a regular mono, hence its pullback j is a subcoalgebra of $\mathcal{G}^K B \in K$. As K is a covariety, the domain $\mathcal{C}$ of the $\mathcal{G}A$-subcoalgebra k belongs to K. But σ_A^K is the largest such subcoalgebra of $\mathcal{G}A$, so k in turn factors through σ_A^K, making these two subcoalgebras equivalent. Hence l is an iso, and therefore the perimeter is also a pullback, making σ_A^K an inverse image of σ_B^K along $\mathcal{G}f$. But $U_{\mathbb{G}}$ preserves inverse images (Theorem 4) so

$$\begin{array}{ccc} G^K A & \xrightarrow{G^K f} & G^K B \\ {\scriptstyle \sigma^K A}\downarrow & & \downarrow{\scriptstyle \sigma^K B} \\ GA & \xrightarrow{Gf} & GB \end{array}$$

is a pullback in $\mathbf{C}$, proving σ^K is cartesian for regular monos.

Finally, if K is a behavioural covariety, then the domain C of j will be in K for any $\mathbb{G}$-morphism j to to $\mathcal{G}^K B$, regardless of whether $\mathcal{G}f$ is regular mono, so the last diagram will be a pullback for every **C**-arrow f, i.e. σ^K is cartesian. $\quad\square$

6 Acceptors

To illustrate some of these ideas we define an *acceptor* space to be a triple $\mathbb{A} = (A, A^{\mathsf{st}}, A^{\mathsf{ac}})$ consisting of two distinguished subsets $A^{\mathsf{st}}, A^{\mathsf{ac}}$ of a set A which is itself thought of as a set of *states*. A^{st} comprises the *starting* states and A^{ac} the *accepting* states. An *acceptor space morphism* $f : \mathbb{A} \to \mathbb{B} = (B, B^{\mathsf{st}}, B^{\mathsf{ac}})$ is a function $f : A \to B$ preserving the subsets, i.e. $f(A^{\mathsf{x}}) \subseteq B^{\mathsf{x}}$ for $\mathsf{x} = \mathsf{st}, \mathsf{ac}$. This defines a category **Asp** of acceptor spaces, in which monos are injective and the *regular* monos are those for which $f(A)^{\mathsf{x}} = f(A) \cap B^{\mathsf{x}}$. This category is complete and cocomplete, and has all the properties required of the category **C** at the start of Section 5. Actually **Asp** is a quasi-topos (see [20, 31.7] for a description of a quasi-topos of sets with a single distinguished subset).

A nondeterministic acceptor within input set I has an I-labelled state-transition relation $x \overset{i}{\mapsto} y$, meaning that y is a possible next state on input of $i \in I$ to state x. Letting $\alpha(x)$ be the map assigning $\{y : x \overset{i}{\mapsto} y\}$ to each $i \in I$ gives a function $\alpha : A \to (\mathcal{P}A)^I$, where $\mathcal{P}A$ is the powerset of A. *Finitely branching* nondeterminism can be modelled by using the finitary powerset operation $\mathcal{P}_\omega$, where $\mathcal{P}_\omega A$ is the set of all finite subsets of A. This determines a functor $\mathcal{P}_\omega : \mathbf{Asp} \to \mathbf{Asp}$ that has $\mathcal{P}_\omega \mathbb{A} = (\mathcal{P}_\omega A, \mathcal{P}_\omega A, \mathcal{P}_\omega A)$ and takes each morphism $f : \mathbb{A} \to \mathbb{B}$ to the function $\mathcal{P}_\omega f$ assigning to each $X \subseteq A$ its image $fX \subseteq B$. A functor $T = (\mathcal{P}_\omega -)^I : \mathbf{Asp} \to \mathbf{Asp}$ is then defined on objects by $T\mathbb{A} = (\mathcal{P}_\omega \mathbb{A})^I = ((\mathcal{P}_\omega A)^I, (\mathcal{P}_\omega A)^I, (\mathcal{P}_\omega A)^I)$ and on arrows by $Tf(g) = (\mathcal{P}_\omega f) \circ g$.

We write **Finac**$_I$ for the category of $(\mathcal{P}_\omega -)^I$-coalgebras over **Asp**. Its objects $\mathcal{A} = (\mathbb{A}, \alpha_\mathcal{A})$ can be identified with the nondeterministic acceptors with input set I that are *image-finite*, i.e. the set $\{y : x \overset{i}{\mapsto} y\}$ of possible next states is finite for all pairs (x, i). Its arrows $f : \mathcal{A} \to \mathcal{B}$ can be characterised as those acceptor space morphisms $f : \mathbb{A} \to \mathbb{B}$ for which $f(x) \overset{i}{\mapsto} z$ iff $\exists y \in A(x \overset{i}{\mapsto} y$ and $f(y) = z)$.

It can be shown that the forgetful functor on **Finac**$_I$ has a right adjoint, and that **Finac**$_I$ is isomorphic to the category of $\mathbb{G}$-coalgebras for the associated adjunction. So there is an exact correspondence between (quasi/virtual/behavioural) covarieties in **Finac**$_I$ and the same kinds of subcategory of the category of $\mathbb{G}$-coalgebras. $(\mathcal{P}_\omega -)^I$ preserves regular monos, so the forgetful functor on **Finac**$_I$ preserves and reflects regular monos. $(\mathcal{P}_\omega -)^I$ preserves inverse images, and so **Finac**$_I$ has inverse images preserved by this forgetful functor.

There are many properties of acceptors that define covarieties in **Finac**$_I$, such as the following:

- Every state x is recurrent, in the sense that there is a transition path $x \overset{i}{\mapsto} y \overset{i'}{\mapsto} \cdots \mapsto x$ returning to x.
- There are no deadlocked states, where x is deadlocked if there is no transition $x \overset{i}{\mapsto} y$ starting from x.

- Every non-deadlocked state can reach a deadlocked one in finitely many transitions.
- Every transition path $x \overset{i}{\mapsto} y \overset{i'}{\mapsto} y \mapsto \cdots$ is finite (i.e. eventually reaches a deadlocked state).

The last three in fact define behavioural covarieties. Virtual covarieties can be defined by considering existential properties of starting and accepting states. For instance, let K be the class $\{\mathcal{A} : A^{\mathsf{ac}} \neq \emptyset\}$ of all coalgebras having at least one accepting state. This property is evidently preserved by coproducts (disjoint unions) and codomains of epis (indeed by codomains of all morphisms). It is also preserved by retracts, for if the underlying **Asp**-arrow of some **Finac**$_I$-arrow $\mathcal{B} \to \mathcal{A}$ has a left inverse in **Asp**, and $\mathcal{A}$ has an accepting state, then this state will be preserved by the left-inverse, i.e. carried to an accepting state in $\mathcal{B}$. However K is not a covariety: let $\mathcal{A} \in K$ be any one-state acceptor whose one state is both starting and accepting, while $\mathcal{B}$ is the empty acceptor. Then the inclusion function is a regular mono $\mathcal{B} \to \mathcal{A}$ giving a subcoalgebra of $\mathcal{A}$ with $\mathcal{B} \notin K$.

Some other properties defining virtual covarieties that are not closed under subcoalgebras are:

- There is a state that is both starting and accepting.
- There exist starting states and all of them can reach an accepting state.
- There exist accepting states and they include all the deadlocked states.

Further examples can be given by various combinations of the properties listed, e.g. "there exists an accepting state but no deadlocked states", and so on.

7   Coequations

Birkhoff's theorem [7] states that the *varieties* of universal algebras are precisely those classes that are definable by *equations*. This has been dualised to a notion of *coequation* giving characterisations of covarieties of coalgebras. In this final Section we briefly review this theory and indicate how it relates to our work with cartesian comonad morphisms.

An algebraic equation $t_1 = t_2$ with variables from a set X is given by a pair of terms that can be taken as elements of the free algebra $\mathbf{F}X$ generated by X. If E is the smallest congruence on $\mathbf{F}X$ containing (t_1, t_2), then the quotient map $e : \mathbf{F}X \twoheadrightarrow \mathbf{F}X/E$ is a regular epi (coequaliser) identifying t_1 and t_2. Moreover, an algebra $\mathcal{A}$ satisfies $t_1 = t_2$ iff every homomorphism $\mathbf{F}X \to \mathcal{A}$ factors as e followed by a homomorphism $\mathbf{F}X/E \to \mathcal{A}$, a property that is expressed by saying that $\mathcal{A}$ is *injective for* e. Abstracting, the notion of an equation became in [14] the notion of a regular epi with free domain, and the class defined by an equation became the class of algebras injective for it.

Dually, a *coequation* associated with a comonad $\mathbb{G}$ can be defined as a regular mono $i : \mathcal{A} \rightarrowtail \mathcal{G}C$ in $\mathbf{C}_\mathbb{G}$ with cofree codomain. Another regular mono $i' : \mathcal{A}' \to \mathcal{G}C$ will be taken to represent the same coequation as i if it represents the same subobject of $\mathcal{G}C$. A coalgebra $\mathcal{B}$ is *projective for* coequation i if every morphism $\mathcal{B} \to \mathcal{G}C$ factors through i:

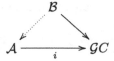

The class $(i)_\perp$ of objects projective for i is invariably a *virtual* covariety [15, 6.16]. If i and i' represent the same coequation, then $(i)_\perp = (i')_\perp$. If i is a *coequation over* 1 (i.e. $C = 1$ is terminal in **C**), then $(i)_\perp$ is a *behavioural* covariety. This is because $\mathcal{G}1$ is terminal in $\mathbf{C}_\mathbb{G}$, so if $\mathcal{B} \in (i)_\perp$, then the unique morphism $\mathcal{B} \to \mathcal{G}1$ is factored through i by some $g : \mathcal{B} \to \mathcal{A}$, so given any $\mathbb{G}$-morphism $f : \mathcal{B}' \to \mathcal{B}$, the unique $\mathcal{B}' \to \mathcal{G}1$ is factored through i by $g \circ f$. Hence $\mathcal{B}' \in (i)_\perp$, and $(i)_\perp$ is closed under domains of $\mathbb{G}$-morphisms.

Now it was shown in [11, 4.2] that if **C** has a terminal 1, then any behavioural covariety K in $\mathbf{C}_\mathbb{G}$ is equal to $(\varepsilon_{\mathcal{G}1}^R)_\perp$, where ε^R is the co-unit of the coreflector $R : \mathbf{C}_\mathbb{G} \to K$ described in Section 5. But by definition $\varepsilon_{\mathcal{G}1}^R = \sigma_1^K$, where σ^K is the comonad morphism to $\mathbb{G}$ determined by K. The maps $i \mapsto (i)_\perp$ and $K \mapsto \sigma_1^K$ provide a bijection between (equivalence classes of) coequations over 1 in $\mathbf{C}_\mathbb{G}$ and behavioural covarieties of $\mathbb{G}$-coalgebras. In fact for any regularly monomorphic cartesian $\sigma : \mathbb{F} \to \mathbb{G}$, there is a $\mathbb{G}$-coalgebra $(F1, \alpha)$ based on $F1$ such that σ_1 is a coequation $(F1, \alpha) \to \mathcal{G}1$. This can be shown from the fact that $\sigma_1 \simeq \sigma_1^K$ where $K = \mathrm{Im}\varphi\sigma$, and the fact that the components of σ^K are $\mathbb{G}$-morphisms. We thus have the picture of correspondences shown in Figure 1. Any virtual covariety K of $\mathbb{G}$-coalgebras is *coequational* in the sense that there is a class $\mathcal{E}$ of coequations $\mathcal{A} \rightarrowtail \mathcal{G}C$ such that $K = \mathcal{E}_\perp$ = the class of all coalgebras that are projective for every member of $\mathcal{E}$ [15, 6.16]. In fact $\mathcal{E}$ can be taken to be the class of all coreflection morphisms $\varepsilon_\mathcal{B}^R$ with $\mathcal{B}$ a cofree coalgebra $\mathcal{G}C$. Since $\varepsilon_{\mathcal{G}C}^R = \sigma_C^K$, we see that the class of coequations defining a virtual covariety K is just the class

$$\{\sigma_C^K : C \text{ is any } \mathbf{C}\text{-object}\} \tag{7.1}$$

of all components of the comonad morphism σ^K.

Now as we saw in Section 6, there are coequational classes (virtual covarieties) that are not covarieties, so to obtain a coequational characterisation of covarieties

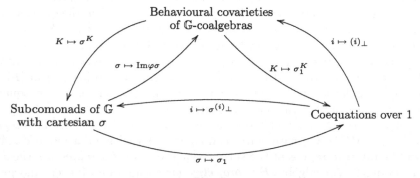

Fig. 1.

themselves we need some refinement of the notion of coequation. For equations, such a refinement was given in [14] by replacing free domains by domains that are *regular-projective*, i.e. projective for every regular epi, this being a property enjoyed by classical free universal algebras. Dually we contemplate coequations as regular monos i whose codomain is *regular-injective*, i.e. injective for every regular mono. Then the class $(i)_\perp$ will be an abstract covariety, i.e. closed under coproducts, codomains of epis and regular subobjects.

For the converse of this to work it is required that the ambient category *has enough injectives*, i.e. each object is a regular subobject of some regular-injective object. Then it can be shown that each abstract covariety is equal to $\mathcal{E}_\perp$ where $\mathcal{E}$ is some class of regular monos with regular-injective codomains [11,12,13,21]. For categories of coalgebras, if $\mathbf{C}$ has enough injectives, then so does $\mathbf{C}_\mathbb{G}$: in fact $\mathcal{G}C$ is regular-injective in $\mathbf{C}_\mathbb{G}$ whenever C is regular-injective in $\mathbf{C}$, and from this it can be shown that $\mathbf{C}_\mathbb{G}$ has enough regular-injectives that are *cofree*. Then each covariety K of $\mathbb{G}$-coalgebras is the coequational class $(\mathcal{E}^K)_\perp$ for some class $\mathcal{E}^K$ of regular monos with cofree regular-injective codomains [11,13]. Indeed, in our present terminology, we can take $\mathcal{E}^K = \{\sigma_C^K : C \text{ is regular-injective in } \mathbf{C}\}$, giving a direct comparison via (7.1) with the case that K is a *virtual* covariety.

Note that in the presence of enough injectives there can still be cocquational classes of coalgebras that are not covarieties. For example, this happens when $\mathbf{C}$ is the category **Asp** of acceptor spaces of Section 6. The regular-injective objects of **Asp** are just those acceptor spaces that have at least one starting state that is also accepting ($A^{st} \cap A^{ac} \neq \emptyset$). We can always expand a space by adding such a state if there is none, which implies that **Asp** has enough injectives.

References

1. Reichel, H.: An approach to object semantics based on terminal co-algebras. Mathematical Structures in Computer Science **5** (1995) 129–152
2. Jacobs, B.: Objects and classes, coalgebraically. In Freitag, B., Jones, C.B., Lengauer, C., Schek, H.J., eds.: Object-Orientation with Parallelism and Persistence. Kluwer Academic Publishers (1996) 83–103
3. Rutten, J.J.M.M.: A calculus of transition systems (towards universal coalgebra). In Ponse, A., de Rijke, M., Venema, Y., eds.: Modal Logic and Process Algebra. CSLI Lecture Notes No. 53. CSLI Publications, Stanford, California (1995) 231–256
4. Rutten, J.: Universal coalgebra: a theory of systems. Theoretical Computer Science **249** (2000) 3–80
5. Jacobs, B., Rutten, J.: A tutorial on (co)algebras and (co)induction. Bulletin of the European Association for Theoretical Computer Science **62** (1997) 222–259
6. Jacobs, B.: Exercises in coalgebraic specification. In Backhouse, R., Crole, R., Gibbons, J., eds.: Algebraic and Coalgebraic Methods in the Mathematics of Program Construction. Volume 2297 of Lecture Notes in Computer Science. Springer (2002) 237–280
7. Birkhoff, G.: On the structure of abstract algebras. Proceedings of the Cambridge Philosophical Society **31** (1935) 433–454

8. Hennessy, M., Milner, R.: Algebraic laws for nondeterminism and concurrency. Journal of the Association for Computing Machinery **32** (1985) 137–161
9. Goldblatt, R.: A comonadic account of behavioural covarieties of coalgebras. Mathematical Structures in Computer Science **15** (2005) 243–269
10. Gumm, H.P., Schröder, T.: Coalgebraic structure from weak limit preserving functors. Electronic Notes in Theoretical Computer Science **33** (2000)
11. Awodey, S., Hughes, J.: The coalgebraic dual of Birkhoff's variety theorem. Technical Report CMU-PHIL-109, Department of Philosophy, Carnegie Mellon University (2000)
12. Hughes, J.: A Study of Categories of Algebras and Coalgebras. PhD thesis, Carnegie Mellon University (2001)
13. Awodey, S., Hughes, J.: Modal operators and the formal dual of Birkhoff's completeness theorem. Mathematical Structures in Computer Science **13** (2003) 233–258
14. Banaschewski, B., Herrlich, H.: Subcategories defined by implications. Houston Journal of Mathematics **2** (1976) 149–171
15. Adámek, J., Porst, H.E.: On varieties and covarieties in a category. Mathematical Structures in Computer Science **13** (2003) 201–232
16. Borceux, F.: Handbook of Categorical Algebra 2. Categories and Structures. Cambridge University Press (1994)
17. Barr, M., Wells, C.: Toposes, Triples and Theories. Springer-Verlag (1985)
18. Mac Lane, S.: Categories for the Working Mathematician. Springer-Verlag (1971)
19. Herrlich, H., Strecker, G.: Category Theory. Allyn and Bacon, Newton, MA (1973)
20. Wyler, O.: Lecture Notes on Topoi and Quasitopoi. World Scientific (1991)
21. Kurz, A.: Logics for Coalgebras and Applications to Computer Science. PhD thesis, Ludwig-Maximilians-Universität München (2000)

Linking Theories of Concurrency

He Jifeng[1],[*] and C.A.R. Hoare[2]

[1] International Institute for Software Technology,
The United Nations University, P.O.Box 3058, Macau
jifeng@iist.unu.edu
[2] Microsoft Research, Cambridge CB3 0FB, UK

Abstract. We construct a Galois connection between the theories that underlie CCS [7] and CSP [4]. It projects the complete transition system for CCS onto exactly the subset that satisfies the healthiness conditions of CSP. The construction applies to several varieties of both calculi: CCS with strong, weak or barbed simulation, and CSP with trace refinement or failures refinement, or failures/divergence. We suggest the challenge of linking other theories of concurrency by Galois connection.

1 Introduction

Process algebra is the branch of mathematics which studies systems, computational or natural, that act and react continuously with each other and with their common environment. A wide variety of process algebra has been developed to meet widely varying needs. They have been comprehensively classified into an elegant hierarchies. This paper contributes to further clarification the close links between the full range of theories of concurrency that underlie apparently disparate process algebra.

In our definition, a theory of concurrency consists of two components. Firstly, it specifies a labelled directed graph, whose nodes represent process states and whose arcs represent transitions between the states. The labels on the arcs are the names of events that trigger or accompany the transition. Secondly, it specifies a pre-ordering relation between the nodes, which permits the replacement of one process state by another that is equivalent to it, or possibly better than it in some interesting sense.

A process algebra based on such a theory adds a syntax of constants and operators, which names particular nodes in the transition system. The local properties of the graph surrounding each named node are specified by the rules of a structured operational semantics. In this paper, we will ignore these important aspects of syntax and semantics of a process algebra, to concentrate on the underlying theories of concurrency. Our results thereby apply to whole classes of algebra based on the same underlying transition system.

---

[*] On leave from the SEI of East China Normal University, Shanghai. The work is partially supported by the 211 Key Project of the MoE, and the 973 project (2002CB312001) of the MoST of China.

D.V. Hung and M. Wirsing (Eds.): ICTAC 2005, LNCS 3722, pp. 303–317, 2005.

Extant theories of concurrency can be classified into two flourishing schools. The first of them owes its origin to CCS [7]. The underlying transition system is a universal graph, containing every other labelled graph as a sub-graph (up to isomorphism). Its pre-ordering relation is called similarity, or bi-similarity if it is symmetric – as it is usually required to be. Similarity is defined co-inductively, as the weakest relation that weakly commutes with all the transitions. It can be efficiently computed by model checking, and it permits elegant manual proofs by induction.

The second of the schools owes its origin to CSP [4]. Its underlying transition system is not universal, but is required to satisfy certain 'healthiness' conditions. Its notion of pre-ordering (called refinement) is defined as inclusion of the sets of observations that can be made of the two processes. An observation consists primarily of a trace of all the events in which a process engages, possibly followed by a 'barb', describing a property of the final state. Refinement represents a correctness relation between processes and their specifications. Failure of the ordering can easily be demonstrated by a single counter-example. Reasoning about correctness may exploit the full power of the mathematics of sets and sequences.

A Galois connection provides an interesting way of comparing two pre-ordered sets. It is like an isomorphism, but weaker and therefore more interesting. It consists of a pair of functions, one from each theory to the other. They are approximate mutual inverses, in the sense that their composition is not an identity, but rather a reducing function in one case, and an increasing function in the other. Each function is interpreted as mapping a member of either set to its closest approximation in the other.

We show how to construct a Galois connection between a pre-order based on simulation and one based on observation sets. We apply the method to three kinds of simulation, strong, weak and barbed, and to three kinds of refinement, traces, failures and failures/divergences. The connection is defined in terms of the familiar automata-theoretic concept of a derivative: If P is a process and a is an event, then 'P after a' denotes the most general process that behaves exactly the way(s) that P would behave after performing the action a.

This connection is of a particularly strong kind, known as a retraction. The function from the observation-based transition system to the simulation-based one is a projection. The other function is the identity function over the range of the projection. This means that the processes of CSP are effectively just a subset of those of CCS. The subset consists exactly of the fixed points of the projection: the fixed point equation expresses the healthiness conditions of CSP. Over this subset simulation agrees exactly with observational inclusion. Furthermore, the projection is a decreasing function, and so it preserves the least fixed point operator of both calculi.

The next section gives a brief tutorial introduction to the notions of pre-order, fixed points, derivatives, and Galois connections. Section 3 introduces the notions of simulation and refinement. It proves the fundamental theorem that is applied in subsequent sections. Section 4 links strong simulation with trace refinement. Section 5 introduces the silent event τ, and links weak simulation with the appropriate redefinition of trace refinement. Section 6 introduces barbs as properties of the final states of a process, and links barbed simulation with barbed trace refinement. Section 7 applies these results to the failures and divergences of CSP. The concluding section suggests that the same techniques might be applied to other varieties of simulation and refinement, perhaps including time or probability.

2 Background

A pre-order is a reflexive and transitive relation over a set. A special case is an equivalence relation, defined as a symmetric pre-order. Another special case is a partial order, which is anti-symmetric. A pre-order set is a set together with a pre-ordering relation over it.

Let $(P, \leq)$ and $(Q, \sqsubseteq)$ be pre-ordered sets. A Galois connection between them is a pair of monotonic functions $(f : P \rightarrow Q, g : Q \rightarrow P)$ such that for all $p \in P$ and for all $q \in Q$:

$$p \leq g(q) \quad \text{iff} \quad f(p) \sqsubseteq q$$

It follows that $f \cdot g$ is a decreasing function in Q, and $g \cdot f$ is increasing in P:

$$p \leq g(f(p)) \quad \text{and} \quad f(g(q)) \sqsubseteq q$$

An interior operator on a pre-ordered set is a function F from the set to itself that is monotonic, decreasing and idempotent in the sense that

$$F(F(x)) = F(x)$$

In this case, (F, id) is a Galois connection, where id is the identity function. The subset of elements in the range of F is called F-healthy.

Relations are sets of ordered pairs. The set of relations over a given set is partially ordered by set inclusion. The graph of a function is a relation, which we will often call by the same name. If r and s are relations, their composition $(r; s)$ is defined as

$$\{(x, z) \mid \exists y \bullet (x, y) \in r \land (y, z) \in s\}$$

Composition is associative and monotonic, and has the identity relation id as its unit. The set of relations over a given set is thereby a monoid.

The Kleene closure of a relation r is defined as the least pre-order that includes r:

$$r^* = id \cup r \cup (r; r) \cup \dots$$

We use u to denote the universal relation over the set. The complement and the converse of a relation are defined as usual

$$r - bar =_{df} \{(x, y) \mid (x, y) \in u \land (x, y) \notin r\}$$

$$r - cup =_{df} \{(x, y) \mid (y, x) \in r\}$$

If s and t are relations, their residual is defined

$$t/s \; = \; (t - bar; s - cup) - bar \; = \; \{(x, y) \mid \forall z \bullet (y, z) \in s \Rightarrow (x, z) \in t\}$$

The pair $(\_; s, \; \_/s)$ forms a Galois connection, because

$$(r; s) \subseteq t \quad \text{iff} \quad r \subseteq (t/s)$$

A complete lattice is an ordered set of which every subset has a greatest lower bound and (consequently) a least upper bound. The bottom of the lattice is the greatest lower bound of the whole lattice. Let G be a monotonic function from a complete lattice to itself. A point x of the set is called a fixed point of G if

$$G(x) \; = \; x$$

By the famous Knaster-Tarski theorem, the set of fixed points of G constitutes a complete lattice; it therefore has a greatest lower bound $\mu X \bullet G(x)$, which itself a fixed point of G.

Let F be an interior operator on a complete lattice S. Then the set T of F-healthy elements of F are just its fixed points, which form a complete lattice. Let G be a monotonic function which commutes with F, in the sense that

$$F \cdot G = G \cdot F$$

Then G maps T to T. Furthermore, the least fixed point of G taken over the complete lattice S is the same as the least fixed point of the function G, when taken over just the F-healthy operands.

Proof. We use $\mu_S G$ and $\mu_T G$ to represent the least fixed points of the function G over the sets S and T respectively.

$$
\begin{array}{lll}
& \mu_S G \; = \; G(\mu_S G) & \\
\Rightarrow & F(\mu_S G) \; = \; F(G(\mu_S G)) & \{F \cdot G = G \cdot F\} \\
\Rightarrow & F(\mu_S G) \; = \; G(F(\mu_S G)) & \{\text{least fixed point}\} \\
\Rightarrow & F(\mu_S G) \; \geq \; \mu_S G & \{F(x) \leq x\} \\
\Rightarrow & F(\mu_S G) \; = \; \mu_S G &
\end{array}
$$

This shows that $\mu_S G$ is a member of the set T. Since $T \subseteq S$, it is the least fixed point in T as well

$$\mu_S G \; = \; \mu_T G$$

In [5], the semantics of a programming language is embedded into a richer space of program specifications by means of healthiness conditions, usually defined as the fixed points of some suitably defined idempotent function F. All the operators G of the programming language are then required to be monotonic and to commute with F. The theorem proved above ensures that the meaning of recursion in the programming language can be defined by Tarski's fixed point construction, and the result will always be healthy. Recursive processes defined in the programming language are therefore guaranteed to be healthy.

3 Refinement and Simulation

Definition 3.1. (Observations)
Let $\mathcal{P}$ be a set of processes. A set $\mathcal{B}$ of binary relations over $\mathcal{P}$ is an observation set if it is a monoid, i.e.,

(1) it is closed under the relational composition.

(2) it has a total relation $id_\mathcal{B}$ as its unit.

Remark 1: The relations b, c,... in $\mathcal{B}$ are usually only partial. It is quite possible that the composition $(b; c)$ is empty; that means only that the observation c is impossible after b.

Remark 2: $id_\mathcal{B}$ is not necessary the identity relation $id_\mathcal{P}$ on $\mathcal{P}$. In the case of weak simulation we will select $id_\mathcal{B} = \xrightarrow{\tau}{}^*$.   □

Definition 3.2. ($\mathcal{B}$-simulation)
A binary relation r is a $\mathcal{B}$-simulation if it satisfies for all $b \in \mathcal{B}$

$$(r; b) \subseteq (b; r)$$

We will use $\leq_\mathcal{B}$ to stand for the greatest $\mathcal{B}$-simulation.   □

$\leq_\mathcal{B}$ can be defined as the greatest fixed point.

Theorem 3.1. $\leq_\mathcal{B} = \mu x \bullet \bigcap_{b \in \mathcal{B}} ((b; x)/b)$

Proof. $RHS; b$ {fixed point theorem}

$\subseteq$ $((b; RHS)/b); b$ $\{(x/y); y \subseteq x\}$

$\subseteq$ $(b; RHS)$

which indicates RHS is a $\mathcal{B}$-simulation. Because $\leq_\mathcal{B}$ is the greatest $\mathcal{B}$ simulation we conclude $RHS \subseteq LHS$. Furthermore one has

      true   {Defining inequations of $\leq_\mathcal{B}$}

$\Rightarrow$ $(LHS; b) \subseteq (b; LHS)$ $\{(x; y) \subseteq z$ iff $x \subseteq (z/y)\}$

$\Rightarrow$ $LHS \subseteq (b; LHS)/b$

which implies that $LHS \subseteq \bigcap_{b \in \mathcal{B}}((b; LHS)/b)$. The conclusion $LHS \subseteq RHS$ follows from Tarski's greatest fixed point theorem [14].   □

$\leq_\mathcal{B}$ is transitive.

Lemma 3.1. $\leq_\mathcal{B}; \leq_\mathcal{B} = \leq_\mathcal{B}$

Proof. From the fact that $(\leq_\mathcal{B}; b \subseteq b; \leq_\mathcal{B})$ we can show prove that LHS is also a $\mathcal{B}$-simulation, which implies $LHS \subseteq RHS$. The opposite inequation follows from the fact that $id_\mathcal{P} \subseteq \leq_\mathcal{B}$.   □

Definition 3.3. ($\mathcal{B}$-refinement)
A binary relation r on $\mathcal{P}$ is a $\mathcal{B}$-refinement if for all $b \in \mathcal{B}$

$$(r; b; \mathcal{U}) \subseteq (b; \mathcal{U})$$

where $\mathcal{U}$ denotes the universal relation over $\mathcal{P}$. We use $\sqsubseteq_\mathcal{B}$ to denote the greatest $\mathcal{B}$-refinement, and define $\equiv_\mathcal{B} =_{df} (\sqsubseteq_\mathcal{B} \cap \sqsubseteq_\mathcal{B} -cup)$.   □

Theorem 3.2. $\sqsubseteq_\mathcal{B} = \bigcap_{b \in \mathcal{B}} ((b; \mathcal{U})/(b; \mathcal{U}))$

Proof. Similar to Theorem 3.1.   □

Lemma 3.2. $\sqsubseteq_\mathcal{B}; b; \mathcal{U} = b; \mathcal{U}$

Proof. The inequation $LHS \supseteq RHS$ follows from the fact $id_\mathcal{P} \subseteq \sqsubseteq_\mathcal{B}$. The opposite one follows from Definition 3.3.   □

Corollary. $\sqsubseteq_\mathcal{B}; \sqsubseteq_\mathcal{B} = \sqsubseteq_\mathcal{B}$ □

Simulation implies refinement.

Theorem 3.3. $\leq_\mathcal{B} \subseteq \sqsubseteq_\mathcal{B}$

Proof.
$\quad \leq_\mathcal{B}; b; \mathcal{U}$ {Definition 3.2}
$\subseteq \quad b; \leq_\mathcal{B}; \mathcal{U}$ $\{\leq_\mathcal{B} \subseteq \mathcal{U}$ and $\mathcal{U}; \mathcal{U} = \mathcal{U}\}$
$\subseteq \quad b; \mathcal{U}$

which implies that $\leq_\mathcal{B}$ is a $\mathcal{B}$-refinement.   □

A process can be identified by a set of observations which it can present during its execution.

Definition 3.4. (Behaviours)
$$\mathbf{beh}_\mathcal{B}(P) =_{df} \{b : \mathcal{B} \mid P \in \mathbf{dom}(b)\}$$
where $\mathbf{dom}(b)$ denotes the domain of b.   □

Lemma 3.3. $(b_1; b_2) \in \mathbf{beh}_\mathcal{B}(P)$ implies $b_1 \in \mathbf{beh}_\mathcal{B}(P)$

Proof. From the fact that
$$\mathbf{dom}(b_1; b_2) = \mathbf{dom}(b_1; b_2; \mathcal{U}) \subseteq \mathbf{dom}(b_1; \mathcal{U}) = \mathbf{dom}(b_1)$$ □

Lemma 3.4. $\mathbf{beh}_\mathcal{B}(P) = \bigcup \{\mathbf{beh}_\mathcal{B}(Q) \mid P \sqsubseteq_\mathcal{B} Q\}$

Proof. From Lemma 3.2.   □

Theorem 3.4.

$P \sqsubseteq_\mathcal{B} Q$ iff $\mathbf{beh}_\mathcal{B}(P) \supseteq \mathbf{beh}_\mathcal{B}(Q)$.

Proof.
$\quad P \sqsubseteq_\mathcal{B} Q$ {Lemma 3.4}
$\Rightarrow \quad \mathbf{beh}_\mathcal{B}(P) \supseteq \mathbf{beh}_\mathcal{B}(Q)$ $\{\{(P, Q)\}; b; \mathcal{U} \subseteq b; \mathcal{U}\}$
$\Rightarrow \quad \{(P, Q)\} \subseteq \sqsubseteq_\mathcal{B}$
$\Rightarrow \quad P \sqsubseteq_\mathcal{B} Q$ □

A deterministic transition system is traditionally defined by a partial binary function (which we denote by \, read as 'after'), mapping nodes and labels to nodes, $p \backslash b$ is the node that describes exactly the behaviour of the process p, after it has engaged in the event b. The process $p\backslash b$ is defined exactly when p is in the domain of b. In the deterministic transition system, there is always just one arrow labelled b from p to $p\backslash b$, whenever the latter is defined. In a non-deterministic system, there may be more than one such arrow. Or there may be none. In order to rule out such a transition system, we have to postulate the existence of an 'after' function with the following properties

(1) $p \in \mathbf{dom}(b; c)$ iff $(p\backslash b, p\backslash(b; c)) \in c$

(2) $p \in \mathbf{dom}(b; c)$ iff $(p\backslash b) \in \mathbf{dom}(c)$

(3) $p\backslash b\backslash c = p\backslash(b; c)$

Lemma 3.5. $\mathbf{dom}(\backslash b) = \mathbf{dom}(b)$

Proof. Let $c = id_{\mathcal{B}}$ in the property (2) of $\backslash$. $\qquad\qquad\square$

Lemma 3.6. If $P \in \mathbf{dom}(b)$, then $\mathbf{beh}_{\mathcal{B}}(P\backslash b) = \{c \mid (b; c) \in \mathbf{beh}_{\mathcal{B}}(P)\}$

Proof. From the property (2) of the definition of $\backslash$. $\qquad\qquad\square$

Corollary 1. If $P\backslash b \sqsubseteq_{\mathcal{B}} Q$ and $Q\, c\, R$ then $P\backslash(b; c) \sqsubseteq R$ $\qquad\qquad\square$

Corollary 2. If $P \sqsubseteq_{\mathcal{B}} Q$, then $P\backslash b \sqsubseteq_{\mathcal{B}} Q\backslash b$ $\qquad\qquad\square$

In the case that $p = p\backslash id_{\mathcal{B}}$, we can derive from the property (1)

$$p \in \mathbf{dom}(c) \quad \text{if and only if} \quad (p, p\backslash c) \in c$$

That suggests that we explore the subset of nodes p of the transition system that satisfy the condition. We will show that on this subset, $\mathcal{B}$-simulation has the same meaning as $\mathcal{B}$-refinement.

Theorem 3.5. $\mathcal{D}\lhd \sqsubseteq_{\mathcal{B}}$ is a $\mathcal{B}$-simulation.
where $\mathcal{D}$ is the range of $\backslash$, and $\mathcal{D}\lhd \sqsubseteq_{\mathcal{B}}$ denotes the sub-relation of $\sqsubseteq_{\mathcal{B}}$ whose domain is restricted to the set $\mathcal{D}$.

Proof. $\mathcal{D}\lhd \sqsubseteq_{\mathcal{B}} ; b$ $\qquad\qquad\qquad\qquad$ {Lemma 3.5}

$= \quad \{(P\backslash c, Q) \mid P \in \mathbf{dom}(c) \wedge P\backslash c \sqsubseteq_{\mathcal{B}} Q\} ; b$ $\qquad$ {Definition of ; }

$= \quad \{(P\backslash c, R) \mid P \in \mathbf{dom}(c) \wedge$

$\qquad\qquad\qquad \exists Q \bullet P\backslash c \sqsubseteq_{\mathcal{B}} Q \wedge (Q\, b\, R)\}$ $\qquad$ {property (2) of $\backslash$}

$\sqsubseteq \quad \{(P\backslash c, P\backslash(c; b) \mid P \in \mathbf{dom}(c; b)\};$

$\qquad \{(P\backslash(c; b), R) \mid P \in \mathbf{dom}(c; b) \wedge$

$\qquad\qquad\qquad \exists Q \bullet P\backslash c \sqsubseteq_{\mathcal{B}} Q \wedge (Q\, b\, R)\}$ $\qquad$ {property (1) of $\backslash$}

$\sqsubseteq \quad c; \{(P\backslash(c; b), R) \mid P \in \mathbf{dom}(c; b) \wedge$

$\qquad\qquad\qquad \exists Q \bullet P\backslash c \sqsubseteq_{\mathcal{B}} Q \wedge (Q\, b\, R)\}$ $\qquad\qquad$ {Corollary 1}

$\sqsubseteq \quad c; \{(P\backslash(c; b), R) \mid P \in \mathbf{dom}(c; b) \wedge$

$\qquad\qquad\qquad\qquad P\backslash(c; b) \sqsubseteq_{\mathcal{B}} R\}$ $\qquad\qquad$ {Definition of $\mathcal{D}$}

$\sqsubseteq \quad c; \mathcal{D}\lhd \sqsubseteq_{\mathcal{B}}$ $\qquad\qquad\qquad\qquad\qquad\qquad\square$

Definition 3.6.
$$\mathcal{H}_B(P) =_{df} (P \backslash id_B)$$

From Lemma 3.5 it follows that $\mathcal{H}_B$ is a total function. $\square$

The following theorem states that $\mathcal{H}_B$ is a link.

Theorem 3.6.

(1) $\mathcal{H}_B$ is monotonic: if $P \sqsubseteq_B Q$ then $\mathcal{H}_B(P) \leq_B \mathcal{H}_B(Q)$

(2) $\mathcal{H}_B$ keeps the behaviour unchanged: $\mathcal{H}_B(P) \equiv_B P$

(3) $\mathcal{H}_B$ is idempotent: $\mathcal{H}_B^2(P) = \mathcal{H}_B(P)$

(4) $\mathcal{H}_B$ is a weakening: $\mathcal{H}_B(P) \leq_B P$

(5) $(id_P, \mathcal{H}_B)$ forms a Galois connection
$$P \sqsubseteq_B Q \text{ iff } \mathcal{H}_B(P) \leq_B Q$$

Proof of (1). $P \sqsubseteq_B Q$ {Corollary 2}

$\Rightarrow$ $\mathcal{H}_B(P) \sqsubseteq_B \mathcal{H}_B(Q)$ {Theorem 3.5}

$\Rightarrow$ $\mathcal{H}_B(P) \leq_B \mathcal{H}_B(Q)$

(2) From Lemma 3.6.

(3) From the property (3) of $\backslash$.

(4) The conclusion follows from the conclusion (2) and Theorem 3.5.

Proof of (5). $P \sqsubseteq_B Q$ {Theorem 3.6(2)}

$\equiv$ $\mathcal{H}_B(P) \sqsubseteq_B Q$ {Theorems 2.3 and 3.5}

$\equiv$ $\mathcal{H}_B(P) \leq_B Q$ $\square$

4   Strong Simulation

We use $\mathcal{L}$ to represent the set of all visible actions which appear at the interface of the system, and λ range over this set. Let τ denote an invisible action, which usually stands for a silent event, and is entirely internal to the system. We will use α to range over the set $\mathcal{A} =_{df} \mathcal{L} \cup \{\tau\}$, and $\mathcal{A}^*$ to denote the set of all finite sequences of elements of $\mathcal{A}$.

Definition 4.1. (Labelled transition system)
A labelled transition system over $\mathcal{A}$ is a pair $(\mathcal{P}, \mathcal{T})$ consisting of

(1) a set $\mathcal{P}$ of processes;

(2) a set $\mathcal{T}$ of binary relations on $\mathcal{P}$: $\mathcal{T} = \{\xrightarrow{\alpha} \mid \alpha \in \mathcal{A}\}$

Define for $s \in \mathcal{A}^*$
$$\xrightarrow{s} =_{df} \begin{cases} id_P & s = \epsilon \\ \xrightarrow{\alpha}; \xrightarrow{t} & s = \langle \alpha \rangle \cdot t \end{cases}$$

where ϵ denotes the empty sequence.

Define $\mathcal{B} =_{df} \mathcal{T}^* = \{\overset{s}{\to} \mid s \in \mathcal{A}^*\}$. $\mathcal{B}$ is a set of observations.

Lemma 4.1.
(1) $\overset{\epsilon}{\to}$ is the unit of $\mathcal{B}$

(2) $\overset{s}{\to}; \overset{t}{\to} = \overset{s \cdot t}{\to}$ □

Definition 4.2. (Strong simulation [8])
The strong simulation $\leq_s$ is defined as the greatest relation r satisfying for all $\alpha \in \mathcal{A}$

$$(r; \overset{\alpha}{\to}) \subseteq (\overset{\alpha}{\to}; r) \qquad \qquad \square$$

Theorem 4.1. $\leq_\mathcal{B} = \leq_s$.

Proof. From the definition of $\mathcal{B}$ it follows that for all $\alpha \in A$ one has $\overset{\alpha}{\to} \in \mathcal{B}$. As a result, one concludes that $\leq_\mathcal{B}$ satisfies

$$(\leq_\mathcal{B}; \overset{\alpha}{\to}) \subseteq (\overset{\alpha}{\to}; \leq_\mathcal{B})$$

which implies that $leq_\mathcal{B}$ is a subset of $\leq_s$.

On the other hand by induction on the length of t one can show that

$$(\leq_s; \overset{t}{\to}) \subseteq (\overset{t}{\to}; \leq_s)$$

from which it follows that $\leq_s \subseteq \leq_\mathcal{B}$. □

A trace of the behaviour of a process is a finite sequence of events in which the process has engaged up to some moment in time. We define $traces_A(P)$ as the set of all possible traces of P:

$$traces_A(P) =_{df} \{s : \mathcal{A}^* \mid P \in \mathbf{dom}(\overset{s}{\to})\}$$

Theorem 4.2.
$P \sqsubseteq_\mathcal{B} Q$ iff $traces_A(P) \supseteq traces_A(Q)$

Proof. From the fact that $s \in traces_A(P)$ iff $\overset{s}{\to} \in \mathbf{beh}_\mathcal{B}(P)$ □

Definition 4.3.
Define $P \backslash \overset{s}{\to} \backslash \overset{t}{\to} =_{df} P \backslash \overset{s \cdot t}{\to}$, and

$$\frac{P \in \mathbf{dom}(\overset{s \cdot \langle \alpha \rangle}{\to})}{(P \backslash \overset{s}{\to}) \overset{\alpha}{\to} (P \backslash \overset{s \cdot \langle \alpha \rangle}{\to})}$$

Theorem 4.3. $\backslash$ satisfies the defining properties of Definition 3.5.

Proof. From Definition 4.3 it follows that that $P \in \mathbf{dom}(\overset{s \cdot t}{\to})$ implies that

$$(P \backslash \overset{s}{\to}) \overset{t}{\to} (P \backslash \overset{s \cdot t}{\to})$$

i.e., the property (1) of Definition 3.5 holds.

Definition 4.3 also indicates

$$(P\backslash \xrightarrow{s}) \in \mathbf{dom}(\xrightarrow{t}) \quad \text{if and only if} \quad P \in \mathbf{dom}(\xrightarrow{s \cdot t})$$

which implies the property (2) of Definition 3.5 $\qquad \square$

Define $\mathcal{H}_s(P) =_{df} P\backslash id_P$.

Theorem 4.4. $traces_A(P) \supseteq traces_A(Q)$ iff $\mathcal{H}_s(P) \leq_s Q$

Proof. From Theorems 3.6(5), 4.1, 4.2 and 4.3. $\qquad \square$

5   Weak Simulation

Define $\Rightarrow =_{df} \xrightarrow{\tau}{}^*$, and $\xRightarrow{\lambda} =_{df} (\Rightarrow; \xrightarrow{\lambda}; \Rightarrow)$ for $\lambda \in \mathcal{L}$.

For $e \in \mathcal{L}^*$, define

$$\xRightarrow{e} =_{df} \begin{cases} \Rightarrow & \text{if } e = \epsilon \\ \xRightarrow{\lambda}; \xRightarrow{e'} & \text{if } e = \langle \lambda \rangle e' \end{cases}$$

Let $\mathcal{B} =_{df} \{\xRightarrow{e} \mid e \in \mathcal{L}^*\}$.

Lemma 5.1. $\mathcal{B}$ is an observation set with $\Rightarrow$ as its unit. $\qquad \square$

Definition 5.1. (Weak simulation [8])
$\leq_w$ is defined as the greatest relation r satisfying

(1) $(r; \xrightarrow{\tau}) \leq (\Rightarrow; r)$

(2) $(r; \xrightarrow{\lambda}) \leq (\xRightarrow{\lambda}; r)$ for all $\lambda \in \mathcal{L}$ $\qquad \square$

Theorem 5.1. $\leq_{\mathcal{B}} = \leq_w$.

	Proof.	$\leq_{\mathcal{B}}; \xrightarrow{\tau}$	$\{\xrightarrow{\tau} \subseteq \Rightarrow\}$
$\subseteq$		$\leq_{\mathcal{B}}; \Rightarrow$	$\{\text{Definition 3.2}\}$
$\subseteq$		$\Rightarrow; \leq_{\mathcal{B}}$	
		$\leq_{\mathcal{B}}; \xrightarrow{\lambda}$	$\{\xrightarrow{\lambda} \subseteq \xRightarrow{\lambda}\}$
$\subseteq$		$\leq_{\mathcal{B}}; \xRightarrow{\lambda}$	$\{\text{Definition 3.2}\}$
$\subseteq$		$\xRightarrow{\lambda}; \leq_{\mathcal{B}}$	

which implies $\leq_{\mathcal{B}} \subseteq \leq_w$. On the other hand, one has

		$\leq_w; \Rightarrow$	$\{\text{Definition 5.1(1)}\}$
$\subseteq$		$\Rightarrow^*; \leq_w$	$\{\Rightarrow^* = \Rightarrow\}$
$=$		$\Rightarrow; \leq_w$	
		$\leq_w; \xRightarrow{\lambda}$	$\{\xRightarrow{\lambda} = (\Rightarrow; \xrightarrow{\lambda}; \Rightarrow)\}$
$=$		$\leq_w; \Rightarrow; \xrightarrow{\lambda}; \Rightarrow$	$\{(\leq_w; \Rightarrow) \subseteq (\Rightarrow; \leq_w)\}$

$$\subseteq \quad \Rightarrow; \leq_w; \xrightarrow{\lambda}; \Rightarrow \qquad\qquad \text{\{Definition 5.1(2)\}}$$

$$\subseteq \quad \Rightarrow; \xrightarrow{\lambda}; \Rightarrow; \leq_w \qquad\qquad \text{\{Lemma 5.1\}}$$

$$= \quad \xrightarrow{\lambda}; \leq_w$$

which indicates $\leq_w$ is a sub-relation of $\leq_\mathcal{B}$. □

Define $traces_\mathcal{L}(P) =_{df} \{e : \mathcal{L}^* \mid P \in \mathbf{dom}(\xrightarrow{e})\}$

Theorem 5.2. $P \sqsubseteq_\mathcal{B} Q$ iff $traces_\mathcal{L}(P) \supseteq traces_\mathcal{L}(Q)$

Proof. From the fact that $e \in traces_\mathcal{L}(P)$ if and only if $\xrightarrow{e} \in \mathbf{beh}_\mathcal{B}(P)$ □

Define $P\backslash \xrightarrow{s} \backslash \xrightarrow{t} =_{df} P\backslash \xrightarrow{s \cdot t}$, and

$$\frac{P \in \mathbf{dom}(\xrightarrow{s \cdot \langle \lambda \rangle})}{(P\backslash \xrightarrow{s}) \xrightarrow{\lambda} P\backslash(s \cdot \langle \lambda \rangle)}$$

Theorem 5.3. $\backslash$ satisfies the defining properties of Definition 3.5. □

Define $\mathcal{H}_w(P) =_{df} P\backslash \Rightarrow$.

Theorem 5.4. $traces_\mathcal{L}(P) \supseteq traces_\mathcal{L}(Q)$ iff $\mathcal{H}_w(P) \leq_w Q$

Proof. From Theorems 3.6(5), 5.1, 5.2 and 5.3. □

6 Barbed Simulation

A *barb* is used to denote a property of states, rather than an action which changes the state. For example, the following barbs have suggestive names.

(1) **candiverge** is a property of states which can engage in an infinite sequence of invisible action τ.

(2) Let X be a subset of $\mathcal{L}$. The barb **canrefuse**(X) indicates a deadlocked state, which cannot perform in any of the actions in the set X.

$$P \text{ has } \mathbf{canrefuse}(X) \text{ if } \mathbf{init}(P) \cap (X \cup \{\tau\}) = \emptyset$$

where $\mathbf{init}(P) =_{df} \{\alpha : \mathcal{A} \mid P \in \mathbf{dom}(\xrightarrow{\alpha})\}$.

In order to treat a barb b in the same way as a labelled transition, we encode it as a binary relation as follows:

$$P \text{ has the barb } b \quad \text{iff} \quad P \xrightarrow{b} \top$$

where the notation $\top$ represents a process which does not engage in any transition, nor lie in the domain of any barb. For convenience, sometimes we will use b to abbreviate $\xrightarrow{b}$ in the later discussion.

Let *Barbs* be a set of barbs. Define

$$\mathcal{B} =_{df} \{\xrightarrow{e} \mid e \in (\mathcal{L} \cup Barbs)^*\}$$

Lemma 6.1. $\mathcal{B}$ is a set of observations, and

$$\mathcal{B} = \{\emptyset\} \cup \{\stackrel{s}{\Rightarrow} \mid s \in \mathcal{L}^*\} \cup \{\stackrel{s\cdot\langle b\rangle}{\Rightarrow} \mid s \in \mathcal{L}^* \wedge b \in Barbs\}$$

Proof. From the fact that for $b \in Barbs$

$$\stackrel{s}{\Rightarrow};\stackrel{e}{\Rightarrow} = \stackrel{s\cdot e}{\Rightarrow} \qquad s \in \mathcal{L}^* \wedge e \in (\mathcal{L} \cup Barbs)^*$$

$$\stackrel{s\cdot\langle b\rangle}{\Rightarrow};\stackrel{e}{\Rightarrow} = \emptyset \qquad s \in \mathcal{L}^* \wedge e \in (\mathcal{L} \cup Barbs)^* \wedge e \neq \epsilon \quad \square$$

Lemma 6.2. $b; \leq_\mathcal{B} = b$ for all $b \in Barbs$

Proof. From the fact that $\mathbf{beh}_\mathcal{B}(\top) = \emptyset$ it follows that

$$\top \leq_\mathcal{B} P \equiv (P = \top) \qquad\qquad\qquad \square$$

Definition 6.2. (Barbed simulation)
The barbed simulation $\leq_{Barbs}$ is defined as the greatest relation r satisfying

(1) $(r; \stackrel{s}{\Rightarrow}) \subseteq (\stackrel{s}{\Rightarrow}; r)$ for all $s \in \mathcal{L}^*$

(2) $(r; b) \subseteq b$ for all $b \in Barbs$ $\qquad\qquad\qquad \square$

Definition 6.2. (Barbed traces)
$Btraces(P) =_{df} \{(s, b) : \mathcal{L}^* \times Barbs \mid P \in \mathbf{dom}(\stackrel{s\langle b\rangle}{\Rightarrow})\}$ $\qquad \square$

In the following discussion we will confine ourselves to those $Barbs$ which satisfy the following properties:

(1) $(\Rightarrow; b) = b$ for all $b \in Barbs$

(2) $\bigcup_{b \in Barbs} \mathbf{dom}(b) = \mathcal{P}$.

where the property (1) requires that the τ event keeps its invisibility in the theory of barbed simulations, while (2) indicates that the set $Barbs$ covers a wide range of properties of states. Section 7 will present the barb set with these two properties.

Theorem 6.1. $\leq_\mathcal{B} = \leq_{Barbs}$

Proof. Because $\stackrel{s}{\Rightarrow} \in \mathcal{B}$ one conclude that $(\leq_\mathcal{B}; \stackrel{s}{\Rightarrow}) \subseteq (\stackrel{s}{\Rightarrow}; \leq_\mathcal{B})$.

We are going to show that $\leq_\mathcal{B}$ also meets the defining property (2) of Definition 6.2., i.e., $\leq_\mathcal{B}$ is a subset of $\leq_{Barbs}$.

Proof.	$\leq_\mathcal{B}; b$	$\{b \subseteq \stackrel{b}{\Rightarrow}\}$
$=$	$\leq_\mathcal{B}; \stackrel{b}{\Rightarrow}$	$\{$Definition 3.2$\}$
$\subseteq$	$\stackrel{b}{\Rightarrow}; \leq_\mathcal{B}$	$\{$Property (1) of $Barbs$ and $\mathbf{range}(b) = \{\top\}\}$
$=$	$b; \leq_\mathcal{B}$	$\{$Lemma 6.2$\}$
$\subseteq$	b	

In the following we will show that for all $b \in Barbs$

$$\leq_{Barbs}; \stackrel{b}{\Rightarrow} \subseteq \stackrel{b}{\Rightarrow}; \leq_{Barbs}$$

which implies that for all $c \in \mathcal{B}$ one has $(\leq_{Barbs}; c) \subseteq (c; \leq_{Barbs})$, i.e., $\leq_{Barbs}$ is a subset of $\leq_w$.

$$
\begin{aligned}
& \leq_{Barbs}; \overset{b}{\Rightarrow} && \{\text{Property (2) } of \ Barbs\} \\
= \quad & \leq_{Barbs}; b; \Rightarrow && \{(2) \text{ of Definition 6.2}\} \\
= \quad & b; \Rightarrow && \{id_P \subseteq \Rightarrow \text{ and } id_P \subseteq \leq_{Barbs}\} \\
\subseteq \quad & \Rightarrow; b; \Rightarrow; \leq_{Barbs} && \{\text{Def of } \overset{b}{\Rightarrow}\} \\
= \quad & \overset{b}{\Rightarrow}; \leq_{Barbs} && \square
\end{aligned}
$$

Theorem 6.2. $P \sqsubseteq_{\mathcal{B}} Q$ iff $Btraces(P) \supseteq Btraces(Q)$

Proof. From the property (2) of the set $Barbs$ one concludes that

$$P \in \mathbf{dom}(\overset{s}{\Rightarrow}) \text{ if and only if } \exists b \in Barbs \bullet P \in \mathbf{dom}(\overset{s\langle b \rangle}{\Rightarrow})$$

which implies

$$\mathbf{beh}_{\mathcal{B}}(P) = \{\overset{s\langle b \rangle}{\Rightarrow}) \mid (s, b) \in Btraces(P)\} \cup \{\overset{s}{\Rightarrow} \mid \exists b \bullet (s, b) \in Btraces(P)\}$$

which leads to the conclusion. $\qquad\square$

Definition 6.3.

Define $P\backslash \overset{s\langle b \rangle}{\Rightarrow} =_{df} \top$ whenever $P \in \mathbf{dom}(\overset{s\langle b \rangle}{\Rightarrow})$. and

$$
\frac{P \in \mathbf{dom}(\overset{s \cdot \langle \lambda \rangle}{\Rightarrow})}{(P\backslash \overset{s}{\Rightarrow}) \overset{\lambda}{\to} (P\backslash \overset{s \cdot \langle \lambda \rangle}{\Rightarrow})} \lambda \in \mathcal{L}, \qquad \frac{P \in \mathbf{dom}(\overset{s\langle b \rangle}{\Rightarrow})}{(P\backslash \overset{s}{\Rightarrow}) \overset{b}{\to} \top}
$$

Define $\mathcal{H}_{Barbs}(P) =_{df} P\backslash \Rightarrow$. $\qquad\square$

Theorem 6.3. $\backslash$ satisfies the defining properties of Definition 3.5. $\qquad\square$

Theorem 6.4. $Btraces(P) \supseteq Btraces(Q)$ iff $\mathcal{H}_{Barbs}(P) \leq_{Barbs} Q$

Proof. From Theorem 3.6(5), 6.1, 6.2 and 6.3.

7 Failures and Divergences Refinement

Let X be a subset of visible actions. Define the barb **mayrefuse** X by

$$\mathbf{mayrefuse}\, X =_{df} \mathbf{candiverge} \vee (\Rightarrow; \mathbf{canrefuse}\, X)$$

Define the barb set

$$RefDiv =_{df} \{\mathbf{candiverge}\} \cup \{\mathbf{mayrefuse}\, X \mid X \subseteq \mathcal{L}\}.$$

Lemma 7.1. $RefDiv$ satisfies the properties of $Barbs$ defined in Section 6.

Proof. From the fact that $(\Rightarrow; \Rightarrow) = \Rightarrow$ it follows that

$$(\Rightarrow; \mathbf{mayrefuse}\, X) = \mathbf{mayrefuse}\, X$$

which implies the property (1) defined in Section 6. The property (2) follows from the fact that **dom**(**mayrefuse** $\emptyset$) = $\mathcal{P}$.   □

Failures/divergences are due to Brookes and Roscoe [2].

Definition 7.1. (Failures/Divergences)

$Failures(P) =_{df} \{(s, X) \mid s \in \mathcal{L}^* \wedge X \subseteq \mathcal{L} \wedge \exists Q \bullet P \overset{s}{\Rightarrow} Q \wedge Q \, \textbf{mayrefuse} \, X\}$

$Divergences(P) =_{df} \{s \mid s \in \mathcal{L}^* \wedge \exists Q \bullet P \overset{s}{\Rightarrow} Q \wedge Q \, \textbf{candiverge}\}$

Define $P \sqsubseteq_{FD} Q =_{df} (Failures(P) \supseteq Failures(Q)) \wedge$

$$(Divergences(P) \supseteq Divergences(Q)) \qquad □$$

Lemma 7.2. $\sqsubseteq_B = \sqsubseteq_{FD}$

Proof. From Theorem 6.2 and the following facts:

(1) $s \in Divergences(P)$ iff $(s, \textbf{candiverge}) \in Btraces(P)$

(2) $(s, X) \in Failures(P)$ iff $(s, \textbf{mayrefuse} \, X) \in Btraces(P)$ □

Notice that the property **candiverge** is undecidable, it is infeasible to refer to the premise $P \in \textbf{dom}(\overset{s\langle\textbf{candiverge}\rangle}{\Rightarrow})$ in a transition rule. In the following we replace the second transition rule of Definition 6.3 by

$$\frac{P \overset{s}{\Rightarrow} Q}{(P\backslash \overset{s}{\Rightarrow}) \overset{\tau}{\to} Q}$$

and show that the new rule does implement the old one.

Lemma 7.3. If $P \in \textbf{dom}(\overset{s\langle b\rangle}{\Rightarrow})$ then $(P\backslash \overset{s}{\Rightarrow})$ has the barb b.

Proof. For all $b \in RefDiv$ one has

$P \in \textbf{dom}(\overset{s\langle b\rangle}{\Rightarrow})$ \hfill $\{\overset{s\langle b\rangle}{\Rightarrow} = (\overset{s}{\Rightarrow}; \overset{b}{\Rightarrow})\}$

$\Rightarrow \exists Q \bullet (P \overset{s}{\Rightarrow} Q \wedge Q \overset{b}{\Rightarrow} \top)$ \hfill {The new transition rule}

$\Rightarrow \exists Q \bullet ((P\backslash \overset{s}{\Rightarrow}) \overset{\tau}{\to} Q \wedge Q \, \text{has the barb } b)$ \hfill $\{\Rightarrow; b = b\}$

$\Rightarrow P\backslash(\overset{s}{\Rightarrow})$ has the barb b \hfill □

Theorem 7.1. $P \sqsubseteq_{FD} Q$ iff $\mathcal{H}_{Barbs}(P) \leq_{Barbs} Q$

Proof. From Theorem 6.4 and Lemmas 7.1 and 7.2.   □

8 Conclusion

Many methods of unifying theories of concurrency have been proposed in the literature. A simple method is by postulation of a sufficient collection of algebraic laws, more than in the usual definition of structural equivalence [7]. An indirect method is by defining a specification language, the modal mu calculus, and then restricting its expression power so that it cannot recognise distinctions that one wishes to ignore. Two processes are equated if they satisfy the same specifications. Gardiner achieved unification by a definition of simulation based on sets of states rather than individual states [3].

This paper aims to unify the study of process algebras, by establishing a Galois connection between similarity and refinement. This is achieved by additional transition rules, suitable for inclusion at will in the operational semantics of any calculus that seeks reconciliation. The new transitions may be interpreted by an implementer of the calculus as permission to be kind to the user of the process, in the sense of giving the user more opportunities to avoid deadlock. The new transitions also offer additional possibilities for resolving non-determinism at compile time; they valid more algebraic laws, so giving more opportunities for optimisations.

References

1. J.A. Bergstra and J.W. Klop. *"Algebra of communicating processes with abstraction"*. Theoretical Computer Sciences, Vol 37(1): 77–121, (1985).
2. S.D. Brookes, C.A.R. Hoare and A.W. Roscoe. *"A theory of communicating sequential processes"*, Journal of the ACM, Vol 31, (1984)
3. P. Gardiner. *"Power simulation and its relation to Traces and Failures Refinement"*. Theoretical Computer Science, 309(1): 157–176, (2003).
4. C.A.R. Hoare. *"Communicating sequential processes"*, Prentice Hall, (1985)
5. C.A.R. Hoare and He Jifeng. *"Unifying theories of programming"*, Prentice Hall, (1998)
6. K.G. Larsen and A. Skou. *"Bisimulation through probabilistic testing"*, Information and control 94(1), (1991)
7. R. Milner. *"Communication and concurrency"*, Prentice Hall, (1989)
8. R. Milner *"Communicating and mobile systems: the π -calculus"* Cambridge University Press, (1999)
9. R. Milner and D. Sangiorgi. *"Barbed simulation"*. Lecture Notes in Computer Science 623, : 685–695, (1992)
10. R. De Nicola and M. Hennessy. *"Testing equivalence for processes"*, Theoretical Computer Science 34, (1983)
11. D.M.R. Park. *"Concurrency and automata on infinite sequences"*, Lecture Notes in Computer Science, Vol 14, (1980)
12. G.D. Plotkin. *"A structural approach to operational semantics"*, Report DAIMI-FN-19, Computer Science Department, Arhus University, Denmark, (1981)
13. A.W. Roscoe. *"The theory and practice of concurrency"*, Prentice Hall, (1998)
14. A. Tarski. *"A lattice-theoretical fixedpoint theorem and its applications"*. Pacific Journal of Mathematics, Vil 5: 285–309, (1955).

On Cool Congruence Formats
for Weak Bisimulations
(Extended Abstract)

Robert Jan van Glabbeek

National ICT Australia and School of Computer Science and Engineering,
The University of New South Wales
rvg@cs.stanford.edu

Abstract. In TCS 146, Bard Bloom presented rule formats for four
main notions of bisimulation with silent moves. He proved that weak
bisimulation equivalence is a congruence for any process algebra defined
by *WB cool rules*, and established similar results for rooted weak bisimulation (Milner's "observational congruence"), branching bisimulation
and rooted branching bisimulation. This study reformulates Bloom's results in a more accessible form and contributes analogues for (rooted)
η-bisimulation and (rooted) delay bisimulation. Moreover, finite equational axiomatisations of rooted weak bisimulation equivalence are provided that are sound and complete for finite processes in any RWB cool
process algebra. These require the introduction of auxiliary operators
with lookahead. Finally, a challenge is presented for which Bloom's formats fall short and further improvement is called for.

Introduction

Structural Operational Semantics [8,10] is one of the main methods for defining
the meaning of operators in system description languages like CCS [8]. A system
behaviour, or *process*, is represented by a closed term built from a collection of
operators, and the behaviour of a process is given by its collection of (outgoing) transitions, each specifying the action the process performs by taking this
transition, and the process that results after doing so. For each n-ary operator
f in the language, a number of *transition rules* are specified that generate the
transitions of a term $f(p_1, \ldots, p_n)$ from the transitions (or the absence thereof)
of its arguments $p_1, \ldots, p_n$.

For purposes of representation and verification, several behavioural equivalence relations have been defined on processes, of which the most well-known is
strong bisimulation equivalence [8], and its variants *weak* and *branching* bisimulation equivalence [8,7], that feature abstraction from internal actions. In order
to allow compositional system verification, such equivalence relations need to be
congruences for the operators under consideration, meaning that the equivalence
class of an n-ary operator f applied to arguments $p_1, \ldots, p_n$ is completely determined by the equivalence classes of these arguments. Although strong bisimulation equivalence is a congruence for the operators of CCS and many other

D.V. Hung and M. Wirsing (Eds.): ICTAC 2005, LNCS 3722, pp. 318–333, 2005.

languages found in the literature, weak bisimulation equivalence fails to be a congruence for the *choice* or *alternative composition* operator + of CCS. To bypass this problem one uses the coarsest congruence relation for + that is finer than weak bisimulation equivalence, characterised as *rooted weak bisimulation equivalence* [8,3], which turns out to be a minor variation of weak bisimulation equivalence, and a congruence for all of CCS and many other languages. Analogously, *rooted branching bisimulation* is the coarsest congruence for CCS and many other languages that is finer than branching bisimulation equivalence [7].

In order to streamline the process of proving that a certain equivalence is a congruence for certain operators, and to guide sensible language definitions, syntactic criteria (*rule formats*) for the transition rules in structural operational semantics have been developed, ensuring that the equivalence is a congruence for any operator specified by rules that meet these criteria. One of these is the *GSOS format* of BLOOM, ISTRAIL & MEYER [5], generalising an earlier format by DE SIMONE [11]. When adhering to this format, all processes are computably finitely branching, and strong bisimulation equivalence is a congruence [5]. BLOOM [4] defines congruence formats for (rooted) weak and branching bisimulation equivalence by imposing additional restrictions on the GSOS format. As is customary in this field, finer equivalences have wider formats, so Bloom's *BB cool* GSOS format, which guarantees that branching bisimulation equivalence is a congruence, is more general than his *WB cool* GSOS format, which suits weak bisimulation equivalence; also his *RWB cool* GSOS format, suiting rooted weak bisimulation, is more general than the WB cool GSOS format, and his *RBB cool* GSOS format, guaranteeing that rooted branching bisimulation equivalence is a congruence, is the finest of all. The prime motivating example for these formats is the structural operational semantics of CCS [8]. All CCS operators are RWB cool, and the CCS operators other than the + are even WB cool.

Bloom's formats involve a fast bookkeeping effort of names of variables, used to precisely formulate the *bifurcation rules* that his formats require. To make his work more accessible, Bloom also presents simpler but less general versions of his formats, obtained by imposing an additional syntactic restriction. This restriction makes it possible to simplify the bifurcation rules to *patience rules*, which do not require such an extensive bookkeeping. FOKKINK [6] generalises Bloom's *simply RBB cool* format to a format he calls *RBB safe*, and writes "The definition of bifurcation rules is deplorably complicated, and we do not know of any examples from the literature that are RBB cool but not simply RBB cool. Therefore, we refrain from this generalisation here." ULIDOWSKI [12,13,14] studies congruence formats for variations of the semantic equivalences mentioned above with a different treatment of divergence. Ulidowski's formats form the counterparts of Bloom's simply cool formats only.

The main aim of the present study is to simplify and further clarify Bloom's work, so as to make it more accessible for the development of applications, variations and extensions. In passing, analogous results are obtained for two equivalences, and their rooted variants, that bridge the gap between weak and branching bisimulation. Moreover, the method of ACETO, BLOOM & VAANDRAGER [1] to extract from any GSOS language a finite equational axiomatisation that is sound and complete for strong bisimulation equivalence on finite processes, is adapted to rooted weak bisimulation equivalence. In the construction fresh function symbols may need be added whose transition rules have *lookahead* and thereby fall outside the GSOS format.

One of the simplifications of Bloom's formats presented here stems from the observation that the operators in any of the cool formats can be partitioned in *principal operators* and *abbreviations*, such that the abbreviations can be regarded as syntactic sugar, adding nothing that could not be expressed with principal operators. For any abbreviation f there exists a principal operator f^* that typically takes more arguments. For instance, $f(x_1, x_2)$ could be an abbreviation of $f^*(x_1, x_1, x_2)$. The rules for the abbreviations are completely determined by the rules for the principal operators, and for principal operators patience rules suffice, i.e. one does not need the full generality of bifurcation rules. Moreover, the simply cool formats can be characterised by the requirement that all operators are principal. These observations make it possible to define the cool formats of Bloom without mentioning bifurcation rules altogether. It also enables a drastic simplification of the congruence proofs, namely by establishing the congruence results for the simply cool formats first, and reducing the general case to the simple case by means of some general insights in abbreviation expansion.

Even though any operation that fits the cool formats can also be defined using merely the simply cool formats, in practice it may be handy to work with the full generality of the cool formats. The unary copying operator cp of [5] (page 257) for instance does not fit the cool formats directly, but can be made to fit by adding an auxiliary binary copying operator to the language, of which the unary one is an abbreviation. Dumping the abbreviation from the language would appear unnatural here, as the unary operator motivates the rules for both itself and its binary expansion, the latter being needed merely to make it work.

Another simplification contributed here is in the description of the RWB cool format. Bloom requires for every operational rule with target t the existence of two terms t_1 and t_2, and seven types of derived operational rules. I show that without limitation of generality it is always possible to choose $t_2 = t$, thereby making four of those seven types of rules redundant. Thus, the same format is obtained by requiring only t_1 and two types of derived rules (the third being a patience rule, that was already required for its own sake).

After defining the basic concepts in Section 1, I present the simply cool congruence formats in Section 2. Section 3 presents the theory of abbreviations that lifts the results from the simple to the general formats, and Sect. 4 deals with the rooted congruence formats. Section 5 compares my definitions of the cool formats with the ones of Bloom. Section 6 recapitulates the method of [1] to provide finite equational axiomatisations of strong bisimulation equivalence that are sound and complete for finite processes on an augmentation of any given GSOS language, and Sect. 7 extends this work to the rooted weak equivalences. Finally, Sect. 8 presents a fairly intuitive GSOS language for which the existing congruence formats fall short and further improvement is called for.

1 Preliminaries

In this paper $V = \{x_1, x_2, \ldots\}$ and *Act* are two sets of *variables* and *actions*.

Definition 1. A *signature* is a collection Σ of *function symbols* $f \notin V$ equipped with a function $ar : \Sigma \to \mathbb{N}$. The set $\mathbb{T}(\Sigma)$ of *terms* over a signature Σ is defined recursively by:

- $V \subseteq \mathbb{T}(\Sigma)$,
- if $f \in \Sigma$ and $t_1, \ldots, t_{ar(f)} \in \mathbb{T}(\Sigma)$ then $f(t_1, \ldots, t_{ar(f)}) \in \mathbb{T}(\Sigma)$.

A term $c()$ is abbreviated as c. For $t \in \mathbb{T}(\Sigma)$, $var(t)$ denotes the set of variables that occur in t. $T(\Sigma)$ is the set of closed terms over Σ, i.e. the terms $p \in \mathbb{T}(\Sigma)$ with $var(p) = \emptyset$. A Σ-*substitution* σ is a partial function from V to $\mathbb{T}(\Sigma)$. If σ is a substitution and S is any syntactic object, then $\sigma(S)$ denotes the object obtained from S by replacing, for x in the domain of σ, every occurrence of x in S by $\sigma(x)$. In that case $\sigma(S)$ is called a *substitution instance* of S. A Σ-substitution is *closed* if it is a total function from V to $T(\Sigma)$.

Definition 2. Let Σ be a signature. A *positive Σ-literal* is an expression $t \xrightarrow{a} t'$ and a *negative Σ-literal* an expression $t \xrightarrow{a}\!\!\!\!\!/\;\;$ with $t, t' \in \mathbb{T}(\Sigma)$ and $a \in Act$. A *transition rule* over Σ is an expression of the form $\frac{H}{\alpha}$ with H a set of Σ-literals (the *premises* of the rule) and α a positive Σ-literal (the *conclusion*). The left- and right-hand side of α are called the *source* and the *target* of the rule, respectively. A rule $\frac{H}{\alpha}$ with $H = \emptyset$ is also written α. A *transition system specification* (*TSS*), written (Σ, R), consists of a signature Σ and a set R of transition rules over Σ. A TSS is *positive* if the premises of its rules are positive.

Definition 3. [5] A *GSOS* rule is a transition rule such that

- its source has the form $f(x_1, \ldots, x_{ar(f)})$ with $f \in \Sigma$ and $x_i \in V$,
- the left-hand sides of its premises are variables x_i with $1 \leq i \leq ar(f)$,
- the right-hand sides of its positive premises are variables that that are all distinct, and that do not occur in its source,
- its target only contains variables that also occur in its source or premises.

A *GSOS language*, or TSS in GSOS format, is a TSS whose rules are GSOS rules.

Definition 4. A *transition* over a signature Σ is a closed positive Σ-literal. With structural recursion on p one defines when a GSOS language $\mathcal{L}$ generates a transition $p \xrightarrow{a} p'$ (notation $p \xrightarrow{a}_{\mathcal{L}} p'$):

$$f(p_1, \ldots, p_n) \xrightarrow{a}_{\mathcal{L}} q \text{ iff } \mathcal{L} \text{ has a transition rule } \frac{H}{f(x_1, \ldots, x_n) \xrightarrow{a} t} \text{ and there is a}$$

closed substitution σ with $\sigma(x_i) = p_i$ for $i = 1, \ldots, n$ and $\sigma(t) = q$, such that $p_i \xrightarrow{c}_{\mathcal{L}} \sigma(y)$ for $(x_i \xrightarrow{c} y) \in H$ and $\neg \exists r (p_i \xrightarrow{c}_{\mathcal{L}} r)$ for $(x_i \xrightarrow{c}\!\!\!\!\!/\;) \in H$.

Henceforth a GSOS language $\mathcal{L}$ over a signature Σ is assumed, and closed Σ-terms will be called *processes*. The subscript $\mathcal{L}$ will often be suppressed. Moreover, $Act = A \;\dot\cup\; \{\tau\}$ with τ the *silent move* or *hidden action*.

Definition 5. Two processes t and u are *weak bisimulation equivalent* or *weakly bisimilar* $(t \leftrightarroweq_w u)$ if $t\mathcal{R}u$ for a symmetric binary relation $\mathcal{R}$ on processes (a *weak bisimulation*) satisfying, for $a \in Act$,

$$\text{if } p\mathcal{R}q \text{ and } p \xrightarrow{a} p' \text{ then } \exists q_1, q_2, q' \text{ such that } q \Longrightarrow q_1 \xrightarrow{(a)} q_2 \Longrightarrow q' \wedge p'\mathcal{R}q'. \quad (*)$$

Here $p \Longrightarrow p'$ abbreviates $p = p_0 \xrightarrow{\tau} p_1 \xrightarrow{\tau} \cdots \xrightarrow{\tau} p_n = p'$ for some $n \geq 0$, whereas $p \xrightarrow{(a)} p'$ abbreviates $(p \xrightarrow{a} p') \vee (a = \tau \wedge p = p')$.

 t and u are *η-bisimilar* $(t \leftrightarroweq_\eta u)$ if in $(*)$ one additionally requires $p\mathcal{R}q_1$;

 t and u are *delay bisimilar* $(t \leftrightarroweq_d u)$ if in $(*)$ one additionally requires $q_2 = q'$;

 t and u are *branching bisimilar* $(t \leftrightarroweq_b u)$ if in $(*)$ one requires both;

 t and u are *strongly bisimilar* $(t \leftrightarroweq u)$ if in $(*)$ one simply requires $q \xrightarrow{a} q'$.

Two processes t and u are *rooted weak bisimulation equivalent* $(t \leftrightarroweq_{rw} u)$, if they satisfy

 if $t \xrightarrow{a} t'$ then $\exists u_1, u_2, u$ such that $u \Longrightarrow u_1 \xrightarrow{a} u_2 \Longrightarrow u'$ and $t' \leftrightarroweq_w u'$, and

 if $u \xrightarrow{a} u'$ then $\exists t_1, t_2, t$ such that $t \Longrightarrow t_1 \xrightarrow{a} t_2 \Longrightarrow t'$ and $t' \leftrightarroweq_w u'$.

They are *rooted η-bisimilar* $(t \leftrightarroweq_{r\eta} u)$ if above one additionally requires $u_1 = u$, $t_1 = t$, and $t' \leftrightarroweq_\eta u'$, they are *rooted delay bisimilar* $(t \leftrightarroweq_{rd} u)$ if one requires $u_2 = u'$, $t_2 = t'$ and $t' \leftrightarroweq_d u'$, and they are *rooted branching bisimilar* $(t \leftrightarroweq_{rb} u)$ if one requires $u_1 = u$, $u_2 = u'$, $t_1 = t$, $t_2 = t'$ and $t' \leftrightarroweq_b u'$.

It is well known and easy to check that the nine relations on processes defined above are equivalence relations indeed [2,7], and that, for $x \in \{\text{weak}, \eta, \text{delay, branching, strong}\}$, x-bisimulation equivalence is the largest x-bisimulation relation on processes. Moreover, $p \leftrightarroweq_{rx} q$ implies $p \leftrightarroweq_x q$.

Definition 6. An equivalence relation $\sim$ on processes is a *congruence* if

$$p_i \sim q_i \text{ for } i = 1, \ldots, ar(f) \quad \Rightarrow \quad f(p_1, \ldots, p_{ar(f)}) \sim f(q_1, \ldots, q_{ar(f)})$$

for all $f \in \Sigma$. This is equivalent to the requirement that for all $t \in \mathbf{T}(\Sigma)$ and closed substitutions $\sigma, \nu : V \to T(\Sigma)$

$$\sigma(x) = \nu(x) \text{ for } x \in var(t) \quad \Rightarrow \quad \sigma(t) = \nu(t).$$

This note, and BLOOM [4], deal with syntactic conditions on GSOS languages that guarantee that the equivalence notions of Definition 5 are congruences.

2   Simply Cool GSOS Languages

In this section I define *simply XB cool* rule formats, for $X \in \{\text{W,D,H,B}\}$, such that on XB cool GSOS languages, X-bisimulation equivalence is a congruence. In [5] it is shown that strong bisimulation equivalence is a congruence on any GSOS language. The proof is pretty straightforward; it consists of showing that the congruence-closure of $\leftrightarroweq$ is a bisimulation. The same idea can be applied almost verbatim to $\leftrightarroweq_w$, $\leftrightarroweq_d$, $\leftrightarroweq_\eta$ and $\leftrightarroweq_b$, once we have lemmas like Lemma 1 below. The simply XB cool formats contain the simplest syntactic requirements that guarantee these lemmas to hold.

Definition 7. Let $\mathcal{L}$ be a positive GSOS language. For an operator f in $\mathcal{L}$, the *rules of f* are the rules in $\mathcal{L}$ with source $f(x_1, ..., x_{ar(f)})$.

- An operator in $\mathcal{L}$ is *straight* if it has no rules in which a variable occurs multiple times in the left-hand side of its premises. An operator is *smooth* if moreover it has no rules in which a variable occurs both in the target and in the left-hand side of a premise.

- An argument $i \in \mathbb{N}$ of an operator f is *active* if f has a rule in which x_i appears as left-hand side of a premise.

- A variable x occurring in a term t is *receiving* in t if t is the target of a rule in $\mathcal{L}$ in which x is the right-hand side of a premise. An argument $i \in \mathbb{N}$ of an operator f is *receiving* if a variable x is receiving in a term t that has a subterm $f(t_1, \ldots, t_n)$ with x occurring in t_i.

- A rule of the form $\dfrac{x_i \xrightarrow{\tau} y}{f(x_1, \ldots, x_n) \xrightarrow{\tau} f(x_1, \ldots, x_n)[y/x_i]}$ with $1 \le i \le n$ is called a *patience rule* for the ith argument of f. Here $t[y/x]$ denotes term t with all occurrences of x replaced by y.

Definition 8. A GSOS language $\mathcal{L}$ is *simply WB cool* if it is positive and

1. all operators in $\mathcal{L}$ are straight,
2. patience rules are the only rules in $\mathcal{L}$ with τ-premises,
3. every active argument of an operator has a patience rule,
4. every receiving argument of an operator has a patience rule,
5. all operators in $\mathcal{L}$ are smooth.

The formats *simply DB cool*, *simply HB cool* and *simply BB cool* are defined likewise, but skipping Clause 4 for DB and BB, and Clause 5 for HB and BB.

The simply WB and BB cool formats above coincide with the ones of [4], whereas the simply DB cool format coincides with the **eb** format of [13].

Lemma 1. *Let $\mathcal{L}$ be simply WB cool, let $\dfrac{H}{s \xrightarrow{a} t}$ be a rule in $\mathcal{L}$, and let ν be a closed substitution such that $\nu(x) \Longrightarrow \xrightarrow{(c)} \Longrightarrow \nu(y)$ for each premise $x \xrightarrow{c} y$ in H. Then $\nu(s) \Longrightarrow \xrightarrow{(a)} \Longrightarrow \nu(t)$.*

Similar lemmas can be obtained for the other three formats, and these yield the following congruence results. The proofs are in the full version of this paper.

Theorem 1. *On any simply WB cool GSOS language, $\underleftrightarrow{}_w$ is a congruence.*
On any simply DB cool GSOS language, $\underleftrightarrow{}_d$ is a congruence.
On any simply HB cool GSOS language, $\underleftrightarrow{}_\eta$ is a congruence.
On any simply BB cool GSOS language, $\underleftrightarrow{}_b$ is a congruence.

3   Cool GSOS Languages

In this section I will extend the simply XB cool rule formats to XB cool rule formats and establish the associated congruence theorems (X$\in$ {W,D,H,B}).

Definition 9. A GSOS language is *two-tiered* if its operators are partitioned into *abbreviations* and *principal operators*, and for every abbreviation f a principal operator $f^\star$ is specified, together with a substitution
$\sigma_f : \{x_1, \ldots, x_{ar(f^\star)}\} \to \{x_1, \ldots, x_{ar(f)}\}$, such that the rules of f are

$$\left\{ \frac{\sigma_f(H)}{f(x_1, \ldots, x_{ar(f)}) \xrightarrow{a} \sigma_f(t)} \;\middle|\; \frac{H}{f^\star(x_1, \ldots, x_{ar(f^\star)}) \xrightarrow{a} t} \text{ is a rule of } f^\star \right\}.$$

Write $f(i)$ for the j such that $\sigma_f(x_i) = x_j$; take $f^\star = f$ and $f(i) = i$ in case f is a principal operator.

Trivially, any positive GSOS language can be extended (*straightened*) to a two-tiered GSOS language whose principal operators are straight and smooth [1].

Example 1. Let $\mathcal{L}$ have an operator f with rule $\dfrac{x_1 \xrightarrow{a} y, \; x_1 \xrightarrow{b} z}{f(x_1, x_2) \xrightarrow{a} f(x_1, (f(y, x_2)))}$.
$\mathcal{L}$ is straightened by adding a operator $f^\star$ with

$$\frac{x_1 \xrightarrow{a} y, \; x_2 \xrightarrow{b} z}{f^\star(x_1, x_2, x_3, x_4) \xrightarrow{a} f(x_3, f(y, x_4))}.$$

In this case $\sigma_f(x_1) = \sigma_f(x_2) = \sigma_f(x_3) = x_1$ and $\sigma_f(x_4) = x_2$.

Equally trivial, $f^\star(p_{f(1)}, \ldots, p_{f(n)}) \xrightarrow{a} t$ iff $f(p_1, \ldots, p_n) \xrightarrow{a} t$;
so $f^\star(p_{f(1)}, \ldots, p_{f(n)}) \leftrightarrow f(p_1, \ldots, p_n)$.

Definition 10. A two-tiered GSOS language $\mathcal{L}$ is *WB cool* if it is positive and

1. all principal operators in $\mathcal{L}$ are straight,

2. patience rules are the only rules of principal operators with τ-premises,

3. every active argument of a principal operator has a patience rule,

4. if argument $f(i)$ of f is receiving, then argument i of $f^\star$ has a patience rule,

5. all principal operators in $\mathcal{L}$ are smooth.

The formats *DB cool*, *HB cool* and *BB cool* are defined likewise, but skipping Clause 4 for DB and BB, and Clause 5 for HB and BB. Clause 4 may be weakened slightly; see Sect. 3.1.

Note that the simply cool formats defined before are exactly the cool formats with the extra restriction that all operators are principal.

Theorem 2. *On any WB cool GSOS language, $\leftrightarrow_w$ is a congruence.*
   On any DB cool GSOS language, $\leftrightarrow_d$ is a congruence.
   On any HB cool GSOS language, $\leftrightarrow_\eta$ is a congruence.
   On any BB cool GSOS language, $\leftrightarrow_b$ is a congruence.

Given that the cool GSOS languages differ from the simply cool GSOS language only by the addition of operators that can be regarded as syntactic sugar, the theorems above are a simple consequence of the corresponding theorems for simply cool GSOS languages. Details are in the full version of this paper.

3.1   A Small Extension

Say that an argument i of an operator f is *ignored* if $f^\star$ has no argument k with $f(k) = i$. In that case there can be no rule with source $f(x_1, \ldots, x_{ar(f)})$ with x_i in its premises or in its target. A subterm u of a term t is *irrelevant* if occurs within an ignored argument t_i of a subterm $f(t_1, \ldots, t_{ar(f)})$ of t. Now Definition 7 of an argument of an operator being receiving may be strengthened by replacing "a subterm $f(t_1, \ldots, t_n)$ with x occurring in t_i" by "a relevant subterm $f(t_1, \ldots, t_n)$ with x a relevant subterm of t_i". This yields a slight weakening of Clause 4 in Definition 10, still sufficient to obtain Theorem 2.

Example 2. Let $\mathcal{L}$ have a rule $\dfrac{x_1 \xrightarrow{a} y}{g(x_1) \xrightarrow{a} f(h(f(x_1, y)), k(y))}$. By Definition 7 both the arguments of h and k are receiving, so Clause 4 in Definition 10 demands patience rules for both $h^\star$ and $k^\star$. Now suppose that $h^\star = h$, $k^\star = k$, $ar(f^\star) = 1$ and $\sigma_f(x_1) = x_1$. This means that $f(x_1, x_2)$ is an abbreviation for $f^\star(x_1)$ and the second argument of f is ignored. In such a case $f(p, q) \bisim f(p, r)$ for all closed terms p, q and r. Now the weakened Clause 4 does not demand a patience rule for either $h^\star$ or $k^\star$, since the arguments of h and k are no longer receiving.

4   Rooted Cool GSOS Languages

In this section I will define the (simply) RWB, RDB, RHB and RBB cool rule formats and establish the associated congruence theorems. In order to formulate the requirements for the RWB and RDB cool GSOS languages I need the concept of a *ruloid*, this being a kind of derived GSOS rule.

Definition 11. For r transition rule, let $\mathrm{RHS}(r)$ denote the set of right-hand sides of its premises. Let $\mathcal{L}$ be a positive GSOS language. The class of $\mathcal{L}$-*ruloids* is the smallest set of rules such that

- $\dfrac{x \xrightarrow{a} y}{x \xrightarrow{a} y}$ is an $\mathcal{L}$-ruloid, for every $x, y \in V$ and $a \in Act$;

- if σ is a substitution, $\mathcal{L}$ has a rule $\dfrac{H}{s \xrightarrow{a} t}$, and for every premise $x \xrightarrow{c} y$ in H there is an $\mathcal{L}$-ruloid $r_y = \dfrac{H_y}{\sigma(x) \xrightarrow{c} \sigma(y)}$ such that the sets $\mathrm{RHS}(r_y)$ are pairwise disjoint and each $\mathrm{RHS}(r_y)$ is disjoint with $var(\sigma(s))$, then $\dfrac{\bigcup_{y \in H} H_y}{\sigma(s) \xrightarrow{a} \sigma(t)}$ is an $\mathcal{L}$-ruloid.

Note that a transition α, seen as a rule $\frac{\emptyset}{\alpha}$, is an $\mathcal{L}$-ruloid iff it is generated by $\mathcal{L}$ in the sense of Definition 4. The left-hand sides of premises of a ruloid are variables that occur in its source, and the right-hand sides are variables that are all distinct and do not occur in its source. Its target only contains variables that also occur elsewhere in the rule.

Example 3. Let $\mathcal{L}$ contain the rule $\dfrac{x_1 \xrightarrow{a} y_1 \quad x_2 \xrightarrow{b} y_2}{f(x_1, x_2) \xrightarrow{a} g(x_1, y_1)}$. Then $\mathcal{L}$ has ruloids

$$\dfrac{x \xrightarrow{a} x' \quad y \xrightarrow{b} y'}{f(x, y) \xrightarrow{a} g(x, x')} \quad \text{and} \quad \dfrac{x \xrightarrow{a} x' \quad y \xrightarrow{b} y' \quad z \xrightarrow{b} z'}{f(f(x, y), z) \xrightarrow{a} g(f(x, y), g(x, x'))}.$$

Definition 12. A GSOS language $\mathcal{L}$ is *RWB cool* if the operators can be partitioned in *tame* and *wild* ones, such that

1. the target of every rule contains only tame operations;

2. the sublanguage $\mathcal{L}^{tame}$ of tame operators in $\mathcal{L}$ is WB cool;

3. $\mathcal{L}$ is positive, and for each rule $\frac{H}{s \xrightarrow{a} t}$ there is a term u and a substitution $\sigma : var(u) \to var(s)$ such that

   – there is an $\mathcal{L}$-ruloid $\frac{K}{u \xrightarrow{a} v}$ with $\sigma(K) = H$ and $\sigma(v) = t$,

   – and for every premise $x \xrightarrow{c} y$ in K, $\mathcal{L}$ has a rule $\frac{\sigma(x) \xrightarrow{\tau} y}{s \xrightarrow{\tau} \sigma(u[y/x])}$;

(4. if argument $f(i)$ of f is receiving, then argument i of f^* has a patience rule.)

The formats *RDB cool*, *RHB cool* and *RBB cool* are defined likewise, adapting "WB cool" in the second clause appropriately, but skipping the third clause for RHB and RBB, and the last one for RDB and RBB. The last clause cannot be skipped for RHB. The *simply RXB cool* rule formats (X$\in$ {W,D,H,B}) are obtained by requiring the sublanguage of tame operators to be simply XB cool.

Note that in the third clause, u, σ and the ruloid can always be chosen in such a way that $v = t$. The instance of this clause with $s = f(x_1, \ldots, x_{ar(f)})$ for a tame operator f is (in the full version of this paper) easily seen to be redundant.

The last clause above appeared before as Clause 4 in Definition 10 of the WB and HB cool formats. Given that a term with a receiving variable cannot contain wild operators, this clause is almost implied by Clause 2 above. All it adds, is that the requirement of Clause 4 for the sublanguage of tame operators applies to "receiving in $\mathcal{L}$" instead of merely "receiving in $\mathcal{L}^{tame}$". Thus, the rules for the wild operators help determine which variables in a term t count as receiving. The following results are obtained in the full version of this paper.

Proposition 1. *In the definition of RWB cool above, Clause 4 is redundant.*

Theorem 3. *On any RWB cool GSOS language, $\underline{\leftrightarrow}_{rw}$ is a congruence.*
On any RDB cool GSOS language, $\underline{\leftrightarrow}_{rd}$ is a congruence.
On any RHB cool GSOS language, $\underline{\leftrightarrow}_{r\eta}$ is a congruence.
On any RBB cool GSOS language, $\underline{\leftrightarrow}_{rb}$ is a congruence.

Example 4. The following fragment of CCS has the constant 0, unary operators $a.\_$, binary operators $+$ and $\|$, and instances of the GSOS rules below. Here a ranges over $Act = \mathcal{N} \,\dot{\cup}\, \overline{\mathcal{N}} \,\dot{\cup}\, \{\tau\}$ with $\mathcal{N}$ a set of *names* and $\overline{\mathcal{N}} = \{\bar{a} \mid a \in \mathcal{N}\}$ the set of *co-names*. The function $\bar{\cdot}$ extends to $\mathcal{N} \cup \overline{\mathcal{N}}$ (but not to Act) by $\bar{\bar{a}} = a$.

$$\frac{x_1 \xrightarrow{a} y_1}{x_1 + x_2 \xrightarrow{a} y_1} \qquad \frac{x_2 \xrightarrow{a} y_2}{x_1 + x_2 \xrightarrow{a} y_2} \qquad a.x_1 \xrightarrow{a} x_1$$

$$\frac{x_1 \xrightarrow{a} y_1}{x_1 \| x_2 \xrightarrow{a} y_1 \| x_2} \qquad \frac{x_2 \xrightarrow{a} y_2}{x_1 \| x_2 \xrightarrow{a} x_1 \| y_2} \qquad \frac{x_1 \xrightarrow{a} y_1 \quad x_2 \xrightarrow{\bar{a}} y_2}{x_1 \| x_2 \xrightarrow{\tau} y_1 \| y_2}$$

The sublanguage without the $+$ is simply WB cool, and the entire GSOS language is simply RWB cool. Clause 3 of Definition 12 applied to the ith rule for the $+$ is satisfied by taking $u = x$, $\sigma(x) = x_i$, and the ruloid $\frac{x \xrightarrow{a} y_i}{x \xrightarrow{a} y_i}$.

5 Comparison with Bloom's Formats

Bloom's definitions of the cool formats differ in five ways from mine.

First of all Bloom requires *bifurcation rules* for all operators in $\mathcal{L}^{tame}$, whereas I merely require patience rules for the principal operators. As principal operators in $\mathcal{L}^{tame}$ are straight, and bifurcation rules for straight operators are exactly patience rules, the difference is that I dropped the bifurcation requirement for abbreviations (non-principal operators). This is possible, because by Definition 9, which corresponds to Definition 3.5.5 in [4], the rules for the abbreviations are completely determined by the rules for their straightenings, and it turns out that a bifurcation rule of an abbreviation f is exactly what is determined by the corresponding patience rule for its straightening $f^\star$.

Bloom requires the existence of bifurcation/patience ruloids for receiving variables in any term, whereas I require them for receiving arguments of operators, which is a more syntactic and easy to check requirement. The two approaches are shown equivalent in the full version of this paper when using the extension of my formats of Sect. 3.1, this being the reason behind that extension.

Bloom's WB and RWB cool formats use a so-called ε-*presentation*. This entails that rules may have premises of the form $x \xrightarrow{\varepsilon} y$. In terms of Definition 4, the meaning of such premises is given by the requirement that $\sigma(x) = \sigma(y)$ for $(x \xrightarrow{\varepsilon} y) \in H$. By using ε-premises, any rule can be given a form in which the target is a univariate term, having no variables in common with the source. This allows a simplification of the statement of the bifurcation ruloids. Any ε-presented GSOS language can be converted to ε-free form by substitution, in each rule r, x for y for every premise $x \xrightarrow{\varepsilon} y$ of r. I believe that my conventions for naming variables improve the ones of [4].

Bloom's rendering of the RWB cool format doesn't feature Clause 4 (and in view of Prop. 1, neither does mine), but Clause 3 is much more involved. For every rule with conclusion $s \xrightarrow{a} t$ Bloom requires the existence of two terms t_1 and t_2 and seven types of derived operational rules, such that the diagram on the right commutes. My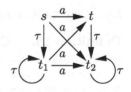
Clause 3 stems from the observation that, given Bloom's other restrictions, t necessarily has the rules required for t_2, so that one may always choose $t_2 = t$. This leaves only t_1 (called u in Definition 12) and three types of rules, one of which (the t_1-loop in the diagram above) is in fact a bifurcation rule whose existence is already implied by the requirements of Definition 10.

In Clause 3 of Definition 12, Bloom requires that

$$var(u) = \{y' \mid y \in var(t)\} \text{ and } \sigma(y') = \begin{cases} x & \text{if } H \text{ contains a premise } x \xrightarrow{c} y \\ y & \text{otherwise.} \end{cases}$$
(1)

In order to match Bloom's format I could have done the same, but this condition is not needed in the proof and reduces the generality of the format.

Proposition 2. *A GSOS language is WB cool, respectively RWB, BB or RBB cool, as defined here, with the extension of Sect. 3.1 and the restriction (1) above, iff it is WB cool, resp. RWB, BB or RBB cool, as defined in* BLOOM [4].

Moreover, my proofs that cool languages are compositional for bisimulation equivalences greatly simplify the ones of Bloom [4] by using a reduction of the general case to the simple case, instead of treating the general formats directly.

6   Turning GSOS Rules into Equations

This section recapitulates the method of [1] to provide finite equational axiomatisations of $\leftrightarrow$ on an augmentation of any given GSOS language.

Definition 13. A process p, being a closed term in a GSOS language, is *finite* if there are only finitely many sequences of transitions $p \xrightarrow{a_1} p_1 \xrightarrow{a_2} \cdots \xrightarrow{a_n} p_n$. The length n of the longest sequence of this form is called the *depth* of p.

Definition 14. An *equational axiomatisation* Ax over a signature Σ is a set of equations $t = u$, called *axioms*, with $t, u \in \mathbf{T}(\Sigma)$. It *respects* an equivalence relation $\sim$ on $T(\Sigma)$ if $\sigma(t) \sim \sigma(u)$ for any closed substitution $\sigma : V \to T(\Sigma)$.

An *instance* of axiom $t = u$ is an equation $\sigma(C[t/x]) = \sigma(C[u/x])$ where σ is a substitution and C a term with $var(C) = \{x\}$, and x occurring only once in C. An equation $p = q$ is *derivable* from Ax, notation $p =_{\text{Ax}} q$, if there is a sequence $p_0, \ldots, p_n$ of terms with $n \geq 0$ such that $p = p_0$, $q = p_n$ and for $i = 1, \ldots, n$ the equation $p_{i-1} = p_i$ is an instance of one of the axioms.

Ax is *sound* for $\sim$ if $p =_{\text{Ax}} q$ implies $p \sim q$ for $p, q \in T(\Sigma)$. Ax is *complete for $\sim$ on finite processes* if $p \sim q$ implies $p =_{\text{Ax}} q$ for finite processes p and q.

Note that Ax is sound for $\sim$ iff Ax respects $\sim$ and $\sim$ is a congruence.

Definition 15. A GSOS language $\mathcal{L}$ *extends BCCS* (*basic* CCS) if it contains the operators 0, $a.\_$ and $+$ of Example 4.
A *basic process* is a closed term build from the operators mentioned above only.
A *head normal form* is a closed term of the form $0 + a_1.p_1 + \cdots + a_n.p_n$ for $n \geq 0$.
An axiomatisation on $\mathcal{L}$ is *head normalising* if any term $f(p_1, \ldots, p_{ar(f)})$ with the p_i basic processes can be converted into head normal form.

Proposition 3. *Let $\mathcal{L}$ be a GSOS language extending BCCS, and Ax a head normalising equational axiomatisation, respecting $\leftrightarrow$, and containing the axioms A1–4 of Table 1. Then Ax is sound and complete for $\leftrightarrow$ on finite processes.*

Proof. Using induction on the depth of p and a nested structural induction, the axioms can convert any finite process p into a basic process. Here one uses that strongly bisimilar processes have the same depth. Now apply the well-known fact that the axioms A1–4 are sound and complete for $\leftrightarrow$ on basic processes [8].

For the parallel composition operator $\parallel$ of CCS no finite equational head normalising axiomatisation respecting strong bisimulation equivalence exists [9].

Table 1. Complete equational axiomatisations of BCCS and the parallel composition

$x + (y + z) = (x + y) + z$	A1	$x \| y = x \mathbin{\underline{\|}} y + y \mathbin{\underline{\|}} x + x\|y$	CM1
$x + y = y + x$	A2	$a.x \mathbin{\underline{\|}} y = a.(x\|y)$	CM2
$x + x = x$	A3	$0 \mathbin{\underline{\|}} y = 0$	CM3
$x + 0 = x$	A4	$(x + y) \mathbin{\underline{\|}} z = x \mathbin{\underline{\|}} z + y \mathbin{\underline{\|}} z$	CM4
		$a.x\|\bar{a}.y = \tau.(x\|y)$	CM5
$a.(\tau.(x + y) + x) = a.(x + y)$	T1	$a.x\|b.y = 0 \quad$ (if $b \neq \bar{a}$)	CM6
$\tau.x + x = \tau.x$	T2	$0\|x = x\|0 = 0$	CM7
$a.(\tau.x + y) + a.x = a.(\tau.x + y)$	T3	$(x + y)\|z = x\|z + y\|z$	CM8
		$x\|(y + z) = x\|y + x\|z$	CM9

However, BERGSTRA & KLOP [3] gave such an axiomatisation on the language obtained by adding two auxiliary operators, the *left merge* $\mathbin{\underline{\|}}$ and the *communication* merge $|$, with rules $\dfrac{x_1 \xrightarrow{a} y_1}{x_1 \mathbin{\underline{\|}} x_2 \xrightarrow{a} y_1\|x_2}$ and $\dfrac{x_1 \xrightarrow{a} y_1 \quad x_2 \xrightarrow{\bar{a}} y_2}{x_1|x_2 \xrightarrow{\tau} y_1\|y_2}$, provided the alphabet *Act* of actions is finite. The axioms are CM1–9 of Table 1, in which $+$ binds weakest and $a.\_$ strongest, and a, b range over *Act*.

ACETO, BLOOM & VAANDRAGER [1] generalise this idea to arbitrary GSOS languages with finitely many rules, each with finitely many premises, and assuming a finite alphabet *Act*. I recapitulate their method for positive languages only.

A smooth operator (Definition 7) only has rules of the form $\dfrac{\{x_i \xrightarrow{c_i} y_i \mid i \in I\}}{f(x_1, \ldots, x_n) \xrightarrow{a} t}$.

The *trigger* of such a rule is the partial function $\uparrow_r: \{i, \ldots, n\} \to$ *Act* given by $\uparrow_r (i) = c_i$ if $i \in I$, and $\uparrow_r (i)$ is undefined otherwise.

Definition 16. [1] A smooth GSOS operator f is *distinctive*, if no two rules of f have the same trigger, and the triggers of all rules of f have the same domain.

All operators of CCS, as well as $\mathbin{\underline{\|}}$ and $|$, are smooth. The operators 0, $a.\_$, $\mathbin{\underline{\|}}$ and $|$ are distinctive, but $\|$ is not. Its triggers have domains $\{1\}$, $\{2\}$ and $\{1, 2\}$.

For every smooth and distinctive operator f, ACETO, BLOOM & VAANDRAGER declare four types of axioms. First of all, for every rule r as above there is an axiom $f(\sigma(x_1), \ldots, \sigma(x_n)) = a.\sigma(t)$, where $\sigma : \{x_1, \ldots, x_n\} \to \mathbf{T}(\Sigma)$ is the substitution given by $\sigma(x_i) = c_i.y_i$ for $i \in I$ and $\sigma(x_i) = x_i$ for $i \notin I$. Such an axiom is called an *action law*. Examples are CM2 and CM5 in Table 1.

Secondly, whenever I is the set of active arguments of f, but f has no rule of the form above (where the name of the variables y_i is of no importance), there is an axiom $f(\sigma(x_1), \ldots, \sigma(x_n)) = 0$, with σ as above (for an arbitrary choice of distinct variables y_i). Such an axiom is an *inaction law*. An example is CM6. If f has k active arguments, in total there are $|Act|^k$ action and inaction laws for f, one for every conceivable trigger with as domain the active arguments of f.

Finally, for any active argument i of f, there are laws

$$f(x_1, \ldots x_{i-1}, 0, x_{i+1}, \ldots, x_n) = 0 \qquad \text{and}$$
$$f(x_1, \ldots, x_i + x_i', \ldots, x_n) = f(x_1, \ldots, x_i, \ldots, x_n) + f(x_1, \ldots, x_i', \ldots, x_n).$$

Examples for the second type of inaction law are CM3 and CM7, and examples of *distributivity laws* are CM4, CM8 and CM9.

It is not hard to see that all axioms above respect $\leftrightarrow$ and that together they bring any term $f(p_1, \ldots, p_{ar(f)})$ with the p_i basic processes in head normal form.

The method of [1] makes three types of additions to a given finite GSOS language $\mathcal{L}$, and provides an equational head normalising axiomatisation on the resulting language, that respects strong bisimulation.

First of all, the operators 0, $a._-$ and $+$ are added, if not already there. The corresponding axioms are A1–4 of Table 1. If all other operators are smooth and distinctive, for each of them the axioms just described are taken, which finishes the job. (In the presence of negative premises, this step is slightly more complex.)

In case there are operators f that are smooth but not distinctive, the set of operational rules of f is partitioned into subsets D such that no two rules in D have the same trigger, and the triggers of all rules in D have the same domain. Note that such a partition can always be found—possibly by taking exactly one rule in each subset D. Now for any subset D in the partition, an operator f_D with $ar(f_D) = ar(f)$ is added to the language, whose rules are exactly the rules in that subset, but with f_D in the source. By definition, f_D is distinctive. Now add an axiom $f(x_1, \ldots, x_{ar(f)}) = \sum f_D(x_1, \ldots, x_{ar(f)})$, where the sum is taken over all subsets in the partition, and apply the method above to the operators f_D. Again, it is trivial to check that the axioms respect $\leftrightarrow$ and are head normalising. Applied to the $\|$ of CCS, this technique yields the left merge and communication merge as auxiliary operators, as well as a right merge, and the axiom CM1.

In case of operators f that are not smooth, a smooth operator f^* is added to $\mathcal{L}$, of which f is an abbreviation in the sense of Definition 9 (cf. Example 1). The treatment of f^* proceeds as above, and the project is finished by the axiom

$$f(p_1, ..., p_n) = f^*(p_{f(1)}, ..., p_{f(n)}).$$

Besides completeness for finite processes, using an infinitary induction principle the method of [1] even yields completeness for arbitrary processes. I will not treat this here, as it does not generalise to weak equivalences.

7   Turning Cool GSOS Rules into Equations

The method of [1] does not apply to $\leftrightarrow_w$, $\leftrightarrow_d$, $\leftrightarrow_\eta$, and $\leftrightarrow_b$, because these equivalences fail to be congruences for the $+$. However, Bloom [4] shows that the method applies more or less verbatim to $\leftrightarrow_{rb}$. This section observes that the same holds for $\leftrightarrow_{r\eta}$, and finds an adaptation to yield finite equational axiomatisations of $\leftrightarrow_{rw}$ (resp. $\leftrightarrow_{rd}$) that are sound and complete for finite processes on an augmentation of any RWB cool (resp. RDB cool) GSOS language.

On basic processes, the axioms A1–4 together with T1–T3 are complete for $\leftrightarrow_{rw}$ [8], whereas complete axiomatisations for $\leftrightarrow_{rd}$, $\leftrightarrow_{r\eta}$ and $\leftrightarrow_{rb}$ are obtained by dropping T3, T2 or both, respectively [7]. So in order to get axiomatisations of these equivalences that are complete for finite processes, all that is needed is head normalisation. The simplest approach is to use the same head normalising axioms as in the previous section, reasoning that axioms that respect $\underline{\leftrightarrow}$ surely respect a coarser equivalence like $\underline{\leftrightarrow}_{rb}$ or $\underline{\leftrightarrow}_{rw}$. The only way this approach could fail is when the auxiliary operators generated by [1] fail to be congruences for the equivalence relation at hand. The operators 0, $a._-$ and $+$ are WB cool, and thus unproblematic. As observed in [4], for any RBB cool GSOS language, the augmented language is also RBB cool. Namely, the new operators do not show up in targets of new rules, so classifying all auxiliary operators as wild is sufficient. Since the auxiliary operators do not increase the collection of receiving arguments of operators either, it follows likewise that for any RHB cool GSOS language, the augmented language is also RHB cool. Hence one obtains

Proposition 4. *The method of [1], together with axiom T1 (and T3), yields finite equational axiomatisations of $\underline{\leftrightarrow}_{rb}$ (resp. $\underline{\leftrightarrow}_{r\eta}$) that are sound and complete for finite processes on an augmentation of any RBB cool (resp. RHB cool) GSOS language.*

For $\underline{\leftrightarrow}_{rw}$ and $\underline{\leftrightarrow}_{rd}$ this approach fails. In particular, these equivalences fail to be congruences for the communication merge: one has $\tau.a.0 \underline{\leftrightarrow}_{rd} \tau.a.0 + a.0$ but

$$0 \underline{\leftrightarrow} (\tau.a.0 | \bar{a}.b.0) \underline{\not\leftrightarrow}_{rd} ((\tau.a.0 + a.0) | \bar{a}.b.0) \underline{\leftrightarrow} \tau.b.0.$$

Conjecture. *There exists no GSOS language including the parallel composition of CCS and ≥ 2 visible actions that admits a finite equational axiomatisation of weak bisimulation equivalence that is sound and complete for finite processes.*

Nevertheless, such an axiomatisation was found by BERGSTRA & KLOP [3], using a variant of the communication merge that is not a GSOS operator. Their axiomatisation of $\|$ is obtained from the one in Table 1 by requiring $a, b \neq \tau$ in CM6, and adding the axioms $\tau.x|y = x|\tau.y = x|y$. Here I generalise their approach to arbitrary RWB cool (or RDB cool) GSOS languages.

The RWB cool format can be extended by allowing wild operators f, besides GSOS rules satisfying Clause 3 of Definition 12, also to have rules of which all premises have the form $x \Longrightarrow \overset{c}{\longrightarrow} y$ with $c \in A$. For such rules Clause 3 is not required, but in fulfilling Clause 4, they do count in determining which arguments are receiving. A similar extension applies to the RDB cool format.

Theorem 4. *On any extended-RWB cool TSS, $\underline{\leftrightarrow}_{rw}$ is a congruence.*
On any extended-RDB cool TSS, $\underline{\leftrightarrow}_{rd}$ is a congruence.

In an RWB (or RDB) cool language, the smooth operators $f^\star$ that are needed to axiomatise a non-smooth operator f are unproblematic. For tame operators f, they are already in the language, and for a wild f it is not hard to define them in such a way that the augmented language remains RWB (or RDB) cool. Of the operators f_D needed to axiomatise a non-distinctive operator f, those that have exactly one active argument can be made to satisfy Clause 3 of Definition 12 by including the relevant τ-rule in D. All operators f_D with another number of active arguments cannot have τ-premises, by Definitions 12 and 10. These operators f_D are replaced by counterparts f'_D, obtained by replacing each premise

$x \xrightarrow{c} y$ in a rule for f_D by $x \Longrightarrow\xrightarrow{c} y$. By Theorem 4, $\underline{\leftrightarrow}_{rw}$ (or $\underline{\leftrightarrow}_{rd}$) is a congruence for f'_D. Furthermore, $f(x_1, \ldots, x_{ar(f)}) \underline{\leftrightarrow}_{rw} \sum f'_D(x_1, \ldots, x_{ar(f)})$. Now the required axiomatisation is obtained by omitting all inaction laws for the modified operators f'_D with $\sigma(x_i) = \tau.y_i$ for some active argument i, and instead adding τ-laws $f'_D(x_1, \ldots, \tau.x_i, \ldots, x_n) = f'_D(x_1, \ldots, x_i, \ldots, x_n)$.

8   A Challenge

All equivalences of Definition 5 are congruences of the GSOS language with rules

$$\frac{x_1 \xrightarrow{a} y}{f(x_1) \xrightarrow{a} g(y)} \qquad \frac{x_1 \xrightarrow{\tau} y}{g(x_1) \xrightarrow{\tau} g(y)} \qquad g(x_1) \xrightarrow{\tau} !x_1$$

$$\frac{x_1 \xrightarrow{a} y}{!x_1 \xrightarrow{a} y \| !x_1} \qquad \frac{x_1 \xrightarrow{a} y_1}{x_1 \| x_2 \xrightarrow{a} y_1 \| x_2} \qquad \frac{x_2 \xrightarrow{a} y_2}{x_1 \| x_2 \xrightarrow{a} x_1 \| y_2}$$

for $a \in Act$. Here, the operator $!x$ can be understood as a parallel composition of infinitely many copies of x. The rules for f, g and $\|$ are WB cool, but the one for $!$ is not. It is not even RBB safe in the sense of [6].

Open problem. Find a congruence format that includes the language above.

Acknowledgement. My thanks to Simone Tini for inspiration.

References

1. L. ACETO, B. BLOOM & F.W. VAANDRAGER (1994): *Turning SOS rules into equations.* Information and Computation 111(1), pp. 1–52.
2. T. BASTEN (1996): *Branching bisimulation is an equivalence indeed!* Information Processing Letters 58(3), pp. 141–147.
3. J.A. BERGSTRA & J.W. KLOP (1985): *Algebra of communicating processes with abstraction.* Theoretical Computer Science 37(1), pp. 77–121.
4. B. BLOOM (1995): *Structural operational semantics for weak bisimulations.* Theoretical Computer Science 146, pp. 25–68.
5. B. BLOOM, S. ISTRAIL & A.R. MEYER (1995): *Bisimulation can't be traced.* Journal of the ACM 42(1), pp. 232–268.
6. W.J. FOKKINK (2000): *Rooted branching bisimulation as a congruence.* Journal of Computer and System Sciences 60(1), pp. 13–37.
7. R.J. VAN GLABBEEK & W.P. WEIJLAND (1996): *Branching time and abstraction in bisimulation semantics.* Journal of the ACM 43(3), pp. 555–600.
8. R. MILNER (1990): *Operational and algebraic semantics of concurrent processes.* In J. van Leeuwen, editor: Handbook of Theoretical Computer Science, chapter 19, Elsevier Science Publishers B.V. (North-Holland), pp. 1201–1242. Alternatively see *Communication and Concurrency,* Prentice-Hall International, Englewood Cliffs, 1989, or *A Calculus of Communicating Systems,* LNCS 92, Springer-Verlag, 1980.
9. F. MOLLER (1990): *The nonexistence of finite axiomatisations for CCS congruences.* In Proceedings 5th Annual Symposium on Logic in Computer Science, Philadelphia, USA, IEEE Computer Society Press, pp. 142–153.

10. G.D. PLOTKIN (2004): *A structural approach to operational semantics. The Journal of Logic and Algebraic Programming* 60–61, pp. 17–139. First appeared in 1981.
11. R. DE SIMONE (1985): *Higher-level synchronising devices in* MEIJE-*SCCS. Theoretical Computer Science* 37, pp. 245–267.
12. I. ULIDOWSKI (1992): *Equivalences on observable processes.* In Proceedings 7th Annual Symposium on Logic in Computer Science, Santa Cruz, California, IEEE Computer Society Press, pp. 148–159.
13. I. ULIDOWSKI & I. PHILLIPS (2002): *Ordered SOS rules and process languages for branching and eager bisimulations. Information & Computation* 178, pp. 180–213.
14. I. ULIDOWSKI & S. YUEN (2000): *Process languages for rooted eager bisimulation.* In C. Palamidessi, editor: Proceedings of the 11th International Conference on Concurrency Theory, CONCUR 2000, LNCS 1877, Springer, pp. 275–289.

Externalized and Internalized Notions of Behavioral Refinement[*]

Michel Bidoit[1] and Rolf Hennicker[2]

[1] Laboratoire Spécification et Vérification (LSV),
CNRS & ENS de Cachan, France
[2] Institut für Informatik,
Ludwig-Maximilians-Universität München, Germany

Abstract. Many different behavioral refinement notions for algebraic specifications have been proposed in the literature but the relationship between the various concepts is still unclear. In this paper we provide a classification and a comparative study of behavioral refinements according to two directions, the *externalized* approach which uses an explicit behavioral abstraction operator that is applied to the specification to be implemented, and the *internalized* approach which uses a built-in behavioral semantics of specifications. We show that both concepts are equivalent under suitable conditions. The formal basis of our study is provided by the COL institution (constructor-based observational logic). Hence, as a side-effect of our study on internalized behavioral refinements, we introduce also a novel concept of behavioral refinement for COL-specifications.

1 Introduction

The investigation of behavioral refinement notions is motivated by the fact that, in general, an implementation does not need to satisfy literally the properties of an abstract specification but it can nevertheless be considered as correct if this implementation respects the observable consequences of the specification to be implemented. In the framework of algebraic specifications this idea has been taken into account in many approaches in the literature proposing behavioral (or observational) refinement (or implementation) concepts; see e.g. [9,17,19,12,13,4] and, for an overview, [16,8]. However, due to the various different formalizations, there is still no clear picture of the relationships between the various approaches.

In this paper we propose a classification based on two principal directions that can be identified when we analyze behavioral refinement concepts. The first direction, in the following called the *externalized view*, uses an explicit behavioral abstraction operator to relax the (semantics of the) specification to be implemented. The general idea is then that the models of an implementing specification not necessarily have to lie in the model class of the specification to be implemented but it is sufficient if they lie in its "abstracted" model class (see

---

[*] This work is partially supported by the German BMBF-project GLOWA-Danube.

D.V. Hung and M. Wirsing (Eds.): ICTAC 2005, LNCS 3722, pp. 334–350, 2005.
© Springer-Verlag Berlin Heidelberg 2005

e.g. [17,19,16,4]). Of course, there is again a variety of proposed behavioral abstraction operators which are either based on observational equivalences between algebras (see, e.g., [17,16]) or on observational equalities between the elements of algebras (see, e.g., [4]). Since in many cases both approaches can be expressed by each other (see [7]), we will restrict here to behavioral abstraction operators that are based on observational equalities between elements. As a concrete formalism we use the notion of observational equality defined in [5] which is based on distinguished sets of constructor operations (determining the relevant values from the user's point of view) and observer operations (determining the indistinguishability of elements). As a first result, we show in Section 3 (Theorem 1) that behavioral refinement relations based on the externalized view can be characterized by standard, non-behavioral refinements if we use a quotient construction as an implementation constructor.

Then, in Section 4, we consider the second direction to behavioral refinement, in the following called the *internalized view*. Here the idea is to use a built-in behavioral semantics that is used both for the specification to be implemented and for the implementing specification. A built-in behavioral semantics is most appropriately obtained by the use of a behavioral institution that provides a logical system focusing on the behavioral aspects of system specifications (as with hidden algebra [10] or the constructor-based observational logic COL [5]). A behavioral refinement concept based on hidden algebra is studied in [13], a behavioral refinement concept for COL-specifications is introduced in Section 4. This refinement concept is based on the notion of a COL-implementation constructor which can be applied to the models of the implementing COL-specification SPI_{COL} to produce models of the COL-specification SP_{COL} to be implemented. A crucial property of COL-implementation constructors is that they have to be compatible with behavioral isomorphisms. We show that under mild assumptions reduct functors along (standard) signature morphisms are indeed COL-implementation constructors (Lemma 1) and we discuss the need for such constructions (in contrast to reduct functors along COL-signature morphisms which are appropriate for encapsulation of specifications but not adequate for refinement).

In Section 5 we discuss the relationships between the externalized and the internalized views on behavioral refinements. We show that the behavioral compatibility assumption of COL-implementation constructors is closely related to the notion of stability (introduced by Schoett [20]) which requires that implementation constructors preserve observational equivalences between algebras. Indeed, considering the externalized view, stability is the crucial criterion to obtain composability of behavioral refinement steps (see [19]), also called *vertical composition*. For the internalized view vertical composition of behavioral refinements is guaranteed by definition, according to the built-in behavioral semantics of the implementing specification. As the central result of this paper we show in Theorem 2 that, under suitable assumptions, externalized and internalized notions of behavioral refinement can be expressed by each other. As pointed out in Section 6, this leads to a useful proof rule for internalized behavioral refinements.

2   Basic Concepts

2.1   Algebraic Preliminaries and Structured Specifications

We assume that the reader is familiar with the basic notions of algebraic specifications (see, e.g., [22,1]), like the notions of (many-sorted) *signature* $\Sigma =$
(S, OP) (where S is a set of *sorts* and OP is a set of *operation symbols op* :
$s_1, \ldots, s_n \rightarrow s$), *signature morphism* $\sigma : \Sigma \rightarrow \Sigma'$, *(total) Σ-algebra* $A =$
$((A_s)_{s \in S}, (op^A)_{op \in \mathrm{OP}})$, The class of all Σ-algebras is denoted by $\mathrm{Alg}(\Sigma)$. Together with Σ-morphisms this class forms a category which, for simplicity, is
also denoted by $\mathrm{Alg}(\Sigma)$. For any signature morphism $\sigma : \Sigma \rightarrow \Sigma'$, the *reduct
functor* $\_|_\sigma : \mathrm{Alg}(\Sigma') \rightarrow \mathrm{Alg}(\Sigma)$ is defined as usual.

The notion of an institution was introduced by Goguen and Burstall [11] to
formalize the general concept of a logical system from a model-theoretic point
of view; see [21] for an overview on the basic definitions and the theory of institutions. Any institution provides a suitable framework for defining a set of
specification-building operators which are independent from the concrete form
of the institution. We will use the following four fundamental operators introduced in [18] for constructing structured specifications over an institution I. The
semantics of a specification SP is always determined by its signature, denoted
by $Sig[\mathrm{SP}]$, and by its class of models, denoted by $Mod[\mathrm{SP}]$.

***presentation*:** Any pair $\langle \Sigma, \Phi \rangle$ consisting of a signature Σ and of a set Φ of
Σ-sentences is a specification with semantics:
$Sig[\langle \Sigma, \Phi \rangle] \overset{\text{def}}{=} \Sigma$
$Mod[\langle \Sigma, \Phi \rangle] \overset{\text{def}}{=} \{ M \in \mathrm{Mod}(\Sigma) \mid M \models_\Sigma \Phi \}$

***union*:** For any two specifications SP_1 and SP_2 with the same signature
$Sig[\mathrm{SP}_1] = Sig[\mathrm{SP}_2] = \Sigma$, the expression $\mathrm{SP}_1 \cup \mathrm{SP}_2$ is a specification with
semantics:
$Sig[\mathrm{SP}_1 \cup \mathrm{SP}_2] \overset{\text{def}}{=} \Sigma$
$Mod[\mathrm{SP}_1 \cup \mathrm{SP}_2] \overset{\text{def}}{=} Mod[\mathrm{SP}_1] \cap Mod[\mathrm{SP}_2]$

***translation*:** For any specification SP and signature morphism $\sigma : Sig[\mathrm{SP}] \rightarrow$
Σ, the expression **translate** SP **by** σ is a specification with semantics:
$Sig[\textbf{translate SP by } \sigma] \overset{\text{def}}{=} \Sigma$
$Mod[\textbf{translate SP by } \sigma] \overset{\text{def}}{=} \{ M \in \mathrm{Mod}(\Sigma) \mid M|_\sigma \in Mod[\mathrm{SP}] \}$

***hiding*:** For any specification SP and signature morphism $\sigma : \Sigma \rightarrow Sig[\mathrm{SP}]$, the
expression **derive from** SP **by** σ is a specification with semantics:
$Sig[\textbf{derive from SP by } \sigma] \overset{\text{def}}{=} \Sigma$
$Mod[\textbf{derive from SP by } \sigma] \overset{\text{def}}{=} \mathrm{Iso}_\Sigma(\{ M|_\sigma \mid M \in Mod[\mathrm{SP}] \})$,
where $\mathrm{Iso}_\Sigma(\_)$ denotes the closure under Σ-isomorphisms in $\mathrm{Mod}(\Sigma)$.

2.2   Observability Concepts

In this section we recall the underlying observability notions that will be used
hereafter to formalize behavioral refinements (see [5] for more details). Note,

however, that the forthcoming study of behavioral refinement notions is in principle independent of the chosen formal basis.

To capture the behavioral aspects of system specifications we consider distinguished sets of constructor and observer operations. Intuitively, the constructor operations determine those elements which are of interest from the user's point of view while the observers determine a set of observable experiments that a user can perform to examine hidden states. Thus we can abstract from junk elements and also from concrete state representations whereby two states are considered to be "observationally equal" if they cannot be distinguished by observable experiments.

Formally, a *constructor operation* is an operation symbol $cons : s_1, \ldots, s_n \rightarrow s$ with $n \geq 0$. The result sort s of $cons$ is called a *constrained sort*. An *observer operation* is a pair (obs, i) where obs is an operation symbol $obs : s_1, \ldots, s_n \rightarrow s$ with $n \geq 1$ and $1 \leq i \leq n$. The distinguished argument sort s_i of obs is called a *state sort* (or *hidden sort*). If $obs : s_1 \rightarrow s$ is a unary observer we simply write obs instead of $(obs, 1)$.

If we consider a standard algebraic signature $\Sigma = (S, \mathrm{OP})$ together with a distinguished set $\mathrm{OP_{Cons}}$ of constructor operations and a distinguished set $\mathrm{OP_{Obs}}$ of observer operations we obtain a so-called COL-*signature* $\Sigma_{\mathrm{COL}} = (\Sigma, \mathrm{OP_{Cons}}, \mathrm{OP_{Obs}})$ with underlying (standard) signature Σ.[1] The set $S_{\mathrm{Cons}} \subseteq S$ of *constrained sorts* (w.r.t. $\mathrm{OP_{Cons}}$) consists of all sorts s such that there exists at least one constructor in $\mathrm{OP_{Cons}}$ with range s. The set $S_{\mathrm{Loose}} \subseteq S$ of *loose sorts* consists of all non-constrained sorts, i.e. $S_{\mathrm{Loose}} = S \setminus S_{\mathrm{Cons}}$. The set $S_{\mathrm{State}} \subseteq S$ of *state sorts* (or *hidden sorts*, w.r.t. $\mathrm{OP_{Obs}}$) consists of all sorts s_i such that there exists at least one observer (obs, i) in $\mathrm{OP_{Obs}}$, $obs : s_1, \ldots, s_i, \ldots, s_n \rightarrow s$. The set $S_{\mathrm{Obs}} \subseteq S$ of *observable sorts* consists of all sorts which are not a state sort, i.e. $S_{\mathrm{Obs}} = S \setminus S_{\mathrm{State}}$.

The set $\mathrm{OP_{Cons}}$ of constructor operations (of a COL-signature Σ_{COL}) determines a set of *constructor terms*. A constructor term is a term t of a constrained sort $s \in S_{\mathrm{Cons}}$ which is built only from constructor operations of $\mathrm{OP_{Cons}}$ and from variables of loose sorts. In particular, if all sorts are constrained, i.e., $S_{\mathrm{Cons}} = S$, the constructor terms are exactly the $(S, \mathrm{OP_{Cons}})$-ground terms which are built by the constructor symbols. The set of constructor terms determines, for any Σ-algebra A, a family of subsets of the carrier sets of A, called the *generated part* and denoted by $\mathrm{Gen}_{\Sigma_{\mathrm{COL}}}(A)$, which consists of those elements that can be constructed by the interpretations of the given constructors (starting from constants and from arbitrary elements of loose sorts, if any). The Σ_{COL}-generated part represents those elements which are of interest from the user's point of view according to the given constructor operations. A Σ-algebra A is *reachable* (w.r.t. Σ_{COL}) if its carrier sets coincide with the carrier sets of its Σ_{COL}-generated part.

---

[1] The terminology "COL-signature" stems from the constructor-based observational logic institution COL. Our study is however independent from the COL institution as long as we do not consider the internalized view of behavioral refinements studied in Section 4.

The set $\mathrm{OP_{Obs}}$ of observer operations determines a set of *observable contexts* which represent the observable experiments that a user can perform. An observable context is a term c of observable sort $s' \in S_{\mathrm{Obs}}$ which is built only from observer operations of $\mathrm{OP_{Obs}}$ and which contains a distinguished variable z_s of some hidden sort $s \in S_{\mathrm{State}}$. s is called the *application sort* and s' is called the *observable result sort* of c. The set of observable contexts determines, for any Σ-algebra A, an indistinguishability relation, called *observational equality* and denoted by $\approx_{\Sigma_{\mathrm{COL}},A}$. For any two elements $a, b \in A$, $a \approx_{\Sigma_{\mathrm{COL}},A} b$ holds if either $a = b$ and a, b are observable (i.e. belong to a carrier set of observable sort $s \in S_{\mathrm{Obs}}$) or if a and b cannot be distinguished by the application of observable contexts. A Σ-algebra A is *fully abstract* if the observational Σ_{COL}-equality coincides with the set-theoretic equality.

The constructor and the observer operations induce certain constraints on Σ-algebras. First, since the constructor operations determine the values of interest, we require that the non-constructor operations should (up to observational equality) respect the constructor-generated part of an algebra, i.e. by the application of non-constructor operations one should at most be able to obtain elements which are observationally equal to some element of the constructor-generated part. Technically this means that for a given Σ-algebra A we first consider the smallest Σ-subalgebra $\langle \mathrm{Gen}_{\Sigma_{\mathrm{COL}}}(A) \rangle_\Sigma$ of A containing the Σ_{COL}-generated part because this subalgebra represents the only elements a user can compute (over the loose carrier sets) by invoking operations of Σ. Then we require that each element of $\langle \mathrm{Gen}_{\Sigma_{\mathrm{COL}}}(A) \rangle_\Sigma$ is observationally equal to some element of the Σ_{COL}-generated part $\mathrm{Gen}_{\Sigma_{\mathrm{COL}}}(A)$ of A. This condition is called *reachability constraint*.

Secondly, since the declaration of observer operations determines a particular observational equality on any Σ-algebra A, the (interpretations of the) non-observer operations should respect this observational equality, i.e. a non-observer operation should not contribute to distinguish non-observable elements. To ensure this we require that the observational equality is a Σ-congruence on the subalgebra $\langle \mathrm{Gen}_{\Sigma_{\mathrm{COL}}}(A) \rangle_\Sigma$. (Note that it is sufficient to consider $\langle \mathrm{Gen}_{\Sigma_{\mathrm{COL}}}(A) \rangle_\Sigma$ instead of A because computations performed by a user can only lead to elements in the Σ-subalgebra $\langle \mathrm{Gen}_{\Sigma_{\mathrm{COL}}}(A) \rangle_\Sigma$.) This condition is called *observability constraint*.

A Σ-algebra A which satisfies both the reachability and the observability constraints induced by a COL-signature $\Sigma_{\mathrm{COL}} = (\Sigma, \mathrm{OP_{Cons}}, \mathrm{OP_{Obs}})$ is called Σ_{COL}-*algebra* (or simply COL-*algebra*). Note that any Σ-algebra A which is reachable and fully abstract w.r.t. Σ_{COL} is a Σ_{COL}-algebra. The class of all Σ_{COL}-algebras is denoted by $\mathrm{Alg_{COL}}(\Sigma_{\mathrm{COL}})$.

The satisfaction of the reachability and observability constraints allows us to construct for each Σ_{COL}-algebra A its *black box view* which is a reachable and fully abstract algebra representing the behavior of A from the user's point of view. The black box view is constructed in two steps. First, we *restrict* to the Σ_{COL}-generated subalgebra $\langle \mathrm{Gen}_{\Sigma_{\mathrm{COL}}}(A) \rangle_\Sigma$ of A thus forgetting junk values. Then, we *identify* all elements of $\langle \mathrm{Gen}_{\Sigma_{\mathrm{COL}}}(A) \rangle_\Sigma$ which are observationally equal. Hence the black box view of a Σ_{COL}-algebra A is given by the quotient algebra of $\langle \text{Gen}_{\Sigma_{\text{COL}}}(A) \rangle_\Sigma$ w.r.t. $\approx_{\Sigma_{\text{COL}},A}$ which, for simplicity, will be denoted by $A/\approx_{\Sigma_{\text{COL}},A}$. Two Σ_{COL}-algebras A and B are *observationally equivalent* (w.r.t. Σ_{COL}), denoted by $A \equiv_{\Sigma_{\text{COL}}} B$, if their black box views $A/\approx_{\Sigma_{\text{COL}},A}$ and $B/\approx_{\Sigma_{\text{COL}},B}$ are isomorphic Σ-algebras.

The observability notions defined above provide a generalization of the approach in [7] which is based on partial observational equalities $\approx_{Obs,In,A}$. The difference here is the declaration of the constructor and observer operations which provide much more flexibility than declaring just observable sorts Obs and input sorts In as done in [7]. In fact, any standard signature $\Sigma = (S, \text{OP})$ together with distinguished sets $In \subseteq S$ of input sorts and $Obs \subseteq S$ of observable sorts induces a COL-signature $\Sigma_{\text{COL}}^{In,Obs} = (\Sigma, \text{OP}_{\text{Cons}}, \text{OP}_{\text{Obs}})$ where OP_{Cons} consists of *all* operation symbols $cons \in \text{OP}$ with range $s \in S \setminus In$ and OP_{Obs} consists of all pairs (obs, i) with $obs \in \text{OP}$, $obs : s_1, \ldots, s_i, \ldots, s_n \to s$ and $s_i \in S \setminus Obs$. Then, for any Σ-algebra A, the partial observational equality $\approx_{Obs,In,A}$ coincides (on $\langle \text{Gen}_{\Sigma_{\text{COL}}}(A) \rangle_\Sigma$) with $\approx_{\Sigma_{\text{COL}},A}$. In particular, in this case each Σ-algebra is also a COL-algebra. Hence the results on behavioral refinements developed in the following sections are also valid for all observability notions based on fixed sets of observable sorts (and input sorts) which are frequently found in the literature, see, e.g., [15,17].

3   Behavioral Refinement: The Externalized View

In this section we consider the institution FOLEq of many-sorted first-order logic with equality (as detailed, e.g., in [3]) and we consider structured specifications over FOLEq built by the specification building operations defined in Section 2.1. A simple refinement relation between two specifications SP (the abstract specification to be implemented) and SPI (the implementing specification) can be defined by requiring that both specifications have the same signature and that the model class of the implementing specification SPI is included in the model class of SP, see, e.g., [22]. To take into account that an implementation usually involves some construction steps the notion of constructor implementation has been introduced in [19] (and similarly in other implementation concepts; see [16,8] for an overview). According to [19] an implementation constructor is a function which maps algebras over the signature of the implementing specification to algebras over the signature of the abstract specification. Since an implementation construction must not necessarily be defined on all algebras but only on the models of the implementing specification we allow partial functions as implementation constructors. (An example of a partial implementation constructor is the formation of observational quotients used below.) On the other hand, we assume that implementation constructions are performed in a uniform way, i.e. preserve isomorphisms.

Definition 1 (Implementation constructor). *Let Σ, ΣI be two signatures. An* implementation constructor *from ΣI to Σ (also simply called a* constructor*)* *is a partial function* $\kappa : \mathrm{Alg}(\Sigma I) \to \mathrm{Alg}(\Sigma)$ *which is iso-preserving, i.e. for all* $AI, BI \in \mathrm{Alg}(\Sigma I)$,

  if AI *is* ΣI-*isomorphic to* BI *and* $\kappa(AI)$ *is defined*
  then $\kappa(BI)$ *is defined and* $\kappa(AI)$ *is* Σ-*isomorphic to* $\kappa(BI)$.
The definition domain of κ *is denoted by* $Dom(\kappa)$.

An example of an implementation constructor is, for a given signature morphism $\sigma : \Sigma \to \Sigma I$ which renames abstract sorts and operations into those offered by the implementation, the reduct functor $\_\!\_|_\sigma : \mathrm{Alg}(\Sigma I) \to \mathrm{Alg}(\Sigma)$ (see also [19]). Note that in FOLEq this constructor can also be expressed by the *derive* specification-building primitive.

Definition 2 (Refinement). *Let* SP, SPI *be two specifications with signatures* Σ, ΣI *resp. and let* κ *be a constructor from* ΣI *to* Σ. SPI *is a refinement of* SP *w.r.t.* κ, *denoted by* SP $\leadsto^\kappa$ SPI, *if*

$$Mod[\mathrm{SPI}] \subseteq Dom(\kappa) \text{ and } \kappa(Mod[\mathrm{SPI}]) \subseteq Mod[\mathrm{SP}].$$

Many examples show that the above refinement definition is too restrictive since an implementation does not need to satisfy literally all requirements of an abstract specification but can nevertheless be considered as correct if the implementation respects the observable properties of the specification to be implemented. This fact has inspired a lot of work on adequate notions of behavioral refinement relations. A popular idea is to relax the model class of the specification SP to be implemented by some behavioral abstraction operation, see, e.g., [17,19,16,4]. We call this direction the *externalized view* of behavioral refinement because, only for the purpose of refinement, a behavioral abstraction operation is applied on top of the given (standard) model class of SP. In contrast to that idea, other approaches use a built-in behavioral semantics which is used for both specifications, the specification to be implemented *and* the implementing specification, see [13]. We call this direction the *internalized view* of behavioral refinement which will be more closely considered in the next section. In this section we focus on the externalized view using as a behavioral abstraction operation the following behavior operator which constructs for a given class C of Σ-algebras the class of all algebras whose black box view belongs to C. The behavior operator is defined according to distinguished sets of constructor operations and observer operations, i.e. w.r.t. a COL-signature.

Definition 3 (Behavior operator). *Let* $\Sigma_{\mathrm{COL}} = (\Sigma, \mathrm{OP}_{\mathrm{Cons}}, \mathrm{OP}_{\mathrm{Obs}})$ *be a* COL-*signature. For any class* C *of* Σ-*algebras,*

$$\mathrm{Beh}_{\Sigma_{\mathrm{COL}}}(C) \stackrel{\mathrm{def}}{=} \{A \in \mathrm{Alg}_{\mathrm{COL}}(\Sigma_{\mathrm{COL}}) \mid A/\!\approx_{\Sigma_{\mathrm{COL}},A} \in C\}.$$

A class C of Σ-algebras is called *behaviorally closed* w.r.t. a COL-signature Σ_{COL} if $C \subseteq \mathrm{Beh}_{\Sigma_{\mathrm{COL}}}(C)$ or, equivalently, if any Σ-algebra $A \in C$ is a COL-algebra and its black box view $A/\!\approx_{\Sigma_{\mathrm{COL}},A}$ belongs also to C. A specification SP is behaviorally closed if its model class $Mod[\mathrm{SP}]$ is behaviorally closed.

When considering the externalized view of behavioral refinement the idea is, of course, to apply the behavior operator to the model class of the specification to be implemented. This leads to the following notion of behavioral refinement.

Definition 4 (Behavioral refinement: the externalized view). *Let* SP, SPI *be two specifications with signatures* Σ, ΣI *resp., let* Σ_{COL} *be a* COL-*signature of the form* $(\Sigma, \text{OP}_{\text{Cons}}, \text{OP}_{\text{Obs}})$ *and let* $\kappa : \text{Alg}(\Sigma I) \to \text{Alg}(\Sigma)$ *be a constructor.* SPI *is a* behavioral refinement *of* SP *w.r.t.* Σ_{COL} *and* κ, *denoted by* SP $\xrightarrow{\Sigma_{\text{COL}}}^{\kappa}$ SPI, *if*

$$\mathcal{M}od[\text{SPI}] \subseteq Dom(\kappa) \text{ and } \kappa(\mathcal{M}od[\text{SPI}]) \subseteq \text{Beh}_{\Sigma_{\text{COL}}}(\mathcal{M}od[\text{SP}]).$$

The given behavioral refinement notion is essentially based on the use of the observational equality of elements induced by a COL-signature. Other approaches in the literature, which follow the externalized view, use for behavioral abstraction not an indistinguishability relation between elements but an abstraction equivalence between algebras, see, e.g., [17,15]. According to the results in [7,4] there is, however, no difference between both approaches if the abstraction equivalence is factorizable (see [7]) and if the specification to be implemented is behaviorally closed.

Example 1. The following specification SET specifies properties of sets of natural numbers.

spec SET =
      sorts *bool, nat, set*
      ops *true, false : bool;*
            0 : nat; succ : nat $\to$ nat; plus : nat $\times$ nat $\to$ nat;
            empty : set; add : nat $\times$ set $\to$ set;
            isin : nat $\times$ set $\to$ bool;
      axioms
      $\forall x, y : nat;\ s : set$
      %% standard axioms for booleans and natural numbers, plus
- $isin(x, empty) = false$
- $isin(x, add(x, s)) = true$
- $x \neq y \Rightarrow isin(x, add(y, s)) = isin(x, s)$
- $add(x, add(x, s)) = add(x, s)$ (1)
- $add(x, add(y, s)) = add(y, add(x, s))$ (2)

end

For the implementation of sets we first abstract from the SET specification by using as an observer operation the membership test *isin* to observe sets. More precisely, we consider the COL-signature $\Sigma\text{SET}_{\text{COL}} = (Sig[\text{SET}], \emptyset, \{(isin, 2)\})$. For the concrete implementation we use the specification LIST shown below and a signature morphism $\sigma_{\text{SET}as\text{LIST}} : Sig[\text{SET}] \to Sig[\text{LIST}]$ such that $\sigma_{\text{SET}as\text{LIST}}(set) = list$, $\sigma_{\text{SET}as\text{LIST}}(add) = cons$ and $\sigma_{\text{SET}as\text{LIST}}(x) = x$ otherwise. Hence the implementation constructor κ is the reduct functor $\_\_|_{\sigma_{\text{SET}as\text{LIST}}} : \text{Alg}(Sig[\text{LIST}]) \to \text{Alg}(Sig[\text{SET}])$.

Thus we obtain the refinement relation SET $^{\Sigma\text{SET}_{\text{COL}}} \leadsto^{\kappa}$ LIST.[2]

spec LIST =

    sorts *bool, nat, list*

    ops   *true, false* : *bool*;

           0 : *nat*; *succ* : *nat* → *nat*; *plus* : *nat* × *nat* → *nat*;

           empty : *list*; *cons* : *nat* × *list* → *list*;

           head : *list* → *nat*; *tail* : *list* → *list*;

           isin : *nat* × *list* → *bool*;

    axioms

    $\forall x, y$: *nat*; l : *list*

    %% standard axioms for booleans and natural numbers, plus

    • *head*(*cons*(x, l)) = x

    • *tail*(*cons*(x, l)) = l

    • *isin*(x, *empty*) = *false*

    • *isin*(x, *cons*(x, l)) = *true*

    • $x \neq y \Rightarrow isin(x, cons(y, l)) = isin(x, l)$

end

Let us still point out that inspired by the results in [3] we can characterize externalized behavioral refinements by standard refinements in the sense of Definition 2 if we use behavioral quotient constructors which are induced by the black box views of COL-algebras.

Definition 5 (Behavioral quotient constructor). *Let Σ_{COL} be a COL-signature with underlying signature Σ. The behavioral quotient constructor (w.r.t. Σ_{COL}) is given by* $\_/\approx_{\Sigma_{\text{COL}}}$: $\text{Alg}(\Sigma) \rightarrow \text{Alg}(\Sigma)$, *where*

$$\_/\approx_{\Sigma_{\text{COL}}}(A) \overset{\text{def}}{=} A/\approx_{\Sigma_{\text{COL}},A} \text{ if } A \text{ is a } \Sigma_{\text{COL}}\text{-algebra,}$$
$$\_/\approx_{\Sigma_{\text{COL}}}(A) \text{ is undefined otherwise.}[3]$$

Theorem 1 (Characterization of externalized behavioral refinements). *Let SP, SPI be two specifications with signatures Σ, ΣI resp., let Σ_{COL} be a COL-signature with underlying signature Σ and let κ : $\text{Alg}(\Sigma I) \rightarrow \text{Alg}(\Sigma)$ be a constructor.*

$$\text{SP } ^{\Sigma_{\text{COL}}} \leadsto^{\kappa} \text{ SPI } \quad \text{if and only if} \quad \text{SP } \leadsto^{\kappa; \ \_/\approx_{\Sigma_{\text{COL}}}} \text{ SPI}.$$

Proof. The proof is a direct consequence of the definitions, in particular of the fact that $\kappa(\mathcal{M}od[\text{SPI}]) \subseteq \text{Beh}_{\Sigma_{\text{COL}}}(\mathcal{M}od[\text{SP}])$ is equivalent to the inclusion $\kappa(\mathcal{M}od[\text{SPI}])/\approx_{\Sigma_{\text{COL}}} \subseteq \mathcal{M}od[\text{SP}]$. □

---

[2] The correctness proof is easy: First, the implementation indeed satisfies the non-observable equations (1) and (2) of SET due to the behavioral abstraction. That the reduct functor yields COL-algebras w.r.t. $\Sigma\text{SET}_{\text{COL}}$ follows from the observer complete form of the axioms; see [6] for more details.

[3] Obviously, $\_/\approx_{\Sigma_{\text{COL}}}$ is iso-preserving.

4   Behavioral Refinement: The Internalized View

The idea of the internalized view of behavioral refinement is to use a built-in behavioral semantics for specifications. For this purpose behavioral institutions which are tailored towards the behavioral aspects of system specifications provide an appropriate basis. Examples of such institutions are the framework of hidden algebra (see [10]) and the constructor-based observational logic institution COL (see [5]). In the following we will consider the COL institution for which no behavioral refinement concept has been investigated yet while for hidden algebra a refinement notion has been discussed in [13]. The COL institution has as signatures COL-signatures and as models COL-algebras as described in Section 2. COL-signature morphisms are standard signature morphisms which fulfill additional properties related to the preservation of constructor and observer operations and COL-morphisms between COL-algebras reflect behavioral relationships (see [5] for details). In particular, two Σ_{COL}-algebras A and B are Σ_{COL}-isomorphic if they are *observationally equivalent* (w.r.t. Σ_{COL}), i.e. if $A \equiv_{\Sigma_{\mathrm{COL}}} B$.

A crucial concept to obtain a built-in behavioral semantics is the *behavioral satisfaction relation*, denoted by $\models_{\Sigma_{\mathrm{COL}}}$, which generalizes the standard satisfaction relation of first-order logic by abstracting with respect to reachability and observability. From the reachability point of view, the valuations of variables are restricted to the elements of the Σ_{COL}-generated part $\mathrm{Gen}_{\Sigma_{\mathrm{COL}}}(A)$ only. From the observability point of view, the equality symbol "$=$" occurring in a first-order formula φ is not interpreted by the set-theoretic equality but by the observational equality $\approx_{\Sigma_{\mathrm{COL}},A}$ of elements.

In the following of this section we consider structured specifications over COL built by the specification building operations defined in Section 2.1. For instance, a basic COL specification $\mathrm{SP}_{\mathrm{COL}} = \langle \Sigma_{\mathrm{COL}}, \mathrm{Ax} \rangle$ consists of a COL-signature Σ_{COL} and a set Ax of Σ-sentences, called axioms. The semantics of $\mathrm{SP}_{\mathrm{COL}}$ is given by its signature Σ_{COL} and by its class of models

$$\mathcal{M}od[\mathrm{SP}_{\mathrm{COL}}] = \{A \in \mathrm{Alg}_{\mathrm{COL}}(\Sigma_{\mathrm{COL}}) \mid A \models_{\Sigma_{\mathrm{COL}}} \mathrm{Ax}\}.$$

In order to define behavioral refinements for COL-specifications we can simply transfer the notions of implementation constructor and refinement used for the FOLEq institution in Definitions 1 and 2 to the COL institution. In particular, this means that COL-implementation constructors are required to preserve COL-isomorphisms, i.e. behavioral equivalences of algebras.

Definition 6 (COL-implementation constructor). *Let Σ_{COL}, ΣI_{COL} be two COL-signatures. A COL-implementation constructor from ΣI_{COL} to Σ_{COL} (also simply called a COL-constructor) is a partial function κ_{COL} : $\mathrm{Alg}_{\mathrm{COL}}(\Sigma I_{\mathrm{COL}}) \to \mathrm{Alg}_{\mathrm{COL}}(\Sigma_{\mathrm{COL}})$ which is COL-iso-preserving, i.e. for all $AI, BI \in \mathrm{Alg}_{\mathrm{COL}}(\Sigma I_{\mathrm{COL}})$,*

if $AI \equiv_{\Sigma I_{\mathrm{COL}}} BI$ and $\kappa_{\mathrm{COL}}(AI)$ is defined

then $\kappa_{\mathrm{COL}}(BI)$ is defined and $\kappa_{\mathrm{COL}}(AI) \equiv_{\Sigma_{\mathrm{COL}}} \kappa_{\mathrm{COL}}(BI)$.

The definition domain of κ_{COL} is denoted by $Dom(\kappa_{\mathrm{COL}})$.

Definition 7 (Behavioral refinement: the internalized view). *Let* SP_{COL}, SPI_{COL} *be two COL-specifications with signatures* Σ_{COL}, ΣI_{COL} *resp. and let* κ_{COL} *be a COL-constructor from* ΣI_{COL} *to* Σ_{COL}. SPI_{COL} *is a behavioral refinement of* SP_{COL} *w.r.t.* κ_{COL}, *denoted by* $SP_{COL} \rightsquigarrow^{\kappa_{COL}} SPI_{COL}$, *if*

$$\mathcal{M}od[SPI_{COL}] \subseteq Dom(\kappa_{COL}) \ and \ \kappa_{COL}(\mathcal{M}od[SPI_{COL}]) \subseteq \mathcal{M}od[SP_{COL}].$$

An important question is, of course, which implementation constructors are appropriate for COL-refinements. As a first approach one could simply consider COL-signature morphisms $\sigma_{COL} : \Sigma_{COL} \rightarrow \Sigma I_{COL}$. Since COL is an institution, the corresponding COL-reduct functor $\_\_|_{\sigma_{COL}} : Alg_{COL}(\Sigma I_{COL}) \rightarrow Alg_{COL}(\Sigma_{COL})$ preserves COL-isomorphisms, i.e. is a COL-implementation constructor. Hence it is tempting to consider COL-refinements where the syntactic relationship between the specification SP_{COL} to be implemented and the implementing specification SPI_{COL} is established by a COL-signature morphism. This approach has, however, a serious drawback because the implementing specification SPI_{COL} usually has constructor and observer operations OPI_{Cons}, OPI_{Obs} which are unrelated to the constructor and observer operations OP_{Cons}, OP_{Obs} of the specification SP_{COL} to be implemented. As a simple example we consider below the implementation of sets by lists where the observer for sets is the membership test *isin* while the observer operations for lists are, as usual, the *head* and *tail* operations. Hence the COL-specifications of sets and lists cannot be related by a COL-signature morphism which would require the preservation of constructor and observer operations. This is the reason why we want to consider standard signature morphisms and their reduct functors as implementation constructors for COL-specifications.

But before let us still point out that from a methodological point of view it is indeed adequate not to stick to COL-signature morphisms when we construct implementations. COL-signature morphisms are the appropriate tool to ensure encapsulation of COL-specifications (formally expressed by the satisfaction condition of an institution) which is indeed important when we construct large specifications in a modular way (often called *horizontal composition*). But when we discuss refinements and compositions of refinement steps (often called *vertical composition*) this is a totally different matter. Indeed, talking about encapsulation when relating abstract and concrete specifications makes no sense. An extensive discussion of this issue can also be found in [13].

Hence, let us consider two COL-specifications SP_{COL}, SPI_{COL} with signatures Σ_{COL}, ΣI_{COL} resp. together with a (standard) signature morphism $\sigma : \Sigma \rightarrow \Sigma I$ (where Σ and ΣI are the underlying standard signatures of Σ_{COL} and ΣI_{COL} resp.). Moreover, let us consider the reduct functor $\_\_|_\sigma : Alg(\Sigma I) \rightarrow Alg(\Sigma)$ as a partial function $\_\_|_\sigma : Alg_{COL}(\Sigma I_{COL}) \rightarrow Alg_{COL}(\Sigma_{COL})$,[4] where

$\_\_|_\sigma(AI) \stackrel{\text{def}}{=} AI|_\sigma$ if $AI|_\sigma$ is a Σ_{COL}-algebra,

$\_\_|_\sigma(AI)$ is undefined otherwise.

---

[4] By abuse of notation we use the same symbol $\_\_|_\sigma$ for the (total) reduct functor on $Alg(\Sigma I)$ and for its induced partial reduct function on $Alg_{COL}(\Sigma I_{COL})$.

The next lemma provides a simple criterion under which the (partial) reduct function on COL-algebras is COL-iso-preserving, i.e. is a COL-implementation constructor.

Lemma 1. *Let $\Sigma_{\text{COL}}, \Sigma I_{\text{COL}}$ be COL-signatures with underlying signatures Σ, ΣI resp. Let $S_{\text{Obs}}, SI_{\text{Obs}}$ be the observable sorts and $S_{\text{Loose}}, SI_{\text{Loose}}$ be the loose sorts induced by $\Sigma_{\text{COL}}, \Sigma I_{\text{COL}}$ resp. (see Section 2). If $\sigma(S_{\text{Obs}}) \subseteq SI_{\text{Obs}}$ and $\sigma(S_{\text{Loose}}) \subseteq SI_{\text{Loose}}$ then $\_\_|_\sigma : \text{Alg}_{\text{COL}}(\Sigma I_{\text{COL}}) \to \text{Alg}_{\text{COL}}(\Sigma_{\text{COL}})$ is a COL-implementation constructor.*

Proof. We have to show that for all $AI, BI \in \text{Alg}_{\text{COL}}(\Sigma I_{\text{COL}})$ the following holds:

1. If $AI \equiv_{\Sigma I_{\text{COL}}} BI$ and $AI|_\sigma$ is a Σ_{COL}-algebra then $BI|_\sigma$ is a Σ_{COL}-algebra.
2. If $AI \equiv_{\Sigma I_{\text{COL}}} BI$ then $AI|_\sigma \equiv_{\Sigma_{\text{COL}}} BI|_\sigma$.

Proof of (1): Let $AI \equiv_{\Sigma I_{\text{COL}}} BI$ and $AI|_\sigma$ be a Σ_{COL}-algebra. Then $AI/\approx_{\Sigma I_{\text{COL}}, AI}$ iso $BI/\approx_{\Sigma I_{\text{COL}}, BI}$. Hence $(AI/\approx_{\Sigma I_{\text{COL}}, AI})|_\sigma$ iso $(BI/\approx_{\Sigma I_{\text{COL}}, BI})|_\sigma$. Due to the assumption $\sigma(S_{\text{Obs}}) \subseteq SI_{\text{Obs}}$ and $\sigma(S_{\text{Loose}}) \subseteq SI_{\text{Loose}}$, we can conclude that $AI|_\sigma$ is a Σ_{COL}-algebra iff $(AI/\approx_{\Sigma I_{\text{COL}}, AI})|_\sigma$ is a Σ_{COL}-algebra. Hence, $(AI/\approx_{\Sigma I_{\text{COL}}, AI})|_\sigma$ is a Σ_{COL}-algebra and so is $(BI/\approx_{\Sigma I_{\text{COL}}, BI})|_\sigma$. Again, by using the assumption, we conclude that $BI|_\sigma$ is a Σ_{COL}-algebra

Proof of (2): Let $In \stackrel{\text{def}}{=} S_{\text{Loose}}, Obs \stackrel{\text{def}}{=} S_{\text{Obs}}, InI \stackrel{\text{def}}{=} SI_{\text{Loose}}$, and $ObsI \stackrel{\text{def}}{=} SI_{\text{Obs}}$. Due to the assumption $\sigma(In) \subseteq InI$, $\sigma(Obs) \subseteq ObsI$ and according to [4] (Example 3.15), the reduct functor $\_\_|_\sigma : \text{Alg}(\Sigma I) \to \text{Alg}(\Sigma)$ is behavior respecting w.r.t. the partial observational equalities $\approx_{Obs,In}$ and $\approx_{ObsI,InI}$ in the sense of [4] (Def. 3.12). Since AI, BI are ΣI_{COL}-algebras, $\approx_{ObsI,InI,AI} = \approx_{\Sigma I_{\text{COL}}, AI}$ and $\approx_{ObsI,InI,BI} = \approx_{\Sigma I_{\text{COL}}, BI}$ and hence $AI \equiv_{\Sigma I_{\text{COL}}} BI$ iff $AI \equiv_{ObI,InI} BI$. Since $\_\_|_\sigma$ is behavior respecting, $AI|_\sigma \equiv_{Obs,In} BI|_\sigma$. Since both reducts are Σ_{COL}-algebras this is equivalent to $AI|_\sigma \equiv_{\Sigma_{\text{COL}}} BI|_\sigma$. □

Example 2. In contrast to Example 1 let us now consider COL-specifications of sets and lists. First, the COL-specification SETCOL of sets is given by including the observer *isin* into the COL-signature of the specification. (For simplicity, we do not consider constructor operations here.)

spec SETCOL =
> **sorts** *bool, nat, set*
> **ops**   *true, false : bool;*
>   *0 : nat; succ : nat $\to$ nat; plus : nat $\times$ nat $\to$ nat;*
>   *empty : set; add : nat $\times$ set $\to$ set;*
>   *isin : nat $\times$ set $\to$ bool;*
> **observer** (*isin, 2*)
> **axioms**
> %% the same axioms as in SET (see Example 1)

end

The following specification LISTCOL provides a COL-specification of lists. As in any usual approach for a behavioral specification of lists we use the operations *head* and *tail* as observers for lists.

spec LISTCOL =
    sorts *bool*, *nat*, *list*
    ops   *true*, *false* : *bool*;
           0 : *nat*; *succ* : *nat* → *nat*; *plus* : *nat* × *nat* → *nat*;
           empty : *list*; *cons* : *nat* × *list* → *list*;
           head : *list* → *nat*; *tail* : *list* → *list*;
           isin : *nat* × *list* → *bool*;
    observers *head*, *tail*
    axioms
    %% the same axioms as in LIST (see Example 1)
end

For the implementation construction we use the same (standard) signature morphism $\sigma_{\text{SET}_{as}\text{LIST}}$ as in Example 1 and the partial function

$$-|_{\sigma_{\text{SET}_{as}\text{LIST}}} : \text{Alg}_{\text{COL}}(\mathit{Sig}[\text{LISTCOL}]) \to \text{Alg}_{\text{COL}}(\mathit{Sig}[\text{SETCOL}])$$

induced by the reduct functor $-|_{\sigma_{\text{SET}_{as}\text{LIST}}}$ on standard algebras. It is important to note that the (image of the) observable sorts of SETCOL are included in the observable sorts of LISTCOL and hence, due to Lemma 1, the reduct functor is indeed a COL-implementation constructor, denoted by κ_{COL}. Thus we obtain the refinement relation SETCOL $\leadsto^{\kappa_{\text{COL}}}$ LISTCOL.[5]

5 Relating the Externalized and the Internalized Views of Behavioral Refinements

Let us first relate the implementation constructors used in the different approaches. Since any COL-algebra is also a (standard) algebra it is obvious that any implementation constructor $\kappa : \text{Alg}(\Sigma I) \to \text{Alg}(\Sigma)$ gives rise to a (partial) function $\kappa_{\text{COL}} : \text{Alg}_{\text{COL}}(\Sigma I_{\text{COL}}) \to \text{Alg}_{\text{COL}}(\Sigma_{\text{COL}})$ where

$\kappa_{\text{COL}}(AI) \stackrel{\text{def}}{=} \kappa(AI)$ if $\kappa(AI)$ is defined and is a Σ_{COL}-algebra,
$\kappa_{\text{COL}}(AI)$ is undefined otherwise.

If this partial function is COL-iso-preserving then κ_{COL} is a COL-implementation constructor *induced* by κ. In particular this means that κ is compatible with observational equivalences between COL-algebras, a property which is frequently used in the literature in different contexts having its origin in the notion of stability introduced by Schoett [20]. Thus constructors κ which induce COL-constructors will synonymously be called *stable* constructors. A criterion for the stability of reduct functors along standard signature morphisms has been provided in Lemma 1. The following lemma states a useful consequence of stable constructors.

---

[5] The correctness proof can be reduced to the proof of the refinement relation of Example 1 due to the forthcoming Theorem 2 which relates externalized and internalized views of behavioral refinements.

Lemma 2. *Let κ be a constructor from ΣI to Σ and κ_{COL} be a COL-constructor from ΣI_{COL} to Σ_{COL} induced by κ. Then, for any class $CI \subseteq \mathrm{Alg}(\Sigma I)$ of ΣI-algebras and for any iso-closed class $C \subseteq \mathrm{Alg}(\Sigma)$ of Σ-algebras, it holds:*
If $CI \subseteq Dom(\kappa)$ and $\kappa(CI) \subseteq \mathrm{Beh}_{\Sigma_{\mathrm{COL}}}(C)$
then $\mathrm{Beh}_{\Sigma I_{\mathrm{COL}}}(CI) \subseteq Dom(\kappa)$ and $\kappa(\mathrm{Beh}_{\Sigma I_{\mathrm{COL}}}(CI)) \subseteq \mathrm{Beh}_{\Sigma_{\mathrm{COL}}}(C)$.

Proof. Let $AI \in \mathrm{Beh}_{\Sigma I_{\mathrm{COL}}}(CI)$. Then $AI/\approx_{\Sigma I_{\mathrm{COL}},AI} \in CI$ and, by assumption, $\kappa(AI/\approx_{\Sigma I_{\mathrm{COL}},AI}) \in \mathrm{Beh}_{\Sigma_{\mathrm{COL}}}(C)$. Hence, in particular, $\kappa(AI/\approx_{\Sigma I_{\mathrm{COL}},AI})$ is a Σ_{COL}-algebra. Thus $\kappa_{\mathrm{COL}}(AI/\approx_{\Sigma I_{\mathrm{COL}},AI})$ is defined. Since $AI \equiv_{\Sigma I_{\mathrm{COL}}} AI/\approx_{\Sigma I_{\mathrm{COL}},AI}$ and κ_{COL} is a COL-constructor, $\kappa_{\mathrm{COL}}(AI)$ is defined as well, i.e. $\kappa(AI)$ is a Σ_{COL}-algebra and thus $\mathrm{Beh}_{\Sigma I_{\mathrm{COL}}}(CI) \subseteq Dom(\kappa)$.

Moreover, since κ_{COL} is COL-iso-preserving, $\kappa(AI) = \kappa_{\mathrm{COL}}(AI) \equiv_{\Sigma_{\mathrm{COL}}} \kappa_{\mathrm{COL}}(AI/\approx_{\Sigma I_{\mathrm{COL}},AI}) = \kappa(AI/\approx_{\Sigma I_{\mathrm{COL}},AI}) \in \mathrm{Beh}_{\Sigma_{\mathrm{COL}}}(C)$. Since C is iso closed, $\mathrm{Beh}_{\Sigma_{\mathrm{COL}}}(C)$ is closed under COL-iso, i.e. under $\equiv_{\Sigma_{\mathrm{COL}}}$. Thus we obtain, as desired, $\kappa(AI) \in \mathrm{Beh}_{\Sigma_{\mathrm{COL}}}(C)$. $\qquad\square$

From Lemma 2 we can easily conclude that for stable constructors, behavioral refinement steps according to the externalized view compose, i.e.

$$\mathrm{SP} \xrightarrow{\Sigma_{\mathrm{COL}}}{}^{\kappa} \mathrm{SPI}, \; \mathrm{SPI} \xrightarrow{\Sigma I_{\mathrm{COL}}}{}^{\kappa'} \mathrm{SPI}' \text{ implies } \mathrm{SP} \xrightarrow{\Sigma_{\mathrm{COL}}}{}^{\kappa'; \, \kappa} \mathrm{SPI}'.$$

Indeed, it has been pointed out already in [19] that the preservation of observational equivalences is crucial to guarantee vertical composition of so-called abstractor implementations which are a variant of the externalized approach. For the internalized approach, vertical composition is trivially guaranteed according to the built-in behavioral semantics which is used for both the specification to be implemented and for the implementing specification, i.e.

$$\mathrm{SP}_{\mathrm{COL}} \xrightarrow{}{}^{\kappa_{\mathrm{COL}}} \mathrm{SPI}_{\mathrm{COL}}, \; \mathrm{SPI}_{\mathrm{COL}} \xrightarrow{}{}^{\kappa'_{\mathrm{COL}}} \mathrm{SPI}'_{\mathrm{COL}} \text{ implies}$$
$$\mathrm{SP}_{\mathrm{COL}} \xrightarrow{\Sigma I_{\mathrm{COL}}}{}^{\kappa'_{\mathrm{COL}}; \, \kappa_{\mathrm{COL}}} \mathrm{SPI}'_{\mathrm{COL}}.$$

In the following of this section we will show that under certain conditions (stability of constructors and behavioral closedness of specifications), externalized behavioral refinements and internalized behavioral refinements are expressible by each other. To relate the two approaches we first define a trivial syntactic translation $Forget_{\mathrm{COL}}$ from COL-specifications into standard specifications over FOLEq according to the structure of specifications:

$Forget_{\mathrm{COL}}(\langle \Sigma_{\mathrm{COL}}, \mathrm{Ax}\rangle) \overset{\mathrm{def}}{=} \langle \Sigma, \mathrm{Ax}\rangle$
where Σ is the underlying standard signature of Σ_{COL}

$Forget_{\mathrm{COL}}(\mathrm{SP}_{1,\mathrm{COL}} \cup \mathrm{SP}_{2,\mathrm{COL}}) \overset{\mathrm{def}}{=}$
$Forget_{\mathrm{COL}}(\mathrm{SP}_{1,\mathrm{COL}}) \cup Forget_{\mathrm{COL}}(\mathrm{SP}_{2,\mathrm{COL}})$

$Forget_{\mathrm{COL}}(\textbf{translate } \mathrm{SP}_{\mathrm{COL}} \textbf{ by } \sigma_{\mathrm{COL}}) \overset{\mathrm{def}}{=}$
$\textbf{translate } Forget_{\mathrm{COL}}(\mathrm{SP}_{\mathrm{COL}}) \textbf{ by } \sigma$
where σ is the underlying standard signature morphism of σ_{COL}

$Forget_{COL}(\textbf{derive from } SP_{COL} \textbf{ by } \sigma_{COL}) \stackrel{\text{def}}{=}$
$\textbf{derive from } Forget_{COL}(SP_{COL}) \textbf{ by } \sigma$
where σ is the underlying standard signature morphism of σ_{COL}

We implicitly assume in the following that for any structured COL-specification SP_{COL} its associated FOLEq-specification $Forget_{COL}(SP_{COL})$ is denoted by SP and similarly for SPI_{COL} etc. The following lemma states that COL-specifications and behavioral abstractions of their associated FOLEq-specifications are semantically equivalent.

Lemma 3. *Let SP_{COL} be a COL-specification with signature Σ_{COL} and let SP be its associated FOLEq-specification. Assume that in the structured specification SP, each occurrence of the derive construct (if any) is applied to a behaviorally closed specification. Then $Mod[SP_{COL}] = Beh_{\Sigma_{COL}}(Mod[SP]).$*[6]

Proof. The proof of the lemma is straightforward by induction on the structure of specifications. For the basic step we use the fact (see [5]) that for any Σ_{COL}-algebra A and Σ-sentence φ, $A \models_{\Sigma_{COL}} \varphi$ iff $A/\approx_{\Sigma_{COL},A} \models \varphi$ (where $\models$ denotes the standard satisfaction relation of first-order logic). The induction step for the union of two specifications is trivial and the induction steps for *translate* and *derive* utilize the fact that reduct functors w.r.t. COL-signature morphisms commute with black box constructions; see Theorem 51 of [5]. □

Theorem 2 (Relating externalized and internalized behavioral refinements). *Let SP_{COL}, SPI_{COL} be two COL-specifications with signatures Σ_{COL}, ΣI_{COL} resp. and let SP, SPI be the associated FOLEq-specifications with signatures Σ, ΣI resp. Again we assume that in the structured specifications SP and SPI, each occurrence of the derive construct (if any) is applied to a behaviorally closed specification. Let κ_{COL} be a COL-constructor from ΣI_{COL} to Σ_{COL} induced by a constructor κ from ΣI to Σ.*

1. If $SP \stackrel{\Sigma_{COL}}{\leadsto}{}^{\kappa} SPI$ then $SP_{COL} \leadsto^{\kappa_{COL}} SPI_{COL}$.
2. If SPI is behaviorally closed w.r.t. ΣI_{COL} then
   $SP \stackrel{\Sigma_{COL}}{\leadsto}{}^{\kappa} SPI$ if and only if $SP_{COL} \leadsto^{\kappa_{COL}} SPI_{COL}$.

Proof. (1): By assumption,
   $Mod[SPI] \subseteq Dom(\kappa)$ and $\kappa(Mod[SPI]) \subseteq Beh_{\Sigma_{COL}}(Mod[SP]).$
Hence, by Lemma 2 (and since $Mod[SP]$ is iso-closed)
   $Beh_{\Sigma I_{COL}}(Mod[SPI]) \subseteq Dom(\kappa)$ and
   $\kappa(Beh_{\Sigma I_{COL}}(Mod[SPI])) \subseteq Beh_{\Sigma_{COL}}(Mod[SP]).$
Since, by Lemma 3,
   $Mod[SPI_{COL}]=Beh_{\Sigma I_{COL}}(Mod[SPI])$ and $Mod[SP_{COL}]=Beh_{\Sigma_{COL}}(Mod[SP])$
we obtain, as desired,
   $Mod[SPI_{COL}] \subseteq Dom(\kappa_{COL})$ and $\kappa_{COL}(Mod[SPI_{COL}]) \subseteq Mod[SP_{COL}].$

---

[6] In this equation the Σ_{COL}-algebras on the left-hand side are considered as standard Σ-algebras.

(2): Conversely, if
$$\mathcal{M}od[\text{SPI}_{\text{COL}}] \subseteq Dom(\kappa_{\text{COL}}) \text{ and } \kappa_{\text{COL}}(\mathcal{M}od[\text{SPI}_{\text{COL}}]) \subseteq \mathcal{M}od[\text{SP}_{\text{COL}}],$$
then we obtain, again by Lemma 3,
$$\text{Beh}_{\Sigma I_{\text{COL}}}(\mathcal{M}od[\text{SPI}]) \subseteq Dom(\kappa) \text{ and}$$
$$\kappa(\text{Beh}_{\Sigma I_{\text{COL}}}(\mathcal{M}od[\text{SPI}])) \subseteq \text{Beh}_{\Sigma_{\text{COL}}}(\mathcal{M}od[\text{SP}]).$$
Since SPI is behaviorally closed w.r.t. ΣI_{COL}, $\mathcal{M}od[\text{SPI}] \subseteq \text{Beh}_{\Sigma I_{\text{COL}}}(\mathcal{M}od[\text{SPI}])$
and therefore $\mathcal{M}od[\text{SPI}] \subseteq Dom(\kappa)$ and $\kappa(\mathcal{M}od[\text{SPI}]) \subseteq \text{Beh}_{\Sigma_{\text{COL}}}(\mathcal{M}od[\text{SP}])$.   □

6   Conclusion

We have studied the relationships between externalized and internalized behavioral refinements which we believe is useful for further elaborations of behavioral refinement notions in the context of particular specification frameworks, like, e.g., the algebraic specification language CASL [2]. Indeed the essential results of our study, in particular the main theorem pointing out the equivalence of the external and the internal views of behavioral refinements (under certain assumptions), are in principle independent of the chosen formalism. Hence, it should be possible to generalize our results to a more abstract category-theoretic setting, e.g. along the lines of [14].

An important further issue concerns proof techniques to verify behavioral refinements. It seems that the most efficient way would be to reduce both, the externalized and the internalized notions, to the proof of refinement relations between standard first-order logic specifications (possibly involving sort generation constraints). Indeed Theorem 1 and 2 induce immediately the following two proof rules:

$$\frac{\text{SP} \leadsto^{\kappa;\ --/\approx_{\Sigma_{\text{COL}}}} \text{SPI}}{\text{SP} \ ^{\Sigma_{\text{COL}}}\leadsto^{\kappa} \text{SPI}}$$

$$\frac{\text{SP} \ ^{\Sigma_{\text{COL}}}\leadsto^{\kappa} \text{SPI}}{\text{SP}_{\text{COL}} \leadsto^{\kappa_{\text{COL}}} \text{SPI}_{\text{COL}}}$$

Then, further proof rules are needed for proving $\text{SP} \leadsto^{\kappa;\ --/\approx_{\Sigma_{\text{COL}}}} \text{SPI}$. A useful source for this purpose are the proof techniques for the validity of first-order sentences in behavioral quotient specifications provided in [3].

References

1. E. Astesiano, H.-J. Kreowski, and B. Krieg-Brückner, editors. *Algebraic Foundations of Systems Specification*. Springer, 1999.
2. E. Astesiano, H. Kirchner M. Bidoit, B. Krieg-Brückner, P.D. Mosses, D.T. Sannella, and A. Tarlecki. CASL: The Common Algebraic Specification Language. *Theoretical Computer Science*, 286(2):153–196, 2002.
3. M. Bidoit, M.-V. Cengarle, and R. Hennicker. Proof systems for structured specifications and their refinements. In *[1]*, chapter 11, pages 385–433. Springer, 1999.

4. M. Bidoit and R. Hennicker. Modular correctness proofs of behavioural implementations. *Acta Informatica*, 35:951–1005, 1998.
5. M. Bidoit and R. Hennicker. Constructor-based observational logic. *Journal of Logic and Algebraic Programming*, 2005, to appear. Preliminary version available at www.lsv.ens-cachan.fr/Publis/PAPERS/PDF/BID-HEN-JLAP.pdf.
6. Michel Bidoit and Rolf Hennicker. Observer complete definitions are behaviourally coherent. In *Proc. OBJ/CafeOBJ/Maude Workshop at Formal Methods'99, Toulouse, France, Sep. 1999*, pages 83–94. THETA, 1999.
7. Michel Bidoit, Rolf Hennicker, and Martin Wirsing. Behavioural and abstractor specifications. *Science of Computer Programming*, 25(2–3):149–186, 1995.
8. H. Ehrig and H.-J. Kreowski. Refinement and implementation. In *[1]*, chapter 7, pages 201–242. Springer, 1999.
9. J. Goguen and J.A. Meseguer. Universal realization, persistent interconnection and implementation of abstract modules. In *Proc. ICALP'82*, volume 140 of *Lecture Notes in Computer Science*, pages 265–281. Springer, 1982.
10. J. Goguen and G. Roşu. Hiding more of hidden algebra. In J.M. Wing, J. Woodcock, and J. Davies, editors, *Proc. Formal Methods (FM'99)*, volume 1709 of *Lecture Notes in Computer Science*, pages 1704–1719. Springer, 1999.
11. Joseph Goguen and Rod Burstall. Institutions: abstract model theory for specification and programming. *Journal of the ACM*, 39(1):95–146, 1992.
12. R. Hennicker. Observational implementation of algebraic specifications. *Acta Informatica*, 35:951–1005, 1998.
13. G. Malcolm and J. Goguen. Proving correctness of refinement and implementation. Technical Report PRG-114, Oxford University Computing Laboratory, 1994.
14. Michal Misiak. Behavioural semantics of algebraic specifications in arbitrary logical systems. In *Recent Trends in Algebraic Development Techniques*, volume 3423 of *LNCS*, pages 144–161. Springer, 2004.
15. M.P. Nivela and F. Orejas. Initial behaviour semantics for algebraic specifications. In *Recent Trends in Data Type Specification*, volume 332 of *LNCS*, pages 184–207. Springer, 1988.
16. F. Orejas, M. Navarro, and A. Sanchez. Implementation and behavioural equivalence. In *Recent Trends in Data Type Specification*, volume 655 of *Lecture Notes in Computer Science*, pages 93–125. Springer, 1993.
17. D. Sannella and A. Tarlecki. On observational equivalence and algebraic specification. *Journal of Computer and System Sciences*, 34:150–178, 1987.
18. Donald Sannella and Andrzej Tarlecki. Specifications in an arbitrary institution. *Information and Computation*, 76:165–210, 1988.
19. D.T. Sannella and A. Tarlecki. Toward formal development of programs from algebraic specifications: implementation revisited. *Acta Informatica*, 25:233–281, 1988.
20. O. Schoett. Data abstraction and correctness of modular programming. Technical Report CST-42-87, University of Edinburgh, 1987.
21. Andrzej Tarlecki. Institutions: An Abstract Framework for Formal Specification. In *[1]*, chapter 4, pages 105–130. Springer, 1999.
22. Martin Wirsing. Algebraic Specification. In J. van Leeuwen, editor, *Handbook of Theoretical Computer Science*, chapter 13, pages 676–788. Elsevier Science Publishers B.V., 1990.

Information Flow Is Linear Refinement of Constancy

Fausto Spoto

Dipartimento di Informatica, Università di Verona, Italy
fausto.spoto@univr.it

Abstract. Detecting information flows inside a program is useful to check non-interference of program variables, an important aspect of software security. Information flows have been computed in the past by using abstract interpretation over an abstract domain IF which expresses sets of flows. In this paper we reconstruct IF as the *linear refinement* C → C of a basic domain C expressing *constancy* of program variables. This is important since we also show that C → C, and hence IF, is closed *w.r.t.* linear refinement, and is hence *optimal* and *condensing*. Then a compositional, input-independent static analysis over IF has the same precision of a non-compositional, input-driven analysis. Moreover, we show that C → C has a natural representation in terms of Boolean formulas, efficiently implementable through binary decision diagrams.

1 Introduction

Language-based security is recognised as an important aspect of modern programming languages design and implementation [11]. One of its aspects is *non-interference*, which determines the pairs of program variables that do not affect each other's values during the execution of a program. From non-interference it is then possible to study the confinement of confidential information injected in the program through some input variables. Non-interference is often implemented above an information-flow analysis, which tracks the flows of information in a program [15,12,3,11,6].

Information flows in a program can be computed through abstract interpretation [4] by using an abstract domain, that we call IF in this paper, which models sets of flows [11,6]. Abstract interpretation consists in executing the program over the description of the concrete data as provided by IF. Correctness states that if a program features a flow, then it must be included in the description that the analysis computes. The domain IF has been implemented by using Boolean formulas [6] to represent sets of flows. This leads to an efficient analysis [7] which uses binary decision diagrams [2] to implement such formulas. Moreover, that analysis is *input-independent i.e.*, it is performed only once, without any assumption on the input provided to the program. The input variables containing confidential information are specified *after* the analysis is performed. An *input-driven* analysis, instead, would require the input to be available *before*

D.V. Hung and M. Wirsing (Eds.): ICTAC 2005, LNCS 3722, pp. 351–365, 2005.

the analysis, so that it must be re-executed for each different input. Hence it is not possible to analyse a library independently from the applications that use it.

In this paper we show that IF coincides with the *linear refinement* C → C of an abstract domain C which expresses *constancy* of program variables *i.e.,* the set of variables that are definitely bound to a constant value in a given program point. Linear refinement [10] is a formal technique which adds input/output relational information to an abstract domain. In our case, the added relational information over C corresponds to the flows of information between variables.

This result is important since

- it shows that an independently developed abstract domain such as IF can be reconstructed through a methodological technique such as linear refinement;
- we later prove that C → C is closed *w.r.t.* linear refinement. This entails that C → C (and hence IF) is an *optimal* and *condensing* abstract domain [9]. This means that IF is the minimal abstract domain which models information flows and all relational information between them (optimality) and that it can be used for a compositional, input-independent static analysis without sacrificing precision *w.r.t.* a non-compositional, input-driven static analysis (condensing). None of these properties was known before for IF;
- we finally show that the elements of C → C, and hence of IF, have a *natural* representation in terms of Boolean formulas. This formally justifies the use of Boolean formulas to implement IF [6].

The rest of this paper is organised as follows. Section 2 presents the preliminaries and defines C. Section 3 formalises the abstract domain IF. Section 4 shows that IF = C → C. Section 5 proves that C → C is closed *w.r.t.* linear refinement, and is hence optimal and condensing. Section 6 provides a representation of the elements of C → C in terms of Boolean formulas. Section 7 concludes.

2   Preliminaries

2.1   Functions and Ordered Sets

A total (partial) function f is denoted by $\mapsto$ ($\rightarrow$). The *domain* of f is $dom(f)$ We denote by $[v_1 \mapsto t_1, \ldots, v_n \mapsto t_n]$ the function f where $dom(f) = \{v_1, \ldots, v_n\}$ and $f(v_i) = t_i$ for $i = 1, \ldots, n$. Its *update* is $f[w_1 \mapsto d_1, \ldots, w_m \mapsto d_m]$, where the domain may be enlarged. By $f|_s$ ($f|_{-s}$) we denote the *restriction* of f to $s \subseteq dom(f)$ (to $dom(f) \setminus s$). The composition $f \circ g$ of functions f and g is such that $(f \circ g)(x) = g(f(x))$. A *poset* is a set S with a reflexive, transitive and antisymmetric relation $\leq$. An *upper (respectively, lower) bound* of $S' \subseteq S$ is an element $u \in S$ such that $u' \leq u$ (respectively, $u' \geq u$) for every $u' \in S'$. A *complete lattice* is a poset where *least* upper bounds ($\sqcup$) and *greatest* lower bounds ($\sqcap$) always exist. The top and bottom elements of a lattice are denoted by $\top$ and $\bot$, respectively.

2.2   Denotations

We model the *state* of an interpreter of a computer program at a given program point as a function from the variables in scope to their *values*. We consider integers as values, but any other domain of values would do. Our state can be seen as the activation frame on top of the activation stack of the interpreter. Since in this paper we use a denotational semantics of programs [16], we do not need to model to whole activation stack. Instead, we assume that procedure calls are resolved by plugging the meaning or *interpretation* of a procedure in the calling point. This is standard in denotational semantics, and has been used for years in the semantics of logic programs [1].

Definition 1 (State). *Let V be a finite set of variables (this will be assumed in the rest of the paper). A* state over V *is a total function from V into integer values. The set of states over V is Σ_V, where V is usually omitted.*

The set V contains only the variables in scope in the program point under analysis.

Example 1. An example of state $\sigma \in \Sigma$ is such that $\sigma(v) = 3$ for each $v \in V$.

A denotational semantics associates a *denotation* to each piece of code *i.e.*, a function from input states to output states. Possible divergence is modelled by using partial functions as denotations.

Definition 2 (Denotation). *A* denotation over V *is a partial function $\delta :$ $\Sigma_V \rightarrow \Sigma_V$. The set of denotations is Δ_V, where V is usually omitted. Let $\sigma \in$ Σ_V. If $v \in V$ and $\delta(\sigma)$ is not defined, then we let $\delta(\sigma)(v) = undef$.*

A *denotational semantics* is a *compositional* (*i.e.*, inductive) definition of the denotations of each language construct. This definition is irrelevant here, since expressivity and precision of a static analysis are domain-related issues [4]. Hence we give complete freedom to the language designer, so that for instance we impose no constraint on the denotations of Definition 2. The interested reader can find in [16] an example of denotational semantics.

Example 2. The denotation for the assignment $y := x+1$ is δ_1 such that $\delta_1(\sigma) = \sigma[y \mapsto \sigma(x) + 1]$ for all $\sigma \in \Sigma$. That is, the successor of the input value of x is stored in the output value of y. The other variables are not modified.

Example 3. The denotation of the assignment $x := 4$ is δ_2 such that $\delta_2(\sigma) = \sigma[x \mapsto 4]$ for all $\sigma \in \Sigma$. That is, the output value of x is constantly bound to 4. The other variables are not modified.

Example 4. The denotation of if $y = 0$ then $x := 4$ else while true do skip is δ_4, *compositionally* defined as

$$\delta_4(\sigma) = \begin{cases} \delta_2(\sigma) & \text{if } \sigma(y) = 0 \\ \delta_3(\sigma) & \text{if } \sigma(y) \neq 0, \end{cases}$$

where δ_2 is the denotation of $x := 4$ (Example 3) and δ_3 is the denotation of while true do skip, which is *always* undefined.

Example 5. The denotation of $x := 4; y := x+1$ is the functional composition $\delta_2 \circ \delta_1$ (Examples 3 and 2). In general, $\circ$ is the semantical counterpart of the sequential composition of commands.

Constancy is a property of denotations. Namely, a variable v is constant in a denotation δ when δ always binds v to a given value.

Definition 3. *Let $\delta \in \Delta$. The set of variables which are* constant *in δ is*

$$const(\delta) = \{v \in V \mid \text{for all } \sigma_1, \sigma_2 \in \Sigma \text{ we have } \delta(\sigma_1)(v) = \delta(\sigma_2)(v)\}.$$

Example 6. The denotation δ_1 of Example 2 copies $x+1$ into y. Hence $const(\delta_1) = \varnothing$. The denotation δ_2 of Example 3 binds x to 4. Then $const(\delta_2) = \{x\}$.

Constancy is closed *w.r.t.* composition of denotations. Namely, for any $\delta, \overline{\delta} \in \Delta$ and $v \in V$, if $v \in const(\delta)$ then $v \in const(\overline{\delta} \circ \delta)$.

2.3   Abstract Domains and Abstract Interpretation

Let C be a complete lattice playing the role of the *concrete* domain. For instance, in this paper C will be the powerset $\wp(\Delta)$ of the *concrete* denotations of Subsection 2.2. Each element of C is an *abstract property*. For instance, the set of concrete denotations which bind x to 4 is an element of $\wp(\Delta)$ expressing the property: "x holds 4 in the output of the denotation". An *abstract domain* A is a collection of abstract properties *i.e.*, a subset of C.

Example 7 (The Abstract Domain C). Let us use $\wp(\Delta_V)$ as concrete domain and let $\mathbf{v_1} \cdots \mathbf{v_n} = \{\delta \in \Delta_V \mid v_i \in const(\delta) \text{ for } 1 \leq i \leq n\}$. An abstract domain of $\wp(\Delta_V)$ is

$$C_V = \{\mathbf{v_1} \cdots \mathbf{v_n} \mid \{v_1, \ldots, v_n\} \subseteq V\}.$$

It expresses the properties of *being constant* for a set of variables in a denotation. Its top element is $\varnothing$. We will usually omit V in C_V. From Example 6 we conclude that $\delta_1 \in \varnothing$ and $\delta_2 \in \mathbf{x}$. However, $\delta_2 \notin \mathbf{xy}$ since y is not constant in δ_2 (Example 3).

Abstract interpretation theory [4] requires A to be meet-closed, which guarantees the existence in A of a *best approximation* for each element of C. That is, A must be a *Moore family* of C *i.e.*, a complete meet-sublattice of C (for any $Y \subseteq A$ we have $\sqcap_C Y \in A$). Note that A is not, in general, a complete sublattice of C, since the join $\sqcup_A$ might be different from $\sqcup_C$.

Example 8. The set C of Example 7 is closed *w.r.t.* intersection *i.e.*, the $\sqcap$ operation on $\wp(\Delta)$. Hence C deserves the name of *abstract domain*. Namely, $(\mathbf{v_1} \cdots \mathbf{v_n}) \cap (\mathbf{w_1} \cdots \mathbf{w_m}) = \mathbf{x_1} \cdots \mathbf{x_p}$ where $\{x_1, \ldots, x_p\} = \{x \mid x \in \{v_1, \ldots v_n\}$ and $x \in \{w_1, \ldots, w_m\}\}$.

For any $X \subseteq C$, we denote by $\lambda X = \{\sqcap_C I \mid I \subseteq X\}$ the *Moore closure* of X *i.e.*, the least Moore family of C containing X. Hence the operation λ *constructs* the smallest abstract domain which includes the set of properties X.

Example 9. We write the set of denotations where x is constant as $\mathbf{x} = \{\delta \in \Delta \mid x \in const(\delta)\}$. The abstract domain of Example 7 can be constructed as $C_V = \lambda\{\mathbf{x} \mid x \in V\}$. We write the elements of C as $\mathbf{v_1} \cdots \mathbf{v_n}$, standing for $\cap\{\mathbf{v_i} \mid 1 \leq i \leq n\}$. If $vs \subseteq V$ then by $\mathbf{vs}$ we mean $\cap\{\mathbf{v} \mid v \in vs\}$.

Once an abstract domain is defined, abstract interpretation theory provides the abstract semantics induced by each given concrete semantics. Hence, from a theoretical point of view, the abstract domain is an exhaustive definition of an abstract semantics for a programming language, which can then be implemented and used for static analysis. For this reason, and for space concerns, we concentrate in this paper on abstract domains only, without any consideration on the induced abstract semantics.

2.4 Linear Refinement

The definition of an appropriate abstract domain for a static analysis is not in general easy. Although a *basic* abstract domain A can be immediately constructed (λ) from the abstract properties one wants to model, there is no guarantee that the induced abstract semantics is precise enough to be useful. The intuition and experience of the abstract domain designer helps in determing what A is missing in order to improve its precision. In alternative, there are more methodological techniques which *refine* A to get a more precise domain.

Reduced product [5] allows one to refine two abstract domains A_1 and A_2 into an abstract domain $A_1 \sqcap A_2 = \lambda(A_1 \cup A_2)$ which expresses the conjunction of properties of A_1 and A_2.

Linear refinement [10] is another domain refinement operator. It allows one to enrich an abstract domain with information relative to the *propagation* of the abstract properties before and after the application of a concrete operator $\boxtimes$. It requires the concrete domain C to be a *quantale w.r.t.* $\boxtimes$ *i.e.,*

1. C must be a complete lattice;
2. $\boxtimes : C \times C \to C$ must be (in general partial and) associative;
3. for any $a \in C$ and $\{b_i\}_{i \in I} \subseteq C$ with $I \subseteq \mathbb{N}$ we must have $a \boxtimes (\sqcup_{i \in I} b_i) = \sqcup_{i \in I}\{a \boxtimes b_i\}$ and $(\sqcup_{i \in I} b_i) \boxtimes a = \sqcup_{i \in I}\{b_i \boxtimes a\}$.

For instance, the complete lattice $\wp(\Delta)$, ordered by set-inclusion, is a quantale *w.r.t.* the composition operator $\circ$, extended to sets of denotations as $d_1 \circ d_2 = \{\delta_1 \circ \delta_2 \mid \delta_1 \in d_1 \text{ and } \delta_2 \in d_2\}$.

Let $a, b \in C$. The abstract property $a \to^\boxtimes b$ which *transforms* every element of a into an element of b is

$$a \to^\boxtimes b = \bigsqcup_C \{c \in C \mid \text{if } a \boxtimes c \text{ is defined then } a \boxtimes c \leq_C b\}.$$

Given $a \in C$, $I \subseteq \mathbb{N}$ and $\{b_i\}_{i \in I} \subseteq C$, we have $a \to^\boxtimes (\sqcap_{i \in I} b_i) = \sqcap_{i \in I}(a \to^\boxtimes b_i)$.

Definition 4 (Linear Refinement). *The (forward) linear refinement of an abstract domain $A_1 \subseteq C$ w.r.t. another abstract domain $A_2 \subseteq C$ is the abstract domain $A_1 \to^\boxtimes A_2 = \lambda\{a \to^\boxtimes b \mid a \in A_1 \text{ and } b \in A_2\}$. That is, it collects all possible arrows between elements of A_1 and elements of A_2.*

The following results hold [10]

1. $\to^{\boxtimes}$ is argument-wise monotonic;
2. $A_1 \to^{\boxtimes} (A_2 \to^{\boxtimes} A_3) = (A_1 \to^{\boxtimes} A_2) \to^{\boxtimes} A_3$, so parentheses are not relevant;
3. $A_1 \to^{\boxtimes} A_2 \to^{\boxtimes} A_3 = (A_1 \sqcap A_2) \to^{\boxtimes} A_3$, where $\sqcap$ is the reduced product.

We now instantiate $\to^{\boxtimes}$ over the quantale $\langle \wp(\Delta), \circ \rangle$. The intuition under the choice of $\circ$ for $\boxtimes$ is that the denotational semantics of an imperative program is defined by *composing* smaller denotations to form larger denotations [16]. Hence we must refine the composition operation if we want to improve the precision of the abstractions of $\wp(\Delta)$.

We first provide an explicit definition for $\to^{\circ}$.

Proposition 1. *Let* $d_1, d_2 \subseteq \Delta$. *Then* $d_1 \to^{\circ} d_2 = \{\delta \in \Delta \mid \text{for every } \overline{\delta} \in d_1 \text{ we have } \overline{\delta} \circ \delta \in d_2\}$.

Proof.

$$d_1 \to^{\circ} d_2 = \bigcup \{d \in \wp(\Delta) \mid \text{if } d_1 \circ d \text{ is defined then } d_1 \circ d \subseteq d_2\}$$

$$= \bigcup \{d \in \wp(\Delta) \mid d_1 \circ d \subseteq d_2\}$$

$$= \bigcup \{d \in \wp(\Delta) \mid \{\overline{\delta} \circ \delta \mid \overline{\delta} \in d_1 \text{ and } \delta \in d\} \subseteq d_2\}$$

$$= \{\delta \in \Delta \mid \{\overline{\delta} \circ \delta \mid \overline{\delta} \in d_1\} \subseteq d_2\}$$

$$= \{\delta \in \Delta \mid \text{for every } \overline{\delta} \in d_1 \text{ we have } \overline{\delta} \circ \delta \in d_2\}.$$

The intuition behind $d_1 \to^{\circ} d_2$ is that it is the set of denotations that when composed with a denotation in d_1 become a denotation in d_2.

Example 10. Consider the abstract domain C of Example 7 and its two elements $\mathbf{x}$ and $\mathbf{y}$. The denotation δ_1 of Example 2 belongs to $\mathbf{x} \to^{\circ} \mathbf{y}$ since δ_1 stores the input value of x plus 1 in the output value of y, so that if x is constant in δ_1's input then y is constant in δ_1's output.

From now on, we will omit $\circ$ in $\to^{\circ}$.

3   A Classical Domain for Information Flow Analysis

We present here a traditional abstract domain for information flow analysis. It expresses which *termination-sensitive* flows [3] are allowed in a denotation.

Definition 5 (Information-Flow). *Let* $\delta \in \Delta$ *and* $x, y \in V$. *We say that* δ *features an information flow from* x *to* y *[11] if there exist* $\sigma_1, \sigma_2 \in \Sigma$ *such that*

1. $\sigma_1|_{V \setminus x} = \sigma_2|_{V \setminus x}$ *(σ_1 and σ_2 agree on x);*
2. $\delta(\sigma_1)(y) \neq \delta(\sigma_2)(y)$ *(the input value of x affects the output value of y).*

Definition 5 entails that $\sigma_1(x) \neq \sigma_2(x)$. Moreover, if exactly one between $\delta(\sigma_1)$ and $\delta(\sigma_2)$ is defined, then by Definition 2 the condition $\delta(\sigma_1)(y) \neq \delta(\sigma_2)(y)$ holds. This is why Definition 5 formalises termination-sensitive information flows.

Example 11. The denotation δ_1 of Example 2 is such that $\delta_1(\sigma) = \sigma[y \mapsto \sigma(x) + 1]$ for every $\sigma \in \Sigma$. Let σ_1 and σ_2 be such that $\sigma_1(v) = 0$ for every $v \in V$, $\sigma_2(x) = 1$ and $\sigma_2(v) = 0$ for every $v \in V \setminus x$. We have $\sigma_1|_{V \setminus x} = \sigma_2|_{V \setminus x}$ and $\delta_1(\sigma_1)(y) = 1 \neq 2 = \delta_1(\sigma_2)(y)$. Then δ_1 features a flow from x to y. Moreover, $\delta_1(\sigma_1)(x) = 0$ and $\delta_1(\sigma_2)(x) = 1$. Then δ_1 features a flow from x to x. These are both *explicit* flows [11] *i.e.*, generated by copying input values into output values in a denotation. They are the only flows featured by δ_1. For instance, δ_1 does not feature any flow from y to y, since for every $\sigma_1, \sigma_2 \in \Sigma$ such that $\sigma_1|_{V \setminus y} = \sigma_2|_{V \setminus y}$ we have $\delta_1(\sigma_1)(y) = \sigma_1(x) + 1 = \sigma_2(x) + 1 = \delta_1(\sigma_2)(y)$.

Example 12. The denotation δ_4 of Example 4 features a flow from y to x. Namely, take σ_1 and σ_2 such that $\sigma_1(v) = 0$ for every $v \in V$, $\sigma_2(v) = 0$ for every $v \in V \setminus y$ and $\sigma_2(y) = 1$. We have $\sigma_1|_{V \setminus y} = \sigma_2|_{V \setminus y}$, $\delta_4(\sigma_1)(x) = 4 \neq undef = \delta_4(\sigma_2)(x)$. Since we consider termination-sensitive flows, the denotation δ_4 actually features a flow from y to *any* variable $v \in V$, since the initial value of y determines the termination of the conditional statement in Example 4. These flows are called *implicit* [11] since they arise from the conditional execution of program statements on the basis of the initial value of some variables.

The abstract domain for information flow analysis is the powerset of the set of flows. Each abstract element expresses which flows a denotation can feature.

Definition 6 (Abstract Domain IF). *Let $x_i, y_i \in V$ for $i = 1, \ldots n$. We define*

$$x_1 \leadsto y_1, \ldots, x_n \leadsto y_n = \left\{ \delta \in \Delta_V \,\middle|\, \begin{array}{l} \text{if } \delta \text{ features a flow from } x \text{ to } y \text{ then} \\ \text{there exists } i \text{ such that } x \equiv x_i \text{ and } y \equiv y_i \end{array} \right\}.$$

The abstract domain for information flow analysis is

$$\mathsf{IF}_V = \{x_1 \leadsto y_1, \ldots, x_n \leadsto y_n \mid n \geq 0 \text{ and } x_i, y_i \in V \text{ for every } i = 1, \ldots, n\}$$

where V is usually omitted. It is ordered by inverse set-inclusion.

Each element of IF is a set of denotations. In order to justify the name of *abstract domain* for IF, we must prove that the set of its elements is closed by intersection.

Proposition 2. *The set IF is a Moore family of $\wp(\Delta)$.*

Proof. Let $f^i = x_1^i \leadsto y_1^i, \ldots, x_{n^i}^i \leadsto y_{n^i}^i \in \mathsf{IF}$ with $I \subseteq \mathbb{N}$ and $i \in I$. We prove that $X = \{x \leadsto y \mid x \leadsto y \in f^i \text{ for all } i \in \mathbb{N}\}$ (which belongs to IF) is their intersection. We have $\delta \in \cap_{i \in I} f^i$ if and only if $\delta \in f^i$ for each $i \in I$, if and only if whenever δ features a flow from x to y then $x \leadsto y \in f^i$ for each $i \in I$, if and only if whenever δ features a flow from x to y then $x \leadsto y \subseteq X$, if and only if $\delta \in X$.

Figure 1 shows the abstract domain $\mathsf{IF}_{\{x,y\}}$. The top of the domain allows denotations to feature any flow, and hence coincides with Δ.

Example 13. Assume $V = \{x, y\}$. The denotation δ_1 of Example 2 belongs to $x \leadsto x, x \leadsto y$ since it only features flows from x to y and from x to x (Example 11). It also belongs to the upper bound $x \leadsto x, x \leadsto y, y \leadsto y$. However, δ_1 does not belong to $x \leadsto x$ since δ_1 features a flow from x to y (Example 11), not allowed in $x \leadsto x$.

4   The Linear Refinement $C \to C$

Example 7 defines a basic domain for constancy C which models the set of variables which are constant in the output of a denotation. Here, we linearly refine C into $C \to C$, which is a new abstract domain for *constancy propagation*. Then we show that IF and $C \to C$ coincide.

The following result shows that $C \to C$ includes C.

Proposition 3. *We have* $C \subseteq C \to C$. *If* $\#V \geq 2$, *the inclusion is strict.*

Proof. Since $\varnothing \in C$ and $\varnothing = \wp(\Delta)$, then for every $v \in V$ we have $\varnothing \to \mathbf{v} \in C \to C$. If we show that $\varnothing \to \mathbf{v} = \mathbf{v}$, we conclude that $C \subseteq C \to C$. Let $\delta \in \varnothing \to \mathbf{v}$ and ι be the identity denotation, such that $\iota(\sigma) = \sigma$ for every $\sigma \in \Sigma$. We have $\iota \in \varnothing = \wp(\Delta)$, so that $\iota \circ \delta = \delta \in \mathbf{v}$. Conversely, let $\delta \in \mathbf{v}$. Constancy is closed by composition, so $\overline{\delta} \circ \delta \in \mathbf{v}$ for every $\overline{\delta} \in \wp(\Delta) = \varnothing$. Hence $\delta \in \varnothing \to \mathbf{v}$.

To prove the strict inclusion, let $x, y \in V$, $x \not\equiv y$. Let ι be the identity denotation. Since no variable is constant in ι, we have $\iota \in \varnothing$ and $\iota \notin c$ for all $c \in C \setminus \{\varnothing\}$. We have $\iota \in \mathbf{x} \to \mathbf{x}$. This is because for all $\overline{\delta} \in \mathbf{x}$ we have $\overline{\delta} \circ \iota = \overline{\delta} \in \mathbf{x}$. To prove that $C \subset C \to C$ is then enough to show that $\mathbf{x} \to \mathbf{x} \neq \varnothing$. Consider δ such that $\delta(\sigma) = \sigma[x \mapsto \sigma(y)]$. We have $\delta \in \varnothing$ since no variable is constant in δ. But $\delta \notin \mathbf{x} \to \mathbf{x}$, since if we take $\overline{\delta} \in \mathbf{x}$ such that $\overline{\delta}(\sigma) = \sigma[x \mapsto 0]$ we have $\overline{\delta} \circ \delta = \delta \notin \mathbf{x}$ (no variable is constant in δ). $\square$

The following lemma states that if a denotation does not feature any flow from a set of variables $V \setminus S$ into a given variable y, then y's value in the output of the denotation depends only on the input values of the variables in S.

Lemma 1. *Let* $\sigma_1, \sigma_2 \in \Sigma$, $y \in V$, $S \subseteq V$ *and* $\delta \in \Delta$ *which does not feature any flow* $v \rightsquigarrow y$ *with* $v \in V \setminus S$. *Then* $\sigma_1|_S = \sigma_2|_S$ *entails* $\delta(\sigma_1)(y) = \delta(\sigma_2)(y)$.

Proof. Let $V \setminus S = \{v_1, \ldots, v_n\}$. Define $\sigma_1^0 = \sigma_1$, $\sigma_2^0 = \sigma_2$ and $\sigma_1^i = \sigma_1^{i-1}[v_i \mapsto \max(\sigma_1(v_i), \sigma_2(v_i))]$, $\sigma_2^i = \sigma_2^{i-1}[v_i \mapsto \max(\sigma_1(v_i), \sigma_2(v_i))]$ for $1 \leq i \leq n$. Note that whether $\sigma_1^i = \sigma_1^{i-1}$ or they differ at $v_i \in V \setminus S$ only. The same holds for σ_2^i and σ_2^{i-1}. Since δ does not feature any flow $v_i \rightsquigarrow y$, in both cases we have $\delta(\sigma_1^i) = \delta(\sigma_1^{i-1})$ and $\delta(\sigma_2^i) = \delta(\sigma_2^{i-1})$. Moreover, $\sigma_1^n = \sigma_2^n$. Hence $\delta(\sigma_1) = \delta(\sigma_1^0) = \delta(\sigma_1^1) = \cdots = \delta(\sigma_1^n) = \delta(\sigma_2^n) = \cdots = \delta(\sigma_2^1) = \delta(\sigma_2^0) = \delta(\sigma_2)$. $\square$

We can now state that IF coincides with $C \to C$. We first prove that $\mathsf{IF} \subseteq C \to C$, by *implementing* each element of IF through an element of $C \to C$.

Lemma 2. *Let* $f = x_1 \rightsquigarrow y_1, \ldots, x_n \rightsquigarrow y_n \in \mathsf{IF}$. *We have*

$$f = \cap\{\mathbf{S}(\mathbf{y}) \to \mathbf{y} \mid y \in V \text{ and } S(y) = \{x_i \mid x_i \rightsquigarrow y \in f\}\}.$$

Proof. Let $\delta \in x_1 \rightsquigarrow y_1, \ldots, x_n \rightsquigarrow y_n$. We prove that $\delta \in \mathbf{S}(\mathbf{y}) \to \mathbf{y}$ for each $y \in V$. Let $\overline{\delta} \in \mathbf{S}(\mathbf{y})$ and $\sigma_1, \sigma_2 \in \Sigma$. We have $\overline{\delta}(\sigma_1)|_{S(y)} = \overline{\delta}(\sigma_2)|_{S(y)}$. Moreover, δ does not feature any flow $v \rightsquigarrow y$ with $v \notin S(y)$. By Lemma 1 we have $(\overline{\delta} \circ \delta)(\sigma_1)(y) = \delta(\overline{\delta}(\sigma_1))(y) = \delta(\overline{\delta}(\sigma_2))(y) = (\overline{\delta} \circ \delta)(\sigma_2)(y)$ *i.e.*, $\overline{\delta} \circ \delta \in \mathbf{y}$.

Conversely, assume that $\delta \in \mathbf{S}(\mathbf{y}) \to \mathbf{y}$ for every $y \in V$. We show that if δ features a flow $v \rightsquigarrow w$ then $v \equiv x_i$ and $w \equiv y_i$ for some $1 \leq i \leq n$.

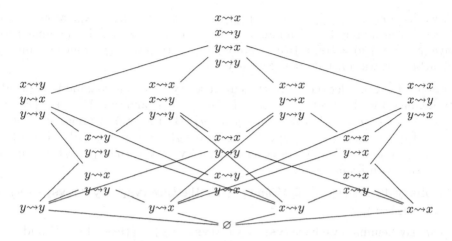

Fig. 1. The abstract domain $\mathsf{IF}_{\{x,y\}}$

$w \in \{y_1, \ldots, y_n\}$. Let by contradiction $w \notin \{y_1, \ldots, y_n\}$. There exist $\sigma_1, \sigma_2 \in \Sigma$ such that $\sigma_1|_{V \setminus v} = \sigma_2|_{V \setminus v}$ and $\delta(\sigma_1)(w) \neq \delta(\sigma_2)(w)$. Since $S(w) = \varnothing$, we have $\delta \in \varnothing \to \mathbf{w} = \mathbf{w}$. Then $\delta(\sigma_1)(w) = \delta(\sigma_2)(w)$, a contradiction.

$v \in \{x_i \mid x_i {\rightsquigarrow} w \in f\}$. Let by contradiction $v \notin \{x_i \mid x_i {\rightsquigarrow} w \in f\}$ i.e., $v \notin S(w)$. There exist $\sigma_1, \sigma_2 \in \Sigma$ such that $\sigma_1|_{V \setminus v} = \sigma_2|_{V \setminus v}$ and $\delta(\sigma_1)(w) \neq \delta(\sigma_2)(w)$. Let $\overline{\delta}$ be such that $\overline{\delta}(\sigma) = \sigma_1[v \mapsto \sigma(v)]$. We have $\overline{\delta}(\sigma_1) = \sigma_1$, $\overline{\delta}(\sigma_2) = \sigma_2$. Moreover, we have $\overline{\delta} \in \mathbf{S}(\mathbf{w})$ since $v \notin S(w)$. We conclude that $\overline{\delta} \circ \delta \in \mathbf{w}$. But $(\overline{\delta} \circ \delta)(\sigma_1)(w) = \delta(\overline{\delta}(\sigma_1))(w) = \delta(\sigma_1)(w) \neq \delta(\sigma_2)(w) = \delta(\overline{\delta}(\sigma_2))(w) = (\overline{\delta} \circ \delta)(\sigma_2)(w)$, which is a contradiction.

Example 14. Consider the abstract element $y {\rightsquigarrow} y$ over $V = \{x, y\}$. We have $S(x) = \varnothing$ and $S(y) = \{y\}$. Then $x {\rightsquigarrow} y = (\varnothing \to \mathbf{x}) \cap (\mathbf{y} \to \mathbf{y}) = \mathbf{x} \cap (\mathbf{y} \to \mathbf{y})$.

We prove now that $\mathsf{C} \to \mathsf{C} \subseteq \mathsf{IF}$. We first show that each single arrow in $\mathsf{C} \to \mathsf{C}$ belongs to IF (Lemma 3) and then lift this result to arbitrary elements of $\mathsf{C} \to \mathsf{C}$ (Proposition 4).

Lemma 3. *Let $x_1, \ldots, x_n, y \in V$. We have*

$$\mathbf{x_1} \cdots \mathbf{x_n} \to \mathbf{y} = \{v {\rightsquigarrow} w \mid v \in V \text{ and } w \in V \setminus y\} \cup \{v {\rightsquigarrow} y \mid v \in \{x_1, \ldots, x_n\}\}.$$

Proof. Let $\delta \in \mathbf{x_1} \cdots \mathbf{x_n} \to \mathbf{y}$. Assume that δ features a flow $v {\rightsquigarrow} w$. If $w \not\equiv y$ then $v {\rightsquigarrow} w \in \{v {\rightsquigarrow} w \mid v \in V \text{ and } w \in V \setminus y\}$. Assume then $w \equiv y$. We must prove that $v \in \{x_1, \ldots, x_n\}$. Let by contradiction $v \notin \{x_1, \ldots, x_n\}$. There are $\sigma_1, \sigma_2 \in \Sigma$ such that $\sigma_1|_{V \setminus v} = \sigma_2|_{V \setminus v}$ and $\delta(\sigma_1)(y) \neq \delta(\sigma_2)(y)$. Let $\overline{\delta}(\sigma) = \sigma_1[v \mapsto \sigma(v)]$. We have $\overline{\delta}(\sigma_1) = \sigma_1$ and $\overline{\delta}(\sigma_2) = \sigma_2$. Moreover, since $v \notin \{x_1, \ldots, x_n\}$, we have $\overline{\delta} \in \mathbf{x_1} \cdots \mathbf{x_n}$. Then $\overline{\delta} \circ \delta \in \mathbf{y}$. But $(\overline{\delta} \circ \delta)(\sigma_1)(y) = \delta(\overline{\delta}(\sigma_1))(y) = \delta(\sigma_1)(y) \neq \delta(\sigma_2)(y) = \delta(\overline{\delta}(\sigma_2))(y) = (\overline{\delta} \circ \delta)(\sigma_2)(y)$, which is a contradiction.

Conversely, let δ feature flows in $\{v {\rightsquigarrow} w \mid v \in V \text{ and } w \in V \setminus y\} \cup \{v {\rightsquigarrow} y \mid v \in \{x_1, \ldots, x_n\}\}$ only. Let $\overline{\delta} \in \mathbf{x_1} \cdots \mathbf{x_n}$. We must prove that $\overline{\delta} \circ \delta \in \mathbf{y}$. Given $\sigma_1, \sigma_2 \in$

Σ, we have $\overline{\delta}(\sigma_1)|_{\{x_1,\ldots,x_n\}} = \overline{\delta}(\sigma_2)|_{\{x_1,\ldots,x_n\}}$ since $\overline{\delta} \in \mathbf{x_1} \cdots \mathbf{x_n}$. Moreover, δ does not feature any flow from any $v \in V \setminus \{x_1,\ldots,x_n\}$ to y. By Lemma 1 we have $(\overline{\delta} \circ \delta)(\sigma_1)(y) = \delta(\overline{\delta}(\sigma_1))(y) = \delta(\overline{\delta}(\sigma_2))(y) = (\overline{\delta} \circ \delta)(\sigma_2)(y)$. Since σ_1 and σ_2 are arbitrary, we conclude that $\overline{\delta} \circ \delta \in \mathbf{y}$.

Example 15. Consider the abstract element $\mathbf{x} \cap (\mathbf{y} \to \mathbf{y})$ and assume $V = \{x, y\}$. By Lemma 3 we have $\mathbf{x} = \varnothing \to \mathbf{x} = \{v \rightsquigarrow w \mid v \in V$ and $w \in V \setminus x\} \cup \{v \rightsquigarrow x \mid v \in \varnothing\} = \{x \rightsquigarrow y, y \rightsquigarrow y\} \cup \varnothing = \{x \rightsquigarrow y, y \rightsquigarrow y\}$. By the same lemma, $\mathbf{y} \to \mathbf{y} = \{v \rightsquigarrow w \mid v \in V$ and $w \in V \setminus y\} \cup \{v \rightsquigarrow y \mid v \in \{y\}\} = \{x \rightsquigarrow x, y \rightsquigarrow x\} \cup \{y \rightsquigarrow y\} = \{x \rightsquigarrow x, y \rightsquigarrow x, y \rightsquigarrow y\}$. The intersection of $\mathbf{x}$ and $\mathbf{y} \to \mathbf{y}$ is then $\{y \rightsquigarrow y\}$. Compare this result with Example 14.

Corollary 1. *Let $vs_1, vs_2 \subseteq V$ and $y \in V$. We have $(\mathbf{vs_1} \to \mathbf{y}) \cap (\mathbf{vs_2} \to \mathbf{y}) = (\mathbf{vs_1} \cap \mathbf{vs_2}) \to \mathbf{y}$.*

Proof. By Lemma 3 we have $(\mathbf{vs_1} \to \mathbf{y}) \cap (\mathbf{vs_2} \to \mathbf{y}) = (\{v \rightsquigarrow w \mid v \in V$ and $w \in V \setminus y\} \cup \{v \rightsquigarrow y \mid v \in vs_1\}) \cap (\{v \rightsquigarrow w \mid v \in V$ and $w \in V \setminus y\} \cup \{v \rightsquigarrow y \mid v \in vs_2\}) = \{v \rightsquigarrow w \mid v \in V$ and $w \in V \setminus y\} \cup (\{v \rightsquigarrow y \mid v \in vs_1\} \cap \{v \rightsquigarrow y \mid v \in vs_2\}) = \{v \rightsquigarrow w \mid v \in V$ and $w \in V \setminus y\} \cup \{v \rightsquigarrow y \mid v \in vs_1 \cap vs_2\} = (\mathbf{vs_1} \cap \mathbf{vs_2}) \to \mathbf{y}$.

We can now prove that the traditional domain for information flow analysis is the linear refinement of the basic domain for constancy.

Proposition 4. *We have $\mathsf{IF} = \mathsf{C} \to \mathsf{C}$.*

Proof. By Lemma 2 we conclude that $\mathsf{IF} \subseteq \mathsf{C} \to \mathsf{C}$. Conversely every element of $\mathsf{C} \to \mathsf{C}$ is the intersection of arrows of the form $\mathbf{vs} \to \mathbf{vs'}$. We can assume that vs' is a single variable, since $\mathbf{vs} \to (\mathbf{vs_1} \cap \mathbf{vs_2}) = (\mathbf{vs} \to \mathbf{vs_1}) \cap (\mathbf{vs} \to \mathbf{vs_2})$ (Subsection 2.4). By Lemma 3 and since IF is closed by intersection (Proposition 2) we conclude that $\mathsf{C} \to \mathsf{C} \subseteq \mathsf{IF}$.

As a consequence, the abstract domain in Figure 1 can be rewritten in terms of elements of $\mathsf{C} \to \mathsf{C}$. The result is in Figure 2. You can pass from Figure 1 to Figure 2 by using Lemma 2 (as in Example 14) and from Figure 2 to Figure 1 by using Lemma 3 (as in Example 15). Note that in Figure 2 there is one variable at most on the left of arrows. This is because, if $V = \{x, y\}$, then $\mathbf{xy} \to \mathbf{x} = \mathbf{xy} \to \mathbf{y} = \wp(\Delta)$, so that these arrows are tautologies (if everything is constant in the input, the output must be constant). This is false for larger V. For instance, in $C_{\{x,y,z\}} \to C_{\{x,y,z\}}$ the arrow $\mathbf{xy} \to \mathbf{x}$ is not a tautology.

5   IF Is Optimal and Condensing

We have just seen that $\mathsf{C} \to \mathsf{C} = \mathsf{IF}$. We show now that, if we linearly refine $\mathsf{C} \to \mathsf{C}$, we end up with $\mathsf{C} \to \mathsf{C}$ itself. Hence $\mathsf{C} \to \mathsf{C}$ already contains all possible dependencies between constancy of variables. This entails [9] that IF is *optimal* and *condensing i.e.,* a compositional, input-independent static analysis over IF, such as that implemented in [7], has the same precision as a non-compositional, input-driven analysis. These results were unknown for IF up to now.

The following result states that an arrow between an element of $\mathsf{C} \to \mathsf{C}$ and an element of C is equal to an element of $\mathsf{C} \to \mathsf{C}$.

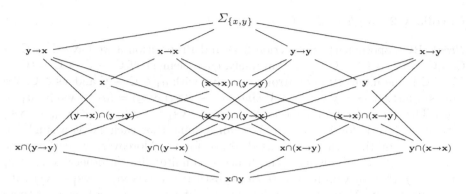

Fig. 2. The abstract domain $C_{\{x,y\}} \to C_{\{x,y\}}$

Lemma 4. *Let $V = \{v_1, \ldots, v_n\}$ and $vs_i \subseteq V$ for $1 \le i \le n$. Then*

$$((\mathbf{vs_1} \to \mathbf{v_1}) \cap \ldots \cap (\mathbf{vs_n} \to \mathbf{v_n})) \to \mathbf{y} = (\cap\{\mathbf{v_i} \mid vs_i = \varnothing\}) \to \mathbf{y}.$$

Proof. Let $\delta \in ((\mathbf{vs_1} \to \mathbf{v_1}) \cap \ldots \cap (\mathbf{vs_n} \to \mathbf{v_n})) \to \mathbf{y}$. Let $vs = \{v_i \mid vs_i = \varnothing\}$ and $\overline{\delta} \in \mathbf{vs}$. We must prove that $\overline{\delta} \circ \delta \in \mathbf{y}$. Assume by contradiction that $\overline{\delta} \circ \delta \notin \mathbf{y}$. Then there are $\sigma_1, \sigma_2 \in \Sigma$ such that $(\overline{\delta} \circ \delta)(\sigma_1)(y) \ne (\overline{\delta} \circ \delta)(\sigma_2)(y)$.

We can assume without any loss of generality that $\overline{\delta}(\sigma)(v) = \sigma(v)$ for every $\sigma \in \Sigma$ and $v \in V \setminus vs$, since otherwise we can take $\overline{\delta}'$ such that $\overline{\delta}'(\sigma) = \sigma[v \mapsto \overline{\delta}(\sigma)(v) \mid v \in vs]$, $\sigma_1' = \overline{\delta}(\sigma_1)$, $\sigma_2' = \overline{\delta}(\sigma_2)$ and still have $\overline{\delta}' \in \mathbf{vs}$, $(\overline{\delta}' \circ \delta)(\sigma_1')(y) = \delta(\overline{\delta}'(\overline{\delta}(\sigma_1)))(y) = \delta(\overline{\delta}(\sigma_1))(y) \ne \delta(\overline{\delta}(\sigma_2))(y) = \delta(\overline{\delta}'(\overline{\delta}(\sigma_2)))(y) = (\overline{\delta}' \circ \delta)(\sigma_2')(y)$.

Let k_1, k_2 be two distinct concrete values. Define δ' such that, for all $\sigma \in \Sigma$,

$$\delta'(\sigma)(v_i) = \begin{cases} \sigma_1(v_i) & \text{if } vs_i \ne \varnothing \text{ and for all } w \in vs_i \text{ we have } \sigma(w) = k_1 \\ \sigma_2(v_i) & \text{if } vs_i \ne \varnothing \text{ and for some } w \in vs_i \text{ we have } \sigma(w) \ne k_1 \\ k_1 & \text{otherwise.} \end{cases}$$

Define the states ς_1, ς_2 such that $\varsigma_1(w) = k_1$ and $\varsigma_2(w) = k_2$ for every $w \in V$.

By construction, we have $\delta' \in ((\mathbf{vs_1} \to \mathbf{v_1}) \cap \ldots \cap (\mathbf{vs_n} \to \mathbf{v_n}))$. Moreover, we have $\delta'(\varsigma_1)(v) = \sigma_1(v)$ and $\delta'(\varsigma_2)(v) = \sigma_2(v)$ for every $v \in V \setminus vs$. Since we assume that $\overline{\delta}$ leaves the variables in $S \setminus vs$ unaffected, we conclude that $\delta' \circ \overline{\delta} \in ((\mathbf{vs_1} \to \mathbf{v_1}) \cap \ldots \cap (\mathbf{vs_n} \to \mathbf{v_n}))$. Moreover, for $i = 1, 2$ we have

$$(\delta' \circ \overline{\delta})(\varsigma_i)(v) = (\overline{\delta}(\delta'(\varsigma_i)))(v) = \begin{cases} \overline{\delta}(\sigma_i)(v) & \text{if } v \in vs \\ \delta'(\varsigma_i)(v) = \sigma_i(v) = \overline{\delta}(\sigma_i)(v) & \text{if } v \notin vs. \end{cases}$$

Then $((\delta' \circ \overline{\delta}) \circ \delta)(\varsigma_1)(y) = (\delta((\delta' \circ \overline{\delta})(\varsigma_1)))(y) = (\delta(\overline{\delta}(\sigma_1)))(y) \ne (\delta(\overline{\delta}(\sigma_2)))(y) = (\delta((\delta' \circ \overline{\delta})(\varsigma_2)))(y) = ((\delta' \circ \overline{\delta}) \circ \delta)(\varsigma_1)(y)$. But by definition of δ, we have $(\delta' \circ \overline{\delta}) \circ \delta \in \mathbf{y}$, which is a contradiction.

Conversely, let $\delta \in (\cap\{\mathbf{v_i} \mid vs_i = \varnothing\}) \to \mathbf{y}$. Let $\overline{\delta} \in ((\mathbf{vs_1} \to \mathbf{v_1}) \cap \ldots \cap (\mathbf{vs_n} \to \mathbf{v_n}))$. We must prove that $\overline{\delta} \circ \delta \in \mathbf{y}$. For each i such that $vs_i = \varnothing$ we have $\overline{\delta} \in \varnothing \to \mathbf{v_i} = \mathbf{v_i}$. We conclude that $\overline{\delta} \in \cap\{\mathbf{v_i} \mid vs_i = \varnothing\}$ and then $\overline{\delta} \circ \delta \in \mathbf{y}$.

Corollary 2. *We have* $C \to C \to C = C \to C$.

Proof. By monotonicity (Subsection 2.4) and Proposition 3 we have $C \to C \to C = C \to (C \to C) \supseteq C \to C$. Conversely, each element of $C \to C \to C = (C \to C) \to C$ is the intersection of arrows $a_1 \to \mathbf{vs}$ with $a_1 \in C \to C$ and $\mathbf{vs} \in C$. We can assume that $\mathbf{vs} = \mathbf{y}$ with $y \in V$ since $a_1 \to (\mathbf{vs_1} \cap \mathbf{vs_2}) = (a_1 \to \mathbf{vs_1}) \cap (a_1 \to \mathbf{vs_2})$. The set a_1 is the intersection of arrows $\mathbf{vs_1} \to \mathbf{vs_1'} \cap \ldots \cap \mathbf{vs_n} \to \mathbf{vs_n'}$ with $vs_i, vs_i' \subseteq V$ for $1 \leq i \leq n$. We can assume that each vs_i' is a singleton variable v_i for the same reason used above for $\mathbf{vs}$. Moreover, we can assume that $v_1, \ldots, v_n$ are all distinct (and hence n is finite) since if otherwise $v_i \equiv v_j$ with $i \neq j$, then by Corollary 1 we can substitute $(\mathbf{vs_i} \to \mathbf{v_i}) \cap (\mathbf{vs_j} \to \mathbf{v_j})$ with $(\mathbf{vs_i} \cap \mathbf{vs_j}) \to \mathbf{v_i}$. Moreover, we can assume that $\{v_1, \ldots, v_n\} = V$ since if there is $v \in V \setminus \{v_1, \ldots, v_n\}$ then we can add the tautological arrow $\cap \{\mathbf{w} \mid w \in V\} \to \mathbf{v} = \Delta$. In conclusion, every element e of $(C \to C) \to C$ is the intersection of arrows of the form $((\mathbf{vs_1} \to \mathbf{v_1}) \cap \ldots \cap (\mathbf{vs_n} \to \mathbf{v_n})) \to \mathbf{y}$ with $v \in V$, $vs_i \subseteq V$ and $v_i \in V$ for each $1 \leq i \leq n$. By Lemma 4, e is equal to the intersection of arrows $(\cap \{\mathbf{v_i} \mid vs_i = \varnothing\}) \to \mathbf{y}$ *i.e.*, to the intersection of elements of $C \to C$. Since $C \to C$ is closed by intersection, we have the thesis.

It is easy now to prove that $C \to C$ is closed *w.r.t.* linear refinement, and is hence optimal and condensing [9].

Proposition 5. *We have* $(C \to C) \to (C \to C) = C \to C$.

Proof. We have $(C \to C) \to (C \to C) = ((C \to C) \sqcap C) \to C$ (Subsection 2.4) and since $C \subseteq C \to C$ (Proposition 3) we conclude that $(C \to C) \sqcap C = C \to C$ [5] and hence $(C \to C) \to (C \to C) = (C \to C) \to C$. The thesis follows by Corollary 2.

6   A Logical Representation for IF

We have seen in Section 4 that IF coincides with $C \to C$. We show here that Boolean formulas can be used to represent elements of $C \to C$.

Since the elements of $C \to C$ express dependencies between the constancy of variables in the input and the constancy of variables in the output, we need to distinguish such variables. Hence we write $\breve{v}$ for the variable v in the input of a denotation, and $\hat{v}$ for the same variable in the output of a denotation [6].

Definition 7 (Denotational Formulas). *The* denotational formulas *over* V *are the Boolean (propositional) formulas over the variables* $\{\breve{v} \mid v \in V\} \cup \{\hat{v} \mid v \in V\}$, *modulo logical equivalence.*

Definition 8. *Let* $vs \subseteq V$. *We define* $\breve{vs} = \{\breve{v} \mid v \in vs\}$ *and* $\hat{vs} = \{\hat{v} \mid v \in vs\}$. *Let* $vs \subseteq \{\breve{v} \mid v \in V\} \cup \{\hat{v} \mid v \in V\}$. *We define* $\wedge vs = \wedge \{v \mid v \in vs\}$.

We specify now the meaning or *concretisation* of a denotational formula ϕ. It is the set of denotations whose behaviour *w.r.t.* constancy is consistent with the propositional models of ϕ.

Definition 9. *The* concretisation *of a denotational formula ϕ is*

$$\gamma(\phi) = \{\delta \in \Delta \mid \text{for all } \overline{\delta} \in \Delta \text{ we have } \overset{\smile}{cons}t(\overline{\delta}) \cup \overset{\wedge}{cons}t(\overline{\delta} \circ \delta) \models \phi\}.$$

Lemma 5. *Let ϕ_1, ϕ_2 be denotational formulas. Then $\gamma(\phi_1 \wedge \phi_2) = \gamma(\phi_1) \cap \gamma(\phi_2)$.*

Proof.

$$\gamma(\phi_1 \wedge \phi_2) = \{\delta \in \Delta \mid \text{for all } \overline{\delta} \in \Delta \text{ we have } \overset{\smile}{cons}t(\overline{\delta}) \cup \overset{\wedge}{cons}t(\overline{\delta} \circ \delta) \models (\phi_1 \wedge \phi_2)\}$$

$$= \left\{\delta \in \Delta \,\middle|\, \begin{array}{l} \text{for all } \overline{\delta} \in \Delta \text{ we have } \overset{\smile}{cons}t(\overline{\delta}) \cup \overset{\wedge}{cons}t(\overline{\delta} \circ \delta) \models \phi_1 \\ \text{and } \overset{\smile}{cons}t(\overline{\delta}) \cup \overset{\wedge}{cons}t(\overline{\delta} \circ \delta) \models \phi_2 \end{array}\right\}$$

$$= \{\delta \in \Delta \mid \text{for all } \overline{\delta} \in \Delta \text{ we have } \overset{\smile}{cons}t(\overline{\delta}) \cup \overset{\wedge}{cons}t(\overline{\delta} \circ \delta) \models \phi_1\}$$

$$\cap \{\delta \in \Delta \mid \text{for all } \overline{\delta} \in \Delta \text{ we have } \overset{\smile}{cons}t(\overline{\delta}) \cup \overset{\wedge}{cons}t(\overline{\delta} \circ \delta) \models \phi_2\}$$

$$= \gamma(\phi_1) \cap \gamma(\phi_2).$$

Lemma 6. *Let $x \in V$. We have $\gamma(\hat{x}) = \mathbf{x}$.*

Proof.

$$\gamma(\hat{x}) = \{\delta \in \Delta \mid \text{for all } \overline{\delta} \in \Delta \text{ we have } \overset{\smile}{cons}t(\overline{\delta}) \cup \overset{\wedge}{cons}t(\overline{\delta} \circ \delta) \models \hat{x}\}$$

$$= \{\delta \in \Delta \mid \text{for all } \overline{\delta} \in \Delta \text{ we have } x \in const(\overline{\delta} \circ \delta)\}$$

$$= \{\delta \in \Delta \mid x \in const(\delta)\} = \mathbf{x},$$

since if $x \in const(\overline{\delta} \circ \delta)$ then $x \in const(\delta)$ since we can choose $\overline{\delta} = \iota$, the identity denotation. Conversely, if $x \in const(\delta)$ then $x \in const(\overline{\delta} \circ \delta)$.

Lemma 7. *Let $\{x_1, \ldots, x_n\} \subseteq V$, $y \in V$ $\check{X} = \wedge_{1 \leq i \leq n} \check{x}_i$ and $\hat{X} = \wedge_{1 \leq i \leq n} \hat{x}_i$. Then $\gamma(\check{X} \Rightarrow \hat{y}) = \gamma(\hat{X}) \rightarrow \gamma(\hat{y})$.*

Proof.

$$\gamma(\check{X} \Rightarrow \hat{y}) = \{\delta \in \Delta \mid \text{for all } \overline{\delta} \in \Delta \text{ we have } \overset{\smile}{cons}t(\overline{\delta}) \cup \overset{\wedge}{cons}t(\overline{\delta} \circ \delta) \models X \Rightarrow y\}$$

$$= \left\{\delta \in \Delta \,\middle|\, \begin{array}{l} \text{for all } \overline{\delta} \in \Delta \\ (x_i \in const(\overline{\delta}) \text{ for all } i \text{ such that } 1 \leq i \leq n) \text{ entails} \\ y \in const(\overline{\delta} \circ \delta) \end{array}\right\}$$

$$= \left\{\delta \in \Delta \,\middle|\, \begin{array}{l} \text{for all } \overline{\delta} \in \Delta \\ (\overline{\delta} \in \gamma(\hat{x}_i) \text{ for all } i \text{ such that } 1 \leq i \leq n) \text{ entails} \\ \overline{\delta} \circ \delta \in \gamma(\hat{y}) \end{array}\right\}$$

$$= \{\delta \in \Delta \mid \text{for all } \overline{\delta} \in \gamma(\hat{X}) \text{ we have } \overline{\delta} \circ \delta \in \gamma(\hat{y})\} = \gamma(\hat{X}) \rightarrow \gamma(\hat{y}).$$

Proposition 6. *The domain $\mathsf{IF} = \mathsf{C} \rightarrow \mathsf{C}$ is isomorphic to the set of denotational formulas of the form $\wedge \check{vs} \Rightarrow \wedge \hat{ws}$ with $vs, ws \subseteq V$.*

Proof. By Lemmas 5, 6 and 7, since $\mathbf{vs} \rightarrow (\mathbf{w_1} \cap \cdots \cap \mathbf{w_m}) = (\mathbf{vs} \rightarrow \mathbf{w_1}) \cap \cdots \cap (\mathbf{vs} \rightarrow \mathbf{w_m})$ and $\wedge \check{vs} \Rightarrow (w_1 \wedge \cdots \wedge w_m) = (\wedge \check{vs} \Rightarrow w_1) \wedge \cdots \wedge (\wedge \check{vs} \Rightarrow w_m)$.

Figure 3 shows the Boolean representation of $\mathsf{IF}_{\{x,y\}} = \mathsf{C}_{\{x,y\}} \rightarrow \mathsf{C}_{\{x,y\}}$.

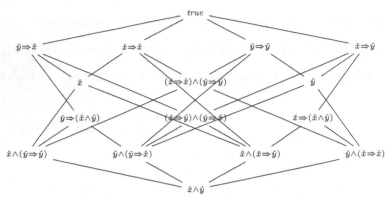

Fig. 3. The representation of $\mathsf{IF}_{\{x,y\}} = \mathsf{C}_{\{x,y\}} \to \mathsf{C}_{\{x,y\}}$ through denotational formulas

7   Conclusion

We have used linear refinement to reconstruct an existing domain for information flow analysis, to prove it optimal and condensing, and to provide an efficient representation in terms of Boolean formulas. The size of the abstract domain $\mathsf{IF}_V = \mathsf{C}_V \to \mathsf{C}_V$ grows exponentially with V, but V only contains the variables in scope in the program point under analysis. Its actual application to the analysis of relatively large programs has been experimentally validated in [7].

Our work has similarities with the reconstruction through linear refinement of abstract domains for groundness analysis of logic programs [13]. In particular, constancy is the imperative counterpart of groundness in logic programming. There, however, two iterations of linear refinement (only one here) are needed to reach an abstract domain which is closed *w.r.t.* further refinements. There might also be relations with strictness analysis of functional programs, which has also been proved to enjoy some optimality property [14]. There, optimality means that precision cannot be improved as long as constant symbols are abstracted away. It is enlightening to observe that the same abstraction is used in groundness analysis of logic programs, where all functor symbols are abstracted away. In information flow analysis, values are abstracted away, and only their constancy is observed. These similarities might not be casual.

We are confident that our work can be generalised to *declassified* forms of non-interference, such as *abstract non-interference* [8]. One should consider a de-classified form of constancy as the basic domain to refine. Declassified constancy means that a variable, in the output of a denotation, is *always* bound to a given *abstract* value, as specified by the declassification criterion.

References

1. A. Bossi, M. Gabbrielli, G. Levi, and M. Martelli. The s-Semantics Approach: Theory and Applications. *Journal of Logic Programming*, 19/20:149–197, 1994.
2. R. E. Bryant. Graph-based Algorithms for Boolean Function Manipulation. *IEEE Transactions on Computers*, 35(8):677–691, 1986.

3. D. Clark, C. Hankin, and S. Hunt. Information Flow for Algol-like Languages. *Computer Languages and Security*, 28(1):3–28, April 2002.
4. P. Cousot and R. Cousot. Abstract Interpretation: A Unified Lattice Model for Static Analysis of Programs by Construction or Approximation of Fixpoints. In *Proc. of the 4th ACM Symposium on Principles of Programming Languages (POPL)*, pages 238–252, 1977.
5. P. Cousot and R. Cousot. Systematic Design of Program Analysis Frameworks. In *Proc. of the 6th ACM Symp. on Principles of Programming Languages*, pages 269–282, 1979.
6. S. Genaim, R. Giacobazzi, and I. Mastroeni. Modeling Secure Information Flow with Boolean Functions. In P. Ryan, editor, *ACM SIGPLAN and GI FoMSESS Workshop on Issues in the Theory of Security*, pages 55–66, April 2004.
7. S. Genaim and F. Spoto. Information Flow Analysis for Java Bytecode. In R. Cousot, editor, *Proc. of the Sixth International Conference on Verification, Model Checking and Abstract Interpretation (VMCAI'05)*, volume 3385 of *Lecture Notes in Computer Science*, pages 346–362, Paris, France, January 2005.
8. R. Giacobazzi and I. Mastroeni. Abstract Non-Interference: Parameterizing Non-Interference by Abstract Interpretation. In *Proc. of the 31st Annual ACM SIGPLAN-SIGACT Symposium on Principles of Programming Languages (POPL'04)*, pages 186–197, Venice, Italy, January 2004. ACM-Press.
9. R. Giacobazzi, F. Ranzato, and F. Scozzari. Making Abstract Domains Condensing. *ACM Transactions on Computational Logic (ACM-TOCL)*, 6(1):33–60, 2005.
10. R. Giacobazzi and F. Scozzari. A Logical Model for Relational Abstract Domains. *ACM Transactions on Programming Languages and Systems*, 20(5):1067–1109, 1998.
11. A. Sabelfeld and A. C. Myers. Language-based Information-Flow Security. *IEEE Journal on Selected Areas in Communications*, 21(1):5–19, 2003.
12. A. Sabelfeld and D. Sands. A PER Model of Secure Information Flow in Sequential Programs. *Higher-Order and Symbolic Computation*, 14(1):59–91, 2001.
13. S. Scozzari. Logical Optimality of Groundness Analysis. *Theoretical Computer Science*, 277(1-2):149–184, 2002.
14. M. C. Sekar, P. Mishra, and I. V. Ramakrishnan. On the Power and Limitation of Strictness Analysis Based on Abstract Interpretation. In *Proc. of the 18th ACM SIGPLAN-SIGACT Symposium on Principles of Programming Languages (POPL'91)*, pages 37–48, Orlando, Florida, January 1991.
15. D. Volpano, G. Smith, and C. Irvine. A Sound Type System for Secure Flow Analysis. *Journal of Computer Security*, 4(2,3):167–187, 1996.
16. G. Winskel. *The Formal Semantics of Programming Languages*. The MIT Press, 1993.

On Typing Information Flow*

Gérard Boudol

INRIA Sophia Antipolis

Abstract. We investigate the issue of typing confidentiality in a language-based information-flow security approach, aiming at improving some previously proposed type systems, especially for higher-order languages with mutable state à la ML. We show that the typing of termination leaks can be largely improved, by particularizing the case where the alternatives in a conditional branching both terminate. Moreover, we also provide a quite precise way of approximating the confidentiality level of an expression, that ignores the level of values used for side-effects only.

1 Introduction

In a world where more and more information is digitalized, and where more and more people have access to it, most often by means of dedicated software, protecting confidential data is a concern of growing importance. Controlling access rights is obviously necessary, and access control techniques have indeed been developed and implemented long ago. However, access control is not enough to ensure confidentiality. One issue is to prevent authorized users to publicly disclose confidential data. For instance, a software dedicated to the selling of articles in electronic journals should obviously have the right to access all the articles – a private information. The selling service must also be accessible to anyone – malicious or not, like a search engine. Still, the selling software could contain programming bugs allowing a client to obtain articles for free. Therefore, one should have means to control that programs do not contain such bugs, that is, that programs do not implement illegal *flow of information*. This is the aim of language-based information-flow security.

Language-based information-flow security is a well established theory, providing static analysis techniques for programs to ensure a security property known as *non-interference* [6] (or *strong independence* [3]). Since the pioneering work of Volpano & al. [18], these static analyses are now implemented by means of *type systems*, which are well-suited for preventing programming errors. This has been applied in particular to languages such as JAVA [10] or CAML [11]. (For a complete review of results and issues – up to year 2002 – in the area of language-based information-flow security, we refer to the survey [12].) However, the theory of information flow security is not yet widely used, and there are still a number of issues to investigate in order to make it practically useful – see [20] for a review of some of the challenges.

* Work partially supported by the CRISS project of the ACI Sécurité Informatique.

D.V. Hung and M. Wirsing (Eds.): ICTAC 2005, LNCS 3722, pp. 366–380, 2005.

One of the challenges is to design new security properties and static analysis techniques to accept programs that intentionally *declassify* information. For instance, although it should not release electronic articles for free, the selling software must deliver information to clients who have paid for it, or who identify themselves as regular subscribers of the journal. That is, although confidential information should normally be kept secret, one should also be able to declassify it when some run-time conditions are met (we refer to [14] for a discussion of this topic). To this end, we introduced in [1] a specific construct for declassifying computations, together with a confidentiality property generalising non-interference, so that a type system ensuring the security property can be designed for a language including the declassification construct. The language we used in [1] is an extension of Core ML, a higher-order language with mutable state, and our type system is a direct generalization of those commonly used for simple imperative languages, such as the ones in [2,15,18].

Another pragmatic concern, which is not specific to typing information flow, is that, to be useful, a type system should not reject too many programs. It is well-known that a decidable static analysis technique cannot, in general, be complete with respect to the property to ensure, like not running into an error of some kind, because the latter is generally undecidable. Then a trade-off has to be found, between the most conservative way – of not accepting any program – and a complete but non-computable method. In this respect, an issue that is specific to language-based security is the typing of *termination leaks*. This kind of leak arises when performing (or not) some public operation depends on the termination of another program which, in turn, terminates or not depending on confidential information. For instance, assume that we have a secret, or *High* memory location u_H, and a public, or *Low* memory address v_L, both containing boolean values *tt* or *ff*. Then the program

$$(\text{while } !u_H \text{ do } ()) \,; v_L := \mathit{ff} \tag{1}$$

(where $!u_H$ is the dereferencing operation of ML, and $()$ means termination) implements a flow of information from u_H to v_L, since the value that can (or cannot) be read from this location depends on secret information. Many research works avoid this issue by only considering *weak*, or *termination insensitive* non-interference. Although this may be acceptable when dealing with sequential programs, one has to seriously take into account termination leaks when dealing with concurrent threads, where a program such as (1) is dangerous (see [2,7,15,16,17]). Similarly, dealing with declassification, as we do in [1], relies on a termination sensitive security property.

Termination leaks may be ruled out using very severe restrictions, like allowing only predicates of the lowest confidentiality level in the while loops [16,17]. This would be even worse in a language, like Core ML, in which while loops are recursively defined by means of conditional branching, since the predicate in the branching construct would then be restricted to be of the lowest confidentiality level only – an unacceptable constraint. Here we will improve on a solution to this issue introduced in [2] (and independently in [15]), which we followed in [1]. This solution essentially consists in recording the confidentiality level of the predicate of a conditional branching as a *"termination level"* that is used to control information flow in sequential composition. In this way, a program such as (1) is rejected, but loops or conditional branchings on high predicates are allowed. However, this typing discipline is still quite inflexible, since for instance any program of the form

$$\text{(if } !u_H \text{ then } P \text{ else } Q) \text{ ; } v_L := \textit{ff} \tag{2}$$

is rejected. Here we show that such a program is secure in the case where both branches P and Q are known to terminate. This provides us with an improved type system for termination leaks, where the termination level of a conditional branching may be ignored when the branches terminate. As far as we can see, such a refined typing has not been previously suggested (the proof of type soundness is quite elaborate).

Another contribution we make in this paper is in the way the typing of information flow in a simple imperative language is extended to a more expressive one, like the higher-order core of ML, with mutable state. In the simple "while" language of [18], which is very often considered as a kernel language in the information flow literature, the typing is as follows: an expression has for "type" an upper bound of the confidentiality level of memory locations that are read to compute the value of the expression, and a program has for "type" a lower bound of the confidentiality level of memory locations it may update. In the system of [2,15], one adds, as we have seen, a "termination level". In a language like Core ML, an expression is a program, and therefore it may have side-effects, and its evaluation may diverge. Then the "security effect" of an expression in such a language is a triple (r, w, t) where r is the *reading effect*, or *confidentiality level*, w is the *writing effect* and t is the *termination effect* of the expression. This is the basis on which we built our type system in [1]. However, the way we generalize in [1] the typing, from "pure" expressions to expressions having side-effects is rather coarse, since we build the reading effect as an upper bound of the confidentiality level of all the memory locations that are read while evaluating the expression. This may be improved, as we will show here. More specifically, we will exploit the fact that some read operations do not contribute to the specific value an expression may have (a similar observation is made in [4] to motivate the "informativeness" predicate). For instance, readings performed while evaluating E do not influence the value of $E \text{ ; } E'$, which is the one of E'. Similarly, the value returned by a reference creation (ref E) does not depend on the readings performed by E, and the same holds for an assignment $E := E'$ or $E' := E$, which returns the value (). In this paper we will show that recording as the *confidentiality level* of an expression only the level of readings that may influence its value is enough to perform a safe information flow analysis. This, together with the improvement in typing termination leaks we suggested above, results in a type system that accepts many more programs than the one of [1], while still ensuring the same security property.

The paper is organized as follows. In the next section we introduce the security lattices we use, and we give the syntax and operational semantics of our language. In Section 3 we define the security property we aim at establishing, and in Section 4 we introduce our type and effect system, formalizing the intuitions we gave above. Finally we explain some of the steps of the type soundness proof, and conclude. For lack of space, the proofs are omitted.

2   The Language

The information flow analysis we are aiming at relies, as usual, on a notion of security level, and on assigning such levels to memory locations – also called *references*. (More generally, one would classify in this way any "container" in which information is stored, like files, database entries, libraries, and so on.) However, instead of using a lattice of security levels as it is standard [5], we will be using a *pre-lattice* structure, which is a pair $(\mathcal{L}, \preceq)$ where $\preceq$ is a preorder on $\mathcal{L}$, such that for any $\ell, \ell' \in \mathcal{L}$ there exist a meet $\ell \curlywedge \ell'$ and a join $\ell \curlyvee \ell'$ for ℓ and ℓ'. More specifically, we assume given a set $\mathcal{P}$ of *principals*, ranged over by $p, q \ldots$, and a *confidentiality level* is any set of principals, that is any subset ℓ of $\mathcal{P}$. The intuition is that whenever ℓ is the confidentiality label of a reference, it represents a set of programs that are allowed to read the reference. From this point of view, a reference labelled $\mathcal{P}$ (also denoted $\perp$) is a most public one – every program is allowed to read it –, whereas the label $\emptyset$ (also denoted $\top$) indicates a secret reference. Reverse inclusion of security levels may be interpreted as indicating allowed flows of information: if a reference u is labelled ℓ, and $\ell \supseteq \ell'$ then the value of u may be transferred to a reference v labelled ℓ', since the programs allowed to read this value from v were already allowed to read it from u.

The declassification construct we introduced in [1] consists in declaring flow relations, or *flow policies* having a local scope. A flow policy is a binary relation over $\mathcal{P}$. We let $F, G \ldots$ range over such relations. A pair $(p, q) \in F$ is to be understood as "information may flow from principal p to principal q". We denote, as usual, by F^* the preorder generated by F (that is, the reflexive and transitive closure of F). Then the security pre-lattices we use are defined as follows:

DEFINITION (SECURITY PRE-LATTICES) 0.1.   *A confidentiality level is any subset ℓ of the set $\mathcal{P}$ of principals. Given a flow policy $F \subseteq \mathcal{P} \times \mathcal{P}$, the confidentiality levels are pre-ordered by the relation*

$$\ell \preceq_F \ell' \quad \Leftrightarrow_{\text{def}} \quad \forall q \in \ell'. \ \exists p \in \ell. \ p \, F^* \, q$$

The meet and join, w.r.t. F, of two security levels ℓ and ℓ' are respectively given by $\ell \cup \ell'$ and

$$\ell \curlyvee_F \ell' = \{\, q \mid \exists p \in \ell. \ \exists p' \in \ell'. \ p \, F^* \, q \ \& \ p' \, F^* \, q \,\}$$

The language we consider is a higher-order language with mutable state à la ML, extended with a construct for dynamically creating concurrent threads, and a construct for declassifying computations. The syntax is given in Figure 1, where x is any variable, and $u_{\ell,\theta}$ is a triple made of a reference u, a type θ (see Section 4 below) and a label ℓ which is a confidentiality level. The type and security label have no operational significance, as can be checked from the description of the semantics given below. They are only used for the purpose of the proof of type soundness. We denote by $\mathsf{loc}(M)$ the set of decorated references occurring

$$M, N \ldots \in \mathcal{E}xpr ::= W \mid (\text{if } M \text{ then } N \text{ else } N') \mid (MN) \qquad \textit{expressions}$$
$$\mid M ; N \mid (\text{ref}_{\ell,\theta} N) \mid (! N) \mid (M := N)$$
$$\mid (\text{thread } M) \mid (\text{flow } F \text{ in } M)$$
$$W \in \mathcal{W} ::= V \mid \varrho x W \qquad\qquad\qquad\qquad\qquad \textit{pseudo-values}$$
$$V \in \mathcal{V}al ::= x \mid u_{\ell,\theta} \mid \lambda x M \mid tt \mid f\!f \mid () \qquad \textit{values}$$

Fig. 1. Syntax

in M. These addresses are regarded as providing the *inputs* of the expression M. Recursive definitions are introduced by the construct $\varrho x W$, which binds the variable x in W. We denote by loop the expression $\varrho x x$, and we may use the following standard abbreviation:

$$(\text{while } M \text{ do } N) =_{\text{def}} (\varrho y \lambda x(\text{if } M \text{ then } N ; (yx) \text{ else } x)())$$

We denote by $\{x \mapsto W\}M$ the capture-avoiding susbtitution of W for the free occurrences of x in M, where $W \in \mathcal{W}$. The evaluation relation is a transition relation between configurations of the form (P, μ) where P is a *process*, written according to the following syntax:

$$P, Q \ldots \in \mathcal{P}roc ::= M \mid (P \parallel Q)$$

and μ, the *memory* (or *heap*), is a mapping from a finite set $\text{dom}(\mu)$ of decorated references to values. In what follows we shall only consider *well-formed* configurations, that is pairs (P, μ) such that $\text{loc}(P) \subseteq \text{dom}(\mu)$ and for any $u_{\ell,\theta} \in \text{dom}(\mu)$ we have $\text{loc}(\mu(u_{\ell,\theta})) \subseteq \text{dom}(\mu)$ (this property will be preserved by the operational semantics). The operation of updating the value of a reference in the memory is denoted, as usual, $\mu[u_{\ell,\theta} := V]$. We say that the name u is *fresh for* μ if $v_{\ell,\theta} \in \text{dom}(\mu) \Rightarrow v \neq u$. The operational semantics consists of a small-step transition relation $(P, \mu) \to (P', \mu')$ between (well-formed) configurations. This is defined by means of an auxiliary transition relation $(M, \mu) \xrightarrow{N} (M', \mu')$, as follows:

$$\frac{(M, \mu) \xrightarrow{0} (M', \mu')}{(M, \mu) \to (M', \mu')} \qquad \frac{(M, \mu) \xrightarrow{N} (M', \mu') \quad N \neq ()}{(M, \mu) \to ((M' \parallel N), \mu')}$$

$$\frac{(P, \mu) \to (P', \mu')}{((P \parallel Q), \mu) \to ((P' \parallel Q), \mu')} \qquad \frac{(P, \mu) \to (P', \mu')}{((Q \parallel P), \mu) \to ((Q \parallel P'), \mu')}$$

As usual we denote by $\xrightarrow{*}$ the reflexive and transitive closure of $\to$. The meaning of $(M, \mu) \xrightarrow{N} (M', \mu')$ is that the expression M, in the context of the memory μ, makes a computing step, possibly spawning a thread with body N, and reconfigures itself as M', while updating the memory into μ'. In order to define this auxiliary transition system, we introduce evaluation contexts:

$$\mathbf{E} ::= [] \mid \mathbf{F}[\mathbf{E}] \mid (\text{flow } F \text{ in } \mathbf{E})$$
$$\mathbf{F} ::= (\text{if } [] \text{ then } M \text{ else } N) \mid ([]N) \mid (V[])$$
$$\mid [] ; N \mid (\text{ref}_{\ell,\theta} []) \mid (! []) \mid ([] := N) \mid (V := [])$$

$$((\text{if } tt \text{ then } M \text{ else } N), \mu) \xrightarrow{\ 0\ } (M, \mu)$$

$$((\text{if } ff \text{ then } M \text{ else } N), \mu) \xrightarrow{\ 0\ } (N, \mu)$$

$$((\lambda x M V), \mu) \xrightarrow{\ 0\ } (\{x \mapsto V\} M, \mu)$$

$$(V \,;\, N, \mu) \xrightarrow{\ 0\ } (N, \mu)$$

$$((\text{ref}_{\ell,\theta}\, V), \mu) \xrightarrow{\ 0\ } (u_{\ell,\theta}, \mu \cup \{u_{\ell,\theta} \mapsto V\}) \quad u \text{ fresh for } \mu$$

$$((!\, u_{\ell,\theta}), \mu) \xrightarrow{\ 0\ } (V, \mu) \qquad\qquad \mu(u_{\ell,\theta}) = V$$

$$((u_{\ell,\theta} := V), \mu) \xrightarrow{\ 0\ } ((), \mu[u_{\ell,\theta} := V])$$

$$((\text{thread } M), \mu) \xrightarrow{\ M\ } ((), \mu)$$

$$((\text{flow } F \text{ in } V), \mu) \xrightarrow{\ 0\ } (V, \mu)$$

$$(\varrho x W, \mu) \xrightarrow{\ 0\ } (\{x \mapsto \varrho x W\} W, \mu)$$

$$\frac{(M, \mu) \xrightarrow{\ 0\ } (M', \mu')}{(\mathbf{E}[M], \mu) \xrightarrow{\ 0\ } (\mathbf{E}[M'], \mu')} \qquad\qquad \frac{(M, \mu) \xrightarrow{\ N\ } (M', \mu') \quad N \neq 0}{(\mathbf{E}[M], \mu) \xrightarrow{(\text{flow } \lceil \mathbf{E} \rceil \text{ in } N)} (\mathbf{E}[M'], \mu')}$$

Fig. 2. Transitions

and we denote by $\lceil \mathbf{E} \rceil$ the flow policy enforced by the context $\mathbf{E}$. This is defined as follows:

$$\lceil [] \rceil = \emptyset$$
$$\lceil \mathbf{F}[\mathbf{E}] \rceil = \lceil \mathbf{E} \rceil$$
$$\lceil (\text{flow } F \text{ in } \mathbf{E}) \rceil = F \cup \lceil \mathbf{E} \rceil$$

The relation $\xrightarrow{\ N\ }$ is given in Figure 2. We shall use, somewhat abusively, the notation $\twoheadrightarrow$ for the transition relation defined as $\exists N \xrightarrow{\ N\ }$. Then we introduce the *strong convergence* predicate $M{\Downarrow}$, meaning that in the context of any memory μ, the evaluation of M, as the main thread, terminates on a value, while possibly spawning some new threads:

$$M{\Downarrow} \quad\Leftrightarrow_{\text{def}}\quad \forall \mu\, \exists V \in \mathit{Val}\, \exists \mu'.\ (M, \mu) \xrightarrow{\ *\ } (V, \mu')$$

It is easy to see that, for instance, the expressions given by the following grammar are strongly converging:

$$T ::= V \mid (\text{if } T \text{ then } T_0 \text{ else } T_1) \mid T \,;\, T' \mid (\text{ref}_{\ell,\theta}\, T) \mid (!\, T) \mid (T := T')$$
$$\mid (\text{thread } M) \mid (\text{flow } F \text{ in } T)$$

3   The Non-disclosure Policy

In this section we introduce our security property. Roughly speaking, it says that a process is secure if, at each step, it satisfies a non-interference property with respect to the flow policy that holds for this particular step. This policy is obtained by extending the given global flow policy G with the flow relations introduced by the flow declarations in the scope of which the computational step is performed. To state this formally, we first introduce a new transition relation $(P, \mu) \xrightarrow{F} (P', \mu')$, where F is the local flow policy that holds for this step. This is defined exactly as $(P, \mu) \to (P', \mu')$, using an auxiliary transition relation $(M, \mu) \xrightarrow[F]{N} (M', \mu')$ given by

$$(M, \mu) \xrightarrow{0} (M', \mu') \qquad\qquad (M, \mu) \xrightarrow{N} (M', \mu') \quad N \neq 0$$

$$\frac{}{(\mathbf{E}[M], \mu) \xrightarrow[\lceil \mathbf{E} \rceil]{0} (\mathbf{E}[M'], \mu')} \qquad\qquad \frac{}{(\mathbf{E}[M], \mu) \xrightarrow[\lceil \mathbf{E} \rceil]{(\text{flow } \lceil \mathbf{E} \rceil \text{ in } N)} (\mathbf{E}[M'], \mu')}$$

The meaning of F in a transition $(P, \mu) \xrightarrow{F} (P', \mu')$ is that what is read by P at confidentiality level ℓ at this step can be regarded as having level ℓ' if information is allowed to flow from ℓ to ℓ' by the global policy G extended with the local flow policy F, that is if $\ell \preceq_{G \cup F} \ell'$. Then P is secure if, for any confidentiality level ℓ, it does not reveal, by writting in the memory at a level lower than ℓ, information that it reads at levels not lower than ℓ. As we just said, from the reading point of view, confidentiality levels are compared with respect to $G \cup F$, whereas from the writing point of view, the levels are to be compared with respect to the global policy G only, because the updates in the memory are read by other expressions that are not, a priori, in the scope of the declarations introducing F.

As usual, the property that a process does not transfer information from a "high" part (not below ℓ) of the memory to a "low" part (below ℓ) is formalized by requiring that the process preserves in a sense the "low equality" of memories. Two memories are equal up to level ℓ if they assign the same value to every location with security level lower than ℓ. Here we have to explicitly indicate which is the flow policy that is used to compare confidentiality levels. The low equality of memories is thus defined:

$$\mu \simeq^{F,\ell} \nu \Leftrightarrow_{\text{def}} \forall u_{\ell',\theta} \in \text{dom}(\mu) \cap \text{dom}(\nu). \ \ell' \preceq_F \ell \implies \mu(u_{\ell',\theta}) = \nu(u_{\ell',\theta})$$

Following [13], our security property is defined in terms of *bisimulations*, which are relations over processes: a process is defined to be secure if it is bisimilar to itself. The notion of a bisimulation we use here is relative not only to a confidentiality level ℓ, determining what is regarded as being "low", but also to the global flow policy G. The definition is as follows:

DEFINITION (BISIMULATION) 0.2. *A (G, ℓ)-bisimulation is a symmetric relation $\mathcal{R}$ on processes such that if*

$$P \mathcal{R} Q \ \& \ (P, \mu) \xrightarrow{F} (P', \mu') \ \& \ \mu \simeq^{F \cup G, \ell} \nu \ \& \ u_{\ell',\theta} \in \text{dom}(\mu' - \mu) \implies u \text{ is fresh for } \nu$$

then there exist Q' and ν' such that

$$(Q, \nu) \xrightarrow{*} (Q', \nu') \ \& \ P' \mathcal{R} Q' \ \& \ \mu' \simeq^{G,\ell} \nu'$$

(It is implicit in this definition that the configurations (P, μ) and (Q, ν) are well-formed.) For instance, the set $\mathcal{V}al \times \mathcal{V}al$ of pairs of values is a (G, ℓ)-bisimulation. Values are just a particular case of "high" processes, which never modify the "low" part of the memory. Let us define:

DEFINITION (OPERATIONALLY HIGH PROCESSES) 0.3.   *A set $\mathcal{H}$ of processes is said to be a set of operationally (G, ℓ)-high processes if the following holds for any $P \in \mathcal{H}$:*

$$(P, \mu) \to (P', \mu') \;\Rightarrow\; \mu' \simeq^{G,\ell} \mu \;\&\; P' \in \mathcal{H}$$

It is easy to see that there exists a largest set of operationally (G, ℓ)-high processes, which we denote by $\mathcal{H}_{G,\ell}$. Then we have:

LEMMA and NOTATION 0.4.   *If $\mathcal{H}$ is a set of (G, ℓ)-high processes, then the relation $\mathcal{H} \times \mathcal{H}$ is a (G, ℓ)-bisimulation. We denote by $\asymp^{G,\ell}$ the (G, ℓ)-bisimulation $\mathcal{H}_{G,\ell} \times \mathcal{H}_{G,\ell}$.*

As we have just seen, (G, ℓ)-bisimulations exist, for any G and ℓ. Moreover, the union of a family of (G, ℓ)-bisimulations is a (G, ℓ)-bisimulation, and therefore there is a largest (G, ℓ)-bisimulation, which we denote $\bowtie^{G,\ell}$. This is the union of all such bisimulations. One should observe that $\bowtie^{G,\ell}$ is not reflexive. Indeed, a process which is not bisimilar to itself, like $v_L := \, ! \, u_H$ if $H \not\preceq_G L$, is not secure. As in [13], our definition states that a program is secure if it is bisimilar to itself:

DEFINITION (THE NON-DISCLOSURE POLICY) 0.5.   *A process P satisfies the non-disclosure policy (or is secure from the confidentiality point of view) with respect to the flow policy G if it satisfies $P \bowtie^{G,\ell} P$ for any ℓ. We then write $P \in \mathcal{ND}(G)$.*

It is easily seen that the set $\mathcal{ND}(G)$ is non-empty. For instance, any value is secure, as well as any "pure" expression, that never touches the memory. As a matter of fact, any "mute" expression, that does not update the memory (like in particular an expression written without using the assignment construct) is secure, and this is intuitively quite natural, since such an expression cannot disclose any information.

4   The Type and Effect System

The analysis of information flow in a program will be done by means of an *effect system* [9], where the effects are, roughly speaking, confidentiality levels at which the program reads or writes. The types for expressions involve confidentiality levels, namely, in the types $\theta \, \mathsf{ref}_\ell$ for references, for classification purposes, and in the types for functions, which record a *latent effect*, that is the effect a function may have when applied to an argument. The functional types also record the "latent flow relation", which is assumed to hold when a function is applied to an argument. The syntax of types is

$$\tau, \; \sigma, \; \theta \ldots \; ::= \; t \mid \mathsf{bool} \mid \mathsf{unit} \mid \theta \, \mathsf{ref}_\ell \mid (\tau \xrightarrow[F]{s} \sigma)$$

where t is any type variable and s is any "security effect" – see below. The judgements of the type and effect system have the form

$$G; \Gamma \vdash M : s, \tau$$

where G is a flow relation, Γ is a typing context, assigning types to variables, s is a security effect, that is a triple (ℓ_0, ℓ_1, ℓ_2) of confidentiality levels, and τ is a type. The intuition is:

- G is the current flow policy that is in force when evaluating M;
- ℓ_0, also denoted by $s.c$, is the *confidentiality level* of M. This is an upper bound (up to the current flow relation) of the confidentiality levels of the references the expression M reads that may influence its resulting *value*;
- ℓ_1, also denoted $s.w$, is the *writing effect*, that is a lower bound (w.r.t. the relation $\preceq$) of the level of references that the expression M may update;
- ℓ_2, also denoted $s.t$, is an upper bound (w.r.t. the current flow relation) of the levels of the references the expression M reads that may influence its *termination*. We call this the *termination effect* of the expression.

There is actually an implicit parameter in the type system, which is a set $\mathcal{T}$ of expressions that is used in the typing of conditional branching. We could make it apparent, writing for instance the judgements as $G; \Gamma \vdash_{\mathcal{T}} M : s, \tau$. The single property that we will assume about this set in our proof of type soundness is that it only contains strongly converging expressions, that is:

$$M \in \mathcal{T} \;\Rightarrow\; M\Downarrow \qquad\qquad (*)$$

The security effects $s = (c, w, t)$ are ordered componentwise, in a covariant manner as regards the confidentiality level c and the termination effect t, and in a contravariant way as regards the writing effect w. Then we abusively denote by $\bot$ and $\top$ the triples $(\bot, \top, \bot)$ and $(\top, \bot, \top)$ respectively. In the typing rules for compound expressions, we will use the join operation on security effects:

$$s \curlyvee_G s' \;=_{\mathrm{def}}\; (s.c \curlyvee_G s'.c, s.w \cup s'.w, s.t \curlyvee_G s'.t)$$

as well as the following convention:

CONVENTION. *In the type system, when the security effects occurring in the context of a judgement $G; \Gamma \vdash M : s, \tau$ involve the join operation $\curlyvee$, it is assumed that the join is taken w.r.t. G, i.e. it is $\curlyvee_G$. Moreover, by $s.r$ we mean $s.c \curlyvee_G s.t$.*

The typing system is given in Figure 3. We refer to [1] for comments explaining the constraints on the flow of information (that is, the inequations involving $\preceq$ in the premises) in the rules. In particular, all the examples given in this paper showing that these constraints are necessary are still valid here. With respect to the system introduced in [1], the main differences are the following:

(i) In the (COND) rule for conditional branching, we do not record the confidentiality level of the predicate M in the termination effect of the compound expression if both branches are in the set $\mathcal{T}$.

(ii) In the rules (SEQ), (REF) and (ASSIGN), we do not record the confidentiality level of the expression M in the effect of the compound expression, and similarly for N in (ASSIGN). Moreover, the constructs for creating a reference and updating the memory do not introduce any non-trivial confidentiality level.

$$\frac{}{G;\Gamma \vdash u_{\ell,\theta} : \bot, \theta\, \mathsf{ref}_\ell} \ (\textsc{Loc}) \qquad \frac{}{G;\Gamma, x : \tau \vdash x : \bot, \tau} \ (\textsc{Var})$$

$$\frac{F;\Gamma, x : \tau \vdash M : s, \sigma}{G;\Gamma \vdash \lambda x M : \bot, (\tau \xrightarrow[F]{s} \sigma)} \ (\textsc{Abs}) \qquad \frac{}{G;\Gamma \vdash () : \bot, \mathsf{unit}} \ (\textsc{Nil})$$

$$\frac{}{G;\Gamma \vdash \mathit{tt} : \bot, \mathsf{bool}} \ (\textsc{BoolT}) \qquad \frac{}{G;\Gamma \vdash \mathit{ff} : \bot, \mathsf{bool}} \ (\textsc{BoolF})$$

$$\frac{G;\Gamma \vdash M : s, \mathsf{bool} \quad G;\Gamma \vdash N_i : s_i, \tau \quad s.\mathsf{r} \preceq_G s_0.\mathsf{w} \cup s_1.\mathsf{w}}{G;\Gamma \vdash (\mathsf{if}\ M\ \mathsf{then}\ N_0\ \mathsf{else}\ N_1) : s \curlyvee s_0 \curlyvee s_1 \curlyvee (\bot, \top, t), \tau} \ (\textsc{Cond})$$

where
$$t = \begin{cases} \bot & \text{if } N_0, N_1 \in \mathcal{T} \\ s.\mathsf{c} & \text{otherwise} \end{cases}$$

$$\frac{G;\Gamma \vdash M : s, \tau \xrightarrow[F]{s'} \sigma \quad G;\Gamma \vdash N : s'', \tau \quad s.\mathsf{t} \preceq_G s''.\mathsf{w} \quad s.\mathsf{r} \curlyvee s''.\mathsf{r} \preceq_G s'.\mathsf{w}}{F, G;\Gamma \vdash (MN) : s \curlyvee s' \curlyvee s'' \curlyvee (\bot, \top, s.\mathsf{c} \curlyvee s''.\mathsf{c}), \sigma} \ (\textsc{App})$$

$$\frac{G;\Gamma \vdash M : s, \tau \quad G;\Gamma \vdash N : s', \sigma \quad s.\mathsf{t} \preceq_G s'.\mathsf{w}}{G;\Gamma \vdash M\,;N : (\bot, s.\mathsf{w}, s.\mathsf{t}) \curlyvee s', \sigma} \ (\textsc{Seq})$$

$$\frac{G;\Gamma \vdash M : s, \theta \quad s.\mathsf{r} \preceq_G \ell}{G;\Gamma \vdash (\mathsf{ref}_{\ell,\theta}\ M) : (\bot, s.\mathsf{w}, s.\mathsf{t}), \theta\, \mathsf{ref}_\ell} \ (\textsc{Ref}) \qquad \frac{G;\Gamma \vdash M : s, \theta\, \mathsf{ref}_\ell}{G;\Gamma \vdash (!M) : s \curlyvee (\ell, \top, \bot), \theta} \ (\textsc{Deref})$$

$$\frac{G;\Gamma \vdash M : s, \theta\, \mathsf{ref}_\ell \quad G;\Gamma \vdash N : s', \theta \quad s.\mathsf{t} \preceq_G s'.\mathsf{w}, \ s.\mathsf{r} \curlyvee s'.\mathsf{r} \preceq_G \ell}{G;\Gamma \vdash (M := N) : (\bot, s.\mathsf{w} \cup s'.\mathsf{w} \cup \ell, s.\mathsf{t} \curlyvee s'.\mathsf{t}), \mathsf{unit}} \ (\textsc{Assign})$$

$$\frac{G;\Gamma \vdash M : s, \mathsf{unit}}{G;\Gamma \vdash (\mathsf{thread}\ M) : (\bot, s.\mathsf{w}, \bot), \mathsf{unit}} \ (\textsc{Thread})$$

$$\frac{G;\Gamma, x : \tau \vdash V : s, \tau}{G;\Gamma \vdash \varrho x V : s, \tau} \ (\textsc{Rec}) \qquad \frac{F, G;\Gamma \vdash M : s, \tau \quad s.\mathsf{c} \preceq_{\mathsf{GUF}} c \quad s.\mathsf{t} \preceq_{\mathsf{GUF}} t}{G;\Gamma \vdash (\mathsf{flow}\ F\ \mathsf{in}\ M) : (c, s.\mathsf{w}, t), \tau} \ (\textsc{Flow})$$

Fig. 3. The Type and Effect System

One should also observe that, since both the confidentiality level and the termination effect of an expression are always smaller in this system than in the one of [1], the flow constraints where these are involved – in the rules (COND), (APP), (SEQ), (REF) and (ASSIGN) – are less constraining here. Indeed, for each of these constraints one can find an expression that is accepted in our system but rejected by the system of [1]. For instance, the expression of Example (2) is accepted, provided that $P, Q \in \mathcal{T}$, and that the writing level of P and Q is not lower than H. One can see also that if M is an expression with side-effects, then $v_L := M$ is generally accepted, provided that the confidentiality level of M is less than L, even though to perform the side-effects of M involves reading in a part of the memory that is not lower than L. Typically, for instance

$$v_L := (u_H := \; ! \, w_H) \; ; \; ! \, v'_L \tag{3}$$

is now accepted, whereas it was rejected by the system of [1].

We conclude this section with some technical definitions and results that are useful for our proof of type soundness. First, we notice that the writing effect of an expression is indeed a lower bound of the level of references that are updated while evaluating the expression:

LEMMA 0.6. $G; \Gamma \vdash \mathbf{E}[(u_{\ell,\theta} := V)] : s, \tau \;\Rightarrow\; s.\mathsf{w} \preceq \ell$.

This justifies the following definition:

DEFINITION (SYNTACTICALLY HIGH EXPRESSIONS) 0.7.   *An expression M is syntactically (G, ℓ)-high if $G; \Gamma \vdash M : s, \tau$ with $s.\mathsf{w} \npreceq_G \ell$. The expression M is a (G, ℓ)-high function if $G; \Gamma \vdash M : s, (\tau \xrightarrow[F]{s'} \sigma)$ with $s'.\mathsf{w} \npreceq_G \ell$.*

Indeed, we have:

LEMMA 0.8.
(i) *A syntactically (G, ℓ)-high expression is operationally (G, ℓ)-high.*
(ii) *If (MN) is typable in the context of the flow relation G, with $M, N \in \mathcal{H}_{G,\ell}$ and M is a (G, ℓ)-high function then $(MN) \in \mathcal{H}_{G,\ell}$.*

5   Type Soundness

Our main result is the type soundness property, stating that typable expressions are secure:

THEOREM (SOUNDNESS).   *If M is typable in the context of a flow policy G, that is if for some Γ, s and τ we have $G; \Gamma \vdash M : s, \tau$, then M satisfies the non-disclosure policy with respect to G, that is $M \in \mathcal{ND}(G)$.*

To prove this result, for any security level ℓ we exhibit a (G, ℓ)-bisimulation that contains the pair (M, M) for any G-typable expression M. A simple but crucial observation regarding the operational semantics of our language is that if the evaluation of an expression M differs in the context of two distinct memories while not creating two distinct references, this is because M is performing a dereferencing operation, which yields different results depending on the memory, that is $M = \mathbf{E}[(!u_{\ell,\theta})]$. Now trying to see to which bisimulation a pair (M, M) where M is G-typable may belong, we see that we have in particular to examine the case where $M = \mathbf{E}[(!u_{\ell',\theta})]$, so that the bisimulation we are seeking would contain the pair $(\mathbf{E}[V_0], \mathbf{E}[V_1])$ where V_0 and V_1 are respectively the values stored

at location $u_{\ell',\theta}$ in memories μ and ν such that $\mu \simeq^{G \cup \lceil \mathbf{E} \rceil, \ell} \nu$, with $\ell' \npreceq_{G \cup \lceil \mathbf{E} \rceil} \ell$.
A case analysis on the evaluation context $\mathbf{E}$ justifies the following definition.
Given a global flow policy G and a confidentiality level ℓ, we define inductively
three mutually recursive binary relations $\mathcal{U}_{G,\ell}$, $\mathcal{S}_{G,\ell}$ and $\mathcal{R}_{G,\ell}$ on expressions,
as follows:

$M \, \mathcal{U}_{G,\ell} \, N$ if M and N are both G-typable with s.r $\preceq_G \ell$, and one of the following
holds:

(Clause 1) $M = N$, or
(Clause 2) $M = (\text{if } M_0 \text{ then } M_1 \text{ else } M_2)$ and $N = (\text{if } N_0 \text{ then } M_1 \text{ else } M_2)$ with
$M_0 \, \mathcal{U}_{G,\ell} \, N_0$, or
(Clause 3) $M = (M_0 M_1)$ and $N = (N_0 N_1)$ with $M_i \, \mathcal{U}_{G,\ell} \, N_i$ $(i = 0, 1)$, or
(Clause 4) $M = M_0 \, ; \, M_1$ and $N = N_0 \, ; \, N_1$ with $M_0 \, \mathcal{S}_{G,\ell} \, N_0$ and $M_1 \, \mathcal{U}_{G,\ell} \, N_1$, or
(Clause 5) $M = (\text{ref}_{\ell',\theta} \, M_0)$ and $N = (\text{ref}_{\ell',\theta} \, N_0)$ with

   (a) either $M_0 \, \mathcal{U}_{G,\ell} \, N_0$, or

   (b) $\ell' \npreceq_G \ell$ and $M_0 \, \mathcal{S}_{G,\ell} \, N_0$, or
(Clause 6) $M = (! \, M_0)$ and $N = (! \, N_0)$ with $M_0 \, \mathcal{U}_{G,\ell} \, N_0$, and both M_0 and N_0 have
type $\theta \, \text{ref}_{\ell'}$ for some θ and ℓ' such that $\ell' \preceq_G \ell$, or
(Clause 7) $M = (M_0 := M_1)$ and $N = (N_0 := N_1)$ with

   (a) either $M_0 \, \mathcal{U}_{G,\ell} \, N_0$ and $M_1 \, \mathcal{U}_{G,\ell} \, N_1$, or

   (b) $M_0 \, \mathcal{S}_{G,\ell} \, N_0$ and $M_1 \, \mathcal{S}_{G,\ell} \, N_1$, and both M_0 and N_0 have type $\theta \, \text{ref}_{\ell'}$ for some θ
and ℓ' such that $\ell' \npreceq_G \ell$, or
(Clause 8) $M = (\text{flow } F \text{ in } M_0)$ and $N = (\text{flow } F \text{ in } N_0)$ with $M_0 \, \mathcal{U}_{F \cup G,\ell} \, N_0$.

$M \, \mathcal{S}_{G,\ell} \, N$ if M and N are both G-typable with s.t $\preceq_G \ell$, and one of the following
holds:

(Clause 1) M and N are both values, or
(Clause 2) $M, N \in \mathcal{H}_{G,\ell} \cap \mathcal{T}$, or
(Clause 3) $M = N$, or
(Clause 4) $M = (\text{if } M_0 \text{ then } M_1 \text{ else } M_2)$ and $N = (\text{if } N_0 \text{ then } M_1 \text{ else } M_2)$ with

   (a) either $M_0 \, \mathcal{U}_{G,\ell} \, N_0$, or

   (b) $M_0 \, \mathcal{S}_{G,\ell} \, N_0$ and $M_1 \, \mathcal{S}_{G,\ell} \, M_2$, or
(Clause 5) $M = (M_0 M_1)$ and $N = (N_0 N_1)$ with $M_i \, \mathcal{U}_{G,\ell} \, N_i$ $(i = 0, 1)$, or
(Clause 6) $M = M_0 \, ; \, M_1$ and $N = N_0 \, ; \, M_1$ with $M_0 \, \mathcal{S}_{G,\ell} \, N_0$, or
(Clause 7) $M = (\text{ref}_{\ell',\theta} \, M_0)$ and $N = (\text{ref}_{\ell',\theta} \, N_0)$ with

   (a) either $M_0 \, \mathcal{U}_{G,\ell} \, N_0$, or

   (b) $\ell' \npreceq_G \ell$ and $M_0 \, \mathcal{S}_{G,\ell} \, N_0$, or
(Clause 8) $M = (! \, M_0)$ and $N = (! \, N_0)$ with $M_0 \, \mathcal{S}_{G,\ell} \, N_0$, or
(Clause 9) $M = (M_0 := M_1)$ and $N = (N_0 := N_1)$ with

   (a) either $M_0 \, \mathcal{U}_{G,\ell} \, N_0$ and $M_1 \, \mathcal{U}_{G,\ell} \, N_1$, or

   (b) $M_0 \, \mathcal{S}_{G,\ell} \, N_0$ and $M_1 \, \mathcal{S}_{G,\ell} \, N_1$, and both M_0 and N_0 have type $\theta \, \text{ref}_{\ell'}$ for some θ
and ℓ' such that $\ell' \npreceq_G \ell$, or
(Clause 10) $M = (\text{flow } F \text{ in } M_0)$ and $N = (\text{flow } F \text{ in } N_0)$ with $M_0 \, \mathcal{S}_{F \cup G,\ell} \, N_0$.

$M \, \mathcal{R}_{G,\ell} \, N$ if M and N are both G-typable and one of the following holds:

(Clause 1) M and N are both values, or
(Clause 2) $M = N$, or

(Clause 3) $M = ($if M_0 then M_1 else $M_2)$ and $N = ($if N_0 then M_1 else $M_2)$ with

    (a) either $M_0\,\mathcal{U}_{G,\ell}\,N_0$, or

    (b) $M_0\,\mathcal{R}_{G,\ell}\,N_0$ and $M_1\,\rtimes^{G,\ell}\,N_1$, or

(Clause 4) $M = (M_0 M_1)$ and $N = (N_0 N_1)$ with

    (a) either $M_0\,\mathcal{U}_{G,\ell}\,N_0$ and $M_1\,\mathcal{U}_{G,\ell}\,N_1$, or

    (b) $M_0\,\mathcal{S}_{G,\ell}\,N_0$ and $M_1\,\mathcal{R}_{G,\ell}\,N_1$ and M_0, N_0 are (G,ℓ)-high functions, or

    (c) $M_0\,\mathcal{R}_{G,\ell}\,N_0$ and $M_1\,\rtimes^{G,\ell}\,N_1$ and M_0, N_0 are (G,ℓ)-high functions, or

(Clause 5) $M = M_0\,;\,M_1$ and $N = N_0\,;\,M_1$ with

    (a) either $M_0\,\mathcal{S}_{G,\ell}\,N_0$, or

    (b) $M_0\,\mathcal{R}_{G,\ell}\,N_0$ and $M_1 \in \mathcal{H}_{G,\ell}$, or

(Clause 6) $M = ($ref$_{\ell',\theta}\,M_0)$ and $N = ($ref$_{\ell',\theta}\,N_0)$ with

    (a) either $M_0\,\mathcal{U}_{G,\ell}\,N_0$, or

    (b) $\ell' \npreceq_G \ell$ and $M_0\,\mathcal{R}_{G,\ell}\,N_0$, or

(Clause 7) $M = (!\,M_0)$ and $N = (!\,N_0)$ with $M_0\,\mathcal{R}_{G,\ell}\,N_0$, or

(Clause 8) $M = (M_0 := M_1)$ and $N = (N_0 := N_1)$ with

    (a) either $M_0\,\mathcal{U}_{G,\ell}\,N_0$ and $M_1\,\mathcal{U}_{G,\ell}\,N_1$, or

    (b) $M_0\,\mathcal{S}_{G,\ell}\,N_0$ and $M_1\,\mathcal{R}_{G,\ell}\,N_1$, and both M_0 and N_0 have type θ ref$_{\ell'}$ for some θ and ℓ' such that $\ell' \npreceq_G \ell$, or

    (c) $M_0\,\mathcal{R}_{G,\ell}\,N_0$ and $M_1\,\rtimes^{G,\ell}\,N_1$, and both M_0 and N_0 have type θ ref$_{\ell'}$ for some θ and ℓ' such that $\ell' \npreceq_G \ell$, or

(Clause 9) $M = ($flow F in $M_0)$ and $N = ($flow F in $N_0)$ with $M_0\,\mathcal{R}_{F\cup G,\ell}\,N_0$.

Finally we may define the bisimulation $\mathcal{R}^\star_{G,\ell}$ we were looking for as follows:

$$\frac{M\,\mathcal{R}_{G,\ell}\,N}{M\,\mathcal{R}^\star_{G,\ell}\,N} \qquad \frac{P\,\rtimes^{G,\ell}\,Q \quad Q\,\mathcal{R}^\star_{G,\ell}\,R}{P\,\mathcal{R}^\star_{G,\ell}\,R} \qquad \frac{P\,\mathcal{R}^\star_{G,\ell}\,Q \quad Q\,\rtimes^{G,\ell}\,R}{P\,\mathcal{R}^\star_{G,\ell}\,R}$$

$$\frac{P\,\mathcal{R}^\star_{G,\ell}\,Q \quad R \in \mathcal{H}_{G,\ell}}{P\,\mathcal{R}^\star_{G,\ell}\,(Q \parallel R)} \qquad \frac{P\,\mathcal{R}^\star_{G,\ell}\,Q \quad R \in \mathcal{H}_{G,\ell}}{(P \parallel R)\,\mathcal{R}^\star_{G,\ell}\,Q} \qquad \frac{P\,\mathcal{R}^\star_{G,\ell}\,P' \quad Q\,\mathcal{R}^\star_{G,\ell}\,Q'}{(P \parallel Q)\,\mathcal{R}^\star_{G,\ell}\,(P' \parallel Q')}$$

6 Conclusion

In this paper we have explored two directions in which type systems for information flow could be improved. Regarding termination leaks, we have shown that there is no such leak in cases where some subexpressions are known to terminate, and the typing discipline can therefore be relaxed accordingly. Moreover, we have shown that the side-effects of an expression are in many cases not a source of information leakage, and, again, this can be reflected in the type system. We believe that these two observations are quite simple and natural, and that they could be adapted to other programming styles than the functional (and imperative) one of ML.

It is not easy to compare the type systems for information flow we find in the literature with the one we have proposed, for various reasons. A first remark is that most type systems for functional languages are not – with the exception of [4] – "store-oriented", but "value-oriented". That is, they most often assign a security level to *values*, whereas we have taken the point of view that the "pure" fragment of the language is secure. Indeed, we think that some communication medium (the references in our case) is needed for implementing the idea that information flows from one place to another. Assigning security levels to values amounts to regarding these levels as channels along which information may be communicated. We think it is better to make the operational existence of such channels explicit, and not to confuse them with the abstract notion of a confidentiality level. Indeed, it is shown in [4] that a typically "value-oriented" approach to typing information flow, as it can be found in [19], can be encoded in a "store-oriented" approach, simply by making any value available as the contents of a reference (a similar result regarding the SLam calculus of [7] is presented in the workshop version of [4]).

Another difference with type systems for functional languages is that these, including the one of [4], are most often only dealing with weak, termination insensitive non-interference, as we already pointed out in the introduction. Then such type systems cannot ensure our "non-disclosure policy", and therefore they are not well-suited to support declassification, as we have formulated it. Then our type system is to be compared with the ones that are used when dealing with termination sensitive non-interference, that is, with type systems for concurrent and imperative languages. As we said in the introduction, our typing of termination leaks improves a lot on the various proposals made regarding concurrent and imperative languages.

We have shown that our type system is sound, whatever choice is made as regards the set T of strongly converging expressions, but obviously to obtain a practical type system, we have to instantiate this parameter into a computable set of expressions. Then an obvious topic of research, which is left open in this paper, is the characterization of a class T of strongly converging expressions which would be as large as possible, including in particular the ability of using functions. This is not the case of the class we mentioned at the end of Section 2, which only contains simple imperative programs. An obvious idea would be to exploit the classical results regarding strong normalization in typed λ-calculi. However, there is a technical difficulty, which is known since a long time but has, as far as I can see, no solution up to now. Namely, it is known since Landin's pioneering work on the implementation of functional languages [8] that circular higher-order references introduce non-termination, like for instance in (using ref without subscripts)

$$(\mathsf{let}\ x = (\mathsf{ref}\ \lambda yy)\ \mathsf{in}\ x := \lambda y((!\,x)y)\,;\,((!\,x)V))$$

This particular expression cannot be typed in our type and effect system, but a variant of it like

$$(\mathsf{let}\ y = \mathsf{ref}\lambda x.(!\mathsf{ref}\lambda x.(!\mathsf{ref}\lambda xx)x)x\ \mathsf{in}\ y := \lambda x.(!\,y)x\,;\,!y)$$

is accepted. Then, to obtain a computable set of strongly converging expressions where functions can be used is still problematic. This issue is left for further work.

References

1. A. ALMEIDA MATOS, G. BOUDOL, *On declassification and the non-disclosure policy*, to appear in the proceedings of the 18th IEEE Computer Security Foundations Workshop (2005).
2. G. BOUDOL, I. CASTELLANI, *Non-interference for concurrent programs and thread systems*, Theoretical Comput. Sci. Vol. 281, No. 1 (2002) 109-130.
3. E. COHEN, *Information transmission in computational systems*, 6th ACM Symp. on Operating Systems Principles (1977) 133-139.
4. K. CRARY, A. KLIGER, F. PFENNING, *A monadic analysis of information flow security with mutable state*, J. of Functional Programming, Vol. 15 No. 2 (2005) 249-291.
5. D. E. DENNING, *A lattice model of secure information flow*, CACM Vol. 19 No. 5 (1976) 236-243.
6. J. A. GOGUEN, J. MESEGUER, *Security policies and security models*, IEEE Symp. on Security and Privacy (1982) 11-20.
7. N. HEINTZE, J. RIECKE, *The SLam calculus: programming with secrecy and integrity*, POPL'98 (1998) 365-377.
8. P. J. LANDIN, *The mechanical evaluation of expressions*, Computer Journal Vol. 6 (1964) 308-320.
9. J. M. LUCASSEN, D. K. GIFFORD, *Polymorphic effect systems*, POPL'88 (1988) 47-57.
10. A. MYERS, *JFlow: practical mostly-static information flow control*, POPL'99 (1999).
11. F. POTTIER, V. SIMONET, *Information flow inference for ML*, ACM TOPLAS Vol. 25 No. 1 (2003) 117-158.
12. A. SABELFELD, A. C. MYERS, *Language-based information-flow security*, IEEE J. on Selected Areas in Communications Vol. 21 No. 1 (2003) 5-19.
13. A. SABELFELD, D. SANDS, *Probabilistic noninterference for multi-threaded programs*, CSFW'00 (2000).
14. A. SABELFELD, D. SANDS, *Dimensions and principles of declassification*, Proceedings of the 18th IEEE Computer Security Foundations Workshop (2005).
15. G. SMITH, *A new type system for secure information flow*, CSFW'01 (2001).
16. G. SMITH, D. VOLPANO, *Secure information flow in a multi-threaded imperative language*, POPL'98 (1998).
17. D. VOLPANO, G. SMITH, *Eliminating covert flows with minimum typings*, CSFW'97 (1997) 156-168.
18. D. VOLPANO, G. SMITH, C. IRVINE, *A sound type system for secure flow analysis*, J. of Computer Security, Vol. 4, No 3 (1996) 167-187.
19. S. ZDANCEWIC, *Programming Languages for Information Security*, PhD Thesis, Cornell University (2002).
20. S. ZDANCEWIC, *Challenges for information-flow security*, PLID'04 (2004).

Representation and Reasoning on RBAC: A Description Logic Approach

Chen Zhao, Nuermaimaiti Heilili, Shengping Liu, and Zuoquan Lin

LMAM, Department of Informatics,
School of Math., Peking University,
Beijing 100871, China
{zchen,nur,lsp,lz}@is.pku.edu.cn

Abstract. Role-based access control (RBAC) is recognized as an excellent model for access control in large-scale networked applications. Formalization of RBAC in a logical approach makes it feasible to reason about a specified policy and verify its correctness. We propose a formalization of RBAC by the description logic language $\mathcal{ALCQ}$. We also show that the RBAC constraints can be captured by $\mathcal{ALCQ}$. Furthermore, we demonstrate how to make access control decision, perform the RBAC functions as well as check the consistency of RBAC via the description logic reasoner RACER.

1 Introduction

Role-Based Access Control (RBAC)[1,2] has been recognized as a strategy which reduces the cost and complexity of security administration in large-scale networked applications. RBAC represents a major advancement in flexibility from traditional discretionary and mandatory access control. In RBAC, permissions are associated with roles, and users are made members of appropriate roles, thereby acquiring the appropriate permissions. Moreover, the use of role hierarchies provides additional advantages since one role may implicitly include the permissions that are associated with another role.

A formal analysis of RBAC will help to design and implement access control policy. Sandhu et al. [1] proposed the RBAC96 model based on set theory, which first formally defined the relations among user, role and permission using the notion of set membership. Koch et al. [3,4] presented a formalization of RBAC using graph transformations.

Moreover, there has been a considerable interest in logical framework for the reasoning of access control models [5,6,7,8,9,10,11,12]. A major advantage of a logical framework is that it becomes feasible to reason about a specified policy and verify its correctness. The first attempt was made by Woo and Lam [5], who proposed a language based on default logic. A logic for reasoning about RBAC is presented by Massacci [7]. It enhances an access control calculus [6] to express role hierarchies, and its semantics is based on the Kripke model of modal logics. Appel and Felten [8] introduced the idea of proof-carrying authorization (PCA),

D.V. Hung and M. Wirsing (Eds.): ICTAC 2005, LNCS 3722, pp. 381–393, 2005.
© Springer-Verlag Berlin Heidelberg 2005

an authorization framework that is based on a higher-order logic (AF logic).
Jajodia *et al.*[9] presented a logic language for specifying security policies and
Bertino *el al.* [11] proposed a formal framework based on C-Datalog language.
Recently Crescini and Zhang [12] presented a logic-based authorization system
by the use of a first-order logic language, $\mathcal{L}$, for defining, updating and querying
of access control policies.

The constraints are an important aspect of RBAC and are always regarded
as one of principal motivations for RBAC, which impose restrictions on acceptable configurations of the different components of RBAC. Nevertheless, it was
discussed informally in the RBAC96 model [1]. There are also some efforts to
express constraints formally. Gligor *el al.* [13] defined a wide variety of separation
of duties (SOD) policies on the basis of first-order logic. Mossakowski *el al.* [14]
used temporal logic to extend the RBAC model and express SOD policies. Ahn
and Sandhu [15] proposed an intuitive formal language for specifying role-based
authorization constraints named *RCL 2000*, and showed that any property written in *RCL 2000* may be translated into an expression written in a restricted
form of first-order logic.

Some of these works are depended upon proprietary languages, which do not
have efficient implementations. The properties of these languages, such as computational complexity, are not well understood by researchers. Others are based
on first-order logic or its extensions. These logic languages have enough expressiveness for representation of access control policies. However, excessively rich expressiveness may bring on complex computation and confusion. For instance, it is
difficult to give a rational interpretation for the expression $\neg read(UserA, doc1) \vee$
$\neg read(UserA, doc2)$.

In this paper, we present a novel formalization of RBAC with a description
logic approach. Description Logics (DLs) [16] are a family of languages used
to describe and classify concepts and their instances. Knowledge representation
systems based on description logics have been proven useful for representing the
terminological knowledge of an application domain in a structured and formally
well understood way. Compared with first-order logic, DLs achieve a better trade-
off between the computational complexity of reasoning and the expressiveness
of the language. We choose a DL language $\mathcal{ALCQ}$ [17] to represent and reason
on RBAC according to the features of RBAC. $\mathcal{ALCQ}$ extends the well-known
description logic $\mathcal{ALC}$ [18] by *qualified number restrictions*. We show how to express constraints in $\mathcal{ALCQ}$ and check the consistency of RBAC with constraints.
In practice there are highly optimized reasoners, such as RACER [19,20], that
handle real problems in a desirable performance. To be intuitive, we develop a
case study about reasoning on RBAC via RACER.

The rest of the paper is organized as follows. In Section 2, we give an overview
of the RBAC96 model. In Section 3, we introduce the description logic language
$\mathcal{ALCQ}$. In Section 4, the representation and reasoning on RBAC in $\mathcal{ALCQ}$ are
developed. In Section 5, we present a case study and show how to perform
some RBAC functions by RACER. In Section 6, we show how to express the
constraints in $\mathcal{ALCQ}$. Finally, conclusions are drawn in Section 7.

2   RBAC96 Model

We review the RBAC96 model which we refer to in this paper. The RBAC96 model includes sets of three basic data elements called users, roles and permissions. A user is a human being in most cases, and may be extended to include autonomous agents. A role is a job function in the context of an organization with some associated semantics regarding the authority and responsibility conferred on a member of the role. A permission is an approval of a particular mode of access to one or more objects in the system or some privilege to carry out specified actions. User assignment and permission assignment are two many-to-many relations in the model, which connect roles to users and permissions respectively. In addition, the model includes a set of sessions where each session is a mapping from a user to an activated subset of roles that are assigned to the user. A user can create a session and choose to activate some subset of the user's roles.

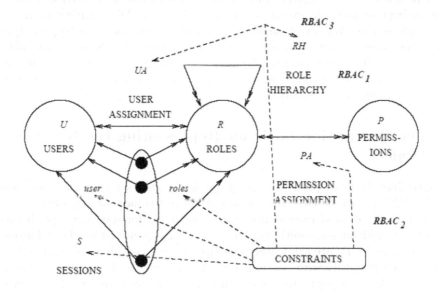

Fig. 1. Summary of the RBAC96 model

There is a family of four conceptual models in the RBAC96 model. $RBAC_0$ is the base model that indicates the minimum requirement for any system that supports RBAC. $RBAC_1$ and $RBAC_2$ both include $RBAC_0$, but add role hierarchies (situations where roles can inherit permissions from other roles) and constraints (which impose restrictions on acceptable configurations of the different components of RBAC) respectively. $RBAC_1$ and $RBAC_2$ are incomparable to one another. $RBAC_3$ is the consolidated model that includes all the essential components of RBAC. Figure 1 illustrates their essential characteristics.

Role hierarchies define an inheritance relation among roles. We say that role r_1 "inherits" role r_2 if all privileges of r_2 are also privileges of r_1, denoted as $r_1 \geq r_2$. The $RBAC_1$ model defined in [1] consists of the following components:

- *Users*, *Roles*, *Perms*, and *Sessions* (users, roles, permissions and sessions respectively),
- $PA \subseteq Perms \times Roles$, a many-to-many permission to role assignment relation,
- $UA \subseteq Users \times Roles$, a many-to-many user to role assignment relation,
- $RH \subseteq Roles \times Roles$ is a partial order on *Roles* (also written as $\geq$),
- *user* : *Sessions* $\rightarrow$ *Users* is a function mapping each session s to the single user $user(s)$ (constant for the session's lifetime), and
- *roles* : *Sessions* $\rightarrow 2^{Roles}$ is a function mapping each session s to a set of roles $roles(s) \subseteq \{rr | \exists\, rr' \geq rr,\ (user(s), rr') \in UA\}$ (which can change with time) and session s has the permissions $\bigcup_{rr \in roles(s)} \{p | \exists\, rr' \leq rr,\ (p, rr') \in PA\}$.

The constraints are introduced informally in $RBAC_2$. Two typical constraints are *separation of duties* (SOD) and *role cardinality constraint*. SOD is achieved by ensuring that mutually exclusive roles must be invoked to complete a sensitive task, such as requiring an accounting clerk and account manager to participate in issuing a check. That is, the same user can be assigned to at most one role in a mutually exclusive set. Role cardinality constraint means that a role can have a maximum number of members. For instance, there is only one person in the role of chairman of a department.

3   The Description Logic for Representing the RBAC96 Model

We introduce the description logic language $\mathcal{ALCQ}$ that will be used to represent the RBAC96 model. In DLs, the domain of interest is modelled by means of *individuals*, *concepts*, and *roles*, denoting objects of the domain, unary predicates, and binary predicates respectively. Atomic concepts (denoted by A) and atomic roles (denoted by R) are elementary descriptions and complex ones can be built from them inductively with constructors. $\mathcal{ALCQ}$ concepts (denoted by C or D, possibly with a subscript) are composed inductively according to the following syntax rule (n denotes a natural number):

$$C ::= A \mid \top \mid \neg C \mid C \sqcap D \mid \exists R.C \mid (\geq nR.C).$$

In DLs, $\top$ is defined as universal concept, and $\bot$ is defined as bottom concept, such that $\bot = \neg\top$. In $\mathcal{ALCQ}$, we also can define the constructors: $\forall R.C = \neg(\exists R.\neg C)$ and $(\leq nR.C) = \neg(\geq (n+1)R.C)$.

From a semantic point of view, concepts are interpreted as subsets of an abstract domain, while roles are interpreted as binary relations over such a domain. More precisely, an *interpretation* $\mathcal{I} = (\Delta^{\mathcal{I}}, \cdot^{\mathcal{I}})$ consists of a *domain of interpretation* $\Delta^{\mathcal{I}}$, and an *interpretation function* $\cdot^{\mathcal{I}}$ mapping every atomic concept A to a subset of $\Delta^{\mathcal{I}}$ and every atomic role R to a subset of $\Delta^{\mathcal{I}} \times \Delta^{\mathcal{I}}$. The syntax and semantics of $\mathcal{ALCQ}$ is summarized in Table 1, where $\#S$ denotes the cardinality of the set S.

Table 1. The syntax and semantics of $\mathcal{ALCQ}$

Constructor	Syntax	Semantics
universal concept	$\top$	$\Delta^{\mathcal{I}}$
atomic concept	A	$A^{\mathcal{I}}$
concept negation	$\neg C$	$\Delta^{\mathcal{I}} - C^{\mathcal{I}}$
intersection	$C \sqcap D$	$C^{\mathcal{I}} \cap D^{\mathcal{I}}$
existential restriction	$\exists R.C$	$\{x \in \Delta^{\mathcal{I}} | \exists y \in \Delta^{\mathcal{I}}, (x,y) \in r^{\mathcal{I}} \wedge y \in C^{\mathcal{I}}\}$
qualified number restriction	$\geq nR.C$	$\{x \in \Delta^{\mathcal{I}} | \#\{y|(x,y) \in r^{\mathcal{I}} \wedge y \in C^{\mathcal{I}}\} \geq n\}$

A Knowledge Base (KB) in description logics comprises two components, the TBox and the ABox. TBox (denoted as $\mathcal{T}$) is a finite set of terminological axioms which make statements about how concepts are related to each other. Generally, they have two forms: $C \equiv D$ or $C \sqsubseteq D$, where C, D are concepts. The first kind is called *equalities* which states that $C^{\mathcal{I}}$ is equivalent to $D^{\mathcal{I}}$, and the second is called *inclusions* which states that $C^{\mathcal{I}}$ is a subset of $D^{\mathcal{I}}$ for all $\mathcal{I}$. Since the $\mathcal{ALCQ}$'s terminology is acyclic, we will focus on the acyclic terminology in the following. ABox (denoted as $\mathcal{A}$) is a finite set of individual assertions in which there are also two kinds: $C(a)$ or $r(a,b)$, where C is a concept, r is a role, a, b are individuals. The first kind is called *concept assertions* which states that $a^{\mathcal{I}} \in C^{\mathcal{I}}$, and the second is called *role assertions* which states that $(a^{\mathcal{I}}, b^{\mathcal{I}}) \in r^{\mathcal{I}}$ for all $\mathcal{I}$.

The basic reasoning services in DL are *satisfiability* and *subsumption*. Determining satisfiability of a concept C in a KB $\mathcal{K}$ amounts to check whether $\mathcal{K}$ admits a model in which the extension of C is nonempty. Determining subsumption between two concepts C and D in $\mathcal{K}$, amounts to check whether $C^{\mathcal{I}} \subseteq D^{\mathcal{I}}$ for every interpretation $\mathcal{I}$ of $\mathcal{K}$, denoted as $\mathcal{K} \models C \sqsubseteq D$. Subsumption can be easily reduced to satisfiability as follows: A concept C is subsumed by a concept D in $\mathcal{K}$ if and only if $C \sqcap \neg D$ is not satisfiable in $\mathcal{K}$. Upon that it is sufficient to consider concept satisfiability only.

4   Representation and Reasoning on the RBAC96 Model in $\mathcal{ALCQ}$

We will now describe how to conceptualize the RBAC96 model and construct a DL knowledge base capturing the characteristics of RBAC. Given a $RBAC_1$ model, we define a DL knowledge base $\mathcal{K}$. We assume that the role set and the permission set are finite. In an access control policy each role and permission must be concretely (one by one) specified, so this assumption is feasible in practise.

The alphabet of $\mathcal{K}$ includes the following atomic concepts and roles:

- the atomic concepts User, CRole, Permission, and Session, represent the users, roles, permissions and sessions respectively,
- for each role $rr \in Roles$, one atomic concept RR,

- for each permission $p \in Perms$, one atomic concept P,
- the atomic role assign, connects the user to the roles assigned to him,
- the atomic role cando, connects the role to the permissions assigned to it,
- the atomic role authorize, connects the user to the permissions authorized through his assigned roles,
- the atomic role founder, connects the user to the sessions established by him,
- the atomic role activate, connects the session to the roles activated in it,
- the atomic role grant, connects the session to the permissions available in it.

Each concept RR is a subconcept of CRole. Similarly, each concept P is a subconcept of Permission. The concept ∃assign.RR describes the concept of "users assigned to the role rr", and ∃cando.P describes the concept of "roles associated with the permission p", and so on.

The TBox of $\mathcal{K}$ includes three catalogs of axioms: *role inclusion axioms*, *permission assignment axioms*, and *authorization axioms*.

Role inclusion axioms express the role hierarchies in RBAC. For each role hierarchy relation $rr_1 \geq rr_2$, $rr_1, rr_2 \in Roles$, role inclusion axioms have the form $RR_1 \sqsubseteq RR_2$, where RR_1 and RR_2 are atomic concepts corresponding to the role rr_1 and rr_2. In addition, we should set up axioms RR $\sqsubseteq$ CRole for each $rr \in Roles$.

Permission assignment axioms express the permission assignments in RBAC. For each permission-role relation $(p, rr) \in PA$, permission assignment axioms have the form $RR \sqsubseteq \exists$cando.P. In RBAC, the senior role inherits the junior one's permissions. Permission assignment axioms can capture this feature. Given a role $rr_1 \in Roles$, a permission $p \in Perms$, if $rr_1 \geq rr_2$ and $(rr_2, p) \in PA$, then we get $RR_1 \sqsubseteq RR_2$, and $RR_2 \sqsubseteq \exists$cando.P, subsequently, $RR_1 \sqsubseteq \exists$cando.P. That is to say that rr_1 is contained in the roles which have the permission p.

Authorization axioms make statements about how user acquire the permissions by assigned roles. For each $p \in Perms$, the associated authorization axioms have the form

$$\exists\text{assign}.(\exists\text{cando.P}) \sqsubseteq \exists\text{authorize.P}$$
$$\exists\text{activate}.(\exists\text{cando.P}) \sqsubseteq \exists\text{grant.P}$$

The concept ∃authorize.P is interpreted as the set of users that are authorized the permission p, and the concept ∃assign.(∃cando.P) is interpreted as the set of users that are assigned to at least one of the roles holding the permission p. The first axiom indicates that a permission can be given to the user who has been assigned to the role associated with that permission. Similarly, the second axiom indicates that in a session a permission can be given to the user who has activated the role associated with that permission.

The ABox of $\mathcal{K}$ includes following six catalogs of axioms: *Role concept assertions* have the form $RR(rr)$ and declare each role to be an instance of corresponding role concept. *User concept assertions* specify users, and *Session concept assertions* specify sessions. *Role activation assertions* have the form activate(s, rr) and indicate that the role rr has been activated by the session s. *Session creation assertions* and have the form founder(u, s), and indicate that the specific session s are created by the user u. *User role assignment assertions* have the form assign(u, rr), and indicate that the user u is assigned to the role rr.

We then show how to use the operations TELL and ASK to achieve some reasoning tasks and make access control decision. TELL is often used to add sentences into KB, and ASK is used to query KB. We can use following query statement to check if a user u is assigned to a role rr:

$$\text{ASK}\{\ \exists\text{assign.RR}(u)\}$$

that refers to assert if u is an instance of $\exists$assign.RR. If we have defined assign(u, rr) in the ABox of $\mathcal{K}$, then $\mathcal{K} \models (\exists\text{assign.RR})(u)$. If assign$(u, rr)$ is not defined in the ABox of $\mathcal{K}$, instead we defined assign(u, rr'), where the role rr' is senior to rr, that is $rr' \geq rr$, then we still get $\mathcal{K} \models (\exists\text{assign.RR})(u)$, because $\exists$assign.RR' $\sqsubseteq$ $\exists$assign.RR. This indicates that if a user u is assigned to a role rr, then u has user role assignment relation with all descendants of the role rr.

We can ask $\mathcal{K}$ to query whether a user u is given permission p:

$$\text{ASK}\{(\exists\text{authorize.P})(u)\}$$

According to authorization axioms $\exists$assign.($\exists$cando.P) $\sqsubseteq$ $\exists$authorize.P, we get that if the user u is assigned anyone role in $\exists$cando.P, there exists authorization relation between the user u and the permission p, i.e. the user u is given the permission p. More reasoning tasks will be discussed in next section with an practical example.

Since there is no knowledge about sessions in $\mathcal{K}$ initially, we should add these information into $\mathcal{K}$ by some TELL operations before we can make access control decision. The set of sentences added by TELL is denoted as $\mathcal{S}$. Firstly, we add session concept assertions and creation assertions into the ABox of $\mathcal{K}$ by

$$\text{TELL}\{\text{Session}(s)\}, \text{TELL}\{\text{founder}(u, s)\}$$

Secondly, users should activate their roles. Before a user activate a role rr, we must judge whether the user is assigned to the role rr. We can use the following query statement:

$$\text{ASK}\{(\exists\text{assign.RR})(u)\}$$

If $\mathcal{K} \not\models (\exists\text{assign.RR})(u)$, we can conclude that there does not exist assignment relation between user u and role rr. Therefore it is not allowed for user u to activate role rr. Otherwise, we can add role activation assertion into the ABox of $\mathcal{K}$ by

$$\text{TELL}\{\text{activate}(s, rr)\}$$

Then, we can query whether the user u is granted the permission p within the session s by

$$\text{ASK}\{(\exists\text{grant.P})(s)\}$$

If $\mathcal{K} \cup \mathcal{S} \models (\exists\text{grant.P})(s)$, the user u has the permission p within the session s. Otherwise, the user's operation is prohibited.

5   A Case Study

In this section, we show a practical example and demonstrate how to accomplish reasoning tasks via RACER and RICE [21] — a RACER interactive client environment.

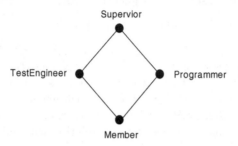

Fig. 2. The role hierarchy in a software development

Suppose, for example, that in a software development there are four roles: *Supervisor*, *TestEngineer*, *Programmer*, *Member*, and three permissions: *Execute*, *WriteSrc*, *ReadDocs*. The role hierarchy is shown in Figure 2. *Supervisor* is senior to *TestEngineer* and *Programmer* which are both senior to *Member*. We suppose that *TestEngineer* has the permission to execute the project, *Programmer* has the permission to write source code, and *Memeber* has the permission to read documents.

To formalize the above policies, we define the concept of roles: CSupervisor, CTestEngineer, CProgrammer, CMember, and the concept of permissions: Execute, WriteSrc, ReadDocs. The inheritance relations among these roles are described by following role inclusion axioms:

$$CSupervisor \sqsubseteq CTestEngineer, CSupervisor \sqsubseteq CProgrammer$$
$$CTestEngineer \sqsubseteq CMember, CProgrammer \sqsubseteq CMember$$

We define permission assignment axioms as follows:

$$CTestEngineer \sqsubseteq \exists cando.Execute$$
$$CProgrammer \sqsubseteq \exists cando.WriteSrc$$
$$CMember \sqsubseteq \exists cando.ReadDocs$$

We define authorization axioms as follows:

$$\exists assign.(\exists cando.Execute) \sqsubseteq \exists authorize.Execute$$
$$\exists assign.(\exists cando.WriteSrc) \sqsubseteq \exists authorize.WriteSrc$$
$$\exists assign.(\exists cando.ReadDocs) \sqsubseteq \exists authorize.ReadDocs$$
$$\exists activate.(\exists cando.Execute) \sqsubseteq \exists grant.Execute$$
$$\exists activate.(\exists cando.WriteSrc) \sqsubseteq \exists grant.WriteSrc$$
$$\exists activate.(\exists cando.ReadDocs) \sqsubseteq \exists grant.ReadDocs$$

We assume that there are four users: *Tom*, *Bob*, *Alice* and *John*, and they are assigned to the role *Supervisor*, *TestEngineer*, *Programmer* and *Member* respectively. We can define the corresponding ABox as follows:

$$\text{User}(Tom), \text{User}(Bob), \text{User}(Alice), \text{User}(John),$$
$$\text{CSupervisor}(Supervisor), \text{CTestEngineer}(TestEngineer),$$
$$\text{CProgrammer}(Programmer), \text{CMember}(Member),$$
$$\text{assign}(Tom, Supervisror), \text{assign}(Alice, TestEngineer),$$
$$\text{assign}(Bob, Programmer), \text{assign}(John, Member).$$

If *Bob* want to login as the role *Programmer*, we should use following RACER command to check *Bob*'s role assignment first:

```
(individual-instance? Bob (some assign CProgrammer))
```

In this example, we can get the result $\top$. Then we go on with TELL operations, adding sentences associated with the session information into KB.

$$\text{TELL}\{\text{Session}(s_1)\}$$
$$\text{TELL}\{\text{founder}(Bob, s_1)\}$$
$$\text{TELL}\{\text{activate}(s_1, Programmer)\}$$

In RACER, it can be written as:

```
(instance s1 Session)
(related Bob s1 founder)
(related s1 programmer activate)
```

We can check whether *Bob* has the permission to read the document in the session s_1 as follows:

```
(individual-instance? s1 (some grant WriteSrc))
```

Table 2. Some reasoning tasks on RBAC performed by RACER

RACER command and description	Result
`(concept-instances (some assign CProgrammer))` fetch all users assigned to the role *Programmer*	(TOM BOB)
`(concept-instances (some authorize Execute))` fetch all users authorized to the permission *Execute*	(TOM ALICE)

`(concept-instances (some founder (some activate`
 `CMember))`
 fetch all users activating the role *Programmer* currently
	(BOB)

`(individual-instance? alice (some assign CMember))` check if *Alice* is assigned to the role *Member* (including implicit assignment)	$\top$
`(individual-fillers alice assign)` fetch the roles which *Alice* is explicitly assigned to	(TESTENGINEER)

We can get the result ⊤. We also can check if *Bob* has the permission to execute the program in the session s_1:

```
(individual-instance? s1 (some grant Execute))
```

The result will be NIL. Then we will assert that *Bob* has no permission to execute the project in the session s_1.

Other related reasoning tasks on RBAC which can performed by RACER are listed in Table 2, and see RACER manual for more.

6   Express Constraints

In this section we will complement the KB $\mathcal{K}$ introduced in Section 4 by adding relevant concepts and constraint axioms to express static SOD, dynamic SOD and role cardinality constraint.

6.1   Static Separation of Duty

Static separation of duty (SSOD) is the simplest mode of SOD. If we define two roles as mutually exclusive, then no user can be assigned to the two roles simultaneously. More generally, if a set of roles which is denoted by CR are mutually exclusive, any user can be assigned to at most k roles in CR simultaneously. A SSOD policy can be denoted as (CR, k).

For each SSOD policy (CR, k), we define a atomic concept CR and a constraint axiom:

$$\geq (k+1) \text{ assign.CR} \sqsubseteq \bot$$

where the complex concept $\geq (k+1)$ assign.CR represents a set of users who have assignment relations with at least $k + 1$ instances of CR. This complex concept is a subconcept of bottom concept. That is to say, the user who is assigned to at least $k + 1$ roles in CR does not exist.

We refer to the above practical example in Section 5, assuming that the roles *Programmer* and *TestEngineer* are mutually exclusive. We should define concept CR_1 and add following sentences into $\mathcal{K}$:

$$\text{CR}_1(Programmer), \text{CR}_1(TestEngineer)$$
$$\geq 2 \text{ assign.CR}_1 \sqsubseteq \bot, \text{CR}_1 \sqsubseteq \text{CRole}$$

If we assign the two roles *Programmer* and *TestEngineer* to the user *Jack* simultaneously:

$$\text{User}(Jack), \text{assign}(Jack, TestEngineer), \text{assign}(Jack, Programmer)$$

It is obvious that the Abox is not consistent. Then following warning will be reported in RACER, and reasoning can not be continued:

```
RACER Exception while retrieving instances: ABox DEV-DEPT is incoherent.
```

6.2   Dynamic Separation of Duty

Dynamic separation of duty (DSOD) refers to restrict the roles activated during a session. If we denote a set of dynamic mutually exclusive roles as CR, a user can be assigned to any roles in CR arbitrarily, but the user can activate at most k roles in CR in a session simultaneously. We still use (CR, k) to define a DSOD policy. For each policy (CR, k), we define a concept CR and another constraint axiom:

$$\geq (k+1)\ \mathsf{activate.CR} \sqsubseteq \bot$$

which means that the user which has activated at least $k + 1$ roles in CR does not exist.

6.3   Role Cardinality Constraint

Role cardinality constraint is used to specify the number of users assigned to or activated a role. Similar to SOD, role cardinality can be differentiated between static and dynamic role cardinality. Static role cardinality specifies the maximum number of users assigned to a role simultaneously, while dynamic role cardinality specifies the maximum number of users activating a role simultaneously.

We introduce the inverse relation of user role assignment "assigned" and add inverse user role assertion for each user role assignment assertion. For example, when assigning the role *Programmer* to *Bob*, we should add the assertion assign(*Bob*, *Programmer*) as well as assigned(*Programmer*, *Bob*).

Given a role rr, if its role cardinality is b, static role cardinality constraint will be expressed as:

$$\geq (b+1)\ \mathsf{assigned.RR} \sqsubseteq \bot$$

Similarly, we need to add the inverse relation of role activation "activated" to express dynamic role cardinality, which can be written as

$$\geq (b+1)\ \mathsf{activated.RR} \sqsubseteq \bot$$

We can also extend $\mathcal{ALCQ}$ by adding the inverse constructor. But this way will increase the computational complexity of reasoning. Moreover, it is unnecessary to define inverse relation for each one. In fact it is easy to add the inverse role assignment assertions and inverse role activation assertions in implementation.

7   Conclusion

The goal of this paper is to demonstrate that expressive description logics are well suited to represent and reason about RBAC. We have provided a formalism of RBAC using the description logic language $\mathcal{ALCQ}$, and demonstrated how to make authorization decision and perform RBAC functions via the description logic reasoner RACER. The query can be done efficiently by taking advantage of the reasoning methods associated to the DLs. We have also represented how to express constraints using $\mathcal{ALCQ}$, including separation of duty and role cardinality constraint. We have showed that the consistency of RBAC with constraints can be checked automatically via RACER. In the future, we will add the negative authorization into RBAC and look for an appropriate solution to handle conflicts in access control.

Acknowledgements. This work was supported by Nation Natural Science Foundation of China (grant numbers 60373002 and 60496322) and by a National Key Basic Research Project of China (2004CB318000). This work was also financially supported by UNU-IIST. We would like to thank Jing Mei and Zhangang Lin for their valuable suggestions on earlier drafts of this paper.

References

1. Sandhu, R., Coyne, E., Feinstein, H., Youman, C.: Role-based access control models. IEEE Computer **29** (1996) 38–47
2. Ferraiolo, D.F., Sandhu, R., Gavrila, S., Kuhn, D.R., Chandramoli, R.: Proposed nist standard for role-based access control. ACM Transactions on Information and System Security (TISSEC) **4** (2001) 224–274
3. Koch, M., Mancini, L.V., Parisi-Presicce, F.: A formal model for role-based access control using graph transformation. In: Proceedings of the 6th European Symposium on Research in Computer Security. (2000) 122–139
4. Koch, M., Mancini, L.V., Parisi-Presicce, F.: A graph-based formalism for rbac. ACM Transactions on Information and System Security (TISSEC) **5** (2002) 332–365
5. Woo, T.Y., Lam, S.S.: Authorization in distributed systems: A new approach. Journal of Computer Security **2** (1993) 107–136
6. Abadi, M., Burrows, M., Lampson, B., Plotkin, G.: A calculus for access control in distributed systems. ACM Transactions on Programming Languages and Systems **15** (1993) 706–734
7. Massacci, F.: Reasoning about security: A logic and a decision method for role-based access control. In: Proceeding of the International Joint Conference on Qualitative and Quantitative Practical Reasoning (ECSQARU/FAPR-97). (1997) 421–435
8. Appel, A.W., Felten, E.W.: Proof-carrying authentication. In: Proceedings of the 6th ACM Conference on Computer and Communications Security, Singapore (1999)
9. Jajodia, S., Samarati, P., Sapino, M., Subrahmanian, V.S.: Flexible support for multiple access control policies. ACM Transactions on Database Systems **26** (2001) 214–260
10. Bacon, J., Moody, K., Yao, W.: A model of oasis role-based access control and its support for active security. ACM Transactions on Information and System Security (TISSEC) **5** (2002) 492–540
11. Bertino, E., Catania, B., Ferrari, E., Perlasca, P.: A logical framework for reasoning about access control models. ACM Transactions on Information and System Security (TISSEC) **6** (2003) 71–127
12. Crescini, V.F., Zhang, Y.: A logic based approach for dynamic access control. In: Proceedings of 17th Australian Joint Conference on Artificial Intelligence (AI 2004), Cairns, Australia (2004)

13. Gligor, V.D., Gavrila, S.I., Ferrailolo, D.: On the formal definition of separation-of-duty policies and their composition. In: Proccedings of IEEE Symposium on Security and Privacy, Oakland, California (1998) 172–185
14. Mossakowski, T., Drouineaud, M., Sohr, K.: A temporal-logic extension of role-based access control covering dynamic separation of duties. In: Proceedings of the 4th International Conference on Temporal Logic. (2003) 83–90
15. Ahn, G.J., Sandhu, R.: Role-based authorization constraints specification. ACM Transactions on Information and System Security (TISSEC) **3** (2000) 207–226
16. Baader, F., McGuinness, D.L., Nardi, D., Patel-Schneider, P.F.: The Description Logic Handbook: Theory, Implementation and Applications. Cambridge University Press (2002)
17. Giacomo, G.D., Lenzerini, M.: A uniform framework for concept definitions in description logics. Journal of Artificial Intelligence Research **6** (1997) 87–110
18. Schmidt-SchauB, M., Smolka, G.: Attributive concept descriptions with complements. Artifical Intelligence **48** (1991) 1–26
19. Haarslev, V., Moller, R.: RACER system description. In: International Joint Conference on Automated Reasoning (IJCAR'2001), Siena, Italy (2001) 18–23
20. Haarslev, V., Moller, R.: Description of the RACER system and its applications. In: International Workshop on Description Logics (DL-2001), Stanford, USA (2001)
21. RICE (RACER Interactive Client Environment),
http://www.b1g-systems.com/ronald/rice/.

Revisiting Failure Detection and Consensus in Omission Failure Environments

Carole Delporte-Gallet[1], Hugues Fauconnier[2], and Felix C. Freiling[3,*]

[1] Institut d'électronique et d'informatique Gaspard-Monge (IGM),
Marne-la-Vallée, France
[2] Laboratoire d'Informatique Algorithmique, Fondements et Applications (LIAFA),
University Paris VII, France
[3] Laboratory for Dependable Distributed Systems,
RWTH Aachen University, Germany

Abstract. It has recently been shown that fair exchange, a security problem in distributed systems, can be reduced to a fault tolerance problem, namely a special form of distributed consensus. The reduction uses the concept of security modules which reduce the type and nature of adversarial behavior to two standard fault-assumptions: message omission and process crash. In this paper, we investigate the feasibility of solving consensus in asynchronous systems in which crash and message omission faults may occur. Due to the impossibility result of consensus in such systems, following the lines of unreliable failure detectors of Chandra and Toueg, we add to the system a distributed device that gives information about the failure of other processes. Then we give an algorithm using this device to solve the consensus problem. Finally, we show how to implement such a device in an asynchronous system using some weak timing assumptions.

1 Introduction

In systems with electronic business transactions, fair exchange is a fundamental problem. In fair exchange, the participating parties start with an item they want to trade for another item. They possess an executable (i.e., machine-checkable) description of the desired item and they know from which party to expect the desired item and which party is expecting their own item. An algorithm that solves fair exchange must ensure three properties: (1) every honest party eventually either delivers its desired item or aborts the exchange (*termination* property). (2) If no party misbehaves and all items match their descriptions then the exchange should succeed (*effectiveness* property). (3) If the desired item of any party does not match its description, then no party can obtain any (useful) information about any other item (*fairness* property). Fair exchange algorithms should guarantee these properties for mutually untrusted parties, i.e., even in the presence of arbitrary (malicious) misbehavior of a subset of participants. Therefore, fair exchange is usually considered a problem in the area of security.

---

* Work by Felix Freiling was performed in part while visiting LIAFA and supported by the French Ministry of Research ACI project FRAGILE.

D.V. Hung and M. Wirsing (Eds.): ICTAC 2005, LNCS 3722, pp. 394–408, 2005.

It has recently been shown [4] that fair exchange, a security problem, can be reduced to a fault-tolerance problem, namely a special form of *consensus*. In the consensus problem, a set of processes must reach agreement on a single value out of a set of values, values which the individual processes have each proposed. The reduction from fair exchange to consensus holds in a model where each participating party is equipped with a tamper proof security module like a smart card. Roughly speaking, the security modules are certified pieces of hardware executing a well-known algorithm so they can establish confidential and authenticated channels between each other. However, since they can only communicate by exchanging messages through their (untrusted) host parties, messages may be intercepted or dropped. Overall, the security modules form a *trusted subsystem* within the overall (untrusted) system. The integrity and confidentiality of the algorithm running in the trusted subsystem is protected by the shield of tamper proof hardware. The integrity and confidentiality of data sent across the network is protected by standard cryptographic protocols. These mechanisms reduce the type and nature of adversarial behavior in the trusted subsystem to message loss and process self-destruction, two standard fault-assumptions known under the names of *omission* and *crash* in the area of fault-tolerance. To summarize, problems from the area of security motivate us to revisit the consensus problem in omission failure environments.

A central assumption for the reduction of fair exchange to consensus to hold is that the system be *synchronous*. A synchronous system has known upper bounds on all important timing parameters of the system like message delivery delay and relative process speeds. Synchronous systems are rare in practice. More common are asynchronous systems, i.e., systems with no or merely uncertain timing guarantees. This holds especially true for systems in which smart cards are used as security modules. Smart cards do not possess any device to reliably measure real-time since they are totally dependent on power supply from their host. If we would like to implement fair exchange using smart cards as security modules, we need an asynchronous consensus algorithm under the assumption of crash and omission faults.

In this paper, we investigate the feasibility of solving consensus in totally asynchronous systems in which crash and message omission faults may occur. Since a result by Fischer, Lynch, and Paterson [11] states that solving consensus deterministically is impossible even if only crash faults can happen, we must strengthen the model so that solutions are possible. We do this using the approach of unreliable failure detectors pioneered by Chandra and Toueg [6]. In this approach, the asynchronous model is augmented with a device that gives information about the failures of other processes. Failure detectors have proven to be a very powerful abstraction of timing assumptions that can express necessary and sufficient conditions for the solvability of problems in the presence of failures. In practice, we want to build a system that solves a certain problem (like consensus). So interesting for practical purposes is the question: What type of failure detector is sufficient to solve that problem? If such a failure detector is found, we only need to implement the failure detector to implement the algorithm in practice, usually reducing the complexity of solving the overall problem substantially. Interesting from a theoretical standpoint is the question: What type of failure detector is necessary to solve a problem? Answers to this question point to the minimum level of timing information which is needed to solve that problem. If only less is available, the problem is impossible to solve.

Here, we focus on the sufficiency part of the question, i.e., what type of failure detector is sufficient to solve consensus in asynchronous systems in which crash and omission faults can occur and what are the timing assumptions needed to solve consensus. Omission faults, meaning that a process drops a message either while sending or while receiving it, were introduced by Hadzilacos [12] and later generalized by Perry and Toueg [16]. We make the following two contributions in this paper:

- We define a new type of failure detector, which we call Ω in analogy to Chandra, Hadzilacos and Toueg [5], and give a protocol that solves consensus in omission failure environments as long as a majority of processes remains fault-free.
- We exhibit a set of weak timing assumptions in the spirit of earlier work [1,3] that allow to implement Ω. More precisely, we show that the existence of some process with which every other process *eventually* can communicate in a timely way is sufficient to implement Ω.

The timing assumptions we exhibit are weaker than any other assumptions proposed up to now for the omission model. They therefore allow to implement consensus, and hence fair exchange, in a larger class of practical systems than before.

This paper is structured as follows: Section 2 introduces the system model, Section 3 specifies the new type of failure detector. Section 4 presents the algorithm to solve consensus using the failure detector from Section 3. Section 5 shows how to implement the failure detector under very weak synchrony assumptions. Finally, Section 6 concludes the paper. For lack of space, some proofs have been omitted and can be found elsewhere [7].

2   Definitions and Model

We model a distributed system by a set of n processes $\Pi = \{p_1, p_2, \ldots, p_n\}$ that communicate using message passing over a network of channels in a fully connected topology. The communication primitives we assume are **send** and **receive**. Communication channels are reliable, i.e., every message sent is eventually received and every received message was previously sent. Processes can be faulty, as explained later.

We assume that the network is asynchronous, i.e., there is neither a bound on the relative process speeds nor on the message delivery delays. This means that while one process takes a single step within the execution of its local algorithm, any other process can take an arbitrary (but finite) number of steps. Also, messages can take an arbitrary (but finite) amount of time to travel from the source to the destination.

2.1   Failure Assumption

There are three ways in which processes can fail: (1) Processes can *crash*, i.e., they stop to execute steps of their local algorithm. Crashed processes never recover. (2) Processes can experience *send omission* failures, i.e., a message which is sent by a process is never placed into the communication channel. (3) Processes can experience *receive omission* failures, i.e., a message which arrives over the communication channel is never actually received by the algorithm of the process. Crash faults model, the usual hardware or operating system crashes, omission faults model overruns of internal I/O buffers within the operating system.

The types of failures result in three distinct failure assumptions:

- the *send omission model*, in which processes can crash and experience only send-omissions (and no receive omissions),
- the *receive omission model* (analogous to the send-omission model), and
- the *send/receive omission model* (sometimes also called *general omission*), in which processes can crash and experience either send-omissions or receive omissions.

A process p is *correct* if it does not make any failure at all, i.e., it never crashes and experiences neither send nor receive omissions. Process p is *crash-correct* if it never crashes. If process p crashes at some time we say it is *crash-faulty*.

Due to the omissions, some processes could be disconnected forever from correct processes. More precisely, we say that process p is *in-connected*, if infinitely often it receives messages from some correct processes. In analogy, we say that process p is *out-connected*, if an infinity of its messages are received by some correct processes. A process is *connected* if it is in-connected and out-connected.

Clearly, in the send-omission failure model every process is in-connected, and in the receive omission failure model every process is out-connected.

2.2   Relations to Crash Model

Transient omissions refer to cases when a process regularly omits a message but equally regularly sends/receives a message over the channel. Such omissions can be masked by piggybacking information about previous messages on every new message sent over a channel.

Since omissions introduce asymmetry in the communication relation, it is also an issue who can communicate with whom. For example, a process with receive omissions may receive messages from a correct process p but may fail to receive messages from another correct process q. We can mask parts of this asymmetry by using the relay algorithm of Figure 1 which defines new primitives **Send** and **Receive**. These primitives ensure that if a process p is in-connected then it receives infinitely often messages from all correct processes. Correspondingly, if a process is out-connected, then infinitely many of its messages are received by all correct processes. However note that the relay algorithm is costly concerning the communication load (each message from p to q generates $2n - 1$ messages).

In the following algorithms we avoid to use this relay algorithm. But it shows that if all crash-correct processes are connected, then by piggybacking old messages and with the relay algorithm all omissions can be masked and the omission

Code for p:

```
1 on receive (m, d) from q
2    if d = p ∧ m not delivered before then Receive m
3    else if d ≠ p then send (m, d) to d

4 to Send(m) to d:
5    send (m, d) to all
```

Fig. 1. Send/Receive with relay

models become equivalent to the crash failure model. Interesting cases arise if not all crash-correct processes are always connected.

2.3 Consensus

We use the standard definition of Uniform Consensus in this paper. The problem is defined using two primitives called *propose* and *decide*, both taking a binary value v. An algorithm solving consensus must satisfy the following properties:

– (Termination) Every correct process eventually decides.
– (Uniform Agreement) No two processes decide differently.
– (Validity) The decided value must have been proposed.

3   Failure Detectors for Omission Failure Environments

In this section we revisit failure detectors in crash environments and give a suitable definition for such a failure detector in omission failure environments.

The definition of failure detectors in the crash model are standard [6] and the literature contains a lot of definitions of failure detectors for crash failures. Among these, the failure detector Ω is particularly interesting: It has been proved to be the weakest failure detector to solve the consensus problem in the crash failure model with a majority of correct processes [5]. The output of Ω for each process p is the identity of one process, the assumed leader for p, such that eventually all correct processes have the same leader forever and this leader is a correct process. Hence Ω implements an *eventual leader election*.

We now extend the definition of failure detector Ω to omission models. In the omission model, the definition of Ω from the crash model would naively translate to an eventual leader election of a *correct* process (i.e., neither does it experience a crash nor any omission). This is generally too restrictive, because it could be impossible to ensure that the chosen eventual leader does not experience permanent omissions. So we consider the following weaker definition:

Definition 1. *Failure detector Ω for omission models is a failure detector that outputs at each time for each process one process, called the leader, such that (1) there is a time after which, this leader is the same forever at all correct processes and (2) this process is crash-correct and connected.*

Note that in contrast to the definition of Ω in the crash model, our definition of Ω allows the eventual leader process to be faulty: The leader may experience send and receive omissions as long as it remains connected.

In the following algorithms the output of the failure detector Ω for process p is given by the value of local variable *Leader*.

4   Solving Consensus

We now show that the failure detector Ω introduced in the previous section is sufficient to solve consensus with a majority of correct processes in the send/receive omission model. Figure 2 depicts our consensus algorithm. It employs the well-known rotating coordinator paradigm, i.e., processes run through asynchronous rounds (counted using the variable r in task 1) and in every such round one process C is chosen as the coordinator. The processes start with v being their proposal value of consensus and spawn three concurrent tasks. In task 0, the coordinator is urged (by using *COORD* messages) to "impose" its value on all processes by sending *ONE* messages (task 1). Processes then evaluate the value they receive from the coordinator (stored in $estfromC$). Unless it comes from the leader (referred to by Ω), a $\perp$ value is stored. In the second part of the algorithm, all processes broadcast their received value to all other processes (*TWO* messages). If such messages are received from a majority of processes, the non-$\perp$ value given in the messages is the decided value and an appropriate decision message is broadcast to all. Task 2 just ensures that eventually all processes who receive the decision message actually do decide.

Proposition 1. *If $Leader_p$ is the output of the failure detector Ω, the algorithm of Figure 2 implements consensus for a majority of correct processes in the send/receive omission model.*

We just give the main lines of the proof here, the full version can be found elsewhere [7]. In the proofs of algorithms, by convention, given a variable x of process p, x_p^τ denotes the value of x in p at time τ.

To prove the proposition, we first state the two following lemmas:

Lemma 1. *If p and q end the first part (lines 13 to 18) of a round r, then:*

(1) if $estFromC_p = x$ for some $x \neq \perp$ then $estFromC_q \in \{\perp, x\}$,

If p and q end line 21 of a round r, then:

(2) if $L_p = \{x\}$ for some $x \neq \perp$ then $L_q = \{x\}$ or $L_q = \{x, \perp\}$,
(3) if $L_p = \{\perp, x\}$ for some $x \neq \perp$ then $L_q = \{x\}$ or $L_q = \{x, \perp\}$ or $L_q = \{\perp\}$.

Lemma 2. *If every process p begins some round r, with variable v equal to the same value d then all processes q ending this round either decide d or have $v_q = d$ at the end of this round.*

Now we show that the algorithm satisfies the properties of consensus.

```
Code for p:
1    Initialization:
2        r := 0                                                    /* round number */
3        v := ⟨proposed value⟩
4    start Task 0 and Task 1 and Task 2
Task 0:
5        upon receive(COORD, *, k) for the first time
6            let (COORD, w, k) be such a message
7            send(ONE, w, k) to all

8        upon receive(ONE, *, k) for the first time from another process
9            let (ONE, w, k) be such a message
10           send(ONE, w, k) to all
Task 1:
11   loop forever
12       C := 1 + r mod n                                          /* coordinator */
13       send(COORD, v, r) to p_C
14       wait until (receive (ONE, *, r) from  p_C) or (p_C ≠ Leader)
15           if (ONE, w, r) is received then
16               estfromC := w
17           else
18               estFromC := ⊥

19       send(TWO, estFromC, r) to all
20       wait until receive(TWO, *, r) from  a majority of processes
21           let L = {w | (TWO, w, r) is received }
22           if L = {rec} for some rec ≠ ⊥ then
23               send (DECIDE, rec) to all
24               decide(rec)
25               halt
26           else
27               if L = {rec, ⊥} for some rec ≠ ⊥ then
28                   v := rec
29       r := r + 1

Task 2:
30       upon received(DECIDE, k) from q
31               send(DECIDE, k) to all
32               decide(k)
33               halt
```

Fig. 2. Consensus algorithm for the send/receive omission model using Ω

Lemma 3. *The algorithm ensures the agreement property.*

Proof. Consider the first time a process, say p, sends a message $(DECIDE, d)$ for some d. By an easy induction, this sending occurs in task 1, say in round r. In this round, after line 21, L_p is $\{d\}$. Let q be any other process ending round r, by Lemma 1, in this round L_q is either $\{d\}$ and q decides in round r, or $\{d, \bot\}$ and q ends the round r with $v = d$.

By Lemma 2 and an easy induction, in every round $r' \geq r$, every process either decides d or ends the round with $v = d$. Hence, all processes which decide in task 1, decide d. If a process decides in task 2, by an easy induction, this decision is issued from a process which has decided in task 1. This proves the agreement property.   □

Lemma 4. *The algorithm ensures the validity property.*

Proof. In the algorithm, all the processes send the values they have just received and by an easy induction they never insert in the algorithm a value of their own.
                                                                               □

Lemma 5. *The algorithm ensures the termination property.*

Proof. If there is no correct process, termination is trivial. If any correct process decides by task 2 or task 1 then clearly all correct processes decide.

Assume that no correct process decides, then we prove that all correct processes participate to an unbounded number of rounds. For this, assume the contrary and let r_0 be the minimal round number in which at least one correct process is blocked forever. Let p be such a process in round r_0:

- p cannot be blocked in Line 14: if the current coordinator p_C is not crash-correct or is not connected, there is a time after which it cannot be leader and then p cannot be blocked. If the current coordinator is crash-correct and connected, by an easy induction p will eventually receive a ONE message from the coordinator.
- p cannot be blocked in Line 20: by an easy induction all correct processes will reach round r and send a TWO message for this round. As there is a majority of correct processes, p will receive a majority of TWO messages.

By the property of the eventual leader election, there is a time τ after which all correct processes have the same leader p_l and this leader is connected. Consider R the set of rounds in which correct processes are at this time τ. Let r_0 be the first round number such that p_l is the coordinator for r_0 and r_0 is greater than all elements of R. When all correct processes are in round r_0, they do not suspect coordinator p_l of the round r_0. Then they adopt for $estFromC$ the value sent by p_l. And so their L set is reduced to one element which is different from $\perp$ and they decide.   □

This concludes the proof of the proposition.

5   Implementing Failure Detectors

In this section we give algorithms to implement eventual leader election in the case of send and send/receive omissions. All these algorithms make some additional assumptions [6,14,2], that are needed if we want to implement consensus deterministically [11]. We also assume that all processes are able to measure time.[1]

---

[1] In fact they can measure time with a very low accuracy: it is sufficient that (1) the time interval measure is not decreasing, (2) for each finite time interval I there is an integer n such that the measure for I is always less than n, and (3) if the measure of interval time I is less than n then I is a finite time interval.

5.1   Partially Synchronous Models and Eventual Leader Election

In the omission models, messages from p to q are not received by q only due to send omissions from p or receive omission from q. Hence all communication links are assumed to be reliable. There is no duplication of messages and every message received has been sent before.

Concerning timeliness, a communication link (p, q) is *eventually timely* if there is a Δ and time τ_0 after which every message sent at time τ by p to q is received by time $\tau + \Delta$. Following previous work [1,3], we define eventual sources and bisources:

Definition 2. *Process p is an* eventual source *if and only if (1) p is a correct process and (2) for all correct processes q, communication link (p, q) is eventually timely. Process p is an* eventual bisource *if and only if (1) p is a source and (2) for all correct processes q, communication link (q, p) is eventually timely.*

Note that if we have at least one eventual bisource in the system, the system is eventually rather synchronous: If all messages are broadcast and relayed one time, as eventually all links from correct processes to the eventual bisource and all the links from this eventual bisource to every correct process are eventually timely, there is a time after which all messages sent by correct processes are received in a timely way by all correct processes. Nevertheless, note that in the partially synchronous model of Dwork, Lynch and Stockmeyer [10], it is assumed that eventually all links between processes are timely. This assumption is strictly stronger than the existence of an eventual bisource in the system. Having an eventual bisource does not exclude that the communication delay between two processes is unbounded if one of these process is faulty but crash-correct. For example, the communication delays from (faulty but crash-correct process) p to (correct process) q are unbounded, if p makes infinitely often send omissions to all processes but q, the communication from p to q (or every other processes to which q could relay messages from p) is not timely.

5.2   Eventual Leader Election

In the following, we assume for the send omission model that there is at least one eventual source and at least one eventual bisource for the send/receive or receive omission model. In these algorithms every process monitors the timeliness of the communication links. For this each process sends "ping" messages regularly and verifies that the messages arrive with a bounded delay. If this is not the case, the origin of the message is suspected to be faulty. But, even if all the ping messages from some process are received, due to the omission model, other messages from this process could not be received. Then in order to simplify the presentation we assume that all messages of the processes are piggybacked in the "ping" messages, in this way, if there is no omission of "ping" messages from p to q then there is no omission of any message from p to q.

Eventual Leader Election in the Send Omission Model. The algorithm in Figure 3 implements Ω for the case of send omission faults under the assumption that there is one eventual source.

In the algorithm, $Timer[q]$ is a special variable that is decremented at each clock tick. When $Timer[q]$ achieves a value equal to zero, we say that $Timer[q]$ expires. The principles of the algorithm are rather simple. Each process maintains a variable δ that is the assumed communication delay. This variable is incremented each time a communication of a process exceeds the assumed communication delay. Each process sends periodically (every η clock ticks) a message to all other processes and maintains a vector V counting the number of times each process p exceeds the assumed communication delay δ. This vector is piggy-backed in each message and each process updates its own vector V accordingly to the received vector (by taking the maximum of the two vectors). In this way, each vector V will evaluate the number of times a process exceeds the assumed communication delay. The leader will be the process having the minimal value in V (in case there is more than one such process, the process with the smallest identity is chosen).

Intuitively, if a process p makes an infinite number of send omission to some out-connected process, then eventually, the $V[p]$ of every out-connected crash-correct process will be unbounded. However, if $V[p]$ is bounded by b for some out-connected crash-correct process, then it will be bounded by b for every out-connected crash-correct process. Then eventually all the $V[p]$ of out-connected crash-correct processes will be equal. Assuming that $V[p]$ is bounded for at least one process, choosing as leader the minimal p with the smallest value in vector V, ensures then that every out-connected crash-correct process eventually chooses p forever.

Then if s is an eventual source, it is straightforward to verify that $V[p]$ is bounded for every crash-correct process ensuring that every crash-correct process eventually chooses forever the same leader.

Note that this leader is not necessarily a correct process: if p makes infinitely often send omission to some process q that is not out-connected, it is possible that p is chosen as leader by all correct processes. In this case, the leader for q could be different from p. However, if there is at least one eventual source in the system, this algorithm implements failure detector Ω:

Proposition 2. *In the algorithm of Figure 3, if there is at least one eventual source then there is a crash-correct out-connected l and a time after which every out-connected process has l as leader. Moreover, all correct processes receive infinitely often messages from l.*

Eventual Leader Election for Send/Receive Omission Models. For the algorithm of Figure 4, we assume that at least a majority of processes are correct and that there is at least one eventual bisource. The principles of this algorithm are similar to the previous one: each process approximates in δ a bound on the communication delay. The main difference here is that processes maintain an array M to count the number of times messages from p to q exceeded the assumed bound. Moreover in order to ensure that the leader is in-connected it penalizes itself if it sees that it does not receive messages in a timely way from a majority of processes.

Initialization:
1 $\delta := 1$
2 **for all** $q : V[q] := 0$
3 **for all** $q : Timer[q] := \delta$

Task 1:
4 **each** η clock ticks
5   **send** V **to all**

Task 2:
6 **on receive** X **from** q
7   **for all** $q : V[q] := \max\{V[q], X[q]\}$
8   **set** $Timer[q]$ **to** δ

Task 3:
9 **on** $Timer[q]$ expired
10     $V[q] := V[q] + 1$
11     $\delta := \delta + 1$
12   **set** $Timer[q]$ **to** δ

Task 4:
13 **forever do**
14        $Leader := \min r$ such that $V[r] := \min\{V[q] | q \in \Pi\}$

Fig. 3. Implementation of Ω in a system with at least one eventual source and a majority of correct processes

As processes may make receive omissions, the value of $M[p, q]$ does not necessarily mean that q has made $M[p, q]$ send omissions, and so the choice of the leader is more intricate. For this, for each process q, we consider all the sets containing a majority of processes and for each such set the maximum value of $M[p, q]$, then the estimate for q is the minimum of these values.

If there is at least one bisource in the system, this algorithm implements Ω:

Proposition 3. *In the Algorithm of Figure 4, if there is at least one eventual bisource there is a crash-correct connected l and a time after which every crash-correct connected process has l as leader.*

We again just give a sketch of the proof: Note first that eventually information from out-connected processes reaches all in-connected and crash-correct processes:

Lemma 6. *If p is out-connected and q is in-connected and crash-correct, then for all τ, there is a time τ' such that $M_p^\tau \leq M_q^{\tau'}$.*

If p is not in-connected and crash-correct, there is a time τ after which p does not receive any message from any correct process, as there is a majority of correct processes after time $\tau + \eta$ strictly less than $n/2$ processes belong to $GoodInputs_p$,

Initialization:

1 $\delta := 1$

2 **for all** $q : Timer[q] := \delta$

3 **for all** $q, r : M[q, r] := 0$

4 $GoodInputs := \emptyset$

Task 1:

5 **each** η clock ticks

6   **if** $(|GoodInput| \leq n/2)$ **then**

7   **for all** $q : M[q, p] := M[q, p] + 1$

8   **send** (M) **to all**

Task 2:

9 **on receive** A **from** q

10   **for all** $x, y : M[x, y] := \max\{M[x, y], A[x, y]\}$

11   **add** q **to** $GoodInputs$

12   **set** $Timer[q]$ **to** δ

Task 3:

13 **on** $Timer[q]$ expired

14   **remove** q **from** $GoodInputs$

15    $M[p, q] := M[p, q] + 1$

16    $\delta := \delta + 1$

17   **set** $Timer[q]$ **to** δ

Task 4:

18 **forever do**

19   **for all** r **do**

20      $V[r] := \min\{\max\{M[q, r]|q \in L\}$ such that $|L| = \lfloor \frac{n}{2} \rfloor + 1\}$

21      $Leader := \min r$ such that $V[r] := \min\{V[q]|q \in \Pi\}$

Fig. 4. Implementation of Ω in a system with at least one eventual bisource and a majority of correct processes

and at each η, p increments for all q $M[q, p]$ and then $\lim_{\tau \to \infty} M_p[q, p] = \infty$ for all q. Then by Lemma 6:

Lemma 7. *If p is crash-correct and not in-connected then for all in-connected and crash-correct processes q and for all r $\lim_{\tau \to \infty} M_q^\tau[r, p] = \infty$.*

If p is crash-faulty or not out-connected, there is a time after which no messages from p are received by correct processes and then for every correct process q $Timer[p]$ expires infinitely often, and $M_q[q, p]$ is incremented infinitely often and $\lim_{\tau \to \infty} M_q^\tau[q, p] = \infty$. By Lemma 6:

Lemma 8. *If p is crash-faulty or not out-connected then for all in-connected and crash-correct q: $\lim_{\tau \to \infty} M_q^\tau[q, p] = \infty$.*

As at least a majority of processes is correct, any subset of more than $n/2$ processes contains at least one correct process, then if p is crash-faulty or not out-connected or not in-connected by the previous lemmas, $\max\{M_q^\tau[r,p]|r \in L$ s.t. $|L| = \lfloor \frac{n}{2} \rfloor + 1\}$ is unbounded for every in-connected and crash-correct process q:

Lemma 9. *If p is crash-faulty or not out-connected or not in-connected then $\lim_{\tau \to \infty} V_q^\tau[p] = \infty$ for every in-connected and crash-correct process q.*

By lemma 6:

Lemma 10. *If $\lim_{\tau \to \infty} V_q^\tau[p] = k$ for some out-connected crash-correct q, then $\lim_{\tau \to \infty} V_r^\tau[p] = k$ for all in-connected crash-correct process r.*

Now let s be an eventual bisource, then there a Δ and a time τ after which, (1) every message sent by a correct process to s and (2) every message sent by s to any correct process p is received within Δ. Then as δ_s is incremented each time a timer expires, there is a time $\tau_s > \tau$ after which every correct process are in $GoodInputs_s$, as there is a majority of correct processes, after time τ_s $|GoodInputs_s| > n/2$ and s will not increment $M_s[p,s]$ for any p. In the same way, there is a time $\tau' > \tau_s$ after which no messages from s will exceed δ_p for any correct process p and then $M_p[p,s]$ will not increase. Then:

Lemma 11. *If s is an eventual bisource then for all in-connected crash-correct process p, $\lim_{\tau \to \infty} V_p^\tau[s] < \infty$.*

Hence, consider the set S of processes q such that for all correct processes p $\lim_{\tau \to \infty} V_p^\tau[q] < \infty$. From Lemma 9, S contains only crash-correct connected processes. By the previous lemma, if there is at least one bisource this set is not empty. By Lemma 10, for every $q \in S$ all the $\lim_{\tau \to \infty} V_p^\tau[q]$ for p correct are equal to, say k_q. Let q_0 be the process belonging to S with minimal identity such that k_q is minimal. It is easy to verify that eventually all correct processes will chose q_0 as leader. This concludes the proof.

6   Comparison with Previous Work and Conclusion

Failure detection and consensus in omission environments have been studied previously in unpublished work by Dolev *et al.* [8,9]. The failure detector $\Diamond S(om)$ which they use to solve consensus is different but rather close in power to our definition of Ω. In contrast to Dolev *et al.* [8,9], we focus on the implementability of that failure detector under weak synchrony assumptions. To the best of our knowledge, our consensus algorithm using Ω is also novel in this model.

Concerning timeliness assumptions enabling to solve consensus, Dwork, Lynch and Stockmeyer [10] proved that consensus is solvable if all correct processes are eventually timely. Other work [2] obtained the same timeliness assumptions as here. Note that in both cases, the authors consider the Byzantine failure model that is strictly stronger than omission faults. Also, these solutions do not use a modular approach with failure detectors.

In this paper we studied consensus in models where processes can crash and experience message omissions. This model was motivated from the area of security problems where omission models can be used to model security problems with smart cards. In this paper we were mainly interested in proving the feasibility of solving consensus in such models, i.e., finding solutions, we were not interested in their efficiency. Hence, most of the algorithms presented here can probably be improved to ensure better performance. For example, in the case of send-omissions and implementation of Ω by algorithm of Figure 3, this algorithm could be improved: In task 0, there is no need to relay the messages ONE because with send-omissions the eventual chosen leader is not only in-connected but already receives infinitely many messages from correct processes.

One interesting open problem is to define the weakest failure detector to solve consensus with omission models, i.e., asking the rather fundamental question on what failure detector is necessary. In particular it is not proved that really the existence of an eventual bisource is needed for receive (and send/receive) omissions models.

The Ω implementation in the send omission model assumes only that there is at least one eventual source in the system, whereas for the receive or send-receive omission model we assume here that there is at least one eventual bisource. We conjecture that in the receive and send-receive omission models an eventual source is not enough.

Another line of future work is to make our "paper and pencil mathematics style" proofs more rigorous and verify them using machine-assisted tools. Previous and ongoing work in the area of fault-tolerant systems is very encouraging [13,15].

References

1. M. Aguilera, C. Delporte-Gallet, H. Fauconnier, and S. Toueg. Stable leader election (extended abstract). In *15th International Symposium on Distributed Computing (DISC)*, LNCS 2180, pages 108–122. Springer-Verlag, 2001.
2. M. Aguilera, C. Delporte-Gallet, H. Fauconnier, and S. Toueg. Communication-efficient leader election and consensus with limited link synchrony. In *23rd ACM Symposium on Principles of Distributed Computing (PODC)*, pages 328–337, St. Johns, Newfoundland, Canada, 2004.
3. M. K. Aguilera, C. Delporte-Gallet, H. Fauconnier, and S. Toueg. On implementing Omega with weak reliability and synchrony assumptions. In *22nd ACM Symposium on Principles of Distributed Computing (PODC)*, pages 306–314, 2003.
4. G. Avoine, F. C. Gärtner, R. Guerraoui, and M. Vukolic. Gracefully degrading fair exchange with security modules. In *In Proceedings of the 5th European Dependable Computing Conference(EDCC)*, pages 55–71, Apr. 2005.
5. T. D. Chandra, V. Hadzilacos, and S. Toueg. The weakest failure detector for solving consensus. *J. ACM*, 43(4):685–722, July 1996.
6. T. D. Chandra and S. Toueg. Unreliable failure detectors for reliable distributed systems. *J. ACM*, 43(2):225–267, Mar. 1996.
7. C. Delporte-Gallet, H. Fauconnier, and F. C. Freiling. Revisiting failure detection and consensus in omission failure environments. Technical Report AIB-2005-13, RWTH Aachen, June 2005.
8. D. Dolev, R. Friedman, I. Keidar, and D. Malkhi. Failure detectors in omission failure environments. Technical Report TR96-1608, Cornell University, Computer Science Department, Sept. 1996.

9. D. Dolev, R. Friedmann, I. Keidar, and D. Malkhi. Failure detectors in omission failure environments (brief announcement). In *16th ACM Symposium on Principles of Distributed Computing (PODC)*, 1997.
10. C. Dwork, N. A. Lynch, and L. Stockmeyer. Consensus in the presence of partial synchrony. *J. ACM*, 35(2):288–323, Apr. 1988.
11. M. J. Fischer, N. A. Lynch, and M. S. Paterson. Impossibility of distributed consensus with one faulty process. *J. ACM*, 32(2):374–382, Apr. 1985.
12. V. Hadzilacos. *Issues of Fault Tolerance in Concurrent Computations*. PhD thesis, Harvard University, 1984. also published as Technical Report TR11-84.
13. Z. Liu and M. Joseph. Specification and verification of fault-tolerance, timing and scheduling. *ACM Transactions on Programming Languages and Systems*, 21(1):46–89, 1999.
14. A. Mostéfaoui, E. Mourgaya, and M. Raynal. Asynchronous implementation of failure detectors. In *Dependable Systems and Networks (DSN)*, pages 351–360. IEEE Computer Society, 2003.
15. U. Nestmann and R. Fuzzati. Unreliable failure detectors via operational semantics. In *Advances in Computing Science - ASIAN 2003 Programming Languages and Distributed Computation, 8th Asian Computing Science Conference*, volume 2896 of *Lecture Notes in Computer Science*, pages 54–71, Mumbai, India, Dec. 2003. Springer-Verlag.
16. K. J. Perry and S. Toueg. Distributed agreement in the presence of processor and communication faults. *IEEE Transactions on Software Engineering*, 12(3):477–482, Mar. 1986.

Congruences and Bisimulations for Continuous-Time Stochastic Logic

Ernst-Erich Doberkat*

Chair for Software Technology, University of Dortmund
ernst-erich.doberkat@udo.edu

Abstract. Continuous stochastic logic (**CSL**) deals with the verification of systems operating in continuous time, it may be traced to the well known tree logic CTL. We propose a probabilistic interpretation of this logic that is based on stochastic relations without making specific assumptions on the underlying distribution, and study the problem of bisimulations in a fairly general context from the viewpoint of congruences for stochastic relations. The goal is finding minimal sets of formulas that permit efficient checking of models.

1 Introduction and Motivation

The logic **CSL** [1] is a stochastic version and variant of the popular logic CTL for model checking. The user is supplied with the usual arsenal of expressions for state formulas, it includes a steady-state operator for modelling asymptotic phenomena, it has the until-, as well as the next-operator, and it has finally a family of path quantifiers that model existential and universal quantification over paths through probabilistic counterparts. The logic has considerable expressive power, as is demonstrated convincingly in [1]. Recently, Desharnais and Panangaden [3] have proposed an interpretation of a fragment of **CSL** over a continuous domain, hereby providing a general framework for the treatment of bisimulations. The originally given interpretation in [1] is based on a finite state space and investigates the computational side of model checking using **CSL**. A comparison with [3] suggests that the wide and well-assorted toolkit provided by probabilities over non-finite state spaces is a welcome addition for investigating the properties of this logic. This is particularly true when it comes to investigating bisimulations. A bisimulation induced by a set F of formulas says that two states are equivalent, provided they behave in the same manner on F (either they both satisfy a formula, or they both don't), and provided the transitions from these states work probabilistically identical on the equivalence classes.

Here the interesting problem arises of determining those states that behave in the same manner, and of factoring the system accordingly. Unfortunately there are infinitely many formulas, so that a direct identification is usually difficult, and one has to investigate ways in which a representing set of formulas can be found: if states behave identical on these representatives, then they will identical on the set of all formulas as well. The bisimulation problem boils down to investigate the problem of identifying such a set. Clearly, a set of formulas yields an equivalence relation on all states by saying the

* Research funded in part by *Deutsche Forschungsgemeinschaft*, grant DO 263/8-1, *Algebraische Eigenschaften stochastischer Relationen*.

D.V. Hung and M. Wirsing (Eds.): ICTAC 2005, LNCS 3722, pp. 409–423, 2005.

two states are equivalent iff they satisfy exactly the same formulas from this set. This very equivalence relation turns out to be the central tool in these investigations: How large can the set of formulas get and still preserve the equivalence relation? This kind of relation has quite an interesting structure the investigation of which will further our understanding of the bisimulation problem.

The present paper observes that [3] does not deal with the full **CSL** but rather with a fragment in which the steady-state operator is missing. It observes structurally that the probabilistic approach is unnecessary restrictive, since the interpretations of **CSL** are based on a rate function. The present paper proposes a more general setting by modelling both, state transitions and transition rates, through stochastic independent probabilistic relations. This permits a more general approach, rendering the probabilistic arguments more transparent. In particular the tools collected from investigating congruences for stochastic relations can be used to some advantage. This requires fitting the probabilistic approach into the framework provided for stochastic relations. This is done explicitly and easily in Section 3, so that we work with a relation between states and paths, i.e., infinite alternating sequences of times and states. Of course, this relation has the rate based relations from [1, 3] as special cases. Given the formulation in terms of transition probabilities, we spend some time for an investigation of sets of infinite paths (Section 3), showing that the sets of states resp. paths in which a formula is valid is measurable indeed. A particular difficulty lies in dealing with those states that satisfy an infinitesimal condition (such as e.g., that the behavior will stabilize asymptotically). Only through showing that these sets are measurable the probabilities for these events to occur could not be computed.

All this preliminary work serves to interpret **CSL** stochastically. This interpretation is introduced in Section 4 by defining the semantics of **CSL**-formulas. Section 5 defines the class of smooth equivalence relations. The class of these relations is well known in the theory of Borel sets.

This leads quite naturally to the investigation of congruences for stochastic relations, and the set of formulas which we need to investigate lead to congruences. Thus subsets of **CSL** and congruences for investigating them are quite intertwined; what happens exactly there is investigated in Section 6 from a rather algebraic point of view. The discussion provides the tools for answering the questions we did start with: given two states x and x' that satisfy the same formulas from a set F of **CSL**-formulas, can we say whether or not they satisfy the same formulas in $\mathsf{cl}(F)$, where $\mathsf{cl}(F)$ is the smallest set of formulas that contains F, and that is closed under the logic's operators? Can we say that for particularly easily described formulas, viz., the atomic propositions AP? Unfortunately, the answer to the latter question is less clearly cut than one would expect (or hope: $\mathsf{cl}(AP)$ is the set of all formulas); criteria for answering the last question are derived. The paper closes in Section 7 with a look at possible further developments which may be pursued. Lack of space prevents giving always complete proofs; the reader is referred to the full paper [6] for a complete discussion.

Related Work. This paper is a companion and an extension to [3]. It extends the latter paper by taking a considerably more general probabilistic approach, by treating the full logic, and by a systematic use of congruences as a tool for investigating the problems at hand.

2   The Logic CSL

Fix AP as a countable set of atomic propositions. We define recursively state formulas and path formulas for **CSL**:

State formulas are defined through the syntax

$$\phi ::= \top \mid a \mid \neg\phi \mid \phi \wedge \phi' \mid \mathcal{S}_{\bowtie p}(\phi) \mid \mathcal{P}_{\bowtie p}(\psi)$$

Here $a \in AP$ is an atomic proposition, ψ is a path formula, $\bowtie$ is one of the relational operators $<, \leq, \geq, >$, and $p \in [0, 1]$ is a rational number.

Path formulas are defined through

$$\psi ::= \mathcal{X}^I \phi \mid \phi \mathcal{U}^I \phi'$$

with ϕ, ϕ' as state formulas, $I \subseteq \mathbb{R}_+$ a closed interval of the non-negative real numbers $\mathbb{R}_+$ with rational bounds (including $I = \mathbb{R}_+$ itself).

We denote the set of all state formulas by $\mathfrak{L}_{AP}$.

The operator $\mathcal{S}_{\bowtie p}(\phi)$ gives the *steady-state probability* for ϕ to hold with the boundary condition $\bowtie p$; the formula $\mathcal{P}$ replaces quantification: the *path-quantifier* formula $\mathcal{P}_{\bowtie p}(\psi)$ holds for a state x iff the probability of all paths starting in x and satisfying ψ is specified by $\bowtie p$. Thus ψ holds on all paths starting from x iff x satisfies $\mathcal{P}_{\geq 1}(\psi)$, a path being an alternating infinite sequence $\sigma = \langle x_0, t_0, x_1, t_1, \ldots \rangle$ of states x_i and of times t_i. The *next-operator* $\mathcal{X}^I \phi$ is assumed to hold on path σ iff x_1 satisfies ϕ, and $t_0 \in I$ holds. Finally, the *until-operator* $\phi_1 \mathcal{U}^I \phi_2$ holds on path σ iff we can find a point in time $t \in I$ such that the state $\sigma@t$ which σ occupies at time t satisfies ϕ_2, and for all times t' before that, $\sigma@t'$ satisfies ϕ_1. Paths and operators on them will be discussed more formally in Section 4.

3   Paths: Probabilities and Measurability

This section collects some of the preparatory work that needs to be done for interpreting **CSL** probabilistically. We will define the probabilistic model as a stochastic relation between states and alternating sequences of times and states. It will be shown that the usual model which is based on rate functions and the exponential distribution is a special case, and it will turn out during the course of the present discussion that many properties which are derived with the specific, exponentially based model in mind hold also in the more general framework.

We fix throughout this paper X as the set of states; X is assumed to be an analytic space, i.e. the Borel image of a Polish space. Polish spaces in turn are topological spaces with a countable dense subset which are metrizable as complete spaces. Recall that a *stochastic relation* $K : X_1 \rightsquigarrow X_2$ between two analytic spaces X_1 and X_2 assigns to each $x_1 \in X_1$ a probability measure $K(x_1)$ on (the Borel sets of) X_2 so that $x_1 \mapsto K(x_1)(B_2)$ constitutes a Borel measurable function on X_1 for each $B_2 \in \mathcal{B}(X_2)$.

We will assume that we work with a family $(K_n)_{n \in \mathbb{N}}$ of stochastic relations $K_n : X \rightsquigarrow X$, so that at the discrete time-point $n \in \mathbb{N}$ the state transitions are governed by

K_n, hence $K_n(x)(D)$ is interpreted as the probability that the new state in step $n + 1$ is a member of the Borel set $D \subseteq X$, provided the state at step n is x. In a similar way we assume that we have a family $(L_n)_{n \in \mathbb{N}}$ of stochastic relations $L_n : X \rightsquigarrow \mathbb{R}_+$ which gives the time in which transitions are triggered: suppose the system is at n in state x, then $L_n(x)([s, t])$ is the probability that jumping from x to another state occurs within the time interval $[s, t]$. Changes of state and times of change are stochastically independent.

Observation 1. The usual approach to interpreting continuous time Markov chains runs via a rate function [1] which is adapted to the case of continuous state spaces through a transition measure [3]. Assume that R represents the rate, then

1. $\forall x \in X : R(x)$ is a finite measure on X such that $E(x) := R(x)(X) > 0$ always holds,
2. $\forall B \in \mathcal{B}(X) : x \mapsto R(x)(B)$ is a measurable function $X \to \mathbb{R}_+$.

The rate function models the transition rate: if the system is in state x, then the transition rate for jumping to a new state that is a member of the Borel set $D \subseteq X$ is given by $R(x)(D)$. This transition rate is assumed to be finite. We also assume in the rate model that there is no blind state, so transitions are assumed to be possible from all states, thus $E(x) > 0$.

Put $K(x)(D) := R(x)(D) \cdot E(x)^{-1}$ and set for the probability of making a transition from state x within t time units $L(x)([0, t]) := 1 - e^{-E(x) \cdot t}$, then $L(x)(F) = E(x)^{-1} \cdot \int_F e^{-E(x) \cdot t} \, dt$ is also independent of n. Consequently, the approach discussed here fits into the usual set up to model continuous time Markov processes, and even generalizes it. —

Fix a state $x \in X$, and proceed inductively: Put $M_1(x) := L_1(x) \otimes K_1(x)$, and set in the inductive step for the Borel set $D \subseteq (\mathbb{R}_+ \times X)^{n+1}$

$$M_{n+1}(x)(D) := \int_{(\mathbb{R}_+ \times X)^n} (L_{n+1}(\pi_{n,X}(\mathbf{w})) \otimes K_{n+1}(\pi_{n,X}(\mathbf{w})) (D_{\mathbf{w}}) \, M_n(x)(d\mathbf{w}),$$

where $D_{\mathbf{w}} := \{\langle t', x' \rangle \mid \langle \mathbf{w}, t', x' \rangle \in D\}$ is the set of all times and states $\langle t', x' \rangle$ such that $\langle \mathbf{w}, t', x' \rangle$ is a member of D, and $\pi_{n,X}(\mathbf{w})$ is just the nth state component of $\mathbf{w}$.

Analyzing the expression, we see that at time $n + 1$ the probability that the pair of timing a transition and changing a state is an element of $D_{\mathbf{w}}$ is computed from the product measure $(L_{n+1}(x_n) \otimes K_{n+1}(x_n)) (D_{\mathbf{w}})$, provided the corresponding times and states that have been run through during steps $1, \ldots, n$ is $\mathbf{w}$ which is captured through $M_n(x)(d\mathbf{w})$ with $x_n := \pi_{n,X}(\mathbf{w})$ as the last state.

Standard arguments show that $M_n : X \rightsquigarrow (\mathbb{R}_+ \times X)^n$ is a stochastic relation which renders the probability for alternating paths of times and states of length n given an initial state. This probability will be extended to infinite paths now.

Lemma 1. *There exists a unique stochastic relation* $M : X \rightsquigarrow (\mathbb{R}_+ \times X)^\infty$ *such that* $M(x)(A \times \prod_{j>n}(\mathbb{R}_+ \times X)) = M_n(x)(A)$ *for each* $A \in \mathcal{B}((\mathbb{R}_+ \times X)^n)$.

We will use this construction for an investigation of path probabilities, because $M(x)(A)$ is the probability for an infinite alternating path constructed from states and transition times that starts at state x to be in the Borel set $A \in \mathcal{B}((\mathbb{R}_+ \times X)^\infty)$. The construction proposed in [1, Section 3.2] and in [3, Definition 3.1] works a wee bit different: it starts with an initial probability π on X and constructs a measure M_π^* on $\mathcal{B}(X \times (\mathbb{R}_+ \times X)^\infty)$, only to specialize π to δ_x, the Dirac measure on x. It is easy to see that $M_{\delta_x}^* = M(x)$, and that vice versa

$$M_\pi^*(A) = \int_X M(x)(A)\, \pi(dx)$$

holds for $A \in \mathcal{B}((\mathbb{R}_+ \times X)^\infty)$. Which way to chose is a matter of taste and of convenience: The approach proposed here makes it easier to use the tools from stochastic relations, as we will see soon.

Let's talk about paths: The logic has path formulas, which will of course be interpreted on paths. A path σ is an element of the set PATHS $:= (X \times \mathbb{R}_+)^\infty$. Path $\sigma = \langle x_0, t_0, x_1, t_1, \ldots \rangle$ is sometimes written as $x_0 \xrightarrow{t_0} x_1 \xrightarrow{t_1} \ldots$ and given the interpretation that t_i is the time spent in state x_i. Given $i \in \mathbb{N}$, denote x_i by $\sigma[i]$ as the $(i+1)$st state of σ, and let $\delta(\sigma, i) := t_i$. Let for $t \in \mathbb{R}_+$ the index i be the smallest index k such that $t < \sum_{i=0}^{k} t_i$, and put $\sigma @ t := \sigma[i]$, if i is defined; set $\sigma @ t := \#$, otherwise (here $\#$ is a new symbol not in $X \cup \mathbb{R}_+$). $X_\#$ denotes $X \cup \{\#\}$; this is an analytic space again (and will be briefly needed only in Lemma 2). The definition of $\sigma @ t$ differs slightly from the one employed by [1]: while that paper takes the smallest index k with $t \le \sum_{i=0}^{k} t_i$, we take in accordance with [3] strict inequality. This has technical reasons which are based on the observation that for any time t we can find a rational time t' with $\sigma @ t = \sigma @ t'$.

We will deal only with infinite paths. This is no loss of generality because events that happen at a certain time with probability 0 will have the effect that the corresponding infinite paths occur only with probability 0. Thus we do not prune the path; this makes the notation somewhat easier to handle without losing anything.

The following Lemma looks innocent, but will turn out as an important device:

Lemma 2. $\langle \sigma, t \rangle \mapsto \sigma @ t$ *is a Borel measurable map from* PATHS $\times \mathbb{R}_+$ *to* $X_\#$. *In particular, the set* $\{\langle \sigma, t \rangle \mid \sigma @ t \in X\}$ *is a measurable subset of* PATHS $\times \mathbb{R}_+$.

We obtain from this the measurability of some sets and maps which will be important for the later development. A notational convention will be observed: the letter σ will always denote a generic element of PATHS, and the letter τ always a generic element of $\mathbb{R}_+ \times$ PATHS, while $t \in \mathbb{R}_+$ is a typical time.

Proposition 1. *We observe the following properties:*

1. $\{\sigma \mid \sum_{i \ge 0} \delta(\sigma, i) \text{ is finite}\}$ *is a measurable subset of* PATHS,
2. $\{\langle \sigma, t \rangle \mid \overline{\lim}_{i \to \infty} \delta(\sigma, i) = t\}$ *is a measurable subset of* PATHS $\times \mathbb{R}_+$,
3. *For each Borel set* $A \subseteq X$, $x \mapsto \liminf_{t \to \infty} M(x)(\{\tau \mid \langle x, \tau \rangle @ t \in A\})$ *and* $x \mapsto \limsup_{t \to \infty} M(x)(\{\tau \mid \langle x, \tau \rangle @ t \in A\})$ *are measurable maps* $X \to \mathbb{R}_+$.

As a consequence we obtain that the set on which the asymptotic behavior of the transition times is reasonable in the sense that it tends probabilistically to a limit is well behaved in terms of measurability:

Corollary 1. *Let $A \subseteq X$ be a Borel set, then*

1. *The set $Q_A := \{x \in X \mid \lim_{t \to \infty} M(x)(\{\tau \mid \langle x, \tau \rangle @t \in A\})$ exists$\}$ on which the limit exists is a Borel subset of X,*
2. *$x \mapsto \lim_{t \to \infty} M(x)(\{\tau \mid \langle x, \tau \rangle @t \in A\}$ is a measurable map $Q_A \to \mathbb{R}_+$.*

Using these results one can prove for example that the set of all Zeno paths (i.e., the set of all paths the timing information of which is summable to a finite sum) constitutes a set of measure zero provided the probabilities given by $(L_n)_{n \in \mathbb{N}}$ are uniformly bounded. The reader is referred to [1], and to the full paper [6] for a discussion.

4   Interpreting the Logic

Now that we know how to describe the behavior of paths probabilistically, we are ready for a probabilistic interpretation of **CSL**. This is done using the sequences $(K_n)_{n \in \mathbb{N}}$ and $(L_n)_{n \in \mathbb{N}}$, from which the stochastic relation $M : X \rightsquigarrow \mathbb{R}_+ \times$ PATHS has been constructed. The interpretations for the formulas are established, and we show that the sets of states resp. paths on which formulas are valid are Borel measurable.

To get started on the formal definition of the semantics, we assume that we know for each atomic proposition which state it is satisfied in, so we fix a map $\mathbf{L} : AP \to \mathcal{B}(X)$.

The semantics is then described recursively through relation $\models$ between states resp. paths, and formulas as follows:

1. $x \models \top$ is true for all $x \in X$.
2. $x \models a$ iff $x \in \mathbf{L}(a)$, provided a is an atomic expression.
3. $x \models \phi_1 \wedge \phi_2$ iff $x \models \phi_1$ and $x \models \phi_2$.
4. $x \models \neg \phi$ iff $x \models \phi$ is false.
5. $x \models S_{\bowtie p}(\phi)$ iff $\lim_{t \to \infty} M(x)(\{\tau \mid \langle x, \tau \rangle @t \models \phi\})$ exists and is $\bowtie p$.
6. $x \models \mathcal{P}_{\bowtie p}(\psi)$ iff $M(x)(\{\tau \mid \langle x, \tau \rangle \models \psi\}) \bowtie p$.
7. $\sigma \models \mathcal{X}^I \phi$ iff $\sigma[1] \models \phi$ and $\delta(\sigma, 0) \in I$.
8. $\sigma \models \phi_1 \mathcal{U}^I \phi_2$ iff $\exists t \in I : \sigma @t \models \phi_2$ and $\forall t' \in [0, t[: \sigma @t' \models \phi_1$.

Denote by $[\![\phi]\!]$ the set of all states for which the state formula ϕ holds, resp. the set of all paths for which the path formula ϕ is valid. We do not distinguish notationally between these sets, as far as the basic domains are concerned, since it should always be clear whether we describe a state formula or a path formula.

We show that we have measurable sets before us. The until-operator requires some attention, thus we single it out, before diving into a general discussion on measurability again.

Lemma 3. *Assume that A_1 and A_2 are Borel subsets of X, and $I \subseteq \mathbb{R}_+$ be an interval, then $U(I, A_1, A_2) \in \mathcal{B}(\text{PATHS})$, where*
$$U(I, A_1, A_2) := \{\sigma \mid \exists t \in I : \sigma @t \in A_2 \wedge \forall t' \in [0, t[: \sigma @t' \in A_1\}.$$

Proof. Remember that, given a path σ and a time $t \in \mathbb{R}_+$ there exists a rational time $t' \leq t$ with $\sigma @t = \sigma @t'$. Consequently, $U(I, A_1, A_2)$ equals the countable union $\bigcup_{t \in \mathbb{Q} \cap I} \left(\{\sigma \mid \sigma @t \in A_1\} \cap \bigcap_{t' \in \mathbb{Q} \cap [0, t]}\{\sigma \mid \sigma @t' \in A_2\}\right)$. The inner intersection is countable and is performed over measurable sets by Lemma 2, thus forms a measurable set of paths. Intersecting it with a measurable set and forming a countable union yields a measurable set again.   ⊣

This is the crucial step towards establishing

Proposition 2. *The set* $[\![\phi]\!]$ *is Borel, whenever* ϕ *is a state formula or a path formula.*

Proof. The proof proceeds by induction on the structure of the formula ϕ. The induction starts with the formula $\top$, for which the assertion is true, and with the atomic propositions, for which the assertion follows from the assumption on L: $[\![a]\!] = \mathbf{L}(a) \in \mathcal{B}(X)$. Assuming for the induction step that we have established that $[\![\phi]\!]$ is Borel measurable we will focus here on the steady state behavior. The until-operator is treated easily through Lemma 3, the other cases are quite straightforward, see [6]. Put $\ell_\phi(x) := \lim_{t\to\infty} M(x)(\{\tau \mid \langle x, \tau \rangle @t \in [\![\phi]\!]\})$, then we infer from Corollary 1 that the set $Q_{[\phi]} := \{x \in X \mid \ell_\phi(x) \text{ exists}\}$ is a Borel set, and that ℓ_ϕ constitutes a Borel measurable function on $Q_{[\phi]}$. Consequently, $[\![S_{\bowtie p}(\phi)]\!] = \{x \in Q_{[\phi]} \mid \ell_\phi(x) \bowtie p\}$ is a Borel set.   ⊣

Measurability of the sets on which a given formula is valid is of course a prerequisite for computing interesting properties. So we can compute e.g.

$$\mathcal{P}_{\geq 0.5}((\neg down)\, \mathcal{U}^{[10,20]}\, \mathcal{S}_{\geq 0.8}(up_2 \vee up_3)))$$

as the set of all states that with probability at least 0.5 will reach a state between 10 and 20 time units so that the system is operational ($up_2, up_3 \in AP$) in a steady state with a probability of at least 0.8; prior to reaching this state, the system must be operational continuously ($down \in AP$) [1, p. 529]. This set can be computed recursively from its components, given the semantics of the logic; for X finite, algorithms for its computation are investigated in [1].

5 Congruences

Suppose that we have a set F of state formulas, then F induces an equivalence relation on the set of states. It would be tremendously practical if one could deduce from the behavior of the states on F properties that holds for the system as a whole. Consider e.g. $F = AP$, then validity for a given state can be decided upon inspection of L. Before going deeper into this issue, we need smooth equivalence relations as a tool from the theory of Borel sets. We will define smooth equivalence relations, and investigate some of their helpful properties. It will become apparent that the notion of an invariant Borel set is quite central to the discussions that will be undertaken later, so we study the σ-algebra of these sets. We use a somewhat surprising property of invariant sets: they uniquely determine the equivalence relation from which they stem, which means that whenever we know the invariant sets, we are able to identify the relation. This will be most helpful later on.

The reader may have wondered why we work in the context of analytic spaces, given that analyticity did not really have an impact for the constructions undertaken so far. This is true: All constructions until now could have been carried out in general measurable spaces. But the notion of a smooth equivalence relation is not particular fruitful in these general spaces, so from now on the assumption of working in an analytic space will become instrumental.

Definition 1. *An equivalence relation ρ on X is called* smooth *iff there exists a sequence $(A_n)_{n\in\mathbb{N}}$ of Borel set in X such that $x \rho x' \Leftrightarrow [\forall n \in \mathbb{N} : x \in A_n \Leftrightarrow x' \in A_n]$. The relation ρ is said to be* determined *by $(A_n)_{n\in\mathbb{N}}$.*

Smooth relations are a helpful tool for the theory of Borel sets [8], for the theory of stochastic relations [5], and, indirectly, for the theory of labelled Markov transition systems [2, 4].

Let ρ be a smooth equivalence relation, denote as usual the equivalence class of $x \in X$ by $[x]_\rho$ and by $\eta_\rho : X \rightarrow X/\rho$ the factor map. Invariant Borel sets will be at the core of the discussion:

Definition 2. *A Borel set A is called ρ-invariant iff $A = \bigcup\{[x]_\rho \mid x \in X\}$, thus $x \in A, x \rho x'$ together imply $x' \in A$. Denote by $\mathcal{INV}(\mathcal{B}(X), \rho)$ the set of all ρ-invariant Borel sets.*

It is well known [8, Lemma 3.1.6] that $\mathcal{INV}(\mathcal{B}(X), \rho)$ forms a σ-algebra, and that $\mathcal{INV}(\mathcal{B}(X), \rho)$ equals $\sigma(\{A_n \mid n \in \mathbb{N}\})$, provided the sequence $(A_n)_{n\in\mathbb{N}}$ determines ρ. The identity relation Δ_X and the universal relation U_X are always smooth equivalence relations. The invariant Borel sets are easy determined: It is not difficult to see that $\mathcal{INV}(\mathcal{B}(X), \Delta_X) = \mathcal{B}(X)$ and $\mathcal{INV}(\mathcal{B}(X), U_X) = \{\emptyset, X\}$.

Invariant Borel sets have some interesting properties:

Lemma 4. *Let ρ be a smooth equivalence relation, then*

1. *X/ρ is an analytic space the Borel sets of which are the final σ-algebra with respect to $\eta_\rho : X \rightarrow X/\rho$.*
2. *The ρ-invariant Borel sets on X are the inverse image of $\mathcal{B}(X/\rho)$ under η_ρ, thus $\mathcal{INV}(\mathcal{B}(X), \rho) = \eta_\rho^{-1}[\mathcal{B}(X/\rho)]$.*
3. *If $C \subseteq \mathcal{B}(X)$ is a countably generated sub-σ-algebra of the Borel sets of X, then there exists a unique smooth equivalence relation ρ_C on X with $C = \mathcal{INV}(\mathcal{B}(X), \rho_C)$.*

Let us have a look at what Lemma 4 entails. The first property is structurally important: it says that factoring through a smooth relation keeps us within the realm of analytic spaces, and it gives a specific procedure telling us how to construct the Borel sets on this analytic space. Polish spaces do not have this property. This is why analytic spaces, being more robust, are of interest here. The second property states that if we take an arbitrary ρ-invariant Borel set $B' \in \mathcal{INV}(\mathcal{B}(X), \rho)$, then we always find a Borel set $B_0 \subseteq X/\rho$ with $B' = \eta_\rho^{-1}[B_0]$. The third property indicates that the equivalence relation is uniquely determined by its invariant sets, thus if we can infer that two smooth equivalence relations have the same invariant sets, then we may conclude that these equivalences coincide. We will investigate below equivalence relations which are defined by a set F of formulas, and through the property 3 in Lemma 4 we are provided with considerable degrees of freedom for selecting a generating set of formulas. This will be capitalized upon later.

For technical reasons we will need to construct the countable product of equivalence relations, and it will be important that smoothness is preserved; the invariant sets of the product relation can be characterized in terms of the individual components.

Lemma 5. *Assume that* $(H_n)_{n\in\mathbb{N}}$ *is a sequence of analytic spaces, and let* ζ_n *be a smooth equivalence relation on* H_n *for each* $n \in \mathbb{N}$. *Define the equivalence relation* $(\times_{n\in\mathbb{N}}\zeta_n)$ *through* $(a_n)_{n\in\mathbb{N}} (\times_{n\in\mathbb{N}}\zeta_n) (a'_n)_{n\in\mathbb{N}}$ *iff* $\forall n \in \mathbb{N} : a_n \zeta_n a'_n$. *Then* $\times_{n\in\mathbb{N}}\zeta_n$ *is a smooth equivalence relation on* $\prod_{n\in\mathbb{N}} H_n$, *and* $\mathcal{INV}\left(\mathcal{B}(\prod_{n\in\mathbb{N}} H_n), \times_{n\in\mathbb{N}}\zeta_n\right) = \bigotimes_{n\in\mathbb{N}}\mathcal{INV}\left(\mathcal{B}(H_n),\zeta_n\right)$.

Thus the $(\times_{n\in\mathbb{N}}\zeta_n)$-invariant Borel sets of the product are just the product of the Borel sets for the components. A finite version is available as well: the product of two smooth equivalence relations is smooth again, and the invariant Borel sets for the product are just the product of the Borel sets for the factors.

Now let V, W be analytic spaces, and $G : V \rightsquigarrow W$ a stochastic relation. Then equivalent behavior is described by a congruence, which is a pair (α, β) of smooth equivalence relations with the following property: if two inputs v and v' cannot be separated through α, then $G(v)$ and $G(v')$ behave in the same way on those Borel sets of W that cannot be separated through β. Here a set B cannot be separated through β iff $w \in B$ and $w\,\beta\,w'$ together imply $w' \in B$, hence iff B is β-invariant. This leads to

Definition 3. *The pair* (α, β) *of smooth equivalence relations on* V *resp.* W *is said to be a* congruence *for the stochastic relation* $G : V \rightsquigarrow W$ *iff the following holds* $v \alpha v'$ *implies* $G(v)(B) = G(v')(B)$ *for each* β-invariant Borel subset $B \subseteq W$. *If* $V = W$, *and* $\alpha = \beta$, *then* α *alone is called a congruence for* G.

Let (α, β) be a congruence for $G : V \rightsquigarrow W$, and define $G_{\alpha,\beta}([v]_\alpha)(D) := G(v)(\eta_\beta^{-1}[D])$ for $v \in A$ and $D \in \mathcal{B}(W/\beta)$, then it can be shown that $G_{\alpha,\beta} : V/\alpha \rightarrow W/\beta$ is a stochastic relation, and that the pair of factor maps $(\eta_\alpha, \eta_\beta)$ constitutes a morphism, see [5]. We will use this construction for a special case when we define bisimulations induced by sets of formulas in Section 6.

We will assume for the rest of the paper that both K_n and L_n are independent of n, so that we work with K resp. L instead. Thus the probabilities for a transition and those governing the time for staying in a state are independent of the step in which we are considering the system. This assumption is still considerably more general than the rate model in [1, 3].

As a first consequence of making the basic probabilities independent of step n we obtain a recursive formulation for the transition law $M : X \rightsquigarrow (\mathbb{R}_+ \times X)^\infty$ that reflects the domain equation $(\mathbb{R}_+ \times X)^\infty = (\mathbb{R}_+ \times X) \times (\mathbb{R}_+ \times X)^\infty$.

Lemma 6. *If* $D \in \mathcal{B}((\mathbb{R}_+ \times X)^\infty)$, *then*

$$M(x)(D) = \int_{\mathbb{R}_+ \times X} M(x')(D_{\langle t,x'\rangle})\, M_1(x)(d\langle t, x'\rangle)$$

holds for all states $x \in X$.

This decomposition indicates that we may first select in state x a new state and a transition time; with these data the system then works just as if the selected new state would have been the initial state. New states and transition times are being averaged over. Lemma 6 may accordingly be interpreted as a Markov property for a process the behavior of which is independent of the specific first step.

6   Bisimulations

Returning to the logic, fix a set F of state formulas, and define the — central — equivalence relation $x \, \rho_F \, x' \Leftrightarrow \forall \phi \in F : [x \models \phi \Leftrightarrow x' \models \phi]$, then ρ_F is smooth due to F being countable. We will investigate in this Section the equivalence ρ_F. First, the closure $\mathsf{cl}(F)$ of F will be defined as the smallest set of formulas containing F and being closed under the logic's operators, and it will be investigated under which conditions $\rho_{\mathsf{cl}(F)} = \rho_F$ holds. An answer to this question makes life easier, since testing satisfaction only on F is presumably much easier than testing on $\mathsf{cl}(F)$, in particular when $F = AP$ (so that $\mathsf{cl}(F) = \mathfrak{L}_{AP}$). We will examine an enabling condition, using smooth equivalence relations and congruences as the decisive tool. This leads to a discussion of bisimulations, the results obtained for congruences will be transported for an investigation of bisimilar states. Conditions under which AP-bisimilarity and the satisfaction of the same formulas will be formulated at the end of this Section.

Definition 4. *The closure* $\mathsf{cl}(F)$ *of* F *is defined as the smallest set of formulas in* $\mathfrak{L}_{AP}$ *which contains* F *and is closed under the defining operations for the logic.*

Thus we start in building up F-formulas from elements of F as the base, just as we started building up $\mathfrak{L}_{AP}$ from the set AP of atomic propositions. Observe that $\mathsf{cl}(AP) = \mathfrak{L}_{AP}$. We will investigate the smooth relations ρ_F and $\rho_{\mathsf{cl}(F)}$ and will establish that under a mildly restrictive condition $\rho_F = \rho_{\mathsf{cl}(F)}$ holds. This result looks rather modest, but it has some interesting consequences in terms of bisimulations which will be discussed right away.

The mild condition that will enable us to establish the relations' equality was detected by Desharnais and Panagaden in [3] for their fragment.

Definition 5. *A set* F *of formulas is said to satisfy the* **DP-condition** *iff* F *has these properties:* F *is closed under conjunctions, and* $\mathcal{P}_{\bowtie p}(\mathcal{X}^I \, \phi) \in F$ *whenever* $\phi \in F, p \in [0, 1]$ *rational,* $I \subseteq \mathbb{R}_+$ *a closed interval with rational endpoints.*

Closedness under conjunction is a technical condition that will enable us to carry a property from a set of generators to the σ-algebra generated from it, in the present case from $\{[\![\phi]\!] \mid \phi \in F\}$ to $\mathcal{INV}\left(\mathcal{B}(X), \rho_F\right)$. Closedness under the next operator will have a special consequence, as we will see in a moment.

The DP-condition makes sure that the probabilities for a transition of ρ_F-equivalent states into a state in which a formula in F is valid are identical. This is quite comparable to the observation one makes for stochastic Kripke models for modal logics: there it can be shown that the probabilities for making a move into a state in which the same formula is satisfied after an action coincide for equivalent states as well, see [2, 4].

Lemma 7. *If $x \, \rho_F \, x'$ and $\phi \in F$, then $K(x)(\llbracket \phi \rrbracket) = K(x')(\llbracket \phi \rrbracket)$, provided F satisfies the DP-condition.*

Proof. Suppose that we find for $x \, \rho_F \, x'$ a formula $\phi' \in F$ such that $K_1(x)(\llbracket \phi' \rrbracket) < r \leq K_1(x')(\llbracket \phi' \rrbracket)$, where r may be assumed to be rational. Since

$$\{\tau \mid \langle x, \tau \rangle \models \mathcal{X}^{\mathbb{R}+} \, \phi'\} = (\mathbb{R}_+ \times \llbracket \phi' \rrbracket) \times (\mathbb{R}_+ \times X)^\infty,$$

we conclude that $K_1(x)(\llbracket \phi' \rrbracket) = M(x)(\{\tau \mid \langle x, \tau \rangle \models \mathcal{X}^{\mathbb{R}+} \, \phi'\})$. But this implies that $x \models \mathcal{P}_{<r}(\mathcal{X}^{\mathbb{R}+} \, \phi')$, similarly, $x' \not\models \mathcal{P}_{<r}(\mathcal{X}^{\mathbb{R}+} \, \phi')$. But the DP-condition implies that $\mathcal{P}_{<r}(\mathcal{X}^{\mathbb{R}+} \, \phi') \in F$, which is a contradiction.   ⊣

This Lemma is actually a first step towards establishing that ρ_F generates a congruence for M. This requires an extension of the equivalence relation ρ_F on X to $(\mathbb{R}_+ \times X)^\infty$. The basic idea is to relate the alternating states in such a sequence through ρ_F, and to leave the times alone, hence to relate them through the identity relation $\Delta_{\mathbb{R}_+}$. Thus $\langle t_0, x_1, t_1, \ldots \rangle$ will be related to $\langle t'_0, x'_1, t'_1, \ldots \rangle$ iff $x_i \, \rho_F \, x'_i$ and $t_i = t'_i$ for all indices i. In view of Lemma 5 we form the product relation $\rho_F^{(\infty)} := \times_{n \in \mathbb{N}} (\Delta_{\mathbb{R}_+} \times \rho_F) = (\Delta_{\mathbb{R}_+} \times \rho_F)^\infty$.

Proposition 3. *Assume that F satisfies the DP-condition, then $c_F := (\rho_F, \rho_F^{(\infty)})$ is a congruence for $M : X \rightsquigarrow (\mathbb{R}_+ \times X)^\infty$.*

Analyzing the proof (see [6]), it becomes apparent that the DP-condition on F is needed to establish the initial step in this induction. This property is also responsible for maintaining invariance in the induction step through the integral representation rendering the Markov property.

The intermediate goal is to prove that $\rho_F = \rho_{\mathrm{cl}(F)}$ holds. Because by construction $F \subseteq \mathrm{cl}(F)$, and because $F \mapsto \rho_F$ is anti-monotonic, for establishing the equality above we need to show that $\rho_F \subseteq \rho_{\mathrm{cl}(F)}$ is true . We will first investigate ρ_F-invariant Borel sets with respect to a smooth equivalence relation on PATHS related to ρ_F and $\Delta_{\mathbb{R}_+}$.

Some auxiliary operators are introduced: let A, A_1, A_2 be subsets of X, B be a subset of PATHS, and $I \subseteq \mathbb{R}_+$ an interval with rational bounds, then

$$P_{\bowtie p}(B) := \{x \in X \mid M(x)(\{\tau \mid \langle x, \tau \rangle \in B\}) \bowtie p\}.$$

$$Q_A := \{x \in X \mid \lim_{t \to \infty} M(x)(\{\tau \mid \langle x, \tau \rangle @t \in A\}) \text{ exists}\}.$$

$$f_A(x) := \lim_{t \to \infty} M(x)(\{\tau \mid \langle x, \tau \rangle \in A\}), \text{ if } x \in Q_A.$$

$$S_{\bowtie p}(A) := \{x \in Q_A \mid f_A(x) \bowtie p\}.$$

$$X(I, A) := \{\sigma \mid \sigma[1] \in A \wedge \delta(\sigma, 0) \in I\}.$$

We observe the following properties:

Lemma 8. *Let F be a set of formulas, and recall that $\rho_F \times \Delta_{\mathbb{R}_+}$ denotes the smooth equivalence relation $\langle x, t \rangle \, (\rho_F \times \Delta_{\mathbb{R}_+}) \, \langle x't' \rangle$ iff $x \, \rho_F \, x' \wedge t = t'$ on $X \times \mathbb{R}_+$. Assume that F satisfies the DP-condition. We observe the following properties:*

1. If $B \in \mathcal{INV}\left(\mathcal{B}(\text{PATHS}), \rho_F^{(\infty)}\right)$, then $P_{\bowtie p}(B) \in \mathcal{INV}\left(\mathcal{B}(X), \rho_F\right)$.

2. If $A \in \mathcal{INV}\left(\mathcal{B}(X), \rho_F\right)$, then both Q_A and $S_{\bowtie p}(A)$ are ρ_F-invariant Borel sets, and $X(I, A) \in \mathcal{INV}\left(\mathcal{B}(\text{PATHS}), \rho_F^{(\infty)}\right)$.

3. $U(I, A_1, A_2) \in \mathcal{INV}\left(\mathcal{B}(\text{PATHS}), \rho_F^{(\infty)}\right)$, provided A_1, A_2 are ρ_F-invariant Borel sets.

This Lemma is instrumental in establishing our main result on bisimulations. Its proof is technically somewhat awkward due to the necessity of keeping track of many smooth relations at once.

Proposition 4. *Let $F \neq \emptyset$ be a set of formulas, denote by ρ_F the equivalence relation on the set of states imposed by F, and let $\text{cl}(F)$ be the closure of F under the logic's operators. Then $\rho_F = \rho_{\text{cl}(F)}$ holds, provided F satisfies the DP-condition.*

Proof. Because $\rho_{\text{cl}(F)} \subseteq \rho_F$ is trivial, and since $\rho_{\text{cl}(F)}$ is determined by the countable set $\{[\![\phi]\!] \mid \phi \in \text{cl}(F)\}$ of Borel sets, it is by Lemma 4, part 3 sufficient to show that $[\![\phi]\!] \in \mathcal{INV}\left(\mathcal{B}(X), \rho_F\right)$ holds for each $\phi \in \text{cl}(F)$. Since for each $\phi \in F$ we have trivially $[\![\phi]\!] \in \mathcal{INV}\left(\mathcal{B}(X), \rho_F\right)$, an inductive reasoning with Lemma 8 on the structure of F-state formulas and of F-path formulas establishes the assertion.   ⊣

As an interesting direct and first consequence of Proposition 4 we obtain that the equivalence of states on the atomic propositions determines their equivalence of all formulas, provided the DP-condition is satisfied. If it is not, we force it: Define for a set F of formulas

$$\text{dp}(F) := \bigcap \{G \subseteq \mathcal{L}_{AP} \mid F \subseteq G, G \text{ has the DP-condition}\}$$

as the smallest set of formulas that satisfy the DP-condition (this construction is sensible because the set $\mathcal{L}_{AP}$ of all formulas satisfies the condition under consideration).

We obtain from Proposition 4 right away:

Corollary 2. $\rho_{\text{dp}(AP)} = \rho_{\mathcal{L}_{AP}}$.

This result is not yet fully satisfying; in practice it means that one has to have a look at the formulas in the DP-closure for concluding whether or not a given property holds for all formulas. It is, however, desirable to restrict oneself to observing properties on the atomic propositions alone, and then to say that this property holds for the entirety of formulas. This is what we want to investigate now.

The basic idea is to find a suitable representation for $\text{dp}(F)$ and then to capitalize on Lemma 4, part 3, for identifying the equivalence relation as $\rho_{\text{dp}(F)}$.

Let F be a non-empty set of formulas. Define for $\Psi \subseteq \mathcal{L}_{AP}$ the set valued map

$$H(\Psi) := F \cup \{ \bigwedge_{1 \le i \le n} \phi_i \mid n \in \mathbb{N}, \phi_1, \ldots, \phi_n \in \Psi\}$$

$$\cup \{\mathcal{P}_{\bowtie p}(\mathcal{X}^{[a,b]} \phi) \mid \phi \in \Psi, a, b, p \text{ rational}\},$$

then the least fixed point $H_* := \mu\Psi.H(\Psi)$ exists by the celebrated Kleene-Knaster-Tarski Fixed Point Theorem, and $H_* = \bigcup_{n \in \mathbb{N}} H^{(n)}(\emptyset)$ holds, with $H^{(n)}$ as the nth iterate of H. Similarly, define for a family $\mathcal{A}$ of Borel sets in X

$$h(\mathcal{A}) := \{ [\![\phi]\!] \mid \phi \in F \} \cup \mathcal{A} \cup \{ P_{\bowtie p}(X([a,b], A)) \mid A \in \mathcal{A}, a, b, p \text{ rational} \}.$$

Again invoking the Kleene-Knaster-Tarski Theorem, we know that the smallest fixed point $\mathcal{C}_* := \mu\mathcal{A}.h(\mathcal{A})$ exists, and can be computed through $\mathcal{C}_* = \bigcup_{n \in \mathbb{N}} h^{(n)}(\emptyset)$. Here $h^{(n)}$ is of course the nth iterate of h.

As witnessed by the use of the path quantifier, both constructs are closely related:

Lemma 9. *Construct the set H_* of formulas and the family $\mathcal{C}_*$ of Borel sets as above. Then $H_* = \mathsf{dp}(F)$, and $\sigma(\mathcal{C}_*) = \mathcal{INV}\left(\mathcal{B}(X), \rho_{\mathsf{dp}(F)}\right)$, thus the $\rho_{\mathsf{dp}(F)}$-invariant sets are generated from H_*.*

Let us define F-bisimulations in order to put these results into the proper context. Define for $F \subseteq \mathcal{L}_{AP}$ and for each state $x \in X$ the set $\mathbf{L}_F(x) := \{ \phi \in F \mid x \models \phi \}$ as the set of all formulas in F that are satisfied by x.

Definition 6. *Let F be a set of formulas, then a smooth equivalence relation $\equiv_F$ is called an F-bisimulation iff*

1. *$\mathbf{L}_F(x) = \mathbf{L}_F(x')$, whenever $x \equiv_F x'$.*
2. *$K(x)(D) = K(x')(D)$, whenever $x \equiv_F x'$ and $D \in \mathcal{INV}\left(\mathcal{B}(X), \equiv_F\right)$.*

An F-bisimulation is concentrated on the behavior that manifests itself on states, rather than on paths. Hence we use for its formulation the relation K rather than M. If $\equiv_F$ is an F-bisimulation, condition 2 tells us that this relation is in particular a congruence, so we may define the factor relation $K_{\equiv_F}([x]_{\equiv_F})(D) := K(x)((\eta_{\equiv_F}^{-1}[D]))$ whenever $D \in \mathcal{B}(X/\equiv_F)$ in a Borel set in the factor space (cp. Lemma 4). It has the additional property that the map $\mathbf{L}_F : X \to F$ is constant on the equivalence classes. This observation yields a characterization of F-bisimulations in terms of congruences:

Proposition 5. *Let ρ be a smooth equivalence relation on X. Then ρ is an F-bisimulation iff ρ is a congruence for K with $x \rho x' \Rightarrow \mathbf{L}_F(x) = \mathbf{L}_F(x')$.*

Consequently, bisimilar states accept exactly the same formulas in F, and they behave in exactly the same way on the $\equiv_F$-invariant Borel sets. As a first result towards relating the results obtained so far to bisimulations, we see that under the mild condition of F being closed under conjunctions, ρ_F is actually one:

Proposition 6. *The relation ρ_F is an F-bisimulation for each $F \subseteq \mathcal{L}_{AP}$ which satisfies the DP-condition.*

The relation ρ_F is provided naturally with F, so it plays a prominent role among all the F-bisimulations (there are other F-bisimulations, e.g., the identity is one, but probably not the most interesting among all the candidates):

Definition 7. *The states $x, x' \in X$ are called F-bisimilar iff $x \rho_F x'$ holds.*

This is a characterization of F-bisimilarity:

Theorem 1. *Let $\emptyset \neq F \subseteq \mathcal{L}_{AP}$ be a set of formulas which satisfy the DP-condition, then two states are F-bisimilar iff they satisfy exactly the same formulas in $\mathsf{cl}(F)$.*

Proof. This follows immediately from Proposition 4 in conjunction with Proposition 6. ⊣

Specializing to the set of atomic formulas, we obtain at once:

Corollary 3. *Two states are* $\mathsf{dp}(AP)$*-bisimilar iff they satisfy exactly the same formulas in* $\mathcal{L}_{AP}$.

This is not yet satisfying for practical purposes, because one has to construct the closure $\mathsf{dp}(AP)$ of the set of all atomic propositions which can be done iteratively through the computation of a fixed point, as the discussion leading to Lemma 9 shows. Nevertheless it leads to an infinite process, handling a countable set of objects. But suppose we are in the situation in which both the state transitions K and the jump times L are determined through a rate function R (cp. Observation 1). Now an easy computation reveals $x \models \mathcal{P}_{\bowtie p}(\mathcal{X}^I \phi) \Leftrightarrow L(x)(I) \cdot K(x)(\llbracket \phi \rrbracket) \bowtie p$. Thus the σ-algebra of $\rho_{\mathsf{dp}(AP)}$-invariant Borel sets is by Lemma 9 determined by the ρ_{AP}-invariant Borel sets and by the smallest σ-algebra $\mathcal{T}_R$ on X that renders the map $x \mapsto R(x)(A)$ measurable for each $A \in \mathcal{INV}(\mathcal{B}(X), \rho_{AP})$. This observation yields

Corollary 4. *If* $x \mapsto R(x)(A)$ *is a* $\mathcal{INV}(\mathcal{B}(X), \rho_{AP})$*-$\mathcal{B}(\mathbb{R}_+)$ -measurable map for each* ρ_{AP}*-invariant Borel set* A, *then the following conditions are equivalent for any two states* $x, x' \in X$:

1. x *and* x' *are AP-bisimilar.*
2. x *and* x' *satisfy exactly the same formulas in* $\mathcal{L}_{AP}$.

The proof capitalizes on the uniqueness of the invariant sets for a smooth equivalence relation: since we are able to identify these sets, we may conclude what shape the relation has. This shows that a closer inspection of the invariant Borel sets bears some — probably unexpected — fruits.

Remark 1. The look at [1, Theorem 5] and [3, Theorem 6.3/6.4], in which a similar equivalence as in Corollary 4 is proposed without additional conditions, is slightly confusing. The paper [1] refers to the paper [3], but the latter paper investigates a logic without a steady state operator (which the former paper has). On the other hand, there is reference in [3, Theorem 6.3/6.4] to a corresponding result in [1, Theorem 5]. —

The condition imposed in the Corollary above is satisfied in the finite case whenever the rate function is constant on the equivalence classes for $\equiv_{AP}$. This can be checked quite efficiently once the classes are computed, as [1] demonstrates.

7 Conclusion

The paper proposes a stochastic interpretation of **CSL** imposing minimal assumptions on the stochastic independence of state changes and residence times. The state space is an analytic space, hence a rather general type of space that includes finite state spaces as well as Polish or compact spaces. This permits understanding the interpretation as a stochastic relation, enabling the use of the tools developed for investigating these relations.

The main contribution of the paper are the incorporation of a steady state operator into the stochastic interpretation, yielding a uniform approach, the investigation of bisimulations as congruences and the development of criteria for the equivalence of different notions of bisimulations, and finally the formulation of a general approach for the investigation of bisimulations for this type of logic through the theory of congruences for stochastic relations.

The investigation of logics with stochastic methods has proven to be useful, both for the logical side and for getting a better understanding of the stochastic issues. While usually computational aspects appear as the foremost concern in these investigations, it becomes evident both from [3] and from the present work that structural properties need to be looked at for their own interest, and from the understanding gained there a deeper understanding of the applications arises [2, 4, 5]. It may be helpful to continue with this programme from both points of view. To mind comes a closer investigation into the probabilistic semantics of logics such as PDL and the incorporation of the μ-calculus into the framework [7].

References

[1] C. Baier, B. Haverkort, H. Hermanns, and J.-P. Koert. Model-checking algorithms for continuous time Markov chains. *IEEE Trans. Softw. Eng.*, 29(6):524 – 541, June 2003.

[2] J. Desharnais, A. Edalat, and P. Panangaden. Bisimulation of labelled Markov-processes. *Information and Computation*, 179(2):163 – 193, 2002.

[3] J. Desharnais and P. Panangaden. Continuous stochastic logic characterizes bisimulation of continuous-time Markov processes. *J. Log. Alg. Programming*, 56(1-2):99 – 115, 2003.

[4] E.-E. Doberkat. Semi-pullbacks and bisimulations in categories of stochastic relations. In *Proc. ICALP'03*, volume 2719 of *Lecture Notes in Computer Science*, pages 996 – 1007, Berlin, 2003. Springer-Verlag.

[5] E.-E. Doberkat. Stochastic relations: congruences, bisimulations and the Hennessy-Milner theorem. *SIAM J. Computing*, 2005. (in print).

[6] E.-E. Doberkat. Zeno paths, congruences and bisimulations for continuous-time stochastic logic. Technical Report 155, Chair for Software Technology, University of Dortmund, March 2005.

[7] M. Narasimha, R. Cleaveland, and P. Iyer. Probabilistic temporal logics via the modal mu-calculus. In W. Thomas, editor, *Proc. FOSSACS'99*, number 1578 in Lecture Notes in Computer Science, pages 288 – 305, Berlin, 1999. Springer-Verlag.

[8] S. M. Srivastava. *A Course on Borel Sets*. Graduate Texts in Mathematics. Springer-Verlag, Berlin, 1998.

A Logic for Quantum Circuits and Protocols[*]
(Extended Abstract)

Manas Patra[1,2]

[1] School of Computer Science and Engineering,
The University of New South Wales, Sydney 2052, Australia
[2] CQCT, Macquarie University, Sydney NSW 2109, Australia
manasp@cse.unsw.edu.au

Abstract. A logic for reasoning about quantum circuits and protocols is proposed. It incorporates the basic features of quantum theory-probability, unitary dynamics, tensor products and measurement. The underlying language could be used for verification and synthesis of quantum circuits. Important algorithms like the quantum search algorithm of Grover are discussed. The logic also forms the foundation on which more elaborate formal systems for reasoning about quantum protocols could be based. A sound and complete axiomatization is presented. Algorithms for circuit verification, circuit equivalence (exact and approximate) are outlined. Some related complexity issues are also discussed.

Keywords: Probability logic, quantum computing, quantum circuits, complexity.

1 Introduction

There exist several equivalent approaches to formal models of computing. Physicists and computer scientists dealing with quantum computation and information have focused on the circuit model [Yao93] or the quantum version of Turing machine model [BV97]. There is another approach to computing, due to Post, viz. formal systems [Smu61]. This paper is about this approach. For formal reasoning, specification and algorithmic verifications a formal approach is often more suitable. By this I mean a deductive system with precise syntax, axioms and rules of inference. It must be concise yet expressive enough to be useful. This paper is an attempt towards that. The resulting logic is more expressive-the quantum circuits correspond to a special class of formulas. For example, it is not only expressible that the Grover search algorithm is correct but also that in any fixed dimension such an algorithm exists. Even for circuits a formal language may be easier to reason with and develop algorithms. Compare the use of formal circuit model and propositional logic (perhaps extended with additional logical/modal operators) for reasoning about classical combinational

---

[*] Work supported by a scholarship from an ARC Discovery Grant to Ron van der Meyden.

D.V. Hung and M. Wirsing (Eds.): ICTAC 2005, LNCS 3722, pp. 424–438, 2005.
© Springer-Verlag Berlin Heidelberg 2005

and sequential circuits. In many cases dealing with decidability and complexity issues, formal models are easier to handle than the corresponding circuit models. Moreover, the axiomatic approach would facilitate the use of powerful theorem provers for reasoning about quantum systems. Finally, it is an alternative viewpoint which complements the quantum circuit model. In an earlier work [MP03b]. Meyden and Patra had laid the foundations of such a language. Although expressive enough to formalise important physical concepts like superposition, the uncertainty principle and quantum state tomography it was lacking two notions crucial for quantum computation and information viz. tensor products and measurement. This was dealt with in [Pat04]. The approach in that paper was somewhat more general. There are two equivalent "pictures" of quantum systems. The first is the Schroedinger picture, in which the dynamics is carried by the state and the bases in which measurements are performed remain unchanged. In contrast, in the Heisenberg picture, the bases carry the dynamics and the state remains unchanged. Of course, both pictures make identical probabilistic predictions. In the works cited above I had followed the Heisenberg picture. The proofs of certain important results are more transparent in that picture. In the present work, I loosely follow the Schroedinger picture favoured by the quantum computing community. The present approach is pragmatic one somewhat akin to the operational approach in quantum measurement theory [PBL95]. Other approaches notably functional programming approach [vT03] and categorical approach [AC04]. The formulation in [MS04] is closer to the current approach. Of these, the categorical semantics of [AC04] is quite elegant. Baltag and Smets [BS04] discuss a *propositional* dynamic logic type semantics for quantum programmes and the "quantum computational logic" gven in [CGL05] exploits the properties of some basic gates (Toffoli, CNOT) to develop a semantics for quantum computation. The present work was motivated by the following considerations.

1. Any logic dealing with probabilities must deal with real expressions[FHM90]. If we also have to include order relations then the theory of real closed fields seems a natural building block because it is a well investigated field with sophisticated decision procedures[BPR03].
2. We can develop algorithms for efficiently translating the formulas of the present logic to those in a real closed field hence any decision procedure for the latter can be used for verification of a large class of formulas in quantum theory which includes quantum circuits and many protocols.
3. As I show later we can use the language for *synthesis* of quantum circuits. Important example are the Grover search circuit[Gro96] and the teleportation circuit. We can formulate and in principle, prove the existence of such circuits. Such formulas are most naturally expressed by quantified formulas.
4. The language is close to the informal language of physicists. Let us remember that the real measurable quantities are the probabilities.
5. It has a relatively small set of axioms (compare with the full scale axiomatization of the Hilbert space formalism). It is not only a logically consistent theory but physically consistent. No counterfactual reasoning is admitted.

A brief outline of the paper follows. I assume some familiarity with the formalism of quantum mechanics in finite dimensional Hilbert spaces. Section II deals with the syntax and semantics of the language. The language components appearing in [MP03b] are only discussed briefly. A symbol for tensor product is introduced which resembles a function symbol in a multi-sorted language. New symbols for two types of measurement is introduced and their properties discussed.

In Section III some applications are presented. An algorithm for translating any combinational quantum circuit to the language is sketched. The important Grover quantum search circuit [Gro96] is discussed including some aspects of synthesis of such circuits.

In the next section (IV) I give a sound and complete axiomatization. Some complexity theorems are stated. As a corollary one obtains yet another proof of the complexity upper bounds discovered in [BV97]. In the conclusion, I discuss some possible extensions of the language and future developments.

2   Syntax and Semantics

Any logic for probabilistic reasoning must deal with real numbers. One could express some concepts using rational integers only. But then one has to restrict to *linear* relations only to ensure that one stays within the domain of integers [FHM90]. However, quantum probabilities are inherently nonlinear as they depend quadratically on certain complex quantities- the amplitudes. Even in the classical case, to express notions like conditional probability we require nonlinear relations (essentially inequalities) and hence the domain has to be expanded to real numbers. More precisely, we have to include the first order theory of real closed fields as in [FHM90]. In case of quantum probabilities it gets more complicated because the *complex* amplitudes, though directly unobservable, give rise to observable probability distributions. Refer to Feynman's excellent discussion on the subtle differences between classical and quantum probabilities [RPFS65]. Hence, a logic designed to capture quantum probabilities has to include a theory that deals with real numbers (probabilities) as a subfield of complex numbers (amplitudes). I briefly outline below one such theory, **RC**, since its properties are crucial in the proof of similar properties of the logic. First, a few well known facts. The first order theory of real *and* algebraically closed fields are decidable (every closed formula or its negation is provable [Sho67]) and complete (every consistent formula is satisfiable). Moreover, both admit the elimination of quantifiers: every formula is provably equivalent to a quantifier free formula.

The language of **RC** consists of two binary function symbols +and · for addition and multiplication. As usual these operations will be written in the infix notation and the symbol · often omitted. There are three basic constants': $0, 1$ and i. There are two predicate symbol R and $<$. Informally, R defines the set of real elements. It is implicit that **RC** is a first order theory with equality. The nonlogical axioms of **RC** are (informally) stated below.

1. All the field axioms. In other words any model of **RC** is a field.
2. The axiom of algebraic closure. A term **t** of **RC** is a polynomial in several variables. The term may also be treated as polynomial in a single variable with variable coefficients. The axiom states that the polynomial equation **t** = 0 has a solution for all values of the coefficients.
3. The real elements, that is all x for which $R(x)$ is true constitute a totally ordered field with respect to the order relation $<$. Two elements can be compared iff both are real. The identity elements 0 and 1 are real.
4. Every element z can be uniquely written as $z = x + iy$ with x and y real, and $i^2 + 1 = 0$

All the important *algebraic* properties of real numbers as a subfield of complex numbers can be deduced from these. For example, sum of squares of reals can not be 0 unless each summand is 0. Any polynomial of odd degree with real coefficients has a real solution. The last property makes the set of reals, a real closed field. One may now define a real number x to be positive if $x > 0$. The real and imaginary parts of a complex numbers are defined as usual. It is convenient to add several defined constants and functions. These defined symbols can always be eliminated. I assume that there is a constant symbol for each positive integer. Thus, the integer k is equivalent to $1 + 1 + \ldots$ (k times). Also there is constant $n^{1/k}$ positive k^{th} root for positive n and k. The usual definition of positive and negative powers will be assumed. The defined function symbols are the complex conjugate, the modulus $|z|^2 = z\bar{z} = x^2 + y^2$ and the square root. Of the two square roots of a complex number we always pick up the one with positive real part if the latter is not 0. If the real part is 0, pick out the one with positive imaginary part. The most important properties of **RC** are summarised below.

Theorem 1. **RC** *is a complete theory that admits elimination of quantifiers.*

The logic presented in this work is a first order interpreted theory [Sho67]. It is interpreted in the theory **RC** which it extends. The language of the logic, denoted by $\mathcal{L}_n(P, t, M, S, \mathbf{U})$. The language $\mathcal{L}_n(P, t, M, S, \mathbf{U})$ consists of the following. It will be convenient to treat it as a sorted language.

The variables of **RC** are written as x, y, z etc. with subscripts possibly. Instead of saying the "real" predicate R holds for some term **t** of **RC** I write that **t** is real. It is clear that one can dispense with the sorted syntax by introducing extra predicates. There is a special basis symbol **b**. Associated with **b** are the 'atomic basis formulas' (b-formulas) $\{\mathbf{b}_0, \ldots, \mathbf{b}_{n-1}\}$. They are also called basis components. Intuitively, the basis symbol **b** will denote a basis in the n-dimensional Hilbert space **C** ^{n} and $\mathbf{b}_0, \ldots, \mathbf{b}_{n-1}$ will denote the corresponding basis vectors. Thus, if B and C are b-formulas then so are $B \vee C$ and $\neg B$. Call **b** the irreducible basis symbol. Now define the composite basis symbol recursively as follows: $t(\mathbf{b}, \mathbf{b})$ is a (composite) basis symbol and if X and Y are basis symbols then so is $t(X, Y)$. Call the number of t-operators appearing in a basis symbol the t-*degree*(for tensor degree) of that symbol. The t-operator will be interpreted as the tensor or direct product of bases. If the t-degree of a basis symbol is k then its interpretation is as a product basis in $(\mathbf{C}^n)^{\otimes k} \cong \mathbf{C}^{n^k}$. The t-operator extends to a map of basis formulas of composite bases. Thus, associated with a composite basis symbol of t-degree k are, n^k atomic basis formulas defined recursively as follows. Assume the components of a basis symbol X, Y of respective t-degrees $r, s < k$ are already defined. These components will always be denoted as subscripts.

$$t(X, Y)_i \equiv t(X, Y)_{j2^r + k} \stackrel{\text{def}}{=} t(X_j, Y_k)$$
$$0 \leq j < n^s \text{ and } 0 \leq k < n^r \tag{1}$$

For a basis symbol X of t-degree k define $\dim(X) = n^k$ It will be seen that due to the associativity of the tensor product several products are semantically equivalent. Again we take the Boolean combination of basis components of a fixed t-degree. Note that Boolean combination of formulas of different t-degrees are not allowed. I assume right associativity:$t(\mathbf{b}, \mathbf{b}, \mathbf{b}) \stackrel{\text{def}}{=} t(\mathbf{b}, t(\mathbf{b}, \mathbf{b}))$. Similarly for higher degree expressions. Note that the basis components of $t(X, Y)$ are uniquely determined by the components X and Y. For example, if $n = 2$ then $t(\mathbf{b}, \mathbf{b}, \mathbf{b})_i = t(\mathbf{b}_{[i/2^2]}, t(\mathbf{bb})_{i \bmod 2^2}) = t(\mathbf{b}_{j_2}, t(\mathbf{b}_{j_1}, \mathbf{b}_{j_0}))$, where $[x]$ denotes the greatest integer $\leq x$ and $j_2 j_1 j_0$ is the binary representation of i as a 3-bit string.

Next we introduce probability terms over b-formulas. If B is any b-formula of t-degree k then $P(B)$ is a probability term of degree k. If $P(B_1), \ldots, P(B_r)$ are probability terms of the *same* degree k and $q(x_1, \ldots, x_m)$ is a polynomial in $\mathbf{RC}$ then the expression obtained by substituting uniformly the $P(B_i)$'s for some of the variables in q is also a probability term. A *probability atom* is an expression of the form $T \geq 0$, where T is a probability term. Intuitively, the probability formulas like $P(\mathbf{b}_i) > a$ asserts that the probability of obtaining the state corresponding to $\mathbf{b}_i$ when the quantum system in some initial state ψ is measured in the basis corresponding to $\mathbf{b}$. These are *a priori* probabilities that we assign to the quantum state ρ. No actual measurement need be performed. A probability formula is a boolean combination of probability atoms of the same degree. It is clear that binary relations like $T < 0$ can be defined as $\neg (T \geq 0)$. Note that, by definition, we do not combine basis or probability formulas of different degrees. The next construction is for the basic unitary operations. An $m \times m$ complex matrix U is called unitary if its entries $U(ij)$ satisfy $UU^\dagger = I_m = \delta_{ij}$, where I_m is the $m \times m$ identity matrix and the Kronecker symbol $\delta_{ij} = 1$ if $i = j$ and 0 otherwise. Call m the order of U. The unitary property can also be written as $UU^\dagger = I_m = \delta_{ij}$. Here $U^\dagger$ is the transposed conjugate of U. It is also called the hermitian conjugate. Sometimes, I quantify over unitary matrices, $\exists U$ or $\forall U$. This is simply a shorthand for the n^2 variables $x_{ij} = U(ij)$ of $\mathbf{RC}$ which satisfy unitary conditions. If Φ is a probability formula of degree k then it is formula of $\mathcal{L}_n(P, t, M, S, \mathbf{U})$. For any such probability formula and any unitary matrix of order 2^k, $[U]\Phi$ is also a formula of $\mathcal{L}_n(P, t, M, S, \mathbf{U})$. The intuition of the $[U]$ operators is that, $[U]\Phi$ is true in a state ρ if Φ is true in the transformed state $U^{-1} \cdot \rho$. This will be further clarified in the section on semantics. The final syntactic constructs are measurement operators, M_X and S_{X_i}, where X is some basis symbol and X_i are its components. Thus, there is one measurement operator for every basis X and the number of *selection* operators S_{X_i} equals

$\dim(X)$. The operator M_X expresses that a complete measurement is performed in the basis X although the outcome may not be known. The operator S_{X_i}, in contrast, captures the situation where the outcome of the above measurement is known or selected to be X_i. One of the X_i,s must occur and $S_{X_i}(\Phi)$ is true if Φ is true *after* the selection of X_i in the measurement. The degree of the measurement operators M_X and S_{X_i} is defined to be the t-degree of X. It must match the degree of Φ on which they operate. Note that the term "operator" is intentionally overloaded. In the context of the syntax the operators $[U], M_X$ are syntactic operators acting on formulas.

The semantics of $\mathcal{L}_n(P, t, M, S, \mathbf{U})$ is described next. As stated above the language is to be ultimately interpreted in **RC**, but an intermediate interpretation in an appropriate Hilbert space will make the connection with quantum theory clear. Since we have to interpret arbitrary tensor formulas a fixed vector space will not suffice. For a positive integer m let H_m denote the vector space $\mathbf{C}^m$ with standard inner product. First, variables of real and complex sort will be interpreted as such in **RC**. I omit the description except for the remark that there are some technical formalities to be observed when deducing properties of an interpreted theory from the properties of the theory which is the domain of interpretation [Sho67].

It is convenient to first consider a simpler fragment of $\mathcal{L}_n(P, t, M, S, \mathbf{U})$ consisting of all formulas without the t-operator, that is, formulas of t-degree 0. Hence, there is only one basis symbol b. Call this fragment $\mathcal{L}_n(P, M, S, \mathbf{U})$. A *structure* for $\mathcal{L}_n(P, M, S, \mathbf{U})$ is made up of an n-dimensional complex Hilbert space H_n and $L(H_n)$ the space of linear operators on H_n. The vectors of H_n, written as $|\alpha\rangle$ are $n \times 1$ matrices with components z_i. The dual $\langle\alpha|$ is a row vector with entries $\overline{z_i}$. The inner product $\langle\alpha|\beta\rangle$ of two vectors is defined to be $\sum_i \overline{\alpha_i}\beta_i$ and the length of a vector $|\alpha\rangle$ is $\||\alpha\rangle\| = \langle\alpha|\alpha\rangle$.

An *interpretation* of $\mathcal{L}_n(P, M, S, \mathbf{U})$ in a structure H_n is function π, such that for the basis variable b, $\pi(\mathbf{b})$ is an orthonormal basis $\psi_0, \dots, \psi_{n-1}$ of H; (we write $\pi(\mathbf{b})_i$ for ψ_i and occasionally suppress the $|\rangle$ notation). If $M = (m_{ij})$ is an $n \times n$ unitary matrix and $B = \{\psi_1, \dots, \psi_n\}$ is a sequence of vectors of H, we write MB for the sequence of vectors $\psi_1', \dots, \psi_n'$, where $\psi_i' = \Sigma_{i=1}^n m_{ik}\psi_i$. If B is an orthonormal basis of H then so is MB. Extend the interpretation π to terms t of various sorts as follows. A (quantum) state ρ is a hermitian matrix with nonnegative eigenvalues such that $\mathrm{Tr}(\rho) = 1$, where Tr denotes the trace of a matrix. It is called a pure state if $\rho^2 = \rho$. If ρ is a pure state then $\rho = |\alpha\rangle\langle\alpha|$ for some unit vector $\alpha \in H_n$. Then it is a projection operator since $|\alpha\rangle\langle\alpha|(|\beta\rangle) = (\langle\alpha|\beta\rangle)|\alpha\rangle$. Given the term t, a state ρ and an interpretation π, define the interpretation $[\![\mathbf{t}]\!]_{\pi,\rho}$ of t with respect to π and ρ as follows. Interpret b-formulas as projection operators on H (these may also be understood as representing the subspaces of H_n onto which they project): $[\![\mathbf{b}_i]\!]_{\pi,\rho} = |\psi_i\rangle\langle\psi_i|$, where $\psi_i = \pi(\mathbf{b})_i$; and $[\![\alpha_1 \wedge \alpha_2]\!]_{\pi,\rho} = [\![\alpha_1]\!]_{\pi,\rho} \cdot [\![\alpha_2]\!]_{\pi,\rho}$ (this is the projection onto intersection of the subspaces of H that are the images of the projectors $[\![\alpha_1]\!]_{\pi,\rho}$ and $[\![\alpha_1]\!]_{\pi,\rho}$). $[\![\neg\alpha]\!]_{\pi,\rho} = [\![\alpha]\!]_{\pi,\rho}^\perp$ is the projection operator projecting onto the orthogonal complement of the image of H under $[\![\alpha]\!]_{\pi,\rho}$. Unitary matrices are interpreted as such, that is, an array of complex numbers satisfying the unitarity condition $\sum_k U(ik)\overline{U(jk)} = \delta_{jk}$.

The interpretation of the probability terms are: $[\![P(\alpha)]\!]_{\pi,\rho} = \text{Tr}([\![\alpha]\!]_{\pi,\rho} \cdot \rho)$. To give semantics to formulas of $\mathcal{L}_n(P, M, S, \mathbf{U})$, we define recursively a relation of satisfaction of a formula Φ at a state ρ in a structure H_n, with respect to an interpretation π, denoted by $H, \pi, \rho \models \Phi$. If Φ is an probability atom it is of the form $q(P(\mathbf{b}_i)) > 0$ for some multivariate real polynomial q. Then,

$$H_n, \pi, \rho \models \Phi \text{ iff } q([\![P(\mathbf{b}_i)]\!]_{\pi,\rho}) > 0$$

If Φ is a Boolean combination of probability atoms then the conditions for satisfiability is standard. Finally,

$$H_n, \pi, \rho \models [U]\Phi \text{ iff } H_n, \pi, [U^{-1}] \cdot \rho[\mathbf{b}] \models \phi$$

Recall that the action of a unitary matrix V on ρ is given by $V \cdot \rho = V\rho V^{-1}$, where the rhs denotes ordinary matrix multiplication. In the above formula I write $\rho[\mathbf{b}]$ to indicate that the matrix ρ is to be written in the basis $\pi(\mathbf{b})$. Thus a numerical matrix may represent different linear operators depending on the interpretation π. The reason for operating the state with $U^{-1} = U^\dagger$ instead of U is that it preserves matrix multiplication. Hence, $U \to [U]$ is a morphism.

The intended interpretation of the t-operator is as a tensor product. Let

$$H = \sum_k H_n^k \stackrel{\text{def}}{=} \overbrace{H \otimes \ldots \otimes H}^{k \text{ times}},$$

where the sum is direct and the inner product is the one induced on each summand. That is, a vector $|\alpha\rangle \in H$ is finite sum of the form $\sum_k |\alpha^k\rangle$ with $|\alpha^k\rangle \in H_n^k$. Then for two such vectors $\langle\alpha|\beta\rangle = \sum_k \langle\alpha^k|\beta^k\rangle$. Since all but a finite number of summands are 0 this is well defined. Note that the subspaces H_m^k are orthogonal for different k. With the above notation define recursively $\pi(t(X_i, Y_j) \equiv \{\pi(X_i) \otimes \pi(Y_j)\}$- the basis in H_m^{k+r} consisting of tensor product of the vectors in two bases. Interpretation of various terms of the full language $\mathcal{L}_n(P, t, M, S, \mathbf{U})$ is now straightforward. A formula of degree k is interpreted in the space $H_n^{\otimes k}$. The definitions are identical to the degree 0 case. We restrict to *homogeneous* formulas, that is, all the atomic formulas are of same degree. This corresponds to the intuition that the dimension of the quantum system under discussion is fixed. Semantics for the general inhomogeneous case can be given. The state in which a (homogeneous) formula is interpreted lives in the appropriate Hilbert space. Note that the t-degree is arbitrary. The associativity of the tensor product $(\alpha \otimes (\beta \otimes \gamma) = (\alpha \otimes \beta) \otimes \gamma)$ has an interesting consequence. Any basis symbol of t-degree k is equivalent to the basis $t(\mathbf{b}, \ldots, \mathbf{b})$(k times). Hence, it is easy to see that the basis component $t(\mathbf{b}, \ldots, \mathbf{b})_i$ corresponds to the product $t(\mathbf{b}_{j_{k-1}}, \ldots, \mathbf{b}_{j_0})$ where $j_{n-1} \cdots j_0$ is the representation of i in base n as a string of length k. I will discuss some examples in the next section to illustrate. Finally, for measurements

$$H, \pi, \rho \models M_X(\Phi) \text{ iff } H, \pi, \sum_i \pi(X_i)\rho\pi(X_i) \models \Phi.$$

i.e. formula $M_X(\Phi)$ is true at a state ρ iff Φ is true in the post-measurement state $\sum_i \pi(\mathbf{b}_i)\rho\pi(\mathbf{b}_i)$. The latter is a convex linear combination of the post-measurement states; the coefficients being the respective probabilities. For the selection operator $H, \pi, \rho \models S_{X_i}(\Phi)$ iff $H, \pi, \pi(X_i) \models \Phi \wedge P(X_i) \neq 0$. Thus, $S_{X_i}(\Phi)$ is true in a state ρ if Φ is true in the state $\pi(X_i)$. This corresponds to the fact that the outcome of the measurement is known to be X_i. The additional condition $P(X_i) \neq 0$ captures the fact in the opposite case $P(X_i) = 0$ and the the state corresponding to X_i is the "impossible" event in the state ρ. This happens when ρ is orthogonal to $\pi(X_i)$.

3 Examples

In this section I discuss examples and applications. The main focus will be on quantum circuits although a lot more can be expressed in the logic. For quantum protocols one needs several other operators to capture various classical actions. I only discuss the amazing quantum teleportation protocol. The dimension n of the irreducible basis will be fixed throughout this section: $n = 2$. In the quantum computing folklore any such 2-dimensional system is a qubit.

Quantum Circuits

In any dimension there are uncountably many unitary operators. Efficient quantum circuits must be built out of a small set of basic operations called gates, involving only a few qubits. Obviously, a finite set of gates can not generate all unitary operations. Hence, we may only approximate an arbitrary operator with the basic gates. A set of gates which is sufficient to approximate any unitary operator is called a universal set. Several such universal set of gate are known to exist [NC01]. First, I introduce some notation. Let $J_m = \{0, \ldots, m-1\}$, for any positive integer m. Let $U = U(i, j)$ be a given unitary matrix in dimension 2^k, $S = \{s_0, \ldots, s_k\} \subset J_m$ and $S' = J_m - S$. Recall that i, j are represented in binary base as $i = r_{n-1}(i) \ldots r_0(i)$ possibly with leading zeroes. Let $N = 2^m$ and $m \geq k$. The notation $V(i, j) = U[s_1, \ldots, s_k]$ means that the operator U acts on the indices $s_0, \ldots, s_k$ leaving the rest unaffected. Explicitly,

$$V(i,j) = V(r_{m-1}(i) \ldots r_0(i), r_{m-1}(j)) \ldots r_0(j) =$$

$$\prod_{l \in S'} \delta_{r_l(i) r_l(j)} \cdot U(r_{s_k}(i) \ldots r_{s_0}(i), r_{s_k}(j) \ldots r_{s_0}(j)).$$

For disjoint $\{q_1, \ldots, q_k\}$ and $\{s_1, \ldots, s_l\}$ one may take the product of commuting unitaries $U[q_1, \ldots, q_k] \cdot V[s_1, \ldots, s_l]$ of appropriate dimension. Let $t^n(\mathbf{b})$ stand for the n-fold tensor product of the basis symbol $\mathbf{b}$ with itself. The examples below make it clear. First, some quantum gates which will treated as "matrix constants".

$$X = \begin{pmatrix} 0 & 1 \\ 1 & 0 \end{pmatrix} \quad H = \begin{pmatrix} 1 & 1 \\ 1 & -1 \end{pmatrix} \quad C = \begin{pmatrix} 1 & 0 & 0 & 0 \\ 0 & 1 & 0 & 0 \\ 0 & 0 & 0 & 1 \\ 0 & 0 & 1 & 0 \end{pmatrix}$$

The matrix X and H are single qubit operators called Pauli-X gate and Hadamard gate respectively. The matrix C is the controlled-not gate [NC01]. Henceforth, I follow tradition and write the interpretation of $\pi(\mathbf{b}_0) = |0\rangle$ and $\pi(\mathbf{b}_1) = |1\rangle$, and the tensor product $\pi(t(\mathbf{b}_{i_{k-1}}, \ldots, \mathbf{b}_{i_0})) = |i_{k-1}\rangle \cdots |i_0\rangle \equiv |i\rangle$, where i is the unique integer whose binary representation of length k is $i_{k-1} \cdots i_0$. A quantum circuit is specified as a labelled graph. The labels on the vertices are the unitary gates and the connecting 'wires' are the edges. This description is similar to the classical case but with a stipulation that the number of in and out edges are equal. Besides, there is a 'measurement' with respect to a specified basis at the output. Starting with specially labelled input vertices as level 0 one recursively defines level k+1 as the vertices connected to level k. In [Pat04] an algorithm for translating a quantum circuit specification into a different logic was given. I briefly sketch a similar algorithm for translation into $\mathcal{L}_2(P, t, M, S, \mathbf{U})$.

1. Initialise input to a basis $t^n(\mathbf{b})$. The formula for the initialisation is $\mathbf{In} \equiv P(t^n(\mathbf{b})) = 1$.
2. Let $\{S_1^1, \ldots, S_{r_1}^1\}$ be a partition of $J_n = \{1, \ldots, n\}$, such that the unitary operators $U_i^{(1)} \in UB$, $1 \le i \le r_1$ is applied to the qubits in S_i. Of course, it is assumed that the order of the matrix $U_i^{(1)}$ is $2^{|S_i^1|}$. The formula corresponding to output of level 1 is

$$\Phi_1 \equiv [U_1^{\dagger(1)}[S_1^1]] \cdots [U_{r_1}^{\dagger(1)}[S_{r_1}^1]](\bigwedge_j (P(t^n(\mathbf{b})_j) \sim x_j)) \tag{2}$$

Here, the symbol $\sim$ is either an equality or inequality. The operator corresponds to $U^\dagger = U^{-1}$ instead of U because then the latter operates on the state. The range of j is as yet unspecified as are the *real* variables x_j. Next, suppose Φ_k is defined as the output of the circuit at level k and let $\{S_1^k, \ldots, S_{r_k}^k\}$ be a partition of J_n such that unitary operator $U^{(i)} \in$ is applied to the qubits in S_i^k. Then,

$$\Phi_{k+1} = [U_1^{\dagger(k)}[S_1^k]] \cdots [U_{r_1}^{\dagger(k)}r_1[S_{r_k}^k]]\Phi_k \tag{3}$$

An important point to be noted is that the matrices $U_i^{(k)}[S_i^k]$, $i = 1, \ldots, r_k$ in level k commute among themselves. Therefore, the ordering of the matrices in a fixed level do no matter. Let Φ be the final formula after all the levels, i.e. , when the output nodes have been reached.
3. The final step is a measurement (if necessary). The circuit C is represented by

$$C \stackrel{\text{def}}{=} \mathbf{In} \wedge \Phi \wedge \mathbf{X}, \tag{4}$$

where $\mathbf{X}$ is a formula of $\mathbf{RC}$, usually in the terms of the matrix entries of the unitary gates.

As an application of the above algorithm consider the Grover search circuit [NC01]. Suppose we have an unstructured set of $2^n = N$ distinct numbers in binary strings of length n and we are looking for a particular number a. Let $r = \sqrt{N}$. a. Let O_q be the unitary 'oracle' given by

$$O_q(ij) = \delta_{r_1(i)r_1(j)}[\delta_{r_0(i)r_0(j)}(1 - \delta_{r_1(i)a}) + (1 - \delta_{r_0(i)r_0(j)})\delta_{r_1(i)a}]$$

The oracle is unitary matrix of order $N + 1$ acting in the space $(\mathbf{C}^2)^{\otimes n} \otimes \mathbf{C}^2$ that sends $|x\rangle|q\rangle \to |x\rangle|q \oplus f(x)\rangle$ where $f(x) = \delta_{xa}$ and $\oplus$ is addition modulo 2. Let V be unitary matrix of order N given by $V(ij) = 2N^{-1} - \delta_{ij}$. The formula for the Grover circuit is

$$\mathbf{G} \equiv P(\mathbf{b}_0) = 1 \Rightarrow [V[S_n]O_q]^k[H[1]] \dots [H[n]][HX[N+1]]$$
$$(P(t^{n+1}(\mathbf{b})_{a0} \vee t^{n+1}(\mathbf{b})_{a1}) > 3/4) \tag{5}$$

First, the probability lower bound can be improved but it serves the purpose of illustration of the application of the logic. Secondly, the formula really corresponds to the Grover *theorem* as it is an assertion about the probability of obtaining a particular state after the application of Grover circuit. Hence, the language serves as a verification language. In the full paper, Grover circuit is treated as an approximation to a unitary transformation and these circuit approximations can be easily expressed in the language.

Let us pretend that we are not aware of the Grover result. Can we *deduce* the existence of such circuits in a given dimension? The answer is, in principle, *yes*. Consider the formula

$$\exists V(P(\mathbf{b}_0) = 1 \Rightarrow \overbrace{[VO_q] \dots [VO_q]}^{k \text{ times}}[H[1]] \dots [H[n]] \tag{6}$$
$$[HX[n+1]](P(t^{n+1}(\mathbf{b})_{a0} \vee t^{n+1}(\mathbf{b})_{a1}) > 1/2)).$$

If the formula is satisfiable, that is, if there is *one* matrix which, if applied k times in conjunction with the oracle, finds the desired item with high probability. In the next section, I state a result which says that corresponding to any formula of $\mathcal{L}_2(P, t, M, S, \mathbf{U})$ there is a formula of **RC** such that satisfiability of one is equivalent to the satisfiability of the other. Now, **RC** is a complete and hence decidable theory (it is recursively axiomatized). Thus, satisfiability of a formula like the above can be done in two steps. First, reduce to the equivalent formula in formula in **RC** and then use an existing decision algorithm for real closed field to test for satisfiability of the latter[BPR03]. The bad news is that the existing decision algorithms for the real closed fields, essentially based on systematic elimination, have at least exponential runtime. However, in some special cases of quantum, circuits it is possible to get an approximate linearisation. Then, it is problem of linear programming and efficient algorithms are available for the latter. Therefore, the logics presented here may be used for *synthesis* of quantum circuits. It is also possible to write a formula for the Shor factorisation algorithm if one makes the effort to encode the language of modular arithmetic.

In the examples considered above I have not used the measurement operators M_X and S_{X_i}. They can be used to express circuits in which measurements, not unitary gates, are used as the primitive unit of computation[Nie03]. They are also necessary in the discussion of quantum protocols [NC01]. For example, in the teleportation protocol Alice and Bob share a qubit each of an entangled pair. Then Alice applies unitary transformation to her share of the pair and another qubit in unknown state and then performs a measurement. Due to entanglement Bob's qubit gets affected. By applying unitary transformations depending on Alice's measurement outcome Bob can change the state of his qubit to that of the unknown one. Since the qubits are entangled Bob's qubit gets affected by the measurement. Alice knows the outcome of the measurement. The corresponding formula is given below. Let $\mathbf{A} \stackrel{\text{def}}{=} H[1]C[1,2]C[2,3]H[2](P(t^3(\mathbf{b})_0)) = 1$ and $\mathbf{B} \stackrel{\text{def}}{=} P(t(\top, \top, \mathbf{b}_0)) = 1$.

$$\Phi \equiv [U](P(t(\mathbf{b}_0, \top, \top)) = 1) \Rightarrow (S_{00}\mathbf{A} \Rightarrow [U]\mathbf{B}) \wedge (S_{01}\mathbf{A} \Rightarrow [U][X]\mathbf{B}) \wedge \\ (S_{10}\mathbf{A} \Rightarrow [U][Z]\mathbf{B}) \wedge (S_{10}\mathbf{A} \Rightarrow [U][ZX]\mathbf{B}) \tag{7}$$

This formula is quite easy to understand actually. Alice has qubits 1 and 2 and Bob has the third. Alice and Bob start with the entangled pair 2 and 3, which is achieved by applying $C[2,3]H[2]$. Then Alice applies $H[1]C[1,2]$ and the four alternatives correspond to the four outcomes of a measurement in the computational basis. after running the protocol the state of the third qubit (Bob's) is identical to that of the unknown qubit they started with. Although this formula is valid it does not capture the actual knowledge or information that the agents have at each stage. Some preliminary work in this direction may be found in [MP03a] where knowledge and temporal operators are introduced. Let $\Phi(V)$ be the formula obtained from Φ by replacing $H[1]C[1,2]$ by V a "unitary" variable. We may ask $\exists V \Phi(V[1,2])$. That is, whether there exist unitary operation on Alice's qubit such that "teleportation" takes place. In fact it can be verified quite easily by a simple procedure. We may formulate and verify more complicated questions. The point is, since the theory is decidable it is not too hard to devise algorithms answer such questions. Alternatively, it is in principle possible to utilise theorem provers like PVS or Isabelle using the axiomatization below.

4 Axiomatization

In this section I present an axiomatization of $\mathcal{L}_n(P, t, M, S, \mathbf{U})$ and some of the general properties of the resulting theory. I also discuss some complexity questions. The axioms are grouped under several headings, one for each of the constructs of the logic. Many of the axioms are dealt with in detail in [MP03b]. Hence, the discussion will be mostly brief. First, for basis formulas. For a basis symbol of degree k let $N = n^k$. By definition, there are N components of X. Call N the dimension of X.

> **B1** $X_0 \vee \ldots \vee X_{n-1}$ **B2** $\neg(X_i \wedge X_j)$ for $i \neq j$

Call a basis formula B is a b-tautology, and write $\vdash_b B$ if it can be derived from these axioms alone. If a basis symbol has dimension N, let $\top^N$ stand for the basis formula $X_0 \vee \ldots X_{n-1}$-the certain event. From **B1** above it is a tautology. The following are axioms for probability operator. I assume that ϕ, ϕ_1 and ϕ_2 are basis formulas:

> **P1** $0 \leq P(\phi) \leq 1$ **P2** $P(\phi) = 1$ if ϕ is a b $-$ tautology
> **P3** $P(\phi_1 \wedge \phi_2) + P(\phi_1 \wedge \neg\phi_2) = P(\phi_1)$ and
> **P4** $P(\phi_1) = P(\phi_2)$ if $\phi_1 \Leftrightarrow \phi_2$ is a b-tautology

As $\mathcal{L}_n(P, t, M, S, \mathbf{U})$ extends **RC** I assume that axioms of **RC** are included in the axiomatization of the former. The axioms for tensor operator are as follows.

Tensor1 $P(t(t(X, Y), Z)_i) = P(t(X, t(Y, Z))_i)$

Tensor2 $P(t(X, Y)_0) = 1 \Rightarrow P(t(X', Y')_{jk} = P(t(X'_j, \top^N))P(t(\top^M, Y_k))$

where M and N are the dimensions of X and Y respectively. The first axiom expresses the associativity of tensor product. The associativity property is expressed in terms of probabilities. Since this is valid, that is, true for every interpretation in all states, we can deduce the actual equality of the corresponding vectors for any interpretation. This axiom combined with the substitution axiom for "=" implies that for a fixed degree k we may fix an arbitrary product basis symbol of that degree, for example $t^k(\mathbf{b})$, since we have to deal only with probability formulas over bases. The second axiom asserts that if the quantum system is in a state which is a tensor product state then the probability of outcome of a measurement in some other *product* basis is the product of measurements done separately to the constituent bases X and Y. Note that the introduction of the $\top$ symbols is to keep the formula homogeneous. Also for the notation $t(X', Y')_{jk}$ refer to equation 1. The only bases I have considered are tensor product bases. Surely, there are bases which are "entangled" that is can not be written as a product basis. These bases are indirectly generated by the unitary operations. The present logic though adequate for quantum computing is slightly less expressive than those considered in [MP03b] and [Pat04]. The formulas corresponding to the unitary operators are presented below. Let Γ_N denote the formula $\sum_{k=0}^{N-1} U(ik)\overline{U(jk)} = \delta_{ij}$, for a unitary matrix of order N. Below Φ is a formula in dimension N and I_N is the unit matrix in that dimension.

Unitary1 $\Phi \Leftrightarrow [I_N]\Phi$ **Unitary2** $[U][V]\Phi \Leftrightarrow [UV]\Phi$

Unitary3 $P(X_i) = 1 \Rightarrow [U]P(X_j) = |U_{ij}|^2 \wedge \Gamma_N$

The first axiom is the normalisation axiom. It states that the unit matrix does not affect the valuation of a formula. The second axiom states that if the system is known to be in a state of a basis $\pi(X_i)$ vector then the application of the unitary operator U transforms it into a state $\sum_k \overline{U(ik)}\pi(X_k)$ and hence the probability of X_j is as stated in the axiom. The third axiom formalises the fact that the map $U \to [U]$ preserves products. The next axiom is the consistency axiom. Let us fix the dimension N and let:

$$\mathbf{U}_k \stackrel{\text{def}}{=} \bigwedge_i (P(X_i) = x_i) \Rightarrow \exists z_{11} z_{12} \ldots z_{NN}$$

$$(\bigwedge_{i=1}^N z_{ii} = x_i \wedge \forall y_1 \ldots y_N (\sum_{ij} \overline{y_i} z_{ij} y_j \geq 0)) \wedge \tag{8}$$

$$\bigwedge_{j=1}^k \bigwedge_{i=1}^n ([U_j]P(X_i) = \Sigma_{r,s=1}^N \overline{U_j(ri)} z_{rs} U_j(is)))$$

This formula simply asserts the existence of a state which satisfies probability formulas for k unitary operators. The consistency axiom is given below.

Cons. In dimension N the formulas $\mathbf{U}_k$ are satisfied for all $k \leq N^2 - N + 1$. This is the most complicated axiom. However, in N-dimensions the following theorem holds.

Theorem 2. *If the formula $\mathbf{U}_k$ are satisfied for any set of k unitary matrices for $k \leq N^2 - N + 1$ then the corresponding formula is satisfiable for all k.*

The theorem states that given an arbitrary number of formulas of the type $[U_i](\wedge_i P(X_i) = a_i)$, for $i = 1, 2, \ldots k$ if every subset of formulas of cardinality $N^2 - N + 1$ are satisfiable ($k \geq N^2 - N + 1$) then the whole set of formulas is satisfiable. This theorem is crucial in the proof of completeness theorem. Finally we have the axioms for measurement operators.

$$\textbf{Measure1} \quad \bigwedge_{ij}[U](P(X_i) = x_i) \Rightarrow M_X([V]P(X_j) = \sum_k |V(jk)|^2 x_k).$$

The axiom captures the fact that measurement of state in a basis yields as outcome the state X_i with probability x_i. A further measurement in some other basis which transforms X_i to VX_i is the sum $\sum_k |V(jk)|^2 x_k$. Note that the $|V(jk)|^2$ is the transition probability of getting an outcome X_i if the system is known to be in a state VX_i.

$$\textbf{Selection} \quad S_{X_i}([V]P(X_j)) = |V(ij)|^2.$$

The motivation of the axiom is clear since the post-measurement state is already known to be X_i. Finally, we have the following axiom and inference rules for both measurement operators.

Denote by L either of the measurement operators. Then the axiom schema for boolean combinations is:

$$\textbf{Measure2} \quad L(\Phi_1 \wedge \Phi_2) \Leftrightarrow L(\Phi_1) \wedge L(\Phi_2) \qquad \textbf{Measure3} \quad L(\neg\Phi) \Leftrightarrow \neg L(\Phi)$$

Moreover, for both measurement operators add the rule

K. From $\vdash \Phi$ infer $L\Phi$.

If a formula is theorem then by the soundness of the theory it is valid and hence true in any state. I call it **K** because a similar rule goes by the same name in modal logic. Let $\mathbf{Ax}_n(P, t, U, M, S)$ be the theory given by the above axioms. Its properties are summarised below.

Theorem 3. $\mathbf{Ax}_n(P, t, U, M, S)$ *is sound and complete.*

The proof of the theorem is rather long. It is sketched in [Pat04]. The detailed proof will appear in my dissertation. The first step is to prove satisfiability of a consistent formula ignoring tensor structures, and then to prove that the constraints imposed by tensor structures are satisfiable if the formula is consistent. Both parts of the proof use a systematic reduction of a given formula of $\mathcal{L}_n(P, t, M, S, \mathbf{U})$ to an equivalent formula in **RC**. I state that as a separate result since it gives us decision procedure for the logic.

Theorem 4. *Given a formula Φ of $\mathcal{L}_n(P, t, M, S, \mathbf{U})$ there is a polynomial time algorithm which results in a formula $\Phi*$ of* **RC** *such that Φ is satisfiable iff $\Phi*$ is satisfiable.*

As an immediate corollary we get a result proved in [BV97].

Theorem 5. *Satisfiability of a formula in $\mathcal{L}_n(P, t, M, S, \mathbf{U})$ can be decided in exponential space. If the formula is quantifier free, then its satisfiability can be decided in polynomial space.*

The proof of this result makes use of results of Ben-Or, Kozen and Reif [BKR86] for the full language, and of Canny [Can88] for the quantifier free case. As in the proof of the theorem the idea is to reduce the formula to that of a real closed field. It is obvious that the reduction algorithm is in **PSPACE**. Using the above theorem, since the algorithm for a quantum circuit yields a quantifier free formula and the validity of a set of equations and inequalities can reduced to satisfiability of the negated formula. The latter is in **PSPACE** by the results in the references cited. Thus we get another proof that classical simulation of quantum circuits is in **PSPACE**.

5   Conclusion

A complete axiomatization of a logic for quantum computation and information is presented. It is expressive enough to write formulas for quantum circuits. The formulas of the language can be used for classical and quantum simulation. This would help facilitate a comparative study of the respective complexity classes. I have illustrated it with some examples. Other cases will be dealt with elsewhere. Another possible application would be to use it as a language for specification, verification and synthesis of quantum circuits possibly with extra modal operators. It would be possible to use the language for verification of quantum hardware (model checking). I am also experimenting with some extensions of the language-in particular, bounded quantifiers over the integer indices and quantified boolean variables-for more efficient representation. Another potential field of application is quantum cryptography. Some preliminary work in this direction has been done. Yet another interesting avenue to explore is the descriptive characterisation[Imm89] of quantum complexity classes[BV97].

I wish to thank R. van der Meyden for many illuminating discussions.

References

[AC04]   S. Abramsky and B. Coecke. A categorical semantics of quantum protocols. Research Report RR-04-02, Oxford University Computing Laboratory, 2004.

[BKR86]   M. Ben-Or, D. Kozen, and J. H. Reif. The complexity of elementary algebra and geometry. *Journal of Computer and System Sciences*, 32(1):251–264, 1986.

[BPR03]   S. Basu, R. Pollack, and M-F. Roy. *Algorithms in real algebraic geometry.* Springer, 2003.

[BS04]   A. Baltag and S. Smets. A logic for quantum programs. In *Proc. of QPL 2004*, pages 39–56, 2004.

[BV97]   E. Bernstein and U. V. Vazirani. Quantum complexity theory. *SIAM. J. Computing*, 26(5):1411–1473, 1997.

[Can88]   J. F. Canny. Some algebraic and geometric computations in PSPACE. In *Proc. 20th ACM Symp. on Theory of Computing*, pages 460–467, 1988.

[CGL05]   M. L. Dalla Chiara, R. Guntini, and R. Leporoni. Quantum computational logics and fock space semantics. *Int. Journal of quantum information*, 3(1):9–16, 2005.

[FHM90]   R. Fagin, J. Y. Halpern, and N. Megiddo. A logic for reasoning about probabilities. *Information and Computation*, 87(1/2):78–128, 1990.

[Gro96]   L. Grover. A fast quantum mechanical algorithm for database search. In *Proc. 28th. annual ACM symposium on Theory of computing*, pages 212–210, New York, 1996. ACM.

[Imm89]   N. Immerman. Descriptive and computational complexity. In *Computational complexity theory, Proc. Symp. App. Math*, pages 75–91. AMS, 1989.

[MP03a]   R. v. Meyden and M. Patra. Knowledge in quantum systems. In *Theoretical aspects of knowledge and rationality*, Bloomington, 2003. ACM.

[MP03b]   R. v. Meyden and M. Patra. A logic for probability in quantum systems. In *Proc. Computer Science Logic and 8th Kurt Gdel Colloquium*, Vienna, 2003. Springer-Verlag.

[MS04]   P. Mateus and A. Serandas. Reasoning about quantum systems. In *Logics in Artificial Intelligence JELIA04*, pages 239–251. Springer-Verlag, 2004.

[NC01]   M. A. Nielsen and I. L. Chuang. *Quantum computation and information.* CUP, 2001.

[Nie03]   M. Nielsen. Universal quantum computation using only projective measurement, quantum memory, and preparation of the 0 state. *Physics Lett. A*, 308(2-3):96–100, 2003.

[Pat04]   M. Patra. Logics for quantum computation and information. *cse.unsw.edu.au/db/staff/info/mansp.html*, 2004.

[PBL95]   M. Grabowski P. Busch and P. J. Lathi. *Operational Quantum Physics.* Springer, Berlin, 1995.

[RPFS65]   R. B. Leighton R. P. Feynman and M. Sands. *Feynman Lectures on Physics Vol.III.* Addison-Wesely, Reading, Mass., 1965.

[Sho67]   J. R. Shoenfield. *Mathematical Logic.* Addison-Wesely, 1967.

[Smu61]   R. M. Smullyan. *Theory of Formal Systems.* Princeton University Press, Princeton, 1961.

[vT03]   A. van Tonder. A lambda calculus for quantum computation. *arXiv e-Print (http://arxiv.org/abs/quant-ph/03071509)*, 2003.

[Yao93]   A. C-C. Yao. Quantum circuit complexity. In *Proc. 34th. Symp. on Foundations of computer science*, pages 352–360, Los Alamitos, 1993. IEEE.

Quantitative Temporal Logic Mechanized in HOL

Orieta Celiku

Åbo Akademi University and Turku Centre for Computer Science,
Lemminkäisenkatu 14 A, 20520 Turku, Finland

Abstract. The paper describes an implementation in the HOL theorem prover of the *quantitative Temporal Logic* (*qTL*) of Morgan and McIver [18,14]. *qTL* is a branching-time temporal logic suitable for reasoning about probabilistic nondeterministic systems. The interaction between probabilities and nondeterminism, which is generally very difficult to reason about, is handled by interpreting the logic over real- rather than boolean-valued functions. In the *qTL* framework many laws of standard branching-time temporal logic generalize nicely giving access to a number of logical tools for reasoning about quantitative aspects of randomized algorithms.

1 Introduction

Randomization is very useful for improving algorithms' efficiency and solving problems where standard methods fail, but reasoning about randomized algorithms is notoriously difficult. As a result the interest in the computer-aided verification of randomized algorithms has been increasing, both in the model-checking as well as in the theorem-proving communities. Recent work on using theorem provers for such verifications includes Hurd et al.'s [9] mechanization in HOL [5] of Morgan's *probabilistic Guarded Command Language* (*pGCL*) [19] and its associated program logic [21]. We extend this work with the mechanization of the *quantitative Temporal Logic* (*qTL*) — the probabilistic generalization of temporal logic — and its associated algebra [18,14].

Our interest in the mechanization of *qTL* is several-fold. To start with, *pGCL* and *qTL* provide a unified framework in which to model, specify temporal properties of, and reason about probabilistic systems. The properties that can be specified and verified are *quantitative* and thus very general. For example, one can reason about "the probability that a walker eventually reaches a position on the number line"; more generally one can reason about the expected value of a random variable of interest when certain strategies for deciding whether to continue executing the program are applied. That *nondeterminism* — the mathematical notion underlying abstraction and refinement — is retained in the framework makes it possible to work at various abstraction levels, including at the level of program code. Moreover, nondeterminism's ability to abstract over probability distributions enables switching from quantitative to *qualitative*

D.V. Hung and M. Wirsing (Eds.): ICTAC 2005, LNCS 3722, pp. 439–453, 2005.

analyses, when one is interested in properties that hold with probability 1 [13]. Another useful application of qTL is provided by the relationship of its operators to McIver's operators for reasoning about performance-related aspects of probabilistic programs [16].

Our newly-mechanized qTL is suitable for both high-level analyses of properties of probabilistic programs, which may make use of the many algebraic laws we verify for qTL, as well as for concrete verifications, which are supported by the HOL interactive correctness tools built for $pGCL$ programs [9].

In this paper we describe how qTL is implemented in HOL. Although we briefly summarize qTL itself, we refer the reader to [14] for a thorough discussion of it. In Sec. 2 we describe the probabilistic semantics and HOL theories [9] on which the implementation of qTL builds. In Sec. 3 the syntax and semantics of qTL is given. We then continue in Sec. 4 with showing the algebra of qTL which supplies many useful properties for verification. A non-trivial result for (non-homogeneous) random walkers satisfying certain properties is verified in Sec. 5. Finally, we conclude with some remarks on the present state of computer-aided verification for probabilistic programs in Sec. 6.

Notation: We use "." for function application. We write α for a (fixed) underlying state space. Functions from α to the non-negative reals are called *expectations*; they are ordered by lifting pointwise the order $\leq$ on the reals — we denote the order on expectations by $\Rrightarrow$. Given two expectations A and B, they are equivalent, denoted $A \equiv B$, exactly when $A \Rrightarrow B$ and $B \Rrightarrow A$. Operations on expectations are pointwise liftings of those on the reals. $\underline{c}$ denotes the constant function returning c for all states. cA denotes $\underline{c} \times A$, where A is an expectation. If pred is a predicate, then we write [pred] for the *characteristic function* which takes states satisfying pred to 1, and to 0 otherwise.

2 Probabilistic Semantics

In this section we briefly describe the *quantitative program logic* [21,14] — the probabilistic semantics that has inspired the choice of semantics for qTL.

Unlike standard programs, probabilistic programs do not produce definite final states — although any *single* execution of such a program will result in the production of some specific state, which one in particular might well be impossible to predict (if its computation is governed by some random event). However over many executions the relative *frequencies* with which final states occur will be correlated with the program's known underlying random behavior. For example executing the *probabilistic choice*

$$b := \mathsf{T} \;_{2/3}\oplus\; b := \mathsf{F} \,, \tag{1}$$

a large number of times results in roughly $2/3$ of the executions setting b to T.

The language $pGCL$ [19] — the *Guarded Command Language* [3] augmented with the probabilistic choice construct mentioned above — and its associated *quantitative logic* [14] were developed to express such programs and to derive their probabilistic properties by extending the classical assertional style of programming [20]. Programs in *pGCL* are modeled (operationally) as functions (or transitions) which map *initial states* in α to (sets of) discrete probability distributions over *final states*, where a probability distribution is a function from α to the interval $[0, 1]$ which is normalized to 1. The program at (1) for instance operates over a state space of size 2, and has a single transition which maps any initial state to a (single) final distribution; we represent that distribution as a normalized function d, evaluating to $2/3$ when $b = \mathsf{T}$ and to $1/3$ when $b = \mathsf{F}$.

Since properties now involve numeric frequencies they are expressed via a logic of (non-negative) *real-valued functions*, or *expectations*. For example the property "the final value of b is T with probability $2/3$" can be expressed as "the *expected value* of $[b = \mathsf{T}]$ with respect to the distribution d above is $2/3 \times 1 + 1/3 \times 0 = 2/3$". However, direct appeal to the operational semantics is often unwieldy — better is the equivalent transformer-style semantics which is obtained by rationalizing calculations in terms of expectations rather than transitions. The *post-expectation* $[b = \mathsf{T}]$ has been transformed to the *pre-expectation* $2/3$ by the program (1) above so that they are in the relation "$2/3$ is the expected value of $[b = \mathsf{T}]$ with respect to the program's result distribution".

More generally, having access to real-valued functions makes it possible to express many properties as "random variables" of interest, which for us are synonymous with expectations. Then given a program P, an expectation A and a state $s \in \alpha$, we define wp.$P.A.s$ to be the expected value of A with respect to the result distribution of program P if executed initially from state s [14]. We say that wp.P is the *expectation transformer* relative to P. In our example that allows us to write

$$\frac{2/3}{} \quad \equiv \quad \mathsf{wp}.(b := \mathsf{T} \ _{2/3}\oplus \ b := \mathsf{F}).[b = \mathsf{T}] \ . \tag{2}$$

When P contains genuine *nondeterminism* its execution results in a set of possible distributions and the definition of wp is modified to take account of this — in fact wp.$P.A.s$ may be defined so that it delivers either the *least*- or *greatest* expected value with respect to all distributions in the result set. Those choices correspond respectively to a *demonic* or *angelic* resolution of the nondeterminism — which interpretation is used depends very much on the application.

With the transformer approach it is possible to express temporal properties of systems. For example, fixing the underlying computation to be the expectation transformer relative to the program at (1), the modal primitive *next time* "○" has a natural interpretation relative to an expectation, say $[b = \mathsf{T}]$ — the intended interpretation of ○$[b = \mathsf{T}]$ is "$2/3$", and expresses as Eqn. 2 does, that the probability of $(b = \mathsf{T})$'s holding after *one execution step* is $2/3$. More generally, given an expectation transformer *step*, and an expectation A, ○A is the expected value of A when transformed as explained above by *step*.

Reachability properties can also be expressed, using while-loops. For example since the following loop

$$\mathsf{do} \ (b = \mathsf{F}) \quad \rightarrow \quad b := \mathsf{T} \ _{2/3}\oplus \ b := \mathsf{F} \ \mathsf{od} \ ,$$

iterates as long as $(b = \mathsf{F})$ holds, its termination probability is in fact the probability of *eventually* establishing $(b = \mathsf{T})$ by repeatedly executing the probabilistic choice. By a simple fact of probability theory this probability is 1. Although many temporal properties can be expressed in the *pGCL* framework, analysis of more complex temporal behavior requires the introduction of an extra logical layer.

The *quantitative Temporal Logic (qTL)* [18,14] — the probabilistic extension of temporal logic — was developed to express such properties and provide a set of logical tools to reason about them. The underlying computation is viewed as an expectation transformer, as described above, and the temporal operators *eventually* ($\Diamond$), *always* ($\Box$), and *unless* ($\triangleright$), are defined in terms of fixed points over expectations. We will set out the formal semantics in Sec. 3; in the remainder of this section we describe the HOL theories of non-negative reals, expectations and their transformers, which are the basis of the *qTL* mechanization.

2.1 Formalized Expectation Transformers

Non-negative reals have been formalized in HOL by Hurd et al. [9] as a type of higher-order logic, called posreal. The posreal type also includes a constant ∞, which dominates other elements of the type with respect to the natural order $\leq$ on posreal. The usual arithmetic operations are defined over this type.

Expectations, formalized in HOL by Hurd et al., are functions of type:

$$(\alpha)\mathsf{expect} \;\hat{=}\; \alpha \to \mathsf{posreal} \;.$$

where α, the type of the state space, is polymorphic and can be instantiated to any type of higher-order logic. The order and operations on posreal are lifted pointwise to operations on expectations. The space of expectations bounded by any constant expectation $\underline{c}$ forms a complete partial order, and fixed points are well-defined for any monotonic function on such expectations.

We define some extra operations on expectations which are needed in the probabilistic context; in Fig. 1 we name a few. These operations generalize standard operations on predicates; however since we are working in the more general context of the reals there may be several suitable generalizations for each operation on predicates. For example, both "$\sqcap$" and "$\&$" are suitable, in different contexts, as generalizations of conjunction. The first sanity check when picking the operators is whether the truth tables are as expected for standard predicates. The choice of the operators is fully-motivated in [14].

Expectation transformers are functions from expectations to expectations:

$$(\alpha)\mathsf{transformer} \;\hat{=}\; (\alpha)\mathsf{expect} \to (\alpha)\mathsf{expect} \;.$$

For us the interesting expectation transformers are those that determine the wp-meaning of *pGCL* programs, that is, describe how *pGCL* commands transform post-expectations into pre-expectations. For example, assignments induce substitutions, and probabilistic choices average according to the specified probabilities. We show in Fig. 2 the definitions for the straight-line commands; the wp-semantics for the complete *pGCL* (including Boolean choice, and while-loops) has been formalized in HOL by Hurd et al. [9].

$$
\begin{aligned}
A \sqcap B &\;\hat{=}\; (\lambda s \bullet A.s \text{ min } B.s) & minimum \\
A \sqcup B &\;\hat{=}\; (\lambda s \bullet A.s \text{ max } B.s) & maximum \\
\neg A &\;\hat{=}\; (\lambda s \bullet 1 - A.s) & complement \\
A \;\&\; B &\;\hat{=}\; (\lambda s \bullet A.s + B.s - 1) & conjunction \\
A \rightarrowtail B &\;\hat{=}\; (\lambda s \bullet 1 - (A.s - B.s)) & implication, \Rrightarrow\text{-}adjoint \text{ of } \& \\
P \rightrightarrows Q &\;\hat{=}\; [P \Rightarrow Q] & \text{``}standard\text{''} implication
\end{aligned}
$$

A, B range over (α)expect; P, Q over standard (boolean-valued) predicates.
$\neg$ binds tightest, whereas the order relations $\Rrightarrow, \equiv$ weakest.
We will also use more general versions of some of the above operations, with β —
a scalar from posreal — substituted for 1. They can be viewed as scaling by β the
corresponding operation. Such operators will be denoted by say $\&_\beta$ instead of $\&$.

Fig. 1. Some operations on expectations

$$
\begin{aligned}
&skip & &\text{wp.skip.}A \;\hat{=}\; A \;, \\
&assignment & &\text{wp.}(x := E).A \;\hat{=}\; A[x := E] \;, \\
&sequential\ composition & &\text{wp.}(r; r').A \;\hat{=}\; \text{wp.}r.(\text{wp.}r'.A) \;, \\
&probabilistic\ choice & &\text{wp.}(r \;{}_p\!\oplus r').A \;\hat{=}\; p \times \text{wp.}r.A + (\underline{1}{-}p) \times \text{wp.}r'.A \;, \\
&multi\text{-}way\ prob.\ choice & &\text{wp.}(r_0 @ p_0 \mid \ldots \mid r_n @ p_n).A \;\hat{=}\; p_0 \times \text{wp.}r_0.A + \ldots + p_n \times \text{wp.}r_n.A, \\
&nondeterm.\ choice & &\text{wp.}(r \;\|\; r').A \;\hat{=}\; \text{wp.}r.A \sqcap \text{wp.}r'.A \;.
\end{aligned}
$$

The state space here is instantiated to string $\rightarrow \mathbb{Z}$.
E is an integer-valued state function, expectation p is 1-bounded, and $p_0 + \ldots + p_n \equiv \underline{1}$.
Nondeterminism is interpreted demonically, that is minimal-seeking.

Fig. 2. Structural definitions of wp for straight-line $pGCL$

$$
\begin{aligned}
\text{feasible } t &\;\hat{=}\; \forall A, c \bullet A \Rrightarrow \underline{c} \;\;\Rightarrow\;\; t.A \Rrightarrow \underline{c} \\
\text{monotonic } t &\;\hat{=}\; \forall A, B \bullet A \Rrightarrow B \;\;\Rightarrow\;\; t.A \Rrightarrow t.B \\
\text{sublinear } t &\;\hat{=}\; \forall A, B, c, c_1, c_2 \bullet t.(c_1 A + c_2 B - \underline{c}) \Rrightarrow c_1(t.A) + c_2(t.B) - \underline{c}
\end{aligned}
$$

t ranges over (α)transformer, A, B over (α)expect, and c, c_1, c_2 over posreal.
Feasibility implies $t.A \Rrightarrow \sqcup A$, so $t.\underline{0} \equiv \underline{0}$.
Sublinearity generalizes *conjunctivity* of standard predicate transformers.
Monotonicity is a consequence of sublinearity.
The wp-operator (part of which is given in Fig. 2) satisfies all three conditions [14,9].

Fig. 3. Healthiness conditions for demonic transformers

We do not discuss the full semantics of $pGCL$ here because the structure of
the wp-operator is not of importance in the development of the qTL theory.[1,2]
More important are the properties characterizing the wp-transformers, which
generalize Dijkstra's *healthiness conditions* characterizing standard programs.

---

[1] It is however imperative when verifying concrete algorithms. For such verifications
correctness tools [9] can be used to reduce reasoning about goals of the form "$A \Rrightarrow$
wp.*Prog*.B" to reasoning about relationships between ordinary expectations.

[2] We will not make any assumptions about how the state space is implemented, which
increases the utility of the mechanized theory.

The healthiness conditions for demonic probabilistic transformers are shown in Fig. 3; they are part of the HOL expectations theory formalized in HOL by Hurd et al. [9]. Monotonicity, for example, ensures that the fixed-points $(\mu X \bullet t.X)$ (least), and $(\nu X \bullet t.X)$ (greatest) are well-defined for a transformer t.

3 qTL and Its Semantics

In this section we show the syntax and semantics of qTL, Morgan and McIver's [18,14] probabilistic extension of temporal logic.

The syntax of qTL formulas, set out in Fig. 4, is defined in HOL as a new datatype called formula. Note that any expectation can be transformed into a qTL formula of the form Atom(A).

$$
\begin{aligned}
\text{formula} \ \hat{=}\ & \text{Atom}(A) \\
| \ & \neg a \mid a \sqcup b \mid a \sqcap b \mid a \ \& \ b \mid a \rightarrow b \mid a \rightrightarrows b \\
| \ & \circ a \mid \Diamond a \mid a \rhd b
\end{aligned}
$$

A is an expectation. Lower-case letters $a, b, \ldots$ range over formulas.

The second row contains state formulas. To improve readability here we use the same symbols as for the operators on expectations.

The third row describes proper temporal formulas, which are read as usual: *next time*, *eventually*, (weak) *unless*. *always* is defined in terms of *unless*:

$$\Box a \ \hat{=}\ a \rhd (\text{Atom}(\text{false}))$$

where false $\hat{=}\ \underline{0}$.

Temporal operators associate to the right, and apart from $\neg$ bind tighter than the rest of the operators.

Fig. 4. The syntax of qTL

As hinted in the previous section, when interpreting the temporal formulas we do so with respect to a fixed expectation transformer *step*, which describes the underlying computation; the intention is that most of the time and whenever convenient *step* is wp.*Step*, where *Step* is a syntactic *pGCL* program.

The formal semantics of qTL is defined on the structure of the formulas and is set out in full in Fig. 5 — it essentially generalizes standard modal μ-calculus [11] from Booleans to reals, and takes the temporal subset of that [14]. We postpone explaining β's appearance in the definitions until further down in this section.

The operational interpretation of the quantitative temporal operators requires thinking in terms of games. Take $\Diamond(\text{Atom}(A))$: if A is a standard expectation — there exists a predicate P such that $A \equiv [P]$ — then the interpretation of $\Diamond(\text{Atom}(A))$ is in fact the probability that P is eventually established. However, in the more general case when A is a proper expectation, thinking in terms of

$$\|\mathsf{Atom}(A)\|_{(\beta,step)} \;\; \hat{=} \;\; A \sqcap \beta$$

$$\|\neg a\|_{(\beta,step)} \;\; \hat{=} \;\; \beta - \|a\|_{(\beta,step)}$$

$$\|a \sqcap b\|_{(\beta,step)} \;\; \hat{=} \;\; \|a\|_{(\beta,step)} \sqcap \|b\|_{(\beta,step)}$$

$$\|a \sqcup b\|_{(\beta,step)} \;\; \hat{=} \;\; \|a\|_{(\beta,step)} \sqcup \|b\|_{(\beta,step)}$$

$$\|a \;\&\; b\|_{(\beta,step)} \;\; \hat{=} \;\; \|a\|_{(\beta,step)} \;\&_\beta\; \|b\|_{(\beta,step)}$$

$$\|a \dashrightarrow b\|_{(\beta,step)} \;\; \hat{=} \;\; \|a\|_{(\beta,step)} \dashrightarrow_\beta \|b\|_{(\beta,step)}$$

$$\|b \Rrightarrow b\|_{(\beta,step)} \;\; \hat{=} \;\; \|a\|_{(\beta,step)} \Rrightarrow_\beta \|b\|_{(\beta,step)}$$

$$\|\bigcirc a\|_{(\beta,step)} \;\; \hat{=} \;\; step.\|a\|_{(\beta,step)}$$

$$\|\Diamond a\|_{(\beta,step)} \;\; \hat{=} \;\; (\mu A \bullet \|a\|_{(\beta,step)} \sqcup step.A)$$

$$\|a \rhd b\|_{(\beta,step)} \;\; \hat{=} \;\; (\nu A \bullet \|b\|_{(\beta,step)} \sqcup (\|a\|_{(\beta,step)} \sqcap step.A))$$

step is a (α)transformer. β is a **posreal** scalar.

The (least μ and greatest ν) fixed points are defined over the complete partial order of expectations bounded by β. For a monotonic *step* the fixed points are well-defined. For finite β, $\sqcup$ and $\sqcap$ are duals: $\|a \sqcup b\|_{(\beta,step)} \equiv \|\neg(\neg a \sqcap \neg b)\|_{(\beta,step)}$.

Fig. 5. The semantics of qTL

"establishing A" does not make sense. The interpretation of $\Diamond(\mathsf{Atom}(A))$ in the general case relies on a game-like analogy, and we quote directly from [13]:

> [I]t is the supremum, over all strategies that determine in each state whether to make another transition or to stop, of the expected value of A when the strategy says "stop"; the strategy "never stop" gives 0 by definition.

The other operators are interpreted similarly. Note for example that non-termination in the case of $\square$ is interpreted as a success, and that the interpretation of $\rhd$ involves a mixture of minimizing and maximizing strategies.

With the game analogy in mind it is clear that there is no need to focus exclusively on expectations bounded by 1 when specifying the semantics of qTL, although admittedly most of the time this is sufficient (since most often than not we are interested in temporal behavior relative to standard expectations). Especially as far as the implementation in HOL is concerned, it is advantageous to parameterize the semantic operator with the bound "β". This is so because proving properties for an arbitrary bound β (although sometimes under the assumption that $\beta \neq \infty$) is no more difficult than in the 1-bounded case. Moreover, specializing to the 1-bounded expectations is trivial, and clearly we also have access to reasoning about unbounded expectations, although as expected the properties available in this case are fewer.

We conclude this section with a few words on the expressibility of qTL. Recall that in the wp-definition (Fig. 2) we interpreted nondeterminism demonically. With such an interpretation we can only describe *universal* versions of the temporal operators, since demonic interpretations give us guarantees on least expected values. For a logic that also admits *existential* versions of the operators the transformer *step* should also allow angelic interpretations. However, the price to pay is that sublinearity does not generally hold for transformers containing angelic nondeterminism [14]. Note however that for the semantics to be well-defined monotonicity is all that is needed.

4   The Algebra of qTL

In this section we show some of the qTL properties [14], which generalize laws of standard branching-time temporal logic [1]. They are essential logical tools when verifying algorithms since often direct appeal to the semantics is impractical. The results have been derived in HOL from the semantics of qTL (Fig. 5) and the main general healthiness assumptions about the transformer $step$ (Fig. 3).

A useful property in concrete verifications is $feasibility$, which can be proved easily if $step$ is feasible:

$$\forall \beta, step, a \bullet \ \|a\|_{(\beta, step)} \Rrightarrow \underline{\beta} \ .$$

From now on to improve readability we identify formulas with their semantics; we identify the semantic bound β when that can be ambiguous, in particular, we mark those properties that assume that the bound is finite. We also pretty-print $\mathsf{Atom}(A)$ as simply A. As far as the computation $step$ is concerned we assume throughout that it is feasible and monotonic. However many of the interesting properties require $step$ be sublinear (i.e. demonic). We will point out when the sublinearity assumption is necessary. Although a (purely) demonic $step$ is in most situations expressive enough, there are some situations when it is more advantageous to interpret nondeterminism angelically. McIver [16], for example, showed how temporal operators working with an angelic transformer can be used to reason about the efficiency of probabilistic programs.

The properties of "$\circ$" are trivially inherited from those of the transformer $step$. In Fig. 6 we show some basic consequences of the monotonicity of $step$.

Next we prove the basic fixed points laws for $\Diamond, \triangleright$, and $\square$, which are shown in Fig. 7. The $greatest$ law for $always$, for example, is a very useful tool for bounding from below the probability that $invariance$ properties hold. Moreover the verification conditions in such cases can be discharged with the help of total correctness calculators [9].

We also note that the usual "double" laws hold in our setting:

$$\Diamond\Diamond a \equiv \Diamond a \qquad double, \ eventually \ ,$$
$$\square\square a \equiv \square a \qquad double, \ always \ .$$

The most challenging and interesting properties are shown in Fig. 8. As noted in [14] it can require some ingenuity to describe the intuition behind some of them. However, what is clear is that these properties allow breaking down the reasoning to more manageable pieces, and achieving modularity of proofs. The example in the next section illustrates the usefulness of such properties.

$$a \Rrightarrow b \quad \Rightarrow \quad \bigcirc a \Rrightarrow \bigcirc b \qquad \textit{monotonic, next time}$$
$$a \Rrightarrow b \quad \Rightarrow \quad \Diamond a \Rrightarrow \Diamond b \qquad \textit{monotonic, eventually}$$
$$a \Rrightarrow b \quad \Rightarrow \quad \Box a \Rrightarrow \Box b \qquad \textit{monotonic, always}$$
$$a \Rrightarrow b \quad \Rightarrow \quad \neg b \Rrightarrow \neg a \qquad \textit{antimonotonic, complement } (*)$$

$(*)$ assumes $\beta \neq \infty$.

Because some of the formulas, e.g. those containing $\rightarrow\!\!\!\triangleright$, are neither "logically positive" nor "negative", a more general result for the (anti)monotonicity of positive (negative) formulas cannot be established.

For op any of the monotonic operators, it is easy to prove:

$$op(a) \sqcup op(b) \Rrightarrow op(a \sqcup b) \qquad \textit{subdistributes } \sqcup$$
$$op(a \sqcap b) \quad \Rrightarrow op(a) \sqcap op(b) \qquad \textit{supdistributes } \sqcap$$

Fig. 6. (Anti)Monotonicity properties

$$\Diamond a \equiv a \sqcup \bigcirc\Diamond a \qquad \textit{fixed point, eventually}$$
$$a \sqcup \bigcirc b \Rrightarrow b \Rightarrow \Diamond a \Rrightarrow b \qquad \textit{least, eventually}$$
$$\bigcirc a \sqcup \bigcirc\Diamond a \Rrightarrow \Diamond a$$
$$a \triangleright b \equiv b \sqcup (a \sqcap \bigcirc(a \triangleright b)) \qquad \textit{fixed point, unless}$$
$$d \Rrightarrow b \sqcup (a \sqcap \bigcirc d) \Rightarrow d \Rrightarrow a \triangleright b \qquad \textit{greatest, unless}$$
$$\Box a \equiv a \sqcap \bigcirc\Box a \qquad \textit{fixed point, always}$$
$$b \Rrightarrow a \sqcap \bigcirc b \Rightarrow b \Rrightarrow \Box a \qquad \textit{greatest, always}$$
$$\Box a \Rrightarrow \bigcirc a \sqcap \bigcirc\Box a$$

The monotonicity of *step* suffices for these properties.

Fig. 7. Fixed point properties of $\Diamond, \triangleright$, and $\Box$

5   Example: The Jumping Bean

The verification of the example presented in this section follows very closely Morgan's presentation of the proof [17]; the same result is also proved in [14], although the presentation there is given in terms of while-loops. Throughout this section we assume that the semantic bound β is 1. Moreover, we assume that the computation step is given in terms of wp.

The Jumping Bean sits on the number line and hops some integer distance, either up or down. Informally, the Bean must move according to the following rules:

1. With some nonzero probability, it *must move* at least one unit up or down.
2. There is a *uniform maximum distance*, arbitrarily large but fixed, that it can travel in one jump.
3. Its *expected movement is never down*: on average, it either moves up or stays where it is.

$$\square a \ \& \ \square b \Rightarrow \square(a \ \& \ b) \qquad \textit{always subdistributes} \ \&$$
$$\square(a \dashrightarrow b) \Rightarrow \square a \dashrightarrow \square b \qquad \textit{always supdistributes} \dashrightarrow$$
$$a \ \& \ \square(a \rightrightarrows \circ a) \Rightarrow \square a$$
$$\square(a \dashrightarrow b) \ \& \ \Diamond a \Rightarrow \Diamond b$$
$$\square a \Rightarrow \neg\Diamond(\neg a) \qquad \textit{always-eventually duality}$$
$$\Diamond a \ \& \ \square(\circ a \rightrightarrows a) \Rightarrow a$$
$$\Diamond a \ \& \ \square b \Rightarrow \Diamond(a \ \& \ b)$$

The properties assume $\beta \neq \infty$, and that *step* is sublinear.

Fig. 8. Duality properties and more

For example, the *symmetric walker*:

$$Symmetric\,Walker \ \hat{=} \ \ n := n - 1 \ _{1/2}\oplus \ n := n + 1 \ , \tag{3}$$

trivially satisfies the required behavior: it moves with probability 1, the maximum distance of each jump is 1, and on average it stays in place. A less trivial example of an acceptable behavior is that of this *demonic walker*:

$$Demonic\,Walker \ \hat{=} \ \begin{pmatrix} n := n + 2 \ @ \ 1/4 \\ \text{skip} \qquad @ \ 5/12 \\ n := n - 1 \ @ \ 1/3 \end{pmatrix} \ \| \ \begin{pmatrix} n := n + 1 \ @ \ 1/2 \\ n := n - 1 \ @ \ 1/2 \end{pmatrix} \tag{4}$$

On each step the walker can choose to move according to the distribution specified in the left statement or the one in the right — which choice will be made cannot be predicted in advance. However, each of the alternatives satisfies the movement conditions set above, thus the *demonic walker*'s behavior is in the acceptable range.

We will prove that under the three assumptions above (which we state formally below), and given any number H on the integer line, the Bean will eventually jump over it with probability 1:

$$\Diamond[H \leq n] \ \equiv \ \underline{1} \ . \tag{5}$$

Here n is the variable recording the current position of the Bean on the line. First we note that we can easily establish $\Diamond[H \leq n] \Rightarrow \underline{1}$ from the feasibility of the formulas. However the other direction is nontrivial to show since the least fixed point property works the other way around. Moreover, since we do not know the exact probabilities involved in the jumps we cannot just solve the fixed-point equation. This is an indication that we need to check whether some *zero-one* law is at work. The next theorem shows an example of such a law for *eventually*.

Theorem 1 (Zero-one law for *eventually*). *If the probability of eventually establishing a standard predicate P is everywhere bounded away from 0 then it is in fact 1:*

$$(\exists c \bullet 0 < c \wedge \underline{c} \Rightarrow \Diamond[P]) \quad \Rightarrow \quad \Diamond[P] \equiv \underline{1}$$

Note that we are assuming that step is nondivergent.[3]

Another *zero-one* law we have available for $\Diamond$ of a standard expectation $[P]$ is a lot like the variant-rule for probabilistic loops [14]. Informally, if we can find an integer-valued function of the state — a *variant* — that

- is bounded from below and above while P is not established,
- and the probability of its increasing on every computation step is bounded away from 0,

then we know that with probability 1, P will eventually be established.

Theorem 2 (Variant-rule for *eventually*). *For any standard predicate P, an integer-valued* state variant V,

$$(\exists c, L, H \bullet$$
$$0 < c \wedge \neg(P \Rightarrow L \leq V < H) \wedge (\forall N \bullet c[\neg P \wedge (V = N)] \Rightarrow \circ[N < V])) \Rightarrow$$
$$\Diamond[P] \equiv \underline{1}$$

From the informal assumptions the position of the Bean must increase with some probability, if the Bean must move on each step and its expected movement is never down. However, we cannot apply Thm. 2 directly to our initial goal because we cannot bound our variant n from below.

Instead we argue that given any (finite) position L to the left of H, if the Bean starts from a position within the interval $[L \ldots H)$ then

- it eventually escapes from that interval with probability 1,
- the probability of its escaping from the right can be bounded away from 0 — this probability depends on how low L is chosen.

The glue to all the pieces is the following lemma.

Lemma 3. *For any H, L*

$$\Diamond[\neg(L \leq n < H)] \quad \& \quad [L \leq n] \rhd [H \leq n] \quad \Rightarrow \quad \Diamond[H \leq n] .$$

The part that needs some explanation is when for the chosen L the initial position of n falls to the left of the interval $[L \ldots H)$. Then trivially the first conjunct of the left-hand side is 1, however since both $[L \leq n]$ and $[H \leq n]$ are 0, by the semantics of $\rhd$ and the definition of $\&$ we get on the left-hand side 0, which in other words means that we cannot say anything nontrivial about the probability of $(H \leq n)$'s establishment. Clearly L should be chosen such that it is lower than n's initial position (when this itself is lower than H). We show that L can be chosen low enough so that the probability of escaping to the right of H is at least $1/2$, which allows us to prove the following:

$$\begin{array}{lll} & \Diamond[\neg(L \leq n < H)] \quad \& \quad [L \leq n] \rhd [H \leq n] & \\ \Leftarrow & \underline{1} \quad \& \quad \underline{1/2} & \text{To show later (6,7)} \\ \equiv & \underline{1/2} \, . & \text{Definition of \&, Fig 1} \end{array}$$

---

[3] For $pGCL$ programs nondivergence means that they *terminate with probability* 1 [14].

Having bounded $\Diamond[H \le n]$ away from 0, by appeal to Thm. 1, we can conclude that the Bean's eventual escape to the right of H is *almost certain*, i.e. occurs with probability 1.

Now we fill in the missing steps, for which we first state the assumptions about the Jumping Bean formally in Fig. 9.

$$\forall L, H \bullet L \le H \Rightarrow$$
$$\exists c \bullet 0 < c \Rightarrow \qquad\qquad JB1$$
$$\forall N \bullet c[L \le n < H \wedge (n = N)] \Rightarrow \circ(N < n)$$

JB1 encodes the requirement that the Bean must move on each step; more precisely that it must move up with some probability.

$$\exists K \bullet 0 < K \wedge$$
$$\forall L, H \bullet L \le H \Rightarrow \qquad\qquad JB2$$
$$\langle L : n : H \rangle \Rightarrow \circ\langle L : n : H + K \rangle$$

where

$$\langle L : n : H \rangle \;\hat{=}\; [L \le n \le H] \times (n - \underline{L}) + [H < n] \times (\underline{H - L}) \;.$$

K in *JB2* is the maximum distance the Bean can travel in one step; recall that in our informal assumption we required that such a distance be bounded. *JB2* also encodes the requirement that the movement never be down: take $L + 1 = H = N$, where N is the Bean's initial position (in state s). Then $\langle L : n : L+1 \rangle$ in s is 1, and the only way for $1 \le \circ\langle L : n : L+1+K \rangle.s$ is if finally $N \le n$.

We also assume that the jump is nondivergent.

Fig. 9. Jumping Bean assumptions

Appealing to Thm. 2 with state-variant n we directly conclude from *JB1* that:

$$\forall L, H \bullet L \le H \;\;\Rightarrow\;\; \Diamond[\neg(L \le n < H)] \equiv \underline{1} \;. \tag{6}$$

Next we prove that under assumption *JB2* the bound L can be chosen such that:

$$\underline{1/2} \;\;\Rightarrow\;\; [L \le n] \triangleright [H \le n] \;. \tag{7}$$

First we note that given an initial position N of the Bean, if $H \le N$ then the right-hand side trivially evaluates to 1, and thus it is enough to choose any $L \le H$ (for which (6) is true). So we can safely assume that $N < H$ initially.

Using the least-fixed point property for *unless*, and some transformations of *JB2* which we do not show here because the details are rather unenlightening, we can prove:

$$\frac{\langle L : n : H + K \rangle}{H + K - L} \;\Rightarrow\; [L \le n] \triangleright [H \le n] \;.$$

For any initial position of the Bean N (to the left of H), we can see that choosing $L = 2N - (H + K)$, makes the left-hand side 1/2.

We have thus proved the claim we set about to:

Theorem 4 (Jumping Bean). *Given any number H on the number line, a Jumping Bean satisfying the assumptions JB1 and JB2 (see Fig. 9) will eventually jump over it with probability 1:*

$$\Diamond[H \le n] \equiv \underline{1} \ .$$

This result is more general than similar ones found in probability textbooks: the actual transition probabilities may vary from place to place since the probability distributions can be functions of state, so our walkers may be non-homogeneous. Allowing nondeterministic moves is a further generalization to traditional such theorems — the transition probabilities may vary not only on different places of the number line but also on different visits to the same place (see *Demonic Walker* (4)). We also note that the state space is infinite, and the theorem is parameterized on the limit on the jump.

To give an idea of the mechanization effort involved in the verification, the proofs of this section (including those for the *zero-one* laws) required around 2000 lines of proof script. However, proving that the *Symmetric Walker* (see (3)) and *Demonic Walker* (see (4)) satisfy the assumptions is by comparison much easier, and the proofs were around 100 and 150 lines respectively. The latter verifications can also be supported by correctness tools built for *pGCL* [9], cutting the verification effort further.

Verifications in a theorem prover are most useful if properties about classes of probabilistic programs can be proved — this is possible either as in our example, by stating the assumptions as generally as possible, or by specifying the syntactic *pGCL* program as abstractly as possible and using refinement to derive the property for concrete programs. The refinement approach is justified by theorems such as the following:

$$\forall \beta, step, step' \bullet step \sqsubseteq step' \quad \Rightarrow \quad \|a\|_{(\beta, step)} \Rrightarrow \|a\|_{(\beta, step')} \ ,$$

where $step \sqsubseteq step'$ denotes that $step'$ *refines* $step$ — formally that $\forall A \bullet$ wp.*Step*.$A \Rrightarrow$ wp.*Step'*.A — and a is a positive formula.

6   Conclusions and Related Work

The importance of having methods suitable for reasoning about randomized algorithms is already widely recognized. A recent survey on a number of approaches used to verify the correctness of such algorithms is presented by Norman [22]. As far as computer-aided verification is concerned much work has been done in the area of model checking, with PRISM [12,23], ETMCC [4], Ymer [24], RAPTURE [10], and ProbVerus [6] being some of the model-checking tools for probabilistic systems. They differ in whether they model-check purely probabilistic systems (ETMCC, Ymer, ProbVerus), or probabilistic nondeterministic systems (PRISM, RAPTURE); the temporal logics used to express the properties to be model-checked also vary, although they mainly fall into two categories:

logics that keep the formulas standard and associate probabilities with computation paths, and those that have formulas denote probabilities rather than truth values. qTL falls into the latter category.

Although impressive work has been done to tackle the problems inherent in model-checking approaches, such as state explosion, model-state finiteness, and the inability to parameterize systems, as concluded in [22] most of the probabilistic model-checking tools are not yet sufficiently developed compared to their non-probabilistic peers; as such they still are applicable to only complete, finite-state models.

Theorem provers can deal with infinite-state systems, and parameterization — our Jumping Bean theorem is one such example. However, verification using theorem provers is still labor-intensive. Compared to model-checking efforts not much work has been done on providing theorem prover support for verifying probabilistic systems. To our knowledge the first work on verifying probabilistic programs using a theorem prover is that of Hurd [8], who formalized probability theory in HOL and implemented tools for reasoning about correctness of (purely) probabilistic algorithms. More recently work on formalizing $pGCL$ and its quantitative logic in HOL has appeared [9,2], and it is this work that we extended. Similarly, support for probabilistic reasoning in the $pGCL$ style is being incorporated in the B method [7,15].

Acknowledgments

I thank Annabelle McIver for answering my questions with regard to qTL and commenting on a draft of this paper. I also thank Carroll Morgan for making available the nice Jumping Bean slides.

References

1. M. Ben-Ari, A. Pnueli, and Z. Manna. The temporal logic of branching time. *Acta Informatica*, 20:207–226, 1983.
2. O. Celiku and A. McIver. Cost-based analysis of probabilistic programs mechanised in HOL. *Nordic Journal of Computing*, 11(2):102–128, 2004.
3. E. W. Dijkstra. *A Discipline of Programming*. Prentice-Hall, 1976.
4. Erlangen-Twente Markov Chain Checker.
   http://www.informatik.uni-erlangen.de/etmcc/.
5. M. J. C. Gordon and T. F. Melham. *Introduction to HOL (A theorem-proving environment for higher order logic)*. Cambridge University Press, 1993.
6. V. Hartonas-Garmhausen, S. V. A. Campos, and E. M. Clarke. Probverus: Probabilistic symbolic model checking. In *Formal Methods for Real-Time and Probabilistic Systems, 5th International AMAST Workshop, Proceedings*, volume 1601 of *Lecture Notes in Computer Science*, pages 96–110. Springer, 1999.
7. T. S. Hoang, Z. Jin, K. Robinson, A. McIver, and C. Morgan. Probabilistic invariants for probabilistic machines. In *ZB 2003: Formal Specification and Development in Z and B,Proceedings*, volume 2651 of *Lecture Notes in Computer Science*, pages 240–259. Springer, 2003.

8. J. Hurd. *Formal Verification of Probabilistic Algorithms.* PhD thesis, University of Cambridge, 2002.
9. J. Hurd, A. McIver, and C. Morgan. Probabilistic guarded commands mechanized in HOL. In *Proc. of QAPL 2004*, Mar. 2004.
10. B. Jeannet, P. D'Argenio, and K. Larsen. RAPTURE: A tool for verifying Markov Decision Processes. In I. Cerna, editor, *Tools Day'02*, Brno, Czech Republic, Technical Report. Faculty of Informatics, Masaryk University Brno, 2002.
11. D. Kozen. Results on the propositional μ-calculus. *Theoretical Computer Science*, 27:333–354, 1983.
12. M. Kwiatkowska, G. Norman, and D. Parker. PRISM: Probabilistic symbolic model checker. In *Proceedings of TOOLS 2002*, volume 2324 of *Lecture Notes in Computer Science*, pages 200–204. Springer, Apr. 2002.
13. A. McIver and C. Morgan. Almost-certain eventualities and abstract probabilities in the quantitative temporal logic qTL. *Theoretical Computer Science*, 293(3):507–534, 2003.
14. A. McIver and C. Morgan. *Abstraction, refinement and proof for probabilistic systems.* Springer, 2004.
15. A. McIver, C. Morgan, and T. S. Hoang. Probabilistic termination in B. In *ZB 2003: Formal Specification and Development in Z and B, Proceedings*, volume 2651 of *Lecture Notes in Computer Science*, pages 216–239. Springer, 2003.
16. A. K. McIver. Quantitative program logic and expected time bounds in probabilistic distributed algorithms. *Theoretical Computer Science*, 282:191–219, 2002.
17. C. Morgan. Probabilistic temporal logic: qTL. *Lectures on Probabilistic Formal Methods for the 2004 RSISE Logic Summer School.* Slides available at *http://www.cse.unsw.edu.au/~carrollm/canberra04/*.
18. C. Morgan and A. McIver. An expectation-transformer model for probabilistic temporal logic. *Logic Journal of the IGPL*, 7(6):779–804, 1999.
19. C. Morgan and A. McIver. pGCL: Formal reasoning for random algorithms. *South African Computer Journal*, 22:14—27, 1999.
20. C. C. Morgan. *Programming from Specifications.* Prentice-Hall, 1990.
21. C. C. Morgan, A. K. McIver, and K. Seidel. Probabilistic predicate transformers. *ACM Transactions on Programming Languages and Systems*, 18(3):325–353, May 1996.
22. G. Norman. Analysing randomized distributed algorithms. In *Validation of Stochastic Systems*, volume 2925 of *Lecture Notes in Computer Science*, pages 384–418. Springer-Verlag, 2004.
23. Probabilistic Symbolic Model Checker. *http://www.cs.bham.ac.uk/dxp/prism/*.
24. Ymer. *http://www.cs.cmu.edu/~lorens/ymer.html*.

Weak Stochastic Bisimulation for Non-Markovian Processes*

Natalia López and Manuel Núñez

Dpt. Sistemas Informáticos y Programación,
Universidad Complutense de Madrid
{natalia, mn}@sip.ucm.es

Abstract. In this paper we introduce a novel notion of bisimulation to properly capture the behavior of stochastic systems with general distributions. The key idea consists in the identification of different sequences of random variables if the *additions* of the random variables of each sequence are identically distributed. That is, we will not only identify sequences of internal actions with one of them (as it is usually done in weak bisimulations) but we will also reduce (in some conditions) sequences of stochastic transitions to only one transition. Therefore, we will identify processes that are considered non-equivalent in previous notions of bisimulation for this kind of languages.

1 Introduction

Process algebras [Hoa85, Hen88, Mil89, BW90] are a powerful mechanism to specify the functional behavior of concurrent and distributed systems. Nevertheless, the original formulations were not able to accurately represent systems where *quantitative* information, such as time and probabilities, played a fundamental role. Therefore, several timed and/or probabilistic extensions of process algebras have been proposed in the literature. In timed process algebras time information is mainly specified in two different forms: Either by adding a delay operator or by including information about the time when actions are enabled. So, no information about the *probability* associated with this temporal information is included. However, there are processes in which we would like to specify that the probability of performing an action changes as time passes. For example, the event of cars arriving to a petrol station follows a Poisson distribution.

A natural evolution has appeared with the introduction of *stochastic process algebras* (e.g. [GHR93, ABC+94, Hil96, Her98, BG98, HS00, LN01, HHK02]) where time information is incremented with some probabilistic information. For example, one may specify a system where a message is expected to be received with probability $\frac{1}{2}$ in the interval $(0, 1]$, with probability $\frac{1}{4}$ in $(1, 2]$, and so on. This is an advantage with respect to timed processes where we could only specify that the message arrives in the interval $(0, \infty)$. There are two main ways of specifying this (stochastic) time information: Either by adding a *timer* to

---

* Research partially supported by the Spanish MCYT project TIC2003-07848-C02-01 and the Junta de Castilla-La Mancha project PAC-03-001.

D.V. Hung and M. Wirsing (Eds.): ICTAC 2005, LNCS 3722, pp. 454–468, 2005.

actions or by specifying (random) delays. In the first case, an expression as
(a, ξ); P indicates that the probability of performing a, before time t has passed,
is equal to the probability that the random variable ξ takes values less than or
equal to t. After a is performed, the process behaves as P. For example, if ξ is
uniformly distributed over the interval $[1, 2]$ the probability of executing a before
time $\frac{2}{3}$ is equal to 0, the probability of executing a before time $\frac{3}{2}$ is equal to $\frac{1}{2}$, and
so on. Examples of such languages are [Hil96, BG98, LN00]. In the second case,
an expression as ξ; P indicates that the process will be delayed according to ξ and
then it will behave as P. Again, if ξ is uniformly distributed over $[1, 2]$, P starts
before time $\frac{5}{4}$ with probability $\frac{1}{4}$, before time 2 with probability 1, etc. Examples
of such languages are [Her98, DKB98, LN01, HHK02, BG02]. In this paper
we have preferred to take the second approach because the separation between
stochastic and functional behaviors makes (semantic) definitions simpler.

With a few exceptions most stochastic models consider that distributions
are restricted to be exponential. This restriction simplifies several of the problems that appear when considering general distributions. In particular, some
quantities of interest, like reachability probabilities or steady-state probabilities,
can be efficiently calculated by using well known methods on Markov chains. Besides, the (operational) definition of the language is usually simpler than the one
for languages allowing general distributions. Nevertheless, this restriction does
not allow to properly specify some kind of systems where time distributions
are not exponential. Moreover, the main weakness of non-exponential models,
the analysis of properties, can be (partially) overcome by restricting the class
of distributions. A good candidate are phase-type distributions. This kind of
distributions has some good properties: they are closed under minimum, maximum, and convolution, and any other distribution over the interval $(0, \infty)$ can
be approximated by arbitrarily accurate phase-type distributions. Moreover, the
analysis of performance measures can be efficiently done in some general cases.

Our aim in this paper is to define an equivalence relation that, on the one
hand, properly captures the branching structure of stochastic processes and that,
on the other hand, it is sufficiently abstract with respect to stochastic transitions.
Even though most of the semantics presented for stochastic process algebras
are bisimulation-like semantics,[1] in our opinion previous definitions do not adequately abstract stochastic transitions because these transitions are (essentially)
treated as *visible* ones. For example, consider the processes depicted in Figure 1
whose initial states are s_1 and s_2. We think that s_1 and s_2 could be equivalent
(for a suitable choice of ξ in the second process) but they are usually considered to be non-equivalent. The reason is that s_1 may consecutively perform two
stochastic transitions while s_2 may perform only one. This situation represents
a big difference with respect to timed process algebras where, for example, the
following process delay(1) ; delay(2) ; Q is always considered to be equivalent to
delay(3) ; Q, where delay(n) indicates that the process is delayed n units of time
(in this case, the delay is fixed). Following this reasoning, we should be able to

---

[1] Two notable exceptions are [BC00, LN01] where testing semantics are defined for
stochastic process algebras.

identify s_1 and s_2 for an appropriate ξ. A good candidate is to consider that ξ is distributed as the addition of ξ_1 and ξ_2. But here appears a drawback of exponential distributions: They are not closed under addition, that is, if ξ_1 and ξ_2 are exponentially distributed, then the random variable $\xi_1 + \xi_2$ is not exponentially distributed. For this reason, the restriction to exponential distributions does not allow to define a semantics with our expected characteristics. However, to the best of our knowledge, even when considering general distributions, such a semantics has not been previously presented.

We propose a new bisimulation semantics for stochastic processes. Regarding the treatment of *usual* actions, our definition follows the classical weak bisimulation. Let us present some simple examples to show which processes we would like to identify according to their stochastic behaviors. Consider s_3, s_4 and s_5 in Figure 1. The first two ones are weakly bisimilar, so we would like to identify them. On the contrary, s_5 is always considered to be *different*. The reason is similar to the case of s_1 and s_2: A stochastic transition may be performed from s_5 while this is not the case for s_3 or s_4. But this transition leads to the same state s_5, so the intended meaning of this process is "If a is offered by the environment, then a is performed; if the delay is consumed, then the process comes back to the initial state". In other words, we should not be able to distinguish between s_4 and s_5 because both can perform a as soon as it is offered by the environment. Using a similar reasoning, s_6 should be also equivalent to the previous processes. Consider now s_7 and s_8. Assuming that ψ_1 and ψ_2 are not identically

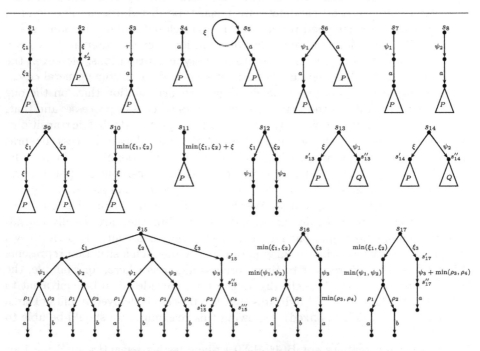

Fig. 1. Examples of stochastic processes

distributed, the probabilities of performing a after n units of time have passed are different. So, s_7 and s_8 should not be identified (and they are usually not). Consider now s_9, s_{10} and s_{11}. The first two processes are usually identified in stochastic bisimulation semantics (so we do). The idea is that the *fastest* delay will be taken, and so we must consider a random variable distributed as the *minimum* of ξ_1 and ξ_2. Besides, following a reasoning similar to that for s_1 and s_2, we also consider that s_{11} is equivalent to both s_9 and s_{10}. This example presents the key point of our semantics: First, we have to check if some transitions may be *joined* (by using the minimum) because they lead to *equivalent* states, and then we have to check if the *continuation* must be added to the resulting random variable. But there are situations where no stochastic transitions are joined at all. For example, if we consider s_{12} and we take into account the previous comments on s_7 and s_8, we should not join the two initial random variables because they lead to non-equivalent states. So, this process will not be equivalent to any other process (up to trivial renaming of random variables).

The combination of *minimums* and *additions*, that we have commented before, produces that the definition of the desired semantics is far from trivial. Consider s_{15}, s_{16}, and s_{17} in Figure 1. All these processes will be identified in our semantics. This example illustrates that the minimum is chosen among all the random variables that lead to equivalent states. The transitions labelled by ξ_1 and ξ_2 are joined by the minimum. Afterwards, there does not exist the possibility of adding the following transition (in this case $\min(\psi_1, \psi_2)$) due to the fact that this would produce a change in the *stochastic* choice at the root. Besides, the states located after ρ_1 and ρ_2 are not equivalent, so they cannot be joined. Finally, we can add ψ_3 and $\min(\rho_3, \rho_4)$ as in s_{10} and s_{11}.

In order to keep the presentation as simple as possible, we have preferred to introduce our semantics on a class of (stochastic) labelled transition systems. As we said before, we will separate between *usual* actions and *stochastic* actions. Random variables associated with stochastic transitions may have any kind of probability distribution. In Section 2 we present this class of labelled transition systems. In Section 3, we define three notions of bisimulation (strong, weak, and weak stochastic). As usually, weak bisimulation is weaker than strong bisimulation. We will also show that the new defined weak stochastic bisimulation is weaker than weak bisimulation. Finally, in Section 4 we present our conclusions and some lines for future work.

2   Stochastic Labelled Transition Systems

In this section we define our model of stochastic processes. We consider a class of labelled transition systems where transitions are labelled either by an action or by a random variable. First, we introduce some concepts on random variables. We will consider that the sample space (that is, the domain of random variables) is the set of real numbers $\mathbb{R}$ and that random variables take positive values only in $\mathbb{R}^+$, that is, given a random variable ξ we have $P(\xi \leq t) = 0$ for all $t < 0$. The reason for this restriction is that random variables are always associated with time distributions. We also introduce the function $\oplus$. This operator will be used when random variables associated with the same state are combined.

Definition 1. Let ξ be a random variable. We define its *probability distribution function*, $F_\xi : \mathbb{R} \to [0,1]$, as the function such that $F_\xi(x) = \mathrm{P}(\xi \le x)$, where $\mathrm{P}(\xi \le x)$ is the probability that ξ assumes values less than or equal to x. We denote by *unit* the random variable such that $F_{unit}(x) = 1$ for all $x \ge 0$.

Let ξ_1, ξ_2 be independent random variables with probability distribution functions F_{ξ_1} and F_{ξ_2}, respectively. We define the *combined addition* of ξ_1 and ξ_2, denoted by $\xi_1 \oplus \xi_2$, as the random variable with probability distribution function $F_{\xi_1 \oplus \xi_2}(x) = F_{\xi_1}(x) + F_{\xi_2}(x) - F_{\xi_1}(x) \cdot F_{\xi_2}(x)$. This operator can be generalized to an arbitrary (finite) number of random variables. Let $\Psi = \{\xi_i\}_{i \in I}$ be a non-empty finite set of independent random variables. We define the *combined addition* of the variables in Ψ, denoted by $\oplus\Psi$, as the random variable such that $F_{\oplus\Psi}(x) = \sum_{\emptyset \subset \Phi \subseteq \Psi} (-1)^{(|\Phi|+1)} F_{\otimes\Phi}(x)$ where $F_{\otimes\Psi}(x) = \prod_{i \in I} F_{\xi_i}(x)$. $\square$

Let us note that for singleton sets, $\Psi = \{\xi\}$, we have $\oplus\Psi = \xi$. Also note that this operator does not correspond to the usual definition of addition of random variables (we will denote the addition of random variables by $+$). Actually, it can be shown that $\oplus$ computes the minimum of a set of random variables.

Lemma 1. Let $\Psi = \{\xi_1, \xi_2, \ldots, \xi_n\}$ be a non-empty set of independent random variables, and let ξ be a random variable distributed as the random variable $\min\{\xi_1, \xi_2, \ldots, \xi_n\}$. For all $x \in \mathbb{R}$ we have $F_\xi(x) = F_{\oplus\Psi}(x)$.

We suppose a fixed set of actions Act $(a, a', \ldots$ to range over Act) and a special action $\tau \notin$ Act to represent internal activity. We denote by Act_τ the set $\mathrm{Act} \cup \{\tau\}$ $(\alpha, \alpha', \ldots$ to range over $\mathrm{Act}_\tau)$. We denote by $\mathcal{V}$ the set of random variables $(\xi, \xi', \psi, \ldots$ to range over $\mathcal{V})$. Finally, $\gamma, \gamma', \ldots$ will denote generic elements in $\mathrm{Act}_\tau \cup \mathcal{V}$.

Definition 2. A *stochastic labelled transition system* P is a pair $(S, \to)$ where S is a finite *set of states*, and $\to \subseteq S \times (\mathrm{Act}_\tau \cup \mathcal{V}) \times S$ is a *transition relation*.

We will use the following conventions: $s \xrightarrow{\gamma} s'$ stands for $(s, \gamma, s') \in \to$; $s \xrightarrow{\gamma}$ stands for there exists $s' \in S$ such that $s \xrightarrow{\gamma} s'$; we write $s \xrightarrow{\gamma}\!\!\!\!/\,$ if there does not exist such an $s' \in S$. We say that s is *stable* if $s \xrightarrow{\tau}\!\!\!\!/\,$. We denote by $\Longrightarrow$ the reflexive and transitive closure of $\xrightarrow{\tau}$; given $\gamma \neq \tau$, we write $s \xRightarrow{\gamma} s'$ if there exist s_1, s_2 such that $s \xRightarrow{\tau} s_1 \xrightarrow{\gamma} s_2 \xRightarrow{\tau} s'$. Given a set $A \subseteq \mathrm{Act}_\tau \cup \mathcal{V}$, we write $s \xrightarrow{A}$ (resp. $s \xRightarrow{A}$) if there exists $\gamma \in A$ such that $s \xrightarrow{\gamma}$ (resp. $s \xRightarrow{\gamma}$), and we write $s \xrightarrow{A}\!\!\!\!/\,$ (resp. $s \xRightarrow{A}\!\!\!\!/\,$) if there does not exist such a γ. $\square$

Intuitively, a transition $s \xrightarrow{a} s'$ indicates that a process may evolve from s to s' by performing the (visible) action a. A transition $s \xrightarrow{\tau} s'$ indicates that a process may internally evolve from s to s'. Finally, a transition $s \xrightarrow{\xi} s'$ expresses that a process may evolve from the state s to the state s' once the (random) delay indicated by ξ has been elapsed. In order to avoid *side effects*, we suppose that all the random variables labeling transitions of a process are independent. In particular, this implies that the same random variable cannot appear in different transitions. Note that this restriction does not forbid to have identically distributed random variables (as far as they have different names). This assumption would not be necessary if we defined stochastic delays by using probability distribution functions. Anyway, for the sake of convenience, we will sometimes use the same random variable in different transitions. For example, two transitions labelled by the same random variable ξ (e.g. s_9 in Figure 1) is a shorthand to indicate that these transitions are labelled by two identically distributed independent random variables ψ_1 and ψ_2.

The following examples show how the *race policy* (i.e. the fastest delay is always taken in a process) identifies some processes that *apparently* should not be equivalent.

Example 1. Consider s_{13} and s_{14} in Figure 1. Suppose that ξ is uniformly distributed over $[0, 2]$, ψ_1 is uniformly distributed over $[1, 5]$, and that the probability distribution function of ψ_2 is given by:

$$F_{\psi_2}(x) = \begin{cases} 0 & \text{if } x \leq 1 \\ \frac{x-1}{4} & \text{if } 1 < x \leq 4 \\ \frac{x}{2} - \frac{5}{4} & \text{if } 4 < x \leq \frac{9}{2} \\ 1 & \text{if } \frac{9}{2} < x \end{cases}$$

Taking into account that ψ_1 and ψ_2 are not identically distributed, we could think that s_{13} and s_{14} are not equivalent. However, as the fastest delay will be taken in these states, after two units of time ξ will be chosen with probability 1 because $P(\xi \leq 2) = 1$. Since we have that ψ_1 and ψ_2 are identically distributed over the interval $[0, 4]$, so are they over $[0, 2]$. Thus, s_{13} and s_{14} should be equivalent.   □

Example 2. Consider again s_{13} and s_{14} in Figure 1, but now suppose that ξ is uniformly distributed over $[0, \frac{1}{2}]$ and that ψ_1 and ψ_2 are defined as in Example 1. We have that the probability of performing either ψ_1 or ψ_2 would be zero. In this case, both s_{13} and s_{14} should be equivalent, and they should be also equivalent to s_2 (also in Figure 1). This is so because the delay associated with ξ is performed with probability 1 after a half of a unit of time, and at that time ψ_1 and ψ_2 cannot be performed.   □

We also consider that internal actions are *urgent*, that is, given the fact that they do not need to interact with the environment, they will be performed as soon as possible, so no delay is allowed. This property, usually known as *maximal progress*, appears in most timed and stochastic models. Moreover, we will consider that if a state can evolve neither internally nor stochastically, this state can *wait* any amount of time before any visible action is performed.

Definition 3. Let $P = (S, \rightarrow)$ be a stochastic labelled transition system, $s, s' \in S$, $\xi, \psi \in \mathcal{V}$, $t_0 \in \mathbb{R}^+$, and $C \subseteq S$. We define the following concepts:

Maximum waiting time. The *maximum waiting time* for a state s, denoted by $maxW(s)$, is defined as

$$maxW(s) = \begin{cases} 0 & \text{if } s \xrightarrow{\tau} \\ \min\{t \mid \exists \xi \in \mathcal{V} \colon s \xrightarrow{\xi} \wedge F_\xi(t) = 1\} & \text{otherwise} \end{cases}$$

Identically distributed random variables. We say that ξ and ψ are *identically distributed with respect to* states s and s', denoted by $\xi \asymp_{s,s'} \psi$, if $maxW(s) = maxW(s')$ and for all $t \leq maxW(s)$ we have $F_\xi(t) = F_\psi(t)$.

Feasible random variable. We say that the random variable ξ is *feasible with respect to* t_0, denoted by $fact_{t_0}(\xi)$, if $t_0 > \min\{t \mid F_\xi(t) > 0\}$.

Set positively reached. We say that s *may positively reach* C, denoted by $s \nearrow C$, if there exist $s' \in C$ and $\xi \in \mathcal{V}$ such that $s \xrightarrow{\xi} s'$ and $fact_{maxW(s)}(\xi)$. $\quad\square$

The function $maxW(s)$ will ensure maximal progress. If the state can evolve internally, it cannot wait to perform any delay, and so $maxW(s) = 0$. If the state is stable, then the function $maxW(s)$ computes the maximum amount of time that s can wait until a delay is performed with probability 1. We have considered $\min \emptyset = \infty$. So, if s is stable and has no stochastic transitions then it can wait as long as one of its transitions is enabled.

The predicate $\asymp_{s,s'}$ will be used to compare random variables. As previous examples illustrate, probability distribution functions associated with random variables are compared only in the interval of time limited by the maximum waiting time of the corresponding states. For example, if we consider Example 1 we have $\psi_1 \asymp_{s_{13},s_{14}} \psi_2$ because $maxW(s_{13}) = maxW(s_{14}) = 2$. For that reason, the states s_{13} and s_{14} should be equivalent. Meanwhile, in Example 2 the transitions ψ_1 and ψ_2 will not be taken into consideration (and so, we will say that they are not feasible).

In order to avoid the computation of the minimum of an empty set of random variables we have defined the predicate $s \nearrow C$. This predicate holds if s can reach $C \subseteq S$ by performing a stochastic transition.

3   Stochastic Bisimulations

Next we define our notions of bisimulation. The first two ones correspond to the typical notions of strong and weak bisimulations for stochastic processes (see for example [Her98, BG98] for similar notions on a Markovian setting). The third notion, that we call *weak stochastic bisimulation*, represents a refinement (i.e. it is *weaker*) of the previous notions. We consider that not only internal actions may be (partially) abstracted but also (in some cases) sequences of random variables may be abstracted.

We start by giving the definition of strong bisimulation. First, we introduce an auxiliary definition to combine random variables that, starting from the same state, reach equivalent states.

Definition 4. Let $P = (S, \to)$ be a stochastic labelled transition system, and $C \subseteq S$. We define the *strong random variable* associated with the execution of stochastic transitions from a state $s \in S$ leading to C, denoted by $\xi_s(s, C)$, as

$$\xi_s(s, C) = \oplus\{\xi \mid \exists s' \in C \colon s \xrightarrow{\xi} s'\}. \qquad\qquad \square$$

The function $\xi_s(s, C)$ combines all the random variables leading from s to a state belonging to C by using the function $\oplus$. Let us remind that $\oplus$ computes the minimum of a set of random variables.

Definition 5. We say that an equivalence relation $\mathcal{R}$ is a *strong bisimulation* on $P = (S, \rightarrow)$ if for all pair of states $s_1, s_2 \in S$ we have that $s_1 \mathcal{R} s_2$ implies:

- For all $\alpha \in \text{Act}_\tau, s_1 \xrightarrow{\alpha} s_1'$ implies $\exists s_2'$ such that $s_2 \xrightarrow{\alpha} s_2'$ and $s_1' \mathcal{R} s_2'$.
- For all $C \in S/\mathcal{R}$, $s_1 \nearrow C$ implies $s_2 \nearrow C$ and $\xi_s(s_1, C) \asymp_{s_1, s_2} \xi_s(s_2, C)$.

We say that two states $s_1, s_2 \in S$ are *strongly bisimilar*, denoted by $s_1 \sim_s s_2$, if there exists a strong bisimulation that contains the pair (s_1, s_2). □

The definition of strong bisimulation mimics the one for non-stochastic systems: A transition from a state must be simulated by the same transition in the other one. The first clause of the definition is the usual one for strong bisimulation. The second clause is used to join several stochastic transitions leading to the same equivalence class. Note that $\xi_s(s_1, C)$ and $\xi_s(s_2, C)$ do not need to be equal for any time value; they have to take equal values for any time lower than or equal to the maximum waiting time of both states. Finally, let us note that the symmetric cases, where s_1 and s_2 exchange roles, are omitted because we already force $\mathcal{R}$ to be an equivalence relation (and so $\mathcal{R}$ is symmetric).

Example 3. Consider the states s_2, s_{13}, and s_{14} from Figure 1 together with the random variables defined in Examples 1 and 2. Let us define the sets of states C_1 and C_2 such that $s_2', s_{13}', s_{14}' \in C_1$ and $s_{13}'', s_{14}'' \in C_2$. Considering the values of the random variables given in Example 1, we have $\xi_s(s_{13}, C_i) \asymp_{s_{13}, s_{14}} \xi_s(s_{14}, C_i)$ for $i \subset \{1, 2\}$ (note that $maxW(s_{13}) = 2 = maxW(s_{14})$). So, $s_{13} \sim_s s_{14}$.
    Let us consider the random variables as defined in Example 2. In this case we have that $\xi_s(s_2, C_1) \asymp_{s_2, s_{13}} \xi_s(s_{13}, C_1) \asymp_{s_{13}, s_{14}} \xi_s(s_{14}, C_1)$. Note that the values $\xi_s(s_j, C_2)$ for $j \in \{2, 13, 14\}$ should not be computed. So, $s_2 \sim_s s_{13} \sim_s s_{14}$. □

Next we present a notion of weak bisimulation for stochastic processes. As in the strong case, we will also impose the condition of reachability (given in Definition 3) before we compute ξ_s. Nevertheless, the corresponding transitions have to reach C^τ instead of C, where $C^\tau = \{s \mid \exists s' \in C : s \xRightarrow{} s'\}$.

Definition 6. We say that an equivalence relation $\mathcal{R}$ is a *weak bisimulation* on a stochastic labelled transition system $P = (S, \rightarrow)$ if for any pair of states $s_1, s_2 \in S$ we have that $s_1 \mathcal{R} s_2$ implies:

- For all $\alpha \in \text{Act}_\tau, s_1 \xrightarrow{\alpha} s_1'$ implies $\exists s_2'$ such that $s_2 \xRightarrow{\alpha} s_2'$ and $s_1' \mathcal{R} s_2'$.
- For all $C \in S/\mathcal{R}$, $s_1 \xRightarrow{} s_1' \nearrow C^\tau$ implies $\exists s_2'$ such that $s_2 \xRightarrow{} s_2' \nearrow C^\tau$ and $\xi_s(s_1', C^\tau) \asymp_{s_1', s_2'} \xi_s(s_2', C^\tau)$.

We say that two states $s_1, s_2 \in S$ are *weakly bisimilar*, denoted by $s_1 \sim_w s_2$, if there exists a weak bisimulation that contains the pair (s_1, s_2). □

As in the definition of strong bisimulation, we distinguish between stochastic transitions and usual action transitions. The first clause of the previous definition is the usual one for weak bisimulation. The last clause checks whether the random variables associated with the states are identically distributed up to the corresponding maximum waiting time. In this case, in order to (partially) abstract internal transitions, it is also allowed the evolution by a (possibly empty) sequence of internal actions.

Strong and weak bisimulations fulfill the usual properties. The proof is an adaptation of the one given in [Mil89] by taking into account that, also in our setting, the relation $\sim_s$ (resp. $\sim_w$) can be defined as the union of all the relations that are strong (resp. weak) bisimulations.

Lemma 2. Let $P = (S, \rightarrow)$ be a stochastic labelled transition system. The strong (resp. weak) bisimilarity relation on P, that is, $\sim_s$ (resp. $\sim_w$) is an equivalence relation on P. Moreover, $\sim_s$ (resp. $\sim_w$) is a strong (resp. weak) bisimulation on P and it is the largest strong (resp. weak) bisimulation on P.

Example 4. Consider Figure 2. States s_{21} and s_{22} are both strong and weak bisimilar. Besides, s_{23} is weakly equivalent (but not strongly) to both s_{21} and s_{22}. In contrast, s_{24} and s_{25} are not equivalent under any of the bisimulations defined in this paper. These examples show that these notions are conservative with respect to the non-stochastic framework (see forthcoming Lemma 3).

Stochastic transitions leading to the same equivalence class must be *joined*. Consider s_{26} and s_{27}. These two states are (strongly and weakly) bisimilar due to the fact that both stochastic transitions outgoing from s_{26} lead to the same equivalence class. In this way, the delay after which P is enabled will be the minimum of both random variables, that is, the same as in s_{27}. Consider now s_2 in Figure 1 and s_{28} in Figure 2. They are not strongly bisimilar because $s_2 \xrightarrow{\tau}\!\!\!\!\!/\,$ while $s_{28} \xrightarrow{\tau}$. However, $s_2 \sim_w s_{28}$. The states s_{28} and s_{29} are not identified. If s_{28} evolves by performing a τ transition then s_{29} cannot simulate this transition. This is a desired result (and standard in stochastic models) because the identification of these two states would produce that a pure internal decision (as in s_{28}) should be treated as a *probabilistic* one.   □

These two notions of bisimulation restricted either to labelled transition systems, or to stochastic labelled transition systems where distributions are always exponential, are equivalent to the classical notions of bisimulation, and to the

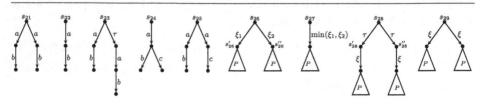

Fig. 2. Examples of strongly/weakly bisimilar processes

notions of bisimulation defined in [Her98], respectively. In the latter case it is enough to take into account that when restricted to exponential distributions we have that, for all $s \in S$, $maxW(s)$ is equal either to 0 or ∞. Besides, for any $C \subseteq S$, we have that $s \nearrow C$ can be simplified as $\exists s' \in C$ such that $s \xrightarrow{\xi} s'$. Unfortunately, it is not easy to compare our definitions with the corresponding to models with general distributions. For example, [BG02] uses a preselection policy (instead of a race policy), while the clocks mechanism of [DKB98] is difficult to compare with our model.

Lemma 3. Restricted to non-stochastic labelled transitions systems, $\sim_s$ (resp. $\sim_w$) is equivalent to the strong (resp. weak) bisimulation defined in [Mil89].
   Restricted to Markovian stochastic labelled transitions systems, $\sim_s$ (resp. $\sim_w$) is equivalent to the strong (resp. weak) bisimulation defined in [Her98].

Nevertheless, this notion of weak bisimulation presents a drawback. Specifically, it considers stochastic transitions almost as visible ones. Obviously, stochastic transitions cannot be considered to be just τ transitions because they carry some information that τ transitions do not. However, as discussed in the introduction, in some situations sequences of stochastic transitions should be identified. This is the case for s_1 and s_2 in Figure 1 for some particular random variables ξ_1, ξ_2, and ξ.
   Next, we define our new notion of bisimulation that we call *weak stochastic bisimulation*. It is needed again an auxiliary function to compute the *probability* of reaching a set of states from a state. First, we introduce some predicates to indicate conditions on the *continuations* after evolving by internal and/or stochastic transitions.

Definition 7. Let $P = (S, \rightarrow)$ be a stochastic labelled transition system, $\mathcal{R}$ be an equivalence relation on S, and $s \in S$. We define the following predicates:
   Equivalence class. We denote by $[s]_\mathcal{R}$ the *equivalence class* induced by $\mathcal{R}$ on S containing s, that is, the set $[s]_\mathcal{R} = \{s' \in S \mid s\mathcal{R}s'\}$.
   Stabilization of a state. We say that s' is a *stabilization of s* with respect to $\mathcal{R}$, denoted by $Stab_\mathcal{R}(s, s')$, if $s' \in [s]_\mathcal{R}$ and $s' \xrightarrow{\tau}\!\!\!\!\!\!/\ $, and for all $r \in S$ we have $s \xRightarrow{\tau} r$ implies $r \in [s]_\mathcal{R}$.
   Stochastically nondeterministic state. We say that s is *stochastically nondeterministic* with respect to $\mathcal{R}$, and we write $Snd_\mathcal{R}(s)$, if there exist $s_1, s_2 \in S$ such that $s \nearrow [s_1]_\mathcal{R}$, $s \nearrow [s_2]_\mathcal{R}$, and $[s_1]_\mathcal{R} \neq [s_2]_\mathcal{R}$.
   Deterministically reached state. We say that s *deterministically reaches s' by stochastic transitions* with respect to $\mathcal{R}$, denoted by $\mathcal{D}_\mathcal{R}(s, s')$, if $[s]_\mathcal{R} \neq [s']_\mathcal{R}$ and exists $s'' \in S$ such that $Stab_\mathcal{R}(s, s'')$ and $s'' \nearrow [s']_\mathcal{R}$, and for all $r \in S$ such that $s'' \nearrow [r]_\mathcal{R}$ we have $[s']_\mathcal{R} = [r]_\mathcal{R}$.
   Stochastically deterministic state. We say that s is *stochastically deterministic* with respect to $\mathcal{R}$, denoted by $Sd_\mathcal{R}(s)$, if for any state $r \in S$ we have $s \xRightarrow{\tau} r$ implies $r \in [s]_\mathcal{R}$ and one of the following two conditions holds:

   - $s \xrightarrow{v}\!\!\!\!\!\!/\ $.
   - For all $s' \in [s]_\mathcal{R}$, $\exists s'' \in S$ such that $s' \nearrow [s'']_\mathcal{R}$ implies $[s'']_\mathcal{R} = [s]_\mathcal{R}$.   □

The predicate $Stab_{\mathcal{R}}(s, s')$ indicates that either s is stable or it stays in its equivalence class after performing any sequence of internal transitions. We will use any stable state s' belonging to the class of s to study its associated random variables.

The predicate $Snd_{\mathcal{R}}(s)$ indicates the case when *continuations* after the performance of a stochastic action should not be added. We reject to (immediately) study the continuations if the states reached after performing stochastic transitions do not belong to the same equivalence class. As we have already say, it is important to note that not all the stochastic transitions outgoing from a state are considered. For example, the state s_{13} appearing in Example 2 is not stochastically nondeterministic. Consider s_{31} in Figure 4. In this case, the continuations after the execution of the initial stochastic transitions, (that is, after ξ_1, ξ_2 and ξ_3) are not equivalent if ψ_1 and ψ_2 are not identically distributed. That is, s'_{31} and s'''_{31} will not be equivalent. Let us consider that ξ_1, ξ_2 and ξ_3 are such that $maxW(s_{31}) > \min\{t \mid F_{\xi_i}(t) > 0\}$ for $i \in \{1, 2, 3\}$. In this case, all the stochastic transitions are considered. So, we have that s_{31} is a stochastically nondeterminist state.

Meanwhile, the predicate $\mathcal{D}_{\mathcal{R}}(s, s')$ represents the reverse case. The continuations will be joined when all the stochastic transitions outgoing from a state lead to states belonging to the same equivalence class. For example, in Figure 4, we have that s'_{37} deterministically reaches the state s''_{37}. So, if $\xi = \psi + (\psi_1 \oplus \psi_2)$ then s_{37} should be equivalent to s_2 in Figure 1.

Finally, the predicate $Sd_{\mathcal{R}}(s)$ represents the case when all the stochastic and internal transitions outgoing either from s or from any state of its equivalence class reach states belonging to $[s]_{\mathcal{R}}$. For example, in Figure 1, we have that s_5 is a stochastically deterministic state.

The following function represents the core of the definition of weak stochastic bisimulation. The key point is the addition of the continuations only when it does not distort the choice in the upper level. A similar approach, that is, to introduce an auxiliary function to define weak bisimulation, is taken in [BH97] although for a much simpler model.

Definition 8. Let $P = (S, \rightarrow)$ be a stochastic labelled transition system, $\mathcal{R}$ an equivalence relation on S, and $C \in S/\mathcal{R}$. We define the *weak stochastic random variable* associated with the stochastic transitions outgoing from a state s_0 of P leading to a state belonging to C, denoted by $\xi_{wst}(s_0, C, \mathcal{R})$, in Figure 3.   □

Let us note that the previous function is partial because not all the classes of a given equivalence relation will be stochastically reached with a weak stochastic random variable. Let us remind that *unit* is the random variable given in Definition 1 and that for any class A, A^τ is the set $\{s \in S \mid \exists s' \in A : s \overset{\tau}{\Longrightarrow} s'\}$. The first clause is applied if s_0 belongs to the class we are interested in (or this class can be reached after the execution of several internal transitions) and it is stochastically deterministic. For example, for s_4 and s_5 in Figure 1, if we consider $\mathcal{R}$ such that $[s_4]_{\mathcal{R}} = [s_5]_{\mathcal{R}}$ then the random variables associated with s_4 to reach $[s_4]_{\mathcal{R}}$ and with s_5 to reach $[s_5]_{\mathcal{R}}$ are identically distributed as *unit*.

$$
\begin{cases}
\quad unit & \text{if } s_0 \in C^\tau \wedge Sd_{\mathcal{R}}(s_0) \\[4pt]
\xi_s(s, C^\tau) & \text{if } s_0 \notin C^\tau \wedge Stab_{\mathcal{R}}(s_0, s) \wedge \\[4pt]
& \quad \left(s \xrightarrow{\text{Act}} \ \vee \ Snd_{\mathcal{R}}(s) \ \vee \right. \\
& \quad \left. \exists s' \in S : \left(\begin{matrix} \mathcal{D}_{\mathcal{R}}(s,s') \wedge \\ \left(s' \xRightarrow{\text{Act}} \vee \\ \exists s'' \in S : (\neg Stab_{\mathcal{R}}(s',s'') \vee Snd_{\mathcal{R}}(s'')) \right) \end{matrix} \right) \right) \\[10pt]
\xi_s(s, [s']_{\mathcal{R}}^\tau) & \text{if } s_0 \notin C^\tau \wedge Stab_{\mathcal{R}}(s_0,s) \wedge s \xcancel{\xrightarrow{\text{Act}}} \wedge \mathcal{D}_{\mathcal{R}}(s,s') \wedge s' \xcancel{\xRightarrow{\text{Act}}} \wedge \\
\quad + \\
\xi_{wst}(s', C, \mathcal{R}) & \quad \exists s'' \in S : \mathcal{D}_{\mathcal{R}}(s', s'')
\end{cases}
$$

Fig. 3. Definition of the weak stochastic random variable $\xi_{wst}(s_0, C, \mathcal{R})$

The other two cases are considered when s_0 is not in C^τ. The second case is applied if there exists a stable state $s \in S$, reached from s_0 after performing internal transitions, and either s may perform a visible action, or not all of the feasible initial stochastic transition (or their continuations) lead to the same equivalence class. In this case, we do not *add* the continuations. Consider Figure 4 and an equivalence relation $\mathcal{R}$ such that $[s_{31}]_{\mathcal{R}} = \{s_{31}\}$, $[s'_{31}]_{\mathcal{R}} = \{s'_{31}, s''_{31}\}$, and $[s'''_{31}] = \{s'''_{31}\}$. We have $\xi_{wst}(s_{31}, [s'_{31}]_{\mathcal{R}}, \mathcal{R}) = \xi_{wst}(s_{31}, [s''_{31}]_{\mathcal{R}}, \mathcal{R}) = \xi_1 \oplus \xi_2$, and $\xi_{wst}(s_{31}, [s'''_{31}]_{\mathcal{R}}, \mathcal{R}) = \xi_3$.

The third clause is taken if all the feasible initial stochastic transitions are joined and their continuations lead to equivalent states. In this case, we should not stop *counting* after the initial transitions. We join the initial stochastic transitions (by using ξ_s) and then we add the results to the random variable corresponding to the continuations. Consider the states s_{15} and s_{17} in Figure 1 and an equivalence relation $\mathcal{R}$ such that $[s_{15}]_{\mathcal{R}} = \{s_{15}, s_{17}\} = [s_{17}]_{\mathcal{R}}$, $[s'_{15}]_{\mathcal{R}} = \{s'_{15}, s'_{17}\} = [s'_{17}]_{\mathcal{R}}$, and $[s'''_{15}]_{\mathcal{R}} = \{s'''_{15}, s^{iv}_{15}, s''_{17}\} = [s''_{17}]_{\mathcal{R}}$. In this case, $\xi_{wst}(s'_{15}, [s'''_{15}]_{\mathcal{R}}, \mathcal{R}) = \xi_{wst}(s'_{17}, [s''_{17}]_{\mathcal{R}}, \mathcal{R}) = \psi_3 + (\rho_3 \oplus \rho_4)$. Finally, it is obvious to check that the three cases are mutually exclusive.

In the previous definitions of bisimulation we have imposed $s \nearrow C$, before computing $\xi_s(s, C)$, to ensure that this function was defined. But this condition

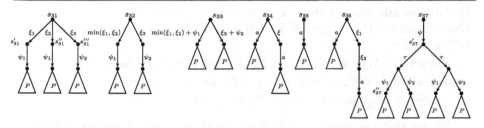

Fig. 4. Examples of weakly stochastic bisimilar processes

is not enough to assure that $\xi_{wst}(s, C, \mathcal{R})$ is defined. There exist two reasons why this function could be indefinite: Either there does not exist a path to reach C from s or there exists a path but it is *illegal*. We will say that a path $p \equiv s \overset{\xi_1}{\Longrightarrow} s_1 \ldots s_{n-1} \overset{\xi_n}{\Longrightarrow} s_n$ is *legal* if the states of the path fulfill the conditions of any of the three clauses of the definition of $\xi_{wst}(s, C, \mathcal{R})$. Intuitively, we need to consider only those paths such that the function ξ_{wst} can be applied in every step of the computation.

Definition 9. Let $P = (S, \rightarrow)$ be a stochastic labelled transition system, $C \subseteq S$, $\mathcal{R}$ an equivalence relation on S, and $s_0, s_i \in S, \xi_i \in \mathcal{V}$ with $1 \leq i \leq n$. We say that $p \equiv s_0 \overset{\xi_1}{\Longrightarrow} s_1 \overset{\xi_2}{\Longrightarrow} s_2 \cdots s_{n-1} \overset{\xi_n}{\Longrightarrow} s_n$ is a *legal path to reach* C with respect to $\mathcal{R}$, denoted by $legal_{\mathcal{R}}(p, C)$, if one of the following conditions hold:

1. $s_0 \in C^\tau$, $Sd_{\mathcal{R}}(s_0)$, and $n = 0$.
2. $s_0 \notin C^\tau$, $n = 1$, there exists $s \in S$ such that $Stab_{\mathcal{R}}(s_0, s)$, $fact_{maxW(s)}(\xi_1)$,
   $s_1 \in C^\tau$, and $\left(\begin{array}{l} s \overset{Act}{\longrightarrow} \ \vee \ Snd_{\mathcal{R}}(s) \ \vee \ (\mathcal{D}_{\mathcal{R}}(s, s_1) \ \wedge \ s_1 \overset{Act}{\Longrightarrow}) \ \vee \\ (\mathcal{D}_{\mathcal{R}}(s, s_1) \ \wedge \ \forall s'' \in S : Stab_{\mathcal{R}}(s_1, s'') \text{ implies } Snd_{\mathcal{R}}(s'')) \end{array} \right)$.
3. $s_0 \notin C^\tau$, there exists $s \in S$ such that $Stab_{\mathcal{R}}(s_0, s)$, $s \overset{Act}{\longrightarrow}\!\!\!\!\!/\,$, $\mathcal{D}_{\mathcal{R}}(s, s_1)$, and for all $1 \leq i \leq n-1$ we have $s_i \overset{Act}{\Longrightarrow}\!\!\!\!\!\!/\,$ and $\mathcal{D}_{\mathcal{R}}(s_i, s_{i+1})$ and, finally, $s_n \in C^\tau$ and $Sd_{\mathcal{R}}(s_n)$.

We say that C is *stochastically reached* from s_0 with respect to $\mathcal{R}$, denoted by $s_0 \nearrow_{\mathcal{R}} C$, if there exists a path p from s_0 such that $legal_{\mathcal{R}}(p, C)$. □

Let us remark that if there exists a legal path p from s to C then all the paths from s to states in C whose stochastic transitions are feasible are also legal. This is so because the condition to be a legal path considers all the stochastic transitions that each state can perform. Actually, the predicate $s \nearrow_{\mathcal{R}} C$ is used to check that one of the clauses in Definition 8 holds.

Lemma 4. Let $P = (S, \rightarrow)$ be a stochastic labelled transition system, $C \subseteq S, \mathcal{R}$ an equivalence relation in S and $s \in S$. If $s \nearrow_{\mathcal{R}} C$ then the function $\xi_{wst}(s, C, \mathcal{R})$ is well defined.

Once we have defined the previous predicate, we present the notion of weak stochastic bisimulation.

Definition 10. We say that an equivalence relation $\mathcal{R}$ is a *weak stochastic bisimulation* on $P = (S, \rightarrow)$ if for any pair of states $s_1, s_2 \in S$ we have that $s_1 \mathcal{R} s_2$ implies:

 – For all $\alpha \in Act_\tau$, $s_1 \overset{\alpha}{\longrightarrow} s_1'$ implies $\exists s_2'$ such that $s_2 \overset{\alpha}{\Longrightarrow} s_2'$ and $s_1' \mathcal{R} s_2'$.
 – For all $C \in S/\mathcal{R}$, $s_1 \overset{\tau}{\Longrightarrow} s_1'$, $s_1' \overset{\tau}{\longrightarrow}\!\!\!\!/\,$, and $s_1' \nearrow_{\mathcal{R}} C$ implies $\exists s_2'$ such that $s_2 \overset{\tau}{\Longrightarrow} s_2' \nearrow_{\mathcal{R}} C$ and $\xi_{wst}(s_1', C, \mathcal{R}) \asymp_{s_1', s_2'} \xi_{wst}(s_2', C, \mathcal{R})$.

We say that two states $s_1, s_2 \in S$ are *weakly stochastic bisimilar*, denoted by $s_1 \sim_{wst} s_2$, if there exists a weak stochastic bisimulation that contains the pair (s_1, s_2). □

The difference between $\sim_w$ and $\sim_{wst}$ comes from the definition of ξ_{wst} and the new condition $(s\not\nearrow_{\mathcal{R}}C)$ to ensure that $\xi_{wst}(s, C, \mathcal{R})$ is computed only if there exists a legal path from s reaching C.

Example 5. Consider s_{31}, s_{32}, and s_{33} in Figure 4. Let us suppose that all the stochastic transitions are feasible with respect to the state they lead from. We have that s_{31} and s_{32} are both weakly and weakly stochastic bisimilar. On the contrary, s_{33} is not equivalent to them. The point is that while the choice appearing in s_{31} and s_{32} is made between ξ_3 and the minimum of ξ_1 and ξ_2, in the case of s_{33} the choice is *distorted* by ψ_1 and ψ_2.

Consider s_{34}, s_{35}, and s_{36}, the first two ones are weakly stochastic bisimilar (they are not weakly bisimilar). However, s_{34} and s_{36} are not weakly stochastic bisimilar because s_{34} is always able to perform a while this is not the case for s_{36}. If the stochastic transition $s_{36} \xrightarrow{\xi_1}$ is performed then this process will not be able to perform a until the delay ξ_2 is elapsed. □

This new bisimulation also fulfills the usual properties. The proof is a little bit more involved than the ones for strong and weak bisimulations because of the definition of ξ_{wst}.

Lemma 5. Let $\Gamma = (S, \rightarrow)$ be a stochastic labelled transition system. Weak stochastic bisimilarity on P (that is, the relation $\sim_{wst}$) is an equivalence relation on P. Moreover, $\sim_{wst}$ is a weak stochastic bisimulation on P and the largest weak stochastic bisimulation on P.

Theorem 1. Let $P = (S, \rightarrow)$ be a stochastic labelled transition system, and $s_1, s_2 \in S$. We have that $s_1 \sim_s s_2$, implies $s_1 \sim_w s_2$. Besides, if $s_1 \sim_w s_2$, then $s_1 \sim_{wst} s_2$.

Corollary 1. $\sim_s \subsetneq \sim_w \subsetneq \sim_{wst}$.

4 Conclusions and Future Work

In this paper we have studied bisimulation semantics for a class of stochastic processes with general distributions. We have presented a notion of weak stochastic bisimulation to solve some of the counterintuitive results that appeared in previous definitions. One key point that we have not addressed in this paper is how our results can be extended to a more complex language. In particular, to define a parallel operator in the context of general distributions is always involved. We obtained some preliminary results in [LNR04], but the formulation of the resulting (weak) bisimulation relation is very involved.

Acknowledgments. We would like to thank David de Frutos for helpful discussions on the topic of this paper.

References

[ABC+94]   M. Ajmone Marsan, A. Bianco, L. Ciminiera, R. Sisto, and A. Valenzano. A LOTOS extension for the performance analysis of distributed systems. *IEEE/ACM Transactions on Networking*, 2(2):151–165, 1994.

[BC00]   M. Bernardo and W.R. Cleaveland. A theory of testing for markovian processes. In *CONCUR'2000, LNCS 1877*, pages 305–319. Springer, 2000.

[BG98]   M. Bernardo and R. Gorrieri. A tutorial on EMPA: A theory of concurrent processes with nondeterminism, priorities, probabilities and time. *Theoretical Computer Science*, 202:1–54, 1998.

[BG02]   M. Bravetti and R. Gorrieri. The theory of interactive generalized semi-Markov processes. *Theoretical Computer Science*, 282(1):5–32, 2002.

[BH97]   C. Baier and H. Hermanns. Weak bisimulation for fully probabilistic processes. In *Computer Aided Verification'97, LNCS 1254*, pages 119–130. Springer, 1997.

[BW90]   J.C.M. Baeten and W.P. Weijland. *Process Algebra*. Cambridge Tracts in Computer Science 18. Cambridge University Press, 1990.

[DKB98]   P.R. D'Argenio, J.-P. Katoen, and E. Brinksma. An algebraic approach to the specification of stochastic systems. In *Programming Concepts and Methods*, pages 126–147. Chapman & Hall, 1998.

[GHR93]   N. Götz, U. Herzog, and M. Rettelbach. Multiprocessor and distributed system design: The integration of functional specification and performance analysis using stochastic process algebras. In *16th Int. Symp. on Computer Performance Modelling, Measurement and Evaluation (PERFORMANCE'93), LNCS 729*, pages 121–146. Springer, 1993.

[Hen88]   M. Hennessy. *Algebraic Theory of Processes*. MIT Press, 1988.

[Her98]   H. Hermanns. *Interactive Markov Chains*. PhD thesis, Universität Erlangen-Nürnberg, 1998.

[HHK02]   H. Hermanns, U. Herzog, and J.-P. Katoen. Process algebra for performance evaluation. *Theoretical Computer Science*, 274(1-2):43–87, 2002.

[Hil96]   J. Hillston. *A Compositional Approach to Performance Modelling*. Cambridge University Press, 1996.

[Hoa85]   C.A.R. Hoare. *Communicating Sequential Processes*. Prentice Hall, 1985.

[HS00]   P.G. Harrison and B. Strulo. SPADES – a process algebra for discrete event simulation. *Journal of Logic Computation*, 10(1):3–42, 2000.

[LN00]   N. López and M. Núñez. NMSPA: A non-markovian model for stochastic processes. In *International Workshop on Distributed System Validation and Verification (DSVV'2000)*, pages 33–40, 2000.

[LN01]   N. López and M. Núñez. A testing theory for generally distributed stochastic processes. In *CONCUR 2001, LNCS 2154*, pages 321–335. Springer, 2001.

[LNR04]   N. López, M. Núñez, and F. Rubio. An integrated framework for the analysis of asynchronous communicating stochastic processes. *Formal Aspects of Computing*, 16(3):238–262, 2004.

[Mil89]   R. Milner. *Communication and Concurrency*. Prentice Hall, 1989.

On Refinement of Software Architectures

Sun Meng[1,3,*], Luís S. Barbosa[2,**], and Zhang Naixiao[3]

[1] School of Computing, National University of Singapore, Singapore
[2] Department of Informatics, Minho University, Portugal
[3] LMAM, School of Mathematical Science, Peking University, China
sunm@comp.nus.edu.sg, lsb@di.uminho.pt, znx@pku.edu.cn

Abstract. Although increasingly popular, software component techniques still lack suitable formal foundations on top of which rigorous methodologies for the description and analysis of software architectures could be built. This paper aims to contribute in this direction: building on previous work by the authors on coalgebraic semantics, it discusses component refinement at three different but interrelated levels: *behavioural, syntactic, i.e.*, relative to component *interfaces*, and *architectural*. Software architectures are defined through component aggregation. On the other hand, such aggregations, no matter how large and complex they are, can also be dealt with as components themselves, which paves the way to a discipline of hierarchical design. In this context, a major contribution of this paper is the introduction of a set of rules for architectural refinement.

Keywords: Software component, software architecture, refinement, coalgebra.

1 Introduction

As the size and complexity of software increase continuously, the design and specification of the overall software architecture [28] becomes a central design problem. Software architecture [28] is an important aspect of software engineering, which has a major impact in system's efficiency, adaptability, reusability, and maintainability. Research on software architecture is still in its progressing phase as witnessed by the emergence, in recent years, of a significant number of approaches and methodologies (see, among many other, [3,10,14,22,27]). In the object-oriented paradigm, where development methods like the Unified Modeling Language (UML) [8,25,23] and the Unified Process (UP) [13] are widely used, architectural design forms a critical element of the whole design process [1].

---

* Partially supported by the National Natural Science Foundation of China, under grant 60473056, and a Public Sector Research grant from the Agency of Science, Technology and Research (A*STAR), Singapore.
** Funded by the Portuguese Foundation for Science and Technology, in the context of the PURE project, under contract POSI/ICHS/44304/2002.

D.V. Hung and M. Wirsing (Eds.): ICTAC 2005, LNCS 3722, pp. 469–484, 2005.

The importance of software architecture for the working software engineer is highlighted by the ubiquitous use of architectural descriptions containing information about systems, subsystems, components and interfaces which comprise the whole architecture. Expressions like 'client-server organization" [7], "layered system", "pipeline", etc., quite popular in the software engineering jargon, denote in fact particular architectural styles.

The primary focus of architecture-driven software development shifted from code organization to the definition and manipulation of coarser-grained architectural elements, their interactions, and the overall interconnection structure. However, there still lacks a systematic approach to the architectural development process encompassing both aggregation and refinement in a coherent way.

Previous work on specification refinement, understood as the the process of transforming an 'abstract' into a more 'concrete' design (see, *e.g.*, Hoare's landmark paper [12]), has concentrated on preservation of invariance properties. There is, however, a wide range of ways of understanding both what substitution means, and what such a transformation should seek for. In *data refinement* [9], for example, the 'concrete' model is required to have *enough redundancy* to represent all the elements of the 'abstract' one. This is captured by the definition of a surjection from the former into the latter (the *retrieve map*). However, these well established refinement approaches [11,21] are of limited use for refinement of component-based systems, since they are based on semantic frameworks that consider only the relational behaviour of sequential programs.

The main contribution in this paper is a methodology for the refinement of software architectures. Our work is based on a coalgebraic model for component based systems [4,5,6] in which components can be aggregated through a number of combinators to build hierarchical models of complex systems. Reference [19] introduces the basic results on interface and behavioural refinement of generic components, including a soundness result, upon which a notion of *architectural refinement* is proposed in this paper. Note that, while interface-level refinement is concerned with the manipulation and adjustment of component interfaces, and behavioural refinement relates blackbox behaviours of components, architectural refinement allows us to refine a component by a subsystem architecture as well as to refine a system by another system with a different architecture.

This paper is organized as follows: The underlying coalgebraic model for components and its calculus are briefly reviewed in sections 2 and 3, respectively. Three kinds of refinement relations are introduced in section 4, followed by a family of refinement rules for refinement of system architectures. The paper closes with a brief discussion on what has been achieved in section 5.

2   Components

A software system is defined in terms of a collection of components and connectors among those components. The components interact with each other by the connectors, exchanging information in terms of messages of specified types. Such systems may in turn be used as components in larger designs.

2.1   Components as Coalgebras

We adopt a coalgebraic model for state-based components which follows closely the "*components as coalgebras*" approach proposed by L. Barbosa *et al* in [4,5]. This approach provides an observational semantics for software components and a generic assembly calculus. Qualificative *generic* means that the proposed constructions are parametric on a (mathematical) model of behaviour.

Components interact with their environment via interfaces. Every interface provides a set of typed channels for receiving and sending messages, acting as a type for the corresponding component. Let $\mathbb{C}$ be a set of channel identifiers. Then a component *interface* is defined as follows: we can define the interface of a component as follows:

Definition 1. *Let $I \subseteq \mathbb{C}$ and $O \subseteq \mathbb{C}$ be sets of typed input and output channels, respectively. The pair (I, O), is called an* interface *and any component p with such an interface is typed as $p : I \to O$.*

In the simplest, deterministic case, the behaviour of a component p is captured by the output it produces, which is determined by the supplied input. But reality is often more complicated, for one may have to deal with components whose behavioural pattern is, *e.g.*, partial or even non deterministic. Therefore, to proceed in a generic way, the behaviour model is abstracted to a strong monad B. Of course, B = Id retrieves the simple deterministic behaviour, whereas B = $\mathcal{P}$ or B = Id + 1 would model non deterministic or partial behaviour, respectively. Therefore, a component $p : I \to O$ can be modelled by a pointed concrete coalgebra

$$\langle n_p, U_p, \overline{\alpha}_p : U_p \to \mathsf{B}(U_p \times O)^I, u_0 \in U_p \rangle \tag{1}$$

for the **Set** endo-functor $\mathsf{T}^\mathsf{B} = \mathsf{B}(\mathsf{Id} \times O)^I$. In detail, n_p is the component's name, a specific value u_0 is taken as its 'initial state' (or 'seed') and the dynamics is captured by currying the state-transition function $\alpha_p : U_p \times I \to \mathsf{B}(U_p \times O)$. Notice that the computation of p will not simply produce an output and a continuation state, but a B-structure of such pairs.

For a component p as given in (1), we define the operators name.p, in.p, out.p and beh.p to return n_p, I, O and α_p respectively. In the following sections, for simplicity, we may sometimes omit the occurrence of n_p and u_0, and just use the T^B-coalgebra $\langle U_p, \overline{\alpha}_p \rangle$ to denote component p.

Successive observations of a component p reveal its allowed behavioural patterns. For each state value $u \in U_p$, the behaviour of p at u (more precisely, from u onwards) organize itself into a tree-like structure, because it depends on the sequences of input items processed. Such trees, whose arcs are labelled with I values and nodes with O values, can be represented by functions from non empty sequences of I to B-structures of output items. In other words, the space of behaviours of a component with interface (I, O) is the set $(\mathsf{B}O)^{I^+}$, which is in fact the carrier ν_T of the final T^B-coalgebra $(\nu_\mathsf{T}, \omega_\mathsf{T} : \nu_\mathsf{T} \to \mathsf{T}^\mathsf{B}\nu_\mathsf{T})$. Therefore, by finality, from any other T^B-coalgebra p, there is a unique morphism $[\![\overline{\alpha}_p]\!]$ making the following diagram to commute:

$$\nu_T \xrightarrow{\omega_T} B(\nu_T \times O)^I$$

$$[\![\overline{\alpha}_p]\!] \uparrow \qquad \qquad \uparrow B([\![\overline{\alpha}_p]\!] \times O)^I$$

$$U_p \xrightarrow{\overline{\alpha}_p} B(U_p \times O)^I$$

Applying morphism $[\![p]\!]$ to a state value $u \in U_p$ gives the observable behaviour of a sequence of p transitions starting at u. By instantiating B with concrete strong monads, such as $\mathcal{P}$ and $\mathsf{Id} + 1$, it is possible to model different behaviour patterns such as non-determinism and partial behaviour respectively.

3   Architectures

This section recalls the basic mechanisms for component aggregation along the lines of [4,5,6]. A simple, but precise, notion of software architecture is introduced as a composition pattern for a number of components.

3.1   Composing Components

In the coalgebraic framework revisited in the previous section, components become *arrows* in a (bicategorical) universe **Cp** whose objects are sets, which provide types to input/output parameters (the components' *interfaces*), and component morphisms $h : p \longrightarrow q$ are functions relating the state spaces of $p = \langle n_p, U_p, \overline{\alpha}_p : U_p \to B(U_p \times O)^I, u_p \in U_p \rangle$ and $q = \langle n_q, U_q, \overline{\alpha}_q : U_q \to B(U_q \times O)^I, u_q \in U_q \rangle$ and satisfying the following *seed preservation* and *homomorphism* conditions:

$$h\, u_p \;=\; u_q \qquad \text{and} \qquad \overline{\alpha}_q \cdot h \;=\; B\, (h \times O)^I \cdot \overline{\alpha}_p \qquad (2)$$

For each triple of objects $\langle I, K, O \rangle$, a composition law is given by functor $;_{I,K,O} :$ **Cp**$(I, K) \times$ **Cp**$(K, O) \longrightarrow$ **Cp**(I, O) whose action on objects p and q is

$$p\,;q \;=\; \langle n_{p;q}, U_p \times U_q, \overline{\alpha}_{p;q}, \langle u_p, u_q \rangle \rangle \qquad \text{with}$$

$$\alpha_{p;q} = U_p \times U_q \times I \xrightarrow{\cong} U_p \times I \times U_q \xrightarrow{\alpha_p \times \mathsf{id}} B(U_p \times K) \times U_q$$
$$\xrightarrow{\tau_r} B(U_p \times K \times U_q) \xrightarrow{\cong} B(U_p \times (U_q \times K))$$
$$\xrightarrow{B(\mathsf{id} \times \alpha_q)} B(U_p \times B(U_q \times O)) \xrightarrow{B\tau_l} BB(U_p \times (U_q \times O))$$
$$\xrightarrow{\cong} BB(U_p \times U_q \times O) \xrightarrow{\mu} B(U_p \times U_q \times O)$$

Similarly, for each object K, an identity law is given by a functor $\mathsf{copy}_K : 1 \longrightarrow$ **Cp**(K, K) whose action is the constant component $\langle * \in 1, \eta_{1 \times K} \rangle$. Note that the definitions above rely solely on the monadic structure of B.

In [5,4] a collection of component *combinators* was defined upon **Cp** in a similar parametric way and their properties studied. In particular it was shown that any function $f : A \longrightarrow B$ can be lifted to **Cp** as

$$\ulcorner f \urcorner = \langle n_{\ulcorner f \urcorner}, 1, \eta_{(1 \times B)} \cdot (\mathrm{id} \times f), * \in 1 \rangle$$

A *wrapping* mechanism $p[f, g]$ which encodes the pre- and post-composition of a component with $\mathbf{Cp}$-lifted functions is defined as a combinator which resembles the *renaming* connective found in process algebras (*e.g.*, [20]). Let $p : I \longrightarrow O$ be a component and consider functions $f : I' \longrightarrow I$ and $g : O \longrightarrow O'$. By $p[f, g]$ we will denote component p wrapped by f and g, typed as $I' \longrightarrow O'$ and defined by input pre-composition with f and output post-composition with g. Formally, the wrapping combinator is a functor

$$-[f, g] : \mathbf{Cp}(I, O) \longrightarrow \mathbf{Cp}(I', O')$$

which is the identity on morphisms and maps a component $\langle n_p, U_p, \overline{\alpha}_p, u_p \rangle$ into $\langle n_{p[f,g]}, U_p, \overline{\alpha}_{p[f,g]}, u_p \rangle$, where

$$\alpha_{p[f,g]} = U_p \times I' \xrightarrow{\mathrm{id} \times f} U_p \times I \xrightarrow{\alpha_p} B(U_p \times O) \xrightarrow{B(\mathrm{id} \times g)} B(U_p \times O')$$

Component aggregation is catered by three generic tensors, capturing, respectively, *external choice* ($\boxplus : I + J \longrightarrow O + R$), *parallel* ($\boxtimes : I \times J \longrightarrow O \times R$) and *concurrent* ($\boxdot : I + J + I \times J \longrightarrow O + R + O \times R$) composition. When interacting with $p \boxplus q : I + J \longrightarrow O + R$, the environment chooses either to input a value of type I or one of type J, which triggers the corresponding component (p or q, respectively), producing the relevant output. In its turn, *parallel* composition corresponds to a synchronous product: both components are executed simultaneously when triggered by a pair of legal input values. Note, however, that the behavioural effect, captured by monad B, propagates. For example, if B expresses component failure and one of the arguments fails, the product will fail as well. *Concurrent* composition combines choice and parallel, in the sense that p and q can be executed independently or jointly, depending on the input supplied. Finally, generalized interaction is catered through a sort of 'feedback' mechanism on a subset of the inputs. This can be defined by a new combinator, called *hook*, which connects some input to some output wires and, consequently, forces *part* of the output of a component to be fed back as input. Formally, for each tuple of objects I, O and Z, we define $- \urcorner_Z : \mathbf{Cp}(I + Z, O + Z) \longrightarrow \mathbf{Cp}(I + Z, O + Z)$. This combinator is the identity on arrows and maps each component $p : I + Z \longrightarrow O + Z$ to $p \urcorner_Z : I + Z \longrightarrow O + Z$ given by

$$p \urcorner_Z = \langle n_{p \urcorner_Z}, U_p, \overline{\alpha}_{p \urcorner_Z}, u_p \rangle$$

where

$$\alpha_{p \urcorner_Z} = U_p \times (I + Z) \xrightarrow{\alpha_p} B(U_p \times (O + Z))$$
$$\xrightarrow{B((\mathrm{id} \times \iota_1 + \mathrm{id} \times \iota_2) \cdot \mathrm{dr})} B(U_p \times (O + Z) + U_p \times (I + Z))$$
$$\xrightarrow{B(\eta + a_p)} B(B(U_p \times (O + Z)) + B(U_p \times (O + Z)))$$
$$\xrightarrow{\mu \cdot B\triangledown} B(U_p \times (O + Z))$$

3.2   Systems

From the architectural point of view, a software system comprises a finite set of interconnected components. In itself such a system can be thought of as a new component, which paves the way to hierarchical decomposition. this motivates the following definition:

Definition 2. *A system is defined as a tuple $S = \langle n_S, I_S, O_S, C, R \rangle$, where n_S is its unique identifier, $I_S \subseteq \mathbb{C}$ and $O_S \subseteq \mathbb{C}$ are the sets of input and output channels, respectively, $C = \{p_k\}_{1 \leq k \leq n}$ denotes a finite set of components $p_k = \langle n_k, U_k, \overline{\alpha}_k : U_k \to B(U_k \times O_k)^{I_k}, u_k \in U_k \rangle$ for $k = 1, 2, \cdots, n$, $R = \{\langle op_j, C_j \rangle\}_{1 \leq j \leq m}$ denotes a finite set of combinators together with the components being combined by them, where $C_j = \{p_{j_1}, p_{j_2}, \cdots \mid \forall i. p_{j_i} \in C\}$.*

Note that it is useful to introduce a notion of (input/output) channels I_S and O_S as system's external interfaces. Therefore, for a given system S, we define the operators name.S, in.S, out.S, comps.S and combs.S to return n_S, I_S, O_S, C and R respectively. Moreover, we have

$$\text{in.}C \triangleq \bigcup_{c \in C} \text{in.}c \quad \text{and} \quad \text{out.}C \triangleq \bigcup_{c \in C} \text{out.}c$$

as the union of input or output channels for the components in S.

In fact, we hope to decompose systems hierarchically, and regard them as ordinary component. Therefore, we introduce the set of channels I_S and O_S as the external interfaces of the system.

3.3   Black-Box and Glass-Box Views of Systems

There are two ways of interpreting a system's specification. The first one emphasises its black-box behaviour and arises from the observation that a system, being composed by component aggregation, is itself a component, actually a (final) coalgebra over its space of behaviours. In other words, as a component whose state space is specified as $(BO_S)^{I_S^+}$. Such component abstracts over all internal structure the system may bear, and is simply defined as

$$p_S = \langle n_S, U_S = (BO_S)^{I_S^+}, \overline{\alpha}_S : U_S \to B(U_S \times O_S)^{I_S}, \langle u_1, u_2, \cdots, u_n \rangle \rangle$$

For a given system S, we use the notation $[\![S]\!]$ to denote p_S which captures only the externally visible behaviour of the system. Thus, its internal architecture and organization is not characterized by such an interpretation. It does not reflect, for example, the internal structural decomposition of the system, the internal communication between its components, its internal states, and so on. Thus, it gives a pure black-box view of the system, which is mainly used in the early stages of a system development.

In later stages of development, the software engineer is also concerned with structural aspects of the design, and a glass-box view is then required. Such a glass-box view is provided by Definition 2, on top of which a hierarchical decomposition function ξ is defined. Formally,

Definition 3. *For a given system* $S = \langle n_S, I_S, O_S, C, R \rangle$, *a decomposition function* $\xi : C \longrightarrow \mathcal{P}(C)$ *is a function which satisfies:*

- $\exists ! \, p \in C . p \notin \bigcup ran(\xi)$, *denoted by* ξ_{root}^S;
- $\bigcup ran(\xi) = C \setminus \{\xi_{root}^S\}$ *and* $\forall p \in C \setminus \{\xi_{root}^S\} . (\exists ! \, p' \in C \setminus \{p\} . p \in \xi(p'))$;
- $\forall C' \subseteq C . (C' \neq \emptyset \Rightarrow (\exists p \in C' . C' \cap \xi(p) = \emptyset))$.

4   Architecture Refinement

From a practical point of view, it is impossible to get a concrete architecture of a large system from the abstract requirements in just one step. Therefore, a stepwise development process is needed where software architectures are refined systematically in a number of steps. In this section, we investigate three kinds of refinement relations, namely, *behavioural*, *interface* and *architectural refinement*.

4.1   Behavioural Refinement

The most fundamental notion of refinement in our approach is behavioural refinement [19], based on a simulation preorder between components with identical interfaces. Since morphisms between such components are in fact coalgebra homomorphisms, therefore entailing bisimilarity, there is a need to seek for a weaker notion of a morphism between components, still preserving the source component dynamics.

We say that a component p behaviourally refines component q if the behavioural patterns observed for p are a structural restriction, with respect to the behavioural model captured by monad B, of those of q. To make such a 'definition' more precise we describe behavioural patterns concretely as *generalized transitions*. Thus a possible (and intuitive) way of regarding component p as a behavioural refinement of q is to consider that p transitions are *preserved* in q. For non deterministic components this is understood simply as set inclusion. But one may also want to consider additional restrictions. For example, to stipulate that if p has no transitions from a given state, q should also have no transitions from the corresponding state(s). Recall that a component morphism from p to q is a seed preserving function $h : U_p \longrightarrow U_q$ such that $B(h \times id) \cdot \alpha_p = \alpha_q \cdot (h \times id)$. In terms of transitions, this equation is translated into the following two requirements (by a straightforward generalization of an argument in [26]):

$$u \xrightarrow{\langle i,o \rangle}_p u' \;\Rightarrow\; h\,u \xrightarrow{\langle i,o \rangle}_q h\,u' \tag{3}$$

$$h\,u \xrightarrow{\langle i,o \rangle}_q v' \;\Rightarrow\; \exists_{u' \in U} \; s.t. \; u \xrightarrow{\langle i,o \rangle}_p u' \wedge v' = h\,u' \tag{4}$$

which captures the fact that, not only p dynamics, as represented by the induced transition relation, is *preserved* by h (3), but also q dynamics is *reflected* back over the same h (4).

To define a weaker notion of coalgebra morphism, let $\leq$ be an order on a **Set** endo-functor T [15] (concretely, mapping every set U into a collection of preorders $\leq_{TU}$), referred to as a *refinement preorder*. Also assume that functor T is stable wrt order $\leq^1$. Then,

Definition 4. *Let* T *be an extended polynomial functor on* **Set** *and consider two* T-*coalgebras* $p = (U, \alpha : U \to T(U))$ *and* $q = (V, \beta : V \to T(V))$. *A forward morphism* $h : p \to q$ *with respect to a refinement preorder* $\leq$, *is a function from* U *to* V *such that*

$$T\, h \cdot \alpha \leq \beta \cdot h$$

The existence of a *forward* morphism connecting two components p and q witnesses a refinement situation whose symmetric closure coincides, as expected, with bisimulation. *Behavioural refinement* is therefore defined as the existence of a forward morphism *up to bisimulation* [2]. Formally,

Definition 5. *Given components* p *and* q, p *is a* behavioural refinement *of* q, *written* $p \sqsubseteq_B q$, *if there exist components* r *and* s *such that* $p \sim r$, $q \sim s$ *and* $r \sqsubseteq_F s$, *where* $r \sqsubseteq_F s$ *stands for the existence of a (seed preserving) forward morphism* h *from* r *to* s.

We refer to p as the *concrete* or *refined* component and q as the *abstract* component.

In [19] we have proved the soundness of simulation for behavioural refinement, which is given in the following lemma[3]:

Lemma 1. *To prove* $p \sqsubseteq_B q$ *it is sufficient to exhibit a simulation* R *relating components* p *and* q.

On the other hand, for two components p and q, if p behaviourally refines q, then we can always get a simulation R between them, which is defined as $\sim \circ Graph(h) \circ \sim$. To prove the result, we first recall from [15] the following result:

Lemma 2. *Let* T *be a functor stable wrt order* $\leq$. *Then,*

- *If* R *is a bisimulation, then both* R *and* R^{op} *are simulations;*
- *Simulations are closed under composition.*

and prove that

---

[1] Given a **Set** endofunctor T and a refinement preorder $\leq$, a lax relation lifting is an operation $Rel_{\leq}(T)$ mapping relation R to $\leq \circ Rel(T)(R) \circ \leq$, where $Rel(T)(R)$ is the lifting of R to T (defined, as usual, as the T-image of inclusion $\langle r_1, r_2 \rangle : R \longrightarrow U \times V$, i.e., $\langle Tr_1, Tr_2 \rangle : TR \longrightarrow TU \times TV$). A functor T is stable wrt a order $\leq$ if the associated lax relation lifting operation $Rel_{\leq}(T)$ commutes with substitution.

[2] In [19] the dual notion of a *backwards* morphism, i.e., one that satisfies $\beta \cdot h \leq T\, h \cdot \alpha$, is also studied, leading to a notion of *backward* refinement which do have some applications, although the underlying intuition seems less familiar.

[3] Here we adopt a generic definition of simulation due to Jacobs and Hughes in [15]: Given T-coalgebras α and β, a simulation is a $Rel_{\leq}(T)$-coalgebra over α and β, i.e., a relation R such that, for all $u \in U, v \in V$, $\langle u, v \rangle \in R \Rightarrow \langle \alpha\, u, \beta\, v \rangle \in Rel_{\leq}(T)(R)$.

Lemma 3. *The graph of a forward morphism h between two T-coalgebras $p =$ (U, α) and $q = (V, \beta)$ is a simulation.*

Proof. Define a relation $R \subseteq U \times V$ as $\langle u, v \rangle \in R$ iff $h(u) = v$. Because h is a forward morphism, for all $u \in U$, the following diagram commutes:

$$
\begin{array}{ccc}
u & \xrightarrow{\ \ h\ \ } & h(u) = v \\[4pt]
\alpha \downarrow & & \downarrow \beta \\[4pt]
\alpha(u) \xrightarrow{\ Th\ } Th(\alpha(u)) & \leq_{\mathsf{TV}} & \beta(v)
\end{array}
$$

Since $\leq$ is a preorder, we have $\alpha(u) \leq_{\mathsf{T}U} \alpha(u)$. Therefore, for any $u \in U$ and $v \in V$, if $\langle u, v \rangle \in R$, then $\langle \alpha(u), \beta(v) \rangle \in \leq \circ Rel(\mathsf{T})(R) \circ \leq$. That means, R is a simulation.

Then,

Theorem 1. *For two components p and q, if p behaviourally refines q, and this is witnessed by a forward morphism h, then $\sim \circ Graph(h) \circ \sim$ is a simulation between them.*

Proof. Immediate by combination of lemmas 2 and 3.

4.2 Properties of Behavioural Refinement

Behavioural refinement of components has a number of pleasant properties. First of all it is a preorder:

$$p \sqsubseteq_B p$$

$$p \sqsubseteq_B q \wedge q \sqsubseteq_B r \Rightarrow p \sqsubseteq_B r$$

Proof. The reflexivity is obvious: we just need to take the identity function id on p as the forward morphism (the graph of id is a bisimulation). For the transitivity, we can first derive two simulations R and R' from $p \sqsubseteq_B q$ and $q \sqsubseteq_B r$ respectively, then from Lemma 2, we can know that $R' \circ R$ is also a simulation. By Lemma 1, p is a behaviour refinement of r.

In the case of a large system consisting of many components, it is not practical to consider the whole system each time one of its components is to be refined. On the contrary, we would like to decompose the original system, perform refinement locally and reconstruct the relevant services from the refined components. To make this possible behavioural refinement should also be a pre-congruence. Formally,

Lemma 4. *For any refinement preorder $\leq$, behavioural refinement $\sqsubseteq_B$ is monotonic with respect to combinators:*

$$p[f,g] \sqsubseteq_B q[f,g]$$
$$p\,;r \sqsubseteq_B q\,;t$$
$$p \boxtimes r \sqsubseteq_B q \boxtimes t$$
$$p \boxplus r \sqsubseteq_B q \boxplus t$$
$$p \boxast r \sqsubseteq_B q \boxast t$$
$$p \,^\curvearrowleft z \sqsubseteq_B q \,^\curvearrowleft z$$

whenever $p \sqsubseteq_B q$ and $r \sqsubseteq_B t$.

Proof. Let R_1 and R_2 be the simulation relations witnessing $p \sqsubseteq_B q$ and $r \sqsubseteq_B t$ respectively. For wrapping and the hook combinator, we just need to define $R = R_1$. Let $\langle u, v \rangle \in R$, then for all $i \in I$, we can easily derive $\langle \alpha_p(u,i), \alpha_q(v,i) \rangle \in \leq \circ Rel_\leq (\mathsf{B}(\mathsf{Id} \times O))(R) \circ \leq$ from $p \sqsubseteq_B q$. Therefore,

$$\langle \overline{\alpha}_{p[f,g]}(u), \overline{\alpha}_{q[f,g]}(v) \rangle \in \leq \circ Rel_\leq (\mathsf{B}(\mathsf{Id} \times O')^{I'})(R) \circ \leq$$
$$\equiv \forall i' \in I'. \langle \alpha_{p[f,g]}(u,i'), \alpha_{q[f,g]}(v,i') \rangle \in \leq \circ Rel_\leq (\mathsf{B}(\mathsf{Id} \times O'))(R) \circ \leq$$
$$\equiv \langle \mathsf{B}(\mathsf{id} \times g) \cdot \alpha_p \cdot (\mathsf{id} \times f)(u,i'), \mathsf{B}(\mathsf{id} \times g) \cdot \alpha_q \cdot (\mathsf{id} \times f)(v,i') \rangle \in$$
$$\leq \circ Rel_\leq (\mathsf{B}(\mathsf{Id} \times O'))(R) \circ \leq$$
$$\equiv \{\text{let } f(i') = i\}$$
$$\langle \mathsf{B}(\mathsf{id} \times g) \cdot \alpha_p(u,i), \mathsf{B}(\mathsf{id} \times g) \cdot \alpha_q(v,i) \rangle \in \leq \circ Rel_\leq (\mathsf{B}(\mathsf{Id} \times O'))(R) \circ \leq$$
$$\equiv \mathsf{B}(\mathsf{id} \times g) \cdot \langle \alpha_p(u,i), \alpha_q(v,i) \rangle \in \leq \circ Rel_\leq (\mathsf{B}(\mathsf{Id} \times O'))(R) \circ \leq$$
$$\equiv \langle \alpha_p(u,i), \alpha_q(v,i) \rangle \in \leq \circ Rel_\leq (\mathsf{B}(\mathsf{Id} \times O))(R) \circ \leq$$
$$\equiv \text{TRUE}$$

The proof for the hook combinator can be similarly obtained. Proofs for the monotonicity of $\sqsubseteq_B$ for other combinators can be found in [18].

4.3 Interface Refinement

Behavioural refinement characterizes the preservation of component behaviour. But if we rely solely on behavioural refinement, the inability to change the syntactic interface will force us to work at the same level of interface abstraction throughout the whole development process. To avoid this, a more general notion of refinement, called interface refinement is introduced, which relates components with different interfaces.

Definition 6. *Let* $p : I \to O$ *and* $q : I' \to O'$ *be components. If there exist functions* $w_1 : I' \to I$ *and* $w_2 : O \to O'$, *such that*

$$p[w_1, w_2] \sqsubseteq_B q$$

then p *is an* interface refinement *of* q *modulo the downwards function* w_1 *and the upwards function* w_2, *written as* $p \sqsubseteq_{(w_1, w_2)} q$.

Interface refinement supports the systematic construction of new components from existing ones. Generally, for any component p, and functions w_1, w_2,

$$p \sqsubseteq_{(w_1, w_2)} p[w_1, w_2]$$

One situation where this technique is useful is when we have an already completed off-the-shelf component and want to adapt the syntactic interface of this component to fit some context requirements. Therefore, interface refinement provides a systematic pattern for interface adaptation of components.

As explained previously, the behavioural refinement relation on components is both reflexive and transitive. Moreover, behavioural refinement is monotonic with respect to the combinators defined in the component calculus. This allows system development in a flexible top-down manner. The following properties show that interface refinement combines nicely with behavioural refinement:

$$p_1 \sqsubseteq_B p_2 \wedge p_2 \sqsubseteq_{(w_1, w_2)} p_3 \Rightarrow p_1 \sqsubseteq_{(w_1, w_2))} p_3$$

$$p_1 \sqsubseteq_{(w_1, w_2)} p_2 \wedge p_2 \sqsubseteq_B p_3 \Rightarrow p_1 \sqsubseteq_{(w_1, w_2))} p_3$$

Furthermore, we have transitivity in the sense that

$$p_1 \sqsubseteq_{(w_1, w_2)} p_2 \wedge p_2 \sqsubseteq_{(w_3, w_4)} p_3 \Rightarrow p_1 \sqsubseteq_{(w_3 \cdot w_1, w_2 \cdot w_4)} p_3$$

4.4   Architectural Refinement

By *architectural* refinement we mean behavioural refinement of a complex system regarded as a component on its own. Formally,

Definition 7. *Let* $S = \langle n_S, I_S, O_S, C, R \rangle$ *and* $S' = \langle n_{S'}, I_{S'}, O_{S'}, C', R' \rangle$ *be two systems. If* $I_S = I_{S'}$, $O_S = O_{S'}$, *and* $[\![S]\!] \sqsubseteq_B [\![S']\!]$, *then we say that* S *is an architectural refinement of* S', *written as* $S \sqsubseteq_A S'$.

From the transitivity of behavioural refinement relation, one gets,

$$S_1 \sqsubseteq_A S_2 \wedge S_2 \sqsubseteq_A S_3 \Rightarrow S_1 \sqsubseteq_A S_3$$

This definition becomes really useful if it can be translated on concrete refinement rules concerned with structural changes in the design. A number of them, easily derived from the definitions, are stated below in the format

$$\frac{precondition}{refinement}$$

where *precondition* is the condition to be satisfied for the refinement relation to hold.

Behavioural refinement. A system can be refined by refining one of its components and leave other components unchanged. For a given system $S = \langle n_S, I_S, O_S, C, R \rangle$, let $p \in C$ be a component and p' is a behavioural refinement of p, then we can get a refinement of the whole system:

$$p \in C$$
$$p' \sqsubseteq_B p$$
$$C' = (C \setminus \{p\}) \cup \{p'\}$$
$$R' = \{\langle op_j, (C_j \setminus \{p\}) \cup \{p'\} \triangleleft p \in C_j \triangleright C_j \rangle\}_{1 \leq j \leq m}$$
$$S' = \langle n_S, I_S, O_S, C', R' \rangle$$
$$\overline{\qquad\qquad\qquad\qquad}$$
$$S' \sqsubseteq_A S$$

Adding output channels. New output channels may be added to a component p if it is neither connected to a system component, nor part of the system interface. For a given system $S = \langle n_S, I_S, O_S, C, R \rangle$, let $p \in C$ be a component, then

$$O' \subseteq \mathbb{C} \setminus (\text{in}.C \cup \text{out}.C)$$
$$p = \langle n_p, U_p, \overline{\alpha}_p : U_p \to \mathsf{B}(U_p \times O_p)^{I_p}, u_p \in U_p \rangle$$
$$p' = \langle n_p, U_p, \overline{\alpha}_{p'} : U_p \to \mathsf{B}(U_p \times (O_p + O'))^{I_p}, u_p \in U_p \rangle$$
$$\forall u \in U_p, i \in I_p \,.\, \alpha_{p'}(u, i) = \alpha_p(u, i)$$
$$C' = (C \setminus \{p\}) \cup \{p'\}$$
$$R' = \{\langle op_j, (C_j \setminus \{p\}) \cup \{p'\} \triangleleft p \in C_j \triangleright C_j \rangle\}_{1 \leq j \leq m}$$
$$S' = \langle n_S, I_S, O_S, C', R' \rangle$$
$$\overline{\qquad\qquad\qquad\qquad}$$
$$S' \sqsubseteq_A S$$

Removing output channels. An output channel of component p being not used in the system can be removed from the component. For a given system $S = \langle n_S, I_S, O_S, C, R \rangle$, let $p \in C$ be a component, then

$$o \notin O_S \cup \text{in}.C$$
$$p = \langle n_p, U_p, \overline{\alpha}_p : U_p \to \mathsf{B}(U_p \times O_p)^{I_p}, u_p \in U_p \rangle$$
$$O'_p = O_p \setminus \{o\}$$
$$p' = \langle n_p, U_p, \overline{\alpha}_{p'} : U_p \to \mathsf{B}(U_p \times O'_p)^{I_p}, u_p \in U_p \rangle$$
$$\forall u \in U_p, i \in I_p \,.\, \alpha_{p'}(u, i) = \alpha_p(u, i)$$
$$C' = (C \setminus \{p\}) \cup \{p'\}$$
$$R' = \{\langle op_j, (C_j \setminus \{p\}) \cup \{p'\} \triangleleft p \in C_j \triangleright C_j \rangle\}_{1 \leq j \leq m}$$
$$S' = \langle n_S, I_S, O_S, C', R' \rangle$$
$$\overline{\qquad\qquad\qquad\qquad}$$
$$S' \sqsubseteq_A S$$

Adding input channels. An input channel can be added to a component p provided that it is already in the output of some other component or input of the system. For a given system $S = \langle n_S, I_S, O_S, C, R \rangle$, let $p \in C$ be a component, then

$$i' \in I_S \cup \text{out}.C$$
$$p = \langle n_p, U_p, \overline{\alpha}_p : U_p \to \mathsf{B}(U_p \times O_p)^{I_p}, u_p \in U_p \rangle$$
$$I'_p = I_p \cup \{i'\}$$
$$p' = \langle n_p, U_p, \overline{\alpha}_{p'} : U_p \to \mathsf{B}(U_p \times O_p)^{I'_p}, u_p \in U_p \rangle$$
$$\forall u \in U_p, i \in I_p \,.\, \alpha_{p'}(u, i) = \alpha_p(u, i)$$
$$C' = (C \setminus \{p\}) \cup \{p'\}$$
$$R' = \{\langle op_j, (C_j \setminus \{p\}) \cup \{p'\} \triangleleft p \in C_j \triangleright C_j \rangle\}_{1 \leq j \leq m}$$
$$S' = \langle n_S, I_S, O_S, C', R' \rangle$$
$$\overline{\qquad\qquad\qquad\qquad}$$
$$S' \sqsubseteq_A S$$

Removing input channels. If the behaviour of a component p does not depend on the input from an input channel, then the channel can be removed. For a given system $S = \langle n_S, I_S, O_S, C, R \rangle$, let $p \in C$ be a component, then[4]

$$p = \langle n_p, U_p, \overline{\alpha}_p : U_p \to (B(U_p \times O_p) + 1)^{I_p}, u_p \in U_p \rangle$$
$$i' \in \mathrm{in}.p$$
$$\forall u \in U_p \ . \ \alpha_p(u, i') = *$$
$$I'_p = I_p \setminus \{i'\}$$
$$p' = \langle n_p, U_p, \overline{\alpha}_{p'} : U_p \to B(U_p \times O_p)^{I'_p}, u_p \in U_p \rangle$$
$$\forall u \in U_p, i \in I'_p \ . \ \alpha_{p'}(u, i) = \alpha_p(u, i)$$
$$C' = (C \setminus \{p\}) \cup \{p'\}$$
$$R' = \{\langle op_j, (C_j \setminus \{p\}) \cup \{p'\} \triangleleft p \in C_j \triangleright C_j \rangle\}_{1 \leq j \leq m}$$
$$\frac{S' = \langle n_S, I_S, O_S, C', R' \rangle}{S' \sqsubseteq_A S}$$

Adding new components. We can simply add a new component $\mathrm{nil} = \ulcorner \mathrm{id}_\emptyset \urcorner$ to a system, which does not change the global system behaviour. For a given system $S = \langle n_S, I_S, O_S, C, R \rangle$, we have

$$\forall p \in C \ . \ \mathrm{name}.p \neq \mathrm{name}.\mathrm{nil}$$
$$C' = C \cup \{\mathrm{nil}\}$$
$$\frac{S' = \langle n_S, I_S, O_S, C', R \rangle}{S' \sqsubseteq_A S}$$

Removing old components. Components may be removed from a system if it does not have output that affects the system. For a given system $S = \langle n_S, I_S, O_S, C, R \rangle$ and a component $p \in C$, we have

$$\mathrm{out}.p = \emptyset$$
$$C' = C \setminus \{p\}$$
$$R' = \{\langle op_j, (C_j \setminus \{p\}) \triangleleft p \in C_j \triangleright C_j \rangle\}_{1 \leq j \leq m}$$
$$\frac{S' = \langle n_S, I_S, O_S, C', R \rangle}{S' \sqsubseteq_A S}$$

Decomposing components. Sometimes we may want to change the hierarchical structure of a system. For example, a lift system might consist of a lift controller, several doors and buttons. Especially, in later phases of a system development, we might consider the glass-box view of the system, and thus need to expand components into architectures. For a given system $S = \langle n_S, I_S, O_S, C, R \rangle$ and a component $p \in C$, which has the same behaviour with the architecture $T = \langle n_T, I_T, O_T, C_T, R_T \rangle$, i.e., p is behaviour equivalent to T, we have

---

[4] The monad $B + 1$ specifies the possibility of partial behaviour of components, where $*$ is the only element in the singleton set **1**.

$$p \sim [\![T]\!]$$
$$\forall q \in C, q' \in C_T . \text{name}.q \neq \text{name}.q'$$
$$\text{out}.C_T \cap \text{out}.C = \text{out}.p$$
$$C' = (C \setminus \{p\}) \cup C_T$$
$$R' = \{\langle op_j, (C_j \setminus \{p\}) \cup \{\xi_{root}^T\} \lhd p \in C_j \rhd C_j\rangle\}_{1 \leq j \leq m} \cup R_T$$
$$S' = \langle n_S, I_S, O_S, C', R'\rangle$$
$$\overline{\hspace{6cm}}$$
$$S' \sqsubseteq_A S$$

Folding components. If $T = \langle n_T, I_T, O_T, C_T, R_T\rangle$ is a subarchitecture of a system $S = \langle n_S, I_S, O_S, C, R\rangle$, then we can fold it into a new component $p = \langle n_p, U_p, \overline{\alpha}_p : U_p \rightarrow \mathsf{B}(U_p \times O_p)^{I_p}, u_p \in U_p\rangle$, which has the same behaviour with T.

$$p \sim [\![T]\!]$$
$$C_T \subseteq C$$
$$\forall q \in C \setminus C_T . \text{name}.q \neq n_p$$
$$C' = (C \setminus C_T) \cup \{p\}$$
$$R'' = (R \setminus (R_T \cup \{\langle op_j, C_j\rangle \mid \exists p' \in C_T \cap C_j\}))$$
$$R' = R'' \cup \{\langle op_j, (C_j \setminus C_T) \cup \{p\}\rangle \mid \exists p' \in C_T \cap C_j . \langle op_j, C_j\rangle \in R\}$$
$$S' = \langle n_S, I_S, O_S, C', R'\rangle$$
$$\overline{\hspace{6cm}}$$
$$S' \sqsubseteq_A S$$

5   Conclusions

This paper discusses refinement of software architectures in the context of a broader research agenda on coalgebraic semantics for componentware. From our experience to date, the appropriateness of the coalgebraic approach for component based systems is driven by the following two key ideas: first, the 'black-box' characterization of software components favors an *observational* semantics; secondly, the proposed constructions are *generic* in the sense that they do not depend on a particular notion of component behaviour. This led both to the adoption of coalgebra theory [26] to capture observational semantics and to the abstract characterization of possible behaviour models (*e.g.*, partiality or different degrees of non-determinism) by strong monads acting as parameters in the resulting calculus [4,5]. Our work provides three basic refinement relations, which can be used for refinement of systems at different granularity.

A large body of work on software architectures using process algebraic ADLs can be found in the literature (see, *e.g.*, [10,28]). These approaches are usually biased towards specific behavioural models and therefore less generic than the one sketched in this paper. An approach closer to ours is that of [22], where a refinement mapping is defined to provide a syntactical translation between abstract and concrete architectures. However, such a mapping is required to be *faithful*, which means that both the positive and the implicit negative facts in the abstract architecture should be preserved in the concrete one. This makes both definition and proof of refinement difficult. Yet another interesting calculus was proposed in [24] to deal with refinement of information flow architectures. However, it only deals with the refinement of system's internal organization.

Our work is based on some preliminary results on behavioural refinement of generic state-based components documented in [19]. In this paper we proved a completeness result connecting simulation to behavioural refinement and provided further insight on refinement at both interface and architectural levels. Both of them can be reduced to the simple behavioural refinement relationship. A family of refinement rules was provided for local, stepwise modification of architectural designs. The genericity of the underlying coalgebraic model makes our approach not limited to any sort of architecture style. Whether it scales up to more sophisticated architectural models, namely the ones based on component coordination by anonymous communication and independent connectors (as in, *e.g.*, [2] or [17,16]), is still an open research question.

References

1. Aynur Abdurazik. Suitability of the UML as an Architecture Description Language with Applications to Testing. Technical Report ISE-TR-00-01, Information and software engineering, George Mason University, 2000.
2. Farhad Arbab. Abstract Behavior Types: A Foundation Model for Components and Their Composition. In Frank S. de Boer, Marcello M. Bonsangue, Susanne Graf, and Willem-Paul de Roever, editors, *Formal Methods for Components and Objects: First International Symposium, FMCO 2002, Leiden, The Netherlands, November 2002, Revised Lectures*, volume 2852 of *LNCS*, pages 33–70. Springer, 2003.
3. Farhad Arbab and Jan Rutten. A coinductive calculus of component connectors. In M. Wirsing, D. Pattinson, and R. Hennicker, editors, *Recent Trends in Algebraic Development Techniques: 16th International Workshop, WADT 2002, Frauenchiemsee, Germany, September 24-27, 2002, Revised Selected Papers*, volume 2755 of *LNCS*, pages 34–55. Springer-Verlag, 2003.
4. Luís Soares Barbosa. Towards a Calculus of State-based Software Components. *Journal of Universal Computer Science*, 9(8):891–909, August 2003.
5. Luís Soares Barbosa and José Nuno Fonseca de Oliveira. State-based components made generic. In H. Peter Gumm, editor, *Elect. Notes in Theor. Comp. Sci. (CMCS'03 - Workshop on Coalgebraic Methods in Computer Science)*, volume 82.1, Warsaw, April 2003.
6. Luís Soares Barbosa, Sun Meng, Bernhard K. Aichernig, and Nuno Rodrigues. On the semantics of componentware: a coalgebraic perspective. In Jifeng He and Zhiming Liu, editors, *Mathematical Frameworks for Component Software.- Models for Analysis and Synthesis*, chapter 2. World Scientific, 2004. To be published.
7. Alex Berson. *Client/Server Architecture*. McGraw-Hill, 1992.
8. Grady Booch, James Rumbaugh, and Ivar Jacobson. *The Unified Modeling Language User Guide*. Addison Wesley, 1999.
9. Willem-Paul de Roever and Kai Engelhardt. *Data Refinement: Model-Oriented Proof Methods and their Comparison*. Cambridge University Press, 1998.
10. David Garlan. Higher-order connectors. Proceedings of Workshop on Compositional Software Architectures, January 1998.
11. C. A. R. Hoare, He Jifeng, and Jeff W. Sanders. Prespecification in data refinement. *Information Processing Letters*, 25:71–76, 1987.
12. Charles Antony Richard Hoare. Proof of correctness of data representations. *Acta Information*, 1:271–281, 1972.

13. John Hunt. *The Unified Process for Practitioners: Object Oriented Design, UML and Java*. Practitioner. Springer, 2001.
14. Paola Inverardi and Alexander L. Wolf. Formal specification and analysis of software architectures using the chemical abstract machine model. *IEEE Transactions on Software Engineering*, 21(4), 1995.
15. Bart Jacobs and Jesse Hughes. Simulations in coalgebra. In H. Peter Gumm, editor, *Elect. Notes in Theor. Comp. Sci. (CMCS'03 - Workshop on Coalgebraic Methods in Computer Science)*, volume 82, pages 245–263, Warsaw, April 2003.
16. M. A. Marco A. Barbosa and Luís Soares Barbosa. A Relational Model for Component Interconnection. *Journal of Universal Computer Science*, 10(7):808–823, July 2004.
17. M. A. Marco A. Barbosa and Luís Soares Barbosa. Specifying software connectors. In K. Araki and Z. Liu, editors, *1st International Colloquium on Theorectical Aspects of Computing (ICTAC'04)*, pages 53–68, Guiyang, China, September 2004. Springer Lect. Notes Comp. Sci. (3407).
18. Sun Meng and Luís Soares Barbosa. On Refinement of Generic Components. Technical Report 281, UNU/IIST, May 2003.
19. Sun Meng and Luís Soares Barbosa. On Refinement of Generic State-based Software Components. In C. Rattray, S. Maharaj, and C. Shankland, editors, *Algebraic Methodology And Software Technology, 10th International Conference, AMAST'04, Proceedings*, volume 3116 of *LNCS*, pages 506–520. Springer, 2004.
20. Robin Milner. *Communication and Concurrency*. Prentice Hall, 1989.
21. Carroll Morgan. *Programming from Specifications, Second Edition*. Prentice Hall, 1994.
22. Mark Moriconi, Xiaolei Qian, and R. A. Riemenschneider. Correct architecture refinement. *IEEE Transactions on Software Engineering*, 21(4):356–372, 1995.
23. OMG. *OMG Unified Modeling Language Specification, Version 1.3* , 2000.
24. Jan Philipps and Bernhard Rumpe. Refinement of information flow architectures. In M. Hinchey, editor, *Proceedings of ICFEM'97*. IEEE CS Press, 1997.
25. James Rumbaugh, Ivar Jacobson, and Grady Booch. *The Unified Modeling Language Reference Manual*. Addison Wesley Longman, 1999.
26. Jan Rutten. Universal coalgebra: a theory of systems. *Theoretical Computer Science*, 249:3–80, 2000.
27. J.-G. Schneider and O. Nierstrasz. Components, scripts, glue. In L. Barroca, J. Hall, and P. Hall, editors, *Software Architectures - Advances and Applications*, pages 13–25. Springer-Verlag, 1999.
28. Mary Shaw and David Garlan. *Software Architecture: Perspectives on an Emerging Discipline*. Prentice Hall, 1996.

POST: A Case Study for an Incremental Development in rCOS*

Quan Long[1], Zongyan Qiu[1], Zhiming Liu[2,**], Lingshuang Shao[3], and He Jifeng[2]

[1] LMAM and Department of Informatics, School of Mathematical Sciences,
Peking University, Beijing, China
{longquan, qzy}@math.pku.edu.cn
[2] International Institute for Software Technology,
United Nations University, Macao, China
{lzm, hjf}@iist.unu.edu
[3] Software Engineering Institute, Peking University, Beijing, China
shaolsh04@sei.pku.edu.cn

Abstract. We have recently developed an object-oriented refinement calculus called rCOS to formalize the basic object-orient design principles, patterns and refactoring as refinement laws. The aim is of rCOS is to provide a formal support to the *use-cased driven, incremental* and *iterative* Rational Unified Process (RUP). In this paper, we apply rCOS to a step-wised development of a Point of Sale Terminal (POST) system, from a requirement model to a design model, and finally, to the implementation in Visual C#.

Keywords: Refinement, Software design, Object-orientation, Refactoring, UML.

1 Introduction

In the imperative paradigm, the *specification* of a problem is mainly concerned with the control and data structures of the program. The program development is the design and implementation of data structures and algorithms through a number of steps of *refinement*. *Verification* is needed to prove that each step preserves the specification of the control and data structures in the previous step. Various formal methods, especially those state-based models [5,10] such as VDM [11] and Z [4], are widely found helpful in correct and reliable construction of such a program.

The object-oriented requirement analysis, design and programming are popular recently in practical software engineering. Recent development and application of UML and the Rational Unified Process (RUP) have led to the use of design patterns and refactoring more effective.

However, the research in the formal aspects and techniques does not reflect or provide enough support to these newly developed objected-oriented engineering principles and development processes. It is still hard to obtain assurance of correctness in object-oriented developing process using old fashioned programming techniques. Model-based formalisms have been extended with object-oriented techniques, via languages such as Object-Z [1], VDM++ [6], and methods such as Syntropy [3] which

---

* Supported by NNSFC(No. 60173003) and NKBRPC(2004CB318000).
** Partly supported as a research task of E-Macao Project funded by the Macao Government.

D.V. Hung and M. Wirsing (Eds.): ICTAC 2005, LNCS 3722, pp. 485–500, 2005.

uses the Z notation, and Fusion [2] that is related to VDM. Whilst these formalisms are effective at modelling data structures as sets and relations between sets, they do not capture the main principles of object-oriented decomposition, including function-ality delegation, class decomposition, and object-oriented refinement. Object-oriented refinement must capture the notation of substitutability of a group of associated classes by another group of associated classes. The development of rCOS is mainly motivated by these problems [8].

In this paper, we use the case study of a Point of Sale Terminal (POST) system, originally from [12] to demonstrate how a system can be formally and systematically developed supported by the rCOS based development process. A POST system is typ-ically used in a retail store or supermarket. It includes hardware components such as a computer and a bar code scanner, and the software to control the system. The case study also shows how the techniques could be used in the development of other systems. It mainly demonstrates how functionality is decomposed in the object-oriented settings by the expert pattern, and how object-oriented structure is refined by refactoring rules.

The rest of this paper is organized as follows. We first briefly introduce rCOS and related development process in Section 2 and Section 3 respectively. And then, in Sec-tion 4, we present the development process, or refinement process of POST software system. The executable product developed from the final refined design is illustrated in Section 5. Finally, in Section 6, we conclude the paper and discuss some future research directions.

2   Overview of rCOS

In this section we give a brief introduction to the rCOS model and our earlier work based on it. We refer the readers to [8,9,15] for more details.

2.1   rCOS Syntax

rCOS is a refinement calculus of *object-oriented sequential systems*. In rCOS, a system (or program) S is of the form *cdecls* • P, consisting of class declaration section *cdecls* and a main method P. The main method P is a pair (glb, c) of a set glb of *global variables declarations* and a command c. P can also be understood as the *main method* in Java. The class declaration section *cdecls* is a sequence of class declarations $cdecl_1; \ldots; cdecl_k$, where each class declaration $cdecl_i$ is of the form

[private] class N extends M {
    private $(U_i\, u_i = a_i)_{i:1..m}$; protected $(V_i\, v_i = b_i)_{i:1..n}$; public $(W_i\, w_i = c_i)_{i:1..k}$;
    method $m_1(\underline{T}_{11}\, \underline{x}_1, \underline{T}_{12}\, \underline{y}_1, \underline{T}_{13}\, \underline{z}_1)\{c_1\}; \cdots; m_\ell(\underline{T}_{\ell 1}\, \underline{x}_\ell, \underline{T}_{\ell 2}\, \underline{y}_\ell, \underline{T}_{\ell 3}\, \underline{z}_\ell)\{c_\ell\}\}$

Note that

- A class can be declared as private or public, but by default it is assumed as public. Only the public classes and primitive types can be used in the global vari-able declarations glb.
- N and M are distinct names of classes, and M is called the direct superclass of N.

- Attributes annotated with `private` are private attributes of the class, and similarly, the `protected` and `public` declarations for the protected and public attributes. Types and initial values of attributes are also given in the declaration.
- The `method` declaration declares the methods, their value parameters ($\underline{T}_{i1}\,\underline{x}_i$), result parameters ($\underline{T}_{i2}\,\underline{y}_i$), value-result parameters ($\underline{T}_{i3}\,z_i$) and bodies (c_i). We sometimes denote a method by $m(\textit{paras})\{c\}$, where $\textit{paras}$ is the list of parameters of m, and c is the body command of m. The method body c_i is a command that will be defined later.

We use Java convention to write a class specification, and assume an attribute `protected` when it is not tagged with `private` or `public`. We have these different kinds of attributes to show how visibility issues can be dealt with. We can also have different kind of methods for a class, however, it is omitted here for simplicity of the theory. Instead, we assume all methods in public classes are public and can be inherited by a subclass and accessed by the main method, and all methods in private classes are protected.

When we write refinement laws, we use the following notation to denote a class declaration of class N.

$$N[M, \texttt{pri}, \texttt{prot}, \texttt{pub}, \texttt{op}]$$

where M is the name of the direct superclass of N, `pri`, `prot` and `pub` are the sets of the private, protected and public attribute declarations, and `op` is the set of the method declarations of N. When there is no confusion, we only explicitly give the parameters that we are concerned. For example, we use $N[\texttt{op}]$ to denote a class with a set `op` of methods, and $N[\texttt{prot}, \texttt{op}]$ a class with a protected attributes `prot` and methods `op`.

Commands.   rCOS supports typical object-oriented programming constructs, but it also allows some commands for the purpose of specification and refinement:

$$c ::=\ skip \mid chaos \mid \textbf{var}\ T\ \text{x=e} \mid \textbf{end}\ x \mid c; c \mid c \lhd b \rhd c \mid c \sqcap c$$
$$\mid b * c \mid le.m(\underline{e}, \underline{v}, \underline{u}) \mid le := e \mid C.new(x)[\underline{e}]$$

where b is a Boolean expression, e is an expression, and le is an expression which may appear on the left side of an assignment and is of the form $le ::= x \mid le.a$, where x is a simple variable and a an attribute of an object. We use $le.m(\underline{e}, \underline{v}, \underline{u})$ to denote a call of method m of the object denoted by le with actual value parameters $\underline{e}$ for input to the method, actual result parameters $\underline{v}$ for the return values, and value-result parameters $\underline{u}$ that can be changed during the execution of the method and with their final values as return values too. The command $C.new(x)[\underline{e}]$ creates a new object of class C with the initial values of its attributes assigned by the values of the expressions in $\underline{e}$ and assigns it to variable x. Thus, $C.new(x)[\underline{e}]$ uses x with type C to refer to the newly created object. The other commands, $c; c$, $c \lhd b \rhd c$, $c \sqcap c$ and $b * c$ denote the conventional commands of sequential composition, choice, non-determined choice, and iteration respectively.

The expressions e appear in the commands are defined in a usual way. We ignore them here.

2.2 Semantics and Refinement of Object Systems

rCOS adopts an observation-oriented and relational semantics. The model describes the behavior of an object-oriented program by a *design* containing seven logical variables as its *free variables* that form the *alphabet* "α" in [10] of the program. They are **cname, attr, op, superclass, Σ, glb** and **locvar**. They record both static structure of the classes and dynamic state of the system.

Commands and class declarations, as well as an object system as a whole, are semantically defined as a *framed design* $D(\alpha, P)$ with the form $\{\alpha\} : pre(x) \vdash Post(x, x')$. That is, the effect of any piece of code are defined by the pre- and post states of the above mentioned *alphabet*. Please see [9] for details if interested.

Based on the relational model, rCOS supports refinement of object-oriented designs at different levels of abstraction during a system development. It includes design refinement, data refinement, refinement of classes and refinement of a whole system.

In [9], the *Design refinement* and *Data refinement* are defined similar to traditional ones. In this section we only present the definitions of *System refinement* and *Class refinement* as follows.

Definition 1. (System refinement) *Let S_1 and S_2 be object programs which have the same set global variables* **glb**. *S_1 is a refinement of S_2, denoted by $S_2 \sqsubseteq_{sys} S_1$, if its behavior is more controllable and predictable than that of S_2:*

$$\forall \underline{x}, \underline{x}' \cdot (S_1 \Rightarrow S_2)$$

where $\underline{x}$ are variables in **glb**.

This indicates the external behavior of S_1, that is, the pairs of pre- and post global states, is a subset of that of S_2. To prove one program S_1 refines another S_2, we require that they have the same set of global variables and the existence of a *refinement mapping* between the variables of S_1 to those of S_2 that is identical on global variables.

Definition 2. (Class refinement) *Let $cdecls_1$ and $cdecls_2$ be two declaration sections. $cdecls_1$ is a refinement of $cdecls_2$, denoted by $cdecls_2 \sqsubseteq_{class} cdecls_1$, if the former can replace the later in any object system:*

$$cdecls_2 \sqsubseteq_{class} cdecls_1 =_{df} \forall P \cdot (cdecls_2 \bullet P \sqsubseteq_{sys} cdecls_1 \bullet P)$$

where P stands for a main method (**glb**, c).

Intuitively, it states that $cdecls_1$ supports at least the same set of services as $cdecls_2$.

As stated in the introduction section, in our earlier work [9] and [16], we have given many useful refinement laws that capture the nature of incremental development in object-oriented programming. Please refer to them if interested.

2.3 Some Refinement Laws

We introduce some laws in [9] and [16] that will be used in the case study.

Law 1 (Law 7. in [9] Introducing a private attribute has no effect). *If neither N nor any of its superclasses and subclasses in* cdecls *has x as an attribute, then*

$$N[pri]; \text{cdecls} \sqsubseteq N[pri \cup \{T\ x = d\}]; \text{cdecls}.$$

Law 2 (Law 8. in [9] Changing private attributes into protected supports more services).

$$N[pri \cup \{T\ x = d\}, prot]; \text{cdecls} \sqsubseteq N[pri, prot \cup \{T\ x = d\}]; \text{cdecls}.$$

Law 3 (Law 9. in [9] Adding a new method refines a declaration). *If m is not in N, let $m(paras)\{c\}$ be a method with distinct parameters paras and a command c, then*

$N[ops];$ cdecls $\sqsubseteq N[ops \cup \{m(paras)\{c\}\}];$ cdecls

Law 4 (Law 10. in [9] Refining a method refines a declaration). *If $c_1 \sqsubseteq c_2$,*

$N[ops \cup \{m(paras)\{c_1\}\}];$ cdecls $\sqsubseteq N[ops \cup \{m(paras)\{c_2\}\}];$ cdecls

Law 5 (Law 1. (Extract Method) in [16]). *Assume that $m_1()\{c\}$ is a method in op of class M. Let* $\text{op}_1 = \text{op}\backslash\{m_1()\{c\}\}$. *Then*

$cdecls; M[\text{op}] \sqsubseteq cdecls; M[\text{op}_1 \cup \{m_1()\{m_2()\}, m_2()\{c\}\}]$

where m_2 is a method name that is not used in cdecls and op.

Law 6 ((Law 10. (Move Method) in [16]). *Let op and op_1 be sets of method declarations. Assume that $N\ b$ is an attribute of M, and $m()\{\hat{c}\}$ is a method of M, $m()$ is not in op_1 of N, and command c only refers attributes $b.x$ and methods $b.n()$ of class N. Define*

- *$\hat{\text{op}}$ to be the methods obtained from op by replacing each occurrence of $m()$ in every method with $b.m()$*
- *command c to be the command obtained from $\hat{c}$ by replacing each attribute $b.x$ with x and each method call $b.n()$ with $n()$.*

    $cdecls; M[N\ b, \text{op} \cup \{m()\{\hat{c}\}\}]; N[\text{op}_1]$
    $\sqsubseteq cdecls; M[N\ b, \hat{\text{op}}]; N[\text{op}_1 \cup \{m()\{c\}\}]$

    provided that $m()$ is not called from outside M on the left-hand-side of $\sqsubseteq$.

Law 7 ((Law 12. (Extract Class) in [16]). *Assume N is a fresh name which is not used in cdecls and $m_2()$ does not refer any attribute of M. Then we have*

$cdecls; M[m_1(), m_2()] \bullet P \sqsupseteq cdecls'; M[N\ n, \hat{m}_1()]; N[m_2()] \bullet P'$

where cdecls' is gain from cdecls by substitute all $M.m_2()$ to $N.m_2()$, P' is gain from P by substitute all $M.m_2()$ to $N.m_2()$, and $\hat{m}_1() = m_1()[n.m_2()/m_2()]$.

Law 8 ((Law 59. (Strategy) in [16]). *Assume all the newly introduced names are fresh ones. We have*

$Context_0[Strategy\ s, op()]; Strategy[algorithm_0()]$
$\sqsubseteq Context[Strategy\ s, op()]; Strategy[algorithm()];$
$\quad StrategyA[algorithm()]; StrategyB[algorithm()]$

where

- $op() =_{df} \{s.algorithm()\}$.
- *In class StrategyA, $algorithm() =_{df} \{c_A\}$, where c_A is a sequence of commands for a particular algorithm.*
- *In class StrategyB, $algorithm() =_{df} \{c_B\}$, where c_B is a sequence of commands for another particular algorithm.*
- *$algorithm_0() =_{df} \{c_A \lhd b \rhd c_B\}$, where b is a boolean variable for making a choice between algorithm c_A and c_B.*

Finally, we have a shorthand notation $\exists o : T$ which stands for the existing of a reference o which refers to an object of type T. It can be formally defined using rCOS semantics. We use it here to replace the standard notations for simplicity and intuition. Also, we do not have *return* keyword in the syntax of rCOS. But it can be defined using local variable declaration. We will use it for intuition.

3   rCOS Support to RUP

Now we discuss how rCOS supports a step-wised, incremental and iterative development process. For more formal details, please refer to [15].

The incremental development initiates in the requirement analysis to reach the *Use Cases* of the system [13], then, the *Conceptual Model* and *Design Model* [15,14] are built sequentially. From an informal view, a *Conceptual Model* can be thought as a class diagram in which all classes have only attributes without methods, and *Design Model* a class diagram in which all classes have attributes and method specifications (not necessarily code) as well.

The process starts with the creation of a requirement model (specification) of the system. The requirement model consists of a *conceptual* class diagram and a *use-case* model. The conceptual model is specified as a rCOS class declaration section without methods. Use cases are specified as use-case controller class with the user operations as its methods. The conceptual model is created by identifying the domain concepts as classes and relations among the concepts as attributes of classes [13,15]. This can be carried out incrementally by adding more and more use cases, classes and attributes. Each incremental step is a refinement in rCOS [9]. This is called the horizontal refinements.

The design can take the use cases in turns, planned according to their significance, urgency, and risks. In the design of a use case, each use case operation is decomposed by delegation its sub-functionalities (responsibilities) to the classes which maintains the information for the realization of the functionalities. These classes are called the experts of the functionalities. This will also transform the conceptual class diagram by adding the specifications or code of these responsibilities to their expert classes, producing a design class model. This activities are also proven to be rCOS refinement.

Then implementation can also take the designs of the tasks in turns, by coding the methods of the classes. The refinement from the requirement specifications to the designs and to the implementations is called the vertical refinement.

4   A Development of POST

In this section, we present our incremental development as a sequence of refinement steps. During the development, we always denote the system as a sequence of class declarations. Initially, *POST1* stands for the first version, the *Conceptual Model*, of the system. And then, with the support of the refinement laws in Section 2, we refine it to *POST2*. Similarly, *POST2* can be refined to *POST3*. At last, the system reaches *POST7* which is the final version of the design. Intuitively, each version of the sequence of class declarations is depicted by a corresponding UML class diagram.

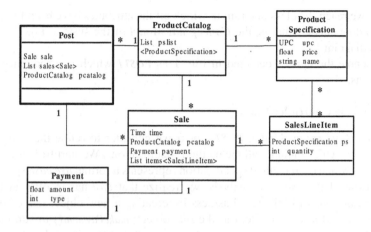

Fig. 1. Conceptual Model

4.1   Conceptual Model

At the beginning, we should determine the basic components of the system. After the requirement analysis, we decide to have the classes as follows: A *Product Catalog* as a database to store the information of all possible on sale products of the given supermarket. Each item of the database is a *Product Specification*. When a sale begins, we need to build a *Sale* object which is composed of many *Sales Line Item* to record all the products purchased. At last, the customer has to make a payment. Thus we need another object *Payment*. During the execution, we will create many instances of *Sale*, *Sales Line Item*, and *Payment*. Finally, we need a class as the user interface which is the *use case controller* of the system. We name it as *Post*.

Our next job is to add the attributes to achieve the *Conceptual Model*. During the requirement analysis, we realize that these classes should have attributes as follows:

- *Post*, which act as the interface of the system, should maintain at least three attributes: *sale* refers to the current sale object, *sales* as a list of sale objects to record all the handled sales, and a reference to the database *ProductCatalog*.
- *ProductCatalog* has a list of references to its *ProductSpecifications*.
- *ProductSpecification* should have a *name*, an attribute *upc* which stands for "Universal Product Code" as its key in the database, and another attribute *price*.
- *Sale* should have at least four attributes: a business time *time*, a reference to *ProductCatalog*, a reference to the *payment* object and a list of its *SalesLineItem*.
- *SalesLineItem* should have a reference to its corresponding *ProductSpecification* and a integer, *quantity*, to record how many products of this kind are purchased.
- The last class, *Payment* should remember how much money the customer should pay in its attribute *amount* and the payment way in *type*. Here we only deal with two kinds of payment: *type* = 0 stands for pay by cash and *type* = 1 for pay by credit card.

In our relational OO model, we can add private attributes and change a private attribute into a protected one by **Law 1** and **Law 2**. We can apply these laws repeatedly to add all the above mentioned attributes to our classes.

Thus we reach the class diagram in which all the attributes have been filled in their corresponding classes, that is, the *Conceptual Model* of the system. Fig. 1 illustrated the class diagram.

We denote the classes depicted in Fig. 1 as *POST1* which is a sequence of class declarations.

4.2   Use Case Controller Class

Having the *Conceptual Model*, *POST1*, next we consider to refine the system to the *Design Model* which includes all the method specifications. We start from the controller class *Post* in which each method specification represents a formal *use case* specification. As the result of the *use case* analysis, we realize that *Post* has to offer at least five methods: *makeSale()* to initiate a business by creating a new object *sale* of type *Sale*; *enterItem()* to add a sale line item to the *sale* object; *makePayment()* to summarize the price and create a *payment* object; *printSale()* and *endSale()* to print and end the business respectively. Further, *endSale()* has another job which is adding the reference of current *sale* object to the *sales* list.

Here we formally give the details of the method specifications as follows:

- *makeSale(Time time)*
  $pcatalog \neq nil \vdash sale'.time = time \wedge sale'.pcatalog = pcatalog$
- *enterItem(UPC upc, int quantity)*
  $pcatalog \neq nil \wedge sale \neq nil \wedge quantity \neq 0 \vdash$
  $\exists item : SalesLineItem \bullet sale.items' = sale.items \cup \{item\}$
  $\wedge item.upc = upc \wedge item.quantity = quantity$
  $\wedge(\exists ps : ProductSpecification \bullet ps \in pcatalog \wedge item.ps = ps \wedge ps.upc = upc)$
- *makePayment(int type)*
  $sale \neq nil \wedge type \in \{0, 1\} \vdash$
  $\exists payment : Payment \bullet sale.payment' = payment$
  $\wedge payment.amount = \sum_{item \in items} item.ps.price \times item.quantity$
  $\wedge((type = 0 \wedge \{\text{Paid by cash}\}) \vee (type = 1 \wedge \{\text{Paid by credit}\}))$
  where {Paid by cash} stands for customer's completion of paying by cash, and {Paid by credit} stands for customer's completion of paying by credit card.
- *printSale()*
  $sale \neq nil \wedge done(makePayment) \vdash \{\text{Print the sales line item report}\}$.
  where the predicate *done(makePayment)* means the customer has made payment, and {Print the sales line item report} stands for printing the receipt for customer.
- *endSale()*
  $sale \neq nil \wedge done(makePayment) \vdash sale' = nil \wedge sales' = sales \cup \{sale\}$

The class diagram is depicted in Fig. 2. We denote the corresponding class declarations as *POST2*. With the support of **Law 3** we can prove that adding a method is a refinement to the system. So, trivially, applying this law five times, we have *POST1* $\sqsubseteq$ *POST2*.

4.3   Design Model

Having added the interface methods to the system, the next task we confront with is to develop all the methods of the classes to complete our *Design Model*.

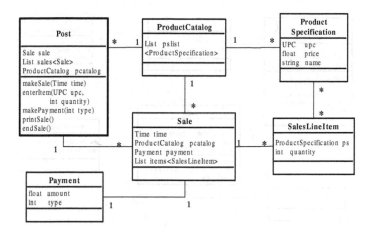

Fig. 2. Use Case Controller

Firstly, we delegate some of the tasks of *Post* to *Sale*. To achieve this, we first develop the following two methods in the class *Sale*. For the same reason to subsection 4.2, the new system added these methods refines the former version.

- *makeLineItem(UPS ups, int quantity)*
  $pcatalog \neq nil \wedge quantity \neq 0 \vdash$
  $\exists item : SalesLineItem \bullet items' = items \cup \{item\} \wedge item.upc = upc \wedge item.quantity = quantity \wedge (\exists ps : ProductSpecification \bullet ps \in pcatalog \wedge item.ps = ps \wedge ps.upc = upc)$
- *makePayment(int type)*
  $type \in \{0, 1\} \vdash \exists payment : Payment \bullet payment' = payment$
  $\wedge payment.amount = \sum_{item \in items} item.ps.price \times item.quantity$
  $\wedge ((type = 0 \wedge \{\text{Paid by cash}\}) \vee (type = 1 \wedge \{\text{Paid by credit}\}))$

Secondly, we can implement, or refine, in our model, the methods *enterItem()*, and *makePayment()* in class *Post* by invoking the above developed methods as follows:

- *enterItem'(UPC upc, int quantity)={sale.makeLineItem(upc, quantity)}*
- *makePayment'(int type)={sale.makePayment(type)}*

Now after adding the methods *makeLineItem()* and *makePayment()* to the class *Sale*, we substitute *enterItem()*, *makePayment()* with *enterItem'()*, *makePayment'()* in class *Post*. We denote the new system as *POST3*.

Using the semantic model of [9], we can prove that in class *Post*, *enterItem()* $\sqsubseteq$ *enterItem'()* and *makePayment()* $\sqsubseteq$ *makePayment'()*. By applying **Law 4** we have *POST2* $\sqsubseteq$ *POST3*.

We will still use unprimed names *enterItem()* and *makePayment()* to denote the newly refined methods in *POST3*. We make this abuse only for avoiding too many notations. In the rest of this paper we will adopt this abuse where no confusion will be made. The corresponding class diagram of *POST3* is depicted in Fig. 3.

Next, we will continue to delegate the tasks of *Sale* to *ProductCatalog* and *Payment*. Similar to the above process, we develop a new method *Search()* in class *ProductCatalog*

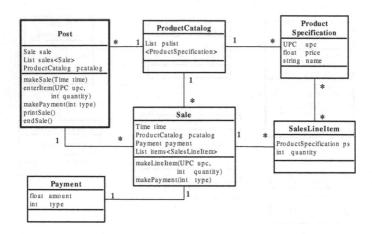

Fig. 3. Primary Design Model

and invoke it in the method *makeLineItem*() of class *Sale*. Let us see the specification of the new method:

Search(UPC upc, ProductSpecification ps):

$pslist \neq nil \vdash (ps' = null) \lhd (\exists ps \in pslist \wedge ps.upc = upc) \rhd (ps' = ps)$

This method searches a valid *Product Specification* from *ProductCatalog* and return it when success. Supported by this method, we can implement the method *makeLineItem* in class *Sale* as follows:

$makeLineItem'(\ UPC\ upc, int\ quantity) =$
$\quad\quad\quad\quad\{\textbf{var} ProductSpecification\ \ ps;$
$\quad\quad\quad\quad Search(upc, ps);$
$\quad\quad\quad\quad (ps \neq null) \rhd \{$
$\quad\quad\quad\quad\quad\quad \textbf{var}\ SalesLineItem\ sli;$
$\quad\quad\quad\quad\quad\quad ProductSpecification.\textbf{new}(sli,[ps,quantity])\}$
$\quad\quad\quad\quad items.Add(sli);$
$\quad\quad\quad\quad \textbf{end}\ ps\}$

Also, motivated by delegating a task of class *Sale* to class *Payment*, we develop a new method *pay*() in the class *Payment*:

$pay() = \{\{\text{Paid by cash}\} \lhd (type = 0) \rhd \{\text{Paid by credit}\}\}$

Supported by this method, we implement *makePayment(int type)* in class *Sale* as

$Sale.makePayment'(\ int\ type) =$
$\quad\quad\quad\quad\quad\quad\{\textbf{skip} \lhd (type = 0 \vee type = 1)\rhd$
$\quad\quad\quad\quad\quad\quad\quad\quad\{$
$\quad\quad\quad\quad\quad\quad\quad\quad \textbf{var}\ float\ amount = 0;$
$\quad\quad\quad\quad\quad\quad\quad\quad foreach\ (SalseLineItem\ item \in items)$
$\quad\quad\quad\quad\quad\quad\quad\quad\quad\quad amount = amount + item.prise*item.quantity;$
$\quad\quad\quad\quad\quad\quad\quad\quad Payment.\textbf{new}(payment,[amount,type]);$
$\quad\quad\quad\quad\quad\quad\quad\quad ayment.pay()$
$\quad\quad\quad\quad\quad\quad\quad\quad\}$
$\quad\quad\quad\quad\quad\quad\}$

In the semantic model we can prove in class *Sale makeLineItem*() $\sqsubseteq$ *makeLineItem'*() and *makePayment*() $\sqsubseteq$ *makePayment'*().

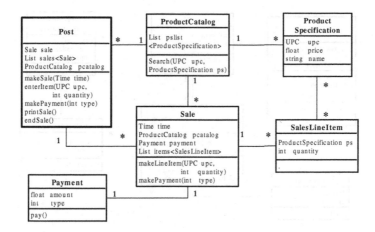

Fig. 4. Design Model

With similar process, we can get a new system as *POST4* by adding *Search()* to class *ProductCatalog* and *pay()* to class *Payment*, substituting old *makeLineItem()*, *makePayment()* with new ones in class *Sale*. And also, we have *POST3* ⊑ *POST4*. The corresponding class diagram of *POST4* is depicted in Fig. 4.

4.4 Refactoring: Extract Method and Move Method

After the efforts, we have reached the *Design Model*. Now we are ready to implement the system with any OO language. But there might be some K. Beck and M. Fowler's *"bad smells"* [7] existing in the design. In the rest of this section we will refactor the model to enhance the flexibility and maintainability.

After carefully reviewing of the design, we find a piece of typical code needed to be refactorred: the method *makePayment()* in class *Sale* uses the attributes of *SalesLineItem* many times. It could be better if the computation happens in *SalesLineItem* itself to reduce the coupling, or interaction, between classes. So we would like to extract a method in class *Sale* and then move it to class *SalesLineItem*.

We formally make the refactoring as follows:
Firstly, supported by the **Law 5 (Extract Method)** we have

$$Sale[makePayment()] \sqsubseteq$$
$$Sale[makePayment()[subtotal() \backslash (item.prise * item.quantity)]]$$

where

- $subtotal() = \{$**return** $item.prise * item.quantity\}$
- $[a \backslash b]$ means to substitute b with a.

The right hand can be refactorred further. With the **Law 6 (Move Method)** we have

$$Sale[makePayment()]; SalesLineItem[\ ] \sqsubseteq$$
$$Sale[makePayment()[item.subtotal() \backslash subtotal()]]; SalesLineItem[subtotal()]$$

where, in the class *SalesLineItem*, $subtotal() = \{$**return** $prise * quantity\}$.

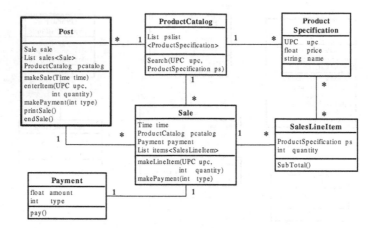

Fig. 5. Extract method and Move method

Thus we get the new class declarations *POST5* whose corresponding class diagram is depicted in Fig. 5. Again, we have *POST4* $\sqsubseteq$ *POST5*.

4.5 Refactoring: Extract Class

Next, we have a closer look at the class *Post*. It has an attribute *sales* which is a list to record all the past sales. For one thing, it is not suitable to let the interface class maintain such a long list. For another, there may be several instances of *Post* working in parallel. They should share the same list[1]. So we need another class to maintain the list. We would like to extract a new class *RecordStore* to do the job instead.

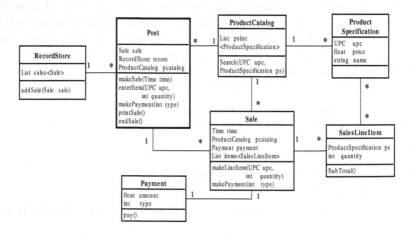

Fig. 6. Extract Class

---

[1] This list can be considered as a database for all the records.

Supported by the **Law 7 (Extract Class)** we have

$Post[List\ sales\langle Sale\rangle] \sqsubseteq Post[RecordStore\ rstore]; RecordStore[List\ sales\langle Sale\rangle]$

Similar to subsection 4.4, we can extract a method *addSale(Sale sale)* in class *Post*, which adds the current *sale* object to the sales list *rstore.sales*. And then, we move it to the newly developed class *RecordStore*, and have the class diagram in Fig. 6. We denote the corresponding class declarations as *POST6* and again *POST5* $\sqsubseteq$ *POST6*.

4.6   Pattern-Directed Refactoring: Strategy

Now it comes to the last phase of the refinement. This is a pattern-directed refactoring in which we introduce *Strategy* design pattern to the existing system.

In method *pay()* of class *Payment*, we have a piece of code "$c_1 \lhd type = 0 \rhd c_2$" in which the value of *type* will affect the behavior of the method. Now, directed by *Strategy Pattern,* we would like to refactor it by replacing the type code with polymorphism.

Supported by **Law 8 (Strategy)** we have

$Sale[makePayment(int\ type)]; Payment[int\ type,pay()] \sqsubseteq$
$\quad Sale[makePayment(int\ type)]; Payment[pay()];$
$\quad CashPayment[Payment,pay()]; CreditPayment[Payment,pay()]$

where

– The method *makePayment(int type)* on the right hand is different to the one on the left hand. We delete the command "*Payment*.**new**(*payment,[amount,type]*);" from the old method and substitute it with another command:
$\quad CashPayment.\textbf{new}(payment,[amount]) \lhd (type = 0)\rhd$
$\quad\quad CreditPayment.\textbf{new}(payment,[amount]);$
– The method body of *pay()* in class *Payment* is empty. It is implemented by its subclasses.
– In class *CashPayment*, method *pay()* = {Paid by cash}, and in class *CreditPayment*, method *pay()* = {Paid by credit}.

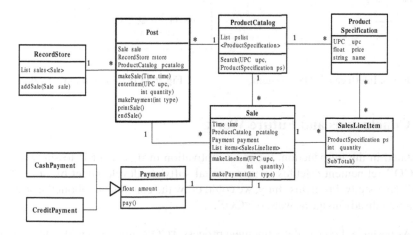

Fig. 7. Strategy Pattern-Directed Refactoring

Now the type code is replaced by polymorphism by introducing two subclasses. We denote the new class declarations as *POST7*, and have *POST6* $\sqsubseteq$ *POST7*. The class diagram is depicted in Fig. 7.

After the above refinement process, we gain the final design *POST7* from *POST0*. This ends our refinement. The classes in the final design is very near to executable code. It is easy to implement it in any OO programming languages. We have implemented it using Visual C# .Net.

5   Implementation

Supported by the $C\sharp$ and the .Net developing environment, we implement an executable software product for the final design model.

The main interface of the system, depicted in Fig. 8, is composed of five "Button"s which represent the five methods in class *Post*. Also we have two "TextBox"s to input the UPC and quantity of the current purchasing product, a "ListBox" to show the content of the current *sale*, and a pair of "RadioButton"s to choose payment ways. After the payment way is chosen, when the "Print Sale" button is pressed, the system will pop-up a form to show the receipt for customers.

An executing snapshot of our software is depicted in Fig. 9.

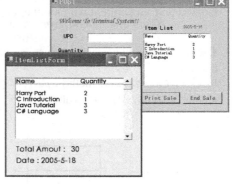

Fig. 8. Interface of POST System   **Fig. 9.** POST System in Execution

6   Conclusions and Future Work

As stated in the introduction, the main motivation of this paper is to show the power of rCOS refinement calculus in incremental software development by presenting the POST case study. From this study, we could draw the conclusions about the advantages, and a tiny disadvantage as well, of rCOS.

- As we have shown in the refinement process, rCOS supports a wide range of object-oriented techniques. So it is a suitable calculus for OO development.

- In the rCOS based software development, we can prove the correctness of each developing step. So at least for highly critical systems, rCOS is a useful supporting model. Further, in teamwork of large scale software development, rCOS also offers a robust support for rigorous correctness formal proof.
- It is proven that rCOS can be used as a formal framework for the *use-cased driven, incremental* and *iterative* Rational Unified Process (RUP). And also, the rCOS based process is practical and scalable in software engineering.
- In practice, rCOS also offers a nice semantic model for correctly refactoring the existing design, and further, might give a choice for refactoring supporting tools development.
- The limitations. During the development of the POST system, we realized that there are some tiny limitations existing in the current version of rCOS. For instance, we do not have exception handling in the syntax of rCOS, making no chance to use such mechanism to deal with dynamic errors in the software development.

As for the future work, we would like to provide tool support for our refinement calculus. We hope, given the proof obligation of a refinement equation, the tool can search whether there is a refinement law syntactically matches. In rCOS, we have not yet had a result about the completeness of the laws. We will look into this problem in future work and discuss the relationship of all of our laws. Another important future work is, as mentioned above, we need to extend the current version of rCOS to support more features, such as exception handling, of OO programming languages. There, we believe, will be no essential difficulty.

References

1. D. Carrington, *et al. Object-Z: an Object-Oriented Extension to Z.* North-Halland, 1989.
2. D. Coleman, *et al. Object-Oriented Development: the FUSION Method.* Prentice-Hall, 1994.
3. S. Cook and J. Daniels. *Designing Object Systems: Object-Oriented Modelling with Syntropy.* Prentice-Hall, 1994.
4. J. Davis and J.P. Woodcock. *Using Z: Specification, Refinement and Proof.* Prentice Hall, 1996.
5. E.W. Dijkstra and C.S. Scholten. *Predicate Calculus and Program semantics.* Springer, 1989.
6. E. Dürr and E.M. Dusink. The role of VDM^{++} in the development of a real-time tracking and tracing system. In J. Woodcock and P. Larsen, editors, *Proc. of FME'93, LNCS 670.* Springer-Verlag, 1993.
7. Martin Fowler. *Refectoring, Improving the Design of Existing Code.* Addison-Wesley, 2000.
8. J. He, Z. Liu, and X. Li.   rCOS: A refinement calculus for object systems.   Technical Report 322, UNU/IIST, P.O. Box 3058, Macao SAR China, 2005. http://www.iist.unu.edu/newrh/III/1/page.html.
9. J. He, Z. Liu, X. Li, and S. Qin. A relational model for object-oriented designs. In *Pro. APLAS'2004, LNCS 3302*, Taiwan, 2004. Springer.
10. C.A.R. Hoare and J. He. *Unifying Theories of Programming.* Prentice-Hall, 1998.
11. C.B. Jones. *Software Development: A Rigorous Approach.* Prentice Hall International, 1980.
12. C. Larman. *Applying UML and Patterns, An Introduction to Object-Oriented Analysis and Design and the Unified Process.* Prentice-Hall, 2001.

13. X. Li, Z. Liu, and J. He. Formal and use-case driven requirement analysis in UML. In *COMPSAC01*, pages 215–224, Illinois, USA, October 2001. IEEE Computer Society.
14. Z. Liu. Object-oriented software development with UML. Technical Report 259, UNU/IIST, P.O. Box 3058, Macao SAR China, 2002. http://www.iist.unu.edu/newrh/III/1/page.html.
15. Z. Liu, J. He, X. Li, and Y. Chen. A relational model for formal requirements analysis in UML. In J.S. Dong and J. Woodcock, editors, *Formal Methods and Software Engineering, ICFEM03, LNCS 2885*, pages 641–664. Springer, 2003.
16. Q. Long, J. He, and Z. Liu. Refactoring and pattern directed refactoring : A formal perspective. Technical Report 318, UNU/IIST, P.O. Box 3058, Macao SAR China, 2005. http://www.iist.unu.edu/newrh/III/1/page.html.

Implementing Application-Specific Object-Oriented Theories in HOL

Kenro Yatake[1], Toshiaki Aoki[1,2], and Takuya Katayama[1]

[1] Japan Advanced Institute of Science and Technology,
1-1 Asahidai Nomi Ishikawa 923-1292, Japan
{k-yatake, toshiaki, katayama}@jaist.ac.jp
[2] PRESTO JST

Abstract. This paper presents a theory of Object-Oriented concepts embedded shallowly in HOL for the verification of OO analysis models. The theory is application-specific in the sense that it is automatically constructed depending on the type information of the application. This allows objects to have attributes of arbitrary types, making it possible to verify models using not only basic types but also highly abstracted types specific to the target domain. The theory is constructed by definitional extension based on the operational semantics of a heap memory model, which guarantees the soundness of the theory. This paper mainly focuses on the implementation details of the theory.

1 Introduction

The Object-Oriented developing method is becoming the mainstream of the software development. In the upstream phase of the development, analysis models are constructed with a language such as UML (Unified Modeling Language [1]). To ensure the correctness of the models, formal semantics must be given to them and verification method such as theorem proving must be applied.

A lot of OO semantics have been implemented in theorem provers of higher-order logic and most of them are for the verification of OO languages such as Java [5][6][7]. In these theories, available types are limited to the primitive ones such as integers and boolean sufficient for the program verification. But for the verification of analysis models, this type restriction is disadvantage as the models are constructed with highly abstracted types specific to the target domain, e.g. tree, stack, date, money. Therefore, an OO semantics which can accommodate various types are required. So, we defined a theory in the HOL system [2] as a semantics of OO concepts in which arbitrary concrete types can be incorporated in the types of object attributes. In general, an object is a data which holds multiple attributes of arbitrary types and even allows referencing and subtyping. This concept is too complex to implement as a general type in the simple first-order type system of HOL. To cope with this problem, we take the approach of automatically constructing the theory depending on the class model of the application which defines the type information of the system.

D.V. Hung and M. Wirsing (Eds.): ICTAC 2005, LNCS 3722, pp. 501–516, 2005.

The theory is constructed by *definitional extension*. This is a standard method to construct sound theories in HOL, where new theories are derived from existing sound theories by only allowing introduction of definition and derivation by sound inference rules. Specifically, the theory is derived from the operational semantics of a heap memory model. If a class model is given in advance, objects and their referencing and subtyping are realized by a linked-tuple structure in the heap memory and the resulting theory becomes quite simple.

In this paper, we present the definition of the theory and its implementation details in HOL. As a verification example, we prove that a UML collaboration diagram satisfies an invariant written in OCL (Object Constraint Language [3]). In this paper, we call the theory ASOOT (for Application-Specific Object-Oriented Theory).

This paper is organized as follows. In section 2 and 3, we explain the definition of the class model and the definition of the theory corresponding to the class model. In section 4, we explain the implementation details. In section 5, we show the example verification. In section 6, we cite related works and section 7 is conclusion and future work.

2   Class Models

The theory depends on the class model of each system which defines the static structure of the system like UML class diagrams. The class model is defined as a six tuple:

$$CM = (C, A, \mathcal{M}_{attr}, \mathcal{M}_{inher}, \mathcal{T}, \mathcal{V})$$

The sets C and A are class names and attribute names which appear in the system, respectively. The mapping $\mathcal{M}_{attr} : C \to Pow(A)$ relates a class to the attributes defined in the class. The mapping $\mathcal{M}_{inher} : C \to Pow(C)$ relates a class to its direct subclasses. We assume single inheritance. The mapping $\mathcal{T} : C \times A \to Type$ relates an attribute to its type. The set $Type$ is a set of arbitrary concrete types in HOL. We assume $C \subset Type$ and define the type of an object to be the name of the class it belongs to. The mapping $\mathcal{V} : C \times A \to Value$ relates an attribute to its default value. The set $Value$ is a set of values of all types in $Type$. By a symbol $\lhd$, we denote the super-sub relationship. The expression $c_1 \lhd c_2$ means c_2 is a direct subclass of c_1, which is equivalent to $c_2 \in \mathcal{M}_{inher}(c_1)$. In addition, $c_1 \lhd^+ c_2$ means c_2 is a descendant class of c_1 and $c_1 \lhd^* c_2$ means $c_1 = c_2$ or $c_1 \lhd^+ c_2$. By $attr(c)$, we denote the attributes and inherited attributes of the class c, i.e. $attr(c) = \{a | a \in \mathcal{M}_{attr}(d), d \lhd^* c\}$.

In the following, we visualize the class models like Fig.1. The class fig is a class of figures which has two attributes x and y as its coordinate position. The

Fig. 1. A class model example

class **rect** is a class of rectangles which has two attributes **w** and **h** as its width and height. The class **crect** is a class of colored-rectangle which has an attribute **c** as its color. The type **color** is an enumeration type which has several colors as its elements.

3   Definition of ASOOT

The theory is defined in HOL by mapping the class model elements to types and constants in the theory and introducing axioms on them. As the embedding policy, we chose a shallow embedding because our verification target is individual applications of the class model (the comparison of a shallow embedding and a deep embedding is found in [4]). We first explain the overview of the theory with the example, and then give the formal definition.

3.1   Overview

In order to implement object referencing, the concept *store* is introduced in the theory. The store is an environment which holds the attribute values of all alive objects in the system and defined as a type **store**. Objects are references to their data in the store and defined as types of their belonging class name. For example, the type of objects of the class **fig** is **fig**. Types of objects are "apparent" types and their type can be transformed to other types by casting.

Several kinds of constants are introduced in the theory by mapping from the elements in the class model as shown in Fig.2. For example, corresponding to the class **fig**, two constants **fig_new** and **fig_ex** are introduced. The function **fig_new** creates a new **fig** instance in the store. It takes a store as an argument and returns a pair of a newly created object and the store after the creation. The predicate **fig_ex** tests if a **fig** object exists in the store. It takes a **fig** object and a store as arguments and return the result as a boolean value. The first axiom is a property about these operators saying "The newly created object is alive in the store after the creation."

Corresponding to the attribute **x** of the class **fig**, read and write operators **fig_get_x** and **fig_set_x** are introduced. The function **fig_get_x** takes a **fig**

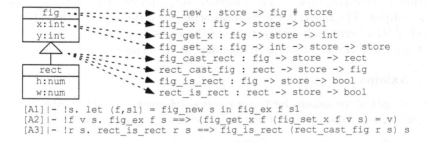

```
    fig
  x:int
  y:int

    rect
  h:num
  w:num
```

```
fig_new : store -> fig # store
fig_ex : fig -> store -> bool
fig_get_x : fig -> store -> int
fig_set_x : fig -> int -> store -> store
fig_cast_rect : fig -> store -> rect
rect_cast_fig : rect -> store -> fig
fig_is_rect : fig -> store -> bool
rect_is_rect : rect -> store -> bool
```

[A1]|- !s. let (f,s1) = fig_new s in fig_ex f s1
[A2]|- !f v s. fig_ex f s ==> (fig_get_x f (fig_set_x f v s)) = v)
[A3]|- !r s. rect_is_rect r s ==> fig_is_rect (rect_cast_fig r s) s

Fig. 2. The mapping from the class model to the theory

object and a store as arguments and returns the current value of the attribute x. The function `fig_set_x` takes a `fig` object, a new integer value and a store as arguments and returns the store after updating the attribute x to the new value. The second axiom says "If the `fig` object is alive in the store, the value of the attribute x of the object obtained just after updating it to v equals to v."

Corresponding to the inheritance relationship between the two classes `fig` and `rect`, type casting operators and instance-of operators are introduced. The function `fig_cast_rect` takes a `fig` object as an argument and casts it downward from `fig` to `rect`. The function `rect_cast_fig` takes a `rect` object and casts it upward from `rect` to `fig`. The predicate `fig_is_rect` tests if a `fig` object is an instance of the class `rect`. After an object is created, its apparent type can be changed by casting operators, but instance-of operators play a role of remembering the actual type of the object. For example, by applying `rect_cast_fig` to the `rect` instance which is created by `rect_new`, its apparent type is changed to `fig`, but as `fig_is_rect` holds for the `fig` object, it is identified as an instance of the class `rect`. The third axiom state this.

3.2   Types and Constants

The store is represented by a type *store*. It has a constant *Emp* as its initial value which represents the empty store. Objects of the class c are represented as a type c. Each type c has a constant $Null^c : c$ which represents the null object.

Following operators are defined on the store:

$$Ex^c : c \rightarrow store \rightarrow bool \ \ (c \in C)$$
$$Get_a^c : c \rightarrow store \rightarrow \mathcal{T}(c, a) \ \ (c \in C, a \in attr(c))$$
$$Set_a^c : c \rightarrow \mathcal{T}(c, a) \rightarrow store \rightarrow store \ \ (c \in C, a \in attr(c))$$
$$Cast_d^c : c \rightarrow store \rightarrow d \ \ (c, d \in C, c \lhd^+ d \text{ or } d \lhd^+ c)$$
$$New^c : store \rightarrow c * store \ \ (c \in C)$$
$$Is_d^c : c \rightarrow store \rightarrow bool \ \ (c, d \in C, c \lhd^* d)$$

The predicate Ex^c tests if the class c object is alive in the store. The function Get_a^c reads the attribute a of the class c object. If it is applied to an object not alive in the store, the constant $Unknown_a^c : \mathcal{T}(c, a)$ which represents the undefined value is returned. The function Set_a^c updates the attribute a of the class c object. The function $Cast_d^c$ transforms the object types from c to d. The function New^c creates a new instance of the class c in the store. The predicate Is_d^c tests if the class c object is an instance of the class d.

3.3   Axioms

Here, we introduce axioms for the operators defined above. There are 36 axioms altogether, but we show only main ones because of space limitations.

1. $\forall o \ s. \ Ex^c \ o \ s = Is_{d_1}^c \ o \ s \vee ... \vee Is_{d_n}^c \ o \ s \ \ (\{d_1, ..., d_n\} = \{d \mid c \lhd^* d\})$
   The c object o alive in the store is an instance of either the class c or one of the descendant-classes of c.

2. $\forall o\ s.\ Is_d^c\ o\ s \Rightarrow \neg(Is_e^c\ o\ s)\ \ (d \neq e)$

If the c object o is an instance of the class d, it is not an instance of the class e different from d, i.e. is-operators are exclusive.

3. $\forall o\ s.\ Is_e^d\ o\ s \Rightarrow Is_e^c\ (Cast_c^d\ o\ s)\ s\ \ (c \lhd^+ d)$

If the d object o is an instance of the class e, the object cast to the superclass c is also the instance of e, i.e. the actual type is invariable by casting.

4. $\forall o\ s.\ Is_c^c\ o\ (Snd\ (New^c\ s)) = (o = Fst\ (New^c\ s)) \vee Is_c^c\ o\ s$

The c object o is an instance of the class c in the store after creating a new instance of the class c iff o is either the newly created object or the object which was already an instance of c before the creation.

5. $\forall o\ s.\ \neg(Ex^c\ (Fst\ (New^c\ s))\ s)$

The newly created object does not exist in the previous store. This axiom implies that the new object is distinct from all previous objects.

6. $\forall o_1\ o_2\ s.\ Ex^d\ o_1\ s \wedge Ex^d\ o_2\ s \Rightarrow$
   $\neg(o_1 = o_2) \Rightarrow \neg(Cast_c^d\ o_1\ s = Cast_c^d\ o_2\ s)\ \ (c \lhd^+ d)$

If two c objects o_1 and o_2 are different objects, the two object obtained by casting to the superclass c are also different objects, i.e. cast-operators are injective.

7. $\forall o\ s.\ Is_e^c\ o\ s \Rightarrow (Cast_c^d\ (Cast_d^c\ o\ s)\ s = o)\ \ (c \lhd^+ d, d \lhd^+ e)$

If the c object o is an instance of the class e which is a descendant class of d, the object obtained by down-casting to d and then up-casting to c equals to o itself.

8. $\forall o\ s.\ Get_a^d\ o\ s = Get_a^c\ (Cast_c^d\ o\ s)\ s\ \ (c \lhd^+ d$ and $a \in \mathcal{M}_{attr}(c))$

When an attribute a is defined in the class c, getting a of the object o of the descendant-class d is the same as getting a by casting o to c.

9. $\forall o\ s.\ Ex^c\ o\ s \Rightarrow (Get_a^c\ o\ (Set_a^c\ o\ x\ s) = x)$

If the object o is alive in the store, the attribute a of o obtained just after updating it to x equals to x.

10. $\forall o_1\ o_2\ s.\ \neg(o_1 = o_2) \Rightarrow (Get_a^c\ o_1\ (Set_a^c\ o_2\ x\ s) = Get_a^c\ o_1\ s)$

If the two objects o_1 and o_2 are different, getting the attribute a of o_1 is not affected by the updating of the same attribute of o_2.

11. $\forall o_1\ o_2\ s.\ Get_a^c\ o_1\ (Set_b^d\ o_2\ x\ s) = Get_a^c\ o_1\ s\ \ ((c \not\lhd^* d$ and $d \not\lhd^* c)$ or $a \neq b)$

If the two classes c and d are not in inheritance relationship or the attribute name a and b are different, getting the attribute is not affected by the updating.

3.4   Modeling OO Concepts in the Theory

Basic OO concepts such as methods, inheritance, overriding and dynamic binding are expressible in the theory. We show a typical way to model these concepts using examples. In HOL, we denote the operators Ex^c, New^c, Get_a^c, Set_a^c, $Cast_d^c$ and Is_d^c as c_ex, c_new, c_get_a, c_set_a, c_cast_d and c_is_d, respectively.

Methods are defined using Get, Set, New, $Cast$ and functions provided in HOL. Let us consider that the class fig has a method move which changes its position by dx and dy. This method is defined as follows.

```
fig_move : fig -> int -> int -> store -> store
fig_move f dx dy s =
  let (x,y) = (fig_get_x f s, fig_get_y f s) in
     fig_set_y f (y+dy) (fig_set_x f (x+dx) s)
```

Method inheritance is modeled by calling the superclass method from the subclass method, i.e. by casting the object to the superclass type and applying the superclass method. If the class `rect` inherits the method `move` of the superclass `fig`, this method is defined as follows.

```
rect_move : rect -> int -> int -> store -> store
rect_move r dx dy s = fig_move (rect_cast_fig r s) dx dy s
```

Method overriding is modeled in the same manner as method inheritance. If the class `crect` overrides the superclass method `move` to change the color to `red` after changing the position, this method is defined as follows.

```
crect_move : crect -> int -> int -> store -> store
crect_move c dx dy s =
  let s1 = rect_move (crect_cast_rect c s) dx dy s in
     crect_set_color c red s1
```

Dynamic binding is a mechanism to dynamically switch method bodies according to which class the applied object is instance of. This is modeled by defining a virtual method which selects the method body using Is. The virtual method `v_fig_move` corresponding to the method `fig_move` is defined as follows.

```
v_fig_move : fig -> int -> int -> store -> store
v_fig_move f dx dy s =
  if fig_is_fig f s then fig_move f dx dy s
  else if fig_is_rect f s then rect_move (fig_cast_rect f s) dx dy s
  else if fig_is_crect f s then crect_move (fig_cast_crect f s) dx dy s
  else s
```

4   Implementing ASOOT in HOL

We implemented a tool called ASOOT generator which inputs a class model and outputs the theory specific to the model. As mentioned in the introduction, the theory is constructed by definitional extension and thus sound. It implements the operational semantics of a heap memory using primitive theories such as natural numbers, lists and pairs and derives the theory from the operational semantics. We first explain the overview of the implementation using the example, and then, explain it formally.

4.1   Overview

The store is represented as a heap memory to store object attributes. Fig.3 shows a snapshot of the heap memory for the example model. The heap memory consists of three sub-heaps which are introduced corresponding to the three classes `fig`, `rect` and `crect`. Each sub-heap is represented by a list and the whole heap is represented by a tuple of them.

Object references are represented by indices of the memory. In the case of the `fig` memory, the reference `f1`, `f2`,... of type `fig` is represented by a natural number 1,2, ... The reference `f0` is used as a null reference `fig_null`. Object instances are represented by a tuple or several tuples in the sub-heaps. For

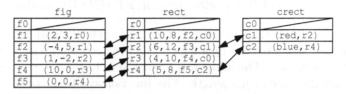

Fig. 3. Representation of the store

example, the tuple in `f_1` represents a `fig` instance whose attribute are x=2 and y=3. Two tuples in `f2` and `r1` together represent a `rect` instance whose attribute are x=-4, y=5, w=10, and h=8. Three tuples in `f3`, `r2`, and `c1` together represent a `crect` instance whose attribute are x=1, y=-2, w=6, h=12, and c=red. Multiple tuples which compose an instance are linked to each other by storing object references. The two tuples in `f2` and `r1` which compose a `rect` instance link to each other by storing the references `r1` and `f2`, respectively. If there are no tuples for a tuple to link, the null references are stored. As the tuple in `f1` does not link to any `rect` tuples, it stores the null reference `r0`. Object subtyping is modeled by this linked-tuple structure. For example, three references `f3`, `r2` and `c1` all point at the same `crect` instance. This means `crect` instance can have three apparent types `fig`, `rect`, and `crect`.

Now, we explain how the operators on the store are implemented in the heap memory. The *New* operator `rect_new` is implemented as a function to add new tuples in the sub-heaps for `fig` and `rect` and connects them to each other. The *Ex* operator `fig_ex` is implemented as a predicate to test if the `fig` reference is not null and not out of bounds of the sub-heap for `fig` . The *Cast* operator `fig_cast_rect` is implemented as a function to read the `rect` reference stored in the tuple pointed by the `fig` reference. The *Get* and *Set* operator `fig_get_x` and `fig_set_x` are implemented as functions to read and update the first element in the tuple pointed by the `fig` reference. The *Is* operator `fig_is_rect` is implemented as a predicate to test if the tuple pointed by the `fig` reference is linked with a tuple in the sub-heap for `rect`.

4.2   Representation of the Store: A Heap Memory Model

A sub-heap is defined independent of the class model and is represented generally as $'a$ *list*. Addresses of data is represented by list indices, or natural numbers 0, 1, 2... The initial value of a sub-heap is defined as [*null*] which is a list with a dummy constant $null : 'a$ in the address 0. Four operators *add*, *valid*, *read* and *write* are defined on the sub-heap as follows.

$add\ x\ l = (Length\ l, Append\ l\ [x])$

$valid\ n\ l = (0 < n) \wedge (n < length\ l)$

$read\ n\ l = if\ valid\ n\ l\ then\ read_1\ n\ l\ else\ unknown$

$(read_1\ 0\ l = Hd\ l) \wedge (read_1\ (Suc\ n)\ l = read_1\ n\ (Tl\ l))$

$write\ n\ x\ l = if\ valid\ n\ l\ then\ write_1\ n\ x\ l\ else\ l$

$(write_1\ 0\ x\ l = x :: (Tl\ l)) \wedge (write_1\ (Suc\ n)\ x\ l = (Hd\ l) :: (write_1\ n\ x\ (Tl\ l)))$

The function add adds the new data x at the tail of the list and returns the new address and the list after the operation. The predicate $valid$ tests if a data is stored in the address n. The address is valid if it is in the range greater than 0 and less than the current list length. The function $read$ reads the data in the address n. If the address is not valid, the constant $unknown$ which represents undefined data is returned. The function $write$ updates the data in the address n by the data x. If the address is not valid, the list is left unchanged.

Sub-heaps are introduced corresponding to each class and each of them stores different types of tuples depending on the class. The type of tuples stored in the sub-heap for the class c is defined as:

$$tuple_c \equiv \mathcal{T}(c, a_1) * \ldots * \mathcal{T}(c, a_n) * d * e_1 * \ldots * e_m \quad (a_i \in \mathcal{M}_{attr}(c), d \lhd c, c \lhd e_j)$$

The first n elements are the attributes defined in c. The next element is a reference of a superclass object. The last m elements are references of subclass objects. The type of the sub-heap storing these tuples is defined as $heap_c \equiv tuple_c\ list$.

The type of object references of the class c is obtained by defining bijections between the type c and natural numbers as follows.

$$HOL\text{\_}datatype\ c = AbsObj_c\ of\ num,\quad RepObj_c\ (AbsObj_c\ n) \equiv n$$

The function $AbsObj_c$ maps a natural number to a c object reference. The function $RepObj_c$ maps a c object reference to a natural number. The null object is represented by 0, i.e. $Null^c \equiv AbsObj_c\ 0$.

The whole heap memory is obtained by gathering sub-heaps into a tuple. The type of the heap memory is defined as:

$$Heap \equiv heap_{c_1} * \ldots * heap_{c_n} \quad (c_i \in C)$$

The four operators on the sub-heap add, $valid$, $read$ and $write$ are extended to operate on the whole heap as follows.

$$Add^c : tuple_c \to Heap \to c * Heap, \quad Valid^c : c \to Heap \to bool$$

$$Read_u^c : c \to Heap \to T, \quad Write_u^c : c \to T \to Heap \to Heap$$

The function Add_c adds a new tuple in the sub-heap of the class c. The predicate $Valid^c$ tests if the c object is valid in the sub-heap of the class c. The function $Read_u^c$ reads the element u in the tuple referenced by the c object. The element u is either one of a_i for attributes, d for the superclass object, or e_j for the subclass object. In the case $u = a_i$, $T = \mathcal{T}(c, a)$ and for other case, $T = u$. The function $Write_u^c$ writes at the same location in the heap as $Read_u^c$ reads. These operators are easily defined using pair functions Fst and Snd and the bijections $AbsObj_c$ and $RepObj_c$.

4.3   Representation of ASOOT Constants

We define constants $EmpRep$, $ExRep^c$, $CastRep_d^c$, $GetRep_a^c$, $SetRep_a^c$, $NewRep^c$ and $IsRep_d^c$ using the operators defined on the heap memory. They are the heap representations of the ASOOT constants Emp, Ex^c, $Cast_d^c$, Get_a^c, Set_a^c, New^c and Is_d^c, respectively.

The constant $EmpRep$ is defined as:

$$EmpRep \equiv ([null : tuple_{c_1}], ..., [null : tuple_{c_n}])\ \ (c_i \in C)$$

The empty store is represented by a tuple of the initial values of the sub-heaps.

The predicate $ExRep^c$ is defined as:

$$ExRep^c\ o\ H \equiv Valid^c\ o\ H$$

The existence of an object in the store is represented by the validity of the object reference in the heap memory.

The function $CastRep_d^c$ is defined as:

$$CastRep_d^c\ o\ H \equiv$$
$$\begin{cases} if\ ExRep^c\ o\ H\ then\ Read_d^c\ o\ H\ else\ Null^d & (c \lhd d\ or\ d \lhd c) \\ CastRep_d^e\ (CastRep_e^c\ o\ H)\ H & ((c \lhd e, e \lhd^+ d)\ or\ (d \lhd^+ e, e \lhd c)) \end{cases}$$

In the case that the two classes c and d are in the direct super-sub relationship, the casting is represented by reading the d object in the tuple referenced by the c object. If the c object does not exists, it is cast to the null object $Null^d$. In the case that c and d are in the ancestor-descendant relationship but not in the direct super-sub relationship, the casting is applied transitively, i.e. first the c object is cast to the direct superclass e and then the e object is cast to the class d.

The functions $GetRep_a^c$ is defined as:

$$GetRep_a^c\ o\ H \equiv$$
$$\begin{cases} if\ ExRep^c\ o\ H\ then\ Read_a^c\ o\ H\ else\ Unknown_a^c & (a \in \mathcal{M}_{attr}(c)) \\ GetRep_a^d\ (CastRep_d^c\ o\ H)\ H & (d \lhd c, a \in attr(d)) \end{cases}$$

In the case that the attribute a is defined in the class c, getting a of a c object is represented by reading the element a in the tuple referenced by the c object. If the c object does not exists, a constant $Unknown_a^c$ which represents the undefined value is returned. In the case that the attribute a is defined in the ancestor-class, the c object is cast to the superclass d and then $GetRep_a^d$ is applied.

The function Set_a^c is defined in the same way as $Read_a^c$:

$$SetRep_a^c \ o \ x \ H \equiv$$
$$\begin{cases} if \ ExRep^c \ o \ H \ then \ Write_a^c \ o \ x \ H \ else \ H & (a \in \mathcal{M}_{attr}(c)) \\ SetRep_a^d \ (CastRep_d^c \ o \ H) \ x \ H & (d \lhd c, a \in attr(d)) \end{cases}$$

If the c object does not exists, the heap is left unchanged.

The function $NewRep^c$ is defined as:

$$NewRep^c \ H \equiv \begin{cases} Add^c \ default_c \ H & (c \text{ is the root class}) \\ let \ (o_1, H_1) = NewRep^d \ H \ in \\ \quad let \ (o_2, H_2) = Add^c \ default_c \ H_1 \ in \\ \quad \quad let \ H_3 = Link_c^d \ o_1 \ o_2 \ H_2 \ in \ (o_2, H_3) & (d \lhd c) \end{cases}$$

$where$
$$Link_c^d \ o_1 \ o_2 \ H \equiv Write_c^d \ o_2 \ o_1 \ (Write_c^d \ o_1 \ o_2 \ H)$$
$$default_c \equiv (\mathcal{V}(c, a_1), ..., \mathcal{V}(c, a_n), Null^d, Null^{e_1}, ..., Null^{e_m})$$
$$(a_i \in \mathcal{M}_{attr}(c), d \lhd c, c \lhd e_j)$$

This function creates a linked-tuple structure recursively on the inheritance chain. As a base step, where the class c is the root class of the inheritance tree, the c instance is created by simply adding a new tuple to the sub-heap for c. As induction steps, first, the instance of the superclass d is created by $NewRep^d$ and then, a new tuple is added to the sub-heap for c, and finally, the newly obtained object o_1 and o_2 is linked by $Link_c^d$. The tuple value $default_c$ added to the sub-heap for c contains default values for attributes and null objects for the superclass and subclass objects.

The predicate $IsRep_d^c$ is defined as:

$$IsRep_d^c \ o \ H \equiv \begin{cases} ExRep^c \ o \ H \wedge \bigwedge_j \neg ExRep^{e_j} \ (CastRep_{e_j}^c \ o \ H) \ H & (c = d, c \lhd e_j) \\ ExRep^c \ o \ H \wedge IsRep_e^d \ (CastRep_d^c \ o \ H) \ H & (c \lhd e, e \lhd^* d) \end{cases}$$

This predicate tests that the c object is the instance of the class d. This is tested by examining if the links are traversed from the c object reference up to a tuple in the sub-heap of d. Link traversing is realized by cast operators. If $c = d$, the c object is the very c instance, so there must not exist any links to any of the subclasses $e_1, ..., e_m$. If c is the ancestor-class of d, the c object is cast to the subclass e and the e object must be an instance of d. In both cases, the c object must exist in the store.

4.4   Abstracting ASOOT from the Heap Memory

Finally, we abstract ASOOT from the heap representation by creating the type *store*, defining ASOOT constants and deriving axioms.

The type *store* is created from a subset of the type *Heap*. In HOL, it takes the following steps to create a new type t_1 from an existing type t_2.

1. Define the predicate $p : t_2 \rightarrow bool$ which determines the subset of t_2.
2. Prove the theorem $\vdash \exists x.\ p\ x$, i.e. the subset is not an empty set.
3. Assert that there are bijections between t_1 and the subset of t_2 determined by p.

The predicate which determines the subset of $Heap$ is defined as $IsStoreRep$ as follows[1].

$$IsStoreRep\ H \equiv \forall P.\ IsInv\ P \Rightarrow P\ H$$

$where$

$$IsInv\ P \equiv P\ EmpRep\ \wedge$$
$$\bigwedge_{c,a} (\forall o\ x\ H.\ P\ H \Rightarrow SetRep_a^c\ o\ x\ H) \wedge \bigwedge_c (\forall H.\ P\ H \Rightarrow Snd\ (NewRep^c\ H))$$

The elements of the subset represented by $IsStoreRep$ are those which satisfy the predicate P which is an invariant proved by the following induction: as a base step, prove that $EmpRep$ satisfies P, and as induction steps, assume that P holds for a heap and prove that the heaps obtained by applying $SetRep_a^c$ and $NewRep^c$ maintain P. The existence of an element is proved as a theorem $th \equiv\ \vdash\ IsStoreRep\ EmpRep$. The existence of bijections between $store$ and the subset is asserted automatically by calling the ML function $new\_type\_definition(store, th)$. Let us say the bijections are $RepStore : store \rightarrow Heap$ and $AbsStore : Heap \rightarrow store$.

ASOOT constants are defined by taking a map with their heap representations as follows.

$$Emp \equiv AbsStore\ EmpRep, \quad Ex^c\ o\ s \equiv ExRep^c\ o\ (RepStore\ s)$$
$$Get_a^c\ o\ s \equiv GetRep_a^c\ o\ (RepStore\ s)$$
$$Set_a^c\ o\ x\ s \equiv AbsStore\ (SetRep_a^c\ o\ x\ (RepStore\ s))$$
$$Cast_d^c\ o\ s \equiv CastRep_d^c\ o\ (RepStore\ s), \quad Is_d^c\ o\ s \equiv IsRep_d^c\ o\ (RepStore\ s)$$
$$New^c\ s \equiv let\ (o, H) = NewRep^c\ (RepStore\ s)\ in\ (o, AbsStore\ H)$$

All the ASOOT axioms are derived from the definition we presented so far. The axioms are divided into two groups according to how they are derived. One is those which are derived simply by expanding the definitions. The axioms 2, 4, 5, 8, 9, 10 and 11 are in this group. The other is those which are proved as invariants on the store. The axioms 1, 3, 6 and 7 are in this group. Invariants are proved by the induction given in $IsInv$. Let us consider the proof of the axiom 1 defined as Inv as follows.

$$Inv\ s \equiv \forall o.\ Ex^c\ o\ s = Is_{d_1}^c\ o\ s \vee ... \vee Is_{d_n}^c\ o\ s \quad (d_i \in \{d\ |\ c \lhd^* d\})$$

First, we define the heap representation of the axiom as follows.

$$InvRep\ H \equiv \forall o.\ ExRep^c\ o\ H = IsRep_{d_1}^c\ o\ H \vee ... \vee IsRep_{d_n}^c\ o\ H$$

---

[1] There is a logically equivalent implementation of the theory where the number of steps of the induction in $IsInv$ becomes only $1 + 2c$.

Then, we prove the theorem $\vdash IsInv\ InvRep$ based on the structural induction. If this holds, the theorem $\vdash \forall H.\ IsStoreRep\ H \Rightarrow InvRep\ H$ is derived from the definition of $IsStoreRep$. And as $IsStoreRep\ (RepStore\ s)$ holds (from the bijection theorem not presented here), we obtain the theorem $\vdash \forall s.\ InvRep\ (RepStore\ s)$. From this theorem and the definitions of Ex^c and Is_d^c, we obtain $\vdash \forall s.\ Inv\ s$.

5 A Verification Example

In this section, we show an example verification using ASOOT, where a UML collaboration diagram is verified to satisfy an invariant written in OCL. The UML class diagram and collaboration diagram of the library system are shown in Fig.4. The system consists of four classes. The class library is the main class of the system and has the methods for operations such as item lending and customer registration. It has association with the classes customer and item which represent the customers and items registered in the library, respectively. There are two kinds of items: books and CDs. They are represented as subclasses book and cd. The class lend keeps the lending information between a customer and an item. In the class model, an association is defined as an attribute whose type is a list of objects, e.g. the association for library with customer is defined as an attribute customerlist of type customer list.

The lending operation is defined as a method lend of the class library and its collaboration proceeds as follows. First, the method is applied to an library object lib with two inputs: a customer ID (cid) and an item ID (iid). Then, it checks if the customer is qualified to lend the item (1.1). The conditions

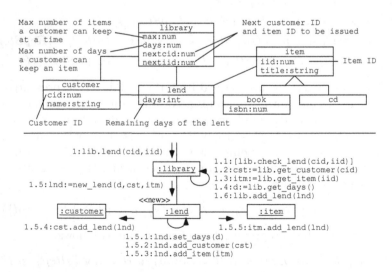

Fig. 4. The class diagram and the lending collaboration

```
Collaboration

library_lend : library -> num -> num -> store -> string # store
library_lend lib cid iid s =                       (* 1 *)
   if library_check_lend lib cid iid s then        (* 1.1 *)
      let cst = library_get_customer lib cid s in  (* 1.2 *)
      let itm = library_get_item lib iid s in      (* 1.3 *)
      let d = library_get_days lib s in            (* 1.4 *)
      let (lnd,s1) = new_lend d cst itm s in       (* 1.5 *)
         library_add_lend lib lnd s1               (* 1.6 *)
   else s

new_lend : num -> customer -> item -> store -> lend # store
new_lend d cst itm s =
   let (lnd,s1) = lend_new s in
   let s2 = lend_set_days lnd d s1 in              (* 1.5.1 *)
   let s3 = lend_add_customer lnd cst s2 in        (* 1.5.2 *)
   let s4 = lend_add_item lnd itm s3 in            (* 1.5.3 *)
   let s5 = customer_add_lend cst lnd s4 in        (* 1.5.4 *)
   let s6 = item_add_lend itm lnd s5 in            (* 1.5.5 *)
      (lnd,s6)

library_get_customer : library -> num -> store -> customer
library_get_customer lib cid s =
   let l = library_get_customerlist lib s in
      HD (FILTER (\x. customer_get_cid x s = cid) l)

lend_add_customer : lend -> customer -> store -> store
lend_add_customer lnd cst s =
   let l = lend_get_customerlist lnd s in
      lend_set_customerlist lnd (cst::l) s
```

```
Invariant

Inv1 : library -> store -> bool
Inv1 lib s = library_ex lib s ==>
   (library_get_customer_lendsum lib s = library_get_item_lendsum lib s)

library_get_customer_lendsum lib s =
   let l = library_get_customerlist lib s in
      LENGTH (FLATTEN (MAP (\x. customer_get_lendlist x s) l))

library_get_item_lendsum lib s =
   let l = library_get_itemlist lib s in
      LENGTH (FILTER (\x. 0 < LENGTH (item_get_lendlist x s)) l)
```

Fig. 5. Definitions of the collaboration (partially) and the invariant in HOL

to check are: if the IDs are valid, if the customer currently keeps at most the maximum number of items specified by the library (max) and if the item is available. If the check is passed, the customer object (cst) and the item object (itm) corresponding to the IDs are obtained (1.2, 1.3) and the maximum number of days for the lent specified by the library (days) is obtained (1.4). Then, a new lend object (lnd) is created by the creation method new_lend (1.5). In this method, the lend object is set the remaining days for the lent (1.5.1) and linked to the customer object and the item object (1.5.2-1.5.5). Finally, the lend object is linked to the library object (1.6).

One of the invariants which must be met by the systems is: "The total number of books lent by all the customers is equal to the number of items unavailable." The OCL expression of this invariant is written as follows.

```
library
customer.lend->size = item->select(lend->size>0)->size
```

The method and the invariant are translated into a function library_lend and a predicate Inv1, respectively, as shown in Fig.5. We have not defined the formal translation, but it is our future work.

The methods in the collaboration is defined as HOL functions and the whole collaboration is represented as their application sequence. This is a merit of ASOOT compared to the UML/OCL verification based on B [13][14] where methods are defined only as as pre- and post-conditions. ASOOT enables to define even the internal operation of the methods using HOL functions. For example, the method call at 1.2 is defined as a function `library_get_customer`. This method returns a `customer` object which has the ID equals to `cid` and is defined making use of the list function `FILTER`. The method call at 1.5 is defined as a function `new_lend` and the collaboration proceeds to the next depth. The method call at 1.5.2 is defined as a function `lend_add_customer`. This function adds the object `cst` to the attribute `customerlist` using the *Get* and *Set* operators. As for the invariant, the left-hand-side is defined as a function `library_get_customer_lendsum`. The navigation `customer.lend` is represented by getting the `lendlist` of all the `customer` object using `MAP`, and then, flattening the nested list using `FLATTEN`. The set operation `size` is represented by `LENGTH`. The predicate `Inv1` takes the `library` object as its first argument. This represents the context object.

The fact that the invariant is maintained by application of the collaboration is proved as the following theorem.

```
|- !lib cid iid s.
   Inv1 lib s /\ Inv2 lib s ==> Inv1 lib (library_lend lib cid iid s)
```

The predicate `Inv2` is another invariant required as lemma which we omit to explain the details. The whole proof proceeds on the abstract level of ASOOT (without expanding the definition of ASOOT constants).

6   Related Work

J. Berg et al. [9] and Claude Marché et al. [10] define memory models for reasoning Java programs annotated with JML specifications. The first work defines the memory with untyped blocks, so that it can store arbitrary Java objects. The second work introduces multiple heap memories for different types in order to statically tell the types of each memory contents. Our memory model differs from them in that it can store values of arbitrary types not limited to the primitive ones in Java. This is important when it comes to the verification on the analysis level as the models are abstracted with high-level types such as list, set, and tree. We made this possible by constructing the memory depending on the type information of the application. Moreover, we can take advantage of the plentiful mathematical libraries and the powerful type definition package provided by HOL to define high-level types. Actually, those types can be implemented using Java classes with primitive types, but it will take additional proof steps to derive type properties from those class implementations compared to use HOL types directly.

A. Poetzsch-Heffer et al. [8] defines a Hoare-style logic for the verification of OO programs. As a logical foundation of the logic, it defines an OO theory based on the store model in HOL. The operators on the store are *get*, *set*, *new*, *alive*. The last one corresponds to *Ex* in our theory. It does not have the operators concerning subtyping like *Cast* and *Is* in our theory, and the axioms about subtyping are defined on the Hoare-logic level. In our theory, we included the axioms about subtyping on the store level by introducing the subtyping operators *Cast* and *Is*. As a result, the store theory becomes independent of the Hoare logic.

W. Naraschewski et al. [11] defines an object as an *extensible record* in Isabelle/HOL. This is a record in which a type variable is embedded as one of its element. Although this record enables structural subtyping of objects, it does not work as a reference. To allow object referencing, we defined our theory based on the store. With the referencing mechanism, verification of object collaboration becomes possible.

T. Aoki et al. [12] defines a semantics for the statechart-based verification of invariants about object attributes in HOL. The semantics is constructed by directly introducing axioms in HOL. The advantage of this axiomatic theory construction is that the mapping between the model elements and the theory element becomes clear, but the problem is that it may weaken the reliability of the theory. On the other hand, the definitional construction adopted in this paper guarantees the soundness of the theory.

7   Conclusion and Future Work

In this paper, we presented an OO theory for the verification of analysis models which we implemented in HOL. In order to allow arbitrary types in object attributes, the theory is automatically constructed depending on the class model of the system. The theory is derived from the operational semantics of a heap memory model and is guaranteed to be sound by definitional extension mechanism. Using the theory, a UML collaboration diagram is verified to satisfy an OCL invariant.

Future work includes the formalization of the UML collaboration diagram and its translation to the theory. We are considering to develop a Hoare-style logic for the verification of collaborations and implementation of a verification condition generator to make proof efficient. One of the future goal is to apply the verification method to collaboration-based designs [15] [16].

References

1. OMG. Unified Modeling Language. URL: http://www.omg.org/.
2. The HOL system. URL: http://hol.sourceforge.net/.
3. J. Warmer and A. Kleppe. The object constraint language: precise modeling with UML. Addison-Wesley, 1999.
4. Tobias Nipkow, David von Oheimb and Cornelia Pusch. μJava: Embedding a Programming Language in a Theorem Prover. In Foundations of Secure Computation. IOS Press, 2000.

5. Bart Jacobs et al. LOOP project, http://www.cs.kun.nl/ bart/LOOP/
6. David von Oheimb. Hoare Logic for Java in Isabelle/HOL. Concurrency and Computation: Practice and Experience, vol.13 pp.1173-1214, 2001.
7. A. Poetzsch-Heffer and P. Muller. A programming logic for sequential Java. Programming Languages and Systems (ESOP'99), vol.1576 LNCS Springer-Verlag, 1999.
8. A. Poetzsch-Heffer and P. Muller. Logical Foundations for Typed Object-Oriented Languages. Programming Concepts and Methods (PROCOMET), 1998.
9. J. van den Berg, M. Huisman, B. Jacobs, and E. Poll. A type-theoretic memory model for verification of sequential Java programs. Techn. Rep. CSI-R9924, Comput. Sci. Inst., Univ. of Nijmegen, 1999.
10. Claude Marché and Christine Paulin-Mohring. Reasoning on Java programs with aliasing and frame conditions. In 18th International Conference on Theorem Proving in Higher Order Logics (TPHOLs 2005), LNCS, August 2005.
11. W. Naraschewski and M. Wenzel. Object-Oriented Verification based on Record Subtyping in Higher-Order Logic. Tecnische Universitat Munchen, 1998.
12. Toshiaki Aoki, Takaaki Tateishi, and Takuya Katayama. An Axiomatic Formalization of UML Models. Practical UML-based Rigorous Development Methods, pp.13-28 2001.
13. Using B formal specifications for analysis and verification of UML/OCL models. Marcano, R. and N. Levy. Workshop on consistency problems in UML-based software development. 5th International Conference on the Unified Modeling Language. Dresden, Germany, October 2002.
14. K. Lano, D. Clark and K. Androutsopoulos. UML to B: Formal Verification of Object-Oriented Models. Integrated Formal Methods: 4th International Conference, IFM 2004, Cnaterbury, UK, April 4-7, 2004.
15. Y. Smaragdakis and D. Batory. Implementing layered designs with mixin layers. Proceedings of the European Conference on Object-Oriented Programming (ECOOP), 1998.
16. Kathi Fisler and Shriram Krishnamurthi. Modular verification of collaboration-based software designs. In Symposium on the Foundation of Software Engineering, 2001.

Constructing Open Systems via Consistent Components

Nguyen Truong Thang and Takuya Katayama

School of Information Science,
Japan Advanced Institute of Science and Technology
{thang, katayama}@jaist.ac.jp

Abstract. Open systems capable of handling unanticipated future changes are very desirable. A common approach towards open systems is based on components. There are some essential issues of the component-based software paradigm. First, the most challenging analysis issue is about *component consistency* - namely a component does not violate some property in another when composed. The paper presents a formal approach to the issue by including consistency semantic to component specification. Based on this semantic information, components can be efficiently cross-checked for the consistency among components. The second issue is on how components are realized from the formal specification. The *layered architecture* is recommended for component-based system design in which component specifications are separated into layers. Subsequently, each layer can be then respectively implemented by a corresponding module via *aspect-oriented programming*. The target system simply involves composing those modules together in a well-defined order.

1 Introduction

Open systems are the ultimate goal of software. Their most vital characteristic is the ability in handling changes, even unanticipated. A system is *open* for further changes in the sense that changes can be consistently integrated into the system; and the overall cost is kept at minimum. Component-based approach is a promising candidate towards those goals of open systems. Component-based software is especially flexible to changes - the vital quality of open systems. If changes can be locally managed within a single or a few related components, the complexity to handle changes is greatly reduced. This paper addresses two essential topics during component-based software development: analysis of component consistency; design and implementation of components from the formal component specification.

First, within the component-based approach, composing components properly is the most important analysis issue. Component-based software idealizes the *plug-and-play* concept. However, usually, components do not *play* after being syntactically *plugged* [1,2]. A main cause of this phenomenon is the violation of

D.V. Hung and M. Wirsing (Eds.): ICTAC 2005, LNCS 3722, pp. 517–531, 2005.

a component to some property inherent to another. To better resolve the composition problem, in this paper, the semantic constraints for *component consistency* are introduced. Associated with a component is a certain set of inherent properties. Another component interacting with that component must preserve constraints at the interface of the former so that those inherent properties continue to hold. Based on the proposed specification, the paper then introduces an efficient and scalable algorithm to analyze consistency between components.

Second, the paper illustrates briefly an approach to realize components based on the corresponding specifications. The *layered architecture* is advocated for component-based software design because it closely links with the way components extend/refine existing systems. Each component is separately encapsulated within a layer. A component refines the system formed by all components of layers on top of it. The layering style is especially resilient with changes. A change to a system is usually kept local to the associated layer or at most to some neighbor layers. As its effect is kept from propagating to system-wide level, the overall layered architecture is not much affected by the change.

Also, the *aspect-oriented programming* technique [3] is utilized to illustrate the implementation of components in separate modules. The target system is then constructed via a well-defined composition of modules.

In this paper, Section 2 introduces a formal dynamic behavior model of components. Section 3 is about component consistency and how to verify it. Later, Section 4 is concerned with specification of components and their composition. Section 5 briefs the connection of the formal component specification with the design (via the layered architecture) and implementation (via aspect-oriented programming) of open systems.

2   A Formal Model of Components

The most common form of components is Commercial-Off-The-Shelf (COTS) on very independent components. The computation paths of these components rarely interleave. The relationship between COTS can be named *functional addition*. Besides COTS, there is another aspect of components, *functional refinement*, in which components interleave their execution paths. Typically, a refinement extends the basic scenarios of a base component. Even though the discussion in this paper focuses on component refinement, the results can be well applied to COTS.

In the typical case of component refinement, there are two interacting components: *base* and *extension (or refinement)*. Between the base and its extension, on the base side, is an interface consisting of *exit* and *reentry* states. An exit state is the state where control is passed to the extension. A reentry state is the point at which the base regains control. Correspondingly, the extension interface contains *in-* and *out*-states at which the refinement component receives and releases system control. Let AP be a set of atomic propositions. The behavior of a component is separately specified by a state transition model.

Definition 1. *A state transition model M is represented by a tuple $\langle S, \Sigma, s_0, R, L \rangle$ where S is a set of states, Σ is the set of input events, $s_0 \in S$ is the initial state, $R \subseteq S \times PL(\Sigma) \to S$ is the transition function (where $PL(\Sigma)$ denotes the set of guarded events in Σ whose conditions are propositional logic expressions), and $L : S \to 2^{AP}$ labels each state with the set of atomic propositions true in that state.*

A base is expressed by a transition model $B = \langle S_B, \Sigma_B, s_{0_B}, R_B, L_B \rangle$ and an *interface* $I = \langle exit, reentry \rangle$, where $exit, reentry \subseteq S_B$. An extension is similarly represented by a model $E = \langle S_E, \Sigma_E, \bot, R_E, L_E \rangle$ ($\bot$ denotes no-care value) and an interface $J = \langle in, out \rangle$.

E can be syntactically plugged with B via *compatible* interface states between I and J. Logically, along the computation flow, when the system is in an exit state $ex \in I.exit$ of B matched with an in-state $i \in J.in$ of E ($ex \leftrightarrow i$), it can only enter E if the conditions to accept extension events, namely the set of atomic propositions at i, are satisfied. In other words, $\bigwedge L_B(ex) \Rightarrow \bigwedge L_E(i)$, where $\bigwedge$ is the inter-junction of atomic propositions. For the matching of a reentry state $re \in I.reentry$ of B and an out-state $o \in J.out$ of E, it is similar, i.e. $re \leftrightarrow o$ if $\bigwedge L_E(o) \Rightarrow \bigwedge L_B(re)$.

Definition 2. *Composing the base B with the extension E, through the interface I produces a composition model $C = \langle S_C, \Sigma_C, s_{0_C}, R_C, L_C \rangle$ as follows:*

- $S_C = S_B \cup S_E$; $\Sigma_C = \Sigma_B \cup \Sigma_E$; $s_{0_C} = s_{0_B}$;
- R_C *is defined from R_B and R_E in which R_E takes precedent, namely any transition in B is overridden by another transition in E if they share the same starting state and input event;*
- $\forall s \in S_B, s \notin I.exit \cup I.reentry : L_C(s) = L_B(s)$;
- $\forall s \in S_E, s \notin J.in \cup J.out : L_C(s) = L_E(s)$;
- $\forall s \in I.exit \cup I.reentry : L_C(s) = L_B(s)$.

Component constraints in this paper belong to temporal logic CTL which is more powerful than constraints in current technology like CORBA, UML and OCL [4]. CTL* logic is formally expressed via two quantifiers **A** ("for all paths") and **E** ("for some path") together with five temporal operators **X** ("next"), **F** ("eventually"), **G** ("always"), **U** ("until") and **R** ("release") [5]. CTL (Computation Tree Logic) is a restricted subset of CTL* in which each temporal operator must be preceded by a quantifier.

Definition 3. *The closure of a property p, $cl(p)$, is the set of all sub-formulae of p including itself.*

- $p \in AP : cl(p) = \{p\}$
- p *is one of* **AX** f, **EX** f, **AF** f, **EF** f, **AG** f, **EG** f : $cl(p) = \{p\} \cup cl(f)$
- p *is one of* **A** $[f \, \mathbf{U} \, g]$, **E** $[f \, \mathbf{U} \, g]$, **A** $[f \, \mathbf{R} \, g]$, **E** $[f \, \mathbf{R} \, g]$: $cl(p) = \{p\} \cup cl(f) \cup cl(g)$
- $p = \neg f : cl(p) = cl(f)$
- $p = f \vee g$ *or* $p = f \wedge g : cl(p) = cl(f) \cup cl(g)$

Definition 4. *The truth values of a state s with respect to a set of CTL proper-ties ps within a model* $M = \langle S, \Sigma, s_0, R, L \rangle$, *denoted as* $\mathcal{V}_M(s, ps)$, *is a function:* $S \times 2^{CTL} \to 2^{CTL}$.

- $\mathcal{V}_M(s, \emptyset) = \emptyset$
- $\mathcal{V}_M(s, \{p\} \cup ps) = \mathcal{V}_M(s, \{p\}) \cup \mathcal{V}_M(s, ps)$
- $\mathcal{V}_M(s, \{p\}) = \begin{cases} \{p\} & \text{if } M, s \models p \\ \{\neg p\} & \text{otherwise} \end{cases}$

Hereafter, $\mathcal{V}_M(s, \{p\}) = \{p\}$ (or $\{\neg p\}$) is written in the shorthand form as $\mathcal{V}_M(s, p) = p$ (or $\neg p$) for individual property p.

An incremental verification technique for CTL properties has been attempted by [6]. It is named *open incremental model checking* (OIMC) for the *open* and *incremental* characteristics of the algorithm. Suppose that a base component is refined by another. The approach consists of the following steps:

1. Deriving a set of *preservation constraints* at the interface states of the base such that if those constraints are preserved, the property inherent to the base under consideration is guaranteed.
2. The refinement preserves the above constraints during its execution.

OIMC is particularly useful for open systems - future extensions are not known in advance. In the typical case of component refinement, the composite model C is regarded as the combination of two sequential components B and E. Besides ex-ecution paths defined in B, a typical execution path in C consists of three parts: initially in B, next in E and then back to B. Associated with each reentry state re of E is a computation tree in B represented by a set of temporal properties. If these properties at re are known, without loss of correctness, we can efficiently derive the properties at the upstream states in E by ignoring model checking in B to find the properties at re. Instead, we start from these reentry states with the associated properties; check the upstream of the extension component, and then the base component if needed [1]. The properties associated with a reentry state re are assumed with truth values from B, $As(re) = \mathcal{V}_B(re, cl(p))$. As is the assumption function of this *assumption model checking* [7]. Of course, this method is reliable if $As(re)$ is proper. Hereafter, As is considered to be proper.

3   Inter-component Consistency

Given a structure $B = \langle S_B, \Sigma_B, s_{0_B}, R_B, L_B \rangle$ as in Definition 1, a property p holding in B is denoted by $B, s_{0_B} \models p$. Later, C is formed by composing B and E. B and E are *consistent* with respect to p if $C, s_{0_B} \models p$.

3.1   A Theorem on Component Consistency

Due to the inherently inside-out characteristic of model checking, after verifying p in B, at each state s, $\mathcal{V}_B(s, cl(p))$ are recorded.

---

[1] There is no need to check the base again if the consistency constraints associated with the exit states of B are preserved at the corresponding in-states of E.

Definition 5. *B and E are in* conformance *at an exit state ex (with respect to cl(p)) if* $\mathcal{V}_B(ex, cl(p)) = \mathcal{V}_E(ex, cl(p))$.

In this definition, $\mathcal{V}_E(ex, cl(p))$ are derived from the assumption model checking within E, and the seeded values at a reentry state re are $As(re) = \mathcal{V}_B(re, cl(p))$.

Theorem 6. *Given a base B and a property p holding on B, an extension E is composed with B. B and E are consistent with respect to p if B and E conform with each other at all exit states.*

The proof details are in [6]. Even though this paper focuses on component refinement, with regards to COTS, the above theorem also holds. A COTS component can be indeed regarded as a special case of refinement in which there is only a single exit state and no reentry state with the base. The computation tree of the COTS deviates from the base and never joins the base again. After being composed with a COTS, instead of an assumption model checking within the COTS, a standard model checking procedure can be executed entirely within the COTS to find the properties at the exit state. The conformance condition to ensure the consistency between the two components can be applied as usual. The only difference in Definition 5 lies in $\mathcal{V}_E(ex, cl(p))$ for each exit state ex. In component refinement, these truth values are derived from the assumption model checking within E with the assumption values $\mathcal{V}_B(re, cl(p))$ at any reentry state re. On the contrary, in COTS, there is no assumption at all. Hence, the model checking procedure in E is then exactly standard CTL model checking.

Figure 1 depicts the composition preserving the property $p = \mathbf{A}\,[f\,\mathbf{U}\,g]$ when B and E are in conformance. The composition is done via a single exit state ex. E overrides the transition $ex\text{-}s_3$ in B. B' is the remainder of B after removing the overridden transition. Within B, $p = \mathbf{A}\,[f\,\mathbf{U}\,g]$ holds at s_1, s_2 and ex. The figure only shows $\mathcal{V}_E(ex, p) = \mathcal{V}_B(ex, p) = \mathbf{A}\,[f\,\mathbf{U}\,g]$. In fact, B and E conform at ex with respect to $cl(p)$. After removing the edge $ex\text{-}s_3$, the new paths in E together with the remaining computation tree in B' still preserve p at ex directly; and consequently s_2 and s_1 indirectly. p is preserved at the initial state s_1, namely B and E are consistent. In this figure, although the reentry state re is not explicitly displayed [2], the arguments are still valid when the downstream of E converges to the reentry state re.

3.2 Open Incremental Model Checking

Component consistency between B and E can be verified via OIMC. Initially, a CTL property p is known to hold in B. We need to check that E does not violate p. From Theorem 6, the incremental verification method only needs to verify the conformance at all exit states between B and E. Corresponding to each exit state ex, within E, the algorithm to verify constraints $\mathcal{V}_B(ex, cl(p))$ can be briefly described as follows:

---

[2] This figure is intended to represent both component refinement and COTS.

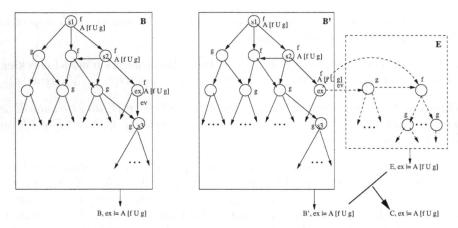

Fig. 1. An illustration of conformance $\mathcal{V}_E(ex, cl(p)) = \mathcal{V}_B(ex, cl(p))$ where E overrides B. The property $p = \mathbf{A}\,[f\,\mathbf{U}\,g]$ is preserved in B due to the conformance.

1. Seeding $\mathcal{V}_B(re, cl(p))$ at any reentry state re. This step defines the assumption function As: $As(re) = \mathcal{V}_B(re, cl(p))$. In case of COTS, there is no assumption function, i.e. no seeding.
2. Executing a CTL assumption model checking procedure within E to check ϕ, $\forall \phi \in cl(p)$.
3. Checking if $\mathcal{V}_E(ex, cl(p)) = \mathcal{V}_B(ex, cl(p))$.

At the end of the algorithm, if the truth values with respect to $cl(p)$ at in-states of E and exit states of B are matched respectively, B and E are consistent with respect to p.

3.3   Scalability of OIMC

We consider the general case of the n-th version of the component (C_n) during software evolution as a structure of components B, E_1, E_2, ..., E_n where E_i is the refining component to the $(i-1)$-th evolved version $(C_{(i-1)})$, $i = \overline{1, n}$. The initial version is $C_0 = B$ and $C_i = C_{i-1} + E_i$. We check for any potential conflict between B and E_i regarding p via OIMC. Theorem 7 claims that OIMC is scalable. The detailed proof is in [6].

Theorem 7. *If all respective pairs of base $(C_{(i-1)})$ and refining (E_i) components conform, the complexity of OIMC to verify the consistency between E_n and B is independent from the n-th version C_n, i.e. it only executes within E_n.*

4   Component Specification and Consistency Verification

This paper advocates the inclusion of an additional semantic aspect of component specification to facilitate proper component composition. Given a base component $B = \langle S_B, \Sigma_B, s_{o_B}, R_B, L_B \rangle$ and an inherent property p, the semantic aspect is represented by consistency constraints $\mathcal{V}_B(s, cl(p))$ at any interface state s of the component (due to Theorem 6 in Section 3).

Component signatures are the fundamental aspect to the component interface. The traditional interface signature of a component contains *attributes* and *operations*. Through attributes, the current state of a software component may be externally observable. The component's clients can observe and even change the values of those attributes. On the other hand, the clients interact with the component through operations.

The interface signature only shows the individual elements of the component for interaction with clients in syntactic terms. Components may be subject to a number of further semantic constraints regarding their use. In general, there are two types of such constraints: internal to individual components and inter-component relationships. The first type is simple [1,2,4]. For example: pre- and post-condition of an operation, or value range of an attribute. Regarding the second type, current component technology such as OMG's CORBA IDL (Interface Definition Language), UML and OCL [4] etc is limited to a simple logic in terms of expressiveness. For example, different attributes in components may be inter-related by their value settings; or an operation of a component can only be invoked when a specific attribute value of another is in a given range etc [1]. The underlying logic only expresses the constraint at the moment an interface element is invoked, i.e. static view, regardless of execution history.

The paper introduces a semantic for inter-component constraint emphasizing on how to make components *play* once they are syntactically *plugged*. This constraint type is expressed in terms of CTL so its scope of expressiveness is enormous. In contrast to the logic above, CTL can describe whole execution paths of a component, i.e. dynamic view. Via OIMC in Section 3.2, a refining client E to a base component B can be efficiently verified on whether it preserves the property p of B.

Component specification can be represented via interface signatures and constraints written in an illustrative specification language. Figure 2 shows the dynamic model of a simple component, while below is the corresponding specification of the component. The interface specification should describe the behavior model of the component including states and transitions among states as formally defined in Definition 1. The next part involves the declaration of static component elements, i.e. attributes and operations, in the object-oriented style. At the end are the semantic constraints of the component for inherent temporal properties at potential interface states. For illustration purpose and due to space limitation, this producer-consumer example is very much simplified so that only

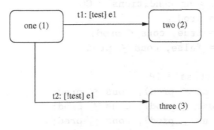

Fig. 2. The dynamic behavior model of the "black" component

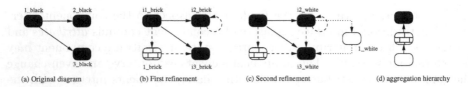

(a) Original diagram   (b) First refinement   (c) Second refinement   (d) aggregation hierarchy

Fig. 3. Component refinements and component composition via class aggregation

some key transitions and states are shown. Because of this over-simplified model, the whole dynamic behavior of the component is visible to clients. In practice, regarding the encapsulation principle, only essential part of the model for future extension is visible. The rest of the model is hidden. In the example, there are three components: "black" (the base B of Figure 3a - supporting the producer function); "brick" (the first refinement E of Figure 3b - allowing variable buffer size; and item-consuming function); and "white" (the second refinement E' of Figure 3c - optimizing data buffer).

```
Component B {
Signature:
   states 1_black, 2_black, 3_black;

   // edge declarations
   edge t1: 1_black -> 2_black
   condition test // OK if adding k items to buffer
   input event e1 // producing k items
   do { produce(k)... }; // t1 action

   edge t2: 1_black -> 3_black;
   ... // similarly defined

   // operations and attributes declaration
   boolean test;
   int cons, prod;// consumed, produced items
   int buffer[];
   init(){ state = 1_black; ...};
   produce(n){ prod = prod + n;...};

Constraint:
   // compatible plugging conditions - CC
   1_black_cc: cons = prod;
   2_black_cc: test = true, cons < prod;
   3_black_cc: test = false, cons ≤ prod;

   // Inherent properties - IP
   1_black_ip: AG (cons ≤ prod), cons ≤ prod;
   2_black_ip: AG (cons ≤ prod), cons ≤ prod;
   3_black_ip: AG (cons ≤ prod), cons ≤ prod;
}
```

```
Component E {// for refining black
Signature:
    states 1_brick, i1_brick, i2_brick, i3_brick;

    // edges declaration
    edge t3: i2_brick -> i3_brick
    condition ... // ready to consume
    input event ... // consuming k items
    do { consume(k)... }; // t3 action

    edge t4: i1_brick -> 1_brick
    condition ... // ready to change buffer size
    input event ... // change the size
    do { changesize();... }; // t4 action

    edge t5: 1_brick -> i3_brick;
    edge t6: i2_brick -> i2_brick;
    ... // similarly defined

    // operations and attributes declaration
    consume(n){ cons = cons + n;...};
    changesize(){ buffer = malloc();...};

Constraint:
    1_brick_cc: cons ≤ prod;
    i1_brick_cc: cons ≤ prod;
    i2_brick_cc: test = true, cons < prod;
    i3_brick_cc: test = false, cons < prod;
}

Component E' {// for refining black + brick
Signature:
    states 1_white, i2_white, i3_white;

    // edges declaration
    edge t7: i2_white -> 1_white
    condition ... // ready to compact buffer
    input event ...// compacting the data buffer
    do { resetbuffer();... }; // t7 action

    edge t8: 1_white -> i3_white;
    ... // similarly defined

    // operations and attributes declaration
    resetbuffer(){ prod = prod - cons; cons = 0;...};
```

Constraint:

```
1_white_cc: cons ≤ prod, cons = 0;
i2_white_cc: test = true, cons ≤ prod;
i3_white_cc: test = false, cons ≤ prod;
```
}

The following explains the preservation of the constraint in B by all subsequent two component refinements E and E'. Informally, the property means that under any circumstance, the number of produced items by the component is always greater or equal to that of consumed items. In terms of CTL notation, $p = \mathbf{AG}\ (cons \leq prod)$. The closure set of p is hence $cl(p) = \{p, a\}$, where $a = (cons \leq prod)$.

Initially, B is composed with E. Interface plugging conditions are used to map compatible interface states among components. The base exposes three interface states 1_black, 2_black and 3_black. On the other hand, the refinement component exposes four interface states, namely 1_brick, $i1\_brick$, $i2\_brick$ and $i3\_brick$. Based on the respective atomic proposition sets at those states, corresponding interface states are mapped accordingly. For instance, as $\bigwedge L_B(1\_black) = (cons = prod) \Rightarrow \bigwedge L_E(i1\_brick) = (cons \leq prod)$, according to the conditions of interface mapping, $i1\_brick \leftrightarrow 1\_black$. Similarly, $i2\_brick \leftrightarrow 2\_black$ and $i3\_brick \leftrightarrow 3\_black$. Here, $i1\_brick$ and $i2\_brick$ perform in-states of E, while $i2\_brick$ and $i3\_brick$ are out-states.

The composite model of the two components $C_1 = B + E$ is shown in Figure 3b. After the modeler decides on the mapping configuration between interface states, and properly resolves any mismatches at the syntactic level between B and E, the consistency between the two components is in focus. The OIMC algorithm in Section 3.2 is applied as follows:

1. Copying $\mathcal{V}_B(s, cl(p))$ to the respectively mapped out-states of E where s is a reentry state such as 2_black ($i2\_brick$) and 3_black ($i3\_brick$).
2. Executing an assumption model checking to check ϕ, $\forall \phi \in cl(p)$, within E only to find $\mathcal{V}_E(i1\_brick, cl(p))$ and $\mathcal{V}_E(i2\_brick, cl(p))$.
3. Checking if the two components conform by comparing $\mathcal{V}_E(i1\_brick, cl(p))$ and $\mathcal{V}_E(i2\_brick, cl(p))$ with the inherent-property constraints at respective exit states 1_black and 2_black (previously written in the specification of B).

The actual model checking is very simple and hence its details are skipped. At the end, B and E components conform at all exit states. According to Theorem 6, p is preserved by E after evolving to $C_1 = B + E$.

C_1 is then extended with E', $C_2 = C_1 + E'$ as shown in Figure 3c. The approach in composing E' with C_1 is similar to the above, the following mapping configuration between interface states is derived: $i2\_white \leftrightarrow 2\_black$, $i3\_white \leftrightarrow 3\_black$. OIMC is similarly applied. The same result is achieved, p is preserved by E'. More importantly, the verification procedure is executed within E' only.

In brief, p is preserved by both extensions E and E'. In this example, the scalability of OIMC is maintained as it only runs on the refinements, independently from the bases B and C_1 respectively.

5   Designing and Implementing Open Systems

This section presents briefly a possible way to realize components from their formal specifications. In particular, there are two topics: design architecture and implementation of component-based systems.

5.1   Layered Architecture for Component-Based Software

The major goal of the illustrative specification language in the example of Section 4 is to minimize the "conceptual distance" between architectural abstractions and their implementation [8]. The specification language is similar to that of [8] for declaring and refining state machines in layering style.

The layered architecture is very effective in separating *concerns* [3]. A system usually consists of several concerns which are essentially high-level abstraction of some system requirements or goals. At the core of software engineering is the *"separation of concerns"* concept. Concerns are the primary motivation for organizing and decomposing software into manageable and comprehensible parts. It is difficult to manage and to evolve several concerns together, especially when they tangle each other. System complexity can be reduced significantly if each concern can be separately managed. In terms of system design, the layered architecture facilitates the concept by assigning each concern to a layer.

Fundamentally, given a system with several concerns, there are several associated *dimensions* of concerns such as: class, function, feature etc [3]. Thus, there could be several layered architectures for the system due to the system partition in different dimensions. The best layered architecture is the one in accordance to the dimension in which the tangling degree among layers is at minimum.

Regarding component refinement as of this paper, the layered architecture resembles the way components refine each other. The base component and each refinement are expressed as separate specifications that are encapsulated in distinct layers. As components are composed with each other, they can be progressively refined/extended in layering manner. The process adds states, transitions and actions to an existing component's behavior model. Figure 3d shows the layering hierarchy for the example in Section 4: the top layer corresponds to the specification from Figure 2 or Figure 3a; the below layers are in turn respectively associated with component specifications in Figures 3b and 3c.

With respect to general component-based software, the layered architecture also plays an important role in terms of both system development and evolution. First, for system development, each component targets a particular system function/service. From the layered architecture's perspective, each layer then corresponds to a component or a group of closely-related components. The layers are ordered from top to bottom according to the sequence of component compositions, i.e. base component on top, and then refinements sequentially. In the example of Section 4, the layers are mapped with the base component B and refinements E, E' from top to bottom in accordance with the dependency among components. The development process then simply involves the composition of layers in a proper order. Because the separation of concerns is achieved, the total development cost is significantly reduced.

Second, with regards to system evolution, the layered architecture is especially resilient to system changes - the vital characteristic of open systems. The changes can arise in the form of either providing new functions/services to or removing some parts from the system. Even so, the system architecture still keeps its layering quality. If each service is encapsulated within a layer, any new service can be positioned into the proper position in the layering hierarchy. On the contrary, a service can be disabled from the system by removing the associated layer from the architecture. The key issue is then about whether system consistency among layers is maintained after some layers are inserted to or removed from the architecture. This issue is in essence about the consistency among components mentioned in Sections 3 and 4.

In brief, with inherent advantages such as the separation of concerns and the resilience to changes, the layered architecture is regarded as a candidate for open systems design, at least in terms of architectural abstraction.

5.2   Implementing Components via Aspect-Oriented Programming

Based on the proposed specification in Section 4, components are usually implemented as classes in typical object-oriented languages. Component composition is then done via class aggregation. All members of the class implementing the base component in Figure 3a are aggregated with the refinement of Figure 3b; and the newly formed class is in turn united with the refinement of Figure 3c.

There are possibly many approaches to implement components from their specifications. For example, traditional object-oriented implementation techniques, *mixin layer* [9] or *aspect-oriented programming* (AOP) [10,11] etc. This paper recommends the use of AOP. Aspect-oriented programming currently attracts a great deal of research from the community for its advantage in handling cross-cutting concerns. In fact, AOP outperforms object-oriented programming in capturing software concerns in modular way. Object-oriented technology focuses on its *dominant* dimension, i.e. class. From the layered architecture's perspective, every layer is associated to exactly a unique class. If concerns crosscut multiple objects as they usually do, the class dimension does not capture system variations well. As a result, corresponding codes for those concerns are scattered among objects. The evolution cost is then certainly high, i.e. a change in any concern will trigger simultaneous updates at cross-cut objects.

The most notable AOP languages are AspectJ [12] and Hyper/J [10]. Their common approach is to capture multi-object crosscutting concerns of a system in separate modules. Each concern corresponds to a module. As their codes are centralized, the cost to handle changes to concerns is significantly improved. The job of the AOP languages is to weave the codes of such concerns into existing object-oriented classes of the system at appropriate places, e.g. *joint points* [12]. The overall result of the approach is the absence of code-tangling among objects.

The example in Section 4 is realized into concrete codes via Java and Hyper/J. Each component is implemented by a Java class which corresponds to a concern or hyperslice among "black", "brick" and "white". The component B is sketched below. Only traditional component attributes and operations are supported by Java classes. The dynamic behavior model of components are ignored in the subsequent implementation.

```
package example.Black;// defined in file Black/ExampleComponent.java
public class ExampleComponent {
// class fragment for the Black (item-producing) concern
   // attributes declaration
   private boolean m_bTest;
   private int m_nCons, m_nProd;// consumed, produced items
   private int m_aBuffer[];
   ...

   // operations declaration
   ExampleComponent(){ m_nCons = m_nProd = 0;...};// constructor
   void Produce(n){ m_nProd = m_nProd + n;...};
   ...

}// END class ExampleComponent
```

The other components E and E' are similarly implemented. The concern mapping files corresponding to the three components are then defined. For example, the first line indicates that all classes, interfaces and members in the example.Black package address the "Black" concern in Feature dimension.

```
package example.Black : Feature.Black
package example.Brick : Feature.Brick
package example.White : Feature.White
```

Three above hyperslices are subsequently mapped by Hyper/J via a hyper-module file. The directive mergeByName indicates that classes, attributes and operations with the same name in different concerns are merged into one.

```
hypermodule BlackBrickWhite
   hyperslices:
      Feature.Black,
      Feature.Brick,
      Feature.White;

   relationships:
      mergeByName;
end hypermodule;
```

6   Related Work

Modular model checking is rooted at assume-guarantee model checking [13,14]. However, unlike the counterpart in hardware verification [13,15] focusing on parallel composition of modules, software modular verification [7] is restricted by its sequential execution nature. Therefore, properties at the interface states are required to be stricter. Incremental model checking inspires verification techniques and the theoretical foundation further. Comparing to some modular verification works such as [13,14,15], there is a fundamental difference in characteristic between those and the proposed approach. Modular verification in those works are rather closed. Even though it is based on component-based modular model checking, it is not prepared for component addition. If a component is added to the system, the whole system of many existing components and the new component are re-checked altogether. On the contrary, the approach in this paper is incrementally modular and hence more open. We only check the new system partially in terms of new component and its interface with the rest of the system. Certainly, this merit comes at the cost of "fixed" preservation constraints at exit states. These constraints can deliver a false negative for some cases of component conformance.

Besides, similar to [16], the proposed specification of component interface in Section 4 is actually a state-full interface specification. Components (or modules) can be checked for consistency before composition. Both approaches are state-based. This paper simply relies on state transition model in the most general sense, while [16] presents a finer realization of state-full model in which states are represented by control points in operations [3] of components; and edges are actually operation calls. In addition, the two approaches target different aspects of consistency. This paper is concerned with component consistency in terms of CTL properties, whereas [16] is involved with the correctness and completeness of operation declarations within components. Instead of the substitution of each other, the two approaches are hence more about complement to each other.

7   Conclusion

This paper presents a formal approach towards open systems via consistent components. There are two important issues during open systems development via component-based approach. They are: component consistency analysis and component realization. First, to overcome the failure of component matching at the syntactic level, the paper advocates the inclusion of *component consistency* written in CTL to the component interface. Based on the proposed specification, an efficient and scalable model checking method is utilized to verify whether components are consistent. Second, regarding the realization of open systems from the proposed formal specification, the aspect-oriented software development is advocated. Specifically, in terms of system design, the layered architecture is recommended due to its advantage and flexibility to changes - the prominent characteristic of open systems. For component-based software implementation, the combination of object-oriented (e.g. Java) and aspect-oriented programming (e.g. Hyper/J) languages are briefly illustrated for the implementation of open systems in modular way.

---

[3] In [16], operations are named as methods.

References

1. Han, J.: An approach to software component specification. In: Proceedings of International Workshop on Component Based Software Engineering. (1999)
2. Liu, Y., Cunningham, H.C.: Software component specification using design by contract. In: Proceedings of the SouthEast Software Engineering Conference. (April 2002)
3. Tarr, P., Ossher, H., Harrison, W., Sutton, S.M.: N-degrees of separation: Multi-dimensional separation of concerns. In: Proc. ICSE. (1999) 109 – 117
4. Warmer, J., Kleppe, A.: The Objects Constraint Language: Precise Modeling with UML. Addison-Wesley (1999)
5. Clarke, E.M., Grumberg, O., Peled, D.A.: Model Checking. The MIT Press (1999)
6. Nguyen, T.T., Katayama, T.: Handling consistency of software evolution in an efficient way. In: Proc. IWPSE. (2004) 121–130
7. Laster, K., Grumberg, O.: Modular model checking of software. In: Conference on Tools and Algorithms for the Constructions and Analysis of Systems. (1998)
8. Batory, D., Johnson, C., MacDonald, B., Heeder, D.V.: Achieving extensibility through product-lines and domain-specific languages: A case study. In: Proc. International Conference on Software Reuse. (2000)
9. Smaragdakis, Y., Batory, D.: Implementing layered designs with mixin layers. In: Proc. ECOOP. (1998)
10. Tarr, P., Ossher, H.: Hyper/J(TM) User and Installation Manual. IBM Research, IBM Corp. (2000)
11. Kiczales, G., Lamping, J., et al.: Aspect-oriented programming. In: Proc. European Conference on Object-Oriented Programming - ECOOP'97, Springer (1997) 220–242
12. The AspectJ Team: The AspectJ(TM) Programming Guide. Xerox Corporation. (2001)
13. Kupferman, O., Vardi, M.Y.: Modular model checking. In: Compositionality: The Significant Difference. Volume 1536 of Lecture Notes in Computer Science., Springer-Verlag (1998)
14. Pasareanu, C.S., Dwyer, M.B., Huth, M.: Assume-guarantee model checking of software: A comparative case study. In: Theoretical and Practical Aspects of SPIN Model Checking. Volume 1680 of Lecture Notes of Computer Science., Springer-Verlag (1999)
15. Grumberg, O., Long, D.E.: Model checking and modular verification. In: International Conference on Concurrency Theory. Volume 527 of Lecture Notes of Computer Science., Springer-Verlag (1991)
16. Chakrabarti, A., de Alfaro, L., Henzinger, T.A., Jurdzinski, M., Mang, F.Y.C.: Interface compatibility checking for software modules. In: Proceedings of the Computer-Aided Verification - CAV, LNCS Springer-Verlag (2002)

A Sub-quadratic Algorithm for Conjunctive and Disjunctive Boolean Equation Systems

Jan Friso Groote[1] and Misa Keinänen[2]

[1] Department of Mathematics and Computer Science,
Eindhoven University of Technology,
P.O. Box 513, 5600 MB Eindhoven, The Netherlands
[2] Laboratory for Theoretical Computer Science,
Department of Computer Science and Engineering,
Helsinki University of Technology,
P.O. Box 5400, FI-02015 TKK, Finland
J.F.Groote@tue.nl, Misa.Keinanen@tkk.fi

Abstract. We present a new algorithm for conjunctive and disjunctive boolean equation systems which arise frequently in the verification and analysis of finite state concurrent systems. In contrast to the previously known $O(e^2)$ time algorithms, our algorithm computes the solution to such a fixpoint equation system with size e and alternation depth d in $O(e \log d)$ time (here $d < e$). We show the correctness and complexity of the algorithm. We discuss heuristics and describe how the algorithm can be efficiently implemented. The algorithm is compared to a previous solution via experiments on verification examples. Our measurements indicate that the new algorithm makes the verification of a large class of fixpoint expressions more tractable.

1 Introduction

A boolean equation system [5,8] is a sequence of boolean equations with minimal and maximal fixpoints. It gives a useful framework for the verification of finite state concurrent systems. This is due to the fact that many interesting properties of systems can naturally be specified in the modal μ-calculus [7], and a μ-calculus formula and a transition system can be straightforwardly translated to a boolean equation system. A pleasant feature of a boolean equation system is that it gives a concise way of representing the model checking problem, laying bare the essential problem of computing the fixpoints.

We examine *conjunctive* and *disjunctive* fragments of boolean equation systems. Many practically relevant properties of systems can be expressed by means of fixed points that lead to boolean equation systems in such forms. It is therefore interesting to develop specific resolution techniques for these particular fragments. The system properties that can be encoded in conjunctive and disjunctive boolean equation systems include, e.g., typical safety, liveness and fairness properties; examples can be can be found in Section 5.

All previous algorithms for solving conjunctive and disjunctive classes, including those from [5,8], take at least quadratic time in the size of a system

D.V. Hung and M. Wirsing (Eds.): ICTAC 2005, LNCS 3722, pp. 532–545, 2005.

in the worst case. For large boolean equations, which are typically encountered in model checking and preorder/equivalence checking of realistic systems, these algorithms may lead to unpleasant running times.

The contribution of this paper is to present an especially fast algorithm for finding a solution to a boolean equation system in either conjunctive or disjunctive form. Given such a system with size e and alternation depth d where $d < e$, our algorithm finds the solution using time $O(e \log d)$ in the worst case. This improves the previously best known upper bound. In addition, our computational experiments indicate that the new algorithm makes the verification of a large class of fixpoint expressions more tractable.

Our algorithm is a variation of Tarjan's hierarchical clustering algorithm [12], and it combines essentially three techniques: binary search, divide-and-conquer, and graph theoretic techniques for finding strong components [11]. King, Kupferman and Vardi [6] gave a related algorithm in the realm of parity word automata which also resorts to the ideas in [12].

We have implemented the new algorithm and have done various computational experiments to show that the theoretical improvement also leads to practical improvements over existing algorithms. In addition, we have investigated various heuristics for speeding up the search for solutions.

The paper is organized as follows. Section 2 introduces basic notions concerning boolean equation systems. Section 3 describes the previously best known algorithm for solving conjunctive and disjunctive boolean equation systems, and discusses its strengths and weaknesses. Section 4 presents our proposed new algorithm, and deals with its correctness and complexity. Section 5 describes experimental results on protocol verification examples. Section 6 deals with heuristics for speeding up the new algorithm. Section 7 presents the conclusions.

2   Boolean Equation Systems

A boolean equation system is an ordered sequence of fixpoint equations over boolean variables, with associated fixpoint signs, μ and ν, specifying the polarity of the fixpoints. The equations are of the form $\sigma x = \alpha$, where α is a positive boolean expression. The sign, σ, is μ if the equation is a least fixpoint equation and ν if it is a greatest fixpoint equation.

Let $\mathcal{X} = \{x_1, x_2, ..., x_n\}$ be a set of boolean variables. The set of *positive boolean expressions* over $\mathcal{X}$ is denoted by $B(\mathcal{X})$, and given by the grammar:

$$\alpha ::= x \mid \alpha \wedge \alpha \mid \alpha \vee \alpha$$

where $x \in \mathcal{X}$. We define the syntax of boolean equation systems as follows.

Definition 1 (The syntax of a boolean equation system). *A boolean equation is of the form $\sigma_i x_i = \alpha_i$, where $\sigma_i \in \{\mu, \nu\}$, $x_i \in \mathcal{X}$, and $\alpha_i \in B(\mathcal{X})$. A boolean equation system is an ordered sequence of boolean equations*

$$(\sigma_1 x_1 = \alpha_1)(\sigma_2 x_2 = \alpha_2) \dots (\sigma_n x_n = \alpha_n)$$

where all left-hand side variables are different. We assume that the order on variables and equations are in synchrony, and that all variables are from $\mathcal{X}$.

The semantics of boolean equation systems is such that each system $\mathcal{E}$ has a uniquely determined solution which is a valuation assigning a constant value in $\{0,1\}$ to variables occurring in $\mathcal{E}$. More precisely, the solution is a truth assignment to the variables $\{x_1, x_2, ..., x_n\}$ satisfying the fixpoint equations such that the right-most equations have higher priority over left-most equations (see e.g. [1,8,9]). In particular, we are interested in the value of the left-most variable x_1 in the solution of a boolean equation system. This is characterized in the following way.

Let α be a closed positive boolean expression (i.e. without occurrences of variables in $\mathcal{X}$). Then α has a uniquely determined value in the set $\{0, 1\}$ which we denote by $\|\alpha\|$. We define a substitution for positive boolean expressions. Given boolean expressions $\alpha, \beta \in B(\mathcal{X})$, let $\alpha[x := \beta]$ denote the expression α where all occurrences of variable x are substituted by β simultaneously.

Similarly, we extend the definition of substitutions to boolean equation systems in the following way. Let $\mathcal{E}$ be a boolean equation system over $\mathcal{X}$, and let $x \in \mathcal{X}$ and $\alpha \in B(\mathcal{X})$. A substitution $\mathcal{E}[x := \alpha]$ means the operation where $[x := \alpha]$ is applied simultaneously to all right-hand sides of equations in $\mathcal{E}$. We suppose that substitution $\alpha[x := \alpha]$ has priority over $\mathcal{E}[x := \alpha]$.

Definition 2 (The solution to a boolean equation system). *The solution to a boolean equation system $\mathcal{E}$, denoted by $[\![\mathcal{E}]\!]$, is a boolean value inductively defined by*

$$[\![\mathcal{E}]\!] = \begin{cases} \|\alpha[x := b_\sigma]\| & \text{if } \mathcal{E} \text{ is of the form } (\sigma x = \alpha) \\ [\![\mathcal{E}'[x := \alpha[x := b_\sigma]]]\!] & \text{if } \mathcal{E} \text{ is of the form } \mathcal{E}'(\sigma x = \alpha) \end{cases}$$

where b_σ is 0 when $\sigma = \mu$, and b_σ is 1 when $\sigma = \nu$.

The following example illustrates the above definition of the solution.

Example 1. Let $\mathcal{X}$ be the set $\{x_1, x_2, x_3\}$ and assume we are given a boolean equation system

$$\mathcal{E} \equiv (\nu x_1 = x_2 \wedge x_1)(\mu x_2 = x_1 \vee x_3)(\nu x_3 = x_3).$$

The solution, $[\![\mathcal{E}]\!]$, is given by
$[\![(\nu x_1 = x_2 \wedge x_1)(\mu x_2 = x_1 \vee x_3)(\nu x_3 = x_3)]\!] =$
$[\![(\nu x_1 = x_2 \wedge x_1)(\mu x_2 = x_1 \vee x_3)[x_3 := 1]]\!] =$
$[\![(\nu x_1 = x_2 \wedge x_1)(\mu x_2 = x_1 \vee 1)]\!] =$
$[\![(\nu x_1 = x_2 \wedge x_1)[x_2 := x_1 \vee 1]]\!] =$
$[\![(\nu x_1 = (x_1 \vee 1) \wedge x_1)]\!] = \|((1 \vee 1) \wedge 1)\| = 1$

There are also alternative characterizations of the solution to a boolean equation system, e.g. Proposition 3.6 in [8] and Definition 1.4.10 in [2], which coincide with the above definition, and may help to provide more insight in the semantics.

In order to formally estimate computational costs we need to define the *size* and the *alternation depth* of boolean equation systems.

Definition 3 (The size of a boolean equation system). *The size of a boolean equation system*

$$(\sigma_1 x_1 = \alpha_1)(\sigma_2 x_2 = \alpha_2) \ldots (\sigma_n x_n = \alpha_n)$$

is

$$\sum_{i=1}^{n} 1 + |\alpha_i|$$

where $|\alpha_i|$ is the number of variables in α_i.

We have taken a definition of alternation depth based on the sequential occurrences of μ's and ν's in a boolean equation system. More formally, the notion of alternation depth can be defined as follows.

Definition 4 (The alternation depth of a boolean equation system). *Let*

$$\mathcal{E} \equiv (\sigma_1 x_1 = \alpha_1)(\sigma_2 x_2 = \alpha_2) \ldots (\sigma_n x_n = \alpha_n)$$

be a boolean equation system. The alternation depth *of $\mathcal{E}$, denoted by $ad(\mathcal{E})$, is the number of variables x_j ($1 \leq j < n$) such that $\sigma_j \neq \sigma_{j+1}$.*

An alternative definition of alternation depth which abstracts from the syntactical appearance can be found in Definition 3.34 of [8]. The idea is that to determine the alternation depth only chains of equations in a boolean equation system must be followed that depend on each other. Using for instance Lemma 3.22 of [8] a boolean equation system can be reordered such that our notion of alternation depth and the notion of [8] coincide. Notice that for each equation system $\mathcal{E}$ with variables from $\mathcal{X}$ we have that $ad(\mathcal{E}) < |\mathcal{X}|$. That is, the alternation depth of a boolean equation system is always less than the number of variables involved.

We define conjunctive and disjunctive boolean equation systems in the following way.

Definition 5 (Disjunctive boolean equation system). *Let $(\sigma x = \alpha)$ be an equation. We call this equation disjunctive if no conjunction symbol $\wedge$ appears in α. Let $\mathcal{E}$ be a boolean equation system. We call $\mathcal{E}$ disjunctive if each equation in $\mathcal{E}$ is disjunctive.*

Definition 6 (Conjunctive boolean equation system). *Let $(\sigma x = \alpha)$ be an equation. We call this equation conjunctive if no disjunction symbol $\vee$ appears in α. Let $\mathcal{E}$ be a boolean equation system. We call $\mathcal{E}$ conjunctive if each equation in $\mathcal{E}$ is conjunctive.*

Given such a conjunctive or disjunctive system, we can view its variables as vertices of a graph and the dependencies between the variables as directed edges, obtaining another representation as defined below.

Definition 7 (The dependency graph of a boolean equation system). *Let $\mathcal{E}$ be a conjunctive or disjunctive boolean equation system*

$$(\sigma_1 x_1 = \alpha_1)(\sigma_2 x_2 = \alpha_2) \ldots (\sigma_n x_n = \alpha_n).$$

The dependency graph of $\mathcal{E}$ is a directed graph $G_\mathcal{E} = (V, E, \ell)$ where

- *$V = \{i \mid 1 \leq i \leq n\}$ is the set of nodes;*
- *$E \subseteq V \times V$ is the set of edges such that, for all equations $\sigma_i\, x_i = \alpha_i$, $(i, j) \in E$ iff a variable x_j occurs in α_i*
- *$\ell : V \to \{\mu, \nu\}$ is a labelling function defined by $\ell(i) = \sigma_i$.*

We now turn to the solution algorithms which refer to the disjunctive case only. The conjunctive case is fully dual and is therefore not treated explicitly.

3   The Depth-First Search Based Algorithm

The following essential lemma comes from [5], and it gives a useful characterization of a solution to a disjunctive boolean equation system.

Lemma 1. *Let $\mathcal{E}$ be a disjunctive boolean equation system*

$$(\sigma_1 x_1 = \alpha_1)(\sigma_2 x_2 = \alpha_2) \ldots (\sigma_n x_n = \alpha_n)$$

and let $G_\mathcal{E} = (V, E, \ell)$ be the dependency graph of $\mathcal{E}$. Let $[\![\mathcal{E}]\!]$ be the solution to $\mathcal{E}$. Then the following are equivalent:

1. *$[\![\mathcal{E}]\!] = 1$*
2. *$\exists j \in V$ with $\ell(j) = \nu$ such that:*
   (a) j is reachable from node 1 in G, and
   (b) G contains a cycle of which the lowest index of a node on this cycle is j.

Based on the above lemma, one can give a relatively simple algorithm to solve disjunctive boolean equation systems which relies on Tarjan's depth-first search algorithm [11] on directed graphs. This kind of approach is presented in [5] and we briefly review it here because in Section 5 we conduct experiments and comparisons with the algorithms.

The essential idea of the approach is to calculate maximal strongly connected components using the algorithm from [11]. A strongly connected component in a graph $G = (V, E, \ell)$ is a set of vertices $W \subseteq V$ such that for each pair of vertices $k, l \in W$ it is possible to reach l from k by following directed edges in E. In the sequel, we assume that all strongly connected components are maximal in the sense that there does not exist a larger set of vertices that is also a strongly connected component. When a strongly connected component is detected, a standard depth-first search is initiated for all ν labelled nodes residing in the component, in order to determine whether the component contains a node which satisfies condition 2 of Lemma 1.

This approach is well suited for many boolean equation systems. Since Tarjan's algorithm performs only a single depth-first search and can detect completed strongly connected components even before the whole graph has been traversed, the algorithm may find the solution by searching only a small portion of the dependency graph. In many cases, this leads to a very early detection of the solution.

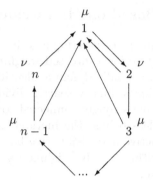

Fig. 1. A worst-case example for the depth-first search based algorithm from [5]

A disadvantage of the approach from [5] is that, in the worst case, it requires quadratic time in the size of an input dependency graph. For instance, consider the following example.

Example 2. For some even $n \in \mathbb{N}$ s.t. $n \geq 4$, consider the boolean equation system:

$$(\mu x_1 = x_2)$$

$$(\nu x_2 = x_1 \vee x_3)$$

$$(\mu x_3 = x_1 \vee x_4)$$

$$\vdots$$

$$(\mu x_{n-1} = x_1 \vee x_n)$$

$$(\nu x_n = x_1)$$

The above equation system is disjunctive, and the solution to variable x_1 is 0. Consider the dependency graph of this system depicted in Figure 1. In order to solve the system with the depth-first search based algorithm from [5] we need at least $O(n^2)$ steps.

Unfortunately, all previously known algorithms for solving conjunctive and disjunctive boolean equation systems take at least quadratic time in the size of a system in the worst case. For large boolean equations, which are typically encountered in model checking and preorder/equivalence checking of realistic systems, this often leads to unpleasant running times.

In the next section, we present a new sub-quadratic algorithm for finding a solution to a boolean equation system in disjunctive form. Then, in Section 5 the new algorithm is compared to the depth-first search based algorithm through experiments on protocol verification examples.

4 The Algorithm Based on Hierarchical Clustering

Tarjan [12] presents a hierarchical clustering algorithm for constructing a strong component decomposition tree for a directed weighted graph. Tarjan's clustering algorithm is an off-line, partially dynamic algorithm which is heavily based on three well-known techniques: binary search, divide-and-conquer, and graph theoretic technique for finding strongly connected components [11].

It turns out that the ideas behind the hierarchical clustering algorithm are also suited to solve conjunctive and disjunctive boolean equation systems. We provide here such an algorithm to solve disjunctive boolean equation systems. The conjunctive case is dual.

4.1 The New Algorithm

To enhance the readability, our presentation is at a high level of description. We chose not to show all the actual details of the implementation of our algorithm because they would substantially impede the clarity of presentation.

Before presenting the algorithm, we define a few useful notions that will be needed.

Definition 8. *Let*

$$\mathcal{E} \equiv (\sigma_1 x_1 = \alpha_1)(\sigma_2 x_2 = \alpha_2)\ldots(\sigma_n x_n = \alpha_n)$$

be a boolean equation system. An index j is a ν-starting point of $\mathcal{E}$ if $\sigma_j = \nu$, and either $j = 1$ or $\sigma_{j-1} = \mu$. If j is a ν-starting point then the ν-segment of j are those indices $j, j + 1, \ldots, j + k$ such that $\sigma_{j+i} = \nu$ $(0 \leq i \leq k)$ and either $j + k = n$ or $\sigma_{j+k+1} = \mu$.

Note that the alternation depth of a boolean equation system is twice the number of ν-starting points of a boolean equation system minus 0, 1 or 2 depending on whether or not there are initial and trailing μ's.

Definition 9. *Let $G = (V, E, \ell)$ be a dependency graph and $k \in V$. We define a restricted graph $G{\restriction}k = (V, E{\restriction}k, \ell)$ by taking*

$- E{\restriction}k = \{\langle i, j \rangle \in E \mid i \geq k \text{ and } j \geq k\}.$

In general, we may assume that a dependency graph of a boolean equation system does not contain any self-loops (i.e. an edge from a node to itself) because such edges can easily be removed from dependency graphs. Furthermore, we may assume that all nodes in a dependency graph of a boolean equation system are reachable from node 1 because the nodes that are not reachable from node 1 do not affect the solution. Thus, by Lemma 1, the condition that needs to be checked is whether there is a cycle in the dependency graph of which the lowest numbered node has label ν. The following algorithm performs this task efficiently.

To apply the algorithm on a boolean equation system $\mathcal{E}$ with n equations, $MinNuLoop(k, n, G)$ must be executed where G is the dependency graph of $\mathcal{E}$ and k is the first ν-starting point of $\mathcal{E}$. If such a starting point does not exist, then it holds that $[\![\mathcal{E}]\!] = 0$ and $\mathcal{E}$ is already solved.

Algorithm. We define the algorithm $MinNuLoop(k_1, k_2, G)$ where k_1 and k_2 are indices such that $k_1 \leq k_2$, $G = (V, E, \ell)$ is a dependency graph, $\ell(k_1) = \nu$ and $|E| \geq |V|$. The algorithm $MinNuLoop$ calculates whether there is an index k with $k_1 \leq k \leq k_2$, $\ell(k) = \nu$ and k is the smallest node on some cycle of G. The algorithm consists of the following steps:

1. Let s be the number of ν-starting points on $k_1, \ldots, k_2$. Let k_3 be the index of the $\lceil \frac{1}{2} s \rceil$-th ν-starting point on $k_1, \ldots, k_2$. Calculate the strongly connected components of $G \restriction k_3$. A strongly connected component is called trivial if it consists of one node and has no self-loop. Check whether any node on the ν-segment of k_3 resides in a non-trivial strongly connected component. If so, report "found" and stop. In the following steps, let $C(k)$ represent the strongly connected component of $G \restriction k_3$ containing node $k \in V$.

2. Here and in 5 below we check nodes in the range $k_1, \ldots, k_3 - 2$. Calculate the graph $G' = (V', E', \ell')$ by

$$
\begin{aligned}
V' &= \{\min\{C(i)\} \mid i \in V \text{ and } \exists j.\langle i, j \rangle \in E \text{ and } C(i) \neq C(j)\}, \\
E' &= \{\langle \min\{C(i)\}, \min\{C(j)\}\rangle \in V' \times V' \mid \langle i, j \rangle \in E, \ C(i) \neq C(j)\} \text{ and} \\
\ell'(\min\{C(i)\}) &= \begin{cases} \ell(i) \text{ if } C(i) \text{ trivial}, \\ \mu \quad \text{otherwise.} \end{cases}
\end{aligned}
$$

3. Let k_4 be the smallest index of a ν-starting point larger than k_3. We check nodes in the range $k_4, \ldots, k_2$ (see also item 6). Calculate the graph $G'' = (V'', E'', \ell)$ by

$$
\begin{aligned}
V'' &= \{i \in V \mid C(i) \text{ is not trivial}\} \text{ and} \\
E'' &= \{\langle i, j \rangle \in V'' \times V'' \mid \langle i, j \rangle \in E \text{ and } C(i) = C(j)\}.
\end{aligned}
$$

4. Forget G.
5. If $k_1 \leq k_3 - 2$, execute $MinNuLoop(k_1, k_3 - 2, G')$.
6. If $k_4 \leq k_2$, execute $MinNuLoop(k_4, k_2, G'')$.

The algorithm stops reporting "found" iff a cycle with a minimal ν-labelled node exists, or in other words iff the solution to the boolean equation system is $[\![\mathcal{E}]\!] = 1$.

Notice that the algorithm $MinNuLoop$ splits up the input dependency graph G into two graphs G' and G'', and then recurs on these new graphs. More precisely, in steps 2 and 5, the graph G' is a condensed version of the graph G, in which nodes belonging to the same strongly connected component of $G \restriction k_3$ (calculated in step 1) are compressed into a single node. In steps 3 and 6, the graph G'' is a subgraph of G, in which edges connecting different strongly connected components of $G \restriction k_3$ (calculated in step 1) are removed.

4.2 Correctness and Complexity

Since the algorithm $MinNuLoop$ is closely related to Tarjan's clustering algorithm, its correctness and complexity can be seen along the lines set out in [12]. However, as our presentation significantly differs from [12] and [6] – in that we work in the setting of boolean equation systems – we sketch the correctness and complexity arguments from scratch.

The correctness of the algorithm can be seen as follows. In step 1 it is straight-forwardly checked whether any node in the ν-segment of k_3 is the smallest ν-labelled node on a cycle.

When investigating whether some of the nodes in the range $k_1, \ldots, k_3 - 2$ (node $k_3 - 1$ is μ-labelled) is the smallest ν-labelled node on a cycle, the internal structures of non-trivial strongly connected components of $G \restriction k_3$ are irrelevant, and can therefore be safely collapsed. Thus, it suffices that all strongly connected components calculated in step 1 occur as compressed nodes of G'. In addition, we can take as edges of G' exactly those edges of E that bridge the strongly connected components of $G \restriction k_3$. Furthermore, nodes in V' without outgoing edges cannot contribute to cycles and can therefore be removed. Note that as all nodes without outgoing edges are removed from G', the precondition that $|E'| \geq |V'|$ to invoke $MinNuLoop$ is met.

When investigating whether some node in the range $k_4, \ldots, k_2$ is the smallest ν-labelled node on a cycle, we do not need to consider edges that connect nodes belonging to different strongly connected components of $G \restriction k_3$ because such edges cannot participate in any cycle whose smallest index is in the range $k_4, \ldots, k_2$.

The time complexity of the algorithm $MinNuLoop(k_1, k_2, G)$ is $O(|E| \log A)$ where $G = (V, E, \ell)$ and A is the number of ν-starting points on $k_1, \ldots, k_2$. As noted elsewhere in this paper $2A$ is approximately the alternation depth of the boolean equation system that corresponds to G.

The time complexity has a nice justification. In step 1 of $MinNuLoop$ it takes $O(|V|) \leq O(|E|)$ to determine k_3. Calculating $G \restriction k_3$, the strongly connected components and checking whether any node on the ν-segment of k_3 resides on a non-trivial strongly connected component requires $O(|E|)$ time.

In step 2, 3 and 4 the graphs G' and G'' are constructed to replace G. This can clearly be done in time $O(|E|)$.

A crucial observation is that for each edge $\langle i, j \rangle \in E$ at most one edge shows up in either E' or E'', depending on whether $C(i) = C(j)$. This means that $|E'| + |E''| \leq |E|$. Furthermore, if the number of ν-starting points in $k_1, \ldots, k_2$ is A, then there are at most $\frac{1}{2}A$ ν-starting points in both $k_1, \ldots, k_3 - 1$ and $k_4, \ldots, k_2$. So $MinNuLoop(k_1, k_3 - 1, G')$ has time complexity $O(|E'| \log \frac{1}{2}A)$ and $MinNuLoop(k_4, k_2, G'')$ has time complexity $O(|E''| \log \frac{1}{2}A)$. So, the time complexity of $MinNuLoop(k_1, k_2, G)$ is

$$O(|E|) + O(|E'| \log \frac{1}{2}A) + O(|E''| \log \frac{1}{2}A) \leq O(|E| + |E| \log \frac{1}{2}A) = O(|E| \log A).$$

The time complexity for solving a boolean equation system also contains the generation of the dependency graph, and is easily seen to be $O(e \log d)$ where e is the size of the boolean equation system and d the alternation depth.

The space complexity of $MinNuLoop(k_1, k_2, G)$ is $O(|E|)$. In order to see this it suffices to note that the graphs constructed in step 2 and 3 are together smaller than the graph G, which is thrown away in step 4. So, the memory footage is only reduced while executing the algorithm. As generating the dependency graph also takes linear space, solving a disjunctive boolean equation system also takes linear space.

5   Experiments with Sliding Window Protocols

We have implemented both the depth-first search based algorithm from [5] and the new algorithm in the C programming language. We have done experiments with models of sliding window protocols described in [10]. To investigate and compare the performance of the algorithms, we have studied three variants of the protocol with different behaviours:

- *Variation 1*: This is an unidirectional version of the protocol where a sender receives data through a channel and passes it to a receiver. There are 2 data elements, window size is 2, and buffer size is 4 at both receiving and sending side.
- *Variation 2*: This is a bidirectional, one bit sliding window protocol where, in addition to the feature of variation 1, also the receiver receives data via a channel and passes it to the sender. There is 1 data element, window size is 1 and buffer size is 2 at both receiving and sending side.
- *Variation 3*: As variation 2, this is a bidirectional version with buffer size 2, window size 1, and 1 data element. However, *piggy backing* is used to guarantee a better bandwidth, i.e. acknowledgements, which are sent between the sender and the receiver, are appended to data elements.

Each of the variations was modelled with the μCRL tool set [3] and its state space, combined with liveness and fairness related formulas, was converted to boolean equation systems for input by our implementations of the solution algorithms. In the conversion, we used the translation from μ-calculus to boolean equation systems as described in [8].

The results of our experiments are shown in Table 1. The first column contains the names of the checked formulas which are given explicitly below the table. The column marked "Equation system" gives the number of left hand side variables and the size of the corresponding boolean equation system. The columns marked "New algorithm" and "Algorithm in [5]" give the execution times in seconds for the algorithms to solve the boolean equation systems measured as cpu time. The reported times are the average of three runs on a 1.0Ghz AMD Athlon running Linux with sufficient main memory.

The checked μ-calculus formulas can be explained as follows[1]. Formula A states unconditional fairness for the reception of data by requiring that reception of data happens infinitely often along every infinite execution. Formula B is related to counting silent actions and states the property that the protocol does only finitely many τ-actions, no matter what else it does. Formula C is a liveness property which states that whenever a message is sent then eventually it is received. Formula D expresses a strong fairness property that delivery of data

---

[1] We use standard syntax and semantics of μ-calculus, see e.g. [4] for detailed definitions.

Table 1. Comparison of the new algorithm and the algorithm from [5] for checking property ϕ for different versions of the sliding window protocol

Variation 1: 44540 states, 183344 transitions			
ϕ	Equation system	New algorithm	Algorithm in [5]
A	54265 193069	0.10	29.69
B	87464 226268	0.32	244.90
C	76348 325660	0.70	0.01
D	69476 269152	1.66	86.29
E	115716 507376	0.51	1.44

Variation 2: 17040 states, 79472 transitions			
ϕ	Equation system	New algorithm	Algorithm in [5]
A	19185 81617	0.08	69.35
B	33904 96336	0.10	44.88
C	30376 146344	0.21	0.00
D	36832 137892	0.79	46.48
E	48600 232648	1.39	4.37

Variation 3: 23728 states, 112960 transitions			
ϕ	Equation system	New algorithm	Algorithm in [5]
A	26337 115569	0.06	14.51
B	47152 136384	0.07	62.81
C	42808 208816	0.11	0.00
D	50560 194356	0.28	407.03
E	70072 338364	2.38	4.37

$r1(x) \equiv$ receive data x
$s4(x) \equiv$ send data x

$A \equiv \nu X.\mu Y.([r1(d1)]X \wedge [\neg r1(d1)]Y)$
$B \equiv \mu X.\nu Y.([\tau]X \wedge [\neg \tau]Y)$
$C \equiv \nu Z.([s4(d1)](\mu Y.\langle-\rangle\top \wedge [\neg r1(d1)]Y) \wedge [-]Z)$
$D \equiv \nu X.\mu Y.\nu Z.([s4(d1)]X \wedge (\langle s4(d1)\rangle\top \Rightarrow [\neg s4(d1)]Y) \wedge [\neg s4(d1)]Z)$
$E \equiv \nu Y.([s4(d1)]\psi \wedge [-]Y)$ where ψ is given below
$\psi \equiv \mu X.\nu Y1.(([s4(d1)]\bot \vee [\neg r1(d1)](\nu Y2.([r1(d1)]\bot \vee X) \wedge [\neg r1(d1)]Y2)) \wedge [\neg r1(d1)]Y1)$

via send action is fairly treated. The last formula is a more involved property which expresses liveness under fairness. More precisely, property E says that, for any execution, if the sender is enabled infinitely often and the receiver is enabled infinitely often, then whenever a message is sent eventually it is received.

In almost all cases the time consumption by the new algorithm was considerably less than by the algorithm from [5]. In only three cases, namely variations 1-3 C, the time consumed by the new algorithm was slightly more than that by the algorithm [5]. For instance, in variation 3 the new algorithm spent less than 3 seconds to solve all formulas A-E while the corresponding total running time for [5] was around 8 minutes. Based on these computational results we may draw the conclusion that the new algorithm substantially outperforms the one from [5] in time.

We were not able to conduct a comparative study with other approaches because our formulas have non-zero alternation depths. All other publicly available tools are for alternation-free boolean equation systems (e.g. [9]).

6   Heuristic Issues

As indicated by the performance measures in the previous section, there exist examples where the new algorithm fares worse than the one from [5]. This suggests to use heuristics to guide the new algorithm to find solutions more quickly.

In steps 5 and 6 of *MinNuLoop* algorithm, two distinct recursive calls are done. It turns out that the order of these recursive calls does not affect the correctness of the algorithm. Steps 5 and 6 might as well be executed in any possible order as long as they are both executed after step 4. But, the differences in the execution order certainly may be reflected in the performance of the algorithm. To investigate the impact of changing the execution order of the recursive calls, various heuristics were used.

The results are shown in Table 2. Only the performance for the new algorithm is described in the table. The meaning of the first two columns is the same as in Table 1. The remaining columns contain the measures for the heuristics; the number indicates the cpu time in seconds to find the solution. Here, the column "None" agrees with the column "New algorithm" in Table 1. Finally, the last row describes the total cpu time in seconds to solve all the problems.

The following heuristics were investigated:

H1 Reversed execution order of the recursive calls in steps 5 and 6; i.e. execute step 6 first, and then execute step 5.

Table 2. Effect of heuristics on the new algorithm

Equation system		Heuristic			
Variation	ϕ	None	H1	H2	H3
1	A	0.10	0.10	0.11	0.09
1	B	0.32	0.17	0.16	0.32
1	C	0.70	0.22	0.23	0.78
1	D	1.66	0.18	0.19	1.69
1	E	0.51	0.36	0.36	0.52
2	A	0.08	0.05	0.05	0.08
2	B	0.20	0.07	0.07	0.09
2	C	0.21	0.09	0.10	0.21
2	D	0.79	0.10	0.10	0.79
2	E	1.39	0.17	0.16	1.39
3	A	0.06	0.06	0.06	0.06
3	B	0.07	0.07	0.07	0.07
3	C	0.11	0.11	0.10	0.10
3	D	0.28	0.13	0.13	0.29
3	E	2.38	0.20	0.20	2.35
Total cpu time		8.86	2.08	2.09	8.83

H2 Selects those recursive calls that lead to smaller graphs first; i.e. if the graph G' constructed in step 2 has less edges than the graph G'' constructed in step 3, execute step 5 first, and then execute step 6. Otherwise, execute step 6 first, and then execute step 5.

H3 Selects those recursive calls that lead to larger graphs first; i.e. if the graph G' constructed in step 2 has more edges than the graph G'' constructed in step 3, execute step 5 first, and then execute step 6. Otherwise, execute step 6 first, and then execute step 5.

As the table shows, heuristics H1 and H2 performed up to a factor 10 better than using no heuristic at all. The performance of heuristic H3, which selects those recursive calls that lead to larger graphs first, was the worst.

One must notice that the differences in the performance are very small and, therefore, they can be influenced by other factors too. Of course, some heuristics might work well on some boolean equation systems, and poorly for others. But, the results indicate that changing the execution order of the recursive calls has a clear impact on the solution times.

7   Conclusions

We have presented an alternative to the algorithms in [5,8] for solving conjunctive and disjunctive boolean equation systems. Our algorithm has better estimation of its worst-case complexity than the previous algorithms. Practical evaluation on protocol verification benchmarks shows that the theoretical improvement also leads to practical improvements over the existing algorithm [5]. The new algorithm is often able to find solutions more quickly, and additional reduction in time consumption can be gained by using suitable heuristics to guide the search.

Acknowledgments. Jaco van de Pol is thanked for providing useful comments. The work of Misa Keinänen was funded by Academy of Finland (project 211025) and Helsinki Graduate School in Computer Science and Engineering.

References

1. H.R. Andersen. Model checking and boolean graphs. Theoretical Computer Science, 126 (1994) 3-30.
2. A. Arnold and D. Niwinski. Rudiments of μ-calculus. Studies in logic and the foundations of mathematics, 146. Elsevier, 2001.
3. S. Blom, W. Fokkink, J. Groote, I. van Langevelde, B. Lisser and J. van de Pol. μCRL: a toolset for analysing algebraic specifications. In Proceedings of the 13th Conference on Computer Aided Verification (CAV'2001), Paris, Lecture Notes in Computer Science 2102, pp. 250-254, Springer-Verlag, July 2001.
4. J. Bradfield and C. Stirling. Modal Logics and mu-Calculi: An introduction. Chapter 4 of Handbook of Process Algebra. J.A. Bergstra, A. Ponse and S.A. Smolka, editors. Elsevier, 2001.

5. J.F. Groote and M.K. Keinänen. Solving Disjunctive/Conjunctive Boolean Equation Systems with Alternating Fixed Points. In K. Jensen and A. Podelski, editors, Proc. 10th International Conference on Tools and Algorithms for the Construction and Analysis of Systems (TACAS'2004), volume 2988 of Lecture Notes in Computer Science, pages 436-450. Springer, 2004.
6. V. King, O. Kupferman and M.Y. Vardi. On the complexity of parity word automata. Proc. of 4th International Conference on Foundations of Software Science and Computation Structures, volume 2030 of Lecture Notes in Computer Science, pages 276–286. Springer, 2001.
7. D. Kozen. Results on the propositional μ-calculus. Theoretical computer Science 27 (1983) 333-354.
8. A. Mader. Verification of Modal Properties using Boolean Equation Systems. PhD thesis, Technical University of Munich, 1997.
9. R. Mateescu. A Generic On-the-Fly Solver for Alternation-Free Boolean Equation Systems. In Proceedings of Conf. on Tools and Algorithms for the Construction and Analysis of Systems, Lecture Notes in Computer Science 2619 (Springer Verlag, 2003) 81-96.
10. A. Tanenbaum. Computer Networks. Prentice Hall PTR, fourth edition, 2003.
11. R.E. Tarjan. Depth first search and linear graph algorithms. SIAM Journal of Computing. 1(2):146-160, 1972.
12. R.E. Tarjan. A hierarchical clustering algorithm using strong components. Information Processing Letters, 14(1):26-29, 1982.

Using Fairness Constraints
in Process-Algebraic Verification

Antti Puhakka

Tampere University of Technology,
Institute of Software Systems,
P.O. Box 553, FIN-33101 Tampere, Finland
antti.puhakka@tut.fi

Abstract. Although liveness and fairness have been used for a long time
in classical model checking, with process-algebraic methods they have
seen far less use. One problem is that it is difficult to combine fairness
constraints with the compositionality of process algebra. Here we show
how a class of fairness constraints can be applied in a consistent way to
processes in the compositional setting. We use only ordinary, but possibly
infinite, LTSs as our models of processes. In many cases the infinite LTSs
are part of a larger system, which can again be represented as a finite
LTS. We show how this finiteness can be recovered, namely, we present
an algorithm that checks whether a finite representation exists and, if
it does, constructs a finite LTS that is equivalent to the infinite system.
Even in the negative case, the system produced by the algorithm is a
conservative estimate of the infinite system. Such a finite representation
can be placed as a component in further compositional analysis just like
any other LTS.

1 Introduction

In the verification of concurrent systems it is often important to show that the
system eventually performs some desired task. Such properties are called *liveness*
properties [2]. For proving liveness properties some *fairness assumptions* [3,9,14]
often have to be added to the system, meaning that the system is not allowed
to continually favour some choices at the expense of others.

Within classical model checking [6,22] liveness and fairness have been used
in one form or another for quite some time. However, in the context of *process-
algebraic* methods such as *CCS* [16] and *CSP* [12,23] they have seen relatively
little use. As shown in [21], one reason for this is that fairness properties are
tricky to combine with the compositionality of process algebra, because outside processes can interfere with the actions used in the fairness constraint. As
also discussed in [21], another problem is that most process-algebraic semantics do not preserve enough fairness-related information about the behaviour of
systems.

In this article we use a variant of CSP called *CFFD* (*Chaos-Free Failures
Divergences*), which is especially well suited for handling liveness properties, because it preserves both divergences (livelocks) and the behaviour after executing

D.V. Hung and M. Wirsing (Eds.): ICTAC 2005, LNCS 3722, pp. 546–561, 2005.
© Springer-Verlag Berlin Heidelberg 2005

a divergence trace. Also, it allows the use of infinite and infinitely branching processes [13,27,26].

Some previous approaches have aimed at using a "global" fairness assumption in a process-algebraic system, meaning that all processes or enabled actions should eventually proceed. This has been done either by changing the operational semantics, as in [8], or by considering only the fair executions in the semantics, as in [5,11,17]. Others have suggested adding some extra constraints to the process to restrict the infinite executions, such as ω-regular expressions [18] or Büchi states [7]. However, a potential problem in such an approach is that a process may be unable to fulfill the requirements of the additional constraint, which creates a situation with no meaningful interpretation. Furthermore, this can happen as the result of the parallel composition of "healthy" subprocesses, as discussed in [21]. These and a number of other references are discussed in more detail in [20].

In this paper we use only ordinary LTSs (Labelled Transition Systems), so processes will always have an unambiguous behaviour, and we can clearly define how fairness constraints should change the behaviour of systems. The fairness requirements are expressed in linear temporal logic, and we allow the resulting LTSs to be infinite, if necessary. However, we will see that such infinite processes are often part of a larger system which can again be represented as a finite LTS. We will describe an algorithm for checking whether a finite representation exists and, if so, for constructing a finite LTS that is equivalent to the original system. The result can then be used as a component in further compositional analysis. In fact, even when no exact finite representation of the fair system exists, the finite model is a conservative estimate of the fair system. However, it turns out that the complexity of deciding whether an exact finite representation exists is higher than that of building the representation. Fortunately, the parameter system of the analysis can be significantly smaller than the full state-space of the system.

This paper extends the earlier work in [21] by using a significantly more general class of fairness constraints, by presenting the above-mentioned algorithm for constructing a finite model of the fair system, and also by extending the set of systems to which such constraints can be applied.

The paper is organised as follows. In the next section we will review the basic definitions concerning LTSs, process operators and behavioural equivalences. In Section 3 we will consider fairness operators that add fairness constraints to systems, and we state the requirements we believe these operators should fulfill in order to be meaningful in process-algebraic verification. Then, in Section 4 we present the class of fairness properties that we will use. These are properties of the form "if something happens infinitely many times, then something else also has to happen infinitely many times". In Section 5 we define a fairness operator that implements the fairness constraints by placing the target system in parallel with a "fairness LTS". We then show that the operator fulfills all the stated requirements. In Section 6 we present an algorithm for constructing a finite representation of the fair system. In Section 7 we present some examples using the approach, and in Section 8 we present our conclusions.

2   Background

The behaviour of a process consists of executing *actions*. There are two kinds of actions: *visible* and *invisible*. Invisible actions are denoted with a special symbol τ. The behaviour of a process is represented as a labelled transition system. This is a directed graph whose edges are labelled with action names, with one state distinguished as the initial state.

Definition 1. *A* labelled transition system, *abbreviated* LTS, *is a four-tuple* $(S, \Sigma, \Delta, \hat{s})$, *where*

- *S is the set of* states,
- *Σ, the* alphabet, *is the set of the* visible actions *of the process; we assume that $\tau \notin \Sigma$,*
- *$\Delta \subseteq S \times (\Sigma \cup \{\tau\}) \times S$ is the set of* transitions, *and*
- *$\hat{s} \in S$ is the* initial state.

We also use Σ_L to denote the alphabet of L, and similarly with S_L, Δ_L and $\hat{s}_L$. Let A^* denote the set of finite and A^ω the set of infinite sequences of elements of a set A. The empty sequence is denoted with ε, and a^ω denotes the infinite sequence of the symbol a. For a finite or infinite sequence ρ, the *restriction* of ρ to B, denoted $restr(\rho, B)$, means the result of removing all actions from ρ that are not in B.

The following notation is useful for talking about the execution of a process. The " $-\rho\rightarrow$ "-notation requires that all actions along the execution path are listed, while the τ-actions are skipped in the " $=\eta\Rightarrow$ "-notation.

Definition 2. *Let* $(S, \Sigma, \Delta, \hat{s})$ *be an LTS, let* $s, s' \in S$, $a, a_1, a_2, \ldots \in \Sigma \cup \{\tau\}$. *We write*

- *$s -a\rightarrow s'$ if and only if $(s, a, s') \in \Delta$,*
- *$s -a_1 a_2 \cdots a_n\rightarrow s'$ if and only if there are $s_0, s_1, \ldots, s_n \in S$ such that $s = s_0$, $s_n = s'$ and $s_{i-1} -a_i\rightarrow s_i$ when $1 \le i \le n$,*
- *$s -a_1 a_2 a_3 \cdots \rightarrow$ is defined similarly for an infinite execution,*
- *$s -a_1 a_2 \cdots a_n\rightarrow$ if and only if there is $s' \in S$ such that $s -a_1 a_2 \cdots a_n\rightarrow s'$.*

We also write $s =\sigma\Rightarrow s'$ for $\sigma \in \Sigma^*$ if and only if there is $\rho \in (\Sigma \cup \{\tau\})^*$ such that $s -\rho\rightarrow s'$ and $restr(\rho, \Sigma) = \sigma$, and similarly for $s =\eta\Rightarrow$, where $\eta \in \Sigma^* \cup \Sigma^\omega$.

We need the following semantic sets extracted from an LTS. A *trace* of an LTS is the sequence of visible actions generated by any finite execution that starts in the initial state. An infinite execution that starts in the initial state generates either an *infinite trace* or a *divergence trace*, depending on whether the number of visible actions in the execution is infinite or finite. The *stable failures* describe the ability of the LTS to refuse actions after executing a particular trace.

Definition 3. *Let* $L = (S, \Sigma, \Delta, \hat{s})$ *be an LTS.*

- *$Tr(L) = \{ \sigma \in \Sigma^* \mid \hat{s} =\sigma\Rightarrow \}$ is the set of* traces *of L.*

- $Inftr(L) = \{ \xi \in \Sigma^\omega \mid \hat{s} = \xi \Rightarrow \}$ *is the set of* infinite traces *of L.*
- $Divtr(L) = \{ \sigma \in \Sigma^* \mid \exists s \in S : \hat{s} = \sigma \Rightarrow s \wedge s - \tau^\omega \rightarrow \}$ *is the set of* divergence
  traces *of L.*
- $Sfail(L) = \{ (\sigma, A) \in \Sigma^* \times 2^\Sigma \mid \exists s \in S : \hat{s} = \sigma \Rightarrow s \wedge \forall a \in A \cup \{\tau\} : \neg(s - a \rightarrow) \}$
  is the set of stable failures *of L.*

The *parallel composition operator* defined below forces precisely those component processes to participate in the execution of a visible action that have the action in their alphabets. The invisible action is always executed by exactly one component process at a time. We first define the product of LTSs as the LTS that satisfies the above description and has as its set of states the Cartesian product of the component state sets. We then define parallel composition by picking the part of the product that is reachable from the initial state of the product.

Definition 4. *Let* $L_1 = (S_1, \Sigma_1, \Delta_1, \hat{s}_1), \ldots, L_n = (S_n, \Sigma_n, \Delta_n, \hat{s}_n)$ *be LTSs. Their product is the LTS* $(S', \Sigma, \Delta', \hat{s})$ *such that the following hold:*

- $S' = S_1 \times \cdots \times S_n$
- $\Sigma = \Sigma_1 \cup \cdots \cup \Sigma_n$
- $((s_1, \ldots, s_n), a, (s'_1, \ldots, s'_n)) \in \Delta'$ *if and only if either*
  - $a = \tau$, *and* $(s_i, \tau, s'_i) \in \Delta_i$ *for some* $1 \leq i \leq n$,
    and $s_j = s'_j$ *for all* $1 \leq j \leq n$, $j \neq i$
  - $a \in \Sigma$, *and for each* $1 \leq i \leq n$ *either* $a \in \Sigma_i$ *and* $(s_i, a, s'_i) \in \Delta_i$, *or*
    $a \notin \Sigma_i$ *and* $s_i = s'_i$
- $\hat{s} = (\hat{s}_1, \cdots, \hat{s}_n)$

The parallel composition $L_1 \| \cdots \| L_2$ *is the LTS* $(S, \Sigma, \Delta, \hat{s})$ *such that*

- $S = \{ s \in S' \mid \exists \sigma \in \Sigma^* : \hat{s} = \sigma \Rightarrow s \}$
- $\Delta = \Delta' \cap (S \times (\Sigma \cup \{\tau\}) \times S)$

It is straightforward to show that "$\|$" is symmetric and associative, so that $L_1 \| L_2 \cong L_2 \| L_1$ and $(L_1 \| L_2) \| L_3 \cong L_1 \| (L_2 \| L_3)$, where "$\cong$" denotes isomorphism. Therefore, if we wish, we can discard the parentheses and write $L_1 \| L_2 \| L_3$, and similarly with any greater number of processes.

The *hiding* operator converts given visible actions into τ-actions and removes them from the alphabet.

Definition 5. *Let* $L = (S, \Sigma, \Delta, \hat{s})$ *be an LTS and* X *any set of action names. Then* **hide** X **in** L *is the LTS* $(S, \Sigma', \Delta', \hat{s})$ *such that the following hold:*

- $\Sigma' = \Sigma - X$
- $(s, a, s') \in \Delta'$ *if and only if*
  $a = \tau \wedge \exists b \in X : (s, b, s') \in \Delta$, *or* $a \notin X \wedge (s, a, s') \in \Delta$.

We now define the CFFD-model and CFFD-equivalence, which will be our main equivalence notion in this article. We also define CFFD-preorder. Intuitively, preorder means that the smaller process is "better" or "more deterministic" than the larger one.

Definition 6. *Let L and L' be LTSs with the same alphabet.*

- *The* CFFD *model of L is the 3-tuple $(Sfail(L), Divtr(L), Inftr(L))$*
- $L \simeq_{\text{CFFD}} L' \iff$
  $[\, Sfail(L) = Sfail(L') \wedge Divtr(L) = Divtr(L') \wedge Inftr(L) = Inftr(L') \,]$
- $L \leq_{\text{CFFD}} L' \iff$
  $[\, Sfail(L) \subseteq Sfail(L') \wedge Divtr(L) \subseteq Divtr(L') \wedge Inftr(L) \subseteq Inftr(L') \,]$

The traces are not included in the CFFD model because they can be determined from *Sfail* and *Divtr* by the equation $Tr(L) = Divtr(L) \cup \{\, \sigma \in \Sigma^* \mid (\sigma, \emptyset) \in Sfail(L) \,\}$ [27].

It should be noted that when certain process-algebraic operators are used, a component called *stability* must be included in the CFFD model. This one bit of information tells whether or not there are τ-transitions from the initial state of the LTS. However, with parallel composition and hiding this component is not needed, so we will not use it here.

An important property of an equivalence is that when a component process in a system is replaced by an equivalent process, the system should remain equivalent to the original one. This is formally captured by the *congruence* property.

Definition 7. *An equivalence "$\simeq$" is a congruence with respect to a process operator $op(L_1, \ldots, L_n)$ if and only if $L_1 \simeq L_1' \wedge \cdots \wedge L_n \simeq L_n'$ implies $op(L_1, \ldots, L_n) \simeq op(L_1', \ldots, L_n')$.*

CFFD-equivalence is a congruence with respect to parallel composition and hiding. Similarly, CFFD-preorder is a *precongruence* (*monotonic*) with respect to parallel composition and hiding. [27]

3   Temporal Logic and Fairness Operators

The desired properties of reactive and concurrent systems are often expressed by using *linear temporal logic* [15,19]. We next present a straightforward adaptation of the logic to our process-algebraic framework.

Definition 8. *A formula is generated by the grammar $\psi ::= \text{true} \mid a \mid \neg\psi \mid \psi \vee \psi \mid \psi\, \mathcal{U}\, \psi$, where a is an action name. We also use the following denotations: $false \equiv \neg true$, $\psi \wedge \phi \equiv \neg(\neg\psi \vee \neg\phi)$, $\psi \Rightarrow \phi \equiv \neg\psi \vee \phi$, $\Diamond\psi \equiv true\, \mathcal{U}\, \psi$ ("eventually"), $\Box\psi \equiv \neg\Diamond\neg\psi$ ("always").*

We will define the semantics of formulas on the infinite executions of systems.

Definition 9. *Let $L = (S, \Sigma, \Delta, \hat{s})$ be an LTS. The set of the infinite executions of L is $infex(L) = \{\, s_0 a_1 s_1 a_2 s_2 a_3 \cdots \mid \hat{s} = s_0 \wedge \forall i \geq 1 : s_{i-1} -a_i \rightarrow s_i \,\}$.*

Below we use the following notation: if $\eta = s_0 a_1 s_1 a_2 s_2 a_3 \cdots$ is an infinite execution, then $acts(\eta)$ is the sequence of actions $a_1 a_2 a_3 \cdots$ and η^i is the ith suffix $s_i a_{i+1} s_{i+1} a_{i+2} \cdots$.

Definition 10. *Let $L = (S, \Sigma, \Delta, \hat{s})$ be an LTS and $\eta = s_0 a_1 s_1 a_2 s_2 a_3 \cdots$ an infinite execution of L. Then*

- $(L, \eta) \models true$
- $(L, \eta) \models a$ *iff* $a_1 = a$
- $(L, \eta) \models \neg \psi$ *iff* $not\ (L, \eta) \models \psi$
- $(L, \eta) \models \psi \lor \phi$ *iff* $(L, \eta) \models \psi$ *or* $(L, \eta) \models \phi$
- $(L, \eta) \models \psi\,\mathcal{U}\,\phi$ *iff* $\exists j \geq 0 : (L, \eta^j) \models \phi$ *and* $\forall k, 0 \leq k < j : (L, \eta^k) \models \psi$

The properties of reactive systems are usually divided into *safety properties*, expressing requirements of the form "nothing bad must ever happen", and *liveness properties*, expressing requirements of the form "something good must eventually happen" [2]. *Fairness properties* are liveness properties which state that even though the system makes nondeterministic choices, it does not infinitely favour some choices at the expense of others.

Often to verify liveness properties we first add *fairness constraints* to the system. These are fairness properties that are assumed to hold of the system, expressing the idea that the modelled system is behaving fairly. To use such assumptions in process-algebraic verification, we want to have, for each fairness constraint ϕ, a corresponding "fairness operator" Φ_ϕ that can be applied to an LTS, and which produces a new LTS having the same finite behaviour, namely traces and stable failures, and precisely those infinite behaviours (infinite traces and divergences) that can be executed while assuming the fairness constraint. We should notice, however, that not every fairness constraint can be applied to every system. This is because the constraint may require something that the system is unable to do without also changing its finite behaviour. For this reason we assume that for each fairness formula we have defined a corresponding set of *compatible* LTSs, denoted by *COMP*, to which ϕ may be applied.

However, it will sometimes be very useful to associate a hiding operation with the fairness operator. Namely, we can apply the fairness constraint to a wider class of systems if there is a guarantee that certain actions in the constraint will be hidden *immediately after* applying the fairness operator. This will be illustrated in Section 7. Therefore, the compatibility set will depend on both ψ and a "hiding set" H, which is to be hidden after applying the fairness operator (notice that the latter is different from [20] and [21]). We formulate the requirement as follows:

Definition 11. *An operator Φ_ϕ is a* fairness operator *for formula ϕ with compatibility set $COMP(\phi, H)$ if and only if for every $L \in COMP(\phi, H)$*

- $Tr(L_1) = Tr(L_2)$ *and* $Sfail(L_1) = Sfail(L_2)$, *and*
- $Divtr(L_1) =$
  $\left\{\, \sigma \in \Sigma_{L_2}^* \mid \exists \eta \in infex(L) : ((L, \eta) \models \phi) \land restr(acts(\eta), \Sigma_{L_2}) = \sigma \,\right\}$, *and*
- $Inftr(L_1) =$
  $\left\{\, \xi \in \Sigma_{L_2}^\omega \mid \exists \eta \in infex(L) : ((L, \eta) \models \phi) \land restr(acts(\eta), \Sigma_{L_2}) = \xi \,\right\}$,

where $L_1 = $ **hide** H **in** $\Phi_\phi(L)$ *and $L_2 = $* **hide** H **in** L.

However, some care must be taken in using fairness in the compositional setting of process algebra, because in such a setting other, yet unknown, processes may interfere with the behaviour of the process for which we define the fairness constraint. Firstly, when we are using a particular behavioural equivalence, we should make sure that this a congruence with respect to the fairness operator. Furthermore, the fairness operator would typically be applied to some subprocess L (e.g., a communication channel) which can be placed in a larger context $C[\cdot]$ (e.g., a protocol system). The property of the underlying system expressed by the fairness constraint should remain the same in the larger context. Therefore, within some reasonable limits, it should make no difference whether the same fairness constraint is assumed of L or of the composition $C[L]$. We will refer to these desired properties of the fairness operator as *context-independence*:

Definition 12. *Let Φ_ϕ be a fairness operator for formula ϕ which is expressed in terms of the actions $\mathcal{F}$. We say that Φ_ϕ is* context-independent *with respect to "$\simeq$", if and only if "$\simeq$" is a congruence with respect to Φ_ϕ, and for all L in $COMP(\psi, H)$ it holds that*

- $\Phi_\phi(L) \parallel L' \simeq \Phi_\phi(L \parallel L')$ *for any LTS L' such that $\Sigma_{L'} \cap H = \emptyset$*
- **hide** X **in** $\Phi_\phi(L) \simeq \Phi_\phi(\textbf{hide } X \textbf{ in } L)$ *for any X such that $X \cap \mathcal{F} = \emptyset$.*

4   A Class of Fairness Constraints

Some types of fairness properties (such as *weak fairness* and *strong fairness*) require the execution of an action if it is sufficiently often enabled. However, as discussed in [21], it is difficult to use such properties with weak behavioural process-algebraic semantics, because these do not preserve information about the enabledness of actions in infinite executions. Therefore, we here concentrate on fairness properties that can be used with such semantics. These will be fairness properties of the form "if something happens infinitely often, then something else also has to happen infinitely often".

In [21], fairness formulas of the form $\Box\Diamond a_1 \vee \cdots \vee \Box\Diamond a_m \Rightarrow \Box\Diamond b_1 \vee \cdots \vee \Box\Diamond b_n$ were used. Here, we consider formulas of the form

$$\alpha \Rightarrow \beta$$

where α and β are any formulas constructed from action names by using the operators "$\vee$", "$\wedge$" and "$\Box\Diamond$" ("infinitely often"), with the restriction that every action name must reside within the scope of at least one "$\Box\Diamond$"-operator (because we are interested in fairness properties, not individual actions).

Formally, α and β are any formulas generated by the grammar $\phi ::= false \mid \phi \wedge \phi \mid \phi \vee \phi \mid \Box\Diamond\phi_1$ and $\phi_1 ::= \phi_1 \wedge \phi_1 \mid \phi_1 \vee \phi_1 \mid \Box\Diamond\phi_1 \mid a$, where a is any visible action name. Because we allow β to be *false*, the complete formula may become $\neg\alpha$.

Let us denote the set of formulas of this form by F. We next transform the fairness formulas into a normal form where, for technical convenience, the left side is in a conjunctive form and the right side in a disjunctive form; the detailed proof is given in [20].

Proposition 1. *Every formula in F that is not trivially true can be given in the form*

$$\mathcal{A}_1 \wedge \mathcal{A}_2 \wedge \cdots \wedge \mathcal{A}_m \;\Rightarrow\; \mathcal{B}_1 \vee \mathcal{B}_2 \vee \cdots \vee \mathcal{B}_n,$$

where $\mathcal{A}_i = \Box\Diamond a_1^i \vee \Box\Diamond a_2^i \vee \cdots \vee \Box\Diamond a_{u_i}^i$, $\mathcal{B}_j = \Box\Diamond b_1^j \wedge \Box\Diamond b_2^j \wedge \cdots \wedge \Box\Diamond b_{v_j}^j$, and a_k^i and b_l^j are names of actions. If $n = 0$, then the formula is $\neg(\mathcal{A}_1 \wedge \mathcal{A}_2 \wedge \cdots \wedge \mathcal{A}_m)$.

From now on we will assume that the fairness formulas have already been given in the above form. We will denote such a formula by

$$\psi(\mathcal{A}_1, \ldots, \mathcal{A}_m; \mathcal{B}_1, \ldots, \mathcal{B}_n).$$

We will use $\mathcal{A}_i$ and $\mathcal{B}_j$ to denote the sets of actions $\{a_1^i, \ldots, a_{u_i}^i\}$ and $\{b_1^j, \ldots, b_{v_j}^j\}$, respectively, and, we will write $\mathcal{A}$ for $\mathcal{A}_1 \cup \cdots \cup \mathcal{A}_m$, and $\mathcal{B}$ for $\mathcal{B}_1 \cup \cdots \cup \mathcal{B}_n$.

As indicated above, we must define a set of LTSs which are compatible with the fairness formula. One intuitive idea could be to require that the actions a_k^i always have an alternative τ-transition or a transition that will be hidden, so that the system can always nondeterministically choose a different route. In fact, it turns out that a closely related but weaker requirement suffices:

Definition 13. *LTS $L = (S, \Sigma, \Delta, \hat{s})$ is in $COMP(\psi, H)$ if and only if $\mathcal{A} \cup \mathcal{B} \subseteq \Sigma$, $H \cap \mathcal{A} = \emptyset$ and $\forall(\sigma, X) \in Sfail(L) : (\sigma, X \cup H) \notin Sfail(L) \vee (\sigma, X \cup \mathcal{A}) \in Sfail(L)$.*

Notice that the given condition can be determined from the CFFD-model of an LTS. It is also straightforward to show that if L is in $COMP(\psi, H)$ then so are $L \| L'$ and **hide** X **in** L with the same restrictions as in Definition 12.

5 Fairness LTS and Fairness Operator

We will next define a "fairness LTS" that corresponds to a fairness formula. We first illustrate the idea with some examples. Figure 1 shows a fairness LTS corresponding to the fairness constraint $\Box\Diamond a \Rightarrow \Box\Diamond b$. It has an infinite number of branches with lengths 1, 2, 3, ... and it can execute any finite number of consecutive a-actions, but not infinitely many, before executing a b-action and returning to the initial state. Then, the same can be repeated.

We can easily add new actions to the formula in a disjunctive manner by simply adding new parallel arcs to the LTS with the new action names. Using conjunctive conditions, on the other hand, requires a more elaborate structure. Figure 2 shows a fairness LTS that corresponds to the fairness constraint

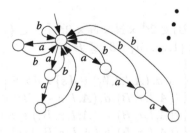

Fig. 1. A fairness LTS for the constraint $\Box\Diamond a \Rightarrow \Box\Diamond b$

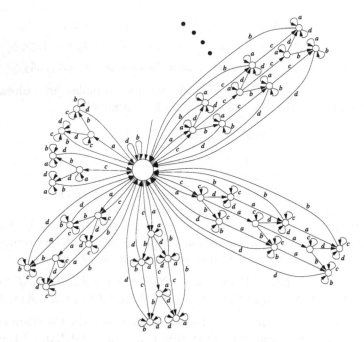

Fig. 2. A fairness LTS for the constraint $\Box\Diamond a \wedge \Box\Diamond c \Rightarrow \Box\Diamond b \wedge \Box\Diamond d$

$\Box\Diamond a \wedge \Box\Diamond c \Rightarrow \Box\Diamond b \wedge \Box\Diamond d$. Like before, there are branches of length 1, 2, 3, and so on. However, now there are two branches of each length, one of which limits action a to the given finite number and the other which limits action c. Furthermore, each branch has an internal structure which keeps track of which of the two actions b and d have been detected so far. Once both b and d have been detected we return to the initial state.

We should point out that the fairness LTS is a theoretical concept that allows us to handle the fairness constraint by using the well-known properties of parallel composition, and, as we will later see, we do not have to construct such LTSs in actual verification. The following gives the formal definition of a fairness LTS.

Definition 14. *For a formula $\psi(\mathcal{A}_1, \ldots, \mathcal{A}_m; \mathcal{B}_1, \ldots, \mathcal{B}_n)$, L_ψ is the LTS $(S, \Sigma, \Delta, \hat{s})$, where*

- $S = \{()\} \cup \big\{ (A, l, r, B) \in 2^{\mathcal{A}} \times \mathbb{N} \times \mathbb{N} \times 2^{\mathcal{B}} \mid \exists i \in \{1, \ldots, m\} : A = \mathcal{A}_i$
  $\wedge\ 0 \leq r \leq l\ \wedge\ \forall j \in \{1, \ldots, n\} : \mathcal{B}_j \not\subseteq B \big\}$
- $\Sigma = \mathcal{A} \cup \mathcal{B}$ *and* $\hat{s} = ()$
- $\Delta = \{\hat{s}\} \times \mathcal{B} \times \{\hat{s}\} \cup \big\{ (\hat{s}, a, (A, l, l, \emptyset)) \in \{\hat{s}\} \times \mathcal{A} \times S \mid l \geq 1 \vee a \in A \big\}$
  $\cup \big\{ ((A, l, r, B), a, (A, l, r-1, B)) \in S \times \mathcal{A} \times S \mid a \in A \big\}$
  $\cup \big\{ ((A, l, r, B), a, (A, l, r, B)) \in S \times \mathcal{A} \times S \mid a \notin A \big\}$
  $\cup \big\{ ((A, l, r, B), b, (A, l, r, B \cup \{b\})) \in S \times \mathcal{B} \times S \mid true \big\}$
  $\cup \big\{ ((A, l, r, B), b, \hat{s}) \in S \times \mathcal{B} \times \{\hat{s}\} \mid \exists j : \mathcal{B}_j \subseteq B \cup \{b\} \big\}$

It can be shown that the fairness LTS has the following properties; the proof is given in [20]. It should be noted that our construction is not unique in the sense that there are many LTSs with the same properties, and, indeed, we could use any such LTS, but our construction shows that at least one such LTS exists.

Proposition 2. *For $L_\psi = (S, \Sigma, \Delta, \hat{s})$ it holds that $Tr(L_\psi) = \Sigma^*$, $Divtr(L_\psi) = \emptyset$, $Sfail(L_\psi) \subseteq \Sigma^* \times 2^A$, and $Inftr(L_\psi) = \{ \eta \in \Sigma^\omega \mid \eta \models \psi \}$.*

Now we define the fairness operator. As indicated above, it works simply by placing the target system in parallel with the fairness LTS.

Definition 15. *Given the formula ψ, operator $\Psi_\psi^{\|}$ is the following mapping from LTSs to LTSs: $\Psi_\psi^{\|}(L) = L \| L_\psi$.*

The following results show that $\Psi_\psi^{\|}$ really is a fairness operator, in the sense of Definition 11, and context-independent with respect to CFFD. The proofs, which are based on the previous proposition and the properties of parallel composition and hiding, can be found in [20], although the former requires some modifications to cater for the hiding set H.

Theorem 1. *$\Psi_\psi^{\|}$ is a fairness operator for ψ with compatibility set $COMP(\psi, H)$.*

Theorem 2. *$\Psi_\psi^{\|}$ is context-independent with respect to "$\simeq_{\text{CFFD}}$".*

It is also straightforward to show that our fairness operators commute, and the compatibility of an LTS is preserved by fairness operators that do not use the actions in the hiding set H.

6   Algorithm for Verification

In this section we will show how the fairness operators can be used in verification without having to construct infinite systems. As a starting point we assume a system P composed by using "$\|$" and "**hide**" from LTSs. Next, we want to add some fairness constraints and we change the system by adding fairness operators $\Psi_1^{\|}, \ldots, \Psi_k^{\|}$ so that each $\Psi_i^{\|}$ is applied to a subsystem that is in $COMP(\psi_i, H_i)$, and which is, if H_i is nonempty, under a hiding operator that hides H_i. The new "fair" system is denoted by P_{fair}.

For technical convenience, we will from now on assume that any actions that are hidden in an expression of the form **hide** X **in** R only occur in the subsystem R. We do not lose any generality in this assumption; if it does not hold we can simply rename the hidden actions in **hide** X **in** R with new, unique names without affecting the end result. Also, we will denote by $\mathcal{F}$ the actions that are used in some fairness formula, and by $\mathcal{F}_h$ those of $\mathcal{F}$ that are also used in some hiding operator.

P_{fair} can be (and typically is) infinite. Therefore, our aim in the following algorithm is to construct a finite representation of P_{fair}, that is, a finite LTS P_{fair}^* such that

$$P^*_{fair} \simeq_{\text{CFFD}} P_{fair}.$$

Step 1: Construct a system $P^\dagger$ in the same way as P except that the actions $\mathcal{F}_h$ are not hidden.

The significance of this step is revealed by the following proposition, which shows that the fairness operators and the hiding of the related actions can be moved to the outmost level in the system, so that we can examine their effect on the remaining finite parameter system $P^\dagger$. The proof is based on the context-independence property and other properties of operators. The (lengthy) details are given in [20].

Proposition 3. $P_{fair} \simeq_{\text{CFFD}} \text{hide } \mathcal{F}_h \text{ in } \Psi_1^{||}(\cdots \Psi_k^{||}(P^\dagger)\cdots).$

Intuitively, any divergence (cycle of τ-actions) that shows up in the complete system is caused by a cycle consisting of actions $\mathcal{F}_h \cup \{\tau\}$ in $P^\dagger$. Furthermore, each such cycle is a part of a unique maximal strongly connected component of actions $\mathcal{F}_h \cup \{\tau\}$. Next we identify all such components (see the next section for illustrating examples), which we will call $\mathcal{F}_h^\tau$-components .

Step 2: Taking into account only the actions $\mathcal{F}_h \cup \{\tau\}$ in $P^\dagger$, identify the maximal nontrivial strongly connected components $C_1, \ldots, C_t$ (e.g., by using Tarjan's algorithm [1]).

For each component C, we remove all transitions and states of C except one state s_C, which can be any state of C, but if C contains the initial state, this is selected as s_C. We redirect transitions in and out of C into s_C. If there are transitions between states of C which themselves are not part of C, those transitions become loops from s_C to itself. We also check (see below) whether C contains an infinite execution (starting from any state) that is allowed by the fairness formulas. If it does, we add a τ-loop from s_C to itself. When this has been done for each C, we hide the actions $\mathcal{F}_h$.

Step 3: **for** C **in** $[C_1, \ldots, C_t]$ **do**
    if $\hat{s}_{P^\dagger} \in S_C$ **then** $s_C := \hat{s}_{P^\dagger}$ **else** choose any $s_C \in S_C$
    $S_{P^\dagger} := S_{P^\dagger} \setminus (S_C \setminus \{s_C\})$
    $\Delta_{P^\dagger} := \{(s_1, b, s_2) \mid \exists (s_1', b, s_2') \in \Delta_{P^\dagger} \setminus \Delta_C :$
        $(s_1' \notin S_C \wedge s_1 = s_1' \vee s_1' \in S_C \wedge s_1 = s_C) \wedge$
        $(s_2' \notin S_C \wedge s_2 = s_2' \vee s_2' \in S_C \wedge s_2 = s_C)\}$
    if C has an infinite execution η such that $\eta \models \psi_1, \ldots, \psi_k$ **then**
        $\Delta_{P^\dagger} := \Delta_{P^\dagger} \cup \{(s_C, \tau, s_C)\}$

Step 4: Hide the actions $\mathcal{F}_h$.

The result of the above steps is our finite model P^*_{fair}. We will show that P^*_{fair} is an exact model of P_{fair} if one exists, and otherwise it is a conservative estimate of it. However, let us first consider the complexity of the construction. Other parts of the algorithm can be done in time linear in the number of states and transitions, except checking for allowed infinite executions in a component. Infinite sequences of τ-actions are allowed by the formulas and can be detected with a depth-first search. One way to detect allowed sequences with infinitely many $\mathcal{F}_h$-actions is by using a variation of the Büchi automata [25] based verification of linear temporal logic [10]. We can construct an automaton with $O(k \prod_{i=1}^{k} |\psi_i|)$ states that accepts precisely the infinite $\mathcal{F}_h$-sequences that fulfill the formulas $\psi_1, \ldots, \psi_k$; here, $|\Delta_C|$ is the number of transitions in C, and $|\psi_i|$ is the length of the formula ψ_i. In this way we can show (see [20] for details) that checking whether an $\mathcal{F}_h^\tau$-component C contains an acceptable infinite execution can be done in time $O(|\Delta_C| \, k \prod_{i=1}^{k} |\psi_i|)$.

The following result states that P_{fair}^* has precisely the same stable failures and divergences as P_{fair}. This can be shown by a modification of the proof of Theorem 40 in [20] to cater for the hiding set H; the proof is based on the fact that replacing the components preserves traces of Σ_P-actions in the system, on the definition of compatibility, and the fact and that our construction adds τ-loops to precisely the states that replace components with allowed infinite executions.

Proposition 4. $Sfail(P_{fair}^*) = Sfail(P_{fair})$ and $Divtr(P_{fair}^*) = Divtr(P_{fair})$

It only remains to consider the set of infinite traces, $Inftr$. It can be shown that our construction preserves both finite and infinite traces, so $Inftr(P_{fair}^*) = Inftr(P)$. Therefore, the question is now whether the fairness operators also preserve infinite traces, that is, whether $Inftr(P_{fair}) = Inftr(P)$. If they do, then our model P_{fair}^* and P_{fair} are equivalent. However, if they do not, then it turns out that a finite model of P_{fair} does not even exist. This is stated in the following; we again refer to the proof of Theorem 40 in [20].

Theorem 3. If $Inftr(P_{fair}) = Inftr(P)$ then $P_{fair}^* \simeq_{\mathsf{CFFD}} P_{fair}$.
If $Inftr(P_{fair}) \neq Inftr(P)$, then there does not exist a finite LTS $Q \simeq_{\mathsf{CFFD}} P_{fair}$.

We still need an algorithm for checking whether $Inftr(P_{fair}) = Inftr(P)$. Unfortunately, it turns out that the complexity of checking this is higher than that of constructing the model P_{fair}^*. By using a similar construction as above we can reduce this problem to language containment of Büchi automata, and solve it by using the Büchi automaton complementation construction in [24] (with a small modification to include τ-actions), as shown in [20]. The result is that the problem can be decided in $PSPACE(|S_{P^\dagger}| \, k \prod_{1 \leq i \leq k} |\psi_i|)$.

Fortunately, even in the negative case, P_{fair}^* can only have some infinite traces that P_{fair} does not have. Therefore, in every case P_{fair}^*, the product of the algorithm, is a conservative estimate of the possibly infinite P_{fair}, and so it is always safe to use it in place of P_{fair} in verification.

Theorem 4. $P_{fair} \leq_{\mathsf{CFFD}} P_{fair}^*$.

It is also important to remember that the system $P^\dagger$ which is used as a parameter in the construction, is not the complete state-space of the original system, but an intermediate system where the actions of the fairness formulas have been left visible. $P^\dagger$ can be constructed by using any semantics-preserving reduced LTS construction method.

7 Examples

As a simple example, consider a semaphore S that controls the access of two processes P_1 and P_2 to a critical region, as shown in Figure 3. We look at the system from the point of view of P_2, and hide all actions except use_res_2, and reduce the system with a CFFD-preserving reduction algorithm. We notice that there is a divergence in the result, so P_2 may never get access to the resource. We therefore add the fairness constraint $\psi \equiv \Box\Diamond p_1 \Rightarrow \Box\Diamond p_2$ which forces S to eventually give access to P_2. Notice that we cannot add the constraint directly to S; intuitively, this is because if S were connected with a different P_2-process that could refuse p_2, this would create a new deadlock. However, when we connect P_1 and P_2 to S, we can see that the system is in $COMP(\psi, \{p_2\})$. We construct the LTS $P^\dagger$, and the result has one $\mathcal{F}_h^\tau$-component, as shown in Figure 4. This $\mathcal{F}_h^\tau$-component does not have an allowed infinite execution, so when we finish the algorithm and reduce the result, we get the rightmost process in Figure 4, and this behaviour is clearly satisfactory.

We will next consider the classic example of the alternating bit protocol [4], which is used for sending data messages over unreliable channels. The protocol is based on retransmitting data messages for which an acknowledgement message does not arrive in time, and using sequence numbers 0 and 1 to distinguish new messages from retransmissions. The sender S, receiver R, data channel DC and acknowledgement channel AC of the protocol are shown in Figure 5.

After receiving a message, DC chooses either the action $passd$ (pass the data message through) or $losed$ (lose it). AC works similarly. When the entire system is constructed and reduced, we see that there are two τ-loops in the behaviour, as shown in Figure 6. We can guess that these represent an infinite sequence of message losses and retransmissions. Therefore, we will first try applying the condition $\psi_{DC} \equiv \Box\Diamond losed \Rightarrow \Box\Diamond passd$ on DC. We notice that $DC \in COMP(\psi_{DC}, \{passd\})$, so we can use it on DC. We obtain a $P^\dagger$ that

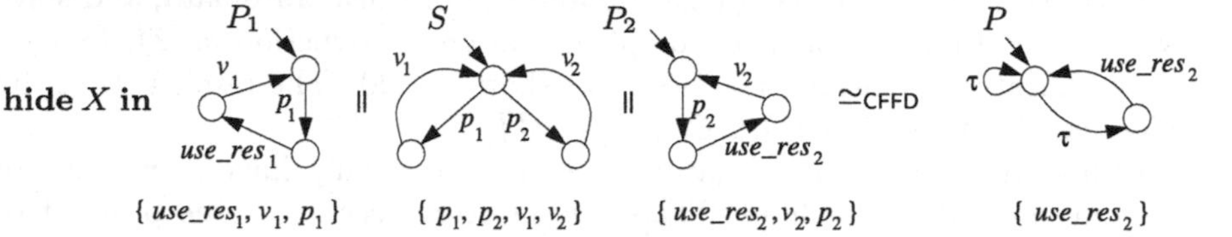

Fig. 3. The semaphore system (alphabets shown), where $X = \{p_1, v_1, use\_res_1, p_2, v_2\}$

Fig. 4. $P^\dagger$ of the semaphore system with an $\mathcal{F}_h^\tau$-component shown, and the final result

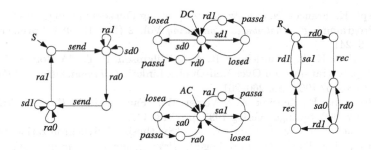

Fig. 5. The processes of the alternating bit protocol

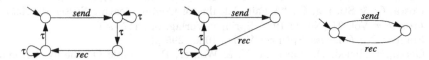

Fig. 6. The reduced behaviour of ABP without fairness, with ψ_{DC}, and with $\psi_{DC} \wedge \psi_{AC}$

has 11 states and four $\mathcal{F}_h^\tau$-components, one of which has an allowed infinite execution. After replacing the components, hiding, and reducing the result, we get the second process in Figure 6. We notice that one of the divergences has disappeared, but one remains. We therefore add a similar requirement for the acknowledgement channel, $\psi_{AC} \equiv \Box\Diamond losea \Rightarrow \Box\Diamond passa$. In the new $P^\dagger$ (with 52 states), none of the $\mathcal{F}_h^\tau$-components contain an allowed infinite execution. The final result is the rightmost LTS in Figure 6, which clearly satisfies any reasonable specification of the behaviour of the protocol.

8   Conclusions

In this article we have shown how a class of fairness constraints can be added to process-algebraic systems in a consistent way. We have presented an algorithm for constructing a finite representation of the resulting system in every case that one exists. The result can be placed as a component in further compositional analysis just like any other LTS. A remaining task is to build the approach into tools supporting LTS-based verification. Also, we believe that the theory can be extended to other types of fairness constraints and a wider class of systems.

References

1. Aho, A. V., Hopcroft, J. E. & Ullman, J. D.: *The Design and Analysis of Computer Algorithms.* Addison-Wesley Publishing Company 1974, 470 p.
2. Alpern, B. & Schneider, F. B.: "Defining Liveness". *Information Processing Letters*, Vol. 21 (No. 4) 1985, North-Holland, pp. 181–185.

3. Apt, K., Francez, N. & Katz, S.: "Appraising Fairness in Languages for Distributed Programming". *Distributed Computing* Vol. 2 (No. 4) 1988, Springer-Verlag, pp. 226–241.
4. Bartlett, K. A., Scantlebury, R. A. & Wilkinson, P. T.: "A Note on Reliable Full-Duplex Transmission Over Half-Duplex Links", *Communications of the ACM* Vol. 12 (No. 5) 1969, pp. 260–261.
5. Brinksma, E., Rensink, A. & Vogler, W.: "Fair Testing". *Proc. CONCUR'95*, LNCS 962, Springer-Verlag 1995, pp. 313–327.
6. Clarke, E. M. & Emerson, E. A.: "Synthesis of Synchronization Skeletons for Branching Time Temporal Logic". *Proc. Logic in Programs: Workshop, 1981*, LNCS 131, Springer-Verlag 1981, pp. 52–71.
7. Cleaveland, R. & Lüttgen, G.: "A Semantic Theory for Heterogeneous System Design". *Proc. FST TCS 2000*. LNCS 1974, Springer-Verlag 2000, pp. 312–324.
8. Costa, G. & Stirling, C.: "A Fair Calculus of Communicating Systems". *Acta Informatica* Vol. 21 (No. 1) 1984, Springer-Verlag, pp. 417–441.
9. Francez, N.: *Fairness*. Springer-Verlag 1986, 295 p.
10. Gerth, R., Peled, D., Vardi M. Y. & Wolper, P.: "Simple On-the-fly Automatic Verification of Linear Temporal Logic". *Proc. Fifteenth IFIP International Symposium on Protocol Specification, Testing and Verification*, 1995, IFIP Conference Proceedings 38, pp. 3–18.
11. Hennessy, M.: "An Algebraic Theory of Fair Asynchronous Communicating Processes". *Theoretical Computer Science* Vol. 49 (Nos 2,3) 1987, North-Holland, pp. 121–143.
12. Hoare, C.A.R.: *Communicating Sequential Processes*. Prentice-Hall 1985, 256 p.
13. Kaivola, R. & Valmari, A.: "The Weakest Compositional Semantic Equivalence Preserving Nexttime-less Linear Temporal Logic". *Proc. CONCUR'92*, LNCS 630, Springer-Verlag 1992, pp. 207–221.
14. Lehmann, D., Pnueli, A. & Stavi, J.: "Impartiality, Justice and Fairness: The Ethics of Concurrent Termination". *Proc. ICALP'81*, LNCS 115, Springer-Verlag 1981, pp. 264–277.
15. Manna, Z. & Pnueli, A.: *The Temporal Logic of Reactive and Concurrent Systems, Volume I: Specification*. Springer-Verlag 1992, 427 p.
16. Milner, R.: *Communication and Concurrency*. Prentice-Hall 1989, 260 p.
17. Older, S.: "Strong Fairness and Full Abstraction for Communicating Processes". *Information and Computation* Vol. 163 (No. 2) 2000, pp. 471–509.
18. Parrow, J.: *Fairness Properties in Process Algebra with Applications in Communication Protocol Verification*. Ph.D. thesis, Uppsala University, 1985, 176 p.
19. Pnueli, A.: "A Temporal Logic of Concurrent Programs". *Theoretical Computer Science*, Vol. 13, 1981, North Holland, pp. 45–60.
20. Puhakka, A.: Using Fairness in Process-Algebraic Verification. Tampere University of Technology, Institute of Software Systems Report 24, 2003. http://www.cs.tut.fi/ohj/VARG/publications/
21. Puhakka, A. & Valmari, A.: "Liveness and Fairness in Process-Algebraic Verification". *Proc. CONCUR'01*, LNCS 2154, Springer-Verlag 2001, pp. 202–217.
22. Queille, J. P. & Sifakis, J.: "Specification and Verification of Concurrent Systems in CESAR". *Proc. Fifth International Symposium on Programming*, LNCS 137, Springer-Verlag 1982, pp. 337–351.
23. Roscoe, A. W.: *The Theory and Practice of Concurrency*. Prentice-Hall 1998, 565 p.
24. Sistla, A. P., Vardi, M. Y. & Wolper, P.: "The Complementation Problem for Büchi Automata with Applications to Temporal Logic". *Theoretical Computer Science* Vol. 49 (Nos 2,3) 1987, North Holland, pp. 217–237.

25. Thomas, W.: "Automata on Infinite Objects". In van Leeuwen, J., editor, *Handbook of Theoretical Computer Science, Volume B*, Elsevier 1990, pp. 133–191.
26. Valmari, A.: "A Chaos-Free Failures Divergences Semantics with Applications to Verification". *Millennial Perspectives in Computer Science: Proceedings of the 1999 Oxford–Microsoft Symposium in honour of Sir Tony Hoare*, Palgrave "Cornerstones of Computing" series, 2000, pp. 365–382.
27. Valmari, A. & Tienari, M.: "Compositional Failure-Based Semantic Models for Basic LOTOS". *Formal Aspects of Computing* Vol. 7 (No. 4) 1995, Springer-Verlag, pp. 440–468.

Maximum Marking Problems with Accumulative Weight Functions

Isao Sasano[1], Mizuhito Ogawa[2], and Zhenjiang Hu[3]

[1] RIEC, Tohoku University,
2-1-1 Katahira, Aoba-ku, Sendai 980-8577, Japan
sasano@riec.tohoku.ac.jp
[2] School of Information Science, JAIST,
1-1 Asahidai, Nomi-shi, Ishikawa 923-1292, Japan
mizuhito@jaist.ac.jp
[3] Department of Mathematical Informatics,
School of Information Science and Technology, University of Tokyo,
7-3-1 Hongo, Bunkyo-ku, Tokyo 113-8656, Japan
hu@mist.i.u-tokyo.ac.jp

Abstract. We present a new derivation of efficient algorithms for a class of optimization problems called maximum marking problems. We extend the class of weight functions used in the specification to allow for weight functions with accumulation, which is particularly useful when the weight of each element depends on adjacent elements. This extension of weight functions enables us to treat more interesting optimization problems such as a variant of the maximum segment sum problem and the fair bonus distribution problem. The complexity of the derived algorithm is linear with respect to the size of the input data.

Keywords: Program derivation, Maximum marking problem, Accumulative weight function, Optimization problem.

1 Introduction

One way to guarantee the correctness of programs is to derive programs from specification [PP96, BdM96]. For this approach to be practical, we need high-level theorems that provide solutions for a wide class of problems. Such theorems should also guide the programmer in casting the specification in a form that fulfills the prerequisite conditions of the theorems.

The optimization theorem presented by Sasano et al. [SHTO00, SHT01] is such a theorem, designed for solving the maximum marking problem [Bir01] (also called the maximum weightsum problem). The core of the theorem is generic dynamic programming; it clarifies a class of problems that can be solved by dynamic programming.

The maximum marking problem, MMP for short, is the problem of marking the entries of some given data structure D to maximize a given weight function w under a given constraint p. This covers a wide variety of problems

D.V. Hung and M. Wirsing (Eds.): ICTAC 2005, LNCS 3722, pp. 562–578, 2005.
© Springer-Verlag Berlin Heidelberg 2005

[BLW87, BPT92] (by instantiating D, p and w), including the well-known maximum segment sum problem [Bir89, Gri90], the maximum independent set problem [SHTO00], some knapsack problems [SHTO01], some optimized range problems in data mining [SHTO02], and the register allocation problem [OHS03].

MMP was first considered in a work on graph algorithms [BLW87], which showed that MMP can be solved in linear time for a certain class of graphs. Borie et al. [BPT92] presented a way to derive a linear time algorithm for MMP from properties described by logical formulae. Their work is elegant in theory; but prohibitive in practice due to the huge constant factor. Our work [SHTO00] facilitated a flexible description of the constraint p by recursive functions and reduced the constant factor drastically. Our subsequent work [SHT01] extended the way the constraint p is described with accumulation. Bird showed a relational derivation for MMP [Bir01], and we demonstrated how to apply the optimization theorem to program analysis [OHS03].

Existing theorems, in a functional [SHTO00], logical [BPT92], or relational [Bir01] setting, can deal with a general data structure D and a powerful constraint p. However, they require the weight function w to be in homomorphic form, and hence do not allow for some simple modifications of the weight functions. For instance, consider a variant of the maximum segment sum problem, where the sum is computed by alternately changing the sign. Even this simple example cannot be dealt with by the existing theorems, because the distributivity condition with respect to maximum does not hold, but is required by the theorems.

In this paper, we present two new optimization theorems (calculational rules) for deriving efficient algorithms for a wider class of MMP, by allowing weight functions to be accumulative both in a top-down and bottom-up way. These weight functions are useful when the weight of each element depends on adjacent elements. This extension enables us to treat more interesting optimization problems such as a variant of the maximum segment sum problem (which requires a top-down accumulative weight function) and the fair bonus distribution problem (which requires a bottom-up accumulative weight function). The derived algorithm is linear in the size of the data.

Throughout the paper we will use the notation of Haskell [PJH99], a functional language, to describe our derivation as well as derived programs.

2   Preliminaries

In this section we define maximum marking problems on polynomial data types.
We describe polynomial data types in the following form:

$$D \, \alpha = A_1 \, (\alpha, D_1, \ldots, D_{n_1}) \mid A_2 \, (\alpha, D_1, \ldots, D_{n_2}) \mid \cdots \mid A_k \, (\alpha, D_1, \ldots, D_{n_k})$$

where every D_i is just $D \, \alpha$, and A_i's are called data constructors, applied to an element of type α and bounded number of recursive components. Though they seem restrictive, these polynomial data types are powerful enough to cover commonly used data types such as lists, binary trees, and rooted trees [BLW87]. Moreover, other data types like rose trees, a regular data type defined by

$$RTree\ \alpha = Node\ \alpha\ [RTree\ \alpha],$$

can be encoded by a polynomial data type (see Section 4.3). The fold operation $foldD$ on $D\ \alpha$ is defined as follows:

$$foldD\ \varphi_1\ \ldots\ \varphi_k = f$$
$$\textbf{where}\ f\ (A_i\ (x,\ t_1,\ldots,t_{n_i})) = \varphi_i\ (x,\ f\ t_1,\ldots,f\ t_{n_i})\quad (i = 1,\ldots,k).$$

Maximum marking problems are specified on polynomial data types in the following form:

$$max\ w \circ filter\ p \circ gen_D\ M.$$

The function gen_D generates all possible markings by using a finite list of marks $M :: [Mark]$:

$$gen_D :: [Mark] \to D\ \alpha \to [D\ (\alpha, Mark)].$$

$Mark$ is the type of marks. We treat data types that have a single type parameter α, and the elements of type α in the input data are the marking targets. We implement marking as a pair of an element and a mark, so the type of marked elements is $(\alpha, Mark)$ and the type of marked data is $D\ (\alpha, Mark)$.

The functions max and gen_D are defined as follows:

$$
\begin{array}{ll}
max\ w\ [] & = error\ \texttt{"No solution."} \\
max\ w\ [x] & = x \\
max\ w\ (x : xs) & = bmax\ w\ x\ (max\ w\ xs) \\
bmax\ f\ a\ b & = \textbf{if}\ f\ a > f\ b\ \textbf{then}\ a\ \textbf{else}\ b \\
gen_D\ M & = foldD\ \xi_1 \ldots \xi_k \\
\xi_i\ (x, ts_1, \ldots, ts_{n_i}) & = [\,A_i\ (x^*, t_1, \ldots, t_{n_i})\mid x^* \leftarrow [\,(x, m)\mid m \leftarrow M\,], \\
& \qquad\qquad\qquad t_1 \leftarrow ts_1, \ldots, t_{n_i} \leftarrow ts_{n_i}\,] \\
& \qquad (i = 1, \ldots, k)
\end{array}
$$

Here we define mutumorphisms on the data type $D\ \alpha$.

Definition 1 (Mutumorphisms). *Functions* $f_1, f_2, \ldots, f_n$ *are mutumorphisms on a recursive data type* $D\ \alpha$ *if each function* f_i *is defined mutually by*

$$f_i\ (A_j\ (x,\ t_1,\ldots,t_{n_j})) = \varphi_{ij}\ (x,\ h\ t_1,\ldots,h\ t_{n_j})$$
$$\textbf{where}\ h = (f_1 \vartriangle f_2 \vartriangle \ldots \vartriangle f_n)\quad (j = 1,\ldots,k).$$

Note that $f_1 \vartriangle f_2 \vartriangle \ldots \vartriangle f_n$ *represents a function defined as follows:*

$$(f_1 \vartriangle f_2 \vartriangle \ldots \vartriangle f_n)\ x = (f_1\ x, f_2\ x, \ldots, f_n\ x).$$

We say that a function f is *finite mutumorphic* [SHTO00] if the function f is defined as mutumorphisms along with other functions, each of which has finite range. A finite mutumorphic function f can be represented as a composition of a projection function π whose domain is finite and a folding function:

$$f = \pi \circ foldD\ \varphi_1\ \varphi_2\ \ldots\ \varphi_k.$$

In the following sections, we use the following fusion theorem:

Theorem 1 (Fusion). *If the following equation holds for $i = 1 \ldots k$,*

$$f\left(\phi_i\left(x,\ t_1, \ldots, t_{n_i}\right)\right) = \psi_i\left(x,\ f\ t_1, \ldots, f\ t_{n_i}\right)$$

then the following equation holds:

$$f \circ foldD\ \phi_1\ \ldots\ \phi_k = foldD\ \psi_1\ \ldots\ \psi_k.$$

3   Top-Down Accumulative Weight Functions

In this section we define top-down accumulative weight functions on polynomial data types and present a new optimization theorem.

3.1   The Top-Down Optimization Theorem

Definition 2 (Top-Down Accumulative Weight Function). *A function w is* top-down accumulative *if it is defined as follows:*

$$
\begin{aligned}
w &\qquad\qquad\quad :: D\ (\alpha, Mark) \to Weight \\
w\ x &\qquad\qquad\quad = w'\ x\ e_0 \\
w' &\qquad\qquad\quad :: D\ (\alpha, Mark) \to Acc \to Weight \\
w'\ (A_i\ (x, t_1, \ldots, t_{n_i}))\ e &= \phi_i\ (x,\ w'\ t_1\ (\delta_{i1}\ x\ e),\ \ldots,\ w'\ t_{n_i}\ (\delta_{in_i}\ x\ e))\ e
\end{aligned}
$$

where the range of δ_{ij} is finite and ϕ_i $(i = 1, \ldots, k)$ satisfies the following distributivity condition wrt maximum:

$$
\begin{aligned}
maximum\ \{\phi_i\ (x,\ w_1, \ldots, w_{n_i})\ e \mid w_1 \in S_1, \ldots, w_{n_i} \in S_{n_i}\} = \\
\phi_i\ (x,\ maximum\ S_1, \ldots, maximum\ S_{n_i})\ e
\end{aligned}
$$

Theorem 2 (Top-Down Optimization Theorem). *If property p is finite mutumorphic:*

$$p = \pi \circ foldD\ \rho_1 \ldots \rho_k$$

and weight function w is top-down accumulative, MMP specified by

$$max\ w \circ filter\ p \circ gen_D\ M$$

has an $O(|Acc|^d \cdot |C|^d \cdot |M| \cdot n)$ algorithm described by

$$opttd\ \phi_1\ \ldots\ \phi_k\ \delta_{11}\ \ldots\ \delta_{kn_k}\ (\lambda(c,e).\ (\pi\ c) \wedge (e = e_0))\ \rho_1\ \ldots\ \rho_k\ M\ Acc$$

where C is the domain of π, M is the list of marks, $d = maximum\ \{n_i \mid 1 \leq i \leq k\}$, and n is the size of the input data. The definition of the function $opttd$ is given in Fig. 1.

3.2   Proof of the Top Down Optimization Theorem

Here we prove Theorem 2 by showing the correctness and complexity of the function *opttd*.

$$
\begin{aligned}
&opttd \; \phi_1 \ldots \phi_k \; \delta_{11} \ldots \delta_{kn_k} \; accept \; \rho_1 \ldots \rho_k \; M \; Acc = \\
&\quad third \; \circ \; max \; second \; \circ \; filter \; (accept \circ first) \; \circ \; foldD \; \zeta_1 \; \ldots \; \zeta_k \\
&\quad \textbf{where} \; \zeta_i \; (x, t_1, \ldots, t_{n_i}) = \\
&\qquad eachmax \; [\,((\rho_i \; (x^*, c_1, \ldots, c_{n_i}), \; e), \\
&\qquad\qquad\quad \phi_i \; (x^*, w_1, \ldots, w_{n_i}) \; e, \\
&\qquad\qquad\quad A_i \; (x^*, r_1, \ldots, r_{n_i})) \mid \\
&\qquad\qquad\qquad\qquad x^* \leftarrow [\,(x, m) \mid m \leftarrow M\,], \\
&\qquad\qquad\qquad\qquad ((c_1, e_1), w_1, r_1) \leftarrow t_1, \cdots, ((c_{n_i}, e_{n_i}), w_{n_i}, r_{n_i}) \leftarrow t_{n_i}, \\
&\qquad\qquad\qquad\qquad e \leftarrow Acc, \; \delta_{i1} \; x^* \; e = e_1, \; \ldots, \; \delta_{in_i} \; x^* \; e = e_{n_i}] \quad (i=1,\ldots,k) \\
&eachmax \; xs = foldl \; f \; [\,] \; xs \\
&\quad \textbf{where} \; f \; [\,] \; (c, w, cand) = [(c, w, cand)] \\
&\qquad\qquad\quad f \; ((c, w, cand) : opts) \; (c', w', cand') = \\
&\qquad\qquad\qquad \textbf{if} \; c == c' \; \textbf{then} \; \textbf{if} \; w > w' \; \textbf{then} \; (c, w, cand) : opts \\
&\qquad\qquad\qquad\qquad\qquad\qquad\qquad\qquad \textbf{else} \; opts + +[(c', w', cand')] \\
&\qquad\qquad\qquad \textbf{else} \; (c, w, cand) : f \; opts \; (c', w', cand') \\
&first \; (x, \_, \_) = x, \qquad second \; (\_, x, \_) = x, \qquad third \; (\_, \_, x) = x
\end{aligned}
$$

Fig. 1. Optimization function *opttd*

Correctness. We show the correctness by transforming the specification into *opttd* as in Fig. 2. In the transformation we use the auxiliary functions ζ_i' ($i = 1, \ldots, k$) and an underline notation for simple representation:

$$
\begin{aligned}
&\zeta_i' \; (x, t_1, \ldots, t_{n_i}) = \\
&\quad [\,((\rho_i \; (x^*, c_1, \ldots, c_{n_i}), \; e), \; \phi_i \; (x^*, w_1, \ldots, w_{n_i}) \; e, \; A_i \; (x^*, r_1, \ldots, r_{n_i})) \\
&\quad \mid x^* \leftarrow [\,(x, m) \mid m \leftarrow M\,], \\
&\qquad ((c_1, e_1), w_1, r_1) \leftarrow t_1, \ldots, ((c_{n_i}, e_{n_i}), w_{n_i}, r_{n_i}) \leftarrow t_{n_i}, \\
&\qquad e \leftarrow Acc, \; \delta_{i1} \; x^* \; e = e_1, \; \ldots, \; \delta_{in_i} \; x^* \; e = e_{n_i}] \\
&\underline{x} = \lambda((\_, y), \_, \_). \; x == y
\end{aligned}
$$

The first step is simply unfoldings of p and gen_D.
The second step is

$$
\forall \epsilon. \; foldD \; \xi_1 \; \ldots \; \xi_k = map \; third \circ filter \; \underline{\epsilon} \circ foldD \; \zeta_1' \; \ldots \; \zeta_k',
$$

which is proved by induction on the structure of input data. In the case of $A_i \; (x, t_1, \ldots, t_{n_i})$,

$$
\begin{aligned}
&RHS \\
&= \; \{ \text{ unfolding of } foldD \; \} \\
&\quad map \; third \; (filter \; \underline{\epsilon} \\
&\quad [\,((\rho_i \; (x^*, c_1, \ldots, c_{n_i}), \; e), \; \phi_i \; (x^*, w_1, \ldots, w_{n_i}) \; e, \; A_i \; (x^*, r_1, \ldots, r_{n_i})) \\
&\quad \mid x^* \leftarrow [\,(x, m) \mid m \leftarrow M\,], \; ((c_1, e_1), w_1, r_1) \leftarrow foldD \; \zeta_1' \; \ldots \; \zeta_k' \; t_1, \ldots, \\
&\qquad ((c_{n_i}, e_{n_i}), w_{n_i}, r_{n_i}) \leftarrow foldD \; \zeta_1' \; \ldots \; \zeta_k' \; t_{n_i}, \\
&\qquad e \leftarrow Acc, \; \delta_{i1} \; x^* \; e = e_1, \; \ldots, \; \delta_{in_i} \; x^* \; e = e_{n_i}])
\end{aligned}
$$

$max\ w \circ filter\ p \circ gen_D\ M$

$=$ { unfold p and gen_D }

$max\ w \circ filter\ (\pi \circ foldD\ \rho_1 \ldots \rho_k) \circ foldD\ \xi_1 \ldots \xi_k$

$=$ { $\forall \epsilon.\ foldD\ \xi_1 \ldots \xi_k = map\ third \circ filter\ \underline{\epsilon} \circ foldD\ \zeta_1' \ldots \zeta_k'$ }

$max\ w \circ filter\ (\pi \circ foldD\ \rho_1 \ldots \rho_k) \circ map\ third \circ filter\ \underline{e_0} \circ foldD\ \zeta_1' \ldots \zeta_k'$

$=$ { $filter\ p \circ map\ f = map\ f \circ filter\ (p \circ f)$ }

$max\ w \circ map\ third \circ filter\ (\pi \circ foldD\ \rho_1 \ldots \rho_k \circ third) \circ filter\ \underline{e_0} \circ foldD\ \zeta_1' \ldots \zeta_k'$

$=$ { $max\ w \circ map\ third \circ foldD\ \zeta_1' \ldots \zeta_k' = third \circ max\ second \circ foldD\ \zeta_1' \ldots \zeta_k'$ }

$third \circ max\ second \circ filter\ (\pi \circ foldD\ \rho_1 \ldots \rho_k \circ third) \circ filter\ \underline{e_0} \circ foldD\ \zeta_1' \ldots \zeta_k'$

$=$ { $filter\ p \circ filter\ q = filter\ q \circ filter\ p$ }

$third \circ max\ second \circ filter\ \underline{e_0} \circ filter\ (\pi \circ foldD\ \rho_1 \ldots \rho_k \circ third) \circ foldD\ \zeta_1' \ldots \zeta_k'$

$=$ { $map\ (foldD\ \rho_1 \ldots \rho_k \circ third) \circ foldD\ \zeta_1' \ldots \zeta_k' =$
    $map\ (fst \circ first) \circ foldD\ \zeta_1' \ldots \zeta_k'$ }

$third \circ max\ second \circ filter\ \underline{e_0} \circ filter\ (\pi \circ fst \circ first) \circ foldD\ \zeta_1' \ldots \zeta_k'$

$=$ { $max\ second = max\ second \circ eachmax$ }

$third \circ max\ second \circ eachmax \circ filter\ \underline{e_0} \circ filter\ (\pi \circ fst \circ first) \circ foldD\ \zeta_1' \ldots \zeta_k'$

$=$ { $filter\ p \circ filter\ q = filter\ (p \wedge q)$ }

$third \circ max\ second \circ eachmax \circ filter\ ((\pi \circ fst \circ first) \wedge \underline{e_0}) \circ foldD\ \zeta_1' \ldots \zeta_k'$

$=$ { $eachmax \circ filter\ ((\pi \circ fst \circ first) \wedge \underline{e_0}) = filter\ ((\pi \circ fst \circ first) \wedge \underline{e_0}) \circ eachmax$ }

$third \circ max\ second \circ filter\ (\pi \circ fst \circ first \wedge \underline{e_0}) \circ eachmax \circ foldD\ \zeta_1' \ldots \zeta_k'$

$=$ { $eachmax \circ foldD\ \zeta_1' \ldots \zeta_k' = foldD\ \zeta_1 \ldots \zeta_k$ }

$third \circ max\ second \circ filter\ ((\pi \circ fst \circ first) \wedge \underline{e_0}) \circ foldD\ \zeta_1 \ldots \zeta_k$

$=$ { fold $opttd$ }

$opttd\ \phi_1\ \ldots\ \phi_k\ \delta_{11}\ \ldots\ \delta_{kn_k}\ (\lambda(c,e).\ (\pi\ c) \wedge (e == e_0))\ \rho_1\ \ldots\ \rho_k\ M\ Acc$

Fig. 2. A proof of the top-down optimization theorem

$=$ { distributing $filter$ }

$map\ third$

$[((\rho_i\ (x^*, c_1, \ldots, c_{n_i}),\ \epsilon),\ \phi_i\ (x^*, w_1, \ldots, w_{n_i})\ \epsilon,\ A_i\ (x^*, r_1, \ldots, r_{n_i}))$
$|\ x^* \leftarrow [(x,m)\ |\ m \leftarrow M],$
$\quad ((c_1, e_1), w_1, r_1) \leftarrow filter\ \underline{\delta_{i1}}\ x^*\ \epsilon\ (foldD\ \zeta_1'\ \ldots\ \zeta_k'\ t_1), \ldots,$
$\quad ((c_{n_i}, e_{n_i}), w_{n_i}, r_{n_i}) \leftarrow filter\ \underline{\delta_{in_i}}\ x^*\ \epsilon\ (foldD\ \zeta_1'\ \ldots\ \zeta_k'\ t_{n_i})]$

$=$ { distributing map }

$[\ A_i\ (x^*, r_1, \ldots, r_{n_i})$
$|\ x^* \leftarrow [(x,m)\ |\ m \leftarrow M],$
$\quad ((c_1, e_1), w_1, r_1) \leftarrow map\ third\ (filter\ \underline{\delta_{i1}}\ x^*\ \epsilon\ (foldD\ \zeta_1'\ \ldots\ \zeta_k'\ t_1)), \ldots,$
$\quad ((c_{n_i}, e_{n_i}), w_{n_i}, r_{n_i}) \leftarrow map\ third\ (filter\ \underline{\delta_{in_i}}\ x^*\ \epsilon\ (foldD\ \zeta_1'\ \ldots\ \zeta_k'\ t_{n_i}))]$

$=$ { induction hypothesis }

$[\ A_i\ (x^*, r_1, \ldots, r_{n_i})$
$|\ x^* \leftarrow [(x,m)\ |\ m \leftarrow M],\ ((c_1, e_1), w_1, r_1) \leftarrow foldD\ \xi_1\ \ldots\ \xi_k\ t_1, \ldots,$
$\quad ((c_{n_i}, e_{n_i}), w_{n_i}, r_{n_i}) \leftarrow foldD\ \xi_1\ \ldots\ \xi_k\ t_{n_i}]$

$$= \{ \text{folding of } foldD \}$$
$$LHS.$$

The third step is the commutativity of map and filter [Bir87].
The fourth step is

$$max\ w \circ map\ third \circ foldD\ \zeta'_1\ \dots\ \zeta'_k = third \circ max\ second \circ foldD\ \zeta'_1\ \dots\ \zeta'_k.$$

This means that the second element is the weight of the third element, which is proved by induction on the structure of the argument of type $D\ \alpha$.

The fifth step is commutativity of filters.

The sixth step is

$$map\ (foldD\ \rho_1 \dots \rho_k \circ third) \circ foldD\ \zeta'_1\ \dots\ \zeta'_k = map\ (fst \circ first) \circ foldD\ \zeta'_1\ \dots\ \zeta'_k.$$

This equation means the first part of the first element is equal to the value of $foldD\ \rho_1\ \dots\ \rho_k$ applied to the third element, which is proved by induction on the structure of the argument of type $D\ \alpha$.

The seventh step is

$$max\ second = max\ second \circ eachmax.$$

This holds because $max\ second$ returns the rightmost optimal solution, and $eachmax$ returns a list which consists of the rightmost optimal solution for each value of the first element, preserving the order.

The eighth step is an equation concerning filter, which can be proved by induction on the structure of the argument list.

The ninth step is

$$eachmax \circ filter\ ((\pi \circ fst \circ first) \wedge \underline{e_0}) = filter\ ((\pi \circ fst \circ first) \wedge \underline{e_0}) \circ eachmax$$

which means the commutativity between the functions $filter$ and $eachmax$. This equation holds because the predicate $((\pi \circ fst \circ first) \wedge \underline{e_0})$ is concerned only with the first elements, and the functions $filter$ and $eachmax$ preserve the order.

The tenth step is

$$eachmax \circ foldD\ \zeta'_1\ \dots\ \zeta'_k = foldD\ \zeta_1\ \dots\ \zeta_k$$

which follows from the fusion theorem (Theorem 1). The prerequisite condition for applying the fusion theorem is that the equations below hold for $i = 1, \dots, k$:

$$eachmax\ (\zeta'_i\ (x, t_1, \dots, t_{n_i})) = \zeta_i\ (x, eachmax\ t_1, \dots, eachmax\ t_{n_i}).$$

Since $eachmax$ and ζ'_i preserve the order, the following equations hold for $i = 1, \dots, k$:

$$\zeta_i\ (x, t_1, \dots, t_{n_i}) = \zeta_i\ (x, eachmax\ t_1, \dots, eachmax\ t_{n_i}).$$

```
msas = third . foldr1 (bmax second) . filter (accept . first) . h
accept ((c1,c2,c3),e) = c1 && e == True
h [] = [((rho1,e), phi1 e, [])| e <- [True,False]]
h (x:xs) = eachmax [((rho2 y c, e), phi2 y w e, y:r)
                   | y <- [(x,True),(x,False)],
                     ((c,e'),w,r) <- h xs,
                     e <- [True,False], delta y e == e']
phi1 e = 0
phi2 y w e = if kind y then (if e then weight y else - weight y) + w
             else w
delta y e = if kind y then not e else e
rho1 = (True, True, True)
rho2 y (c1,c2,c3) = if kind y then (c2,c2,False) else (c1,c3,c3)
```

Fig. 3. A linear-time Haskell program for the MSAS problem

Since $\zeta_i = eachmax \circ \zeta_i'$, the prerequisite condition holds.
The eleventh step is simply the folding of *opttd*.

Complexity. The complexity of the function *opttd*:

$$opttd \ \phi_1 \ \dots \ \phi_k \ \delta_{11} \ \dots \ \delta_{kn_k} \ (\lambda(c,e).\ (\pi \ c) \wedge (e = e_0)) \ \rho_1 \ \dots \ \rho_k \ M \ Acc$$

is $O(|Acc|^{d+1} \cdot |C|^{d+1} \cdot |M| \cdot n)$ where C is the domain of π, M is the list of marks, $d = maximum \ \{n_i \mid 1 \le i \le k\}$, and n is the size of the input data. The complexity follows from that the complexity of the function

$$\zeta_i \ (x, t_1, \dots, l_{n_i})$$

is $O(|Acc|^d \cdot |C|^d \cdot |M| \cdot n)$ and it is computed n times. The function ζ_i firstly generates a list that contains at most $|Acc| \cdot |C| \cdot |M|$ elements. Next, the function *eachmax* reduces it to a list that has at most $|Acc| \cdot |C|$ elements. With a list implementation (as in Fig. 1), this reduction takes $O(|Acc|^{d+1} \cdot |C|^{d+1} \cdot |M|)$ time; however, with an array implementation (as in [SHT01]), it is reduced to $O(|Acc|^d \cdot |C|^d \cdot |M|)$ time. For readability, throughout the paper, we describe algorithms by list implementations.

3.3 The Maximum Segment Alternate Sum Problem

Consider the following list problem: find a consecutive sublist from the input list such that the selected sublist has the maximum alternate sum, where the alternate sum is computed by alternately changing the sign. For example, given a list $[-3, 5, 2, 7, 6]$, the sublist $[5, 2, 7]$ gives the maximum alternate sum of $5 + (-2) + 7 = 10$ among all the consecutive sublists (segments) in the input list. We call this the *maximum segment alternate sum problem* (MSAS for short).

The property p and the weight function w are written as follows:

$p = \pi_0 \circ foldr\ \rho\ (True, True, True)$
$\quad$ **where** $\rho\ x\ (r_0, r_1, r_2) = $ **if** $kind\ x$ **then** $(r_1, r_1, False)$ **else** (r_0, r_2, r_2)
$\qquad \pi_0\ (r_0, r_1, r_2) = r_0$
$w\ xs = w'\ xs\ True$
$w'\ [\,]\ e = 0$
$w'\ (x : xs)\ e = \phi_{cons}\ x\ e\ (w'\ xs\ (\delta\ x\ e))$
$\phi_{cons}\ x\ e\ r = $ **if** $kind\ x$ **then**
$\qquad\qquad\qquad$ (**if** e **then** $weight\ x$ **else** $-\ weight\ x) + r$
$\qquad\qquad$ **else** r
$kind\ (x, m) = m$
$weight\ (x, m) = x$

where ϕ_{cons} satisfies the following distributivity condition:

$$maximum\ \{\phi_{cons}\ x\ e\ w \mid w \in S\} = \phi_{cons}\ x\ e\ (maximum\ S).$$

The function $foldr$ is a folding function on lists [Bir98]. Applying Theorem 2 immediately yields the linear algorithm in Fig. 3. Note that the weight function written in the following homomorphic form

$$
\begin{aligned}
w\ [\,] \quad &= 0 \\
w\ (x : xs) &= \textbf{if } kind\ x \textbf{ then } weight\ x - w\ xs \textbf{ else } w\ xs
\end{aligned}
$$

does not meet the prerequisite of the theorems in previous work of MMP.

4 Bottom-Up Accumulative Weight Functions

In some cases as shown in Section 4.3, we need weight functions that accumulate in bottom-up way.

4.1 The Bottom-Up Optimization Theorem

Definition 3 (Bottom-up Accumulative Weight Function). *A weight function w on D is* bottom-up accumulative *if w is defined as follows:*

$$
\begin{aligned}
w \quad &:: D\ (\alpha, Mark) \to Weight \\
w\ (A_i\ (x, t_1, \ldots, t_{n_i})) &= \eta_i\ x\ (w\ t_1) \ldots (w\ t_{n_i})\ (q\ t_1) \ldots (q\ t_{n_i}) \\
&\qquad\qquad\qquad\qquad\qquad\qquad (i = 1, \ldots, k) \\
q \quad &:: D\ (\alpha, Mark) \to Acc \\
q \quad &= foldD\ \sigma_1 \ldots \sigma_k
\end{aligned}
$$

where Acc is a finite set and $\eta_i\ (i = 1, \ldots, k)$ satisfies the following distributivity condition:

$$
\begin{aligned}
maximum\ \{\eta_i\ x\ w_1 \ldots w_{n_i}\ e_1 \ldots e_{n_i} \mid w_1 \in S_1, \ldots, w_{n_i} \in S_{n_i}\} = \\
\eta_i\ x\ (maximum\ S_1) \ldots (maximum\ S_{n_i})\ e_1 \ldots e_{n_i} \quad (j = 1, \ldots, n_i)
\end{aligned}
$$

Theorem 3 (Bottom-up Optimization Theorem). *If property p is finite mutumorphic:*

$$\begin{aligned}
&optbu \; \eta_1 \ldots \eta_k \; \sigma_1 \ldots \sigma_k \; accept \; \rho_1 \ldots \rho_k \; M = \\
&\quad third \circ max \; second \circ filter \; (accept \circ first) \circ foldD \; \psi_1 \; \ldots \; \psi_k \\
&\quad \textbf{where} \; \psi_i \; (x, t_1, \ldots, t_{n_i}) = \\
&\quad\quad eachmax \; [\, ((\rho_i \; (x^*, c_1, \ldots, c_{n_i}), \sigma_i \; (x^*, q_1, \ldots, q_{n_i})), \\
&\quad\quad\quad\quad \eta_i \; (x^*, (w_1, q_1), \ldots, (w_{n_i}, q_{n_i})), \\
&\quad\quad\quad\quad A_i \; (x^*, r_1, \ldots, r_{n_i})) \mid \\
&\quad\quad\quad\quad\quad x^* \leftarrow [\, (x, m) \mid m \leftarrow M\,], \\
&\quad\quad\quad\quad\quad ((c_1, q_1), w_1, r_1) \leftarrow t_1, \cdots, ((c_{n_i}, q_{n_i}), w_{n_i}, r_{n_i}) \leftarrow t_{n_i}\,] \\
&\quad (i = 1, \ldots, k)
\end{aligned}$$

Fig. 4. Optimization function *optbu*

$$p = \pi \circ foldD \; \rho_1 \ldots \; \rho_k$$

and weight function w is bottom-up accumulative, MMP specified by

$$max \; w \circ filter \; p \circ gen_D \; M$$

has an $O(|Acc|^d \cdot |C|^d \cdot |M| \cdot n)$ *algorithm described by*

$$optbu \; \eta_1 \; \ldots \; \eta_k \; \sigma_1 \; \ldots \; \sigma_k \; (\lambda(c, q). \; \pi \; c) \; \rho_1 \; \ldots \; \rho_k \; M$$

where Acc is the range of q, C *is the domain of* π, M *is the list of marks,* $d = maximum \; \{n_i \mid 1 \le i \le k\}$, *and* n *is the size of the input data. The definition of the optimization function optbu is given in Fig. 4.*

4.2 Proof of the Bottom-Up Optimization Theorem

Here we prove Theorem 3 by showing the correctness and complexity of the function *optbu*.

Correctness. We show the correctness by transforming the specification into *optbu* as in Fig. 5. In the transformation we use the auxiliary functions ψ'_i ($i = 1, \ldots, k$) defined by

$$\begin{aligned}
\psi'_i \; (x, t_1, \ldots, t_{n_i}) = [\,&((\rho_i \; (x^*, c_1, \ldots, c_{n_i}), \sigma_i \; (x^*, q_1, \ldots, q_{n_i})), \\
&\eta_i \; (x^*, (w_1, q_1), \ldots, (w_{n_i}, q_{n_i})), \\
&A_i \; (x^*, r_1, \ldots, r_{n_i})) \\
&\mid x^* \leftarrow [\, (x, m) \mid m \in M\,], \\
&((c_1, q_1), w_1, r_1) \leftarrow t_1, \cdots, ((c_{n_i}, q_{n_i}), w_{n_i}, r_{n_i}) \leftarrow t_{n_i}\,].
\end{aligned}$$

The transformation is simpler than that in the proof of Theorem 2, so we omit the detail.

Complexity. Similarly to *opttd*, the complexity is $O(|Acc|^{d+1} \cdot |C|^{d+1} \cdot |M| \cdot n)$, but $O(|Acc|^d \cdot |C|^d \cdot |M| \cdot n)$ is achieved if we use array implementation.

$$
\begin{aligned}
&max\ w \circ filter\ p \circ gen_D\ M \\
=\ &\{\ unfold\ p\ and\ gen_D\ \} \\
&max\ w \circ filter\ (\pi \circ foldD\ \rho_1 \ldots \rho_k) \circ foldD\ \xi_1 \ldots \xi_k \\
=\ &\{\ foldD\ \xi_1 \ldots \xi_k = map\ third \circ foldD\ \psi_1' \ \ldots\ \psi_k'\ \} \\
&max\ w \circ filter\ (\pi \circ foldD\ \rho_1 \ldots \rho_k) \circ map\ third \circ foldD\ \psi_1' \ \ldots\ \psi_k' \\
=\ &\{\ filter\ p \circ map\ f = map\ f \circ filter\ (p \circ f)\ \} \\
&max\ w \circ map\ third \circ filter\ (\pi \circ foldD\ \rho_1 \ldots \rho_k \circ third) \circ foldD\ \psi_1' \ \ldots\ \psi_k' \\
=\ &\{\ max\ w \circ map\ third \circ foldD\ \psi_1' \ \ldots\ \psi_k' = third \circ max\ second \circ foldD\ \psi_1' \ \ldots\ \psi_k'\ \} \\
&third \circ max\ second \circ filter\ (\pi \circ foldD\ \rho_1 \ldots \rho_k \circ third) \circ foldD\ \psi_1' \ \ldots\ \psi_k' \\
=\ &\{map\ (foldD\ \rho_1 \ldots \rho_k \circ third) \circ foldD\ \psi_1' \ \ldots\ \psi_k' = \\
&\quad map\ (fst \circ first) \circ foldD\ \psi_1' \ \ldots\ \psi_k'\} \\
&third \circ max\ second \circ filter\ (\pi \circ fst \circ first) \circ foldD\ \psi_1' \ \ldots\ \psi_k' \\
=\ &\{\ max\ second = max\ second \circ eachmax\ \} \\
&third \circ max\ second \circ eachmax \circ filter\ (\pi \circ fst \circ first) \circ foldD\ \psi_1' \ \ldots\ \psi_k' \\
=\ &\{\ eachmax \circ filter\ (\pi \circ fst \circ first) = filter\ (\pi \circ fst \circ first) \circ eachmax\ \} \\
&third \circ max\ second \circ filter\ (\pi \circ fst \circ first) \circ eachmax \circ foldD\ \psi_1' \ \ldots\ \psi_k' \\
=\ &\{\ eachmax \circ foldD\ \psi_1' \ \ldots\ \psi_k' = foldD\ \psi_1 \ \ldots\ \psi_k\ \} \\
&third \circ max\ second \circ filter\ (\pi \circ fst \circ first) \circ foldD\ \psi_1 \ \ldots\ \psi_k \\
=\ &\{\ fold\ optbu\ \} \\
&optbu\ \eta_1 \ldots \eta_k\ \sigma_1 \ldots \sigma_k\ (\pi \circ fst)\ \rho_1 \ldots \rho_k\ M
\end{aligned}
$$

Fig. 5. A proof of the bottom-up optimization theorem

4.3   The Fair Bonus Distribution Problem

As an example for the bottom-up accumulative optimization theorem, we consider the *fair bonus distribution problem*. There is some profit T to distribute to people in a company. The company has a hierarchical structure; that is, supervisor relationships form a tree rooted at the president. As a natural requirement, the bonus of a supervisor should be more than that of a subordinate. In order to reduce employee complaints, the sum of the difference in bonus between an employee and his/her immediate supervisor should be minimized.

Fig. 6 shows an optimal distribution for $T = 6$. It is not easy to give an optimal distribution, as there are many possibilities. A naive solution is to generate all the distributions, filter out the invalid distributions, and then select the optimal one. Though this naive solution is exponential, we can reduce it to $O(T^4 n)$ by specifying it as MMP and applying our new theorem.

Specification. Before we give the specification, we define the trees as follows:

$$RTree\ \alpha = Node\ \alpha\ [RTree\ \alpha].$$

This data type is called a rose tree and is used to represent a general tree, each node of which can have arbitrarily many children.

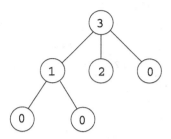

Fig. 6. Fair bonus distribution (total = 6)

To specify the problem as MMP we need to define a finite list of marks M, property p, and weight function w.

We use marks to represent the amount of bonus given to each person, so

$$M = [0, 1, \ldots, T].$$

Property p checks whether the sum of the distributed bonuses is T and whether the bonus of each person is more than those of his/her subordinates. Checking the sum can be written as follows:

$$
\begin{aligned}
csum\ t &= (bonusSum\ t = T) \\
bonusSum\ (Node\ x\ [\,]) &= bonus\ x \\
bonusSum\ (Node\ x\ (t:ts)) &= bonusSum\ t + bonusSum\ (Node\ x\ ts)
\end{aligned}
$$

Checking to determine whether the bonus of a supervisor is more than those of his/her subordinates can be written as follows:

$$
\begin{aligned}
more\ (Node\ x\ [\,]) &= True \\
more\ (Node\ x\ (t:ts)) &= bonus\ x > bonus\ (root\ t)\ \wedge\ more\ t \\
&\quad \wedge\ more\ (Node\ x\ ts) \\
root\ (Node\ x\ ts) &= x
\end{aligned}
$$

Using these functions, property p can be defined as follows:

$$p\ t = csum\ t\ \wedge\ more\ t.$$

Weight function w sums up the difference of amount of bonus between an employee and his or her immediate supervisor. In order to minimize the sum of the difference, w returns a negative value.

$$
\begin{aligned}
w\ (Node\ x\ [\,]) &= 0 \\
w\ (Node\ x\ (t:ts)) &= bonus\ (root\ t) - bonus\ x + w\ t + w\ (Node\ x\ ts)
\end{aligned}
$$

Therefore, we can specify the problem as follows:

$$fbd = max\ w \circ filter\ p \circ gen_{RTree}\ M.$$

When total T is not enough, there may be no solution. In such a case the result is "No solution." by the definition of $max\ w$.

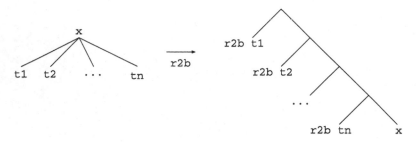

Fig. 7. Isomorphism between rose trees and leaf-labeled binary trees

Derivation. We have specified the bonus problem as an MMP. Rose tree is not a polynomial data type, so we encode it by leaf-labeled binary tree as in [SHTO00]:

$$BTree \; \alpha = Tip \; \alpha$$
$$| \;\; Bin \; (BTree \; \alpha) \; (BTree \; \alpha)$$

Rose trees and leaf-labeled binary trees are isomorphic and we exploit the isomorphism between them, as illustrated in Fig. 7, for converting functions on rose trees into functions on leaf-labeled binary trees. Transformations between the two structures can be implemented in linear time as follows:

$$
\begin{aligned}
r2b \; (Node \; x \; []) \quad &= Tip \; x \\
r2b \; (Node \; x \; (t : ts)) &= Bin \; (r2b \; t) \; (r2b \; (Node \; x \; ts)) \\
b2r \; (Tip \; x) \quad &= Node \; x \; [] \\
b2r \; (Bin \; t_1 \; t_2) \quad &= \mathbf{let} \; Node \; x \; ts = b2r \; t_2 \; \mathbf{in} \; Node \; x \; ((b2r \; t_1) : ts)
\end{aligned}
$$

Meanwhile, we would like to convert $p :: RTree \; (\alpha, M) \rightarrow Bool$ into $p' :: BTree \; (\alpha, M) \rightarrow Bool$, which satisfies the following equation:

$$p' \; t = p \; (b2r \; t)$$

By fusion, we get the following:

$$
\begin{aligned}
p' \; t \quad &= csum' \; t \; \wedge \; more' \; t \\
csum' \; t \quad &= bonusSum' \; t == T \\
bonusSum' \; (Tip \; x) \quad &= bonus \; x \\
bonusSum' \; (Bin \; t_1 \; t_2) &= bonusSum' \; t_1 + bonusSum' \; t_2 \\
more' \; (Tip \; x) \quad &= True \\
more' \; (Bin \; t_1 \; t_2) \quad &= bonus \; (root' \; t_2) > bonus \; (root' \; t_1) \; \wedge \\
& \quad \; more' \; t_1 \; \wedge \; more' \; t_2 \\
root' \; (Tip \; x) \quad &= x \\
root' \; (Bin \; t_1 \; t_2) \quad &= root' \; t_2
\end{aligned}
$$

Similarly, we convert w into w', which satisfies $w' \; t = w \; (b2r \; t)$. By fusion, we get the following:

$$
\begin{aligned}
w' \; (Tip \; x) \quad &= 0 \\
w' \; (Bin \; t_1 \; t_2) &= bonus \; (root' \; t_1) - bonus \; (root' \; t_2) + w' \; t_1 + w' \; t_2
\end{aligned}
$$

Using these functions we get the following form:

$$fbd = b2r \circ max\ w' \circ filter\ p' \circ gen_{BTree}\ M \circ r2b.$$

Property p' is defined as mutumorphisms with $csum'$, $bonusSum'$, $more'$, $root'$, but $bonusSum'$ and $root'$ do not have finite range. As for $bonusSum'$, we use the cutting method [SHTO01] by introducing the function cut.

$$csum'\ t = cut\ (bonusSum'\ t) == T$$
$$cut\ s\quad = \textbf{if } s \leq T \textbf{ then } s \textbf{ else } T + 1$$

Let $cbs = cut \circ bonusSum'$, and we get

$$csum'\ t\quad\quad = cbs\ t == T$$
$$cbs\ (Tip\ x)\quad = cut\ (bonus\ x)$$
$$cbs\ (Bin\ t_1\ t_2) = cut\ (cbs\ t_1 + cbs\ t_2).$$

As for $root'$, we let $br = bonus \circ root'$. By fusion we get

$$br\ (Tip\ x)\quad\ = bonus\ x$$
$$br\ (Bin\ t_1\ t_2) = br\ t_2.$$

Using these functions the property p' is described as finite mutumorphisms.
The weight function w' is described using the above function br as follows:

$$w'\ (Tip\ x)\quad\quad = \eta_{tip}\ x$$
$$w'\ (Bin\ t_1\ t_2)\quad = \eta_{bin}\ (w'\ t_1)\ (w'\ t_2)\ (br\ t_1)\ (br\ t_2)$$
$$\eta_{tip}\ x\quad\quad\quad\quad = 0$$
$$\eta_{bin}\ w_1\ w_2\ e_1\ e_2 = e_1 - e_2 + w_1 + w_2$$

This is bottom-up accumulative, because η_{bin} satisfies the monotonicity:

$$w_{11} \leq w_{12} \wedge w_{21} \leq w_{22}\ \Rightarrow\ \eta_{bin}\ w_{11}\ w_{21}\ e_1\ e_2 \leq \eta_{bin}\ w_{12}\ w_{22}\ e_1\ e_2$$

and hence satisfies the distributivity condition. By applying Theorem 3, we get an $O(T^6 n)$ algorithm (by an array implementation, it is reduced to $O(T^4 n)$) in Fig. 8, where n is the size of the input tree. When total = 6, the expression

```
fbd (Node 'a' [Node 'b' [Node 'c' [], Node 'd' []],
            Node 'e' [], Node 'f' []])
```

computes the following result:

```
Node ('a',3) [Node ('b',1) [Node ('c',0) [],Node ('d',0) []],
            Node ('e',2) [],Node ('f',0) []].
```

```
fbd = b2r . third . foldr1 (bmax second) .
      filter (accept . first) . h . r2b
h (Tip x) = [(((m,True),m),0,Tip (x,m)) | m <- [0..total]]
h (Bin t1 t2) = eachmax [(((cut (c1+c2),q2 > q1 && m1 && m2),q2),
                          q1-q2+w1+w2,Bin r1 r2)
                       | (((c1,m1),q1),w1,r1) <- h t1,
                         (((c2,m2),q2),w2,r2) <- h t2]
accept ((a,b),c) = a == total && b
```

Fig. 8. An $O(T^6 n)$ Haskell program for the bonus problem

5 Comparison with the Relational Approach

One of the studies that is closely related to our work is derivation by relational calculus [BdM96]. This work showed many optimization problems can be dealt with in a uniform way by relational calculus. Bird showed that MMP can be dealt with by relational calculus [Bir01]. Bird and de Moor gave theorems for deriving efficient greedy, dynamic programming, and thinning algorithms, which cover our optimization theorems. Though they are general, they are not good guides for programmers to write specifications that meet their prerequisite condition. For example, see the thinning theorem [BdM96]:

Theorem 4. [BdM96] *If* $Q \subseteq R$ *and* S *is monotonic on* Q°, *then*

$$min\ R \circ fold_\mathsf{F}(thin\ Q \circ \Lambda(S \circ \mathsf{F} \in)) \quad \subseteq \quad min\ R \circ \Lambda(fold_\mathsf{F}\ S).$$

This roughly means that the right side, $min\ R \circ \Lambda(fold_\mathsf{F}\ S)$, is the specification, where S is a generating function and $min\ R$ selects the optimal results, and the left side is the derived algorithm. In the example of MMP, $filter\ p \circ gen$ corresponds to $\Lambda(fold_\mathsf{F}\ S)$ and $max\ w$ corresponds to $min\ R$. In order to apply this theorem, we have to find Q to satisfy the required conditions with respect to S and R; this may be a little burdensome for programmers using the theorem.

Our target is less general, but still includes a useful class of problems called MMP; we provide theorems to automatically derive efficient algorithms with a more friendly interface that guides programmers in writing specifications.

6 Conclusions and Future Work

We have presented a new method for deriving efficient algorithms for a class of optimization problems called maximum marking problems. The main contribution of this work is two new powerful optimization theorems, which allow weight functions to be accumulative both in a top-down and bottom-up way. The examples, which cannot be handled by existing approaches, are variants of the maximum segment sum problem and the fair bonus distribution problem. For simplicity, we focused on weight functions and used only finite mutumorphisms as property descriptions; however, the extension for the property description with accumulators (as in [SHT01]) is straightforward.

Our problem remained, as demonstrated in the fair bonus distribution problem, is that the derived algorithm may have a relatively large constant factor. We expect reduction of the constant factor by using automata compression to eliminate unnecessary states; our current method may produce redundant states due to simple tupling of the property description functions.

Another plan is to apply our new method to more practical real-world problems such as program analysis. Our work [OHS03] solved register allocation without rescheduling as a maximum marking problem. When taking into account the rescheduling of instructions, we will need accumulative information and we expect that the new theorem would play a key role in deriving efficient algorithms for solving these problems.

References

[BdM96]   Richard Bird and Oege de Moor. *Algebra of Programming*. Prentice Hall, 1996.

[Bir87]   Richard Bird. An introduction to the theory of lists. In Manfred Broy, editor, *Logic of Programming and Calculi of Discrete Design*, volume F36 of *NATO ASI Series*, pages 5–42. Springer-Verlag, 1987.

[Bir89]   Richard Bird. Algebraic identities for program calculation. *The Computer Journal*, 32(2):122–126, 1989.

[Bir98]   Richard Bird. *Introduction to Functional Programming using Haskell (second edition)*. Prentice Hall, 1998.

[Bir01]   Richard Bird. Maximum marking problems. *Journal of Functional Programming*, 11(4):411–424, 2001.

[BLW87]   Marshall W. Bern, Eugene L. Lawler, and A. L. Wong. Linear-time computation of optimal subgraphs of decomposable graphs. *Journal of Algorithms*, 8:216–235, 1987.

[BPT92]   Richard B. Borie, R. Gary Parker, and Craig A. Tovey. Automatic generation of linear-time algorithms from predicate calculus descriptions of problems on recursively constructed graph families. *Algorithmica*, 7:555–581, 1992.

[Gri90]   D. Gries. The maximum-segment-sum problem. In E. W. Dijkstra, editor, *Formal Development of Programs and Proofs*, pages 33–36. Addison-Wesley, 1990.

[OHS03]   Mizuhito Ogawa, Zhenjiang Hu, and Isao Sasano. Iterative-free program analysis. In *Proceedings of the 8th ACM SIGPLAN International Conference on Functional Programming (ICFP'03)*, pages 111–123, Uppsala, Sweden, August 2003. ACM Press.

[PJH99]   Simon Peyton Jones and John Hughes, editors. *The Haskell 98 Report*. February 1999. Available from http://www.haskell.org/definition/.

[PP96]   Albert Pettrossi and Maurizio Proietti. Rules and strategies for transforming functional and logic programs. *ACM Computing Surveys*, 28(2):360–414, June 1996.

[SHT01]   Isao Sasano, Zhenjiang Hu, and Masato Takeichi. Generation of efficient programs for solving maximum multi-marking problems. In Walid Taha, editor, *Semantics, Applications, and Implementation of Program Generation (SAIG'01)*, volume 2196 of *Lecture Notes in Computer Science*, pages 72–91, Firenze, Italy, September 2001. Springer-Verlag.

[SHTO00]   Isao Sasano, Zhenjiang Hu, Masato Takeichi, and Mizuhito Ogawa. Make it practical: A generic linear-time algorithm for solving maximum-weightsum problems. In *Proceedings of the 5th ACM SIGPLAN International Conference on Functional Programming (ICFP'00)*, pages 137–149, Montreal, Canada, September 2000. ACM Press.

[SHTO01]   Isao Sasano, Zhenjiang Hu, Masato Takeichi, and Mizuhito Ogawa. Solving a class of knapsack problems on recursive data structures (in Japanese). *Computer Software*, 18(2):59–63, 2001.

[SHTO02]   Isao Sasano, Zhenjiang Hu, Masato Takeichi, and Mizuhito Ogawa. Derivation of linear algorithm for mining optimized gain association rules. *Computer Software*, 19(4):39–44, 2002.

Toward an Abstract Computer Virology

G. Bonfante, M. Kaczmarek, and J.-Y. Marion

Loria, Calligramme project, B.P. 239, 54506 Vandœuvre-lès-Nancy, Cédex, France
and École Nationale Supérieure des Mines de Nancy, INPL, France

Abstract. We are concerned with theoretical aspects of computer viruses. For this, we suggest a new definition of viruses which is clearly based on the iteration theorem and above all on Kleene's recursion theorem. We show that we capture in a natural way previous definitions, and in particular the one of Adleman. We establish generic constructions in order to construct viruses, and we illustrate them by various examples. We discuss the relationship between information theory and viruses and we propose a defense against a kind of viral propagation. Lastly, we show that virus detection is Π_2-complete. However, since we are able to deal with system vulnerability, we exhibit another defense based on controlling system access.

1   Introduction

Computer viruses seem to be an omnipresent issue of information technology; there are a lot of books, see [14] or [17], discussing practical issues. But, as far as we know, there are only a few theoretical studies. This situation is even more amazing because the word "computer virus" comes from the seminal theoretical works of Cohen [4,5,6] and Adleman [1] in the mid-1980's. We do think that theoretical point of view on computer viruses may bring some new insights to the area, as it is also advocated for example by Filiol [8], an expert on computer viruses and cryptology. Indeed, a deep comprehension of mechanisms of computer viruses is from our point of view a promising way to suggest new directions on virus detection and on defence against attacks. On theoretical approach to virology, there is an interesting survey of Bishop [2] and we are aware of the paper of Thimbleby, Anderson and Cairns [10] and of Chess and White paper [3].

This being said, the first question is what is a virus? In his Phd-thesis [4], Cohen defines viruses with respect to Turing Machines. Roughly speaking, a virus is a word on a Turing machine tape such that when it is activated, it duplicates or mutates on the tape. Adleman took a more abstract formulation of computer viruses based on recursive function in order to have a definition independent from computation models. A recent article of Zuo and Zhou [22] completes Aldeman's work, in particular in formalizing polymorphic viruses. In both approaches, a virus is a self-replicating device. So, a virus has the capacity to act on a description of itself. That is why Kleene's recursion theorem is central in the description of the viral mechanism.

D.V. Hung and M. Wirsing (Eds.): ICTAC 2005, LNCS 3722, pp. 579–593, 2005.

This paper is an attempt to use computability and information theory as a vantage point from which to understand viruses. We suggest a definition which embeds Adelman's as well as Zuo and Zhou's definitions in a natural way.

A virus is a program $\mathbf{v}$ which is solution of the fixed point equation

$$\varphi_{\mathbf{v}}(\mathbf{p}, x) = \varphi_{\mathcal{B}(\mathbf{v}, \mathbf{p})}(x) , \qquad (1)$$

where $\mathcal{B}$ is a function which describes the propagation and mutation of the virus in the system. The intuition behind the definition is given in Section 3. This approach has at least three advantages compared with others mentioned above. First, a virus is a program and not a function. Thus, we switch from a purely functional point of view to a programming perspective.

Second, we consider the propagation function, unlike others. So, we are able to have another look at virus replications. All the more so since $\mathcal{B}$ corresponds also to a system vulnerability. Lastly, since the definition is clearly based on recursion theorem, we are able to describe a lot of types of virus smoothly. To illustrate our work, we establish a general construction of trigger virus in Section 3.3.

The results and the organization of this paper is as follows. Section 2 presents the theoretical tools needed to define viruses. We will focus in particular on the s-m-n theorem and the recursion theorem. In section 3, we propose a virus definition and we pursue by a first approach to self-duplication. Section 4 is devoted to Adleman's virus definition. Then, we explore another duplication methods by mutations. We compare our work with the Zuo and Zhou definition of polymorphic viruses. Lastly, Section 6 ends with a discussion on the relation with information theory. From that, we deduce an original defense against some particular kind of viruses, see 6.3. The last Section is about virus search complexity which turns out to Π_2-complete. It is worth to mention that we conclude the paper on some research direction to study system flaws, see Theorem 8.

2   Iteration and Recursion Theorems

2.1   Programming Languages

We are not taking a particular programming language but we are rather considering an abstract, and so simplified, definition of a programming language. However, we shall illustrate all along the theoretical constructions by bash programs. The examples and analogies that we shall present are there to help the reader having a better understanding of the main ideas but also to show that the theoretical constructions are applicable to any programming language.

We briefly present the necessary definitions to study programming languages in an independent way from a particular computational model. We refer to the book of Davis [7], of Rogers [16] and of Odifreddi [15].

Throughout, we consider that we are given a set $\mathcal{D}$, the domain of the computation. As it is convenient, we take $\mathcal{D}$ to be the set of words over some fixed alphabet. But we could also have taken natural numbers or any free algebra as domains. The size $|u|$ of a word u is the number of letters in u.

A programming language is a mapping φ from $\mathcal{D} \to (\mathcal{D} \to \mathcal{D})$ such that for each program $\mathbf{p}$, $\varphi(\mathbf{p}) : \mathcal{D} \to \mathcal{D}$ is the partial function computed by $\mathbf{p}$. Following the convention used in calculability theory, we write $\varphi_{\mathbf{p}}$ instead of $\varphi(\mathbf{p})$. Notice that there is no distinction between programs and data.

We write $f \approx g$ to say that for each x, either $f(x)$ and $g(x)$ are defined and $f(x) = g(x)$ or both are undefined on x.

A total function f is computable wrt φ if there is a program $\mathbf{p}$ such that $f \approx \varphi_{\mathbf{p}}$. If f is a partial function, we shall say that f is semi-computable. Similarly, a set is computable (resp. semi-computable) if its characteristic function is computable (semi-computable).

We also assume that there is a pairing computable function $(\_, \_)$ such that from two words x and y of $\mathcal{D}$, we form a pair $(x, y) \in \mathcal{D}$. A pair (x, y) can be decomposed uniquely into x and y by two computable projection functions. Next, a finite sequence $(x_1, \ldots, x_n)$ of words is built by repeatedly applying the pairing function, that is $(x_1, \ldots, x_n) = (x_1, (x_2, (\ldots, x_n) \ldots))$.

So, from now on, we won't make the distinction between a n-uple and its encoding. Every function is formally considered unary even if we have in mind a binary one. The context will always be clear.

It is worth to mention that the pairing function may be seen as an encryption function and the projections as decryption function.

Following Uspenski [20] and Rogers [16], a programming language φ is acceptable if

1. For each semi-computable function f, there is a program $\mathbf{p} \in \mathcal{D}$ such that $\varphi_{\mathbf{p}} \approx f$.
2. There is an universal program $\mathbf{u}$ which satisfies that for each program $\mathbf{p} \in \mathcal{D}$, $\varphi_{\mathbf{u}}(\mathbf{p}, x) \approx \varphi_{\mathbf{p}}(x)$. item There is a program $\mathbf{s}$ such that

$$\forall \mathbf{p}, x, y \in \mathcal{D} \quad \varphi_{\mathbf{p}}(x, y) \approx \varphi_{\varphi_{\mathbf{s}}(\mathbf{p}, x)}(y) \ .$$

Of course, the function $\varphi_{\mathbf{s}}$ is the well-known s-m-n function written S.

The existence of an acceptable programming language was demonstrated by Turing [19]. The existence of the s-m-n function is also known as the Iteration Theorem [12].

Kleene's Iteration Theorem yields a function S which specializes an argument in a program. The self-application that is $S(\mathbf{p}, \mathbf{p})$ corresponds to the construction of a program which can read its own code $\mathbf{p}$. By analogy with bash programs, it means that the variable \$0 is assigned to the text, that is $\mathbf{p}$, of the executed bash file.

We present now a version of the second recursion theorem which is due to Kleene. This theorem is one of the deepest results in theory of recursive functions. As it is the cornerstone of the paper, we write its proof. We could also have presented Rogers's recursion theorem but we have preferred to focus on only one recursion theorem in order not to introduce any extra difficulties. It is worth also to cite the paper [11] in which the s-m-n function and the recursion theorem are experimented;

Theorem 1 (Kleene's second recursion Theorem). *If g is a semi- computable function, then there is a program* **e** *such that*

$$\varphi_{\mathbf{e}}(x) = g(\mathbf{e}, x) \ . \tag{2}$$

Proof. Let **p** be a program of the semi-computable function $g(S(y, y), x)$. We have

$$g(S(y, y), x) = \varphi_{\mathbf{p}}(y, x)$$
$$= \varphi_{S(\mathbf{p}, y)}(x) \ .$$

By setting $\mathbf{e} = S(\mathbf{p}, \mathbf{p})$, we have

$$g(\mathbf{e}, x) = g(S(\mathbf{p}, \mathbf{p}), x)$$
$$= \varphi_{S(\mathbf{p}, \mathbf{p})}(x)$$
$$= \varphi_{\mathbf{e}}(x) \ .$$

3   The Viral Mechanism

3.1   A Virus Definition

A virus may be thought of as a program which reproduces, and executes some actions. Hence, a virus is a program whose propagation mechanism is described by a computable function $\mathcal{B}$. The propagation function $\mathcal{B}$ searches and selects a sequence of programs $\mathbf{p} = (\mathbf{p}_1, \ldots, \mathbf{p}_n)$ among inputs $(\mathbf{p}, x)$. Then, $\mathcal{B}$ replicates the virus inside **p**. In other words, $\mathcal{B}$ is the vector which carries and transmits the virus to a program. On the other hand, the function $\mathcal{B}$ can be also seen as a flaw in the programming environment. Indeed, $\mathcal{B}$ is a functional property of the programming language φ which is used by a virus **v** to enter and propagate into the system. We suggest below an abstract formalization of viruses which reflects the picture that we have described above.

Definition 1. *Assume that $\mathcal{B}$ is a semi-computable function. A virus wrt $\mathcal{B}$ is a program* **v** *such that for each* **p** *and x in $\mathcal{D}$,*

$$\varphi_{\mathbf{v}}(\mathbf{p}, x) = \varphi_{\mathcal{B}(\mathbf{v}, \mathbf{p})}(x) \ . \tag{3}$$

The function $\mathcal{B}$ is called the propagation function of the virus **v***.*

Throughout, we call *virus* a program, which satisfies the above definition.

As we have said above, we make no distinction between programs and data. However we write in bold face words of $\mathcal{D}$, like **p**, **v**, which are intended to denote programs. On the other hand, the argument x does not necessarily denote a data. Nevertheless, in both cases, **p** or x refer either to a single word or a sequence of words. (For example $x = (x_1, \ldots, x_n)$.)

3.2   Self-reproduction

A distinctive feature of viruses is the self-reproduction property. This has been well developed for cellular automata from the work of von Neumann [21]. Hence, Cohen [4] demonstrated how a virus reproduces in the context of Turing machines.

We show next that a virus can copy itself in several ways. We present some typical examples which in particular illustrate the key role of the recursion Theorem.

We give a first definition of self-reproduction. (A second direction will be discussed in Section 5.) A duplication function Dup is a total computable function such that $Dup(\mathbf{v}, \mathbf{p})$ is a word which contains at least an occurrence of $\mathbf{v}$. A duplicating virus is a virus, which satisfies $\varphi_{\mathbf{v}}(\mathbf{p}, x) = Dup(\mathbf{v}, \mathbf{p})$. The existence of duplicating viruses is a consequence of the following Theorem by setting $f = Dup$.

Theorem 2. *Given a semi-computable function f, there is a virus $\mathbf{v}$ such that*
$$\varphi_{\mathbf{v}}(\mathbf{p}, x) = f(\mathbf{v}, \mathbf{p})$$

Proof. For set $g(y, \mathbf{p}, x) = f(y, \mathbf{p})$. Recursion Theorem implies that the semi-computable function g has a fixed point that we call $\mathbf{v}$. We have $\varphi_{\mathbf{v}}(\mathbf{p}, x) = g(\mathbf{v}, \mathbf{p}, x) = f(\mathbf{v}, \mathbf{p})$.

Next, let $\mathbf{e}$ be a code of g, that is $g \approx \varphi_{\mathbf{e}}$. The propagation function $\mathcal{B}$ induced by $\mathbf{v}$ is defined by $\mathcal{B}(\mathbf{v}, \mathbf{p}) = S(\mathbf{e}, \mathbf{v}, \mathbf{p})$, since

$$\begin{aligned}
\varphi_{\mathcal{B}(\mathbf{v}, \mathbf{p})}(x) &= \varphi_{S(\mathbf{e}, \mathbf{v}, \mathbf{p})}(x) \\
&= g(\mathbf{v}, \mathbf{p}, x) = \varphi_{\mathbf{v}}(\mathbf{p}, x) \ .
\end{aligned}$$

It is worth saying that the propagation function lies on the s-m-n S function. The s-m-n S function specializes the program $\mathbf{e}$ to $\mathbf{v}$ and $\mathbf{p}$, and thus it drops the virus in the system and propagates it. So, in some sense, the s-m-n S function should be considered as a flaw, which is inherent to each acceptable programming language.

To illustrate behaviors of duplicating viruses, we consider several examples, which correspond to known computer viruses.

Crushing

A duplication function Dup is a crushing if $Dup(\mathbf{v}, \mathbf{p}) = \mathbf{v}$.

This basic idea is in fact the starting point of a lot of computer viruses.

Most of the email worms use this methods, copying their script to many directories. The e-mail worm "loveletter" copies itself as "MSKernel32.vbs". Lastly, here is a tiny bash program which copies itself.

```
cat $0 > $0.copy
```

Cloning

Suppose that $\mathbf{p} = (\mathbf{p}_1, \dots, \mathbf{p}_n)$. Then, a virus is cloning wrt Dup, if $Dup(\mathbf{v}, \mathbf{p}) = (d(\mathbf{v}, \mathbf{p}_1), \dots, d(\mathbf{v}, \mathbf{p}_n))$ where d is a duplication function. A cloning virus keeps the structure of the program environment but copies itself into some parts. For example, we can think that **p** is a directory and $(\mathbf{p}_1, \ldots, \mathbf{p}_n)$ are the files inside. So a cloning virus infects some files in the directory.

Moreover, a cloning virus should also verify that $|d(\mathbf{v}, \mathbf{p}_i)| \leq |\mathbf{p}_i|$. Then, the virus does not increase the program size, and so the detection of such non-size increasing virus is harder.

A cloning virus is usually quite malicious, because it overwrites existing program. A concrete example is the virus named "4870 Overwriting". The next bash program illustrates of a cloning virus.

```
for FName in $(ls *.infect.sh);do
  LENGTH='wc -m ./$FName'
  if [ ./$FName != $0 -a "193" -le "${LENGTH%*./$FName}"
     ]; then
    echo [$0 infect ./$FName]
    cat $0 > ./$FName
  fi
done
```

Ecto-Symbiosis
A virus is ecto-symbiotic if it lives on the body surface of the program **v**. For example, $Dup(\mathbf{v}, \mathbf{p}) = \mathbf{v} \cdot \mathbf{p}$ where $\cdot$ is the word concatenation.

The following bash code adds its own code at the end of every file.

```
for FName in $(ls *.infect.sh);do
  if [ ./$FName != $0 ]; then
    echo [$0 infect ./$FName]
    tail $0 -n 6 | cat >> ./$FName
  fi
done
```

The computer virus "Jerusalem" is ecto-symbiotic since it copies itself to executable file (that is, ".COM" or ".EXE" files).

3.3   Implicit Viruses

We establish a result which constructs a virus which performs several actions depending on some conditions on its arguments. This construction of trigger viruses is very general and embeds a lot of practical cases.

Theorem 3. *Let* $C_1, \ldots, C_k$ *be* k *semi-computable disjoint subsets of* $\mathcal{D}$ *and* $V_1, \ldots, V_k$ *be* k *semi-computable functions There is a virus* **v** *which satisfies for all* **p** *and* x, *the equation*

$$\varphi_{\mathbf{v}}(\mathbf{p}, x) = \begin{cases} V_1(\mathbf{v}, \mathbf{p}, x) & (\mathbf{p}, x) \in C_1 \\ \vdots & \\ V_k(\mathbf{v}, \mathbf{p}, x) & (\mathbf{p}, x) \in C_k \end{cases} . \tag{4}$$

Proof. Define

$$F(y, \mathbf{p}, x) = \begin{cases} V_1(y, \mathbf{p}, x) & (\mathbf{p}, x) \in C_1 \\ \vdots \\ V_k(y, \mathbf{p}, x) & (\mathbf{p}, x) \in C_k \end{cases} .$$

The function F is computable and has a code $\mathbf{e}$ such that $F \approx \varphi_e$. Again, recursion Theorem yields a fixed point $\mathbf{v}$ of F which satisfies the Theorem equation. The induced propagation function is $V(\mathbf{v}, \mathbf{p}) = S(\mathbf{e}, \mathbf{v}, \mathbf{p})$.

4 Comparison with Adleman's Virus

Adleman's modeling is based on the following scenario. For every program, there is an "infected" form of the program.

The virus is a computable function from programs to "infected" programs. An infected program has several behaviors which depend on the input x. Adleman lists three actions. In the first (5) the infected program ignores the intended task and executes some "destroying" code. That is why it is called *injure*. In the second (6), the infected program infects the others, that is it performs the intended task of the original, a priori sane, program, and then it contaminates other programs. In the third and last one (7), the infected program imitates the original program and stays quiescent.

We translate Adleman's original definition into our formalism.

Definition 2 (Adleman's viruses). *A total computable function A is said to be a A-viral function (virus in the sense of Adleman) if for each $x \in \mathcal{D}$ one of the three following properties holds:*

Injure

$$\forall \mathbf{p}, \mathbf{q} \in \mathcal{D} \quad \varphi_{A(\mathbf{p})}(x) = \varphi_{A(\mathbf{q})}(x) . \tag{5}$$

This first kind of behavior corresponds to the execution of some viral functions independently from the infected program.

Infect

$$\forall \mathbf{p}, \mathbf{q} \in \mathcal{D} \quad \varphi_{A(\mathbf{p})}(x) = A(\varphi_{\mathbf{p}}(x)) . \tag{6}$$

The second item corresponds to the case of infection. One sees that any part of $\varphi_{\mathbf{p}}(x)$ is rewritten according to A.

Imitate

$$\forall \mathbf{p}, \mathbf{q} \in \mathcal{D} \quad \varphi_{A(\mathbf{p})}(x) = \varphi_{\mathbf{p}}(x) . \tag{7}$$

The last item corresponds to mimic the original program.

Our definition respects Adleman's idea and implies easily the original infection definition. In Adleman's paper, the infection definition is very close to the crushing virus as they have defined previously. However, our definition of the infect case is slightly stronger. Indeed, there is no condition or restriction on the application of the A-viral function to A to $\varphi_{\mathbf{p}}(x)$ unlike Adleman's definition. Indeed, he assumes that $\varphi_{\mathbf{p}}(x) = (\mathbf{d}, \mathbf{p}_1, \ldots, \mathbf{p}_n)$ and that $A(\varphi_{\mathbf{p}}(x)) = (\mathbf{d}, a(\mathbf{p}_1), \ldots, a(\mathbf{p}_n))$ where a is a computable function which depends on A.

Theorem 4. *Assume that A is a A-virus. Then there is a virus that performs the same actions as A.*

Proof. Let $\mathbf{e}$ be the code of A, that is $\varphi_{\mathbf{e}} \approx A$. There is a semi-computable function App such that $App(x, y, z) = \varphi_{\varphi_x(y)}(z)$. Suppose that $\mathbf{q}$ is the code of App. Take $\mathbf{v} = S(\mathbf{q}, \mathbf{e})$. We have

$$\begin{aligned}
\varphi_{A(\mathbf{p})}(x) &= \varphi_{\varphi_{\mathbf{e}}(\mathbf{p})}(x) \\
&= App(\mathbf{e}, \mathbf{p}, x) \\
&= \varphi_{\mathbf{q}}(\mathbf{e}, \mathbf{p}, x) \\
&= \varphi_{S(\mathbf{q}, \mathbf{e})}(\mathbf{p}, x) \\
&= \varphi_{\mathbf{v}}(\mathbf{p}, x) \ .
\end{aligned}$$

We conclude that the propagation function is $\mathcal{B}(\mathbf{v}, \mathbf{p}) = A(\mathbf{p})$.

5   Polymorphic Viruses

Until now, we have considered viruses which duplicate themselves without modifying their code. Now, we consider viruses which mutate when they duplicate. Such viruses are called polymorphic; they are common computer viruses. The appendix gives more "practical information" about them.

This suggests a second definition of self-reproduction. A mutation function *Mut* is a total computable function such that $Mut(\mathbf{v}, \mathbf{p})$ is a word which contains at least an occurrence of a virus $\mathbf{v}'$. The difference with the previous definition of duplication function in Subsection 3.2 is that $\mathbf{v}'$ is a mutated version of $\mathbf{v}$ wrt $\mathbf{p}$.

5.1   On Polymorphic Generators

Theorem 2, and the implicit virus Theorem 3, shows that a virus is essentially a fixed point of a semi-computable function. In other words, a virus is obtained by solving the equation: $\varphi_{\mathbf{v}}(\mathbf{p}, x) = f(\mathbf{v}, \mathbf{p}, x)$. And solutions are fixed points of f. Rogers [16] established that a computable function has an infinite number of fixed points. So, a first mutation strategy could be to enumerate fixed points of f. However, the set of fixed points of a computable function is Π_2, and worst it is Π_2-complete for constant functions.

So we can not enumerate all fixed points because it is not a semi-computable set. But, we can generate an infinite number of fixed points.

To illustrate it, we suggest to use a classical padding function '*Pad*' which satisfies

1. *Pad* is a one-one function.
2. For each program $\mathbf{q}$ and each y, $\varphi_{\mathbf{q}} \approx \varphi_{Pad(\mathbf{q},y)}$.

Lemma 1. *There is a computable padding function Pad.*

Proof. Take $T : \mathcal{D} \times \mathcal{D} \to \mathcal{D}$ as a computable bijective encoding of pairs. Let π_1 be first projection function of T. Define $Pad(\mathbf{q}, y)$ as the code of $\pi_1(T(\mathbf{q}, y))$.

Theorem 5. *Let f be a computable function. Then there is a computable function Gen such that*

$$Gen(i) \ \ is \ a \ virus \tag{8}$$
$$\forall i \neq j, \quad Gen(i) \neq Gen(j) \tag{9}$$
$$\varphi_{Gen(i)}(\mathbf{p}, x) = f(Gen(i), \mathbf{p}) \ . \tag{10}$$

Proof. In fact, $Gen(i)$ is the ith fixed point of f wrt to a fixed point enumeration procedure. A construction of a fixed point enumeration procedure is made by padding Kleene's fixed point given by the proof of the recursion Theorem.

For this, suppose that $\mathbf{p}$ is a program of the semi-computable function $g(S(y, y), x)$. We have

$$g(S(y, y), x) = \varphi_{\mathbf{p}}(y, x) \ .$$

By setting $Gen(i) = S(Pad(\mathbf{p}, i), Pad(\mathbf{p}, i))$, we have

$$\begin{aligned} g(S(Pad(\mathbf{p}, i), Pad(\mathbf{p}, i)), x) &= \varphi_{\mathbf{p}}(Pad(\mathbf{p}, i), x) \\ &= \varphi_{Pad(\mathbf{p},i)}(Pad(\mathbf{p}, i), x) \quad\quad Pad\text{'s dfn} \\ &= \varphi_{S(Pad(\mathbf{p},i),Pad(\mathbf{p},i))}(x) \ . \end{aligned}$$

Remark 1. For a virus writer, a mutation function is a polymorphic engine, such as the well known "Dark Avenger". A polymorphic engine is a module which gives the ability to look different on replication most of them are encryptor, decryptor functions.

5.2   Zuo and Zhou's Viral Function

Polymorphic viruses were foreseen by Cohen and Adleman. As far as we know, Zuo and Zhou's are the first in [22] to propose a formal definition of the virus mutation process. They discuss on viruses that evolve into at most n forms, and then they consider polymorphism with an infinite numbers of possible mutations.

Definition 3 (Zuo and Zhou viruses). *Assume that T and I are two disjoint computable sets. A total computable function ZZ is a ZZ-viral polymorphic function if for all n and $\mathbf{q}$,*

$$\varphi_{ZZ(n,\mathbf{q})}(x) = \begin{cases} D(x) & x \in T & Injure \\ ZZ(n+1, \varphi_{\mathbf{q}}(x)) & x \in I & Infect \\ \varphi_{\mathbf{q}}(x) & & Imitate \end{cases} \tag{11}$$

This definition is close to the one of Adleman, where T corresponds to a set of arguments for which the virus injures and I is a set of arguments for which the virus infects. The last case corresponds to the imitation behavior of a virus. So, the difference stands on the argument n which is used to mutate the virus in the infect case. Hence, a given program $\mathbf{q}$ has an infinite set of infected forms which are $\{ZZ(n, \mathbf{q}) \mid n \in \mathcal{D}\}$. (Technically, n is an encoding of natural numbers into $\mathcal{D}$.)

Theorem 6. *Assume that ZZ is a ZZ-viral polymorphic function. Then there is a virus which performs the same actions as ZZ wrt a propagation function.*

Proof. The proof is a direct consequence of implicit virus Theorem 3 by setting $\mathbf{p} = (n, \mathbf{q})$. $\qquad\blacksquare$

6   Information Theory

There are various ways to define a mutation function. A crucial feature of a virus is to be as small as possible. Thus, it is much harder to detect it. We now revisit clone and symbiote virus definitions.

6.1   Compressed Clones

A compressed clone is a mutated virus $Mut(\mathbf{v}, \mathbf{p})$ such that $|Mut(\mathbf{v}, \mathbf{p})| < |\mathbf{v}|$. A compression may use information inside the program $\mathbf{p}$. There are several compression algorithms which perform such replications.

6.2   Endo-Symbiosis

An endo-symbiote is a virus which hides (and lives) in a program. A spyware is a kind of endo-symbiote. For this, it suffices that

1. We can retrieve $\mathbf{v}$ and $\mathbf{p}$ from $Mut(\mathbf{v}, \mathbf{p})$. That is, there are two inverse functions V and P such that $\varphi_{V(Mut(\mathbf{v},\mathbf{p}))} \approx \varphi_{\mathbf{v}}$ and $\varphi_{P(Mut(\mathbf{v},\mathbf{p}))} \approx \varphi_{\mathbf{p}}$
2. To avoid an easy detection of viruses, we impose that

$$|Mut(\mathbf{v}, \mathbf{p})| \le |\mathbf{p}| \ .$$

3. We suppose furthermore that

$$|V(Mut(\mathbf{v}, \mathbf{p}))| + |P(Mut(\mathbf{v}, \mathbf{p}))| \le |Mut(\mathbf{v}, \mathbf{p})| \ .$$

Both examples above show an interesting relationship with complexity information theory. For this, we refer to the book of Li and Vitányi [13]. Complexity information theory leans on Kolmogorov complexity. The Kolmogorov complexity of a word $x \in \mathcal{D}$ wrt φ_e and knowing y is $K_{\varphi_e}(x|y) = \min\{|\mathbf{q}| : \varphi_e(\mathbf{q}, y) = x\}$. The fundamental Theorem of Kolmogorov complexity theory yields: There is an universal program $\mathbf{u}$ such that for any program $\mathbf{e}$, we have $K_{\varphi_u}(x|y) \leq K_{\varphi_e}(x|y) + c$ where c is some constant. This means that the minimal size of a program which computes a word x wrt y is $K_{\varphi_u}(x|y)$, up to an additive constant.

Now, suppose that the virus $\mathbf{v}$ mutates to $\mathbf{v}'$ from $\mathbf{p}$. That is $Mut(\mathbf{v}, \mathbf{p}) = \mathbf{v}'$. An interesting question is then to determine the amount of information which is needed to produce the virus $\mathbf{v}'$. The answer is $K_{\varphi_u}(\mathbf{v}'|(\mathbf{v}, \mathbf{p}))$ bits, up to an additive constant.

The demonstration of the fundamental Theorem implies that the shortest description of a word x is made of two parts. The first part $\mathbf{e}$ encodes the word regularity and the second part $\mathbf{q}$ represents the "randomness" side of x. And, we have $\varphi_e(\mathbf{q}, y) = x$. Here, the program $\mathbf{e}$ plays the role of an interpreter which executes $\mathbf{q}$ in order to print x. Now, let us decompose $\mathbf{v}'$ into two parts (i) an interpreter $\mathbf{e}$ and (ii) a random data part $\mathbf{q}$ such that $\varphi_{\mathbf{v}'} = \varphi_{\varphi_e(\mathbf{q}, \mathbf{v}, \mathbf{p})}$. In this construction, the virus introduces an interpreter for hiding itself. This is justified by the fundamental Theorem which says that it is an efficient way to compress a virus. In [9], Goel and Bush use Kolmogorov complexity to make a comparison and establish results between biological and computer viruses.

6.3   Defense Against Endo-Symbiotes

We suggest an original defense (as far as we know) against some viruses based on information Theory. We use the notations introduced in Section 6 about endo-symbiosis and Kolmogorov complexity.

Our defense prevents the system to be infected by endo-symbiote. Suppose that the programming environment is composed of an interpreter $\mathbf{u}$ which is a universal program. We modify it to construct $\mathbf{u}'$ in such way that $\varphi_{\mathbf{u}'}(\mathbf{p}, x) = \varphi_{\varphi_u(\mathbf{p})}(x)$. Hence, intuitively a program for $\varphi_{\mathbf{u}'}$ is a description of a program wrt $\varphi_{\mathbf{u}}$.

Given a constant c, we define a c-compression of a program $\mathbf{p}$ as a program $\mathbf{p}'$ such that $\varphi_u(\mathbf{p}') = \mathbf{p}$ and $|\mathbf{p}'| \leq K_{\varphi_u}(\mathbf{p}) + c$. Observe that $\varphi_{\mathbf{u}'}(\mathbf{p}', x) = \varphi_{\mathbf{p}}(x)$.

Now, suppose that $\mathbf{v}$ is an endo-symbiote. So, there is a mutation function Mut and two associated projections V et P. We have by definition of endo-symbiotes that $|V(Mut(\mathbf{v}, \mathbf{p}'))| + |P(Mut(\mathbf{v}, \mathbf{p}'))| \leq |Mut(\mathbf{v}, \mathbf{p}')| \leq |\mathbf{p}'|$. By definition of P, we have $\varphi_{\mathbf{p}'} = \varphi_{P(Mut(\mathbf{v}, \mathbf{p}'))}$. As a consequence, $\varphi_u(\mathbf{p}') = \varphi_u(P(Mut(\mathbf{v}, \mathbf{p}'))) = \mathbf{p}$. So, $|P(Mut(\mathbf{v}, \mathbf{p}'))| \geq K_{\varphi_u}(\mathbf{p})$. Finally, the space $|V(Mut(\mathbf{v}, \mathbf{p}'))|$ to encode the virus is bounded by c. Notice that it is not difficult to forbid $\varphi_{\mathbf{u}'}$ to execute programs which have less than c bits. In this case, no endo-symbiote can infect $\mathbf{p}'$. Therefore, c-compressed programs are safe from attack by endo-symbiotes.

Of course, this defense strategy is infeasible because there is no way to approximate the Kolmogorov complexity by mean of a computable function. In consequence, we can not produce c-compressed programs. However, we do think this kind of idea shed some light on self-defense programming systems.

7 Detection of Viruses

Let us first consider the set of viruses wrt a function $\mathcal{B}$. It is formally given by $V_{\mathcal{B}} = \{\mathbf{v} \mid \forall \mathbf{p}, x : \exists y : \varphi_{\mathbf{v}}(\mathbf{p}, x) = y \land \varphi_{\mathcal{B}(\mathbf{v}, \mathbf{p})}(x) = y\}$. As the formulation of $V_{\mathcal{B}}$ shows it, we have:

Proposition 1. *Given a recursive function $\mathcal{B}$, $V_{\mathcal{B}}$ is Π_2.*

Theorem 7. *There are some functions $\mathcal{B}$ for which $V_{\mathcal{B}}$ is Π_2-complete.*

Proof. Suppose now given a computable function t, it has an index $\mathbf{q}$. It is well known that the set $T = \{i \mid \varphi_i = t\}$ is Π_2-complete. Define now $\mathcal{B}(y, p) = S(\mathbf{q}, p)$. Observe that a virus $\mathbf{v}$ verify: $\forall \mathbf{p}, x : \varphi_{\mathbf{v}}(\mathbf{p}, x) = t(\mathbf{p}, x)$. The pairing procedure being surjective, $\mathbf{v}$ is an index of t. Conversely, suppose that $\mathbf{e}$ is not a virus. In that case, there is some $\mathbf{p}, x$ for which $\varphi_{\mathbf{e}}(\mathbf{p}, x) \neq \varphi_{\mathcal{B}(\mathbf{e}, \mathbf{p})}(x) = t(\mathbf{p}, x)$. As a consequence, it is not an index of t. So, $V_{\mathcal{B}} = T$.

Theorem 8. *There are some functions $\mathcal{B}$ for which it is decidable whether $\mathbf{p}$ is a virus or not.*

Proof. Let us define $f(y, \mathbf{p}, x) = \varphi_y(\mathbf{p}, x)$. Being recursive, it has a code, say $\mathbf{q}$. Application of s-m-n Theorem provides $S(\mathbf{q}, y, \mathbf{p})$ such that for all $y, \mathbf{p}, x$, we have $\varphi_{S(\mathbf{q}, y, \mathbf{p})}(x) = f(y, \mathbf{p}, x)$. Let us define $\mathcal{B}(y, \mathbf{p}) = S(\mathbf{q}, y, \mathbf{p})$. It is routine to check that for all $\mathbf{d}$, $\mathbf{d}$ is a virus for $\mathcal{B}$. So, in that case, any index is a virus.

A consequence of this is that there are some weakness for which it is decidable whether a code is a virus or not. This is again, as far as we know, one of the first positive results concerning the detection of viruses.

References

1. L. Adleman. An abstract theory of computer viruses. In *Advances in Cryptology — CRYPTO'88*, volume 403. Lecture Notes in Computer Science, 1988.
2. M. Bishop. An overview of computer viruses in a research environment. Technical report, Hanover, NH, USA, 1991.
3. D. Chess and S. White. An undetectable computer virus.
4. F. Cohen. *Computer Viruses*. PhD thesis, University of Southern California, January 1986.
5. F. Cohen. Computer viruses: theory and experiments. *Comput. Secur.*, 6(1):22–35, 1987.
6. F. Cohen. Models of practical defenses against computer viruses: theory and experiments. *Comput. Secur.*, 6(1), 1987.

7. M. Davis. *Computability and unsolvability.* McGraw-Hill, 1958.
8. E. Filiol. *Les virus informatiques: théorie, pratique et applications.* Springer-Verlag France, 2004.
9. S. Goel and S. Bush. Kolmogorov complexity estimates for detection of viruses in biologically inspired security systems: a comparison with traditional approaches. *Complex.*, 9(2):54–73, 2003.
10. S. Anderson H. Thimbleby and P. Cairns. A framework for medelling trojans and computer virus infection. *Comput. J.*, 41:444–458, 1999.
11. N. Jones. Computer implementation and applications of kleene's S-m-n and recursive theorems. In Y. N. Moschovakis, editor, *Lecture Notes in Mathematics, Logic From Computer Science*, pages 243–263. 1991.
12. S. C. Kleene. *Introduction to Metamathematics.* Van Nostrand, princeton, nj edition, 1964.
13. M. Li and P. Vitányi. *An Introduction to Kolmogorov Complexity and its Application.* Springer, 1997. (Second edition).
14. M. Ludwig. *The Giant Black Book of Computer Viruses.* American Eagle Publications, 1998.
15. P. Odiffredi. *Classical recursion theory.* North-Holland, 1989.
16. H. Rogers. *Theory of Recursive Functions and Effective Computability.* McGraw Hill, New York, 1967.
17. P. Szor. *The Art of Computer Virus Research and Defense.* Addison-Wesley Professional, 2005.
18. A. Turing and J.-Y. Girard. *La machine de Turing.* Seuil, 1995.
19. A. M. Turing. On computable numbers with an application to the entscheidungsproblem. *Proc. London Mathematical Society*, 42(2):230–265, 1936. Traduction [18].
20. V.A. Uspenskii. Enumeration operators ans the concept of program. *Uspekhi Matematicheskikh Nauk*, 11, 1956.
21. J. von Neumann and A. W. Burks. Theory of self-reproducing automata. University of Illinois Press, Champaign, IL, 1966.
22. Z. Zuo and M. Zhou. Some further theorical results about computer viruses. In *The Computer Journal*, 2004.

A   Polymorphic Viruses

A method widely used for virus detection is file scanning. It uses short strings, refered as signatures, resulting from reverse engineering of viral codes. Those signatures only match the considered virus and not healthy programs. Thus, using a search engine, if a signature is found a virus is detected.

To avoid this detection, one could consider and old virus and change some instructions in order to fool the signature recognition. As an illustration, consider the following signature of a viral bash code

```
for FName in $( ls *.infect.sh );do
  if [ ./$FName != $0 ];then
   cat $0 > ./$FName
  fi
done
```

The following code denotes the same program but with an other signature

```
OUT=cat
for FName in $(ls *.infect.sh);do
 if [ ./$FName != $0 ];then
  $OUT $0 > ./$FName
 fi
done
```

Polymorphic viruses use this idea, when it replicates, such a virus changes some parts of its code to look different.

Virus writers began experimenting with such techniques in the early nineties and it achieved with the creation of mutation engines. Historically the first one was "Dark Avenger". Nowadays, many mutation engines have been released, most of them use encryption, decryption functions. The idea, is to break the code into two parts, the first one is a decryptor responsible for decrypting the second part and passing the control to it. Then the second part generates a new decryptor, encrypts itself and links both parts to create a new version of the virus.

A polymorphic virus could be illustrated by the following bash code, it is a simple virus which use as polymorphic engine a swap of two characters.

```
SPCHAR=007
LENGTH=17
ALPHA=
    azertyuiopqsdfghjklmwxcvbnAZERTYUIOPQSDFGHJKLMWXCVBN
CHAR1=${ALPHA:'expr $RANDOM % 52':1}
CHAR2=${ALPHA:'expr $RANDOM % 52':1}
#add the decryptor
echo "SPCHAR=007" > ./tmp
echo "tail -n $LENGTH \$0 | sed -e \"s/$CHAR1/\$SPCHAR/g\
    " -e \"s/$CHAR2/$CHAR1/g\" -e \"s/\$SPCHAR/$CHAR2/g\"
    -e \"s/SPCHAR=$CHAR2/SPCHAR=$SPCHAR/g\"> ./vx" >> ./
    tmp
echo "./vx" >> ./tmp
echo "exit 0" >> ./tmp
#encrypt and add viral code
cat $0 | sed -e "s/$CHAR1/$SPCHAR/g" -e "s/$CHAR2/$CHAR1/
    g" -e "s/$SPCHAR/$CHAR2/g" -e "s/SPCHAR=$CHAR2/SPCHAR=
    $SPCHAR/g" >> ./tmp
#infect
for FName in $(ls *.infect.sh);do
  cat ./tmp >> ./$FName
done
rm -f ./tmp
```

B   Metamorphic Viruses

To detect polymorphic computer viruses, antivirus editors have used code emulation techniques and static analysers. The idea of emulation, is to execute programs in a controled fake environment. Thus an encrypted virus will decrypt itself in this environment and some signature detection can be done. Concerning static analysers, they are improved signature maching engines which are able to recognize simple code variation.

To thward those methods, since 2001 virus writers has investigated metamorphism. This is an enhanced morphism technique. Where polymorphic engines generate a variable encryptor, a metamorhic engine generates a whole variable code using some obfuscation functions. Moreover, to fool emulation methods metamorphic viruses can alter their behavior if they detect a controled environment.

When it is executed, a metamorphic virus desassembles its own code, reverse engineers it and transforms it using its environment. If it detects that his environment is controled, it transforms itself into a healthy program, else it recreates a new whole viral code using reverse ingineered information, in order to generate a replication semantically indentical but programmatically different.

Such a virus is really difficult to analyse, thus it could take a long period to understand its behavior. During this period, it replicates freely.

Intuitively, polymorphic viruses mutates without concidering their environment whereas metamophic viruses spawn their next generation using new information. As a matter of fact, to capture this notion, one must consider the equation $\varphi_{\mathbf{v}}(\mathbf{p}, x) = f(\mathbf{v}, \mathbf{p}, x)$ in its entirety.

On Superposition-Based Satisfiability Procedures and Their Combination

Hélène Kirchner, Silvio Ranise, Christophe Ringeissen, and Duc Khanh Tran

LORIA & INRIA-Lorraine

Abstract. We study how to efficiently combine satisfiability procedures built by using a superposition calculus with satisfiability procedures for theories, for which the superposition calculus may not apply (e.g., for various decidable fragments of Arithmetic). Our starting point is the Nelson-Oppen combination method, where satisfiability procedures cooperate by exchanging entailed (disjunction of) equalities between variables. We show that the superposition calculus deduces sufficiently many such equalities for convex theories (e.g., the theory of equality and the theory of lists) and disjunction of equalities for non-convex theories (e.g., the theory of arrays) to guarantee the completeness of the combination method. Experimental results on proof obligations extracted from the certification of auto-generated aerospace software confirm the efficiency of the approach. Finally, we show how to make satisfiability procedures built by superposition both incremental and resettable by using a hierarchic variant of the Nelson-Oppen method.

1 Introduction

Satisfiability procedures for theories of data types such as arrays, lists, and integers are at the core of many state-of-the-art verification tools. The task of designing, proving correct, and implementing satisfiability procedures is far from simple. One of the main problem is proving the correctness of satisfiability procedures. Furthermore, data structures and algorithms for each new procedure are implemented from scratch, with little software reuse and high risk of errors.

To overcome these difficulties, an approach to flexibly build satisfiability procedures based on superposition has been proposed in [2] and it has been shown competitive with *ad hoc* satisfiability procedures in [3,1]. Following this approach, the correctness proof of a procedure for a theory T reduces to show the termination of the fair and exhaustive application of the rules of the superposition calculus [12] on an axiomatization of T and an arbitrary set of literals. Furthermore, the implementation of the satisfiability procedure for T becomes easy by using (almost) off-the-shelf an available prover implementing the superposition calculus. In this way, years of careful engineering and debugging can be effortlessly reused. Unfortunately, this approach does not allow one to build satisfiability procedures for the fragments of Arithmetic which are required by most (if not all) verification problems. Hence, there is a need to combine satisfiability procedures obtained by superposition with satisfiability procedures for the various fragments of Arithmetic based on *ad hoc* techniques (see e.g., [8]).

D.V. Hung and M. Wirsing (Eds.): ICTAC 2005, LNCS 3722, pp. 594–608, 2005.

The method proposed by Nelson and Oppen (N-O) [11] allows one to combine satisfiability procedures for theories (satisfying some requirements) by exchanging equalities or disjunction of equalities between variables. Such equalities (or their disjunction) must be entailed by the input set of literals in each component theory. Since a set S of literals entails an equality (or a disjunction of equalities) ϕ if and only if the conjunction of S and the negation of ϕ is unsatisfiable, there does not seem to be any problem in using a satisfiability procedure based on superposition in a N-O combination. However, as it is well known (see e.g. [6]), to implement the combination method efficiently, the satisfiability procedure for the component theories must be capable of deriving the formulae to exchange with other procedures. This is not obvious for satisfiability procedures obtained by superposition since latter is not known to be complete for consequence finding, i.e. we are not guaranteed that a clause which is a logical consequence of a set of clauses will be eventually derived by applying the rules of the calculus. The **first contribution** of this paper is to show that satisfiability procedures obtained by superposition deduce sufficiently many equalities between variables for convex theories (e.g., the theory of lists) or disjunction of equalities between variables for non-convex theories (e.g., the theory of arrays) to guarantee the completeness of the N-O combination method.

The capability of detecting entailed equalities is not the only requirement to efficiently implement the N-O method: the component satisfiability procedures must be incremental and resettable, i.e. it must be possible to add and remove literals to and from the state of the procedure without restarting it. Actual state-of-the-art theorem provers based on superposition do not satisfy these two requirements and each time a literal is added or removed, provers must be invoked from scratch. This may result in an unacceptable overhead. To overcome this difficulty, the **second contribution** of this paper is to propose a hierarchic variant of the N-O combination method, where the superposition prover is used as a front-end of a congruence closure algorithm which is then combined with a satisfiability procedure for Arithmetic by the standard N-O method.

Our motivation for this work is to give a firm basis to a theorem proving system, called **haRVey** [3], which we are currently developing. Experimental results on a set of benchmarks [4] extracted from program verification problems clearly show the advantages of the proposed approach.

Plan of the paper. In Section 2, we introduce some basic notions. In Section 3, we show how to directly extract entailed (disjunction of) equalities between variables from satisfiability procedures built by superposition for various theories, we discuss some experimental results, and we conclude by describing a refinement of the N-O method. In Section 4, we discuss some related work. In Section 5, we conclude and sketch the future work. All omitted proofs can be found in [9].

2 Background

We assume the usual first-order syntactic notions of signature, term, position, and substitution, as defined, e.g., in [5]. If l and r are two terms, then $l = r$

is an *equality* and $\neg(l = r)$ (also written as $l \neq r$) is a *disequality*. A literal is either an equality or a disequality. A first-order *formula* is built in the usual way over the universal and existential quantifiers, Boolean connectives, and symbols in a given first-order signature. We call a formula *ground* if it has no variable. A *clause* is a disjunction of literals. A *unit* clause is a clause with only one disjunct, equivalently a literal. The *empty* clause is the clause with no disjunct, equivalently an unsatisfiable formula.

We also assume the usual first-order notions of model, satisfiability, validity, logical consequence, and theory. A *first-order theory* is a set of first-order formulae with no free variables. When T is a finitely axiomatized theory, $Ax(T)$ denotes the set of axioms of T. All the theories in this paper are first-order theories *with equality*, which means that the equality symbol $=$ is always interpreted as the equality relation. The theory of equality is denoted with $\mathcal{E}$. A formula is *satisfiable in a theory* T if it is satisfiable in a model of T. Two formulas φ and ψ are *equisatisfiable in* T if for every model $\mathcal{A}$ of T, φ is satisfiable in $\mathcal{A}$ iff ψ is satisfiable in $\mathcal{A}$. The *satisfiability problem* for a theory T amounts to establishing whether any given finite conjunction of literals (or equivalently, any given finite set of literals) is T-satisfiable or not. A *satisfiability procedure* for T is any algorithm that solves the satisfiability problem for T (the satisfiability of any quantifier-free formula can be reduced to the satisfiability of sets of literals by converting to disjunctive normal form and then splitting on disjunctions). The reader should observe that free variables in a formula φ behave as (Skolem) constants when φ is checked for satisfiability. In the rest of the paper, we use variables and constants interchangeably when the context allows us to do so, i.e. when combining satisfiability procedures.

2.1   The Superposition Calculus $\mathcal{SP}$

In the following, $=$ is (unordered) equality, $\equiv$ is identity, $\bowtie$ is either $=$ or $\neq$, l, r, u, t are terms, v, w, x, y, z are variables, all other lower case letters are constant or function symbols. The rules of the superposition calculus $\mathcal{SP}$ used in [2] and in this paper are depicted in Figures 1 and 2.

Given a set S of clauses, an expansion inference in Figure 1 adds the clause in its conclusion to S while a contraction inference rule in Figure 2 either simplifies (e.g. *Simplification* reduces to (ordered) rewriting when C is a unit clause) or deletes a clause from S. Notice that the premises and conclusion of an expansion rule are clauses while those of a contraction rule are sets of clauses. The rules in Figures 1 and 2 are well-known in the theorem proving literature (see e.g., [12]). A fundamental feature of $\mathcal{SP}$ is the usage of a *total reduction ordering (TRO)* $\succ$ [5] on terms. The ordering $\succ$ is extended to literals in such a way that only maximal sides of maximal instances of literals are considered when applying the expansion rules of Figure 1. Since later we need a total reduction ordering $\succ_c$ on clauses, we extend the TRO $\succ$ on terms to clauses as follows: $C \succ_c D$ if $ms(C) \; (\succ_{mul})_{mul} \; ms(D)$, where C and D are clauses, $\succ_{mul}$ is the multiset extension of the TRO $\succ$ over terms (see [5] for details), and $ms(s_1 \neq s_1' \lor \ldots \lor s_n \neq s_n' \lor t_1 = t_1' \lor \ldots t_m = t_m')$ returns the multi-

Superposition (SP)	$\dfrac{\Gamma \Rightarrow \Delta, l[u'] = r \quad \Pi \Rightarrow \Sigma, u = t}{\sigma(\Gamma, \Pi \Rightarrow \Delta, \Sigma, l[t] = r)}$ (i), (ii), (iii), (iv)
Paramodulation (PM)	$\dfrac{\Gamma, l[u'] = r \Rightarrow \Delta \quad \Pi \Rightarrow \Sigma, u = t}{\sigma(l[t] = r, \Gamma, \Pi \Rightarrow \Delta, \Sigma)}$ (i), (ii), (iii), (iv)
Reflection (R)	$\dfrac{\Gamma, u' = u \Rightarrow \Delta}{\sigma(\Gamma \Rightarrow \Delta)} \forall L \in \Gamma \cup \Delta : \sigma(u' = u) \not\succ \sigma(L)$
Eq. Factoring (EF)	$\dfrac{\Gamma \Rightarrow \Delta, u = t, u' = t'}{\sigma(\Gamma, t = t' \Rightarrow \Delta, u = t')}$ (i), $\forall L \in \Gamma : \sigma(u) \not\preceq \sigma(L)$, $\forall L \in \{u' = t'\} \cup \Delta : \sigma(u = t) \not\succ \sigma(L)$

where a clause $\neg A_1 \vee \cdots \vee \neg A_n \vee B_1 \vee \cdots \vee B_n$ is written in sequent style as $\{A_1, \ldots, A_n\} \Rightarrow \{B_1, \ldots, B_m\}$ (where the A_i's and B_j's are literals), equality is the only predicate symbol, σ is the most general unifier of u and u', u' is not a variable in Superposition and Paramodulation, L is a literal, and the following hold:

(i) $\sigma(u) \not\preceq \sigma(t)$, (ii) $\forall L \in \Pi \cup \Sigma : \sigma(u = t) \not\succ \sigma(L)$, (iii) $\sigma(l[u']) \not\preceq \sigma(r)$, and (iv) $\forall L \in \Gamma \cup \Delta : \sigma(l[u'] = r) \not\succ \sigma(L)$.

Fig. 1. Expansion inference rules of $\mathcal{SP}$

Subsumption	$\dfrac{S \cup \{C, C'\}}{S \cup \{C\}}$	if for some substitution θ, $\theta(C) \subseteq C'$ and for no substitution ρ, $\rho(C') \equiv C$
Simplification	$\dfrac{S \cup \{C[l'], l = r\}}{S \cup \{C[\theta(r)], l = r\}}$	if $l' \equiv \theta(l)$, $\theta(l) \succ \theta(r)$, and $\forall L \in C[\theta(l)] : L \succ (\theta(l) = \theta(r))$
Deletion	$\dfrac{S \cup \{\Gamma \Rightarrow \Delta, t = t\}}{S}$	

where C and C' are clauses and S is a set of clauses.

Fig. 2. Contraction inference rules of $\mathcal{SP}$

set $\{\{s_1, s_1, s_1', s_1'\}, \ldots, \{s_n, s_n, s_n', s_n'\}, \{t_1, t_1'\}, \ldots, \{t_m, t_m'\}\}$. (By abuse of notation, we abbreviate $\succ_c$ with $\succ$.)

A clause C is *redundant* with respect to a set S of clauses if either $C \in S$ or S can be obtained from $S \cup \{C\}$ by a sequence of application of the contraction rules of Figure 2. An inference is *redundant* with respect to a set S of clauses if its conclusion is redundant with respect to S. A set S of clauses is *saturated* with respect to $\mathcal{SP}$ if every inference of $\mathcal{SP}$ with a premise in S is redundant with respect to S. A *derivation* is a sequence $S_0, S_1, \ldots, S_i, \ldots$ of sets of clauses where at each step an inference of $\mathcal{SP}$ is applied to generate and add a clause (cf. expansion rules in Figure 1) or to delete or reduce a clause (cf. contraction rules in Figure 2). A derivation is characterized by its *limit*, defined as the set of persistent clauses $S_\infty = \bigcup_{j \geq 0} \bigcap_{i > j} S_i$.

Lemma 1 ([12]). *Let $S_0, S_1, \ldots, S_n, \ldots$ be a derivation and let C be a clause in $(\bigcup_i S_i) \backslash S_\infty$. Then C is redundant with respect to S_∞.*

A derivation $S_0, S_1, \ldots, S_i, \ldots$ with limit S_∞ is *fair* with respect to $\mathcal{SP}$ if for every inference in $\mathcal{SP}$ with premises in S_∞, there is some $j \geq 0$ such that the inference is redundant in S_j.

Theorem 1 ([12]). *If $S_0, S_1, \ldots$ is a fair derivation of $\mathcal{SP}$, then (i) its limit S_∞ is saturated with respect to $\mathcal{SP}$, (ii) S_0 is unsatisfiable iff the empty clause is in S_j for some j, and (iii) if such a fair derivation is finite, i.e. it is of the form $S_0, \ldots, S_n$, then S_n is saturated and logically equivalent to S_0.*

We say that $\mathcal{SP}$ is *refutation complete* since it is possible to derive the empty clause with a finite derivation from an unsatisfiable set of clauses (cf. (*ii*) of Theorem 1).

2.2   A Superposition Approach to Satisfiability Procedures

The rewrite-based methodology [2] uses $\mathcal{SP}$ to build in an uniform way satisfiability procedures for theories which can be finitely axiomatized by a set of clauses. For a term t, $depth(t) = 0$, if t is a constant or a variable, and $depth(f(t_1, \ldots, t_n)) = 1 + max\{depth(t_i) \mid 1 \le i \le n\}$. A term is *flat* if its depth is 0 or 1. For a literal, $depth(l \bowtie r) = depth(l) + depth(r)$. A positive literal is *flat* if its depth is 0 or 1. A negative literal is *flat* if its depth is 0. A flat clause is a clause containing only flat literals. Let V be a set of variables. A *V-elementary equality* is an equality of the form $x = y$ for $x, y \in V$. A *V-elementary clause* is a disjunction of V-elementary equalities.

The rewrite-based methodology for T-satisfiability consists of two phases:

1. *Flattening:* all ground literals are flattened by introducing new constants, yielding an equisatisfiable T-reduced *flat* problem.
2. *Ordering selection and termination:* any fair derivation of $\mathcal{SP}$ is shown to be finite when applied to a T-reduced flat problem, provided that the TRO $\succ$ satisfies a few properties depending on T.

If T is a theory to which the rewrite-based methodology applies, a T-satisfiability procedure can be built by implementing the flattening (this can be done once and for all), and by using a prover mechanizing $\mathcal{SP}$ with a suitable TRO $\succ$. If the final set of clauses returned by the prover contains the empty clause, then the T-satisfiability procedure returns unsat; otherwise, it returns sat.

2.3   The Nelson-Oppen Method

The N-O combination method allows us to solve the problem of checking the satisfiability of a conjunction Φ of quantifier-free literals in the union of two signature-disjoint theories T_1 and T_2 for which two satisfiability procedures are available. Since the literals in Φ may be built over symbols in T_1 or in T_2, we need to *purify* them by introducing fresh variables to name subterms. This process leaves us with a conjunction $\Phi_1 \wedge \Phi_2$ which is equisatisfiable to Φ where Φ_i contains only literals with symbols of T_i, for $i = 1, 2$. In this way, literals in Φ_i can be *dispatched* to the available decision procedure for T_i.

To show the correctness of the N-O method [10,13], the theories T_1 and T_2 must be stably-infinite. Roughly, a theory is *stably infinite* if any satisfiable quantifier-free formula is satisfiable in a model having an infinite cardinality. All theories considered in this paper (the theory of equality, the theory of lists, the theory of arrays, and the theory of Linear Arithmetic) are stably infinite.

An efficient description of the N-O method is based on the availability of satisfiability procedures with the following properties (see [6] for an in depth discussion on these issues):

Deduction completeness. It must be capable of efficiently detecting elementary clauses which are implied by the input conjunction of literals.

Incrementality & resettability. It must be possible to add and remove literals to and from the state of the procedure without restarting it. Also, processing each literal must be computationally cheap.

The N-O method for satisfiability procedures satisfying the requirements above is depicted in Figure 3 when T_1 is the theory of equality for which the superposition calculus is known to be a satisfiability procedure (see e.g., [2]) and T_2 is Linear Arithmetic (LA) for which various satisfiability procedures are available (see e.g., [8]). Such a combination method simply consists of exchanging elementary clauses between the two procedures until either unsatisfiability is derived by one of the two, or no more elementary clauses can be exchanged. In the first case, we derive the unsatisfiability of the input formula; in the second case, we derive its satisfiability. N-O method terminates because only finitely many elementary clauses can be constructed by using the variables of both Φ_1 and Φ_2.

It is sufficient to exchange only elementary equalities when combining convex theories. A theory is *convex* if for any conjunction Γ of equalities, a disjunction D of equalities is entailed by Γ if and only if some disjunct of D is entailed by Γ. Examples of convex theories are the theory of equality, the theory of lists, and the theory of Linear Arithmetic over the Rationals ($LA(\mathcal{R})$). Since both procedures are assumed to be deduction complete, the combination method only needs to

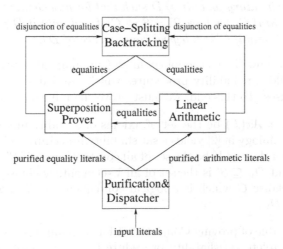

Fig. 3. The Nelson-Oppen Combination Method

pass around elementary equalities between the procedures as soon as they detect them. Adding the newly detected equalities can be done efficiently as long as the procedures are also assumed to be incremental.

When combining at least one non-convex theory such as the theory of arrays or the theory of Linear Arithmetic over the Integers $(LA(\mathcal{I}))$, the combination method is more complex since the procedures should exchange elementary clauses. Although the procedures are capable of deriving the entailed elementary clauses, their processing is problematic since they are only capable of handling conjunctions of literals. The standard solution, as depicted in Figure 3, is to case-split on the derived elementary clauses and then consider each disjunct in turn by using a backtracking procedure; this can be efficiently done (see e.g., [6] for details) since both procedures are assumed to be incremental and resettable.

3   Deduction Complete, Incremental, and Resettable Satisfiability Procedures Based on Superposition

As discussed in Section 2.3, satisfiability procedures must be deduction complete, incremental, and resettable to be efficiently combined à la N-O. Here, we show how to extend the satisfiability procedures based on superposition of [2] with such capabilities.

3.1   Deduction Completeness

First, we need a formal definition of deduction completeness to precisely state our results.

Definition 1. *A T-satisfiability procedure is* deduction complete with respect to elementary clauses (resp. elementary equalities) *if for any T-satisfiable set S of clauses (resp. unit clauses), it returns, in addition to* sat, *a set of elementary clauses (resp. elementary equalities) D such that for any elementary clause (resp. elementary equality) C, we have $T \models S \Rightarrow C$ if and only if $D \models C$ (i.e. $S \Rightarrow C$ is T-valid if and only if C is a logical consequence of D).*

We now show how the methodology in [2] (summarized in Section 2.2) can be extended to build satisfiability procedures which are deduction complete w.r.t. elementary clauses. To this end, we must prove the following conjecture.

Conjecture 1. Let $Ax(T)$ be the set of axioms of a stably infinite theory T for which the methodology in [2] yields a satisfiability procedure, S be a T-satisfiable set of ground literals, and V be the set of all constants in S. If S' is the saturation of $Ax(T) \cup S$ and $D_V \subseteq S'$ is the set of all V-elementary clauses, then for every V-elementary clause C which is a logical consequence of $T \cup S$, C is a logical consequence of D_V.

If we are capable of proving Conjecture 1 for a certain theory T, we can build a deduction complete satisfiability procedure for T by simply extracting from a saturated set S' of clauses (not containing the empty clause) the elementary clauses which entail all elementary clauses entailed by S'. Indeed, this is sufficient for the completeness of the N-O method depicted in Figure 3.

Since Conjecture 1 must be proved for each theory T for which the methodology of [2] (cf. Section 2.2) yields a superposition-based satisfiability procedure, we extend such a methodology with the following phase:

3. *Deduction completeness*: any set of clauses saturated by $\mathcal{SP}$ (not containing the empty clause) is shown to contain a set of elementary clauses entailing all elementary clauses which are logical consequences of the initial set of clauses.

Below, **we assume that $\succ$ is a TRO such that $t \succ c$ for each constant c and term t containing a function symbol of arity bigger than** 0. This requirement is easy to realize in practice (see [2] for more details). We also assume that the contraction rules of $\mathcal{SP}$ have higher priority than expansion rules. This is a reasonable assumption: before enlarging the search space by adding a new clause via the application of an expansion rule, one would try to reduce it as much as possible via the application of as many contraction rules as possible.

Theory of Equality $\mathcal{E}$. Let S be a set of ground literals and $Ax(\mathcal{E})$ be the empty set since equality is built-in the rules of $\mathcal{SP}$. For any TRO $\succ$, the fair and exhaustive applications of the rules of $\mathcal{SP}$ on $Ax(\mathcal{E}) \cup S$ always terminates and so $\mathcal{SP}$ can be used to build a satisfiability procedure for $\mathcal{E}$ (see [2] for details). Here, for the sake of generality, we consider S to be a set of clauses and not simply of literals.

Theorem 2. *Let S be a satisfiable set of ground clauses and V be the set of all constants occurring in S. Let S' be a saturation of S with respect to $\mathcal{SP}$ and D_V be the set of all V-elementary clauses in S'. Then for every V-elementary clause C, $S \models C$ implies $D_V \models C$.*

Proof. Since S and S' are logically equivalent, $S \models C$ if and only if $S' \models C$. Let $C \equiv c_1 = c_1' \vee c_2 = c_2' \vee \ldots \vee c_n = c_n'$, then $S' \models c_1 = c_1' \vee c_2 = c_2' \vee \ldots \vee c_n = c_n'$ is equivalent to $S' \cup \{c_1 \neq c_1', c_2 \neq c_2', \ldots, c_n \neq c_n'\}$ is unsatisfiable.

By the refutation completeness of $\mathcal{SP}$, we can derive the empty clause from $S' \cup \{c_1 \neq c_1', c_2 \neq c_2', \ldots, c_n \neq c_n'\}$ using the inference system $\mathcal{SP}$. Since S' is already saturated, only inferences between clauses in S' and clauses in $\{c_1 \neq c_1', c_2 \neq c_2', \ldots, c_n \neq c_n'\}$ could derive the empty clause. But then, only *Paramodulation*, *Simplification* and *Reflection* can apply since clauses in $\{c_1 \neq c_1', \ldots, c_n \neq c_n'\}$ are all negative. Now let us analyze the form of clauses used by these three rules to derive the empty clause.

- *Paramodulation*: a clause of the form $c_1 = c_1' \vee c_2 = c_2' \vee \ldots \vee c_m = c_m'$ ($m \in \{1, \ldots, n\}$) in S' and $c_1 \neq c_1'$ are used to derive in one step $c_2 = c_2' \vee \ldots \vee c_m = c_m'$. The rule repeatedly applies until the empty clause is obtained. That means the clause $c_1 = c_1' \vee c_2 = c_2' \vee \ldots \vee c_m = c_m'$ must be in S' and hence in D_V. But $c_1 = c_1' \vee c_2 = c_2' \vee \ldots \vee c_m = c_m' \models C$, consequently $D_V \models C$.

- *Simplification*: a clause $c_j \neq c'_j$ in $\{c_1 \neq c'_1, c_2 \neq c'_2, \ldots, c_n \neq c'_n\}$ is simplified (by one or many steps) to the clause $a \neq a$; and *Reflection* applies to derive the empty clause. But *Simplification* uses equalities to simplify clauses. In addition, these equalities must be elementary since they are used to simplify a disequality between constants. In other word $c_j = c'_j$ is a consequence of a set of elementary equalities which is itself a subset of D_V. Thus we have $D_V \models C$.
- *Reflection*: $a \neq a$ is used in *Reflection* and hence either $a \neq a \in S'$ or $a \neq a \in \{c_1 \neq c'_1, c_2 \neq c'_2, \ldots, c_n \neq c'_n\}$. But that type of clause cannot be in S' that is saturated and does not contain the empty clause. If it is in $\{c_1 \neq c'_1, c_2 \neq c'_2, \ldots, c_n \neq c'_n\}$, this simply means that $c_1 = c'_1 \vee c_2 = c'_2 \vee \ldots \vee c_n = c'_n$ is a tautology clause; and we have $D_V \models C$.

In all cases, we have $D_V \models C$.   □

Corollary 1. *Let S be a satisfiable set of ground literals and V be the set of all constants occurring in S. Let S' be a saturation of S with respect to SP and Γ_V be the set of all V-elementary equalities in S'. Then for every V-elementary equality $c = c'$, $S \models c = c'$ implies $\Gamma_V \models c = c'$.*

Corollary 2. *SP is a deduction complete (with respect to elementary equalities) satisfiability procedure for $\mathcal{E}$.*

Proof. By Corollary 1, it is immediate to see that a deduction complete satisfiability procedure for $\mathcal{E}$ is obtained by computing a saturation of the input set of literals (unit clauses) and then collecting the elementary equalities in such a saturated set of clauses.   □

Theory of Lists à la Shostak. The (convex) theory $\mathcal{L}$ of lists à la Shostak [16] is axiomatized by the following set $Ax(\mathcal{L})$ of axioms:

$$car(cons(X, Y)) = X \tag{L1}$$
$$cdr(cons(X, Y)) = Y \tag{L2}$$
$$cons(car(X), cdr(X)) = X \tag{L3}$$

where X and Y are implicitly universally quantified variables.

Lemma 2 ([2]). *Let S be a finite set of ground flat $\mathcal{L}$-literals. The clauses occurring in the saturation of $Ax(\mathcal{L}) \cup S$ w.r.t. SP are of the following types only, where X, Y are variables, a, b, c are constants, and $\bowtie \in \{=, \neq\}$:*

i) *the empty clause;*
ii) *the axioms in $Ax(\mathcal{L})$: 1) $car(cons(X, Y)) = X$; 2) $cdr(cons(X, Y)) = Y$; and 3) $cons(car(X), cdr(X)) = X$;*
iii) *ground flat literals of the forms: 1) $c \bowtie c'$; 2) $car(a) = b$; 3) $cdr(a) = b$; and 4) $cons(a, b) = c$;*
iv) *equalities of the form $cons(b, cdr(a)) = a$ or $cons(car(a), b) = a$, where a, b are constants.*

A consequence of this lemma [2] is that $\mathcal{SP}$ is a satisfiability procedure for $\mathcal{L}$. This is so because all saturations of $Ax(\mathcal{L}) \cup S$ are finite, since only finitely many literals of types $i)$–$iv)$ can be built out of a finite signature.

Lemma 3. *Let S be a finite $\mathcal{L}$-satisfiable set of ground flat $\mathcal{L}$-literals and V be the set of constants occurring in S. Let S_g be the set of all ground clauses in the saturation of $Ax(\mathcal{L}) \cup S$ w.r.t. $\mathcal{SP}$. Then, for every V-elementary equality $c = c'$, we have that*
A) if $\mathcal{L} \cup S \models c = c'$ then $S_g \models c = c'$, and
B) $\mathcal{L} \cup S \cup \{c = c'\}$ is unsatisfiable iff $S_g \cup \{c = c'\}$ is unsatisfiable.

Proof. Let S' be a saturation of $Ax(\mathcal{L}) \cup S$. Since S is $\mathcal{L}$-satisfiable, S' does not contain the empty clause.

A) Notice that $\mathcal{L} \cup S \models c = c'$ is equivalent to $S' \cup \{c \neq c'\}$ is unsatisfiable; that also means we can derive the empty clause from $S' \cup \{c \neq c'\}$ using $\mathcal{SP}$. Since S' is saturated, we only consider inferences between clauses in S' and $c \neq c'$. For that, we consider all possible inferences between clauses listed in Lemma 2 and $c \neq c'$. We can easily see that only inferences between clauses of type $(iii.1)$ and $c \neq c'$ are possible. In other words, $c = c'$ is a consequence of a subset of S_g; consequently, $S_g \models c = c'$.

B) We have that $\mathcal{L} \cup S \cup \{c = c'\}$ is unsatisfiable if and only if $S' \cup \{c = c'\}$ is unsatisfiable. Since S' is saturated, we only consider inferences between clauses in S' and $c = c'$. Again, we consider all possible inferences between clauses listed in Lemma 2 and $c = c'$ to derive the empty clause. We can see that only the following inferences are possible: (iii) and $c = c'$, (iv) and $c = c'$. This simply means $c = c'$ is a consequence of S_g. □

Theorem 3. *Let S be a finite $\mathcal{L}$-satisfiable set of ground flat $\mathcal{L}$-literals and V be the set of constants occurring in S. Let Γ_V be the set of V-elementary equalities that belong to the saturation of $Ax(\mathcal{L}) \cup S$ w.r.t. $\mathcal{SP}$. Then for every V-elementary equality $c = c'$ which is a logical consequence of $Ax(\mathcal{L}) \cup S$, $c = c'$ is a logical consequence of Γ_V.*

Proof. It follows from Lemma 3 that the subset S_g containing the ground clauses in the saturation of S is sufficient to derive V-elementary equalities, i.e. for every ground V-elementary equality $c = c'$, $S \models c = c'$ implies $S_g \models c = c'$. By Corollary 1, $S_g \models c = c'$ implies $\Gamma_V \models c = c'$. □

Corollary 3. *$\mathcal{SP}$ is a deduction complete (with respect to elementary equalities) satisfiability procedure for $\mathcal{L}$.*

Other convex theories. The result obtained for $\mathcal{L}$ can be extended to other convex theories considered in [2,1], namely the theory of lists à la N-O, a theory of encryption, or a theory of records by proceeding along the lines of what has been done for $\mathcal{L}$: show that only the ground clauses in a saturation are sufficient to derive entailed elementary equalities and then use Corollary 1 to conclude that the elementary equalities in the saturation are sufficient to derive all entailed elementary equalities. We do not do this here for lack of space.

Theory of Arrays. The (non-convex) theory $\mathcal{A}$ of arrays (see e.g., [2]) is axiomatized by the following finite set $Ax(\mathcal{A})$ of axioms:

$$select(store(A, I, E), I) = E \qquad \qquad (\text{A}1)$$
$$I \neq J \Rightarrow select(store(A, I, E), J) = select(A, J) \qquad (\text{A}2)$$

where A, I, J, E are implicitly universally quantified variables.

Lemma 4 ([2]). *Let S be a finite set of ground flat $\mathcal{A}$-literals. Then, the clauses occurring in the saturation of $Ax(\mathcal{A}) \cup S$ with respect to $\mathcal{SP}$ are of the following types only, where X is a variable, and $a, a', e, e', i, i_1, i'_1, \ldots, i_n, i'_n, j_1, j'_1 \ldots, j_m,$ j'_m for $n \geq 0$, $m \geq 0$ are constants, and $\bowtie \in \{=, \neq\}$:*

  i) the empty clause;
  ii) the axioms in $Ax(\mathcal{A})$;
  iii) ground flat literals;
  iv) non-unit clauses of the form:
      a) clauses of the form $select(c, X) = select(c', X) \vee X = i_1 \vee \ldots X = i_n \vee j_1 \bowtie j'_1 \vee \ldots \vee j_m \bowtie j'_m$;
      b) $select(a, i) \bowtie e \vee i_1 \bowtie i'_1 \vee \ldots \vee i_n \bowtie i'_n$;
      c) $t = a' \vee i_1 \bowtie i'_1 \vee \ldots \vee i_n \bowtie i'_n$, where t is either a or $store(a, i, e)$;
      d) $e \bowtie e' \vee i_1 \bowtie i'_1 \vee \ldots \vee i_n \bowtie i'_n$;
      e) $i_1 \bowtie i'_1 \vee i_2 \bowtie i'_2 \vee \ldots \vee i_n \bowtie i'_n$;

A consequence of this lemma [2] is that $\mathcal{SP}$ is a satisfiability procedure for $\mathcal{A}$.

Lemma 5. *Let S be a finite $\mathcal{A}$-satisfiable set of ground flat $\mathcal{A}$-literals and V be the set of constants occurring in S. Let S_g be the set of all ground clauses in the saturation of $Ax(\mathcal{A}) \cup S$ with respect to $\mathcal{SP}$. Then, for every V-elementary clause D, we have that*
A) $Ax(\mathcal{A}) \cup S \models D \Rightarrow S_g \models D$, and
B) $Ax(\mathcal{A}) \cup S \cup \{D\}$ is unsatisfiable if and only if $S_g \cup \{D\}$ is unsatisfiable.

Theorem 4. *Let S be a finite $\mathcal{A}$-satisfiable set of ground flat $\mathcal{A}$-literals and V be the set of constant occurring in S. Let D_V be the set of V-elementary clauses that belong to the saturation of $Ax(\mathcal{A}) \cup S$ with respect to $\mathcal{SP}$. Then for every V-elementary clause C which is a logical consequence of $Ax(\mathcal{A}) \cup S$, C is a logical consequence of D_V.*

Proof. It follows from Lemma 5 that the subset S_g containing the ground clauses in the saturation of S is sufficient to derive V-elementary clauses, i.e. for every ground V-elementary clause C, $S \models C$ implies $S_g \models C$. By Theorem 2, $S_g \models C$ implies $D_V \models C$. $\qquad\square$

Corollary 4. *$\mathcal{SP}$ is a deduction complete (with respect to elementary clauses) satisfiability procedure for $\mathcal{A}$.*

Other non-convex theories. The result obtained for $\mathcal{A}$ can be extended to the theory of arrays with extensionality and a simple theory of sets with and without extensionality considered in [2]. For lack of space, we do not develop this further.

3.2   Experiments

In order to show the efficiency of the deduction complete satisfiability procedures based on superposition presented above, we have implemented the combination method described in Figure 3 in the theorem prover **haRVey** [3]. In particular, the E prover [15] implements $\mathcal{SP}$ and we have implemented a module to inspect the saturated sets of clauses computed by the E prover and extract the elementary clauses. We have also implemented a deduction complete procedure for $LA(\mathcal{R})$ along the lines of [8].

For benchmarks, we used a selection of proof obligations from those generated to certify auto-generated aerospace software in [4]. We selected 107 (out of 356) unsatisfiable proof obligations expressing the property that each access to an array element are within the appropriate range. For example, an array variable a is modeled as the constant a and its i-element a[i] is written as $sel(a, i)$; hence, we need to reason about a combination of $\mathcal{E}$ and $LA(\mathcal{I})$. As it is common in software verification, we use the decision procedure for $LA(\mathcal{R})$ as a semi-decision procedure for $LA(\mathcal{I})$. On these benchmarks, this is sufficient since all proof obligations have been checked unsatisfiable already over the rationals. In [4], the proof obligations come with a set of axioms which approximates $LA(\mathcal{I})$ and should be sufficient to discharge (almost) all of them. Since **haRVey** is capable of handling virtually any theory which can be finitely axiomatized, we compared the behavior of the system **haRVey**$(\mathcal{SP})$ with the E prover alone handling the supplied axioms for $LA(\mathcal{I})$ and the system **haRVey**$(\mathcal{SP} + LA(\mathcal{R}))$ featuring the combination between the decision procedure for $LA(\mathcal{R})$ and the superposition prover without axioms for $LA(\mathcal{I})$.

Table 1. Experimental results

	time-out	don't know	unsat
haRVey$(\mathcal{SP})$	5	17	85
haRVey$(\mathcal{SP} + LA(\mathcal{R}))$	0	0	107

Experiments were performed on a Pentium-IV 2 GHz running Linux with 256 Kb of RAM and 1 Gb of disk space. We set a time-out of 60 seconds. A comparison of **haRVey**$(\mathcal{SP})$ and **haRVey**$(\mathcal{SP} + LA(\mathcal{R}))$ is shown in Table 1. The column "don't know" means that the prover returned with satisfiable but since the axiomatization of $LA(\mathcal{I})$ is necessarily incomplete we interpreted it as non conclusive. From Table 1, it is clear that the incorporation of $LA(\mathcal{R})$ in **haRVey** is successful since it both eliminates the need of an explicit axiomatization of the background theory and makes the system more reliable. We believe that these results clearly show that Arithmetic reasoning has been efficiently combined with superposition theorem proving to discharge the proof obligations arising in typical software verification problems.

3.3   Incrementality and Resettability

Although the combination method in Figure 3 is already efficient in practice to tackle interesting proof obligations arising in verification (as shown in Sec-

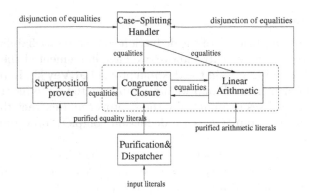

Fig. 4. The Hierarchic Nelson-Oppen Combination Method

tion 3.2), there is still room for improvement. In fact, Lemmas 3.B) and 5.B)
allow us to observe that when new elementary clauses (deduced from another
satisfiability procedure) must be added to a saturated set of clauses, it is only
necessary to consider the ground clauses in the saturated set. This implies that
it is sufficient to use the superposition calculus as a front-end for the congruence
closure algorithm, which can be turned into a deduction complete, incremental,
and resettable satisfiability procedure for $\mathcal{E}$ (see e.g., [6]). So, the superposition calculus must be applied only once before the combination loop in which
the congruence closure algorithm and another satisfiability procedure exchange
elementary clauses. Figure 4 depicts the hierarchic combination method which
allows us to obtain satisfiability procedures which are both incremental and resettable. We are currently implementing the method in **haRVey** and we expect
further improvements in performances. It is interesting to notice that this approach can be used in any theorem proving system featuring a combination of
satisfiability procedures à la N-O, offering an easy and efficient way to incorporate procedures for a variety of theories extending $\mathcal{E}$.

4   Related Work

Our approach to efficiently combine a theory processed by superposition with a
procedure for $LA(\mathcal{R})$ is based on the N-O method. An alternative combination
method has been proposed by Shostak [16]. Such a method assumes that the
theories to be combined are such that there exist functions for reducing terms
to canonical form (*canonizers*) and for solving equations (*solvers*) [13]. There
are essentially two different ways to use canonizers and solvers for deciding the
satisfiability problem in unions of disjoint theories.

First, one can use a solver and a canonizer to build a satisfiability procedure having the capability of computing entailed elementary equalities. Then,
this satisfiability procedure can be combined with others using the N-O method.
So, combining theories à la Shostak can be directly viewed as a refinement of
the Nelson-Oppen combination method [13]. In this way, solvers and canonizers

can be readily integrated with the satisfiability procedures based on superposition described in this paper. A second approach consists in extending the use of canonizers and solvers in order to deal with terms built over the union of the signatures of the component theories. In contrast to the N-O method, one does not need to purify the input literals. Rather, the input literals are processed directly by solvers and canonizers having the capability of transforming heterogeneous terms. This approach was initiated by Shostak and has been followed by many other papers revisiting this combination method (see again [13] for details). Recently, this approach has been used in [7] to integrate a canonizer and a solver in the superposition calculus. This yields a refutationally complete calculus on *ground* clauses whose terms are built over the union of the signatures of the component theories. This is particularly interesting to integrate some form of Arithmetic reasoning with superposition. The main drawback of this approach is the ordering relation used to restrict the applicability of the inference rules which is quite complex. Instead, our approach uses the standard and well understood framework of the superposition calculus (including the standard techniques to define ordering relations) which allows us to re-use a wide range of existing results.

5 Conclusion

In [2], the authors give a general and flexible approach to derive satisfiability procedures by superposition. In this work, we have shown that such satisfiability procedures deduce sufficiently many (disjunctions of) equalities between variables to be combined *à la* Nelson and Oppen with other satisfiability procedures without loosing completeness. Experimental results on typical software verification problems show the efficiency of the proposed approach. Moreover, it is possible to obtain a certain degree of incrementality and resettability by using a hierarchic variant of the N-O method.

There are several main lines for future work. First, we want to derive a more precise characterization of the theories for which deduction complete superposition based satisfiability procedures can be built with the methodology of [2]. Second, we intend to empirically evaluate the efficiency of our hierarchic variant of N-O combination method by conducting some experiments in **haRVey** [3]. Finally, we plan to study, along the line of [14], the combination of superposition based satisfiability procedures with satisfiability procedures for non stably infinite theories, for which the N-O method does not directly apply.

References

1. A. Armando, M. P. Bonacina, S. Ranise, and S. Schulz. On a rewriting approach to satisfiability procedures: extension, combination of theories and an experimental appraisal. In *Proc. of the 5th Int. Workshop on Frontiers of Combining Systems (FroCos'05)*, LNCS. Springer-Verlag, 2005. To appear.
2. A. Armando, S. Ranise, and M. Rusinowitch. A Rewriting Approach to Satisfiability Procedures. *Info. and Comp.*, 183(2):140–164, June 2003.

3. D. Déharbe and S. Ranise. Light-Weight Theorem Proving for Debugging and Verifying Units of Code. In *Proc. of the Int. Conf. on Software Engineering and Formal Methods (SEFM03)*. IEEE Comp. Soc. Press, 2003.
4. E. Denney, B. Fischer, and J. Schumann. Using automated theorem provers to certify auto-generated aerospace software. In *Proc. of Int. Joint Conf. On Automated Reasoning (IJCAR'04)*, volume 3097 of *LNCS*, 2004.
5. N. Dershowitz and J.-P. Jouannaud. *Handbook of Theoretical Computer Science*, volume B, chapter 6: Rewrite Systems, pages 244–320. Elsevier Science Publishers B. V. (North-Holland), 1990.
6. D. Detlefs, G. Nelson, and J. B. Saxe. Simplify: A Theorem Prover for Program Checking. Technical Report HPL-2003-148, HP Laboratories, 2003.
7. H. Ganzinger, T. Hillenbrand, and U. Waldmann. Superposition modulo a Shostak theory. In F. Baader, editor, *Automated Deduction — CADE-19*, volume 2741 of *LNAI*, pages 182–196. Springer-Verlag, 2003.
8. D. Kapur and X. Nie. Reasoning about Numbers in Tecton. In *Proc. 8th Inl. Symp. Methodologies for Intelligent Systems*, pages 57–70, 1994.
9. H. Kirchner, S. Ranise, C. Ringeissen, and D. K. Tran. On Superposition-Based Satisfiability Procedures and their Combination (Full Version). Available at http://www.loria.fr/~ranise/pubs/long-ictac05.ps.gz.
10. G. Nelson. Techniques for program verification. Technical Report CS-81-10, Xerox Palo Research Center California USA, 1981.
11. G. Nelson and D. C. Oppen. Simplification by cooperating decision procedures. *ACM Trans. on Programming Languages and Systems*, 1(2):245–257, Oct. 1979.
12. R. Nieuwenhuis and A. Rubio. Paramodulation-based theorem proving. In A. Robinson and A. Voronkov, editors, *Hand. of Automated Reasoning*. 2001.
13. S. Ranise, C. Ringeissen, and D.-K. Tran. Nelson-Oppen, Shostak and the Extended Canonizer : A Family Picture with a Newborn. In *First International Colloquium on Theoretical Aspects of Computing — ICTAC 2004, Guiyang, China*, volume 3407 of *LNCS*, pages 372–386. Springer, Sep 2004.
14. S. Ranise, C. Ringeissen, and C. G. Zarba. Combining data structures with non-stably infinite theories using many-sorted logic. In *Proc. of the 5th Int. Workshop on Frontiers of Combining Systems (FroCos'05)*, LNCS. Springer-Verlag, 2005. To appear.
15. S. Schulz. E – A Brainiac Theorem Prover. *Journal of AI Communications*, 15(2/3):111–126, 2002.
16. R. E. Shostak. Deciding combinations of theories. *J. of the ACM*, 31:1–12, 1984.

A Summary of the Tutorials at ICTAC 2005

Dang Van Hung*

International Institute for Software Technology,
The United Nations University, P.O. Box 3058, Macau
dvh@iist.unu.edu

Abstract. Five tutorials were provided by ICTAC 2005. They were conducted by internationally recognised experts. A brief summary of each tutorial is include here.

1 Introduction

One of the aims of ICTAC is to bridge the digital divide between the developing world and the developed world. The tutorial program at ICTAC is an efficient way toward the achievement of this aim. It provides opportunities for the conference attendees, many of whom are from developing countries, to get knowledge, insights and abilities on key subjects on theoretical aspects of computing and software engineering.

The tutorial program at ICTAC 2005 has five tutorials which cover advanced topics in theories, practical formal engineering methods and tools that we believe to be very popular, useful and relevant to the audience. Two of the five tutorials introduce model checking techniques and tools from different approaches. The others give a theory for dynamic component composition, coalgebraic structures and their application, and answer set programming. The abstracts of these five tutorials are given in the following section.

2 The Tutorials

Tutorial 1A: Compositional Models for Dynamic Component Composition

Lecturer: Farhad Arbab, Center for Mathematics and Computer Science (CWI), Amsterdam, The Netherlands.

Abstract: This tutorial has two parts. In the first part of this tutorial, a formal model of components is introduced which extends object-orientation with additional structuring and abstraction mechanisms to support a modeling discipline based on interfaces. This component model formalizes the concepts of roles, ports, interfaces, and connectors. Components in this model encapsulate their internal structure and interact only through ports. The behavior of ports is

---

* On leave from the Institute of Information Technology, Hanoi, Vietnam.

D.V. Hung and M. Wirsing (Eds.): ICTAC 2005, LNCS 3722, pp. 609–612, 2005.

generically described by roles. Roles export information about required and provided operations by means of interfaces. Finally, connectors wire roles of different components together to form a component-based application.

Next, a fully abstract trace semantics for this object-oriented component model is discussed. This semantics is formalized in terms of a new notion of abstract behavior types for components, which provides a description of the externally observable behavior of a component, inspired by UML sequence diagrams. Such a description abstracts from the actual implementation given, for example, by UML state-machines. The full abstraction result is based on a may-testing semantics of abstract behavior types which involves a composition of components in terms of cross-border dynamic class instantiation through component interfaces. This is the first such result for a concurrent object-oriented language with dynamic class instantiation.

In the second part of this tutorial, models for dynamic component composition using mobile channels are discussed. The notion of mobile channels is introduced, and their implementation and utility in distributed platforms is shown.

Next the lecture describes how mobile channels form the basis for a surprisingly expressive distributed coordination model, called Reo. Reo is an exogenous coordination language wherein complex coordinators, called connectors are compositionally built out of simpler ones, based on a calculus of channel composition. Reo offers a "glue language" for compositional construction of reusable connectors that orchestrate component instances in a component based system. Each connector in Reo imposes a specific coordination pattern on the entities (e.g., component instances) that perform I/O operations through that connector, without the knowledge of those entities.

Tutorial 1B: Answer Set Programming

Lecturer: Tran Cao Son, New Mexico State University, USA.

Abstract: Answer set programming is a new programming paradigm based on Logic Programming under answer set semantics. In this paradigm, a problem to be solved is translated to a program whose answer sets correspond one-to-one to the solutions of the original problem, and can be computed using an answer set solver. Answer set programming has become popular recently. This tutorial provides an overview of answer set programming and its applications, and pointers to state-of-the-art answer set solvers. This tutorial also discusses the current issues and research problems in the area of answer set programming.

Tutorial 2A: Model Checking with SPIN and Its Industrial Applications

Lecturer: Jay S. Bagga and Adrian Heinz, Ball State University, USA, and Dang Van Hung, UNU-IIST, Macao.

Abstract: Industrial use of software has grown rapidly in the last few decades. Industries such as telecommunications, automotive, manufacturing, defense, and aerospace use software to run and control their applications, processes, and systems. Many critical applications in such industries require that the software be accurate and highly reliable, since a malfunction can lead to catastrophic losses. Formal methods are used to improve the reliability of software and hardware systems. A formal method called *model checking* uses efficient search techniques to check that a model of the system being developed satisfies the specifications (properties).

The specifications that the system must have can be generally written in terms of logical propositions. A verification technique called *temporal logic model checking* was developed in the 1980s by Clarke, Emerson, Quielle and Sifakis. Specifications are expressed as formulas in propositional temporal logic. A finite state-transition model of the system is formed, and the model is checked by using efficient search procedures for the validity of the formulas. Over the last two decades, various model-checking tools have been developed and used. One such popular model-checker is SPIN, a tool developed by Holzmann. SPIN has been used in verification of several types of software systems including communication protocols, and some hardware verification.

This tutorial aims to provide academic faculty members, students, and practicing IT professionals a formal training in software verification methods. The tutorial consists of four sessions, each approximately one hour-long, as described below.

- Session 1: Introduction to Model Checking: This session will provide the basic notions of model checking, temporal logic, LTL and CTL, and model checking algorithms.
- Session 2: SPIN and PROMELA: This session will introduce SPIN and PROMELA and provide hands-on training with examples.
- Session 3: Case Study: An assembly line simulator. This model is composed of several components to load, transport and process mechanical pieces. Every component works independently of the other components and communicates with the rest of the system by the use of channels. An implementation of the assembly line simulator in SPIN will be presented.
- Session 4: Case Study: The second case study used for this tutorial is a telephone switch system taken from the SPIN Modelchecker book with some improvements for modeling the system and its desired properties. We show in this case study how to model the essential elements of a system in incremental way using the language PROMELA, and how to manage the complexity by using abstraction techniques.

Tutorial 2B: Coinductive Reasoning by Calculation

Lecturer: Luis Barbosa, Universidade do Minho, Portugal.

Abstract: Both initial algebras and final coalgebras are devices which provide abstract descriptions of a variety of phenomena in programming, particularly data and behavioural structures. Both initiality and finality, as universal properties, entail definitional and proof principles, i.e., a basis for the development of program calculi directly based on (actually driven by) type specifications. Moreover, such properties can be turned into programming combinators and used, not only to calculate programs, but also to program with. In functional programming the role of such universals has been fundamental to a whole discipline of algorithm derivation and transformation. On the coalgebraic side, coalgebraic modelling of dynamical systems and reasoning by coinduction has recently emerged as active area of research. This tutorial provides an introduction to coalgebraic structures and their application to systems construction. Its main focus, however, is placed on reasoning principles for such structures developing an entirely calculational approach to coinduction which avoids the explicit construction of bisimulations, and therefore, promotes a reasoning style closer to the actual program construction practice. The presentation of basic concepts is illustrated by discussion of small examples in reactive programing.

Tutorial 3: Regular Model Checking: Application to the Analysis of Parametrized Systems and Multithreaded Recursive Programs

Lecturer: Tayssir Touili, LIAFA, CNRS & University of Paris 7, France.

Abstract: This tutorial presents the framework of regular model checking where sets of configurations of a system are represented by regular word/tree languages and its dynamics is modeled by a word/term rewrite system. In this framework, the verification of safety properties is reduced to computing the reachability set $R^*(L)$ where R is a rewrite system and L is a regular language representing the initial configurations. The construction of this set is not possible in general. Therefore, this lecture presents:

1. A general acceleration technique, called regular widening which allows to speed up the convergence of iterative fixpoint computations in regular modelchecking; and which can be applied uniformly to various kinds of transformation. In particular, the lecture shows the application of this technique to the verification of parametrized systems. Moreover, it proves that the widening technique can emulate many existing algorithms for special significant classes of transformation.

2. Exact and approximate algorithms that compute the reachability sets for a special class of rewrite system called Process Rewrite System (PRS). This tutorial shows how these results can be applied to the analysis of programs with complex features such as recursion and dynamic thread creation.

Author Index

Lecture Notes in Computer Science

For information about Vols. 1–3637

please contact your bookseller or Springer

Vol. 3683: R. Khosla, R.J. Howlett, L.C. Jain (Eds.), Knowledge-Based Intelligent Information and Engineering Systems, Part III. LXXX, 1397 pages. 2005. (Subseries LNAI).

Vol. 3682: R. Khosla, R.J. Howlett, L.C. Jain (Eds.), Knowledge-Based Intelligent Information and Engineering Systems, Part II. LXXIX, 1371 pages. 2005. (Subseries LNAI).

Vol. 3681: R. Khosla, R.J. Howlett, L.C. Jain (Eds.), Knowledge-Based Intelligent Information and Engineering Systems, Part I. LXXX, 1319 pages. 2005. (Subseries LNAI).

Vol. 3679: S.d.C. di Vimercati, P. Syverson, D. Gollmann (Eds.), Computer Security – ESORICS 2005. XI, 509 pages. 2005.

Vol. 3678: A. McLysaght, D.H. Huson (Eds.), Comparative Genomics. VIII, 167 pages. 2005. (Subseries LNBI).

Vol. 3677: J. Dittmann, S. Katzenbeisser, A. Uhl (Eds.), Communications and Multimedia Security. XIII, 360 pages. 2005.

Vol. 3676: R. Glück, M. Lowry (Eds.), Generative Programming and Component Engineering. XI, 448 pages. 2005.

Vol. 3675: Y. Luo (Ed.), Cooperative Design, Visualization, and Engineering. XI, 264 pages. 2005.

Vol. 3674: W. Jonker, M. Petković (Eds.), Secure Data Management. X, 241 pages. 2005.

Vol. 3673: S. Bandini, S. Manzoni (Eds.), AI*IA 2005: Advances in Artificial Intelligence. XIV, 614 pages. 2005. (Subseries LNAI).

Vol. 3672: C. Hankin, I. Siveroni (Eds.), Static Analysis. X, 369 pages. 2005.

Vol. 3671: S. Bressan, S. Ceri, E. Hunt, Z.G. Ives, Z. Bellahsène, M. Rys, R. Unland (Eds.), Database and XML Technologies. X, 239 pages. 2005.

Vol. 3670: M. Bravetti, L. Kloul, G. Zavattaro (Eds.), Formal Techniques for Computer Systems and Business Processes. XIII, 349 pages. 2005.

Vol. 3669: G.S. Brodal, S. Leonardi (Eds.), Algorithms – ESA 2005. XVIII, 901 pages. 2005.

Vol. 3668: M. Gabbrielli, G. Gupta (Eds.), Logic Programming. XIV, 454 pages. 2005.

Vol. 3666: B.D. Martino, D. Kranzlmüller, J. Dongarra (Eds.), Recent Advances in Parallel Virtual Machine and Message Passing Interface. XVII, 546 pages. 2005.

Vol. 3665: K. S. Candan, A. Celentano (Eds.), Advances in Multimedia Information Systems. X, 221 pages. 2005.

Vol. 3664: C. Türker, M. Agosti, H.-J. Schek (Eds.), Peer-to-Peer, Grid, and Service-Orientation in Digital Library Architectures. X, 261 pages. 2005.

Vol. 3663: W.G. Kropatsch, R. Sablatnig, A. Hanbury (Eds.), Pattern Recognition. XIV, 512 pages. 2005.

Vol. 3662: C. Baral, G. Greco, N. Leone, G. Terracina (Eds.), Logic Programming and Nonmonotonic Reasoning. XIII, 454 pages. 2005. (Subseries LNAI).

Vol. 3661: T. Panayiotopoulos, J. Gratch, R. Aylett, D. Ballin, P. Olivier, T. Rist (Eds.), Intelligent Virtual Agents. XIII, 506 pages. 2005. (Subseries LNAI).

Vol. 3660: M. Beigl, S. Intille, J. Rekimoto, H. Tokuda (Eds.), UbiComp 2005: Ubiquitous Computing. XVII, 394 pages. 2005.

Vol. 3659: J.R. Rao, B. Sunar (Eds.), Cryptographic Hardware and Embedded Systems – CHES 2005. XIV, 458 pages. 2005.

Vol. 3658: V. Matoušek, P. Mautner, T. Pavelka (Eds.), Text, Speech and Dialogue. XV, 460 pages. 2005. (Subseries LNAI).

Vol. 3657: F.S. de Boer, M.M. Bonsangue, S. Graf, W.-P. de Roever (Eds.), Formal Methods for Components and Objects. VIII, 325 pages. 2005.

Vol. 3656: M. Kamel, A. Campilho (Eds.), Image Analysis and Recognition. XXIV, 1279 pages. 2005.

Vol. 3655: A. Aldini, R. Gorrieri, F. Martinelli (Eds.), Foundations of Security Analysis and Design III. VII, 273 pages. 2005.

Vol. 3654: S. Jajodia, D. Wijesekera (Eds.), Data and Applications Security XIX. X, 353 pages. 2005.

Vol. 3653: M. Abadi, L. de Alfaro (Eds.), CONCUR 2005 – Concurrency Theory. XIV, 578 pages. 2005.

Vol. 3652: A. Rauber, S. Christodoulakis, A M. Tjoa (Eds.), Research and Advanced Technology for Digital Libraries. XVIII, 545 pages. 2005.

Vol. 3651: R. Dale, K.-F. Wong, J. Su, O.Y. Kwong (Eds.), Natural Language Processing – IJCNLP 2005. XXI, 1031 pages. 2005. (Subseries LNAI).

Vol. 3650: J. Zhou, J. Lopez, R.H. Deng, F. Bao (Eds.), Information Security. XII, 516 pages. 2005.

Vol. 3649: W.M. P. van der Aalst, B. Benatallah, F. Casati, F. Curbera (Eds.), Business Process Management. XII, 472 pages. 2005.

Vol. 3648: J.C. Cunha, P.D. Medeiros (Eds.), Euro-Par 2005 Parallel Processing. XXXVI, 1299 pages. 2005.

Vol. 3646: A. F. Famili, J.N. Kok, J.M. Peña, A. Siebes, A. Feelders (Eds.), Advances in Intelligent Data Analysis VI. XIV, 522 pages. 2005.

Vol. 3645: D.-S. Huang, X.-P. Zhang, G.-B. Huang (Eds.), Advances in Intelligent Computing, Part II. XIII, 1010 pages. 2005.

Vol. 3644: D.-S. Huang, X.-P. Zhang, G.-B. Huang (Eds.), Advances in Intelligent Computing, Part I. XXVII, 1101 pages. 2005.

Vol. 3643: R. Moreno Díaz, F. Pichler, A. Quesada Arencibia (Eds.), Computer Aided Systems Theory – EUROCAST 2005. XIV, 629 pages. 2005.

Vol. 3642: D. Ślezak, J. Yao, J.F. Peters, W. Ziarko, X. Hu (Eds.), Rough Sets, Fuzzy Sets, Data Mining, and Granular Computing, Part II. XXIII, 738 pages. 2005. (Subseries LNAI).

Vol. 3641: D. Ślezak, G. Wang, M. Szczuka, I. Düntsch, Y. Yao (Eds.), Rough Sets, Fuzzy Sets, Data Mining, and Granular Computing, Part I. XXIV, 742 pages. 2005. (Subseries LNAI).

Vol. 3639: P. Godefroid (Ed.), Model Checking Software. XI, 289 pages. 2005.

Vol. 3638: A. Butz, B. Fisher, A. Krüger, P. Olivier (Eds.), Smart Graphics. XI, 269 pages. 2005.